W9-AQV-836

ELENCHUS OF BIBLICAL BIBLIOGRAPHY

21

ROBERT ALTHANN S.J.

# ELENCHUS OF BIBLICA

# 2005

Ref
051
E39b
v. 21

WITHDRAWN

Kenrick-Glennon
Seminary Library
Charles L. Souvay Memorial

EDITRICE PONTIFICIO ISTITUTO BIBLICO
ROMA 2008

© 2008 E.P.I.B. – Roma
ISBN: 978-88-7653-639-7

---

EDITRICE PONTIFICIO ISTITUTO BIBLICO
Piazza della Pilotta, 35 - 00187 Roma, Italia
periodicals@biblicum.com

## *Urbes editionis*—**Cities of publication**

| | | | |
|---|---|---|---|
| AA | Ann Arbor | Lv(N) | Leuven (L-Neuve) |
| Amst | Amsterdam | M/Mi | Madrid/Milano |
| B | Berlin | Mkn | Maryknoll/ |
| Ba/BA | Basel/Buenos Aires | Mp | Minneapolis |
| Barc | Barcelona | Mü/Müns | München/Münster |
| Bo/Bru | Bologna/Brussel | N | Napoli |
| C | Cambridge, England | ND | NotreDame IN |
| CasM | Casale Monferrato | Neuk | Neukirchen/Verlag |
| Ch | Chicago | NHv | New Haven |
| CinB | Cinisello Balsamo | Nv | Nashville |
| CM | Cambridge, Mass. | NY | New York |
| ColMn | Collegeville MN | Oxf | Oxford |
| Da:Wiss | Darmstadt, WissBuchg | P/Pd | Paris/Paderborn |
| DG | Downers Grove | Ph | Philadelphia |
| Dü | Düsseldorf | R/Rg | Roma/Regensburg |
| E | Edinburgh | S | Salamanca |
| ENJ | EnglewoodCliffs NJ | Sdr | Santander |
| F | Firenze | SF | San Francisco |
| Fra | Frankfurt/M | Shf | Sheffield |
| FrB/FrS | Freiburg-Br/Schweiz | Sto | Stockholm |
| Gö | Göttingen | Stu | Stuttgart |
| GR | Grand Rapids MI | T/TA | Torino/Tel Aviv |
| Gü | Gütersloh | Tü | Tübingen |
| Ha | Hamburg | U/W | Uppsala/Wien |
| Heid | Heidelberg | WL | Winona Lake IN |
| Hmw | Harmondsworth | Wmr | Warminster |
| J | Jerusalem | Wsb | Wiesbaden |
| K | København | Wsh | Washington D.C. |
| L/Lei | London/Leiden | Wsz | Warszawa |
| LA | Los Angeles | Wu | Wuppertal |
| Lp | Leipzig | Wü | Würzburg |
| LVL | Louisville KY | Z | Zürich |

**Punctuation**: To separate a subtitle from its title, we use a COLON (:). The *semicolon* (;) serves to separate items that in other respects belong together. Hence, at the end of an entry a *semicolon* indicates a link with the following entry. This link may consist in the two entries having the same author or in the case of multiauthor works having the same book title; the author will be mentioned in the first entry of such a group, the common book title in the last entry, that is the one which concludes with a fullstop [period] (.).
**Abbreviations**: These follow S.M. Schwertner, **IATG**[2] (De Gruyter; Berlin 1992) as far as possible. A list of abbreviations **not found** in Schwertner appears below.
* The asterisk after a book review or an article indicates a reference to an electronic version.
**Price of books**: This is sometimes rounded off ($10 for $9.95).

## Index systematicus — Contents

The present volume contains all the 2005 material of the Elenchus. It is, as always, a pleasant duty to thank the staff of the Editrice Pontificio Istituto Biblico which assures the publication of the Elenchus. Graduates of the Institute have also helped materially in its preparation for which we sincerely thank them.

The materials for this volume were gathered principally from the libraries of the Pontifical Biblical Institute, the Pontifical Gregorian University and the University of Innsbruck. I thank the staff of these libraries for their invariable patience and readiness to help. The Department for Biblical Studies and Historical Theology of the University of Innsbruck continues to be an invaluable source of bibliographical information. We in turn supply the Department with lists of book reviews which may be accessed through the University's electronic catalogue, BILDI, at the following address: http://bildi.uibk.ac.at.

We hope that in the course of 2009, the centennial year of the Institute, it may finally be possible to begin accessing the Elenchus through electronic media.

**Acronyms: Periodica** - Series (small). *8 fig.*=ISSN; *10 or 13 fig.*=ISBN.

A: in Arabic.
**ABIG**: Arbeiten zur Bibel und ihrer Geschichte; Lp.
**AcBib**: Acta Pontificii Instituti Biblici; R.
Al-Machriq; Beyrouth.
**ACCS**: Ancient Christian Commentary on Scripture; DG.
**ACPQ**: American Catholic Philosophical Quarterly; Wsh.
Acta Philosophica; R.
**ActBib**: Actualidad Bibliográfica; Barc.
**AcTh(B)**: Acta Theologica; Bloemfontein.
Ad Gentes; Bo.
Adamantius; Pisa.
**AETSC**: Annales de l'Ecole Théologique Saint-Cyprien; Yaoundé, Cameroun.
**AfR**: Archiv für Religionsgeschichte; Stu.
Afrika Yetu; Nairobi.
**AGWB**: Arbeiten zur Geschichte und Wirkung der Bibel; Stu.
**AHIg**: Anuario de historia de la iglesia; Pamplona.
**AJBS**: African Journal of Biblical Studies; Ado-Ekiti, Nigeria.
**AJEC**: Ancient Judaism & Early Christianity; Lei.
**AJPS**: Asian Journal of Pentecostal Studies;
**AJSR**: Association for Jewish Studies Review; Waltham, MA.
**Ä&L**: Ägypten und Levante; Wien.
Alpha Omega; R.
**AltOrF**: Altorientalische Forschungen; B.
**AMIT**: Archäologische Mitteilungen aus Iran und Turan; B.
AnáMnesis; México.
**AnBru**: Analecta Bruxellensia; Bru.
Ancient West & East; Lei.
**ANESt** [<Abr-n]: Ancient Near Eastern Studies; Melbourne.
Annals of Theology [**P.**]; Krákow.
**AnnTh**: Annales Theologici; R.
**AnScR**: Annali di Scienze Religiose; Mi.
**AnStR**: Annali di studi religiosi; Trento.
Antiphon; Greenville.
**APB**: Acta Patristica et Byzantina; Pretoria.
**AramSt**: Aramaic Studies; L.
Archaeology and History in Lebanon; L.
Archaeology in the Biblical World; Shafter, CA.
**ARET**: Archivi reali di Ebla, testi; R.
**ARGU**: Arbeiten zur Religion und Geschichte des Urchristentums; Fra.
**ARJ**: The Annual of Rabbinic Judaism; Lei.
**AsbJ**: The Asbury Journal; Wilmore, KY.
**ASJ**: Acta Sumerologica; Kyoto, Japan.
**ATM**: Altes Testament und Moderne; Münster.
**ATT**: Archivo teologico torinese; Leumann (Torino).
**AtT**: Atualidade teológica; Rio de Janeiro.
Atualizaçâo; Belo Horizonte.
**AuOr**: Aula Orientalis (**S**: Supplement); Barc.
**AUPO**: Acta Universitatis Palackianae Olomucensis; Olomouc.
Auriensia; Ourense, Spain.
Aviso; Mü.
**AWE**: Ancient West & East; Lei.
**B&B**: Babel und Bibel; Moscow.
**BAChr**: The Bible in Ancient Christianity; Lei.
**BAIAS**: Bulletin of the Anglo-Israel Archaeological Society; L.
Bailamme; Mi.
Barnabiti Studi; R.
Bazmavep; Venise.
**BBR**: Bulletin for Biblical Research; WL.
**BCSMS**: Bulletin of the Canadian Society for Mesopotamian Studies; Toronto.
**BEgS**: Bulletin of the Egyptological Seminar; NY.
**BHQ**: Biblia Hebraica Quinta; Stu.

**Bib(L)**: Bíblica; Lisboa.
**BiblInterp** (**BiblInterp**): Biblical Interpretation; Lei.
**Biblioteca EstB**: Biblioteca de Estudios Bíblicos; S.
**BiCT**: The Bible and Critical Theory; Monash University, ePress.
**BnS**: La bibbia nella storia; Bo.
Bobolanum [**P.**]; Wsz.
Bogoslovni Vestnik [**S.**]; Ljubljana.
**BolT**: Boletín teológico; BA.
**BoSm**: Bogoslovska Smotra; Zagreb.
**BOTSA**: Bulletin for Old Testament Studies in Africa; Stavanger.
**BSÉG**: Bulletin de la Société d'Égyptologie; Genève.
**BSGJ**: Bulletin der Schweizerischen Gesellschaft für Judaistische Forschung; Z.
**BSLP**: Bulletin de la Société de Linguistique de Paris; P.
**BuBB**: Bulletin de bibliographie biblique; Lausanne.
Bulletin of Judaeo-Greek Studies; C.
**BWM**: Bibelwissenschaftliche Monographien; Gießen.
**C**: in Chinese.
Cahiers de l'Atelier; P.
**CamArchJ**: Cambridge Archaeological Journal; C.
Camillianum; R.
Carmel(T); Toulouse.
Carmel(V); Venasque.
Carthaginensia; Murcia.
Cathedra; Bogotá.
Cathedra [**H.**]; J.
**CBET**: Contributions to biblical exegesis and theology; Lv.
**CCO**: Collectanea Christiana Orientalia; Córdoba.
Centro pro unione, Bulletin; R.
Chakana; Fra.
**CHANE**: Culture and History of the Ancient Near East; Lei.
**ChDial**:Chemins de Dialogue; Marseille.
Ching Feng; Hong Kong.
Choisir; Genève.
Christus(M); México.
**CMAO**: Contributi e Materiali di Archeologia Orientale; R.
Colloquium; Brisbane.
**CoMa**: Codices Manuscripti; Purkersdorf.
Comunidades; S.
**ConAss**: Convivium Assisiense; Assisi.
Confer; M.
**ConnPE**: Connaissances des Pères de l'Église; Montrouge.
Contacts; Courbevoie.
Contagion; Rocky Mount.
**CoSe**: Consacrazione e Servizio; R.
**CQuS**: Companion to the Qumran Scrolls; L.
**CR&T**: Conversations in Religion and Theology; Oxf.
**CredOg**: Credereoggi; Padova.
Crkva u Svijetu; Split.
Croire aujourd'hui; P.
**CSMSJ**: The Canadian Society for Mesopotamian Studies Journal; Toronto. 1911-8643.
**CTrB**: Cahiers de traduction biblique; Pierrefitte, France.
**CuBR**: Currents in biblical research; L.
**CuesTF**: Cuestiones Teológicas y Filosóficas; Medellin.
Cultura e libri; R.
**CurResB**: Currents in Research: Biblical Studies; Shf.
[D]: Director dissertationis.
Direction; Fresno, CA.
**DiscEg**: Discussions in Egyptology; Oxf.
Doctor Angelicus; Bonn.
Doctor Seraphicus; R.
**DosArch**: Les Dossiers de l'Archéologie; Dijon.
**DosB**: Les Dossiers de la Bible; P.
**DQ**: Documenta Q; Leuven.
**DSBP**: Dizionario di spiritualità biblico-patristica; R.
**DSD**: Dead Sea Discoveries; Lei.
**DT(B)**: Divus Thomas; Bo.
[E]: Editor, Herausgeber, a cura di.
**EBM**: Estudios Bíblicos Mexicanos; México.
Ecclesia orans; R.
**Eccl(R)**: Ecclesia; R.
**EfMex**: Efemérides Mexicana; Tlalpan.

**EgArch**: Egyptian Archaeology, Bulletin of the Egypt Exploration Society; L.
Elenchos; R.
Emmanuel; Cleveland, OH.
Emmaus; Gozo, Malta.
Encounters; Markfield, U.K.
Epimelia; BA.
**ERSY**: Erasmus of Rotterdam Society Yearbook; Lexington.
**EscrVedat**: Escritos del Vedat; Valencia.
Esprit; P.
**EThF**: Ephemerides Theologicae Fluminenses; Rijeka.
Ethical Perspectives; Lv.
**ETJ**: Ephrem's Theological Journal; Satna, India.
**EurJT**: European Journal of Theology; Carlisle.
Evangel; E.
Evangelische Aspekte; Stu.
Evangelizzare; Bo.
**EyV**: Evangelio y Vida; León.
Exchange; Lei.
F: Festschrift.
Faith & Mission; Wake Forest, NC.
**FCNT**:The feminist companion to the New Testament and early christian writings; L.
Feminist Theology; Shf.
**FgNT**: Filologia Neotestamentaria; Córdoba.
Filosofia oggi; Genova.
**FIOTL**: Formation and interpretation of Old Testament literature; Lei.
Firmana; Fermo.
Florensia; S. Giovanni in Fiore (CS).
**FolTh**: Folia theologica; Budapest.
Forum. Sonoma, CA.
Forum Religion; Stu.
**FoSub**: Fontes et Subsidia ad Bibliam perinentes; B.
Furrow; Maynooth.
**G**: in Greek.
Georgica; Konstanz.
Gnosis; SF.
Graphè; Lille.
**H**: in Hebrew.
Hagiographica; F.
**HBM**: Hebrew Bible Monographs; Shf.
**HBO**: Hallesche Beiträge zur Orientwissenschaft; Halle.
Hekima Review; Nairobi.
Henoch; T.
Hermeneutica; Brescia.
Hermenêutica; Cachoeira, Brasil.
**HlL**: Das Heilige Land; Köln.
History of European Ideas; Oxf.
Ḥokhma; Lausanne.
Holy Land; J.
Horeb; Pozzo di Gotto (ME).
Horizons; Villanova, PA.
**HorWi**: Horizonty Wiary; Kraków.
Ho Theológos; Palermo.
**HPolS**: Hebraic Political Studies; J.
**HTSTS**: HTS Teologiese Studies/ Theological Studies; Pretoria.
**IAJS**: Index of Articles on Jewish Studies; J.
**ICMR**: Islam and Christian-Muslim Relations; Birmingham.
**ICSTJ**: ICST Journal; Vigan, Philippines.
Igreja e Missão; Valadares, Cucujaes.
**IHR**: International History Review; Burnaby, Canada.
**IJCT**: International Journal of the Classical Tradition; New Brunswick, NJ.
**IJSCC**: International Journal for the Study of the Christian Church; E.
**IJST**: International journal of systematic theology; Oxf.
Image; Seattle.
Immaculata Mediatrix; Frigento (Av).
**IncW**: The Incarnate Word; NY.
**INTAMS.R**: INTAMS [International Academy for Marital Spirituality] review; Sint-Genesius-Rode, Belgium.
Interpretation(F). Journal of Political Philosophy; Flushing.
Iran; L.
**IRBS**: International Review of Biblical Studies; Lei.
Isidorianum; Sevilla.

**IslChr**: Islamochristiana; R.
**ITBT**: Interpretatie; Zoetermeer.
**ITE**: Informationes Theologiae Europae; Fra.
Iter; Caracas.
**Itin(L)**: Itinerarium; Lisboa.
**Itin(M)**: Itinerarium; Messina.
**J**: in Japanese.
**JAAT**: Journal of Asian and Asian American Theology; Claremont, Calif.
**JANER**: Journal of Ancient Near Eastern Religions; Lei.
**JAnS**: Journal of Anglican Studies; L.
Japan Mission Journal; Tokyo.
**JATS**: Journal of the Adventist Theological Society; Collegedale, Tennessee.
**JBMW**: Journal for Biblical Manhood and Womanhood; LVL.
**JBSt**: Journal of Biblical Studies; http://journalofbiblicalstudies.org.
**JBTSA**: Journal of Black Theology in South Africa; Atteridgeville.
**JCoS**: Journal of Coptic Studies; Lv.
**JECS**: Journal of Early Christian Studies; Baltimore.
Jeevadhara; Alleppey, Kerala.
**JEGTFF**: Jahrbuch der Europäischen Gesellschaft für theologische Forschung von Frauen; Mainz.
**JEMH**: Journal of Early Modern History; Lei.
**JGRChJ**: Journal of Greco-Roman Christianity and Judaism; Shf.
**JHiC**: Journal of Higher Criticism; Montclair, NJ.
**JHScr**: Journal of Hebrew Scriptures [electr. journal]; Edmonton.
Jian Dao; Hong Kong.
**JIntH**: Journal of interdisciplinary history; CM.
**JISt**: Journal of Interdisciplinary Studies; Pasadena, CA.
**JJSS**: Jnanatirtha. (International) Journal of Sacred Scriptures; Ujjain, India.
**JSSEA**: Journal of the Society for the Study of Egyptian Antiquities; Toronto.
**JTrTL**: Journal of Translation and Textlinguistics; Dallas.
**Jud.**: Judaism; NY.
**K**: in Korean.
Kairos(G); Guatemala.
**KaKe**: Katorikku-Kenkyu [J.]; Tokyo
Kerux; Escondido, CA.
**KUSATU (KUSATU)**: Kleine Untersuchungen zur Sprache des Alten Testaments und seiner Umwelt; Waltrop.
Kwansei-Gakuin-Daigaku; Japan.
Landas. Journal of Loyola School of Theology; Manila.
Laós; Catania.
**LecDif**: Lectio Difficilior [electr. journal]; Bern.
**LeD**: Lire et Dire; Donneloye.
Leqach; Lp.
Levant; L.
**LHBOTS**: Library of Hebrew Bible/ Old Testament studies; NY.
**LingAeg**; Lingua Aegyptia; Gö.
Literary and linguistic computing; Oxf.
**L&S**: Letter and Spirit; Steubenville.
**LNTS**: Library of New Testament studies; L.
**LSDC**: La Sapienza della Croce; R.
Luther-Bulletin; Amst.
Luther Digest; Crestwood, Miss.
[M]: Memorial.
**MastJ**: Master's Seminary Journal; Sun Valley, CA.
Mayéutica; Marcilla (Navarra).
**MEAH**: Miscellánea de Estudios Árabes y Hebraicos (**MEAH.A**: Árabe-Islam. **MEAH.H**: Hebreo); Granada.
Medieval Encounters; Lei.
Meghillot; J.
Mélanges carmélitains; P.
**MESA.B**: Middle East Studies Association Bulletin; Muncie, IN.
**MillSt**: Milltown Studies; Dublin.
Mission de l'Église; P.
Missionalia; Menlo Park, South Africa.
**MissTod**: Mission Today; Shillong, India.
**MoBe**: Modern Believing; Liverpool.
Monde des religions, Le; P.

Mondo della Bibbia, Il; T.
Moralia; M.
**MSJ**: Master's Seminary Journal; Sun Valley, CA.
MST Review; Manila.
**MTSR**: Method and Theory in the Study of Religion; Lei.
Muslim World Book Review; Markfield, UK.
**NAC(SBT)**: New American Commentary (Studies in Bible and Theology); Nv.
**NEA**: Near Eastern Archaeology; Boston.
Neukirchener Theologische Zeitschrift; Neuk.
**NET**: Neutestamentliche Entwürfe zur Theologie; Ba.
**NewTR**: New Theology Review; Ch.
**NHMS**: Nag Hammadi and Manichaean Studies; Lei.
**NIBC**: New International Biblical Commentary; Peabody.
**NICNT**: New International Commentary on the New Testament; GR.
**NIDB**: New Interpreter's Dictionary of the Bible; Nv.
**NIGTC**: The New International Greek Testament Commentary; GR.
**NIntB**: The New Interpreter's Bible; Nv.
**NSK.AT**:Neuer Stuttgarter Kommentar: Altes Testament; Stu.
**NTGu**: New Testament Guides; Shf.
**NTMon**: New Testament Monographs; Shf.
**NTTRU**: New Testament Textual Research Update; Ashfield NSW, Australia. 1320-3037.
Nuova Areopago, Il; Forlì.
Nuova Europa, La; Seriate (Bg).
Nuova Umanità; R.
**NV(Eng)**:Nova et Vetera, English edition; Naples, FL.
Obnovljeni Život; Zagreb.
Omnis Terra; R.
**OrBibChr**: Orbis biblicus et christianus; Glückstadt.
**OrExp**: Orient-Express, Notes et Nouvelles d'Archéologie Orientale; P.
Orient; Tokyo.
Orientamenti pastorali; Bo.
Orientamenti pedagogici; R.
**P**: in Polish.
Pacifica. Australian Theological Studies; Melbourne.
Paginas; Lima.
**PaiC.**: Paideia Cristiana; Rosario, ARG.
Paléorient; P.
Parabola; NY.
**PaRe**: The Pastoral Review; L.
Path; Città del Vaticano.
Pensiero politico, Il; F.
People on the Move; R.
Phase; Barc.
Philosophiques; Montréal.
**PJBR**: The Polish Journal of Biblical Research; Kraków.
**PKNT**: Papyrologische Kommentare zum Neuen Testament; Gö.
**PoST**: Poznańskie studia teologiczne; Poznán.
**PredOT**: Prediking van het Oude Testament; Baarn.
Presbyteri; Trento.
Presbyterion; St. Louis.
**PresPast**: Presenza Pastorale, R.
Prism; St. Paul, MN.
**ProcGLM**: Proceedings of the Eastern Great Lakes and Midwest Bible Societies; Buffalo.
Pro dialogo; Città del Vaticano.
**ProEc**: Pro ecclesia; Northfield, MN.
Prooftexts; Baltimore.
Proverbium; Burlington, VT.
Proyección; Granada.
**ProySal**: Proyecto Centro Salesiano de Estudios; BA.
Prudentia [.S]; Auckland, NZ.
Przegląd Tomistyezny; Wsz.
**PzB**: Protokolle zur Bibel; Klosterneuburg.
Qol; México.
Qol(I); Novellara (RE).
Quaderni di scienze religiose; Loreto.
Qumran Chronicle; Kraków.
**QVC**: Qüestions de Vida Cristiana; Barc.
**R**: in Russian.
[R]: *recensio*, book-review.
**RANL.mor.**: Rendiconti dell'Accademia Nazionale dei Lincei, Cl. di scienze morali; R.
**RANT**: Res Antiquae; Bru.

**RBBras**: Revista Bíblica Brasileira; Fortaleza.
**RBLit**: Review of Biblical Literature; Atlanta.
**REAC**: Ricerche di egittologia e di antichità copte; Bo.
**REAug**: Revue d'études augustiniennes et patristiques; P.
Recollectio; R.
Reformation, The; Oxf (Tyndale Society).
Religion; L.
Religious Research; Wsh.
**RelT**: Religion and Theology; Pretoria.
**RenSt**: Renaissance Studies; Oxf.
**ResB**: Reseña Bíblica; Estella.
**RevCT**: Revista de cultura teológica; São Paulo.
Revista católica; Santiago de Chile.
Revue d'éthique et de théologie morale; P.
**RF(UI)**: Revista de filosofia; México.
**RGRW**: Religions in the Graeco-Roman World; Lei.
**Ribla**: Revista de interpretação biblica latino-americana; Petrópolis.
Ricerche teologiche; Bo.
**RiSCr**: Rivista di storia del cristianesimo; Brescia.
Rivista di archeologia; R.
Rivista di science religiose; R.
Rivista de storia della miniatura; F.
Roczniki Teologiczne; Lublin
Romania; P.
**RRJ**: Review of Rabbinic Judaism; Lei.
**RRT**: Reviews in Religion and Theology; L.
**R&T**: Religion and theology = Religie en teologie; Pretoria.
**RTE**: Rivista di teologia dell'evangelizzazione; Bo.
**RTLit**: Review of Theological Literature; Leiderdorp.
**RTLu**: Rivista Teologica di Lugano; Lugano.
**S**: Slovenian.
**SAA Bulletin**: State Archives of Assyria Bulletin; Padova.
**SAAS**: State Archives of Assyria, Studies; Helsinki.
Sacrum Ministerium; R.
Saeculum Christianum; Wsz.
San Juan de la Cruz; Sevilla.
Sapientia Crucis; Anápolis.
**SaThZ**: Salzburger Theologische Zeitschrift; Salzburg.
**SBL.SCSt**: Society of Biblical Literature, Septuagint and Cognate Studies; Atlanta.
**SBSl**: Studia Biblica Slovaca; Svit.
Scriptura; Stellenbosch.
Scriptura(M): Scriptura; Montréal.
**SdT**: Studi di Teologia; R.
**SEAP**: Studi di Egittologia e di Antichità Puniche; Pisa.
Search; Dublin.
**SECA**: Studies on early christian Apocrypha; Lv.
Sedes Sapientiae; Chéméré-le-Roi.
**SeK**: Skrif en Kerk; Pretoria.
Semeia; Atlanta.
Seminarios; M.
Semiotica; Amst.
**Sen.**: Sendros; Costa Rica.
**SetRel**: Sette e Religioni; Bo.
Sewanee Theological Review; Sewanee, TN.
Shofar; West Lafayette, IN.
**SiChSt**: Sino-Christian Studies, Taiwan.
**SIDIC**: Service International de Documentation Judéo-Chrétienne; R.
Silva–Estudios de humanismo y tradición clásica; León.
**SLJTR**: Sri Lanka Journal of Theological Reflection; Pilimatalawa.
**SMEA**: Studi micenei ed egeo-anatolici; R.
**SMEBT**: Serie Monográfica de Estudios Bíblicos y Teológicos de la Universidad Adventista del Plata; Libertador San Martín, Argentina.
Società, La; Verona.
Soleriana; Montevideo.
Sources; FrS.
Spiritual Life; Wsh.
Spiritus(B); Baltimore.
Spiritus; P.
**SRATK**: Studia nad Rodzina, Akademia Teologii Katolickiej; Wsz, 1429-2416.

**STAC**: Studien und Texte zu Antike und Christentum; Tü.
Stauros; Pescara.
**StBob**: Studia Bobolanum; Wsz.
**StEeL**: Studi epigrafici e linguistici; Verona.
St Mark's Review; Canberra.
**StPhiloA**: Studia Philonica Annual; Providence, RI.
**StSp(N)**: Studies in Spirituality; Lv.
Studi Fatti Ricerche; Mi.
Studi sull'Oriente Cristiano; R.
**StWC**: Studies in World Christianity; E.
Sudan & Nubia; L.
Synaxis; Catania.
T: Translator.
**TA**:Tel Aviv; TA.
**TBAC**: The Bible in Ancient Christianity; Lei.
**TC.JBTC**: TC: a journal of biblical textual criticism [http://purl.org/TC].
**TENTS**: Texts and editions for New Testament study; Lei.
**TFE**: Theologische Frauenforschung in Europa; Müns.
**TGr.T**: Tesi Gregoriana, Serie Teologia; R.
**TEuph**: Transeuphratène; P.
Themelios; L.
Theoforum; Ottawa.
Theologia Viatorum; Potenza.
Théologiques; Montréal.
Theologisches; Siegburg.
**ThEv(VS)**: Théologie évangélique; Vaux-sur-Seine.
**ThLi**: Theology & Life; Hong Kong.
Theotokos; R.
**ThirdM**: Third Millennium: Pune, India.
**T&K**: Texte und Kontexte; Stu.
**TKNT**: Theologischer Kommentar zum Neuen Testament; Stu.
**TMA**: The Merton Annual; Shf.
**TrinJ**: Trinity Journal; Deerfield, IL.
Una Voce-Korrespondenz; Köln.
**VeE**: Verbum et Ecclesia; Pretoria.
**VeVi**: Verbum Vitae; Kielce. **P.**
Viator; Turnhout.
Vie Chrétienne; P.
Vie, La: des communautés religieuses; Montréal.
**Vivar(C)**: Vivarium; Catanzaro.
**Vivar(L)**: Vivarium; Lei.
**VivH**: Vivens Homo; F.
**VO**: Vicino Oriente; R.
Volto dei volti, Il; R.
Vox Patrum; Lublin.
**VoxScr**: Vox Scripturae; São Paulo.
**WAS**: Wiener alttestamentliche Studien; Fra.
**WaW**: Word and World; St. Paul, Minn.
Way, The; L.
**WBC**: Word Biblical Commentary; Waco.
**WGRW**: Writings from the Greek and Roman World; Atlanta.
**WUB**: Welt und Umwelt der Bibel; Stu.
**YESW**: Yearbook of the European Society of Women in Theological Research; Lv.
**ZAC**: Zeitschrift für antikes Christentum; B.
**ZAR**: Zeitschrift für altorientalische und biblische Rechtsgeschichte; Wsb.
Zeitzeichen; Stu.
**ZNT**: Zeitschrift für Neues Testament; Tü.
**ZNTG**: Zeitschrift für neuere Theologiegeschichte; B.

# I. Bibliographica

## A1 Opera collecta .1 **Festschriften**, memorials

1 AEJMELAEUS, Lars J.T.: Lux humana, lux aeterna: essays on biblical and related themes in honor of Lars Aejmelaeus. [E]**Mustakallio, Antti**, *al.*: SESJ 89: Gö 2005, Vandenhoeck & R. x; 555 pp. 3-525-53606-2.

2 ALONSO SCHÖKEL, Luis: Palabra, prodigio, poesía: in memoriam P. Luis Alonso Schökel, S.J. [E]**Collado Bertomeu, Vicente**: AnBib 151: 2003 ⇒19,3; 20,4. [R]Cart. 21 (2005) 227-229 (*Alvarez Barredo, M.*).

3 ÅKERSTRÖM-HOUGEN, Gunilla: Kairos: Studies in art history and literature in honour of professor Gunilla Åkerström-Hougen. [E]**Åström, Paul; Piltz, Elisabeth**: Studies in Mediterranean Archaeology and Literature, Pocket-book 147: Jonsered 1998, Åströms 188 pp. 91-7081-1806.

4 BAILEY, Donald; JOHNS, Catherine: Image, craft and the classical world: essays in honour of Donald Bailey and Catherine Johns. [E]**Crummy, Nina** Monographies instrumentum 29: Montagnac 2005, Mergoil 304 pp. 29073-03910.

5 BARTH, Hermann: Von der Anmut des Anstandes: das Buch Jesus Sirach. [E]**Gundlach, Thies; Markschies, Christoph**: Lp 2005, Evangelische 168 pp. €24. 3-374-02336-3.

6 BEKER, Johan Christiaan: Biblical theology. [E]**Ollenburger, Ben C.; Myers, Charles Davison; Kraftchick, Steven John**: 1995 ⇒11/2,16 ... 15,10. [R]ThR 70 (2005) 160-163 (*Reventlow, Henning Graf*).

7 BERGANT, Dianne: The wisdom of creation. [E]**Foley, Edward; Schreiter, Robert**: 2004 ⇒20,9. [R]RBLit (2005)* (*Brown, William; De Wet Oosthuizen, Rudolph*).

8 BERNARD, Charles André: Esperienza e spiritualità: miscellanea in onore del R.P. Charles André Bernard, S.J. [E]**Alphonso, Herbert**: R 2005, E.P.U.G. 413 pp. 88-7839-036-4.

9 BEUTLER, Johannes H.: Israel und seine Heilstraditionen im Johannesevangelium: [E]**Labahn, Michael; Scholtissek, Klaus; Strotmann, Angelika**: 2004 ⇒20,11. [R]ThGl 95 (2005) 495-496 (*Kowalski, Beate*).

10 BOCCALI, Giovanni M.: Domini vestigia sequi: [E]**Vaiani, Cesare**: Studi e Ricerche 15: 2003 ⇒19,9. [R]AFH 98 (2005) 849-850 (*Guidi, Remo L.*); CFr 75 (2005) 362-364 (*Maranesi, Pietro*).

11 BORSE, Udo: Studien zur Entstehung und Auslegung des Neuen Testaments. [E]**Börschel, Regina; Fischer, Wolfgang; Helfmeyer, Franz-Josef**: SBAB 21: 1996 ⇒12,9. [R]Bijdr. 66 (2005) 114 (*Koet, Bart J.*).

12 BOTHMER, Dietrich von: Essays in honor of Dietrich von Bothmer. [E]**Clark, Andrew J.; Gaunt, Jasper**: Allard Pierson 14: 2002 ⇒19,14. [R]AJA 109 (2005) 108-110 (*Barringer, Judith M.*).

13 BOVON, François: Early christian voices: in texts, traditions, and symbols. [E]**Warren, David H.; Brock, Graham; Pao, David W.** : BiblInterp 66: 2003 ⇒19,15. [R]CBQ 67 (2005) 386-388 (*Kloppenborg, John S.*); NT 47 (2005) 301-304 (*Foster, Paul*); RBLit (2005)* (*Williams, H.H.*).

14 BÖCHER, Otto: Studien zur Johannesoffenbarung und ihrer Auslegung: Festschrift für Otto Böcher zum 70. Geburtstag. [E]**Horn, Friedrich W.; Wolter, Michael**: Neuk 2005, Neuk xi; 460 pp. €35. 3-7887-2093-X.

15 BROWN, Raymond E.: Life in abundance: studies of John's gospel in tribute to Raymond E. Brown. [E]**Donahue, John R.**: ColMn 2005, Liturgical xiv; 313 pp. $30. 0-8146-3011-1. Bibl. Brown 259-289. [R]America 193/9 (2005) 25-26 (*Harrington, D.J.*).

16 BRUEGGEMANN, Walter; COUSAR, Charles B.: Shaking heaven and earth: essays in honor of Walter Brueggemann and Charles B. Cousar. [E]**Yoder, Christine R.**, *al.*: LVL 2005, Westminster xi; 170 pp. $30. 0664227775.

17 BURNEY, Charles: A view from the highlands: archaeological studies in honour of Charles Burney. [E]**Sagona, Antonio**: ANESt.S 12: 2004 ⇒20, 14. [R]Paléorient 31/2 (2005) 173-177 (*Meyer, Jan-Waalke*).

18 BÜMLEIN, Klaus: Gott im Wort—Gott im Bild: Bilderlosigkeit als Bedingung des Monotheismus?. [E]**Wagner, Andreas; Hörner, Volker; Geisthardt, Günter**: Neuk 2005, Neuk xii; 212 pp. 3-7887-2111-1.

19 CAMPBELL, Antony F.: Seeing signals, reading signs: the art of exegesis. [E]**O'Brien, Mark A.; Wallace, Howard N.**: JSOT.S 415: 2004 ⇒20,15. [R]RBLit (2005)* (*Christian, Mark*).

20 CAMPBELL, Edward F.: Realia Dei: essays in archaeology and biblical interpretation. [E]**Williams, Prescott H.; Hiebert, Theodore**: 1999 ⇒15, 15; 17,16. [R]JNES 64 (2005) 292-294 (*Klingbeil, Gerald A.*).

21 CANCIK, Hubert; CANCIK-LINDEMAIER, Hildegard: 'Επ τομή τῆς οἰκουμένης: Studien zur römischen Religion in Antike und Neuzeit. [E]**Auffarth, Christoph; Rüpke, Jörg**: 2002 ⇒18,12. [R]SCI 24 (2005) 209-211 (*Klein, Richard*).

22 CAQUOT, André: La bible et l'héritage d'Ougarit: mélanges bibliques et orientaux en hommage posthume à Monsieur André Caquot. [E]**Michaud, Jean-Paul**: Proche-Orient et littérature ougaritique: Sherbrooke 2005, G.G.C. x; 244 pp. CAD30. 2-89444-201-7. [R]Syria 82 (2005) 352-353 (*Briquel-Chatonnet, Françoise*).

23 CARR, Wesley: The character of wisdom: essays in honour of Wesley Carr. [E]**Percy, Martyn; Lowe, Stephen**: 2004 ⇒20,17. [R]RRT 12/1 (2005) 113-116 (*Platten, Stephen*).

24 CATHCART, Kevin James: Biblical and Near Eastern essays: studies in honour of Kevin J. Cathcart. [E]**McCarthy, Carmel; Healey, John F.**: JSOT.S 375: 2004 ⇒20,19. [R]RRT 12 (2005) 501-504 (*Bury, Benjamin*).

25 CLINES, David J.A.: Reading from right to left: essays on the Hebrew Bible. [E]**Williamson, Hugh G.M.; Exum, J. Cheryl**: JSOT.S 373: 2003 ⇒19,21. [R]HeyJ 46 (2005) 209-210 (*Briggs, Richard S.*); BiblInterp 13 (2005) 423-426 (*MacDonald, Nathan*).

26 COHEN, David: Mélanges David Cohen, études sur le langage, les langues, les dialectes, les littératures. [E]**Lentin, Jérôme; Lonnet, Antoine**: 2003 ⇒19,22; 20,21. [R]OLZ 100 (2005) 103-107 (*Oelsner, J.*).

27 CONRAD, Joachim: Das Alte Testament—ein Geschichtsbuch?!: Geschichtsschreibung oder Geschichtsüberlieferung im antiken Israel. [E]**Becker, Uwe; Van Oorschot, Jürgen**: ABIG 17: Lp 2005, Evangelische 240 pp. €49.40. 3-374-02288-X. Joachim Conrad zum 70. Geburtstag.

28 CROSS, Frank Moore, Jr.: Frank Moore Cross volume. [E]**Levine, Baruch A.**: ErIs 26: 1999 ⇒15,20...18,19. [R]JNES 64 (2005) 196-199 (*Pardee, Dennis*).

29 CUNCHILLOS, Jesús-Luis: De la tablilla a la inteligencia artificial. 2003 ⇒19,27. [R]RA 99 (2005) 187-188 (*Charpin, Dominique*).

30 DAN, Joseph: Creation and re-creation in Jewish thought: Festschrift in honor of Joseph Dan on the occasion of his seventieth birthday. [E]**Elior, Rachel; Schäfer, Peter**: Tü 2005, Mohr S. vii; 415 (Eng) + v; 264 (Heb) pp. €199. 3-16-1487-141.

31 DANKER, Frederick William: Biblical Greek language and lexicography. [E]**Taylor, Bernard**, *al.*: 2004 ⇒20,26. [R]ThR 70 (2005) 132-133 (*Du Toit, David S.*); Neotest. 39 (2005) 461-464 (*Stander, H.F.*); TJT

21 (2005) 278-280 (*Baker, Murray*); RBLit 7 (2005) 513-516 (*Litwak, Kenneth*).

32 DAVID, Yona: Studies in Hebrew literature of the Middle Ages and Renaissance. [E]**Rosen, T.; Holtzman. A.**: Te'uda 19: 2002 ⇒18,22. [R]BiOr 62 (2005) 585-589 (*Schippers, Arie*).

33 DE VRIES, Simon John: God's word for our world. [E]**Ellens, J. Harold; Ellens, Deborah L.**: JSOT.S 388-389: 2004 ⇒20,28. [R]RBLit (2005)* (*Klein, Ralph*).

34 DENAUX, Adelbert: Luke and his readers: Festschrift A. Denaux. [E]**Bieringer, Reimund; Van Belle, Gilbert; Verheyden, Joseph**: BEThL 182: Lv 2005, Peeters xxviii; 470 pp. 90-429-1561-7.

35 DI LELLA, Alexander A.: Intertextual studies in Ben Sira and Tobit: essays in honor of Alexander A. Di Lella. [E]**Corley, Jeremy; Skemp, Vincent**: CBQ.MS 38: Wsh 2005, Cath. Biblical Assoc. of America xvi; 319 pp. $25. 0-915170-37-X. [R]RBLit (2005)* (*Legrand, Thierry*).

36 DIAKONOFF, Igor M.: Memoriae Igor M. Diakonoff. [E]**Kogan, Leonid; Loesov, S.; Tishchenko, S.**: B&B 2; Orientalia et classica 8: WL 2005, Eisenbrauns xii; 792 pp. 978-1-57506-123-8.

37 DION, Paul E.: The world of the Aramaeans. [E]**Daviau, Michèle; Wevers, John William; Weigl, Michael**: JSOT.S 324-326: 2001 ⇒17,25... 19,32. [R]HeyJ 46 (2005) 214-216 (*McNamara, Martin*).

38 **Dunn, James D.G.**: The Holy Spirit and christian origins. [E]**Longenecker, Bruce W.; Stanton, Graham N.; Barton, Stephen C.**: 2004 ⇒20,33. [R]SNTU 30 (2005) 268-269 (*Giesen, Heinz*); RBLit (2005)* (*Pahl, Michael; Sweeney, James*).

39 ESSE, Douglas L.: Studies in the archaeology of Israel and neighboring lands. [E]**Wolff, Samuel R.**: SAOC 59; ASOR Books 5: 2001 ⇒17,28. [R]IEJ 55 (2005) 122-125 (*Tadmor, Miriam*).

40 FINET, André: Si un homme...: textes offerts en hommage à André Finet. [E]**Talon, Philippe; Van der Stede, Véronique**: Subartu 16: Turnhout 2005, Brepols iii; 174 pp. 2-503-51878-8.

41 FIORENZA, Elisabeth Schüssler: On the cutting edge: the study of women in biblical worlds. [E]**Schaberg, Jane; Balch, Alice; Fuchs, Esther**: 2003 ⇒19,37; 20,37. [R]RRT 12 (2005) 367-369 (*Guest, Deryn*) RBLit (2005)* (*Gelardini, Gabriella*);

42 Toward a new heaven and a new earth. [E]**Segovia, Fernando F.**: 2003 ⇒19,38. [R]NewTR 18/2 (2005) 88-89 (*Bergant, Dianne*).

43 FOX, Michael Vass: Seeking out the wisdom of the ancients: essays offered to honor Michael V. Fox on the occasion of his sixty-fifth birthday. [E]**Friebel, Kelvin G.; Magary, Dennis R.; Troxel, Ronald**: WL 2005, Eisenbrauns xxviii; 507 pp. $59.50. 1-57506-105-8. Bibl. Fox xiii-xxiv.

44 GARCÍA-MORENO, Antonio: Signum et testimonium. [E]**Chapa, Juan**: 2003 ⇒19,47; 20,46. [R]RivBib 53 (2005) 95-100 (*Tábet, Michelangelo*).

45 GAWLIKOWSKI, Michal: Aux pays d'Allat: mélanges offerts à Michal Gawlikowski. [E]**Bielinski, Piotr; Stepniowski, Franciszek M.**: Wsz 2005, Instytut Archeologii xx; 347pp. 83-87496-22-7. Bibl. Gawlikowski xi-xix.

46 GENEST, Olivette: 'Christ est mort pour nous': études sémiotiques, féministes et sotériologiques en l'honneur d'Olivette Genest. [E]**Gignac, Alain; Fortin, Anne**: Montréal 2005, Médiaspaul 549 pp. 2-89420-632-1.

47 GHIBERTI, Giuseppe: "Il vostro frutto rimanga" (Gv 16,16): miscellanea per il LXX compleanno di Giuseppe Ghiberti. [E]**Passoni Dell'Acqua, Anna**: RivBib.S 46: Bo 2005, EDB 395 pp. 88-10-30234-6. Bibl. Ghiberti 11-21.

48 GILL, Athol: Prophecy and passion: essays in honour of Athol Gill. Adelaide 2002, Australian Theological Forum xix; 424 pp. $30. [R]RBLit (2005)* (*Stott, Katherine*).

49 GOPHNA, Ram: In quest of ancient settlements and landscapes. [E]**Van den Brink, Edwin C.M.; Yannai, Eli**: 2002 ⇒18,49; 20,49. [R]ArOr 73 (2005) 378-381 (*Vlčková, Petra*).

50 GREER, Rowan A.: Reading in christian communities: essays on interpretation in the early church. [E]**Bobertz, Charles A.; Brakke, David**: Christianity and Judaism in Antiquity 14: 2002 ⇒18,51; 19,51. [R]ChH 75 (2005) 170-172 (*Chin, Catherine M.*); HeyJ 46 (2005) 230-231 (*McNamara, Martin*).

51 GROS, Pierre: Théorie et pratique de l'architecture romaine: la norme et l'expérimentation: études offertes à Pierre Gros. [E]**Lafon, Xavier; Sauron, Gilles**: Aix-en-Provence 2005, Publications de l'Université de Provence 342 pp. 2-85399-599-2.

52 GROTTANELLI, Cristiano: Il saggio Ahiqar: fortuna e trasformazioni di uno scritto sapienziale: il testo più antico e le sue versioni. [E]**Contini, Riccardo**: StBi 148: Brescia 2005, Paideia 325 pp. €29.50. 88-394-07-09-X. Bibl. ahiqariana 290-325.

53 GÜTERBOCK, Hans Gustav: Recent developments in Hittite archaeology and history. [E]**Yener, K. Aslihan; Hoffner, Harry Angier**: 2002 ⇒18, 54. [R]OLZ 100 (2005) 162-165 (*Hazenbos, Joost*); BASOR 337 (2005) 95-97 (*Collins, Billie Jean*); RA 99 (2005) 177-178 (*Mouton, A.*).

54 HAAS, Volkert: Kulturgeschichten: altorientalistische Studien. [E]**Richter, Thomas; Prechel, Doris; Klinger, Jörg**: 2001 ⇒17,39. [R]BiOr 62 (2005) 303-307 (*Hutter, Manfred*).

55 HAIKAL, Fayza: Hommages à Fayza Haikal. [E]**Grimal, Nicolas-Christophe; Kamel, Amr; May-Sheikholeslami, Cynthia**: BEt 138: 2003 ⇒19,54. [R]BiOr 62 (2005) 215-219 (*Kockelmann, H.*).

56 HANSEN, Donald P.: Leaving no stones unturned: essays on the ancient Near East and Egypt. [E]**Ehrenberg, Erica**: 2002 ⇒18,58; 20,54. [R]BiOr 62 (2005) 129-131 (*Duistermaat, Kim*); RA 99 (2005) 179-180 (*Amiet, Pierre*).

57 HARRIS, William V.: A tall order: writing the social history of the ancient world: essays in honor of William V. Harris. [E]**Aubert, Jean-Jacques; Várhelyi, Zsuzsanna**: Beiträge zur Altertumskunde 216: Mü 2005, Saur xxiv; 378 pp. €88. 3598-77828-7.

58 HAWTHORNE, Gerald F.: New Testament Greek and exegesis. [E]**Donaldson, Amy M.; Sailors, Timothy B.**: 2003 ⇒19,55; 20,57. [R]BS 162 (2005) 123-127 (*Fantin, Joe*); Neotest. 39 (2005) 194-196 (*Van Rensburg, Fika J.*); BiTr 56 (2005) 59-61 (*Bullard, Roger A.*).

59 HEIM, François: Antiquité tardive et humanisme de TERTULLIEN à BEATUS Rhenanus: mélanges offerts à François Heim à l'occasion de son 70e anniversaire. [E]**Freyburger, Gérard; Hirstein, James; Lehmann, Yves**: Studia humanitatis rhenana: Turnhout 2005, Brepols xiii; 550 pp. 2-503-52061-8.

60 HILHORST, A.: Jerusalem, Alexandria, Rome: studies in ancient cultural interaction. [E]**García Martínez, Florentino; Luttikhuizen, Gerard P.**:

JSJ.S 82: 2003 ⇒19,57. [R]CDios 218 (2005) 252-253 (*Gutiérrez, J.*); RBLit (2005)* (*Noffke, Eric*).

61 HILLERS, Delbert R.: A journey to Palmyra: collected essays to remember Delbert R. Hillers. [E]**Cussini, Eleonora**: Culture and history of the ancient Near East 22: Lei 2005, Brill xxii; 258 pp. €133/$179. 90-04-12418-7. Bibl. 227-247, of Hillers xvii-xxii.

62 HOLTZ, Traugott; WALTER, Nikolaus: Frühjudentum und Neues Testament im Horizont Biblischer Theologie. [E]**Kraus, Wolfgang; Niebuhr, Karl-Wilhelm**: WUNT 162: 2003 ⇒19,60; 20,59. [R]ThG 48 (2005) 234-236 (*Giesen, Heinz*); NT 47 (2005) 409-412 (*Stenschke, Christoph*).

63 HOOGEWOUD, F.J.: Om voor te lezen—miqra: bundel voor F.J. Hoogewoud. [E]**Blok, H.; Deurloo, K.A.**, *al.*: Maastricht 2005, Shaker 197 pp. 90423-02755.

64 HURST, André: κορυφαίῳ ἀνδρί: Mélanges offerts à André Hurst. [E]**Kolde, Antje; Lukinovich, Alessandra; Rey, André-L.**: Recherches et rencontres 22: Genève 2005, Droz 765 pp. FS75. 2600-009-442.

65 HUSS, Werner: Punica—Libyca—Ptolemaica. [E]**Geus, Klaus; Zimmermann, Klaus**: OLA 104: 2001 ⇒17,51... 20,62. [R]AWE 4 (2005) 196-198 (*Sagona, Claudia*).

66 IMMERWAHR, Sara A.: Χαρις. [E]**Chapin, Anne P.**: 2004 ⇒20,63. [R]AJA 109 (2005) 567-568 (*Thomas, Carol G.*); RAr (2005/2) 398-399 (*Bradfer-Burdet, Isabelle*).

67 IRSIGLER, Hubert: "Erforsche mich, Gott, und erkenne mein Herz!": Beiträge zur Syntax, Sprechaktanalyse und Metaphorik im Alten Testament. Schülerfestschrift für Hubert Irsigler zum 60. Geburtstag. [E]**Diller, Carmen; Mulzer, Martin; Ólason , Kristinn**: ATSAT 76: St. Ottilien 2005, EOS-Verl. 212 pp. 3-8306-7222-5. Bibl. Irsigler 207-210.

68 JACOBSEN, Thorkild: Riches hidden in secret places: ancient Near Eastern studies. [E]**Abusch, I. Tzvi**: 2002 ⇒18,62; 19,63. [R]JNES 64 (2005) 71-72 (*Biggs, Robert D.*); OLZ 100 (2005) 49-53 (*Oelsner, J.*).

69 JANSSEN, Jack J.: Deir El-Medina in the third millennium BC. [E]**Demarée, Robert J.; Egberts, Arno**: Egyptologische uitgaven 14: 2000 ⇒16, 56. [R]JESHO 48 (2005) 597-604 (*Müller, Matthias*).

70 JASTROW, Otto: 'Sprich doch mit deinen Knechten aramäisch, wir verstehen es!': 60 Beiträge zur Semitistik. [E]**Arnold, Werner; Bobzin, Hartmut**: 2002 ⇒18,64; 19,64. [R]OLZ 100 (2005) 99-103 (*Oelsner, J.*).

71 JEWETT, Robert: Celebrating Romans: template for Pauline theology. [E]**McGinn, Sheila E.**: 2004 ⇒20,66. [R]RBLit (2005)* (*Fogg, Julia*).

72 JOHANNES PAULUS II: Shepherding: essays in honor of Pope John Paul II. [E]**Vadakumpadan, Paul; Varickasseril, José**: Shillong 2005, Vendrame 456 pp. 81-85408-00-33.

73 JUEL, Donald Harrisville: The ending of Mark and the ends of God: essays in memory of Donald Harrisville Juel. [E]**Gaventa, Beverly R.; Miller, Patrick D.**: LVL 2005, Westminster xii; 184 pp. $25. 0-664-22739-2. [R]RBLit (2005)* (*Iverson, Kelly; Kealy, Sean; Nicklas, Tobias*).

74 JUNCO Garza, Carlos: Palabra no encadenada y pro-vocativa: miscelánea bíblica en honor de Carlos Junco Garza. [E]**Landgrave Gándara, Daniel R.**: Estudios Bíblicos Mexicanos 4: México 2005, Univ. Pont. de México 541 pp. 968-5448-264.

75 JÜNGEL, Eberhard: Denkwürdiges Geheimnis: Beiträge zur Gotteslehre: Festschrift für Eberhard Jüngel zum 70. Geburtstag. [E]**Dalferth, Ingolf U.; Fischer, Johannes; Grosshans, Hans-Peter**: 2004 ⇒20,68. [R]ThGl 95 (2005) 503-504 (*Fuchs, Gotthard*).

76 KIENAST, Burkhart: Festschrift für Burkhart Kienast: zu seinem 70. Geburtstage dargebracht von Freunden, Schülern und Kollegen. [E]**Selz, Gebhard J.**: AOAT 274: 2003 ⇒19,68. [R]AfO 51 (2005-2006) 340-343 (*Charvát, Petr*).

77 KLAIBER, Walter: Bibel—Kirche—Ökumene: Festschrift für Walter Klaiber zum 65. Geburtstag. emk Studien 7: Stu 2005, Medienwerk der Evangelisch-methodistischen Kirche 302 pp. 3-89725-087-X.

78 KLAPPERT, Bertold: Momente der Begegnung: Impulse für das christlich-jüdische Gespräch: Bertold Klappert zum 65. Geburtstag. [E]**Haarmann, Michael; Lüpke, Johannes von; Menn, Antje**: 2004 ⇒20,74. [R]FrRu 12 (2005) 130-131 (*Hoffmann, Klaus*).

79 KLEIN, Jacob: 'An experienced scribe who neglects nothing': ancient Near Eastern studies in honor of Jacob Klein. [E]**Sefati, Yitschak**, *al*: CDL 2005, Bethesda, MD xxvi; 771 pp. 1-883053-838. al.

80 KLEIN, Ralph W.: The Chronicler as theologian. [E]**Graham, M. Patrick; McKenzie, Steven L.; Knoppers, Gary N.**: JSOT.S 371: 2003 ⇒19, 69; 20,75. [R]CBQ 67 (2005) 371-372 (*Van Seters, John*); HebStud 46 (2005) 437-440 (*Klingbeil, Gerald A.*).

81 KNIERIM, Rolf: Problems in biblical theology. [E]**Sun, Henry T.C.; Eades, Keith L.**: 1997 ⇒13,48... 16,62. [R]ThR 70 (2005) 30-34 (*Reventlow, Henning Graf*).

82 KUGEL, James L.: The idea of biblical interpretation. [E]**Najman, Hindy; Newman, Judith Hood**: JSJ.S 83: 2004 ⇒20,78. [R]HebStud 46 (2005) 390-392 (*Kaminsky, Joel*); RBLit (2005)* (*Nicklas, Tobias*).

83 KYSAR, Robert: Word, theology, and community in John. [E]**Painter, John; Culpepper, R. Alan; Segovia, Fernando F.**: 2002 ⇒18,70; 20, 80. [R]RBLit 7 (2005) 338-341 (*Hunt, Steven A.*).

84 LAMBRECHT, Jan: Resurrection in the New Testament. [E]**Bieringer, Reimund; Koperski, Veronica; Lataire, Bianca**: BEThL 165: 2002 ⇒18, 72... 20,81. [R]NT 47 (2005) 75-77 (*Stenschke, Christoph*).

85 LARSON, Gerald James: Theory and practice of yoga: essays in honour of Gerald James Larson. [E]**Jacobsen, Knut A.**: SHR 110: Lei 2005, Brill ix; 478 pp. 90-04-14757-8. Bibl. Larson 449-464.

86 LASH, Nicholas: Fields of faith: theology and religious studies for the twenty-first century. [E]**Ford, David F.; Quash, Ben; Soskice, Janet**: C 2005, CUP xvii; 230 pp. £45/$75. 0-521-84737-0.

87 LAUB, Franz: Was die Bibel mir erzählt: aktuelle exegetische und religionsdidaktische Streiflichter auf ausgewählte Bibeltexte: Festschrift für Prof. Dr. Franz Laub. [E]**Stettberger, Herbert**: Bibel—Schule—Leben 6: Mü 2005, LIT 210 pp. 3-8258-8694-8.

88 LODER, James E., Jr.: Redemptive transformation in practical theology. [E]**Wright, Dana R.; Kuentzel, John D.**: 2004 ⇒20,88. [R]TJT 21 (2005) 314-315 (*Redcliffe, Gary L.*).

89 LOFFREDA, Stanislao: One land—many cultures: archaeological studies. [E]**Bottini, Giovanni C.; Di Segni, Leah; Chrupcala, L. Daniel**: SBF. CMa 41: 2003 ⇒19,76. [R]BiOr 62 (2005) 146-147 (*Geus, C.H.J. de*).

90 LÖNING, Karl: Die Weisheit—Ursprünge und Rezeption. [E]**Faßnacht, Martin; Leinhäupl-Wilke, Andreas; Lücking, Stefan**: NTA 44:

2003 ⇒19,78. RThLZ 130 (2005) 921 (*Niebuhr, Karl-Wilhelm*); ThRv 101 (2005) 473-475 (*Blum, Matthias*).

91 LUKE, K.: 'Going to the roots': a multi-disciplinary study, Festschrift in honour of Dr. K. Luke, o.f.m.cap. E**Puthenpurackal, Johnson J.**: Bangalore 2005, Asian Trading 361 pp. Rs220. RITS 42 (2005) 337-338 (*Legrand, Lucien*).

92 LUST, Johan: Interpreting translation: studies on the LXX and Ezekiel in honour of Johan Lust. E**García Martínez, Florentino; Vervenne, Marc**: BEThL 192: Lv 2005, Peeters xlii; 512 pp. €75. 90-429-1689-3. Collab. *Brian Doyle*.

93 LUTTIKHUIZEN, Gerard P.: The wisdom of Egypt: Jewish, early christian, and gnostic essays in honour of Gerard P. Luttikhuizen. E**Hilhorst, Anthony; Van Kooten, George H.**: AGJU 59: Lei 2005, Brill xii; 558 pp. €117/$158. 90-04-14425-0. Bibl. Luttikhuizen 537-543. RRBLit (2005)* (*Nicklas, Tobias*).

94 LUZ, Ulrich: Die prägende Kraft der Texte: Hermeneutik und Wirkungsgeschichte des Neuen Testaments: ein Symposium zu Ehren von Ulrich Luz. E**Mayordomo, Moisés**: SBS 199: Stu 2005, Katholisches Bibelwerk 177 pp. €25.90. 3-460-04991-X. RJETh 19 (2005) 255-259 (*Buchegger, Jürg*).

95 MALAISE, Michel: La langue dans tous ses états: Michel Malaise in honorem. E**Cannuyer, Christian**: Acta Orientalia Belgica 18: Bru 2005, Belgian Society of Oriental Studies xxviii; 356 pp. Bibl. Malaise xii-xxiv.

96 MARBÖCK, Johannes: Auf den Spuren der schriftgelehrten Weisen. E**Fischer, Irmtraud; Rapp, Ursula; Schiller, Johannes**: BZAW 331: 2003 ⇒19,81. RCBQ 67 (2005) 545-546 (*Crenshaw, James L.*); RivBib 53 (2005) 222-227 (*Milazzo, Maisa*); OLZ 100 (2005) 512-515 (*Delkurt, Holger*); ThRv 101 (2005) 476-477 (*Scoralick, Ruth*); BiOr 62 (2005) 576-578 (*Van Peursen, W.T.*); Gr. 86 (2005) 673-674 (*Calduch-Benages, Nuria*).

97 MAYER, Marc; STYLOW, Armin U.; VELÁZQUEZ SORIANO, Isabel: La cultura latina en la cueva negra: en agradecimiento y homenaje a los profs. A. Stylow, M. Mayer, I. Velázquez y a todos los colaboradores. E**González Blanco, Antonino; Matilla Séiquer, Gonzalo**: Antigüedad y cristianismo 20: Murcia 2003, Universidad de Murcia 643 pp.

98 MCBRIDE, Samuel Dean: Constituting the community: studies on the polity of ancient Israel in honor of S. Dean McBride Jr. E**Strong, John T.; Tuell, Steven S.**: WL 2005, Eisenbrauns xi, 331 pp. $49.50. 1-575-06-078-7.

99 MCCANN, Anna M.: Terra marique: studies in art history and marine archaeology in honor of Anna Marguerite McCann. E**Pollini, John**: Oxf 2005, Oxbow xii; 266 pp. 1-84217-148-8.

100 MERRILL, Eugene: Giving the sense: understanding and using Old Testament historical texts. E**Howard, David M., Jr.; Grisanti, Michael A.**: 2003 ⇒19,87. RFaith & Mission 22/3 (2005) 108-109 (*Bush, L. Russ, III*).

101 MICHEL, Otto: 'Ich bin ein Hebräer'. E**Lindner, Helgo**: 2003 ⇒19,89; 20,90. RThLZ 130 (2005) 747-749 (*Neuer, Werner*).

102 MILLARD, Alan Ralph: Writing and ancient Near Eastern society: papers in honour of Alan R. Millard. E**Mee, Christopher; Bienkowski, Piotr A.; Slater, Elizabeth**: JSOT.S 426; Library of Hebrew Bible, Old Testament Studies 426: NY 2005, Clark 319 pp. $135.

103 MOKROSCH, Reinhold: Friede als Gabe und Aufgabe: Beiträge zur theologischen Friedensforschung. [E]**Ammermann, Norbert; Ego, Beate; Merkel, Helmut**: Gö 2005, Vandenhoeck & R. 291 pp. €34.90. 3-89971-211-0.

104 MOLONEY, Francis J.: Transcending boundaries: contemporary reading of the New Testament: essays in honor of Francis J. Moloney. [E]**Chennattu, Rekha M.; Coloe, Mary L.**: BSRel 187: R 2005, LAS 320 pp. 88-213-0565-1. Bibl. Moloney (1976-2004) 19-35.

105 MONAT, Pierre: Autour de LACTANCE: hommages à Pierre Monat. [E]**Guillaumin, J.-Y.; Ratti, S.**: 2003 ⇒19,96. [R]REAug 51 (2005) 198-199 (*Colot, Blandine*).

106 MOOREY, Peter Roger Stuart: Culture through objects: ancient Near Eastern studies. [E]**Potts, Timothy C.; Roaf, Michael; Stein, Diana L.**: 2003 ⇒19,98; 20,93. [R]BiOr 62 (2005) 596-601 (*Meyer, Jan-Waalke*).

107 MORAN, William L.: Biblical and oriental essays in memory of William L. Moran. [E]**Gianto, Agustinus**: BibOr 48: R 2005, E.P.I.B. ix; 203 pp. €20. 88-7653-351-6. Bibl. 193-203. [R]BiOr 62 (2005) 570-576 (*Gzella, Holger*).

108 MOUSSAIEFF, Shlomo: Shlomo, studies in epigraphy, iconography, history and archaeology. [E]**Deutsch, Robert**: 2003 ⇒19,100; 20,95. [R]WO 35 (2005) 239-240 (*Röllig, Wolfgang*).

109 MÜLLER, Karlheinz: Paradigmen auf dem Prüfstand: Exegese wider den Strich. [E]**Ebner, Martin; Heininger, Bernhard**: NTA 47: 2004 ⇒ 20,98. [R]ThRv 101 (2005) 36-38 (*Kowalski, Beate*); ThLZ 130 (2005) 922 (*Niebuhr, Karl-Wilhelm*); RBLit (2005)* (*Nicklas, Tobias*).

110 NICHOLSON, Ernest Wilson: Covenant as context: essays in honour of E.W. Nicholson. [E]**Mayes, A.D.H.; Salters, Robert B.**: 2003 ⇒19, 104; 20,100. [R]ZAR 11 (2005) 361-369 (*Otto, Eckart*); IBSt 26 (2005) 194-197 (*Alexander, T.D.*); RBLit (2005)* (*Stulman, Louis*).

111 NICOLE, Roger: The glory of the atonement: biblical, historical and practical perspectives. [E]**Hill, E. Charles; Frank, A. James, III**: 2004 ⇒20,101. [R]MissTod 7 (2005) 379-380 (*Thaikadan, Joseph*).

112 NIEDERWIMMER, Kurt: Theologie in der Spätzeit des Neuen Testaments: Vorträge auf dem Symposion zum 75. Geburtstag von Kurt Niederwimmer. [E]**Pratscher, Wilhelm; Öhler, Markus**: Gutachten und Studien 2: W 2005, Evangelisch-Theologische Fakultät 115 pp.

113 NORIN, Stig I.L.: Nomen et nomina: festskrift till Stig Norin. U 2005, Uppsala exegetiska sällskap 387 pp.

114 OATES, David: Of pots and plans: papers on the archaeology and history of Mesopotamia and Syria. [E]**Werr, Lamia Al-Gailani**: 2002 ⇒ 19,108. [R]BiOr 62 (2005) 129-132 (*Duistermaat, Kim*).

115 OLLEY, John: Text & task: scripture & mission. [E]**Parsons, Michael**: Waynesboro, GA 2005, Paternoster 243 pp. $23 [BiTod 45,327—Dianne Bergant].

116 OLTHUIS, James H.: The hermeneutics of charity: interpretation, selfhood, and postmodern faith. [E]**Smith, James K.A.; Venema, Henry I.**: 2004 ⇒20,104. [R]RRT 12 (2005) 512-516 (*Daniel-Smith, Christopher*).

117 OOSTHUIZEN, G.C.: Study of religion in southern Africa: essays in honour of G.C. Oosthuizen. [E]**Kumar, P. Pratap; Smit, Johannes A.**: SHR: Lei 2005, Brill vi; 291 pp. 90-04-14384-X.

118 PACHECO, Maria Cândida: Itinéraires de la raison: études de philosophie médiévale offertes à Maria Cândida Pacheco. [E]**Meirinhos, J.F.**:

Textes et études du moyen âge 32: LvN 2005, Fédération Internationale des Instituts d'Études Médiévales xxv; 444 pp. 2503-51987-3.

119 PATHRAPANKAL, Joseph: Indian interpretation of the bible. [E]**Thottakara, Augustine**: 2000 ⇒16,85; 17,84. [R]VJTR 69 (2005) 627-629 (*Meagher, P.M.*).

120 PETTINATO, Giovanni: Von Sumer nach Ebla und zurück. [E]**Waetzoldt, Harmut**: Heidelberger Studien zum Alten Orient 9: 2004 ⇒20,106. [R]BiOr 62 (2005) 287-290 (*Stol, M.*).

121 PHILIPPART, Guy: Scribere sanctorum gesta: recueil d'études d'hagiographie médiévale offert à Guy Philippart. [E]**Renard, Etienne**, *al.*: Hagiologia 3: Turnhout 2005, Brepols 781 pp. 2-503-51256-9.

122 PIERIS, Aloysius: Encounters with the word. [E]**Crusz, Robert; Fernando, Marshal; Tilakaratna, Asanga**: 2004 ⇒20,107. [R]EAPR 42 (2005) 402-414 (*Mees, Luc*).

123 PINGREE, David: Studies in the history of the exact sciences. [E]**Burnett, Charles**, *al.*: IPTS 54: 2004 ⇒20,110. [R]WZKM 95 (2005) 407-428 (*Brown, David*).

124 PRINZING, L.: Zwischen Polis, Provinz und Peripherie: Beiträge zur byzantinischen Geschichte und Kultur. [E]**Hoffmann, L.M.**: Wsb 2005, Harrassowitz xix; 968 pp. 34470-51701. Mitarbeit *A. Monchizadeh*.

125 PUZA, Richard: Kulturgutschutz und Kirche, Bibel und Kirchenrecht. [E]**Weiss, Andreas; Ihli, Stefan**: Adnotationes in Ius Canonicum 31: 2004 ⇒20,116. [R]ITS 42 (2005) 217-219 (*Kurianal, James*).

126 REDFORD, Donald Bruce: Egypt, Israel, and the ancient Mediterranean world. [E]**Knoppers, Gary N.; Hirsch, Antoine**: PÄ 20: 2004 ⇒20, 118. [R]RBLit (2005)* (*Branch, Robin G.*).

127 RIES, Julien: La figure du prêtre dans les grandes traditions religieuses: actes du colloque organisé en hommage à M. l'abbé Julien Ries.... [E]**Marchetti, P.; Motte, A.**: Collection d'études classiques 20: Lv 2005, Peeters vi; 229 pp. 90429-1596X.

128 ROBERTS, J.J.M.: David and Zion: biblical studies. [E]**Batto, Bernard F.; Roberts, Kathryn L.**: 2004 ⇒20,121. [R]CBQ 67 (2005) 363-365 (*Clifford, Richard J.*); RBLit (2005)* (*Heard, Christopher; Hendel, Ronald*).

129 ROBINSON, Gnana: Bible speaks today. [E]**Muthunayagom, D.J.**: 2000 ⇒16,99. [R]VJTR 69 (2005) 626-627 (*Meagher, P.M.*).

130 ROFÉ, Alexander: On the border line: textual meets literary criticism: proceedings of a conference in honor of Alexander Rofé on the occasion of his seventieth birthday. [E]**Talshir, Zipora; Amara, Dalia**: Beer-Sheva Studies 18: Beer Sheva 2005, Ben Gurion Univ. Pr. 270; xx pp. 0334-2255.

131 RUZÉ, Françoise: Le législateur et la loi dans l'antiquité: hommage à Françoise Ruzé: actes du colloque de Caen, mai 2003. [E]**Sineux, Pierre**: Caen 2005, Presses universitaires de Caen 262 pp. 28413-32373.

132 SALDARINI, Anthony J.: When Judaism and christianity began. [E]**Avery-Peck, Alan J.; Harrington, Daniel J.; Neusner, Jacob**: 2004 ⇒20, 122. [R]JSJ 36 (2005) 324-326 (*Setzer, Claudia*).

133 SCHENKE, Hans-Martin: For the children, perfect instruction. [E]**Bethge, Hans-Gebhard**: NHS 54: 2002 ⇒18,108; 20,125. [R]ThLZ 130 (2005) 1292-1294 (*Schröter, Jens*).

134 SCHENKER, Adrian: L'écrit et l'esprit: études d'histoire du texte et de théologie biblique en hommage à Adrian Schenker. [E]**Böhler, Dieter;**

**Himbaza, Innocent; Hugo, Philippe**: OBO 214: FrS 2005, Academic xxxi; 472 pp. €84.60. 3-7278-1518-3. Bibl. Schenker xiv-xxxi.

135 SCHMID, Johannes Heinrich: Der Erneuerung von Kirche und Theologie verpflichtet: Freundesgabe für Johannes Heinrich Schmid. [E]**Nanz, Philipp**: Riehen 2005, ArteMedia 430 pp. FS25/€16.

136 SCHMITHALS, Walter: Paulus, die Evangelien und das Urchristentum. [E]**Breytenbach, Cilliers**: AGJU 54: 2004 ⇒20,127. [R]ThLZ 130 (2005) 916-917 (*Müller, Ulrich B.*).

137 SEIDL, Theodor: Vom Ausdruck zum Inhalt, vom Inhalt zum Ausdruck: Beiträge zur Exegese und Wirkungsgeschichte alttestamentlicher Texte: Festschrift der Schülerinnen und Schüler für Theodor Seidl zum 60. Geburtstag. [E]**Häusl, Maria; Volgger, David**: ATSAT 75: St. Ottilien 2005, EOS-Verl. x; 257 pp. 3-8306-7221-7.

138 STANTON, Graham: The written gospel. [E]**Bockmuehl, Markus; Hagner, Donald A.**: C 2005, CUP xxvi; 360 pp. £19/$29. 0-521-54040-2. Bibl. 301-336.

139 STEGEMANN, Ekkehard W.: Kontexte der Schrift, 1: Text: Ethik: Judentum und Christentum: Gesellschaft. [E]**Gelardini, Gabriella**: Stu 2005, Kohlhammer 512 pp. €35. 317-018877-7

STEGEMANN, Wolfgang: Kontexte der Schrift, 2: Kultur, Politik, Religion, Sprache—Text. [E]**Strecker, Christian**: Stu 2005, Kohlhammer 480 pp. €35. 317-0188-836.

140 STEMBERGER, Günter: "The words of a wise man's mouth are gracious" (Qoh 10,12): Festschrift for Günter Stemberger on the occasion of his 65th birthday. [E]**Perani, Mauro**: SJ 32: B 2005, De Gruyter xxxiii; 503 pp. €128/$172.80. 3-11-018849-X. Bibl. Stemberger xix-xxxi.

141 STENDEBACH, Franz Josef: Wohin du auch gehst: Festschrift für Franz Josef Stendebach OMI. [E]**Klosterkamp, Thomas; Lohfink, Norbert**: Stu 2005, Katholisches Bibelwerk 376 pp. 3-460-32867-3.

142 STOCK, Klemens: On his way. [E]**Malina, Artur**: Studia i Materialy 21: 2004 ⇒20,135. [R]CoTh 75/4 (2005) 219-22 (*Chrostowski, Waldemar*).

143 STOLLE, Volker: Gottes Wort in der Zeit: verstehen—verkündigen—verbreiten: Festschrift für Volker Stolle. [E]**Barnbrock, Christoph; Klän, Werner**: Theologie: Forschung und Wissenschaft 12: Müns 2005, Lit iv; 616 pp. 3-8258-7132-0. [R]LuThK 29 (2005) 138-142 (*Rothfuchs, Wilhelm*).

144 STONE, Michael E.: Things revealed: studies in early Jewish and christian literature. [E]**Chazon, Esther G.; Satran, David; Clements, Ruth**: JSJ.S 89: 2004 ⇒20,136. [R]ThLZ 130 (2005) 1294-5 (*Beyerle, Stefan*).

145 TADMOR, Hayim; TADMOR, Miriam: Hayim and Miriam Tadmor volume. [E]**Eph'al, Israel; Ben-Tor, Amnon; Machinist, Peter**: ErIs 27: 2003 ⇒19,140; 20,137. [R]BiOr 62 (2005) 300-303 (*Stol, M.*).

146 TAL, Abraham: Samaritan, Hebrew and Aramaic studies presented to Professor Abraham Tal. [E]**Bar-Asher, M:; Florentin, M.**: J 2005, Bialik xx; 387 (H); xii*; 173* (Eng., Fr.) pp. $32.70. 96534-28845. Bibl. Tal xiii-xx.

147 TANNEHILL, Robert C.: Literary encounters with the reign of God. [E]**Ringe, Sharon H.; Kim, H.C. Paul**: 2004 ⇒20,138. [R]RBLit (2005)* (*Fay, Ron*).

148 THELAMON, Françoise: Dieu(x) et hommes: histoire et iconographie des sociétés païennes et chrétiennes de l'antiquité à nos jours: mélanges en l'honneur de Françoise Thelamon. [E]**Crogiez-Pétrequin, Sylvie**:

Publications des Universités de Rouen et du Havre 379: Caen 2005, CRAHM 686 pp. 2-87775-393X.

149 THOMPSON, William G.: The gospel of Matthew in current study. ^E^**Aune, David E.**: 2001 ⇒17,108... 19,144. ^R^RSR 93 (2005) 91-92 (*Miler, Jean*).

150 THRALL, Margaret: Paul and the Corinthians: studies on a community in conflict. ^E^**Burke, Trevor J.; Elliott, J. Keith**: NT.S 109: 2003 ⇒ 19,145. ^R^ThLZ 130 (2005) 615-617 (*Wolff, Christian*); NT 47 (2005) 184-186 (*Kloha, Jeffrey*).

151 TONIOLO, Ermanno Maria: Fons lucis. ^E^**Barbieri, Rosella; Calabuig Adan, Ignacio; Di Angelo, Ornella**: SPFTM 30: 2004 ⇒20,140. ^R^Mar. 67 (2005) 680-681 (*Di Girolamo, Luca M.*).

152 TOV, Emanuel: Emanuel: studies in Hebrew Bible, Septuagint and Dead Sea scrolls. ^E^**Paul, Shalom M.**: VT.S 94: 2003 ⇒19,146. ^R^JSJ 36 (2005) 364-366 (*García Martínez, Florentino*); DSD 12 (2005) 216-219 (*Davila, J.R.*); JJS 56 (2005) 142-144 (*Salvesen, Alison G.*); ThLZ 130 (2005) 918-919 (*Kreuzer, Siegfried*).

153 TWERSKY, Isadore: Be'erot Yitzhak: studies in memory of Isadore Twersky. ^E^**Harris, J.M.**: CM 2005, Harvard Univ. Center for Jewish Studies x; 453; 93* pp. $55/£35. 06740-18079 [NTAb 50,619].

154 ULLENDORFF, Edward: Semitic studies in honour of Edward Ullendorff. ^E^**Khan, Geoffrey**: SStLL 47: Lei 2005, Brill vi; 367 pp. €149/ $201. 90-04-14834-5.

155 VAN TILBORG, Sjef: One text, a thousand methods: studies in memory of Sjef van Tilborg. ^E^**Counet, Patrick Chatelion; Berges, Ulrich**: BiblInterp 71: Lei 2005, Brill viii; 367 pp. 0-391-04230-0. Bibl. Van Tilborg 357-360. ^R^EThL 81 (2005) 504-506 (*Van Belle, G.*).

156 VANNI, Ugo: Apokalypsis: percorsi nell'Apocalisse in onore di Ugo Vanni. ^E^**Colacrai, Angelo; Bosetti, Elena**: Assisi 2005, Cittadella 879 pp. €65. 88-308-0794-X. Pres. *Carlo M. Martini*; Bibl. Vanni 841-853. ^R^ATG 68 (2005) 299-300 (*Contreras Molina, Francisco*).

157 VIDAL, Marciano: La ética cristiana hoy. ^E^**Rubio, M.; García, V.; Gómez Mier, V.**: 2003 ⇒19,152. ^R^RelCult 51 (2005) 513-518 (*Noriega, Roberto*).

158 VOIGT, Rainer Maria: Studia Semitica et Semitohamitica: Festschrift für Rainer Voigt anläßlich seines 60. Geburtstages am 17. Januar 2004. ^E^**Burtea, Bogdan; Tropper, Josef; Younansardaroud, Helen**: AOAT 317: Müns 2005, Ugarit-Verlag xi; 539 pp. 3-934628-73-7.

159 VYCICHL, Werner: Egyptian and Semito-Hamitic (Afro-Asiatic) studies. ^E^**Takács, Gábor**: SStLL 39: 2004 ⇒20,147. ^R^OLZ 100 (2005) 542-546 (*Oelsner, J.*); WO 35 (2005) 185-188 (*Breyer, Francis*); JSSt 50 (2005) 357-359 (*Lipiński, Edward*); LingAeg 13 (2005) 265-271 (*Peust, Carsten*).

160 WALLIS, Gerhard: Ideales Königtum: Studien zu David und Salomo. ^E^**Lux, Rüdiger**: ABIG 16: Lp 2005, Evangelische 179 pp. €48. 3-374-02273-1 [ThLZ 131,365s—Bernd U. Schipper].

161 WEDDERBURN, Alexander J.M.: Paul, Luke and the Graeco-Roman world. ^E^**Christophersen, Alf**, *al.*: JSNT.S 217: 2002 ⇒18,132; 20, 151. ^R^JThS 56 (2005) 168-170 (*Barrett, C.K.*).

162 WEINFELD, Moshe: Sefer Moshe: the Moshe Weinfeld jubilee volume: studies in the bible and the ancient Near East, Qumran, and post-biblical Judaism. ^E^**Cohen, Chaim; Hurvitz, Avi; Paul, Shalom M.**:

2004 ⇒20,152. [R]CBQ 67 (2005) 365-367 (*Sweeney, Marvin A.*); BiOr 62 (2005) 333-337 (*Achenbach, Reinhard*).

163 WEIPPERT, Manfred: Kein Land für sich allein: Studien zum Kulturkontakt in Kanaan, Israel/Palästina und Ebirnâri. [E]**Hübner, Ulrich; Knauf, Ernst Axel**: OBO 186: 2002 ⇒18,133; 20,153. [R]JNES 64 (2005) 304-305 (*Handy, Lowell K.*).

164 WICKS, Jared: Sapere teologico e unità della fede. [E]**Aparicio Valls, Carmen; Dotolo, Carmelo; Pasquale, Gianluigi**: 2004 ⇒20,154. [R]CFr 75 (2005) 712-713 (*De Armellada, Bernardino*).

165 WILCKE, Claus: Literatur, Politik und Recht in Mesopotamien. [E]**Sallaberger, Walther; Volk, Konrad; Zgoll, Annette**: Orientalia Biblica et Christiana 14: 2003 ⇒19,159; 20,155. [R]OLZ 100 (2005) 36-41 (*Schmidt, Karin S.*); JNES 64 (2005) 315-317 (*Biggs, Robert D.*).

166 WINTER, Bruce W.: The New Testament in its first century setting: essays on context and background. [E]**Clarke, Andrew D.; Williams, Peter J.**: 2004 ⇒20,158. [R]CBQ 67 (2005) 555-556 (*Hagner, Donald A.*); RBLit (2005)* (*Donahoe, Kate; Van der Horst, Pieter*).

167 WIRE, Antoinette C.: Distant voices drawing near. [E]**Hearon, Holly E.**: 2004 ⇒20,159. [R]CBQ 67 (2005) 381-383 (*Blickenstaff, Marianne*).

168 YOUNG, Frances: Wilderness: essays in honour of Frances Young. [E]**Sugirtharajah, R.S.**: JSNT.S 295; Library of NT Studies 295: L 2005, Clark xiv; 209 pp. $124. 0-567-04142-5.

169 YOUNGBLOOD, Ronald F.: The challenge of bible translation: communicating God's word to the world. [E]**Scorgie, Glen G.; Strauss, Mark L.; Voth, Steven M.**: 2003 ⇒19,162; 20,161. [R]BiTr 56 (2005) 63-64 (*Omanson, Roger L.*).

170 ZAUZICH, Karl-Theodor: Res severa verum gaudium. [E]**Hoffmann, F.; Thissen, H.J.**: Studia Demotica 4: 2004 ⇒20,162. [R]APF 51 (2005) 179-186 (*Quack, Joachim Friedrich*).

171 ZENGER, Erich: Das Manna fällt auch heute noch: Beiträge zur Geschichte und Theologie des Alten, Ersten Testaments. [E]**Hossfeld, Frank-L.; Schwienhorst-Schönberger, Ludger**: Herders biblische Studien 44: 2004 ⇒20,163. [R]ThPh 80 (2005) 596-598 (*Hofmann, P.*).

172 ZMIJEWSKI, Josef: "Licht zur Erleuchtung der Heiden und Herrlichkeit für dein Volk Israel": Studien zum lukanischen Doppelwerk. [E]**Müller, Christoph G.**: BBB 151: B 2005, Philo xvii; 361 pp. 3-86572-571-6. Bibl. Zmijewski 357-361.

### A1.2 **Miscellanea** *unius* auctoris

173 **Albertz, Rainer** Geschichte und Theologie: Studien zur Exegese des Alten Testaments und zur Religionsgeschichte Israels. [E]*Kottsieper, Ingo; Wöhrle, Jakob:* BZAW 326: 2003 ⇒19,163; 20,164. [R]RBLit (2005)* (*Oeming, Manfred*).

174 **Alexander, Loveday C.A.** Acts in its ancient literary context: a classicist looks at the Acts of the Apostles. LNTS 298: L 2005, Clark xi; 290 pp. $130. 05670-82091. Bibl. 253-271.

175 **Allison, Dale C.** Resurrecting Jesus: the earliest christian tradition and its interpreters. NY 2005, Clark xi; 404 pp. $35. 0-56702-9107.

176 **Auld, A. Graeme** Samuel at the threshold. 2004 ⇒20,167. [R]ET 117 (2005) 19-21 [Resp. 21-22] (*Williamson, H.G.M.*).

177 **Aune, David E.** Apocalypticism, prophecy and magic in early christianity: collected essays. WUNT 199: Tü 2005, Mohr S. xi; 482 pp. 978-31614-90200.

178 **Baarlink, Heinrich** Verkündigtes Heil: Studien zu den synoptischen Evangelien. WUNT 168: 2004 ⇒20,169. [R]SNTU 30 (2005) 246-247 (*Fuchs, Albert*).

179 **Barbiero, Gianni** Studien zu alttestamentlichen Texten. SBAB 34: 2002 ⇒18,139. [R]ThRv 101 (2005) 295-297 (*Paganini, Simone*).

180 **Barrett, C.K.** On Paul: essays on his life, work and influence in the early church. 2003 ⇒19,165; 20,170. [R]DR 431 (2005) 153-155 (*Brumwell, Anselm*); HeyJ 46 (2005) 363-365 (*Hill, Robert C.*).

181 **Barton, Stephen C.** Life together: family, sexuality and community in the New Testament and today. 2001 ⇒17,121... 19,168. [R]NBl 86 (2005) 121-122 (*Edwards, Adrian*).

182 **Baumbach, Günther** JOSEPHUS—Jesusbewegung—Judentum: gesammelte Aufsätze. ANTZ 9: B 2005, Institut Kirche und Judentum vi; 268 pp. €15. 3-923095-35-X.

183 **Beauchamp, Paul** Pages exégétiques. LeDiv 202: P 2005, Cerf 448 pp. €35. 2-204-07168-4. Préf. d'*Yves Simoens*.

184 **Beckwith, Roger T.** Calendar, chronology and worship: studies in ancient Judaism and early christianity. AGJU 61; AJEC 61: Lei 2005, Brill x; 255 pp. €89/$127. 90-04-14603-2.

185 BENEDICTUS XVI Caminos de Jesucristo. 2004 ⇒20,175. [R]Augustinus 50 (2005) 250 (*Oldfield, J.*);

186 Convocados en el camino de la fe. 2004 ⇒20,176. [R]Augustinus 50 (2005) 251-252 (*Gómez, Enrique*).

187 **Bergmeier, Roland** Das Gesetz im Römerbrief und andere Studien zum Neuen Testament. WUNT 121: 2000 ⇒16,132... 19,171. [R]JThS 56 (2005) 162-164 (*Dunn, James D.G.*).

188 **Berschin, Walter** Mittellateinische Studien. Heid 2005, Mattes 456 pp. €75. 3-930978-75-X.

189 **Bingen, Jean** Pages d'épigraphie grecque, 2: Egypte (1983-2002). Epigraphica Bruxellensia 3: Bru 2005, Epigraphica Bruxellensia xii; 204 pp. €35. 296000-1052. 5 pl.

190 **Blenkinsopp, Joseph** Treasures old and new: essays in the theology of the pentateuch. 2004 ⇒20,178. [R]ThLZ 130 (2005) 1309-1311 (*Schmitt, Hans-Christoph*); RBLit (2005)* (*Dozeman, Thomas B.*).

191 **Boesch Gajano, Sofia** GREGORIO Magno: alle origini del medioevo. Collana Sacro/Santo 8: R 2004, Viella 358 pp. €22. 88-8334-1260.

192 **Bovon, François** Studies in early christianity. WUNT 161: 2003 ⇒19, 175. [R]RB 112 (2005) 444-448 (*Devillers, Luc*); JThS 56 (2005) 607-609 (*Elliott, J.K.*);

193 Studies in early christianity. GR 2005 <2003>, Baker viii; 336 pp. $35. 0-8010-2935-X.

194 **Brooke, George J.** The Dead Sea scrolls and the New Testament. Ph 2005, Fortress xxii; 314 pp. £20. 0-8006-3723-2. Bibl. 298-301. [R]RBLit (2005)* (*Frey, Joerg; Kraus, Thomas*).

195 **Buber, Martin** Écrits sur la bible. [T]*Meur, Diane*: 2003 ⇒19,178. [R]Theoforum 36 (2005) 198-199 (*Vogels, Walter*);

196 Werkausgabe 8: Schriften zu Jugend, Erziehung und Bildung. [E]*Jacobi, Juliane; Mendes-Flohr, Paul; Schäfer, Peter*: Gü 2005, Kaiser 464 pp. 3-579-02684-4.

197 **Cardona Ramírez, Hernán** El grano de mostaza. Medellín 2005, Univ. Pont. Bolivariana 230 pp. 958-696-360-8. Bibl. 217-230.

198 **Ceresko, Anthony R.** Prophets and Proverbs: more studies in Old Testament poetry and biblical religion. 2002 ⇒18,154; 20,188. $^{R}$VJTR 69 (2005) 634-635 (*Meagher, P.M.*).

199 **Clines, David J.A.** The Bible and the modern world. BiSe 51: Shf 2005 <1997>, Sheffield Phoenix 116 pp. £13.50/$19. 1-90504-8165. Bibl.

200 **Collins, John J.** Encounters with biblical theology. Mp 2005, Fortress ix; 243 pp. $22. 0-8006-3780-1.

201 **Crüsemann, Frank** Maßstab: Tora?: Israels Weisung für christliche Ethik. 2003 ⇒19,183; 20,191. $^{R}$ThR 70 (2005) 130-131 (*Krüger, Thomas*);

202 Kanon und Sozialgeschichte: Beiträge zum Alten Testament. 2003 ⇒ 19,182. $^{R}$BiKi 60 (2005) 246-247 (*Hieke, Thomas*).

203 **De Benedetti, P.** La morte di Mosè a altri esempi. Il pellicano rosso 27: Brescia $^{3}$2005 <1971, 1979>, Morcelliana 202 pp. €14. 88-372-2042-1.

204 **Dietrich, Walter** Von David zu den Deuteronomisten: Studien zu den Geschichtsüberlieferungen des Alten Testaments. BWANT 156: 2002 ⇒18,160; 20,194. $^{R}$ThR 70 (2005) 218-230 (*Mathys, Hans-Peter*).

205 **Dubois, Marcel** Jérusalem: dans le temps et l'éternité. P 2005, Parole et S. 130 pp. €16. 28457-32643. $^{R}$EstTrin 39 (2005) 589-590 (*Vázquez Allegue, Jaime*).

206 **Ehrlich, Carl S.** Bibel und Judentum: Beiträge aus dem christlich-jüdischen Gespräch. 2004 ⇒20,197. $^{R}$TJT 21 (2005) 235-37 (*Scott, Ian*).

207 **Epp, Eldon Jay** Perspectives on New Testament textual criticism: collected essays, 1962-2004. NT.S 116: Lei 2005, Brill xl; 849 pp. $238. 90-04-14246-0. Bibl. 803-807.

208 **Fee, Gordon D.** To what end exegesis?: essays textual, exegetical, and theological. 2001 ⇒17,143... 20,198. $^{R}$RBLit 7 (2005) 483-487 (*Given, Mark D.*).

209 **Fiedler, Peter** Studien zur biblischen Grundlegung des christlich-jüdischen Verhältnisses. SBAB 35: Stu 2005, Katholisches Bibelwerk x; 291 pp. €48. 3-460-06351-3.

210 **Frankemölle, Hubert** Studien zum jüdischen Kontext neutestamentlicher Theologien. SBAB 37: Stu 2005, Katholisches Bibelwerk x; 316 pp. €49.90. 34600-63718. $^{R}$ThG 48 (2005) 233-4 (*März, Claus-Peter*).

211 **Fuchs, Ottmar** Praktische Hermeneutik der Heiligen Schrift. Praktische Theologie heute 57: 2004 ⇒20,203. $^{R}$ThLZ 130 (2005) 833-836 (*Winkler, Eberhard*).

212 **Fusco, Vittorio** Euanghelion: discussioni neotestamentarie. Quad. della Riv. di Scienze Religiose 3: Roma-Monopoli 2005, Vivere In 450 pp. €40. $^{R}$Rivista di science religiose 19/1 (2005) 227-228 (*Pinto, Sebastiano*).

213 **Garuti, Paolo** Apostolica romana quaedam: études philologiques sur le Nouveau Testament dans le monde gréco-romain. EtB 51: 2004 ⇒ 20,205. $^{R}$Gr. 86 (2005) 407-408 (*Bosetti, Elena*); RB 112 (2005) 277-280 (*Taylor, Justin*).

214 **Georgi, Dieter** The city in the valley: biblical interpretation and urban theology. Studies in biblical literature 7: Atlanta 2005, SBL xxviii; 370 pp. $35. 1-58983-099-7.

215 **Giesen, Heinz** Jesu Heilsbotschaft und die Kirche: Studien zur Eschatologie und Ekklesiologie bei den Synoptikern und im ersten Petrusbrief. BEThL 179: 2004 ⇒20,209. [R]ThPh 80 (2005) 598-600 (*Baumert, N.*).
216 **Grech, Prosper** Il messaggio biblico e la sua interpretazione: saggi di ermeneutica, teologia ed esegesi. RivBib.S 44: Bo 2005, EDB 385 pp. €30. 88-10-30233-8. [R]Aug. 45 (2005) 571-581 (*Simonetti, Manlio*).
217 **Greenfield, Jonas C.** 'Al kanfei Yonah. [E]*Paul, Shalom M.; Stone, Michael Edward; Pinnick, Avital*: 2001 ⇒17,153... 20,211. [R]JQR 95 (2005) 321-323 (*Fassberg, Steven E.*).
218 **Grego, Igino** La Terra Santa e le origini cristiane—luoghi, figure, testimonianze. N 2005, Pont. Fac.Teol. Ital. Merid. 284 pp. [R]MF 105 (2005) 331-333 (*Iammarrone, Luigi*).
219 **Grosby, Steven** Biblical ideas of nationality: ancient and modern. 2002 ⇒18,172...20,212. [R]BiOr 62 (2005) 108-12 (*Vos, J. Cornelis de*).
220 **Gundry, Robert H.** The old is better: New Testament essays in support of traditional interpretations. WUNT 178: Tü 2005, Mohr S. xiii; 454 pp. €109. 3-16-148551-3.
221 **Haight, Roger** The future of christology. NY 2005, Continuum 224 pp. $28.
222 **Hardmeier, Christof** Erzähldiskurs und Redepragmatik im Alten Testament: unterwegs zu einer performativen Theologie der Bibel. FAT 46: Tü 2005, Mohr S. viii; 444 pp. €89. 3-16-148772-9. Bibl. 385-399.
223 **Hays, Richard B.** The conversion of the imagination: Paul as interpreter of Israel's scripture. GR 2005, Eerdmans xx; 213 pp. $20. 0-802-8-1262-7.
224 **Hengel, Martin** Paulus und Jakobus: Kleine Schriften III. WUNT 141: 2002 ⇒18,178... 20,213. [R]NT 47 (2005) 191-193 (*Stenschke, Christoph*).
225 **Henrix, Hans Hermann** Gottes Ja zu Israel: ökumenische Studien christlicher Theologie. Studien zu Kirche und Israel 23: B 2005, Institut Kirche u. Judentum 262 pp. €15. 3-923095-333.
226 **Höffken, Peter** 'Fürchte dich nicht, denn ich bin mit dir!' (Jesaja 41, 10): gesammelte Aufsätze zu Grundtexten des Alten Testaments. Beiträge zum Verstehen der Bibel 14: Müns 2005, LIT 352 pp. €29.90. 3-8258-9106-2.
227 **Hurtado, Larry W.** How on earth did Jesus become a God?: historical questions about earliest devotion to Jesus. GR 2005, Eerdmans xii; 234 pp. £12. 0-8028-2861-2. [R]LASBF 55 (2005) 554-558 (*Chrupcała, Lesław D.*).
228 **Hübner, Hans** Biblische Theologie als Hermeneutik. [E]*Labahn, Antje; Labahn, Michael*: 1995 ⇒11/2,272; 12,130. [R]ThR 70 (2005) 163-166 (*Reventlow, Henning Graf*);
229 Wahrheit und Wirklichkeit: Exegese auf dem Weg zur Fundamentaltheologie: gesammelte Aufsätze. [E]*Labahn, Antje*: Neuk 2005, Neuk 192 pp. €24.90. 3-7887-2108-1.
230 **Jacobs, Louis** Judaism and theology: essays on the Jewish religion. L 2005, Mitchell viii; 262 pp. 0-85303-563-6.
231 **Jeffrey, David Lyle** Houses of the interpreter: reading scripture, reading culture. 2003 ⇒19,212; 20,215. [R]SBET 23 (2005) 125-127 (*Elliott, Mark W.*).
232 **Jenni, Ernst** Studien zur Sprachwelt des Alten Testaments, 2. [E]*Luchsinger, Jürg; Mathys, Hans-Peter; Saur, Markus*: Stu 2005, Kohlhammer 351 pp. €45. 3-17-0187-465.

233 **Jeremias, Joachim** Jesus and the message of the New Testament. [E]*Hanson, K.C.*: 2002 ⇒18,184; 20,216. [R]RBLit (2005)* (*Van der Watt, Jan G.*).

234 **Kaiser, Otto** Zwischen Athen und Jerusalem: Studien zur griechischen und biblischen Theologie, ihrer Eigenart und ihrem Verhältnis. BZAW 320: 2003 ⇒19,215; 20,219. [R]Gn. 77 (2005) 169-171 (*Dietrich, Christine*); BiOr 62 (2005) 330-333 (*Schoors, Antoon*); RBLit 7 (2005) 196-198 (*Römer, Thomas*).

235 **Kasper, Walter** Non ho perduto nessuno: comunione, dialogo ecumenico, evangelizzazione. I libri de 'Il Regno': Bo 2005, EDB 240 pp. €18.90.

236 **Käsemann, Ernst** In der Nachfolge des gekreuzigten Nazareners: Aufsätze und Vorträge aus dem Nachlass. [E]*Landau, Rudolf; Kraus, Wolfgang*: Tü 2005, Mohr S. x; 328 pp. €24. 3-16-148747-8.

237 **Kim, Seyoon** Paul and the new perspective: second thoughts on the origin of Paul's gospel. WUNT 140: 2002 ⇒18,190... 20,7157. [R]BiblInterp 13 (2005) 104-106 (*Thompson, Michael B.*); RBLit (2005)* (*Keay, Robert*); RBLit 7 (2005) 414-417 (*Reasoner, Mark*).

238 **Klauck, Hans-Josef** Religion und Gesellschaft im frühen Christentum: neutestamentliche Studien. WUNT 152: 2003 ⇒19,216; 20,221. [R]LTP 61 (2005) 175-178 (*Lavoie, Jean-Michel*); ThLZ 130 (2005) 44-46 (*Schröter, Jens*).

239 **Klein, Hans** Lukasstudien. FRLANT 209: Gö 2005, Vandenhoeck & R. 219 pp. €69.60. 3-525-53073-0. Bibl. 202-216. [R]SNTU 30 (2005) 282-283 (*Fuchs, Albert*).

240 **Kratz, Reinhard Gregor** Das Judentum im Zeitalter des zweiten Tempels. FAT 42: 2004 ⇒20,225. [R]BiLi 78 (2005) 146-147 (*Hieke, Thomas*); RBLit (2005)* (*Grabbe, Lester*).

241 **Lambert, Mayer** Termes massorétiques, prosodie hébraïque et autres études: appendices à la grammaire hébraïque. [E]*Ellenberger, Yaffa; Weil, Rachel*: HEO 39; Moyen et Proche-Orient 2: Genève 2005, Droz xvi; 165 pp. €92. 2-600-00918-3. Avant-propos de *Colette Sirat*, Introduction de *Philippe Cassuto*; Bibl. 131-158.

242 **Lambrecht, Jan** Understanding what one reads: New Testament essays. [E]*Koperski, Veronica*: ANL 46: 2003 ⇒19,219; 20,226. [R]BZ 49 (2005) 280-282 (*Klumbies, Paul-Gerhard*).

243 **Latte, Kurt** Opuscula inedita zusammen mit Vorträgen und Berichten von einer Tagung zum vierzigsten Todestag von Kurt Latte. [E]*Classen, Carl J.*: Beiträge zur Altertumskunde 219: Mü 2005, Saur vii; 102 pp. 3598-77831-7.

244 **Legrand, Lucien** The word is near you: collected papers of Lucien Legrand, MEP, vol. 1-3. [E]*Xavier, A. Aloysius, al.* 2001-2004 ⇒20,228. [R]VJTR 69 (2005) 625-626 (*Meagher, P.M.*).

245 **Léon-Dufour, Xavier** Un biblista cerca Dio. [T]*Filippi, A.; Pusceddu, R.*: Collana biblica: Bo 2005, Dehoniane 324 pp. €15.50. 8810221273.

246 **Lieu, Judith** Neither Jew nor Greek?: constructing early christianity. 2003 ⇒19,225; 20,230. [R]ThLZ 130 (2005) 271-274 (*Alkier, Stefan*); RBLit 7 (2005) 291-293 (*Inowlocki, Sabrina*); JThS 56 (2005) 604-607 (*Hurtado, L.W.*); SJTh 58 (2005) 363-365 (*Pak, G. Sujin*);

247 Neither Jew nor Greek?: constructing...christianity. E 2005 <2003>, Clark xiii; 265 pp. £20. 0-567-083268. Bibl. 233-255 [NTAb 50,214].

248 **Lilla, Salvatore** DIONIGI l'Areopagita e il platonismo cristiano. Letteratura cristiana antica 4: Brescia 2005, Morcelliana 270 pp. €18.50. 88372-20146.

249 **Loader, James Alfred** Begegnung mit Gott: gesammelte Studien im Bereich des Alten Testaments. Wiener alttestamentliche Studien 3: 2001 ⇒17,175. [R]ThR 70 (2005) 220-222 (*Mathys, Hans-Peter*).

250 **Lohfink, Norbert** Studien zum Deuteronomium und zur deuteronomistischen Literatur V. SBAB 38: Stu 2005, Katholisches Bibelwerk 303 pp. €48/FS83. 3-460-06381-5;

251 Haragos Visszatekintés az Államra: elöadások a Sámuel és Királyok könyveinek válaszott kulcsszövegeiröl: Héber scószedettel [Rückblick im Zorn auf den Staat]. [T]*Kocsi, György*: Budapest 2005, Scent István Társulat az Apostoli Scentszék Könyvkiadója 165; cxi pp.

252 **Luz, Ulrich** Studies in Matthew. [T]*Selle, Rosemary*: GR 2005, Eerdmans xii; 385 pp. $30/£19. 0-8028-3964-9.

253 **Manicardi, Ermenegildo** Gesù, la cristologia, le scritture: saggi esegetici e teologici. [E]*Marcheselli, Maurizio*: Biblioteca di teologia dell' evangelizzazione 1: Bo 2005, EDB 493 pp. €35. 88-10-45001-9. Bibl. Manicardi (1981-2004) 469-475. [R]MF 105 (2005) 765-767 (*Uricchio, Francesco*).

254 **Marböck, Johannes** Weisheit und Frömmigkeit: Studien zur alttestamentlichen Literatur der Spätzeit. ÖBS 29: Fra 2005, Lang 269 pp. €45.50. 3-631-54298-4.

255 **Martyn, J. Louis** Theological issues in the letters of Paul. Studies of the New Testament and Its World: L 2005 <1997>, Clark xviii; 334 pp. £25/$35. 0567-030318. Bibl. [NTAb 50,418].

256 **May, Gerhard** MARKION: gesammelte Aufsätze. VIEG.Abendländische Religionsgeschichte 68: Mainz 2005, Von Zabern viii; 136 pp. €24.80. 3-8053-3593-8.

257 **Meeks, Wayne A.** In search of the early christians: selected essays. [E]*Hilton, Allen R.; Snyder, H. Gregory*: 2002 ⇒18,208; 19,238. [R]JAAR 73 (2005) 940-942 (*BeDuhn, Jason David*).

258 **Meyer, Paul W.** The word in this world: essays in New Testament exegesis and theology. [E]*Carroll, John T.*: 2004 ⇒20,243. [R]ThTo 62 (2005) 266, 268 (*Cousar, Charles B.*).

259 **Millar, Fergus** Rome, the Greek world, and the east, 2: government, society, and culture in the Roman Empire. [E]*Cotton, H.M.; Rogers, G.M.*: 2004 ⇒20,244. [R]SCI 24 (2005) 297-301 (*Shaw, Brent D.*).

260 **Miller, Patrick D.** Israelite religion and biblical theology: collected essays. JSOT.S 267: 2000 ⇒16,191... 19,241. [R]ThR 70 (2005) 34-37 (*Reventlow, Henning Graf*);

261 The way of the Lord: essays in Old Testament theology. FAT 39: 2004 ⇒20,245. [R]OLZ 100 (2005) 500-506 (*Liwak, Rüdiger*); JETh 19 (2005) 252-254 (*Weber, Beat*); RBLit (2005)* (*Branch, Robin G.*).

262 **Moran, William L.** The most magic word: essays on Babylonian and biblical literature. [E]*Hendel, Ronald S.*: CBQ.MS 35: 2002 ⇒18,212... 20,248. [R]CBQ 67 (2005) 546-548 (*Batto, Bernard F.*);

263 Amarna studies: collected writings. [E]*Huehnergard, John; Izre'el, Shlomo*: HSS 54: 2003 ⇒19,243; 20,247. [R]ArOr 73 (2005) 146-147 (*Mynářová, Jana*); RBLit 7 (2005) 60-61 (*Hess, Richard S.*).

264 **Mosis, Rudolf** Gesammelte Aufsätze zum Alten Testament. FzB 93: 1999 ⇒15,156; 16,192. [R]ThR 70 (2005) 222-5 (*Mathys, Hans-Peter*).

265 **Muffs, Yochanan** The personhood of God: biblical theology, human faith and the divine image. Woodstock, Vt. 2005, Jewish Lights xvi; 221 pp. 1-58023-265-5. Foreword by *David Hartman*.

266 **Na'aman, Nadav** Ancient Israel and its neighbors: interaction and counteraction: collected essays vol. 1. WL 2005, Eisenbrauns xiii; 431 pp. 1-57506-108-2. Bibl. 412-414.
267 **Nancy, Jean-Luc** La déclosion: déconstruction du christianisme, 1. P 2005, Galilée 230 pp. 27186-06681.
268 **Nickelsburg, George W.E.** George W.E. Nickelsburg in perspective: an ongoing dialogue of learning. [E]*Neusner, Jacob; Avery-Peck, Alan Jeffery*: JSJ.S 80: 2003 ⇒19,248. [R]RBLit (2005)* (*Argall, Randal*); RRJ 8 (2005) 249-266 (*Horsley, R.A.*).
269 **Novak, David** Talking with christians: musings of a Jewish theologian. Radical traditions: GR 2005, Eerdmans xiv; 269 pp. $25. 0802828426.
270 **Ohly, Friedrich** Sensus spiritualis: studies in medieval significs and the philology of culture. [T]*Northcott, Kenneth J.*: Ch 2005, Univ. of Chicago Pr. xviii; 403 pp. $55.
271 **Onuki, Takashi** Heil und Erlösung: Studien zum Neuen Testament und zur Gnosis. WUNT 165: 2004 ⇒20,253. [R]ThLZ 130 (2005) 1326-1328 (*Nagel, Titus*).
272 **Oppenheimer, Aharon** Between Rome and Babylon: studies in Jewish leadership and society. [E]*Oppenheimer, Nili*: TSAJ 108: Tü 2005, Mohr S. xv; 499 pp. €129. 3-16-148514-9.
273 **Paul, Shalom M.** Divrei Shalom: collected studies of Shalom M. Paul on the bible and the ancient Near East: 1967-2005; [Divre Shalom (Devarim 2,26: Ester 9,30)]. CHANE 23: Lei 2005, Brill xix; 339 pp. 90-04-14367-X. Bibl. 489-490.
274 **Pearson, Birger Albert** Gnosticism and christianity in Roman and Coptic Egypt. 2004 ⇒20,254. [R]JR 85 (2005) 497-498 (*Brakke, David*); HeyJ 46 (2005) 543-545 (*Madigan, Patrick*).
275 **Peterson, Erik** Ausgewählte Schriften, 3: Johannesevangelium und Kanonstudien. [E]*Nichtweiß, Barbara*: 2003 ⇒19,253; 20,255. [R]ThRv 101 (2005) 422-424 (*Söding, Thomas*);
276 Ausgewählte Schriften, 4: Offenbarung des Johannes und politisch-theologische Texte. [E]*Nichtweiß, Barbara; Löser, Werner*: 2004 ⇒20,256. [R]ThLZ 130 (2005) 396-398 (*Lohse, Eduard*);
277 Ausgewählte Schriften, 5: Lukasevangelium und Synoptica. [E]*Bendemann, Reinhard von*: Wü 2005, Echter cvi; 446 pp. €58. 3429-027470.
278 **Pieris, Aloysius** Prophetic humour in Buddhism and christianity. Colombo 2005, Ecumenical Institute for Study and Dialogue vi; 140 pp. 1391-1201. = Dialogue 31 (2004).
279 **Pilhofer, Peter** Die frühen Christen und ihre Welt: ...Aufsätze 1996-2001. [E]*Frey, Jörg; Hengel, Martin; Hofius, Otfried*: WUNT 145: 2002 ⇒18,225...20,258. [R]NT 47 (2005) 196-200 (*Stenschke, Christoph*).
280 **Plaskow, Judith** The coming of Lilith: essays on feminism, Judaism, and sexual ethics, 1973-2003. Boston 2005, Beacon 244 pp. $19. 0-80-70-3623-4.
281 **Plümacher, Eckhard** Geschichte und Geschichten: Aufsätze zur Apostelgeschichte und zu den Johannesakten. [E]*Schröter, Jens; Brucker, Ralph*: WUNT 170: 2004 ⇒20,259. [R]ThRv 101 (2005) 300-301 (*Dormeyer, Detlev*).
282 **Rabello, Alfredo M.** The Jews in the Roman Empire: legal problems, from Herod to Justinian. CStS 645: 2000 ⇒16,202... 19,259. [R]Latomus 64 (2005) 217-219 (*Williams, Margaret H.*).
283 **Rad, Gerhard von** From Genesis to Chronicles: explorations in Old Testament theology. [E]*Hanson, Kenneth C.*: Mn 2005 <1966>, Fortress

xix (2); 286 pp. $18. 0800637186. Bibl. 267-273 [R]RBLit (2005)* (*Cathey, Joseph; Groenewald, Alphonso; Reventlow, Henning; West, James*).

284 **Reinink, G.J.** Syriac christianity under Late Sasanian and Early Islamic rule. Aldershot 2005, Ashgate xii; pag. var. £60. 086078-9756.

285 **Remaud, Michel** Vangelo e tradizione rabbinica. CSB 47: Bo 2005, Dehoniane 206 pp. 88-10-40748-2.

286 **Rhoads, David** Reading Mark, engaging the gospel. 2004 ⇒20,264. [R]RBLit (2005)* (*Driggers, Ira B.; Kealy, Sean; Verheyden, Joseph*).

287 **Rigato, Maria Luisa** Raccolta dei saggi su s. Giovanni Apostolo: per i Simposi di Efeso: III-X (1993-2005). n.p. 2005, n.p. pag. var.

288 **Roberts, Jimmy J.M.** The bible and the ancient Near East. 2002 ⇒18, 230; 20,266. [R]JNES 64 (2005) 295-297 (*Barrick, W. Boyd*).

289 **Robinson, James M.** The sayings gospel Q: collected essays. [E]*Heil, Christoph; Verheyden, Joseph*: BEThL 189: Lv 2005, Peeters xviii; 937 pp. €90. 90-429-1652-4.

290 **Rooker, Mark F.** Studies in Hebrew language, intertextuality, and theology. Text and Studies in Religion 98: 2003 ⇒19,264. [R]Faith & Mission 22/2 (2005) 119-121 (*Madden, Shawn*).

291 **Rordorf, Bernard** Liberté de parole: esquisses théologiques. Actes et Recherches: Genève 2005, Labor et F. 242 pp. 28309-11709. Préf. *Michel Grandjean*.

292 **Russell, James R.** Armenian and Iranian studies. HATS 9: CM 2005, Dept. of Near Eastern Languages, Harvard xxix, 1462 pp. $74.37. 0-9-35411-19-4. Bibl.

293 **Sanz Giménez-Rico, Enrique** Un recuerdo que conduce al don: teología de Dt 1-11. Biblioteca de Teología Comillas 11: 2004 ⇒20,268. [R]SalTer 93 (2005) 423-425 (*Ramírez Fueyo, Francisco*).

294 **Saporetti, Claudio** Saggi su il Ghilgames. Il piacere di raccontare: I libri de l'istrice 2: Mi 2003, Simonelli 207 pp. 88-86792-45-X. Bibl. 188-206.

295 **Schenker, Adrian** Studien zu Propheten und Religionsgeschichte. SBAB 36: 2003 ⇒19,270; 20,269. [R]TS 66 (2005) 442-444 (*Clifford, Richard J.*).

296 **Schner, George P.** Essays catholic and critical. [E]*Ziegler, Philip G.; Husbands, Mark*: 2002 ⇒18,237. [R]MoTh 21/1 (2005) 185-187 (*Buckley, James J.*).

297 **Schweitzer, Albert** Vorträge, Vorlesungen, Aufsätze. [E]*Güntzler, C.; Luz, U.; Zürcher, J.*: Werke aus dem Nachlaß: 2003 ⇒19,276. [R]SNTU 30 (2005) 270 (*Fuchs, Albert*).

298 **Schwienhorst-Schönberger, Ludger** Studien zum Alten Testament und seiner Hermeneutik. SBAB 40: Stu 2005, Katholisches Bibelwerk 312 pp. €50. 3-460-06401-3.

299 **Seeligmann, Isac Leo** The Septuagint version of Isaiah and cognate studies. [E]*Hanhart, Robert; Spieckermann, Hermann*: FAT 40: 2004 ⇒20,274. [R]RBLit (2005)* (*Van der Kooij, Arie*).

300 **Seitz, Christopher R.** Word without end: the Old Testament as abiding theological witness. 1998 ⇒14,200... 20,275. [R]ThR 70 (2005) 143 (*Reventlow, Henning Graf*).

301 **Seland, Torrey** Strangers in the light: Philonic perspectives on christian identity in 1 Peter. BiblInterp 76: Lei 2005, Brill x; 216 pp. 90-04-14491-9. Bibl. 193-203.

302 **Ska, Jean-Louis** El camino y la casa: itinerarios bíblicos. [T]*Montes, Miguel*: El mundo de la Biblia, Horizontes 5: Estella (Navarra) 2005, Verbo Divino 250 pp. 84-8169-662-5.

303 **Skeat, Theodore Cressy** The collected biblical writings of T.C. Skeat. [E]*Elliott, James Keith*: NT.S 113: 2004 ⇒20,279. [R]RBLit (2005)* (*Kraft, Robert*); JThS 56 (2005) 179-184 (*Foster, Paul*); ET 116 (2005) 374-376 (*Kruger, Michael J.*).

304 **Smith, Jonathan Z.** Relating religion: essays in the study of religion. 2004 ⇒20,281. [R]JBL 124 (2005) 584-587 (*Van der Toorn, Karel*); RRJ 8 (2005) 315-328 (*Neusner, J.*).

305 **Soares-Prabhu, George** The dharma of Jesu. [E]*D'Sa, Francis X.*: 2003 ⇒19,5626; 20,282. [R]CBQ 67 (2005) 383-385 (*Reid, Barbara E.*); VJTR 69 (2005) 474-475 (*Meagher, P.M.*).

306 **Soloveitchik, Joseph B.** (Dov) Insights of Rabbi Joseph B. Soloveitchik: discourses on fundamental theological issues in Judaism. [E]*Weiss, Saul*: Lanham 2005, Rowman & L. xviii; 177 pp. 07425-44680. Bibl. 173-177.

307 **Spieckermann, Hermann** Gottes Liebe zu Israel: Studien zur Theologie des Alten Testaments. FAT 33: 2001 ⇒17,215; 19,281. [R]Sal. 67 (2005) 594-595 (*Vicent, Rafael*).

308 **Stanton, Graham N.** Jesus and gospel. 2004 ⇒20,4890. [R]RRT 12 (2005) 370-372 (*Seddon, Philip*); CBQ 67 (2005) 385-386 (*Harrington, Daniel J.*); ScrB 35 (2005) 109-111 (*Boxall, Ian*).

309 **Stegemann, Ekkehard W.** Paulus und die Welt: Aufsätze. [E]*Tuor, Christina; Wick, Peter*: Z 2005, Theologischer 308 pp. €22.50. 3-290-17364-X.

310 **Stolz, Fritz** Religion und Rekonstruktion: ausgewählte Aufsätze. [E]*Pezzoli-Olgiati, Daria, al.*: 2004 ⇒20,285. [R]ThRv 101 (2005) 77-79 (*Arens, Edmund*).

311 **Stuhlmacher, Peter** Biblische Theologie und Evangelium. WUNT 146: 2002 ⇒18,245; 19,282. [R]NT 47 (2005) 193-196 (*Stenschke, Christoph*); JETh 19 (2005) 288-290 (*Haubeck, Wilfrid*).

312 **Sugirtharajah, R.S.** Postcolonial reconfigurations: an alternative way of reading the bible and doing theology. 2003 ⇒19,283. [R]Theol. 108 (2005) 206-208 (*Wingate, Andrew*).

313 **Sweeney, Marvin A.** Form and intertextuality in prophetic and apocalyptic literature. FAT 45: Tü 2005, Mohr S. xiii; 295 pp. €79/$101. 3-16-148655-2.

314 **Tamez, Elsa** Bajo un cielo sin estrellas. 2001 ⇒19,284. [R]ThX 55 (2005) 108-110 (*Sitges, Ana María*).

315 **Tannehill, Robert C.** The shape of Luke's story: essays on Luke-Acts. Eugene, OR 2005, Cascade xvii; 297 pp. $30. 1-59752-3356.

316 **Thiel, Winfried** Gedeutete Geschichte: Studien zur Geschichte Israels und ihrer theologischen Interpretation im Alten Testament. [E]*Mommer, Peter; Pottmann, Simone; Scherer, Andreas*: Biblisch-theologische Studien 71: Neuk 2005, Neuk viii; 167 pp. 3-7887-2089-1.

317 **Van der Horst, Pieter Willem** Japheth in the tents of Shem: studies on Jewish Hellenism in antiquity. CBET 32: 2002 ⇒18,251... 20,291. [R]ThLZ 130 (2005) 624-626 (*Sänger, Dieter*); OLZ 100 (2005) 78-82 (*Galley, Susanne*).

318 **Van Dijk-Hemmes, Fokkelien** The double voice of her desire: texts by Fokkelien van Dijk-Hemmes. [E]*Dröes, Freda; Bekkenkamp, Jonne-*

*ke;* [T]*Orton, David E.*: Tools for Biblical Study 6: 2004 ⇒20,3987. [R]RBLit (2005)* (*Brenner, Athalya*).

319 **Vollenweider, Samuel** Horizonte neutestamentlicher Christologie: Studien zu Paulus und zur frühchristlichen Theologie. WUNT 144: 2002 ⇒18,257; 19,295. [R]NT 47 (2005) 406-09 (*Stenschke, Christoph*).

320 **Wacker, Marie-Theres** Von Göttinnen, Göttern und dem einzigen Gott: Studien zum biblischen Monotheismus aus feministisch-theologischer Sicht. TFE 14: Müns 2005 <2004>, LIT 200 pp. €14.90. 3-8258-6829-X.

321 **Wenz, Armin** Sana doctrina: Heilige Schrift und theologische Ethik. Kontexte 37: 2004 ⇒20,299. [R]JETh 19 (2005) 334-339 (*Meier, Ralph*).

322 **Wénin, André** L'homme biblique: lectures dans le premier Testament. [2]2004 <1995> ⇒20,300. [R]REJ 164 (2005) 329-333 (*Couteau, Élisabeth*); EstB 63 (2005) 130-131 (*Granados, C.*);

323 Dalla violenza alla speranza: cammini di umanizzazione nelle scritture. [T]*Marino, Laura*: Spiritualità biblica: Magnano (Bi) 2005, Qiqajon 252 pp. €13.50. 88-8227-174-9.

324 **Whybray, Norman** Wisdom: the collected articles of Norman Whybray. [E]*Barker, Margaret; Dell, Katharine J.*: Aldershot 2005, Ashgate xxxii; 337 pp. £65. 0-7546-3917-7. [R]ScrB 35 (2005) 102 (*Corley, Jeremy*).

325 **Wifstrand, Albert** Epochs and styles: selected writings on the New Testament, Greek language and Greek culture in the post-classical era. [E]*Rydbeck, Lars; Porter, Stanley E.;* [T]*Searby, Denis*: WUNT 179: Tü 2005, Mohr S. viii; 241 pp. €74. 3-16-148627-7.

326 **Williamson, Hugh G.M.** Studies in Persian period history and historiography. FAT 38: 2004 ⇒20,301. [R]Sal. 67 (2005) 179-180 (*Vicent, Rafael*); RBLit (2005)* (*Edelman, Diana*).

327 **Wischmeyer, Oda** Von Ben Sira zu Paulus: gesammelte Aufsätze zu Texten, Theologie und Hermeneutik des Frühjudentums und des Neuen Testaments. [E]*Becker, Eve-Marie*: WUNT 173: 2004 ⇒20,302. [R]ThLZ 130 (2005) 789-790 (*Niebuhr, Karl-Wilhelm*).

328 **Wyatt, Nick** The mythic mind: essays on cosmology and religion in Ugaritic and Old Testament literature. L 2005, Equinox xiv; 305 pp. 1-84553-043-8. Bibl. 256-285;

329 'There's such divinity doth hedge a king': selected essays of Nicolas Wyatt on royal ideology in Ugaritic and Old Testament literature. MSSOTS: Aldershot 2005, Ashgate xiii; 298 pp. 0-7546-5330-7.

330 **Zanetti, Paolo S.** Imitatori di Gesù Cristo: scritti classici e cristiani. [E]*Cacciari, Antonio, al.*: Bo 2005, Dehoniane 672 pp. 88-10-92815-6.

331 **Zimmerli, Walther** The fiery throne: the prophets and Old Testament theology. [E]*Hanson, K.C.*: 2003 ⇒19,299; 20,304. [R]CBQ 67 (2005) 520-521 (*Van Dyke Parunak, H.*): RBLit 7 (2005) 165-168 (*McEntire, Mark*); JR 85 (2005) 650-651 (*Schuele, Andreas*).

### A1.3 *Plurium compilationes* **biblicae**

332 [E]**Aichele, George; Walsh, Richard G.** Those outside: noncanonical readings of canonical gospels. NY 2005, Clark xvi; 215 pp. $35. 0-567-02650-7. Bibl. 183-201.

333 [E]**Alkier, Stefan; Hays, Richard B.** Die Bibel im Dialog der Schriften: Konzepte intertextueller Bibellektüre. NET 10: Ba 2005, Francke x; 281 pp. 3-7720-8098-7.

334 [E]**Aragione, Gabriella; Junod, Éric; Norelli, Enrico** Le canon du Nouveau Testament: regards nouveaux sur l'histoire de sa formation. MoBi 54: Genève 2005, Labor et F. 322 pp. €26/FS42. 2-8309-1177-6. [R]FgNT 17 (2004) 114-118 (*Amphoux, Christian-B.*).

335 [E]**Arblaster, Paul; Juhász, Gergely; Latré, Guido** TYNDALE's testament. 2002 ⇒18,268. [R]SCJ 36 (2005) 492-494 (*Balserak, Jon*).

336 Archa Verbi: Yearbook for the study of medieval theology, 2. [E]**Roloff, H.-G.**: Müns 2005, Aschendorf 224 pp. 34020-08416.

337 [E]**Auffarth, Christoph; Stuckenbruck, Loren T.** The fall of the angels. Themes in biblical narrative 6: 2004 ⇒20,650. [R]JSJ 36 (2005) 84-86 (*Sullivan, K.P.*); RBLit (2005)* (*Collins, John*) [Gen 6,1-4].

338 [E]**Auwers, Jean-Marie** Regards croisés sur le Cantique des cantiques. Le livre et le rouleau 22: Bru 2005, Lessius 173 pp. €20. 28729-91395.

339 [E]**Bachmann, Michael** Lutherische und neue Paulusperspektive: Beiträge zu einem Schlüsselproblem der gegenwärtigen exegetischen Diskussion. WUNT 182: Tü 2005, Mohr S. xiv; 460 pp. €99. 3-16-148712-5.

340 [E]**Bailey, Randall C.** Yet with a steady beat: contemporary U.S. Afrocentric biblical interpretation. SBL.Semeia studies 42: 2003 ⇒19,305; 20,310. [R]RBLit (2005)* (*Enis, Larry*): RBLit 7 (2005) 478-479 (*Wimbush, Vincent L.*).

341 [E]**Ballard, Paul; Holmes, Stephen R.** The bible in pastoral practice: readings in the place and function of scripture in the church. L 2005, Darton, L. & T. xxiii; 316 pp. £18. 0-232-52611-7.

342 [E]**Barker, Gregory A.** Jesus in the world's faiths: leading thinkers from five religions reflect on his meaning. Mkn 2005, Orbis ix; 198 pp. $18. 1-57075-573-6. [R]LouvSt 30 (2005) 238-239 (*Mendoza, Ruben C.*).

343 **Bartholomew, Craig G.; Green, Joel B.; Thiselton, Anthony C.** Reading Luke: interpretation, reflection, formation. Scripture and hermeneutics 6: GR 2005, Zondervan xxii; 484 pp. 1-84227-070-2.

344 [E]**Barton, John** The biblical world, 1-2. 2002 ⇒18,273...20,313. [R]JRH 29/1 (2005) 77-78 (*Strelan, Rick*);

345 2004 <2002> ⇒20,314. pb. [R]RRT 12/1 (2005) 177-78 (*Guest, Deryn*).

346 [E]**Baumgart, Norbert C.; Ringshausen, Gerhard** Die Sintflut: zwischen Keilschrift und Kinderbuch: das neue Interesse an der alten Erzählung als religionspädagogische Herausforderung. Lüneburger Theologische Beiträge 2: Müns 2005, Lit 160 pp. €16.90. 3825-87931-3.

347 [E]**Becker, Eve-Marie** Neutestamentliche Wissenschaft: autobiographische Essays aus der Evangelischen Theologie. UTB 2475: 2003 ⇒19, 308. [R]ThBeitr 36/3 (2005) 152-157 (*Baum, A.D.*);

348 Die antike Historiographie und die Anfänge der christlichen Geschichtsschreibung. BZNW 129: B 2005, De Gruyter xiv; 308 pp. €88. 3-11-018208-4.

349 [E]**Becker, Eve-Marie; Pilhofer, Peter** Biographie und Persönlichkeit des Paulus. WUNT 187: Tü 2005, Mohr S. viii; 392 pp. €94. 978-3-16-148662-3.

350 [E]**Becker, Hans-Jürgen; Ruzer, Serge** The Sermon on the Mount and its Jewish setting. CRB 60: P 2005, Gabalda xii; 263 pp. €45. 2-85021-165-5.

351 [E]**Ben Zvi, Ehud; Floyd, Michael H.** Writings and speech in Israelite and ancient Near Eastern prophecy. 2000 ⇒16,238; 18,274. [R]JNES 64 (2005) 60-63 (*Sparks, Kent*).

352 [E]**Bianchi, Enzo** Il lavoro opera delle nostre mani. PSV 52: Bo 2005, EDB 295 pp.
353 **Bigarelli, Alberto**, *al.* Libertà va cercando. Sussidi biblici 87: Reggio Emilia 2005, San Lorenzo 124 pp. 88-8071-157-1.
354 [E]**Bland, Dave; Fleer, David** Performing the Psalms. St. Louis, MO 2005, Chalice xii; 195 pp. $20. 0-8272-2983-6.
355 [E]**Blasi, Anthony J.; Duhaime, Jean; Turcotte, Paul-André** Handbook of early christianity: social science approaches. 2002 ⇒18,275... 20,319. [R]JRH 29 (2005) 314-315 (*Jacobs, Andrew S.*); Sociology of Religion 66 (2005) 432-434 (*Berquist, Jon L.*); RBLit (2005)* (*Van der Watt, Jan G.*); RBLit 7 (2005) 487-491 (*Clark, Ron*).
356 [E]**Bordeyne, P.** Bible et morale. LeDiv: 2003 ⇒19,315; 20,323. [R]RTL 36 (2005) 112-113 (*Gaziaux, E.*).
357 [E]**Bortone, Giuseppe** Il bello della bibbia: visione poliedrica del "bello ideale": XXV corso biblico. L'Aquila 2005, ISSRA xiii; 356 pp.
358 [E]**Bouthors, Jean-François** La bible sans avoir peur. P 2005, Lethielleux 322 pp. €23. [R]EeV 135 (2005) 26 (*Cothenet, Edouard*).
359 [E]**Bradfield, Bill** On reading the bible: thoughts and reflections of over 500 men and women, from St. AUGUSTINE to Oprah Winfrey. Mineola, NY 2005, Dover v; 196 pp. $7. 0-486-43708-6 [ThD 52,281—*W. Charles Heiser*].
360 **Braulik, Georg; Lohfink, Norbert** Liturgie und Bibel: gesammelte Aufsätze. ÖBS 28: Fra 2005, Lang 638 pp. €74.30. 3-631-54513-4.
361 [E]**Brown, William P.** The ten commandments: the reciprocity of faithfulness. 2004 ⇒20,325. [R]RBLit (2005)* (*Becking, Bob; Johnstone, William*); RBLit 7 (2005) 141-142 (*Becking, Bob*); HBT 27/1 (2005) 114-115 (*Dearman, J. Andrew*).
362 [E]**Bultmann, Christoph; März, Claus-Peter; Makrides, Vasilios N.** Heilige Schriften: Ursprung, Geltung und Gebrauch. Müns 2005, Aschendorff 255 pp. €14.80. 3-402-03415-8.
363 [E]**Busse, Ulrich** Die Bedeutung der Exegese für Theologie und Kirche. QD 215: FrB 2005, Herder 240 pp. €25. 3-451-02215-X.
364 [E]**Butting, Klara; Minnaard, Gerard; Wacker, Marie T.** Ester. Die Bibel erzählt: Wittingen 2005, Erev-Rav 100 pp. €11. 3-9328-1030-9.
365 [E]**Campbell, Ken M.** Marriage and family in the biblical world. 2003 ⇒19,321. [R]CBQ 67 (2005) 378-379 (*Osiek, Carolyn*).
366 [E]**Carson, D.A.; O'Brien, Peter Thomas; Seifrid, Mark A.** Justification and variegated nomism, 1: the complexities of second temple Judaism. WUNT 2/140: 2001 ⇒17,251...20,326. [R]BibInterp 13 (2005) 91-93 (*Barclay, John*); TrinJ 26 (2005) 329-331 (*Bolt, Peter G.*).
367 [E]**Chazelle, Celia; Edwards, Burton Van Name** The study of the bible in the Carolingian era. Medieval church studies 3: 2003 ⇒19,325; 20, 328. [R]Spec. 80 (2005) 204-206 (*Morrison, Karl F.*).
368 [E]**Cherubini, Paolo** Forme e modelli della tradizione manoscritta della bibbia. Littera Antiqua 13: Città del Vaticano 2005, Scuola Vaticana di Paleografia xv; 562 pp. €45. 88-8505-4153.
369 [E]**Chilton, Bruce; Evans, Craig A.** The missions of James, Peter, and Paul: tensions in early christianity. NT.S 115: Lei 2005, Brill xiv; 534 pp. €133/$179. 90-04-14161-8.
370 [E]**Cosgrove, Charles H.** The meanings we choose: hermeneutical ethics, indeterminacy and the conflict of interpretations. JSOT.S 411: 2004 ⇒20,331. [R]RBLit (2005)* (*Bridgeman-Davis, Valerie*).

371 ECoulton, Nicholas The bible, the church and homosexuality. L 2005, Darton, L. & T. x; 136 pp. £11. 0232-5260-60.
372 ECourt, John M. Biblical interpretation: the meanings of scripture—past and present. 2004 ⇒20,332. RJThS 56 (2005) 184-186 (*Houlden, J.L.*); RRT 12/1 (2005) 138-139 (*Bury, Benjamin*).
373 EDebergé, Pierre; Nieuviarts, Jacques Guide de lecture du Nouveau Testament. 2004 ⇒20,336. RATT 11 (2005) 454-455 (*Ghiberti, Giuseppe*).
374 Le déluge et ses récits: points de vue sémiotiques. Québec 2005, Presses de l'Univ. Laval 190 pp. $25. 27637-82655. Groupe de recherche ASTER.
375 EDietrich, Walter David und Saul im Widerstreit: Diachronie und Synchronie im Wettstreit: Beiträge zur Auslegung des ersten Samuelbuches. OBO 206: 2004 ⇒20,338. RRBLit (2005)* (*Hamilton, Mark*).
376 EDobbeler, Axel von; Theurich, Henning Kanzelreden—quergedacht: prominente Zeitgenossen legen biblische Texte aus. Neuk 2005, Neuk 158 pp. 3-7975-0113-7.
377 EDozzi, Dino Paolo: le prime parole su Gesù. La Bibbia di San Francesco 3: Bo 2005, Dehoniane 208 pp. 88-10-62123-9.
378 EDraper, Jonathan A. The eye of the storm: Bishop John William COLENSO and the crisis of biblical inspiration. JSOT.S 386: 2003 ⇒19, 334. RSvTK 81 (2005) 183-184 (*Booth, Roger P.*).
379 EDunn, James D.G.; McKnight, Scot The historical Jesus in recent research. Sources for biblical and theological study 10: WL 2005, Eisenbrauns xvi; 592 pp. $44.60. 1-57506-100-7.
380 EEbner, Martin, *al.*, Leben trotz Tod. JBTh 19: Neuk 2005, Neuk xiii; 463 pp. €44. 3-7887-2063-8;
381 Der Himmel. JBTh 20: 2005, xii; 472 pp. 3-7887-2103-0.
382 Gott und Geld. JBTh 21: Neuk 2005 <2007>, Neuk xiv; 336 pp. 978-3-7887-2165-7.
383 EEdelman, Diana Vikander The triumph of Elohim: from Yahwisms to Judaisms. 1995 ⇒11/1,79... 15,217. RThR 70 (2005) 427-429 (*Reventlow, Henning Graf*).
384 EEgo, Beate; Merkel, Helmut Religiöses Lernen in der biblischen, frühjüdischen und frühchristlichen Überlieferung. WUNT 180: Tü 2005, Mohr S. xii; 336 pp. €95. 3-16-148562-9.
385 EEvans, Craig A. Of scribes and sages: early Jewish interpretation and transmission of scripture, volume 2: later versions and traditions. Library of Second Temple Studies 51: 2004 ⇒20,347. RRBLit (2005)* (*Liss, Hanna; Martone, Corrado*);
386 From prophecy to Testament: the function of the Old Testament in the New. 2004 ⇒20,345. RCBQ 67 (2005) 369-370 (*Bernas, Casimir*); Theoforum 36 (2005) 203-204 (*Vogels, Walter*); TJT 21 (2005) 237-239 (*Wettlaufer, Ryan D.*); RBLit 7 (2005) 256-259 (*Menken, Maarten J.J.*); JThS 56 (2005) 524-526 (*Moyise, Steve*).
387 EFee, Gordon D.; Groothuis, Rebecca M.; Pierce, Ronald W. Discovering biblical equality: complementarity without hierarchy. 2004 ⇒20,348. RJournal for Biblical Manood and Womanhood 10/1 (2005) 1-125 (*Schemm, P.R., al.*);
388 DG 22005 <2004>, InterVarsity 528 pp. 0-8308-2834-6. Bibl.
389 EFitzgerald, John T.; Obbink, Dirk; Holland, Glenn S. Philodemus and the New Testament world. NT.S 111: 2004 ⇒20,351. RRBLit

KENRICK SEMINARY LIBRARY
5200 GLENNON DRIVE
ST. LOUIS, MO. 63119

(2005)* (*Geyer, Douglas; Jackson-McCabe, Matt*); ET 116 (2005) 390-391 (*Edwards, Ruth B.*).

390 [E]**Flint, Peter W.; Miller, Patrick D., Jr.** The book of Psalms: composition and reception. VT.S 99; FIOTL 4: Lei 2005, Brill xx; 680 pp. €179. 90-04-13642-8. [R]EThL 81 (2005) 512-514 (*Auwers, Jean-Marie*); RBLit (2005)* (*Kraus, Thomas*).

391 [E]**Flint, Peter W.** The bible at Qumran: text, shape, and interpretation. 2001 ⇒17,267 ... 19,342. [R]BiOr 62 (2005) 338-341 (*Cook, Johann*); JSSt 50 (2005) 388-390 (*Herbert, Edward D.*).

392 [E]**Frey, Jörg; Schröter, Jens** Deutungen des Todes Jesu im Neuen Testament. WUNT 181: Tü 2005, Mohr S. xii; 707 pp. €109. 3-16-14-8581-5.

393 [E]**Gaca, Kathy L.; Welborn, Laurence L.** Early patristic readings of Romans. Romans through history and cultures: NY 2005, Clark vi; 237 pp. $40. 0-567-02931-X.

394 [E]**Garhammer, Erich; Zelinka, Udo** 'Brennender Dornbusch und pfingstliche Feuerzungen': biblische Spuren in der modernen Literatur. 2003 ⇒19,344. [R]ThLZ 130 (2005) 1215-1217 (*Maur, Andreas*).

395 [E]**Gelardini, Gabriella** Hebrews: contemporary methods–new insights. BiblInterp 75: Lei 2005, Brill viii; 304 pp. $129. 90-04-14490-0.

396 [E]**Gemünden, Petra von; Weissenrieder, Annette; Wendt, Friederike** Picturing the New Testament: studies in ancient visual images. WUNT 2/193: Tü 2005, Mohr S. xvii; 445 pp. €99. 3-16-148574-2.

397 [E]**Good, Deirdre** Mariam, the Magdalen, and the mother. Bloomington 2005, Indiana Univ. Pr. xvii; 240 pp. $50/23.

398 [E]**Gorman, Michael J.** Scripture: an ecumenical introduction to the bible and its interpretation. Peabody 2005, Hendrickson xvi; 288 pp. $20. 1-56563-927-8.

399 [E]**Grabbe, Lester L.** Did Moses speak Attic?: Jewish historiography and scripture in the Hellenistic period. JSOT.S 317: 2001 ⇒17,270... 20,356. [R]RBLit 7 (2005) 225-228 (*Gruen, Erich S.*).

400 [E]**Greenman, Jeffrey P.; Larsen, Timothy** Reading Romans through the centuries: from the early church to Karl BARTH. GR 2005, Brazos 223 pp. $30. 1-587-43156-4.

401 [E]**Hagedorn, Anselm C.** Perspectives on the Song of Songs = Perspektiven der Hoheliedauslegung. BZAW 346: B 2005, De Gruyter xxii; 373 pp. €98. 3-11-017632-7. [R]UF 37 (2005) 825-26 (*Loretz, Oswald*).

402 [E]**Hauser, Alan J.; Watson, Duane F.** A history of biblical interpretation, 1: the ancient period. 2003 ⇒19,350; 20,360. [R]Cart. 21 (2005) 231-232 (*Sanz Valdivieso, R.*); Faith & Mission 22/2 (2005) 112-115 (*Kellum, L.S.*); CBQ 67 (2005) 184-185 (*McDonald, Lee Martin*); OLZ 100 (2005) 485-491 (*Reventlow, Henning Graf*); RBLit 7 (2005) 474-475 (*Kealy, Seán P.*).

403 [E]**Hieke, Thomas** Tod—Ende oder Anfang?: was die Bibel sagt. Stu 2005, Kath. Bibelwerk 128 pp. €12.90. 3-460-33173-9.

404 The historical Jesus goes to church. 2004 ⇒20,437. By members of the Jesus Seminar. [R]Sewanee Theological Review 48/3 (2005) 341-347 (*Edwards, O.C.*).

405 [E]**Holzem, Andreas** Normieren, Tradieren, Inszenieren: das Christentum als Buchreligion. 2004 ⇒20,368. [R]ThRv 101 (2005) 23-25 (*Beinert, Wolfgang*).

406 [E]**Horsley, Richard A.** Paul and the Roman imperial order. 2004 ⇒20, 369. [R]CBQ 67 (2005) 186-187 (*Pascuzzi, Maria*); RBLit 7 (2005) 419-422 (*Verbrugge, Verlyn D.*).

407 [E]**Horstmann, Kai** Zwischen Bibel und Wissenschaft: gottesdienstliche Reden. Glauben und Leben 31: Müns 2005, LIT 112 pp. 38258-91461.

408 [E]**Human, Dirk J.; Vos, Cas J.A.** Psalms and liturgy. JSOT.S 410: 2004 ⇒20,371. [R]RBLit (2005)* (*Tucker, W. Dennis*).

409 [E]**Janowski, Bernd; Ego, Beate** Das biblische Weltbild und seine altorientalischen Kontexte. FAT 32: 2001 ⇒17,285... 20,373. [R]FrRu 12 (2005) 142 (*Kinet, Dirk*); OLZ 100 (2005) 474-481 (*Dietrich, Jan*); RBLit 7 (2005) 228-230 (*Klein, Ralph W.*).

410 [E]**Janowski, Bernd** Theologie und Exegese des Alten Testaments / der Hebräischen Bibel: Zwischenbilanz und Zukunftsperspektiven. SBS 200: Stu 2005, Katholisches Bibelwerk 238 pp. €29.90. 3460-03004-6.

411 [E]**Jonker, Louis C.; Lawrie, Douglas G.** Fishing for Jonah (anew): various approaches to biblical interpretation. Study guides in religion and theology 7: Stellenbosch 2005, Sun i; 265 pp. R140. 1-919-980-601. [R]BOTSA 19 (2005) 23-24 (*Lavik, Marta Høyland*).

412 [E]**Kampling, Rainer** Ausharren in der Verheißung: Studien zum Hebräerbrief. SBS 204: Stu 2005, Kathol. Bibelwerk 164 pp. 3-460-03044-5.

413 [E]**Keck, Leander E.** Old Testament survey. NIntB: Nv 2005, Abingdon xv; 577 pp. €19.74. 0-687-053-447;

414 New Testament survey. NIntB: Nv 2005, Abingdon xi; 402 pp. 0-687-05434-6.

415 [E]**Kinsler, Gloria; Kinsler, Ross** God's economy: biblical studies from Latin America. Mkn 2005, Orbis xxx; 250 pp. $28. 1-570-75587-6.

416 [E]**Kirk, Alan K.; Thatcher, Tom** Memory, tradition, and text: uses of the past in early christianity. SBL.Semeia Studies 52: Lei 2005, Brill ix; 282 pp. $39. 90-04-13760-2.

417 [E]**Kirk-Duggan, Cheryl A.** Pregnant passion: gender, sex, and violence in the bible. SBL.Semeia studies 44: 2003 ⇒20,377. [R]CBQ 67 (2005) 173-174 (*Glancy, Jennifer A.*); RBLit (2005)* (*Ashman, Ahuva*); BiCT 1/3 (2005)* (*Upson-Saia, Kristi*).

418 [E]**Kitzberger, Ingrid R.** <Autobiographical biblical criticism: between text and self. 2003 ⇒19,358. [R]BibInterp 13 (2005) 418-420 (*Moore, Stephen D.*).

419 [E]**Kizhakkeyil, Sebastian** In the footsteps of Jesus. Ujjain 2003, Ruhalaya 176 pp. [R]JJSS 4 (2004) 103-104 (*Koikkattil, Claris*).

420 [E]**Korpel, Marjo C.A.; Oesch, Josef M.** Delimitation criticism: a new tool in biblical scholarship. Pericope 1: 2000 ⇒16,283; 19,360. [R]JSSt 50 (2005) 207-209 (*Sweeney, Marvin A.*);

421 Studies in scriptural unit division. Pericope 3: 2002 ⇒18,339; 19,361. [R]JSSt 50 (2005) 207-209 (*Sweeney, Marvin A.*);

422 Layout markers in biblical manuscripts and Ugaritic tablets. Pericope 5: Assen 2005, Van Gorcum vii; 227 pp. €69.50. 90-232-4178-9.

423 [E]**Kuhlmann, Helga** Die Bibel—übersetzt in gerechte Sprache?: Grundlagen einer neuen Übersetzung. Gü 2005, Gü 238 pp. €20. 3-57-9-05499-6. [R]Christ und Sozialist 57/58/1/2 (2005) 229-233 (*Dieckmann, Detlef*).

424 [E]**Kügler, Joachim: Ritter, Werner H.** Auf Leben und Tod oder völlig egal: Kritisches und Nachdenkliches zur Bedeutung der Bibel. TRANSIT 3: Müns 2005, LIT 208 pp. €19.90. 3-8258-8476-7. Ringvorlesung Bayreuth 2003/2004. [R]BiKi 60 (2005) 247-248 (*Bauer, Dieter*).

425 [E]**Laato, Antti; Moor, Johannes C. de** Theodicy in the world of the bible. 2003 ⇒19,365; 20,382. [R]Anton. 80 (2005) 359-366 (*Volgger,*

*David*); CBQ 67 (2005) 175-177 (*Gnuse, Robert*); JThS 56 (2005) 123-125 (*Clements, Ronald E.*).

426 [E]**LaCocque, André C.** Guide des nouvelles lectures de la bible. [T]*Prévost, Jean-Pierre*: P 2005, Bayard 370 pp. €45. 2-227-47173-5.

427 [E]**Larkin, William J., Jr.; Williams, Joel F.** Mission in the New Testament: an evangelical approach. 2003 ⇒19,368. [R]IRM 94 (2005) 602-603 (*Nottingham, William J.*).

428 [E]**Leuba, Jean-Louis** Temps et eschatologie: données bibliques et problématiques contemporaines. 2004 ⇒20,387. [R]Brot. 160 (2005) 286-288 (*Silva, Isidro Ribeiro da*).

429 [E]**Levine, Amy-Jill; Blickenstaff, Marianne** A feminist companion to the Deutero-Pauline epistles. FCNT 7: 2003 ⇒19,373; 20,388. [R]RBLit (2005)* (*Stepp, Perry*);

430 A feminist companion to Paul. The feminist companion to the NT 6: 2004 ⇒20,389. [R]RBLit (2005)* (*Heen, Erik; Maccammon, Linda; Pascuzzi, Maria*); ET 117 (2005) 22 (*Collins, Cecelia*).

431 [E]**Levine, Amy-Jill; Robbins, Maria Mayo** A feminist companion to mariology. FCNT 10: L 2005, Clark x; 225 pp. $130. 0-8264-6662-1. Bibl. 194-212.

432 [E]**Levoratti, Armando J.** I vangeli. R 2005, Borla 1026 pp. 88-263-15-66-3.

433 [E]**Linafelt, Tod** A shadow of glory: reading the New Testament after the Holocaust. 2002 ⇒19,347; 20,393. [R]RBLit (2005)* (*Schaberg, Jane D.*); BiCT 1/4 (2005)* (*Walsh, Richard*).

434 **Loba-Mkole, Jean-Claude; Wendland, Ernst R.** Interacting with scriptures in Africa. Nairobi 2005, Action 206 pp.

435 [E]**Lowder Jefferey Jay; Price, Robert M.** The empty tomb: Jesus beyond the grave. Amherst, NY 2005, Prometheus 545 pp. $30. 1-59102-286-X. Bibl. 493-509.

436 [E]**Luttikhuizen, Gerard P.** Eve's children: the biblical stories retold and interpreted in Jewish and Christian traditions. 2003 ⇒19,377. [R]RBLit (2005)* (*Nicklas, Tobias*) [Gen 4].

437 [E]**Maritano, Mario; Zevini, Giorgio** La lectio divina nella vita della chiesa. Studi di Spiritualità 15: R 2005, LAS 224 pp. 88-213-0602-X. Bibl. 209-217.

438 **Marshall, I. Howard**, *al.*, Beyond the bible: moving from scripture to theology. 2004 ⇒20,399. [R]RBLit (2005)* (*Vest, John W.*); ChrTo 49/11 (2005) 92-93 (*Neff, D.*).

439 [E]**Matthews, Shelly; Gibson, Leigh E.** Violence in the New Testament. NY 2005, Clark vii; 160 pp. $28. 0-567-02500-4.

440 [E]**McGinn, Bernard J.; Collins, John J.; Stein, Stephen J.** The Continuum history of apocalypticism. 2003 ⇒19,378. [R]ThLZ 130 (2005) 1302-1305 (*Karrer, Martin*).

441 [E]**McKim, Donald K.** L'interprétation de la bible au fil des siècles, 1: du IIe au XVe siècle. [T]*Triqueneaux, Paya; Triqueneaux, Sylvain*: Ouvrages de Référence: Cléon-d'Andran 2005, Excelsis 167 pp.

442 [E]**McKnight, Scot; Osborne, Grant R.** The face of New Testament studies: a survey of recent research. 2004 ⇒20,400. [R]CBQ 67 (2005) 549-551 (*Barram, Michael*); TrinJ 26 (2005) 327-329 (*Fay, Ron C.*); JETh 19 (2005) 259-261 (*Stenschke, Christoph*).

443 [E]**Menken, Maarten J.J.; Moyise, Steve** Isaiah in the New Testament. L 2005, Clark xii; 217 pp. $50. 0-567-03030-X.

444 [E]**Mies, F.** Bible et économie: servir Dieu ou l'argent. Le livre et le rouleau 17: 2003 ⇒19,382. [R]EeV 115 (2005) 21-22 (*Tabournel, Jean-S.*);

445 Bible et sciences des religions: Judaïsme, christianisme, Islam. Le livre et le rouleau 23; Connaître et croire 12: Bru 2005, Lessius 177 pp. €20. 2-87299-141-7.

446 Mikra: text, translation, reading & interpretation of the Hebrew Bible in ancient Judaism and early christianity. [E]*Mulder, Martin Jan; Sysling, Harry*: 2004 <1988> ⇒20,403. [R]HeyJ 46 (2005) 525-526 (*Briggs, Richard S.*); RBLit (2005)* (*Stenstrup, Ken*).

447 [E]**Miller, Althea S. ; Wicker, Kathleen O.; Dube, Musa S.** Feminist New Testament studies: global and future perspectives. NY 2005, Palgrave xix; 268 pp. 1-403-96870-5.

448 [E]**Moore, Stephen D.; Anderson, Janice C.** New Testament masculinities. SBL.Semeia studies 45: 2003 ⇒19,386; 20,405. [R]SvTK 81 (2005) 41-42 (*Ivarsson, Fredrik*); BiCT 1/2 (2005)* (*Townsley, Gillian*).

449 [E]**Moore, Stephen D.; Segovia, Fernando F.** Postcolonial biblical criticism: interdisciplinary intersections. L 2005, Clark vii; 206 pp. £40. 0-567-08439-6. [R]RBLit (2005)* (*Staley, Jeffrey*).

450 Neues Testament und antike Kultur, 3: Weltauffassung–Kult–Ethos. [E]*Erlemann, Kurt, al.*: Neuk 2005, Neuk viii; 253 pp. €29.90. 3788720-387.

451 [E]**Noel, James A.; Johnson, Matthew V.** The passion of the Lord: African American reflections. Mp 2005, Fortress x; 190 pp. $6. 0-800-6-3730-5 [ThD 52,182—W. Charles Heiser].

452 [E]**Oakes, Peter** Rome in the bible and the early church. 2002 ⇒18,363; 19,389. [R]BS 162 (2005) 379-381 (*Fantin, Joseph D.*).

453 [E]**Oegema, Gerbern S.** Einführung zu den Jüdischen Schriften aus hellenistisch-römischer Zeit: Unterweisung in erzählender Form. JSHRZ 6, Supplementa, Lief. 1, Fasz. 2: Gü 2005, Gü ix; 209 pp. €98. 35790-42734.

454 [E]**Oeming, Manfred; Schmid, Konrad** Der eine Gott und die Götter: Polytheismus und Monotheismus im antiken Israel. AThANT 82: 2003 ⇒19,391. [R]ThLZ 130 (2005) 505-507 (*Schmidt, Werner H.*); ThR 70 (2005) 431-439 (*Reventlow, Henning Graf*).

455 [E]**Oeming, Manfred** Theologie des Alten Testaments aus der Perspektive von Frauen. Beiträge zum Verstehen der Bibel 1: Müns 2003, LIT 325 pp. 3-8258-6386-3.

456 [E]**Otto, Eckart; Achenbach, Reinhard** Das Deuteronomium zwischen Pentateuch und Deuteronomistischem Geschichtswerk. FRLANT 206: 2004 ⇒20,411. [R]RSR 93 (2005) 573-576 (*Artus, Olivier*); RBLit (2005)* (*Auld, A.G.*).

457 [E]**Otto, Eckart; Le Roux, Jurie** A critical study of the pentateuch: an encounter between Europe and Africa. Altes Testament und Moderne 20: Müns 2005, Lit x; 198 pp. 3-8258-8982-3.

458 [E]**Panimolle, Salvatore A.** Maria di Nazaret nella bibbia. DSBP 40: R 2005, Borla 395 pp. €21.50. 88-2631-5442;

459 Il matrimonio nella bibbia. DSBP 42: R 2005, Borla 299 pp. €23.50. 88-263-15787.

460 **Pate, C. Martin**, *al.*, The story of Israel: a biblical theology. 2004 ⇒ 20,414. [R]RBLit (2005)* (*Jones, Brian*).

461 [E]**Patte, Daniel; Grenholm, Cristina** Gender, tradition and Romans: shared ground, uncertain borders. NY 2005, Clark 297 pp. $40. 0-567-02911-5.

462 [E]**Penna, Romano** Le origini del cristianesimo: una guida. 2004 ⇒20, 415. [R]ConAss 7 (2005) 97-100 (*Testaferri, Francesco*).

463 [E]**Penner, Todd C.; Vander Stichele, Caroline** Moving beyond New Testament theology?: essays in conversation with *Heikki Räisänen*. SESJ 88: Helsinki 2005, Finnish Exegetical Society xiii; 490 pp. 951-9217-43-6.

464 [E]**Phillips, Thomas E.** Acts and ethics. New Testament Monographs 9: Shf 2005, Sheffield Academic xi; 161 pp. $85. 9781-9050-48229. Bibl. 135-149.

465 [E]**Piper, John; Taylor, Justin; Helseth, Paul Kjoss** Beyond the bounds: open theism and the undermining of biblical christianity. 2003 ⇒19,400; 20,416. [R]SBET 23 (2005) 227-228 (*Williams, Stephen N.*).

466 [E]**Platone, Giuseppe** La bibbia e l'Italia. 2004 ⇒20,417. [R]RivBib 53 (2005) 252-253 (*Vetrali, Tecle*).

467 [E]**Poorthuis, Marcel; Schwartz, Joshua** Saints and role models in Judaism and christianity. Jewish and Christian Perspectives 7: Lei 2004, Brill xii; 485 pp. 90-04-12614-7.

468 [E]**Porter, Stanley E.; Roo, Jacqueline C.R. de** The concept of the covenant in the Second Temple period. JSJ.S 71: 2003 ⇒19,401; 20,419. [R]JSJ 36 (2005) 366-371 (*Nitzan, Bilhah*);

469 [E]**Porter, Stanley E.** Paul and his opponents. Pauline Studies 2: Lei 2005, Brill xi; 257 pp. €79. 90-04-14701-2.

470 **Puig i Tàrrech, Armand**, *al.* El text: lectures i història. Scripta Biblica 3: 2001 ⇒17,310... 20,716. [R]RivBib 53 (2005) 341-347 (*Passoni Dell'Acqua, Anna*).

471 [E]**Puig i Tàrrech, Armand** La bíblia i els immigrants. Scripta Biblica 6: Montserrat 2005, Montserrat 328 pp. €18. 84-8415-677-X. [R]EstTrin 39 (2005) 386-387 (*Pujana, Juan*).

472 [E]**Rhoads, David** From every people and nation: the book of Revelation in intercultural perspective. Grove City 2005, Augsburg F. 282 pp. $22. 08006-37216. Bibl. 249-277. [R]RBLit (2005)* (*Villiers, Pieter de*).

473 [E]**Sampley, J. Paul** Paul in the Greco-Roman world: a handbook. 2003 ⇒19,406. [R]CBQ 67 (2005) 193-194 (*Brink, Laurie*); RBLit (2005)* (*Nicklas, Tobias; Donahoe, Kate*); RBLit 7 (2005) 368-370 (*Donahoe, Kate*).

474 [E]**Sandlin, P. Andrew** Backbone of the bible: covenant in contemporary perspective. 2004 ⇒20,423. [R]TrinJ 26 (2005) 149-150 (*Karlberg, Mark W.*).

475 [E]**Sánchez Navarro, L.; Granados, C.** Escritura e interpretación: los fundamentos de la interpretación bíblica. 2003 ⇒19,409; 20,426. [R]AnnTh 19 (2005) 286-292 (*Tábet, M.*).

476 [E]**Schenke, Ludger** Jesus von Nazaret—Spuren und Konturen. 2004 ⇒ 20,428. [R]ThLZ 130 (2005) 955-958 (*Schröter, Jens*).

477 [E]**Schenker, Adrian; Hugo, P.** L'enfance de la bible hébraïque: l'histoire du texte de l'Ancien Testament à la lumière des recherches récentes. MoBi 52: Genève 2005, Labor et F. 318 pp. 2-8309-1172-5.

478 [E]**Schertz, Mary H.; Friesen, Ivan** Beautiful upon the mountains: biblical essays on mission, peace, and the reign of God. 2003 ⇒19,410. [R]RBLit (2005)* (*Stenschke, Christoph*).

479 [E]**Schmid, Konrad** Prophetische Heils- und Herrschererwartungen. SBS 194: Stu 2005, Katholisches Bibelwerk viii; 119 pp. €22.80. 3-460-04941-3.

480 [E]**Scholtissek, Klaus** Christologie in der Paulus-Schule: zur Rezeption des paulinischen Evangeliums. SBS 181: 1999 ⇒15,281... 17,316. [R]ScEs 57 (2005) 270-273 (*Doutre, Jean*).

481 [E]**Scholz, Susanne** Biblical studies alternatively: an introductory reader. 2003 ⇒19,412. [R]CBQ 67 (2005) 551-553 (*McMahon, Christopher*).

482 Secrets of the bible: from the editors of Archaeology Magazine. NY 2005, Hatherleigh xvii; 217 pp. 1-57826-172-4. Introd. *Neil Asher Silberman*; Bibl. 209-210.

483 [E]**Sherwood, Yvonne; Bekkenkamp, Jonneke** Sanctified aggression: legacies of biblical and post biblical vocabularies of violence. JSOT.S 400; Bible in the Twenty-First Century Series 3: 2003 ⇒19,416. [R]RBLit (2005)* (*Mandolfo, Carleen*).

484 [E]**Sim, David C.; Riches, John Kenneth** The gospel of Matthew in its Roman imperial context. JSNT.S 276: L 2005, Clark viii; 202 pp. $50. 0-567-08448-5. Bibl. 170-183. [R]RBLit (2005)* (*Carson, Donald*).

485 [E]**Smith, D.E.; Williams, M.E.** Stories about Jesus in the synoptic gospels. Storyteller's companion to the bible 9: Nv 2005, Abingdon 199 pp. $20. 06870-01013. Bibl. [NTAb 49,604].

486 Springs of living water: bible studies on grace and transformation. Geneva 2005, WCC 60 pp. FS12/$9.75. 28254-14204.

487 [E]**Steins, Georg; Untergaßmair, Franz G.** Das Buch, ohne das man nichts versteht: die kulturelle Kraft der Bibel. Vechtaer Beiträge zur Theologie 11: Müns 2005, LIT 245 pp. €20. 3-8258-7969-0.

488 [E]**Strawbridge, Gregg** The case for covenantal infant baptism. 2003 ⇒ 19,418. [R]BS 162 (2005) 372-374 (*Zuck, Roy B.*).

489 [E]**Stuckenbruck, Loren T.; North, Wendy E.S.** Early Jewish and Christian monotheism. JSNT.S 263; Early christianity in context: 2004 ⇒20, 434. [R]RBLit (2005)* (*Calvert-Koyzis, Nancy*).

490 [E]**Stuhlmacher, Peter; Janowski, Bernd** The suffering servant: Isaiah 53 in Jewish and christian sources. [T]*Bailey, Daniel P.*: 2004 ⇒20,436. [R]RBLit (2005)* (*Barker, William; Nam, Roger*).

491 [E]**Uríbarri, G.** Biblia y nueva evangelización. Biblioteca de teología 12: M 2005, UPComillas 158 pp. 84-8468-158-0.

492 [E]**Van Kooten, George H.** The creation of heaven and earth: re-interpretations of Genesis 1 in the context of Judaism, ancient philosophy, christianity, and modern physics. Themes in biblical narrative, Jewish and Christian traditions 8: Lei 2005, Brill xiv; 284 pp. €109/ $147. 90-04-14235-5. [R]JSJ 36 (2005) 381-385 (*Klostergaard Petersen, Anders*).

493 [E]**Vander Stichele, Caroline; Penner, Todd C.** Her master's tools?: feminist and postcolonial engagements of historical-critical discourse. Global perspectives on biblical scholarship 9: Lei 2005, Brill xiii; 390 pp. $40. 1-58983-1195. Bibl. 339-372. [R]RBLit (2005)* (*Coloe, Mary*).

494 [E]**West, Gerald O.; Dube, Musa W.** The bible in Africa: transactions, trajectories and trends. 2000 ⇒16,342... 20,441. [R]RBLit (2005)* (*Wilson, Alistair*).

495 [E]**Wills, Lawrence Mitchell; Wright, Benjamin Givins** Conflicted boundaries in wisdom and apocalypticism. SBL.Symposium 35: Atlanta, GA 2005, SBL viii; 240 pp. $33. 1-58983-184-5. Bibl. 215-219.

496 [E]**Wilt, Timothy** Bible translation: frames of reference. 2003 ⇒19,425. [R]BiTr 56 (2005) 261-265 (*Stine, Philip C.*); 265-267 (*Matos, Francisco Gomes de*); 267-268 (*Albert, Sándor*); 268-271 & JOT 1/3 (2005) 77-79 (*Hill, Ralph*).

497 [E]**Wirtz, Hans G.** Der Fremde aus Nazareth–Jesus Christus in Kinderbibeln. SIKG 20: Weimar 2004, Bertuch 100 pp. €12.80. 3937601066.
498 [E]**Wolter, Michael** Ethik als angewandte Ekkelesiologie: der Brief an die Epheser. SMBen.BE 17: R 2005, Abtei St. Paul vor den Mauern vi; 227 pp. €30.
499 [E]**Yoder, P.B.** Take this word to heart: the shema in torah and gospel. Occasional Papers 23: Elkhart, IN 2005, Institute of Mennonite Studies viii; 137 pp. $15. 09362-73380 [NTAb 50,410].

## A1.4 *Plurium compilationes* theologicae

500 **Aleixandre, Dolores**, *al.* La interioridad: un paradigma emergente. 2004 ⇒20,445. [R]RF 251 (2005) 267-268 (*Irazabal, Juan Antonio*).
501 [E]**Ascough, Richard S.** Religious rivalries and the struggle for success in Sardis and Smyrna. SCJud 14: Waterloo, Ontario 2005, Laurier Univ. Pr. xv; 355 pp. $39. 0-88920-472-1 [ThD 52,285–W.C. Heiser].
502 [E]**Barrow, S.; Bartley, J.** Consuming passion: why the killing of Jesus really matters. L 2005, Darton, L. & T. vii; 136 pp. £11. 02325-26079. Bibl. [NTAb 50,586].
503 [E]**Bataglia, Vicenzo; Dotolo, Carmelo** Gesù Cristo, Figlio di Dio e Signore. 2004 ⇒20,451. [R]Carthaginensia 21 (2005) 510-511 (*Martínez Fresneda, F.*).
504 **Belayche, Nicole**, *al.* Nommer les dieux: théonymes, épithètes, épiclèses dans l'antiquité. Recherches sur les rhétoriques religieuses 5: Turnhout 2005, Brepols 665 pp. 2503-51686-6.
505 **Benvenuti, A.**, *al.* Storia della santità nel cristianesimo occidentale. Sacro/Santo n.s. 9: R 2005, Viella 427 pp.
506 [E]**Berner, Ulrich; Bochinger, Christoph; Flasche, Rainer** Opfer und Gebet in den Religionen. Veröffentlichungen der Wissenschaftlichen Gesellschaft für Theologie 26: Gü 2005, Gü 180 pp. 3-579-01842-6.
507 [E]**Bigarelli, Alberto; Peri, Aldo** L'aldilà: la risurrezione nel testo biblico e nella visione del magistero. Sussidi biblici 85: Reggio Emilia 2005, San Lorenzo 115 pp. 88-8071-163-6.
508 **Biguzzi, Giancarlo**, *al.* Il potere. PSV 51: Bo 2005, Dehoniane 305 pp.
509 [E]**Blankenhorn, David; Browning, Don; Van Leeuwen, Mary** Does christianity teach male headship?: the equal-regard marriage and its critics. 2004 ⇒20,453. [R]RBLit (2005)* (*Hood, Renate V.*).
510 [E]**Block, Ed, Jr.** Glory, grace, and culture: the work of Hans Urs VON BALTHASAR. Mahwah, NJ 2005, Paulist x; 224 pp. $25. 0-8091-4305-4 [ThD 52,162—W. Charles Heiser].
511 [E]**Borowski, Irvin J.** Defining new christian/Jewish dialogue. 2004 ⇒ 20,454. [R]RBLit (2005)* (*Feldman, Louis*).
512 [E]**Bouche, Anne-Marie; Hamburger, Jeffrey H.** The mind's eye: art and theological argument in the Middle Ages. Princeton, NJ 2005, Princeton University Pr. 464 pp. $95. 978-06911-24766.
513 [E]**Boureux, Christophe; Theobald, Christoph** Le péché originel: heurs et malheurs d'un dogme. P 2005, Bayard 210 pp [Etudes (juillet-août 2005), 143—Geneviève Comeau].
514 [E]**Brakmann, Heinzgerd; Gerhards, Albert; Klöckener, Martin** Prex eucharistica, vol. III: Studia, pars prima: ecclesia antiqua et occidentalis. SpicFri 42: FrS 2005, Academic viii; 310 pp. 3-7278-1487-X.

515 [E]**Braun, Willi** Rhetoric and reality in early christianities. Studies in Christianity and Judaism 16: Waterloo, Ontario 2005, Canadian Corporation for Studies in Religion 257 pp. 0-88920-462-4.

516 [E]**Brunner-Traut, Emma** I fondatori delle grandi religioni: Akhenaton, Mosè, Zarathustra, Gesù, Mani, Muhammed, Buddha, Confucio, Lao Tzu. Introduzioni e trattati 26: Brescia 2005, Queriniana 214 pp. €20. [R]CredOg 25/5 (2005) 151-152 (*Rigopoulos, Antonio*).

517 [E]**Burrus, Virginia** Late ancient christianity. A people's history of christianity 2: Mp 2005, Fortress xv; 318 pp. $35. 0-8006-3412-8.

518 [E]**Chareire, Isabelle; Joly, Dominique** La fête, parabole du royaume. 2004 ⇒20,461. [R]Cahiers de l'Atelier 507 (2005) 125-127 (*Durand, Xavier*).

519 [E]**Chilton, Bruce D.; Neusner, Jacob** Altruism in world religions. Wsh 2005, Georgetown Univ. Pr. xiv; 202 pp. $27/£17. 15890-10655 [NTAb 50,443].

520 [E]**Christianson, Eric S.; Francis, Peter; Telford, William R.** Cinéma divinité: religion, theology and the bible in film. L 2005, SCM 373 pp. £20. 0-334-02988-0.

521 [E]**Cobb, Paul M.; Van Bekkum, Wout J.** Strategies of medieval communal identity: Judaism, Christianity and Islam. Mediaevalia Groningana n.s. 5: Lv 2004, Peeters x, 186 pp. 90-429-1492-0. Bibl. 163-180.

522 [E]**Coda, F.; Gavazzi, L.** L'immagine del divino: nelle tradizioni cristiane e nelle grandi religioni. Mi 2005, Mondadori 375 pp.

523 [E]**Crossley, James G.; Karner, Christian** Writing history, constructing religion. Aldershot 2005, Ashgate vii; 233 pp. 0-7546-5183-5.

524 [E]**Dekoninck, Ralph; Watthee-Delmotte, Myriam** L'idole dans l'imaginaire occidental. Structures et pouvoirs des imaginaires: P 2005, L'Harmattan 395 pp. 27475-87983.

525 [E]**Della Pasqua, Biagio; Valentini, Natalino** Mistero di Cristo, mistero dell'uomo: la nuova "questione antropologica" e le radici della fede. Saggistica Paoline 29: Mi 2005, Paoline 201 pp. 88315-28246. Bibl. 195-197.

526 [E]**Dempsey, Carol J.; Pazdan, Mary Margaret** Earth, wind, and fire: biblical and theological perspectives on creation. 2004 ⇒20,466. [R]RBLit (2005)* (*De Wet Oosthuizen, Rudolph; Shields, Mary E.*).

527 [E]**Dexinger, Ferdinand; Hartmann, Gerhard; Hierzenberger, Gottfried** Grundwissen Religion. TOPOS-plus-Taschenbücher 559: Mainz 2005, Matthias-Grünewald 1956 pp. 3-7867-8559-7.

528 [E]**Dodd, David B.; Faraone, Christopher A.** Initiation in ancient Greek rituals and narratives: new critical perspectives. L 2005, Routledge xix; 294 pp. £65.

529 [E]**Ellens, J. Harold; Rollins, Wayne G.** Psychology and the bible: a new way to read the scriptures. Westport (Conn.) 2004, Praeger 4 vols. 0-275-98347-1. Vol 1, From FREUD to Kohut, 2: From Genesis to apocalyptic vision, 3: From gospel to Gnostics, 4: From Christ to Jesus. Foreword by *Donald Capps*.

530 [E]**Erickson, Victoria Lee; Farrell, Susan A.** Still believing: Jewish, Christian, and Muslim women affirm their faith. Mkn 2005, Orbis x; 154 pp. 1-570-75582-5. Bibl. 151-154.

531 [E]**Evans, Gillian R.** The first christian theologians: an introduction to theology in the early church. Great theologians: 2004 ⇒20,476. [R]HeyJ 46 (2005) 545 (*Meconi, David Vincent*); LouvSt 30 (2005) 235-236 (*Leemans, Johan*).

532 [E]**Ewell, C. Rosalee V.; Jones, L. Gregory; Hütter, Reinhard** God, truth, and witness: engaging Stanley HAUERWAS. GR 2005, Brazos 336 pp. 1-58743-151-3.

533 [E]**Feldmeier, Reinhard** Wiedergeburt. BTSP 25: Gö 2005, Vandenhoeck & R. 248 pp. €19.70. 3-525-61584-1.

534 [E]**Ferri, R.; Manganaro, P.** Gesto e parola: ricerche sulla rivelazione. R 2005, Città N. 435 pp. €34.

535 [E]**Frankemölle, Hubert** Juden und Christen im Gespräch über 'Dabru emet–redet Wahrheit'. Pd 2005, Bonifatius 250 pp. €15.90. 3-89710-323-0.

536 **Frankl, Viktor E.; Lapide, Pinchas** Gottsuche und Sinnfrage: ein Gespräch. Gü 2005, Gü 144 pp. 3-579-05428-7.

537 [E]**Freedman, David N.; McClymond, Michael** The rivers of paradise: Moses, Buddha, Confucius, Jesus...Muhammad as religious founders. 2001 ⇒17,354; 19,441. [R]JNES 64 (2005) 145-6 (*Sparks, Kent*).

538 [E]**Geerlings, Wilhelm** Theologen der christlichen Antike: eine Einführung. 2002 ⇒18,405; 19,443. [R]ThRv 101 (2005) 224-225 (*Merkt, Andreas*).

539 [E]**Georgoudi, Stella; Koch Piettre, Renée; Schmidt, Francis** La cuisine et l'autel: les sacrifices en questions dans les sociétés de la Méditerranée ancienne. BEHE.R 124: Turnhout 2005, Brepols xvii; 460 pp. €75. 2-503-51739-0.

540 [E]**Gerhards, Albert; Wahle, Stephan** Kontinuität und Unterbrechung: Gottesdienst und Gebet in Judentum und Christentum. Studien zu Judentum und Christentum: Pd 2005, Schöningh 285 pp. €39.90. 3-506-71338-8.

541 [E]**Gestrich, Christof; Wabel, Thomas** Freier oder unfreier Wille?: Handlungsfreiheit und Schuldfähigkeit im Dialog der Wissenschaften. BThZ.B: B 2005, Wichern 130 pp. 3-88981-181-7. Bibl. 125-128.

542 [E]**Haehling, Raban von** Griechische Mythologie und frühes Christentum. Da:Wiss. 2005, xiii; 401 pp. €59.90. 3-534-18528-5.

543 [E]**Halpérin, Jean; Ucko, Hans** Worlds of memory and wisdom: encounters of Jews and African Christians. Geneva 2005, World Council of Churches vii; 161 pp. 2-8254-1429-8. Bibl.

544 [E]**Harries, Richard; Solomon, Norman; Winter, Tim J.** Abraham's children: Jews, Christians and Muslims in conversation. L 2005, Clark xiv, 338 pp. $40. 0-567-08161-3.

545 [E]**Harris, William Vernon** The spread of christianity in the first four centuries: essays in explanation. CSCT 27: Lei 2005, Brill xiv; 176 pp. €99/$129. 90-04-14717-9. Bibl. 161-172.

546 [E]**Hell, Silva; Lies, Lothar** Amt und Eucharistiegemeinschaft: ökumenische Perspektiven und Probleme. 2004 ⇒20,488. [R]ÖR 54 (2005) 405-407 (*Böttigheimer, Christoph*).

547 [E]**Hinnells, John Russell** The Routledge companion to the study of religion. L 2005, Routledge xii; 556 pp. 0-415-33310-5. Bibl.

548 [E]**Holmes, Stephen R.; Rae, Murray A.** The person of Christ. L 2005, Clark 206 pp. £50.

549 [E]**Hoping, Helmut; Tück, Jan-Heiner** Streitfall Christologie: Vergewisserungen nach der Shoah. QD 214: FrB 2005, Herder 263 pp. €26. 3-451-02214-1.

550 [E]**Horsley, Richard A.** Christian origins. A people's history of Christianity 1: Mp 2005, Fortress xv; 318 p. $35. 0-8006-3411-X.

551 [E]**Jacobson, Yoram; Mach, Michael F.** Historiosophy and the science of Judaism. Te'uda 20: TA 2005, Tel Aviv Univ. xxx; 333 pp.

552 [E]**Johnston, Sara Iles** Religions of the ancient world: a guide. 2004 ⇒ 20,493. [R]RBLit (2005)* (*Arnold, Bill*).

553 [E]**Johnston, Sarah Iles; Struck, Peter T.** Mantikê: studies in ancient divination. RGRW 155: Lei 2005, Brill 322 pp. €97/$132. 90-04-144-97-8.

554 [E]**Jule, Allyson** Gender and the language of religion. L 2005, Palgrave M. xi; 281 pp. 1-403-94862-3.

555 [E]**Kögerler, Reinhart; Schörghofer, Gustav** Wie wirkt Gott in der Welt?: theologische Zugänge und naturwissenschaftliche Sichtweisen. Forum St. Stephan 15: W 2005, Wagner 193 pp. 3-902330-10-4.

556 [E]**Kuefler, M.** The Boswell thesis: essays on christianity, social tolerance, and homosexuality. Ch 2005, Univ. of Chicago Pr. viii; 348 pp. $75/£47.50; $27.50/£17.50. 022654-57400/19 [NTAb 50,441].

557 [E]**Lane, Dermot A.** Catholic theology facing the future: historical perspectives. 2003 ⇒19,453. [R]IThQ 70 (2005) 89-90 (*Boland, Vivian*).

558 [E]**Lange, Armin; Lichtenberger, Hermann; Römheld, K.F.Diethard** Die Dämonen—Demons: die Dämonologie der israelitisch-jüdischen und frühchristlichen Literatur im Kontext ihrer Umwelt—the Demonology of Israelite-Jewish and early christian literature in context of their environment. 2003 ⇒19,454; 20,499. [R]NT 47 (2005) 94-96 (*Stenschke, Christoph*); Numen 52 (2005) 513-516 (*Schipper, Bernd U.*); ThR 70 (2005) 417-419 (*Reventlow, Henning Graf*).

559 [E]**Lee, Sang Hyun** The Princeton companion to Jonathan EDWARDS. Princeton 2005, Princeton Univ. Pr. xxviii; 331 pp. £30. 06911-21087.

560 [E]**Leemans, Johan** More than a memory: the discourse of martyrdom and the construction of christian identity in the history of christianity. ANL 51: Lv 2005, Peeters xvi; 471 pp. 90-429-1688-5. Collab. Jurgen Mettepenningen.

561 [E]**Lietaert Peerbolte, Bert J.; Tigchelaar, Eibert** Kennis van het kwaad: zeven visies uit jodendom en christendom. De bijbel 3: Zoetermeer 2004, Meinema 176 pp. €15.90. 90211-39723.

562 [E]**Linzey, Andrew; Kirker, Richard** Gays and the future of Anglicanism: responses to the Windsor Report. Winchester 2005, O Books xxxviii; 338 pp. $30.

563 [E]**Long, Lynne** Translation and religion: holy untranslatable?. Topics in Translation 28: Clevedon 2005, Multilingual M. vi; 209 pp. 1-85359-8186.

564 [E]**Malek, Roman** The Chinese face of Jesus Christ, 3a: modern faces and images of Jesus Christ. Monograph 50/3a: Sankt Augustin 2005, Institut Monumenta Serica xvi; 847-1311 pp. €60. 3-8050-0524-5 [ThD 52,250—W. Charles Heiser].

565 [E]**Marin, Marcello** Studi e testi di letteratura cristiana antica. Auctores nostri 1: 2004 ⇒20,506. [R]Rivista di science religiose 19/1 (2005) 247-248 (*Dell'Osso, Carlo*).

566 [E]**Mariña, Jaqueline** The Cambridge companion to Friedrich SCHLEIERMACHER. Cambridge Companions to Religion: C 2005, CUP xiv; 348 pp. $30. 0-521-89137X [ThD 53,57–W. Charles Heiser].

567 [E]**Marjanen, Antti; Luomanen, Petri** A companion to second-century christian 'heretics'. VigChr.S 76: Lei 2005, Brill xiii; 385 pp. €118/ $169. 90-04-14464-1.

568 [E]**Marmion, Declan; Thiessen, Gesa E.** Theology in the making: biography contexts methods. Dublin 2005, Veritas 170 pp. 18539-09459.

569 [E]**McGhee, Glen S.; O'Leary, Stephen D.** War in heaven / heaven on earth: theories of the apocalyptic. Millennialism and Society 2: L 2005, Equinox xxvi; 290 pp. £16/$27. 1-90476-881-1.

570 [E]**McNamara, Martin** Apocalyptic and eschatological heritage: the Middle East and Celtic realms. 2003 ⇒20,508. [R]Journal of Medieval Latin 15 (2005) 304-306 (*Calkin, Siobhain Bly*).

571 [E]**Miller, Patrick D.; McCann, Dennis P.** In search of the common good: theology for the twenty-first century. Harrisburg 2005, Clark 360 pp. $40. 0-5670-2770-8.

572 [E]**Miller, William R.; Delaney, Harold D.** Judeo-Christian perspectives on psychology: human nature, motivation, and change. 2005, American Psychological Assoc. xvi; 329 pp. $50. 1-59147-161-3.

573 Il ministero episcopale. Firmana 38-39: Fermo 2005, n.p. 210 pp.

574 [E]**Minnema, L.; Van den Burg, C.** In de ban van het kwaad: het kwaad in religieuze verhalen wereldwijd. De bijbel 3: Zoetermeer 2004, Meinema 315 pp. €20. 90211-40314.

575 [E]**Mintz, Adam; Schiffman, Lawrence H.** Jewish spirituality and divine law. NY 2005, Yeshiva University Press xxi; 534 pp. 0-88125-865-2.

576 Miscellanea Bibliothecae Apostolicae Vaticanae XII. Studi e testi 433: Città del Vaticano 2005, Biblioteca Apostolica Vaticana 532 pp.

577 [E]**Moltmann-Wendel, Elisabeth; Kirchhoff, Renate** Christologie im Lebensbezug. Gö 2005, Vandenhoeck & R. 240 pp. €30. 35255-69580.

578 [E]**Neubrand, Maria** "Lebendige Gemeinde": Beiträge aus biblischer, historischer, systematischer und praktischer Theologie. ESt 54: Rg 2005, Pustet 337 pp. €39.90. 3-7917-1982-3.

579 [E]**Panimolle, Salvatore A.** Maria, madre del Signore, nei padri della chiesa. DSBP 41: R 2005, Borla 388 pp. €23.50. 88-2631-5450;

580 Male–Maligno–peccato nei padri della chiesa. DSBP 39: R 2005, Borla 388 pp. €21.50. 88-263-1540X.

581 [E]**Parratt, John** An introduction to third world theologies. 2004 ⇒20, 518. [R]RBLit (2005)* (*Duggan, Michael*).

582 [E]**Pfeiderer, Georg; Stegemann, Ekkehard W.** Politische Religion: Geschichte und Gegenwart eines Problemfeldes. Basler Studien zur Theologie 3: 2004, ⇒20,519. [R]ZKG 116 (2005) 379-381 (*Meier, Kurt*).

583 [E]**Poorthuis, Marcel; Roggema, Barbara; Valkenberg, Pim** The three rings: textual studies in the historical trialogue of Judaism, Christianity, and Islam. Publications of the Thomas Instituut te Utrecht, n.s. 11: Lv 2005, Peeters xxii; 297 pp. €35. 90-429-1563-3.

584 A Quarant'anni dal Concilio: VI Forum del Progetto Culturale. Oggi e domani, II/41: Bo 2005, EDB 374 pp. 88-10-14025-7. Servizio Nazionale per il Progetto Culturale della Conferenza episcopale italiana.

585 [E]**Ritter, Werner H.; Wolf, Bernhard** Heilung—Energie—Geist: Heilung zwischen Wissenschaft, Religion und Geschäft. Biblisch-theologische Schwerpunkte 26: Gö 2005, Vandenhoeck & R. 284 pp. 3525-61-585-X.

586 [E]**Saturnino, Mario** Rooting faith in Asia. Source book for inculturation: Bangalore 2005, Claretian 435 pp. Rs380.

587 **Siniscalco, Paolo**, *al.* Le antiche chiese orientali: storia e letteratura. R 2005, Città N. 458 pp.

588 [E]**Soskice, Janet Martin; Lipton, Diana** Feminism and theology. Oxford readings in feminism: 2003 ⇒19,476. [R]AThR 87 (2005) 368-370 (*Nemazee, Rowshan*).
589 [E]**Sotomayor, Manuel; Fernández Ubiña, José** Historia del cristianismo, 1: el cristianismo en el mundo antiguo. 2003 ⇒19,477. [R]StMon 47 (2005) 175-177 (*Tragán, P.-R.*).
590 [E]**Staubli, Thomas** Vertikale Ökumene: Erinnerungsarbeit im Dienst des interreligiösen Dialogs. FrS 2005, Academic 72 pp. 37278-1516-7.
591 [E]**Stivers, Robert L.; Stone, Ronald H.** Resistance and theological ethics. Lanham 2004, Rowman & L. 334 pp. $72. [R]HBT 27/1 (2005) 118-121 (*Martin, Dhaum B.*).
592 [E]**Thumma, Scott; Gray, Edward R.** Gay religion. Walnut Creek, Calif. 2004, AltaMira xvi;453 pp. $29. [R]RBLit (2005)* (*De George, Susan*).
593 [E]**Van Harn, Roger H.** Exploring and proclaiming the Apostles' Creed. GR 2004, Eerdmans 320 pp. £16. 978-08192-81166. [R]Sewanee Theological Review 48/3 (2005) 341-347 (*Edwards, O.C.*).
594 [E]**Van Nieuwenhove, Rik; Wawrykow, Joseph** The theology of Thomas AQUINAS. ND 2005, Univ. of ND Pr. xx; 472 pp. $37.50. 0-268-0-4363-9 [ThD 52,190—W. Charles Heiser].
595 [E]**Vanhoozer, Kevin J.** The Cambridge companion to postmodern theology. Cambridge Companions to Religion: 2003 ⇒19,482; 20,539. [R]RBLit 7 (2005) 502-503 (*Jobling, David; Schweitzer, Donald S.*).
596 [E]**Veltri, Giuseppe; Wolf, Hubert; Schuller, Florian** Katholizismus und Judentum: Gemeinsamkeiten und Verwerfungen vom 16. bis zum 20. Jahrhundert. Rg 2005, Pustet 310 pp. €26.90. 3-7917-1955-6.
597 [E]**Wallraff, Martin** Welt-Zeit: christliche Weltchronistik aus zwei Jahrtausenden in Beständen der Thüringer Universitäts- und Landesbibliothek Jena. B 2005, De Gruyter xi; 140 pp. 31101-8480X.
598 [E]**Welker, Michael; Schweitzer, Friedrich** Reconsidering the boundaries between theological disciplines—Zur Neubestimmung der Grenzen zwischen den theologischen Disziplinen. Theologie: Forschung und Wissenschaft 8: Müns 2005, Lit iv; 232 pp. 3-8258-7471-0.
599 [E]**Young, Frances; Ayres, Lewis; Louth, Andrew** The Cambridge history of early christian literature. 2004 ⇒20,541. [R]SR 34 (2005) 604-606 (*Tuzlak, Ayse*); RBLit 7 (2005) 274-280 (*Norelli, Enrico*).

## A1.5 *Plurium compilationes* **philologicae vel archaeologicae**

600 [E]**Abusch, Tzvi; Van der Toorn, Karel** Mesopotamian magic: textual, historical, and interpretive perspectives. 1999 ⇒15,332; 18,444. [R]RA 99 (2005) 184-185 (*Charpin, Dominique*).
601 [E]**Adams, J.N.; Janse, M.; Swain, S.** Bilingualism in ancient society: language contact and the written text. 2002 ⇒18,445; 19,486. [R]REG 118 (2005) 622-623 (*Samama, Evelyne*).
602 [E]**Aitken, Ellen B.; Maclean, Jennifer K.B.** PHILOSTRATUS's Heroikos: religion and cultural identity in the third century C.E. WGRW 6: 2004 ⇒20,544. [R]RBLit (2005)* (*Wills, Lawrence*).
603 [E]**Alexander, Philip S.**, *al.* Studia semitica: the Journal of Semitic Studies jubilee volume. JSSt.S 16: Oxf 2005, OUP vii; 303 pp. 01985-70929.

604 [E]**Alkier, Stefan; Zangenberg, Jürgen** Zeichen aus Text und Stein: Studien auf dem Weg zu einer Archäologie des Neuen Testaments. TANZ 42: 2003 ⇒19,489. [R]ThLZ 130 (2005) 1181-4 (*Tilly, Michael*).

605 [E]**Archibald, Zofia H.; Davies, John K.; Gabrielsen, Vincent** Making, moving and managing: the new world of ancient economies, 323-31 BC. Oxf 2005, Oxbow viii; 368 pp. 1-84217-1577.

606 [E]**Babcock, Robert G.** New studies on Yale manuscripts from the late antique to the early modern period. Yale Univ. Library...Suppl 7: NHv 2005, Beinecke Library viii; 165 pp. 0044-0175.

607 [E]**Badr, Habib** Christianity: a history in the Middle East. Beirut 2005, Middle East Council of Churches 933 pp. 99530-03432.

608 [E]**Bar-Asher, Moshe; Dimant, Devorah** Meghillot: studies in the Dead Sea scrolls, volume 3. Haifa 2005, Univ. of Haifa 262; xxiv pp. 965-342-903-5. **H.**

609 [E]**Beck, Herbert; Bol, Peter C.; Bückling, Maraike** Ägypten–Griechenland–Rom: Abwehr und Berührung: Städelsches Kunstinstitut und Städtische Galerie, 26. November 2005 - 26. Februar 2006. Tü 2005, Wasmuth 757pp. 38030-10578.

610 [E]**Belayche, Nicole; Mimouni, Simon Claude** Les communautés religieuses dans le monde gréco-romain: essai de définition. BEHE.R 117: 2003 ⇒19,493. [R]REJ 164 (2005) 336-337 (*Maraval, Pierre*); AnCl 74 (2005) 411-412 (*Pirenne-Delforge, Vinciane*).

611 [E]**Ben-Tor, Amnon** La arqueología del Antiguo Israel. 2004 ⇒20,551. [R]ATG 68 (2005) 302-303 (*Vílchez, José*).

612 [E]**Bermann, Sandra; Wood, Michael** Nation, language, and the ethics of translation. Princeton, NJ 2005, Princeton University Press vi; 413 pp. 0-691-11608-3.

613 [E]**Biale, David** Cultures of the Jews: a new history. 2002 ⇒18,448. [R]JQR 95 (2005) 119-130 (*Fredriksen, P.*).

614 **Bickel, Susanne**, *al.* In ägyptischer Gesellschaft: Aegyptiaca der Sammlungen Bibel+Orient an der Universität Freiburg Schweiz. 2004 ⇒20, 553. [R]RBLit 7 (2005) 53-54 (*Gee, John*).

615 [E]**Bintliff, John** A companion to archaeology. 2004 ⇒20,554. [R]AJA 109 (2005) 794-795 (*Pullen, Daniel J.*).

616 **Bottero, Jean; Herrenschmidt, Clarisse; Vernant, Jean-Pierre** Ancestor of the west: writing, reasoning and religion in Mesopotamia, Elam and Greece. 2000 ⇒16,386... 20,557. [R]Mes. 40 (2005) 186-187 (*Gianotti, Gian Franco*).

617 [E]**Bowes, Kim; Kulikowski, Michael** Hispania in late antiquity: current perspectives. The Medieval and Early Modern Iberian World 24: Lei 2005, Brill xii; 645 pp. 9004-143912.

618 [E]**Boys, Mary C.** Seeing Judaism anew: christianity's sacred obligation. Lanham, MD 2005, Rowman & L. xxiv; 285 pp. 0-7425-4882-1.

619 [E]**Boys-Stones, G.R.** Metaphor, allegory, and the classical tradition: ancient thought and modern revisions. 2003 ⇒19,495. [R]RFNS 97 (2005) 174-178 (*Ramelli, Ilaria*).

620 [E]**Branham, R. Bracht** The Bakhtin Circle and ancient narrative. Ancient Narrative.S 3: Groningen 2005, Barkhuis xxiv; 347 pp. 90-77-922-008.

621 **Breyer, Francis** Staatsverträge, Herrscherinschriften und andere Dokumente zur politischen Geschichte. [E]*Lichtenstein, Michael*: TUANT 2: Gü 2005, Gü xviii; 406 pp. 978-3-579-05288-5.

622 [E]**Briend, Jacques** La Terre Sainte: cinquante ans d'archéologie, 1: du Jourdain à la Samarie, 2: de la Judée au Sinaï. 2003 ⇒19,496. [R]CDios 218 (2005) 253-255 (*Gutiérrez, J.*).

623 [E]**Bruns, Peter** Grosse Gestalten der Alten Welt. Bamberger Theologische Studien 26: Fra 2005, Lang 137 pp. 3631-53424-8.

624 [E]**Bruun, Otto; Corti, Lorenzo** Les *Catégories* et leur histoire. Bibliothèque d'histoire de la philosophie n.s.: P 2005, Vrin 396 pp. 271-161-7084.

625 [E]**Cébeillac-Gervasoni, Mireille; Lamoine, Laurent** Les élites et leurs facettes: les élites locales dans le monde hellénistique et romain. CEFR 309: 2003 ⇒19,500. [R]AnCl 74 (2005) 487-490 (*Raepsaet-Charlier, Marie-Thérèse*).

626 [E]**Chazon, Esther G.; Bakhos, Carol** Ancient Judaism in its Hellenistic context. JSJ.S 95: Lei 2005, Brill vii; 244 pp. €83/$112. 90-04-138-71-4.

627 [E]**Clarke, Joanne** Archaeological perspectives on the transmission and transformation of culture in the eastern Mediterranean. Levant Supplementary Series 2: Oxf 2005, Oxbow xii; (2), 218 pp. 1-84217-168-2.

628 [E]**Cleland, Liza; Harlow, Mary; Llewellyn-Jones, Lloyd** The clothed body in the ancient world. Oxf 2005, Oxbow x; 192 pp. 1-84217-1658.

629 [E]**Coates, Jennifer; Thornborrow, Joanna** The sociolinguistics of narrative. Studies in narrative 6: Amst 2005, Benjamins vi; 299 pp. 90-272-2646-6. Bibl. 279-293.

630 [E]**Cohen, David J.; Gagarin, Michael** The Cambridge companion to ancient Greek law. C 2005, CUP xiii; 480 pp. $30/£19. 0-521-81840-0. Bibl. 431-456.

631 [E]**Cohn-Sherbok, Dan; Court, John M.** Religious diversity in the Graeco-Roman world: a survey of recent scholarship. BiSe 79: 2001 ⇒ 17,398... 20,565. [R]BTB 35 (2005) 151-152 (*Crook, Zeba A.*).

632 [E]**Collins, John J.; Sterling, Gregory E.** Hellenism in the land of Israel. Christianity and Judaism in Antiquity 13: 2001 ⇒17,399... 19,502. [R]RBLit 7 (2005) 266-271 (*Levine, Lee I.*); AWE 4 (2005) 484-487 (*Fischer, Moshe*).

633 [E]**Colvin, Stephen** The Greco-Roman east: politics, culture, society. YCS 31: C 2004, CUP 278 pp. 978-05218-28758.

634 [E]**Conca, Fabrizio; Gualandri, Isabella; Passarella, Raffaele** Nuovo e antico nella cultura greco-latina di IV-VI secolo. Quaderni di Acme 73: Mi 2005, Cisalpino xvii; 817 pp.

635 [E]**Cooke, Ashley; Simpson, Fiona** Current research in egyptology II: January 2001. BAR Intern. Ser. 1380: Oxf 2005, Archaeopress iv; 80 pp. 1-84171-820-3.

636 [E]**Coşkun, Altay** Roms auswärtige Freunde in der späten Republik und im frühen Prinzipat. Göttinger Forum für Altertumswissenschaft.B 19: Gö 2005, Duehrkohp & R. x; 300 pp. 38974-42523. Bibl.

637 [E]**Cowey, James M.S.; Kramer, Bärbel** Paramone: Editionen und Aufsätze von Mitgliedern des Heidelberger Instituts für Papyrologie zwischen 1982 und 2004. APF.B 16: 2004 ⇒20,9826. [R]BiOr 62 (2005) 270-272 (*Boyaval, Bernard*).

638 [E]**Cunliffe, Barry; Osborne, Robin** Mediterranean urbanization 800-600 BC. PBA 126: Oxf 2005, OUP xvi; 280 pp. £40. 019-726-3259. 64 ill.

639 [E]**Dueck, D.; Lindsay, H.; Pothecary, S.** STRABO's cultural geography: the making of a kolossourgia. C 2005, CUP xvi; 286 pp. 05218-5-3060. Bibl.

640 [E]**Edwards, Douglas R.** Religion and society in Roman Palestine: old questions, new approaches. 2004 ⇒20,570. [R]PEQ 137 (2005) 184-185 (*Jacobson, David M.*).
641 [E]**Egelhaaf-Gaiser, Ulrike; Schäfer, Alfred** Religiöse Vereine in der römischen Antike: Untersuchungen zu Organisation, Ritual und Raumordnung. STAC 13: 2002 ⇒18,468... 20,571. [R]AnCl 74 (2005) 425-426 (*Raepsaet, Georges*).
642 [E]**Erskine, Andrew** A companion to the Hellenistic world. Blackwell Companions to the Ancient World: Malden 2005, Blackwell xxviii; 595 pp. 0631-22537-4.
643 [E]**Eshel, Hanna** The Qumran scrolls and the Hasmonean state. 2004 ⇒ 20,574. [R]Qad. 38 (2005) 57 (*Broshi, M.*).
644 [E]**Falk, Harry** Wege zur Stadt: Entwicklung und Formen urbanen Lebens in der alten Welt. Vergleichende Studien zu Antike und Orient 2: Bremen 2005, Hempen 215 pp. 3-934106-307.
645 [E]**Frei-Stolba, Regula; Bielman, Anne; Bianchi, Olivier** Les femmes antiques entre sphère privée et sphère publique: actes du diplôme d'études avancées, Univ. de Lausanne et Neuchâtel, 2000-2002. 2003 ⇒ 19,514. [R]AnCl 74 (2005) 490-92 (*Raepsaet-Charlier, Marie-Thérèse*).
646 [E]**Frevel, Christian** Medien im antiken Palästina: materielle Kommunikation und Medialität als Thema der Palästinaarchäologie. FAT 2/10: Tü 2005, Mohr S. viii; 276 pp. €54. 3-16-148512-2. Bibl. 262-268.
647 [E]**Galinsky, Karl** The Cambridge companion to the age of Augustus. C 2005, CUP xvii; 407 pp. £47/18. 0521-807964/003938. Num. ill.
648 [E]**Gawlikowski, Michal; Daszewski, Andrzej Wiktor** Polish archaeology in the Mediterranean: XV, Reports 2003. 2004 ⇒20,577. [R]Syria 82 (2005) 371-372 (*Sartre, Maurice*).
649 [E]**Gignoux, Philippe** Ressembler au monde: nouveaux documents sur la théorie du macro-microcosme dans l'antiquité orientale. BEHE.R 106: 1999 ⇒15,356; 18,473. [R]Or. 74 (2005) 443 (*Contini, Riccardo*).
650 [E]**Gourinat, Jean-Baptiste; Romeyer Dherbey, Gilbert** Les Stoïciens. P 2005, Vrin 622 pp. 27116-17785.
651 [E]**Gómez Acebo, Isabel** La mujer en los orígenes del cristianismo. En clave de mujer: Bilbao 2005, Desclée de B. 289 pp. 84-330-1938-4. [R]Studium 45 (2005) 319-320 (*López, L.*).
652 [E]**Gruen, Erich S.** Cultural borrowings and ethnic appropriations in antiquity. Oriens et Occidens 8: Stu 2005, Steiner 314 pp. 3515-08735-4.
653 [E]**Gunter, Ann Clyburn; Hauser, Stefan R.** Ernst Herzfeld and the development of Near Eastern Studies, 1900-1950. Lei 2005, Brill xv; 636 pp. 90-04-14153-7. Bibl. 617-623.
654 [E]**Gyselen, Rika** Charmes et sortilèges: magie et magiciens. Res Orientales 14: 2002 ⇒18,477... 20,581. [R]JRAS 15 (2005) 99-100 (*Kitchen, Kenneth A.*).
655 [E]**Harris, W.V.** Rethinking the Mediterranean. Oxf 2005, OUP xxii; 414 pp. 019-920772-0.
656 [E]**Heinz, M.; Bonatz, Dominik** Bild—Macht—Geschichte: visuelle Kommunikation im Alten Orient. 2002 ⇒18,480; 20,583. [R]Mes. 40 (2005) 193-194 (*Lippolis, Carlo*).
657 [E]**Hoffman, Yair** Studies in Judaica. Te'uda 16-17: 2001 ⇒17,408. [R]JSSt 50 (2005) 399-401 (*Outhwaite, Ben*).
658 [E]**Hopkins, David C.** Across the Anatolian Plateau. AASOR 57: 2002 ⇒18,486; 20,586. [R]AWE 3 (2004) [2005] 403-404 (*Glatz, Claudia; Matthews, Roger*).

659 [E]**Humbert, Jean-Baptiste; Gunneweg, Jan** Khirbet Qumrân et 'Aïn Feshkha II: études d'anthropologie, de physique et de chimie: studies of anthropology, physics and chemistry. NTOA.Archaeologica 3: 2003 ⇒19,521; 20,590. [R]ThLZ 130 (2005) 626-629 (*Zangenberg, Jürgen*).
660 [E]**Inglebert, Hervé** Histoire de la civilisation romaine. P 2005, Nouvelle Clio 512 pp. [R]CRAI (2005/2) 913-915 (*Gros, Pierre*).
661 [E]**Janowski, Bernd; Wilhelm, Gernot; Lichtenstein, Michael** Staatsverträge, Herrscherinschriften und andere Dokumente zur politischen Geschichte. TUAT N.F. 2: Gü 2005, Gü xviii; 406 pp. €148. 3579-05-2888.
662 [E]**Katzoff, Ranon; Schaps, David** Law in the documents of the Judaean Desert. JSJ.S 96: Lei 2005, Brill viii; 244 pp. €89/$120. 90-04-113-576.
663 [E]**Kessler, Martin; Leppin, Volker** Johann Gottfried HERDER: Aspekte seines Lebenswerkes. AKG 92: B 2005, De Gruyter 31101-84273.
664 [E]**Kiss, Katalin É.** Universal grammar in the reconstruction of ancient languages. Studies in generative grammar 83: B 2005, De Gruyter vi; 526 pp. €98. 3-11-018550-4. Bibl.
665 [E]**Koschel, Ansgar** Katholische Kirche und Judentum im 20. Jahrhundert. 2002 ⇒18,491. [R]FrRu 12 (2005) 144-145 (*Sajak, Clauß Peter*).
666 [E]**Long, V. Philips; Baker, David W.; Wenham, Gordon J.** Windows into Old Testament history: evidence, argument, and the crisis of 'Biblical Israel'. 2002 ⇒18,500... 20,11673. [R]HeyJ 46 (2005) 208-209 (*Briggs, Richard S.*); JSSt 50 (2005) 371-372 (*Tomes, Roger*).
667 [E]**Maas, Michael** The Cambridge companion to the age of Justinian. C 2005, CUP xxvii; 626 pp. 0521-52071-1.
668 [E]**Maier, A.M.; Dar, S.; Safrai, S.** The rural landscape of ancient Israel. BArR.Intern. Ser. 1121: 2003 ⇒19,529. [R]BASOR 340 (2005) 86-88 (*Joffe, Alexander H.*); AWE 4 (2005) 494-495 (*Tal, Oren*).
669 [E]**Malkin, Irad** Mediterranean paradigms and classical antiquity. NY 2005, Routledge vi; 149 pp. $125.
670 [E]**Martin, Dale B.; Miller, Patricia Cox** The cultural turn in late ancient studies: gender, asceticism, and historiography. Durham, NC 2005, Duke Univ. Pr. 364 pp. 0-8223-3422-4. Bibl. 317-354.
671 [E]**McHardy, Fiona: Marshall, Eireann** Women's influence on classical civilization. 2004 ⇒20,608. [R]AnCl 74 (2005) 492-494 (*Raepsaet-Charlier, Marie-Thérèse*).
672 [E]**Meissner, Burkhard; Schmitt, Oliver; Sommer, Michael** Krieg, Gesellschaft, Institutionen: Beiträge zu einer vergleichenden Kriegsgeschichte. B 2005, Akademie 448 pp. 3-05-004097-1.
673 **Merkyte, Inga**, *al.* Lîga: copper age strategies in Bulgaria. [E]*Randsborg, Klavs*: AcAr.S 6; AcAr 76.1: K 2005, Blackwell 194 pp. 0065-101X. Bibl. 189-194.
674 [E]**Mouze, Létitia** Rationnel et irrationnel en philosophie ancienne. Kairos 25 Toulouse 2005, Presses universitaires du Mirail 361 pp. 2-8581-6-800-8.
675 Neues Testament und antike Kultur, 1: Prolegomena—Quellen—Geschichte. [E]**Erlemann, Kurt; Noethlichs, Karl Leo**, *al.* 2004 ⇒20,613. [R]JETh 19 (2005) 285-287 (*Schnabel, Eckhard*);
676 2: Familie—Gesellschaft—Wirtschaft. [E]**Erlemann, Kurt; Noethlichs, Karl Leo; Zangenberg, Jürgen**, *al.* Neuk 2005, Neuk ix; 263 pp. €29.90. 3-7887-2037-9 [EuA 81,329—Benedikt Schwank];

677 3: Weltauffassung—Kult—Ethos. [E]**Erlemann, Kurt**, *al.* Neuk 2005, Neuk 253 pp. €29.90. 3-7887-2038-7.

678 [E]**Oden, Amy G.** And you welcomed me: a sourcebook on hospitality in early christianity. 2001 ⇒18,512. [R]RBLit (2005)* (*Fiore, Benjamin*).

679 [E]**Olsson, Birger O.; Mitternacht, Dieter; Brandt, Olof** The synagogue of ancient Ostia and the Jews of Rome: interdisciplinary studies. 2001 ⇒17,427... 20,615. [R]AJA 109 (2005) 810-813 (*Porter, Adam L.*).

680 [E]**Osborne, Robin** Studies in ancient Greek and Roman society. 2004 ⇒20,618. [R]AnCl 74 (2005) 485-486 (*Raepsaet-Charlier, Marie-Thérèse*).

681 [E]**Perkams, Matthias; Piccione, Rosa M.** Selecta colligere, II: Beiträge zur Technik des Sammelns und Kompilierens griechischer Texte von der Antike bis zum Humanismus. Hellenica 18: Alessandria 2005, Orso x; 483 pp. 88-7694-8856.

682 [E]**Pintaudi, Rosario** Papyri graecae Schøyen (PSchøyen I): Greek Papyri, Volume I. Papyrologica Florentina 35; Manuscripts in the Schøyen Collection 5: F 2005, Gonnelli xiii; XLI; 259 pp. 88-7468-0260.

683 [E]**Pollock, Susan; Bernbeck, Reinhard** Archaeologies of the Middle East: critical perspectives. Blackwell studies in global archaeology 4: Oxf 2005, Blackwell xiii; 363 pp. $35. 0-631-23001-7.

684 [E]**Raunig, Walter** Das christliche Äthiopien: Geschichte—Architektur—Kunst. Rg 2005, Schnell & S. 319 pp. €59. 3-7954-1541-1. Fotokampagne von *Basilio Rodella*; Num. ill.

685 [E]**Ravasi, Guido; Scialoja, Mario** Le leggi dell'antica Europa. Fondazione europea Dragàn 23: Mi 2005, Nagard 121 pp. 88-85010-98-9.

686 **Retief, François P.; Cilliers, Louise** Health and healing, disease and death in the Greco-Roman world. AcTh(B).S 7: Bloemfontein 2005, UFS xxv; 310 pp. 0-86886-695-4.

687 [E]**Riemer, Peter ; Riemer, Ulrike** Xenophobie–Philoxenie: vom Umgang mit Fremden in der Antike. Potsdamer Altertumswissenschaftliche Beiträge 7: Stu 2005, Steiner xi; 276 pp. 3-515-08195-X.

688 [E]**Routledge, Christopher; Chapman, Siobhan** Key thinkers in linguistics and the philosophy of language. E 2005, Edinburgh University Press xii; 282 pp. 0-7486-1757-4.

689 [E]**Sagona, Antonio; Sagona, Claudia** Archaeology at the north-east Anatolian frontier, I: an historical geography and a field survey of the Bayburt province. ANESt.S 14: 2004 ⇒20,627. [R]Paléorient 31/2 (2005) 177-179 (*Marro, Catherine*).

690 [E]**Signore, Mario; Scarafile, Giovanni** Libertà e comunità. Padova 2005, Messaggero 653 pp. 88-250-1567-4.

691 [E]**Snell, Daniel C.** A companion to the ancient Near East. Blackwell Companions to the Ancient World: Oxf 2005, Blackwell xix; 504 pp. $40. 14051-60012.

692 [E]**Streck, Michael P.** Sprachen des Alten Orients. Da:Wiss 2005, 184 pp. €34.90. 978-534-17996-0.

693 [E]**Suter, Claudia E.; Uehlinger, Christoph** Crafts and images in contact: studies on eastern Mediterranean art of the first millennium BCE. OBO 210: FrS 2005, Academic xxxi; 395 pp. €85. 3727815094. 54 pl.

694 [E]**Thür, Gerhard** Antike Rechtsgeschichte: Einheit und Vielfalt. Veröffentlichungen der Kommission für antike Rechtsgeschichte 11; ÖAW. PH Sitzungsberichte 726: W 2005, Verlag der Österreichischen Akademie der Wissenschaften viii; 95 pp. 3-7001-3481-9.

695 [E]**Van Ginkel, J.J.; Van Lint, Theo M.; Murre-van den Berg, H.L.** Redefining christian identity: cultural interaction in the Middle East since the rise of Islam. OLA 134: Lv 2005, Peeters xiv; 420 pp. 90429-14181.

696 [E]**Vandendorpe, Christian** Le récit de rêve: fonctions, thèmes et symboles. Québec 2005, Nota bene 377 pp. 2-89518-212-4.

697 [E]**Vazquez Allegue, J.** I manoscritti del Mar Morto. R 2005, Borla 423 pp.

698 [E]**Virgilio, Biagio** Studi ellenistici XVI. Pisa 2005, Giardini 564 pp. 88-427-07953.

699 [E]**Witte, Markus; Fögen, Marie Theres** Kodifizierung und Legitimierung des Rechts in der Antike und im Alten Orient. ZAR.B 5: Wsb 2005, Harrassowitz 150 pp. 3-447-05180-9. Bibl. 146-150.

700 [E]**Young, Ian** Biblical Hebrew: studies in chronology and typology. JSOT.S 369: 2003 ⇒19,559; 20,640. [R]CBQ 67 (2005) 181-182 (*Cook, John A.*); HebStud 46 (2005) 377-384 (*Schniedewind, William M.*); JThS 56 (2005) 125-130 (*Millard, Alan*).

701 [E]**Zerbst, Uwe; Van der Heen, Peter G.** Keine Posaunen vor Jericho?: Beiträge zur Archäologie der Landnahme. Holzgerlingen 2005, Hänssler 155 pp. €18.

## A2.1 Acta *congressuum* biblica

702 [E]**Alston, Wallace M.; Möller, Christian; Schwier, Helmut** Die Predigt des Alten Testaments: Beiträge d. Symposiums anlässlich des 100. Geburtstags Gerhard VON RADs, Heidelberg, 2001. AT und Moderne 16: 2003 ⇒19,564; 20,646. [R]OLZ 100 (2005) 298-301 (*Grünwaldt, Klaus*); WO 35 (2005) 246-247 (*Schäfer-Lichtenberger, Christa*).

703 [E]**Amphoux, Christian-Bernard; Elliott, James K.** The New Testament text in early christianity: proceedings Lille colloquium, 2000. Histoire du texte biblique 6: 2003 ⇒19,565; 20,647. [R]CBQ 67 (2005) 182-3 (*Timbie, Janet A.*); MSR 62/2 (2005) 91-2 (*Clavier, Michèle*).

704 [E]**Attias, Jean-Christophe; Gisel, Pierre** De la bible à la littérature. RePe 15: 2003 ⇒19,567. Colloque Lausanne nov. 2002. [R]Vies consacrées 77 (2005) 210-211 (*Luciani, Didier*); ETR 80 (2005) 113-124 (*Couteau, Elisabeth*).

705 [E]**Attridge, Harold W.; Fassler, Margot E.** Psalms in community: Jewish and christian textual, liturgical, and artistic traditions. Symposium 25: 2003 ⇒19,568; 20,649. Conf. Yale 2002. [R]CBQ 67 (2005) 361-363 (*Kuntz, J. Kenneth*).

706 [E]**Avemarie, Friedrich; Lichtenberger, Hermann** Auferstehung—Resurrection: the fourth Durham-Tübingen research symposium (Tübingen, September 1999). WUNT 135: 2001 ⇒17,452... 19,569. [R]BZ 49 (2005) 277-280 (*Klumbies, Paul-Gerhard*).

707 [E]**Ayán Calvo, Juan José; Navascués Benlloch, Patricio; Aroztegui Esnaola, Manuel** Filiación: cultura pagana, religión de Israel, orígenes del cristianismo: actas de las I y II Jornadas de Estudio. Estructuras y procesos: M 2005, Trotta 386 pp. 84-8164-800-0.

708 [E]**Ådna, Jostein** The formation of the early church. WUNT 183: Tü 2005, Mohr S. xii; 451 pp. $175. 3-16-148561-0. 7th Nordic NT Conf., Stavanger 2003.

709 [E]**Bartholomew, Craig G.; Evans, C. Stephen** "Behind" the text: history and biblical interpretation. Scripture and Hermeneutics 4: 2003 ⇒19,571. Seminar [R]Evangel 23 (2005) 63-64 (*McKay, W. David J.*).

710 [E]**Bartholomew, Craig G.; Green, Joel B.; Thiselton, Anthony C.** Reading Luke: interpretation, reflection, formation. Carlisle 2005, Paternoster 484 pp. £20. 1-84227-0707.

711 [E]**Barton, John; Exum, J. Cheryl; Oeming, Manfred** Das Alte Testament und die Kunst: Beiträge des Symposiums "Das Alte Testament und die Kultur der Moderne" anlässlich des 100. Geburtstags Gerhard VON RADs (1901-1971), Heidelber, Okt. 2001. Altes Testament und Moderne 15: Müns 2005, Lit x; 272 pp. 38258-54620. Bibl. 227-252.

712 [E]**Becker, Adam H.; Reed, Annette Y.** The ways that never parted: Jews and christians in late antiquity and the early middle ages. TSAJ 95: 2003 ⇒19,572; 20,654. Congress Princeton 9-11.1.2002. [R]Zion 70 (2005) 242-247 (*Limor, Ora*).

713 [E]**Bellia, Giuseppe; Passaro, Angelo** The book of Wisdom in modern research: studies on tradition, redaction, and theology. Deuterocanonical and Cognate Literature Yearbook 2005: B 2005, De Gruyter xix; 363 pp. €98. 31101-86594. Introd.*J.J. Collins*; Congr. Palermo 2002.

714 [E]**Bellis, Alice Ogden; Grabbe, Lester L.** The priests in the prophets: the portrayal of priests, prophets and other religious specialists in the latter prophets. JSOT.S 408: 2004 ⇒20,656. SBL Toronto 2002. [R]RBLit (2005)* (*Wiley, Henrietta; Wright, Jacob*).

715 [E]**Berder, Michel** Les Actes des Apôtres: histoire, récit, théologie: XXe congrès de l'Association catholique française pour l'étude de la bible (Angers, 2003). LeDiv 199: P 2005, Cerf 281 pp. €31. 2-204-07416-0. [R]RBLit (2005)* (*Dupertuis, Ruben*).

716 Bibles en français: traduction et tradition: actes du colloque de l'Ecole Cathédrale, 5-6 décembre 2003. 2004 ⇒20,658. [R]RICP 94 (2005) 211-213 (*Asurmendi, Jesús*); RBLit (2005)* (*Inowlocki, Sabrina*).

717 **Blanchard, Yves-Marie**, *al.* Raconter, voir, croire: parcours narratifs du quatrième évangile. CRB 61: P 2005, Gabalda 90 pp. €30. 2-85021-166-7. Sém. Paris 2003; Bibl. 119-144.

718 [E]**Blum, Erhard; Johnstone, William; Markschies, Christoph** Das Alte Testament–ein Geschichtsbuch?: Beiträge des Symposiums "Das Alte Testament und die Kultur der Moderne" anlässlich des 100. Geburtstags Gerhard VON RADs (1901-1971), Heidelberg 2001. Altes Testament und Moderne 10: Müns 2005, Lit x; 207 pp. 38258-54574.

719 [E]**Boccaccini, Gabriele** Il Messia tra memoria e attesa. Biblia 9: Brescia 2005, Morcelliana 225 pp. €18. 88372-20499. Atti del Convegno "Il Messia tra memoria e attesa", Venezia, 4-6 luglio 2003.

720 [E]**Boda, Mark J.; Floyd, Michael H.** Bringing out the treasure: inner biblical allusion in Zechariah 9-14. JSOT.S 370: 2003 ⇒19,574; 20,659. 2 colloquia. [R]RBLit (2005)* (*Serandour, Arnaud*).

721 [E]**Brant, Jo-Ann A.; Hedrick, Charles W.; Shea, Chris** Ancient fiction: the matrix of early Christian and Jewish narrative. SBL.Symposium 32: Lei 2005, Brill xvii; 372 pp. $40. 90041-37688. Bibl. 317-344.

722 [E]**Cameron, Ron; Miller, Merrill P.** Redescribing christian origins. SBL.Symposium 28: 2004 ⇒20,660. [R]RBLit (2005)* (*Dunn, James; Pettipiece, Timothy*).

723 [E]**Chazon, Esther G.; Dimant, Devorah; Clements, Ruth A.** Reworking the bible: apocryphal and related texts at Qumran: symposium by the Orion Center for the Study of the DSS and the Hebrew University

Institute for Advanced Studies Research Group on Qumran, 15-17 January, 2002. StTDJ 58: Lei 2005, Brill x; 245 pp. 9004-14703-9.

724 [E]**Clines, David J.A.; Lichtenberger, Hermann; Müller, Hans-Peter** Weisheit in Israel: Beiträge des Symposiums [⇒718]. Altes Testament und Moderne 12: 2003 ⇒19,583. [R]ThRv 101 (2005) 29-30 (*Kaiser, Otto*); WO 35 (2005) 243-245 (*Schäfer-Lichtenberger, Christa*); JETh 19 (2005) 235-236 (*Kupfer, Christian D.*).

725 [E]**Cremascoli, Giuseppe; Santi, Francesco** La bibbia del XIII secolo: storia del testo, storia dell'esegesi. Millennio medievale 49: 2004 ⇒20, 665. Conv. 2001. [R]RivBib 53 (2005) 372-376 (*Barbaglio, Giuseppe*).

726 [E]**Dal Covolo, Enrico; Fusco, Roberto** Il contributo delle scienze storiche allo studio del Nuovo Testamento. Pontificio Comitato di Scienze Storiche, Atti e Documenti 19: Città del Vaticano 2005, Libreria Editrice Vaticana 354 pp. €40. 88209-77494. Atti convegno, Roma, 2002.

727 [E]**Dauphinais, Michael; Levering, Matthew W.** Reading John with St. Thomas AQUINAS: theological exegesis and speculative theology. Wsh 2005, Catholic Univ.of America Pr. $80. 08132-1405X. Bibl. Aquinas 351-362; Conf.

728 [E]**David, Robert; Jinbachian, Manuel** Traduire la Bible hébraïque: de la Septante á la Nouvelle Bible Segond = Translating the Hebrew Bible: from the Septuagint to the Nouvelle Bible Segond. Sciences bibliques 15: Montreal 2005, Médiaspaul 428 pp. International symposium Canadian Bible Society, Montréal, May 30-June 1st, 2004.

729 [E]**Davis, Ellen F.; Hays, Richard B.** The art of reading scripture. 2003 ⇒19,586; 20,666. [R]ThTo 61 (2005) 548, 550, 552 (*Lincoln, Andrew T.*); CThMi 32 (2005) 207-208 (*Linss, Wilhelm*); CBQ 67 (2005) 380-381 (*Matties, Gordon*).

730 [E]**Day, John** In search of pre-exilic Israel: Oxford OT Seminar. JSOT.S 406: 2004 ⇒20,667. [R]RBLit (2005)* (*Cathey, Joseph; Grabbe, Lester*);

731 Temple and worship in Biblical Israel: Oxford OT Seminar. JSOT.S 422; LHB/OTS 422: L 2005, Clark xviii; 559 pp. £100. 05670-42626.

732 [E]**De Troyer, Kristin; Lange, Armin** Reading the present in the Qumran library: the perception of the contemporary by means of scriptural interpretations. SBL.Symposium 30: Atlanta, GA 2005, SBL viii; 236 pp. 1-58983-1500. Bibl. 203-217.

733 [E]**Debié, Muriel**, *al.* Les apocryphes syriaques. Etudes syriaques 2: P 2005, Geuthner 231 pp. Table ronde CNRS.

734 [E]**Deines, Roland; Niebuhr, Karl-Wilhelm** PHILO und das Neue Testament: wechselseitige Wahrnehmungen, 1: Internationales Symposium zum Corpus Judaeo-Hellenisticum 1.-4. Mai 2003, Eisenach/Jena. WUNT 172: 2004 ⇒20,668. [R]RHPhR 85 (2005) 431-32 (*Grappe, C.*).

735 [E]**Dever, William G.; Gitin, Seymour** Symbiosis, symbolism, and the power of the past: Canaan, Ancient Israel, and their neighbors from the Late Bronze Age through Roman Palaestina: centennial symposium, Albright Institute and ASOR, Jerusalem 2000. 2003 ⇒19,590; 20,669. [R]CBQ 67 (2005) 168-70 (*Launderville, Dale*); BiOr 62 (2005) 326-29 (*Schoors, Antoon*); JESHO 48 (2005) 593-597 (*Crowell, Bradley L.*).

736 [E]**Dimitrov, Ivan Z.**, *al.* Das Alte Testament als christliche Bibel in orthodoxer und westlicher Sicht: Konferenz, Rilakloster 2001. WUNT 174: 2004 ⇒20,670. [R]ETR 80 (2005) 557-558 (*Vincent, Jean M*arcel).

737 [E]**Dorival, Gilles** Qu'est-ce qu'un corpus littéraire?: recherches sur le corpus biblique et les corpus patristiques. Coll. REJ: LvN 2005, Pee-

ters 141 pp. €80. 90429-16338. Conf. Oxf 2003. [R]REG 118 (2005) 634-635 (*Pouderon, Bernard*).

738 [E]**Eriksson, Anders; Olbricht, Thomas H.** Rhetoric, ethic, and moral persuasion in biblical discourse: essays from the 2002 Heidelberg Conference. Emory Studies in Early Christianity 11: L 2005, Clark xiv; 401 pp. $70. 05670-28119 [OTA 29,344].

739 Ethical dimensions in the teaching of Jesus and Paul: proceedings 5th annual convention, Phinma Training Center, Tagaytay City, 2004. Manila 2005, Catholic Biblical Association of the Philippines x; 148 pp.

740 [E]**Firth, David; Johnston, Philip S.** Interpreting the Psalms: issues and approaches. DG 2005, InterVarsity 336 pp. $26. 0-8308-2833-8. 2004 Tyndale Fellowship OT Study Group.

741 [E]**Fischer, Irmtraud; Schmid, Konrad; Williamson, Hugh G.M.** Prophetie in Israel: Beiträge des Symposiums [⇒718]. Altes Testament und Moderne 11: 2003 ⇒19,595; 20,672. [R]ThRv 101 (2005) 124-127 (*Kaiser, Otto*); WO 35 (2005) 241-243 (*Schäfer-Lichtenberger, Christa*); JETh 19 (2005) 240-242 (*Renz, Thomas*).

742 [E]**Focant, Camille; Wénin, André** Analyse narrative et bible: deuxième colloque international du RRENAB, Louvain-La-Neuve, Avril 2004. BEThL 191: Lv 2005, Peeters xvi; 593 pp. €75. 90-429-1654-0;

743 [E]**Focant, Camille** Quelle maison pour Dieu?. LeDiv: 2003 ⇒19,596. Conf. LvN 1998-2002. [R]CBQ 67 (2005) 170-171 (*Patton, Corrine*); RBLit (2005)* (*West, James E.*).

744 [E]**Ford, David F.; Stanton, Graham** Reading texts, seeking wisdom: scripture and theology. 2003 ⇒19,597; 20,673. Conference Cambridge 2002. [R]AThR 87 (2005) 694-695 (*Deller, Walter*); TJT 21 (2005) 322-324 (*Yenson, Mark L.*); RBLit (2005)* (*Carrell, Peter*).

745 [E]**Frevel, Christian; Konkel, Michael; Schnocks, Johannes** Die Zehn Worte: der Dekalog als Testfall der Pentateuchkritik. QD 212: FrB 2005, Herder 122 pp. €19.90. 3-451-02212-5. Koll. Bonn 2002.

746 [E]**Galli, Carlos M.; Fernández, Víctor M.** La palabra viva y actual: estudios de actualización bíblica. BA 2005, San Benito 150 pp. 987-1177-178. Seminarios.

747 [E]**García Martínez, Florentino** Wisdom and apocalypticism in the Dead Sea scrolls and in the biblical tradition. BEThL 168: 2003 ⇒19, 4191; 20,675. Colloquium Biblicum Lovaniense 51, 2002. [R]JNSL 31/1 (2005) 119-125 (*Cook, Johann*).

748 [E]**Garribba, Dario; Tanzarella, Sergio** Giudei o cristiani?: quando nasce il cristianesimo?. Oí Chrístianoí 2: Trapani 2005, Il Pozzo di Giacobbe 195 pp. 88-87324-670. Giornata di studio Dic. 2004, Napoli.

749 [E]**Gordon, Robert P.; Moor, Johannes C. de** The Old Testament in its world. Meeting, January 2003 Society for OT Study and joint meeting, July 2003 with Het Oudtestamentisch Werkgezelschap in Nederland en België. OTS 52: Lei 2005, Brill x; 293 pp. €90. 90-04-14322-X.

750 [E]**Grabbe, Lester L.; Haak, Robert D.** Knowing the end from the beginning: the prophetic, the apocalyptic and their relationships. JSPE.S 46: 2003 ⇒19,600. SBL Meeting 2001. [R]CBQ 67 (2005) 171-173 (*Redditt, Paul L.*); BiblInterp 13 (2005) 429-432 (*Murphy, Frederick J.*); RBLit (2005)* (*Schmid, Konrad*).

751 [E]**Grabbe, Lester L.** Good kings and bad kings. JSOT.S 393; European Seminar in Historical Methodology 5; LHB/OTS 393: L 2005, Clark xi; 371 pp. 0-8264-6976-0.

752 [E]**Gregory, Andrew F.; Tuckett, Christopher M.** The New Testament and the Apostolic Fathers, 1: the reception of the New Testament in the Apostolic Fathers. Oxf 2005, OUP xiii; 375 pp. £55. 0-19-926782-0;
753 2: trajectories through the New Testament and the Apostolic Fathers. Oxf 2005, OUP xvii; 506 pp. £65. 0-19-926783-9. Conf. Oxford 2004; Bibl. 433-465.
754 Grudem, W. Translating truth: the case for essentially literal bible translation. Wheaton, IL 2005, Crossway 157 pp. $15. 15813-47553. al.; Conf. Evangelical Theological Society 2004; [NTAb 50,377].
755 [E]**Hahn, Johannes** Zerstörungen des Jerusalemer Tempels: Geschehen —Wahrnehmung—Bewältigung. WUNT 147: 2002 ⇒18,559... 20, 680. [R]CDios 218 (2005) 241-242 (*Gutiérrez, J.*); BiOr 62 (2005) 116-117 (*Tromp, Joh.*).
756 [E]**Hanson, Paul; Janowski, Bernd; Welker, Michael** Biblische Theologie: Beiträge des Symposiums [⇒718]. Altes Testament und Moderne 14: Müns 2005, Lit x; 176 pp. €31. 38258-54612. [R]BiLi 78 (2005) 274-275 (*Hieke, Thomas*).
757 [E]**Heffernan, Thomas J.; Burman, Thomas E.** Scripture and pluralism: reading the bible in the religiously plural worlds of the Middle Ages and Renaissance: first annual symposium Marco Institute for Medieval and Renaissance Studies, University of Tennessee, Knoxville, February 21-22, 2002. Studies in the history of Christian traditions 123: Lei 2005, Brill ix; 246 pp. €114. 90-04-14415-3.
758 [E]**Helmer, Christine; Petrey, Taylor G.** Biblical interpretation: history, context, and reality. SBL.Symposium 26: Atlanta, Ga. 2005, SBL xii; 181 pp. 1-58983-089-X. Bibl. 165-167.
759 [E]**Henze, Matthias** Biblical interpretation at Qumran. Studies in the Dead Sea Scrolls and Related Literature: GR 2005, Eerdmans xiii; 214 pp. $25. 0-8028-3937-1. Conf. Rice, Houston; Bibl. 194-199. [R]OTEs 18 (2005) 935-937 (*Naudé, J.A.*); RBLit (2005)* (*Nicklas, Tobias*).
760 [E]**Hess, Richard S.; Carroll R., M. Daniel** Israel's messiah in the bible and the Dead Sea scrolls. 2003 ⇒19,605; 20,681. Papers deliv. at Denver Sem. 2001 [R]RBLit 7 (2005) 211-215 (*Arav, Rami*).
761 Holy texts: authority and language = Heilige Texte: Autorität und Sprache = Textes sacrés: autorité et langue. [E]**Methuen, Charlotte**, *al.* YESW 12: Lv 2004, Peeters 312 pp. 90429-1582X. Conf. Netherlands 2003.
762 Hope for a suffering people: proceedings of the fourth annual convention, Phinma Training Center, Tagaytay City, 25-27 July 2003. Manila 2003, Catholic Biblical Association of the Philippines viii; 144 pp.
763 [E]**Horton, Charles** The earliest gospels: the origins and transmission of the earliest christian gospels—the contribution of the Chester Beatty Gospel Codex P45. JSNT.S 258: 2004 ⇒20,682. Conf. Dublin 2000; Bibl. 161-173. [R]RBLit (2005)* (*Raquel, Sylvie*).
764 [E]**Joosten, Jan; Le Moigne, Philippe** L'apport de la Septante aux é-tudes sur l'antiquité. LeDiv 203: P 2005, Cerf 308 pp. €35. 22040781-58. Actes du colloque de Strasbourg, 8-9 novembre 2002. [R]MoBi 167 (2005) 69 (*Boyer, Frédéric*); LASBF 55 (2005) 537-9 (*Cignelli, Lino*).
765 [E]**Kevers, P.; Maex, J.** Toekomst voor verhalen en rituelen?: op het snijpunt von bijbel en geloofscommunicatie. Lv 2005, Acco 287 pp. €22.20. 90-334-5977-9. Symp. Aug. 2004 Leuven.
766 [E]**Klingbeil, Gerald A.** Misión y contextualización: llevar el mensaje biblico a un mundo multicultural. SMEBT 2: Libertador San Martín

2005, Univ. Adventista del Plata xxii; 388 pp. Conf. Univ. Adventista del Plata, 2004 [OTA 28,364].

767 [E]**Kloppenborg, John S.; Marshall, John W.** Apocalypticism, anti-semitism and the historical Jesus: subtexts in criticism. JSNT.S 275; JSHS.S: L 2005, Clark x; 141 pp. $110. 0-567-08428-0. Symposium, Toronto; Bibl. 131-139. [R]RBLit (2005)* (*Kraus, Thomas; Smith, Daniel*).

768 [E]**Klutz, Todd E.** Magic in the biblical world: from the rod of Aaron to the ring of Solomon. JSNT.S 245: 2003 ⇒19,613. Colloquium Manchester, Sheffield 1999. [R]CBQ 67 (2005) 187-189 (*Thompson, Leonard L.*); Jdm 54 (2005) 272-275 (*Jassen, Alex*); RBLit (2005)* (*Bloch, René*); BiCT 1/3 (2005)* (*Carden, Michael*).

769 [E]**Korpel, Marjo C.A.; Oesch, Josef M.** Unit delimitation in Biblical Hebrew and Northwest Semitic literature. Pericope 4: 2003 ⇒19,614; 20,690. 3rd Pericope Meeting, Berlin 2002. [R]CBQ 67 (2005) 174-175 (*Laberge, Léo*).

770 [E]**Kügler, Joachim** Impuls oder Hindernis?: mit dem Alten Testament in multireligiöser Gesellschaft. Symposion Bayreuth 2002. 2004 ⇒20, 691. [R]BZ 49 (2005) 303-307 (*Baumgart, Norbert C.*).

771 L'unité de l'un et l'autre Testament dans l'oeuvre de Paul Beauchamp: colloque octobre 2004. P 2005, Fac. jésuites de Paris 200 pp. €14.

772 [E]**Lee-Linke, Sung-Hee** Paulus der Jude: seine Stellung im christlich-jüdischen Dialog heute. Fra 2005, Lembeck 127 pp. €12. 38747-6468-0. Tagung Ev. Akademie im Rheinland.

773 [E]**Leonardi, Claudio; Orlandi, Giovanni** Biblical studies in the early Middle Ages. Millennio Medievale 52; Atti di Convegni 16: F 2005, SISMEL xii; 352 pp. €60. 88-8450-125-3. Conf. Gargnano 2001.

774 [E]**Lindemann, Andreas** The sayings source Q and the historical Jesus. BEThL 158: 2001 ⇒17,477; 18,573. [R]TJT 21 (2005) 247-49 (*Derrenbacker, Robert*).

775 [E]**Longenecker, Richard N.** Contours of christology in the New Testament. McMaster New Testament Studies: GR 2005, Eerdmans xiv; 346 pp. $28/€18. 0-8028-1014-4. Coll. McMaster 2001. [R]EThL 81 (2005) 521-523 (*Van Belle, G.*).

776 [E]**Mahoney, Edward J.** Scripture as the soul of theology. ColMn 2005, Liturgical 96 pp. $11. 0-8146-5155-0. Symposium 2002 Colchester.

777 [E]**Marguerat, Daniel L.** La bible en récits: l'exégèse biblique à l'heure du lecteur. MoBi 48: 2003 ⇒19,616; 20,697. Colloque Lausanne mars 2002. [R]RivBib 53 (2005) 336-341 (*Romanello, Stefano*); Theoforum 36 (2005) 199-202 (*Vogels, Walter*); RBLit (2005)* (*Millard, Matthias; Racine, Jean-Francois*).

778 [E]**Meyer, Marvin; Hughes, Charles** Jesus then and now: images of Jesus in history and christology. 2001 ⇒17,483... 19,617. Conf. Chapman Univ., 1999. [R]RBLit (2005)* (*Williams, Joel*).

779 [E]**Moor, Johannes C. de** The elusive prophet: the prophet as a historical person, literary character and anonymous artist. Eleventh joint meeting of the Society for OT Study and Het Oudtestamentisch Werkgezelschap in Nederland en België, Soesterberg 2000. OTS 45: 2001 ⇒17,485...20,701. [R]BiblInterp 13 (2005) 88-91 (*Freedman, David N.*).

780 [E]**Norelli, Enrico** Recueils normatifs et canons dans l'Antiquité: perspectives nouvelles sur la formation des canons juif et chrétien dans leur contexte culturel. Colloque Genève avril 2002. Public. de l'Institut

Romand des Sciences Bibliques 3: 2004 ⇒20,707. [R]RHPhR 85 (2005) 468-470 (*Prieur, J.-M.*); JThS 56 (2005) 586-590 (*Wyrick, Jed*).

781 [E]**O'Kane, Martin** Borders, boundaries and the bible. 2002 ⇒18,585; 19,623. Conferences Newman College: [R]BiblInterp 13 (2005) 83-85 (*Øklund, Jorunn*).

782 [E]**Oeming, Manfred; Schmid, Konrad; Schüle, Andreas** Theologie in Israel und in den Nachbarkulturen: Beiträge des Symposiums [⇒718] Altes Testament und Moderne 9: 2004 ⇒20,708. [R]ThZ 61 (2005) 174-176 (*Witte, Markus*).

783 [E]**Otto, Eckart; Levinson, Bernard Malcolm** Recht und Ethik im Alten Testament: Beiträge des Symposiums [⇒718] Altes Testament und Moderne 13: 2004 ⇒20,710. [R]ThZ 61 (2005) 369-370 (*Wright, Jacob L.*).

784 [E]**Padovese, Luigi** Atti dell' VIII Simposio di Efeso su S. Giovanni Apostolo. 2001 ⇒17,488; 19,626. [R]BeO 47 (2005) 185-186 (*Sardini, Davide*);

785 Atti del X Simposio di Efeso su S. Giovanni Apostolo. Turchia: la chiesa e la sua storia 19; Simposio di Efeso su S. Giovanni Apostolo 10: R 2005, Istituto Francescano di Spiritualità 372 pp.

786 [E]**Pastor, Jack; Mor, Menachem** The beginnings of christianity: a collection of articles. J 2005, Yad Ben-Zvi 387 pp. $49. 965-217-151-329. Proc. Conf. Tel Aviv & Jerusalem 1997.

787 [E]**Pipa, Joseph A.** The worship of God: reformed concepts of biblical worship. Fearn, Ross-shire 2005, CFP Mentor 240 pp. £11. 1-8455-00-55-5. Conf. Greenville.

788 [E]**Porter, Stanley E.** Reading the gospels today. 2004 ⇒20,714. Colloquium McMaster 2002. [R]SNTU 30 (2005) 253-254 (*Fuchs, Albert*); RExp 102 (2005) 325-327 (*Kuhl, Roland G.*); ScrB 35 (2005) 49-51 (*Boxall, Ian*); TJT 21 (2005) 262-263 (*Leske, Adrian M.*); PIBA 28 (2005) 134-135 (*Mangan, Céline*).

789 [E]**Prinzivalli, Emanuela** Il commento a Giovanni di ORIGENE: il testo e i suoi contesti: atti dell'VIII Convegno di Studi del Gruppo Italiano di Ricerca su Origene e la tradizione alessandrina (Roma, 28-30 settembre 2004). Biblioteca di Adamantius 3: Verucchio (Rimini) 2005, Pazzini 651 pp. 88-89198-62-1.

790 [E]**Reventlow, Henning Graf; Hoffman, Yair** Creation in Jewish and christian tradition. JSOT.S 319: 2002 ⇒18,593; 19,634. Symposia Tel Aviv—Bochum. [R]WThJ 67 (2005) 173-176 (*Estelle, Bryan D.*).

791 [E]**Sartorio, Ugo** Annunciare il vangelo oggi: è possibile?. Padova 2005, Messagero 187 pp. Atti convegno Padova, feb. 2004.

792 [E]**Schenker, Adrian** The earliest text of the Hebrew Bible: the relationship between the Masoretic Text and the Hebrew base of the Septuagint reconsidered. SBL.SCSt 52: 2003 ⇒19,639; 20,721. Congress 2001 Basel. [R]CBQ 67 (2005) 376-8 (*Wright, Benjamin G., III*); EThL 81 (2005) 219-21 (*Auwers, J.-M.*); RBLit 7 (2005) 115-7 (*Young, Ian*).

793 [E]**Schlosser, Jacques** The Catholic Epistles and the tradition. BEThL 176: 2004 ⇒20,722. 52nd Colloquium Biblicum Lovaniense. [R]EstAg 40 (2005) 381-2 (*Cineira, D.A.*); ThLZ 130 (2005) 958-959 (*Niebuhr, Karl-Wilhelm*); ZKTh 127 (2005) 504-506 (*Nicklas, Tobias*).

794 [E]**Starr, James; Engberg-Pedersen, Troels** Early christian paraenesis in context. BZNW 125: 2004 ⇒20,726. Conf. Lund (2000) & Oslo (2001). [R]ThLZ 130 (2005) 1335-1337 (*Wischmeyer, Oda*).

795 [E]**Stegemann, Wolfgang; Malina, Bruce J.; Theissen, Gerd** Jesus in neuen Kontexten. 2002 ⇒18,602... 20,728. [R]RBL 58 (2005) 307-309 (*Pindel, Roman*).

796 [E]**Van Belle, Gilbert; Van der Watt, Jan Gabriël; Maritz, Petrus** Theology and christology in the fourth gospel: essays by the members of the SNTS Johannine Writings Seminar. BEThL 184: Lv 2005, Peeters xii; 561 pp. €70. 90-429-1571-4.

797 [E]**Van de Sandt, Huub** Matthew and the Didache: two documents from the same Jewish-Christian milieu?. Assen 2005, Van Gorcum vi; 310 pp. €49.50. 90232-40774. Conf. Tilburg 2003. [R]RBLit (2005)* (*Nicklas, Tobias; Witetschek, Stephan*).

798 [E]**Van der Watt, Jan G.** Salvation in the New Testament: perspectives on soteriology. NT.S 121: Lei 2005, Brill xiv; 529 pp. €250. 9004142-975. Conf. Pretoria 2003. [R]EThL 81 (2005) 523-524 (*Van Belle, G.*).

799 [E]**Van Hecke, Pierre** Metaphor in the Hebrew Bible. BEThL 187: Lv 2005, Peeters x; 308, [9] pp. €65. 90-429-1640-0.

800 [E]**Vicent Saera, Rafael; Pastore, Corrado** Ripartire da Cristo, parola di Dio: lectio divina e vita salesiana oggi: atti del V Convegno mondiale Associazione biblica salesiana, Kraków, 27 dicembre 2004 - 3 gennaio 2005. R 2005, n.p. 313 pp.

801 [E]**Walls, Neal H.** Cult image and divine representation in the ancient Near East. ASOR 10: Boston 2005, American Schools of Oriental Research xvii; 115 pp. $25. 0-89757-068-5. SBL Congress 2000.

802 [E]**Welker, Michael; Oeming, Manfred; Schmid, Konrad** Das Alte Testament und die Kultur der Moderne: Beiträge des Symposiums [⇒718] Altes Testament und Moderne 8: 2004 ⇒20,734. [R]ThZ 61 (2005) 176-178 (*Witte, Markus*).

803 [E]**Wells, Paul** Bible et sexualité, l'un et l'autre: la sexualité à la lumière de la bible. Terre nouvelle: Cléon d'Andran 2005, Excelsis 160 pp. Rencontre 2004, Aix-en-Provence.

804 [E]**Weren, Wim; Koch, Dietrich-Alex G.** Recent developments in textual criticism: New Testament, other early christian and Jewish literature. NOSTER Conference in Münster, January, 4-6, 2001. Studies in Theology and Religion 8: 2003 ⇒19,650; 20,735. [R]NT 47 (2005) 291-293 (*Foster, Paul*); JThS 56 (2005) 613-617 (*Parker, D.C.*).

805 [E]**Wischmeyer, Oda** Herkunft und Zukunft der neutestamentlichen Wissenschaft. NET 6: 2003 ⇒19,651. Erlanger NT Kolloquium Jan. 2002. [R]ThLZ 130 (2005) 1194-1197 (*Stenschke, Christoph*).

### A2.3 **Acta *congressuum* theologica**

806 **Alexandre, Jérôme,** *al.* Penser le Christ aujourd'hui. Conférences du Studium Notre-Dame: P 2005, Parole et S. 139 pp. €16. 2-84573-3402.

807 [E]**Alkier, Stefan; Witte, Markus** Die Griechen und das antike Israel. OBO 201: 2004 ⇒20,740. Symp. Frankfurt April 2003. [R]RBLit (2005)* (*Pury, Albert de*).

808 [E]**Aranda, Gonzalo; Caballero, Juan L.** La sagrada escritura, palabra actual. Simposios internacionales de teología 25: Pamplona 2005, Univ. de Navarra xxix; 547 pp. 848081-0173. Simposium Univ. of Navarre 2004.

809 [E]**Arnold, Matthieu; Prieur, Jean-Marc** Dieu est-il violent?: la violence dans les représentations de Dieu. Strasbourg 2005, Presses universitaires 160 pp. €15. 2-868-20-277-2. Strasbourg-Heidelberg 2004.

810 [E]**Baslez, Marie-Françoise; Prévot, Françoise** Prosopographie et histoire religieuse: actes du colloque tenu en l'Université Paris XII-Val de Marne les 27 et 28 octobre 2000. De l'archéologie à l'histoire: P 2005, De Boccard 474 pp. 27018-01869.

811 [E]**Bird, Darlene; Sherwood, Yvonne** Bodies in question: gender, religion, text. Aldershot 2005, Ashgate 202 pp. $100. 978-07546-35307. Conf. Glasgow-Mainz 2001-2.

812 **Blocher, H.**, *al.* Pour une éthique biblique. 2004 ⇒20,743. Congrès, Montmeyran, 2004. [R]SdT 17 Suppl. 3 (2005) 56-57 (*Guerra, Alberto*).

813 [E]**Boudon-Millot, Véronique; Pouderon, Bernard** Les Pères de l'Église face à la science médicale de leur temps. ThH 117: P 2005, Beauchesne xix; 582 pp. 27010-14840. Actes du troisième colloque d'études patristiques (Paris, 9-11 septembre 2004).

814 [E]**Boustan, Ra'anan S.; Reed, Annette Yoshiko** Heavenly realms and earthly realities in late antique religions. 2004 ⇒20,746. [R]ChH 75 (2005) 172-174 (*Frank, Georgia*); RBLit (2005)* (*Noffke, Eric*).

815 [E]**Braaten, Carl E.; Jenson, Robert W.** Mary, mother of God. 2004 ⇒ 20,747. Conf. St Olaf 2002. [R]JETh 19 (2005) 339-340 (*Eber, Jochen*).

816 [E]**Braaten, Carl E.; Seitz, Christopher R.** I am the Lord your God: christian reflections on the ten commandments. GR 2005, Eerdmans xi; 275 pp. $22. 0-8028-2812-4. Conf. on Decalogue 2003. [R]RExp 102 (2005) 743-745 (*Biddle, Mark E.*).

817 [E]**Braekman, Emile M.** ERASME et les théologiens réformés. CEH 11: Bru 2005, Société royale d'histoire du protestantisme belge 254 pp. 2-87240-002-8. Actes du colloque international, Bruxelles avril 2004.

818 [E]**Brakke, David; Satlow, Michael L.; Weitzman, Steven** Religion and the self in antiquity. Indiana 2005, Indiana Univ. Pr. vii; 268 pp. $25. 0-253-21796-2. Conf. Indiana 2003.

819 [E]**Breid, Franz** Die heilige Eucharistie: Referate der 17. 'Internationalen Theologischen Sommerakademie 2005' des Linzer Priesterkreises in Aigen/M. Augsburg 2005, Stella M. 296 pp. €12.80. 3-934225-381.

820 [E]**Brodersen, Kai; Kropp, Amina** Fluchtafeln: neue Funde und neue Deutungen zum antiken Schadenzauber. Fra 2004, Antike 160 pp. 978-3-9380-32046. Symp. Mannheim 2003.

821 [E]**Carruthers, Iva E.; Haynes, Frederick D., III; Wright, Jeremiah A., Jr.** Blow the trumpet in Zion: global vision and action for the 21st-century Black church. Mp 2005, Fortress xiii; 180 pp. $16. 0-8006-37-12-7. Conf. Atlanta 2004; Pref. *Dwight N. Hopkins*.

822 [E]**Coda, Piero; Crociata, Mariano** Il crocifisso e le religioni: compassione di Dio e sofferenza dell'uomo nelle religioni monoteiste. 2002 ⇒ 18,620. [R]RevSR 79 (2005) 417-418 (*Boespflug, François*).

823 [E]**Corley, Jeremy; Egger-Wenzel, Renate** Prayer from Tobit to Qumran: inaugural conference of the ISDCL at Salzburg, 5-9 July 2003. 2004 ⇒20,755. [R]Gr. 86 (2005) 672-673 (*Calduch-Benages, Nuria*).

824 [E]**Dal Covolo, Enrico; Uglione, Renato** Chiesa e impero: da AUGUSTO a GIUSTINIANO. BSRel 170: 2001 ⇒17,517... 19,665. Atti, Prime e Seconde Giornate Patristiche Torinesi, 1994, 1996. [R]Anton. 80 (2005) 387-388 (*Stamm, Heinz-Meinolf*).

825 [E]**Davis, Stephen T.; Kendall, Daniel; O'Collins, Gerald** The incarnation. 2002 ⇒18,624... 20,758. Symposium, Easter 2000, NY. [R]JR 85 (2005) 142-143 (*Tanner, Kathryn*).

826 [E]**De Troyer, Kristin**, *al.* Wholly woman holy blood: a feminist critique of purity and impurity. Studies in Antiquity and Christianity: 2003

⇒19,667; 20,760. Symposium 1999. [R]RBLit 7 (2005) 480-482 (*Fontaine, Carole R.*).

827 [E]**Draper, Jonathan A.** Orality, literacy, and colonialism in antiquity. Semeia Studies 47: 2004 ⇒20,763. [R]RBLit (2005)* (*Loader, James*).

828 [E]**Embry, Brad; Hayward, Robert** Studies in Jewish prayer. JSSt.S 17: Oxf 2005, OUP vi; 223 pp. 0-19-929641-3.

829 [E]**Filoramo, Giovanni; Gianotto, Claudio** Verus Israel: nuove prospettive sul giudeocristianesimo. BCR 65: 2001 ⇒17,524... 19,674. Colloq. Torino, nov. 1999. [R]RTL 36 (2005) 227-229 (*Auwers, J.-M.*).

830 [E]**Gajek, Bernhard** Die Gegenwärtigkeit Johann Georg HAMANNs: Acta des achten Internationalen Hamann-Kolloquiums an der Martin Luther Univ. Halle-Wittenberg. Fra 2005, Lang 659 pp. 3631-52418-8.

831 [E]**Gargano, Innocenzo** L'eredità spirituale di GREGORIO Magno tra Occidente e Oriente: atti del Simposio internazionale Gregorio Magno 604-2004, Roma, 10-12 marzo 2004. Negarine di S. Pietro in Cariano (Verona) 2005, Il Segno dei Gabrielli 386 pp. 88-88163-54-9.

832 [E]**Garhammer, Erich; Langenhorst, Georg** Schreiben ist Totenerweckung: Theologie und Literatur. Wü 2005, Echter 191 pp. €19.80. 342-9-02692-X.

833 [E]**Garibba, Dario; Tanzarella, Sergio** Giudei o cristiani?: quando nasce il cristianesimo?. Oi christianoi: Trapani 2005, Il pozzo di Giacobbe 196 pp. €20. 88-87778-67-0. Giorno di studio, Napoli, 2004.

834 [E]**Gelardini, Gabriella; Schmid, Peter** Theoriebildung im christlich-jüdischen Dialog: kulturwissenschaftliche Reflexionen zur Deutung, Verhältnisbestimmung und Diskursfähigkeit von Reiigionen. Judentum und Christentum 15: 2004 ⇒20,766. Symposion Mai 2003. [R]ThZ 61 (2005) 179-180 (*Gräbe, Uwe*).

835 [E]**Gerhards, Albert; Doeker, Andrea; Ebenbauer, Peter** Identität durch Gebet: zur gemeinschaftsbildenden Funktion institutionalisierten Betens in Judentum und Christentum. Studien zu Judentum und Christentum: 2003 ⇒19,9109; 20,767. Symposion Bonn 2001. [R]TS 66 (2005) 217-218 (*Duffy, Regis A.*).

836 [E]**Grant, Jamie A.; Wilson, Alistair I.** The God of covenant: biblical, theological and contemporary perspectives. Leicester 2005, Apollos 256 pp. £17. 1-8447-4065-X. Congress Tyndale Fellowship 2003.

837 [E]**Gronchi, Maurizio** La salvezza degli alteri: soteriologia e religioni. 2004 ⇒20,769. [R]ConAss 7/1 (2005) 263-266 (*Testaferri, Francesco*).

838 [E]**Halpérin, Jean; Ucko, Hans** Sagesses et mémoires croisées: rencontres entre Juifs et Africains chrétiens. Genève 2005, Conseil oecuménique des Eglises xi; 179 pp. 2-204-07997-9.

839 [E]**Hart, Kevin; Sherwood, Yvonne** DERRIDA and religion: other testaments. L 2005, Routledge 424 pp. £37.50. 0–415–96889–5. Conf. Toronto 2002.

840 [E]**Härle, Wilfried; Neuner, Peter** Im Licht der Gnade Gottes: zur Gegenwartsbedeutung der Rechtfertigungsbotschaft. Symposion Wittenberg, Oktober 2002.. Studien zur systematischen Theologie und Ethik 42: 2004 ⇒20,772. [R]ThZ 61 (2005) 171-172 (*Weber, Beat*).

841 [E]**Herms, E.** Leben: Verständnis—Wissenschaft—Technik: Kongreßband des 9. Europ. Kongr. f. Theol 15.-19. September 2002, Zürich. Veröffentl. d. Wissenschaftl. Gesellsch. f. Theol. 24: Gü 2005, Gü 597 pp. €65. 3-579-05352-3.

842 [E]**Hezser, Catherine** Rabbinic law in its Roman and Near Eastern context. TSAJ 97: 2003 ⇒19,681; 20,776. [R]ThLZ 130 (2005) 623-624 (*Lehnardt, Andreas*).

843 [E]**Hofmann, Norbert J.; Sievers, Joseph; Mottolese, Maurizio** Chiesa ed ebraismo oggi: percorsi fatti, questioni aperte. R 2005, E.P.U.G. xii; 267 pp. €20. 88-7839-046-1. Conf. Centro Cardinal Bea.

844 [E]**Korn, Eugene B.; Pawlikowski, John** Two faiths, one covenant?: Jewish and Christian identity in the presence of the other. Lanham 2005, Rowman & L. viii; 172 pp. 0-7425-3227-5. Rabbi Hayim Perelmutter Conference, 2003 Chicago.

845 [E]**Köstenberger, Andreas** Whatever happened to truth?. Wheaton, IL 2005, Crossway 173 pp. $16. 56th annual meeting, Evangelical Theological Society, San Antonio, 2004.

846 [E]**Lancel, Serge** Saint AUGUSTIN, la Numidie et la société de son temps: Actes du Colloque SEMPAM-AUSONIUS, Bordeaux, 10-11 octobre 2003. Scripta Antiqua 14: Bordeaux 2005, Ausonius 182 pp. 2910-02-3664.

847 [E]**Lancellotti, Maria Grazia; Xella, Paolo** Angelo Brelich e la storia delle religioni: temi, problemi e prospettive. Storia delle religioni 1: Verona 2005, Essedue (8), 197 pp. 88-85697-60-7. Convegno di Roma, C.N.R. (2002); Bibl. Brelich 189-197.

848 [E]**Langer, Ruth; Fine, Steven** Liturgy in the life of the synagogue: studies in the history of Jewish prayer. Duke Judaic Studies 2: WL 2005, Eisenbrauns xii; 280 pp. $49.50. 1-57506-097-3. Proc. conference Baltimore Hebrew College; Bibl.

849 [E]**Lebecq, Stéphane; Perrin, Michel; Szerwiniack, Olivier** BÈDE le Vénérable, entre tradition et modernité: the Venerable Bede: tradition and posterity. Villeneuve d'Ascq 2005, Univ. Ch. de Gaulle 338 pp. €23. 2-905-63739-0. Coll. juillet 2002.

850 [E]**Luisier, Philippe** Studi su CLEMENTE Romano. OCA 268: 2003 ⇒19,690; 20,788. Atti degli incontri di Roma, 29.3 e 22.11.2001. [R]JThS 56 (2005) 195-197 (*Edwards, M.J.*).

851 [E]**McAuliffe, Jane D.; Walfish, Barry; Goering, Joseph W.** With reverence for the word: medieval scriptural exegesis in Judaism, Christianity, and Islam. 2003 ⇒19,691; 20,791. Conf. Toronto 1997. [R]RRT 12 (2005) 353-355 (*Thomas, David*).

852 [E]**Noegel, Scott B.; Wheeler, Brannon M.; Walker, Joel T.** Prayer, magic, and the stars in the ancient and late antique world. Magic in history: 2003 ⇒19,697; 20,794. Conf. Univ. of Washington, 2000. [R]JR 85 (2005) 347-350 (*Betz, Hans Dieter*).

853 [E]**Prieur, Jean-Marc** La croix: représentations théologiques et symboliques. 2004 ⇒20,799. Journée d'étude 19 sept. 2002, Strasbourg. [R]RBLit (2005)* (*Nicklas, Tobias*).

854 [E]**Renner, Paul; Bidese, Ermenegildo; Fidora, Alexander** Ramon LLULL und NIKOLAUS von Kues: eine Begegnung im Zeichen der Toleranz: Akten des Internationalen Kongresses zu Ramon Llull und Nikolaus von Kues (Brixen und Bozen, 25.-27. November 2004). IP 46; Subsidia Lulliana 2: Turnhout 2005, Brepols xi; 300 pp. 2503-51846X.

855 [E]**Schmidinger, Heinrich; Hoff, Gregor M.** Ethik im Brennpunkt. Innsbruck 2005, Tyrolia 208 pp. 3-7022-2710-5. Salzburger Hochschulwochen 2005.

856 [E]**Semplici, Stefano** Pace, sicurezza, diritti umani. Padova 2005, Messaggero 223 pp. 88-250-1395-7. Convegno, Roma 23 maggio 2004.

857 [E]**Senn, Felix** Welcher Gott?: eine Disputation mit Thomas Ruster: Jubiläumsschrift 50 Jahre 'Theologie für Laien'. 2004 ⇒20,804. [R]ThRv 101 (2005) 137-140 (*Werbick, Jürgen*).

858 [E]**Sfameni Gasparro, Giulia**, *al.* Modi di comunicazione tra il divino e l'umano: tradizioni profetiche, divinazione, astrologia e magia nel mondo mediterraneo antico: II Seminario internazionale, Messina, marzo 2003. Themes and problems of the history of religions in contemporary Europe 2; Hierá 7: Cosenza 2005, Giordano 383 pp. €22. 8886919204.

859 [E]**Shaked, Shaul** Officina magica: essays on the practice of magic in antiquity. Studies in Judaica 4: Lei 2005, Brill x; 320 pp. €149/$213. 90-04-14459-5. Conf. Warburg Inst., London 1999.

860 [E]**Sievers, Joseph; Lembi, Gaia** JOSEPHUS and Jewish history in Flavian Rome and beyond. JSJ.S 104: Lei 2005, Brill xiii; 454 pp. $170/ €119. 90-04-14179-0. Conf. Rome 2003.

861 [E]**Sluzewska, Zuzanna; Urbanik, Jakub** Marriage: ideal–law–practice: proceedings of a conference held in memory of Henryk Kupiszewski. JJP.S 5: Wsz 2005, Warsaw University 83918-25043.

862 [E]**Vergani, W.; Chialà, S.** Le chiese sire tra il IV e il VI secolo: dibattito dottrinale e ricerca spirituale: atti del 2° incontro sull'Oriente Cristiano di tradizione siriaca. Mi 2005, Centro Ambrosiano 168 pp. €13. Milano 2003. [R]LASBF 55 (2005) 566-569 (*Pazzini, Massimo*).

863 [E]**Walter, Peter** Das Gewaltpotential des Monotheismus und der dreieine Gott. FrB 2005, Herder 240 pp. €24.90. 3-451-02216-8. Kongress Freising Sept. 2004. [R]SaThZ 9 (2005) 244-250 (*Halbmayr, Alois*).

864 [E]**Weth, Rudolf** Das Kreuz Jesu: Gewalt—Opfer—Sühne. 2001 ⇒17, 552; 19,711. Tagung Gesellschaft für evangelische Theologie. [R]ThRv 101 (2005) 478-479 (*Beinert, Wolfgang*).

## A2.5 *Acta* **philologica** et **historica**

866 [E]**Alroth, Brita; Hägg, Robin** Greek sacrificial ritual: Olympian and Chthonian. Acta Instituti Atheniensis Regni Sueciae, 8°, 18: Sto 2005, Åström 230 pp. SEK400. 917916-0492. Proc. 6th Internat. Sem. on ancient Greek cult, Göteborg 1997.

867 [E]**Anastasiadis, Vasilis I.; Doukellis, Panagiotis L.** Esclavage antique et discriminations socioculturelles. Berne 2005, Lang xi; 358 pp. €55. 40. 3039-1082-47. Actes du 28e Colloque international du Groupement internat. de recherche sur l'esclavage antique, Mytilène 2003.

868 [E]**Basset, L.; Biville, F.** Les jeux et les ruses de l'ambiguité volontaire dans les textes grecs et latins. CMOM 33: Lyon 2005, Maison de l'Orient 248 pp. 2-903264-26-0. Table Ronde, Lyon, Nov. 2000; Bibl.

869 [E]**Bertolini, Francesco; Gasti, F.** Dialetti e lingue letterarie nella Grecia arcaica. Pavia 2005, Ibis 158 pp. 88716-41973. IV Giornata ghisleriana di filologia classica, Pavia April 2004.

870 [E]**Bertrand, J.M.** La violence dans les mondes grec et romain. Histoire ancienne et médiévale 80: P 2005, Sorbonne 467 pp. €28. 2-85944-530-7. Colloq. Paris mai 2002.

871 [E]**Bessone, Federica; Malaspina, Ermanno** Politica e cultura in Roma Antica: atti dell'incontro di studio in ricordo di Italo Lana, Torino, 16-17 ottobre 2003. Bo 2005, Pàtron 171 pp. 88555-28289.

872 [E]**Boulogne, Jacques** Les Grecs de l'antiquité et les animaux: le cas remarquable de PLUTARQUE. Villeneuve d'Ascq 2005, Université Charles-de-Gaulle 205 pp. 2-84467-0733.

873 [E]**Cancik, Hubert; Hitzl, Konrad** Die Praxis der Herrscherverehrung in Rom und seinen Provinzen. 2003 ⇒19,717. Tagung 2002. [R]BZ 49

(2005) 297-298 (*Klauck, Hans-Josef*); RivCC 81 (2005) 329-331 (*Heid, Stefan*).

874 [E]**Dahan, Gilbert; Goulet, Richard** Allégorie des poètes: allégorie des philosophes: études sur la poétique et l'herméneutique de l'allégorie de l'Antiquité à la Réforme: table ronde, l'Institut des traditions textuelles (Féderation de recherche 33 du C.N.R.S.). Textes et traditions 10: P 2005, Vrin 346 pp. €28. 2-7116-1762-9. [R]ASEs 22 (2005) 531-535 (*Villani, Andrea*).

875 [E]**De Carvalho, Paulo; Lambert, Frédéric** Structures parallèles et corrélatives en grec et en latin: actes du colloque de linguistique grecque et latine. Saint-Etienne 2005, Université 278 pp. Bordeaux Sept. 2002.

876 [E]**Desmulliez, Janine; Hoët-van Cauwenberghe, Christine** Le monde romain à travers l'épigraphie: méthodes et pratiques: actes du XXIVe Colloque international de Lille (8-10 novembre 2001). Villeneuve d'Ascq 2005, Université Charles-de-Gaulle 411 pp. 2-84467-0679.

877 [E]**Edzard, L.; Retsö, J.** Current issues in the analysis of Semitic grammar and lexicon I. AKM 56/3: Wsb 2005, Harrassowitz 253 pp. €48. 3447-052686.

878 [E]**Frede, Dorothea; Inwood, Brad** Language and learning: philosophy of language in the Hellenistic Age. C 2005, CUP xi; 353 pp. £50. 0-521-84181-X. Proc. 9th Symposium Hellenisticum, Hamburg 2001.

879 [E]**Hekster, Olivier; Fowler, Richard** Imaginary kings: royal images in the ancient Near East, Greece and Rome. Oriens et Occidens 11: Stu 2005, Steiner 231 pp. €63. 3515-087656. Sem. Oxford 2003; Num. ill.

880 [E]**Hirsch-Luipold, Rainer** Gott und die Götter bei PLUTARCH: Götterbilder—Gottesbilder—Weltbilder. B 2005, De Gruyter x; 287 pp. €88. 3-11-018479-6. Tagung 2005, Göttingen.

881 [E]**Houston, Stephen D.** The first writing: script invention as history and process. 2004 ⇒20,814. Symposium Sundance, 2000. [R]CamArchJ 15 (2005) 275-279 (*Postgate, Nicholas*).

882 [E]**Jansohn, Christa; Plachta, Bodo** Varianten—variants—variantes. Tü 2005, Niemeyer vi; 254 pp. €110. 3484-29522-8. Tagung.

883 [E]**Lachenaud, Guy; Longrée, Dominique** Grecs et Romains aux prises avec l'histoire: représentations, récits et idéologie. 2003 ⇒19,727. Colloque de Nantes et Angers 12-15 septembre 2001. [R]AnCl 74 (2005) 684-686 (*Poucet, Jacques*).

884 [E]**MacDonald, Dennis R.** Mimesis and intertextuality in antiquity and christianity. 2001 ⇒17,568; 18,575. Conf. Claremont Univ. [R]JBL 124 (2005) 715-732 (*Sandnes, Karl O.*).

885 [E]**Mengozzi, Alessandro** Studi afroasiatici: XI incontro italiano di linguistica camitosemitica = Afro-Asiatic studies: 11th Italian meeting of Afro-Asiatic linguistics, 2003 Bergamo. Materiali linguistici 52: Mi 2005, FrancoAngeli 423 pp. 88-464-7155-5.

886 [E]**Moreau, A.; Turpin, J.C.** La magie. Montpellier mars 1999. 2000 ⇒ 16,550...19,731. [R]OLZ 100 (2005) 176-180 (*Christiansen, Birgit*).

887 [E]**Muraoka, Takamitsu; Elwolde, J.F.** Diggers at the well: proceedings of the third international symposium on the Hebrew of the Dead Sea scrolls and Ben Sira. StTDJ 36: 2000 ⇒16,552... 20,818. [R]RdQ 22 (2005) 287-289 (*Puech, Émile*).

888 [E]**Nebes, Norbert** Neue Beiträge zur Semitistik. Jenaer Beiträge zum Vorderen Orient 5: 2002 ⇒18,692; 20,819. [R]ZA 95 (2005) 153-154 (*Metzler, Kai Alexander*); JNES 64 (2005) 226-227 (*Biggs, Robert D.*).

889 [E]**Pouderon, Bernard** Lieux, décors et paysages de l'ancien roman des origines à Byzance: actes du 2e Colloque de Tours, 24-26 octobre 2002. CMOM 34: Lyon 2005, Maison de l'Orient et de la Méditerranée 400 pp. 2-903264-27-9.
890 [E]**Ryholt, Kim S.B.** Acts of the seventh International Conference of Demotic Studies: Copenhagen, 23-27 August 1999. CNI publications 27: K 2002, Carsten Niebuhr Institute of Near Eastern Studies 401 pp. 87-7289-648-5. Num. ill.
891 [E]**Schiffman, Lawrence H.** Semitic papyrology in context: a climate of creativity. Culture and history of the ANE 14: 2003 ⇒19,742. [R]SCI 24 (2005) 313-315 (*Kaizer, Ted*); OLZ 100 (2005) 199-203 (*Oelsner, J.*).
892 [E]**Schneider, Thomas** Das Ägyptische und die Sprachen Vorderasiens, Nordafrikas und der Ägäis. Basler Kolloquium Juli 2003. AOAT 310: 2004 ⇒20,820. [R]LingAeg 13 (2005) 285-295 (*Schweitzer, Simon D.*).
893 [E]**Troiani, Lucio; Zecchini, Giuseppe** La cultura storica nei primi due secoli dell'impero romano: Milano, 3-5 giugno 2004. Alle radici della casa comune europea 5: R 2005, Bretschneider 310 pp. 88-8265-3420.
894 [E]**Ugolini, Gherardo** Die Kraft der Vergangenheit: Mythos und Realität der klassischen Kultur / La forza del passato: mito e realtà della cultura classica. Convegno Centrum Latinitatis Europae, Berlino, novembre 2003. Hildesheim 2005, Olms 256 pp [At. 95,554—Dario Mantovani].
895 [E]**Wagner, Andreas** Bote und Brief: sprachliche Systeme der Informationsübermittlung im Spannungsfeld von Mündlichkeit und Schriftlichkeit. Nordostafrikanisch-westasiatische Studien 4: 2003 ⇒19,745. Symp. Mainz 1999-2000. [R]JSSt 50 (2005) 368-370 (*Watson, Wilfred*).
896 [E]**Weber, Gregor; Zimmermann, Martin** Propaganda—Selbstdarstellung—Repräsentation im römischen Kaiserreich des 1. Jhs. n.Chr. Historia Einzelschriften 164: 2003 ⇒19,746. Coll. Tübingen 2000. [R]AnCl 74 (2005) 536-537 (*Birley, Anthony R.*); REA 107 (2005) 840-843 (*Hurlet, Frédéric*).

## A2.7 *Acta* orientalistica

897 [E]**Andreu, Guillemette** Deir el-Médineh et la Vallée des Rois: la vie en Égypte au temps des pharaons du Nouvel Empire. 2003 ⇒19,747. Colloque musée du Louvre 2002. [R]BiOr 62 (2005) 474-477 (*Peden, A.J.*).
898 [E]**Bricault, Laurent** Isis en occident: actes du IIème colloque international sur les études isiaques, Lyon III 16-17 mai 2002. RGRW 151: 2004 ⇒20,825. [R]AnCl 74 (2005) 424-425 (*Van Haeperen, Françoise*).
899 [E]**Brosius, Maria** Ancient archives and archival traditions: concepts of record-keeping in the ancient world. 2003 ⇒19,750. [R]SCI 24 (2005) 281-283 (*Wasserman, Nathan*).
900 [E]**Cirillo, Luigi; Van Tongerloo, Alois** Quinto congresso internazionale di studi sul manicheismo: atti: il manicheismo: nuove prospettive della richerca. Manichaean Studies 5: Turnhout 2005, Brepols xix; 416 pp. 25035-16467. Dipartimento Studi Asiatici: Univ. di Napoli.
901 [E]**Collon, Dominique; George, Andrew** Nineveh: Papers of the XLIX° Rencontre Assyriologique Internationale: London, 7-11 July 2003. L 2005, British School of Archaeology in Iraq 2 vols; xiv; 427 pp. $140. 233 fig. = IRAQ 66 (2004) & 67/1 (2005).
902 [E]**Fischer, B.**, *al.* Identifying changes: the transition from Bronze to Iron Ages in Anatolia and its neighbouring regions. Istanbul 2003,

Institutum Turcicum Scientiae Antiquitatis viii; 317 pp. 97580-70630. Workshop Istanbul 2002. [R]AWE 3 (2004) 419-420 (*Burney, Charles*).

903 [E]**Fronzaroli, Pelio; Marrassini, Paolo** Proceedings of the 10th Meeting of Hamito-Semitic (Afroasiatic) Linguistics: (Florence, 18-20 april 2001). Quaderni di semitistica 25: F 2005, Dipartimento di Linguistica Universitá di Firenze xviii; 427 pp. 88-901340-1-1.

904 [E]**Gundlach, Rolf; Rößler-Köhler, Ursula** Das Königtum der Ramessidenzeit: Voraussetzungen—Verwirklichung—Vermächtnis. 3. Symposium zur Ägyptischen Königsideologie, Bonn 2001. ÄAT 36: 2003 ⇒19,753; 20,829. [R]BiOr 62 (2005) 35-37 (*Peden, A.J.*).

905 [E]**Immerzeel, Mat; Van der Vliet, Jacques** Coptic studies on the threshold of a new millennium. Congress Leiden 2000. OLA 133: 2004 ⇒20,832. [R]MSR 62/1 (2005) 68-70 (*Cannuyer, Christian*).

906 [E]**Lanfranchi, Giovanni Battista; Rollinger, Robert; Roaf, Michael** Continuity of empire (?): Assyria, Media, Persia. 2003 ⇒19,757. International meeting 2001, Padova. [R]Or. 74 (2005) 436-440 (*Koch, Heidemarie*); AMIT 37 (2005) 445-452 (*Jacobs, Bruno*).

907 [E]**Love, Serena; Piquette, Kathryn** Current Research in Egyptology 2003: proceedings of the fourth annual symposium, London, 18-19 January 2003. Oxf 2005, Oxbow xiii; 200 pp. 1-8421-7133-X.

908 [E]**Panaino, Antonio; Pettinato, Giovanni** Ideologies as intercultural phenomena. Third annual symposium, Assyrian and Babylonian Intellectual Heritage Project, Chicago 2000. Melammu Symposia 3: 2002 ⇒19,760. [R]BSOAS 68 (2005) 113-118 (*Geller, M.J.*).

909 [E]**Pecchioli Daddi, Franca; Guidotti, Maria Cristina** Narrare gli eventi: atti del convegno degli egittologi e degli orientalisti italiani in margine alla mostra "La battaglia di Qadesh". Studia Asiana 2: R 2005, Herder 353 pp. 88-89670-01-0.

910 [E]**Pruzsinszky, Regine; Hunger, Hermann** Mesopotamian dark age revisited. Conference of SCIEM 2000 (Vienna 2002). DÖAW 32: 2004 ⇒20,836. [R]BSOAS 68 (2005) 105-107 (*George, A.R.*); ZA 95 (2005) 149-152 (*Klinger, Jörg*).

911 [E]**Van Soldt, W.H.** Ethnicity in Ancient Mesopotamia : papers read at the 48th Rencontre assyriologique internationale, Leiden 1-4 July 2002. UNHAII 102: Lei 2005, Nederlands Instituut voor het Nabije Oosten viii; 455 pp. 90-6258-313-X.

912 [E]**Whiting, Robert M.** Mythology and mythologies: methodological approaches to intercultural influences. 2nd symp. Assyrian & Babylonian Intellectual Heritage Project, Paris 1999. Melammu Symposia 2: 2001⇒17,589...19,763. [R]BSOAS 68 (2005) 113-8 (*Geller, M.J.*).

## A2.9 *Acta* **archaeologica**

913 [E]**Amenta, Alessia; Luiselli, Maria M.; Sordi, Maria N.** L'acqua nell'antico Egitto: vita, rigenerazione, incantesimo, medicamento. Egitto antico: R 2005, L'Herma 444 pp. Proc. 1st Intern. Conf. for young Egyptologists, Chianciano Terme, Oct. 15-18, 2003.

914 [E]**Andersen, Helle D.** Urbanization in the Mediterranean in the ninth to sixth centuries B.C.. 1997 ⇒13,380; 15,518. [R]AWE 3 (2004) 411-413 (*Dominguez, Adolfo J.*).

915 [E]**Baker, Heather D.; Jursa, Michael** Approaching the Babylonian economy: proceedings of the START Project Symposium held in Vien-

na, 1-3 July 2004. Veröffentlichungen zur Wirtschaftsgeschichte Babyloniens im 1. Jahrtausend v. Chr. 2; AOAT 330: Müns 2005, Ugarit-Verlag x; 448 pp. 3-934628-79-6. Bibl. 393-416.

916 [E]**Barbet, Alix** La peinture funéraire antique: IVe siècle av. J.-C. - IVe siècle ap. J.-C. VIIe colloque de l'Assoc. internat. pour la peinture murale antique (AIPMA) octobre 1998 Saint-Romain-en-Gal - Vienne. 2001 ⇒17,594. [R]AWE 4 (2005) 181-182 (*Ridgway, F.R. Serra*).

917 [E]**Barrett, John C.; Halstead, Paul** The emergence of civilisation revisited. Sheffield studies in Aegean archaeology 6: Oxf 2004, Oxbow xiv; 274 pp. 1-8421-7166-6. Sheffield Centre for Aegean Archaeology.

918 [E]**Bietak, Manfred** The Middle Bronze Age in the Levant. Conf. on MB IIA ceramic material, Vienna 2001. DÖAW 26: 2002 ⇒19,772. [R]BiOr 62 (2005) 592-595 (*Iamoni, Marco*); JNES 64 (2005) 208-209 (*Burke, Aaron A.*);

919 The synchronisation of civilisations in the eastern Mediterranean in the second millennium B.C. SCIEM 2000-EuroConference, Haindorf 2nd of May-7th of May 2001. DÖAW 29: 2003 ⇒16,576... 20,849. [R]WO 35 (2005) 221-223 (*Gamer-Wallert, Ingrid*).

920 [E]**Blenkinsopp, Joseph; Lipschits, Oded** Judah and the Judeans in the Neo-Babylonian period. 2003 ⇒19,776; 20,850. Conf. Tel Aviv 2001. [R]CBQ 67 (2005) 177-179 (*Endres, John C.*); BiOr 62 (2005) 563-566 (*Halpern, Baruch*); RBLit 7 (2005) 206-208 (*Becking, Bob*).

921 [E]**Boccaccini, Gabriele**, *al.* Enoch and Qumran origins: new light on a forgotten connection. GR 2005, Eerdmans xviii; 454 pp. $40/£24. 0-8028-2878-7. Seminar 2: 2003: Venice, Italy.

922 [E]**Bonfante, Larissa; Karageorghis, Vassos** Italy and Cyprus in antiquity: 1500-450 BC. International symposium, Columbia Univ., Nov. 16-18, 2000. 2001 ⇒17,598. [R]IEJ 55 (2005) 113-116 (*Maeir, Aren M.*); Syria 82 (2005) 357-363 (*Cassimatis, Hélène*).

923 [E]**Bourriau, Janine; Phillips, Jacke** Invention and innovation: the social context of technological change, 2: Egypt, the Aegean and the Near East, 1650-1150 BC. 2004 ⇒20,851. Conf. Cambridge Sept. 2002. [R]JESHO 48 (2005) 323-325 (*Nicholson, Paul T.*); DiscEg 63 (2005) 111-113 (*Nibbi, Alessandra*).

924 [E]**Braund, David** Scythians and Greeks: cultural interactions in Scythia, Athens and the early Roman Empire (sixth century BC-first century AD). Exeter 2005, Univ. of Exeter Pr. xi; 254 pp. £50. 0-85989-746-X. Coll. Exeter 2000; 46 fig.

925 [E]**Bresson, A; Cocula, A.-M.; Pébarthe, C.** L'écriture publique du pouvoir. Etudes 10: Bordeaux 2005, Ausonius 219 pp. 29100-23494. Coll. Bordeaux 2002; Bibl.

926 [E]**Briant, Pierre; Boucharlat, Rémy** L'archéologie de l'empire achéménide: nouvelles recherches. Persika 6: P 2005, De Boccard 356 pp. €63. 27018-01958. Colloq. nov. 2003; Bibl.

927 [E]**Caccamo Caltabiano, M.; Castrizio, D.; Puglisi, M.** La tradizione iconica come fonte storica: il ruolo della numismatica negli studi di iconografia. Reggio 2004, Falzea 528 pp. 88296-132X. Atti del I incontro di studio del Lexicon Iconographicum Numismaticae, Messina marzo 2003; Ill.; Bibl.

928 [E]**Campbell, Jonathan G.; Lyons, William J.; Pietersen, Lloyd K.** New directions in Qumran studies. Bristol colloquium on the Dead Sea scrolls, September 2003. L 2005, Clark ix; 226 pp. £50. 0567-04131X.

929 [E]**Ciraolo, Leda; Seidel, Jonathan** Magic and divination in the ancient world. Ancient magic and divination 2: 2002 ⇒18,729; 19,783. Colloquium Berkeley 1994. [R]OLZ 100 (2005) 171-76 (*Christiansen, Birgit*).

930 [E]**Clark, Douglas R.; Matthews, Victor H.** One hundred years of American archaeology in the Middle East. ASOR centennial, Washington, DC, 2000. 2003 ⇒19,784. [R]BiOr 62 (2005) 602-607 (*Collins, S.*).

931 [E]**Cleland, Liza; Stears, Karen** Colour in the ancient Mediterranean world. BAR-IS 1267: Oxf 2004, Archaeopress x; 154 pp. £51. 1-841-71-3732. Collab. *Glenys Davies*; Conf. Edinburgh 2001.

932 [E]**Collins, John J.; Sterling, Gregory E.; Clements, Ruth A.** Sapiential perspectives: wisdom literature in light of the Dead Sea scrolls. 6th Internat. Symp. Orion Center, May 2001. StTDJ 51: 2004 ⇒20,854. [R]JSJ 36 (2005) 101-104 (*Hempel, Charlotte*); DSD 12 (2005) 229-231 (*Harrington, Daniel J.*); Numen 52 (2005) 395-398 (*Schipper, Bernd*).

933 [E]**Dasen, Véronique** Naissance et petite enfance dans l'antiquité. Colloque de Fribourg, 28 novembre - 1er décembre 2001. OBO 203: 2004 ⇒20,856. [R]DiscEg 62 (2005) 111-116 (*Warburton, David*).

934 [E]**Davila, James R.** The Dead Sea scrolls as background to postbiblical Judaism and early christianity. Conference St. Andrews 2001. StTDJ 46: 2002 ⇒18,732; 19,788. [R]RdQ 22 (2005) 296-298 (*Rey, Jean-S.*).

935 [E]**Dekeyzer, B.; Van der Stock, Jan** Manuscripts in transition: recycling manuscripts, texts and images. Corpus of illuminated manuscripts from the Low Countries: Lv 2005, Peeters 446 pp. £67. 90-429-1562-5. Conf. Brussels 2002.

936 [E]**Draper, Jonathan A.** Orality, literacy, and colonialism in Southern Africa. Semeia Studies 46: 2003 ⇒19,789; 20,857. Colloquium Pietermaritzburg 2001. [R]RBLit (2005)* (*Duggan, Michael*).

937 [E]**Duyrat, Frédérique; Picard, Olivier** L'exception égyptienne?: production et échanges monétaires en Egypte hellénistique et romaine. Etudes alexandrines 10: Le Caire 2005, Institut français d'archéologie orientale 391 pp. €51. 978-27247-04105. Actes du colloque d'Alexandrie, 13-15 avril 2002.

938 [E]**Edmondson, Jonathan; Mason, Steve; Rives, James** Flavius JOSEPHUS and Flavian Rome. Oxf 2005, OUP xvi; 400 pp. £75. 0-19926-212-8. Conf. Toronto 2001.

939 [E]**Eichmann, Ricardo; Hickmann, Ellen** Studien zur Musikarchäologie IV: Musikarchäologische Quellengruppen. Orient-Archäologie 15: 2004 ⇒20,12293. Symposium 2002: Kloster Michaelstein. [R]Mes. 40 (2005) 190 (*Menegazzi, Roberta*).

940 [E]**Endesfelder, E.** Von Berlin nach Meroe: Erinnerungen an den Ägyptologen Fritz Hintze. Asien und Afrika-Studien 3: 2003 ⇒19,793. Colloquium 1995. [R]OLZ 100 (2005) 138-142 (*Zibelius-Chen, Karola*).

941 [E]**Favier, René; Granet-Abisset, Anne-Marie** Récits et représentations des catastrophes depuis l'antiquité. Grenoble 2005, CNRS 408 pp. 2-914242-18-2.

942 [E]**Fitzenreiter, Martin** Genealogie—Realität und Fiktion von Identität. Internet Beiträge zur Ägyptologie und Sudanarchäologie 5: L 2005, Golden House xiv; 206 pp. £25. 0-9547-2188-8. Colloq. June 2004.

943 [E]**Follet, Simone** L'hellénisme d'époque romaine, nouveaux documents, nouvelles approches (1er s. a.C.-III[e] s. p.C.). Colloq. L. Robert, Paris 2000. 2004 ⇒20,863. [R]RAr (2005/2) 412-3 (*Le Roy, Christian*).

944 [E]**Foster, Karen P.; Laffineur, Robert** METRON: measuring the Aegean Bronze Age. 9th Int. Aegean Conf., New Haven 2002. Aegeum 24: 2003 ⇒19,795. [R]RAr (2005/1) 132-5 (*Rougemont, Françoise*).

945 [E]**Frey, Jörg; Stegemann, Hartmut** Qumran kontrovers: Beiträge zu den Textfunden vom Toten Meer. 2003 ⇒19,796; 20,865. [R]ThLZ 130 (2005) 928-929 (*Zangenberg, Jürgen*).

946 [E]**Halperin, Jean; Hanson, N.** Ethique du jubilé: vers un réparation du monde?: actes du XXXIXe colloque des intellectuels juifs de langue française. Présences du judaïsme: P 2005, Michel 182 pp. €20.

947 [E]**Hägg, Robin** Peloponnesian sanctuaries and cults. 9th internat. symp. Swedish Institute at Athens 1994. Acta Inst. Athen. Regni Sueciae 48: 2002 ⇒18,746; 20,868. [R]AJA 109 (2005) 308-11 (*Antonaccio, Carla*).

948 [E]**Hersberg, Henner von; Freyberger, Klaus S.; Henning, Agnes** Kulturkonflikte im Vorderen Orient an der Wende vom Hellenismus zur römischen Kaiserzeit. Orient-Archäologie 11: 2003 ⇒19,802. Kolloquium Köln Feb. 2000. [R]OLZ 100 (2005) 611-616 (*Oelsner, J.*).

949 [E]**Hoffmeier, James K.; Millard, Alan R.** The future of biblical archaeology: reassessing methodologies and assumptions. Symposium 2001 Trinity International University. 2004 ⇒20,869. [R]Kerux 20/3 (2005) 47-8 (*Dennison, James T., Jr.*); TrinJ 26 (2005) 321-323 (*Beitzel, Barry J.*); RBLit 7 (2005) 103-110 (*Edelman, Diana*).

950 [E]**Hurst, Henry; Owen, Sara** Ancient colonizations: analogy, similarity and difference. L 2005, Duckworth viii; 165 pp. £17. 0-7156-3298-1. Seminar, Cambridge; Bibl. 141-159.

951 [E]**Kyrieleis, Helmut** Olympia 1875-2000: 125 Jahre deutsche Ausgrabungen: internationales Symposium, Berlin 9-11 November 2000. 2002 ⇒19,805. [R]AJA 109 (2005) 110-111 (*Bookidis, Nancy*).

952 [E]**Levy, Thomas E.; Higham, Thomas** The bible and radiocarbon dating: archaeology, text and science. L 2005, Equinox xii; 450 pp. £75/$135; £25/$40. 1-84553-056-X/7-8. Conf. Oxford 2004; Num. ill.

953 [E]**Moreland, Milton C.** Between text and artifact: integrating archaeology in biblical studies teaching. SBL.Archaeology and Biblical Studies 8: 2003 ⇒19,813. Meetings Duke and Oregon 2000-2001. [R]CBQ 67 (2005) 179-180 (*Fulco, William J.*); ThLZ 130 (2005) 1334-1335 (*Zwickel, Wolfgang*); RBLit 7 (2005) 110-112 (*Brookman, Buzz*).

954 [E]**Neudecker, Richard; Zanker, Paul** Lebenswelten, Bilder und Räume in der römischen Stadt der Kaiserzeit. Wsb 2005, Reichert 254 pp. Symp. 2002.

955 [E]**Nielsen, Inge** The royal palace institution in the first millennium BC. Monographs of the Danish Institute at Athens 4: 2001 ⇒17,631... 20, 884. Coll. Athens 1999. [R]VDI (2005/1) 241-248 (*Koshelenko, G.A.*).

956 [E]**Olsson, Birger; Zetterholm, Magnus** The ancient synagogue from its origins until 200 C.E. Lund 2001. CB.NT 39: 2003 ⇒19,817; 20, 886. [R]RRT 12/1 (2005) 140-41 (*Bury, Benjamin*); CBQ 67 (2005) 191-193 (*Meyers, Eric M.*) AJA 109 (2005) 810-813 (*Porter, Adam L.*).

957 [E]**Papadopoulos, John K.; Leventhal, Richard M.** Theory and practice in Mediterranean archaeology: old world and new world perspectives. Cotsen Advanced Seminars 1: 2003 ⇒19,818. [R]AJA 109 (2005) 95-96 (*German, Senta C.*).

958 [E]**Rutherford, Ian; Elsner, Jas** Pilgrimage in Graeco-Roman & early christian antiquity: seeing the gods. Oxf 2005, OUP xvii; 513 pp. $125. 0-19-925079-0. Conference Reading July 2000.

959 [E]**Spanò Giammellaro, Antonella** Atti del V Congresso internazionale di studi fenici e punici : Marsala-Palermo, ottobre 2000. Palermo 2005, Università degli Studi di Palermo 3 vols; xlviii + xxii + xxii; 1408 pp.

960 [E]**Stampolidis, Nicholas Chr.; Karageorghis, Vassos** Πλόες... sea routes... interconnections in the Mediterranean 16th -6th c. BC. Symposium, Rethymnon, Crete 2002. 2003 ⇒19,824. [R]RAr (2005/2) 374-376 (*Hermary, Antoine*); CRAI (2005/1) 354-355 (*Desanges, Jehan*).
961 [E]**Starkey, Janet C.M.** People of the Red Sea: proceedings of Red Sea Project II held in the British Museum October 2004. BAR Int. Ser. 1395: Oxf 2005, Archaeopress vi; 176 pp. £30. 35 fig.
962 [E]**Strudwick, Nigel; Taylor, J.H.** The Theban necropolis. 2003 ⇒19, 826. [R]BiOr 62 (2005) 245-252 (*Engelmann-von Carnap, B.*).
963 [E]**Uehlinger, Christoph** Images as media: sources for the cultural history of the Near East and the eastern Mediterranean (Ist millennium BCE). OBO 175: 2000 ⇒16,611... 19,828. [R]BZ 49 (2005) 317-319 (*Weigl, Michael*).
964 [E]**Viard, Georges** L'abbaye cistercienne de Morimond: histoire et rayonnement. Langres 2005, Assoc. amis de l'abbaye de Morimond 358 pp. Colloque Langres 2003.
965 [E]**Villing, A.** The Greeks in the east. L 2005, British Museum 123 pp. $50. 0861-59157-7. Colloq. British Museum 1997; 109 fig.; 44 pl.
966 [E]**Wermelinger, Otto**, *al.* Akten des internationalen Kolloquiums Freiburg, Saint-Maurice, Martigny, 17.-20. September 2003: Mauritius und die Thebäische Legion. Paradosis 49: FrS 2005, Academic (8); 481 pp. 3-7278-1527-2.
967 [E]**Zaccagnini, Carlo** Mercanti e politica nel mondo antico. Saggi di storia antica 21: 2003 ⇒19,835. Simposio Roma 2000. [R]OLZ 100 (2005) 445-446 (*Klengel, Horst*); WO 35 (2005) 232-235 (*Faist, Betina*).

## A3.1 *Opera consultationis*—Reference works *plurium* infra

968 Augustinus-Lexikon, 3/1-2: Figura(e)-Hieronymus. [E]**Mayer, Cornelius**: 2004 ⇒20,902. [R]REAug 51 (2005) 417-418 (*Duval, Yves-Marie*).
969 Catholicisme, hier, aujourd'hui, demain. Tables compléments et mises à jour. [E]**Mathon, Gérard**: P 2005, Letouzey et Ané 253-764 col. 270-63-02313. Fasc. 76-77: C-D-E.
970 **DBS:** Supplément au dictionnaire de la bible, 13: Sophonie-Targum. [E]**Briend, Jacques; Quesnel, Michel**: P 2005, Letouzey & A. 1-907; 1*-344* col. €200.
971 [E]**Perdue, Leo G.** The Blackwell companion to the Hebrew Bible. 2001 ⇒17,653... 20,905. [R]JNES 64 (2005) 130-133 (*Clemens, David M.*).
972 **RAC:** Reallexikon für Antike und Christentum: Lieferung 164: Kommentar [Forts.]-Konstantinopel. [E]**Schöllgen, Georg**, *al.*: Stu 2005, Hiersemann 321-480 col.. 3-7772-0524-9;
973 Lieferung 165/166: Konstantinopel[Forts.]-Kot (Latrine). [E]**Schöllgen, Georg**, *al.*: Stu 2005, Hiersemann 481-800 col.. 3-7772-0525-7.
974 **RGG:** Religion in Geschichte und Gegenwart, 8: T-Z. [E]**Betz, Hans Dieter**, *al.*: Tü [4]2005, Mohr lxxxviii; 1966 col. €192.60. 31614-69488.
975 **RLA:** Reallexikon der Assyriologie 10: Oannes-Priesterverkleidung. [E]**Edzard, D.O.**: B 2005, De Gruyter xxxvi; 648 pp. €298. 978-31101-85355.
976 **TRE:** Theologische Realenzyklopädie, 33-34. [E]**Müller, Gerhard** 2002 ⇒18,799-800. [R]ThR 70 (2005) 237-242 (*Gräßer, Erich*);
977 36: Wiedergeburt - Zypern. [E]**Müller, Gerhard**: De-Gruyter-Studienbuch: B 2005, De Gruyter 872 pp. €150. 3-11-017842-7.

### A3.3 *Opera consultationis* **biblica** *non excerpta infra*—**not subindexed**

978 [E]**Alter, Robert; Kermode, Frank** Encyclopédie littéraire de la bible. [T]*Dauzat, Pierre-Emmanuel*: 2003 ⇒19,855; 20,917. [R]EeV 125 (2005) 21-23 (*Chauvin, Charles*); Theoforum 36 (2005) 188-191 (*Vogels, Walter*).

979 [E]**Arnold, Bill T.; Williamson, Hugh G.M.** Dictionary of the Old Testament: historical books. DG 2005, InterVarsity xxiii: 1060 pp. $50. 0-8308-1782-4.

980 **Aune, David E.** The Westminster dictionary of New Testament and early christian literature and rhetoric. 2003 ⇒19,856; 20,918. [R]RBLit 7 (2005) 491-493 (*Matson, Mark A.*).

981 [E]**Betz, Otto; Ego, Beate; Grimm, Werner** Calwer Bibellexikon. 2003 ⇒19,858; 20,921. [R]GlLern 20 (2005) 91-92 (*Gendreissig, Börries*).

982 [E]**Bruce, Frederick F.; Harrison, Roland K.; Youngblood, Ronald F.** Nelson's student bible dictionary: a complete guide to understanding the world of the bible. Nv 2005, Nelson vi; 275 pp. 1-418-50331-2.

983 [E]**Coenen, Lothar; Haacker, Klaus** Theologisches Begriffslexikon zum Neuen Testament. Wu 2005, Brockhaus xlvi; 2106 pp. €50. 3-41-7-24845-0. Neubearb. Ausgabe.

984 [E]**Dohmen, Christoph** Das große Sachbuch zur Welt und Umwelt der Bibel. Stu [2]2005 <1996>, Kathol. Bibelwerk 360 pp. €29.90. 3-46030-2089 [EuA 81,329].

985 **Evans, Craig A.** Ancient texts for New Testament studies: a guide to the background literature. Peabody, MASS 2005, Hendrickson xxxvi; 539 pp. $35. 1-565-63409-8.

986 [E]**Freedman, David N.** Eerdmans dictionary of the bible. 2000 ⇒16, 633... 18,806. [R]JNES 64 (2005) 285-287 (*Pardee, Dennis*).

987 **GLAT** 5: Grande lessico dell'Antico Testamento, 5: מים – נשר. [E]**Botterweck, G. Johannes**, *al.*; [T]*Asciutto, Liborio, al.*: Brescia 2005, Paideia xvi pp; 1136 col. 88-394-0712X.

988 **Heller, Jan** Výkladový slovnik biblických jmen [Wörterbuch der biblischen Eigennamen]. 2003 ⇒19,868. [R]OLZ 100 (2005) 63-64 (*Thiel, Winfried*).

989 **Heriban, Jozef** Dizionario terminologico-concettuale di scienze bibliche e ausiliarie. R 2005, LAS 1495 pp. €65. 88213-05678. Bibl. 1325-1385 [R]OrdKor 46 (2005) 506-507 (*Wahl, Otto*); SBSl (2005) 86-88 (*Felici, Sergio*).

990 **Holloman, Henry W.** Kregel dictionary of the bible and theology. GR 2005, Kregel 600 pp. $33.

991 [E]**Houlden, Leslie** Jesus: the complete guide. NY 2005, Continuum xxxvii; 922 pp. $50. 08264-8011X [BiTod 44,264—Donald Senior].

992 **Losch, Richard R.** The uttermost parts of the earth: a guide to places in the bible. GR 2005, Eerdmans xi; 260 pp. $16. 08028-28051 [MissTod 7,380s—Shaji Joseph].

993 **Maurer, Helmar** Bibel-Navigator: wo steht was—was steht wo?. Bibel, Kirche, Gemeinde: Neuk [2]2005, Aussaat 237 pp. 3-7615-5438-9.

994 Nuovo dizionario enciclopedico illustrato della bibbia. CasM 2005, Piemme xxvii; 1167 pp.

995 [E]**Reid, Daniel G.** The IVP dictionary of the New Testament: a one-volume compendium of contemporary biblical scholarship. 2004 ⇒

20,940. [R]SNTU 30 (2005) 270-271 (*Fuchs, Albert*); RBLit (2005)* (*Sweeney, James*).

996 [E]**Renn, Stephen D.** Expository dictionary of bible words: word studies for key English bible words based on the Hebrew and Greek texts: coded to the revised Strong's numbering system. Peabody, MASS 2005, Hendrickson x; 1171 pp. 1565-636732. Incl. CD-ROM.

997 **TDOT**: Theological Dictionary of the Old Testament, 12: pâsaḥ-qûm. [E]**Botterweck, G. Johannes; Ringgren, Helmer; Fabry, Heinz-J.**; [T]*Stott, Douglas W.*: 2003 ⇒19,876; 20,945. [R]BS 162 (2005) 241-242 (*Chisholm, Robert B., Jr.*);

998 14: שָׁכַן-רָשַׁע. 2004 ⇒20,944. [R]RBLit (2005)* (*Finlay, Timothy D.; Kaminsky, Joel S.*);

999 12-14. 2003-2004 ⇒19,976; 20,943-4. [R]VJTR 69 (2005) 389-391 (*Meagher, P.M.*);

1000 [E]**Vanhoozer, Kevin J.**, *al.* Dictionary for theological interpretation of the bible. GR 2005, Baker 896 pp. $50. 0-8010-2694-2. [R]HBT 27/1 (2005) 104-105 (*Dearman, J. Andrew*).

1001 **Vermes, Geza** Who's who in the age of Jesus. L 2005, Penguin ix; 285 pp. 0-14-051565-8. Bibl. 265-271.

1002 **Vigni, Giuliano** Dizionario del Nuovo Testamento: concetti fondamentali, parole-chiave, termini ed espressioni caratteristiche, 2: B-custodire. Bibbia Paoline: Mi 2005, Paoline 181 pp. €13.50. 97888-31-528-641.

1003 **Vine, William E.** Vine's concise dictionary of bible. Nv 2005, Nelson v; 426 pp. 1-418-50151-4.

1004 WORDsearch life application study bible library. 2003 ⇒19,877. CD-ROM. [R]Evangel 23 (2005) 62-63 (*Baxter, Tony*).

## A3.5 *Opera consultationis* **theologica** *non excerpta infra*

1005 **Bosch Navarro, Juan** Diccionario de teólogos/as contemporáneos. 2003 ⇒20,951. [R]EstTrin 39 (2005) 144-145 (*Pujana, Juan*).

1006 [E]**Bowden, John** Encyclopedia of christianity. NY 2005, OUP xli; 1364 pp. $125. 0-19-522393-4 [ThD 52,256—W. Charles Heiser].

1007 **Denzinger, Heinrich** Enchridion symbolorum definitionum et declarationum de rebus fidei et morum: Kompendium der Glaubensbekenntnisse und kirchlichen Lehrentscheidungen. [E]*Hünermann, Peter*: FrB 2005, Herder xxxviii; 1811 pp. €98. 3-451-28520-7. Lateinisch-Deutsch.

1008 [E]**Eicher, P.** Neues Handbuch theologischer Grundbegriffe. Mü 2005, Kösel 4 vols; 526+526+528+528 pp. €112. 3-466-20456.

1009 Encyclopedia of religion. [E]**Jones, Lindsay** Farmington Hills, MI [2]2005 <1987>, Macmillan R 15 vols; cxlvi; 10735 pp. $1,295. 0-02-865733-0. Num. ill. [ThD 52,43—W. Charles Heiser].

1010 **Esquerda Bifet, Juan** Dizionario dell'evangelizzazione. N 2005, EDI 969 pp. €100. 88-89094-12-5.

1011 Eucharistia: enciclopedia dell'eucaristia. [E]**Brouard, Maurice** 2004 ⇒20,964. [R]Asp. 52 (2005) 262-264 (*Petti, Angelo*); Crkva u Svijetu 40 (2005) 399-403 (*Mateljan, Ante*).

1012 [E]**Fahlbusch, Erwin; Bromiley, Geoffrey W.** The encyclopedia of christianity, 3: J-O. 2003 ⇒19,886; 20,966. [R]ET 116 (2005) 124-126 (*Court, John M.*);

1013 The encyclopedia of christianity, 4: P-Sh. GR 2005, Eerdmans xxix; 884 pp. $100. 0-8028-2416-1.

1014 **Gonzalez, Justo L.** Essential theological terms. LVL 2005, Westminster 187 pp. $25. 0-664-22810-0.

1015 [E]**Graf, Friedrich W.** Klassiker de Theologie, 1: von TERTULLIAN bis CALVIN, 2: von Richard SIMON bis Karl RAHNER. Becksche Reihe 1630-1631: Mü 2005, Beck 288; 320 pp. 3-406-52800-7/1-5.

1016 Handbuch Religionswissenschaft: Religionen und ihre zentralen Themen. [E]**Figl, Johann** 2003 <2005> ⇒19,890. [R]ThRv 101 (2005) 244-246 (*Elsas, Christoph*).

1017 [E]**Hauerwas, Stanley; Wells, Samuel** The Blackwell companion to christian ethics. 2004 ⇒20,969. [R]RRT 12/1 (2005) 102-106 (*D'Costa, Gavin*).

1018 **Hermann, Uwe** Taschenbuch theologischer Fremdwörter. Gü 2005, Gü 272 pp. €15. 3-579-06421-5.

1019 [E]**Hillerbrand, Hans J.** The encyclopedia of protestantism. 2004 ⇒ 20, 970. [R]TS 66 (2005) 192-194 (*Dabney, D. Lyle*).

1020 [E]**Lacoste, Jean-Yves** Dizionario critico di teologia. [E]*Coda, Piero*: R 2005, Borla 1545 pp. €160. 88-263-1496-9.

1021 [E]**Lacoste, Jean-Yves** Encyclopedia of christian theology. L 2005, Routledge 3 vols; xxxiii; 601 + xxxiii; 603-1174 + xxxiii; 1175-1816 pp. £310. 1-57958-2508. Translated from the *Dictionnaire critique de théologie* ⇒16,1523.

1022 **Langenhorst, Georg** Theologie und Literatur: ein Handbuch. Da: Wiss 2005, 271 pp. €39.90.

1023 **McGuckin, John A.** The SCM Press A-Z of patristic theology. L [2]2005, SCM xxiii; 367 pp. £30. 0-334-04010-8;

1024 The Westminster handbook to patristic theology. 2004 ⇒20,975. [R]CTJ 40 (2005) 370-372 (*Payton, James R., Jr.*); JECS 12 (2004) 548-550 (*Harvey, Paul B., Jr.*).

1025 **Mesotten, Bart** Van Aalmoes tot Zwitserse garde: etymologie en betekenis van duizend woorden rond religie. 2004 ⇒20,976. [R]Coll. 35 (2005) 221-223 (*De Voght, Karel*).

1026 [E]**Moeller, Bernd; Jahn, Bruno** Deutsche biographische Enziklopädie der Theologie und der Kirchen (DBETh). Mü 2005, Saur 2 vols; 1785 pp. €328. 3-598-11666-7.

1027 **Noegel, Scott B.; Wheeler, Brannon M.** Historical dictionary of prophets in Islam and Judaism. 2002 ⇒18,844; 20,977. [R]JSSt 50 (2005) 238-240 (*Meri, Josef*).

1028 [E]**Potin, J.; Zauber, V.** Dizionario dei monoteismi. Bo 2005, EDB 473 pp.

1029 **Ramons-Lissón, Domingo** Patrología. Manuales de teología 35: Pamplona 2005, EUNSA 525 pp. €26.94. 84-313-2297-7.

1030 [E]**Sheldrake, Philip** The new Westminster[/SCM] dictionary of christian spirituality. LVL 2005, Westminster xix; 680 pp. $50. 0-664-23-003-2. Bibl. [R]Worship 80/1 (2005) 84-85 (*Seasoltz, R. Kevin*); VJTR 69 (2005) 713-715 (*Mangai, Poulose*); ER 57 (2005) 520-521 (*Longchar, A. Wati*).

1031 [E]**Strumia, Alberto; Tanzella-Nitti, Giuseppe** Dizionario interdisciplinare di scienza e fede: cultura scientifica, filosofia e teologia. Città del Vaticano: Urbaniana Univ. Pr. 2002, 2 vol; 2340 pp. 88-401-105-0-X.

1032 [E]**Swarat, Uwe** Fachwörterbuch für Theologie und Kirche. Wu [3]2005, Brockhaus 252 pp. €10.90.

1033 [E]**Taylor, Bron R.** The encyclopedia of religion and nature. NY 2005, Thoemmes 2 vols; xliv; 1877pp. $450. 1-84371-138-9 [ThD 52,257—W. Charles Heiser].

1034 Thesaurus cultus et rituum antiquorum (ThesCRA), 3-5. LA 2005, Getty Museum xviii; 434 + xiv; 485 + xix; 502 pp. 0-89236-7873. Num. ill.

1035 [E]**Viganò, Dario E.** Gesù e la macchina da presa: dizionario ragionato del cinema cristologico. Città del Vaticano 2005, Pont. Univ. Lateranense 384 pp. €30. 978-88465-04982. [R]Cultura e libri 151 (2005) 133-135 (*Dal Bello, Mario*).

1036 **Vorgrimler, Herbert** Nuovo dizionario teologico. 2004 ⇒20,983. [R]EstTrin 39 (2005) 602-604 (*Miguel, José María de*).

## A3.6 *Opera consultationis* generalia

1037 **Anselmo, Daniele,** *al.* Lessico delle libertà: percorso tra 15 parole chiave. Saggistica Paoline 31: T 2005, Paoline 166 pp. 88315-29145.

1038 Brill's new Pauly: encyclopaedia of the ancient world, antiquity, 6: Hat-Jus. [E]**Cancik, Hubert; Schneider, Helmuth** Lei 2005, Brill xvi pp; 1232 col. 90-04-12269-9;

1039 7: K-Lyc. Lei 2005, Brill lvi pp; 942 col.. €196. 90-04-12270-2.

1040 Encyclopaedia aethiopica, 2: D-Ha. [E]**Uhlig, Siegbert** Wsb 2005, Harrassowitz xxxix; 1082 pp. €78. 3447-052384.

1041 The encyclopaedia of Judaism, 1-4: A-E; F-K; L-Ra; Re-Z. [E]**Neusner, Jacob; Avery-Peck, Alan J.; Green, William S.** Lei [2]2005, Brill xlv; 808 + 809-1533 + 1535-2246 + 2247-2948 pp. €359. 90-0-4-14787-X;

1042 5, Suppl. 2. 2004 ⇒20,1000. [R]RBLit (2005)* (*Garber, Zev*).

1043 Encyclopédie de l'Islam, 11: V - Z. [E]**Bearman, P.J.,** *al.* Lei 2005, Brill xiii; 621 pp. 90-04-13951-6.

1044 **Fant, M.B.; Lefkowitz, M.** Women's life in Greece and Rome: a source book in translation. Baltimore 2005 <1982, 1992>, Johns Hopkins Univ. Pr. xxvii; 420 pp. $60/23. 08018-8309/105. Bibl. [NTAb 50,630].

1045 **Frier, Bruce W.; McGinn, Thomas A.J.** A casebook on Roman family law. Oxf 2004, OUP xxi; 506 pp. 01951-61858.

1046 [E]**Hanegraaff, Wouter J.** Dictionary of gnosis and western esotericism. Lei 2005, Brill 2 vols; 1228 pp. €289. 90-04-141871. [R]ThLZ 130 (2005) 1300-1302 (*Frenschkowski, Marco*).

1047 Historisches Wörterbuch der Rhetorik, 7: Pos-Rhet. [E]**Ueding, Gert** Tü 2005, Niemeyer vi; 1768 Sp.. 3-484-68107-1.

1048 **Hughes, Aaron W.** Jewish philosophy A-Z. E 2005, University Press xvii; 180 pp. 0-7486-2218-7. Bibl. 176-180.

1049 [E]**Kilcher, Andreas B.; Fraisse, Otfried** Metzler Lexikon jüdischer Philosophen: philosophisches Denken des Judentums von der Antike bis zur Gegenwart. 2003 ⇒19,911; 20,996. [R]REJ 164 (2005) 396-398 (*Rothschild, Jean-Pierre*).

1050 [E]**Kotowski, Elke-Vera; Schoeps, Julius H.; Wallenborn, Hiltrud** Handbuch zur Geschichte der Juden in Europa,1: Länder und Regionen; 2: Religion, Kultur, Alltag. 2001 ⇒19,912. [R]FrRu 12 (2005) 216-217 (*Ehrlich, Ernst Ludwig*).

1051 [E]**Leclant, Jean** Dictionnaire de l'antiquité. Quadrige: P 2005, PUF xlviii; 2389 pp. €49. 2-13-0550-18-5.

1052 **Matras, Yaron** Romani: a linguistic introduction. C 2005, CUP xiv, 291pp. 0-521-02330-0. Bibl. 260-278.

1053 The Oxford handbook of Jewish studies. [E]**Goodman, Martin** Oxf 2005, OUP xiv; 1037 pp. 0-19-928032-0.

1054 [E]**Po-chia Hsia, R.** A companion to the Reformation world. 2004 ⇒ 20,999. [R]RRT 12/1 (2005) 149-151 (*Holder, R. Ward*).

1055 **Rodriguez Carmona, A.** La religione ebraica: storia e teologia. CinB 2005, San Paolo 603 pp.

1056 [E]**Schmitt, Hatto H.; Vogt, Ernst** Lexikon des Hellenismus. Wsb 2005, Harrassowitz xii; 616 pp. €99. 3-447-04842-5. [R]Syria 82 (2005) 368-369 (*Sartre, Maurice*).

1057 **Sedley, David** The Cambridge companion to Greek and Roman philosophy. 2003 ⇒19,914. [R]AnCl 74 (2005) 394 (*Stevens, Annick*).

1058 **Thiselton, Anthony C.** A concise encyclopedia of the philosophy of religion. GR 2005, Baker viii; 344 pp. $25. 0-8010-3120-6 [RRT 13, 262s—Owen Anderson].

1059 [E]**Vetter, Helmuth** Wörterbuch der phänomenologischen Begriffe. Hamburg 2005, Meiner 699 pp.

1060 [E]**Woodard, Roger D.** The Cambridge encyclopedia of the world's ancient languages. 2004 ⇒20,1002. [R]BiOr 62 (2005) 620-623 (*Jongeling, K.*); RBLit (2005)* (*Daniels, Peter T.*).

## A3.8 *Opera consultationis* **archaeologica** et **geographica**

1061 [E]**Bienkowski, Piotr; Millard, Alan** Dictionary of the ancient Near East. 2000 ⇒16,679... 19,916. [R]AsbTJ 60/1 (2005) 125-127 (*Strawn, Brent A.*).

1062 [E]**Garrett, Duane A.; Kaiser, Walter C.** The NIV archaeological study bible. GR 2005, Zondervan 2306 pp.

1063 **Höcker, Christoph** Metzler Lexikon antiker Architektur, Sachen und Begriffe. 2004 ⇒20,1003. [R]RAr (2005/2) 389-390 (*Hellmann, Marie-Christine*).

1064 Lexicon of the Greek and Roman cities and place names in antiquity: ca. 1500 B.C.-ca. A.D. 500, 7: Artanissa-Augusta Rauricorum. [E]**Zahariade, Mihail** Amst 2005, Hakkert 961-1120 col. 90-256-0985-6.

1065 Lexicon topographicum urbis Romae: suburbium, 3: G-L. [E]**La Regina, Adriano** R 2005, Quasar 370 pp. 213 fig.

1066 **Neusner, Jacob** The Halakhah: an encyclopaedia of the law of Judaism. Reference Library of Ancient Judaism 1/1-5: 2000 ⇒16,686... 20,1006. [R]RBLit (2005)* (*Pérez Fernández, Miguel*).

## A4.0 **Bibliographiae**, *computers* **biblicae**

1067 *Bergant, Dianne; Senior, Donald* The bible in review. BiTod 43 (2005) 56-67, 125-136, 194-204, 261-272, 324-335, 395-406.

1068 (a) BibleWorks 6. 2003 ⇒19,933; 20,1014. Software Program. [R]Faith & Mission 22/3 (2005) 105-107 (*Kellum, L. Scott*);

(b) BibleWorks 6.1: software for biblical exegesis and research. Norfolk, VA 2005, BibleWorks $300. [R]OTEs 18 (2005) 928-930 (*Wessels, W.J.*); RBLit (2005)* (*Van der Watt, Jan*).

1069 (a) [E]**Brooke, George J.** The Society for Old Testament Study: Book List 2005. JSOT 29/5 (2005) 1-237 [also: L: Sage].
(b) **BuBB**: Bulletin de bibliographie biblique. [E]**Kaestli, Jean Daniel** Lausanne 2005, Institut des sciences bibliques de l'Université de Lausanne. 3 issues a year. From November *Thomas Naef* responsible.

1070 *Debergé, Pierre* Écrits du Nouveau Testament et naissance du christianisme. BLE 106 (2005) 401-420.

1071 (a) **IRBS (IZBG)**: International review of biblical studies, 51: 2004-2005. [E]**Lang, Bernhard**: Lei 2006, Brill xii; 596 pp. €134/$200. 97-8-90041-48963.
(b) JSNT Booklist 2005. [E]**Oakes, Peter** JSNT 27/5: L 2005, Sage 1-184 0142-064X.

1072 *Klingbeil, Gerald A.* El escritorio digital: *software* esencial para el que hacer teológico. DavarLogos 4/1 (2005) 65-80.

1073 Logos bible software series X—scholar's library silver edition. 2004 ⇒20,1022. [R]BS 162 (2005) 366-367 (*Blackmon, Matt; Harris, W. Hall, III*); RBLit 7 (2005) 37-43 (*Van der Watt, Jan*).

1074 **Longo Valentino; Magrini, Sabina; Palma, Marco** Bibliografia della Bibbia Amiatina (1990-1999). R 2000, Viella 56 pp. Univ. degli Studi di Cassino [RBen 112,154—Bogaert, P.-M].

1075 *Luciani, Didier* Chronique d'Écriture Sainte (A.T.). Vies consacrées 77 (2005) 195-212.

1076 *Meagher, P.M.* Reading the bible in India: introducing recent significant publications. VJTR 69 (2005) 625-629.

1077 [E]**Mills, Watson E.** Index to periodical literature for the study of the New Testament. NTTS 31: 2004 ⇒20,1025. [R]ThLZ 130 (2005) 164-165 (*Frenschkowski, Marco*); RivBib 53 (2005) 333-336 (*Fabris, Rinaldo*).

1078 (a) **NTAb**: New Testament Abstracts 49. [E]**Harrington, Daniel J.; Matthews, Christopher R.** CM 2005, Weston Jesuit School of Theology. 3 issues a year.
(b) **OTA**: Old Testament Abstracts 28. [E]**Begg, Christopher T.**: Wsh 2005, Catholic Biblical Association. 3 issues a year.

1079 *Pieri, Francesco* Percorsi digitali nell'antichità cristiana. Adamantius 11 (2005) 268-272.

1080 *Roig Lanzillotta, Lautaro* New Testament philology bulletin n° 35-36. FgNT 18 (2005) 185-237.

1081 **Schwarzfuchs, Lyse** Le livre hébreu à Paris au XVIe siècle: inventaire chronologique. 2002 ⇒19,968. [R]RHE 100 (2005) 994-995 (*Gilmont, Jean-François*).

1082 **Sparks, Kenton L.** Ancient texts for the study of the Hebrew Bible: a guide to the background literature. Peabody 2005, Hendrickson xxxviii; 514 pp. $40. 1-56563-407-1. Bibl. 303-304.

1083 The United Bible Society's [sic] New Testament handbook series. 2003 ⇒19,970; 20,1052. CD-ROM. [R]BiTr 56 (2005) 61-63 (*Graham, Susan Lochrie*).

1084 Virtuelle Keilschrift. WUB 35 (2005) 67.

1085 *Wansbrough, Henry* New Testament chronicle 2005. PaRe 1/4 (2005) 72-77 [NTAb 50,252].

1086 (a) *Woyke, Johannes* Die Stuttgarter Elektronische Studienbibel (SESB). ThBeitr 36 (2005) 272-276.
(b) Zeitschriften und Bücherschau. ZAW 117. [E]*Köckert, Matthias; Van Oorschot, Jürgen*: B 2005, De Gruyter. 98-168, 281-328, 420-484.

### A4.2 *Bibliographiae* **theologicae**

1087 **Alarcón, Enrique; Berger, David; Vijgen, Jörgen** Bibliographia thomistica 2004. Doctor Angelicus 5 2005, 237-314.
1088 Bibliografia internationalis spiritualitatis, 37: bibliografia anni 2002. [E]**Astigarraga, Juan L.** R 2005, Teresianum xxxi; 502 pp. 00847834.
1089 [E]*Cregheur, Eric* Littérature et histoire du christianisme ancien. LTP 61 (2005) 175-205.
1090 Elenchus bibliographicus. [E]**Auwers, J.-M.**, *al.* EThL 80: Lv 2004, Peeters 854* pp. 0013-9513.;
1091 EThL 81: Lv 2005, Peeters 845* pp. 0013-9513.
1092 *Froschauer, Harald* Bibliographische Notizen zum christlichen Ägypten (2003-2004). ByZ 98 (2005) 97-111.
1093 *Gordon, R.* Religion. GaR 52/2 (2005) 272-282 [NTAb 50,535].
1094 International bibliography of sociology of religions 2004. SocComp 52 (2005) 355-405.
1095 **Kranz, Dirk K.** Bibliografia della bibliografie patristiche e materie affini: un sussidio didattico e di ricerca. Sussidi e strumenti didattici 3: R 2005, Ateneo Pontificio Regina Apostolorum 280 pp. €12. 88-89174-30-7.
1096 *Krüger, Klaus* Bibliographische Hinweise zur ökumenischen Theologie. Cath(M) 59 (2005) 154-166.
1097 [E]*Langlois, Luc* Histoire, bilan et index: 60e anniversaire (1945-2005). LTP Supplément (2005) 3-120
1098 [E]*Poirier, Paul-Hubert* Littérature et histoire du christianisme ancien. LTP 61 (2005) 363-393.
1099 **Žitnik, Maksimilijian** Sacramenta: bibliographia internationalis: continuatio, 5: A-K; 6: L-Z; 7: Indices. 2002, ⇒18,921; 19,982. [R]De Processibus matrimonialibus 12 (2005) 543-544 (*Selge, Karl-Heinz*).

### A4.3 *Bibliographiae* **philologicae** et **generales**

1100 **Aneziri, Sophia; Giannakopoulos, N.; Paschidis, P.** Index du Bulletin Epigraphique (1987-2001), 1: les publications. Μελετηματα 43: Athens 2005, Research Centre for Greek and Roman Antiquity 398 pp. €44. 960-7905-253;
1101 2: les mots grecs. Μελετηματα 43: Athens 2005, Research Centre for Greek and Roman Antiquity 686 pp. €68. 960-7905-261;
1102 3: les mots français. Μελετηματα 43: Athens 2005, Research Centre for Greek and Roman Antiquity 570 pp. €62. 960-7905-27X.
1103 Bibliographie annuelle du Moyen-Âge Tardif, 15. Turnhout 2005, Brepols 678 pp. 2-503-51748-X.
1104 Bibliographie de l'année 2003 et compléments d'années antérieures. [E]**Corsetti, Pierre-Paul** AnPh 74: P 2005, Société internationale de bibliographie classique lxv; 2019 pp. 0184-6949.

1105 **Ceresa, Massimo** Bibliographfia dei fondi manoscritti della Biblioteca Vaticana (1991-2000). Studi e Testi 426: Biblioteca Apostolica Vaticana 2005, Città del Vaticano 737 pp. 88210-07820.

1106 *Gauthier, Philippe; Dubois, Laurent, al.* Bulletin épigraphique. REG 118 (2005) 436-591.

1107 General index 1 (1975) - 30 (2004). IslChr 31 (2005) 25-200.

1108 [E]**Offenberg, Adrian K.** Catalogue of books printed in the XVth century now in the British Library, part XIII: Hebraica. 't Goy Houten 2004, Hes & De Graaf lxxi; 288 pp. €1325. 90-6194-2594. [R]Materia giudaica 10 (2005) 437-441 (*Perani, Mauro*).

1109 **Schäfer, Dorothea; Deissler, Johannes** Bibliographie zur antiken Sklaverei, 1: Bibliographie, II: Abkürzungsverzeichnis und Register. FASk.B 4: [3]2003 <1971, 1983> ⇒19,991. [R]AnCl 74 (2005) 494-495 (*Straus, Jean A.*).

### A4.5 *Bibliographiae* **orientalisticae** et **archaeologicae**

1110 Jakab, Attila Chronique alexandrine III. Adamantius 11 (2005) 211-226.

1111 *Pietras, Henryk; Szram, Mariusz* Bibliografia polacca sulla tradizione alessandrina. Adamantius 11 (2005) 236-254.

1112 *Faist, Betina I.; Justel, Josué-Javier; Vita, Juan-Pablo* Bibliografía de los estudios de Emar (2). UF 37 (2005) 329-340.

1113 *Rubiato, María T.* Arqueología en tierras de la biblia. Sef. 65 (2005) 171-192.

1114 **Vartavan, Christian de** Anubis: bibliography on mummies and related subjects. 2004 ⇒20,1087. [R]BiOr 62 (2005) 409-430 (*Vanlathem, Marie-Paule*).

## II. Introductio

### B1.1 *Introductio tota vel VT*—**Whole Bible or OT**

1115 **Ammanathukunnel, K.; Kizhakkeyil, S.** Guide to biblical studies. Ujjain 2003, Ruhalaya 312 pp. [R]JJSS 4 (2004) 101-102 (*Athikalam, James*).

1116 **Barton, John; Bowden, Julia** The original story: God, Israel and the world. GR 2005, Eerdmans xii; 318 pp. $20. 0-8028-2900-7.

1117 **Benjamin, Don C.** The Old Testament story: an introduction with CD-ROM. 2004 ⇒20,1092. [R]AThR 87 (2005) 490-491 (*Christian, Mark A.*); CBQ 67 (2005) 106-108 (*Kaltner, John*).

1118 **Berlinerblau, Jacques** The secular bible: why nonbelievers must take religion seriously. C 2005, CUP xiii; 217 pp. $55. 05218-53141.

1119 **Birch, Bruce C.**, *al.* A theological introduction to the Old Testament. Nv [2]2005, Abingdon xviii; 485 pp. $40. 0-687-06676-X. Bibl.

1120 **Blasi i Bisbe, Ferran** Conèixer la bíblia. Barc 2005, Montserrat 331 pp. 84-8415-724-5.

1121 **Borghi, Ernesto** "Di soltanto una parola": linee introduttive alla lettura della bibbia. Vicenza 2005, Monte Berico 282 pp. 88-87483-11-6. Bibl. 274-278.

1122 **Bormann, Lukas** Bibelkunde: Altes und Neues Testament. UTB Medium-Format 2674; UTB basics: Gö 2005, Vandenhoeck & R. 293 pp. €20. 3-525-03611-6.

1123 **Bravo, Arturo** Palabra de Dios en palabras humanas: introducción didáctica al contexto histórico-cultural y literario de la biblia. Santiago 2005, Tiberiades 194 pp.

1124 **Brettler, Marc Zvi** How to read the bible: translating the culture of the bible. Ph 2005, Jewish Publication Society of America xiv; 384 pp. $35. 0-8276-0775-X. Bibl. 339-360.

1125 **Brueggemann, Walter** An introduction to the Old Testament: the canon and christian imagination. 2003 ⇒19,1010; 20,1095. [R]RBLit 7 (2005) 117-121 (*Hieke, Thomas*).

1126 **Brueggemann, Walter** Introduzione all'Antico Testamento: il canone e l'immaginazione cristiana. [E]*Malerba, Carla* Strumenti 21: T 2005, Claudiana 471 pp. €35. 88-7016-539-6. Bibl. 421-438.

1127 **Ceresko, Anthony R.** Introduction to the Old Testament: a liberation perspective. 2001 <1992> ⇒17,802; 18,949. [R]ITS 42 (2005) 343-344 (*Legrand, Lucien*).

1128 **Collins, John J.** Introduction to the Hebrew Bible. 2004 ⇒20,1097. [R]TrinJ 26 (2005) 131-132 (*Rata, Tiberius*); RRT 12 (2005) 605-606 (*Guest, Deryn*); CBQ 67 (2005) 109-112 (*Davies, Philip R.*).

1129 **Dauphinais, Michael; Levering, Matthew W.** Holy people, holy land: a theological introduction to the bible. GR 2005, Baker 266 pp. $20. 1-587-43123-8.

1130 **Dohmen, Christoph; Hieke, Thomas** Das Buch der Bücher: die Bibel—eine Einführung. Topos plus Taschenbücher 524: Rg 2005, Pustet 208 pp. 3-7867-8524-4.

1131 **Drane, John W.** Introducing the bible. Mp [2]2005 <1999-2000>, Fortress 730 pp. $49. 0-8006-3672-4. With CD-ROM [ThD 52,157—W. Charles Heiser].

1132 **Faley, Roland J.** From Genesis to Apocalypse: introducing the bible. NY 2005, Paulist 272 pp. $20. 0-8091-4217-1.

1133 **Galley, Susanne**, *al.* Die hebräische Bibel: eine Einführung. Abenteuer Wissen Band 1: 2004 ⇒20,1099. [R]FJB 32 (2005) 207-10 (*Lehnardt, Andreas*).

1134 **Harbin, Michael A.** The promise and the blessing: a historical survey of the Old and New Testaments. GR 2005, Zondervan 681 pp. 0-310-24037-9. Bibl. 601-606.

1135 **Hill, Andrew E.; Walton, John H.** Old Testament today: a journey from original meaning to contemporary significance. GR 2004, Zondervan xx; 412 pp. 0-310-23826-9.

1136 **Holdsworth, John** SCM study guide to the Old Testament. L 2005, SCM xiv; 239 pp. £15. 0-334-02985-6. Bibl. 227-231.

1137 **Lambert, Christian Yohanan** Au commencement: la bible hébraïque. P 2005, Desclée de B. 244 pp. €24. 22200-53938 [Vies consacrées 77,207—Luciani, Didier].

1138 **Levin, Christoph** Introduzione all'Antico Testamento. 2004 ⇒20,1106. [R]EstTrin 39 (2005) 580-582 (*Vázquez Allegue, Jaime*);

1139 The Old Testament: a brief introduction. [T]*Kohl, Margaret* Princeton, NJ 2005, Princeton Univ. Pr. xiii; 191 pp. 0-691-11394-7. Bibl. 187-191.

1140 **Liss, Hanna** Tanach: Lehrbuch der jüdischen Bibel. Schriften der Hochschule für Jüdische Studien Heidelberg 8: Heid 2005, Winter x; 393 pp. €25. 3-8253-5116-5.

1141 **Matthews, Victor H.; Moyer, James C.** The Old Testament: text and context. Peabody, MASS $^{2}$2005 <1997>, Hendrickson xv; 357 pp. €20. 1-565-63358-X.

1142 **Moyise, Steve** Introduction to biblical studies. Cassell Biblical Studies: L $^{2}$2004 <1998>, Clark 152 pp. £18. 0567083977. $^{R}$RBLit (2005)* (*Donahoe, Kate*).

1143 **Neuhaus, Volker** Bibel. DuMont Taschenbücher 560; DuMont-Schnellkurs: Köln 2005, DuMont 191 pp. 3-8321-7635-7.

1144 **Nigosian, Solomon A.** From ancient writings to sacred texts: the Old Testament and Apocrypha. 2004 ⇒20,1108. $^{R}$RBLit (2005)* (*Arnold, Russell; Linville, James*).

1145 **Paprocki, Joe** God's library: a catholic introduction to the world's greatest book. Chicago (Ill.) 2005, Loyola ix; 122 pp. 0-8294-2069-X. Bibl. 121-122.

1146 **Rogerson, John; Davies, Philip R.** The Old Testament world. L $^{2}$2005, Clark x; 250 pp. $30. 0-567-08488-4.

1147 **Rogerson, John W.** An introduction to the bible. L $^{2}$2005 <1999>, Equinox xvii; 176 pp. £15/$25. 18455-3039X. Bibl. [NTAb 50,383].

1148 $^{E}$**Römer, Thomas; Macchi, Jean-Daniel; Nihan, Christophe** Introduction à l'Ancien Testament. MoBi 49: 2004 ⇒20,1109. $^{R}$ThLZ 130 (2005) 262-265 (*Bauks, Michaela*); RSR 93 (2005) 571-573 (*Artus, Olivier*); RBLit (2005)* (*Lemaire, André*).

1149 **Sanders, James A.** Torah and canon. Eugene, OR $^{2}$2005 <1972>, Cascade xxxii; 156 pp. $17.

1150 $^{E}$**Sánchez Caro, J.M.** Storia, narrativa, apocalittica. Introduzione allo studio della bibbia 3/2: Brescia 2004, Paideia 440 pp.

1151 **Sánchez Navarro, Luis** Acercarse a la palabra: breve iniciación al disfrute de la biblia. Pastoral 67: Valencia 2005, EDICEP 110 pp. 84-7050-833-4.

1152 **Schmitt, Hans-Christoph** Arbeitsbuch zum Alten Testament: Grundzüge der Geschichte Israels und der alttestamentlichen Schriften. UTB 2146: Gö 2005, Vandenhoeck & R. 478 pp. €25. 3-525-03-250-1.

1153 **Shillington, V. George** Reading the sacred text: an introduction to biblical studies. 2002 ⇒18,961; 19,1031. $^{R}$VJTR 69 (2005) 630-631 (*Meagher, P.M.*).

1154 **Sproul, Robert C.; Wolgemuth, Robert** What's in the Bible: the story of God through time & eternity. Nv 2000, Word xxii; 400 pp. 0-8499-1612-7.

1155 **Swindoll, Charles R.** Fascinating stories of forgotten lives: rediscovering some Old Testament characters. Nv 2005, Nelson xiv; 251 pp. 0-8499-0016-6.

1156 **Tosaus Abadía, José Pedro** El octógono sagrado: breve introducción a la biblia en cuatro lecciones. Estella 2005, Verbo Divino 91 pp [ResB 50,68—Juan Carlos García Domene].

1157 *Zenger, Erich* La sacra scrittura degli ebrei e dei cristiani. Introduzione AT. 2005 ⇒1159. 9-45.

1158 **Zenger, Erich**, *al.* Einleitung in das Alte Testament. Kohlhammer-Studienbücher Theologie 1/1: $^{5}$2004 ⇒20,1121. $^{R}$ZKTh 127 (2005)

123-124 (*Siquans, Agnethe*); RivBib 53 (2005) 100-103 (*Paganini, Simone*).

1159 [E]**Zenger, Erich** Introduzione all'Antico Testamento. Brescia 2005, Queriniana 926 pp. €78. 88-399-0108-6.

### B1.2 'Invitations' to Bible or OT

1160 **Arnold, Bill T.; Beyer, Bryan E.** Readings from the ancient Near East. 2002 ⇒18,967... 20,1123. [R]JNES 64 (2005) 294-295 (*Chavalas, Mark W.*).

1161 **Ausloos, Hans; Lemmelijn, Benedicte** De bijbel: een (g)oude(n) gids: bijbelse antwoorden op menslijke vragen. Lv 2005, Acco 192 pp.

1162 **Bartholomew, Craig G.; Goheen, Michael W.** The drama of scripture: finding our place in the biblical story. 2004 ⇒20,1124. [R]TJT 21 (2005) 221-2 (*Dunn, Matthew W.I.*); RBLit (2005)* (*Lamp, Jeffrey*).

1163 **Binz, Stephen J.** The books of the bible: a simple guide. New London, CT 2005, Twenty-Third 47 pp. $5 [BiTod 43,325—Dianne Bergant];

1164 Angels of God; Eucharist; Mysteries of the rosary. Threshold Bible Study: New London, CT 2005, Twenty-Third 128 + 128 + 112 pp. $13 [BiTod 43,400—Donald Senior].

1165 [E]**Bouthors, Jean-François** La bible sans avoir peur. P 2005, Lethielleux 322 pp. €23. [R]EeV 135 (2005) 26 (*Cothenet, Edouard*).

1166 [E]**Davies, Philip R.** Yours faithfully: virtual letters from the bible. 2004 ⇒20,1127. [R]RBLit (2005)* (*Bach, Alice*).

1167 **Dowley, T.** The Kregel pictorial guide to bible facts & figures. GR 2005, Kregel 32 pp. $10. 08254-24526 [NTAb 49,381].

1168 **Fischer, Georg** Wege in die Bibel: Leitfaden zur Auslegung. 2000 ⇒16,790... 19,1050. [R]RBL 58 (2005) 304-307 (*Pindel, Roman*); Materia giudaica 10/1 (2005) 183-185 (*Paganini, Simone*).

1169 **Hann, Martin** Die Bibel. KulturKompakt; UTB 2591: Pd 2005, Schöningh 243 pp. €17. 3-506-71719-7.

1170 **Janssen, Kolet** Het grote aventuur van God en mens: kinderbijbel met meer dan 150 verhalen. 2004 ⇒20,1132. [R]Str. 72 (2005) 278-279 (*Beentjes, Panc*).

1171 **Kalas, J. Ellsworth** Grace in a tree stump: Old Testament stories of God's love. LVL 2005, Westminster 141 pp. 0-664-22900-X. Bibl. 139-141.

1172 **Martínez-Galdeano, F.** Descubre la biblia. 2004 ⇒20,1136. [R]RF 251/1 (2005) 89-90 (*Sanjosé, Jesús*); CDios 218 (2005) 555-556 (*Gutiérrez, J.*).

1173 **Matthews, Victor H.** Old Testament turning points: the narratives that shaped a nation. GR 2005, Baker 208 pp. $19. 0-8010-2774-8. Bibl. 187-198.

1174 **McKenzie, Steven L.** How to read the bible: history, prophecy, literature — why modern readers need to know the difference, and what it means for faith today. Oxf 2005, OUP 204 pp. $26. 0-195161-491. Bibl. 195-203. [R]America 193/20 (2005) 22-24 (*Endres, John C.*).

1175 **Meynet, Roland** La bible: histoire & civilisations. Idées reçues 94: P 2005, Cavalier Bleu 126 pp. €9. 2-84670-105-9.

1176 **Nürnberger, Christian** Die Bibel: was man wirklich wissen muss. B [4]2005, Rowohlt 224 pp. €16.50. 3-87134-5342.

1177 **O'Grady, John F.** Men in the bible: the good, the bad & the ugly. Mahwah, NJ 2005, Paulist xi; 199 pp. $19. 0-8091-4262-7. [R]RBLit (2005)* (*Davies, Philip*).

1178 **Orr-Ewing, Amy** Is the bible intolerant?. DG 2005, IVP 142 pp.

1179 **Pohl-Patalong, Uta** Bibliolog: gemeinsam die Bibel entdecken im Gottesdienst—in der Gemeinde—in der Schule. Stu 2005, Kohlhammer 152 pp. €19.80.

1180 **Rooney, Don** Journeying with the bible. ColMn 2005, Liturgical 114 pp. $11. 0-8146-2896-6.

1181 *Scoralick, Ruth* Von Mehltöpfen, die nicht leer werden, und Gästen, die nicht schlürfen dürfen. KatBl 130 (2005) 204-207.

1182 [E]**Silvano, Renu Rita; Mascarenhas, Fio** For people of all faiths, inspiring teachings of Jesus Christ (from the holy bible). Mumbai 2005, Catholic Bible Institute 213 pp.

1183 **Smith, Charles Merrill; Bennett, James W.** How the bible was built. GR 2005, Eerdmans xi; 97 pp. $12. 0-8028-2943-0.

1184 **Trainor, Michael** Journeying: a beginner's guide to the bible. Strathfield 2005, St Paul's 71 pp. AUS$10.

## B1.3 *Pedagogia biblica*—**Bible-teaching techniques**

1185 *Adam, Gottfried* "Sünde" in Kinderbibeln: exemplarische Beispiele und unterrichtliche Verwendung. GlLern 20 (2005) 164-177.

1186 [E]**Adam, Gottfried; Lachmann, Rainer; Schindler, Regine** Das Alte Testament in Kinderbibeln: eine didaktische Herausforderung in Vergangenheit und Gegenwart. 2003 ⇒19,1065. [R]ThLZ 130 (2005) 702-4 (*Erne, Thomas*); ThZ 61 (2005) 190-1 (*Kellenberger, Edgar*).

1187 *Adamo, David Tuesday* Decolonizing the teaching of the Old Testament in Africa. BOTSA 19 (2005) 3-10.

1188 **Babin, Pierre; Zukowski, Angela** El evangelio en el ciberespacio. M 2005, PPC 235 pp.

1189 **Bagrowicz, J.; Jankowski, S.** 'Pan, Bóg twój, wychowuje ciebie' (Pwt 8,5): studia z pedagogiki biblijnej [Il Signore tuo Dio corregge te' (Dtr 8,5): studi sulla pedagogia biblica]. Toruń 2005, Uniw. Kopernika 243 pp. **P.**

1190 *Baldermann, Ingo* Les enfants se découvrent eux-mêmes dans la bible. LV.F 60 (2005) 165-177.

1191 *Ballhorn, Egbert* Hören auf die Bibel: neue Akzente für die Bibelarbeit aus dem "Hildesheimer Bibelkurs". BiLi 78 (2005) 20-27.

1192 **Barbon, G.; Paganelli, R.** Narrar a Jesús. Recursos catequéticas: Sdr 2005, Sal Terrae 102 pp.

1193 *Bastes, Arturo M.* The present trends of the biblical apostolate. ICSTJ 7 (2005) 16-31.

1194 **Bazylinski, Stanislaw** Guida alla ricerca biblica: note introduttive. SubBi 24: R [2]2005 <2004>, EPIB 151 pp. 88-7653-624-8.

1195 *Beard, Luna; Du Toit, Jacqueline S.* 'Room of requirement': the interplay of visual and conceptual space in biblical literature for children. OTEs 18 (2005) 567-578 [Gen 6,9-9,17; Exod 2,1-10; Jonah 1,1-2,10].

1196 *Beauchemin, Colette* Une catéchèse qui ouvre la 'parole' pour ouvrir la 'Parole'. LV.F 60 (2005) 207-218.

1197 **Becker, U.; Johannsen, F.; Noormann, H.** Neutestamentliches Arbeitsbuch für Religionspädagogen. Stu [3]2005 <1993>, Kohlhammer 267 pp. €20. 31701-83338. Bibl. [NTAb 49,581].

1198 **Bieringer, Reimund; Pollefeyt, Didier** The role of the bible in religious education reconsidered: risks and challenges in teaching the bible. International Journal of Practical Theology 9/1 (2005) 117-39.

1199 *Bin, Y.* Literacy, canon and social reality: socio-cultural dimension of the reception of the bible among ethnic groups in southwest China. Ching Feng 6/2 (2005) 179-192 [NTAb 52,2].

1200 *Bissoli, Cesare* La catéchèse biblique aujourd'hui: bilan de la recherche de ces vingt dernières années. LV.F 60 (2005) 307-324.

1201 **Brost, Corey** Gospel connections for teens: reflections for Sunday Mass Cycle B. Winona, MN 2005, St Mary's 129 pp. $5.

1202 *Brownell, Kenneth* Prospettive storiche sulla catechesi evangelistica. SdT 17 (2005) 23-35.

1203 **Brunelli, Stefan** Meine Kinderbibel. Insbruck 2005, Tyrolia 240 pp. €24.90.

1204 *Campbell, Michael-M.* Corps de passions et vérité: de la réception d'un témoignage de foi. Théologiques 13 (2005) 109-131.

1205 *Cardona Ramírez, Hernán* La pastoral bíblica en medio de los jóvenes. El grano. 2005 <2002> ⇒197. 99-114.

1206 *Chancey, M.A.* Lesson plans: the bible in the classroom. CCen 122/17 (2005) 18-19, 21 [NTAb 50,3].

1207 *Chrostowski, Waldemar* Uniwersytet jako kontekst studiów biblijnych [University as the context of biblical studies]. CoTh 75/1 (2005) 97-114 [NTAb 50,19].

1208 *Copley, Terence* Young people, biblical narrative and "theologizing": a UK perspective. RelEd 100/3 (2005) 254-265.

1209 **Douma, Jochem** Job, Psalmen. Gaan in het spoor van het Oude Testament: Kampen 2005, Kok 116 pp. €10. 90-435-11757.

1210 *Du Toit, Jaqueline S.* Teaching Biblical Hebrew at a historically disadvantaged institution in South Africa in the mid-1990s. BOTSA 18 (2005) 11-16.

1211 *Dubied, Pierre-Luigi* Diversità dei linguaggi biblici, varietà delle predicazioni. RTLu 10 (2005) 453-462.

1212 *Dufour, Georges* Fécondité des Écritures. Cahiers de l'atelier 506 (2005) 26-37.

1213 **Duval-Poujol, Valérie** Les dix clés pour comprendre la bible. 2004 ⇒20,1158. [R]EeV 136 (2005) 24-25 (*Roure, P. David*).

1214 **Dyas, Dee; Hughes, Esther S.** The bible in western culture: the student's guide. L 2005, Routledge ix; 260 pp. £10. 0-415-32617-6. Bibl. 259-260.

1215 [E]**Edwards, Cenwyn; Greene, Colin** Who wrote the New Testament?. 2004, Bible Society £20. DVD 180 min. [R]ET 117 (2005) 120-121 (*Foster, Paul*).

1216 **Essex, B.J.** Bad boys of the New Testament: exploring men of questionable virtue. Cleveland, OH 2005, Pilgrim 127 pp. $16. 0829-8-16720. Bibl.

1217 [E]**Farmer, David A.** The pastor's bible study volume two: New Interpreter's Bible study. Nv 2005, Abingdon xii; 318 pp. 0-687-05520-2. With a CD-ROM; Bibl. 299-303.

1218 *Finsterbusch, Karin* "Wenn dein Kind dich morgen fragt ...": Lehren, Lernen und die nächste Generation. BiHe 41/163 (2005) 4-6.

1219 *Förster, Stefan* Vom "Jahr mit der Bibel 1992" zum "Jahr der Bibel 2003": elf Jahre "bibeln" in der SELK. [F]STOLLE, V. Theologie: Forschung und Wissenschaft 12: 2005 ⇒143. 485-499.

1220 **Fricke, Michael** "Schwierige" Bibeltexte im Religionsunterricht: theoretische und empirische Elemente einer alttestamentlichen Bibeldidaktik für die Primarstufe. ARPäd 26: Gö 2005, V & R Unipress 616 pp. €62. 3-89971-190-4.

1221 **Fry, C. George** Teaching the bible as a cross-cultural classic in a Middle Eastern society: the world literature curriculum at Damavand College in Tehran, Iran. Lewiston, NY 2005, Mellen xxx; 261 pp. 0-7734-6111-6. Bibl. 219-247.

1222 *Galli, M.* The beginning of education. ChrTo 49/10 (2005) 78-81 [NTAb 50,4].

1223 **Girardet, Maria; Soggin,Thomas** Racconta la bibbia ai tuoi ragazzi. T 2005, Claudiana 307 pp. €14. 88704-66015. Ill. *Silvia Gastaldi.*

1224 *Goldoni, Lidia; Marra, Vitaliana* Alcune proposte evangeliche per la catechesi. SdT 17 (2005) 67-79.

1225 [E]**Grassi, Riccardo; Pollet, Enrico** Alla scoperta della bibbia, 1: l'Antico Testamento. Rivoli 2005, Elledici 191 pp. €9.50.

1226 **Hahn, Scott** Understanding the scriptures: a complete course on bible study. Didache: Woodridge, IL 2005, Midwest Theological Forum 548 pp. $40 [HPR 106/4,73s—Donald H.Calloway].

1227 *Hanisch, Helmut* Himmelsvorstellungen von Kindern und Jugendlichen. JBTh 20 (2005) 359-380.

1228 *Haokip, P.* The bible as the source and model for catechesis. India Journal of Family Studies [Thuruthy, Kerala] 3/3 (2005) 59-67 [NTAb 50,234].

1229 [E]**Hess, Richard S.; Wenham, Gordon H.** Make the Old Testament live: from curriculum to classroom. 1998 ⇒14,668... 16,834. [R]AsbTJ 60/2 (2005) 136-138 (*Hunt, Joel H.*).

1230 *Holmås, Geir O.* Noen utfordringer til et forbedret studieopplegg: praksishorisonten og den interdisiplinaere integrasjon i profesjonsstudiet belyst ut fra NT-faget. Ung teologi 38/4 (2005) 57-61.

1231 **Johannsen, Friedrich** Alttestamentliches Arbeitsbuch für Religionspädagogen. Stu [3]2005, Kohlhammer 291 pp. €22.

1232 *Keifert, Patrick R.* The bible and theological education: a report and reflections on a journey. [M]JUEL, D. 2005⇒73. 165-182.

1233 **Koh, Won Seok** Kindgemäß, lebendig, dialektisch: Martin Rangs Bibeldidaktik des tua res agitur. [D]*Meyer-Blanck, M.* 2005, Diss. Bonn.

1234 *König, Klaus* Vom Nutzen der Bibeldidaktik für die Bibelarbeit in der Gemeinde. "Lebendige Gemeinde". ESt 54: 2005 ⇒578. 93-111.

1235 **Kreuzer, Siegfried**, *al.* Proseminar I Altes Testament: ein Arbeitsbuch. Stu [2]2005 <1999>, Kohlhammer 228 pp. €22. 3-17-019-063-6.

1236 *Kropac, Ulrich* Bibelarbeit in der Postmoderne: zur Gestalt einer dekonstruktiven Bibeldidaktik. rhs 48 (2005) 160-169.

1237 *Kuld, Lothar* "Ich fand gut, dass der Engel gekommen ist"—Kinder lesen Genesis 22. KatBl 130 (2005) 82-84.

1238 **Lehnen, Julia** Internationale Bibelauslegung im Religionsunterricht. [D]*Steinkamp, Hermann* 2005, Diss. Münster [ThRv 102,i].

1239 *Lehtinen, Esa* Achieved similarity: describing experience in Seventh-Day Adventist bible study. Text 25 (2005) 341-371.

1240 *Léon-Dufour, Xavier* Il buon uso della bibbia. Un biblista cerca Dio. Collana biblica: 2005 <1974> ⇒245. 115-124.

1241 *Lombaard, Christo* Die oudste boodskap via die nuutste massamedium: evaluering van 'n e-pos dagstukkiediens. VeE 26 (2005) 412-31.

1242 **Mennen, Claudia** Bibliodrama—religiöse Erfahrungen im Kontext der Lebensgeschichte: eine qualitativ-empirische Studie. Praktische Theologie im Dialog 26: 2004 ⇒20,1176. [R]ThRv 101 (2005) 407-408 (*Lohkemper, Gudrun*).

1243 *Mercer, Joyce* Teaching the bible in congregations: a congregational studies pedagogy for contextual education. RelEd 100/3 (2005) 280-295.

1244 **Milstein, Werner; Oedeven, Kadia** Und wie geht es Jakob?: Menschen der Bibel begegnen. Kinder glauben praktisch 7: Gö 2005, Vandenhoeck & R. 126 pp. 3-525-61537-X. 25 ill.

1245 *Muema, Peter* The biblical apostolate and its relevance to evangelization in Africa. African christian studies 21/1 (2005) 5-45.

1246 *Niehl, Franz W.* Wann sind Väter bereit, ihre Söhne zu opfern?. KatBl 130 (2005) 89-96 [Gen 22].

1247 **Oberthür, Rainer** Die Bibel für Kinder und alle im Haus. [2]2004 ⇒ 20,1184. [R]BiHe 41/162 (2005) 24-25 (*Wellmann, Bettina*).

1248 **Osmer, Richard R.** The teaching ministry of congregations. LVL 2005, Westminster 347 pp. $30. 0-664-22547-0.

1249 **Ponessa, Joseph; Manhardt, Laurie W.** Come and see: catholic bible study: prophets and apostles. Steubenville, OH 2005, Emmaus R. 208 pp. $20 [HPR 106/1,76—Madeleine Grace].

1250 *Popović, Anto* Sveto pismo u teologiji i pastoralu Crkve. BoSm 75 (2005) 713-744. **Croatian.**

1251 **Puttkammer, Annegret; Puttkammer, Detlef** Lauter Lebeworte: lebensbezogene Bibelarbeit—Grundlagen und Methoden. Bausteine Gemeindeaufbau 6: Neuk 1999, Aussaat 190 pp. €11.15. 3-7615-36-36-4.

1252 *Reichert, Jean-Claude* Servir l'expérience de la révélation de l'instruction à l'initiation. LV.F 60 (2005) 179-191.

1253 *Reil, Elisabeth* David gegen Goliath. KatBl 130 (2005) 450-456 [1 Sam 17].

1254 **Renz, Irene** Kinderbibeln als theologisch-pädagogische Herausforderung unter Bezugnahme auf die 'Analytische Psychologie' nach G. G. JUNG. [D]*Kürzdörfer, Klaus* 2005, Diss. Kiel [ThLZ 131,339].

1255 [E]**Roncace, Mark; Gray, Patrick** Teaching the bible: practical strategies for classroom instruction. SBL.Resources for Biblical Study 49: Lei 2005, Brill xxvii; 440 pp. $40. 1-58983-171-3.

1256 **Ryrie, Charles** Ryrie's practical guide to communicating bible doctrine. Nv 2005, Broadman & H. v; 88 pp. $13.

1257 **Schall, Norbert** Die Bibel verstehen. 2004 ⇒20,1187. [R]ThRv 101 (2005) 203-204 (*Dormeyer, Detlev*).

1258 *Schmid, Hansjörg* Die Bibeldidaktik vor einem neuen Aufbruch?. KatBl 130 (2005) 85-88.

1259 *Sterzinger, Harald* Per Mausklick den Zugang zum Glauben finden?. BiHe 41/161 (2005) 26-27.

1260 *Stettberger, Herbert* Von der Beispielerzählung zur tätigen Nächstenliebe: Ansätze empathisch-transformativen Lernens im Religionsunterricht auf der Basis der Perikope vom barmherzigen Samariter (Lk 10,25-37). [F]LAUB, F.: Bibel-Schule-Leben 6: 2005 ⇒87. 67-87.

1261 *Taschner, Johannes* "... dass sie es hören und lernen" (5. Mose 31, 24): zum Stellenwert des Lernens in der Geschichte Gottes mit seinem Volk. JK 66/4 (2005) 1-4.

1262 **Theis, Joachim** Biblische Texte verstehen lernen: eine bibel-didaktische Studie mit einer empirischen Untersuchung zum Gleichnis vom barmherzigen Samaritaner. PTHe 64: Stu 2005, Kohlhammer 302 pp. €20. 3-17-018078-9 [Lk 10,29-37].

1263 **Theissen, Gerd** Motivare alla bibbia: per una didattica aperta della bibbia. Introd. allo studio della bibbia, suppl. 22: Brescia 2005, Paideia 315 pp. 88-394-0703-0;

1264 Zur Bibel motivieren: Aufgaben, Inhalte und Methoden einer offenen Bibeldidaktik. 2003 ⇒19,1147. [R]BZ 49 (2005) 282-284 (*Dormeyer, Detlev*); GlLern 20 (2005) 88-90 (*Schoberth, Ingrid*).

1265 *Turrey, Christian* Bibel für Kinder im TV. BiHe 41/163 (2005) 26-8.

1266 *Van der Merwe, C.N.; Venter, C.J.H.* Verseëling met die Heilige Gees as element in die kerklike kategese: basisteoretiese perspektiewe. VeE 26 (2005) 571-592.

1267 *Wainwright, E.* Looking both ways or in multiple directions: doing/teaching theology in context into the twenty-first century. Pacifica 18 (2005) 123-40.

1268 *Wegenast, Philipp* Neue Bibeln für Kinder und Jugendliche. KatBl 130 (2005) 128-131.

1269 *Wuckelt, Agnes* Weichei und Patriarch. KatBl 130 (2005) 102-105 [Gen 22].

1270 *Zimmermann, Mirjam; Zimmermann, Ruben* 'Hermeneutische Kompetenz' und Bibeldidaktik: durch Unverständnis der Bibel das Verstehen lernen. GlLern 20 (2005) 72-87.

1271 *Zimmermann, Mirjam* Die (Be-)Deutung des Todes Jesu in der Religionspädagogik: eine Skizze. Deutungen. WUNT 181: 2005 ⇒392. 609-647.

## B2.1 Hermeneutica

1272 *Abel, Olivier* Le clos et l'ouvert: RICOEUR et le néokantisme de l'"école de Paris". ETR 80 (2005) 469-482.

1273 **Adamczewski, Wojciech H.** Il significato del dialogo nell'incontro interumano alla luce della filosofia di LEVINAS. T.Gr.Filosofia 27: R 2005, E.P.U.G. 370 pp. 978-88-7839-105-5.

1274 *Akper, G.I.* The role of the 'ordinary reader' in Gerald O. West's hermeneutics. Scriptura 88 (2005) 1-13 [NTAb 50,1].

1275 *Alaribe, Gilbert N.* The Bible as scripture and as literature: questions and approaches in some modern philosophical vis-à-vis critical scholarships. [F]IRSIGLER, H. ATSAT 76: 2005 ⇒67. 185-206.

1276 *Aleaz, K.P.* The *Sabda-Dhvani* methods of biblical-theological hermeneutics. BTF 37/2 (2005) 130-151 [NTAb 50,456].

1277 *Alkier, Stefan* Neutestamentliche Wissenschaft—ein semiotisches Konzept. [F]STEGEMANN, W. 2005 ⇒139. 343-360.

1278 **Alonso Schökel, Luis; Bravo Aragón, José María** A manual of hermeneutics. BiSe 54: 1998 ⇒14,693... 19,1159. [R]ThR 70 (2005) 305-307 (*Reventlow, Henning Graf*).

1279 *Attridge, H.W.* Can we trust the bible?. Reflections [NHv] 92/1 (2005) 4-9 [NTAb 50,1].

1280 *Aymer, M.P.* Empire, alter-empire, and the twenty-first century. USQR 59/3-4 (2005) 140-146 [NTAb 50,229].
1281 *Baptist, Damico, N.; Theoharis, L.* Responses of the poor to empire, then and now. USQR 59/3-4 (2005) 162-171 [NTAb 50,230].
1282 *Barton, John* Biblical criticism and the harmonization of texts. PSB 26 (2005) 144-156 [NTAb 50,230].
1283 *Batholomew, Craig* In front of the text: the quest of hermeneutics. Bible in pastoral practice. 2005 ⇒341. 135-152.
1284 **Bauckham, Richard** God and the crisis of freedom: biblical and contemporary perspectives. 2002 ⇒18,142... 20,172. [R]ThR 70 (2005) 324-329 (*Reventlow, Henning Graf*).
1285 *Bauer, Uwe F.W.* Gedenken in der Nacht: Liturgie der Antizipation. TeKo 28/1 (2005) 5-15.
1286 *Bedenbender, Andreas* Logik des Phantastischen—Bibel und Science Fiction. TeKo 28 (2005) 43-48 [NTAb 50,2].
1287 **Behrens, Achim** Verstehen des Glaubens: eine Einführung in Fragestellungen evangelischer Hermeneutik. Neuk 2005, Neuk xiii; 242 pp. 3-7887-2084-0.
1288 *Benson, B.E.* Text messages: GADAMER, DERRIDA and how we read. CCen 122/6 (2005) 30-32 [NTAb 49,462].
1289 *Betcher, H.V.* Resurrecting christianities: critical theories and constructive postcolonial, postmodern christianities. AThR 87 (2005) 319-328.
1290 *Betz, John R.* Hamann's London writings: the hermeneutics of trinitarian condescension. ProEc 14 2005, 191-234.
1291 **Beuchot, Mauricio** Hermenéutica, analogía y simbolo. 2004 ⇒20, 1203. [R]Teol. 4r2 (2005) 207-209 (*Baliña, Luis M.*).
1292 **Blomberg, Craig L.; Hubbard, Robert L.; Klein, William W.** Introduction to biblical interpretation. Nv 2004, Nelson xxvii, 563 pp. 0-7852-5225-8. Rev. ed.; Bibl. 505-543.
1293 *Boecker, Hans Jochen* Bibel lesen. GlLern 20 (2005) 5-18.
1294 *Boer, Roland* MARX, postcolonialism and the bible. Postcolonial biblical criticism. The bible and postcolonialism: 2005 ⇒449. 166-183.
1295 **Boer, Roland** Last stop before Antarctica: the bible and postcolonialism in Australia. The Bible and postcolonialism 6: 2001 ⇒17,1742. [R]BiblInterp 13 (2005) 56-58 (*Brett, Mark*).
1296 *Bossart, Rolf* Rückgewinnung einer theologischen Exegese: Kornelis Heiko Miskottes (1894-1976) Entscheidung für das Spezifische der Schrift. Orien. 69/15/16 (2005) 170-176.
1297 *Botha, P.J.J.* New Testament texts in the context of reading practices of the Roman period: the role of memory and performance. Scriptura 90 (2005) 621-640 [NTAb 51,223].
1298 *Breuer, Mordechai* Glaube und wissenschaftliche Bibelauslegung. Jud. 61/1 (2005) 1-19.
1299 *Brewster, Paul* The perspicuity of scripture. Faith & Mission 22/2 (2005) 16-34.
1300 *Bruncz, Dariusz* Hermeneutyka chrześcijańska w zarysie [Esquisse de l'herméneutique chrétienne]. PrzPow 122 (2005) 94-110. **P.**
1301 *Burkhardt, Helmut* Die Bibel verstehen. JETh 19 (2005) 35-48.
1302 *Buscemi, Maria S.* Errando ... entre homens e textos ... editando o inédito!. Estudos bíblicos 86 (2005) 7-15.
1303 **Buzzetti, Carlo** "Estemeca": ermeneutica biblica completa. 2003 ⇒ 19,1183. [R]RBL 58 (2005) 239-240 (*Jędrzejewski, Sylwester*).

1304 *Bühler, Pierre* Freiheit des Lesers und Grenzen der Interpretation nach Umberto ECO—am Beispiel von Martin LUTHERs Auslegung der Bergpredigt. [F]LUZ, U. SBS 199: 2005 ⇒94. 125-141 [Mt 5-7].

1305 *Cardona Ramírez, Hernán* La hermenéutica bíblica hoy—algunas resonancias. El grano. 2005 <2003> ⇒197. 115-132.

1306 *Chia, P.P.* Biblical hermeneutics and the construction of biblical theology. CGSTJournal 38 (2005) 123-142 [NTAb 49,463].

1307 *Childs, Brevard S.* Speech-act theory and biblical interpretation. SJTh 58 (2005) 375-392.

1308 *Chuecas Saldías, Ignacio* "¿Entiendes, con seguridad, lo que lees?" Hch 8,30: caminos de la hermenéutica de [en] la escritura. TyV 46 (2005) 75-102.

1309 **Clauson, Marc A.** A study of Scottish hermeneutical method from John KNOX to the early twentieth century: from christian to secular. TST 94: Lewiston, NY 2005, Mellen 416 pp. £79. 0-7734-6416-6. Diss. [R]SBET 23 (2005) 251-252 (*Quinn, Jack*).

1310 *Collins, John J.* The politics of biblical interpretation. Encounters. 2005 <2004> ⇒200. 34-44.

1311 *Combet-Galland, Corina* La bible, une oeuvre capable de monde: reconnaissance à Paul RICOEUR. ETR 80 (2005) 499-514.

1312 *Counet, Patrick C.* Introduction. [M]VAN TILBORG, S.: BiblInterp 71: 2005 ⇒155. 1-18.

1313 **Countryman, Louis W.** Interpreting the truth: changing the paradigm of biblical studies. 2003 ⇒19,1190. [R]ThTo 61 (2005) 545-546, 548 (*Hull, Robert F., Jr.*); CBQ 67 (2005) 137-138 (*Kittredge, Cynthia B.*); AThR 87 (2005) 683-684, 686 (*Floyd, Michael H.*).

1314 *Crossley, James G.; Karner, Christian* Writing history, constructing religion. Writing history. 2005 ⇒523. 3-8.

1315 *Cudby, Paul* Openness theology: a new evangelical approach to the Epicurean paradox. MoBe 46/2 (2005) 13-21;

1316 Openness theology part two—dealing with the shortcomings. MoBe 46/3 (2005) 15-23.

1317 **Dalferth, Ingolf U.** Die Wirklichkeit des Möglichen: hermeneutische Religionsphilosophie. 2003 ⇒19,1192. [R]ZNT 8/2 (2005) 59-62 (*Hübner, Hans*).

1318 **Davies, Philip R.** Whose bible is it anyway?. JSOT.S 204: 1995 ⇒ 11/2,1158... 20,1221. [R]ThR 70 (2005) 41-43 (*Reventlow, Henning Graf*); BiCT 1/3 (2005)* (*Aichele, George*).

1319 *Davis, R.F.* African-American interpretation of scripture. JRT 58/1-2 (2005) 93-105 [NTAb 50,457].

1320 **De La Torre, Miguel** Reading the bible from the margins. 2002 ⇒ 18,1133; 19,1196. [R]CBQ 67 (2005) 338-339 (*Segovia, Fernando F.*).

1321 *deClaissé-Walford, Nancy L.* Confessions of a canonical critic. PRSt 32/2 (2005) 87-92.

1322 *Decock, Paul B.* On the value of pre-modern interpretation of scripture for contemporary biblical studies. Neotest. 39 (2005) 57-74.

1323 *Djaballah, Amar* L'herméneutique selon Hans-Georg GADAMER. ThEv(VS) 4/2 (2005) 63-78.

1324 *Dohmen, Christoph* Grenzen der Interpretation für die von Gott zur Auslegung gegebene Torah?. [F]STEMBERGER G.: SJ 32: 2005 ⇒140. 1-5.

1325 **Dohmen, Christoph; Stemberger, Günter** Hermeneutik der jüdischen Bibel und des Alten Testaments. KStTh 1/2: 1996 ⇒12,604... 16,919. [R]ThR 70 (2005) 312-314 (*Reventlow, Henning Graf*).

1326 **Dohmen, Christoph** Die Bibel und ihre Auslegung. 1998 ⇒14,740; 17,959. [R]ThR 70 (2005) 311-312 (*Reventlow, Henning Graf*).
1327 *Donaldson, Laura E.* Gospel hauntings: the postcolonial demons of New Testament criticism. Postcolonial biblical criticism. The bible and postcolonialism: 2005 ⇒449. 97-113.
1328 **Döbert, Marcus** Die erloschene Stimme: biblische Hermeneutik und postmoderner Wissensdiskurs. [D]*Sparn, Walter* 2005, Diss. Erlangen-Nürnberg [ThLZ 131,335].
1329 *Dubovský, Peter* Výklad Svätého písma: hermeneutický model založený na teórii štyroch kultúr [Explanation of the sacred scripture: a hermeneutical model based on the theory of the four cultures]. SBSl (2005) 17-38 [Gen 1].
1330 *Durrer, Marcel* Le lecteur face à la Parole: illusion de la proximité et/ou irréductible écart?. LV.F 60 (2005) 139-151.
1331 *Enns, P.* To what does the bible refer?: on metaphor and analogy. Conrad Grebel Review [Waterloo, ON] 23/3 (2005) 63-73 [NTAb 50,233].
1332 *Fee, Gordon D.* Hermeneutics and the gender debate. Discovering biblical equality. 2005 ⇒387. 364-381.
1333 **Ferraris, M.** La hermenéutica. [T]*Sanz, Lázaro* 2004 ⇒20,1235. [R]EfMex 67 (2005) 138-139 (*López García, Francisco Manuel*).
1334 *Fiorenza, E. Schüssler* Empire and christian Testament studies. USQR 59/3-4 (2005) 131-139 [NTAb 50,240];
1335 Wissenschaftsrhetorik und Interpretationsethik. [F]STEGEMANN, E. 2005 ⇒139. 282-295.
1336 *Fiorenza, Francis S.* The challenge of Brown's hermeneutics: fidelity to both historical criticism and the church's tradition: a response to Robert Leavitt. [M]BROWN, R. 2005 ⇒15. 231-237.
1337 *Fishbane, Michael* Bible interpretation. The Oxford handbook of Jewish studies. 2005 ⇒1053. 680-704.
1338 *Ford, D.F.* Reading scripture with intensity: academic, ecclesial, interfaith, and divine. PSB 26 (2005) 22-35 [NTAb 50,4].
1339 *Fortin, Anne* Bible sans Parole, bible sans paroles?: de la recherche d'identité à l'écoute de la Parole. LV.F 60 (2005) 125-137.
1340 *Fowl, Stephen* Theological and ideological strategies of biblical interpretation. Scripture. 2005 ⇒398. 163-175.
1341 **Gadamer, Hans-Georg** Esquisses herméneutiques: essais et conférences. 2004 ⇒20,1241. [R]LTP 61 (2005) 398-401 (*Lafrance, Yvon*).
1342 *García-Jalón de la Lama, Santiago* Literatura e historia. Salm. 52 (2005) 421-447.
1343 *Garrone, Daniele* Categorie interpretative de la crisi secondo la bibbia. FilTeo 19 (2005) 269-284.
1344 *Geffré, Claude* Exégèse et pluralisme. ChDial 26 (2005) 111-122.
1345 **Geffré, Claude J.** Credere e interpretare: la svolta ermeneutica della teologia. Giornale di teologia 288: 2002 ⇒18,1150. [R]StPat 52 (2005) 666-668 (*Sartori, Luigi*).
1346 *Georgi, Dieter* Preface. xi-xxviii;
1347 Personal reflections on an American theological perspective. 1-9;
1348 Reason, religion, responsibility: reflections on the Frankfurt Tillich. 323-336;
1349 Praxis and theory in theological education: is scholarship "hot" or "cold"?. 337-342;

1350 En route to an urban theology: can theology help us understand urban society?. 343-366;
1351 On sojourning. The city in the valley. Studies in biblical literature 7: 2005 ⇒214. 367-370.
1352 [E]**Gerstenberger, Erhard; Schoenborn, Ulrich** Hermeneutik 1999 ⇒15,232. [R]ThR 70 (2005) 316-319 (*Reventlow, Henning Graf*).
1353 *Gessmann, Martin* Hermeneutik und Dekonstruktion. PhR 52/1 (2005) 1-20.
1354 *Gorman, Michael J.* The interpretation of the bible in Protestant churches. Scripture. 2005 ⇒398. 177-193.
1355 *Grasso, Emilio* Sacra scrittura e regole di lettura. VitaCon 41/1 (2005) 63-72.
1356 *Grech, Prosper* L'ermeneutica biblica nel XX secolo. <1994> 189-200;
1357 Ermeneutica biblica: breve prospetto storico. <1990> 9-21;
1358 La reinterpretazione intra-biblica e l'ermeneutica moderna. <2002> 89-108;
1359 Problemi di interpretazione dell'Antico Testamento nei primi secoli. <2002> 115-127;
1360 Interpretazioni patristiche del Nuovo Testamento. <2000> 129-136;
1361 The *regula fidei* as hermeneutical principle yesterday and today. Il messaggio biblico <2001>. SRivBib 44: 2005 ⇒216. 147-161.
1362 *Green, Garrett* FEUERBACH and the hermeneutics of imagination. Biblical interpretation. SBL.Symp. 26: 2005 ⇒758. 155-163;
1363 Hermeneutics. Routledge companion to the study of religion. 2005 ⇒ 547. 392-406.
1364 **Grenholm, Cristina** The Old Testament, christianity and pluralism. BGBE 33: 1996 ⇒17,969. [R]ThR 70 (2005) 314-316 (*Reventlow, Henning Graf*).
1365 *Grohmann, Marianne* "The word is very near to you!" (Deuteronomy 30:14): reader-oriented intertextuality in Jewish and Christian hermeneutics. OTEs 18 (2005) 240-252.
1366 *Gundry, Robert H.* Hermeneutic liberty, theological diversity, and historical occasionalism in the biblical canon. The old is better. WUNT 178: 2005 ⇒220. 1-17.
1367 *Hardmeier, Christof* Bible reading AND critical thinking. Erzähldiskurs. FAT 46: 2005 <2004> ⇒222. 355-369.
1368 *Harkins, Angela K.* Theological attitudes toward the scriptural text: lessons from the Qumran and Syriac exegetical traditions. TS 67 (2005) 498-516.
1369 **Hass, Andrew W.** Poetics of critique: the interdisciplinarity of textuality. 2003 ⇒19,1222. [R]RRT 12 (2005) 522-525 (*Hancock, Brannon*).
1370 *Hauge, Martin R.* Lesning: Gjenkjennelse: gjenkjennelse: deltagelse (om hellighet og dusker med blå snorer). NTT 106/1 (2005) 3-15 [Num 15,37-41].
1371 *Heimbrock, Hans-Günter* Bibellektüre im Kontext "dichter Beschreibung": Überlegungen eines Praktischen Theologen zu einem phänomenologischen Begriff von Kontextualität. Die Bibel im Dialog. NET 10: 2005 ⇒333. 237-253.
1372 **Hernando, James D.** Dictionary of hermeneutics: a concise guide to terms, names, methods, and expressions. Springfield, MO 2005, Gospel 186 pp. $30 [BiTod 44,55—Dianne Bergant].

1373 **Herrero Hernández, Francisco Javier** De HUSSERL a LEVINAS: un camino en la fenomonología. S 2005, Universidad de Salamanca 437 pp. Extr. Diss.; Bibl. 405-433.
1374 *Holland, Tom* Individualism and the people of God. Evangel 23 (2005) 86-91.
1375 *Huelin, Scott* Toward a theological ontology of textual meaning. CScR 34 (2005) 217-233.
1376 *Hunt, C. Anthony* The interpretation of the bible in African-American churches. Scripture. 2005 ⇒398. 217-227.
1377 *Hübner, Hans* Zuspruch des Seyns und Zuspruch Gottes: die Spätphilosophie Martin HEIDEGGERs und die Hermeneutik des Neuen Testaments. Wahrheit und Wirklichkeit. 2005 <2002> ⇒229. 109-138.
1378 **Jasper, David** A short introduction to hermeneutics. 2004 ⇒20, 1258. [R]AThR 87 (2005) 698, 700 (*Adam, A.K.M.*); RBLit (2005)* (*Newsom, Carol*).
1379 *Jin Hee Han* Homi K. Bhabha and the mixed blessing of hybridity in biblical hermeneutics. BiCT 1/4 (2005)*.
1380 *Jobling, David* 'Very limited ideological options': Marxism and biblical studies in postcolonial scenes. Postcolonial biblical criticism. The bible and postcolonialism: 2005 ⇒449. 184-201.
1381 *Karner, Christian* Postmodernism and the study of religions. Writing history. 2005 ⇒523. 31-46.
1382 *Klingbeil, Gerald A.* Cultural criticism and biblical hermeneutics: definition, origins, benefits, and challenges. BBR 15/2 (2005) 261-277.
1383 *Ko Ha Fong, Maria* Towards an Asian biblical hermeneutics. Japan Mission Journal 59 (2005) 102-112.
1384 *Körtner, Ulrich H.J.* Exegese, Tod und Leben: zur Hermeneutik des Todes und der Auferstehung biblischer Texte. ZThK 102 (2005) 312-332.
1385 *Kvanvig, Helge S.* Å se leseren med teksten. NTT 106/1 (2005) 16-17 [Num 15,37-41].
1386 **Lanci, John R.** Texts, rocks, and talk: reclaiming biblical christianity to counterimagine the world. 2002 ⇒18,1199; 20,1267. [R]ACR 82 (2005) 122 (*Trainor, Michael*).
1387 *Lämmlin, Georg* Die Kunst des Bibellesens: ein rezeptionstheoretisches Lektüremodell. GlLern 20 (2005) 49-60.
1388 *Leavitt, Robert F.* Raymond BROWN and Paul RICOEUR on the surplus of meaning. [M]BROWN, R. 2005 ⇒15. 207-230.
1389 *Lehnert, Volker A.* Die 'Verstockung Israels' und biblische Hermeneutik: ein exegetisches Kabinettstückchen zur Methodenfrage. ZNT 8/16 (2005) 13-19.
1390 *Leonardi, Giovanni* Il sapere teologico del biblista. StPat 52 (2005) 447-449.
1391 **Levenson, Jon D.** The Hebrew Bible, the Old Testament, and historical criticism: Jews and Christians in biblical studies. 1993 ⇒9,211... 14,1204. [R]ThR 70 (2005) 287-291 (*Reventlow, Henning Graf*).
1392 *Léon-Dufour, Xavier* La domanda: "per voi, chi sono?". Un biblista cerca Dio. Collana biblica: 2005 ⇒245. 109-112.
1393 *Liew, Tat-siong B.* Margins and (cutting-)edges: on the (il)legitimacy and intersections of race, ethnicity and (post)colonialism. Postcolonial biblical criticism. 2005 ⇒449. 114-165.

1394 **Lim, Johnson T.K.** A strategy for reading biblical texts. Studies in Biblical Literature 29: 2002 ⇒18,983. [R]BiblInterp 13 (2005) 61-63 (*Powell, Mark Allan*).
1395 *Lohfink, Norbert* Das Alte Testament christlich ausgelegt: eine Reflexion im Anschluß an die Osternacht. Liturgie und Bibel. ÖBS 28: 2005 <1988> ⇒360. 53-64.
1396 *Luz, Ulrich* Wirkungsgeschichtliche Hermeneutik und kirchliche Auslegung der Schrift. [F]LUZ, U.: SBS 199: 2005 ⇒94. 15-37;
1397 Reflections on the appropriate interpretation of New Testament texts. Studies in Matthew. 2005 <1982> ⇒252. 265-289;
1398 The significance of the church fathers for biblical interpretation in western Protestant perspective. <2000> 290-312;
1399 Hermeneutics of 'effective history' and the church. Studies in Matthew. 2005 ⇒252. 349-369.
1400 *Maggioni, Bruno* Scrittura: verità, interpretazione, confronto con l'esistenza. Lectio divina. 2005 ⇒ 9-16.
1401 *Mariano de la Maza, Luis* Fundamentos de la filosofía hermenéutica: HEIDEGGER y GADAMER. TyV 46 (2005) 122-138.
1402 *Marshall, John W.* Postcolonialism and the practice of history. Her master's tools?. 2005 ⇒493. 93-108.
1403 *Martínez-Vázques, Hjamil A.* Breaking the established scaffold: imagination as a resource in the development of biblical interpretation. Her master's tools?. 2005 ⇒493. 71-91.
1404 *Matlock, R. Barry* Beyond the great divide?: history, theology, and the secular academy. Moving beyond NT theology?. Ment. *Räisänen H.* SESJ 88: 2005 ⇒463. 369-399.
1405 *Mayordomo, Moisés* Wirkungsgeschichte als Erinnerung an die Zukunft der Texte (Hinführung). [F]LUZ, U. SBS 199: 2005 ⇒94. 11-14.
1406 *Meadowcroft, Tim* Between authorial intent and indeterminacy: the incarnation as an invitation to human-divine discourse. SJTh 58 (2005) 199-218.
1407 *Meeks, Wayne A.* Why study the New Testament?. NTS 51 (2005) 155-170.
1408 **Meschonnic, Henri** Un coup de bible dans la philosophie. 2004 ⇒ 20,1284. [R]REJ 164 (2005) 590-593 (*Osier, Jean-Pierre*).
1409 *Mihoc, Vasile* Basic principles of Orthodox hermeneutics. [F]LUZ, U. SBS 199: 2005 ⇒94. 38-64.
1410 *Minto, A.L.* The charismatic renewal and the spiritual sense of scripture. Pneuma [Lei] 27/2 (2005) 256-272 [NTAb 50,238].
1411 *Mizell, Stephen* The integration of general and special revelation in applied hermeneutics. Faith & Mission 22/3 (2005) 51-86.
1412 *Moore, Stephen D.; Segovia, Fernando F.* Postcolonial biblical criticism: beginnings, trajectories, intersections. Postcolonial biblical criticism. 2005 ⇒449. 1-22.
1413 *Moore, Stephen D.* Questions of biblical ambivalence and authority under a tree outside Delhi: or, the postcolonial and the postmodern. Postcolonial biblical criticism. 2005 ⇒449. 79-96.
1414 *Mulloor, Augustine* Towards a scientific, life transforming and pastoral interpretation of the bible. BiBh 31 (2005) 248-260.
1415 **Mura, Gaspare** Introduzione all'ermeneutica veritativa. Prospettive filosofiche 4: R 2005, Univ. della Santa Croce 287 pp. 88-8333-111-7. Bibl. 263-281.

1416 *Muthunayagom, D.J.* Biblical hermeneutics in the context of the life experience of Dalits and Burakumin communities. BTF 37/1 (2005) 1-26 [NTAb 50,462].

1417 *Müller, Sascha* Kritik und Theologie: christliche Glaubens- und Schrifthermeneutik nach Richard SIMON (1638-1712). MThZ 56 (2005) 212-224.

1418 *Nicole, Roger* Biblical hermeneutics: basic principles and questions of gender. Discovering biblical equality. 2005 ⇒387. 355-363.

1419 **Nikolakopoulos, Konstantin** Die 'unbekannten' Hymnen des Neuen Testaments: die orthodoxe Hermeneutik und die historisch-kritische Methode. 2000 ⇒16,1001; 18,1227. [R]ThRv 101 (2005) 61-62 (*Petzolt, Martin*).

1420 *Nortjé-Meyer, L.* Critical principles for a homosexual reading of biblical texts: an introduction. Scriptura 88 (2005) 174-82 [NTAb 50,7].

1421 **Oeming, Manfred** Biblische Hermeneutik. 1998 ⇒14,802... 17, 1018. [R]ThR 70 (2005) 307-311 (*Reventlow, Henning Graf*).

1422 *Page, H.* Performance as interpretive metaphor: the bible as *libretto* for research, translation, preaching,and spirituality in the 21st century —prolegomenon. Memphis Theological Seminary Journal [Memphis, TN] 41 (2005) 11-33 [NTAb 50,7].

1423 *Palu, M.* Contextualisation as bridging the hermeneutical gap: some biblical paradigms. PJT 34 (2005) 22-43 [NTAb 51,10].

1424 *Pambrun, James R.* The relationship between theology and philosophy: AUGUSTINE, RICOEUR and hermeneutics. Theoforum 36/3 (2005) 293-319.

1425 **Pani, Giancarlo** Paolo, AGOSTINO, LUTERO: alle origini del mondo moderno. Ermeneutica: Soveria Mannelli (Catanzaro) 2005, Rubbettino 209 pp. €18. 88-498-1175-6. Bibl. 235-270.

1426 **Parmentier, Élisabeth** L'Écriture vive: interprétations chrétiennes de la bible. MoBi 50: 2004 ⇒20,1301. [R]Vies consacrées 77 (2005) 205-206 (*Luciani, Didier*); RevSR 79 (2005) 424-426 (*Fricker, Denis*); EstTrin 39 (2005) 595-596 (*Vázquez Allegue, Jaime*).

1427 **Pelikan, Jaroslav** Interpreting the bible and the constitution. 2004 ⇒20,1303. [R]MoTh 21 (2005) 532-535 (*Powell, H. Jefferson*); AUSS 43 (2005) 367-369 (*Miller, Nicholas*); RBLit (2005)* (*Smith, Wade*).

1428 *Pellauer, David* Temps historique, connaissance historique. Ment. *Ricoeur P.*: ETR 80 (2005) 515-524.

1429 **Pelletier, Anne-Marie** D'âge en âge, les écritures: la bible et l'herméneutique contemporaine. Le livre et le rouleau 18: 2004 ⇒20, 1304. [R]CBQ 67 (2005) 505-507 (*Laffey, Alice L.*).

1430 [E]**Pokorny, Petr; Roskovec, Jan** Philosophical hermeneutics and biblical exegesis. WUNT 153: 2002 ⇒18,367; 20,1308. [R]ThLZ 130 (2005) 752-756 (*Kammler, Hans-Christian*).

1431 *Poythress, Vern S.* Truth and fullness of meaning: fullness versus reductionist semantics in biblical interpretation. WThJ 67 (2005) 211-227.

1432 *Prasad, Jacob* A response to the paper 'Towards a scientific, life transforming and pastoral interpretation of the bible'. BiBh 31 (2005) 261-272.

1433 *Prendergast, Terrence T.* The church's great challenge: proclaiming God's word in the new millennium. [M]BROWN, R. 2005 ⇒15. 1-15.

1434 *Probst, A.* Penser la bible. RRef 56/231 (2005) 59-66 [NTAb 49, 240].

1435 *Pyysiäinen, Ilkka* Intuition, reflection, and the evolution of traditions. Moving beyond NT theology?. Ment. *Räisänen H.*: SESJ 88: 2005 ⇒ 463. 282-307.

1436 **Rae, Murray A.** History and hermeneutics. L 2005, Clark 168 pp. £25. 0-567-08092-7. Bibl. 157-163.

1437 *Raiter, Michael; Wilson, Michael K.* Culture, human identity, and cross-cultural ministry: some biblical reflections. RTR 64/3 (2005) 121-134.

1438 *Ranieri, Aldo A.* La intertextualidad como perspectiva hermenéutica: un desafio para la exégesis bíblica. La palabra viva. 2005 ⇒746. 99-111.

1439 *Reinmuth, Eckart* In der Vielfalt der Bedeutungen: Notizen zur Interpretationsaufgabe neutestamentlicher Wissenschaft. Die Bedeutung. QD 215: 2005 ⇒363. 76-96.

1440 **Reinmuth, Eckart** Hermeneutik des Neuen Testaments. UTB 2310: 2002 ⇒18,1247; 19,1291. [R]ThLZ 130 (2005) 1067-1068 (*Söding, Thomas*).

1441 *Reiser, Marius* Die Prinzipien der biblischen Hermeneutik und ihr Wandel unter dem Einfluss der Aufklärung. [F]LUZ, U. SBS 199: 2005 ⇒94. 65-102.

1442 **Reyes, Xaé A.** How the language and culture of scholars affects their choice of subjects and methods of research: investigating the researcher's habit of mind. Lewiston, NY 2005, Mellen vi; 104 pp. 0-7-734-5987-1. Bibl. 93-99.

1443 *Ridderbos, Jan; Spronk, Klaas* Lees—en preekroosters. Theologisch debat 2/2 (2005) 26-28.

1444 *Rivas García, Ricardo M.* Replanteamiento crítico de la cienca a partir de la hermenéutica. EfMex 23 (2005) 59-79.

1445 *Rordorf, Bernard* La bible: une lecture à inventer. Liberté de parole. 2005 <1997> ⇒291. 11-29.

1446 *Rose, Martin* Une herméneutique de l'Ancien Testament: comprendre—se comprendre—faire comprendre. MoBi 46: 2003 ⇒19, 1297; 20,1319. [R]EeV 125 (2005) 19-21 (*Gruson, Philippe*); ThLZ 130 (2005) 33-35 (*Vincent, Jean Marcel*); ThR 70 (2005) 320-322 (*Reventlow, Henning Graf*).

1447 *Salvioli, M., al.* Note su esegesi ed ermeneutica a partire da 'Ermeneutica filosofica ed ermeneutica biblica' di P. RICOEUR. SapDom 58 (2005) 323-350 [NTAb 50,239].

1448 *Schneider, Michael* Texte–Intertexte–Schrift: Perspektiven intertextueller Bibellektüre. [F]STEGEMANN, W. 2005 ⇒139. 361-376.

1449 *Schreiter, Johannes* Bildende Kunst und Evangelium. GlLern 20 (2005) 61-71.

1450 *Schuman, Nick* Verrassingen en verwarringen: de bijbel multicultureel. ITBT 13/1 (2005) 8-9.

1451 *Schutte, P.J.W.* When *they, we*, and *the passive* become *I*—introducing autobiographical biblical criticism. HTSTS 61/1-2 (2005) 401-416 [NTAb 50,240].

1452 *Schwienhorst-Schönberger, Ludger* Einheit statt Eindeutigkeit: Paradigmenwechsel in der Bibelwissenschaft. Studien zum AT. SBAB 40: 2005 <2003> ⇒298. 271-279.

1453 *Schwier, Helmut* Verschiedene Arten des Bibelgebrauchs. GlLern 20 (2005) 19-31.

1454 *Segovia, Fernando F.* Mapping the postcolonial optic in biblical criticism: meaning and scope. Postcolonial biblical criticism. The bible and postcolonialism: 2005 ⇒449. 23-78.

1455 *Silva Arévalo, Eduardo* Paul RICOEUR y los desplazamientos da la hermenéutica. TyV 46 (2005) 167-205.

1456 *Silva Soler, Joaquín* Hermenéutica y verdad teológica. TyV 46 (2005) 206-253.

1457 **Simon, Josef** Écriture sainte et philosophie critique. [T]*Launay, Marc de:* P 2005, Bayard 206 pp. €26. 2-227-47415-7.

1458 *Simpson, Theo* Doctrine as canonical exegesis. Theol. 108/841 (2005) 23-31.

1459 *Smith, Susan* "Biblical interpretation: a power for good or evil?". IRM 94 (2005) 524-534.

1460 *Snyman, Gerrie* Social identity and South African biblical hermeneutics: a struggle against prejudice?. JTSA 121 (2005) 34-55;

1461 Racial performance and religious complicity: racialised discourse and perpetrator culture. Scriptura 90 (2005) 595-607 [NTAb 51,233].

1462 *Söding, Thomas* Exegetische und systematische Theologie im Dialog über den Schriftsinn. ThPh 80 (2005) 490-516.

1463 **Stadelmann, Helge** Evangelikales Schriftverständnis: die Bibel verstehen, der Bibel vertrauen, der Bibel folgen. Hammerbrücke 2005, Jota 398 pp. €20. [R]JETh 19 (2005) 331-334 (*Hille, Rolf*).

1464 *Steiner, Erich* Wo liegt die Bedeutung im Text—und kann man sie übersetzen?. Zwischen Bibel und Wissenschaft. 2005 ⇒407. 61-77.

1465 *Stell, Stephen L.* The ends of New Testament studies and the effects of those ends. Moving beyond NT theology?. Ment. *Räisänen H.*: SESJ 88: 2005 ⇒463. 61-104.

1466 *Storie, Deborah* Reading between places: participatory interpretive praxis. Pacifica 18 (2005) 281-301.

1467 *Sugirtharajah, R.S.* Scripture, scholarship, empire: putting the discipline in its place. ET 117 (2005) 2-11.

1468 **Teevan, Donna** LONERGAN, hermeneutics, & theological method. [D]*Doran, R.*: Marquette Studies in Theology 45: Milwaukee, WI 2005, Marquette University Press 226 pp. $27. 0-87462-697-8. Diss. Research Institute of Toronto; Bibl. 213-219.

1469 *Thomasset, Alain* L'imagination dans la pensée de Paul RICOEUR: fonction poétique du langage et transformation du sujet. ETR 80 (2005) 525-541.

1470 *Tomson, Peter J.* "Theological implications" of the "Semitic background": conversing with James BARR. AnBru 10 (2005) 89-109.

1471 *Twomey, Jay* Reading DERRIDA's New Testament: a critical appraisal. BiblInterp 13 (2005) 374-403.

1472 *Vaage, Leif E.* Learning to read the bible with disease: contextual theology in an era of HIV/AIDS. Journal of constructive theology 11/2 (2005) 107-119.

1473 *Van Aarde, A.G.* Cultural criticism as an imperative for christians. HTSTS 61 (2005) 683-708 [NTAb 50,466].

1474 *Van Leeuwen, Mary* Gender relations and the biblical drama. JPsT 33 (2005) 122-126.

1475 *Vanhoozer, K.J.* Lost in interpretation?: truth, scripture, and hermeneutics. JETS 48 (2005) 89-114 [NTAb 49,471].

1476 *Venattumattam, J.* Truth as reflected in the sacred scriptures. JJSS 5 (2005) 92-104.

1477 *Villefranche, Henry de* Histoire et vérité. Com(F) 30/5-6 (2005) 161-169.

1478 *Voderholzer, Rudolf* "Die Heilige Schrift wächst irgenwie mit den Lesern" (Gregor der Große): Dogmatik und Rezeptionsästhetik. MThZ 56 (2005) 162-175;

1479 Die biblische Hermeneutik Joseph RATZINGERS. MThZ 56 (2005) 400-414.

1480 *Vorster, J.N.* 'And God became human': conversations within the humanities. R&T 12 (2005) 239-261 [NTAb 50,466].

1481 *Walùs, Monika* Interpretation und Auslegung: Bibelrezeption am Beispiel der polnischen "Befreiungstheologie". AnStR 6 (2005) 407-15.

1482 **Watson, Brenda** Truth and scripture: challenging underlying assumptions. 2004 ⇒20,1352. [R]RRT 12/1 (2005) 19-22 (*Smith-Christopher, Daniel L.*); Theol. 108 (2005) 211-212 (*Harvey, A.E.*).

1483 *Webb, William J.* A redemptive-movement hermeneutic: the slavery analogy. Discovering biblical equality. 2005 ⇒387. 382-400;

1484 A redemptive-movement hermeneutic: encouraging dialogue among four evangelical views. JETS 48 (2005) 331-349 [NTAb 50,12].

1485 *Weber, Beat* Verbum, theologia et ecclesia: some hermeneutical reflections and methodological considerations towards an integrated interpretation of the bible. VeE 26 (2005) 593-613.

1486 *Wellmann, Bettina* Lies mich!: Bibel lesen als Gespräch mit dem Text. BiHe 41/162 (2005) 8-11.

1487 *West, Gerald O.* Articulating, owning and mainstreaming local theologies: the contribution of contextual bible study. JTSA 122 (2005) 23-35;

1488 Shifting perspectives on the comparative paradigm in (South) African biblical scholarship. R&T 12 (2005) 48-72.

1489 *West, Jim* The bible in the pew: congregations and critical scholarship from the pastor's perspective. ET 116 (2005) 330-333.

1490 *Weyde, Karl W.* Inner-biblical interpretation: methodological reflections on the relationship between texts in the Hebrew Bible. SEÅ 70 (2005) 287-300.

1491 *White, S.R.* The problem with scripture and the trouble with metaphysics. Search 28/2 (2005) 100-113 [NTAb 50,13].

1492 *Wick, Peter* Exegese und Realität: über das Wirklichkeitsverständnis eines multimethodischen Ansatzes. [F]STEGEMANN, E. 2005 ⇒139. 267-281.

1493 **Wilke, Matthias** Die KIERKEGAARD-Rezeption Emanuel Hirschs: eine Studie über die Voraussetzungen der Kommunikation christlicher Wahrheit. HUTh 49: Tü 2005, Mohr S. xiii; 568 pp. 31614-877-7-X. Bibl. 543-559.

1494 *Wilken, Robert L.* Interpreting the New Testament. ProEc 14 (2005) 15-25.

1495 *Witherup, Ronald D.* The interpretation of the bible in the Roman Catholic Church and the Orthodox churches. Scripture. 2005 ⇒398. 195-215.

1496 **Yarchin, William** History of biblical interpretation: a reader. 2004 ⇒20,1362. [R]Gr. 86 (2005) 671-672 (*Taylor, Richard J.*); EThL 81 (2005) 215-217 (*Van Belle, G.*); AUSS 43 (2005) 381-384 (*Reeve, John W.*); RBLit (2005)* (*Edwards, Richard M.; Odell, Margaret; Sparks, Kenton*).

1497 *Young, Frances M.* The "mind" of scripture: theological readings of the bible in the Fathers. IJST 7/2 (2005) 126-141.

1498 *Young, William W., III* The identity of the literal sense: midrash in the work of Hans FREI. JR 85 (2005) 609-633.

1499 **Zimmerman, Jen** Recovering theological hermeneutics: an incarnational-trinitarian theory of interpretation. 2004 ⇒20,1364. [R]RRT 12 (2005) 493-500 (*Chittom, Thom*); Faith & Mission 23/1 (2005) 106-108 (*Lenow, Evan C.*); RBLit (2005)* (*Finlan, Stephen*); BTB 35 (2005) 113-114 (*Yong, Amos*).

1500 *Zwingenberger, Uta* Begreifen, was uns ergreift: Bibel lesen zwischen Autoren, Texten und Lesern. BiHe 41/162 (2005) 18-21.

## B2.4 *Analysis* **narrationis** *biblicae*

1501 *Agua, Agustín del* Identidad narrativa de los christianos según el NT. Qol 38 (2005) <2000> 23-33 ⇒16,1081.

1502 **Bar-Efrat, Shimon** El arte de la narrativa en la biblia. [T]*Moncó, Beatriz* 2003, ⇒19,1341; 20,1366. [R]Augustinus 50 (2005) 222-223 (*Eguiarte, Enrique*);

1503 Narrative art in the bible. 2004 ⇒20,1367. [R]RBLit (2005)* (*Ska, Jean-Louis*); BiCT 1/3 (2005)* (*Aichele, George*).

1504 *Bartelmus, Rüdiger* Von Eselinnen mit Durchblick und blinden Sehern: Numeri 22,20-35 als Musterbeispiel narrativer Theologie im Alten Testament. ThZ 61 (2005) 27-43.

1505 *Beaude, Pierre M.* L'exégèse narratologique: quels enjeux?. FV 104/4 (2005) 92-105.

1507 *Bourquin, Yvan* Vers une nouvelle approche de la focalisation. Analyse narrative. BEThL 191: 2005 ⇒742. 497-506.

1508 [E]**Brooke, George J.; Kaestli, Jean-Daniel** Narrativity in biblical and related texts; La narrativité dans la bible et les textes apparentés. BEThL 149: 2000 ⇒16,1084... 19,1342. [R]RivBib 53 (2005) 218-222 (*De Virgilio, Giuseppe*).

1509 **Craig, Kenneth M.** Asking for rhetoric: the Hebrew Bible's Protean interrogative. BiblInterp 73: Boston 2005, Brill xii; 228 pp. 039-104-231-9. Bibl. 211-215.

1510 *Delorme, Jean* Les évangiles dans le texte. SémBib 119 (2005) 32-49.

1511 **Finlay, Timothy D.** The birth report genre in the Hebrew Bible. FAT 2/12: Tü 2005, Mohr S. xi; 292 pp. €59. 31614-87451. Bibl. 254-80.

1512 *Hardmeier, Christof* Old Testament exegesis and linguistic narrative research. Erzähldiskurs. FAT 46: 2005 <1986> ⇒222. 57-76.

1513 *House, Paul R.* Examining the narratives of Old Testament narrative: an exploration in biblical theology. WThJ 67 (2005) 229-245.

1514 *Latacz, Joachim* Zur modernen Erzählforschung in der HOMER-Interpretation. ThZ 61 (2005) 92-111.

1515 **Lee, Han Young** From history to narrative hermeneutics. Studies in Biblical Literature 64: 2004 ⇒20,1373. [R]Faith & Mission 23/1 (2005) 99-101 (*Köstenberger, Andreas J.*).

1516 **Navarro Puerto, Mercedes** Quand la bible raconte: clés pour une lecture narrative, 1: approche des textes bibliques. ConBib 41: Bru 2005, Lumen V. 78 pp. €9. 28732-42639.

1517 *Osborne, G.R.* Historical narrative and truth in the bible. JETS 48 (2005) 673-688 [NTAb 50,238].
1518 **Resseguie, James L.** Narrative criticism of the New Testament: an introduction. GR 2005, Baker 288 pp. $23. 0-8010-2789-6. Bibl. 255-271.
1519 *Ricoeur, Paul* La fonction narrative. ETR 80 (2005) 57-78.
1520 *Ritschl, Dietrich* Nachgedanken zum "Story"-Konzept: die Koagulation wiedererzählter "Stories" auf dem Weg zu differierenden theologischen Lehren. ThZ 61 (2005) 78-91.
1521 *Robert, Francine* Lire des récits, parler son histoire. LV.F 60 (2005) 153-164.
1522 *Seybold, Klaus* Erzählen vom Erzählen: Beobachtungen zu einer biblischen Erzähltheorie. ThZ 61 (2005) 14-26 [Gen 24].
1523 **Ska, Jean-Louis** A Palavra de Deus nas narrativas dos homens. [T]*Machado, Alda da Anunciaçao*: Sao Paulo 2005, Loyola 143 pp. 85150-29766. Bibl. 139.
1524 *Verrecchia, Jean-Claude* Narratology and the bible: the French experience. ScrB 35 (2005) 18-30.
1525 **Welke-Holtmann, Sigrun** Die Kommunikation zwischen Frau und Mann: Dialogstrukturen in den Erzähltexten der Hebräischen Bibel. Exegese in unserer Zeit 13: Müns 2005, Lit 320 pp. 3-8258-7198-3.

## B3.1 *Interpretatio ecclesiastica* Bible and Church

1526 *Alvarez Verdes, Lorenzo* La constituzione Dei Verbum: contenuti e risvolti liturgici. RivLi 92 (2005) 423-436.
1527 **Armstrong, Dave** A biblical defense of catholicism. Manchester, NH 2003, Sophia 295 pp.
1528 *Artus, Olivier* Dei Verbum: l'exégèse catholique entre critique historique et renouveau des sciences bibliques. Gr. 86 (2005) 76-91.
1529 *Balaguer, Vicente* La economía de la palabra de Dios: a los 40 años de la constitución dogmática Dei Verbum. ScrTh 37 (2005) 407-439.
1530 *Bathrellos, Demetrios* The eastern Orthodox tradition for today. Bible in pastoral practice. 2005 ⇒341. 32-58.
1531 [ET]**Béchard, Dean P.** The scripture documents: an anthology of official catholic teachings. 2002 ⇒18,1333... 20,1385. [R]ACR 82 (2005) 382-383 (*Daniel, Michael E.*).
1532 *Bowe, Barbara E.* Conceived by the Holy Spirit, born of the Virgin Mary. BiTod 43 (2005) 309-313.
1533 *Boys, Mary C.* The covenant in contemporary ecclesial documents. Two faiths. 2005 ⇒844. 81-110.
1534 *Brueggemann, Walter* Counterscript: living with the elusive God. CCen 122/24 (2005) 22-28 [NTAb 50,231].
1535 **Brugnaro, Francesco G.** Teologia: metodo e strumenti, secondo il Concilio Vaticano II: ricerca sul n. 24 della costituzione 'Dei Verbum' e sul n. 16 del decreto 'Optatam totius'. [D]*O'Collins, Gerald:* R 2005, Diss. Gregoriana [RTL 37,606].
1536 **Buzzetti, Carlo; Cimosa, Mario** 'Dei Verbum': testo e commento. 2004 ⇒20,1390. [R]MTh 56/1 (2005) 103-104 (*Abela, Anthony*).
1537 *Carvalho, José Carlos* A sagrada escritura na vida da igreja a quarenta anos da *Dei Verbum*. Did(L) 35 (2005) 751-784.

1538 *Castellucci, Erio* La recezione del metodo storico-critico di interpretazione della bibbia del magistero cattolico. DT(P) 108/41 (2005) 55-92.

1539 *Cifrak, Mario* Kongres o Svetom pismu u zivotu Crkve: 40 godina dogmatske konstitucije "Dei Verbum". BoSm 75 (2005) 627-629. **Croatian**.

1540 *Ciruli, Giacomo* La sacra scrittura nella vita della chiesa. Rivista di science religiose 19/1(2005) 193-202.

1541 *Colwell, John* The church as ethical community. Bible in pastoral practice. 2005 ⇒341. 212-224.

1542 *De Mey, Peter* Authority in the church: the appeal to Lk 22,21-34 in Roman Catholic magisterial teaching and in the ecumenical dialogue. [F]DENAUX, A.: BEThL 182: 2005 ⇒34. 307-323.

1543 *De Zan, Renato* Obiettivi e limiti di Liturgiam authenticam. RivLi 92 (2005) 73-90.

1544 *Debergé, Pierre* Les fondements bibliques de la laïcité?. BLE 106/3 (2005) 219-238.

1545 **Díaz Sariego, Jesús** Palabra-fundación y palabras-glosa: escritura y renovación eclesial. CTom 132 (2005) 473-502.

1546 Documentos sobre a bíblia e sua interpretação. São Paulo 2005, Paulus 287 pp. 85-349-2269-1.

1547 **Ehrman, Bart D.** Misquoting Jesus: the story behind who changed the bible and why. NY 2005, HarperSanFrancisco ix; 242 pp. 00607-3817-0.

1548 *Fabris, Rinaldo* A quarant'anni dalla *Dei Verbum*: il cammino biblico della chiesa. Rivista di science religiose 19/1 (2005) 157-171.

1549 *Feldkämper, Ludger* Die Heilige Schrift im Leben der Kirche: Erfahrungen um die Umsetzung von DEI VERBUM VI. BiKi 60 (2005) 234-238.

1550 **Ferrari, Pier L.** La Dei Verbum. Interpretare la Bibbia oggi 1,1: Brescia 2005, Queriniana 269 pp. €15. 88399-24515. Bibl. 257-266.

1551 *Fiedler, Peter* Israel und unsere Hoffnung: bibeltheologische Überlegungen zum Israel-Abschnitt im Synodenbeschluß 'Unsere Hoffnung'. Studien zur biblischen Grundlegung. SBAB 35: 2005 <1986> ⇒209. 88-102.

1552 *Fisher, Eugene J.* Catholic teaching on Jews and Judaism: an evolution in process. Seeing Judaism anew. 2005 ⇒618. 252-262.

1553 **Fragnito, Gigliola** Proibito capire: la chiesa e il volgare nella prima età moderna. Saggi 640: Bo 2005, Il Mulino 325 pp. 8815-107916. Bibl.

1554 *Frankemölle, Hubert* Fortschritt und Stillstand: Entwicklungen seit 1965. BiKi 60 (2005) 173-177;

1555 Zehn Gebote für die Kirche im dritten Jahrtausend: biblische Impulse aus dem Neuen Testament. Studien zum jüdischen Kontext. SBAB 37: 2005 <2001> ⇒210. 303-311.

1556 **Franz, Ansgar** Wortgottesdienst der Messe und Altes Testament: katholische und ökumenische Lektionarrefor. PiLi 14: 2002 ⇒19,1391. [R]ThRv 101 (2005) 142-144 (*Braulik, Georg*).

1557 *Giavini, Giovanni* La bibbia nella vita della chiesa e la "Dei Verbum": storia di un cammino, acquisizioni, nodi problematici, esigenze: riflessi sulla pastorale, sulla catechesi e nell'IRC. Ambrosius 81/3 (2005) 445-466.

1558 The gift of scripture. L 2005, Catholic Truth Society. A teaching document of the Bishops' Conferences of England and Wales, and of Scotland.

1559 *Giraudo, Cesare* Traduzione e tradizione: dinamica e implicanze di un rapporto alla luce dell'istruzione Liturgiam authenticam. RivLi 92 (2005) 91-110.

1560 *Graffy, A. Dei verbum*: before and after. PaRe 1/6 (2005) 48-55 [NTAb 50,233].

1561 *Grasso, Emilio* Sacra Scrittura e regole di lettura. VitaCon 41 (2005) 63-72.

1562 *Harrington, Wilfrid* Scripture as the soul of theology: a reprise. Scripture as the soul of theology. 2005 ⇒776. 84-89.

1563 *Henrix, Hans H.* Das Vatikandokument "Das jüdische Volk und seine Heilige Schrift in der christlichen Bibel": ein Text von Tragweite für Theologie und Dialog. [F]STEGEMANN, E. 2005 ⇒139. 336-349.

1564 *Hofmann, Norbert J.* Worte und Taten: das Konzilsdokument Nostra Aetate und seine Wirkungsgeschichte. Dialog/60 (2005) 9-15.

1565 *Hoppe, Leslie J.* I believe in God. BiTod 43 (2005) 176-181.

1566 *Izquierdo, Antonio* En el cuarenta aniversario de la *Dei Verbum*. Eccl(R) 19 (2005) 511-517.

1567 *Jamourlian, Serop* Dei Verbum: dogmatic constitution on divine revelation. Bazmavep 163 (2005) 308-329. **Armenian.**

1568 *Karimattom, Michael* 40 years of bible apostolate in the catholic church of Kerala. BiBh 31 (2005) 273-289.

1569 *Kasper, Walter* 'Dei verbum audiens et proclamans': the constitution on divine revelation *Dei verbum*. BDV 76-77 (2005) 14-19, 22-24 [NTAb 50,460].

1570 *King, Nicholas* The New Testament as holy ground. Way 44/2 (2005) 57-69.

1571 *Kirchschläger, Walter* Das Studium der Bibel als Seele der Theologie: der Einfluss von Bibel und Exegese auf das Zweite Vatikanische Konzil. BiKi 60 (2005) 112-116.

1572 *Kosch, Daniel* "Um unseres Heiles willen": eine relecture von "Dei Verbum" nach 40 Jahren. BiKi 60 (2005) 45-51. Summary in: Dei verbum [Stu] 74-75 (2005) 13-16: 'For the sake of our salvation': a re-reading of *Dei verbum* after 40 years from a European perspective [NTAb 50,236].

1573 *Kowalski, Beate* The relationship between the OT and the NT according to *Dei Verbum*—response to Jan Lambrecht SJ, The significance of *Dei Verbum* for biblical studies today. PIBA 28 (2005) 21-27.

1574 *Körtner, Ulrich J.H.* Concilio Vaticano II/40°: sola scrittura. Il Regno 50 (2005) 451-458.

1575 *Kügler, Joachim* Die Gegenwart ist das Problem!: Thesen zur Rolle der neutestamentlichen Bibelwissenschaft in Theologie, Kirche und Gesellschaft. Die Bedeutung. QD 215: 2005 ⇒363. 10-37.

1576 *Lambiasi, Francesco* "Dei Verbum": tra parola e storia: a quarant'anni dalla promulgazione. Ricerche teologiche 16 (2005) 205-218.

1577 *Lambrecht, Jan Dei Verbum* forty years later. PIBA 28 (2005) 1-20.

1578 *Lefebvre, Jean-François* S'aventurer dans la parole de Dieu avec *Dei Verbum*. Carmel(T) 118 (2005) 9-25.

1579 *Lehmann, Karl* Schrift—Überlieferung—Kirche: das Zweite Vatikanische Konzil von nahem betrachtet, am Beispiel der Dogmatischen Konstitution über die göttliche Offenbarung. IKaZ 34 (2005) 559-71.

1580 *Lesch, Karl J.* "Nimm und lies!": zum Stellenwert des Bibellesens in der katholischen Tradition. Das Buch. 2005 ⇒1130. 210-223.

1581 *Levering, Matthew* Ecclesial exegesis and ecclesiastical authority: Childs, fowl, and AQUINAS. Thom. 69 (2005) 407-467.

1582 *Lodge, J.G. Dei verbum* on scripture and tradition forty years later. ChiSt 44 (2005) 238-249 [NTAb 50,236].

1583 *Löser, Werner* Die Lehre von der Kirche in den Dekreten des Konzils von Trient. [F]STOLLE, V.: Theologie 12: 2005 ⇒143. 339-358.

1584 *Lyall, David* The bible, worship and pastoral care. Bible in pastoral practice. 2005 ⇒341. 225-240.

1585 *Maës, Bernard* Sull'immagine della Trasfigurazione in "Vita consecrata". VitaCon 41 (2005) 391-406.

1586 *Manakatt, Matthew Dei verbum*—a challenge to Indian exegetes. BiBh 31 (2005) 217-223.

1587 *Martini, Carlo M.* The central role of the word of God in the life of the church: biblical animation of the entire pastoral ministry. BDV 76-77 (2005) 33-38 [NTAb 50,462];

1588 L'avventura della bibbia nella chiesa a quarantt' anni dalla "Dei Verbum". ScC 133 (2005) 385-402.

1589 *Mendoza, Claudia* Logros y tareas: a 40 años de la promulgación de la constitución dogmática sobre la divina revelación. Teol. 42 (2005) 557-571.

1590 *Mitchell, Nathan* The Amen corner. Worship 79 (2005) 357-369.

1591 **Montaldi, Gianluca** In fide essentia revelationis completur: il tema della fede nell'evolversi del Concilio Vaticano II: la genesi DV 5-6 e i suoi riflessi su ulteriori ambiti conciliari. [D]*Wicks, Jared*: TGr.T 126: R 2005, E.P.U.G. 624 pp. 88-7839-043-7. Bibl. 575-603.

1592 *Morrison, Craig* Rooted in the bible: a reflection on the use of the Old Testament in the documents of Pope JOHN PAUL II. CIW 45 (2005) 33-42 [AcBib 11,32].

1593 *Nellickal, Abraham* A response to the paper 'The church: the interpreter of the bible'. BiBh 31 (2005) 241-247.

1594 *Onaiyekan, J.* From *Dei verbum* to *Novo Millennio ineunte*: the reception process of *Dei verbum* in the light of the change of paradigm in the past 40 years. BDV 76-77 (2005) 24-32 [NTAb 50,463].

1595 **Pelikan, Jaroslav** À qui appartient la bible?: le livre des livres à travers les âges. [T]*Canal, Denis-Armand*: P 2005, Table Ronde 336 pp. €22. 2-7103-2767-8;

1596 Whose bible is it?: a history of the scriptures through the ages. NY 2005, Viking xi; 274 pppp. $25. 0-670-03385-5. Bibl. 257-274 [R]New York Times Book Review [NY] (March 27, 2005) 22 (*Kugel, James*); Commonweal [NY] 132/10 (2005) 23-25 (*Perkins, P.*).

1597 *Phan, Peter C.* Jesus as the universal savior in the light of God's eternal covenant with the Jewish people: a Roman Catholic perspective. Seeing Judaism anew. 2005 ⇒618. 127-137.

1598 *Pinto, Porfirio José dos Santos* L'évolution de la 'pastorale biblique' après *Dei Verbum*. VSVD 46 (2005) 9-26.

1599 **Pock, Johann I.** Gemeinden zwischen Idealisierung und Planungszwang: biblische Gemeindetheologien in ihrer Bedeutung für gegenwärtige Gemeindeentwicklungen: eine kritische Analyse von Pastoralplänen und Leitlinien der Diözesen Deutschlands und Österreichs. [D]*Fuchs, Ottmar*: 2005, Diss.-Habil. Tübingen [ThRv 102,xvi].

1600 The Pontifical Biblical Commission: The Jewish people and their sacred scriptures in the christian bible. 2002 ⇒18,1364. [R]BTB 35 (2005) 34-39 (*Miller, Charles H.*).

1601 **Popovic, Anto** Nacela i metode za tumacenje Biblije: komentar Papina govora i dokumenta Biblijske komisije Tumacenje Biblije u Crkvi. Biblica 1: Zagreb 2005, Krscanska sadasnjost 416 pp. 953-11-0177-9. Bibl. 375-385.

1602 *Prato, Ezio* I quarant'anni di Dei Verbum: invito alla lettura. Orientamenti bibliografici [Brescia] 26 (2005) 12-16.

1603 [T]**Price, Richard; Gaddis, Michael** The acts of the Council of Chalcedon. Translated texts for historians 45: Liverpool 2005, Liverpool University Press 3 vols. 0-85323-039-0. Bibl.

1604 *Ratzinger, Josef* The dogmatic constitution on divine revelation: a commentary. BDV 74-75 (2005) 4-6. German 1967 [NTAb 50,239].

1605 *Rivas, Luis H.* Presentación del documento de la Pontificia Comisión Bíblica 'El pueblo judío y sus escrituras sagradas en la biblia cristiana'. La palabra viva. 2005 ⇒746. 13-35.

1606 **Robinson, A.** The Apostles' Creed: God's special revelation. Brighton 2005, Alpha viii; 113 pp. £10/$18. 18985-95461 [NTAb 49,427].

1607 **Salza, John** The biblical basis for the catholic faith. Huntington, IN 2005, Our Sunday Visitor 254 pp. $14. 15927-61461 [ThD 52,388—W. Charles Heiser].

1608 *Sander, Hans-Joachim* Die kritische Autorität der Exegese für die Dogmatik: Theologie im Zeichen einer prekären Differenz über die Heilige Schrift. Die Bedeutung. QD 215: 2005 ⇒363. 38-75.

1609 *Sanz, Rafael* Cuarenta años de la constitución "Dei Verbum". VyV 63/242 (2005) 223-232.

1610 *Sixtus, Bernd* Bridging the gap?: on some suggestions towards solving the normative problem in ecclesial exegesis. SJTh 58 (2005) 13-38.

1611 *Tábet, Michelangelo* Nel 40° anniversario della "Dei Verbum": una riflessione storica. RivBib 53 (2005) 385-421.

1612 *Tupayupanki, Nicanor S.* Il magistero di GIOVANNI PAOLO II. I vangeli. 2005 ⇒432. 117-120.

1613 *Vanhoye, Albert* I fondamenti biblici dell'Istruzione '*Erga migrantes caritas Christi*'. People on the Move 37/98 (2005) 31-38.

1614 *Velamparampil, Cyrus* A response to the paper 40 years of bible apostolate in the catholic church of Kerala. BiBh 31 (2005) 290-305.

1615 *Vellanickal, Matthew* Church: the interpreter of the bible. BiBh 31 (2005) 224-240.

1616 *Villemin, Laurent* Les Actes des Apôtres dans l'ecclésiologie de Vatican II. Les Actes des Apôtres. LeDiv 199: 2005 ⇒715. 213-230.

1617 *Wanke, Joachim* Bibel und Kirche: eine katholische Perspektive. Die Bedeutung. QD 215: 2005 ⇒363. 227-240.

1618 *Wolf, Hubert* Gegen Rassismus und Antisemitismus?: der Heilige Stuhl und die NS-Ideologie im Spiegel der neu zugänglichen vatikanischen Quellen. ThG 48 (2005) 82-100.

## B3.2 *Homiletica*—**The Bible in preaching**

1619 **Aaron, Charles L., Jr.** Preaching Hosea, Amos, & Micah. St. Louis 2005, Chalice 148 pp. $19. 9780-8272-29822.

1620 **Allen, Ronald James; Williamson, Clark M.** Preaching the gospels without blaming the Jews: a lectionary commentary. 2004, ⇒20, 1442. [R]RBLit (2005)* (*Haber, Susan; Lawrence, Jonathan*).

1621 *Arterbury, Andrew E.* Between text & sermon: Psalm 86:11-17. Interp. 59 (2005) 290-292.

1622 *Barram, Michael* Colossians 3:1-17. Interp. 59 (2005) 188-190.

1623 *Beach-Verhey, Kathy* Exodus 3:1-12. Interp. 59 (2005) 180-182.

1624 *Becker, Hans* Unsterblichkeitsmedizin. Zwischen Bibel und Wissenschaft. Glauben und Leben 31: 2005 ⇒407. 45-50.

1625 *Bohle, Evamaria* Das Unmögliche glauben. zeitzeichen 6/9 (2005) 58-59 [Lam 3,21-22].

1626 **Bos, Rein** Wij hebben gehoord dat God met u is: preken vanuit het Oude Testament. 2004 ⇒20,1451. [R]VeE 26 (2005) 654-656 (*Vos, C. J.A.*).

1627 *Böckler, Annette* 5. Mose 7,6-12: Noblesse oblige: Predigttext für den 6. Sonntag nach Trinitatis. JK 66/2 (2005) 58-61.

1628 **Brueggemann, Walter** Inscribing the text: sermons and prayers of Walter Brueggemann. [E]*Florence, Anna Carter* 2004 ⇒20,1452. [R]PSB 26 (2005) 240-241 (*Davis, David A.*).

1629 *Bruske, Wolf* Die Christen und der Staat: Predigt über 1. Petrus 2,13-17. Zeitschrift für Theologie und Gemeinde 10 (2005) 292-297.

1630 *Butting, Klara* Gesegnetes Leben: Überlegungen zu 1. Mose 1,26-31. JK 66/2 (2005) 1-5.

1631 **Cantalamessa, Raniero** Le passage à ce qui ne passe pas. [T]*Garoche, Sylvie* 2004 ⇒20,1456. [R]RTL 36 (2005) 265-266 (*Houdart, M.-A.*).

1632 **Davis, Ellen F.** Wondrous depth: preaching the Old Testament. LVL 2005, Westminster xvii; 162 pp. $20. 0-664-22859-3.

1633 **De Klerk, Ben; Van Rensburg, Fika J.** Making a sermon: a guide for reformed exegesis and preaching applied to 1 Peter 2:11-12, 18-25. Potchefstroom 2005, Potchefstroom Theological Publications 145 pp. R92. 0-620-34290-0/1-9. Afrikaans: Preekgeboorte: 'n handleiding vir Gereformeerde eksegese en prediking toegepas op 1 Petrus 2:11-12, 18-25. [R]VeE 26 (2005) 913-915 (*Smith, Eben*); VeE 26 (2005) 916-917 (*Forster, Dion A.*).

1634 *DeBona, Guerric* Classical rhetoric and the contemporary preacher. NewTR 18/3 (2005) 66-76.

1635 **Deeg, Alexander** Predigt und Derascha: homiletische Textlektüre im Dialog mit dem Judentum. [D]*Nicol* 2005, Diss. Erlangen-Nürnberg; [ThRv 102,iv].

1636 **Dever, Mark** The message of the New Testament: promises kept. Wheaton, IL 2005, Crossway 559 pp. $30. 158134-7162 [ThD 53,65 –W. Charles Heiser].

1637 *Donahue, John R.* "A whisper from the grave": homily at the final liturgy of the Raymond Brown Conference: twenty-ninth Sunday in ordinary time, October 18, 2003. [M]BROWN, R. 2005 ⇒15. 297-300.

1638 *Dreßler-Kromminga, Sabine* Predigt zum Ende eines Kirchenasyls. JK 66/2 (2005) 46-47 [Prov 13,12].

1639 *Duke, William H.* Jeremiah 1:4-18. Interp. 59 (2005) 184-186.

1640 **Dunn-Wilson, D.** A mirror for the church: preaching in the first five centuries. Gr 2005, Eerdmans xvi; 224 pp. $22/£14. 08028-28663. Bibl. [NTAb 49,630].

1641 **Edwards, J. Kent** Effective first-person biblical preaching. Grand Rapids 2005, Zondervan 192 pp. $25. 0-3102-6311-5.

1642 *Eschmann, Holger* Predigt zu 1. Korinther 4,1-5. ThFPr 31/1 (2005) 95-98.
1643 *Fangmeier, Jürgen* "Mit großer Freude". Predigt zu Lukas 24,50-53. ThBeitr 36 (2005) 57-59.
1644 **Fernández, J.** Les espejos de la palabra 2: anécdotas y narraciones para la homilía y la catequesis. M 2005, CCS 234 pp [Iter 17/1,172 —Javier Tello Vegas].
1645 *Ford, Elizabeth B.* Matthew 26:6-13. Interp. 59 (2005) 400-402.
1646 **Gordis, Lisa M.** Opening scripture: bible reading and interpretive authority in Puritan New England. 2003 ⇒19,1466; 20,1472. [R]JAAR 73 (2005) 922-924 (*Hall, David D.*).
1647 *Grümbel, Ute* Die Christusbeziehung als Grund und Horizont für Geschlechtergerechtigkeit (nicht nur) in der Kirche: Predigt über Gal 3, 26-28 im Kontext gegenwärtiger Fragestellungen. Christologie im Lebensbezug. 2005 ⇒577. 183-211.
1648 *Harmon, Steven R.* Hebrews 2:10-18. Interp. 59 (2005) 404-406.
1649 *Härtling, Peter* Nicht verstummen: eine österliche Predigt zu Psalm 22. BiLi 78 (2005) 34-36.
1650 **Hendrie, Robert** Go tell them: thoughts towards a theology of preaching. L 2005, St Paul's 256 pp. £11. 0854-397205.
1651 *Hinson-Hasty, Elizabeth* Psalm 8. Interp. 59 (2005) 392-394.
1652 *Hoffmann, Michael* Solidarität mit den Leidenden: eine Karfreitagspredigt. [F]STEGEMANN, W. 2005 ⇒139. 232-234.
1653 *Horstmann, Kai* Leben im Schatten: Predigt zu Eph 5,1-14. Zwischen Bibel und Wissenschaft. 2005 ⇒407. 99-107.
1654 [T]**Isebaert-Cauuet, Isabelle** JACQUES de Saroug: La fin du monde: homélies eschatologiques. CPF 91: P 2005, Migne 217 pp. 29085-8-7521.
1655 **Jensen, R.A.** Envisioning the word: the use of visual images in preaching. Mp 2005, Fortress xi; 155 pp. $20. 08006-37291. Bibl.; CD-ROM [NTAb 50,378].
1656 *Johnson, Janell* Genesis 1:26-28. Interp. 59 (2005) 176-178.
1657 **Jonaitis, Dorothy** Unmasking apocalyptic texts: a guide to teaching and preaching. NY 2005, Paulist vii; 198 pp. $19 [NewTR 19/2,92s —Dianne Bergant].
1658 *Kaiser, Jürgen* Von Gott überrascht. zeitzeichen 6/3 (2005) 24-25 [Gen 22,12].
1659 **Kaiser, Walter C., Jr.** Preaching and teaching from the Old Testament: a guide for the church. 2003 ⇒19,1477; 20,1489. [R]SdT 17 (2005) 104-105 (*De Blasi, Sergio*); OTEs 18 (2005) 937-940 (*Van Deventer, H.J.M.*).
1660 *Käßmann, Margot* Mine eyes have seen the glory of the coming Lord: Predigt zum Halbzeitfest der Dekade zur Überwindung von Gewalt auf dem Kirchentag 2005 in Hannover. JK 66/3 (2005) 58-60 [Mt 17,1-8].
1661 *King, Rosemary* Preaching through narrative. ET 117 (2005) 100-104.
1662 *Kissel-Ito, Cindy* Exodus 8-11. Interp. 59 (2005) 54-56.
1663 *Koranyi, Max* Fremdkörper in der Welt. zeitzeichen 6/10 (2005) 24-25 [Gen 8,22].
1664 *Krabbe, Dieter* Wo bleibst du, Trost der ganzen Welt?: Offenbarung des Johannes 5,1-14: Predigttext für den 1. Sonntag im Advent. JK 66/4 (2005) 61-64.

1665 *Krause, Rainer* Was tut der Seele gut?: Seelsorge und Psychotherapie. Zwischen Bibel und Wissenschaft. 2005 ⇒407. 37-44.

1666 **MacPherson, Duncan** Pilgrim preacher: Palestine, pilgrimage and preaching. 2004 ⇒20,1499. [R]Theol. 108 (2005) 391-392 (*Need, Stephen W.*).

1667 *Marin, Pascal* La parole, sacrement du réel dans la prédication: une approche de philosophie contemporaine. LV(L) 54/4 (2005) 71-85.

1668 *Minnaard, Gerard* Predigt nach dem Tod eines Freundes. JK 66/1 (2005) 67-69 [Deut 30,19-20].

1669 *Molthagen, Joachim* Wie anders sollen Christen sein?: Predigt über Philipper 3,20-4,3. Zeitschrift für Theologie und Gemeinde 10 (2005) 286-291.

1670 *Müller, Ulrich B.* Jesus, Menschensohn oder Gottessohn?: ein Übermensch?. Zwischen Bibel und Wissenschaft. 2005 ⇒407. 19-26.

1671 *Neef, Heinz-Dieter* Schuld und Gerechtigkeit: Predigt zu Ez 18,1-4. 21-25.30-32. ThBeitr 36 (2005) 225-228.

1672 *Nierop, Jantine* 'Maak ze impotent!': een ongewone preek over Psalm 10. ITBT 13/3 (2005) 19-20.

1673 **Old, Hughes O.** The reading and preaching of the scriptures in the worship of the christian church, 5: moderatism, pietism and awakening. 2004 ⇒20,1513. [R]SBET 23 (2005) 216-217 (*Ward, Rowland S.*); ET 117 (2005) 111 (*Armstrong, C.D.C.*).

1674 *Olimón Nolasco, Manuel* Héroes bíblicos y héroes de la patria mexicana: un sermón patriótico de 1823. [F]GARZA, C.: Estudios Bíblicos Mexicanos 4: 2005 ⇒74. 47-72.

1675 *Olyott, S.* La prédication biblique: une prédication 'ciblée'. RRef 56/232 (2005) 78-87 [NTAb 49,467].

1676 *Oosterhuis, Huub* Nimm das Kind mit: Predigt über Matthäus 2,1-15 im Schlussgottesdienst des Kirchentages. JK 66/3 (2005) 68-69.

1677 *Owen, John M.* Karl BARTH and his Advent sermon, 1933. Colloquium 37/1 (2005) 3-25 [Rom 15,5-13].

1678 *Page, H.* Moving from theory to praxis. Memphis Theological Seminary Journal [Memphis, TN] 41 (2005) 34-56 [NTAb 50,7].

1679 *Parsons, Mikeal Carl* Mark 2:23-28. Interp. 59 (2005) 57-60.

1680 *Pidcock-Lester, Karen* John 5:1-9. Interp. 59 (2005) 61-63.

1681 *Plantinga, Cornelius* Arise, shine: a sermon on Isaiah 60:1. CTJ 40 (2005) 104-107.

1682 **Prugar, Andrzej** Les passages mariaux de l'évangile selon saint Jean (2,1-12; 19,25-27) dans la prédication polonaise postconciliaire: étude exégétique et homilétique. [D]*Kudasiewicz, J.* 2005, 291 pp. Diss. Lublin [RTL 37,617].

1683 *Pugh, Elizabeth A.* Communion across the ages (Luke 20:27-38). RExp 102 (2005) 507-511.

1684 *Quanbeck, Philip A.* Preaching apocalyptic texts. Word and world 25 (2005) 317-327.

1685 *Quicke, Michael* The scriptures in preaching. Bible in pastoral practice. 2005 ⇒341. 241-257.

1686 [T]**Righi, Davide** SEVERIANUS Gabalensis: In apostolos: testo, traduzione, introduzione e note. 2004 ⇒20,9691. [R]Muséon 118 (2005) 177-178 (*Brankaer, Joanna*).

1687 *Roberts, Raymond R.* Matthew 3:1-12. Interp. 59 (2005) 396-398.

1688 *Schächtele, Traugott* Regeln außer Kraft. zeitzeichen 6/4 (2005) 24-25 [Ezek 34].

1689 *Schmid, Peter* Das Volk mit Milch tränken: die Predigt als öffentliche Rede. [F]STEGEMANN, E. 2005 ⇒139. 116-125.
1690 *Schmidtchen, Dieter* "Kirche, Geld und Seelenheil";
1691 *Scholz, Christian* Neue Arbeitswelt und alte Tugenden. Zwischen Bibel und Wissenschaft. 2005 ⇒407. 13-18/27-36.
1692 *Schöttler, Heinz-Günther* Biblisch predigen heißt: offen predigen. ThG 48 (2005) 265-274.
1693 *Schreur, Jutta* Lust am Billardspiel. zeitzeichen 6/1 (2005) 24-25 [Mt 4,17];
1694 Trotz allem: Ja. zeitzeichen 6/12 (2005) 44-45 [Rom 15,7];
1695 Das Nein wird zum Ja. zeitzeichen 6/7 (2005) 60-61 [John 6,33].
1696 *Schulz, Otmar* Ende der Tyrannei. zeitzeichen 6/8 (2005) 24-25 [Isa 29,20; 29,24].
1697 *Steiger, Lothar* Über uns selbst und unsre Kinder oder "Denk es, o Seele": Lukas 23,26-49 / Karfreitag: Predigt am 25. März 2005 in der Alten Aula der Universität Heidelberg während der Innenrenovierung der Peterskirche daselbst. [F]STEGEMANN, W. 2005 ⇒139. 443-454.
1698 **Stewart-Sykes, Alistair** From prophecy to preaching: a search for the origins of the christian homily. SVigChr 59: 2001 ⇒17,1176... 20,1553. [R]RSR 93 (2005) 151-152 (*Sesboüé, Bernard*).
1699 *Strittmatter, Peter* Kann man Glauben lernen?. Zwischen Bibel und Wissenschaft. Glauben und Leben 31: 2005 ⇒407. 51-59.
1700 *Strübind, Kim* Ist Gott liberal?: Predigt über Römer 2,4 und Hebräer 10,35-36. Zeitschrift für Theologie und Gemeinde 10 (2005) 261-68.
1701 *Thiedemann, Volker* Bekenntnis aus persönlicher Verantwortung: Predigt über "Das Bekenntnis des Petrus" (Markus 8,27-30; Matthäus 16,13-20; Lukas 9,18-21; Johannes 6,67-69). LKW 52 (2005) 14-18.
1702 *Trible, Phyllis* 'A striving after wind': St. Mary's Seminary and University October 17, 2003. [M]BROWN, R. 2005 ⇒15. 292-296 [Qoh 3,10-15; John 16,20-24]
1703 *Tuell, Steven S.* Genesis 2:1-3. Interp. 59 (2005) 51-53.
1704 *Van Rooy, H.F.* Messiasverwagting en prediking uit die Ou Testament. In die Skriflig 39 (2005) 615-630 [OTA 30,69].
1705 *Vos, C.J.A.* Drivers for the writing of a sermon about reconciliation. VeE 26 (2005) 293-307.
1706 **Wallace, James A.; Waznak, Robert P.; DeBona, Guerric** Lift up your hearts: homilies for the 'A' cycle. 2004 ⇒20,1558. [R]NewTR 18/3 (2005) 90-91 (*Sloyan, Gerald*).
1707 *Wandel, Jürgen* Lamm oder Wolf. zeitzeichen 6/11 (2005) 24-25 [Lk 11,23];
1708 Lob des Fleisches. zeitzeichen 6/2 (2005) 22-23 [Gen 3,4-5];
1709 Jenseits der Nationen. zeitzeichen 6/6 (2005) 24-25 [Luke 15,7].
1710 *Weber, E.A. Wilhelm* Vom Wort zum Gebrauch gereinigt. [F]STOLLE, V.: Theologie: Forschung und Wissenschaft 12: 2005 ⇒143. 453-63.
1711 **Wells, C. Richard; Luter, A. Boyd** Inspired preaching: a survey of preaching found in the New Testament. 2002 ⇒19,1532. [R]RExp 102 (2005) 180-181 (*Quicke, Michael J.*).
1712 **Wells, David A.** The 'Central Franconian rhyming bible' ('Mittelfränkische Reimbibel'). APSL 155: 2004 ⇒20,1562. [R]MAe 74/1 (2005) 153-154 (*Harris, Nigel*).
1713 **Willimon, William H.** Proclamation and theology. Nv 2005, Abingdon 106 pp. $9. 0-687-49343-9.

1714 **Wilson, David D.** A mirror for the church: preaching in the first five centuries. GR 2005, Eerdmans 224 pp. $22. 0-8028-2866-3.

1715 *Ziemer, Christof* Predigt beim Requiem für Herbert Froehlich. JK 66/2 (2005) 62-64 [Isa 38,10-20].

1716 *Zuurmond, Rochus* Von menschlicher Klage und Gottes Treue: Klagelieder 3,22-32: Predigttext vom 11. September. JK 66/3 (2005) 65-67.

### B3.3 **Inerrantia, inspiratio**

1717 *Bärend, Hartmut* Schutz vor Beliebigkeit: die Ursache vieler Probleme liegt darin, dass die Bibel nicht mehr die einzige Autorität ist. zeitzeichen 6/11 (2005) 30-32.

1718 *Blanchard, Yves-Marie* "Toute Écriture est inspirée" (2 Tm 3,16): les problématiques de la canonisation et de l'inspiration, avec leurs enjeux respectifs. RSR 93 (2005) 497-515.

1719 **Blomberg, Craig L.** Making sense of the New Testament: three crucial questions. 2004 ⇒20,1566. [R]RBLit (2005)* (*Scott, Mark*).

1720 *Claussen, Johann H.* Poetische Schönheit: warum hat die Bibel heute noch Autorität?. zeitzeichen 6/11 (2005) 26-29.

1721 *Dirscherl, Erwin* In-spiration angesichts des Anderen. Diak. 36 (2005) 103-109.

1722 **Enns, Peter** Inspiration and incarnation: evangelicals and the problem of the Old Testament. GR 2005, Baker 197 pp. £10. 0-8010-2730-6.

1723 *Freitag, Josef* Wie ist die Heilige Schrift Alten und Neuen Testaments als "Wort Gottes" zu verstehen?. Heilige Schriften. 2005 ⇒ 362. 55-71, 237-238.

1724 *Gestrich, Christof* Schriftauslegung und Macht—ein unerledigtes Problem von "sola scriptura": ein Beitrag zur evangelisch-katholischen Verständigung. BThZ 22 (2005) 250-266.

1725 *Gifford, Paul* Religious authority: scripture, tradition, charisma. Routledge companion to the study of religion. 2005 ⇒547. 379-391.

1726 *Gisel, Pierre* Lire théologiquement et spirituellement les Écritures: une contrepoint à l'article de Jean-Louis Chrétien "Se laisser lire avec autorité par les Saintes Écritures". RSR 93 (2005) 533-543.

1727 *Grech, Prosper* Che cosa significa oggi 'ispirazione'?: una visione globale. Il Messaggio biblico. SRivBib 44: 2005 <2002> ⇒216. 287-298.

1728 *Guevara, Junkal* A los cuarenta años de la *Dei Verbum*: ¿la palabra recuperada?. Proyección 52 (2005) 349-370.

1729 *Guthrie, C.F.* So human a book: pragmatism and scriptural authority. QR 25/3 (2005) 254-273 [NTAb 50,5].

1730 *Hathaway, William L.* Scripture and psychological science: integrative challenges & callings. JPsT 33 (2005) 89-97.

1731 *Hill, Peter C.* Living on the boundary: scriptural authority and psychology. JPsT 33 (2005) 98-112.

1732 *Karrer, Martin* Die Schrift gewinnt durch Kritik: eine Replik auf Reinhard Slenczka. KuD 51/3 (2005) 197-206.

1733 **Lauster, Jörg** Prinzip und Methode: die Transformation des protestantischen Schriftprinzips durch die historische Kritik von SCHLEIERMACHER bis Gegenwart. HUTh 46: 2004 ⇒20,1585. [R]Protest. 60

(2005) 84-85 (*Ferrario, Fulvio*); JETh 19 (2005) 313-316 (*Felber, Stefan*).

1734 *Liefeld, D.R.* God's word or male words?: postmodern conspiracy culture and feminist myths of christian origins. JETS 48 (2005) 449-473 [NTAb 50,236].

1735 *Makrides, Vasilios N.* Die Autorität und Normativität der Tradition: zum Umgang mit Heiligen Schriften im Orthodoxen Christentum. Heilige Schriften. 2005 ⇒362. 72-85, 238-240.

1736 **Malley, Brian** How the bible works: an anthropological study of evangelical biblicism. 2004 ⇒20,1587. [R]RRT 12/1 (2005) 23-25 (*Bury, Benjamin*); RStR 31 (2005) 173-174 (*Brown, Robert E.*).

1737 *Paré, Marc D.* L'inerrance chez les évangéliques. Scriptura(M) 7/2 (2005) 47-67.

1738 *Rogerson, John* Authority without infallibility: the bible today. MoBe 46/1 (2005) 6-15 [Mt 25,31-46].

1739 *Roth, Michael* Das Verhältnis von Glaube und Schrift: Überlegungen zu einer protestantischen Bestimmung der "Autorität" der Schrift. BThZ 22 (2005) 230-249.

1740 *Satta, Ronald F.* The case of Professor Charles A. Briggs: inerrancy affirmed. TrinJ 26 (2005) 69-90.

1741 *Scaer, David P.* Biblical inspiration in trinitarian perspective. Ment. *Luther, Martin*: ProEc 14 (2005) 143-160.

1742 *Sonnet, Jean-Pierre* De Moïse et du narrateur: pour une pensée narrative de l'inspiration. RSR 93 (2005) 517-531.

1743 **Sproul, R.C.** Scripture alone: the evangelical doctrine. Phillipsburg 2005, P&R 210 pp. £11. 1-59638-010-1.

1744 *Theobald, Christoph* La réception des Écritures inspirées. RSR 93 (2005) 545-570.

1745 *Village, Andrew* Assessing belief about the bible: a study among Anglican laity. RRelRes 46/3 (2005) 243-254.

1746 **Ward, Timothy** Word and supplement: speech acts, biblical texts, and the sufficiency of scripture. 2002 ⇒18,1509... 20,1598. [R]MoTh 21 (2005) 516-518 (*Wolterstorff, Nicholas*); BiblInterp 13 (2005) 321-324 (*MacDonald, Neil B.*); JThS 56 (2005) 802-805 (*Loughlin, Gerard*); SJTh 58 (2005) 485-489 (*Brown, Colin*).

1747 *Watts, James W.* Ritual legitimacy and scriptural authority. JBL 124 (2005) 401-417.

1748 *Welker, Michael* Sola Scriptura?: die Autorität der Bibel in pluralistischen Umgebungen und die interdisziplinäre Biblische Theologie. Reconsidering the boundaries. 2005 ⇒598. 15-29.

1749 **Whitlock, Jonathan** Schrift und Inspiration. WMANT 98: 2002 ⇒ 18,1510... 20,1599. [R]ThLZ 130 (2005) 287-288 (*Reiser, Marius*).

1750 **Wright, Nicholas T.** The last word: beyond the bible wars to a new understanding of the authority of scripture. NY 2005, HarperSanFrancisco xiv; 146 pp. $20. 0-06-081609-0;

1751 = Scripture and the authority of God. L 2005, SPCK xv; 107 pp. £8. 0-281-05722-2.

## B3.4 **Traditio**

1752 *Grech, Prosper* La tradizione presso i padri della chiesa;

1753 Le tradizioni neotestamentarie e la 'traditio catholica' <1990>. Il messaggio biblico. SRivBib 44: 2005 ⇒216. 137-146/109-114.
1754 *Jackson, Peter* Retracing the path: gesture, memory, and the exegesis of tradition. HR 45 (2005) 1-28.
1755 *Mekkattukunnel, Andrews G.* The word of God in tradition and scripture. BiBh 31 (2005) 306-324.
1756 *Stolle, Volker* Persönliches Zeugnis und schriftliche Tradition: zwei Dimensionen christlicher Identität. LuThK 29/2 (2005) 79-106.
1757 *Thondiparampil, Joseph* A response to the paper 'The word of God in tradition and scripture'. BiBh 31 (2005) 325-328.
1758 **Williams, D.H.** Evangelicals and tradition: the formative influence of the early church. Evangelical Ressourcement: GR 2005, Baker 192 pp. $17. 0-8010-2713-6.

## B3.5 Canon

1759 *Aichele, George* Kanon als Intertext: Einschränkung oder Befreiung?. Die Bibel im Dialog. NET 10: 2005 ⇒333. 159-178.
1760 **Aichele, George** The control of biblical meaning: canon as semiotic mechanism. 2001 ⇒17,1223... 20,1607. [R]BiCT 1/3 (2005)* (*Jobling, David*).
1761 *Aletti, Jean-Noël* Les finales des récits évangéliques et le statut du livre et des lecteurs. RevSR 79 (2005) 23-37 [Mt 28,18-20; Mk 16; Lk 24; John 20,30-31; 21,24-25].
1762 **Barton, John** The spirit and the letter: studies in the biblical canon. 1997 ⇒13,942... 15,1095. [R]ThR 70 (2005) 279-281 (*Reventlow, Henning Graf*).
1763 *Beckwith, Roger T.* The significance of the 364-day calendar for the Old Testament canon. Calendar, chronology. AGJU 61: 2005 ⇒184. 54-66.
1764 **Bokedal, Tomas** The scriptures and the LORD: formation and significance of the christian biblical canon: a study in text, ritual and interpretation. [D]*Jeanrond, W.G.* Lund 2005, Univ. of Lund 374 pp. Diss. Lund [StTh 60,115].
1765 *Brooke, George J.* Between authority and canon: the significance of reworking the bible for understanding the canonical process. Reworking the bible. StTDJ 58: 2005 ⇒723. 85-104.
1766 *Bultmann, Christoph* Heiliges Schreiben und Heilige Schriften: zum Ursprung von "Gesetz und Propheten". Heilige Schriften. 2005 ⇒ 362. 41-54, 236-237.
1767 **Chapman, Stephen B.** The law and the prophets: a study in Old Testament canon formation. FAT 27: 2000 ⇒16,1226... 20,1617. [R]ThR 70 (2005) 281-283 (*Reventlow, Henning Graf*); BiOr 62 (2005) 118-119 (*Van der Kooij, Arie*).
1768 (a) *Childs, Brevard S.* The canon in recent biblical studies: reflections on an era. ProEc 14 (2005) 26-45.
(b) *Cova, Gian Domenico* Note preliminari per l'apprezzamento della natura canonica dei testi biblici. RTE 9/1 (2005) 59-78.
1769 *Ebach, Jürgen* Verbindliche Vielfalt: über die "Schrift" als Kanon. KuI 20 (2005) 109-119.
1770 *Elgvin, Torleif* Different bibles for different groups?. Enoch and Qumran origins. 2005 ⇒921. 408-413.

1771 *Fernández E., P. Samuel* Regulæ fidei et rationis: tradición, razón y escritura en los primeros siglos. TyV 46 (2005) 103-121.

1772 *Frankemölle, Hubert* Juden und Christen: "eine Bibel?". Studien zum jüdischen Kontext. SBAB 37: 2005 <2003> ⇒210. 23-27.

1773 *Gilbert, Maurice* Bible et christianisme. Bible et sciences des religions. 2005 ⇒445. 95-121.

1774 **Gosse, Bernard** La constitution du corpus des écritures à l'époque perse, dans la continuité de la tradition biblique. TEuph.S 10: 2003 ⇒19,14244; 20,1624. [R]Theoforum 36 (2005) 196-98 (*Laberge, Léo*).

1775 *Gundry, Robert H.* Hermeneutic liberty, theological diversity, and historical occasionalism in the biblical canon. The old is better. WUNT 178: 2005 ⇒220. 1-17.

1776 [E]**Helmer, Christine; Landmesser, Christof** One scripture or many?: canon from biblical, theological, and philosophical perspectives. 2004 ⇒20,361. [R]CBQ 67 (2005) 373-374 (*Gnuse, Robert*); Jud. 61 (2005) 74-75 (*Eißler, Friedmann*); Theol. 108 (2005) 204-205 (*Brett, Mark*).

1777 *Hübner, Hans* Kanon–Geschichte–Gott. Wahrheit und Wirklichkeit. 2005 <2003> ⇒229. 18-37.

1778 *Janowski, Bernd* Kanonhermeneutik: eine problemgeschichtliche Skizze. BThZ 22 (2005) 161-180.

1779 *Junod, Eric* D'EUSÈBE de Césarée à ATHANASE d'Alexandrie en passant par CYRILLE de Jérusalem: de la construction savante du Nouveau Testament à la clôture ecclésiastique du canon. Le canon du NT. MoBi 54: 2005 ⇒334. 169-195.

1780 *Lafitte, Serge* Les choix de l'église. Le monde des religions 14 (2005) 26-29.

1781 *Lander, Shira* The formation of the biblical canon(s). Scripture. 2005 ⇒398. 103-117.

1782 *Lange, Armin* Authoritative literature and scripture in the Chronistic corpus: the use of כתוב-formulas in Ezra-Nehemiah and 1-2 Chronicles. [F]STEMBERGER G.: SJ 32: 2005 ⇒140. 29-52.

1783 *Leppä, Outi* Debates within the New Testament canon. The formation of the early church. WUNT 183: 2005 ⇒708. 211-237.

1784 **Lips, Hermann von** Der neutestamentliche Kanon: seine Geschichte und Bedeutung. Zürcher Grundrisse zur Bibel: 2004 ⇒20,1636. [R]ThLZ 130 (2005) 656-658 (*Heckel, Theo K.*).

1785 *Loader, James A.* The canon as text for a biblical theology. HTS 61 (2005) 1027-1048 [OTA 29,259] [Ps 69,10].

1786 *Löhr, Winrich* Norm und Kontext—Kanonslisten in der Spätantike. BThZ 22 (2005) 202-229.

1787 *Marjanen, Antti* Montanism and the formation of the New Testament canon. The formation of the early church. WUNT 183: 2005 ⇒708. 239-263.

1788 *Markschies, Christoph* Époques de la recherche sur le canon du Nouveau Testament en Allemagne: quelques remarques provisoires. Le canon du NT. MoBi 54: 2005 ⇒334. 11-34.

1789 **McDonald, Lee M.** The formation of the christian biblical canon. [3]2003 <1988> ⇒19,1643. [R]CV 47/1 (2005) 90-93 (*Korečková, Andrea*).

1790 [E]**McDonald, Lee Martin; Sanders, James A.** The canon debate. 2002 ⇒18,1551... 20,1640. [R]RBLit (2005)* (*Young, Ian*).

1791 **Miller, John Wolf** How the bible came to be: exploring the narrative and message. 2004 ⇒20,1641. [R]CBQ 67 (2005) 152-154 (*Matson, Mark A.*); RBLit (2005)* (*Keith, Pierre*).
1792 *Morra, Stella* Testi, letture e discorsi fra sacro e modernità. AnStR 6 (2005) 307-319.
1793 *Müllner, Ilse* Dialogische Autorität: feministisch-theologische Überlegungen zur kanonischen Schriftauslegung. AnStR 6 (2005) 371-83.
1794 *Nicklas, Tobias* Neutestamentliche Texte als Teil des Buches "Bibel" lesen. rhs 48 (2005) 151-159.
1795 *Norelli, Enrico* Étude critique: le canon biblique: nouvelles perspectives. Apocrypha 16 (2005) 253-262.
1796 **Ohme, Heinz** Kanon ekklesiastikos: die Bedeutung des altkirchlichen Kanonbegriffs. AKG 67: 1998 ⇒14,1018; 16,1244. [R]JThS 56 (2005) 638-662 (*Kinzig, Wolfram*).
1797 *Pate, C.M.* Current challenges to the christian canon. Criswell Theological Review [Dallas] 3/1 (2005) 3-10 [NTAb 50,229].
1798 *Piper, Ronald A.* The one, the four and the many. [F]STANTON, G. 2005 ⇒138. 254-273.
1799 *Poirier, John C.* The canonical approach and the idea of 'scripture'. ET 116 (2005) 366-370.
1800 *Schmithals, Walter* Der Kanon, die Apostolische Sukzession und die Ökumene. BThZ 22 (2005) 267-283.
1801 **Schniedewind, William M.** How the bible became a book: the textualization of ancient Israel. 2004 ⇒20,1654. [R]CBQ 67 (2005) 324-325 (*Hoppe, Leslie J.*); SR 34 (2005) 293-294 (*Patterson, Dilys N.*); RBLit 7 (2005) 125-126 (*Amit, Yairah*); JThS 56 (2005) 509-512 (*Millard, Alan*); ET 116 (2005) 391 (*Southwell, P.J.M.*).
1802 *Schröter, Jens* "Die Kirche besitzt vier Evangelien, die Häresie viele": die Entstehung des Neuen Testaments im Kontext der frühchristlichen Geschichte und Literatur. BiKi 60 (2005) 68-74.
1803 **Söding, Thomas** Einheit der Heiligen Schrift?: zur Theologie des biblischen Kanons. QD 211: FrB 2005, Herder 402 pp. €32. 3-451-02211-7. Bibl. 398-402.
1804 *Steinberg, Julius* Literatur, Kanon, Theologie: ein strukturell-kanonischer Ansatz für eine Theologie des Alten Testaments. JETh 19 (2005) 93-122.
1805 *Stenschke, Christoph* Das Neue Testament als Dokumentensammlung urchristlicher Mission: alter Hut oder neue Perspektive?. JETh 19 (2005) 167-190.
1806 *Stone, Michael E.* L'étude du canon arménien. Le canon du NT. MoBi 54: 2005 ⇒334. 283-295.
1807 *Tilly, Michael* Des livres controversés. MoBi 168 (2005) 28-29.
1808 *Voss, Florian* Kampf gegen Ketzer: die Kirche legte fest, welche Schriften in das Neue Testament gehören und welche nicht. zeitzeichen 6/11 (2005) 33-35.
1809 *Williams, Daniel H.* The patristic tradition as canon. PRSt 32/4 (2005) 357-379.
1810 **Witherington, Ben, III** The New Testament story. 2004 ⇒20,1662. [R]AUSS 43 (2005) 380-381 (*Paroschi, Wilson*); RBLit 7 (2005) 284-285 (*Kealy, Seán P.*); ET 117 (2005) 34-35 (*Draper, Jonathan A.*).
1811 **Wyrick, Jed** The ascension of authorship: attribution and canon formation in Jewish, Hellenistic, and christian traditions. Harvard

Studies in Comparative Literature 49: 2004 ⇒20,1664. [R]JThS 56 (2005) 515-517 (*Beckwith, Roger*).

1812 *Zilonka, Paul P.* The bible as book and as library. Scripture. 2005 ⇒ 398. 3-21.

## B4.1 *Interpretatio humanistica* **The Bible—man; health, toil, age**

1813 *Anderson, Herbert* The bible and pastoral care. Bible in pastoral practice. 2005 ⇒341. 195-211.

1814 *Báez, S.J.* La sanación física y espiritual en la biblia. REsp 255 (2005) 183-213 [NTAb 50,326].

1815 **Brighton, L.A.** Where is the holy family today?: marriage a holy covenant before God—the biblical role of man and woman. ConJ 31/3 (2005) 260-268 [NTAb 50,92] [Gen 2,16-24].

1816 *Brossier, François* La bible et la famille. LV.F 60 (2005) 385-390.

1817 *Bruckner, James K.* A theological description of human wholeness in Deuteronomy 6. ExAu 21 (2005) 1-19 [OTA 30,310].

[E]**Campbell, K.** Marriage and family...biblical world 2003 ⇒365.

1818 *Garzon, Fernando* Interventions that apply scripture in psychotherapy. JPsT 33 (2005) 113-121.

1819 *Haacker, Klaus* Krankheit, Gebet und Heilung. ThBeitr 36 (2005) 60-79.

1820 **Hinsen, Peter** Vom Wort, das alles heilt: Meditationen zur therapeutischen Botschaft Gottes. 2004 ⇒20,1672. [R]OrdKor 46 (2005) 254 (*Bopp, Karl*).

1821 *Kaveny, M.C.* The order of widows: what the early church can teach us about older women and health care. Christian Bioethics [Ph] 11/1 (2005) 11-34 [NTAb 50,532] [Acts 6,1-7; 1 Tim 5,3-16].

1822 **Milani, Marcello** A immagine del Cristo 'paziente': sofferenza, malattia e salvezza nella scrittura. 2004 ⇒20,1678. [R]PaVi 50/2 (2005) 62-63 (*Cappelletto, Gianni*).

1823 *Otto, Eckart* Magie–Dämonen–göttliche Kräfte: Krankheit und Heilung im Alten Orient und im Alten Testament. Heilung. BTSP 26: 2005 ⇒585. 208-225.

1824 *Parvis, S.* The open family: kinship in the bible and the pre-Reformation church. PaRe 1/3 (2005) 28-35 [NTAb 50,330].

1825 *Ruiz, J.-P.* Of walls and words: twenty-first century empire and New Testament studies. USQR 59/3-4 (2005) 122-130 [NTAb 50,239].

1826 **Schroer, Silvia; Staubli, Thomas** Die Körpersymbolik der Bibel. Gü [2]2005 <1998>, Gü xiv; 192 pp. €30. 3-579-05207-1. Num. ill.

1827 *Simoens, Yves* La famille à la lumière des données bibliques. NRTh 127 (2005) 354-372 [Gen 1-2; Dt 6,4-9; Isa 54,5].

1828 *Ska, Jean Louis* El trabajo en la biblia. El camino. 2005 <1995> ⇒ 302. 75-101.

1829 *Strobel, Katja* Der neue Mensch nach Hartz—wo bleiben die Gegenstimmen der Frauen?. BiKi 60 (2005) 60-61.

1830 *Vaux, Kenneth* Response to Bruckner. ExAu 21 (2005) 20-23 [OTA 30,383] [Dt 6].

### B4.2 *Femina, familia*; **Woman in the Bible** [⇒B4.1; H8.8s]

1831 *Adamo, David T.; Eghwubare, Erivwierho F.* The African wife of Abraham (Gn 16:1-16; 21:8-21). OTEs 18 2005, 455-471.

1832 [E]**Adelman, Penina** Praise her works: conversations with biblical women. Ph 2005, Jewish Publication Society of America xxii; 228 pp. 0-8276-0823-3. Includes selections from Midrash ha-Gadol in Hebrew and English translation [Prov 31,10-31].

1833 *Avanzinelli, Milka Ventura* Le donne e la violenza del sacro: storie dalla bibbia. ReSo 20 (2005) 22-36.

1834 *Baumann, Gerlinde* Von Ohnmacht bis Heldinnentum: die biblischen Geschichten vermitteln kein einheitliches Mutterbild. zeitzeichen 6/12 (2005) 29-31.

1835 *Belleville, Linda L.* Women leaders in the bible. Discovering biblical equality. 2005 ⇒387. 110-125.

1836 **Bodi, Daniel; Donnet-Guez, Brigitte** The Michal affair: from Zimri-Lim to the rabbis. HBM 3: Shf 2005, Shf Phoenix ix; 169 pp. €75. 1-90504-817-3. Bibl. 146-161.

1837 [E]**Brenner, Athalya** Are we amused?: humour about women in the biblical worlds. JSOT.S 383; The Bible in the 21st century 2: 2003 ⇒19,1719. [R]RBLit (2005)* (*Reinhartz, Adele; Schearing, Linda*).

1838 *Claassens, L.J.* Laughter and tears: carnivalistic overtones in the stories of Sarah and Hagar. Ment. *Bakhtin, M.*: PRSt 32/3 (2005) 295-308 [Gen 16; 21,09-21].

1839 *Duran, Nicole* Having men for dinner: deadly banquets and biblical women. BTB 35 (2005) 117-124 [Judg 4,17-22; Esther 4-7; Mk 6,14-30].

1840 **Dutcher-Walls, Patricia** Jezebel: portrait of a queen. Interfaces: 2004 ⇒20,1700. [R]RBLit (2005)* (*Scholz, Susanne*).

1841 **Fischer, Irmtraud** Women who wrestled with God: biblical stories of Israel's beginnings. [T]*Maloney, Linda M.*: ColMn 2005, Liturgical 149 pp. $17. 0-8146-5160-7. [R]RBLit (2005)* (*Shemesh, Yael*).

1842 *Green, Yosef* Our mother Rachel: *prima inter pares*. JBQ 33 (2005) 166-173.

1843 **Havea, Jione** Elusions of control: biblical law on the words of women. SBL.Semeia 41: 2003 ⇒19,1729; 20,1708. [R]CBQ 67 (2005) 318-319 (*Patrick, Dale*).

1844 [E]**Hecht, Anneliese** 'Böse' Frauen. FrauenBibelArbeit 15: Stu 2005, Kath. Bibelwerk 96 pp. €9.50. 3-460-25295-2.

1845 *Hyman, Ronald* Comment on 'the God of Abraham, Rebekah, and Jacob'. JBQ 33 (2005) 61-64.

1846 *Kaiser, W.C.* Correcting caricatures: the biblical teaching on women. Priscilla Papers [Mp] 19/2 (2005) 5-11 [NTAb 51,320].

1847 [E]**Kampling, Rainer** Sara lacht: eine Erzmutter und ihre Geschichte. 2004 ⇒20,595. [R]FrRu 12 (2005) 48-51 (*Brockmöller, Katrin*).

1848 **Lapsley, Jacqueline E.** Whispering the word: hearing women's stories in the Old Testament. LVL 2005, Westminster xii; 154 pp. $20. 0-664-22435-0. Bibl. 137-145.

1849 **Marsman, Hennie J.** Women in Ugarit and Israel: their social and religious position in the context of the ancient Near East. OTS 49: 2003 ⇒19,1736. [R]ThLZ 130 (2005) 1169-1172 (*Krispenz, Jutta*); Bib. 86 (2005) 448-451 (*Meyers, Carol*).

1850 *McKinlay, Judith E.* Sarah and Hagar: what have I to do with them?. Her master's tools?. 2005 ⇒493. 159-177 [Gen 16; 21].

1851 **McKinlay, Judith E.** Reframing her: biblical women in postcolonial focus. The Bible in the Modern World 1: 2004 ⇒20,1720. [R]BTB 35 (2005) 156-7 (*Bartusch, Mark*); BiCT 1/4 (2005)* (*Kirova, Milena*).

1852 **Meyers, Carol** Households and holiness: the religious culture of Israelite women. Facets: Mp 2005, Fortress viii; 106 pp. $6. 08006-37-31-3.

1853 *Michel, Thomas* Hagar: mother of faith in the compassionate God. ICMR 16 (2005) 99-105 [Gen 16; 21].

1854 **Motté, Magda** 'Esthers Tränen, Judiths Tapferkeit': biblische Frauen in der Literatur des 20. Jahrhunderts. 2003 ⇒19,1740. [R]ThLZ 130 (2005) 1220-1222 (*Mauz, Andreas*).

1855 *Müller, Monika* Von Herrinnen, Mägden und ungleichen Schwestern: weibliche Konkurrenz im Alten Orient und in der Hebräischen Bibel. WuD 28 (2005) 27-51.

1856 **Ochs, Vanessa L.** Sarah laughed: modern lessons from the wisdom & stories of biblical women. NY 2005, McGraw-Hill xxii; 229 pp. 0-07-140290-X.

1857 *Pierce, Ronald W.* From Old Testament law to New Testament gospel. Discovering biblical equality. 2005 ⇒387. 96-109.

1858 **Rapp, Ursula** Mirjam: eine feministisch-rhetorische Lektüre der Mirjamtexte in der hebräischen Bibel. BZAW 317: 2002 ⇒18,1614 ... 20,1730. [R]ThR 70 (2005) 404-407 (*Schmidt, Ludwig*) [Exod 15, 19-21; Num 12; 20,1-13; 26,59; Dt 24,8-9; 1 Chr 5,29].

1859 **Schneider, Tammi Joy** Sarah: mother of nations. 2004 ⇒20,1733. [R]RBLit (2005)* (*Dempsey, Carol*).

1860 *Tezza, Maristela* Memória da ocultação e revelação: sobre mulheres em textos bíblicos. Fragmenta de Cultura [Goías] 15 (2005) 1385-1399 [OTA 29,4].

1861 *Thiel, Winfried* Rizpa und das Ritual von Gibeon. Gedeutete Geschichte. BThSt 71: 2005 <1994> ⇒316. 121-139 [2 Sam 21,1-4].

1862 **Thompson, John Lee** Writing the wrongs: women of the Old Testament among biblical commentators from PHILO through the Reformation. 2001 ⇒17,1313... 20,1737. [R]JR 85 (2005) 301-302 (*Baskin, Judith R.*); HeyJ 46 (2005) 226-227 (*Hill, Robert C.*).

1863 *Trevett, Christine* Wilderness woman: the taming of Miriam. [F]YOUNG, F.: JSNT.S 295: 2005 ⇒168. 26-44.

1864 **Yee, Gale A.** Poor banished children of Eve: woman as evil in the Hebrew Bible. 2003 ⇒19,1759; 20,1744. [R]ThTo 61 (2005) 582, 584, 586 (*Sakenfeld, Katharine D.*); CBQ 67 (2005) 332-334 (*Brenner, Athalya*); BiblInterp 13 (2005) 421-423 (*Maier, Christl M.*); OTEs 18 (2005) 955-956 (*Klopper, Frances*); RBLit (2005)* (*Jobling, David*); BiCT 1/1 (2004)* (*McKinlay, Judith E.*).

1865 **Zlotnick, Helena** Dinah's daughters: gender and Judaism from the Hebrew Bible to late antiquity. 2002 ⇒18,1627. [R]JAAR 73 (2005) 955-958 (*Sheres, Ita*).

1866 **Zolli, Eugenio** Da Eva a Maria. Frigento (Avellino) 2005 <1954>, Casa Mariana 77 pp.

### B4.4 *Exegesis litteraria*—**The Bible itself as literature**

1867 **Aaron, David H.** Biblical ambiguities: metaphor, semantics and divine imagery. 2001 ⇒17,1317. [R]ThR 70 (2005) 332-335 (*Reventlow, Henning Graf*).

1868 *Bar-Efrat, Shimon* Aesthetic as the key for understanding the Old Testament. Das AT und die Kunst. ATM 15: 2005 ⇒711. 1-9.

1869 *Böckler, Annette M.* Unser Vater. Metaphor in the Hebrew Bible. BEThL 187: 2005 ⇒799. 249-261.

1870 **Dorsey, David A.** The literary structure of the Old Testament: a commentary on Genesis-Malachi. 1999 <2004> ⇒15,1664... 17, 1331. [R]AsbTJ 60/2 (2005) 134-136 (*Hunt, Joel H.*); RBLit (2005)* (*Shapira, Amnon*).

1871 *Engel, Ulrich* Unglücksglück: zur Beziehung zwischen Literatur, Ethik und Theologie;

1872 *Garhammer, Erich* Schreiben ist Totenerweckung: Theologie und Literatur;

1873 *Gellner, Christoph; Henneke-Weischer, Andrea* Bibel und Literatur. Schreiben ist Totenerweckung. 2005 ⇒832. 168-171/13-16/157-167.

1874 *Gorman, Michael J.* The character and composition of the books of the New Testament. Scripture. 2005 ⇒398. 71-90.

1875 *Huizing, Klaas* Ästhetischer Protestantismus: Wiedererkennen und Konstruktion oder: Theologie als Gespielin der Literatur. Schreiben ist Totenerweckung. 2005 ⇒832. 99-115.

1876 *Hunziker-Rodewald, Regine* Hirt aus Barmherzigkeit: zu einer als Symbol wahrgenommenen Metapher. Metaphor in the Hebrew Bible. BEThL 187: 2005 ⇒799. 233-247.

1877 *Knauf, Ernst A.* Der Text als Artefakt. Das AT und die Kunst. ATM 15: 2005 ⇒711. 51-66.

1878 *Kotzé, Zacharias* A cognitive linguistic methodology for the study of metaphor in the Hebrew Bible. JNSL 31/1 (2005) 107-117.

1879 **Kövecses, Zoltàn** Metaphor in culture: universality and variation. C 2005, CUP xvii; 314 pp. 0-521-84447-9. Bibl. 295-305.

1880 *Krašovec, Jože* Etimološka razlaga svetopisemskih imen kot lingvistično in literarno izrazno sredstvo v izvirniku in v prevodih [Etymological explanation of biblical names as linguistic and literary devices in the original and in translations]. Bogoslovni Vestnik 65/1 (2005) 5-42. S.

1881 *Kuschel, Karl-Josef* Literatur und Theologie als gegenseitige Herausforderung: Bilanz, Ertrag, Entwicklung 1984-2004;

1882 *Langenhorst, Annegret; Meurer, Thomas* Literarische Texte im Religionsunterricht;

1883 *Langenhorst, Georg* Ertrag und Perspektiven. Schreiben ist Totenerweckung. 2005 ⇒832. 19-42/145-150/175-189.

1884 *Leiner, Martin* Eindeutiges Wort und vieldeutiges Bild?: auf dem Weg zu einer neuen Theologie des Bildes. [F]BÜMLEIN, K. 2005 ⇒18. 189-200.

1885 *Leiter, David A.* The character and composition of the books of the Old Testament. Scripture. 2005 ⇒398. 45-69.

1886 *Martin, François* "Les feuilles mortes" de Jacques Prévert: approches de l'énonciation. SémBib 117 (2005) 5-29.

1887 *Moser, Antônio* Para além dos genes: a metáfora do "livro da vida". REB 65/257 (2005) 25-45.
1888 *Muffs, Yochanan* Image and imagination in the bible. Personhood of God. 2005 ⇒265. 97-102.
1889 *Newsom, Carol A.* Spying out the land: a report from genology. [F]FOX, M. 2005 ⇒43. 437-450.
1890 *Nielsen, Kirsten* Metaphors and biblical theology. Metaphor in the Hebrew Bible. BEThL 187: 2005 ⇒799. 263-273 [Dt 32; 2 Sam 22].
1891 *Orosz, Magdolna* Literarische Bibellektüre(n): Aspekte einer semiotischen Intertextualitätskonzeption und intertextueller Textanalyse. Die Bibel im Dialog. NET 10: 2005 ⇒333. 217-236.
1892 *Parker, David* The mountain and the desert. [F]YOUNG, F. JSNT.S 295: 2005 ⇒168. 59-65.
1893 *Pervo, Richard I.* Introduction. Ancient fiction. SBL.Symp. 32: 2005 ⇒721. 1-12.
1894 **Pyper, Hugh S.** An unsuitable book: the bible as scandalous text. The bible in the modern world 7: Shf 2005, Sheffield Phoenix viii; 186 pp. $85. 1-905048-32-7. Bibl. 169-181.
1895 **Schmidt, Karl L.** The place of the gospels in the general history of literature. [T]*McCane, Byron R.* 2002 ⇒18,1662; 19,1785. [R]CoTh 75/3 (2005) 243-246 (*Kręcidło, Janusz*).
1896 *Seip, Jörg* Anker lichten: Fährten für einen Dialog zwischen Praktischer Theologie und Literatur. Schreiben ist Totenerweckung. 2005 ⇒832. 151-156.
1897 **Sharpes, Donald K.** Lords of the scrolls: literary traditions in the bible and gospels. NY 2005, Lang xvi; 394 pp. 0-8204-7849-0. Bibl. 365-384.
1898 *Sonnet, Jean-Pierre* "C'est moi qui, pour YHWH, c'est moi qui veux chanter" (Jg 5,3): la poésie lyrique au sein du récit biblique. Analyse narrative. BEThL 191: 2005 ⇒742. 373-387.
1899 **Strawn, Brent A.** What is stronger than a lion?: leonine image and metaphor in the Hebrew Bible and the ancient Near East. OBO 212: Gö 2005, Vandenhoeck & R. xix; 587 pp. FS175. 3-525-53006-4. Bibl. 501-553.
1900 *Van Hecke, Pierre* Metaphor in the Hebrew Bible: an introduction;
1901 Conceptual blending: a recent approach to metaphor: illustrated with the pastoral metaphor in Hos 4,16. Metaphor in the Hebrew Bible. BEThL 187: 2005 ⇒799. 1-17/215-231;
1902 Pastoral metaphors in the Hebrew Bible and in its ancient Near Eastern context. The OT in its world. OTS 52: 2005 ⇒749. 200-217.
1903 *Vette, Joachim* Methods in dialogue: a response to Shimon Bar-Efrat. Das AT und die Kunst. ATM 15: 2005 ⇒711. 11-13.
1904 **Vriezen, Theodorus C.; Van der Woude, Adam S.** Ancient Israelite and early Jewish literature. [T]*Doyle, Brian*: Lei 2005, Brill x; 766 pp. €59/$59. 90-04-14181-2.
1905 *Wall, Lynne* Finding identity in the wilderness. [F]YOUNG, F. JSNT.S 295: 2005 ⇒168. 66-77.
1906 *Wright, Terry* Von der Moderne zur Postmoderne: internationale Entwicklungslinien von "Literatur und Theologie". Schreiben ist Totenerweckung. 2005 ⇒832. 70-98.
1907 *Yona, Shamir* Repetition and variation in biblical texts. UF 37 (2005) 729-740.

### B4.5 **Influxus biblicus in litteraturam profanam**, *generalia*

1908 *Aichele, George* Artificial bodies: Blade Runner and the death of man. Cinéma divinité. 2005 ⇒520. 137-148.

1909 *Albersmeier, Franz-Josef* "In den Tod gehen" (Lk 22,33): Todesauffassung und Todesdarstellung in der Lyrik des europäischen Barock. FZMIJEWSKI, J. BBB 151: 2005 ⇒172. 339-355.

1910 *Beaude, Pierre-Marie* La bible en post-modernité: l'exemple de la littérature. LV.F 60 (2005) 219-230.

1911 *Bernbeck, Reinhard* The past as fact and fiction: from historical novels to novel histories. Archaeologies of the Middle East. 2005 ⇒ 683. 97-121.

1912 **Boyle, Nicholas** Sacred and secular scriptures: a catholic approach to literature. Erasmus Institute Books: Notre Dame 2005, Univ. of Notre Dame Pr. xi; 299 pp. $55/22.50. 0-268-02178-3/80-5 [ThD 52, 149—W. Charles Heiser].

1913 *Brock, Sebastian* Dinah in a Syriac poem on Joseph. FULLENDORFF, E.: SStLL 47: 2005 ⇒154. 222-235 [Gen 30,21].

1914 *Castellani, Marie M.* La Jérusalem céleste dans les textes littéraires des XII et XIII siècles, un modèle descriptif?. Graphè 14 (2005) 103-117 [Rev 21].

1915 *Christianson, Eric S.* A fistful of shekels: Ehud the judge (Judges 3. 12-30) and the spaghetti western. Cinéma divinité. 2005 ⇒520. 199-213.

1916 *Ehninger, Eva; Feß, Eike; Müller, Jens-Oliver* Das Alte Testament in Bildender Kunst, Musik und Film des 20. Jahrhunderts: eine Werkauswahl mit bibliographischen Hinweisen. Das AT und die Kunst. ATM 15: 2005 ⇒711. 227-252.

1917 *Engelbrecht, Martin* Transformationsmotive in Science Fiction und Fantasy. Wiedergeburt. BTSP 25: 2005 ⇒533. 165-208.

1918 *Fiorini, Pierluigi* Riflessi letterari delle tentazioni di Cristo. Com(I) 199 (2005) 49-54 [Mt 4,1-11].

1919 E**Fischer, Michael; Rothaug, Diana** Das Motiv des Guten Hirten in Theologie, Literatur und Musik. Mainzer Hymnologische Studien 5: 2002 ⇒18,402. RThPh 80 (2005) 472-473 (*Sievernich, M.*).

1920 *Franz, Ansgar* 'Weißt du, wo der Himmel ist?': Himmelsvorstellungen im Kirchenlied. JBTh 20 (2005) 381-411.

1921 *Gabel, Michael* Biblische Texte für nichtchristliche Leser: Franz Fühmann über die Bibel und Dichtung. Heilige Schriften. 2005 ⇒ 362. 172-187, 248-249.

1922 **Hamlin, Hannibal** Psalm culture and early modern English literature. 2004 ⇒20,1781. RReformation 10 (2005) 177-180 (*Swift, Daniel*).

1923 *Heil, Stefan* Religion im Werk deutschsprachiger Autorinnen und Autoren I (20./21. Jahrhundert). Schreiben ist Totenerweckung. 2005 ⇒832. 133-138.

1924 *Hill, Thomas D.* The 'palmtwigede' Pater noster: horticultural semantics and the Old English *Solomon and Saturn* I. Mae 74/1 (2005) 1-9 [Mt 6,9-13].

1925 **Hussher, Cécile** L'ange et la bête: Caïn et Abel dans la littérature. Littérature: P 2005, Cerf 220 pp. €24. 2-204-07686-4. Cf. Diss. Marne-la-Vallé 2002 [Gen 4,1-16].

1926 **Klaghofer-Treitler, Wolfgang** Sha'ul König von Israel. 2003 ⇒19, 1814; 20,1786. [R]FrRu 12 (2005) 143 (*Winklehner, Herbert*).
1927 **Kling, David W.** The bible in history: how the texts have shaped the times. 2004 ⇒20,1787. [R]ChH 75 (2005) 242-244 (*Duff, Paul B.*).
1928 *Kreitzer, Larry* Matthew 11:28-30 and 'rest' from heavy burdens: Bunyan and De Niro meet Jesus. Those outside. 2005 ⇒332. 65-84.
1929 *Langenhorst, Georg* 'Veruntreut', 'versiegelt', geteilt': die Rede vom Himmel in der Literatur unserer Zeit. JBTh 20 (2005) 413-432.
1930 *Llewellyn-Jones, Lloyd* The fashioning of Delilah: costume design, historicism and fantasy in Cecil B. DeMille's *Samson and Delilah* (1949). The clothed body. 2005 ⇒628. 14-29 [Judg 16,1-31].
1931 **Marchal, Bertrand** Salomé: entre vers et prose: Baudelaire, Mallarmé, Flaubert et Huysmans. P 2005, Corti 298 pp. 2-7143-0889-9.
1932 *Nitsche, Stefan A.* Grenzüberschreitungen: Prometheussage und biblische Urgeschichte als Ursprungserzählungen der westlichen Kultur. EvTh 65 (2005) 444-458 [Gen 1-11];
1933 Gott goes Hollywood: mit den Mitteln des Films von Gottesbegegnungen erzählen: Chancen und Fallen der Verfilmung biblischer Texte. Das AT und die Kunst. ATM 15: 2005 ⇒711. 165-97 [Exod 3-4].
1934 *Pippin, Tina* The end of Jesus. Those outside. 2005 ⇒332. 43-63 [Mk 13].
1935 *Prudký, Martin* Tschechische Lyriker der Moderne und das Alte Testament. Das AT und die Kunst. Ment. *Seifert, J.*: ATM 15: 2005 ⇒711. 207-226.
1936 *Salvarani, Brunetto* La letteratura e l'assenza: a proposito di bibbia, grande codice della cultura occidentale. Horeb 14/3 (2005) 73-80.
1937 *Schwens-Harrant, Brigitte* Religion im Werk deutspracher Autorinnen und Autoren II: offene Fragen rund ums Thema "Religion und Literatur". Schreiben ist Totenerweckung. 2005 ⇒832. 139-144.
1938 *Staley, Jeffrey L.* Reading 'this woman' back into John 7:1-8:59: *Liar Liar* and the 'Pericope adulterae' in intertextual tango. Those outside. 2005 ⇒332. 85-107.
1939 *Telford, William R.* The two faces of betrayal: the characterization of Peter and Judas in the biblical epic or Christ film;
1940 'His blood be upon us, and our children': the treatment of Jews and Judaism in the Christ film;
1941 Ritual recast and revisioned: Hollywood remembers the first passover and the last supper [Exod 12-13; Mt 26]. Cinéma divinité. 2005 ⇒ 520. 214-235/266-288/289-309
1942 *Wiegand, Wilfried* Das Buch der Bücher—im neuen Jahrtausend. Das Buch. Vechtaer Beiträge zur Theologie 11: 2005 ⇒1130. 7-8.
1943 *Wifstrand, Albert* Son of fortune, son of affliction. Epochs and styles. WUNT 179: 2005 <1959, 1976> ⇒325. 197-203.
1944 **Zierler, Wendy I.** And Rachel stole the idols: the emergence of modern Hebrew women's writing. 2004 ⇒20,1803. [R]Jdm 54 (2005) 280-285 (*Aschkenasy, Nehama*).

## B4.6 *Singuli auctores*—Bible influence on individual authors

1945 AMICHAI Y: *Ferrari, Sara* Alcune note su un particolare caso d'intertestualità nella poesia di Yehuda Amichai. Materia giudaica 10/2 (2005) 375-385 [Gen 48,10].

1946 AZRIEL Y: **Azriel, Yakov** Threads from a coat of many colors: poems on Genesis. St. Louis 2005, Time Being 115 pp.

1947 BLAKE W: *Rowland, Christopher* Blake and the bible: biblical exegesis in the work of William Blake. IJST 7/2 (2005) 142-154.

1948 BORGES J: *Walsh, Richard* Three versions of ~~Judas~~ Jesus. Those outside. 2005 ⇒332. 155-181.

1949 BRECHT B; MARX K: *Boer, Dick* Die Gewalt, die Armut und das gute Leben: Bertolt Brecht und die Religion. TeKo 28/1 (2005) 30-42.

1950 CELAN P: *Wiesmüller, Wolfgang* Paul Celans Gedicht "Psalm" und der jüdische Gottesname JHWH. PzB 14 (2005) 23-34.

1951 CHANDIEU A DE: *Di Mauro, Damon* Antoine de Chandieu, auteur d'un drame biblique?. BSHPF 151 (2005) 219-229 [Dan 3].

1952 CHRISTINE DE P: **Birk, Bonnie A.** Christine de Pizan and biblical wisdom: a feminist-theological point of view. Marquette Studies in Theology 47: Milwaukee 2005, Marquette Univ. Pr. 202 pp. $23. 08-746-26994.

1953 CLAUDEL P: **Claudel, Paul** Le poète et la bible, II: 1945-1955. 2004 ⇒20,1804. [R]Com(F) 30/3 (2005) 91-93 (*Tilliette, Xavier*); NRTh 127 (2005) 681-683 (*Lebeau, P.*); RThom 105 (2005) 694-695 (*Boudaroua, Joël-Marie*);

1954 *Millet-Gérard, Dominique* Dieu parle: la figure de prosopopée dans l'exégèse claudélienne. RSHum 279 (2005) 123-140.

1955 COETZEE J: *Ammicht-Quinn, Regina* Aus der Gnade gefallen: J.M. Coetzee's "Disgrace" und der ethische "Mehrwert" des Ästhetischen. Schreiben ist Totenerweckung. 2005 ⇒832. 116-130.

1956 CONSTANTINUS STILBES: [E]**Hörandner, Wolfram; Diethart, Johannes** Poemata Constantinus Stilbes. Monachii 2005, Saur xxx; 73 pp. 3-598-71235-9. Bibl. xxviii-xxix.

1957 DANTE: *Fasolini, Diego* 'Illuminating' and 'illuminated' light: a biblical-theological interpretation of God-as-light in Canto XXXIII of Dante's Paradiso. JLT 19/4 (2005) 297-310;

1958 *Orlandi, Stefania* Il cosmo di Dante: note per una lettura della *Commedia*. Com(I) 202 (2005) 58-70.

1959 DOSTOEVSKY F: *Maddison, Bula* A Bakhtinian reading of biblical allusion in Dostoevsky's novel "Crime and punishment". PRSt 32/3 (2005) 267-279;

1960 **Plasencia Moncayo, José Luis** Nada más humano que Cristo: el misterio del hombre a la luz de Cristo en Fiodor M. Dostoyevski. BSRel 193: R 2005, LAS 506 pp. €33. 88-213-0596-1;

1961 **Salvestroni, Simonetta** Dostoïevski et la bible. 2004 ⇒20,1808. [R]Contacts 57 (2005) 282-284 (*Evdokimov, Michel*);

1962 *Venier, Elio* Il volto di Gesù in Dostoevskij: inquisito o inquisitore?. Volto dei volti 8/1 (2005) 63-69.

1963 DYLAN B: **Gilmour, Michael J.** Tangled up in the bible: Bob Dylan and scripture. 2004 ⇒20,1809. [R]TJT 21 (2005) 305-306 (*Donaldson, Andrew*).

1964 ELIOT T: *Clément, Olivier* Le voyage des Mages. Contacts 57 (2005) 302-306.

1965 GIDE A: **Gide, André** El regreso del hijo pródigo. 2003 ⇒19,1849. [R]EE 80 (2005) 619-620 (*Millán Romeral, Fernando*) [Lk 15,11-32].

1966 GOETHE J: *Einboden, Jeffrey* The genesis of Weltliteratur: Goethe's West-Östlicher Divan and kerygmatic pluralism. JLT 19/3 (2005) 238-250;

1967 **Hübner, Hans** Goethes Faust und das Neue Testament. 2003 ⇒19, 1850. RThLZ 130 (2005) 672-674 (*Degler, Frank*).

1968 *Rechenmacher, Hans* Goethes Mosebild. MThZ 56 (2005) 318-326.

1969 GREEN G: *Aitken, Tom* Was Judas The Third Man?: the lost childhood in the cinema of Graham Green. Cinéma divinité. 2005 ⇒520. 124-136.

1970 HEIDEGGER M: **Giustozzi, Gianfilippo** La riabilitazione del 'ciarlatano': Heidegger lettore di San Paolo. Firmana.S 4: Fermo 2005, Istituto Teologico Marchigiano 116 pp. €12. Bibl. 103-112;

1971 **Sommer, Christian** Heidegger, ARISTOTE, LUTHER: les sources aristotéliciennes et néo-testamentaires d'*Etre et Temps*. P 2005, PUF 335 pp.

1972 HOBBES T: **Hobbes, Thomas** Leviathan. E*Tuck, Richard*: C 2005, CUP xciii; 519 pp. 0-521-39641-7. Revised student edition.

1973 JOHN T: T*Stone, Michael E.* On the creation of the world (stanzas 1-150): John of T'lkuran. Saint Nersess theological review 10 (2005) 51-75.

1974 KAFKA F: *Braungart, Wolfgang* Literaturwissenschaft und Theologie: Versuch zu einem schwierigen Verhältnis, ausgehend von Kafkas Erzählung "Ein Hungerkünstler". Schreiben ist Totenerweckung. 2005 ⇒832. 43-69.

1975 KELLER G: *Pestalozzi, Karl* "Blüh' auf, gefrorner Christ [...]": zum Kapitel IV/13 in Gottfried Kellers Roman Der grüne Heinrich (1854/1855). FSTEGEMANN, E. 2005 ⇒139. 74-86.

1976 KOSMAN A: *Kosman, Admiel* Sieben Psalmen: unterschiedliche Anfänge eines Briefes an Gott: aus dem Hebräischen übersetzt von Edna Brocke. FSTEGEMANN, E. 2005 ⇒139. 153-167.

1977 LE FÈVRE DE LA BODERIE G: *Victoria, Thierry* Évocation du Royaume et messianisme politique: le thème de la Jérusalem céleste chez Guy Le Fèvre de La Boderie. Graphè 14 (2005) 129-44 [Rev 21].

1978 LEVIN H: *Naumann, Matthias* Yiṣḥaqs rettende Stimme—zu Hanoch Levins satirischer Fassung der 'Aqeda. FJB 32 (2005) 73-114 [Gen 22,1-19].

1979 MARITAIN R: *Mayaux, Catherine; Bercot, Martine* Bible et liturgie dans les poèmes de Raïssa Maritain. Cahiers Jacques Maritain 51 (2005) 33-47.

1980 MASTENA M: *Venier, Elio* Il volto sorridente di Gesù in Maria Pia Mastena. Volto dei volti 8/1 (2005) 70-73.

1981 MELVILLE H: *Vogel, Dan* The legacy of two Adams. JBQ 33 (2005) 3-12.

1982 MIÉVILLE C: *Aichele, George* Jesus' two fathers: an afterlife of the gospel of Luke. Those outside. 2005 ⇒332. 17-41 [Lk 1,35].

1983 MORUS T: *Vincette, Pascale* L'Utopie de Thomas More: médiation entre la cité historique et la Jérusalem céleste. Graphè 14 (2005) 119-128 [Rev 21].

1984 O'CONNOR F: *Maddison, Bula* Where a story can take you: reading "The bible in the river" by Flannery O'Connor. Listening 40/2 (2005) 131-137.

1985 PRUDENTIUS C: ET**Garuti, Giovanni** Clemens Aurelius Prudentius: Apotheosis. Collana di Studi 26: Modena 2005, Mucchi 179 pp. €20. 88-7000-4104. Bibl. 9-11.

1986 ROMANO M: *Frank, Georgia* Dialogue and deliberation: the sensory self in the hymns of Romanos the Melodist. Religion and the self in antiquity. 2005 ⇒818. 163-179;

1987 [ET]**Maisano, Riccardo** Romano il Melodo: Cantici. Classici greci: 2002 ⇒18,9448... 20,1822. [R]Rhetorica 23 (2005) 205-207 (*Pernot, Laurent*).

1988 ROTH P: [E]**Langenhorst, Georg** Patrick Roth—Erzähler zwischen Bibel und Hollywood. Müns 2005, LIT 208 pp. €24.90.

1989 SAND G: **Christophe, Paul** George Sand et Jésus. Histoire: 2003 ⇒ 19,1868. [R]EeV 123 (2005) 25-26 (*Dubray, Jean*).

1990 SITUMORANG, S.: *Hoekema, Alle* De verloren zoon in gedichten van Sitor Situmorang. ITBT 13/1 (2005) 12-15 [Lk 15,11-32].

1991 WESLEY C: *Watson, J.R.* Pitying tenderness and tenderest pity: the hymns of Charles Wesley and the writings of Saint Luke. EpRe 32/3 (2005) 33-38 [NTAb 50,45].

### B4.7 *Interpretatio* materialistica, psychiatrica

1992 **Beier, Matthias** A violent God-image: an introduction to the work of Eugen DREWERMANN. 2004 ⇒20,1831. [R]CTJ 40 (2005) 394-396 (*Ellens, J. Harold*); RBLit (2005)* (*Rollins, Wayne*).

1993 **Boer, Roland** Marxist criticism of the bible: a critical introduction to Marxists literary theory and the bible. 2003 ⇒19,1875. [R]BiCT 1/3 (2005)* (*Jobling, David*).

1994 *Francis, L.J.; Village, A.* The relationship of psychological type preferences to biblical interpretation. JET 18/1 (2005) 74-89 [NTAb 50, 10].

1995 *Garzon, Fernando* Interventions that apply scripture in psychotherapy. JPsT 33/2 (2005) 113-121.

1996 *Gemünden, Petra von* Methodische Überlegungen zur historischen Psychologie exemplifiziert am Themenkomplex der Trauer. EvTh 65 (2005) 86-102.

1997 *Hathaway, William L.* Scripture and psychological science: integrative challenges and callings. JPsT 33/2 (2005) 89-97.

1998 *Hill, Peter C.* Living on the boundary: scriptural authority and psychology. JPsT 33/2 (2005) 98-112.

1999 *Vollenweider, Samuel* Außergewöhnliche Bewusstseinszustände und die urchristliche Religion: eine alternative Stimme zur psychologischen Exegese. EvTh 65 (2005) 103-117.

2000 **Wolf, Marc-Alain** Un psychiatre lit la bible. LiBi 141: P 2005, Cerf 185 pp. €18. 2-204-07570-1. [R]CEv 134 (2005) 59-60 (*Escaffre, Bernadette*).

2001 *Wynne, Vincent W.* Abraham's gift: a psychoanalytic christology. JAAR 73 (2005) 759-780.

## B5 Methodus exegeticus

2002 *Aletti, Jean-Noël* Lecture rhétorique: difficultés et enjeux d'une nouvelle approche. Guide des nouvelles lectures. 2005 ⇒426. 40-66.

2003 **Aletti, Jean-Noël**, *al.* Vocabulaire raisonné de l'exégese biblique: les mots, les approches, les auteurs. P 2005, Cerf 159 pp. 2204-07380-6.

2004 **Armstrong, Karen** Le combat pour Dieu: une histoire du fondamentalisme juif, chrétien et musulman (1492-2001). [T]*Trierweiler, Denis:* P 2005, Seuil 616 pp. €27. 2-02-058862-5.
2005 *Artus, Olivier* L'approche de l'exégète. CEv 131 (2005) 20-35.
2006 **Bar-Ilan, Meir** Biblical numerology. Rehovot 2005, Association for Jewish astrology and numerology 239; xvii pp. 965-90620-1-X. Bibl. 229-239.
2007 *Beauchamp, Paul* L'analyse structurale et l'exégèse biblique. Pages exégétiques. LeDiv 202: 2005 <1972> ⇒183. 37-54;
2008 Exégèse typologique, exégèse d'aujourd'hui. Pages exégétiques. LeDiv 202: 2005 <1993> ⇒183. 407-412.
2009 **Becker, Uwe** Exegese des Alten Testaments: ein Methoden- und Arbeitsbuch. UTB 2664: Tü 2005, Mohr S. x; 216 pp. €13.90. 3-8252-2664-6 [ZKTh 128,136s—Markl, Dominik].
2010 *Belmonte García, Olga* El fundamentalismo: la negación del próximo (desde la lectura de F. ROSENZWEIG). MCom 63 (2005) 439-455.
2011 *Bernstein, Moshe J.* "Rewritten bible": a generic category which has outlived its usefulness?. Textus 22 (2005) 169-196.
2012 *Blum, Erhard* "Wie jede andere fiktionale Literatur ..."?: Einwürfe eines Exegeten zum Beitrag von Jochen Teuffel. NZSTh 47/3 (2005) 251-258;
2013 Notwendigkeit und Grenzen historischer Exegese: Plädoyer für eine alttestamentliche "Exegetik". Theologie und Exegese. SBS 200: 2005 ⇒410. 11-40.
2014 *Burnett, Carole C.* The interpretation of the bible before the modern period. Scripture. 2005 ⇒398. 133-145.
2015 **Carr, David M.** Writing on the tablet of the heart: origins of scripture and literature. Oxf 2005, OUP xiv; 330 pp. £39.50. 0-19-51729-73. Bibl. 307-317. [R]RBLit (2005)* (*Singer, Itamar*).
2016 *Charlier, Pascal* Les mots et le texte: esquisses de réponses aux théologiens qui ne sont pas philologues. [F]FINET, A.: Subartu 16: 2005 ⇒ 40. 25-29.
2017 *Collins, John J.* Historical criticism in a postmodern age: the case of the Old Testament. PIBA 28 (2005) 28-47;
2018 **Collins, John Joseph** The bible after Babel: historical criticism in a postmodern age. GR 2005, Eerdmans x; 201 pp. $18. 0-8028-2892-2. Bibl. 162-192.
2019 *Davis, Ellen F.* Salvific surprise: the shared and complementary tasks of exegetical and critical or constructive theologians. Reconsidering the boundaries. 2005 ⇒598. 35-44.
2020 *Donahue, John R.* Modern and postmodern critical methods of biblical study. Scripture. 2005 ⇒398. 147-162.
2021 **Ebner, Martin; Heininger, Bernhard** Exegese des Neuen Testaments: ein Arbeitsbuch für Lehre und Praxis. UTB 2677: Pd 2005, UTB xiii; 419 pp. €19.90. 3-8252-2677-8.
2022 *Elliott, John H.* Lecture socioscientifique: illustration par l'accusation du mauvais oeil en Galatie. Guide des nouvelles lectures. 2005 ⇒426. 141-167 [Gal 4,12-15].
2023 **Erickson, Richard J.** A beginner's guide to New Testament exegesis: taking the fear out of critical method. DG 2005, InterVarsity 239 pp. $18. 0-8308-2771-4. Bibl. 225-232.
2024 *Eriksson, LarsOlov* Några kommentarer om kommentarer. SEÅ 70 (2005) 43-52.

2025 *Estévez López, Elisa* La escritura en el centro de la evangelización: los métodos exegéticos a examen. Biblia y nueva evangelización. 2005 ⇒491. 109-158.

2026 *Gargano, Guido I.* 'Senza di me non potete far nulla': mistagogia della parola e dell'eucaristia (NMI 35-39). Path 4/1 (2005) 57-84.

2027 *Ghiberti, Giuseppe* Orientamenti odierni dell'esegesi biblica. Rivista di science religiose 19/1 (2005) 173-192.

2028 *Groenewald, Alphonso* Synchrony and/or diachrony: is there a way out of the methodological labyrinth?. Critical study. ATM 20: 2005 ⇒457. 50-61.

2029 *Hall, S.* Historical-critical methods of bible study: too academically-minded to be of any pastoral use?. Theology in Scotland 12/2 (2005) 39-55 [NTAb 50,234].

2030 *Hardmeier, Christof* New relations between systematic theology and exegesis and the perspectives on practical theology and ethics. Reconsidering the boundaries. 2005 ⇒598. 71-80.

2031 *Jobling, David* Lecture idéologique: la guérison du centurion. Guide des nouvelles lectures. 2005 ⇒426. 222-245 [Lk 7,2-10].

2032 *Jonker, Louis* 'Contextuality' in (South) African exegesis: reflections on the communality of our exegetical methodologies. OTEs 18 (2005) 637-650.

2033 *Kalman, Jason* Biblical criticism in the service of Jewish theology: a case study in post-Holocaust biblical exegesis. OTEs 18 (2005) 93-108.

2034 *Kambou, Sié Daniel* Bible et sociétés à tradition orale. LV.F 60 (2005) 193-205.

2035 *Kandler, Karl H.* Abschied von einem falschen Konsens: Gedanken zur gegenwärtigen Auslegung der Heiligen Schrift. LuthBei 10/4 (2005) 246-249.

2036 **Kennedy, George A.** Retórica y Nuevo Testamento: la interpretación del Nuevo Testamento mediante la crítica retórica. 2003 ⇒19, 1906; 20,1864. [R]CTom 133 (2005) 398-399 (*Huarte, Juan*).

2037 *Kim, Micah E.* A new approach to biblical criticism: spiritual interpretation. AJTh 19/2 (2005) 241-255.

2038 *Leiner, Martin* Neutestamentliche Exegese zwischen "Psycholatrie" und "Psychophobie". EvTh 65 (2005) 148-154.

2039 *Léon-Dufour, Xavier* L'esegeta e l'evento storico. Un biblista cerca Dio. Collana biblica: 2005 <1970> ⇒245. 79-89.

2040 **Longenecker, Bruce W.** Rhetoric at the boundaries: the art and theology of the New Testament chain-link transitions. Waco, Texas 2005, Baylor x; 305 pp. 1-932792-24-4. Bibl. 259-282.

2041 *Luz, Ulrich* Can the bible still be the foundation for a church today?: the task of exegesis in a society of religious pluralism <1998>;

2042 Canonical exegesis and hermeneutics of 'effective history' <2003>. Studies in Matthew. 2005 ⇒252. 313-332/333-348.

2043 [E]**Malina, Artur; Kucz, Anna** Interpretacja (w) dialogu: tozsamosc egzegezy biblijnej. Studia Biblica 10: Kielce 2005, Instytut Teologii Biblijnej Verbum 144 pp. 83-919505-3-0. **P.**

2044 **Marshall, I. Howard**, *al.* Beyond the bible: moving from scripture to theology. 2004 ⇒20,399. [R]RBLit (2005)* (*Vest, John W.*); ChrTo 49/11 (2005) 92-93 (*Neff, D.*).

2045 *Mathieu, Yvan* Les livres historiques du Premier Testament: la synchronie ouvre-t-elle de nouvelles pistes de recherche?. Traduire la Bible hébraïque. 2005 ⇒728. 375-411.

2046 *Maurer, Ernstpeter; Schmidt, Werner H.* Theologische Exegese und Systematische Theologie. GlLern 20 (2005) 32-48.

2047 *Moore, Mary E.M.* Systematic theology and exegesis: multifarious conversations with God and creation. Reconsidering the boundaries. 2005 ⇒598. 45-63.

2048 **Mortara Garavelli, Bice** Manuale di retorica. Tascabili Bompiani, Saggi 94: Mi [9]2005, Bompiani 368 pp. 88-452-4750-3.

2049 *Nasta, Mihaïl* Effigies helléniques du prototype dans un langage figural du christianisme. [F]HURST, A. 2005 ⇒64. 473-487.

2050 **Ossandón Widow, Juan Carlos** Los sentidos de la escritura: aproximación a una definición teológica del sentido literal. [D]*Balaguer Beltrán, V.C.* 2005, 645 pp. Diss. Pampelune [RTL 37,607].

2051 *Peden, Alison* Contextual bible study at Cornton Vale women's prison, Stirling. ET 117 (2005) 15-18.

2052 *Penner, Todd; Vander Stichele, Caroline* Mastering the tools or retooling the masters?: the legacy of historical-critical discourse. Her master's tools?. 2005 ⇒493. 1-29.

2053 *Perrot, Charles* L'exégèse aujourd'hui. ChDial 26 (2005) 123-144.

2054 **Reis, Pamela Tamarkin** Reading the lines: a fresh look at the Hebrew Bible. 2002 ⇒18,1798... 20,1878. [R]RBLit (2005)* (*Mcentire, Mark*); JThS 56 (2005) 520-523 (*Rooke, Deborah*).

2055 *Riches, John* Worship resources: contextual bible study: some reflections. ET 117 (2005) 23-26 [Mt 25; Eph 1,15-23].

2056 *Sanders, James A.* Lecture canonique: histoire, canon et débuts du christianisme. Guide des nouvelles lectures. 2005 ⇒426. 67-94.

2057 [E]**Sánchez Navarro, Luis; Granados, Carlos** <ed> Escritura e interpretación: los fundamentos de la interpretación bíblica. Libros Palabra 42: M [2]2005, Palabra 204 pp.

2058 *Schieder, Rolf* Historische Kritik als Lebensstil: das Beispiel Michel Foucaults. [F]STEGEMANN, W. 2005 ⇒139. 107-119.

2059 *Schneider, Jörg* Über den Umgang mit biblischen und juristischen Quellen: Disziplinübergreifendes und -trennendes am Beispiel der wissenschaftlichen Bibelexegese sowie der Interpretation juristischer Texte hinsichtlich Auslegung undTextänderung. ARSP 91 (2005) 188-220.

2060 *Scholz, Susanne* "Tandoori Reindeer" and the limitations of historical criticism. Her master's tools?. 2005 ⇒493. 47-69.

2061 *Segovia, Fernando* Lecture postcoloniale: Jean ou la vision d'un monde alternatif. Guide des nouvelles lectures. 2005 ⇒426. 246-272 [John 1,1-18].

2062 *Ska, Jean-Louis* A plea on behalf of the biblical redactors. StTh 59 (2005) 4-18.

2063 **Söding, Thomas; Münch, Christian** Kleine Methodenlehre zum Neuen Testament. FrB 2005, Herder 173 pp. €9.90. 3-451-28782-X.

2064 *Strecker, Christian* Das Gewesene, das Fremde und die Exegese: die jüngeren Grundlagendebatten in Geschichtswissenschaft und Kulturanthropologie und ihre Bedeutung für die biblische Wissenschaft. [F]STEGEMANN, W. 2005 ⇒139. 120-131.

2065 [E]**Sweeney, Marvin; Ben Zvi, Ehud** The changing face of form criticism for the twenty-first century. 2003 ⇒19,420; 20,1890. [R]JQR 95 (2005) 331-335 (*Di Vito, Robert A.*); Faith & Mission 22/3 (2005) 113-115 (*Rooker, Mark F.*); BS 162 (2005) 367-369 (*Chisholm,*

*Robert B., Jr.*); JJS 56 (2005) 138-139 (*Williamson, H.G.M.*); RBLit 7 (2005) 496-502 (*Hoffman, Yair*).

2066 *Teuffel, Jochen* Geschichten, Historik und die Theologie. NZSTh 47/3 (2005) 233-250.

2067 *Theißen, Gerd* Exegese und Wahrheit: Überlegungen zu einer Interpretationsethik für die Auslegung der Bibel. Reconsidering the boundaries. 2005 ⇒598. 81-96.

2068 *Tichý, Ladislav* Wie genau muss man die Gattung eines neutestamentlichen Textes bestimmen?: geprüft und dargestellt an 1 Kor 13 und Röm 8,31-39. AUPO 6 (2005) 53-64.

2069 *Tov, Emanuel* The writing of early scrolls: implications for the literary analysis of Hebrew scripture. [F]SCHENKER, A.: OBO 214: 2005 ⇒134. 355-371.

2070 *Van Deventer, H.J.M.* Pardon my paradigm: on the paradigmatic nature of methods and paradigm changes in biblical studies. OTEs 18 (2005) 847-862.

2071 [E]**Van Leeuwen, M.** De bijbel in context: oecumenische toenadering rond de schriften. 2004 ⇒20,1895. [R]Str. 72 (2005) 182-183 (*Beentjes, Panc*).

2072 *Vander Stichele, Caroline* Historical-criticism and interreligious dialogue: a conversation with Räisänen. Moving beyond NT theology?. SESJ 88: 2005 ⇒463. 308-335.

2073 *Welzen, Huub* Intertextuality: traces of mysticism. [M]VAN TILBORG, S.: BiblInterp 71: 2005 ⇒155. 317-347.

2074 *Wilken, Robert L.* Allegory and the interpretation of the Old Testament in the 21st century. L&S 1 (2005) 11-21;

2075 The inevitability of allegory. Gr. 86 (2005) 742-753.

## III. Critica Textus, Versiones

### D1 Textual Criticism

2076 *Barré, Michael L.* The transmission and translation of the bible. Scripture. 2005 ⇒398. 119-130.

2077 *Baur, Wolfgang* Ägypten: Katharinenkloster: Streit um die zweitälteste Bibelhandschrift der Welt. WUB 37 (2005) 69.

2078 *Berschin, Walter* Griechisches in der Klosterschule des alten St. Gallen. Mittellateinische Studien. 2005 <1991-2> ⇒188. 179-192 [RBen 116,137—P.-M. Bogaert].

2079 [E]**Delaveau, Martine; Hillard, Denise** Bibles imprimées du XV$^{e}$ au XVIII$^{e}$ siècle conservées à Paris: catalogue collectif. 2003 ⇒19,1946; 20,1901. [R]JQR 95 (2005) 732-737 (*Schwarzbach, Bertram E.*).

2080 **Jongkind, Dirk** Studies in the scribal habits of Codex Sinaiticus. [D]*Head, Peter M.* 2005, Diss. Cambridge [TynB 56,155-156].

2081 [E]**McKendrick, Scot; O'Sullivan, Orlaith A.** The bible as book: the transmission of the Greek text. 2003 ⇒19,379; 20,1906. [R]NT 47 (2005) 162-163 (*Hurtado, L.W.*).

## D2.1 *Biblia Hebraica* Hebrew text

2082 *Bedenbender, Andreas* Die Leiblichkeit des Textes: Notizen zu den Namen und den Anfangsversen einiger biblischer Bücher. TeKo 28/4 (2005) 49-52 [Qoh, Est, Jb, Cant].

2083 *Cathcart, Kevin J.* The comparative philological approach to the text of the Old Testament. The OT in its world. OTS 52: 2005⇒749. 1-13.

2084 **Chiesa, Bruno** Filologia storica della bibbia ebraica, 1-2. StBi 125, 135: 2000-2002 ⇒16,1833... 20,1927. [R]RSIt 117 (2005) 610-614 (*Catastini, Alessandro*).

2085 *Cogan, Mordechai* Some text-critical issues in the Hebrew Bible from an assyriological perspective. Textus 22 (2005) 1-20.

2086 *Contreras, E. Martin* Continuity of the tradition: midrashic explanations. JSSt 50 (2005) 329-339.

2087 *DeCaen, Vincent* On the distribution of major and minor pause in Tiberian Hebrew in the light of the variants of the second person independent pronouns. JSSt 50 (2005) 321-327.

2088 **Dotan, Aron** The awakening of word lore: from the masora to the beginnings of Hebrew lexicography. Sources and Studies 7: J 2005, Academy of the Hebrew Language xvi; 222; viii* pp. 965-481-022-0. H.

2089 [E]**Ellenberger, Y.; Weil, R.** Termes massorétiques, prosodie hébraïque et autres études: appendices à la grammaire hébraïque. Sciences historiques II, hautes études orientales 39: Genève 2005, Droz xvi; 158 pp. 26000-09183.

2090 *Fabry, Heinz J.* Il testo e la sua storia. Introduzione AT. 2005 ⇒ 1159. 47-90.

2091 **Fernández Marcos, Natalio; Spottorno Díaz-Caro, María V.; Cañas Reíllo, José M.** Índice griego-hebreo del texto antioqueno en los libros históricos, I: Índice general. TECC 75: M 2005, Consejo Superior de Investigaciones Científicas xl; 616 pp. 84-00-08383-0;

2092 II: Índice de nombres propios. TECC 75: M 2005, Consejo Superior de Investigaciones Científicas xx; 210 pp. 84-00-08384-9.

2093 **Francisco, Edson de Faria** Manual da Biblia Hebraica: introdução ao texto massorético: guia introdutório para a *Biblia Hebraica Stuttgartensia*. São Paulo [2]2005, Vida Nova 568 pp [REB 65,1017].

2094 *Geiger, Gregor* Die Pausalformen der Segolata und die Mitte des biblischen Verses. LASBF 55 (2005) 59-111.

2095 *Gzella, Holger* New ways in textual criticism: Isa 42,1-4 as a paradigm case. EThL 81 (2005) 387-423.

2096 *Heckl, Raik* Ist die Alttestamentliche Exegese ein Spiel mit mehreren Variablen?: zur Anwendung der Begriffe "Kohärenz" und "Inkohärenz" in der alttestamentlichen Exegese. BN 124 (2005) 51-56.

2097 *Himbaza, Innocent* La conscience des problèmes textuels de l'Ancien Testament: état de la question hier et aujourd'hui;

2098 *Hugo, Philippe; Schenker, Adrian* Histoire du texte et critique textuelle de l'Ancien Testament dans la recherche récente. L'enfance de la Bible hébraïque. MoBi 52: 2005 ⇒477. 34-61/11-33.

2099 **Kelley, Page H.; Mynatt, Daniel S.; Crawford,Timothy G.** Die Masora der Biblia Hebraica Stuttgartensia: Einführung und kommentiertes Glossar. 2003 ⇒20,1932. [R]JETh 19 (2005) 211-212 (*Siebenthal, Heinrich von*).

2100 **Kogman-Appel, Katrin** Jewish book art between Islam and christianity: the decoration of Hebrew bibles in medieval Spain. Medieval and early modern Iberian world 19: 2004 ⇒20,1933. [R]Scr. 59 (2005) 212*-213* (*Sirat, C.*).

2101 *Lambert, Mayer* Les termes massorétiques (Appendice I);

2102 De la prosodie hébraïque (Appendice II);

2103 Lettres employés comme chiffres (Appendice IV, XI);

2104 Les systèmes des points voyelles (Appendice V);

2105 Les accents de pause (Appendice VI). Termes massorétiques. 2005 ⇒2089. 1-7/9-10/13, 75/15-16/17-38.

2106 *Lamprecht, A.* The setting of the *makkeph* in an idea-cluster: on homonymy and metonymy. JNSL 31/2 (2005) 107-127.

2107 *Migsch, Herbert* Huldreich ZWINGLIs hebräische Bibel. Zwingliana 32 (2005) 39-44.

2108 *Ofer, Yosef* Abraham FIRKOVICH and the dedication inscription of the Aleppo codex. HUCA 76 (2005) 259-272.

2109 *Ortega Monasterio, Maria Teresa* Los códices modelo y los manuscritos hebreos bíblicos españoles. Sef. 65 (2005) 353-383 [1 Kgs 2, 1-9].

2110 *Richardson, M.E.J.* Textual modification: some examples from Egypt. The OT in its world. OTS 52: 2005 ⇒749. 168-182.

2111 *Samuel, Leonora* Accentuation: a tool for interpreting the text of the Hebrew Bible. JBQ 33 (2005) 174-183.

2112 [E]**Schenker, Adrian**, *al.* Biblia Hebraica Quinta, 18: general introduction and Megilloth. 2004 ⇒20,1943. [R]ThEv(VS) 4/2 (2005) 93-96 (*Nicole, Émile*); RBLit (2005)* (*Sanders, James*).

2113 *Tov, Emanuel* The *Biblia Hebraica Quinta*: an important step forward. JNSL 31/1 (2005) 1-21;

2114 Implications of Qumran finds for the literary analysis of Hebrew scripture. Meghillot III. 2005 ⇒608. 191-204. **H.**;

2115 L'écriture des anciens manuscrits: implications pour l'analyse littéraire des Écritures hébraïques. Traduire la Bible hébraïque. 2005 ⇒728. 29-53.

2116 *Van der Kooij, Arie* Ancient emendations in MT. [F]SCHENKER, A.: OBO 214: 2005 ⇒134. 152-59 [Deut 32,8; 32,43; Isa 10,32; 19,18].

## D2.2 Targum

2117 [T]**Alexander, Philip S.** The Targum of Canticles: translated with a critical introduction, apparatus, and notes. The Aramaic Bible 17A: 2003 ⇒19,1985. [R]StBob 2 (2005)227-230 (*Baraniak, Marek*).

2118 *Bernstein, Moshe J.* A Jewish reading of Psalms: some observations on the method of the Aramaic targum. The book of Psalms. VT.S 99: 2005 ⇒390. 476-504.

2119 Bibliography of the Aramaic Bible. AramSt 3/1 (2005) 127-131.

2120 *Hayward, Robert* The temple as a place of prayer in the pentateuchal targumim. Studies in Jewish prayer. JSSt.S 17: 2005 ⇒828. 151-161 [Gen 28,17].

2121 *Houtman, Alberdina* The role of Abraham in Targum Isaiah. AramSt 3 (2005) 3-14;

2122 Wat is er met de lijdende knecht gebeurd?: de lezing van Jesaja 52: 13-53:12 volgens Targoem Jonathan. NedThT 59/3 (2005) 235-251;

2123 [E]**Houtman, Alberdina; Moor, Johannes de** A bilingual concordance to the targum of the prophets, 21: Introduction, additions and corrections, indices. Lei 2005, Brill 453 pp. €140/$200. 90-04-13107-8.

2124 *Kant, Laurence H.* Arguing with God and *Tiqqum Olam*: a response to André LaCocque. LexTQ 40 (2005) 203-219 [Gen 22].

2125 *Kuntzmann, Raymond* Le targum des Chroniques I,1 (TC I,1) et la géographie synagogale. RevSR 79 (2005) 147-161.

2126 *Kuty, Renaud J.* Determination in Targum Jonathan to Samuel. AramSt 3 (2005) 187-201.

2127 *LaCocque, André* About the "Aqedah" in Genesis 22: a response to Laurence A. Kant. LexTQ 40 (2005) 191-201 [Gen 22].

2128 *Legrand, Thierry* Les targums du pentateuque: leur rapport aux documents inscrits, aux livres et à la Torah. RevSR 79 (2005) 127-146.

2129 [T]**Lenzi, Giovanni** Il targum Yonathan, 1: Isaia: traduzione a confronto con il testo masoretico. Genova 2004, Marietti lvi; 290 pp. €38.

2130 *Lorein, Geert W.* malkûta in the Targum of the Prophets. AramSt 3 (2005) 15-42.

2131 *Ribera i Florit, Josep* El targum de los profetas y el Nuevo Testamento. ResB 47 (2005) 23-31;

2132 La congregació d'Israel (כנשתא דישראל) reflectida en el targum dels profetes. RCatT 30/1 (2005) 1-15.

2133 **Shepherd, David** Targum and translation: a reconsideration of the Qumran Aramaic version of Job. SSN 45: 2004 ⇒20,1968. [R]Bib. 86 (2005) 297-300 (*Joosten, Jan*); CBQ 67 (2005) 327-328 (*Morrison, Craig E.*); TJT 21 (2005) 273-274 (*Hu, Wesley*); HebStud 46 (2005) 430-433 (*Gold, Sally L.*).

2134 *Van Staalduine-Sulman, Eveline* Vowels in the trees: the role of vocalisation in stemmatology. AramSt 3 (2005) 215-240.

2135 **Van Staalduine-Sulman, Eveline** The Targum of Samuel. 2002 ⇒ 18,1893... 20,1970. [R]JSSt 50 (2005) 391-394 (*Stec, David M.*).

## D3.1 *Textus graecus*—**Greek NT**

2136 *Arcieri, Mike* Preliminary examination of McGill New Testament manuscripts. Arc 33 (2005) 401-415.

2137 [E]**Black, David Alan** Rethinking New Testament textual criticism. 2002 ⇒18,1897... 20,1974. [R]BiTr 56 (2005) 222-224 (*Omanson, Roger L.*).

2138 *Brock, Ann G.* Scribal blunder or textual plunder?: Codex Bezae, textual-rhetorical analysis, and the diminished role of women. Her master's tools?. 2005 ⇒493. 253-264.

2139 **Brodie, Thomas L.** The birthing of the New Testament: the intertextual development of the New Testament writings. NT Monographs 1: 2004 ⇒20,1975. [R]Ang. 82 (2005) 481-484 (*Jurič, Stipe*); ScrB 35 (2005) 105-107 (*O'Loughlin, Thomas*).

2140 **Chase, Frederic H.** The Old Syriac element in the text of Codex Bezae. Piscataway (N.J.) 2004 <1893>, Gorgias xvi; 160 pp. 1-593-33-166-5.

2141 **Comfort, Philip** Encountering the manuscripts: an introduction to New Testament paleography and textual criticism. Nv 2005, Broadman & H. 393 pp. $35.

2142 *Crisci, Edoardo* Note sulla più antica produzione di libri cristiani nell'oriente greco. Segno e Testo [Cassino] 3 (2005) 93-145.

2143 *Elliott, J. Keith* Absent witnesses?: the critical apparatus to the Greek New Testament and the apostolic fathers. The reception of the NT. 2005 ⇒752. 47-58.

2144 *Epp, Eldon J.* The Claremont profile method for grouping New Testament minuscule manuscripts <1967, 1993> 41-57;

2145 The twentieth century interlude in New Testament textual criticism. <1974, 1993> 59-100;

2146 Toward the clarification of the term 'textual variant' <1976, 1993> 101-124;

2147 The eclectic method in New Testament textual criticism: solution or symptom? <1976, 1993> 125-173;

2148 New Testament textual criticism in America: requiem for a discipline <1979> 75-184;

2149 A continuing interlude in New Testament textual criticism? <1980, 1993> 185-209;

2150 Decision points in past, present, and future New Testament textual criticism <1989, 1993> 227-283;

2151 New Testament textual criticism past, present, and future: reflections on the Alands' *Text of the New Testament*. <1989> 285-307;

2152 The New Testament papyrus manuscripts in historical perspective <1989> 309-343;

2153 The significance of the papyri for determining the nature of the New Testament text in the second century: a dynamic view of textual transmission <1989, 1993> 345-381;

2154 New Testament papyrus manuscripts and letter carrying in Greco-Roman times <1991> 383-409;

2155 The papyrus manuscripts of the New Testament <1995> 411-435;

2156 The International Greek New Testament Project: motivation and history <1997> 437-459;

2157 Textual criticism in the exegesis of the New Testament <1997> 461-495;

2158 The New Testament papyri at Oxyrhynchus in their social and intellectual context <1997> 497-520;

2159 The multivalence of the term 'original text' in New Testament textual criticism <1999> 551-593;

2160 Issues in the interrelation of New Testament textual criticism and canon <2002> 595-639;

2161 Issues in New Testament textual criticism: moving from the nineteenth century to the twenty-first century <2002> 641-697;

2162 Introduction: a half-century adventure with New Testament textual criticism. Perspectives on NT textual criticism. NT.S 116: 2005 ⇒207. xxvii-xl.

2163 *Förster, Hans* 7Q5=Mark 6.52-53: a challenge for textual criticism?. JGRChJ 2 (2005) 27-35.

2164 **Goodrich, Richard J.; Lukaszewski, Albert L.** A reader's Greek New Testament. GR 2004, Zondervan 585 pp. $30. 03102-48884.

2165 *Grech, Prosper* La filologia neotestamentaria nel secolo XX. Il messaggio biblico. SRivBib 44: 2005 <1993> ⇒216. 179-188.

2166 *Güting, E.* Offene Fragen in der Methodendiskussion der neutestamentlichen Textkritik. Editio [Tü] 19 (2005) 77-98 [NTAb 50,244].

2167 *Head, Peter M.* Is P4, P64 and P67 the oldest manuscript of the four gospels?: a response to T.C. SKEAT. NTS 51 (2005) 450-457.

2168 **Kannaday, Wayne C.** Apologetic discourse and the scribal tradition: evidence of the influence of apologetic interests on the text of the canonical gospels. SBL.Text-Critical Studies 5: 2004 ⇒20,1984. $^{R}$RBLit (2005)* (*Haines-Eitzen, Kim; Kaler, Michael*); ET 116 (2005) 387-388 (*Foster, Paul*).

2169 *Kruger, Michael J.* Bridging the gap between New Testament and textual criticism: the legacy of T.C. SKEAT. ET 116 (2005) 374-376.

2170 *Lee, John A.L.* Dimitrios Doukas and the accentuation of the New Testament text of the Complutensian Polyglot. NT 47 (2005) 250-90.

2171 *Martin, Michael W.* Defending the "western non-interpolations": the case for an anti-separationist Tendenz in the longer Alexandrian readings. JBL 124 (2005) 269-294 [Lk 22,19-20].

2172 **Metzger, Bruce; Ehrman, Bart D.** The text of the New Testament: its transmission, corruption, and restoration. Oxf $^{4}$2005 <1964>, OUP xvi; 366 pp. $85. 0-1951-6667-5.

2173 **Nicklas, Tobias** Fragmente christlicher Apokryphen und die Textgeschichte des Neuen Testaments. ZNW 96 (2005) 129-142.

2174 Novum Testamentum Graece. Stu $^{27}$2005, Deutsche Bibelgesellschaft xiii; 93*; 812; 207 pp. $90. 34380-5115X. With A concise Greek-English dictionary of the New Testament, by *B.M. Newman*.

2175 *Osburn, Carroll D.* Methodology in identifying patristic citations in NT textual criticism. NT 47 (2005) 313-343.

2176 *Parker, David C.* Greek gospel manuscripts in Bucharest and Sofia. BJRL 85/1 (2003) 3-12.

2177 $^{E}$**Pierpont, William G.; Robinson, Maurice A.** The New Testament in the original Greek: Byzantine Textform 2005. Southborough, MA 2005, Chilton xxiii; 587 pp. $18. 0-7598-00774.

2178 *Porter, Stanley E.* Pericope markers in some early Greek New Testament manuscripts. Layout markers. Pericope 5: 2005 ⇒422. 161-76.

2179 *Taylor, Justin* The Western text of the New Testament: its nature and interest. Beginnings of christianity. 2005 ⇒786. 53-63.

2180 **Timpanaro, S.** The genesis of LACHMANN's method. $^{ET}$*Most, G.W.*: Ch 2005, Univ. of Chicago Pr. vii; 252 pp. $47.50/£30. 02268-0405-4. Bibl. [NTAb 50,385].

2181 *Trobisch, David* Structural markers in New Testament manuscripts with special attention to observations in Codex Boernerianus (G 012) and Papyrus 46 of the Letters of Paul. Layout markers. Pericope 5: 2005 ⇒422. 177-190.

2182 *Voicu, Sever J.* Le rôle des centres de copie dans la fixation du canon du Nouveau Testament. Le canon du NT. MoBi 54: 2005 ⇒334. 221-235.

2183 *Wachtel, Klaus* Varianten in der handschriftlichen Überlieferung des Neuen Testaments. Varianten. 2005 ⇒882. 25-38 [Scr. 60,266*—G. Hendrix].

2184 *Wasserman, Tommy* Papyrus 72 and the Bodmer Miscellaneous Codex. NTS 51 (2005) 137-154.

2185 **Williams, Peter J.** Early Syriac translation technique and the textual criticism of the Greek gospels. Texts and Studies 3.2: 2004 ⇒20, 1999. $^{R}$JThS 56 (2005) 622-624 (*Brock, Sebastian*).

## D3.2 *Versiones graecae*—**VT, Septuaginta etc.**

2186 *Boyd-Taylor, Cameron* Calque-culations — loan words and the lexicon. BIOSCS 38 (2005) 79-100.
2187 *Cardona Ramírez, Hernán* La biblia: una mediación hermenéutica. El grano. 2005 <2002> ⇒197. 55-81.
2188 *Casiday, Augustine* EVAGRIUS Ponticus' use of different versions of scripture with special reference to his *Scholia on Job*. Adamantius 11 (2005) 143-157.
2189 *Cook, Johann* Reconsiderung Septuagintal origins. JSem 14 (2005) 441-461;
2190 Novel developments in Septuagint research. OTEs 18 (2005) 531-41.
2191 **Cousin, Hugues** A Bíblia Grega—a Setenta. Fátima 2005, Bíblica 120 pp.
2192 **De Troyer, Kristin** Die Septuaginta und die Endgestalt des Alten Testaments: Untersuchungen zur Entstehungsgeschichte alttestamentlicher Texte. [T]*Robinson, Gesine S.*: UTB S (Small-Format) 2599: Gö 2005, Vandenhoeck & R. 206 pp. €20. 3525-03606-X. Bibl. 188-99.
2193 **Dines, Jennifer M.** The Septuagint. [E]*Knibb, Michael A.* 2004, ⇒20,2009. [R]RBLit (2005)* (*Shaw, Frank*);
2194 The Septuagint. Understanding the Bible and its World: L 2005, Clark xvii; 196 pp. 0-567-08464-7.
2195 *Dorival, Gilles* L'originalité de la Bible grecque des Septante en matière de sacrifice. La cuisine et l'autel. BEHE.R 124: 2005 ⇒539. 309-315 [Gen 4,1-8].
2196 *Evans, T.V.* Approaches to the language of the Septuagint. JJS 56 (2005) 25-33.
2197 *Fernández Marcos, Natalio* Un manuscrito complutense redivivo Ms. griego 442 = Villa-Amil 22. Sef. 65 2005, 65-83 [1 Kgs 17,13-25; 2 Kgs 18,24-28; 19,1-5; 1 Macc 5,27-33];
2198 Certidumbres y enigmas del texto antioqueno en I-IV Reyes. AnScR 10 (2005) 155-168;
2199 **Fernández Marcos, Natalio** Introducción a las versiones griegas de la Biblia. TECC 64: [2]1998 ⇒14,1302... 18,1936. [R]NatGrac 52 (2005) 206-208 (*Sanz Acera, José María*).
**Fernández Marcos, Natalio**, *al.* Indice griego-hebreo del texto antioqueno en los libros históricos I-II 2005 ⇒2091-2092.
2200 **Field, Frederick** Frederick FIELD's Prolegomena to Origenis Hexaplorum quae supersunt, sive veterum interpretum graecorum in totum vetus testamentum graecorum. [E]*Norton, Gerard J.*: CRB 62: P 2005, Gabalda 202 pp. 2-85021-167-9. Bibl. 189-202.
2201 *García Martínez, Florentino* La Bible d'Alexandrie au miroir de Qumrân. RdQ 22 (2005) 253-268;
2202 La Genèse d'Alexandrie, les rabbins et Qumran. [F]LUTTIKHUIZEN, G.: AGJU 59: 2005 ⇒93. 21-41 [Gen 1,1; 1,26-27; 2,2].
2203 *Greenspoon, Leonard* Texts and contexts: perspectives on Jewish translations of the Hebrew Bible. Translation and religion. Topics in Translation 28: 2005 ⇒563. 54-64.
2204 *Hacham, Noah* The letter of Aristeas: a new Exodus story?. JSJ 36 (2005) 1-20.
2205 *Hanhart, Robert* Rechenschaftsbericht zur Editio altera der Handausgabe der Septuaginta von Alfred RAHLFS. VT 55 (2005) 450-460.

2206 **Hanhart, Robert** Studien zur Septuaginta und zum hellenistischen Judentum. [E]*Kratz, Reinhard G.*: FAT 24: 1999 ⇒15,1493... 17,1642. [R]OLZ 100 (2005) 194-198 (*Willi-Plein, Ina*).

2207 **Harl, Marguerite** La bible en Sorbonne ou la revanche d'ÉRASME. L'histoire à vif: 2004 ⇒20,2016. [R]RHPhR 85 (2005) 488-489 (*Prieur, J.-M.*); Sef. 65/1 (2005) 198-201 (*Fernández Marcos, Natalio*).

2208 *Hartman, Lars* Psychae-"själ"?: att läsa Septuaginta som grekisk text. SEÅ 70 (2005) 89-99.

2209 **Hengel, Martin** The Septuagint as christian scripture: its prehistory and the problem of its canon. [T]*Biddle, Mark E.*: 2004 <2002> ⇒ 18, 1939... 20,2019. [R]RBLit (2005)* (*De Troyer, Kristin*); HeyJ 46 (2005) 210-211 (*McNamara, Martin*).

2210 **Honigman, Sylvie** The Septuagint and Homeric scholarship in Alexandria: a study in the narrative of the Letter of Aristeas. 2003 ⇒19, 2058. [R]RSR 93 (2005) 609-611 (*Berthelot, Katell*); JJS 56 (2005) 146-148 (*Aitken, James*).

2211 *Jędrzejewski, Sylwester* Septuaginta—biblia helleńskiego judaizmu [Septuaginta—die Bibel des hellenistischen Judaismus]. RBL 58 (2005) 245-262. **P.**

2212 *Jinbachian, Manuel* The Septuagint, the first translation of its kind in history. Traduire la Bible hébraïque. 2005 ⇒728. 85-102.

2213 *Kranz, Dirk Kurt* Die theologischen Argumente der Kirchenväter (2.-4. Jh.) zugunsten der Inspiration der griechischen Übersetzung der Septuaginta (LXX). Alpha Omega 8 (2005) 231-262.

2214 *Larson, Erik W.* The LXX and Enoch: influence and interpretation in early Jewish literature. Enoch and Qumran origins. 2005 ⇒921. 84-89.

2215 **Léonas, Alexis** Recherches sur le langage de la Septante. [D]*Alexandre, Monique*: OBO 211: FrS 2005, Academic x; 340 pp. FS98. 3-7278-1510-8. Diss. Paris; Bibl. 254-324.

2216 **Loader, William R.G.** The Septuagint, sexuality, and the New Testament: case studies on the impact of the LXX in PHILO and the New Testament. 2004 ⇒20,2025. [R]CBQ 67 (2005) 355-356 (*Danker, Frederick W.*); AUSS 43 (2005) 219-221 (*Miller, James E.*); TJT 21 (2005) 250-252 (*Richards, William*); RBLit (2005) (*Hiebert, Robert; McEntire, Mark*); JThS 56 (2005) 596-598 (*Thiselton, Anthony C.*).

2217 *Lust, Johan* La syntaxe et le grec de traduction. L'apport de la Septante. LeDiv 203: 2005 ⇒764. 37-55.

2218 **McLay, Tim** The use of the Septuagint in New Testament research. 2003 ⇒19,2066; 20,2030. [R]ThLZ 130 (2005) 658-660 (*Kraus, Wolfgang*); WThJ 67 (2005) 176-179 (*Silva, Moisés*); AUSS 43 (2005) 363-364 (*Reeve, Teresa L.*); Neotest. 39 (2005) 454-457 (*Steyn, Gert J.*); VeE 26 (2005) 650-653 (*Steyn, Gert J.*).

2219 *Mélèze Modrzejewski, Joseph* The Septuagint as nomos: how the torah became a 'civic law' for the Jews in Egypt. ZSRG.R 120 (2005) 183-199.

2220 *Muraoka, Tahamitsu* Apports de la LXX dans notre compréhension de l'hébreu et du grec et de leur vocabulaire. L'apport de la Septante. LeDiv 203: 2005 ⇒764. 57-68;

2221 Gleanings of a Septuagint lexicographer. BIOSCS 38 (2005) 101-08;

2222 Why not a Morgenthaler for the Septuagint?. [F]LUST, J.: BEThL 192: 2005 ⇒92. 301-309.

2223 **Muraoka, Takamitsu** A Greek-English lexicon of the Septuagint: chiefly of the pentateuch and twelve prophets. 2002 ⇒18,1944; 20,2033. [R]REJ 164 (2005) 334-335 (*Rothschild, Jean-Pierre*); RSR 93 (2005) 606-607 (*Berthelot, Katell*).

2224 *Oegema, Gerbern S.* Aristeasbrief. Einführung zu den jüdischen Schriften. JSHRZ 2/1: 2005 ⇒453. 49-65.

2225 *Roukema, Riemer* L'interprétation patristique de quelques mots hébraïques de la Septante. L'apport de la Septante. LeDiv 203: 2005 ⇒ 764. 269-288.

2226 *Siegert, Folker* La bible des premiers chrétiens. ASEs 22/2 (2005) 409-419.

2227 **Siegert, Folker** Zwischen Hebräischer Bibel und Altem Testament: eine Einführung in die Septuaginta. Münster. judaistische Studien 9: 2001 ⇒17,1670...20,2041. [R]BZ 49 (2005) 312-314 (*Maier, Johann*).

2228 **Tilly, Michael** Einführung in die Septuaginta. Da:Wiss 2005, 135 pp. €15. 3-534-15631-5. [R]BiLi 78 (2005) 279-280 (*Hieke, Thomas*).

2229 *Tov, Emanuel* The evaluation of the Greek scripture translations in rabbinic sources. [F]LUST, J.: BEThL 192: 2005 ⇒92. 385-399;

2230 Les traducteurs des Écritures grecques et leurs approches des Écritures. Traduire la Bible hébraïque. 2005 ⇒728. 103-126.

2231 *Tremblay, Hervé* Autonomie de la Septante. Traduire la Bible hébraïque. 2005 ⇒728. 57-84.

2232 *Verwijs, Petra* The Septuagint in the Peshitta and Syro-Hexapla translations of Amos 1:3–2:16. BIOSCS 38 (2005) 25-40.

2233 *Voitila, Anssi* La Septante: un document linguistique de la koiné grecque antique?. L'apport de la Septante. LeDiv 203: 2005 ⇒764. 17-35.

2234 *Wevers, John W.* The Dead Sea scrolls and the Septuagint. BIOSCS 38 (2005) 1-24.

## D4 Versiones orientales

2235 **Avishur, Yitzhak** תַּרְגּוּם קָדוּם לִנְבִיאִים אַחֲרוֹנִים בַּעֲרָבִית-יְהוּדִית בַּבְלִית וְסוּרִית [A medieval translation of the latter prophets into Babylonian and Syrian Judaeo-Arabic]. יְשַׁעְיָהוּ וְיִרְמְיָהוּ כְּתַב יָד בּוֹדְלַיָנָה עִם מָבוֹא וְהֶעָרוֹת [Isaah and Jeremiah according to a manuscript of the Bodleian (Ms. Hunt 206)]. 1998 ⇒14,1321. [R]HebStud 46 (2005) 410-413 (*Hary, Benjamin*).

2236 *Behlmer, Heike* Paul de LAGARDE and the Coptic New Testament: a short note on archival material in the Lagarde papers. Arc 33 (2005) 23-31.

2237 *Cox, Claude E.* Biblical studies and the Armenian Bible, 1980-2002. RB 112 (2005) 355-368.

2238 *Greenberg, Gillian* The faith of the translator of the Peshitta: some indications in P-Isaiah. Studies in Jewish prayer. JSSt.S 17: 2005 ⇒ 828. 117-134.

2239 *Juckel, Andreas* Septuaginta and Peshitta: JACOB of Edessa quoting the Old Testament in Ms BL Add 17134. Hugoye 8/2 (2005)*.

2240 **Lange, Christian** The portrayal of Christ in the Syriac commentary on the Diatessaron. [D]*Brock, Sebastian*: CSCO 616; CSCO.S 118: Lv 2005, Peeters viii; 224 pp. 9042915692. Diss. Oxford; Bibl. 174-202.

2241 *Morrison, Craig E.* The relationship of the Peshitta text of Second Samuel with the Peshitta text of First Chronicles. AramSt 3 (2005) 59-81.

2242 The new covenant community called the New Testament: Aramaic Peshitta text with a Hebrew translation. J [2]2005 <1887-1891; 1951>, Bible Society; The Aramaic Research Society in Israel. [R]Ang. 82 (2005) 484-485 (*Mirri, Luciana Maria*).

2243 *Pasini, Cesare* Per la storia della siro-esaplare Ambrosiana (alla luce delle annotazioni siriache e copta recentemente rinvenute sul codice). OCP 71 (2005) 21-58.

2244 *Petersen, William L.* Canonicité, autorité ecclésiastique et *Diatessaron* de TATIEN. Le canon du NT. MoBi 54: 2005 ⇒334. 87-116.

2245 *Pztikian, Haroutiun* Hebräismen in der armenischen Übersetzung der Bibel. HandAm 118/1-12 (2005) 147-166.

2246 [E]**Schüssler, Karlheinz** Das sahidische Alte und Neue Testament: vollständiges Verzeichnis mit Standorten, Bd. 3: Lfg.2: sa 521-540. Biblia Coptica 3/2: 2003 ⇒19,2095. [R]OLZ 100 (2005) 405-408 (*Feder, Frank*); RBLit 7 (2005) 78-80 (*Seesengood, Robert P.*).

2247 **Shedinger, Robert F.** TATIAN and the Jewish scriptures: a textual and philological analysis of the Old Testament citations in Tatian's Diatessaron. CSCO 591; CSCO.Sub 109: 2001 ⇒17,1699... 20,2060. [R]RBLit (2005)* (*Petersen, William*).

2248 *Ter Haar Romeny, Robert B.* Choosing a textual basis for the new English annotated translation of the Syriac Bible. AramSt 3 (2005) 167-186.

2249 [T]**Weinberg, Joanna** Azariah de' ROSSI's Observation on the Syriac New Testament: a critique of the Vulgate by a sixteenth-century Jew. Warburg Institute Studies and Texts 3: L 2005, Warburg Institute vi; 109 pp.

2250 *Yousif, P.* Syriaques (versions): bibliographie 1955-2000. DBS 13/75. 2005 ⇒970. 828-875.

## D5.0 **Versiones latinae**; *Citationes apud Patres*—**The Patristic Bible**

2251 AVL 38. FrB 2005, Herder 63 pp.

2252 *Bandera, Sandrina* Les premiers manuscrits de l'abbaye de Morimondo et leurs relations avec la région d'origine: l'histoire des filles aide à construire l'histoire des mères. L'abbaye cistercienne de Morimond: histoire et rayonnement. [E]**Viard, Georges**: Langres 2005, Assoc. amis de l'abbaye de Morimond. 279-309. Coll. Langres 2003.

2253 *Bassetti, Massimiliano* Le bibbie imperiali d'età carolingia ed ottoniana. Forme e modelli. 2005 ⇒368. 175-265 [RBen 118,153—P.-M. Bogaert].

2254 *Beall, Barbara A.* Entry point to the scriptorium BEDE knew at Wearmouth and Jarrow: the canon tables of the Codex Amiatinus. Bède le Vénérable. 2005 ⇒849. 187-197 [RBen 116,161—P.-M. Bogaert].

2255 **Boeckler, Albert** Das Goldene Evangeliumbuch Heinrichs III. Lp 2004 <1933>, Holzminden 158 pp. €30. 38262-0221X. Vorwort *Johannes G. Mayer* [Scr. 60,149*—F.O. Büttner].

2256 *Bouton-Touboulic, Anne-Isabelle* Autorité et tradition: la traduction latine de la bible selon Saint JÉRÔME et Saint AUGUSTIN. Aug. 45 (2005) 231-258.

2257 *Brown, Michele P.* Predicando con la penna: il contributo insulare alla trasmissione dei testi sacri dal VI al IX secolo. Forme e modelli. 2005 ⇒368. 61-108 [RBen 118,151—P.-M. Bogaert].

2258 *Brown, Virginia* I libri della bibbia nell'ìItalia meridionale longobarda. Forme e modelli. 2005 ⇒368. 281-307 [RBen 118,154—P.-M. Bogaert].

2259 *Buzzetti, Carlo* Presenza plurale e simbolo unificante: il latino nella storia delle traduzioni della bibbia. RivLi 92 (2005) 225-238.

2260 *Cherubini, Paolo* Le bibbie spagnole in visigotica. Forme e modelli. 2005 ⇒368. 109-173 [RBen 118,152—P.-M. Bogaert].

2261 *Condello, Emma* La bibbia al tempo della riforma gregoriana. Forme e modelli. 2005 ⇒368. 347-372 [RBen 118,154—P.-M. Bogaert].

2262 *Dahan, Gilbert* Les éditions des commentaires bibliques de Saint THOMAS d'Aquin: leur apport à la connaissance du texte de la bible au XIIIe siécle. RSPhTh 89 (2005) 9-15.

2263 *Elder, Marcus* New leaves for the Tours Bible of Saint MAXIMIN at Trier. New studies on Yale manuscripts. 2005 ⇒606. 45-60 [Scr. 60/1,46*—M. Huglo].

2264 *Elsakkers, Marianne* Gothic Bible, Vetus Latina and Visigothic law: evidence for a Septuagint-based Gothic version of Exodus. SE 44 (2005) 37-76 [Exod 21,22-23].

2265 *Eymann, Hugo S.* Zur Textüberlieferung der Schriften des EUTROPIUS. BVLI 49 (2005) 51-54.

2266 **Frede, Hermann; Gryson, Roger** Kirchenschriftsteller, Verzeichnis und Sigel: Aktualisierungsheft 2004 - Compléments 2004. VL.AGLB 1/1D: 2004 ⇒20,2075. [R]JThS 56 (2005) 618-620 (*Elliott, J.K.*).

2267 **Goins, Scott E.** A Vulgate Old Testament reader. Gorgias handbooks 1: Piscataway, NJ 2005, Gorgias xx; 153 pp. 1-593-33215-7.

2268 *Lobrichon, Guy* Le bibbie ad immagini, secoli XII-XV. Forme e modelli. 2005 ⇒368. 423-457 [RBen 118,155—P.-M. Bogaert].

2269 *Lowden, John* The *Bible moralisée* in the fifteenth century and the challenge of the *Bible historiale*. JWCI 68 (2005) 73-136 [RBen 118, 155–P.-M. Bogaert].

2270 *Magrini, Sabina* La bibbia di Matheus de Planisio (Vat. lat. 3550, I-III): documenti e modelli per lo studio della produzione scritturale in età angioina. Codices Manuscripti 50-51 (2005) 1-16;

2271 La bibbia all'università (secoli XII-XIV): la 'Bible de Paris' e la sua influenza sulla produzione scritturale coeva. Forme e modelli. 2005 ⇒368. 407-421 [RBen 118,156—P.-M. Bogaert].

2272 *Manfredi, Antonio* Manoscritti biblici nelle biblioteche umanistiche tra Firenze e Roma: una prima recognizione. Forme e modelli. 2005 ⇒368. 459-501 [RBen 118,156—P.-M. Bogaert].

2273 *Marone, Paola* Note sul testo biblico di OTTATO. SMSR 29 (2005) 309-336.

2274 *Martins, Maria Manuela B. Habitatio* e *aedificatio* na bíblia latina. Did(L) 35 (2005) 685-699.

2275 *Moussy, C.* Nouveaux préverbés en *com-* dans la Vetus Latina et dans la Vulgate. Latin et langues romanes: études de linguistique offertes à József Herman de son 80ème anniversaire. [E]**Kiss, Sándor; Mondin, Luca; Salvi, Giampaolo** Tü 2005, Niemeyer. €154. 3-484-50508-7. 327-336 [RBen 116,147—P.-M. Bogaert.

2276 **Mundó, A.M.** Les bíblies de Ripoll: estudi dels mss. Vaticà, lat. 5729 i París, BNF, lat.6. StT 408: 2002 ⇒19,2111. [R]RCatT 30/1 (2005) 241-242 (*Gros i Pujol, Miquel S.*).

2277 *Noble, Thomas F.X.* The bible in the *Codex Carolinus*. Biblical studies in the early Middle Ages. 2005 ⇒773. 61-74 [RBen 116,146 —P.-M. Bogaert].

2278 *Petrucci Nardelli, Franca* L'evangeliario de S. Maria in Via Lata et la sua legatura: nuovi dati e nuove ipotesi. Miscellanea Bibliothecae Apostolicae Vaticanae 10. Studi e Testi 416: Città del Vaticano 2003, Biblioteca Apostolica Vaticana. 207-225. 88210-07596.

2279 *Schaab, Rupert* Die Heiligen Schriften der Karolinger. Heilige Schriften. 2005 ⇒362. 101-117, 242-243.

2280 *Schmid, Ulrich* "Unum ex quattuor": eine Geschichte der lateinischen Tatianüberlieferung. BVLI 49 (2005) 47-51.

2281 **Schmid, Ulrich** Unum ex quattuor: eine Geschichte der lateinischen Tatianüberlieferung. VL.AGLB 37: FrB 2005, Herder xiv; 401 pp. €68. 3-451-21955-7. Bibl. 379-393.

2282 *Tischler, Matthias* Die glossierten Bibeln von Saint-Victor. Schrift, Schreiber, Schenker: Studien zur Abtei Sankt Viktor und den Viktorinern. Corpus Victorinum, Instrumenta 1: B 2005, Akademie. 67-74 [RBen 118,156–P.-M. Bogaert].

2283 *Vezin, Jean* I libri dei Salmi e dei vangeli durante l'alto medioevo. Forme e modelli. 2005 ⇒368. 267-279 [RBen 118,153—P.-M. Bogaert].

2284 *Vogtherr, Thomas* Auf der Suche nach dem rechten Text: die Bibel und ihr Wortlaut in der Zeit der Karolinger. Das Buch. Vechtaer Beiträge zur Theologie 11: 2005 ⇒1130. 49-62.

2285 *Zanna, Paolo* La bibbia in Dúngal. Biblical studies in the early Middle Ages. 2005 ⇒773. 127-142 [RBen 116,146—P.-M. Bogaert].

## D6 Versiones modernae .1 *romanicae*, romance

2286 **Alves, Herculano** A bíblia de Joao Ferreira Annes D'Almeida. Tesis 28: S 2005, Univ. Pont. 96 pp. 972-652-227-7. Extr. Diss.

2287 **Avenoza, G.** La Biblia de Ajuda y la Megl.lat Antiochus en romance. Biblioteca de filología hispánica 25: 2001 ⇒18,2006. [R]CDios 218 (2005) 255-256 (*Gutiérrez, J.*).

2288 Bíblia de Jerusalém. 2003 ⇒18,2012; 19,2125. nova edição. [R]REB 65 (2005) 207-209 (*Pereira, Ney Brasil*).

2289 Bíblia sagrada: nova tradução na linguagem de hoje. São Paulo 2005, Paulinas 1472 pp.

2290 La biblia. [E]**Ausejo, Serafín de; Villanueva, Marciano** Barc 2005, Herder 1866 pp. 84-254-2432-1.

2291 [E]**Blanchi, Antonin** Le Nouveau Testament de Jacques Lefèvre d'Etaples, Nice 1525. Nice 2005, Serre 400 pp. 2-86410-421-0. Edition intégrale de l'exemplaire de Nice, dans une orthographe et une ponctuation d'aujourd'hui, augmentée de numéro de versets de soustitres...[BHR 67,767s—Engammare, Max].

2292 *Bonilla Acosta, Plutarco* Reina-Valera, una versione di oggi o di ieri?. I vangeli. 2005 ⇒432. 177-183.

2293 *Buzzetti, Carlo* La bibbia in "lingua corrente" si usa nella liturgia?. RivLi 92 (2005) 262-265.

2294 [E]**Casanellas i Bassolo, Pere** Corpus Biblicum Catalanicum, 3: Èxode; Levític. 2004 ⇒20,2105. [R]AST 78-79 (2005-2006) 642-644 (*Ferrer, Joan*).

2295 *Casciaro, José María* La biblia de la Universidad de Navarra. ScrTh 37 (2005) 595-603.

2296 *Chapa, Juan* Breve historia de un proyecto. ScrTh 37 (2005) 569-572.

2297 *Contessa, Andreina* Facta sunt coelum, maria [et] terrae: la creazione nelle bibbie catalane di Ripoll e Roda. Miscellanea Bibliothecae Apostolicae Vaticanae 12. Studi e Testi 430: Città del Vaticano 2005, Biblioteca Apostolica Vaticana. 83-156.

2298 *Fontán, Antonio* La Biblia de Navarra y la historia de la biblia. ScrTh 37 (2005) 573-583.

2299 **Fragnito, Gigliola** La bibbia al rogo: la censura ecclesiastica e i volgarizzamenti della Scrittura (1471-1605). Saggi 460: Bo 2005, Il Mulino 345 pp. 88150-57498.

2300 [E]**Gomez-Géraud, M.-C.** La bible nouvellement translatée: avec la suite de l'histoire depuis le temps d'Esdras jusqu'aux Maccabées: et depuis les Maccabées jusqu'à Christ: item avec des annotations sur les passages difficiles. [T]*Castellion, Sebastian*: P 2005 <1555>, Bayard 2974 pp. €179. 22274-75447. Préf. de *J. Roubaud*; Introd. de *Pierre Gibert*.

2301 **Lassave, Pierre** Bible: la traduction des alliances: enquête sur un événement littéraire. Logiques sociales: P 2005, L'Harmattan 267 pp. €24.50. 2-7475-9481-5. La Bible des écrivains.

2302 Nouveau Testament: La Bible de Jérusalem. P 2002, Cerf 510 pp. [R]ScEs 57 (2005) 173-175 (*Gourgues, Michel*).

2303 *Romero Pose, Eugenio* Una biblia en la tradición de la iglesia. ScrTh 37 (2005) 585-593.

## D6.2 *Versiones anglicae*—**English Bible Translations**

2304 *Arblaster, Paul; Juhász, Gergely* Can translating the bible be bad for your health?: William TYNDALE and the falsification of memory. More than a memory. ANL 51: 2005 ⇒560. 315-340.

2305 **Armstrong, D.; Thigpen, P.** The new catholic answer bible. Huntington, IN 2005, Our Sunday Visitor xxix; 1,395; 88 pp. $30. 1-592-76-140-2. New American Bible; Inserts [ThD 52,247—W.C. Heiser].

2306 *Beck, Norman* Translations of the New Testament for our time. Seeing Judaism anew. 2005 ⇒618. 200-210 [Rom 11,11-32].

2307 *Blomberg, Craig L.* Today's New International Version: the untold story of a good translation. BiTr 56 (2005) 187-211.

2308 *Byassee, J.* Beautiful words: the St. John's Bible project. CCen 122/16 (2005) 20-21, 23 [NTAb 50,15].

2309 **Calderhead, Christopher** Illuminating the word: making the Saint John's Bible. 2004 ⇒20,2113. [R]ABenR 56 (2005) 315-321 (*Kardong, Terrence*).

2310 The Catholic comparative New Testament. NY 2005, OUP xxxviii; 1762 pp. $33 [BiTod 44,197—Donald Senior].

2311 **Daniell, David** The bible in English: its history and influence. 2003 ⇒19,2147; 20,2114. [R]BiTr 56 (2005) 214-216 (*Ellingworth, Paul*); RBLit (2005)* (*Shavit, Yaakob*).

2312 **Dewey, David** Which bible?: a guide to English translations. 2004 ⇒20,2115. [R]VeE 26 (2005) 647-648 (*Venter, P.M.*).

2313 *Greenspoon, Leonard J.* The holy bible: a buyer's guide. BiRe 21/4 (2005) 37-44 [OTA 29,9].
2314 **Grudem, Wayne A.; Poythress, Vern S.** The TNIV and the gender-neutral bible controversy. Nv 2004, Broadman & H. xxxiii; 494 pp. $25. [R]RBLit (2005)* (*Matos, Joseph*).
2315 **Jackson, Donald** The Saint John's Bible: Gospels and Acts. 2004 ⇒20,2118. [R]BiTod 43 (2005) 256-260 (*Bergant, Dianne*).
2316 **Katz, David S.** God's last words: reading the English Bible from the Reformation to fundamentalism. 2004 ⇒20,2119. [R]JEH 56 (2005) 384-386 (*Gribben, Crawford*); ChH 74 (2005) 378-380 (*Thuesen, Peter J.*); RBLit (2005)* (*Shavit, Yaakob*); JThS 56 (2005) 267-269 (*Oliver, P.M.*).
2317 [T]**King, Nicholas** The New Testament, freshly translated. Stowmarket 2005, Mayhew 654 pp. £20. 1-84417-324-0. [R]ScrB 35 (2005) 103-104 (*Wansbrough, Henry*).
2318 [E]**Law, Philip J.** Testament: the bible odyssey. NY 2005, Continuum 704 pp. $17. 0-8264-7734-8. Abridgement of whole bible.
2319 *Lloyd Jones, Gareth* People of the book: King James' men. ScrB 35 (2005) 31-41.
2320 *McClymond, Michael J.* Through a gloss darkly: biblical annotations and theological interpretation in modern Catholic and Protestant English-language bibles. TS 67 (2005) 477-497.
2321 *Naudé, Jacobus A.* Twentieth-century English bible translations. AcTh(B) 25/2 (2005) 70-89.
2322 New International Version: faith in action study bible: living God's word in a changing world. GR 2005, Zondervan xvi; 2315 pp. $40. 0-310-92862-1. With World Vision [ThD 52,368—W. Charles Heiser].
2323 **Norton, David** A textual history of the King James Bible. C 2005, CUP xii; 387 pp. $95. 0-521-77100-5. Bibl. 362-367.
2324 [E]**Norton, David** The New Cambridge Paragraph Bible: with the Apocrypha, King James Version. C 2005, CUP xxxvi; 1868 pp. £45. 0-521-84386-3.
2325 *Patella, Michael* The Saint John's Bible: text, metaphor, and exegesis. Council of Societies for the Study of Religion Bulletin [Houston, TX] 34/1-2 (2005) 22-26 [NTAb 50,17].
2326 *Schemm, P.R., al.* JBMW responds to the TNIV. JBMW 10/2 (2005) 1-65 [NTAb 50,247].
2327 [E]**Sproul, R.C.** The Reformation study bible: English Standard Version: containing the Old and New Testaments. Orlando, FL 2005, Ligonier M. xvii; 1948 pp. $40. 08755-26438. [NTAb 50,157].
2328 *Strauss, Mark L.* Form, function, and the 'literal meaning': fallacy in English bible translation. BiTr 56 (2005) 153-168.
2329 **Walden, W.** Encyclopedia of the formation of the Bible: manuscripts and translations. Nv 2005, Walden, W. vi; 159 pp. $40. Bibl. [NTAb 50,158].

### D6.3 *Versiones germanicae*—**Deutsche Bibelübersetzungen**

2330 [E]**Arenhoevel, Heinrich** Die Bibel: mit umfassenden Informationen zur Welt und Umwelt der Bibel; [Einheitsübersetzung]. Stu 2005, Katholisches Bibelwerk 360; 1454 pp. 978-3-460-31944-8.

2331 *Baumann, Gerlinde* Eine neue Stimme im Chor der Bibelübersetzungen: die "Bibel in gerechter Sprache" im Vergleich mit neuen deutschen Bibelübersetzungen. Die Bibel—übersetzt. 2005 ⇒423. 186-199.

2332 **Bechtoldt, Hans-Joachim** Jüdische deutsche Bibelübersetzungen vom ausgehenden 18. bis zum Beginn des 20. Jahrhunderts. [D]*Mayer, Günter*: Stu 2005, Kohlhammer 682 pp. €60. 3-17-018667-1. Diss.-Habil. Mainz.

2333 *Brecht, Martin; Peters, Robert* Theodor Smedeckens niederdeutsche Übertragung von LUTHERs Neuem Testament: dorch M. Theodoricum Smedecken yn der Sassen dudesch vorwandelt. LuJ 72 (2005) 49-76.

2334 *Butting, Klara; Janssen, Claudia* Die Bibel in gerechter Sprache am Beispiel der Begriffe Sünde und Gnade: ein Interview mit Klara Butting und Claudia Janssen. JK 66/1 (2005) 45-49.

2335 *Crüsemann, Marlene* Zur Übersetzung und graphischen Gestaltung des Gottesnamens in beiden Testamenten der "Bibel in gerechter Sprache". Die Bibel—übersetzt. 2005 ⇒423. 173-177.

2336 *Dieckmann, Detlef* "Die neue Bibelübersetzung soll dem gegenwärtigen Gespräch mit Jüdinnen und Juden gerecht werden": Die Bibel in gerechter Sprache und der christlich-jüdische Dialog. Dialog-Du Siach 59 (2005) 10-17.

2337 *Ebach, Jürgen; Steffensky, Fulbert* Die Bibel in gerechter Sprache: ein Briefwechsel zwischen Jürgen Ebach und Fulbert Steffensky. JK 66/1 (2005) 49-52.

2338 [E]**Fricke, Klaus Dietrich; Meurer, Siegfried** Die Geschichte der Lutherbibelrevision: von den Anfängen 1850 bis 1984. Arbeiten zur Geschichte und Wirkung der Bibel 1: 2001 ⇒17,1763; 18,2063. [R]ThR 70 (2005) 383-384 (*Lindemann, Andreas*).

2339 *Kürschner, Wilfried* "Biblia: das ist: Die gantze Heilige Schrifft: Deudsch / Auffs new zugericht. D. Mart. Luth.": sprachliche Erkundungen zu LUTHERs Bibelübersetzung und ihren "neuen Zurichtungen" (Revisionen). Das Buch. 2005 ⇒1130. 63-78.

2340 Leben mit der Bibel in vier Jahrhunderten. Schwerin 2005, Heinrich-Theissing-Institut 180 pp. €14.90. 3-9810-1690-4. Exhibition 2005.

2341 *Migsch, Herbert* Eine zielsprachliche Kohärenzstörung in der Wiedergabe von Jer 35Vulg,8-9 in der vorreformatorischen deutschen Bibel: ein Beitrag zur Erforschung der vorausliegenden handschriftlichen Überlieferung. BN 124 (2005) 19-27.

2342 *Mokrosch, Reinhold* Struwwelpeter oder die Bibel—was war die bessere Moralfibel?: Kinderbibeln im 19. und 20. Jahrhundert;

2343 *Nauerth, Thomas* In welcher Reihenfolge soll ich servieren?: Anmerkungen zu Komposition und Aufbau neuerer Kinderbibeln. Das Buch. 2005 ⇒1130. 101-113/202-209.

2344 *Ortkemper, Franz-Josef* EKD und Einheitsübersetzung. BiHe 41/164 (2005) 26-27.

2345 *Pilvousek, Josef* Gedruckte deutsche Bibeln vor LUTHER: Anmerkungen zur deutschen Bibelrezeption. Heilige Schriften. 2005 ⇒362. 118-131, 243-244.

2346 *Wachinger, Lorenz* 80 Jahre BUBER-ROSENZWEIG-Bibel. StZ 223 (2005) 601-612.

2347 *Wellmann, Bettina* Der Streit um die Einheitsübersetzung. BiHe 41/164 (2005) 25-27.

## D6.4 **Versiones nederlandicae** *et variae*

2348 *Abela, Anthony* What is 'new' in the new edition of *Il-Bibbja*?. MTh 56/2 (2005) 3-12.
2349 *Becking, Bob* Het boek Jeremia in de NBV: zwakte en sterkte van een eigenzinnige "versio moderna". NedThT 59/4 (2005) 274-284.
2350 **Besten, Leen den** Het uitgelezen boek: de bijbel in Nederland. Zoetermeer 2005, Meinema 260 pp. €18.90. 90-211-4041-1.
2351 *Bouwer, Johan* De Nieuwe Bijbelvertaling en geestelijke zorgverlening: een kritische evaluatie. NedThT 59/4 (2005) 329-342.
2352 *Buitenwerf, Rieuwerd* The new Dutch translation of the bible: principles, problems, and solutions. BiTr 56 (2005) 253-261.
2353 *Buitenwerf, Rieuwerd* Twee literaire bijbelvertalingen. Theologisch debat 2/1 (2005) 52-57.
2354 *Burger, Hilde* De taal van het verhaal. ITBT 13/2 (2005) 27-29.
2355 De bijbel: de nieuwe bijbelvertaling: complete katholieke editie met inleidingen. 's-Hertogenbosch 2005, Katholieke Bijbelstichting 2092 pp. 90-6173-800-8.
2356 *Desnitsky, Andrei S.* The Septuagint as a base text for bible translations in Russia. BiTr 56 (2005) 245-252.
2357 *Drieënhuizen, Tineke* Jona in de herhaling. ACEBT 22 (2005) 59-70. Repetition in the New Dutch Bible Translation [OTA 30,368].
2358 *Ďurica, Ján* Boetkov preklad písma s komentármi Jeruzalemskej Biblie [Botek's translation of the scripture with the commentaries of Jerusalem Bible]. SBSl (2005) 89-93. **Slovak.**
2359 *Falluomini, Carla* sagi[]o und nicht sau[]o: zu 1 Kor. 15,2 in der gotischen Bibel. ZDA 133 (2004) 75-79 [Scr. 60,175*—B. Gullath].
2360 *François, Wim* Jacob van Liesvelt, martyr for the evangelical belief?. More than a memory. ANL 51: 2005 ⇒560. 341-369.
2361 **François, Wim** Bijbelvertalingen in de Lage Landen (1477-1553): een kerkhistorische en theologische benadering. [D]*Lamberigts, M.* 2005, xliii; 652 pp. Diss. Leuven.
2362 [E]**Gillaerts, Paul** Boanerges: beschouwingen over bijbel(vertaling) en retorica. 2004 ⇒20,2158. [R]Streven 72 (2005) 657-658 (*Beentjes, Panc*).
2363 *Heikens, Henk* Namen in de NBV: meer consistentie nodig in vertaling. ITBT 13/2 (2005) 7-10.
2364 *Jobsen, Aarnoud* Geitensater en runderzoon: impressies bij de introductie van de Naardense Bijbel en de Nieuwe Bijbelvertaling. ITBT 13/1 (2005) 26-28.
2365 **Lambrecht, Jan** 'Recht op de waarheid af': bijdragen over Paulus, de evangeliën en de Nieuwe Bijbelvertaling. Lv 2005, Acco 192 pp. €18.60. 90-334-5805-5.
2366 [E]**Larsson, T.; Olsson, B.** Den gamla översättningen: Karl XII:s bibel och dess receptionshistoria: föredrag vid en konferens i Lund den 21-25 februari 2003 anordnad av Kung,. Humanistiska Vetenskapssamfundet i Lund. Acta Regiae Societatis Humaniorum Litterarum Lundensis 84: Sto 2005, Almqvist & W. 350 pp. SKr346. 91220-21272. [NTAb 50,153].
2367 *Loden, L.* Two Hebrew New Testaments–a survey. Mishkan [J] 43 (2005) 71-74 [NTAb 50,17].

2368 *Maluleke, T.S.* The next phase in the vernacular bible discourse: echoes from Hammanskraal. Missionalia 33 (2005) 355-374 [NTAb 50,247].

2369 Naardense bijbel. Vught 2005, Skandalon €39.50. 90-765-6413-2. CD-ROM [ITBT 13/7,34—Joep Dubbink].

2370 *Pander, Halina Urszula* Bibbia e testi liturgici nella pastorale per gli zingari. People on the move 37 (2005) 89-99.

2371 Pismo Swiete Nowego Testamentu i Psalmy: najnowszy przekład z jezyków oryginalnych z komentarzem. Czestochowa 2005, Swiety Paweł 827 pp. 83-7424-076-8. Opracował Zespół Biblistów Polskich z inicjatywy Towarzystwa Swietego Pawła. [R]CoTh 75/3 (2005) 231-235 (*Wojciechowski, Michał*). **P.**

2372 *Pritz, R.* Peculiarities of translating the NT into Hebrew. Mishkan [J] 43 (2005) 63-70 [NTAb 50,17].

2373 *Reidar Osnes, Egil* Er NTR et skritt i riktig retning?: et forsøk på vurdering av NTRs kvaliteter som bibeloversettelse. Ung teologi 38/3 (2005) 23-35.

2374 *Roest, Henk de* De Nieuwe Bijbelvertaling en de schriftlezing: een kleine praktisch-theologische evaluatie. NedThT 59/4 (2005) 312-328.

2375 *Schmidt, Peter* Het kan ook anders: beschouwingen bij De Nieuwe Bijbelvertaling. Coll. 35/2 (2005) 115-134.

2376 *Schoors, Antoon* Bijbel en bijbelvertalingen. AnBru 10 (2005) 13-29.

2377 *Smelik, Klaas A.* De Nieuwe Bijbelvertaling nader bekeken. AnBru 10 (2005) 30-37.

2378 *Tigchelaar, Eibert J.* Herleven de Dode-Zeerollen in De Nieuwe Bijbelvertaling?. NedThT 59/4 (2005) 285-296.

2379 **Timm, Erika** Historische jiddische Semantik: die Bibelübersetzungssprache als Faktor der Auseinanderentwicklung des jiddischen und des deutschen Wortschatzes. Tü 2005, Niemeyer viii; 736 pp. €112. 3-484-73063-3.

2380 *Van Oyen, Geert* De NBV: meer dan een vertaling. NedThT 59/4 (2005) 297-311 [Mk 1,1-15].

2381 *Vlieger, Jan de* De Naardense Bijbel: verzilvering van een Amsterdams/Brusselse erfenis. AnBru 10 (2005) 51-54.

### D7 *Problema vertentis*—**Bible translation techniques**

2382 *Bail, Ulrike* Wie Gott und Mensch zur Sprache kommen ... Überlegungen zu einer Bibel in gerechter Sprache. Die Bibel—übersetzt. 2005 ⇒423. 61-76.

2383 *Barnard, Benno* Iemand sta God bij: over de methode van een nieuwe bijbelvertaling. AnBru 10 (2005) 38-44.

2384 *Blight, Richard C.* Footnotes for meaningful translations of the New Testament. JOT 1/1 (2005) 7-46.

2385 *Bock, Darrell L.* You make the call: are gender-sensitive translations safe or out?. BiTr 56 (2005) 169-187.

2386 [E]**Brenner, Athalya; Van Henten, Jan W.** Bible translation on the threshold of the twenty-first century: authority, reception, culture and religion. JSOT.S 353; The Bible in the 21st century 1: 2002 ⇒18, 281... 20,2183. [R]BiTr 56 (2005) 211-214 (*Ellington, John*).

2387 *Brumlik, Micha* Jüdische Erwartungen an eine christliche Bibelübersetzung. Die Bibel—übersetzt. 2005 ⇒423. 132-147 [κύριος].

2388 [E]**Bussmann, Britta; Hausmann, Albrecht** Übertragungen, Formen und Konzepte von Reproduktion in Mittelalter und früher Neuzeit. B 2005, De Gruyter 478 pp. £78. 3-110-18339-0.

2389 *Buzzetti, Carlo* Translator training: a European perspective. BiTr 56 (2005) 87-91.

2390 *Clark, David J.* 'Surnames' in the Old Testament?: or: how to be rude politely. BiTr 56 (2005) 232-238.

2391 *David, Robert* L'analyse syntaxique, outil pour la traduction biblique: le cas des cohortatifs. Traduire la Bible hébraïque. 2005 ⇒728. 275-318.

2392 *De Benedetti, Paolo* Del tradurre la scrittura: ovvero alla ricerca dei sensi perduti. [F]GHIBERTI, G.: SRivBib 46: 2005 ⇒47. 277-281.

2393 *Desnitsky, Andrei S.* Training translation teams. BiTr 56 (2005) 98-105.

2394 *Dooley, Robert A.* Source-language versus target-language discourse features in translating the word of God. JOT 1/2 (2005) 1-18.

2395 *Ebach, Jürgen* Wie kann die Bibel gerecht(er) übersetzt werden?;

2396 Zur Wiedergabe des Gottesnamens in einer Bibelübersetzung oder: welche "Lösungen" es für ein unlösbares Problem geben könnte. Die Bibel—übersetzt. 2005 ⇒423. 36-60/150-158.

2397 *Elliott, John H.* Deuteronomy 25:11-12 LXX: no tweaking the twins: more on a biblical euphemism and its translations. [F]STEGEMANN, W. 2005 ⇒139. 323-342.

2398 *Erbele-Küster, Dorothea* Ungerechte Texte und gerechte Sprache: Überlegungen zur Hermeneutik des Bibelübersetzens. Die Bibel—übersetzt. 2005 ⇒423. 222-234;

2399 Ungerechte (biblische) Texte und gerechte Sprache: Überlegungen zur Hermeneutik des Übersetzens. AnStR 6 (2005) 357-369.

2400 *Hess, Richard S.* Adam, father, he: gender issues in Hebrew translation. BiTr 56 (2005) 144-153.

2401 *Holter, Knut* Recent literature on Old Testament translation in Africa. BOTSA 18 (2005) 20-23.

2402 *Horrell, David G.* Familiar friend or alien stranger?: on translating the bible. ET 116 (2005) 402-408.

2403 *Janssen, Claudia; Schottroff, Luise* Übersetzungsfragen zu Herrschaft und Sklaverei. Die Bibel—übersetzt. 2005 ⇒423. 212-221.

2404 *Jasper, David* Settling *Hoti*'s business: the impossible necessity of biblical translation [Mk 4];

2405 *Kirk, Peter* Holy communicative?: current approaches to bible translation worldwide. Translation and religion. Topics in Translation 28: 2005 ⇒563. 105-114/89-101.

2406 *Kuhlmann, Helga* In welcher Weise kann die Sprache einer Bibelübersetzung "gerecht" sein?;

2407 *Leutzsch, Martin* Dimensionen gerechter Bibelübersetzung. Ment. *Ragaz, L.* [Gen 3,16; Mt 5,9];

2408 Inklusive Sprache in der Bibelübersetzung. Die Bibel—übersetzt. 2005 ⇒423. 77-98/16-35/200-209.

2409 *Levoratti, Armando J.* La traduzione e le traduzioni della bibbia: introduzione. I vangeli. 2005 ⇒432. 159-167;

2410 Traduzione e transculturazione. I vangeli. 2005 ⇒432. 168-172.

2411 **Long, Lynne** Translating the Bible: from the 7th to the 17th century. 2001 ⇒17,1833... 20,2199. RScrB 35 (2005) 95-97 (*King, Nicholas*).

2412 E**Long, Lynne** Translation and religion: holy untranslatable?. Topics in Translation 28: Clevedon 2005, Multilingual M. vi; 209 pp. 1-853-59-8186.

2413 *McElhanon, Kenneth A.* From word to scenario: the influence of linguistic theories upon models of translation. JOT 1/3 (2005) 29-67.

2414 **Munteanu, Stefan** Les traductions interconfessionnelles de la bible: étude critique et comparative d'un phenomène moderne. D*Henn, William*: R 2005, 442 pp. Diss. Gregoriana; Bibl. 413-431.

2415 *Noss, Philip A.* A translator's trail: from engagement to ideophones through ideophones to engagement. Traduire la Bible hébraïque. 2005 ⇒728. 351-374.

2416 *Pattemore, Stephen; Ogden, Graham S.* Translator training in the UBS Asia-Pacific region. BiTr 56 (2005) 105-108.

2417 **Poythress, Vern; Grudem, Wayne** The gender neutral bible controversy. 2003 ⇒19,2223. RSBET 23 (2005) 91-2 (*Maciver, James*).

2418 *Redzich, Carola* Mittelalterliche Bibelübersetzung und der Übersetzungsbegriff. Übertragungen. 2005 ⇒2388. 259-278 [Scr. 60/1, 106*—G. Hendrix].

2419 *Salevsky, Heidemarie* Auf der Suche nach der Wahrheit bei der Bibelübersetzung: ein Beitrag aus translationswissenschaftlicher Sicht am Beispiel der Hagar-Geschichte, Gen 16; 21; 25. Die Bibel—übersetzt. 2005 ⇒423. 100-131.

2420 *Sánchez Sánchez, Edesio* Traduzione della bibbia e cultura indigena. I vangeli. 2005 ⇒432. 173-176.

2421 *Shackle, Christopher* From gentlemen's outfitters to hyperbazaar: a personal approach to translating the sacred. Translation and religion. Topics in Translation 28: 2005 ⇒2412. 19-32.

2422 *Steinacker, Peter* Geleitwort. Die Bibel—übersetzt. 2005 ⇒423. 7-12.

2423 *Tauberschmidt, Gerhard* Considerations for OT translation. JOT 1/1 (2005) 61-73.

2424 *Voinov, Vitaly* Pronominal apostasy?: or: whose God do you mean?. BiTr 56 (2005) 239-245.

2425 *Voth, Esteban* Training program for translators in Latin America. BiTr 56 (2005) 91-97.

2426 *Weber, David J.* A tale of two translation theories. JOT 1/2 (2005) 35-74.

2427 *Zaborski, Andrzej* Jak przekazać przykazania i inne teksty biblijne? [How to translate the ten commandments and other biblical texts]. Oriental languages in translation No. 2. Publications of the Oriental Committee 26: Cracow 2005, Polish Acad. of Sciences Pr. 121-42. **P.**

2428 *Zinkuratire, Victor* Introducing bible translation skills in Hebrew courses. BOTSA 18 (2005) 16-20.

2429 *Zuurmond, Rochus* Dynamisch equivalent. FHOOGEWOUD, F. 2005 ⇒ 63. 151-158 [OTA 29,11].

## D8 *Concordantiae, lexica specialia*—**Specialized dictionaries, synopses**

2430 **Konings, Johan** Sinopse dos evangelhos de Mateus, Marcos e Lucas e da 'Fonte Q'. Bíblica Loyola 45: São Paulo 2005, Loyola 340 pp. 85-15-03056-X. RPerTeol 37 (2005) 443-444 (*Paul, Claudio*).

2431 **Militarev, Alexander; Kogan, Leonid**, *al*. Semitic etymological dictionary, vol. 2: animal names. AOAT 278/2: Münster 2005, Ugarit-Verlag xl; 415 pp. 3-934628-57-5.

2432 **Odelain, Olivier; Séguineau, Raymond** Concordance thématique de la bible: les prophètes. Bégrolles en Mauges 2005, Abbaye de Bellefontaine 793 pp. 2-85589-974-5.

2433 E**Stonier, Geoffrey** The new thematic concordance. 2004, ⇒20, 2216. RMTh 56/1 (2005) 101-102 (*Abela, Anthony*).

2434 Stuttgarter elektronische Studienbibel / Stuttgart electronic study bible. E**Hardmeier, C.; Talstra, W.** 2004 ⇒20,2218. RTrinJ 26 (2005) 135-137 (*Schnabel, Eckhard J.*); Neotest. 39 (2005) 210-212 (*Van der Watt, J.G.*); ZKTh 127 (2005) 506-510 (*Repschinski, Boris*); JETh 19 (2005) 212-215 (*Hilbrands, Walter*); HIPHIL 2 (2005)* (*Kummerow, David*).

2435 E**Tov, Emanuel** The parallel aligned Hebrew-Aramaic and Greek texts of Jewish scripture. 2005, Logos Bible Software.

## IV. Exegesis generalis VT vel cum NT

### D9 Commentaries on the whole Bible or OT

2436 E**Berlin, Adele; Brettler, Marc Zvi** The Jewish study bible. 2004 ⇒20,317. RTS 66 (2005) 441-442 (*Walsh, J.P.M.*); AThR 87 (2005) 347-348, 350 (*Sharp, Carolyn J.*); RBLit 7 (2005) 13-19 (*Garber, Zev*).

2437 E**Dunn, James D.G.; Rogerson, John W.** Eerdmans commentary on the bible. 2003 ⇒19,2243; 20,2223. RThLZ 130 (2005) 487-489 (*Bergmeier, Roland*); HeyJ 46 (2005) 352-353 (*Briggs, Richard S.*); RBLit (2005)* (*Römer, Thomas*); JThS 56 (2005) 122-123 (*Bash, Anthony*).

2438 *Ferrari, Michele C.* Before the Glossa ordinaria: the Ezekiel fragment in Irish minuscule Zürich, Staatsarchiv W3.19.XII and other experiments towards a Bible commentée in the early Middle Ages. Biblical studies in the early Middle Ages. 2005 ⇒773. 283-310 [RBen 116,141—P.-M. Bogaert].

2439 E**Foster, Richard J.** The Renovaré Spiritual Formation Bible. SF 2005, HarperSanFrancisco 2400 pp. $40. 978-00606-71082. NRSV. RCCen 122/21 (2005) 26-27, 29 (*Rensberger, D.*).

2440 **Harvey, Anthony E.** A companion to the New Testament: the New Revised Standard Version. 22004 <1970> ⇒20,2225. RRBLit (2005)* (*Fogg, Julia*).

2441 Miedzynarodowy komentarz do Pisma Swietego: komentarz katolicki i ekumeniczny na XXI wiek. E**Farmer, William R.; Chrostowski, Waldemar** Wsz 2000, Verbinum xxxv; 1877 pp. 83-7192-105-5. Wspólredaktorzy *Sean McEvenue*, *Armando J. Levoratti*, *David L. Dungan*; Bibl. 1775-1835. **P**.

2442 Nuevo comentario bíblico San Jerónimo. E**Brown, Raymond E.; Fitzmyer, Joseph A.; Murphy, Roland E.** Estella (Navarra) 2004-2005, Verbo Divino 2 vols. 84-8169-401-0.

2443 [E]**Patte, Daniel** Global bible commentary. Nv 2005, Abingdon xxxvi; 570 pp. 0-687-06403-1. [R]African Christian Studies 21/2 (2005) 76-100 (*Patte, Daniel*).
2444 *Zán, Ján P.* Vypracovanie odborného komentára písma svätého v slovenskom jazyku [Project of the exegetical commentary on sacred scripture in Slovak]. SBSl (2005) 96-97. **Slovak.**
2445 [E]**Zenger, Erich** Stuttgarter Altes Testament: Einheitsübersetzung mit Kommentar und Lexikon. 2004 ⇒20,2232. [R]ThPQ 153 (2005) 88-90 (*Marböck, Johannes*);
2446 Stu [3]2005, Kath. Bibelwerk 1962 pp. 3-460-31959-3.

## V. Libri historici VT

### E1.1 Pentateuchus, Torah *Textus, commentarii*

2447 [E]**Alexander, T. Desmond; Baker, David W.** Dictionary of the Old Testament: pentateuch. 2002 ⇒18,2178; 20,2234. [R]JRTI 7/1 (2005) 81-82 (*Arbino, Gary P.*).
2448 [E]**Blumenthal, Jacob; Liss, Janet L.** Etz Hayim: study companion. Ph 2005, Jewish Publication Society of America 394 pp. 0-8276-082-2-5. Foreword by *David Wolpe*; The Rabbinical Assembly the United Synagogue of Conservative Judaism.
2449 **Cox, Howard H.** The pentateuch: history or story?. Lanham 2005, University Press of America xvi; 126 pp. 0-7618-3096-0.
2450 [E]**Klingbeil, Gerald** Inicios, paradigmas y fundamentos: estudios teológicos y exegéticos en el pentateuco. Monográf. de Estud. Bíblicos 1: 2004 ⇒20,378. [R]HebStud 46 (2005) 402-5 (*Hubbard, Robert L.*).
2451 **Krochmalnik, Daniel** Schriftauslegung: die Bücher Levitikus, Numeri, Deuteronomium im Judentum. NSK.AT 33/5: Stu 2005, Kathol. Bibelwerk 314 pp. 34600-73357.
2452 [E]**Lienhard, Joseph T.** La biblia comentada por los padres le la iglesia: Antiguo Testamento, 3: Éxodo, Levítico, Números, Deuteronomio. 2003 ⇒19,2262. [R]RelCult 51 (2005) 801-802 (*Langa, Pedro*).
2453 *Martone, Corrado* Qumran readings in agreement with the Septuagint against the Masoretic Text, part one: the pentateuch. Henoch 27/1-2 (2005) 53-113.
2454 *Moura, Ozeas C.* Adições ao pentateuco. Hermenêutica 5 (2005) 21-32.
2455 *Oesch, Josef* Drei Torarollen der Sammlungen BIBEL + ORIENT am Departement für Biblische Studien der Universität Fribourg. [F]SCHENKER, A.: OBO 214: 2005 ⇒134. 248-265;
2456 Kodikologisches zu den Sifre Tora: zwei unveröffentlichte Torarollenfragmente aus Innsbruck. PzB 14 (2005) 3-16.
2457 [E]**Paul, Mart-J.; Van den Brink, G.; Bette, J.C.** Bijbelcommentaar: Leviticus; Numeri; Deuteronomium. Studiebijbel Oude Testament 2: Veendendaal 2005, Centrum voor Bijbelonderzoek 23; 1264 pp. €72.
2458 [T]**Scharfstein, Sol** The five books of Moses an easy-to-read torah. Hoboken, NJ 2005, KTAV 534 pp. $20. 0-88125-853-9.
2459 *Sollamo, Raija* Repetitions of prepositions in the Septuagint of Genesis. [F]LUST, J.: BEThL 192: 2005 ⇒92. 371-384.

## E1.2 *Pentateuchus* **Introductio: Fontes JEDP**

2460 *Achenbach, Reinhard* Pentateuch, Hexateuch, und Enneateuch: eine Verhältnisbestimmung. ZAR 11 (2005) 122-154;

2461 The story of the revelation at the mountain of God and the redactional editions of the hexateuch and the pentateuch;

2462 *Arneth, Martin* "And by these were the nations divided in the earth": redactional techniques in the primeval history [Gen 3,17-19; 9,18-27]. Critical study. ATM 20: 2005 ⇒457. 126-151/116-125.

2463 *Auneau, Joseph* Le pentateque, 1: introduction générale; 2: les patriarches; 3: le livre de l'Exode, 4: le Lévitique et les Nombres. EeV 123,125,126,127 (2005) 15-21, 12-18, 19-26, 12-18.

2464 **Aurelius, Erik** Zukunft jenseits des Gerichts: eine redaktionsgeschichtliche Studie zum Enneateuch. BZAW 319: 2003 ⇒19,2271; 20,2250. [R]ZAR 11 (2005) 323-345 (*Otto, Eckart*).

2465 *Bauks, M.* Les notions de "peuple" et de "terre" dans l'oeuvre sacerdotale (Pg). TEuph 30 (2005) 19-36.

2466 *Blenkinsopp, Joseph* Introduction to the pentateuch. NT survey. 2005 ⇒414. 1-16.

2467 **Campbell, Antony F.; O'Brien, Mark A.** Rethinking the pentateuch: prolegomena to the theology of ancient Israel. LVL 2005, Westminster xiii; 183 pp. $30. 0-664-22809-7. Bibl. 157-162.

2468 *Carr, David M.* No return to WELLHAUSEN. Bib. 86 (2005) 107-114.

2469 **Couto, Antônio** Pentateuco: caminho da vida agraciada. 2003 ⇒19, 2317; 20,2254. [R]Burgense 46 (2005) 268-70 (*Otero Lázaro, Tomás*).

2470 *De Villiers, Gerda* Gilgamesh, Africa and the pentateuch. Critical study. ATM 20: 2005 ⇒457. 184-192.

2471 **Douglas, Mary** Jacob's tears: the priestly work of reconciliation. 2004 ⇒20,2255. [R]RRT 12 (2005) 363-365 (*Bury, Benjamin*).

2472 *Fischer, Georg* Wege zu einer neuen Sicht der Tora. ZAR 11 (2005) 93-106;

2473 The need for a new vision of the Torah. Critical study. ATM 20: 2005 ⇒457. 62-73 [Exod 3-4].

2474 *Friedman, Richard E.* Taking the biblical text apart. BiRe 21/4 (2005) 19-23, 48-50 [OTA 29,25].

2475 **García Lopez, Félix** Comment lire le pentateuque. Genève 2005, Labor et F. 378 pp. €26;

2476 El pentateuco: introducción a la lectura de los cinco primeros libros... biblia. Introd. al estud....biblia 3a: 2003 ⇒19,2284; 20,2258. [R]Theologica 40/1 (2005) 211-3 (*Correia, João A.S.*); Burgense 46 (2005) 265-7 (*Otero Lázaro, Tomás*); RB 112 (2005) 291-4 (*Loza Vera, J.*).

2477 [E]**Gertz, Jan C.; Schmid, Konrad; Witte, Markus** Abschied vom Jahwisten: die Komposition des Hexateuch in der jüngsten Diskussion. BZAW 315: 2002 ⇒18,2189... 20,2261. [R]TS 66 (2005) 178-179 (*Anderson, Thomas*); BiOr 62 (2005) 315-317 (*Davies, G.I.*).

2478 **Goldberg, Oskar** Die Wirklichkeit der Hebräer: Einleitung in das System des Pentateuch, erster Band: deutsche Texte zur hebräischen Ausgabe, wissenschaftliche Neuausgabe. [E]*Voigts, Manfred*: Jüdische Kultur 15: Wsb 2005 <1925>, Harrassowitz xxii; 385 pp. Geleitwort *Eleasar Benyoetz*; Nachwort *Roland Goetschel*.

2479 *Graupner, Axel* Die Erzählkunst des Elohisten: zur Makrostruktur und Intention der elohistischen Darstellung der Gründungsgeschichte Israels. Das AT und die Kunst. ATM 15: 2005 ⇒711. 67-89.

2480 **Graupner, Axel** Der Elohist: Gegenwart und Wirksamkeit des transzendenten Gottes in der Geschichte. WMANT 97: 2002 ⇒18,2203; 19,2286. [R]ThLZ 130 (2005) 757-759 (*Oeming, Manfred*); Bib. 86 (2005) 107-114 (*Carr, David M.*).

2481 *Guillaume, Philippe* Tracing the origin of the sabbatical calendar in the Priestly narrative (Genesis 1 to Joshua 5). JHScr 5/13 (2005)*.

2482 **Hamilton, Victor P.** Handbook on the pentateuch: Genesis, Exodus, Leviticus, Numbers, Deuteronomy. GR [2]2005 <1982>, Baker 468 pp. $33. 0-8010-2716-0.

2483 **Kizhakkeyil, Sebastian** The pentateuch: an interpretative study of the first five books of the bible. Ujjain 2004, Ruhalaya 312 pp. [R]JJSS 5 (2005) 105-106 (*Koottumkal, Sebastian*).

2484 **Kratz, Reinhard G.** The composition of the narrative books of the Old Testament. [T]*Bowden, John*: L 2005, Clark xii; 361 pp. $140. 0-567-08920-7. [R]RBLit (2005)* (*Johnstone, William*).

2485 *Le Roux, Jurie* Die Pentateug tussen deel en geheel. OTEs 18 (2005) 265-280;

2486 Pro Pent: a project for the study of the pentateuch in South Africa. Critical study. ATM 20: 2005 ⇒457. 1-21.

2487 *Leveen, Adriane B.* Reading the seams. JSOT 29 (2005) 259-287.

2488 **McDermott, John J.** Reading the pentateuch: a historical introduction. 2002 ⇒18,2213; 19,2291. [R]VJTR 69 (2005) 631-32 (*Meagher, P.M.*).

2489 *Milgrom, Jacob* Systemic differences in the priestly corpus: a response to Jonathan Klawans. RB 112 (2005) 321-329.

2490 **Moenikes, Ansgar** Tora ohne Mose: zur Vorgeschichte der Mose-Tora. BBB 149: 2004 ⇒20,2274. [R]ZAR 11 (2005) 346-350 (*Otto, Eckart*).

2491 *Nocquet, D.* La mort des patriarches, d'Aaron et de Moïse: l'apport de l'écriture sacerdotale à la constitution du Pentateuque à l'époque perse. TEuph 29 (2005) 133-153.

2492 *O'Keefe, Richard A.* Critical remarks on Houk's 'Statistical analysis of Genesis sources'. JSOT 29 (2005) 409-437 ⇒18,2204.

2493 *Otto, Eckart* The Pentateuch between synchrony and diachrony: perspectives for the encounter between Africa and Europe. Critical study. ATM 20: 2005 ⇒457. 22-49.

2494 *Rad, Gerhard von* The form-critical problem of the hexateuch. From Genesis. 2005 <1938> ⇒283. 1-58.

2495 *Rofé, Alexander* The formcritical problem of the Hexateuch—revisited. Das Alte Testament...Beiträge. Ment. *Rad, G. von*: ATM 10: 2005 ⇒802. 41-46 [Dt 26; Josh 24].

2496 *Sanz Giménez Rico, Enrique* El exilio y el postexilio de Israel y la nueva evangelización. Biblia y nueva evangelización. 2005 ⇒491. 79-107.

2497 **Sklar, Jay** Sin, impurity, sacrifice, atonement: the priestly conceptions. Hebrew Bible Monographs 2: Shf 2005, Sheffield Phoenix xi; 212 pp. $42.50. 1-905048-12-2. Bibl. 196-199.

2498 [E]**Terra, João E.M.** Introdução ao pentateuco. RCB 113-116 (2005) 1-295.

2499 *Van Seters, John* The pentateuch as torah *and* history: in defense of G. VON RAD. Das Alte Testament...Beiträge. ATM 10: 2005 ⇒802. 47-63.

2500 **Van Wijk-Bos, Johanna W.H.** Making wise the simple: the torah in christian faith and practice. GR 2005, Eerdmans xxiv; 329 pp. £17. 0-8028-0990-1. Bibl. 306-315.

2501 [E]**Watts, James W.** Persia and torah: the theory of imperial authorization of the pentateuch. SBL.Symposium 17: 2001 ⇒17,1919... 20, 2290. [R]BiblInterp 13 (2005) 67-69 (*Hagedorn, Anselm C.*).

2502 **Wright, Richard M.** Linguistic evidence for the pre-exilic date of the Yahwistic source. Library of Hebrew Bible, OT Studies 419; JSOT.S 419: L 2005, Clark x; 208 pp. $105. 0-567-04121-2. Bibl. 165-176.

2503 *Zenger, Erich* La torah/il pentateuco nel suo insieme;

2504 Ipotesi sull'origine del pentateuco e sviluppi dell'indagine scientifica;

2505 Il processo della redazione del pentateuco;

2506 L'opera (scritta) sacerdotale (P);

2507 L'opera (scritta) pre-sacerdotale. Introduzione AT. 2005 ⇒1159. 93-116/117-186/187-203/236-264/265-281.

2508 **Zucker, David J.** The torah: an introduction for christians and Jews. NY 2005, Paulist 230 pp. $19. 0-8091-4349-6. Bibl. 207-213 [BiTod 44,126—Dianne Bergant].

## E1.3 *Pentateuchus*, **themata**

2509 *Azerrad, David* The two ways: Egypt and Israel in the torah. Interpretation(F) 33/1 (2005) 3-18.

2510 **Caldelari, C.** La bibbia del dì di festa: pensieri familiari su Esodo,Levitico e Numeri. Shemà: Padova 2005, Messagero 159 pp. €9.80.

2511 **Greifenhagen, F.V.** Egypt on the pentateuch's ideological map: constructing Biblical Israel's identity. JSOT.S 361: 2002 ⇒18,2229; 20,2297. [R]JSSt 50 (2005) 209-211 (*McConville, J.G.*); RBLit 7 (2005) 132-136 (*Sherman, Phillip M.*).

2512 **Quintana Fresno, Felipe José** La roca que da agua en el desierto: desarrollo literario y teológico de esta tradición en el Pentateuco y en los Salmos. [D]*Varo Pineda, F.* 2005, 275 pp. Diss. Pampelune [RTL 37,611].

2513 *Rad, Gerhard von* The promised land and Yahweh's land in the hexateuch. From Genesis. 2005 <1943> ⇒283. 59-69.

2514 *Römer, Thomas* La fin du livre de la Genèse et la fin des livres des Rois: ouvertures vers la diaspora: quelques remarques sur le pentateuque, l'hexateuque et l'ennéateuque. [F]SCHENKER, A.: OBO 214: 2005 ⇒134. 285-294 [Gen 50,24-25; 2 Kgs 25,27-30].

2515 **Schmidt, Ludwig** Gesammelte Aufsätze zum Pentateuch. BZAW 263: 1998 ⇒14,195; 16,1818. [R]ThR 70 (2005) 225-227 (*Mathys, Hans-Peter*).

2516 [E]**Zenger, Erich** Die Tora als Kanon für Juden und Christen. 1996 ⇒ 12,1308; 14,1605. [R]ThR 70 (2005) 284-285 (*Reventlow, Henning*).

## E1.4 **Genesis**; *textus, commentarii*

2517 *Amos, Clare* Genesis. Global bible commentary. 2005 ⇒2443. 1-16.

2518 **Amos, Clare** The book of Genesis. 2004 ⇒20,2309. [R]IBSt 26 (2005) 197-199 (*McKeown, James*).

2519 **Brodie, Thomas L.** Genesis as dialogue: a literary, historical, & theological commentary. 2001 ⇒17,1938... 20,2310. [R]RB 112 (2005) 136-138 (*Sonek, Krzysztof P.*).

2520 **Cotter, David W.** Genesis. Berit Olam: 2003 ⇒19,2317; 20,2313. [R]RBLit 7 (2005) 129-131 (*Petersen, David L.*).

2521 *Fretheim, Terence E.* The book of Genesis. OT survey. 2005⇒413. 17-24.

2522 **Kessler, Martin; Deurloo, Karel A.** A commentary on Genesis: the book of beginnings. 2004 ⇒20,2320. [R]RBLit 7 (2005) 136-38 (*Bosworth, David*).

2523 **Longman, Tremper** How to read Genesis. DG 2005, InterVarsity 192 pp. $15. 0-87784-943-9. Bibl. 181-187.

2524 **Loza, José; Aparicio Rodríguez, Ángel** Génesis 1-11; Salmos 1-41. Bilbao 2005, Desclée de B. 1-111; 112-397 pp. €9. 84-330-1952X. One author for each book.

2525 **Mathews, Kenneth A.** Genesis 11:27-50:26. NAC 1B: Nv 2005, Broadman & H. 960 pp. $33. [R]RBLit (2005)* (*Hieke, Thomas*).

2526 **Pirson, R.** Genesis. Belichting van het Bijbelboek: 's-Hertogenbosch 2005, KBS 384 pp.

2527 **Riskin, Shlomo** Torah lights: Genesis confronts life, love and family. J 2005, Ohr Torah Stone 309 pp. 965-7108-63-2. Bibl. 299-301.

2528 **Rogerson, John** Genesis 1-11. Study Guides: 2004 ⇒20,2323. [R]RBLit (2005)* (*Petersen, David*).

2529 **Ruppert, Lothar** Genesis: ein kritischer und theologischer Kommentar, 3. Teilband: Gen 25,19—36,43. FzB 106: Wü 2005, Echter 536 pp. €40. 3-429-02734-9.

2530 **Schorch, Stefan** Die Vokale des Gesetzes: die samaritanische Lesetradition als Textzeugin der Tora, 1: das Buch Genesis. BZAW 339: 2004 ⇒20,2326. [R]ThLZ 130 (2005) 643-644 (*Witte, Markus*); CBQ 67 (2005) 325-327 (*Althann, Robert*); BiOr 62 (2005) 120-124 (*Tal, Abraham*).

2531 [E]**Sheridan, Mark** La biblia comentada por los padres le la iglesia: Antiguo Testamento, 2: Génesis 12-50. [T]*Merino Rodríguez, Marcelo* M 2005, Ciudad N. 501 pp. 84-9715-072-4. [R]EstTrin 39 (2005) 574-575 (*Miguel, José María de*).

2532 *Sollamo, Raija* An example of consistency: interpretation by the translator of the Greek Genesis in rendering the Hebrew semipreposition לפני. [F]AEJMELAEUS, L.: SESJ 89: 2005 ⇒1. 3-12.

2533 **Walton, John H.** Genesis . GR 2001, Zondervan 759 pp. 0-310-20617-0. Bibl. 61-64.

2534 *Wénin, André* La Genesi come racconto. Dalla violenza. 2005 <2003> ⇒323. 15-52.

2535 **Zipor, Moshe A.** The Septuagint version of the book of Genesis. Ramat-Gan 2005, Bar-Ilan Univ. Pr. 651 pp. $86. 965-226-240-4. Bibl. 627-651.

## E1.5 *Genesis*, topics

2536 **Bar-Ilan, Meir** Genesis' numerology. [2]2003 ⇒19,2337. [R]CBQ 67 (2005) 306-308 (*Hillmer, Mark*); RBLit (2005)* (*Valler, Shulamit*).

2537 *Burger, Hilde* Uitgepapegaaid. ITBT 13/7 (2005) 18-20.

2538 *Carden, Michael* Endangered ancestress revisited: Sarah's miraculous motherhood and the restoration of Eden. BiCT 1/3 (2005 *.

2539 **Groote, Lukas de** Isaak, Jakob en de kinderen van Jakob: onderzoek naar de hiaten, haperingen en verrassingen in de bijbeltekst. 2005, Lukas de Groote 257 pp. €17.70. 90-810-1091-3 [Gen 24-37].

2540 *Hendel, Ronald* Genesis 1-11 and its Mesopotamian problem. Cultural borrowings. Oriens et Occidens 8: 2005 ⇒652. 23-36.

2541 *Holmes, Jeremy* Die Genesis ist ein Buch. Theologisches 35 (2005) 235-246.

2542 **Kaminski, Carol M.** From Noah to Israel: realization of the primaeval blessing after the Flood. JSOT.S 413: 2004 ⇒20,2333. [R]RBLit (2005)* (*Leuenberger, Martin*).

2543 **Maalouf, Tony** Arabs in the shadow of Israel: the unfolding of God's prophetic plan for Ishmael's line. 2003 ⇒19,2353; 20,2337. [R]CTJ 40 (2005) 153-155 (*Madany, Bassam M.*); Miss. 33 (2005) 237-238 (*Fisher, Robert B.*).

2544 *Petersen, David L.* Genesis and family values. JBL 124 (2005) 5-23;

2545 Polities in Genesis 12-36. [F]McBRIDE, D. 2005 ⇒98. 75-88.

2546 *Reymond, Bernard* Prêcher sur la Genèse. LeD 66 (2005) 4-5.

2547 *Ska, Jean-Louis* Le genealogie della Genesi e le risposte alle sfide della storia. RStB 17/1 (2005) 89-111.

2548 *Thibault, Danielle* Le travail dans la Genèse. Cahiers de spiritualité ignatienne 29/1 (2005) 59-68.

2549 *Wénin, André* La fraternité, "projet éthique" dans les récits de la Genèse. FV 104/4 (2005) 24-35.

2550 *Wyatt, Nick* The problem of the 'God of the fathers'. Mythic mind. 2005 <1978> ⇒328. 1-5.

## E1.6 **Creatio**, *Genesis 1s*

2551 *Auld, Graeme imago dei* in Genesis: speaking in the image of God. ET 116 (2005) 259-262 [Gen 1,26].

2552 *Beauchamp, Paul* Création et fondation de la loi en Gn 1,1-2,4a: le don de la nourriture végétale en Gn 1,29s. Pages exégétiques. LeDiv 202: 2005 <1986> ⇒183. 105-144.

2553 **Beauchamp, Paul** Création et séparation: étude exégétique du chapitre premier de la Genèse. LeDiv 201: P 2005 <1969>, Cerf 430 pp. €35. 2-204-07825-5.

2554 *Bozung, Douglas C.* An evaluation of the biosphere model of Genesis 1. BS 162/648 (2005) 406-423.

2555 **Capon, Robert F.** Genesis: the movie. 2003 ⇒19,2370; 20,2351. [R]OTEs 18 (2005) 932-934 (*Maré, L.P.*).

2556 **Castilla Cortazar, Bl.** ¿Fue creado el varón antes que la mujer?: reflexiones en torno a la antropología de la creación. M 2005, Rialp 116 pp [Studium 45,315—López, L].

2557 *Den Dulk, Maarten* Het zwijgen van Breukelman. ITBT 13/7 (2005) 25-27.

2558 *Detienne, Claude* Un comentário siríaco inédito do Antigo Testamento: Gênesis 1,1 no comentário de Dionísio BAR SALIBI (+1171). Fragmenta de Cultura [Goías] 15 (2005) 1353-1360 [OTA 29,27].

2559 *Ego, Beate* Schöpfung als Gabe und Aufgabe. BiKi 60 (2005) 3-9.

2560 **Fretheim, Terence E.** God and world in the Old Testament: a relational theology of creation. Nv 2005, Abingdon xvii; 398 pp. $29. 0-687-34296-1.

2561 **Froebe, Dieter** Die Erkenntnis von Gut und Böse macht den Menschen zum Bild und Gleichnis Gottes: die Würdigung der Erzählkomposition von Gen. 1,1-11,32 als kritische Anfrage an die christliche Lehrtradition. Theologie 57: Müns 2005, LIT iv; 159 pp. €17.90. 3-8258-8517-8 [Gen 1,26-27].

2562 *Gounelle, André* Genèse 1: au commencement. LeD 66 (2005) 5-13.

2563 *Hurowitz, Victor A.* The genesis of Genesis: is the creation story Babylonian?. BiRe 21/1 (2005) 36-48, 52-54.

2564 *Jančovič, Jozef* Imago Dei (Gn 1,27)—biblický koncept úplnosti a dokonalosti človeka [*Imago Dei* (Gen 1,27)—biblical concept of completeness and perfection of human being]. SBSl (2005) 36-59 **[Slovak]**.

2565 **Johns, Warren H.** Revelation and creation in the thought of Bernard L. Ramm and Carl F.:H. Henry: the creation 'days' as a case study. D*Jiš, Miroslav* 2005, Diss. Andrews [AUSS 44,174].

2566 **Klaiber, Walter** Schöpfung: Urgeschichte und Gegenwart. BTSP 27: Gö 2005, Vandenhoeck & R. 230 pp. €19.90. 3-525-61589-2.

2567 *Klopper, Frances* Aspects of creation: the water in the wilderness motif in the Psalms and the Prophets. OTEs 18 (2005) 253-264.

2568 *Launay, Marc de* L'analyse de Genèse I dans *L'étoile de la rédemption*. ArPh 68 (2005) 447-464.

2569 *Lundager Jensen, Hans J.* Skabelse og frelse i det Gamle Testamente. Kritisk forum for praktisk teologi 25/102 (2005) 15-29.

2570 **McGrath, Alister** Creation. Truth and christian imagination 1: Mp 2005, Fortress vii; 85 pp. $15. 0-8006-3700-3 [ThD 51,375–Heiser, W. Charles].

2571 **Middleton, J. Richard** The liberating image: the *Imago Dei* in Genesis 1. D*Leene, H.* <dir> GR 2005, Brazos 304 pp. $22. 1-58743-11-06. Diss. Amsterdam, V.U. RInterp. 59 (2005) 408-410 (*Towner, W. Sibley*); RBLit (2005)* (*MacDonald, Nathan*).

2572 *Minamino, Hironori* Genesis 1 as critique of Japanese culture. Direction 34 (2005) 159-169 [OTA 29,27].

2573 **Minamino, Hironori** Interpretation of the biblical first creation account within the Japanese context. D*Aitken, K.* 2005, Diss. Aberdeen [RTL 37,610].

2574 *Noort, Ed* The creation of light in Genesis 1:1-5: remarks on the function of light and darkness in the opening verses of the Hebrew Bible. Creation of heaven and earth. 2005 ⇒492. 3-20.

2575 *Persoz, Henri* Genèse 2: l'homme, entre la terre et la femme. LeD 66 (2005) 14-24.

2576 **Petiau, Marie-Catherine; Wiame, Bernadette** Parole et regards créateurs: Genèse 1,1-2,4a. À l'école de la bible 1: Bru 2005, Lumen Vitae 92 pp. €10. 2-87324-245-0.

2577 *Rad, Gerhard von* The theological problem of the Old Testament doctrine of creation. From Genesis. 2005 <1936> ⇒283. 177-186.

2578 *Ravasi, Gianfranco* La bellezza della creazione nell'Antico Testamento. PATH 4 (2005) 323-335 [Sir 42,15-43,33].

2579 *Rordorf, Bernard* Dominez la terre" (Genèse 1,29): essai sur les résonances historiques de ce commandement biblique. Liberté de parole. 2005 <1979> ⇒291. 41-67.

2580 *Scalabrini, Patrizio R.* Il dono della creazione. Com(I) 202 (2005) 12-23.

2581 *Schüle, Andreas* Made in the "image of God": the concepts of divine images in Gen 1-3. ZAW 117 (2005) 1-20.

2582 *Schwambach, Cristiane V.* Gênesis 1.1-2.4a: observações exegéticas e relevância atual. VoxScr 13/1 (2005) 7-52.

2583 *Ska, Jean Louis* La vida como bendición. El camino. 2005 <1994> ⇒302. 41-64 [Gen 1,28].

2584 *Talmon, Shemaryahu* The biblical understanding of creation and the human commitment. Worlds of memory. 2005 ⇒543. 39-55;

2585 Compréhension biblique de la création et engagement de l'être humain. Sagesses et mémoires croisées. 2005 ⇒838. 43-62.

2586 *Towner, W. Sibley* Clones of God: Genesis 1:26-28 and the image of God in the Hebrew Bible. Interp. 59 (2005) 341-356.

2587 *Van Heerden, Willie* Norman Habel se interpretasie van Genesis 1:1-2:4a binne die raamwerk van die Earth Bible project. OTEs 18 (2005) 371-393.

2588 *Vanoni, Gottfried* Wie stabil ist die Schöpfung?: bibeltheologische Erwägungen. Wie wirkt Gott. 2005 ⇒555. 151-172.

2589 **Watson, Rebecca S.** Chaos uncreated: a reassessment of the theme of "chaos" in the Hebrew Bible. [D]*Joyce, Paul M.*: BZAW 341: B 2005, De Gruyter xix; 504 pp. $159.30. 3-11-017993-8. Diss. Oxford; Bibl. 400-449.

2590 *Wénin, André* Un dominio mite?: la responsabilità umana di fronte al creato (Gen 1-2). PSV 51 (2005) 17-32.

2591 **Wénin, André** Le sabbat dans la bible. ConBib 38: Bru 2005, Lumen V. 80 pp. €9. 2-87324-246-9.

2592 **Wodecki, Bernard** Morze w Piśmie Świętym [Il mare nella Santa Scrittura]. RBL 58 (2005) 97-118. **P.**

2593 *Wyatt, Nick* The darkness of Genesis 1.2. Mythic mind. 2005 <1993> ⇒328. 92-101.

## E1.7 *Genesis 1s*: **Bible and myth** [⇒M3.8]

2594 *Briffard, Colette* Comment lire les mythes?. FV 104/4 (2005) 6-13.

2595 **Dubianetskaya, Iryna** Cosmos and chaos in the Hebrew Bible and ancient Near Eastern mythologies. [D]*Vervenne, M.* 2005, lxxxvi; 338 pp. Diss. Leuven.

2596 *Engel, Tony* Laisser parler les mythes bibliques. RNouv 119/4 (2005) 75-81.

2597 *Evers, Dirk* Chaos im Himmel: die Entwicklung der modernen Kosmologie und ihre Tragweite für die christliche Rede vom Himmel. JBTh 20 (2005) 35-58.

2598 *Fetz, Reto L.* Der Himmel als Symbol: die moderne Umdeutung eines mythischen Raumes. JBTh 20 (2005) 59-82.

2599 *Kok, Johnson L.* Genesis 1-11 and its ancient Near Eastern parallels. AJTh 19/1 (2005) 68-78.

2600 *Molina, Jean P.* L'événement trop vrai: mythe et événement. FV 104/4 (2005) 83-88.

2601 *Schwindt, Rainer* Weltbilder im Umbruch: Himmelsvorstellungen in der Antike. JBTh 20 (2005) 3-34.

2602 *Smyth, Françoise* Bible, mythe et vérité. FV 104/4 (2005) 14-23.

2603 **Stitt, Frederick H.** Adam to Ahab: myth and history in the bible. St. Paul, MN 2005, Paragon xxii; 138 pp. $17. 1-557-78852-9. Bibl.

2604 **Tsumura, David Toshio** Creation and destruction: a reappraisal of the chaoskampf theory in the Old Testament. WL 2005, Eisenbrauns xviii; 214 pp. $32.50. 1-575-06106-6. Rev. and expanded ed. of: The earth and the waters in Genesis 1 and 2 (1989).

2605 **Tworuschka, Monika; Tworuschka, Udo** Als die Welt entstand... Schöpfungsmythen der Völker und Kulturen in Wort und Bild. FrB 2005, Herder 184 pp. €29.90. 3-451-28597-5.

2606 *Van Dyk, Peet* Mythical linkage and mythical frameworks. OTEs 18 (2005) 863-878.

2607 *Wyatt, Nicolas* Arms and the king: the earliest allusions to the *Chaoskampf* motif and their implications for the interpretation of the Ugaritic and biblical traditions <1998>;

2608 The theogony motif in Ugarit and the bible <1994>. 'There's such divinity'. 2005 ⇒329. 151-189/85-101.

### E1.8 *Gen 1s, Jos 10,13...*: The Bible, the Church and science

2609 **Acar, Rahim** Talking about God and talking about creation: AVICENNA's and Thomas AQUINAS' positions. ITPS 58: Lei 2005, Brill x; 250 pp. 90-04-14477-3. Bibl. 235-241.

2610 **Bonting, Sjoerd L.** Creation and double chaos: science and theology in discussion. Theology and the sciences: Mp 2005, Fortress x; 275 pp. $22. 0-8006-3759-3 [ThD 52,370—W. Charles Heiser].

2611 **Burge, Ted** Science and the bible: evidence-based christian belief. Ph 2005, Templeton xii;193 pp. $17. 1-932031-936 [ThD 52,371—W. Charles Heiser].

2612 **Copan, Paul; Craig, William L.** Creation out of nothing: a biblical, philosophical, and scientific exploration. 2004 ⇒20,2389. [R]Phil. 80 (2005) 455-9 (*Mawson, T.J.*); IPQ 45 (2005) 408-10 (*Milem, Bruce*).

2613 *De Rosa, Giuseppe* L'origine dell'uomo secondo la bibbia. CivCatt 156/4 (2005) 319-329.

2614 **Finocchiaro, Maurice A.** Retrying GALILEO, 1633-1992. Berkeley, CA 2005, Univ. of California Pr. 492 pp. $50. 0-520-24261-0 [ThD 52,260—W. Charles Heiser].

2615 *Groessens-Van Dyck, Marie Claire* TEILHARD de Chardin e DE DORLODOT: conciliando a teoria de DARWIN e a cultura bíblica. RPF 61 (2005) 203-210.

2616 *Gruber, Franz J.* Theologie und Naturwissenschaften–Überlegungen zu einem schwierigen Dialog. Wie wirkt Gott. 2005 ⇒555. 29-50.

2617 **Harrison, Peter** The Bible, Protestantism, and the rise of natural science. 1998 ⇒14,1703... 17,2035. [R]JEMH 9 (2005) 445-448 (*Legaspi, Michael C.*).

2618 **Howell, Kenneth J.** God's two books: Copernican cosmology and biblical interpretation in early modern science. 2002 ⇒18,2355... 20, 2394. [R]HeyJ 46 (2005) 72-73 (*Klaver, Jan M.I.*); JThS 56 (2005) 261-267 (*Mandelbrote, Scott*).

2619 *Kenner, Thomas* Anfragen und Randbemerkungen eines Naturwissenschaftlers. Wie wirkt Gott. 2005 ⇒555. 173-182.

2620 *Kögerler, Reinhart* Verstehen und Begreifen—Anmerkungen des Naturwissenschaftlers. Wie wirkt Gott. 2005 ⇒555. 105-115.

2621 **Mayaud, Pierre-Noël** Le conflit entre l'astronomie nouvelle et l'écriture sainte aux XVIe et XVIIe siècles: un moment de l'histoire des idées: autour de l'affaire GALILÉE. Bibliothèque littéraire de la Renaissance 55: P 2005, Champion 6 vols; 440; 404; 1330; 574; 259; 409 pp. €563. 2-7453-1126-3. Bibl.

2622 [E]**McMullin, Ernan** The church and GALILEO. ND 2005, Univ. of ND Pr. xii; 391 pp. $30. 0-268-03484-2.

2623 *Ottati, Douglas F.* Which way is up?: an experiment in christian theology and modern cosmology. Interp. 59 (2005) 370-381.

2624 **Pesce, Mauro** L'ermeneutica biblica di GALILEO e le due strade della teologia cristiana. Uomini e dottrine 43: R 2005, Edizioni di storia e letteratura vii; 240 pp. 88-8498-2073.

2625 **Schmitz-Moormann, Karl; Salmon, James F.** Teología de la creación de un mundo en evolución. [T]*Pérez, Noemi*: Estella 2005, Verbo Divino 295 pp. 84-8169-5890.

2626 *Van Woudenberg, René* Design in nature: some current issues. Creation of heaven and earth. 2005 ⇒492. 245-261.

2627 *Wimmer, Joseph F.* The bible and the awesomeness of creation. NewTR 18/4 (2005) 40-47.

2628 **Witham, Larry A.** Where DARWIN meets the bible: creationists and evolutionists in America. 2002 ⇒18,2370; 20,2401. [R]HeyJ 46 (2005) 275-276 (*Klaver, Jan Marten Ivo*).

2629 *Zauner, Wilhelm* Zur Person Gernot Eder—Absichten und Wirkungen. Wie wirkt Gott. 2005 ⇒555. 183-190.

## E1.9 *Peccatum originale*, the sin of Eden, *Genesis 2-3*

2630 **Abraham, Joseph** Eve: accused or acquitted?: an analysis of feminist readings of the creation narrative texts in Genesis 1-3. 2002 ⇒ 19,2448. [R]CBQ 67 (2005) 104-106 (*Landes, George M.*).

2631 *Arens, Eduardo* El trabajo según Génesis... y hoy. Páginas 30/195 (2005) 12-26.

2632 *Awwad, Johnny* Satan in biblical imagination. ThRev 26/2 (2005) 111-126.

2633 [E]**Boureux, Christophe; Theobald, Christoph** Le péché originel: heurs et malheurs d'un dogme. P 2005, Bayard 210 pp [Etudes (juillet-août 2005),143—Geneviève Comeau].

2634 [E]**Capelli, Piero** Il diavolo e l'Occidente. Biblia 10: Brescia 2005, Morcelliana 158 pp. €12.50. 88372-20960.

2635 *Dieckmann, Detlef* Von Sünde keine Rede: die Paradiesgeschichte in Gen 2-3. Sexuologie 12 (2005) 78-81.

2636 [E]**Goris, H.; Hennecke, S.** Adam en Eva in het paradijs: actuele visies op man en vrouw uit 2000 jaar christelijke theologie. Utr. Studies 7: Zoetermeer 2005, Meinema 200 pp. €18.50. 90-211-4032-2.

2637 *Hartenstein, Friedhelm* "Und sie erkannten, dass sie nackt waren ..." (Gen 3,7): Beobachtungen zur Anthropologie der Paradieserzählung. EvTh 65 (2005) 277-293.

2638 *Hess, Richard S.* Equality with and without innocence: Genesis 1-3. Discovering biblical equality. 2005 387. 79-95.

2639 *Jacobs, Maretha M.* Eve: influential glimpses from her story. Scriptura 90 (2005) 765-778 [OTA 30,25].

2640 *Jayachitra, L.* Adam and Eve in Genesis 1-3 revisited. BiBh 31 (2005) 168-182.

2641 *Jesudasan, Ignatius* Adam: a psychological reading of the myth of man-making. JDh 30 (2005) 271-277.

2642 *Kułaczkowski, Jerzy* Następstwa grzechu pierworodnego dla relacji pomiędzy mężczyzną i kobietą w świetle Księgi Rodzaju (rozdz. 3) [Conséquences du péché originel pour la relation entre l'homme et la femme d'après le livre de la Genèse (ch. 3)]. AtK 145 (2005) 450-459. **P.**

2643 *Manelli, Settimio M.* Gen 3,15 e l'immacolata corredentrice. Immaculata Mediatrix 5 (2005) 17-64.

2644 *Mazzinghi, Luca* La libertà spezzata: l'uomo dopo Genesi 3. Libertà va cercando. Sussidi biblici 87: 2005 ⇒353. 21-45.

2645 *Porath, Renatus* O ser humano em meio a astros, animais e uma serpente esperta!: a antropologia em prosa e verso nos primeiros capítulos da bíblia. VoxScr 13/1 (2005) 53-56.

2646 *Schwienhorst-Schönberger, Ludger* Als Mann und Frau erschaffen: Aspekte biblischer Anthropologie. Studien zum AT. SBAB 40: 2005 <2000> ⇒298. 79-97.

2647 **Shuster, Marguerite** The fall and sin: what we have become as sinners. 2004 ⇒20,2435. [R]SBET 23 (2005) 98-99 (*Jenson, Matt*).

2648 *Simian-Yofre, Horacio* Pecado del hombre, justicia divina. [F]JUNCO GARZA, C.: Estudios Bíblicos Mexicanos 4: 2005 ⇒74. 417-435.

2649 *Ska, Jean Louis* 'Voy a proporcionarle una ayuda adecuada' (Gn 2, 18): a propósito del término 'ezer–'ayuda'. El camino. 2005 <1984, 1998> ⇒302. 149-159.

2650 *Tengström, Sven* Man och kvinna i Genesis 2-3. SEÅ 70 (2005) 281-285.

2651 *Terrinoni, Ubaldo* La bibbia e le realtà ultime dell'uomo: il paradiso. RVS 59 (2005) 247-274.

2652 [E]**Van Wolde, E.** Het paradijs. De bijbel 4: Zoetermeer 2005, Meinema 157 pp. €14.90. 90-211-4067-5.

2653 **Vaz, Eurides** Divino Para o homem Deus criou uma mulher: alusao à Gn 2,18. Goiania, Brasil 2004, Ed. da UCG 98 pp. 85-7103-251-3. Bibl. 95-98.

2654 **Williams, Patricia A.** Doing without Adam and Eve: sociobiology and original sin. Theology and the sciences: 2001 ⇒17,2079. [R]CThMi 32 (2005) 142, 144 (*Mattes, Mark C.*).

2655 **Wray, T.J.; Mobley, Gregory** The birth of Satan: tracing the devil's biblical roots. NY 2005, Palgrave M. xix; 211 pp. $25. 1-403-96933-7. Bibl. 198-203.

2656 *Wyatt, Nicolas* When Adam delved: the meaning of Genesis 3:23. 'There's such divinity'. 2005 <1988> ⇒329. 55-59.

## E2.1 Cain and Abel; *gigantes, longaevi; Genesis 4s*

2657 *Cardona Ramírez, Hernán* La ofrenda agradable a YHWH. El grano. 2005 <2004> ⇒197. 191-199 [Gen 4,3-5; Isa 1,13-15].

2658 *Chrostowski, Waldemar* U źródeł przemocy: Kain i Abel (Rdz 4,1-16) [At the sources of violence: Cain and Abel (Gen 4:1-16)]. StBob 2 (2005) 5-19. **P.**

2659 **Hieke, Thomas** Die Genealogien der Genesis. Herder's Biblical Studies 39: 2003 ⇒19,2485. [R]BZ 49 (2005) 103-107 (*Fischer, Irmtraud*); RivBib 53 (2005) 103-106 (*Paganini, Simone*); Bib. 86 (2005) 416-419 (*Stordalen, Terje*); JETh 19 (2005) 223-225 (*Koorevaar, Hendrik*).

2660 *Jacobson, Howard* Genesis iv 8. VT 55 (2005) 564-565.

2661 *Moko, José* Le mythe caïnite: une lecture de Genèse 4,1-26. Théophilyon 10 (2005) 177-207.

2662 *Northcote, Jeremy* The schematic development of Old Testament chronography: towards an integrated model. JSOT 29 2005, 3-36.

2663 *Raiser, Elisabeth* Gewalt und Gewaltüberwindung (1. Mose, 4,1-17). Kanzelreden. 2005 ⇒376. 11-22.

2664 **Wright, Archie T.** The origin of evil spirits: the reception of Genesis 6,1-4 in early Jewish literature. Ment. *Philo*: WUNT 2/198: Tü 2005, Mohr S. xvi; 260 pp. €49. 3161486560. Diss. Durham; Bibl. 224-40.

2665 *Wyatt, Nicolas* Cain's wife. 'There's such divinity'. 2005 <1986> ⇒ 329. 23-30 [Gen 4,1].

2666 *Zwilling, Anne-Laure* Caïn versus Abel (Gn 4,1-16). Analyse narrative. BEThL 191: 2005 ⇒742. 507-516.

## E2.2 *Diluvium*, the Flood; *Gilgameš (Atrahasis)*; Genesis 6...

2667 *Abusch, Tzvi* The courtesan, the wild man, and the hunter: studies in the literary history of the epic of Gilgamesh. [F]KLEIN, J. 2005 ⇒79. 413-433.

2668 *Alvarez Valdés, Ariel* ¿Por qué Noé maldijo a su hijo Cam que lo vio desnudo?. Eccl(R) 19/1 (2005) 97-105 [Gen 9,18-27].

2669 *Baumgart, Norbert C.* Einleitung: Sintflut—ein Allerweltsthema neben und in der Religion. Die Sintflut. 2005 ⇒346. 1-7;

2670 Dokumentarfilme zum Thema Sintflut und große Flut;

2671 Nicht nur Theologen schreiben Bücher über die Sintflut;

2672 Zuversicht und Hoffnung in Verbindung mit der biblischen Fluterzählung. Die Sintflut. 2005 ⇒346. 9-27/29-51/73-102.

2673 *Bergsma, John S.; Hahn, Scott W.* Noah's nakedness and the curse on Canaan (Genesis 9:20-27). JBL 124 (2005) 25-40.

2674 *Berlyn, Patricia* The journey of Terah: to Ur-Kasdim or Urkesh?. JBQ 33 (2005) 73-80 [Gen 11].

2675 **Bosshard-Nepustil, Erich** Vor uns die Sintflut: Studien zu Text, Kontexten und Rezeption der Fluterzählung Genesis 6-9. [D]*Dietrich, Walter*: BWANT 165: Stu 2005, Kohlhammer 336 pp. €45. 3-17-018557-8. Diss.-Habil. Bern; Bibl. 300-326 [Isa 24-27].

2676 *Breyne, Jean-François* Genèse 6-9: autour de l'arche de Noé. LeD 66 (2005) 25-35.

2677 *Davison, Graeme* The fallen towers: pride, envy and judgement in the modern city. BiCT 1/3 (2005) [Gen 11,1-9].

2678 Le déluge et ses récits: points de vue sémiotiques. Québec 2005, Presses de l'Univ. Laval 190 pp. $25. 27637-82655. Groupe de recherche ASTER.

2679 *Dohmen, Christoph* Mose, das leuchtende Angesicht der Tora. Bib. 86 (2005) 583-591.

2680 *Ferreira, João C.L.* Tornemos célebre nosso nome! Gn 11:1-9. RTel 65 (2005) 47-61 [OTA 29,139].

2681 **George, Andrew R.** The Babylonian Gilgamesh Epic: introduction, critical edition and cuneiform texts. 2003 ⇒19,2511; 20,2475. [R]BSOAS 68 (2005) 111-113 (*Gadotti, Alhena*); StEeL 22 (2005) 125-126 (*Seminara, Stefano*); JAOS 125 (2005) 59-65 (*Foster, Benjamin R.*).

2682 *Guillaume, Philippe; Najm, S.* Jubilee calendar rescued from the Flood narrative. JHScr 5/1 2004*.

2683 **Hirsch, Hans** Gilgamesch-Epos und Erra-Lied: zu einem Aspekt des Verbalsystems. AfO.B 29: 2002 ⇒18,2434... 20,2476. [R]BiOr 62 (2005) 292-293 (*Deutscher, Guy*).

2684 *Höffken, Peter* Zuversicht und Hoffnung in Verbindung mit babylonischen Fluttraditionen. Die Sintflut. 2005 ⇒346. 53-72.

2685 *Kotzé, Zacharias* Conceptual metaphors for anger in the Biblical Hebrew story of the flood. JSem 14/1 (2005) 149-164.

2686 *Leveau, Philippe* Mythe, référence à l'antique et mémoire des catastrophes dans les médias scientifiques: le déluge de la bible à PLATON: les scientifiques croient-ils aux mythes antiques?. Récits et représentations des catastrophes. 2005 ⇒941. 145-159.

2687 *Lüpke, Johannes von* Das Drama der Schöpfung: Gen 6-9 in systematisch-theologischer Perspektive. Die Sintflut. 2005 ⇒346. 109-127.

2688 [T]**Maul, Stefan M.** Das Gilgamesch-Epos. Mü 2005, Beck 191 pp. €19.90. 3-406-52870-8. Bibl. 19-20.

2689 *Nicole, Émile* Babel et la culture. ThEv(VS) 4/2 (2005) 13-22 [Gen 11,1-9].

2690 *Ouro, Roberto* The term t[e]hora in Genesis 7:2: a linguistic study. JATS 16 (2005) 21-29 [OTA 29,261].

2691 **Park, Chun Sik** Theology of judgment in Genesis 6-9. [D]*Davidson, Richard M.* 2005, Diss. Andrews [AUSS 44,172].

2692 **Petrosino, Silvano** Babele: architettura, filosofia e linguaggio di un delirio. 2003 ⇒19,2518; 20,2482. [R]StPat 52 (2005) 640-641 (*De Carolis, Francesco*) [Gen 11].

2693 *Pleitgen, Fritz* Das Internet zu Babel (1. Mose 11,1-9);

2694 *Plöger, Sven* Überflutet (1. Mose 7,11 und 8,22). Kanzelreden. 2005 ⇒376. 35-43/23-33.

2695 *Prinsloo, G.T.M.; Villiers, G.G. de* Unterstanding Gilgamesh: his world and his story. JSem 14/1 (2005) 165-181.

2696 *Pury, Albert de* Sem, Cham et Japhet: de la fraternité à l'esclavage?. [F]HURST, A.: 2005 ⇒64. 495-508 [Gen 9,18-10,32].

2697 *Ringshausen, Gerhard* Noach im Bilderbuch: ein reiches Angebot als didaktische und methodische Herausforderung. Die Sintflut. Lüneburger Theologische Beiträge 2: 2005 ⇒346. 129-150.

2698 [TE]**Sanmartín Ascaso, Joaquín** Epopeya de Gilgames, rey de Uruk. Pliegos de Oriente, Próximo Oriente 10: M 2005, Trotta 427 pp. 84-8164-732-2. Bibl. 14-28.

2699 *Schmid, Vincent* Genèse 11: la tour de Babel ou la dérive totalitaire. LeD 66 (2005) 36-44 [Gen 11,1-9].

2700 *Shaw, Benjamin* The chronogenealogies of Genesis 5 and 11. BVp 39/1 (2005) 107-116.

2701 *Wasserman, Nathan* Offspring of silence, spawn of a fish, son of a gazelle ... Enkidu's different origins in the epic of Gilgameš. [F]KLEIN, J. 2005 ⇒79. 593-599.

## E2.3 **Patriarchae, Abraham**; *Genesis 12s*

2702 *Beauchamp, Paul* Abram et Saraï: la soeur-épouse, ou l'énigme du couple fondateur. Pages exégétiques. LeDiv 202: 2005 <1994> ⇒ 183. 145-180 [Gen 12,10-13,4].

2703 *Boissieu, Emmanuel* Abraham: chevalier de la foi ou figure inhumaine?. Ment. *Kierkegaard, S.*: LV(L) 54/2 (2005) 57-66.

2704 *Carroll Rodas, M. Daniel* La mision integral: ser bendicion: un aporte desde el Antiguo Testamento. Kairós 37 (2005) 25-38 [OTA 29, 81] [Gen 12,1-3].

2705 *Costacurta, Bruna* Abramo e l'esperienza della fede. [F]BERNARD, C. 2005 ⇒8. 15-28 [Gen 12; 22].

2706 *Deurloo, Karel* Abraham van Dan tot Berseba. ITBT 13/2 (2005) 13-14.

2707 *Dion, Marie-France* Du projet à la promesse: analyse syntaxique et critique de la forme de Genèse 12,1-3 et 12,7. SR 34 (2005) 99-118.

2708 *Gelander, Shamai* Abraham's conversations vs. Jacob's conversations. BetM 181 (2005) 125-145 Sum 199. **H.**

2709 *Geoghegan, Jeffrey C.* The exodus of Abraham. BiRe 21/2 (2005) 16-25, 43-46.

2710 *Graham, Helen R.* 'In you all the families of the earth shall be blessed': some initial thoughts on mission in the Old Testament. EAPR 42 (2005) 369-386.

2711 **Grüneberg, Keith N.** Abraham, blessing and the nations: a philological and exegetical study of Genesis 12:3 in its narrative context. BZAW 332: 2003 ⇒19,2551; 20,2502. [R]ThLZ 130 (2005) 258-260 (*Seebass, Horst*); OLZ 100 (2005) 187-191 (*Ruppert, Lothar*); Bib. 86 (2005) 554-557 (*Giuntoli, Federico*).

2712 *Guillaume, Philippe* État de la question historique. LV(L) 54/2 (2005) 5-11.

2713 **Heither, Theresia; Reemts, Christiana** Biblische Gestalten bei den Kirchenvätern: Abraham. Müns 2005, Aschendorff 399 pp. €39. 3-4-02-04385-8 [EuA 81,252—Schwank, Benedikt].

2714 *Hepner, Gershon* The seperation between Abram and Lot reflects the Deuteronomic law prohibiting Ammonites and Moabites. ZAW 117 (2005) 36-52 [Gen 13,6-9; 36,6-8; Dt 23,4].

2715 *Joyce, Paul* Abraham from a christian perspective. Abraham's children. 2005 ⇒544. 18-27.

2716 *Niclós Albarracín, Josep-Vicent* Abraham, com a *gêr* a la terra. La bíblia i els immigrants. 2005 ⇒471. 11-31.

2717 *Ntumba Kapambu, Valentin* Abraham, un paradigme de l'obéissance religieuse. Telema 123/4 (2005) 69-81.

2718 **Pagolu, Augustine** The religion of the patriarchs. JSOT.S 277: 1998 ⇒14,1841; 17,2143. [R]ThR 70 (2005) 439-42 (*Reventlow, Henning*).

2719 *Pardo, José J.* Abrahán, huésped y anfitrión. ResB 46 (2005) 4-12.

2720 *Pelleschi, Christiane* Quand Abraham fait passer sa femme pour sa soeur. LV(L) 54/2 (2005) 23-31.

2721 *Salzmann, Jorg C.* Der Rekurs auf Abraham im Alten Testament. [F]STOLLE, V. 2005 ⇒143. 245-260.

2722 *Sheridan, Sybil* Abraham from a Jewish perspective. Abraham's children. 2005 ⇒544. 9-17.

2723 **Ska, Jean Louis** Abrahán y sus huéspedes: el patriarca y los creyentes en el Dios único. Estella (Navarra) 2004, Verbo Divino 167 pp. 84-8169-637-4. Bibl. 135-149.

2724 *Ska, Jean Louis* Abraham, père de croyants différents. LV(L) 54/2 (2005) 43-56.

2725 *Tollington, J.E.* Abraham and his wives: culture and status. The OT in its world. OTS 52: 2005 ⇒749. 183-199.

2726 *Warner, Megan* Genesis 20-22:19: Abraham's test of allegiance. ABR 53 (2005) 13-30.

2727 *Wénin, André* Abraham: au-delà de l'idolâtrie. LV(L) 54/2 (2005) 13-22.

2728 *Winter, Tim* Abraham from a Muslim perspective. Abraham's children. 2005 ⇒544. 28-35.

### E2.4 **Melchisedech**: *Genesis 14*

2729 *Rossi, Lanfranco* La storia di Mechisedec [!]: re, bestia e angelo: antiche tradizioni giudaiche e cristiane. Studi sull'Oriente Cristiano 9/2 (2005) 21-45.

2730 *Szczepaniak, Michal* Midrasz eschatologiczny o Melchizedeku (11QMelch=11Q13) i jego reminiscencje w Nowym Testamencie. CoTh 75/3 (2005) 125-138. **P.**

2731 **Ziemer, Benjamin** Abram—Abraham: kompositionsgeschichtliche Untersuchungen zu Genesis 14, 15 und 17. BZAW 350: B 2005, De Gruyter xiv; 449 pp. €118. 3-11-018294-7. Bibl. 397-420.

### E2.5 **The Covenant** (alliance, Bund): *Foedus, Genesis 15...*

2732 **Weinfeld, Moshe** Normative and sectarian Judaism in the second temple period. Library of Second Temple Studies 54: L 2005, Clark xiii; 329 pp. £70. 0-567-04441-6.

2733 *Altman, Amnon* Provisions for a case of conflicting commitments in fifteenth-century B.C.E. treaties. $^{F}$KLEIN, J. 2005 ⇒79. 434-445.

2734 *Beauchamp, Paul* Proposition sur l'alliance de l'Ancien Testament comme structure centrale. Pages exégétiques. LeDiv 202: 2005 <1970> ⇒183. 55-86.

2735 *Bolin, Thomas M.* The role of exchange in ancient Mediterranean religion and its implications for reading Genesis 18-19. JSOT 29 (2005) 37-56.

2736 *Castello, Gaetano* Sangue dell'alleanza e banchetto nel contesto di Es 24,1-11. Asp. 52 (2005) 11-40.

2737 *Fiedler, Peter* Zum theologischen Gebrauch von 'Bund' (b$^{e}$rit) in der Hebräischen Bibel. Studien zur biblischen Grundlegung. SBAB 35: 2005 <1981> ⇒209. 1-21.

2738 **Glick, Leonard B.** Marked in your flesh: circumcision from ancient Judea to modern America. NY 2005, OUP xiv; 370 pp. 0-19-517674-X. Bibl. 335-360.

2739 *Olafsson, Gudmundur* God's eternal covenant and the sabbath. JATS 16 (2005) 155-163 [OTA 29,325].

2740 *Rad, Gerhard von* Faith reckoned as righteousness. From Genesis. 2005 <1951> ⇒283. 70-74 [Gen 15,6].

2741 **Rendtorff, Rolf** Die "Bundesformel": eine exegetisch-theologische Untersuchung. SBS 160: 1995 ⇒11/1,425... 14,1874. RThR 70 (2005) 7-8 (*Reventlow, Henning Graf*).

2742 *Stipp, Hermann-Josef* "Meinen Bund hat er gebrochen" (Gen 17,14): die Individualisierung des Bundesbruchs in der Priesterschrift. MThZ 56 (2005) 290-304.

2743 *Van der Horst, Pieter W.* Aan Abrahams dis: Joodse interpretaties van Genesis 18:8. NedThT 59/3 (2005) 207-214.

2744 **Weeks, Noel** Admonition and curse: the ancient Near Eastern treaty/covenant form as a problem in inter-cultural relationships. JSOT.S 407: 2004 ⇒20,2549. RRBLit (2005)* (*Engle, John*).

2745 *Weinfeld, Moshe* The loyalty oath in the ancient Near East;

2746 Sarah and Abimelech (Genesis 20) against the background of an Assyrian law and the Genesis Apocryphon;

2747 The covenantal aspect of the promise of the land to Israel. Normative and sectarian Judaism. 2005 ⇒2732. 2-44/194-198/200-226.

2748 *Wyatt, Nicolas* The meaning of El Roi and the mythological dimension in Genesis 16. 'There's... divinity'. 2005 <1994> ⇒329. 77-84.

## E2.6 The ʿAqedâ, Isaac, Genesis 22...

2749 *Ausloos, Hans; Lemmelijn, Bénédicte* 'Your only son, your beloved one' (Genesis 22): when Septuagint and messianism meet. FLUST, J.: BEThL 192: 2005 ⇒92. 19-31.

2750 *Bergant, Dianne* The binding of Isaac: hermeneutical reflections. Two faiths. 2005 ⇒844. 29-34.

2751 *Boom, Ulrich* Dies ist die Nacht. KatBl 130 (2005) 122-23 [Gen 22].

2752 **Burger, Hilde** De zandloper van Genesis: de visie van Benno Jacob op Genesis 22 in het licht van zijn tijd en van de traditie. 2002 ⇒18, 2527. RKeTh 56 (2005) 159-160 (*Den Dulk, Maarten*).

2753 *Crotty, Robert* The literary structure of the binding of Isaac in Genesis 22. ABR 53 (2005) 31-41.

2754 **Gellman, Jerome I.** Abraham! Abraham! KIERKEGAARD and the Hasidim on the binding of Isaac. 2003 ⇒19,2618; 20,2554. RRelSt 41/1 (2005) 116-120 (*Rynhold, Daniel*) [Gen 22].

2755 **Ghauri, Abdus S.** The only son offered for sacrifice: Isaac or Ishmael?: with Zamzam, Al-Marwah, and Makkah in the bible. 2004 ⇒20, 2556. RVJTR 69 (2005) 159-160, 151 (*Roborgh, Herman*) [Gen 22].

2756 *Greve, Astrid* Bindung Isaaks: Impulse aus der jüdisch-rabbinischen Auslegung. KatBl 130 (2005) 111-116 [Gen 22].

2757 *Kassel, Maria* Gott im Wandel: Imaginationen zu Genesis 22. KatBl 130 (2005) 117-121.

2758 **Kessler, Edward** Bound by the bible: Jews, christians and the sacrifice of Isaac. 2004 ⇒20,2557. RRRT 12 (2005) 358-360 (*Newby, Mark*); Religion 35 (2005) 266-267 (*McClymond, Kathryn*); RBLit (2005)* (*Kalimi, Isaac*) [Gen 22,1-19].

2759 **Keuchen, Marion** Die "Opferung Isaaks" im 20. Jahrhundert auf der Theaterbühne: Auslegungsimpulse im Blick auf "Abrahams Zelt" (Theater Musentümpel–Andersonn) und "Gottesvergiftung" (Choralgraphisches Theater Heidelberg–Grasmück). Altes Testament und Moderne 19: Müns 2005, Lit viii, 296 pp. 38258-71967 [Gen 22].

2760 *Michel, Andreas* Isaaks Opferung, exegetisch gelesen. KatBl 130 (2005) 97-101 [Gen 22].

2761 *Nault, François* Jouissance et engendrement: à propos de Genèse vingt-deux. [F]GENEST, O. 2005 ⇒46. 523-545.

2762 [E]**Noort, Edward; Tigchelaar, Eibert** The sacrifice of Isaac: the Aqedah (Genesis 22) and its interpretations. 2002 ⇒18,2524... 20, 2559. [R]BiblInterp 13 (2005) 194-197 (*Moberly, Walter*).

2763 *Steinacker, Peter* "Das Opfer Abrahams", Gen 22,1-14: eine Predigtstudie. [F]STEGEMANN, W. 2005 ⇒139. 250-259.

2764 *Steins, Georg* Den Sohn opfern?: eine biblische Story als Vermächtnis. Das Buch. 2005 ⇒1130. 163-180.

2765 **Steins, Georg** Die "Bindung Isaaks" im Kanon (Gen 22). Herders Biblische Studien 20: 1999 ⇒15,2011... 20,2563. [R]ThR 70 (2005) 330-332 (*Reventlow, Henning Graf*).

2766 *Swetnam, James* The sacrifice of Isaac in Genesis and Hebrews: a study in the hermeneutic of faith. L&S 1 (2005) 23-40 [Gen 22].

2767 **Teugels, Lieve M.** Bible and midrash: the story of 'The wooing of Rebekah' (Gen. 24). CBET 35: 2004 ⇒20,2567. [R]RBLit (2005)* (*Sherman, Phillip*) [Gen 24].

2768 *Varsam, Maria* "If Isaac could speak...": redefining sacrifice. Writing history. 2005 ⇒523. 163-178 [Gen 22,1-19].

2769 *Zanetti, Paolo S.* Una nota su *Gen.* 24,63. Imitatori di Gesù Cristo. 2005 <1995> ⇒330. 509-516.

### E2.7 **Jacob** and Esau: ladder dream; *Jacob, somnium, Gen 25...*

2770 *Agyenta, Alfred* The Jacob cycle narratively speaking: the question of the extent of the Jacob cycle in the book of Genesis. JNSL 31/1 (2005) 59-74.

2771 **Claypool, John R.** God the ingenious alchemist: transforming tragedy into blessing. Harrisburg, PA 2005, Morehouse 80 pp. $15 [BiTod 45,54—Dianne Bergant].

2772 **Dieckmann, Detlef** Segen für Isaak: eine rezeptionsästhetische Auslegung von Gen 26 und Kotexten. BZAW 329: 2003 ⇒19,2639; 20, 2571. [R]ThZ 61 (2005) 173-174 (*Klein, Renate*).

2773 *Dieckmann, Detlef* Gen 26 als Segenserzählung. BZ 49 (2005) 264-274.

2774 *Fokkelman, Jan P.* Jacob as a character. Analyse narrative. BEThL 191: 2005 ⇒742. 3-17.

2775 **Giuntoli, Federico** L'officina della tradizione: studio di alcuni interventi redazionali post-sacerdotali e del loro contesto nel ciclo di Giacobbe (Gn 25,19-50,26). AnBib 154: 2003 ⇒19,2642; 20,2572. [R]CBQ 67 (2005) 116-117 (*Pilch, John J.*); ZKTh 127 (2005) 128-129 (*Paganini, Simone*); RB 112 (2005) 449-455 (*Loza Vera, J.*); ATG 68 (2005) 311-312 (*Vílchez, José*); Bib. 86 (2005) 115-119 (*Sicre, José Luis*).

2776 *Matysiak, Bogdan W.* Pozabiblijne paralele do 'Drabiny Jakibowej' z Rdz 28,12n [Extra-biblical parallels to 'Jacob's Ladder' in Gen 28: 12ff]. STV 43/2 (2005) 147-154 [Isa 34]. **P.**

2777 *Ortkemper, Franz-Josef* Gottesbegegnungen in der Jakobsgeschichte. FSTENDEBACH, F. 2005 ⇒141. 363-369 [Gen 28,10-22].

2778 *Paganini, Simone* "Wir haben Wasser gefunden": Beobachtungen zur Erzählanalyse von Gen 25,19-26,35. ZAW 117 (2005) 21-35.

2779 *Peleg, Yitzhak* "Going up and going down": a key to interpreting Jacob's dream. HUCA 76 (2005) *33-*47 [Gen 28,10-22]. **H.**

2780 *Roubach, Sharon* 'Two who donned the veil': the image of twins in the bible. BetM 183 (2005) 366-90. Sum 392 [Gen 25; 38,27-30]. **H.**

2781 *Van Wolde, Ellen* Cognitive linguistics and its application to Genesis 28:10-22. MVAN TILBORG, S.: BiblInterp 71: 2005 ⇒155. 125-148.

## E2.8 **Jacob's wrestling, the Angels**: *Gen 31-36 & 38*

2782 *Fewell, Danna N.* Lecture féministe: viol, lecture et représentation en Genèse 34. Guide des nouvelles lectures. 2005 ⇒426. 97-114.

2783 **Hilbrands, Walter** Heilige oder Hure?: Juda und Tamar (Genesis 38) in jüdischer und christlicher Auslegungsgeschichte. D*Houtman, Cornelis* 2005, Diss. Kampen [RTL 37,609].

2784 **Jennings, Theodore W.** Jacob's wound: homoerotic narrative in the literature of ancient Israel. NY 2005, Continuum xv; 288 pp. $27. 0-8264-1712-4. Bibl. 263-269 [Gen 32,25-33].

2785 *Musskopf, André S.; González Hernández, Yoimel* Homens e ratos!: desconstruindo o modelo hegemônico de masculinidade e visibilizando modelos alternativos construídos nos corpos de homens em Gênesis 38. Estudos bíblicos 86 (2005) 57-65.

2786 **Parry, Robin** Old Testament story and Christian ethics: the rape of Dinah as a case study . Milton Keynes 2004, Paternoster xx; 350 pp. 1842272101. Foreword *Craig Bartholomew*; Bibl. 299-338 [Gen 34].

2787 *Rofé, Alexander* Defilement of virgins in biblical law and the case of Dinah (Genesis 34). Bib. 86 (2005) 369-375.

2788 *Scardelai, Donizete* A luta de Jacó como paradigma de violênciao Gn 32,23-33: do simbolismo à realidade. Espaços 13 (2005) 117-131 [OTA 29,140].

2789 *Sharon, Diane M.* Some results of a structural semiotic analysis of the story of Judah and Tamar. JSOT 29 (2005) 289-318 [Gen 38].

2790 *Smelik, Klaas A.D.* Genesis 38 revisited. FHOOGEWOUD, F. 2005 ⇒ 63. 114-120 [OTA 29,30].

2791 **Sullivan, Kevin P.** Wrestling with angels: a study of the relationship between angels and humans in ancient Jewish literature and the NT. AGJU 55: 2004 ⇒20,2589. RRdQ 22 (2005) 291-94 (*Puech, Émile*).

2792 *Winter, Franz* Dimensionen weiterer zentraler religiöser Vorstellungen: Zwischenwesen (Engel, Dämonen, Geister). Handbuch Religionswissenschaft. 2003 ⇒1016. 651-662.

2793 **Yamada, Frank Masao** Configurations of rape in the Hebrew Bible: a literary analysis of three rape narratives. 2005, Diss. Princeton, Sem. [RTL 37,612] [Gen 34].

2794 *Yoreh, Tzemah* Jacob's struggle. ZAW 117 (2005) 95-97 [Gen 32,2-3; 32,24-30].

## E2.9 **Joseph**; Jacob's blessings; *Genesis 37; 39-50*

2795 *Boecker, Hans J.* Eine Überlegung zu Gen 47,2. BN 124 (2005) 5-8.

2796 *Gitay, Y.* The role of the rhetoric in the rise of leadership: the case of Judah. JSem 14/1 (2005) 112-148.

2797 *Gleeson, Len J.* Difficulties with identifying the Pharaoh in Genesis 40-47. BN 123 (2005) 103-104.

2798 *Golka, Friedemann* Biblische Josephserzählung und Josephsroman: Thomas MANN, Gerhard VON RAD und die neuere Bibelexegese. Das AT und die Kunst. ATM 15: 2005 ⇒711. 199-205.

2799 *Guevara Llaguno, Junkal* La historia de José: releyendo a un personaje. ResB 47 (2005) 41-49.

2800 **Krauss, Heinrich; Küchler, Max** Erzählungen der Bibel III: das Buch Genesis in literarischer Perspektive: die Josef-Erzählung. Gö 2005, Vandenhoeck & R. 171 pp. €19.80. 3-525-531044.

2801 **Lanckau, Jörg** Der Herr der Träume: eine Studie zur Funktion des Traumes in der Josefsgeschichte der Hebräischen Bibel. [D]*Rüterswörden, U.* 2005, Diss. Bonn.

2802 *Loren, Aaron Q.* Un'analisi lessicale di Genesi 37-50 della LXX: annotazioni per la comprensione di una traduzione. Materia giudaica 10/1 (2005) 73-84.

2803 *Miller, Patrick D.* The end of the beginning: Genesis 50. [M]JUEL, D. 2005 ⇒73. 115-126.

2804 *Naumann, Thomas* Der Vater in der biblischen Josefserzählung: Möglichkeiten der Charaktermodellierung in biblischen Erzählungen. ThZ 61 (2005) 44-64.

2805 *Newman, Hillel I.* A hippodrome on the road of Ephrath. Bib. 86 (2005) 213-228 [Gen 48,7].

2806 *Niehoff, Maren* New garments for biblical Joseph. Biblical interpretation. Ment. *Josephus; Philo*: SBL.Symp. 26: 2005 ⇒758. 33-56.

2807 **Pirson, Ron** The lord of the dreams: a semantic and literary analysis of Genesis 37-50. JSOT.S 355: 2002 ⇒18,2589; 20,2617. [R]JSSt 50 (2005) 211-213 (*Nolan, Caroline*).

2808 *Rad, Gerhard von* The Joseph narrative and ancient wisdom. From Genesis. 2005 <1953> ⇒283. 75-81.

2809 *Shupak, Nili* A reexamination of the dreams of the Egyptian officials and of Pharaoh in the Joseph narrative (Gen 40-41). Shnaton 15 (2005) 55-95.

2810 *Ska, Jean Louis* Judah, Joseph, and the reader (Gen 42:6-9 and 44:18-34). Das Alte Testament...Beiträge. Ment. *Rad, G. von*: ATM 10: 2005 ⇒802. 27-39.

2811 *Smith, Bryan* The central role of Judah in Genesis 37-50. BS 162/646 (2005) 158-174.

2812 *Weimar, Peter* Gen 46,1-5—Ein fremdkörper im Rahmen der Josefsgeschichte. BN 123 (2005) 5-23;

2813 Gen 46,2-4 und die Jakobgeschichte: eine Spurensuche. RB 112 (2005) 481-510.

2814 *Weisberg, David B.* Jacob wards off endangerment. [F]KLEIN, J. 2005 ⇒79. 764-771 [Gen 47,7-9].

2815 **Wénin, André** Joseph ou l'invention de la fraternité: lecture narrative et anthropologique de Genèse 37-50. Le livre et le rouleau 21: P 2005, Lessius 352 pp. €32. 2-87299-134-4. Bibl. 343-349. [R]Vies consacrées 77 (2005) 195-196 (*Luciani, Didier*); RSR 93 (2005) 580-582 (*Artus, Olivier*); EThL 81 (2005) 508-511 (*Lichtert, C.*); RBLit (2005)* (*Vogels, Walter*).

### E3.1 **Exodus event and theme**; *textus, commentarii*

2816 *Becker, Uwe* Das Exodus-Credo: historischer Haftpunkt und Geschichte einer alttestamentlichen Glaubensformel. FCONRAD, J.: ABIG 17: 2005 ⇒27. 81-100.

2817 *Benzi, Guido* Esodo: dalla servitù al servizio: 'libera il mio popolo perché mi serva nel deserto' (Es 7,16). Libertà va cercando. Sussidi biblici 87: 2005 ⇒353. 47-80.

2818 *Bosman, Hendrik* Origin and identity: rereading Exodus as a polemical narrative then (Palestine) and now (Africa). Scriptura 90 (2005) 869-877 [OTA 30,31].

2819 *Brueggemann, Walter* The book of Exodus. OT survey. 2005 ⇒413. 25-32.

2820 ET**Carasik, Michael** The commentators' bible: the JPS Miqra'ot gedolot: Exodus. Ph 2005, Jewish Publication Society of America xix, 349 pp. 0-8276-0812-8.

2821 *Cardona Ramírez, Hernán* Las raíces de la comunidad en el éxodo. El grano. 2005 ⇒197. 145-160.

2822 **Cherian, George Edayadiyil** From Exodus event and beyond: historical, theological, and interpretative dynamics of the Exodus as an event. D*Boschi, B.G.*: R 2005, Pont. Univ. S. Thoma xix; 118 pp. Pars Diss.; Bibl. 67-110.

2823 **Coats, George W.** Exodus 1-18. FOTL 2A: 1999 ⇒15,2066... 17, 2298. ROTEs 18 (2005) 137-138 (*Stassen, S.L.*).

2824 *Collins, John J.* The development of the Exodus tradition <2001>;

2825 The Exodus and biblical theology <1995>. Encounters. 2005 ⇒200. 59-66/67-77.

2826 **Dohmen, Christoph** Exodus 19-40. HThK.AT: 2004 ⇒20,2631. RThLZ 130 (2005) 933-934 (*Reventlow, Henning Graf*); ThRv 101 (2005) 373-5 (*Oswald, Wolfgang*); IThQ 70 (2005) 289-291 (*Maher, Michael*); JETh 19 (2005) 225-227 (*Kürle, Stefan*).

2827 **Enns, Peter** Exodus. NIV Application Comm.: GR 2000, Zondervan 620 pp. $30. 0-310-20607-3. Bibl. 37-38.

2828 *Fischer, Irmtraud* Aufbruch zu Neuem. BiHe 41/161 (2005) 6-9.

2829 **Galpaz-Feller, Pnina** יציאת מצרים [The Exodus from Egypt (Exodus 1-15)]. 2002 ⇒19,2697. RRBLit (2005)* (*Barmash, Pamela*).

2830 *Himbaza, Innocent* Voir Dieu: LXX d'Exode contre TM et LXX du Pentateuque. FSCHENKER, A.: OBO 214: 2005 ⇒134. 100-111 [Exod 16,7-10; 24,10-11; 33,20].

2831 **Larsson, Göran** Bound for freedom: the book of Exodus in Jewish and Christian traditions. 1999 ⇒15,2088... 18,2617. RRBLit (2005)* (*Burke, Donald*).

2832 *Levy, Yamin Derekh hokhma*, part II: theological implications of the Exodus narrative. JBQ 33 (2005) 53-60.

2833 **Meyers, Carol L.** Exodus. New Cambridge Bible Commentary: C 2005, CUP xxiii; 311 pp. £35/13. 0-521-80781-6/00291-5.

2834 **Motyer, Alec** The message of Exodus. Leicester 2005, IVP 327 pp. 0-8308-2427-8.

2835 **Nepi, Antonio** Esodo: capitoli 16-40. Dabar: 2004 ⇒20,2643. REstTrin 39 (2005) 582-583 (*Vázquez Allegue, Jaime*).

2836 **Oblath, Michael D.** The Exodus itinerary sites: their locations from the perspective of the biblical sources. Studies in biblical literature 55: 2004 ⇒20,2644. RRBLit (2005)* (*Dozeman, Thomas*).

2837 **Phillips, David** Hebrew-English Paleo Exodus: scripture at the end of the Iron II period. ANETS 14: Lewiston, NY 2005, Mellen xxiii; 339 pp. 0-7734-6315-1. Bibl. 323-336.

2838 *Pixley, Jorge* Exodus. Global bible commentary. 2005 ⇒2443. 17-29.

2839 *Salvesen, Alison* JACOB of Edessa's version of Exodus 1 and 28. Hugoye 8/1 (2005)*.

2840 [T]**Vannini, Marco** Meister ECKHART: Commento all'Esodo. Fonti Medievali: R 2004, Città Nuova 200 pp. €18.

2841 *Weor, Jonathan* The narratives of origin and migration of the Tiv people (of Nigeria) as an indigenous interpretative resource for the interpretation of the book of Exodus. Scriptura 90 (2005) 885-891 [OTA 30,31].

2842 **Zornberg, Avivah Gottlieb** The particulars of rapture: reflections on Exodus. 2001 ⇒17,2330... 19,2719. [R]ThLZ 130 (2005) 631-633 (*Graupner, Axel*).

2843 *Zulu, Edwin* Interpreting Exodus from the perspective of Ngoni narratives concerning origins. Scriptura 90 (2005) 892-98 [OTA 30,31].

### E3.2 **Moyses**—Pharaoh, Goshen—*Exodus 1...*

2844 *Barton, John* Moses from a christian perspective. Abraham's children. 2005 ⇒544. 49-54.

2845 *Bordreuil, Pierre* Moïse réformateur religieux. [M]CAQUOT, A. 2005 ⇒22. 101-114.

2846 **Britt, Brian M.** Rewriting Moses: the narrative eclipse of the text. Gender, Culture, Theory 14; JSOT.S 402: 2004 ⇒20,2657. [R]RBLit (2005)* (*McEntire, Mark*).

2847 **Buckenmaier, Achim** Moses: Geschichte einer Rettung. Augsburg 2005, Sankt Ulrich 160 pp. €16.90. 3-936484-554.

2848 **Ferrada Moreira, Andres Gabriel** Nacimiento de Moisés: historia y teología. [D]*Breton, Santiago* 2005, Diss. Gregoriana.

2849 *Gerhards, Meik* Über die Herkunft der Frau des Mose. VT 55 (2005) 162-175.

2850 **Gerhards, Meik** Aussetzungsgeschichte des Mose und Babelerzählung: ein Beitrag zur Frage themenübergreifender literarischer Zusammenhänge im nichtpriesterschriftlichen Tetrateuch. [D]*Jeremias, Jörg* 2005, Diss. Marburg [ThLZ 130,888] [Gen 11,1-9; Exod 2,1-10].

2851 *Gorsky, Jonathan* Moses from a Jewish perspective. Abraham's children. 2005 ⇒544. 40-48.

2852 *Gosse, Bernard* L'écriture d'Ex 2,1-10 en relation avec les rédactions des livres de la Genèse et de l'Exode. BN 123 (2005) 25-30.

2853 *Huizenga, Leroy A.* The incarnation of the Servant: the "Suffering Servant" and Matthean christology. HBT 27/1 (2005) 25-58.

2854 *Keeler, Annabel* Moses from a Muslim perspective. Abraham's children. 2005 ⇒544. 55-66.

2855 *Kiesow, Klaus* Im Netzwerk des Exodus: die Eröffnungskapitel des Buches Exodus intertextuell gelesen. rhs 48 (2005) 185-192 [Exod 1-2].

2856 *Kugler, Rob* Hearing the story of Moses in Ptolemaic Egypt: Artapanus accomodates the tradition. [F]LUTTIKHUIZEN, G.: AGJU 59: 2005 ⇒93. 67-80.

2857 **Otto, Eckart** Mose: Geschichte und Legende. Beck'sche Reihe Wissen 2400: Mü 2004, Beck 128 pp. €7.90. 3406-53600X;

2858 Die Tora des Mose: die Geschichte der literarischen Vermittlung von Recht, Religion und Politik durch die Mosegestalt. 2001 ⇒17,2341; 20,2664. [R]RBLit 7 (2005) 138-140 (*Hamilton, Mark W.*).

2859 *Paul, Shalom M.* Exodus 1:21: ‘to found a family’: a biblical and Akkadian idiom. Divrei Shalom. 2005 <1992> ⇒273. 177-180.

2860 *Reiss, Moshe* The women around Moses. JBQ 33 (2005) 127-130.

2861 *Römer, Thomas C.* The construction of the figure of Moses according to biblical and extrabiblical sources. AJBI 30-31 (2004-2005) 99-116.

2862 **Widmer, Michael** Moses, God, and the dynamics of intercessory prayer: a study of Exodus 32-34 and Numbers 13-14. FAT 2/8: 2004 ⇒20,2670. [R]TrinJ 26 (2005) 323-325 (*Timmer, Daniel C.*); OLZ 100 (2005) 630-633 (*Schmitt, Hans-Christoph*); RBLit (2005)* (*Heard, Christopher*); HBT 27/1 (2005) 125-128 (*Dearman, J. Andrew*).

2863 **Winslow, Karen S.** Early Jewish and christian memories of Moses' wives–exogamist marriage and ethnic identity. Lewiston, NY 2005, Mellen iv; 493 pp. £140/85. 0-7734-6032-2. Bibl. 455-480.

### E3.3 **Nomen divinum, Tetragrammaton**; *Exodus 3,14*...**Plagues**

2864 *Cohen, Jeremy M. Hatan damim*—the bridegroom of blood. JBQ 33 (2005) 120-126 [Exod 4,24-26].

2865 *De Troyer, Kristin* The names of God: their pronunciation and their translation: a digital tour of some of the main witnesses. LecDif 2 (2005)*.

2866 **Diesel, Anja** Ich bin Jahwe: der Aufstieg der ’$^{a}$ni Yhwh-Aussage im Alten Testament zum Schlüsselwort monotheistischer Gotteskonzeption. [D]*Zwickel, Wolfgang* 2005, Diss. Mainz [ThLZ 130,888].

2867 *Gericke, J.W.* Beyond reconciliation—monistic Yahwism and the problem of evil in philosophy of religion. VeE 26 (2005) 64-92;

2868 Deconstructed sacred space and the ontological status of Yahweh: the case for anti-realism. JSem 14/2 (2005) 361-383.

2869 **Gnuse, Robert Karl** No other gods: emergent monotheism in Israel. JSOT.S 241: 1997 ⇒13,1990... 17,2359. [R]ThR 70 (2005) 423-425 (*Reventlow, Henning Graf*).

2870 *Guillaume, Philippe* Only six plagues in the Priestly narrative. BN 123 (2005) 31-33 [Exod 7-12].

2871 *Hempelmann, Heinzpeter* Die "mosaische Unterscheidung" als Geburtsstunde und Verhängnis des jüdisch-christlichen Monotheismus (Jan Assmann). ThBeitr 36 (2005) 117-132.

2872 **Humphreys, Colin J.** The miracles of Exodus: a scientist's discovery of the extraordinary natural causes of the biblical stories. 2003 ⇒19,2740. [R]JSSt 50 (2005) 373-379 (*Johnstone, William*).

2873 *Kessler, Hans* Töten für Gott?: die neue Monotheismuskritik, oder: was monotheistische Religionen pluralismusfähig (und authentisch) macht. [F]STENDEBACH, F. 2005 ⇒141. 256-269.

2874 *Krem, John David K.* The rendering of the divine name *Yhwh* in some Ghanaian bible translation projects. BiTr 56 (2005) 71-76.

2875 **Kusuhara, Hiroyuki** Die Komposition der Plagenerzählung (Ex 7-11) und die gegenwärtige Pentateuchdiskussion. [D]*Utzschneider, Helmut* 2005, Diss. Augustana [ThLZ 130,889].

2876 *Lemaire, André* The universal God: how the God of Israel became a God for all. BArR 31/6 (2005) 57-59, 67.

2877 **Lemaire, André** Naissance du monothéisme: point de vue d'un historien. 2003 ⇒19,2745. [R]REJ 164 (2005) 327-329 (*Rothschild, Jean-Pierre*); RB 112 (2005) 138-139 (*Tarragon, J.-M. de*).

2878 *Medina, Richard W.* La estructura sintáctica y la interpretación de Éxodo 6:2- 9. DavarLogos 4/2 (2005) 101-115.

2879 **Orenstein, Walter** Teach me about God: the meaning and significance of the name of God . Northvale, NJ 2005, Aronson xxvii; 263 pp. 0-7657-6188-2.

2880 *Pertini, Miguel Ángel* Apuntes para la exégesis y la teología de LXX Ex 3,14. EstB 63 (2005) 147-173.

2881 **Pfeiffer, Henrik** Jahwes Kommen von Süden: Jdc 5; Hab 3; Dtn 33 und Ps 68 in ihrem literatur- und theologiegeschichtlichen Umfeld. [D]*Köckert, Matthias*: FRLANT 211: Gö 2005, Vandenhoeck & R. 313 pp. €98. 3-525-53074-9. Diss.-Habil. Humboldt; Bibl. 272-296.

2882 *Ricoeur, Paul* Nommer Dieu. ETR 80/4 (2005) 37-56.

2883 **Rösel, Martin** Adonaj—warum Gott 'Herr' genannt wird. FAT 29: 2000 ⇒16,2244... 20,2693. [R]ThR 70 (2005) 446-447 (*Reventlow, Henning Graf*).

2884 *Ska, Jean Louis* La vocación de Moisés. El camino. 2005 <1993> ⇒ 302. 9-21 [Exod 3].

2885 **Trevisanato, Siro Igino** The plagues of Egypt: archaeology, history and science look at the Bible. Piscataway, NJ 2005, Euphrates vii; 196 pp. 1-593-33234-3.

2886 *Wyatt, Nick* The development of the tradition in Exodus 3<1979>;

2887 The significance of the burning bush <1986>. Mythic mind. 2005 ⇒ 328. 6-12/13-17 [Exod 3].

2888 *Zalcman, Lawrence* Shield of Abraham, Fear of Isaac, Dread of Esau. ZAW 117 (2005) 405-410 [2 Chr 25,14-15; Jer 49,16].

## E3.4 *Pascha, sanguis, sacrificium*: **Passover, blood, sacrifice,** *Ex 11...*

2889 **Albert, Jean-Pierre; Midant-Reynes, Béatrix** Le sacrifice humain en Egypte ancienne et ailleurs. Études d'égyptologie 6: P 2005, Soleb 284 pp. 2-9523726-0-8.

2890 *Böckler, Annette Mirjam* Eine Nacht, anders als alle Nächte: Gedanken zu Sederfeiern in Kirchen. FrRu 12 (2005) 94-107.

2891 *Briend, Jacques* La Pâque, de Moïse à Jésus. MoBi 164 (2005) 24-9.

2892 *Brooke, George J.* Songs of revolution: the Song of Miriam and its counterparts. Dead Sea scrolls and the NT. 2005 <1994> ⇒194. 272-281 [Exod 15,21].

2893 **Dahm, Ulrike** Opferkult und Priestertum in Alt-Israel: ein kultur- und religionswissenschaftlicher Beitrag. BZAW 327: 2003 ⇒19, 2764; 20,2706. [R]ETR 80 (2005) 126-127 (*Bauks, Michaela*).

2894 **Davies, John A.** A royal priesthood: literary and intertextual perspectives on an image of Israel in Exodus 19.6. JSOT.S 395: 2004 ⇒ 20,2707. [R]L&S 1 (2005) 179; CBQ 67 (2005) 487-488 (*Gnuse, Robert Karl*); RBLit (2005)* (*Ska, Jean-Louis*).

2895 *Doan, William; Giles, Terry* The songs of Israel: Exodus 15:1-18. ProcGLM 25 (2005) 29-42.

2896 **Eberhart, Christian** Studien zur Bedeutung der Opfer im Alten Testament: die Signifikanz von Blut- und Verbrennungsriten im kultischen Rahmen. WMANT 94: 2002 ⇒18,2689... 20,2710. [R]OLZ 100 (2005) 72-75 (*Thiel, Winfried*).

2897 **Frankel, David** The murmuring stories of the priestly school: a retrieval of ancient sacerdotal lore. VT.S 89: 2002 ⇒18,2690... 20, 2711. [R]ThR 70 (2005) 399-402 (*Schmidt, Ludwig*) [Exod 16; Num 16-18; 20].

2898 *Geller, Stephen A.* Manna and sabbath: a literary-theological reading of Exodus 16. Interp. 59 (2005) 5-16.

2899 **Gilders, William K.** Blood ritual in the Hebrew Bible: meaning and power. 2004 ⇒20,2712. [R]Religion 35 (2005) 132-134 (*Doak, Brian R.*); SR 34 (2005) 581-582 (*Bergen, David A.*); RBLit (2005)* (*McEntire, Mark*).

2900 *Human, Dirk J.* Africa in need of an exodus?: perspectives on the theology of Exodus 15:1-21. Critical study. ATM 20: 2005 ⇒457. 74-96.

2901 **Laufer, Nathan** Leading the Passover journey: the Seder's meaning revealed, the Haggadah's story retold. Woodstock, VT 2005, Jewish Lights xxi; 185 pp. 1-580-23211-6. Bibl. 173-176.

2902 *Lüling, G.* The Passover lamb and the hyena, the old Arab 'mother of blood vengeance'. JHiC 11/2 (2005) 24-38 [NTAb 50,532].

2903 *Marx, Alfred* Pourquoi sacrifie-t-on?: sur les traces d'un mythe fondateur. [F]SCHENKER, A.: OBO 214: 2005 ⇒134. 215-228;

2904 Tuer, donner, manger dans le culte sacrificiel de l'Ancien Israël. La cuisine et l'autel. BEHE.R 124: 2005 ⇒539. 3-13.

2905 **Marx, Alfred** Les systèmes sacrificiels de l'Ancien Testament: formes et fonctions du culte sacrificiel à Yhwh. VT.S 105: Lei 2005, Brill vi; 263 pp. €90. 90-04-14286-X. Bibl. 226-241.

2906 *Palumbieri, Sabino* Ira, castigo e sacrificio. una lettura comparata in chiave antropologica. Sal. 67 (2005) 27-73.

2907 **Prosic, Tamara** The development and symbolism of Passover until 70 CE. JSOT.S 414: 2004 ⇒20,2726. [R]RBLit (2005)* (*Gilders, William; Wagenaar, Jan*).

2908 *Schmidt, Ludwig* Die vorpriesterliche Darstellung in Ex 11,1-13,16. ZAW 117 (2005) 171-188.

2909 *Schonfield, Jeremy* The four-fold structure of the Passover Haggadah. Studies in Jewish prayer. JSSt.S 17: 2005 ⇒828. 185-205 [Exod 12].

2910 *Ska, Jean Louis* El paso del mar Rojo. El camino. 2005 <1993> ⇒ 302. 23-39 [Exod 14];

2911 Il Cantico de Mosè (Es 15,1-21) e la regalità di Yhwh, Dio d'Israele: riflessione sulla poetica ebraica. Il bello della bibbia. 2005 ⇒357. 3-34.

2912 **Stroumsa, Guy G.** La fin du sacrifice: les mutations religieuses de l'antiquité tardive. P 2005, Jacob 213 pp. 2-7381-1634-5. Préf. *Scheid, John.*

2913 *Winther-Nielsen, Nicolai* Towards the peak of Mount Sinai: a discourse-pragmatic analysis of Exodus 19. HIPHIL 2 (2005)*;

2914 Appendix: a hierarchical display of Exodus 19. HIPHIL 2 (2005)*.

## E3.5 **Decalogus**, *Ex 20=Dt 5; Ex 21ss*; **Ancient Near Eastern Law**

2915 *Baker, David L.* The finger of God and the forming of a nation: the origin and purpose of the decalogue. TynB 56/1 (2005) 1-24 [Exod 20,1-17; Deut 5,6-21].

2916 *Dohmen, Christoph* "Es gilt das gesprochene Wort": zur narrativen Logik der Verschriftung des Dekalogs. Die Zehn Worte. QD 212: 2005 ⇒745. 43-56.

2917 *Guillaume, Jean-Marie* 'Tu ne te feras pas d'idole': du décalogue aux béatitudes. Spiritus 180 (2005) 304-313.

2918 **Himbaza, Innocent** Le décalogue et l'histoire du texte: études des formes textuelles du décalogue et leurs implications dans l'histoire du texte de l'Ancien Testament. OBO 207: 2004 ⇒20,2737. [R]BOTSA 19 (2005) 21-22 (*Holter, Knut*); RBLit (2005)* (*Sanders, Paul*).

2919 *Hossfeld, Frank-Lothar* Vom Horeb zum Sinai: der Dekalog als Echo auf Ex 32-34. Die Zehn Worte. QD 212: 2005 ⇒745. 87-93.

2920 *Hütter, Reinhard* The Ten Commandments as a mirror of sin(s): Anglican decline—Lutheran eclipse. ProEc 14 (2005) 46-57.

2921 **John de Taizé** A caminho da terra da liberdade: uma releitura dos dez mandamentos. Braga 2005, A.O. 160 pp.

2922 *Konkel, Michael* Was hörte Israel am Sinai?: methodische Anmerkungen zur Kontextanalyse des Dekalogs [Exod 24; Dt 5,6-21];

2923 *Kratz, Reinhard G.* "Höre Israel" und Dekalog. Die Zehn Worte. QD 212: 2005 ⇒745. 11-42/77-86.

2924 **Kuntz, Paul Grimley** The ten commandments in history: Mosaic paradigms for a wellordered society. [E]*D'Evelyn, Thomas* 2004 ⇒20, 2742. [R]RRT 12 (2005) 360-362 (*Vinten, Gerald*); OTEs 18 (2005) 942-944 (*Branch, Robin G.*).

2925 *Oden, Thomas C.* No other gods. I am the Lord your God. 2005 ⇒ 816. 41-54 [OTA 28,280].

2926 *Otto, Eckart* Der Dekalog in den deuteronomistischen Redaktionen des Deuteronomiums. Die Zehn Worte. QD 212: 2005 ⇒745. 95-108.

2927 *Schwienhorst-Schönberger, Ludger* Die Zehn Gebote—der Freiheit eine Form geben. Studien zum AT. SBAB 40: 2005 <2000> ⇒298. 33-41;

2928 Das Verhältnis von Dekalog und Bundesbuch. Die Zehn Worte. QD 212: 2005 ⇒745. 57-75 = Studien zum AT 43-60.

2929 *Seitz, Christopher R.* The ten commandments: positive and natural law and the covenants old and new—christian use of the decalogue and moral law. I am the Lord your God. 2005 ⇒816. 18-38 [OTA 28,279].

2930 **Soler, Jean** L'invention du monothéisme: aux origines du Dieu unique, 2: la loi de Moïse. Pluriel: P 2005, Hachette 347 pp. €9. 2-012-7920-06.

2931 *Turner, Philip* The ten commandments in the church in a postmodern world. I am the Lord your God. 2005 ⇒816. 3-17 [OTA 28,279].

2932 *Vilarassau, Marc* El cos, ídol o icona?. QVC 220 (2005) 44-58.

2933 *Wilken, Robert L.* Keeping the commandments. I am the Lord your God. 2005 ⇒816. 239-252 [OTA 28,280].

2934 *Frevel, Christian* Jeden dla wszystkich?: blaski i cienie monoteizmu biblijnego [Einer für alle?: Leistung und Schwächen des biblischen Monotheismus]. ACra 37 (2005) 201-223 [Exod 20,3]. **P.**
2935 *Miller, Patrick D.* What do you do with the God you have?: the first commandment as political axiom. FBRUEGGEMANN, W.—COUSAR, C. 2005 ⇒16. 33-41 [Exod 20,3].
2936 **Miller, Patrick D.** The God you have: politics and the first commandment. 2004 ⇒20,2762. ROTEs 18 (2005) 149-151 (*Branch, Robin G.*).
2937 *Rahner, Johanna* Du wirst keine anderen Götter neben mir haben: theologische und (religions-)philosophische Implikationen der Mosaischen Unterscheidung Jan Assmanns. ZKTh 127 (2005) 57-76 [Exod 20,3].
2938 *Cottin, Jérôme* L'interdit biblique sur les images. Sources 31 (2005) 240-246 [Exod 20,4-5].
2939 *Molinski, Waldemar* Das biblische Bilderverbot und die kirchliche Bilderverehrung. LebZeug 60 (2005) 85-99 [Exod 20,4-5].
2940 *Tilly, Michael* Antijüdische Instrumentalisierungen des biblischen Bilderverbots. FBÜMLEIN, K. 2005 ⇒18. 23-30 [Exod 20,4-5].
2941 *Rad, Gerhard von* Some aspects of the Old Testament worldview. From Genesis. 2005 <1964> ⇒283. 205-222 [Exod 20,4-6].
2942 *Radner, Ephraim* Taking the Lord's name in vain. I am the Lord your God. 2005, 77-94 [OTA 28,281] [Exod 20,7].
2943 *Bockmuehl, Markus* 'Keeping it holy': Old Testament commandment and New Testament faith. I am the Lord your God. 2005 ⇒816. 95-124 [OTA 28,281] [Exod 20,8-11].
2944 **Bailey, Wilma A.** "You shall not kill" or "You shall not murder"?: the assault on a biblical text. ColMn 2005, Liturgical ix; 94 pp. $11. 0-8146-5214-X [Exod 20,13].
2945 *Cavanaugh, William T.* Killing in the name of God. I am the Lord your God. 2005 ⇒816. 127-147 [OTA 28,282] [Exod 20,13].
2946 **Hossfeld, Frank-Lothar** "Du sollst nicht töten!": das fünfte Dekaloggebot im Kontext alttestamentlicher Ethik. 2003 ⇒19,2801. RStMor 43 (2005) 332-334 (*Alvarez Verdes, Lorenzo*) [Exod 20,13].
2947 *Wannenwetsch, Bernd* You shall not kill—what does it take?: why we need the other commandments if we are to abstain from killing. I am the Lord your God. 2005 ⇒816. 148-174 [OTA 28,282] [Exod 20,13].
2948 *Braaten, Carl E.* Sins of the tongue. I am the Lord your God. 2005 ⇒816. 206-217 [OTA 28,283] [Exod 20,16].
2949 *Hütter, Reinhard* The tongue—fallen and restored: some reflections on the three voices of the eighth commandment. I am the Lord your God. 2005 ⇒816. 189-205 [OTA 28,283] [Exod 20,16].
2950 *Baker, David L.* Last but not least: the tenth commandment. HBT 27/1 (2005) 3-24 [Exod 20,17].
2951 *Reno, R.R.* God or Mammon. I am the Lord your God. 2005 ⇒816. 218-236 [OTA 28,284] [Exod 20,17].

2952 **Anderson, Cheryl B.** Women, ideology, and violence: critical theory and the construction of gender in the book of the Covenant and the Deuteronomic law. JSOT.S 394: 2004 ⇒20,2784. RJThS 56 (2005) 492-494 (*Guest, Deryn*); BiCT 1/3 (2005)* (*McKinlay, Judith E.*).
2953 *Artus, O.* Talion. DBS 13/75. 2005 ⇒970. 881-908.

2954 *Bretherton, Donald J.* An invitation to murder?: a re-interpretation of Exodus 22:18. 'You shall not suffer a witch to live'. ET 116 (2005) 145-152.

2955 *Buzon, Emanuel* Algumas observações sobre Ex 21,22-25 à luz do direito cuneiforme. AtT 9 (2005) 137-155.

2956 *Graupner, Axel* Vergeltung oder Schadensersatz?: Erwägungen zur regulativen Idee alttestamentlichen Rechts am Beispiel des ius talionis und der mehrfachen Ersatzleistung im Bundesbuch. EvTh 65 (2005) 459-477.

2957 *Ionescu, Laurentiu* Las leyes הַמִּשְׁפָּטִים y la contextualización de la Torá. Misión y contextualización. SMEBT 2: 2005 ⇒766. 213-231 [OTA 28,284] [Exod 21].

2958 *Kapambu, Valentin N.* Enjeux et implication de la loi du talion: essai de lecture évolutive de Hammourabi à Moïse. Ter. 56/115 (2005) 531-543.

2959 *Klein, Joel T.* A comment on *You shall not boil a kid in its mother's milk.* JBQ 33 (2005) 196-197 [Exod 23,19].

2960 *Maier, Johann* Berechtigung und Grenzen der Notwehr und Selbstverteidigung im jüdischen Recht. [F]STEMBERGER G.: SJ 32: 2005 ⇒ 140. 331-384.

2961 *Paul, Shalom M.* Exod 21:10: a threefold maintenance clause. Divrei Shalom. CHANE 23: 2005 <1969> ⇒273. 27-35.

2962 **Recinella, Dale S.** The biblical truth about America's death penalty. Boston, MA 2005, Northeastern Univ. Pr. xxviii; 433 pp. $22.50. 1-55553-632-8. Bibl. 393-407.

2963 *Reimer, Haroldo* A time of grace in order to begin anew: the sabbatical year in Exodus 21:2-11 and Deuteronomy 15:1-18. God's economy. 2005 <1999> ⇒415. 71-88.

2964 *Schwienhorst-Schönberger, Ludger* 'Auge um Auge, Zahn um Zahn': zu einem antijüdischen Klischee. Studien zum AT. SBAB 40: 2005 <1990> ⇒298. 13-31 [Mt 5,38-39].

2965 *Solé i Auguets, M. Claustre* La figura de l'immigrant comtemplada a la llum dels grans codis legislatius de l'Antic Testament. La bíblia i els immigrants. 2005 ⇒471. 33-56.

2966 **Van Seters, John** A law book for the diaspora: revision in the study of the covenant code. 2003 ⇒19,2807; 20,2792. [R]ZAR 11 (2005) 388-392 (*Otto, Eckart*); RBLit 7 (2005) 144-148 (*Otto, Eckart*).

2967 **Artus, Olivier** Les lois du pentateuque: points de repère pour une lecture exégétique et théologique. LeDiv 200: P 2005, Cerf 214 pp. €25. 2-204-07379-2. Bibl. 195-201 [R]RICP 95 (2005) 250-252 (*Noël, Damien*); RSR 93 (2005) 582-583 (*Gibert, Pierre*); SR 34 (2005) 569-570 (*Vogels, Walter*).

2968 **Barmash, Pamela** Homicide in the biblical world. C 2005, CUP xvi; 253 pp. £16. 0-5215-4773-3. Diss. Harvard 1999; Bibl. 221-237. [R]ChH 75 (2005) 163-164 (*Kelley, Nicole*); RBLit (2005)* (*Bartor, Assnat*).

2969 **Brague, Rémi** La loi de Dieu: histoire philosophique d'une alliance. L'esprit de la cité: P 2005, Gallimard 400 pp. 20707-35206.

2970 **Burnside, Jonathan P.** The signs of sin: seriousness of offence in biblical law. JSOT.S 364: 2003 ⇒19,2814; 20,2802. [R]BiblInterp 13 (2005) 426-429 (*Bechtel, Lyn M.*).

2971 *Chinitz, Jacob* Ten terms in the torah for teachings, commandments and laws. JBQ 33 (2005) 113-119.

2972 **Dauvillier, Jean** Le Nouveau Testament et les droits de l'antiquité. [E]*Bruguière, Marie-Bernadette*: Etudes d'histoire du droit 9: Toulouse 2005, Presses de l'Université 506 pp. €30. 2-915699-11-9. Préf. *Germain Sicard.*

2973 *Davydov, Ivan P.* Die Behandlung von Straftaten nach israelitisch-jüdischem Recht. BN 127 (2005) 11-19.

2974 **Dorff, Elliot N.** The unfolding tradition: Jewish law after Sinai. NY 2005, Aviv xvi; 566 pp. 0-916219-29-1. Bibl. 515-524.

2975 **Friedmann, Daniel** To kill and take possession: law, morality, and society in biblical stories. 2002 ⇒18,2756... 20,2803. [R]CBQ 67 (2005) 114-116 (*Smith-Christopher, Daniel L.*); TS 66 (2005) 663-664 (*Rosenblatt, Eloise*); RBLit (2005)* (*De George, Susan*).

2976 *Gerstenberger, Erhard S.* Women in Old Testament legal procedures. LecDif 1 (2005)* [Exod 12,49].

2977 **Hasel, Michael G.** Military practice and polemic: Israel's laws of warfare in Near Eastern perspective. Berrien Springs 2005, Andrews Univ. Pr. xx; 194 pp. $25. 1-883925-479. Bibl. 139-184.

2978 *Heger, Paul* Source of law in the biblical and Mesopotamian law collections. Bib. 86 (2005) 324-342.

2979 [E]**Hezser, Catherine** Rabbinic law in its Roman and Near Eastern context. TSAJ 97: 2003 ⇒19,681; 20,776. [R]ThLZ 130 (2005) 623-624 (*Lehnardt, Andreas*).

2980 *Lohfink, Norbert* Prolegomena zu einer Rechtshermeneutik des Pentateuchs. Studien zum Deuteronomium V. SBAB 38: 2005 <2003> ⇒250. 181-231.

2981 *Markl, Dominik* Narrative Rechtshermeneutik als methodische Herausforderung des Pentateuch. ZAR 11 (2005) 107-121.

2982 **McIlroy, David** A biblical view of law and justice. 2004 ⇒20,2811. [R]Anvil 22/2 (2005) 109-112 (*Millar, Ian*).

2983 *Nobile, Marco* Il rapporto tra la legge e la sapienza: un dono della rivelazione divina. RivBib 53 (2005) 463-467.

2984 *Otto, Eckart* Der Zusammenhang von Herrscherlegitimation und Rechtskodifizierung in altorientalischer und biblischer Rechtsgeschichte. ZAR 11 (2005) 51-92;

2985 Die Rechtshermeneutik des Pentateuch und die achämenidische Rechtsideologie in ihren altorientalischen Kontexten. Kodifizierung. ZAR.B 5: 2005 ⇒699. 71-116.

2986 *Paul, Shalom M.* Formulaic patterns of law in Israel and Mesopotamia. Divrei Shalom. CHANE 23: 2005 <1970> ⇒273. 39-50;

2987 Unrecognized biblical legal idioms in the light of comparative Akkadian expressions <1979>;

2988 Adoption formulae: a study of cuneiform and biblical legal clauses <1979-1980>;

2989 Biblical analogues to Middle Assyrian law <1990>. Divrei Shalom. CHANE 23: 2005 ⇒273. 99-108/ 109-119/159-176.

2990 **Phillips, Anthony C.J.** Essays on biblical law. JSOT.S 344: 2002 ⇒ 18,4268... 20,2815. [R]ZAR 11 (2005) 383-384 (*Otto, Eckart*).

2991 *Quensel, Bernhard K.* Der 'spekulative Paria-Kapitalismus' des Judentums: Max WEBERs These in wirtschaftsrechtlicher Rekonstruktion. ZAR 11 (2005) 214-273.

2992 **Radkau, Joachim** Max WEBER: die Leidenschaft des Denkens. Mü 2005, Hanser 1007 pp.

2993 **Rée, Paul** Gesammelte Werke 1875-1885. [E]*Treiber, Hubert*: Supplementa Nietzscheana 7: 2004 ⇒20,2819. [R]ZAR 11 (2005) 384-386 (*Otto, Eckart*).

2994 *Scholz, Susanne* 'Back then it was legal': the epistemological imbalance in readings of biblical and ancient Near Eastern rape legislation. BiCT 1/4 (2005)* [Dt 21,10-14; 22,22-29].

2995 *Shemesh, Yael* Punishment of the offending organ in biblical literature. VT 55 (2005) 343-365.

2996 *Ska, Jean Louis* La ley en Israel. El camino. 2005 <2000> ⇒302. 161-191;

2997 La legislazione biblica e la sua influenza sulle legislazioni europee. Le leggi dell'antica Europa. 2005 ⇒685. 17-32.

2998 **Weinfeld, Moshe** The place of the law in the religion of ancient Israel. Ment. *Wellhausen, J.*: VT.S 100: 2004 ⇒20,2824. [R]RBLit (2005)* (*Otto, Eckart*).

2999 **Wells, Bruce** The law of testimony in the pentateuchal codes. ZAR.B 4: 2004 ⇒20,2825. [R]RSR 93 (2005) 576-577 (*Artus, Olivier*); ZAR 11 (2005) 392-395 (*Hagedorn, Anselm C.*).

3000 **Altman, Amnon** The historical prologue of the Hittite vassal treaties: an inquiry into the concepts of Hittite interstate law. 2004 ⇒20,2827. [R]BiOr 62 (2005) 553-556 (*De Martino, Stefano*).

3001 *Charpin, Dominique* Le statut des 'Codes de lois' des souverains babyloniens. [F]RUZÉ, F. 2005 ⇒131. 93-108.

3002 *Démare-Lafont, Sophie* Second-millennium arbitration;

3003 *Edzard, Dietz O.* Das Wechselverhältnis von Richter und Gesellschaft: Mesopotamien und Peripherie bis Ur III. Maarav 12 (2005) 69-81/19-26.

3004 **Faist, Betina I.** Neuassyrische Rechtsurkunden III. WVDOG 110: Ausgrabungen in Tall Munbaqa - Ekalte 8: Saarbrücken 2005, Saarbrücker xv; 138 pp. 39308-43951. Beitrag *Evelyn Klengel-Brandt*; 111 pl.

3005 *Fleischman, Joseph* Continuity and change in some provisions of the code of Hammurabi's family law. [F]KLEIN, J. 2005 ⇒79. 480-496.

3006 *Fögen, Marie T.* Das römische Zwölftafelgesetz: eine imaginierte Wirklichkeit. Kodifizierung. ZAR.B 5: 2005 ⇒699. 45-70.

3007 *Giorgieri, Mauro* Zu den Treueiden mittelhethitischer Zeit. AltOrF 32 (2005) 322-346.

3008 *Haase, Richard* Darf man den sog. Telipinu-Erlaß eine Verfassung nennen?. WO 35 (2005) 56-61;

3009 Nekromantie in der hethitischen Rechtssatzung?. WO 35 (2005) 62-67;

3010 Fälle von Doppelverkauf in der hethitischen Rechtssatzung (§§ 146 bis 148). ZAR 11 (2005) 1-3.

3011 *Jin, Shoufu* Vier Formen der Gesetzgebung des Königs im alten Ägypten. DiscEg 62 (2005) 67-80.

3012 **Loretz, Oswald** Götter—Ahnen—Könige als gerechte Richter: der 'Rechtfall' des Menschen vor Gott nach altorientalischen und biblischen Texten. AOAT 290: 2003 ⇒19,2871. [R]ThRv 101 (2005) 204-06 (*Buysch, Christoph*); ThLZ 130 (2005) 1311-3 (*Grätz, Sebastian*).

3013 *Loscalzo, Donato* Le leggi dell'antica Grecia. Le leggi dell'antica Europa. 2005 ⇒685. 53-83.

3014 **Lupu, Eran** Greek sacred law: a collection of new documents (NGSL). RGRW 152: Lei 2005, Brill xx; 499 pp. €118/$159. 90-04-13959-1. Bibl.p. 423-433.

3015 *Maehler, Herwig* Greek, Egyptian and Roman law. JJP 35 (2005) 121-140.

3016 *Maffi, Alberto* Klassisches griechisches und hellenistisches Recht. Antike Rechtsgeschichte. 2005 ⇒694. 11-16.

3017 [E]**Manthe, Ulrich** Die Rechtskulturen der Antike: vom Alten Orient bis zum Römischen Reich. 2003 ⇒19,2874. [R]ZSRG.R 120 (2005) 429-431 (*Hengstl, Joachim*).

3018 *Markiewicz, Tomasz* Security for debt in the demotic papyri. JJP 35 (2005) 141-167.

3019 **Mayer-Maly, Theo** Rechtsgeschichtliche Bibelkunde. 2003 ⇒19, 2876. [R]ZSRG.R 120 (2005) 418-420 (*Bauer, Johannes B.*).

3020 **Müller-Wollermann, Renate** Vergehen und Strafen: zur Sanktionierung abweichenden Verhaltens im alten Ägypten. PÄ 21: 2004 ⇒20, 2849. [R]ZAR 11 (2005) 312-322 (*Otto, Eckart*).

3021 *Otto, Eckart* Recht ohne Religion: zur "Romanisierung" der altorientalischen Rechtsgeschichte im "Handbuch der Orientalistik". ZAR 11 (2005) 296-303.

3022 *Pecchioli Daddi, Franca* Die mittelhethitischen *išḫiul*-Texte. AltOrF 32 (2005) 280-290.

3023 *Ponchia, Simonetta* Notes on the legal conventions and on the practice of the *adê* in the early Neo-Babylonian letters from Nippur. SAA Bulletin 14 (2002-2005) 133-167.

3024 *Radner, Karen* The reciprocal relationship between judge and society in the Neo-Assyrian period. Maarav 12 (2005) 41-68.

3025 *Rupprecht, Hans-A.* Griechen und Ägypter–Vielfalt des Rechtslebens nach den Papyri. Antike Rechtsgeschichte. 2005 ⇒694. 17-25.

3026 *Saporetti, Claudio* Le antiche leggi della Mesopotamia. Le leggi dell' antica Europa. 2005 ⇒685. 13-16.

3027 *Skaist, Aaron* Introduction to: Judge and society in antiquity. Maarav 12 (2005) 11-14.

3028 **Tetlow, Elisabeth M.** Women, crime, and punishment in ancient law and society, 2: ancient Greece. NY 2005, Continuum 353 pp. $35.

3029 *Thür, Gerhard* Gab es 'Rechtscorpora' im archaischen Griechenland?. Kodifizierung. ZAR.B 5: 2005 ⇒699. 9-27.

3030 *Thür, Gerhard* Rechtsstreit im archaischen Griechenland: Parallelen im Alten Orient. Kodifizierung. ZAR.B 5: 2005 ⇒699. 29-43.

3031 **Traulsen, Christian** Das sakrale Asyl in der alten Welt. JusEcc 72: 2004 ⇒20,2860. [R]ThLZ 130 (2005) 618-620 (*Grethlein, Jonas*).

3032 **Viel, Dieter** The complete Code of Hammurabi. Mü 2005, Lincom E. 2 vols; 799 pp. €104/$124.80. 3-89586-860-4.

3033 *Westbrook, Raymond* Judges in the cuneiform sources. Maarav 12 (2005) 27-39.

3034 [E]**Westbrook, Raymond** A history of ancient Near Eastern law. HO 1/72: 2003 ⇒19,2897. [R]ThLZ 130 (2005) 853-858 (*Otto, Eckart*); JRAS 15 (2005) 355-356 (*Kitchen, Kenneth A.*); BiOr 62 (2005) 532-543 (*Hertel, Thomas*).

### E3.6 **Cultus**, *Exodus 24-40*

3035 **Balentine, Samuel E.** The Torah's vision of worship. 1999 ⇒15, 2274...18,2795. [R]ThR 70 (2005) 168-69 (*Reventlow, Henning Graf*).

3036 *Beard, Luna* From barefootedness to sure-footedness: contrasts involving sacred space and movement in the bible. JSem 14/2 (2005) 235-260 [Exod 3,5].

3037 *Bloch-Smith, Elizabeth Maṣṣēbôt* in the Israelite cult: an argument for rendering implicit cultic criteria explicit;

3038 *Brooks, Simcha S.* From Gibeon to Gibeah: high place of the kingdom. Temple and worship. LHBOTS 422: 2005 ⇒731. 28-39/40-59.

3039 **Chilton, Bruce David** Redeeming time: the wisdom of ancient Jewish and Christian festal calendars. 2002 ⇒18,2800... 20,8921. [R]AUSS 43 (2005) 334-335 (*Lake, Judd*).

3040 *Day, John* Whatever happened to the ark of the covenant?. Temple and worship. LHBOTS 422: 2005 ⇒731. 250-270.

3041 *Dohmen, Christoph* Zuerst tun, dann hören?. BiLi 78 (2005) 31-34 [Exod 24,7].

3042 *Du Toit, J.S.; Lamprecht, A.; Schmidt, N.F.* Constructing and deconstructing sacred space. JSem 14/2 (2005) 227-234.

3043 *Ellington, Scott A.* Who shall lead them out?: an exploration of God's openness in Exodus 32.7-14. JPentec 14/1 (2005) 41-60.

3044 **Franz, Matthias** Der barmherzige und gnädige Gott: die Gnadenrede vom Sinai (Exodus 34, 6-7) und ihre Parallelen im Alten Testament und seiner Umwelt. BWANT 160: 2003 ⇒19,2913. [R]ThLZ 130 (2005) 633-635 (*Wagner, Thomas*); CBQ 67 (2005) 313-314 (*Dozeman, Thomas B.*); OLZ 100 (2005) 301-307 (*Schöpflin, Karin*).

3045 *Fross, Frank M.* The priestly houses of early Israel. [F]MCBRIDE, D. 2005 <1973> ⇒98. 35-55.

3046 **Gruenwald, Ithamar** Rituals and ritual theory in ancient Israel. 2003 ⇒19,2917. [R]ThLZ 130 (2005) 372-375 (*Schenker, Adrian*).

3047 *Kroeze, J.H.; Phahlamohlaka, L.J.* Sacred space in cyberspace: an African perspective. JSem 14/2 (2005) 413-440.

3048 *Lamprecht, A.* Experience eternity: on sacred space and holy places. JSem 14/2 (2005) 336-360.

3049 **LaRocca-Pitts, Elizabeth C.** "Of wood and stone": the significance of Israelite cultic items in the bible and its early interpreters. HSM 61: 2001 ⇒17,2491; 18,2807. [R]JQR 95 (2005) 324-327 (*Ackerman, Susan*).

3050 *Le Roux, Magdel* African light on the new moon ceremony. OTEs 18 (2005) 281-295.

3051 **Lee, Young-Jae** A study in the composition of the unit Exodus 31, 18-34,45 as the centre of the pentateuch. [D]*Aitken, K.* 2005, Diss. Aberdeen [RTL 37,610].

3052 *Makujina, John* Additional considerations for determing the meaning of *ʿanôt* and *ʿannôt* in Exod xxxii 18. VT 55 (2005) 39-46.

3053 **Munro-Hay, Stuart C.H.** The quest for the ark of the covenant: the true history of the tablets of Moses. L 2005, Tauris xi; 276 pp. 1-850-43-668-1.

3054 *Olyan, Saul M.* Exodus 31:12-17: the sabbath according to H, or the sabbath according to P and H?. JBL 124 (2005) 201-209.

3055 **Paximadi, Giorgio** E io dimorerò in mezzo a loro: composizione e interpretazione di Es 25-31. Retorica biblica 8: 2004 ⇒20,2878. $^{R}$Ang. 82 (2005) 237-240 (*Garuti, Paolo*).

3056 **Price, Randall** Searching for the ark of the covenant. Eugene, OR 2005, Harvest 226 pp. $12.

3057 *Rad, Gerhard von* The tent and the ark. From Genesis. 2005 <1931> ⇒283. 99-114.

3058 *Rooke, Deborah W.* The Day of Atonement as a ritual of validation for the high priest. Temple and worship. LHBOTS 422: 2005 ⇒731. 342-364 [Lev 16].

3059 *Siebert-Hommes, Jopie* Hij maakt het wasvat met de 'spiegels' der dienstdoende vrouwen (Exodus 38:8). $^{F}$HOOGEWOUD, F. 2005 ⇒63. 109-114 [OTA 29,32].

3060 *Steinberg, Theodore* A God who cares. JBQ 33 (2005) 198-199 [Exod 32].

3061 **Suomala, Karla R.** Moses and God in dialogue: Exodus 32-34 in postbiblical literature. Studies in biblical literature 61: 2004 ⇒20, 2884. $^{R}$RBLit (2005)* (*Dozeman, Thomas B.*).

3062 *Talstra, Eep* Ik en uw volk: syntaxis en dialoog in Exodus 33. $^{F}$HOOGEWOUD, F. 2005 ⇒63. 129-136 [OTA 29,32].

3063 **Wade, Martha Lynn** Consistency of translation techniques in the tabernacle accounts of Exodus in the Old Greek. SBL.SCSt 49: 2003 ⇒19,2940; 20,2886. $^{R}$RBLit 7 (2005) 521-530 (*Marquis, Galen*).

3064 *Wagenaar, J.A.* The priestly festival calender and the Babylonian New Year festivals: origin and transformation of the ancient Israelite festival year. The OT in its world. OTS 52: 2005 ⇒749. 218-252.

3065 **Wagenaar, Jan A.** Origin and transformation of the ancient Israelite festival calendar. ZAR.B 6: Wsb 2005, Harrassowitz ix; 225 pp. €68. 3-447-05249-X. Bibl. 209-215.

## E3.7 **Leviticus,** *Jubilee*

3066 **Bailey, Lloyd R.** Leviticus-Numbers. Macon 2005, Smyth & H. 648 pp. $65. 1-57312-060-X.

3067 **Balentine, Samuel E.** Leviticus. 2002 ⇒18,2820; 19,2944. $^{R}$Interp. 59 (2005) 67-69 (*Anderson, Gary A.*).

3068 *Barrientos-Parra, Jorge* La notion de jubilé comme principe applicable dans la résolution du surendettement dans l'antiquité. RIDA 52 (2005) 13-23.

3069 *Bergsma, John S.* Once again, the Jubilee, every 49 or 50 years?. VT 55 (2005) 121-125.

3070 **Bibb, Bryan Donald** This is the thing that the Lord commanded you to do: ritual words and narrative worlds in the book of Leviticus. 2005, Diss. Princeton, Sem. [RTL 37,608].

3071 *Cooper, Alan; Scholz, Susanne* Leviticus. Global bible commentary. 2005 ⇒2443. 30-42.

3072 *Cothey, Antony* Ethics and holiness in the theology of Leviticus. JSOT 30 (2005) 131-151.

3073 *Croatto, José S.* From the Leviticus jubilee year to the prophetic liberation time: exegetical reflections on Isaiah 61 and 58 in relation to the jubilee. God's economy. 2005 <1999> ⇒415. 89-111.

3074 **Currid, John D.** A study commentary on Leviticus. Webster, NY 2005, Evangelical 400 pp. $27.

3075 **Deiana, Giovanni** Levitico. I Libri Biblici, Primo Testamento 3: Mi 2005, Paoline 364 pp. €127. 88-315-2818-1. Bibl. 326-344. RStPat 52 (2005) 649-650 (*Lorenzin, Tiziano*); RBL 58 (2005) 303-304 (*Bazyliński, Stanisław*).

3076 **Gane, Roy** Leviticus, Numbers. GR 2004, Zondervan 846 pp. 0-310-21088-7;

3077 Cult and character: purification offerings, Day of Atonement, and theodicy. WL 2005, Eisenbrauns xxi; 394 pp. $39.50. 1575-06101-5.

3078 *Hentrich, Thomas* The purity laws as a source for conflict in the Old and New Testament. AJBI 30-31 (2004-2005) 5-21.

3079 *Kaiser, Walter C., Jr.* The book of Leviticus. OT survey. 2005 ⇒413. 33-46.

3080 *Luciani, Didier* Le Lévitique: pause ou temps mort?. RTL 36 (2005) 72-88.

3081 **Luciani, Didier** Le Lévitique: éthique et esthétique. ConBib 40: Bru 2005, Lumen V. 74 pp. €9. 2-87324-260-4;

3082 Sainteté et pardon, 1: structure littéraire du Lévitique. BEThL 185A: Lv 2005, Univ. Press xiii; 353 pp. €120. 90-5867-500-9;

3083 Sainteté et pardon, 2: guide technique. BEThL 185B: Lv 2005, Univ. Press 356-656, [9] pp. 90-5867-500-9.

3084 **Milgrom, Jacob** Leviticus 23-27. AncB 3B: 2001 ⇒17,2522... 20, 2898. RIEJ 55 (2005) 244-245 (*Aḥituv, Shmuel*);

3085 Leviticus: a book of ritual and ethics. Continental commentaries: 2004 ⇒20,2899. RThLZ 130 (2005) 640-642 (*Reventlow, Henning Graf*); IThQ 70 (2005) 181-183 (*Maher, Michael*); RBLit (2005)* (*Howell, J. Dwayne*); ET 117 (2005) 120 (*Auld, Graeme*).

3086 E**Rendtorff, Rolf; Kugler, Robert A.** The book of Leviticus: composition and reception. VT.S 93: 2003 ⇒19,405; 20,2902. ROLZ 100 (2005) 291-298 (*Reventlow, Henning Graf*); ThLZ 130 (2005) 1055-7 (*Gerstenberger, Erhard S.*); TJT 21 (2005) 265-7 (*Lee, Bernon P.*).

3087 *Richard, Pablo* Now is the time to proclaim the biblical jubilee. God's economy. 2005 <1999> ⇒415. 43-58.

3088 **Ruane, Nicole Jeanne** Male without blemish: sacrifice and gender ideologies in priestly ritual law. D*Cooper, A.* 2005, Diss. NY, Union [RTL 37,611].

3089 **Sherwood, Stephen K.** Leviticus, Numbers, Deuteronomy. Berit Olam: 2002 ⇒18,2840; 20,2907. RRBLit 7 (2005) 126-129 (*Cushman, Beverly W.*).

3090 *Ska, Jean Louis* Algunas observaciones sobre los fundamentos bíblicos del jubileo. El camino. 2005 <1998> ⇒302. 127-147.

3091 **Tidball, Derek** The message of Leviticus. Leicester 2005, IVP 327 pp.

3092 *Venter, P.M.* Atonement through blood in Leviticus. VeE 26 (2005) 275-292.

3093 **Zipor, Moshe** תרגום הפשיטתא לספר ויקרא [The Peshitta version of Leviticus]. 2003 ⇒19,2973. RJSSt 50 (2005) 401-403 (*Williams, P.J.*). **H.**

3094 *Zipor, Moshe A.* Some textual and lexical notes to the Peshitta of Leviticus. EThL 81 (2005) 468-476.

3095 **Bergen, Wesley J.** Reading ritual: Leviticus in postmodern culture. JSOT.S 417: L 2005, Clark 140 pp. $95. 0-5670-4081-X. Bibl. 124-136 [Lev 1-7].

3096 *Mirguet, Françoise* Essai d'interprétation de Lévitique 10: le bouc brûlé et non mangé. ETR 80 (2005) 261-271.

3097 *Wyatt, Nick* Symbols of exile. Mythic mind. 2005 <1990> ⇒328. 55-71 [Lev 11; Dt 14].

3098 *Bertoncel, Mojca* Obred koala za Azazela v 3 Mz 16 in judovskem izročilu: oddaljitev Izraela od prvotnih obredov grešnega kozla v luči teorije Renéja Girard [The rite of the goat for Azazel in Lev 16 and in Jewish tradition: departure of Israel from original scapegoat rites in the light of the theory of René Girard]. Bogoslovni Vestnik 65 (2005) 175-193. **Slovenian.**

3099 **Girard, René** O bode expiatório. [T]*Storniolo, Ivo*: São Paulo 2005, Paulus 280 pp. [R]Estudos Bíblicos 84 (2004) 80-82 (*Beckhäuser, Alberto*) [Lev 16].

3100 *Mohrmann, Doug C.* Making sense of sex: a study of Leviticus 18. JSOT 29 (2005) 57-79.

3101 *Wagner, Volker* Lev 19—Warnung vor irreparabler Unreinheit durch das Zusammenbringen unvereinbarer Dinge und Handlungen. BN 126 (2005) 5-18.

3102 *Lefebvre, Jean-François* Circoncire les arbres?: la portée symbolique d'un précepte: à propos de Lv 19,23-25. [F]SCHENKER, A.: OBO 214: 2005 ⇒134. 183-197.

3103 **Weyde, Karl William** The appointed festivals of YHWH: the festival calendar in Leviticus 23 and the sukkôt festival in other biblical texts. FAT 2/4: 2004 ⇒20,2927. [R]Anton. 80 (2005) 355-9 (*Volgger, David*); ThLZ 130 (2005) 1057-1059 (*Sauer, Georg*); Sal. 67 (2005) 185-186 (*Vicent, Rafael*); RBLit (2005)* (*Achenbach, Reinhard*).

3104 **Lefebvre, Jean-François** Le jubilé biblique: Lv 25–exégèse et théologie. OBO 194: 2003 ⇒19,3004; 20,2930. [R]ThLZ 130 (2005) 31-33 (*Reventlow, Henning Graf*); RSR 93 (2005) 577-578 (*Artus, Olivier*); RB 112 (2005) 456-457 (*Loza Vera, J.*).

3105 *Weinfeld, Moshe* The day of atonement and freedom (Deror): the redemption of the soul. Normative and sectarian Judaism. Library of Second Temple Studies 54: 2005 ⇒2732. 227-231 [Lev 25].

3106 *Levinson, Bernard M.* The birth of the Lemma: the restrictive reinterpretation of the covenant code's manumission law by the holiness code (Leviticus 25:44-46). JBL 124 (2005) 617-639 [Exod 21,2-6].

3107 *Barrick, William D.* The eschatological significance of Leviticus 26. MSJ 16 (2005) 95-126 [OTA 28,286].

## E3.8 *Numeri*; **Numbers, Balaam**

3108 **Achenbach, Reinhard** Die Vollendung der Tora: Studien zur Redaktionsgeschichte des Numeribuches im Kontext von Hexateuch und Pentateuch. ZAR.B 3: 2003 ⇒19,3006; 20,2932. [R]ThLZ 130 (2005) 22-25 (*Seebass, Horst*); OLZ 100 (2005) 278-285 (*Frevel, Christian*); RSR 93 (2005) 573 (*Artus, Olivier*); ThR 70 (2005) 398-399 (*Schmidt, Ludwig*).

**Bailey, Lloyd R.** Leviticus-Numbers 2005 ⇒3066.

3109 *Clark, David J.* Delimitation markers in the book of Numbers. Layout markers. Pericope 5: 2005 ⇒422. 1-20.
3110 *Dozeman, Thomas B.* The book of Numbers. OT survey. 2005 ⇒ 413. 47-60.
**Gane, Roy** Leviticus, Numbers. 2004 ⇒3076.
3111 *Havea, Jione* Numbers. Global bible commentary. 2005 ⇒2443. 43-51.
3112 **Hoffmeier, James Karl** Ancient Israel in Sinai: the evidence for the authenticity of the wilderness tradition. NY 2005, OUP xxii; 336 pp. £27. 0-19-515546-7.
3113 **Knierim, Rolf P.; Coats, George W.** Numbers. FOTL 4: GR 2005, Eerdmans xii; 367 pp. $55. 0-8028-2231-2. [R]RBLit (2005)* (*Achenbach, Reinhard*); LASBF 55 (2005) 525-532 (*Niccacci, Alviero*).
3114 **Lee, Won W.** Punishment and forgiveness in Israel's migratory campaign. 2003 ⇒19,3012; 20,2936. [R]ThLZ 130 (2005) 155-158 (*Seebass, Horst*); JThS 56 (2005) 494-498 (*Davies, Eryl W.*).
3115 **Levine, Baruch A.** Numbers 21-36. AncB 4A: 2000 ⇒16,2501; 17,2553. [R]ThR 70 (2005) 390-391 (*Schmidt, Ludwig*).
3116 *Lohfink, Norbert* Die Landübereignung in Numeri und das Ende der Priesterschrift: zu einem rätselhaften Befund im Buch Numeri. Studien zum Deuteronomium V. SBAB 38: 2005 ⇒250. 273-292.
3117 *Rapp, Ursula* Zahlenspiele in der Wüste?: Numeri—ein Buch auch für Christinnen und Christen. Dialog/60 (2005) 27-29.
3118 *Schmidt, Ludwig* Neuere Literatur zum Buch Numeri (1996-2003). ThR 70 (2005) 389-407.
3119 **Schmidt, Ludwig** Das vierte Buch Mose: Numeri, Kapitel 10,11-36, 13. ATD 7/2: 2004 ⇒20,2939. [R]ThLZ 130 (2005) 764-768 (*Seebaß, Horst*); RBLit (2005)* (*Achenbach, Reinhard*).
3120 **Seebass, Horst** Numeri 10,11-22,1. BK.AT 4/2: 2003 ⇒19,3015; 20,2940. [R]ThR 70 (2005) 391-392 (*Schmidt, Ludwig*);
3121 Numeri 22,2ff. BK.AT 4/3/2: Neuk 2005, Neuk'er 81-160 pp. 3-788-7-2066-2.
**Sherwood, Stephen K.** Leviticus, Numbers...2002 ⇒3089.

3122 *Kopciowski, Clara Costa* La benedizione sacerdotale e il dono della pace. Studi Fatti Ricerche 110 (2005) 6-8 [Num 6,22-26].
3123 *Muffs, Yochanan* The priestly benediction. Personhood of God. 2005 ⇒265. 151-156 [Gen 12,2; Num 6,23-27].
3124 *Gorringe, Tim* Numbers: chapter 11. ET 117 (2005) 12-14.
3125 *Reis, Pamela T.* Numbers xi: seeing Moses plain. VT 55 (2005) 207-231.
3126 **Artus, Olivier** Études sur le livre des Nombres: récit, histoire et loi en Nombres 13,1-20,13. OBO 157: 1997 ⇒13,2217... 18,2876. [R]ThR 70 (2005) 394-395 (*Schmidt, Ludwig*).
3127 *Mirguet, Françoise* Interprétation de récit, récit d'interprétations: l'exemple de Nombres 16. BiblInterp 13 (2005) 404-417;
3128 Le motif des cassolettes en Nb 16,1-17,5: une riposte théâtralisée. EstB 63 (2005) 3-19.
3129 **Gass, Erasmus** "Ein Stern geht auf aus Jakob": sprach- und literaturwissenschaftliche Analyse der Bileampoesie. ATSAT 69: 2001 ⇒17, 2572; 19,3038. [R]ThR 70 (2005) 402-404 (*Schmidt, Ludwig*) [Num 22-24].

3130 *McIvor, Robert S.* The oracles of Balaam and the banners of Israel. IBSt 26 (2005) 158-169 [Num 22-24].

3131 *Way, Kenneth C.* Balaam's hobby-horse: the animal motif in the Balaam traditions. UF 37 (2005) 679-693 [Num 22-24].

3132 *Dorival, Gilles* Moïse est-il le fruit d'un inceste?: à propos de Nombres 26,59. [F]LUST, J.: BEThL 192: 2005 ⇒92. 97-108.

## E3.9 Liber Deuteronomii

3133 "Du kannst nicht so tun, als ginge dich das nichts an": Sozialgesetzgebung im Buch Deuteronomium. BiHe 41/164 (2005) 18-19.

3134 *Alter, Robert* Critique littéraire: rhétorique du Deutéronome et construction de la mémoire collective. Guide des nouvelles lectures. 2005 ⇒426. 23-39.

3135 **Barker, Paul** The triumph of grace in Deuteronomy : faithless Israel, faithful Yahweh in Deuteronomy. Biblical Monographs: Milton Keynes 2004, Paternoster xxi; 269 pp. $31. 1-8422-7226-8. Foreword *Gordon J. Wenham*; Bibl. 223-252.

3136 *Braulik, Georg* Il libro del Deuteronomio. Introduzione AT. 2005 ⇒ 1159. 204-235.

3137 *Clements, Ronald E.* The book of Deuteronomy. OT survey. 2005 ⇒ 413. 61-72.

3138 *Crawford, Sidnie W.* Textual criticism of the book of Deuteronomy and the *Oxford Hebrew Bible* project. [F]FOX, M. 2005 ⇒43. 315-326.

3139 *Finsterbusch, Karin* "Du sollst sie lehren, auf dass sie tun ...": Mose als Lehrer der Tora im Buch Deuteronomium. Religiöses Lernen. WUNT 180: 2005 ⇒384. 27-45.

3140 **Finsterbusch, Karin** Weisung für Israel: Studien zu religiösem Lehren und Lernen im Deuteronomium und in seinem Umfeld. [D]*Janowski, Bernd*: FAT 44: Tü 2005, Mohr S. xi; 349 pp. €99. 31614-8623-4. Diss.-Habil. Tübingen; Bibl. 317-346.

3141 *García Bachmann, Mercedes* Deuteronomy. Global bible commentary. 2005 ⇒2443. 52-63.

3142 *Hagedorn, Anselm C.* Wie flucht man im östlichen Mittelmeer?: kulturanthropologische Einsichten in die *Dirae Teiae* und das Deuteronomium. Kodifizierung. ZAR.B 5: 2005 ⇒699. 117-150.

3143 *Levinson, Bernard M.* Deuteronomy's conception of law as an "ideal type": a missing chapter in the history of constitutional law. Maarav 12 (2005) 83-119.

3144 *Lohfink, Norbert* Die An- und Absageformel in der Hebräischen Bibel: zum Hintergrund des deuteronomischen Vierüberschriftensystems. [M]MORAN, W.: BibOr 48: 2005 ⇒107. 47-77 [Dt 1,1; 4,44; 28,69; 33,1];

3145 Der Neue Bund im Buch Deuteronomium. Studien zum Deuteronomium V. SBAB 38: 2005 <1998> ⇒250. 9-36.

3146 *Loza Vera, José* La alianza en el Deuteronomio: nota sobre un problema urgente. [F]JUNCO GARZA, C.: 2005 ⇒74. 103-111.

3147 **MacDonald, Nathan** Deuteronomy and the meaning of "monotheism". FAT 2/1: 2003 ⇒19,3074; 20,2976. [R]Bib. 86 (2005) 558-560 (*Gnuse, Robert*); RBLit (2005)* (*Amit, Yairah*); SJTh 58 (2005) 237-240 (*Levenson, Jon D.*).

3148 *McBride, S. Dean, Jr.* Polity of the covenant people: the book of Deuteronomy. [F]MCBRIDE, D. 2005 <1987> ⇒98. 17-33.

3149 *Miller, Patrick D.* Constitution or instruction?: the purpose of Deuteronomy. [F]MCBRIDE, D. 2005 ⇒98. 125-141.

3150 [E]**Otto, Eckart; Achenbach, Reinhard** Das Deuteronomium zwischen Pentateuch und Deuteronomistischem Geschichtswerk. FRLANT 206: 2004 ⇒20,411. [R]RSR 93 (2005) 573-576 (*Artus, Olivier*); RBLit (2005)* (*Auld, A.G.*).

3151 *Otto, Eckart* Das Deuteronomium: politische Theologie und Rechtsreform in Juda und Assyrien. BZAW 284: 1999 ⇒15,2417... 19, 3077. [R]BiOr 62 (2005) 204-213 (*Morrow, William S.*).

3152 **Otto, Eckart** Das Deuteronomium im Pentateuch und Hexateuch: Studien zur Literaturgeschichte von Pentateuch und Hexateuch im Lichte des Deuteronomiumrahmens. FAT 30: 2000 ⇒16,2550... 20, 2983. [R]ThR 70 (2005) 396-398 (*Schmidt, Ludwig*);

3153 Gottes Recht als Menschenrecht: rechts- und literaturhistorische Studien zum Deuteronomium. ZAR.Beiheft 2: 2002 ⇒18,2914...20, 2982. [R]VT 55 (2005) 277-278 (*Hagedorn, A.C.*).

3154 *Paganini, Simone* Settenari nel testo finale del Deuteronomio. RivBib 53 (2005) 313-323.

3155 *Rad, Gerhard von* Ancient word and living word—Deuteronomy. From Genesis. 2005 <1961, 1973> ⇒283. 89-98.

3156 **Rofé, Alexander** Deuteronomy: issues and interpretation. Old Testament Studies: 2002 ⇒18,231... 20,2985. [R]RBLit 7 (2005) 142-144 (*Römer, Thomas*).

**Sherwood, Stephen K.** Leviticus...Deuteronomy 2002 ⇒3089.

3157 [E]**Siquans, Agnethe** Der Deuteronomiumkommentar des THEODORET von Kyros. ÖBS 19: 2002 ⇒18,2925. [R]Materia giudaica 10/1 (2005) 185-187 (*Paganini, Simone*).

3158 *Ska, Jean Louis* Recordar para vivir: el estilo de la parénesis deuteronómica. El camino. 2005 <2001> ⇒302. 65-74.

3159 *Stott, Katherine* Finding the lost book of the law: re-reading the story of 'The book of the Law' (Deuteronomy-2 Kings) in light of classical literature. JSOT 30 (2005) 153-169 [2 Kgs 22-23].

3160 *Van Rooy, H.F.* Reconciliation in Deuteronomy. VeE 26 (2005) 263-274.

3161 **Veijola, Timo** Das fünfte Buch Mose: Deuteronomium, Kapitel 1,1-16,17. ATD 8/1: 2004 ⇒20,2995. [R]ThLZ 130 (2005) 940-942 (*Finsterbusch, Karin*); JETh 19 (2005) 227-228 (*Riebesehl, Klaus*).

3162 *Weitzman, Steven* Sensory reform in Deuteronomy. Religion and the self in antiquity. 2005 ⇒818. 123-139.

3163 *Wilson, Robert R.* Deuteronomy, ethnicity, and reform: reflections on the social setting of the book of Deuteronomy. [F]MCBRIDE, D. 2005 ⇒98. 107-123.

3164 **Sanz Giménez-Rico, Enrique** Un recuerdo que conduce al don: teología de Dt 1-11. Biblioteca de Teología Comillas 11: 2004 ⇒20, 268. [R]SalTer 93 (2005) 423-425 (*Ramírez Fueyo, Francisco*).

3165 *Lohfink, Norbert* Deuteronomium 1,5 באר את התורה הזאת: "er verlieh dieser Tora Rechtskraft". Studien zum Deuteronomium V. SBAB 38: 2005 <2003> ⇒250. 233-251.

3166 *Otto, Eckart* Mose, der erste Schriftgelehrte: Deuteronomium 1,5 in der Fabel des Pentateuch. [F]SCHENKER, A.: OBO 214: 2005 ⇒134. 273-284.

3167 *Lohfink, Norbert* Narrative Analyse von Dtn 1,6-3,29 <2000>;
3168 Deuteronomium 1,9-18: Gerichtsverfassung und Militär <2004>. Studien zum Deuteronomium V. SBAB 38: 2005 ⇒250. 57-110/253-72.
3169 *Beauchamp, Paul* Pour une théologie de la lettre. Pages exégétiques. LeDiv 202: 2005 <1979> ⇒183. 87-101 [Deut 4].
3170 *Sternberger, J.-P.* Un écho aux pratiques cultuelles zoroastriennes en Dt 4-5?. TEuph 29 (2005) 189-199.
3171 *Block, Daniel I.* The grace of Torah: the Mosaic prescription for life (Deut. 4:1-8; 6:20-25). BS 162/645 (2005) 3-22.
3172 *Hardmeier, Christof* Die Weisheit der Tora (Dtn 4,5-8): Respekt und Loyalität gegenüber JHWH allein und die Befolgung seiner Gebote–ein performatives Lehren und Lernen. Erzähldiskurs. FAT 46: 2005 <2004> ⇒222. 155-184.
3173 *Lohfink, Norbert* Deuteronomium 5 als Erzählung. Studien zum Deuteronomium V. SBAB 38: 2005 <2003> ⇒250. 111-130.
3174 *Rüterswörden, Udo* Die Dekalogstruktur des Deuteronomiums: Fragen an eine alte Annahme. Die Zehn Worte. QD 212: 2005 ⇒745. 109-121 [Dt 5].
3175 *Vaux, Kenneth* Response to Bruckner. ExAu 21 (2005) 20-23 [OTA 30,383] [Dt 6].
3176 *Hardmeier, Christof* Das *Schema' Jisra'el* in Dtn 6,4 im Rahmen der Beziehungstheologie der deuteronomistischen Tora. Erzähldiskurs. FAT 46: 2005 <2000> ⇒222. 123-154.
3177 *Braulik, Georg* Zwei Kleinformen im Buch Deuteronomium. [F]SCHENKER, A.: OBO 214: 2005 ⇒134. 38-57 [Dt 8-9].
3178 *Hardmeier, Christof* Wirtschaftliche Prosperität und Gottvergessenheit: die theologische Dimension wirtschaftlicher Leistungskraft nach Dtn 8. Erzähldiskurs. FAT 46: 2005 <2004> ⇒222. 185-207.
3179 *Lohfink, Norbert* Deuteronomium 9,1-10,11 und Exodus 32-34: zu Endstruktur, Intertextualität, Schichtung und Abhängigkeiten. Studien zum Deuteronomium V. SBAB 38: 2005 <2001> ⇒250. 131-180.
3180 *Wilson, Ian* Merely a container?: the ark in Deuteronomy. Temple and worship. LHBOTS 422: 2005 ⇒731. 212-249 [Dt 10,1-5].
3181 *Block, Daniel I.* The joy of worship: the Mosaic invitation to the presence of God (Deut. 12:1-14). BS 162/646 (2005) 131-149.
3182 *Giercke, Annett* Zwischen Verheißung und Realität: Inkrafttreten und Einschränkung der Kultgesetzgebung in Dtn 12. PzB 14 (2005) 141-148.
3183 *Hagedorn, Anselm C.* Placing (a) God: central place theory in Deuteronomy 12 and at Delphi. Temple and worship. LHBOTS 422: 2005 ⇒731. 188-211.
3184 *Scheffler, Eben* Deuteronomy 15:1-18 and poverty in (South) Africa. Critical study. ATM 20: 2005 ⇒457. 97-115.
3185 *Ska, Jean-Louis* Divisione e condivisione dei poteri secondo il Deuteronomio (Dt 16,18-18,22). PSV 51 (2005) 63-80.
3186 *Block, Daniel I.* The burden of leadership: the Mosaic paradigm of kingship (Deut. 17:14-20). BS 162/647 (2005) 259-278.
3187 **Baraniak, Marek** Prorok jak Mojzesz (Pwt 18,9-22): hermeneutyka prawa o urzedzie proroka w Izraelu. Rozprawy i studia biblijne 19: Wsz 2005, "Vocatio" 459 pp. 83-7146-241-7. Bibl. 397-437. **P**.
3188 *Havea, Jione* Stor[y]ing Deuteronomy 22:13–19 in missionary positions. BiCT 1/2 2005*.

3189 *Wells, Bruce* Sex, lies, and virginal rape: the slandered bride and false accusation in Deuteronomy. JBL 124 (2005) 41-72 [Dt 22,13-21].
3190 *Block, Daniel I.* The privilege of calling: the Mosaic paradigm for missions (Deut. 26:16-19). BS 162/648 (2005) 387-405.
3191 *Michel, Andreas* Wem nützen Glaubensbekenntnisse?: eine Reflexion auf das heilsgeschichtliche Credo in Deuteronomium 26. ThQ 185 (2005) 38-51.
3192 *Kübel, Paul* Zum Aufbau von Dtn 28. BN 122 (2005) 5-9 [Dt 28,25-30].
3193 *Joosten, Jan* The interpretation of Deut. 29:18 in the Qumran scrolls. Meghillot III. 2005 ⇒608. 231-238. **H.**
3194 *Claassens, L. Juliana M.* 'I kill and I give life': contrasting depictions for God in Deuteronomy 32. OTEs 18 (2005) 35-46.
3195 *Chalmers, Aaron* 'There is no deliverer (from my hand)'—a formula analysis. VT 55 (2005) 287-292 [Dt 32,39; Job 10,7; Ps 50,22; Isa 43,13; Hos 5,14].
3196 *Olson, Dennis T.* Between disappointment and hope at the boundary: Moses' death at the end of Deuteronomy. [M]JUEL, D. 2005 ⇒73. 127-138 [Dt 34].

### E4.1 *Origo Israelis in Canaan: Deuteronomista*; **Liber Josue**

3197 *Davies, Philip R.* The origin of Biblical Israel. JHScr 5/17 2005*.
3198 **Dever, William G.** Who were the early Israelites and where did they come from?. 2003 ⇒19,3135; 20,3039. [R]OLZ 100 (2005) 185-187 (*Scherer, Andreas*); JJS 56 (2005) 358-359 (*Curtis, Adrian*); Bib. 86 (2005) 578-582 (*Liverani, Mario*);
3199 Aux origines d'Israël: quand la bible dit vrai. [T]*Ghirardi, Patrice*: P 2005, Bayard 288 pp. €24. 2-227-47427-0.
3200 **Finkelstein, Israel; Silberman, Neil Asher** The bible unearthed: the making of a religion. NY 2001, Free $490. DVD produced by First Run Films; 4 episodes [SJOT 21, 308ss–West, James E.].
3201 *Borgonovo, Gianantonio* La memoria fondatrice: storia e ideologica, identità e costituzione di un popolo: il caso della "ricapitolazione" deuteronomica. ScC 133 (2005) 323-350.
3202 *Braulik, Georg* Le teorie sull'opera storica deuteronomistica e gli sviluppi nella ricerca. Introduzione AT. 2005 ⇒1159. 290-307.
3203 **Campbell, Antony F.** Joshua to Chronicles: an introduction. 2004 ⇒ 20,3052. [R]RBLit (2005)* (*Becking, Bob; McKenzie, Steven*).
3204 *Cardellini, Innocenzo* Il contributo e la responsibilità del movimento deuteronomistico per la coscienza di elezione. RStB 17/1 (2005) 137-166.
3205 **Dziadosz, Dariusz** Gli oracoli divini in 1 Sam 8-2 Re 25: redazione e teologia nella storia deuteronomistica dei re. 2002 ⇒18,2988... 20, 3054. [R]CBQ 67 (2005) 489-491 (*Duggan, Michael W.*).
3206 *Geoghegan, Jeffrey C.* Additional evidence for a deuteronomistic redaction of the "Tetrateuch". CBQ 67 (2005) 405-421.
3207 *Hardmeier, Christof* "Geschichten" und "Geschichte" in der Hebräischen Bibel: zur Tora-Form von Geschichtstheologie im kulturwis-

senschaftlichen Kontext. Das Alte Testament...Beiträge. Ment. *Rad, G. von*: ATM 10: 2005 ⇒802. 1-25 = Erzähldiskurs 97-121 ⇒222.

3208 **Harvey, John E.** Retelling the torah: the Deuteronomistic historian's use of tetrateuchal narratives. JSOT.S 403: 2004 ⇒20,3058. [R]HebStud 46 (2005) 405-407 (*Gurtner, Daniel M.*).

3209 **Hutton, Jeremy M.** The Transjordanian palimpsest: the overwritten texts of personal exile and transformation in the Deuteronomistic History. 2005, Diss. Harvard [HThR 98,497].

3210 **Kim, Uriah Y.** Decolonizing Josiah: toward a postcolonial reading of the Deuteronomistic History. The Bible in the Modern World 5: Shf 2005, Phoenix xii; 265 pp. £25/$42.50. 1905-04813-0. Bibl. 246-261 [R]SJOT 19 (2005) 302-303 (*Lemche, Niels Peter*) [2 Kgs 22-23].

3211 *Konings, Johan* A Obra Histórica Deuteronomista: uma narrativa da (in)fidelidade. Estudos bíblicos 88 (2005) 7-10.

3212 *Lohfink, Norbert* Der Zorn Gottes und das Exil: Beobachtungen am deuteronomistischen Geschichtswerk. Studien zum Deuteronomium V. SBAB 38: 2005 <2000> ⇒250. 37-55.

3213 **Miller, Robert D., II** Chieftains of the highland clans: a history of Israel in the 12th and 11th centuries B.C.. The bible in its world: GR 2005, Eerdmans xx; 186 pp. $28; €18. 0-8028-0988-X. Bibl. 137-182. [R]SJOT 19 (2005) 304-305 (*Lemche, Niels Peter*).

3214 *Nelson, Richard* The double redaction of the deuteronomistic history: the case is still compelling. JSOT 29 (2005) 319-337.

3215 **Person, Raymond Franklin, Jr.** The Deuteronomic School: history, social setting, and literature. Studies in Biblical Literature 2: 2002 ⇒ 18,2994... 20,3061. [R]JSSt 50 (2005) 213-214 (*Mayes, A.D.H.*).

3216 *Scaiola, Donatella* Il modello del re giusto: Giosia, Giosuè e la tradizione deuteronomista. PSV 51 (2005) 51-62.

3217 *Silva, Airton J. da* O contexto da Obra Histórica Deuteronomista. Estudos bíblicos 88 (2005) 11-27.

3218 *Vitorio, Jaldemir* Proclamar la esperanza en medio del fracaso: teología bíblica del exilio. Christus(M) 747 (2005) 10-16.

3219 *Abadie, Philippe* Le livre de Josué: critique historique. CEv 134 (2005) 3-49.

3220 **Auld, A. Graeme** Joshua: Jesus son of Naue in Codex Vaticanus. Septuagint commentary 1: Lei 2005, Brill xxix; 236 pp. €86. 90-04-13842-0. Bibl. xxvii-xxix.

3221 **Berman, Joshua A.** Narrative analogy in the Hebrew Bible: battle stories and their equivalent non-battle narratives. VT.S 103: 2004 ⇒ 20,3066. [R]RBLit (2005)* (*Branch, Robin G.*).

3222 *Coote, Robert B.* The book of Joshua. OT survey. 2005 ⇒413. 88-108.

3223 **Creach, Jerome F.D.** Joshua. Interpretation: 2003 ⇒19,3179; 20, 3069. [R]OTEs 18 (2005) 138-140 (*Maré, L.P.*).

3224 *De Troyer, Kristin* "And they did so": following orders given by old Joshua. Her master's tools?. 2005 ⇒493. 145-157.

3225 *Dray, Stephen* The book of Joshua. Evangel 23 (2005) 2-6, 34-39, 66-71.

3226 *Earl, Douglas* Reading the book of Joshua theologically: the problem of violence. ScrB 35 (2005) 61-84.

3227 [E]**Franke, John R.** Joshua, Judges, Ruth, 1-2 Samuel. ACCS.OT 4: DG 2005, InterVarsity xxxi; 458 pp. $40. 0830814744. Bibl. 428-45.

3228 *Greenspoon, Leonard* The book of Joshua, part 1: texts and versions. CuBR 3 (2005) 229-261.
3229 *Hentschel, Georg* Il libro di Giosuè. Introduzione AT. 2005 ⇒1159. 308-322.
3230 *Mbuwayesango, Dora* Joshua. Global bible commentary. 2005 ⇒ 2443. 64-73.
3231 *Miscall, Peter D.* Introduction to narrative literature. OT survey. 2005 ⇒413. 73-87.
3232 *Pikor, Wojciech* Święta wojna w biblii: ludzka ideologia czy Boża wola? [Holy war in the bible: human ideology or God's will?]. StBob 2(2005) 21-44. **P.**
3233 *Prado, José L.* A invasão/ocupação da terra em Josué: duas leituras, duas faces. Estudos bíblicos 88 (2005) 28-36.
3234 *Prior, John* Le conquérant et le crucifié: une lecture du livre de Josué en un temps de terrorisme. Spiritus 178 (2005) 53-67.
3235 *Seleznev, Mikhail G.* The origin of the tribal boundaries in Joshua: administrative documents or sacral geography?. [M]DIAKONOFF, M. 2005 ⇒36. 330-361.
3236 *Soggie, Neil A.* Proto-Israelite mythopoeics: a perspective from neuroscience on the book of Joshua. SJOT 19 (2005) 267-289.
3237 *Trebolle Barrera, Julio* The text-critical value of the Old Latin and Antiochean Greek texts in the books of Judges and Joshua. [F]LUST, J.: BEThL 192: 2005 ⇒92. 401-413.
3238 **Van der Meer, Michaël N.** Formation and reformulation: the redaction of the book of Joshua in the light of the oldest textual witnesses. VT.S 102: 2004 ⇒20,3082. [R]JSJ 36 (2005) 133-135 (*Auld, Graeme*); RBLit (2005)* (*McKenzie, Steven*).

3239 *Bailey, Randall C.* He didn't even tell us the worst of it!. USQR 59/1-2 (2005) 15-24 [OTA 28,291] [Josh 1-12].
3240 *Van Midden, Piet* Het kaasmeisje van Kanaän. [F]HOOGEWOUD, F. 2005 ⇒63. 81-92 [OTA 29,39] [Josh 2].
3241 *Beck, John A.* Why do Joshua's readers keep crossing the river?: the narrative-geographical shaping of Joshua 3-4. JETS 48(2005) 689-699 [OTA 30,37].
3242 *Noort, Ed* The disgrace of Egypt: Joshua 5.9a and its context. [F]LUTTIKHUIZEN, G.: AGJU 59: 2005 ⇒93. 3-19.
3243 *Klauck, Hans-Josef* Erinnerung–Übergang–Alltag: eine Besinnung zu Josua 5,9-12. [F]LAUB, F.: Bibel-Schule-Leben 6: 2005 ⇒87. 33-39.
3244 *Mallau, Hans H.* Einbrecher ins Gottesvolk: der Bericht über die Gibeoniten in Josua 9. Zeitschrift für Theologie und Gemeinde 10 (2005) 55-71.
3245 *Marín i Torner, Joan R.* 'Venim d'un país llunyà a demanar-vos que feu una aliança amb nosaltres' (Js 9). La bíblia i els immigrants. 2005 ⇒471. 57-72.
3246 *De Troyer, Kristin* LXX, *Joshua* IX 33 - XI 3 (MS 2648). Greek Papyri, Volume I. 2005 ⇒682. 81-145.
3247 *Vita, Juan-Pablo* Der biblische Ortsnamen Zaphon und die Amarnabriefe EA 273-274. UF 37 (2005) 673-677 [Josh 13,27; Judg 12,1].
3248 *Wieser, Friedrich E.* Josua 22 und das Problem gemeinschafts(zer)-störender Fantasien: Bibelarbeit über Josua 22. Zeitschrift für Theologie und Gemeinde 10 (2005) 251-260.

3249 *Taggar-Cohen, Ada* The covenant as contract: Joshua 24 and the legal Aramaic texts from Elephantine. ZAR 11 (2005) 27-50.

E4.2 *Liber Judicum*: **Richter, Judges**

3250 *Abadie, Philippe* Au souffle de l'ironie. Théophilyon 10/1 (2005) 167-176.
3251 **Assis, Eliyahu** Self-interest or communal interest: an ideology of leadership in the Gideon, Abimelech and Jephthah narratives (Judg. 6-12). VT.S 106: Lei 2005, Brill xiv; 263 pp. 90-04-14354-8.
3252 *Davidson, E.T.A.* Can sources of *Judges* be found in the Ugaritic myths?. ProcGLM 25 (2005) 43-57.
3253 *Faria, Jacir F.* Juízes: utopia ou invenção de uma sociedade igualitária?. Estudos bíblicos 88 (2005) 37-45.
3254 *Fernández Marcos, Natalio* L'histoire textuelle: les livres historiques (Juges). L'enfance de la Bible hébraïque. 2005 ⇒477. 148-169.
[E]**Franke, J.** Joshua, Judges... 2005 ⇒3227.
3255 **Gass, Erasmus** Die Orstnamen des Richterbuchs in historischer und redaktioneller Perspektive. ADPV 35: Wsb 2005, Harrassowitz xii; 683 pp. €98. 3-447-05108-6. Bibl. 511-647. [R]OLZ 100 (2005) 636-640 (*Scherer, Andreas*); RBLit (2005)* (*Becker, Uwe; Knauf, Ernst*).
3256 **Guillaume, Philippe** Waiting for Josiah: the Judges. JSOT.S 385: 2004 ⇒20,3095. [R]RRT 12 (2005) 365-367 (*Guest, Deryn*); ThLZ 130 (2005) 1051-1053 (*Scherer, Andreas*); HeyJ 46 (2005) 527-529 (*Madigan, Patrick*); RBLit (2005)* (*Edelman, Diana*); JThS 56 (2005) 498-501 (*Tollington, Janet E.*).
3257 **Gunn, David M.** Judges. Blackwell Bible Commentaries: Oxf 2005, Blackwell xiii; 329 pp. $28. 06312-22529. Bibl. 276-295. [R]RBLit (2005)* (*Wright, Jacob*).
3258 *Hentschel, Georg* Il libro dei Giudici. Introduzione AT. 2005 ⇒1159. 323-336.
3259 *Isaksson, Bo* Infinitiven som adverbiellt komplement i Domarboken: en komparativ studie. SEÅ 70 (2005) 107-118.
3260 *Kwasi, Fidèle U.* Judges. Global bible commentary. 2005 ⇒2443. 74-85.
3261 *Lanoir, Corinne* Sommes-nous nés d'une catastrophe ou allons-nous à la catastrophe?. FV 104/4 (2005) 48-55.
3262 **Lanoir, Corinne** Femmes fatales, filles rebelles: figures féminines dans le livre des Juges. Actes et recherches: Genève 2005, Labor et F. 369 pp. €34. 2-8309-1157-1. Bibl. 327-356 [R]Vies consacrées 77 (2005) 198-199 (*Luciani, Didier*).
3263 **Matthews, Victor Harold** Judges and Ruth. 2004 ⇒20,3099. [R]CBQ 67 (2005) 122-123 (*Yee, Gale A.*).
3264 **McCann, J. Clinton** Judges. Interpretation: 2002 ⇒18,3032... 20, 3100. [R]BS 162 (2005) 496-497 (*Constable, Thomas L.*); AsbTJ 60/2 (2005) 146-147 (*Matthews, Victor H.*).
3265 **Mobley, Gregory** The empty men: the heroic tradition of ancient Israel. AncB Reference LIbrary: NY 2005, Doubleday xix; 294 pp. $36. 0-385-49851-9. Bibl. 247-266.
3266 *Olson, Dennis* The book of Judges. OT survey. 2005 ⇒413. 109-12.
3267 *Steinmann, Andrew E.* The mysterious numbers of the book of Judges. JETS 48 (2005) 491-500 [OTA 30,38].

*Trebolle Barrera, J.* The text-critical value... 2005 ⇒3237.

3268 *Wong, Gregory T.K.* Is there a direct pro-Judah polemic in Judges?. SJOT 19 (2005) 84-110.

3269 **Scherer, Andreas** Überlieferungen von Religion und Krieg: exegetische und religionsgeschichtliche Untersuchungen zu Richter 3-8 und verwandten Texten. WMANT 105: Neuk 2005, Neukirchener xi; 468 pp. €59. 3-7887-2067-0. Diss.-Habil. Bochum; Bibl. 429-463.

3270 *Deurloo, Karel A.* Net als het lemmer: Ehud. [F]HOOGEWOUD, F. 2005 ⇒63. 57-62 [OTA 29,39] [Judg 3,12-30].

3271 *Snyman, S.D.* Shamgar ben Anath: a farming warrior or a father at war?. VT 55 (2005) 125-129 [Judg 3,31; 5,6].

3272 *Assis, Elie* "The hand of a woman": Deborah and Yael (Judges 4). JHScr 5/19 (2005)*.

3273 *Reis, Pamela T.* Uncovering Jael and Sisera: a new reading. SJOT 19 (2005) 24-47 [Judg 4,7-22; 5,24-31].

3274 **Echols, Charles L.** The eclipse of God in the Song of Deborah (Judges 5): the role of YHWH in the light of heroic poetry. [D]*Davies, Graham I.* 2005, Diss. Cambridge [TynB 56,149-152].

3275 *Knauf, Ernst Axel* Deborah's language: Judges ch. 5 in its Hebrew and Semitic context. [F]VOIGT, R.: AOAT 317: 2005 ⇒158. 167-182.

3276 *Basser, Herbert W.* History of interpretation to Judges 5:4-5 with special attention to Rabbi Yosef KARA. REJ 164 (2005) 9-32.

3277 *Scherer, Andreas* Der Rhythmus der Schlacht: die poetische Sprachgestalt von Jdc 5,19-22. ZAW 117 (2005) 529-542.

3278 *Bovon, François* La dame à sa fenêtre: un cas d'intertextualité entre ESCHYLE et le livre des Juges. [F]HURST, A. 2005 ⇒64. 587-594 [Judg 5,28-30].

3279 *Rofé, Alexander* Lo studio del testo biblico alla luce della critica storico-letteraria: la reprimenda dell'uomo-profeta ('iš nabi') in Gdc 6,7-10. Henoch 27/1-2 (2005) 137-148.

3280 *Niesiołowski-Spanò, Lukasz* Where should one look for Gideon's Ophra?. Bib. 86 (2005) 478-493 [Josh 18,23; Judg 6,11; 1 Sam 13, 17; 1 Chr 1,19; Mic 1,10].

3281 *Zanetti, Paolo S.* Note sulle traduzioni greche e latine di *Giudici* 6, 11.24. Imitatori di Gesù Cristo. 2005 <2001, 2004> ⇒330. 605-617.

3282 *Scherer, Andreas* Gideon—ein Anti-Held?: ein Beitrag zur Auseinandersetzung mit dem sog. 'flawed hero approach' am Beispiel von Jdc. vi 36-40. VT 55 (2005) 269-273.

3283 *Winther-Nielsen, Nicolai* Tracking the world of Judges: the use of contextual resources in narration and conversation. HIPHIL 2 (2005) [Judg 8,18-25; 13,8-14].

3284 **Álvarez Barredo, Miguel** La iniciativa de Dios: estudio literario y teológico de Jueces 9-21. 2004 ⇒20,3115. [R]Burgense 46 (2005) 271-272 (*Otero Lázaro, Tomás*); EstTrin 39 (2005) 584-585 (*Vázquez Allegue, Jaime*); EE 80 (2005) 187-188 (*Yebra, Carme*).

3285 *Smith, Michael J.* The failure of the family in Judges, part 1: Jephthah. BS 162/647 (2005) 279-298 [Judg 10,6-12,7].

3286 *Martin, Lee R.* God at risk: divine vulnerability in Judges 10:6-16. OTEs 18 (2005) 722-740.

3287 *Miller, Barbara* Tell it on the mountain: the daughter of Jephthah in Judges 11. Interfaces: ColMn 2005, Liturgical xxiv; 144 pp. $15. 0-8146-5843-1. Bibl. 134-138.

3288 *Bauks, Michaela* "Sakrale Sprache" und "heilige Worte": die Erzählung von Jephtas Tochter (Ri 11,29-40) ein "text of terror"?. AnStR 6 (2005) 417-428.
3289 *Berman, Joshua* Medieval monasticism and the evolution of Jewish interpretation to the story of Jephthah's daughter. JQR 95 (2005) 228-256 [Judg 11,29-40].
3290 *Houtman, Cornelis* Rewriting a dramatic Old Testament story: the story of Jephthah and his daughter in some examples of christian devotional literature. BiblInterp 13 (2005) 167-190 [Judg 11,29-40];
3291 "Rewritten Bible" in Kinder- und Familienbibeln: beleuchtet am Beispiel der Geschichte von Jefta und seiner Tochter (Ri 11,29-40). BN 122 (2005) 11-33.
3292 *Janzen, David* Why the deuteronomist told about the sacrifice of Jephthah's daughter. JSOT 29 (2005) 339-357 [Judg 11,29-40].
3293 *Schwartzmann, Julia* The vow of Jephthah: a typology of interpretations in traditional exegesis. BetM 182 (2005) 261-280. Sum 293 [Judg 11,30-31]. **H.**
3294 *Hugo, Philippe* "J'ai ouvert la bouche pour YHWH" (Jg 11,36): parole et identité dans le voeu de Jephté. [F]SCHENKER, A.: OBO 214: 2005 ⇒134. 112-127.
3295 *Assis, Elie* The significance of the narrative concerning the annunciation of Samson's birth (Judg 13). Shnaton 15 (2005) 21-38. **H.**
3296 *Blumenthal, Fred* Samson and Samuel: two styles of leadership. JBQ 33 (2005) 108-112 [Judg 13; 1 Sam 1].
3297 *Böhler, Dieter* Was macht denn Simson in der Bibel?. ThPh 80 (2005) 481-489 [Judg 13].
3298 *Fernández Marcos, Natalio* Héros et victime: Samson dans la LXX. L'apport de la Septante. 2005 ⇒764. 119-133 [Judg 13-16].
3299 *Lemardelé, Christophe* Samson le "nazir": un mythe du jeune guerrier. RHR 222/3 (2005) 259-286 [Judg 13-16].
3300 *Smith, Michael J.* The failure of the family in Judges, part 2: Samson. BS 162/648 (2005) 424-436 [Judg 13-16].
3301 *Houtman, Cees* Simson en de leeuw: Richteren 14:6 verwoord en verbeeld. [F]HOOGEWOUD, F. 2005 ⇒63. 73-80 [OTA 29,40].
3302 *Sonnet, Jean-Pierre; Wénin, André* La muerte de Sansón: ¿bendice Dios el atentado suicida?. SelTeol 44 (2005) 200-208 <RTL 35 (2004) 372-381 [Judg 16,21-31].
3303 *Na'aman, Nadav* The Danite campaign northward (Judges xvii-xviii) and the migration of the Phocaeans to Massalia (Strabo IV 1,4). VT 55 2005, 47(2005) -60.
3304 *Faraone, C.A.; Garnand, B.; López-Ruiz, C.* Micah's mother (Judg. 17:1-4) and a curse from Carthage (KAI 89): Canaanite precedents for Greek and Latin curses against thieves?. JNES 64 (2005) 161-86.
3305 *Eynikel, Erik* Judges 19-21, an "appendix": rape, murder, war and abduction. CV 47/2 (2005) 101-115.

## E4.3 **Liber Ruth**, '*V Rotuli*', the Five Scrolls

3306 **Bengtsson, Per Å.** Translation techniques in two Syro-Arabic versions of Ruth. Studia orientalia lundensia n.s. 3: 2003 ⇒19,3241; 20, 3136. [R]BiOr 62 (2005) 582-584 (*Van Peursen, W.T.*).

3307 *Blotz, Joseph W.* Bitterness and friendship: a feminist exegesis of the book of Ruth. CThMi 32 (2005) 47-54.

3308 **Canopi, Anna Maria** Bajo las alas del Dios de Israel. M 2005, Paulinas 76 pp.

3309 **D'Angelo, Cristiano** Il libro di Rut: la forza delle donne: commento teologico e letterario. 2004 ⇒20,3139. [R]Vivens Homo 16 (2005) 189-190 (*Mazzinghi, Luca*); Gr. 86 (2005) 182-183 (*Calduch-Benages, Nuria*).

3310 [T]**Davis, Ellen F.** Who are you my daughter?: reading Ruth through image and text. 2003 ⇒19,3244; 20,3140. Woodcuts *Margaret Adams Parker*. [R]OTEs 18 (2005) 934-935 (*Klopper, Frances*).

3311 *Dearman, J. Andrew; Pussman, Sabelyn A.* Putting Ruth in her place: some observations on canonical ordering and the history of the book's interpretation. HBT 27/1 (2005) 59-86.

3312 *Farmer, Kathleen A.R.* The book of Ruth. OT survey. 2005 ⇒413. 113-117.

[E]**Franke, J.** Joshua, Judges, Ruth 2005 ⇒3227.

3313 *Fuchs, Esther* The history of women in ancient Israel: theory, method, and the book of Ruth. Her master's tools?. 2005 ⇒493. 211-231.

3314 *Gesche, Bonifatia* Ruth. BVLI 49 (2005) 11-16.

3315 [E]**Gesche, Bonifatia** VL 4/5. Ruth. FrB 2005, Herder 83 pp. €64. 34-51-00132-2.

3316 *Grätz, Sebastian* Zuwanderung als Herausforderung: das Rutbuch als Modell einer sozialen und religiösen Integration von Fremden im nachexilischen Judäa. EvTh 65 (2005) 294-309.

3317 **Hausmann, Jutta** Rut: miteinander auf dem Weg. Biblische Gestalten 11: Lp 2005, Evangelische Verlagsanstalt 162 pp. €14.80. 3-374-02278-2. Bibl. 154-162.

3318 **LaCocque, André** Le livre de Ruth. CAT 17: 2004 ⇒20,3147. [R]Vies consacrées 77 (2005) 196-97 (*Luciani, Didier*); RBLit (2005)* (*Korpel, Marjo*);

3319 Ruth: a continental commentary. 2004 ⇒20,3148. [R]Kerux 20/3 (2005) 48-50 (*Dennison, James T., Jr.*); OTEs 18 (2005) 944-945 (*Maré, L.P.*); RBLit (2005)* (*Hubbard, Robert*).

3320 *Masenya, Madipoane* Ruth. Global bible commentary. 2005 ⇒2443. 86-91.

**Matthews, V.** Judges and Ruth 2004 ⇒3263.

3321 **Meier, Levi** Second chances: transforming bitterness to hope and the story of Ruth. J 2005, Urim 158 pp. 965-7108-67-5.

3322 [T]**Pieterse, W.; Yele, M.** The book of Ruth: a translation in English and Pidgin with clarifying notes and articles. Kumba 2005, Presbyterean Theological Seminary x; 95 pp [BOTSA 19,24—Knut Holter].

3323 *Pitzen, Marianne* Naomi und Ruth, zwei Wirtschaftsmigrantinnen im alten Israel (Ruth 1-4 in Auswahl). Kanzelreden. 2005 ⇒376. 45-58.

3324 *Ramis i Darder, Francesc* El llibre de Rut: realitat i simbologia de la presentació dels immigrants i emigrants. La bíblia i els immigrants. 2005 ⇒471. 121-141.

3325 *Silva, José J. da* Rute e Noemi: o resgate das leis na defesa das relações afetivas e a união civil entre pessoas do mesmo sexo. Estudos bíblicos 87 (2005) 46-56.

3326 *Spangenberg, Sakkie* Constructing a historical context for the Ruth novelette: dovetailing the views of J A Loader and R Albertz. OTEs 18 (2005) 345-355.

3327 *Van den Eynde, Sabine* Blessed by God—blessed be God: εὐλογέω and the concept of blessing in the LXX with special attention to the book of Ruth. [F]LUST, J.: BEThL 192: 2005 ⇒92. 415-436.
3328 *Zenger, Erich* Il libro di Rut. Introduzione AT. 2005 ⇒1159. 337-48.
3329 *Zevit, Ziony* Dating Ruth: legal, linguistic and historical observations. ZAW 117 (2005) 574-600.

3330 *Stassen, S.L.* Wie se grond koop Boas (Rut 4:9)?. AcTh(B) 25/2 (2005) 104-119.

### E4.4 1-2 Samuel

3331 **Arnold, Bill T.** 1 and 2 Samuel. GR 2003, Zondervan 681 pp. 0-310-21086-0.
**Auld, A. Graeme** Samuel at the threshold 2004 ⇒176.
3332 *Balancin, Euclides M.* Sobre juízes, sacerdotes, reis e ... profetas. Estudos bíblicos 88 (2005) 46-55.
3333 *Birch, Bruce C.* The first and second books of Samuel. OT survey. 2005 ⇒413. 118-129.
3334 **Brown, George H.** BEDE's Commentary on 1 Samuel. Biblical studies. 2005 ⇒773. 77-90 [Scr. 60/1,28*—G. Michiels].
3335 **Brueggemann, Walter** I e II Samuele. [T]*Girardet, Maria:* Strumenti 22: T 2005, Claudiana 471 pp. €33. 88701-65450. Bibl. 369-74.
3336 **Campbell, Antony F.** 1 Samuel. FOTL 7: 2003 ⇒19,3270; 20,3166. [R]ThLZ 130 (2005) 153-5 (*Adam, Klaus-Peter*); CBQ 67 (2005) 308-309 (*White, Marsha*); RBLit 7 (2005) 148-150 (*Klein, Ralph W.*);
3337 2 Samuel. FOTL 8: GR 2005, Eerdmans xiv; 242 pp. $50/£30. 0-80-28-2813-2. [R]NV 80/4 (2005) 106-107 (*Borel, Jean*); RBLit (2005)* (*Auld, A. Graeme; Vermeylen, Jacques*).
3338 **Dietrich, Walter** Samuel. BK.AT 8/1/2: Neuk 2005, Neuk 81-160 pp. 3-7887-2105-7.
[E]**Dietrich, Walter** David und Saul im Widerstreit 2004 ⇒375.
3339 *Firth, David G.* "Play it again, Sam": the poetics of narrative repetition in 1 Samuel 1-7. TynB 56/2 (2005) 1-17.
[E]**Franke, J.** Joshua...1-2 Samuel 2005 ⇒3227.
3340 *Hentschel, Georg* I libri di Samuele. Introduzione AT. 2005 ⇒1159. 349-362.
3341 **Lefebvre, Philippe** Livres de Samuel et récits de résurrection: le messie ressuscité "selon les écritures". LeDiv 196: 2004 ⇒20,3172. [R]Vies consacrées 77 (2005) 200-201 (*Luciani, Didier*); CBQ 67 (2005) 352-353 (*Branick, Vincent P.*); RB 112 (2005) 101-107 (*Nodet, Etienne*); Theoforum 36 (2005) 191-193 (*Laberge, Léo*); RBLit (2005)* (Rogland, Max); RSPhTh 89 (2005) 563-573 (*Pelletier, Anne-Marie*).
3342 **Mazzinghi, Luca** 1-2 Samuele. Padova 2005, Messaggero 248 pp. 88-250-1353-1. Bibl. 239-240.
3343 **Naastepad, Th.J.M.** Verborgen midden. Kampen 2005, Kok 406 + 332 pp. €21.50. 90-435-11030-0/1-9.
3344 *Peleg, Yaron* Love at first sight?: David, Jonathan, and the biblical politics of gender. JSOT 30 (2005) 171-189.
3345 *West, Gerald* 1 and 2 Samuel. Global bible commentary. 2005 ⇒ 2443. 92-104.

3346 **Frolov, Serge** The turn of the cycle: 1 Samuel 1-8 in synchronic and diachronic perspectives. BZAW 342: 2004 ⇒20,3180. [R]JBL 124 (2005) 533-536 (*Arnold, Bill T.*).

3347 *Esler, Philip F.* The role of Hannah in 1 Samuel 1:1-2:21: understanding a biblical narrative in its ancient context. [F]STEGEMANN, W. 2005 ⇒139. 15-36.

3348 *Leite, Leyde M.* "A solidão da mulher de fé": 1 Sm 1,4-5. Estudos bíblicos 88 (2005) 56-62.

3349 *Grohmann, Marianne* Psalm 113 und das Lied der Hanna (1Sam 2,1-10)–Paradebeispiele für eine intertextuelle Lektüre?. Die Bibel im Dialog. NET 10: 2005 ⇒333. 137-156.

3350 *Papaconstantinou , Arietta* La prière d'Anne dans la version sahidique du premier livre des Règnes: quelques témoins méconnus. Adamantius 11 (2005) 227-231 [1 Sam 2,1-10].

3351 **Brueggemann, Walter** Ichabod toward home: the journey of God's glory. 2002 ⇒18,3118... 20,3184. [R]ThR 70 (2005) 11-13 (*Reventlow, Henning Graf*) [1 Sam 4,6].

### E4.5 *1 Sam 7...Initia potestatis regiae*, **Origins of kingship**

3352 **Brooks, Simcha Shalom** Saul and the monarchy: a new look. [D]*Barton, John*: MSSOTS: Aldershot 2005, Ashgate xvi; 222 pp. £50. 0-7546-5204-1. Diss. University College, London; Bibl. 197-210.

3353 **Green, Barbara** King Saul's asking. 2003 ⇒19,3289; 20,3188. [R]RBLit (2005)* (*Jobling, David*); BiCT 1/3 (2005)* (*Miscall, Peter*);

3354 How are the mighty fallen?: a dialogical study of King Saul in 1 Samuel. JSOT.S 365: 2003 ⇒19,3290; 20,3189. [R]CBQ 67 (2005) 118-20 (*Dutcher-Walls, Patricia*); RBLit 7 (2005) 150-4 (*Frolov, Serge*).

3355 **Hamilton, Mark W.** The body royal: the social poetics of kingship in ancient Israel. BiblInterp 78: Lei 2005, Brill xv; 316 pp. 90-04-14-541-9. Bibl. 275-299.

3356 *Klement, Herbert H.* Monarchiekritik und Herrscherverheißung: alttestamentlich-theologische Aspekte zur Rolle des Königs in Israel. JETh 19 (2005) 49-72.

3357 **Launderville, Dale** Piety and politics: the dynamics of royal authority in Homeric Greece, biblical Israel, and Old Babylonian Mesopotamia. 2003 ⇒19,3292; 20,3191. [R]BASOR 340 (2005) 88-90 (*Rubio, Gonzalo*); JSSt 50 (2005) 361-362 (*West, Martin*); OTEs 18 (2005) 147-149 (*Gericke, J.W.*).

3358 *Mathew, K.V.* Israel, a nation and state: a historical biblical perspective. BiBh 31 (2005) 3-17.

3359 **Müller, Reinhard** Königtum und Gottesherrschaft: Untersuchungen zur alttestamentlichen Monarchiekritik. FAT II/3: 2004 ⇒20,3192. [R]OLZ 100 (2005) 491-495 (*Kessler, R.*); JBL 124 (2005) 536-538 (*Hamilton, Mark W.*); RBLit (2005)* (*Hamilton, Mark W.*).

3360 *Schäfer-Lichtenberger, Christa* Die Herrschaft Sauls. WuD 28 (2005) 53-64.

3361 **Wagner, David** Geist und Tora: Studien zur göttlichen Legitimation und Delegitimation von Herrschaft im Alten Testament anhand der Erzählungen über König Saul. ABIG 15: Lp 2005, Evangelische xi; 452 pp. 3-374-02272-3.

3362 *Wénin, André* Gli inizi della monarchia in Israele: racconti per riflettere sul potere. PSV 51 (2005) 33-49.
3363 *Wyatt, Nicolas* Degrees of divinity: some mythical and ritual aspects of West Semitic kingship;
3364 The hollow crown: ambivalent elements in West Semitic royal ideology <1986>. 'There's such divinity'. 2005 ⇒329. 191-220/31-48.

3365 *Beck, John A.* The narrative-geographical shaping of 1 Samuel 7:5-13. BS 162/647 (2005) 299-309.
3366 **Vette, Joachim** Samuel und Saul: ein Beitrag zur narrativen Poetik des Samuel-Buches. [D]*Oeming, Manfred*: Beiträge zum Verstehen der Bibel 13: Müns 2005, LIT 264 pp. €24.90. 3-8258-8897-5. Diss. Heidelberg [1 Sam 8-12].
3367 *Leuchter, Mark* A king like all the nations: the composition of 1 Sam 8,11-18. ZAW 117 (2005) 543-558.
3368 *Paul, Shalom M.* 1 Samuel 9:7: an interview fee. Divrei Shalom. CHANE 23: 2005 <1978> ⇒273. 95-97.
3369 *Sousa, Mário José Rodrigues de* La importancia del encuentro de Saúl con las jóvenes, en el contexto de su unción por Samuel (*1Sm* 9, 11-13). Did(L) 35 (2005) 117-148.
3370 *Vartejanu-Joubert, Madalina* Les "anciens du peuple" et Saül: temps, espace et rite de passage dans Nombres xi et 1 Samuel x. VT 55 (2005) 542-563.
3371 *Rofé, Alexander* Wave breads for King Saul: 1 Sam. 10:4 in 4QSam[a] and in the Septuagint. Meghillot III. 2005 ⇒608. 245-250. **H.**
3372 *Avioz, Michael* Could Saul rule forever?: a new look at 1 Samuel 13: 13-14. JHScr 5/16 (2005)*.
3373 *Butts, Aaron Michael* P.Duk.Inv. 797 (U)—1 Kingdoms 14:24-50 in Sahidic. Muséon 118 (2005) 7-19.
3374 *Viberg, Åke* Saul exposed by irony: a new understanding of 1 Samuel 15:27 based on two symbolic acts. SEÅ 70 (2005) 301-308.

## E4.6 *1 Sam 16...2 Sam: Accessio Davidis*. **David's Rise**

3375 **Ackerman, Susan** When heroes love: the ambiguity of eros in the stories of Gilgamesh and David. NY 2005, Columbia Univ. Pr. xvi; 353 pp. $45/€29.50. 0-231-13260-3. Bibl. 301-326.
3376 **Adam, Klaus-Peter** Die Saul-David-Geschichten in den Samuelbüchern. [D]*Jeremias, Jörg* 2005, Diss.-Habil. Marburg [ThLZ 131,340].
3377 **Bodner, Keith** David observed: a king in the eyes of his court. HBM 5: Shf 2005, Shf Academic xii; 198 pp. $85. 1-905048-23-8. Bibl. 177-190.
3378 **Eschelbach, Michael A.** Has Joab foiled David?: a literary study of the importance of Joab's character in relation to David. Studies in biblical literature 76: NY 2005, Lang xii; 122 pp. €50. 0-8204-7460-6. Bibl. 113-118. [R]RBLit (2005)* (*Hunziker-Rodewald, Regine*).
3379 *Halpern, Baruch* David did it, others did not: the creation of ancient Israel. The bible and radiocarbon dating. 2005 ⇒952. 422-438.
3380 **Halpern, Baruch** David's secret demons: messiah, murderer, traitor, king. 2001 ⇒17,2791... 20,3214. [R]SJOT 19 (2005) 146-147 (*Lemche, Niels Peter*); BiOr 62 (2005) 560-563 (*Hentschel, Georg*);

3381 I demoni segreti di David: messia, assassino, traditore, re. Introd. allo studio della bibbia, Suppl 19: 2004 ⇒20,3215. [R]Sal. 67 (2005) 593-594 (*Vicent, Rafael*); Anton. 80 (2005) 742-743 (*Nobile, Marco*); Protest. 60 (2005) 74-76 (*Noffke, Eric*).

3382 *Malamat, Abraham* David and Uriah: the consolidation of power in Jerusalem by the Israelites. [F]KLEIN, J. 2005 ⇒79. 742-745.

3383 *Neuenfeldt, Elaine G.; Schinelo, Edmilson* As relações de gênero na casa de Davi. Estudos bíblicos 86 (2005) 16-25.

3384 **Pinsky, Robert** The life of David. NY 2005, Schocken ix; 209 pp. $20. 0-8052-4203-1.

3385 *Pistone, Gioachino* Davide al di fuori dei libri storici. Studi Fatti Ricerche 109 (2005) 6-9.

3386 *Puykunnel, Shaji J.* From shepherd-boy to shepherd-king: David in pastoral terms in the books of Samuel. [M]JOHN PAUL II. 2005 ⇒72. 37-49.

3387 **Rudnig, Thilo Alexander** Davids Thron: redaktionskritische Studien zur Geschichte von der Thronnachfolge Davids. [D]*Pohlmann, Karl-Friedrich* 2005, Diss.-Habil. Münster [ThLZ 131,341].

3388 **Schipper, Jeremy** David 'Why do you still speak of your affairs?': Mephibosheth, disability, and national identity in the David story. 2005, Diss. Prnceton, Sem. [RTL 37,612].

3389 **Suchanek-Seitz, Barbara** 'So tut man nicht in Israel': Kommunikation und Interaktion zwischen höfischen Männern und Frauen in der Erzählung von der Thronnachfolge Davids. [D]*Kessler, R.* 2005, Diss. Marburg [RTL 37,612].

3390 *Thiel, Winfried* Die Davidgeschichten im Alten Testament. Gedeutete Geschichte. BThSt 71: 2005 <1977> ⇒316. 39-63.

3391 **Vogels, Walter** David et son histoire: 1 Samuel 16,1–1 Rois 2,11. 2003 ⇒19,3346. [R]Theoforum 36 (2005) 194 (*Laberge, Léo*).

3392 **Wohl, Louis de** David de Jerusalén: el conquistador del reino. Arcaduz: M 2005, Palabra 319 pp. Historia novelada.

3393 *Vanschoonwinkel, Jacques* L'achéen Achille est-il l'ancêtre du philistin Goliath?: à propos de l'armement et de la technique de combat du Philistin. RANT 2 (2005) 347-361 [1 Sam 17].

3394 *Hayes, J. Daniel* Reconsidering the height of Goliath. JETS 48 (2005) 701-714 [OTA 30,40] [1 Sam 17,4].

3395 *Taggar-Cohen, Ada* Political loyalty in the biblical account of 1 Samuel xx-xxii in the light of Hittite texts. VT 55 (2005) 251-268.

3396 *Duarte Castillo, Raúl* Gad, el vidente. [F]JUNCO GARZA, C.: Estudios Bíblicos Mexicanos 4: 2005 ⇒74. 113-124 [1 Sam 22,1-5; 2 Sam 24,11-19].

3397 *Conrad, Joachim* Die Unschuld der Tollkühnen: Überlegungen zu 1 Sam 24. [M]WALLIS, G.: ABIG 16: 2005 ⇒160. 23-42.

3398 **Ramond, Sophie** Dessin divin et récalcitrance humaine en 1 Samuel 24-26: affrontement et connivence. [D]*Nieuviarts, J.* 2005, 552 pp. Diss.Toulouse [RTL 37,611].

3399 *Paul, Shalom M.* Gleanings from the biblical and talmudic lexica in light of Akkadian. Divrei Shalom. CHANE 23: 2005 <1993> ⇒273. 181-194 [1 Sam 24,13; Cant 8,2; Dan 9,27; Zech 8,23].

3400 *Klein, Johannes* Davids Flucht zu den Philistern (1 Sam. xxi 11ff.; xxvii-xxix). VT 55 (2005) 176-184.

3401 *Mitchell, Margaret M.* Patristic rhetoric on allegory: ORIGEN and EUSTATHIUS put 1 Samuel 28 on trial. JR 85 (2005) 414-445.

3402 *Smelik, Klaas* De dodenbezweerster uit Endor: 1 Samuel 28. ITBT 13/7 (2005) 8-10.

3403 *Vermeylen, Jacques* "Comment sont tombés les héros?": une lecture de 1 S 31 et 2 S 1,1-2,7. Analyse narrative. BEThL 191: 2005 ⇒742. 99-116.

3404 *Piedad Sánchez, Jorge* Añadidos sacerdotales en el relato de la muerte de Saúl: análisis de 2Sam 1,1-16. [F]JUNCO GARZA, C.: Estudios Bíblicos Mexicanos 4: 2005 ⇒74. 125-163.

3405 *Branch, Robin G.* Rizpah—catalyst in king-making: an analysis of 2 Samuel 3:6-11. JSem 14/1 2005, 1-16.

3406 *Orji, Chukwuemeka* Scene doubling structure in 2Sam 5-8. Afrika Yetu 8 (2005) 1-5.

3407 **Orji, Chukwuemeka** Scene doubling structure in 2Sam 5-8. Afrika Yetu Mon.Ser. 1: Nairobi 2005, African Jesuit Publications 78 pp. 9966-70430-2.

3408 *Garbini, Giovanni* Problemi di storiografia nei libri di Samuele-Re tra TM e LXX: la conquista di Gerusalemme. AnScR 10 (2005) 169-178 [2 Sam 5,6-9].

3409 *Schipper, Jeremy* Reconsidering the imagery of disability in 2 Samuel 5:8b. CBQ 67 (2005) 422-434 [2 Kgs 25].

3410 *Haase, Ingrid M.* Uzzah's rebellion. JHScr 5/3 2004* [2 Sam 6,6-8].

3411 *Abadie, Philippe* Pérennité dynastique ou éternité du temple?: deux lectures d'un même oracle (2 S 7 et 1 Ch 17). Analyse narrative. BEThL 191: 2005 ⇒742. 117-130.

3412 **Avioz, Michael** Nathan's oracle (2 Samuel 7) and its interpreters. Bible in history 5: NY 2005, Lang xx; 230 pp. €43.40. 08204-80266.

3413 *Mettinger, Tryggve N.D.* Cui bono?: the prophecy of Nathan (2 Sam. 7) as a piece of political rhetoric. SEÅ 70 (2005) 193-214.

3414 *Leith, Mary J.W.* When forever isn't forever. BiRe 21/2 (2005) 10, 46 [2 Sam 7,12-16].

3415 *Fischer, Alexander A.* Die literarische Entstehung des Großreichs Davids und ihr geschichtlicher Hintergrund: zur Darstellung der Kriegs-Chronik in 2 Sam 8,1-14(15). [F]CONRAD, J.: ABIG 17: 2005 ⇒27. 101-128.

3416 *Zhu-En Wee, John* Maacah and Ish-Tob. JSOT 30 (2005) 191-199 [2 Sam 10,6].

3417 *Combes, Alain* 'Désir du danger' ou 'danger du désir'?. ThEv(VS) 4/3 (2005) 39-44 [2 Sam 11; John 14,12-13].

3418 *Wyatt, Nicolas* Echoes of the king and his Ka: an ideological motif in the story of Solomon's birth. 'There's such divinity'. 2005 <1987> ⇒ 329. 49-59 [2 Sam 11-12].

3419 *Gardner, Anne E.* The identity of Bath-Sheba. RB 112 (2005) 521-535 [2 Sam 11,3; 20,1-22; 1 Chr 3,5].

3420 *Ravid, Dalia* An analysis of inner conflicts experienced by King David when forced to flee from his son Absalom. BetM 183 (2005) 297-312. Sum 392 [2 Sam 15-18].

3421 *Fischer, Alexander A.* Flucht und Heimkehr Davids als integraler Rahmen der Abschalomerzählung. [M]WALLIS, G.: ABIG 16: 2005 ⇒ 160. 43-69 [2 Sam 15-20].

3422 *Pisano, Stephen* Alcune osservazioni sul racconto di Davide e Golia: confronto tra TM e LXX. AnScR 10 (2005) 129-137 [2 Sam 17].

3423 *Branch, Robin G.* Rizpah: activist in nation-building: an analysis of 2 Samuel 21:1-14. JSem 14/1 (2005) 74-94.

3424 *Quiroga, Raúl* La venganza gabaonita a la luz de los conceptos actuales de justicia: un estudio interpretativo de 2 Samuel 21:1-14. DavarLogos 4/2 (2005) 117-129.

3425 *Waschke, Ernst-Joachim* Die Königsvorstellung nach den "letzten Worten Davids" (2 Sam 23,1-7). [F]CONRAD, J.: ABIG 17: 2005 ⇒27. 129-144.

3426 *Wyatt, Nicolas* 'Araunah the Jebusite' and the throne of David. 'There's such divinity'. 2005 <1985>, 1-12 [2 Sam 24,15-17];

3427 'Jedidiah' and cognate forms as a title of royal legitimization. 'There's such divinity'. 2005 <1985> ⇒329. 13-22 [2 Sam 24,15-17].

## E4.7 *Libri Regum*: **Solomon, Temple: 1 Kings...**

3428 *Avioz, Michael* The book of Kings in recent research (part I). CuBR 4 (2005) 11-55.

3429 **Beach, Eleanor F.** The Jezebel letters: religion and politics in ninth-century Israel. Mp 2005, Fortress 220 pp. $19. 0-8006-3754-2 [BiTod 44,323—Dianne Bergant].

3430 *Emerton, John A.* A questionable theory of Egyptian influence on a genre of Hebrew literature. [F]ULLENDORFF, E.: SStLL 47: 2005 ⇒ 154. 189-202 [Sources of Kings].

3431 **Fritz, Volkmar** 1 & 2 Kings: a continental commentary. [T]*Hagedorn, Anselm*: Continental commentaries: 2003 ⇒19,3393; 20,3290. [R]HeyJ 46 (2005) 217-218 (*Hill, Robert C.*); NV 80/4 (2005) 107-108 (*Borel, Jean*); RBLit 7 (2005) 156-158 (*Auld, A. Graeme*).

[E]**Grabbe, L.** Good kings and bad kings 2005 ⇒751.

3432 *Hentschel, Georg* I libri dei Re. Introduzione AT. 2005 ⇒1159. 363-377.

3433 **Inrig, Gary** I & II Kings. 2003 ⇒19,3394; 20,3293. [R]RBLit 7 (2005) 158-159 (*Bostock, David*).

3434 **Kucová, Lydie** Common source theory and composition of the story of the divided monarchy in Kings, with special emphasis on the account of Josiah's reform. [D]*Auld, A.G.* 2005, Diss. Edinburgh [RTL 37,610] [2 Kgs 22-23].

3435 *Lee, Kyung S.* 1 and 2 Kings. Global bible commentary. 2005 ⇒ 2443. 105-118.

3436 *Na'aman, Nadav* Ahab's chariot force at the battle of Qarqar. Ancient Israel. 2005 <1976> ⇒266. 1-12.

3437 **Podany, Amanda H.** The land of Hana: Kings, chronology, and scribal tradition. 2002 ⇒18,11407. [R]BiOr 62 (2005) 290-292 (*Graef, K. de*).

3438 *Rad, Gerhard von* The Deuteronomic theology of history in 1 and 2 Kings. From Genesis. 2005 <1947> ⇒283. 154-166.

3439 **Schenker, Adrian** Älteste Textgeschichte der Königsbücher: die hebräische Vorlage der ursprünglichen Septuaginta als älteste Textform der Königsbücher. OBO 199: 2004 ⇒20,3297. [R]BZ 49 (2005) 307-312 (*Stipp, Hermann-Josef*).

3440 *Seow, Choon-Leong* The first and second books of Kings. OT survey. 2005 ⇒413. 130-135.

3441 **Tetley, M. Christine** The reconstructed chronology of the divided kingdom. WL 2005, Eisenbrauns xiv; 194 pp. $39.50. 1-57506-072-8. RRBLit (2005)* (*Singletary, Jennifer; Steinmann, Andrew*).

3442 *Thiel, Winfried* Böses im Buch der Könige <2004>;

3443 Geschichtliche, innenpolitische und religiöse Entwicklungen in Israel im 9. Jahrhundert v. Chr. <2003>. Gedeutete Geschichte. BThSt 71: 2005 ⇒316. 90-106/151-167.

3444 *Vitório, Jaldemir* O livro dos reis: redação e teologia. Estudos bíblicos 88 (2005) 63-83.

3445 ET**Vogüé, Adalbert de** GRÉGOIRE le Grand (Pierre de Cava): commentaire sur le premier livre des Rois, V (V,1-212). SC 469: 2003 ⇒ 19,3402. RREAug 51 (2005) 215-216 (*Weiss, Jean-Pierre*);

3446 VI (VI,1-116). SC 482: 2004 ⇒20,3303. RRMab 16 (2005) 280-282 (*Lebigue, Jean-Baptiste*); RevSR 79 (2005) 282-283 (*Vinel, Françoise*); JThS 56 (2005) 722-723 (*Winterbottom, Michael*).

3447 *Young, Rodger C.* Tables of reign lengths from the Hebrew court recorders. JETS 48 (2005) 225-248 [OTA 30,291].

3448 **Brueggemann, Walter** Solomon: Israel's ironic icon of human achievement. Columbia, South Carolina 2005, University of South Carolina Press xiii; 301 pp. $45. 1-570-03578-4. Bibl. 255-280.

3449 *Bultmann, Christoph* Dichtung und Weisheit der Blütezeit: zum Salomobild im 18. Jahrhundert. MWALLIS, G.: ABIG 16: 2005 ⇒160. 153-174.

3450 *Charpin, Dominique* Salomon: roi modèle, modèle des rois: en Mésopotamie, aux origines de la royauté. MoBi 163 (2005) 24-27.

3451 *Gillmayr-Bucher, Susanne* Salomo in all seiner Pracht;

3452 Auf der Suche nach dem geschichtlichen Salomo. MWALLIS, G.: ABIG 16: 2005 ⇒160. 127-152/91-105.

3453 **Johnson, Janell Anne** The trouble with Solomon: competing characterizations in the Solomonic narrative. 2005, Diss. Princeton, Sem. [RTL 37,609].

3454 *Kunz-Lübcke, Andreas* Die Komposition der Salomogeschichten. MWALLIS, G.: ABIG 16: 2005 ⇒160. 107-125.

3455 *Lemaire, André* Salomon, la bible et l'histoire. MoBi 163 (2005) 18-23.

3456 *Lory, Pierre* Salomon, personnage du Coran. MoBi 163 (2005) 38-43.

3457 *Mimouni, Simon C.* Salomon : roi modèle, modèle des rois: un messie dans la bible?. MoBi 163 (2005) 28-33.

3458 *Noël, D.* Le surdimensionnement du royaume de Salomon en 1 R 5,1.4. TEuph 29 (2005) 155-170.

3459 *Pasala, Solomon* Archaeological evidences for Solomonic period. FolTh 16 (2005) 125-142.

3460 *Rad, Gerhard von* The royal ritual in Judah. From Genesis. 2005 <1947> ⇒283. 167-173.

3461 *Robin, Christian Julien* Salomon vu du Yémen héros national ou roi étrange. MoBi 163 (2005) 34-37.

3462 **Torijano, Pablo A.** Solomon the esoteric king: from king to magus, development of a tradition. JSJ.S 73: 2002 ⇒18,3197; 20,3315. RJSJ 36 (2005) 127-129 (*Johnston, Sarah Iles*).

3463 **Ariel, Israel; Richman, Chaim** Carta's illustrated encyclopedia of the holy temple in Jerusalem. ᵀ*Wertheimer, Yehoshua*: J 2005, Carta 270 pp. 965-220-530-3.

3464 *Avioz, Michael* The date of the destruction of the first temple in ancient versions and in early biblical interpretation. Textus 22 (2005) 87-94 [2 Kgs 25,8; Jer 52,12].

3465 **Barker, Margaret** Temple theology: an introduction. 2004 ⇒20, 3316. ᴿTheol. 108 (2005) 213-214 (*Økland, Jorunn*).

3466 *Bäumer, Bettina* Praxis-Dimensionen (Ritual, religiöse Erfahrung, Ethik): sakraler Raum und heilige Zeit. Handbuch Religionswissenschaft. 2005 ⇒1016. 690-701.

3467 **Beale, Gregory K.** The temple and the church's mission: a biblical theology of the dwelling place of God. New Studies in Biblical Theology 17: 2004 ⇒20,3317. ᴿRBLit (2005)* (*Fay, Ron*).

3468 *Buchanan, George W.* The area of the temple of Zion. ET 116 (2005) 181-189.

3469 **Decharneux, Baudouin** Du temple à l'homme. Paroles retrouvées: P 2005, Dervy 174 pp. €18. 2-84454-320-0.

3470 *Goodman, Martin* The temple in first century CE Judaism;

3471 *Hayward, C.T.R.* Understandings of the temple service in the Septuagint pentateuch;

3472 *Hurowitz, Avigdor* Yhwh's exalted house—aspects of the design and symbolism of Solomon's temple. Temple and worship. LHBOTS 422: 2005 ⇒731. 459-468/385-400/63-110.

3473 *Janowski, Bernd* Der Himmel auf Erden: zur kosmologischen Bedeutung des Tempels in Israel und in seiner Umwelt. JBTh 20 (2005) 85-110.

3474 **Kamlah, Jens** 'Und es herrschte Friede zwischen Hiram und Salomo': Studien zum Tempelkult in Phönizien und in Israel/Juda. ᴰ*Hübner, Ulrich* 2005, Diss.-Habil. Kiel [ThLZ 130,887].

3475 **Kaufman, Asher S.** The Temple Mount: where is the Holy of Holies?. 2004 ⇒20,3322. ᴿCBQ 67 (2005) 321-323 (*Ritmeyer, Leen*).

3476 **Keel, Othmar; Knauf, Ernst Axel; Staubli, Thomas** Salomons Tempel. Bibel+Orient Museum: 2004 ⇒20,3323. ᴿWZKM 95 (2005) 430-432 (*Jaroš, Karl*).

3477 *Kunin, Seth D.* Neo-structuralism and the contestation of sacred place in biblical Israel. Tem. 41/2 (2005) 203-224.

3478 *Lux, Rüdiger* Der zweite Tempel von Jerusalem—ein persisches oder prophetisches Projekt?. ᶠCONRAD, J.: ABIG 17: 2005 ⇒27. 145-172.

3479 **McCormick, Clifford M.** Palace and temple: a study of architectural and verbal icons. BZAW 313: 2002 ⇒18,3213; 20,12230. ᴿJNES 64 (2005) 193-196 (*Smith, Mark S.*).

3480 *Mettinger, Tryggve N.D.* JHWH-Statue oder Anikonismus im ersten Tempel?: Gespräch mit meinen Gegnern. ZAW 117 (2005) 485-508.

3481 *Murphy-O'Connor, Jerome* The temple and the Antonia. ET 116 (2005) 325-329.

3482 *Netzer, E.* The form and function of courts and gates that surrounded the second temple. Qad. 38 (2005) 97-106. **H.**

3483 **Pitkänen, Pekka** Central sanctuary and the centralization of worship in ancient Israel: from the settlement to the building of Solomon's temple. 2003 ⇒19,3432; 20,3328. ᴿRBLit 7 (2005) 219-22 (*Reventlow, Henning Graf*).

3484 *Plummer, R.L.* Something awry in the temple?: the rending of the temple veil and early Jewish sources that report unusual phenomena in the temple around AD 30. JETS 48 (2005) 301-16 [NTAb 50,28].

3485 *Rothenbusch, Ralf* Die Finanzierung des Jerusalemer Kultes in nachexilischer Zeit und die Mitgliedschaft in einer religiösen Gruppe. [F]IRSIGLER, H.: ATSAT 76: 2005 ⇒67. 159-184.

3486 *Rowland, Christopher* The temple in the New Testament. Temple and worship. LHBOTS 422: 2005 ⇒731. 469-483.

3487 *Schenker, Adrian* Une nouvelle lumière sur l'architecture du temple grâce à la Septante?: la place de l'arche d'alliance selon 1 Rois 6:16-17 et 3 Règnes 6:16-17. AnScR 10 (2005) 139-154 [1 Kgs 6,16-17].

3488 **Souza, Elias Brasil de** The heavenly sanctuary/temple motif in the Hebrew Bible: function and relationship to the earthly counterparts. [D]*Davidson, Richard M.* 2005, Diss. Andrews [AUSS 44,173].

3489 **Van Keulen, Percy S.F.** Two versions of the Solomon narrative: an inquiry into the relationship between MT 1 Kgs. 2-11 and LXX 3 Reg. 2-11. VT.S 104: Lei 2005, Brill vii; 338 pp. 90-04-13895-1. Bibl. 306-312.

3490 *Delfour, Jean-J.* Pouvoir de vie et pouvoir de mort: à propos du 'jugement de Salomon'. Esprit 313 (2005) 191-207 [1 Kgs 3,16-4,1].

3491 *Avioz, Michael* The characterization of Solomon in Solomon's prayer ( 1 Kings 8). BN 126 (2005) 19-28.

3492 *Croatto, Severino* Lecture 'libérationniste': schisme ou processus de libération?: 'l'envers de l'histoire' dans 1 Rois 12. Guide des nouvelles lectures. 2005 ⇒426. 201-221.

3493 *Botta, Alejandro F.* 1 Reyes 12:1-20: análisis estructural. Cuadernos de teología 24 (2005) 9-16.

3494 *Cochell, Trevor* The religious establishments of Jeroboam I. Stone-Campbell Journal [Joplin, MS] 8 (2005) 85-97 [OTA 29,149] [1 Kgs 12,26-33].

3495 *Gosse, Bernhard* Salomon et le Pharaon de la sortie d'Egypte. BZ 49 (2005) 81-85 [Exod 32; 1 Kgs 12,28].

## E4.8 *1 Regum 17-22: Elias*, **Elijah**

3496 **Ackerman, Jane** Elijah, prophet of Carmel. 2003 ⇒19,3450. [R]REsp 64 (2005) 315-316 (*Husillos Tamarit, Ignacio*).

3497 **Beck, Martin** Elia und die Monolatrie. BZAW 281: 1999 ⇒15,2737 ... 19,3452. [R]ThR 70 (2005) 429-431 (*Reventlow, Henning Graf*).

3498 *Den Dulk, Maarten* Elia's levensverhaal: wegbereider voor messiaanse mensen. ITBT 13/2 (2005) 4-6.

3499 *Ebach, Jürgen* Die Elia-Erfahrung. JK 66/4 (2005) 48-50.

3500 *Morrison, Craig* Elijah on Horeb. Carmel 44 (2005) 184-191.

3501 **Tourn, Giorgio** Elia. Piccola collana moderna 116: T 2005, Claudiana 156 pp. €9.50. 88-7016-587-6.

3502 *Villota Herrero, Salvador* Elías, profeta orante: algunas características de la oración eliana desde la perspectiva bíblica. Carmelus 52 (2005) 47-64.

3503 *Wacker, Marie-Theres* Cibo in mezzo alla violenza: i racconti biblici su Elia. Conc(I) 41 (2005) 214-224; Conc(D) 41,146-154.

3504 *Galley, Susanne* Elija: eine Exkursion durch die jüdische Religionsgeschichte. Jud. 61/1 (2005) 20-41 [1 Kgs 17-2 Kgs 2; Mal 3].

3505 *Steenkamp, Yolande* King Ahazia, the widow's son and the theology of the Elijah cycle: employing ancient social values in a comparative reading. OTEs 18 (2005) 811-825 [1 Kgs 17-2 Kgs 2].

3506 *Antista, Aurelio* La voce di un sottile silenzio. Horeb 14/1 (2005) 35-39 [1 Kgs 17-21].

3507 *Overholt, Thomas W.* Lecture culturelle et anthropologique: Elie et Elisée, guérisseurs et hommes de Dieu. Guide des nouvelles lectures. 2005 ⇒426. 115-140 [1 Kgs 17,8-16; 2 Kgs 4,8-37].

3508 *Tonstad, Sigve* The limits of power: revisiting Elijah at Horeb. SJOT 19 (2005) 253-266 [1 Kgs 19,3-18].

3509 **Cronauer, Patrick** The stories about Naboth the Jezreelite: a source, composition, and redaction investigation of 1 Kings 21 and passages in 2 Kings 9. LHBOTS 424; JSOT.S 424: NY 2005, Clark xi; 244 pp. $140. 0-567-02940-9. Bibl. 217-228.

3510 *Thiel, Winfried* Der Todesrechtsprozeß Nabots in 1 Kön 21. Gedeutete Geschichte. BThSt 71: 2005 <1999> ⇒316. 140-150.

3511 *Vitório, Jaldemir* Monarquia e profetismo: duas instituições em conflito : 1 Rs 21,1-29-a vinha de Nabot. Estudos bíblicos 88 (2005) 84-95.

3512 *Farisani, Elelwani* A sociological reading of the confrontation between Ahab and Elijah in 1 Kings 21:1-29. OTEs 18 (2005) 47-60.

3513 *Na'aman, Nadav* Was Ahab killed by an Assyrian arrow in the battle of Qarqar?. UF 37 (2005) 461-474 [1 Kgs 22,1-37].

### E4.9 **2 Reg 1**... *Elisaeus, Elisha*... Ezechias, Josias

3514 **Cohn, Robert L.** 2 Kings. Berit Olam: 2000 ⇒16,2902; 18,3268. [R]RBLit 7 (2005) 154-156 (*Barrick, W. Boyd*).

3515 **Davis, Dale Ralph** 2 Kings. Fearn 2005, Christian Focus 344 pp.

3516 **Ernst, Stephanie** Ahas, König von Juda: ein Beitrag zur Literatur und Geschichte des Alten Israel. [D]*Seidl, Theodor* 2005, Diss. Würzburg [ThRv 102,xiii].

3517 *Grabbe, Lester L.* The kingdom of Judah from Sennacherib's invasion to the fall of Jerusalem: if we had only the bible...;

3518 Reflections on the discussion;

3519 *Knauf, Ernst A.* The glorious days of Manasseh. Good kings. LHBOTS 393: 2005 ⇒751. 164-188/339-350/78-122.

3520 *Na'aman, Nadav* Hezekiah and the kings of Assyria. Ancient Israel. 2005 <1994> ⇒266. 98-117.

3521 *Stavrakopoulou, Francesca* The blackballing of Manasseh;

3522 *Sweeney, Marvin A.* King Manasseh of Judah and the problem of theodicy in the Deuteronomistic History;

3523 *Warburton, David A.* The importance of the archaeology of the seventh century. Good kings. LHBOTS 393: 2005 ⇒751. 248-263/264-278/317-335.

3524 *Alexandre, Jean* Des enfants et du pain: deux récits de purification dans le cycle d'Élisée: II Rois 2,19-25 et 4,38-44. FV 104/4 (2005) 36-47.

3525 *Ska, Jean-Louis* Il carro di fuoco (2Re 2,11). Firmana 38-39 (2005) 35-46 [2 Kgs 2,1-18].

3526 *Westbrook, Raymond* Elisha's true prophecy in 2 Kings 3. JBL 124 (2005) 530-532.

3527 *Asurmendi, Jesus* Elisée et la guerre. 2 R 3:4-27. BiblInterp 13 (2005) 1-12.

3528 *Kim, Jean Kyoung* Reading and retelling Naaman's story (2 Kings 5). JSOT 30 (2005) 49-61.

3529 *Shemesh, Abraham Ofir* "וְהֵנִיף יָדוֹ אֶל הַמָּקוֹם וְסַף הַמְּצֹרָע": touch and hand motions as magic techniques for leprosy cure. BetM 183 (2005) 329-344 Sum 392 [2 Kgs 5,11]. **H.**

3530 *Irvine, Stuart A.* The last battle of Hadadezer. JBL 124 (2005) 341-347 [2 Kgs 9].

3531 *Na'aman, Nadav* Jehu son of Omri: legitimizing a loyal vassal by his overlord. Ancient Israel. 2005 <1998> ⇒266. 13-15 [2 Kgs 9-10].

3532 *Leshem, Yossi* "She painted her eyes with kohl and dressed her hair" 2 Kings 9:30. HUCA 76 (2005) *1-*10. **H.**

3533 *Eskhult, Mats* Kung Joash och pilarna. SEÅ 70 (2005) 53-61 [2 Kgs 13,14-21].

3534 *Yamaga, Tetsuo* The so-called Syro-Ephraimite war in the books of Kings and in the books of Chronicles. AJBI 30-31 (2004-2005) 31-60 [2 Kgs 15-16; 2 Chr 27-28].

3535 *Schenker, Adrian* La cause de la chute du royaume d'Israël selon le Texte Massorétique et selon la Septante ancienne: une différence et ses conséquences pour l'histoire du texte des livres des Rois. Traduire la Bible hébraïque. 2005 ⇒728. 151-171 [2 Kgs 17,1-19].

3536 *Na'aman, Nadav* The historical background to the conquest of Samaria (720 BCE). Ancient Israel. 2005 <1990> ⇒266. 76-93 {2 Kgs 17,3-6].

3537 *Paul, Shalom M.* Sargon's administrative diction in 2 Kings 17:27. Divrei Shalom. CHANE 23: 2005 <1969> ⇒273. 37-38.

3538 **Dubovsky, Peter** A study of the Neo-Assyrian intelligence services and their significance for 2 Kings 18-19. 2005, Diss. Harvard [HThR 98,493. Cf. BibOr 49].

3539 *Na'aman, Nadav* New light on Hezekiah's second prophetic story (2 Kgs 19,9b-35). Ancient Israel. 2005 <2000> ⇒266. 179-192;

3540 The kingdom of Judah under Josiah. Ancient Israel. 2005 <1991> ⇒ 266. 329-398 [2 Kgs 21-23].

3541 *Schenker, Adrian* The relationship between the earliest Septuagint and the Masoretic Text in the books of Kings in light of 2 Kgs 21:2-9. Traduire la Bible hébraïque. 2005 ⇒728. 127-149.

3542 *McKinlay, Judith E.* Gazing at Huldah. BiCT 1/3 (2005)* [2 Kgs 22].

3543 **Barrick, W. Boyd** The king and the cemeteries: toward a new understanding of Josiah's reform. VT.S 88: 2002 ⇒18,3284; 19,3499. [R]RB 112 (2005) 417-425 (*Monroe, Lauren A. Shedletsky*) [1 Kgs 13; 2 Kgs 22-23; 2 Chr 34,1-36,1].

3544 *Albertz, Rainer* Why a reform like Josiah's must have happened;

3545 *Ben Zvi, Ehud* Josiah and the prophetic books: some observations;

3546 *Davies, Philip R.* Josiah and the law book;

3547 *Hardmeier, Christof* King Josiah in the climax of the Deuteronomic History (2 Kings 22-23) and the pre-Deuteronomic document of a cult reform at the place of residence (23.4-15*): criticism of sources, reconstruction of literary pre-stages and the theology of history in 2 Kings 22-23;

3548 *Na'aman, Nadav* Josiah and the kingdom of Judah;

3549 *Uehlinger, Christoph* Was there a cult reform under King Josiah?: the case for a well-grounded minimum. Good kings. LHBOTS 393: 2005 ⇒751. 27-46/47-64/65-77/123-163/189-247/279-316 [2 Kgs 22-23].

3550 *Schipper, Jeremy* "Significant resonances" with Mephibosheth in 2 Kings 25:27-30: a response to Donald F. Murray. JBL 124 (2005) 521-529.

### E5.2 *Chronicorum libri*—**The books of Chronicles**

3551 *Allen, Leslie C.* The first and second books of Chronicles. OT survey. 2005 ⇒413. 136-143.

3552 **Bae, Hee-Sook** Vereinte Suche nach JHWH—die hiskianische und josianische Reform in der Chronik. [D]*Albertz, Rainer*: BZAW 355: B 2005, De Gruyter xii; 242 pp. €78. 3-11-018451-6. Diss. Münster; Bibl. 202-225.

3553 *Boshoff, W.S.* New politics, new stories, new history: the Chronicler as historian for a new generation. VeE 26 (2005) 1-15.

3554 **Dirksen, Peter B.** 1 Chronicles. Lv 2005, Peeters xvii; 358 pp. 90-429-1619-2. Bibl. xiii-xvii.

3555 *Duke, Rodney K.* The ethical appeal of the Chronicler. Rhetoric, ethic. 2005 ⇒738. 33-51 [OTA 29,283].

3556 **Hill, Andrew E.** 1 & 2 Chronicles. GR 2003, Zondervan 699 pp. 0-310-20610-3. Ill.

3557 **Hognesius, Kjell** The text of 2 Chronicles 1-16: a critical edition with textual commentary. CB.OT 51: 2003 ⇒19,3518. [R]CBQ 67 (2005) 121-122 (*Graham, M. Patrick*).

3558 *Japhet, Sara* Chronicles: a history. Das Alte Testament...Beiträge. Ment. *Rad, G. von*: ATM 10: 2005 ⇒802. 129-146.

3559 **Jarick, John** 1 Chronicles. Readings: L 2005, Sheffield Academic xii; 167 pp. £60/18.

3560 *Jarick, John* The temple of David in the book of Chronicles. Temple and worship. LHBOTS 422: 2005 ⇒731. 365-381.

3561 **Kalimi, Isaac** The reshaping of ancient Israelite history in Chronicles. WL 2005, Eisenbrauns xiii; 473 pp. $44.50. 1-57506-058-2. Bibl. 413-444. [R]RBLit (2005)* (*Grabbe, Lester*);

3562 An ancient Israelite historian: studies in the Chronicler, his time, place and setting. SSN 46: Assen 2005, Van Gorcum x; 212 pp. €79.50. 90-232-4071-5. Bibl. 161-180.

3563 *Klein, Ralph W.* Psalms in Chronicles. CThMi 32 (2005) 264-275.

3564 **Knoppers, Gary N.** 1 Chronicles 1-9, 10-29. AncB 12-13: 2004 ⇒ 20,3400. [R]RSR 93 (2005) 593-595 (*Abadie, Philippe*); RivBib 53 (2005) 489-494 (*Balzaretti, Claudio*); SR 34 (2005) 590-591 (*Van Seters, John*); AUSS 43 (2005) 358-360 (*Li, Tarsee*); TJT 21 (2005) 246-247 (*McKenzie, Steven L.*); RBLit (2005)* (*Cathey, Joseph; Hieke, Thomas*).

3565 *Mathias, Dietmar* Der König auf dem Thron JHWHs: Überlegungen zur chronistischen Geschichtsdarstellung. [F]CONRAD, J.: ABIG 17: 2005 ⇒27. 173-202.

3566 *Mitchell, Christine* BAKHTIN and the ideal ruler in 1-2 Chronicles and the *Cyropaedia*. The Bakhtin Circle. 2005 ⇒620. 297-319.
3567 *Rad, Gerhard von* The Levitical sermon in 1 and 2 Chronicles. From Genesis. 2005 <1934> ⇒283. 232-242.
3568 **Royar, Stefan** 'Denn der HERR, eurer Gott ist gnädig und barmherzig...': die Gebete in den Chronikbüchern und ihre Bedeutung für die chronistische Theologie. [D]*Oeming, Manfred*: Beiträge zum Verstehen der Bibel 10: Müns 2005, LIT 200 pp. 3-8258-8387-6. Diss. Heidelberg [ThLZ 130,886].
3569 **Schweitzer, Steven** Reading Utopia in Chronicles. [D]*VanderKam, James* 2005, 506 pp. Diss. Notre Dame [RTL 37,612].
3570 **Selman, M.J.** 1 Cronache: introduzione e commentario. 2004 ⇒20, 3408. [R]RivBib 53 (2005) 494-496 (*Balzaretti, Claudio*).
3571 *Steins, Georg* Chronistisches Geschichtsbild und "levitische Predigt": Überlegungen zur Eigenart der Chronik im Anschluss an Gerhard VON RAD. Das Alte Testament...Beiträge. ATM 10: 2005 ⇒802. 147-173;
3572 I libri delle Cronache. Introduzione AT. 2005 ⇒1159. 378-398.
3573 *Willi, Thomas* Das davidische Königtum in der Chronik. [M]WALLIS, G.: ABIG 16: 2005 ⇒160. 71-87.
3574 *Wong, Fook-Kong* 1 and 2 Chronicles. Global bible commentary. 2005 ⇒2443. 119-126.

3575 *Galil, Gershon* The formation of 1 Chr 2:3-4:23 and the election of King David. [F]KLEIN, J. 2005 ⇒79. 707-717.
3576 *Willi, Thomas* "Den Herrn aufsuchen...": Einsatz und Thema des narrativen Teils der Chronikbücher. [F]SCHENKER, A.: OBO 214: 2005 ⇒ 134. 432-444 [Lev 26,34-35; 1 Chr 10; 2 Chr 36,21].
3577 *Ristau, Kenneth A.* Breaking down unity: an analysis of 1 Chronicles 21.1-22.1. JSOT 30 (2005) 201-221.
3578 *Olson, Dan* What got the gatekeepers into trouble?. JSOT 30 (2005) 223-242 [2 Kgs 23,11; 1 Chr 26,17-18; Ezek 8,16].
3579 *Lucca, Paolo* Note on Armenian [vsestak] (II Chronicles 2:10). Muséon 118 (2005) 315-319.
3580 *Na'aman, Nadav* Hezekiah's fortified cities and the *LMLK* stamps. Ancient Israel. 2005 <1986> ⇒266. 153-178 [2 Chr 11,05-10].
3581 **So, Hyeong-Geun** Die Justizreform des Josaphat. [D]*Rüterswörden, U.*: 2005, Diss. Bonn [ThLZ 130,882] [2 Chr 19,4-11].
3582 *Knuteson, Roy E.* Elijah's little-known letter in 2 Chronicles 21:12-15. BS 162/645 (2005) 23-32.

## E5.4 *Esdrae libri*—**Ezra, Nehemiah**

3583 *Bianchi, F.* "La semence sacrée": la polémique sur les mariages mixtes dans les textes bibliques d'époque achéménide et hellénistique. TEuph 29 (2005) 83-102 [Exod 34,14-16; Dt 7,16; Ezra 9-10; Neh 13,27].
3584 *Boer, Roland* No road: on the absence of feminist criticism of Ezra-Nehemiah. Her master's tools?. 2005 ⇒493. 233-252.
3585 *Brown, A. Philip* Nehemiah and narrative order in the book of Ezra. BS 162/646 (2005) 175-194.

3586 **Dahlen, Kathy; Larson, Knute** Ezra, Nehemiah, Esther. Holman Old Testament Commentary: Nv 2005, Broadman & H. xiii; 381pp. $20. [R]RBLit (2005)* (*Becking, Bob*).

3587 *Fewell, Danna N.* Ezra and Nehemiah. Global bible commentary. 2005 ⇒2443. 127-134.

3588 **Hieke, Thomas** Die Bücher Esra und Nehemia. Neuer Stuttgarter Kommentar: AT 9,2: Stu 2005, Kath. Bibelwerk 264 pp. €25. 3-460-07092-7.

3589 *Johnson, Sylvester* New Israel, new Canaan: the bible, the people of God, and the American holocaust. USQR 59/1-2 (2005) 25-39 [OTA 28,300].

3590 *Klein, Ralph W.* The book of Ezra & Nehemiah. OT survey. 2005 ⇒ 413. 144-151.

3591 **Min, Kyung-jin** The levitical authorship of Ezra-Nehemiah. JSOT.S 409: 2004 ⇒20,3437. [R]RBLit (2005)* (*Becking, Bob*).

3592 *Na'aman, Nadav* Royal vassals or governors?: on the status of Sheshbazzar and Zerubbabel in the Persian Empire. Ancient Israel. 2005 <2000> ⇒266. 403-414.

3593 **Noss, Philip A.; Thomas, Kenneth J.** A handbook on Ezra and Nehemiah. NY 2005, United Bible Societies xii; 611 pp. $50. 08267-01159 [OTA 29,209].

3594 **Schaper, Joachim** Priester und Leviten im achämenidischen Juda: Studien zur Kult- und Sozialgeschichte Israels in persischer Zeit. FAT 31: 2000 ⇒16,2971...20,3440. [R]JSJ 36 (2005) 121-24 (*Grabbe, Lester L.*).

3595 *Steins, Georg* I libri di Esdra e Neemia. Introduzione AT. 2005 ⇒ 1159. 399-420.

3596 *Usue, Emmanuel* Theological perspectives on the concept of 'Yahwe's people' in Ezra and Nehemia during the early post-exilic period (539-350 BC)—part 1. OTEs 18 (2005) 826-846.

3597 **Van Wijk-Bos, Johanna W.H.** Ezra, Nehemiah, and Esther. Westminster Bible companion: 1998 ⇒14,2611. [R]OTEs 18 (2005) 953-955 (*Maré, L.P.*).

3598 *Avishur, Y.; Heltzer, M.* The scribe and priest Ezra: a leader under Achaemenian rule. TEuph 29 (2005) 17-36.

3599 *Brown, A. Philip* Chronological anomalies in the book of Ezra. BS 162/645 (2005) 33-49;

3600 Point of view in the book of Ezra. BS 162/647 (2005) 310-330;

3601 The problem of mixed marriages in Ezra 9-10. BS 162/648 (2005) 437-458.

3602 *Fröhlich, I.* *Mamzēr* in Qumran texts—the problem of mixed marriages from Ezra's time: law, literature and practice. TEuph 29 (2005) 103-115 [Dt 23,3; Zech 9,6].

3603 *Gesche, Bonifatia* Esdras. BVLI 49 (2005) 16-20.

3604 **Grätz, Sebastian** Das Edikt des Artaxerxes: eine Untersuchung zum religionspolitischen und historischen Umfeld von Esra 7,12-26. BZAW 337: 2004 ⇒20,3457. [R]ThLZ 130 (2005) 934-936 (*Reinmuth, Titus*); JBL 124 (2005) 541-543 (*Siedlecki, Armin*).

3605 *Joyce, Paul M.* The poor wise man and the cacophony of voices. [F]YOUNG, F. JSNT.S 295: 2005 ⇒168. 101-105 [Ezra 3,11-13; Qoh 9,13-16].

3606 **Pakkala, Juha** The development of the Ezra material. [D]*Levin, C.* 2005, Diss.-Habil. München [ThLZ 131,340].

3607 **Schwiderski, Dirk** Handbuch des nordwestsemitischen Briefformulars: ein Beitrag zur Echtheitsfrage der aramäischen Briefe des Esrabuches. BZAW 295: 2000 ⇒16,2978... 19,3573. [R]JNES 64 (2005) 133-137 (*Clemens, David M.*) [Ezra 4].

3608 *Castelbajac, I. de* Les sources deutéronomistes de la figure royale de Néhémie. TEuph 30 (2005) 65-76.

3609 *Fried, L.S.* A religious association in second temple Judah?: a comment on Nehemiah 10. TEuph 30 (2005) 77-96.

3610 *Paul, Shalom M.* Nehemiah 6:19—counterespionage. Divrei Shalom. CHANE 23: 2005 <1977> ⇒273. 75-76.

3611 **Reinmuth, Titus** Der Bericht Nehemias: zur literarischen Eigenart, traditionsgeschichtlichen Prägung und innerbiblischen Rezeption des Ich-Berichts Nehemias. OBO 183: 2002 ⇒18,3341... 20,3468. [R]ThRv 101 (2005) 297-300 (*Steins, Georg*); BiOr 62 (2005) 566-569 (*Karrer-Grube, Christiane*) [Neh 1-7; 11].

3612 *Shepherd, David* Prophetaphobia: fear and false prophecy in Nehemiah vi. VT 55 (2005) 232-250.

3613 *Steins, Georg* Inszenierung des Lesens und Lernens in Neh 8,1-12. Religiöses Lernen. WUNT 180: 2005 ⇒384. 83-97.

3614 *Večko, Terezija* Snežna Prayer at the start of action: Neh 1:5-11. Bogoslovni Vestnik 65/1 (2005) 43-57.

3615 **Wright, Jacob L.** Rebuilding identity: the Nehemiah-Memoir and its earliest readers. [D]*Kratz, Reinhard G.*: BZAW 348: B 2005, De Gruyter xiii; 372 pp. 3-11-018319-6. Diss. Göttingen; Bibl. 341-354.

3616 *Metzger, Paul* Esra und das vierte Esra-Buch: die Bedeutung des Pseudonyms für die Interpretation einer apokalyptischen Schrift. [F]BÖCHER, O. 2005 ⇒14. 263-290.

3617 [E]**Talshir, Zipora** I Esdras: a text critical commentary. SBL.SCSt 50: 2001 ⇒17,3015; 19,3594. [R]JNES 64 (2005) 59-60 (*Klein, Ralph W.*); RBLit (2005)* (*De Troyer, Kristin*).

3618 *Viviés, Pierre de Martin* La littérature intertestamentaire, 4: le quatrième Esdras. EeV 122 (2005) 10-17.

## E5.5 Libri Tobiae, Judith, Esther

3619 **Otzen, Benedikt** Tobit and Judith. Guides to the Apocrypha and Pseudepigrapha 11: 2002 ⇒18,3394... 20,3474. [R]JSSt 50 (2005) 386-388 (*Muehlberger, Ellen*).

3620 [E]**Xeravits, Géza G.; Zsengeller, József** The book of Tobit text, tradition, theology: papers of the first international conference on the deuteronomical [!] books, Pápa, Hungary, 20-21 May, 2004. JSJ.S 98: Lei 2005, Brill x; 234 pp. €79/$113. 90-04-14376-9.

3621 *Auwers, Jean-Marie* Tobit. BVLI 49 (2005) 20-22;

3622 La tradition vieille latine du livre de Tobie: un état de la question. Book of Tobit. JSJ.S 98: 2005 ⇒3620. 1-21.

3623 *Barría Iroumé, Christián* El matrimonio de Tobías y la sexualidad: un estudio psicológico. TyV 46 (2005) 675-697.

3624 *Beyerle, Stefan* "Release me to go to my everlasting home..." (Tob 3: 6): a belief in an afterlife in late wisdom literature;

3625 *Bolyki, János* Burial as an ethical task in the book of Tobit, in the bible and in the Greek tragedies;

3626 *Collins, John J.* The Judaism of the book of Tobit;. Book of Tobit. JSJ.S 98: 2005 ⇒3620. 71-88/89-101/23-40.

3627 *Contini, Riccardo; Grottanelli, Cristiano* Introduzione. Il saggio Ahiqar. StBi 148: 2005 ⇒52. 11-89.

3628 *Ego, Beate* Mit dem Engel unterwegs—Tradition und Transformation des biblischen Motivs. Das Buch. 2005 ⇒1130. 23-34;

3629 The book of Tobit and the diaspora. Book of Tobit. JSJ.S 98: 20055 ⇒3620. 41-54;

3630 Buch Tobit. Einführung zu den jüdischen Schriften. JSHRZ 2/6: 2005 ⇒453. 115-150.

3631 *Engel, Helmut* Il libro di Tobia. Introduzione AT. 2005 ⇒1159. 421-437.

3632 *Evans, Trevor V.* Periphrastic tense forms in the Greek Tobit. [F]LUST, J.: BEThL 192: 2005 ⇒92. 109-119.

3633 *Faßbeck, Gabriele* Tobit's religious universe between kinship loyalty and the law of Moses. JSJ 36 (2005) 173-196.

3634 **Fitzmyer, Joseph A.** Tobit. Commentaries on Early Jewish Literature: 2003 ⇒19,3610; 20,3478. [R]JSJ 36 (2005) 347-349 (*Xeravits, Géza*); JNES 64 (2005) 139-140 (*Collins, John J.*); RdQ 22 (2005) 294-296 (*Puech, Émile*).

3635 *Fröhlich, Ida* Tobit against the background of the Dead Sea scrolls;

3636 *Jacobs, Naomi S.* "You did not hesitate to get up and leave the dinner": food and eating in the narrative of Tobit with some attention to Tobit's shavuot meal. Book of Tobit. JSJ.S 98: 2005 ⇒3620. 55-70/ 121-138.

3637 *Nicklas, Tobias* 'Denn der Herr kennt den Weg der Gerechten...' (Ps 1,6a): Lesespaziergänge vom Buch Tobit in den Psalter. SJOT 19 (2005) 61-73;

3638 Marriage in the book of Tobit: a synoptic approach. Book of Tobit. JSJ.S 98: 2005 ⇒3620. 139-154.

3639 *Nowell, Irene* The book of Tobit: an ancestral story. [F]DI LELLA, A.: CBQ.MS 38: 2005 ⇒35. 3-13;

3640 The book of Tobit. OT survey. 2005 ⇒413. 470-479.

3641 *Portier-Young, Anathea* "Eyes to the blind": a dialogue between Tobit and Job. [F]DI LELLA, A. CBQ.MS 38: 2005 ⇒35. 14-27.

3642 *Reiterer, Friedrich V.* Prophet und Prophetie in Tobit und Ben Sira: Berührungspunkte und Differenzen. Book of Tobit. JSJ.S 98: 2005 ⇒3620. 155-175 [Sir 44-50].

3643 *Ryan, Stephen* The Psalms and the book of Tobit. [F]DI LELLA, A.: CBQ.MS 38: 2005 ⇒35. 28-42 [Ps 77,18].

3644 *Skemp, Vincent* Avenues of intertextuality between Tobit and the New Testament. [F]DI LELLA, A.: CBQ.MS 38: 2005 ⇒35. 43-70.

3645 *Stuckenbruck, Loren; Weeks, Stuart* The medieval Hebrew and Aramaic texts of Tobit. [F]DI LELLA, A.: CBQ.MS 38: 2005 ⇒35. 71-86;

3646 The "Fagius" Hebrew version of Tobit: an English translation based on the Constantinople text of 1519. Book of Tobit. JSJ.S 98: 2005 ⇒ 3620. 189-219.

3647 *Toloni, Giancarlo* Tobi e Ahiqar. Il saggio Ahiqar. StBi 148: 2005 ⇒52. 141-165.

3648 **Toloni, Giancarlo** L'originale del libro di Tobia: studio filologico-linguistico. TECC 71: 2004 ⇒20,3484. [R]CBQ 67 (2005) 516-517 (*Laberge, Léo*); Sef. 65/1 (2005) 205-207 (*Ribera Florit, J.*); RBLit (2005)* (*Noffke, Eric*).

3649 *Van den Eynde, Sabine* One journey and one journey makes three: the impact of the reader's knowledge in the book of Tobit. ZAW 117 (2005) 273-280;

3650 Prayer as part of characterisation and plot: an analysis of its narrative function in Tobit 3. Analyse narrative. BEThL 191: 2005 ⇒742. 527-536.

3651 *Velcic, Bruna* The significance of the relation of 4QTobit fr. 6 with Greek texts. Henoch 27/1-2 (2005) 149-162.

3652 [E]**Weeks, Stuart; Gathercole, Simon J.; Stuckenbruck, Loren T.** The book of Tobit: texts from the principal ancient and medieval traditions. FoSub 3: 2004 ⇒20,3485. [R]ThRv 101 (2005) 32-34 (*Nicklas, Tobias*); CBQ 67 (2005) 329-331 (*Di Lella, Alexander*); EThL 81 (2005) 511-512 (*Auwers, J.-M.*).

3653 *Wojciechowski, Michał* Ksiega Tobita jako swiadectwo o diasporze Izraelskiej w Asyrii. CoTh 75/4 (2005) 17-33. **P.**

3654 **Wojciechowski, Michał** Ksiega Tobiasza czyli Tobita: opowiesc o miosci rodzinnej: wstep przeklad z oryginalu, komentarz. Nowy komentarz biblijny, Stary Testament 12: Czestochowa 2005, Swiety Paweł 218 pp. 83-7168-959-4. Bibl. 199-205. **P.**

3655 *Zsengellér, József* Topography as theology: theological premises of the geographical references in the book of Tobit. Book of Tobit. JSJ.S 98: 2005 ⇒3620. 177-188.

3656 *Bremer, Kai* Gottes Kraft und das "schwache Weib": Judith auf der Bühne der frühen Neuzeit. Das Buch. 2005 ⇒1130. 87-100.

3657 *Doré, Daniel* Le livre de Judith ou La guerre et la foi. CEv 132 (2005) 3-52.

3658 **Efthimiadis-Keith, Helen** The enemy is within: a Jungian psychoanalytic approach to the book of Judith. BiblInterp 67: 2004 ⇒20, 3490. [R]RBLit (2005)* (*Kille, D.*).

3659 *Engel, Helmut* Il libro di Giuditta. Introduzione AT. 2005 ⇒1159. 438-456.

3660 **Kobelt-Groch, Marion** Judith macht Geschichte: zur Rezeption einer mythischen Gestalt vom 16. bis 19. Jahrhundert. Mú 2005, Fink 310 pp. €34.90. 3-7705-3959-1.

3661 **Mosis, Rudolf** Welterfahrung und Gottesglaube: drei Erzählungen aus dem Alten Testament. 2004 ⇒20,3162. Jona; Judit. [R]TThZ 114 (2005) 260-261 (*Brandscheidt, Renate*); RBLit (2005)* (*Gerstenberger, Erhard S.*) [1 Sam 4-6].

3662 *Mullally, Erin* The cross-gendered gift: weaponry in the Old English Judith. Exemplaria 17 (2005) 255-284.

3663 **Rakel, Claudia** Judit—über Schönheit, Macht und Widerstand im Krieg: eine feministisch-intertextuelle Lektüre. BZAW 334: 2003 ⇒ 19,3626; 20,3495. [R]CBQ 67 (2005) 509-510 (*Corley, Jeremy*).

3664 *Ramos, José Augusto M.* Percepções de identidade no judaísmo helenístico, segundo o livro de Judite. Did(L) 35 (2005) 49-64.

3665 *Rocca, Samuele* The *Book of Judith*, Queen Sholomzion and King Tigranes of Armenia: a Sadducee appraisal. Materia giudaica 10/1 (2005) 85-98.

3666 *Schmitz, Barbara* "Hört mir zu!" (Jdt 8,11): Einleitendes zum Buch Judit (1). BiLi 78 (2005) 37-42;

3667 "Wer kann dieses Volk verachten, das solche Frauen in seiner Mitte hat?" (Jdt 10,19): die Frau, die dem Buch Judit seinen Namen gibt (2). BiLi 78 (2005) 139-143;

3668 "Achior aber glaubte aus ganzem Herzen an Gott" (Jdt 14,10): der Ammoniter Achior im Buch Judit (3). BiLi 78 (2005) 215-219;

3669 "... denn mit ihnen ist ein Gott, der das Unrecht hasst" (Jdt 5,17): das Gottes-Porträt im Buch Judit (4). BiLi 78 (2005) 263-266.

3670 **Schmitz, Barabara** Gedeutete Geschichte: die Funktion der Reden und Gebete im Buch Judit. Herders Biblische Studien 40: 2004 $\Rightarrow$20, 3500. [R]Jud. 61 (2005) 69-70 (*Morgenstern, Matthias*).

3671 *Steiner, Richard C.* On dating of Hebrew sound changes (°Ḫ > Ḥ and °Ġ > ʿ) and Greek translations (2 Esdras and Judith). JBL 124 (2005) 229-267.

3672 *Wills, Lawrence M.* The book of Judith. OT survey. 2005 $\Rightarrow$413. 480-492.

3673 **Bankson, Marjory Zoet** Braided streams: Esther and a woman's way of growing. Women to walk with: Mp 2005, Augsburg 152 pp. $13 [BiTod 44,191—Dianne Bergant].

3674 **Butting, Klara; Minnaard, Gerard; Wacker, Marie T.** Ester. Die Bibel erzählt: Wittingen 2005, Erev-Rav 100 pp. €11. 39328-1030-9.

3675 **Candido, Dionisio** I testi del libro di Ester: il caso dell'introitus TM 1,1-22–LXX A1-17; 1,1-22—Ta A1,18; 1,1-21. [D]*Pisano, Stephen*: AnBib 160: R 2005, E.P.I.B. iii; 3-483 pp. €30. 88-7653-160-2. Diss. Pont. Ist. Biblico; Bibl. 371-417.

3676 **Chalupa, Petr** Královna Ester: kniha Ester v pohledu synchronnim a diachronnim [Königin Ester: das Buch Ester in synchroner und diachroner Sicht]. 1999 $\Rightarrow$19,3636. [R]ThG 48 (2005) 230-231 (*Hentschel, Georg*). **Czech**.

3677 *Crawford, Sidnie W.* The book of Esther;

3678 The additions to Esther. OT survey. 2005 $\Rightarrow$413. 152-166/493.

3679 [E]**Crawford, Sidnie White; Greenspoon, Leonard Jay** The book of Esther in modern research. JSOT.S 380: 2003 $\Rightarrow$19,585. [R]RRT 12/1 (2005) 25-27 (*Smith-Christopher, Daniel L.*); CBQ 67 (2005) 367-368 (*Cook, Joan E.*); HeyJ 46 (2005) 357-358 (*Hill, Robert C.*).

**Dahlen, Kathy; Larson, Knute** Ezra...Esther 2005 $\Rightarrow$3586.

3680 **Day, Linda** Esther. Nv 2005, Abingdon xi; 177 pp. $24. 0-687-497-92-2. Bibl. 171-177.

3681 **De Troyer, Kristin** The end of the alpha text of Esther: translation and narrative technique in MT 8:1-17, LXX 8:1-17, and AT 7:14-41. SBL.SCSt 48: 2000 $\Rightarrow$17,3045... 20,3528. [R]HebStud 46 (2005) 433-437 (*Cook, Johann*);

3682 Rewriting the sacred text. SBL.Text-Critical Studies 4: 2003 $\Rightarrow$19, 3642; 20,3509. [R]RBLit 7 (2005) 482-483 (*Auld, A. Graeme*).

3683 *Haelewyck, Jean-Claude* Hester. BVLI 49 (2005) 22-31.

3684 **Harvey, Charles** Finding morality in the diaspora?: moral ambiguity and transformed morality in the books of Esther. BZAW 328: 2003 $\Rightarrow$19,3656; 20,3517. [R]ThLZ 130 (2005) 499-502 (*Wahl, Harald*).

3685 *Jaramago, Miguel* ¿Onomástica bíblica en una pieza egipcia de Madrid?. EstB 63 (2005) 313-322.

3686 *Johnson, Sara R.* Novelistic elements in Esther: Persian or Hellenistic, Jewish or Greek?. CBQ 67 (2005) 571-589.
3687 **Kahana, Hanna** Esther: juxtaposition of the Septuagint translation with the Hebrew text. CBET 40: Lv 2005, Peeters l; 474 pp. €48. 90-429-1580-3.
3688 *Kim, Jin Yang* The two eunuchs in the LXX version of the book of Esther. ProcGLM 25 (2005) 87-96 [Esther 2,21-23].
3689 **Limardo Daturi, Elisabetta** Représentations d'Esther entre écritures et images. Liminaires 3: 2004 ⇒20,3519. [R]RSR 93 (2005) 592-593 (*Abadie, Philippe*).
3690 *Macchi, Jean-Daniel* Le livre d'*Esther*: regard hellénistique sur le pouvoir et le monde perses. TEuph 30 (2005) 97-135;
3691 Haman l'orgueilleux dans les livres d'Esther. [F]SCHENKER, A.: OBO 214: 2005 ⇒134. 198-214.
3692 *Marböck, Johannes* Das Gebet der Ester—zur Bedeutung des Gebetes im griechischen Esterbuch. Weisheit und Frömmigkeit. ÖBS 29: 2005 <2002> ⇒254. 237-255.
3693 *Masenya, Madipoane* Their hermeneutics was strange!: ours is a necessity!: rereading Vashti as African-South African women. Her master's tools?. 2005 ⇒493. 179-194.
3694 *Menn, Esther* Prayer of the queen: Esther's religious self in the Septuagint. Religion and the self in antiquity. 2005 ⇒818. 70-90.
3695 *Stefani, Piero* Ester, la parola di Dio nascosta. Horeb 14/2 (2005) 5-10.
3696 *Vialle, Catherine* L'ombre de la reine Vashti: la fonction du chapitre 1 du livre d'Esther dans le texte massorétique. Analyse narrative. BEThL 191: 2005 ⇒742. 517-525;
3697 Mordocaï ou les tentations du pouvoir: étude de la caractérisation du personnage de Mordocaï dans le Texte Massorétique. ScEs 57 (2005) 125-139.
3698 *Wong, Wai* Esther. Global bible commentary. 2005 ⇒2443. 135-140.
3699 *Zenger, Erich* Il libro di Ester. Introduz. AT. 2005 ⇒1159. 457-470.

## E5.8 *Machabaeorum libri*, **1-2[3-4] Maccabees**

3700 **Balzaretti, Claudio** 1-2 Maccabei. Dabar—Logos—Parola: 2004 ⇒ 20,3532. [R]CredOg 25/2 (2005) 148-149 (*Cappelletto, Gianni*).
3701 *Baslez, Marie-Françoise* Les Maccabées: guerre coloniale et évènement fondateur. MoBi 168 (2005) 19-23.
3702 *Brändle, Rudolf* Jüdische Märtyrer als christliche Heilige. [F]STEGEMANN, E. 2005 ⇒139. 328-335.
3703 *Dobbeler, Stephanie von* Les secrets d'une victoire: art militaire et identité religieuse. MoBi 168 2005, 30-35.
3704 *Engel, Helmut* I libri dei Maccabei. Introduzione AT. 2005 ⇒1159. 471-493.
3705 *Lichtenberger, Hermann* Geschichtsschreibung und Geschichtserzählung im 1. und 2. Makkabäerbuch. Antike Historiographie. BZNW 129: 2005 ⇒348. 197-212.
3706 *Nisula, Timo* 'Time has passed since you sent your letter': letter phraseology in 1 and 2 Maccabees. JSPE 14/3 (2005) 201-222 [2 Macc 9].

3707 *Nodet, Etienne* Les pharisiens sont les héritiers des Maccabées. ELaurant, Sophie: MoBi 168 (2005) 24-27.
3708 **Nodet, Étienne** La crise maccabéenne: historiographie juive et traditions bibliques. Josèphe et son temps 6: P 2005, Cerf x; 446 pp. €32. 2-204-07641-4.
3709 *Nongbri, Brent* The motivations of the Maccabees and Judean rhetoric of ancestral tradition. Ancient Judaism. JSJ.S 95: 2005 ⇒626. 85-111.
3710 *Rouwhorst, Gerard* The emergence of the cult of the Maccabean martyrs in late antique christianity. More than a memory. ANL 51: 2005 ⇒560. 81-96.
3711 **Scolnic, Benjamin** Alcimus, enemy of the Maccabees. Lanham 2005, University Pr. of America 184 pp. 07618-30448. Bibl. 174-81.
3712 *Triebel, Lothar* Die angebliche Synagoge der makkabäischen Märtyrer in Antiochia am Orontes. ZAC 9 (2005) 464-495.
3713 *Troiani, Lucio* STRABONE e la cosiddetta riforma ellenistica. FSTEMBERGER G.: Ment. *Strabo*: SJ 32: 2005 ⇒140. 121-128.

3714 *Doran, Robert* The first book of Maccabees. OT survey. 2005 ⇒413. 544-560.
3715 *Hidal, Sten* Rombilden i 1 Mackabeerboken 8. SEÅ 70 (2005) 101-5.
3716 *Hoover, Oliver D.* Eleazar Auaran and the elephant: killing symbols in Hellenistic Judaea. SCI 24 (2005) 35-44 [1 Macc 6,43-47].
3717 **Rappaport, Uriel** Sefer Maqabim A: the first book of Maccabees: introduction, Hebrew translation and commentary. 2004 ⇒20,3540. RREJ 164 (2005) 335-336 (*Hadas-Lebel, Mireille*). **H.**
3718 *Schipper, Friedrich* Mattatias und Josua: eine Beobachtung zur Typologie in der jüdisch-hellenistischen Geschichtsschreibung. BN 125 (2005) 95-96.

3719 *Doran, Robert* The second book of Maccabees. OT survey. 2005 ⇒ 413. 561-563.
3720 *Freire, Anízio* O corpo na mística dos Macabeus: um enfoque a partir de 2 Macabeus 7. Estudos bíblicos 87 (2005) 24-45.
3721 *Kennell, Nigel M.* New light on 2 Maccabees 4:7-15. JJS 56 (2005) 10-24.
3722 *Mariano, Antonio* L'episodio di Eliodoro al tempio (2 Mac 3,1-40) nel contesto dello scontro tra ellenismo e giudaismo. Sal. 67 (2005) 421-456.
3723 **Pizzolato, Luigi F.; Somenzi, Chiara** I sete fratelli Maccabei nella chiesa antica d'Occidente. SPMed 25: Mi 2005, Vita e P. ix; 261 pp. €20. 88-343-1237-6 [2 Macc 7].
3724 *Shaw, F.* Χορηγία at 2 Maccabees 4:14. Bulletin of Judaeo-Greek Studies [C] 35 (2004-2005) 34-36 [NTAb 49,566].

3725 *Hacham, Noah* 3 Maccabees: an anti-Dionysian polemic;
3726 *Johnson, Sara R.* Third Maccabees: historical fictions and the shaping of Jewish identity in the Hellenistic period. Ancient fiction. SBL. Symp. 32: 2005 ⇒721. 167-183/185-197.
3727 *Modrzejewski, Joseph Mélèze* La diaspora face aux tyrans païens: Maccabées 3 et 4 dans la Septante. MoBi 168 (2005) 36-40.
3728 *Hiebert, Robert J.V.* Preparing a critical edition of IV Maccabees: the Syriac translation and *Passio Sanctorum Machabaeorum* as witnes-

ses to the original Greek. [F]LUST, J.: BEThL 192: 2005 ⇒92. 193-216.

3729 *Scarpat, Giuseppe* Il porto della vittoria immortale (4Mac 7,3). [F]GHIBERTI, G.: SRivBib 46: 2005 ⇒47. 213-217.

# VI. Libri didactici VT

## E6.1 *Poesis metrica*, **Biblical** and Semitic **versification**

3730 *Bauer, Uwe F.* Biblische Texte und konkrete Poesie. WuD 28 (2005) 65-71.

3731 *Berlin, Adele* Introduction to Hebrew poetry. OT survey. 2005 ⇒ 413. 167-181.

3732 **Fokkelman, Johannes** Major poems of the Hebrew Bible: at the interface of hermeneutics & structural analysis, 3: the remaining 65 pss. SSN 43: 2003 ⇒19,3705. [R]Bib. 86 (2005) 560-564 (*Berry, Donald*).

3733 *Freedman, David N.; Miano, David* Non-acrostic alphabetic psalms. The book of Psalms. VT.S 99: 2005 ⇒390. 87-96.

3734 **Loretz, Oswald** Psalmstudien: Kolometrie, Strophik und Theologie ausgewählter Psalmen. BZAW 309: 2002 ⇒18,201; 20,3558. [R]ThLZ 130 (2005) 638-640 (*Schöpflin, Karin*).

3735 *Miller, Cynthia* Ellipsis involving negation in biblical poetry. [F]FOX, M. 2005 ⇒43. 37-52.

3736 *Naudé, Jacobus A.* The representation of parallelisms in the Afrikaans Bible translations of the Psalms: a corpus-based analysis. OTEs 18 (2005) 763-776.

3737 *Noegel, Scott* Geminate ballast and clustering: an unrecognized literary feature in ancient Semitic poetry. JHScr 5/8 (2004)* [Ps 74,13-14].

3738 *Paul, Shalom M.* Polysensuous polyvalency in poetic parallelism. Divrei Shalom. CHANE 23: 2005 <1992> ⇒273. 457-476;

3739 Polysemous pivotal punctuation: more Janus *double entendres*. Divrei Shalom. 2005 <1996> ⇒273. 477-483 [Cant 7,6; Isa 49,7.17].

3740 **Renz, Thomas** Colometry and accentuation in Hebrew prophetic poetry. KUSATU 4: 2003 ⇒19,3713; 20,3559. [R]JSSt 50 (2005) 384-385 (*Collins, Terry*).

3741 *Schwantes, Milton* Repetições e paralelismõs: observações em un debate hermenêutico, exemplificado em Provérbios 10,1. Fragmenta de Cultura [Goías] 15 (2005) 1361-1369 [OTA 29,62].

3742 **Seybold, Klaus** Poetik der Psalmen. PSAT 1: 2003 ⇒19,3716; 20, 3560. [R]CBQ 67 (2005) 513-514 (*Nowell, Irene*).

3743 *Trebolle Barrera, Julio* Paralelismo de género en la poesía hebrea bíblica: la mujer del "Cantar de los Cantares" y el hombre del libro de "Job". 'Ilu 10 (2005) 225-247.

3744 **Van der Lugt, Pieter** Cantos and strophes in Biblical Hebrew poetry: with special reference to the first book of the Psalter. OTS 53: Lei 2005, Brill xv; 581 pp. 90-04-14322-X.

3745 **Watson, Wilfred G.E.** Classical Hebrew poetry: a guide to its techniques. NY 2005 <1984>, Clark xviii; 460 pp. $55. 0-567-08388-8. [R]RBLit (2005)* (*Dempsey, Carol*).

3746 *Weber, B.* Einige poetologische Überlegungen zur Psalmeninterpretation verbunden mit einer exemplarischen Anwendung an Psalm 130. OTEs 18 (2005) 891-906.

### E6.2 Psalmi, textus

3747 *Agosti, Gianfranco* LXX, *Ps.* 117.26-27 (MS 2632);
3748 LXX, *Ps.* 118.22-29 (MS 2631). Greek Papyri, Volume I. 2005⇒682. 57-58/59-62.
3749 *Albrektson, Bertil* Två psaltarställen i den nya bibelöversättningen. SEÅ 70 (2005) 11-20 [Ps 22,11; 23,2].
3750 *Andrist, Patrick; Lukinovich, Alessandra Poesis et mores*: Florent Chrestien, Joseph-Juste Scaliger et les *Psaumes* en vers grecs du *Bernensis* A 69. FHURST, A. 2005 ⇒64. 673-715.
3751 **Austermann, Frank** Von der Tora zum Nomos: Untersuchungen zur Übersetzungsweise und Interpretation im Septuaginta-Psalter. MSU 27: 2003 ⇒19,3718. RThLZ 130 (2005) 141-144 (*Dafni, Evangelia*).
3752 **Barthélemy, Dominique** Critique textuelle de l'Ancien Testament, tome 4: Psaumes. E*Ryan, Stephen D.; Schenker, Adrian*: OBO 50/4: FrS 2005, Academic xlvii; 931 pp. €216. 2-8271-0991-3.
3753 **Devens, Monica S.** A concordance to Psalms in the Ethiopic version. ÄthF 59: 2001 ⇒17,3105... 20,3572. RJSSt 50 (2005) 405-407 (*Knibb, Michael A.*).
3754 *Dorival, Gilles* Les titres des psaumes en hébreu et en grec: les écarts quantitatifs. FSCHENKER, A.: OBO 214: 2005 ⇒134. 58-70.
3755 **Eaton, John** The Psalms: a historical and spiritual commentary with an introduction and new translation. L 2005, Continuum vi; 536 pp. 0-8264-8895-1.
3756 *Emmenegger, Gregor* Le texte du psautier copte d'al Mudil: observations de critique et d'histoire du texte. FSCHENKER, A.: OBO 214: 2005 ⇒134. 71-86.
3757 **Emmenegger, Gregor** Die textkritische Einordnung des koptischen Psalters aus al-Mudil (Mudil-Codex): ein Beitrag zur Textgeschichte der Septuaginta und zur Textkritik koptischer Bibelhandschriften. D*Schenker, Adrian* 2005, Diss. Fribourg [ThRv 102,v].
E**Flint, P.** The book of Psalms 2005 ⇒390.
3758 **Fokkelman, Jan P.** The Psalms in form: the Hebrew Psalter in its poetic shape. 2002 ⇒18,3446. RRBLit (2005)* (*Wilson, Gerald H.*).
3759 *Geddes, Jane* The St. Albans psalter: the abbot and the anchoress. Christina of Markyale: a twelfth-century holy woman. E**Fanous, Samuel; Leyser, Henrietta** L 2005, Routledge 197-216 [RBen 116, 154—P.-M. Bogaert.]
3760 E**Geddes, Jane** Der Albani-Psalter: eine englische Prachthandschrift des 12. Jahrhunderts für Christina von Markyate. Rg 2005, Schnell & S. 136 pp. €29.80. 3-7954-1751-1. 89 ill.;
3761 The St. Albans psalter: a book for Christina Markyate. L 2005, British Library 136 pp. [RBen 118,165: P.M. Bogaert].
3762 **Haney, Kristin** The St. Albans psalter: an Anglo-Norman song of faith. StHu 60: 2002 ⇒18,3447. RCCMéd 48 (2005) 62-63 (*Palazzo, Éric*); MÂ 111 (2005) 164-165 (*L'Hermite-Leclercq, Paulette*).
3763 *Hiebert, Robert J.V.* The place of the Syriac versions in the textual history of the Psalter. The book of Psalms. VT.S 99: 2005 ⇒390. 505-536 [Ps 4,7; 9,9; 24; 25,7].

3764 I canti di lode dei Padri (Sap 18,9): i salmi attraverso tre millenni: salterio ebraico...greco...latino...traduzione letterale. 2004 ⇒20, 3579. [R]ATT 11 (2005) 453-454 (*Ghiberti, Giuseppe*).
3765 The inclusive Psalms. Walnut Creek, CA 2005, Alta Mira xxiv; 204 pp. 0-7591-0765-3. Priests for equality.
3766 **Ladouceur, David J.** The Latin psalter: introduction, selected text and commentary. L 2005, Bristol Classical 126 pp. 1-85399-683-1.
3767 *Lohfink, Norbert* Der Münsterschwarzacher Psalter. Liturgie und Bibel. ÖBS 28: 2005 <2003> ⇒360. 549-560.
3768 *Niebrzydowski, Sue* From scriptorium to internet: the implication of audience on the translation of the Psalms of the St Albans Psalter. Translation and religion. Topics in Translation 28: 2005 ⇒2412. 151-161.
3769 *Pietersma, Albert* Septuagintal exegesis and the superscriptions of the Greek Psalter. The book of Psalms. VT.S 99: 2005 ⇒390. 443-475.
3770 *Pintaudi, Rosario* Amuleto cristiano: LXX, *Ps.* 90.4-13 (MS 244/4). Greek Papyri, Volume I. 2005 ⇒682. 55-56.
3771 *Powell, Morgan* Making the Psalter of Christina of Markyate (the St. Albans Psalter). Viator 36 (2005) 293-335.
3772 Die Psalmen: Einheitsübersetzung. Stu 2005, Kathol. Bibelwerk 296 pp. €22. 3-460-32073-7. Großdruck mit Bildern von *Sieger Köder*.
3773 *Van Rooy, Harry F.* The Syro-hexaplaric headings of the Psalms in manuscript 12t3. AramSt 3 (2005) 109-126;
3774 The Psalms in early Syriac tradition. The book of Psalms. VT.S 99: 2005 ⇒390. 537-550.
3775 *Zanetti, Paolo S.* Vnusquisque vestrum psalmum habet. Imitatori di Gesù Cristo. 2005 <1963> ⇒330. 115-155.

## E6.3 Psalmi, introductio

3776 *Cappelletto, Gianni* Lode e lamento: i generi letterari dei salmi. PaVi 50/1 (2005) 34-40.
3777 **Fallon, Michael** The Psalms: an introduction. Kensington, NSW 2005, Chevalier xxvi; 512 pp. 0-86940312-5.
[E]**Firth, D.** Interpreting the Psalms 2005 ⇒740.
3778 **Gilles, Dominique L.** El libro de los salmos. M 2005, San Pablo 296 pp.
3779 *Lorenzin, Tiziano* I salmi come libro: introduzione a una lettura continua del salterio. PaVi 50/1 (2005) 26-33;
3780 Itinerario attraverso il primo libro dei salmi. PaVi 50/2 (2005) 3-10;
3781 Itinerario attraverso il secondo libro dei salmi. PaVi 50/3 (2005) 4-11;
3782 Itinerario attraverso il terzo libro dei salmi (Salmi 73-89). PaVi 50/4 (2005) 4-7;
3783 Itinerario attraverso il quarto libro dei salmi (Salmi 90-106). PaVi 50/4 (2005) 23-25;
3784 Itinerario attraverso il quinto libro dei salmi (I parte). PaVi 50/5 (2005) 4-10;
3785 Itinerario attraverso il quinto libro dei salmi (II parte). PaVi 50/6 (2005) 4-11.

3786 **Mailhiot, Gilles-Dominique** El libro de los Salmos: rezar a Dios con palabras de Dios. [T]*Martin-Peralta, Carlos*: Sicar: M 2005, San Pablo 295 pp. 84285-28047. [R]MisEx 209 (2005) 681-82 (*Almansa, Ángel*).

3787 *McCann, J. Clinton, Jr.* The book of Psalms. OT survey. 2005 ⇒ 413. 197-221.

3788 *Priotto, Michelangelo* Nascita e storia del salterio. PaVi 50/1 (2005) 41-45.

3789 **Rose, Martin**, *al.* Vivre, prier, comprendre: explorations dans les Psaumes. Cours biblique par correspondance 56: Fontaines 2005, Office Protestant de la Formation 124 pp.

3790 *Shute, Dan* On "flexus", "oleh we-yored", and "the murky world of psalmody". Arc 33 (2005) 448-461.

3791 **Vos, Cas J.A.** Theopoetry of the Psalms. [T]*Mills, Sandra*: Pretoria/L 2005, Protea/Clark 423 pp. $50/R180. 1-86919-098-X. [R]AcTh(B) 25 (2005) 204-206 (*Van den Berg, Jan-Albert*); VeE 26 (2005) 656-658 (*Le Roux, Jurie*).

3792 **Wendland, Ernst R.** Analyzing the psalms: with exercises for bible students and translators. [2]2002, 256 pp. $24. 1-55671-1298. Distributed by Eisenbrauns in conjunction with the Summer Institute of Linguistics. [R]OTEs 18 (2005) 151-153 (*Botha, Phil J.*).

3793 *Zenger, Erich* Il libro dei Salmi. Introduz. AT. 2005 ⇒1159. 527-60.

### E6.4 Psalmi, commentarii

3794 *Adamo, David T.* Psalms. Global bible commentary. 2005 ⇒2443. 151-162.

3795 [E]**Baker-Smith, Dominic** ERASMUS: expositions of the Psalms: Concionalis interpretatio in Psalmum 85 in Psalmum 22 enarratio triplex consultatio de bello turcis inferendo, et obiter enarratus Psalmus 28 enarratio Psalmi 33. Collected works of Erasmus 64: Toronto 2005, Univ. of Toronto Pr. xv; 416 pp. 0-8020-3584-1.

3796 [T]**Boulding, Maria** Expositions of the Psalms (*Enarrationes in Psalmos*), 121-150. Works of St Augustine, 3: Books 20: 2004 ⇒20, 3610. [R]AugSt 36 (2005) 459-460 (*Cunningham, Lawrence S.*).

3797 [T]**Caruso, Antonio** Flavio Magno Aurelio CASSIODORO: Spaccati di vita, 1: I salmi di Gesù. Tradizione e Vita 15: R 2005, Vivere In 204 pp. €18.50.

3798 **Clifford, Richard J.** Psalms 73-150. Abingdon OT Commentaries: 2003 ⇒19,3752; 20,3612. [R]CBQ 67 (2005) 309-310 (*Day, Linda*); IThQ 70 (2005) 179-181 (*Maher, Michael*).

3799 **Eaton, John H.** The Psalms: a historical and spiritual commentary with an introduction and new translation. 2003 ⇒19,3753. [R]CBQ 67 (2005) 311-2 (*Limburg, James*); OTEs 18 (2005) 140-1 (*Maré, L.P.*).

3800 [E]**Gori, Franco** Enarrationes in Psalmos 141-150. CSEL 95/5; Sancti Augustini Opera: W 2005, Verlag der ÖAW 304 pp. €73.36. 3-7001-3486-X. Adiuv. *Iuliana Spaccia*.

3801 *Gretsch, Mechtild* The Roman psalter, its Old English glosses and the English Benedictine reform. The liturgy of the late Anglo-Saxon church. [E]**Bedingfield, M. Bradford; Gittos, Helen**: Henry Bradshaw Society, Subsidia 5: L 2005, Boydell. 13-28 [RBen 116,153—P.-M. Bogaert].

3802 T**Gruber, Mayer Irvin** RASHI's commentary on Psalms. 2004 ⇒20, 3615. RRBLit (2005)* (*Gottlieb, Isaac B.*).

3803 T**Hill, Robert C.** DIODORE of Tarsus: commentary on Psalms 1-51. SBL.Writings from the Ancient World 9: Atlanta, GA 2005, Society of Biblical Literature xxxvii; 179 pp. $25. 1-58983-094-6. Bibl. 171-174. RRBLit (2005)* (*Albl, Martin; Human, Dirk*).

3804 **Hossfeld, Frank L.; Zenger, Erich** Die Psalmen, 2: Psalm 51-100. NEB.AT 40: 2002 ⇒18,3487; 20,3617. RTJT 21 (2005) 243-244 (*Williams, Tyler F.*);

3805 Psalms 2: a commentary on Psalms 51-100. T*Maloney, Linda M.*: Hermeneia: Mp 2005, Fortress xxvi; 553 pp. $65. 0-8006-6061-7. Bibl. xvii-xxv.

3806 **Limburg, James** Psalms. Westminster Bible companion: 2000 ⇒16, 3131... 18,3491. RAsbTJ 60/1 (2005) 127-128 (*Strawn, Brent A.*).

3807 **Lorenzin, Tiziano** I salmi. 2000 ⇒16,3132; 17,3159. RED 55/3 (2002) 171-173 (*Bazyliński, Stanisław*); Anton. 78 (2003) 715-716 (*Nobile, Marco*).

3808 **Loza, José; Aparicio Rodríguez, Ángel** Génesis 1-11; Salmos 1-41. Bilbao 2005, Desclée de B. 1-111; 112-397 pp. €9. 84-330-1952X. 1 author for each book.

3809 **Mowinckel, Sigmund** The Psalms in Israel's worship. T*Ap-Thomas, D.R.*: 2004 <1962> ⇒20,3618. RRBLit (2005)* (*Brown, William; Gerstenberger, Erhard*).

3810 T**Orazzo, Antonio** ILARIO di Poitiers: commento ai salmi/1 (1-91); 2 (118); 3 (119-150). CTePa 185-187: R 2005, Città Nuova 473 +234 + 440 pp. €29 + 16.50 + 32. 88-311-3185-0/6-9/7-7.

3811 **Schaefer, Konrad** Psalms. Berit Olam: 2001 ⇒17,3165... 20,3621. RBZ 49 (2005) 117-119 (*Zenger, Erich*); CBQ 67 (2005) 510-512 (*Williams, Tyler F.*).

3812 **Scippa, Vincenzo** Salmi, 2: salmi messianici/1. Dabar AT: 2003 ⇒ 19,3762. REstTrin 39 (2005) 585-587 (*Vázquez Allegue, Jaime*);

3813 Salmi, 2-3: salmi messianici. Dabar AT: 2003 ⇒ 19,3762-3. RRivBib 53 (2005) 231-233 (*Linder, Agnes*).

3814 **Steussy, Marti J.** Psalms. 2004 ⇒20,3623. RRExp 102 (2005) 159-160 (*deClaissé-Walford, Nancy L.*).

3815 **Terrien, Samuel** The Psalms: strophic structure and theological commentary. Eerdmans Critical Commentary: 2003 ⇒19,3765; 20, 3624. RBZ 49 (2005) 114-7 (*Zenger, Erich*); HebStud 46 (2005) 422-425 (*Prinsloo, Gert*); Bib. 86 (2005) 269-271 (*Auwers, Jean-Marie*).

3816 **Wilson, Gerald H.** Psalms, 1. NIV Application Commentary: GR 2002, Zondervan 1024 pp. 0-310-20635-9. Bibl.

## E6.5 Psalmi, themata

3817 E**Büttner, F.O.** The illuminated psalter: studies in the content, purpose and placement of its images. Turnhout 2005, Brepols xii; 615 pp. €93.40. 25035-14650. 472 ill. [RBen 116,152—P.-M. Bogaert].

3818 *Antony, Abraham M.* God the shepherd in the book of Psalms, with special reference to Psalm 23. MJOHN PAUL II. 2005 ⇒72. 50-107.

3819 **Auffret, Pierre** Que seulement de tes yeux...étude structurelle de treize psaumes. BZAW 330: 2003 ⇒19,3771. RETR 80 (2005) 432-3

(*Hüllstrung, Wolfgang*); RivBib 53 (2005) 483-4 (*Lorenzin, Tiziano*) [Ps 18; 35; 9-10; 35; 37; 46-48; 68; 106; 143; 78; 105].

3820 *Barker, David G.* Voices for the pilgrimage: a study in the psalms of ascent. ET 116 (2005) 109-116.

3821 **Bautch, Richard J.** Developments in genre between post-exilic penitential prayers and the Psalms of communal lament. Academia biblica 7: 2003 ⇒19,3775; 20,3634. [R]HebStud 46 (2005) 425-427 (*Ryan, Stephen D.*); RBLit (2005)* (*Falk, Daniel*) [Isa 63,7-64,11; Ezra 9,6-15; Neh 9,6-37].

3822 *Beckwith, Roger T.* Factors bearing on the early history of the psalter. Calendar, chronology. AGJU 61: 2005 ⇒1763. 147-170.

3823 *Bennett, Adelaide* The transformation of the Gothic Psalter in thirteenth century France. The illuminated psalter. 2005 ⇒3817. 211-221 Ill. 190-196 [RBen 118,164–P.-M. Bogaert].

3824 *Berlin, Adele* Psalms and the literature of exile: Psalm 137, 44, 69, and 78. The book of Psalms. VT.S 99: 2005 ⇒390. 65-86.

3825 *Berschin, Walter* Neun Psalteria quadrupartita Salomons III. von Konstanz (Abt von St. Gallen 890-920). Mittellateinische Studien. 2005 <1991> ⇒188. 203-213 [RBen 116,153—P.-M. Bogaert].

3826 *Braulik, Georg* Psalter und Messias: zum christologischen Verständnis der Psalmen im Alten Testament und bei den Kirchenvätern: ein Brückenschlag. Liturgie und Bibel. ÖBS 28: 2005 ⇒ 360. 481-502.

3827 *Bräm, Andreas* Neapolitanische Trecento-Psalterien. The illuminated psalter. 2005 ⇒3817. 193-209 [RBen 118,164–P.-M. Bogaert].

3828 *Brown, William P.* 'Come, O children... I will teach you the fear of the Lord' (Psalm 34:12): comparing Psalms and Proverbs. [F]FOX, M. 2005 ⇒43. 85-102.

3829 **Brown, William P.** Seeing the Psalms: a theology of metaphor. 2002 ⇒18,3504... 20,3639. [R]TS 66 (2005) 179-181 (*Endres, John C.*).

3830 *Broyles, Craig C.* Psalms concerning the liturgies of temple entry. The book of Psalms. VT.S 99: 2005 ⇒390. 248-287 [Isa 33,14-16; Ps 15; 24,3-6].

3831 *Brucker, Ralph* La *Wirkungsgeschichte* de la Septante des Psaumes dans le judaïsme ancien et dans le christianisme primitif. L'apport de la Septante. LeDiv 203: 2005 ⇒764. 289-308.

3832 *Brueggemann, Walter* The psalms in theological use: on incommensurability and mutuality. The book of Psalms. VT.S 99: 2005⇒390. 581-602.

3833 **Buby, Bertrand A.** With a listening heart: biblical and spiritual reflections on the Psalms. NY 2005, St Paul's 234 pp. $17 [BiTod 44,192—Dianne Bergant].

3834 *Büttner, F.O.* Der illuminierte Psalter im Westen. The illuminated psalter. 2005 ⇒3817. 1-106 [RBen 118,164–P.-M. Bogaert].

3835 *Camille, Michael* Bodies, names and gender in a Gothic psalter (Paris, BNF, ms. Laat. 10435). The illuminated psalter. 2005⇒3817. 377-386. Ill. 272, 360-367 [RBen 118,164–P.-M. Bogaert].

3836 *Chazelle, Celia* Violence and the virtuous ruler in the Utrecht Psalter. The illuminated psalter. 2005⇒3817. 337-348. Ill. 311-320, 445-446, 449-450 [RBen 118,164–P.-M. Bogaert].

3837 **Cortese, Enzo** La preghiera del re: formazione, redazione e teologia dei "Salmi di Davide". RivBib.S 43: 2004 ⇒20,3640. [R]Ang. 82 (2005) 231-3 (*Garuti, Paolo*); RevBib 67 (2005) 103-108 (*Blunda, Jorge*).

3838 *Dahmen, Ulrich* "Gepriesen sei der Herr, der Gott Israels, vom Anfang bis zum Ende der Zeiten" (Ps 106,48): Beobachtungen zur Entstehungsgeschichte des Psalters im vierten und fünften Psalmenbuch. BZ 49 (2005) 1-25 [Ps 108-110].

3839 **Day, John** Crying for justice: what the psalms teach us about mercy and vengeance in an age of terrorism. GR 2005, Kregel 199 pp. $15.

3840 **Doeker, Andrea** Die Funktion der Gottesrede in den Psalmen: eine poetologische Untersuchung. BBB 135: 2002 ⇒18,3513. RThLZ 130 (2005) 25-27 (*Saur, Markus*).

3841 *Eidevall, Göran* Images of God, self, and the enemy in the Psalms: on the role of metaphor in identity construction. Metaphor in the Hebrew Bible. BEThL 187: 2005 ⇒799. 55-65.

3842 **Eissler, Friedmann** Königspsalmen und karäische Messiaserwartung: Jefet BEN ELIs Auslegung von Ps 2.72.89.110.132 im Vergleich mit SAADJA Gaons Deutung. TSMJ 17: 2002 ⇒18,3515; 20,3644. RThLZ 130 (2005) 1173-1175 (*Siegert, Folker*).

3843 *Engelhart, Helmut* Der Hornplatteneinband: eine charakteristische Form der Einbandgestaltung illuminierter Psalterhandschriften des 13. Jahrhunderts: mit einem Verzeichnis der Hornplatteneinbände. The illuminated psalter. 2005 ⇒3817. 441-456. Ill. 456-459 [RBen 118,165–P.-M. Bogaert].

3844 *Euw, Anton von* Die Darstellungen zum 90. (91.) Psalm in der frühmittelalterlichen Psalter- und Evangelienillustration mit Ergänzungen und Kommentaren. The illuminated psalter. 2005⇒3817. 405-411. Ill. 406-417 [RBen 118,164–P.-M. Bogaert].

3845 *Evans, Craig A.* Praise and prophecy in the Psalter and in the New Testament. The book of Psalms. VT.S 99: 2005 ⇒390. 551-579.

3846 **Firth, David G.** Surrendering retribution in the psalms: responses to violence in individual complaints. D*Prinsloo, Willem S.*: Paternoster Biblical Monographs: Carlisle 2005, Paternoster xvi; 154 pp. £20. 1-84227-337X. Diss. Pretoria 1996.

3847 *Freeman-Sandler, Lucy* Word imagery in English Gothic psalters: the case of Vienna Bohun manuscripts (ÖNB, cod. 1826*). The illuminated psalter. 2005⇒3817. 387-395. Ill. 368-397 [RBen 118,164–P.-M. Bogaert].

3848 *Gerstenberger, Erhard S.* Life situations and theological concepts of Old Testament Psalms. OTEs 18 (2005) 82-92;

3849 Theologies in the book of Psalms. The book of Psalms. VT.S 99: 2005 ⇒390. 603-625.

3850 *Gillingham, Susan* The Zion tradition and the editing of the Hebrew psalter. Temple and worship. LHBOTS 422: 2005 ⇒731. 308-341.

3851 *Gillmayr-Bucher, Susanne* Glücklich, wer gebahnte Wege im Herzen hat: Raumbilder in den Psalmen. PzB 14 (2005) 67-79;

3852 "Meine Zunge—ein Griffel eines geschickten Schreibers": der kommunikative Aspekt der Körpermetaphern in den Psalmen. Metaphor in the Hebrew Bible. BEThL 187: 2005 ⇒799. 197-213.

3853 *Goulder, Michael* The social setting of book II of the Psalter. The book of Psalms. VT.S 99: 2005 ⇒390. 349-367.

3854 **Grant, Jamie A.** The king as exemplar: the function of Deuteronomy's kingship law in the shaping of the book of Psalms. SBL.Academia Biblica 17: 2004 ⇒20,3651. RCBQ 67 (2005) 494-5 (*Nelson, Richard*); RBLit (2005)* (*Brin, Gershon; Dutcher-Walls, Patricia*) [Deut 17,14-20].

3855 *Helberg, J.L.* Geïntegreedheid van die psalms volgens die verband tussen Psalm 1 (en 2) en die res van die psalms. In die Skriflig 39 (2005) 673-679 [OTA 29,287].

3856 **Hilber, John** Cultic prophecy in the Psalms. D*Davies, Graham I.*: BZAW 352: B 2005, De Gruyter xiv; 268 pp. €84. 3-11-018440-0. Diss. Cambridge 2004; Bibl. 227-251.

3857 *Hilber, John W.* Cultic prophecy in the Psalms in the light of Assyrian prophetic sources. TynB 56/1 (2005) 141-145.

3858 **Jacobson, Rolf** 'Many are saying': the function of direct discourse in the Hebrew Psalter. JSOT.S 397: 2004 ⇒20,3656. RRBLit (2005)* (*Howell, J. Dwayne*).

3859 **Janowski, Bernd** Konfliktgespräche mit Gott: eine Anthropologie der Psalmen. 2003 ⇒19,3799; 20,3657. RThLZ 130 (2005) 759-762 (*Oeming, Manfred*); ThZ 61 (2005) 172-173 (*Schüle, Andreas*); OrthFor 19 (2005) 317-321 (*Dafni, Evangelia G.*).

3860 **Johnson, Vivian L.** David in distress: the transformation of David through the historical Psalm titles. 2005, Diss. Harvard [HThR 98, 498].

3861 *Johnston, Philip S.* Ordeals in the Psalms?. Temple and worship. LHBOTS 422: 2005 ⇒731. 271-291.

3862 *Kahsnitz, Rainer* Frühe Initialpsalter. The illuminated psalter. 2005 ⇒3817. 137-155 [RBen 118,164–P.-M. Bogaert].

3863 *Klemm, Elisabeth* Die Darstellung der Heiligen als Thema der Psalterillustration. The illuminated psalter. 2005 ⇒3817. 361-376. Ill. 343-359 [RBen 118,164–P.-M. Bogaert].

3864 *Knowles, Melody D.* The flexible rhetoric of retelling: the choice of David in the texts of the Psalms. CBQ 67 (2005) 236-249 [Ps78; 89; 132].

3865 *Koch, Klaus* Königspsalmen und ihr ritueller Hintergrund: Erwägungen zu Ps 89,20-38 und Ps 20 und ihren Vorstufen. The book of Psalms. VT.S 99: 2005 ⇒390. 9-52.

3866 **Körting, C.** Zion in den Psalmen. D*Spieckermann, Hermann*: 2005, Diss.-Habil. Göttingen [ThLZ 131,336].

3867 *Kuder, Ulrich* Illuminierte Psalter von den Anfängen bis um 800. The illuminated psalter. 2005 ⇒3817. 107-135 [RBen 118,164–P.-M. Bogaert].

3868 **Kwakkel, Gert** 'According to my righteousness': upright behaviour as grounds for deliverance in Psalms 7, 17, 18, 26, and 44. OTS 46: 2002 ⇒18,3527... 20,3659. RRBLit (2005)* (*Bautch, Richard*).

3869 *Lee, Sung-Hun* Lament and the joy of salvation in the lament psalms. The book of Psalms. VT.S 99: 2005 ⇒390. 224-247.

3870 *Lorenzin, Tiziano* I salmi e il Nuovo Testamento: introduzione: tutta la teologia dei salmi orienta a Cristo. PaVi 50/1 (2005) 51-53.

3871 **Mandolfo, Carleen** God in the dock: dialog tension in the psalms of lament. JSOT.S 357: 2002 ⇒18,3533; 20,3665. RJSSt 50 (2005) 216-217 (*Eaton, J.H.*); OTEs 18 (2005) 948-949 (*Maré, L.P.*).

3872 **Mascarenhas, Theodore** The missionary function of Israel in Psalms 67, 96, and 117. D*Althann, Robert*: Lanham 2005, Univ. Pr. of America xxvi; 380 pp. $48. 0-7618-2930-X. Diss. Pontifical Biblical Institute; Bibl. 299-333.

3873 *McCann, J. Clinton, Jr.* The shape of book 1 of the Psalter and the shape of human happiness. The book of Psalms. VT.S 99: 2005 ⇒ 390. 340-348.

3874 *Morgan, Nigel* Patrons and their devotions in the historical initials and full page miniatures of 13th century psalters. The illuminated psalter. 2005 ⇒3817. 309-319. Liste de 80 psautiers [RBen 118,164 –P.-M. Bogaert].

3875 *Nasuti, Harry P.* The interpretive significance of sequence and selection in the book of Psalms. The book of Psalms. VT.S 99: 2005 ⇒ 390. 311-339.

3876 *Nilgen, Ursula* Psalter für Gelehrte und Ungelehrte im hohen Mittelalter. The illuminated psalter. 2005 ⇒3817. 239-247 [RBen 118,164 –P.-M. Bogaert].

3877 *Oliver, Judith* A primer of thirteenth century German convent life: the psalter as office and mass book (London, BL, ms. Add. 60629). The illuminated psalter. 2005 ⇒3817. 259-270. Ill. 244-251 [RBen 118,164–P.-M. Bogaert].

3878 *Orth, Myra D.* The primacy of the word in French Renaissance psalm manuscripts. The illuminated psalter. 2005 ⇒3817. 397-403 [RBen 118,164–P.-M. Bogaert].

3879 *Peterson, Elizabeth A.* Scholastic hermeneutics in historical initials of 13th century French psalters. The illuminated psalter. 2005 ⇒3817. 349-359 [RBen 118,164–P.-M. Bogaert].

3880 *Peterson, Erik* Die "Armen" in der Psalmenliteratur. Peterson: Lukasevangelium und Synoptica. 2005 ⇒277. 420-423.

3881 *Pfändtner, Karl G.* Zwei Bologneser Psalter des 13. Jahrhunderts und ihr Illustrationsystem (Bologna, Bibl. Univ. cod. 346 und Paris, BNF, Ms Smith-Lesouëf 21). The illuminated psalter. 2005 ⇒3817. 181-192 [RBen 118,164–P.-M. Bogaert].

3882 *Prinsloo, Gert T.M.* The role of space in the שירי דמעלות (Psalms 120-134). Bib. 86 (2005) 457-477.

3883 *Rad, Gerhard von* 'Righteousness' and 'life' in the cultic language of the Psalms. From Genesis. 2005 <1950> ⇒283. 187-204.

3884 *Raeber, Judith* Illuminierte Psalterien aus den innerschweizer Doppelklöstern Muri und Engelberg. The illuminated psalter. 2005 ⇒ 3817. 223-238 [RBen 118,164–P.-M. Bogaert].

3885 *Rendtorff, Rolf* The psalm of David: David in the Psalms. The book of Psalms. VT.S 99: 2005 ⇒390. 53-64.

3886 *Riede, Peter* Die Sprache der Bilder: zur Bedeutung und Funktion der Metaphorik in den Feindpsalmen des Alten Testaments am Beispiel der Psalmen 57 und 59. Metaphor in the Hebrew Bible. BEThL 187: 2005 ⇒799. 19-40.

3887 *Roberts, J.J.M.* MOWINCKEL's enthronement festival: a review. The book of Psalms. VT.S 99: 2005 ⇒390. 97-115.

3888 *Ruiz, Eleuterio Ramón* El silencio en el primer libro del salterio (Salmos 1-41). RevBib 67 (2005) 31-83, 163-178.

3889 **Saur, Markus** Die Königspsalmen: Studien zur Entstehung und Theologie. BZAW 340: 2004 ⇒20,3681. [R]ZKTh 127 (2005) 132-133 (*Paganini, Simone*); RHPhR 85 (2005) 316-317 (*Heintz, J.-G.*).

3890 *Schaefer, Konrad R.* Hacia la celebración litúrgica de la justicia social. [F]JUNCO GARZA, C.: 2005 ⇒74. 223-241.

3891 **Schnocks, Johannes** Vergänglichkeit und Gottesherrschaft: Studien zu Psalm 90 und dem vierten Psalmenbuch. BBB 140: 2002 ⇒18, 3545. [R]ThLZ 130 (2005) 27-29 (*Saur, Markus*).

3892 *Shveka, Avi* A trace of the tradition of diplomatic correspondence in royal psalms. JSSt 50 (2005) 297-320 [Ps 21,2; 61,6].

3893 *Stahl, Harvey* Bathsheba and the kings: the Beatus initial in the psalter of Saint Louis (Paris, BNF, ms lat. 10525). The illuminated psalter. 2005 ⇒3817. 427-434 [RBen 118,164–P.-M. Bogaert].

3894 **Starbuck, Scott R.A.** Court oracles in the Psalms: the so-called royal psalms in their ancient Near Eastern context. SBL.DS 172: 1999 ⇒ 15,3039... 18,3546. [R]JNES 64 (2005) 199-201 (*Pardee, Dennis*).

3895 *Steenbock, Frauke* Psalterien mit kostbaren Einbänden. The illuminated psalter. 2005 ⇒3817. 435-40 [RBen 118,164–P.-M. Bogaert].

3896 *Steymans, Hans U.* Die Gottesbezeichnung Kyrios im Psalter der Septuaginta. [F]SCHENKER, A.: OBO 214: 2005 ⇒134. 325-338.

3897 **Sticher, Claudia** Die Rettung der Guten durch Gott und die Selbstzerstörung der Bösen: ein theologisches Denkmuster im Psalter. BBB 137: 2002 ⇒18,3547... 20,3687. [R]CBQ 67 (2005) 128-130 (*Floyd, Michael H.*); ETR 80 (2005) 433-435 (*Hüllstrung, Wolfgang*).

3898 *Stirnemann, Patricia* The Copenhagen Psalter (Kongel. Bibl. ms Thott 143 2°) reconsidered as a coronation present for Canute VI. The illuminated psalter. 2005 ⇒3817. 323-328 [RBen 118,164–P.-M. Bogaert].

3899 *Stones, Alison* The full-page miniatures of the Psalter-Hours New York PML, ms. M 729: programme and patron, with a table for the distribution of full page miniatures within text in some thirteenth-century psalters. The illuminated psalter. 2005 ⇒3817. 281-307. Ill. 268-282 [RBen 118,164–P.-M. Bogaert].

3900 *Strola, Germana* Il simbolismo dei salmi: Dio creatore: vita e luce 'nella tua luce vediamo la luce'. PaVi 50/1 (2005) 48-50;

3901 : Dio padre: tenerezza e pedagogia. PaVi 50/2 (2005) 47-49;

3902 : Dio re: quale re è grande come il nostro Dio?'. PaVi 50/3 (2005) 51-53;

3903 : Dio maestro: 'fammi conoscere, Signore, le tue vie'. PaVi 50/4 (2005) 47-49;

3904 : Dio salvatore: 'il nostro Dio è un Dio che salva'. PaVi 50/5 (2005) 48-50;

3905 : il Dio con noi: 'Dio sta in essa non potrà vacillare'. PaVi 50/6 (2005) 45-47.

3906 *Suckale, Gude* Zwei Bilderpsalter für Frauen aus dem frühen 13. Jahrhundert. The illuminated psalter. 2005 ⇒3817. 249-258 [RBen 118,164–P.-M. Bogaert].

3907 **Süssenbach, Claudia** Der elohistische Psalter: Untersuchungen zu Komposition und Theologie von Ps 42-93. [D]*Spieckermann, Hermann*: FAT 2/7: Tü 2005, Mohr S. x; 415 pp. €74. 316-148356-1. Diss. Göttingen; Bibl. 395-405.

3908 **Tomes, Roger** 'I have written to the King, my Lord': secular analogies for the Psalms. HBM 1: Shf 2005, Shf Phoenix xii; 145 pp. $27. 50. 1-905048-092. Bibl. 116-125.

3909 **Travers, Michael E.** Encountering God in the Psalms. 2003 ⇒19, 3826. [R]Faith & Mission 22/2 (2005) 116-117 (*Bush, L. Russ, III*).

3910 *Tull, Patricia K.* BAKHTIN's confessional self-accounting and psalms of lament. BiblInterp 13 (2005) 41-55.

3911 *Vogt, Colleen* Reclaiming the prayer of lament. RfR 64 (2005) 37-46.

3912 **Vos, Christiane de** Klage als Gotteslob aus der Tiefe: der Mensch vor Gott in den individuellen Klagepsalmen. FAT 2/11: Tü 2005, Mohr S. 260 pp. €49. 3-16-148700-1. Bibl. 229-237 [Ps 38; 56; 88].

3913 *Weeks, Stuart* Wisdom Psalms. Temple and worship. LHBOTS 422: 2005 ⇒731. 292-307.
3914 *Whybray, Norman* The wisdom psalms. Wisdom. MSSOTS: 2005 <1995> ⇒324. 290-298.
3915 *Wilson, Gerald H.* King, messiah, and the reign of God: revisiting the royal psalms and the shape of the Psalter. The book of Psalms. VT.S 99: 2005 ⇒390. 391-406.
3916 *Wit, Hans de* Het gelaat van de messiaanse gemeenschap: Psalmen multicultureel gelezen. ITBT 13/1 (2005) 4-7.
3917 *Wolter von dem Knesebeck, Harald* Die Beatus Seiten der sog. thüringisch-sächsischen Malereischule. The illuminated psalter. 2005 ⇒ 3817. 413-426 [RBen 118,164–P.-M. Bogaert].
3918 *Zenger, Erich* JHWH als Lehrer des Volkes und der Einzelnen im Psalter. Religiöses Lernen. WUNT 180: 2005 ⇒384. 47-67.
3919 **Zenger, Erich** Un Dio di vendetta?: sorprendente attualità dei salmi 'imprecatori'. Mi 2005, Ancora 176 pp.

## E6.6 *Psalmi: oratio, liturgia*—**Psalms as prayer**

3920 [E]**Arocena, Félix M.; Goñi, J.A.** Psalterium liturgicum: psalterium crescit cum psallente ecclesia, I: Psalmi in missale romano et liturgia horarum. Città del Vaticano 2005, Libreria Editrice Vaticana lxxii; 575 pp. €28. 88-2097-6765. Pres. J. López Martín.
3921 **Arocena, Félix María** Psalterium liturgicum: psalterium crescit cum psallente ecclesia, II: psalmi in missalis romani lectionario. Città del Vaticano 2005, Libreria Editrice Vaticana lxii; 150 pp. €16. 88-209-7-7613. Pres. J. López Martín.
3922 *Awad, Magdi Rashidi Beshai* Die koptische Jahrespsalmodie. HBO 40 (2005) 15-39.
3923 *Barbiero, Gianni* "Mi ricordo di te dalla terra del Giordano e dell'Ermon ...". Il Sal 42-43 come preghiera di un esule. Horeb 14/3 (2005) 47-53.
3924 **Barnard, Willem** Lofzang is geen luxe: gepeins bij psalmen. Zoetermeer 2005, Meinema 164 pp. €15.90. 90-211-4038-1 [KeTh 58,181 —Rein Brouwer] [Ps 107-150].
3925 *Bortolini, José* Salmos violentos: por que não rezá-los?. Espaços 13 (2005) 155-165 [OTA 29,152].
3926 *Braulik, Georg* Rezeptionsästhetik, kanonische Intertextualität und die Meditation unseres Psalters. Liturgie und Bibel. ÖBS 28: 2005 <2003> ⇒360. 523-547.
3927 *Brueggemann, Walter* Psalms in narrative performance;
3928 The Psalms as limit expressions. Performing the Psalms. 2005 ⇒354. 9-29/31-50.
3929 **Buzzetti, Carlo; Cimosa, Mario** Con i salmi in mano: una guida particolare. Città del Vaticano 2005, Libreria Ed. Vaticana 131 pp.
3930 *Capill, Murray* Preaching the passion of the Psalms;
3931 Preaching the spirituality of the Psalms. VR 70 (2005) 45-55/35-44.
3932 *Cappelletto, Gianni* Rilettura della storia nei salmi. PaVi 50/4(2005) 40-46.
3933 *Clifford, Richard J.* What kind of psalter do we want in the new lectionary?. Worship 79 (2005) 258-262.

3934 *Cox, Ronald* The New Testament preaches the Psalms. Performing the Psalms. 2005 ⇒354. 83-104.

3935 *Driebergen, Annette* Aangesproken door de Psalmen. ITBT 13/2 (2005) 19-21.

3936 **Eaton, John** Meditating on the Psalms: a selection with new translation and inspirational commentary. 2004 ⇒20,3712. [R]RBLit (2005)* (*Botha, Philippus J.; Russell, Brian; Wilson, Gerald*).

3937 **Escoyez, Louis** Cris et louange: psaumes pour aujourd'hui. Prières: Namur 2005, Fidélité 168 pp. €10.

3938 *Fuchs, Ottmar* Die jüdisch-christliche Spiritualität der Klage: Worte in der Not und über den Tod hinaus. AnzSS 114/1 (2005) 20-23 [Ps 22].

3939 **Geßner, Georg** Meine Stärke und mein Lied ist der Herr: ein Psalmengebetbuch. WUNT 139: 2004 ⇒20,3717. [R]OrdKor 46 (2005) 107-108 (*Wahl, Otto*).

3940 **Harasta, Eva** Lob und Bitte: der Begriff des Gebetes aus den Psalmen und dem Vater Unser begründet sowie anhand von Johannes CALVIN und Karl BARTH systematisch-theologisch dargestellt. [D]*Welker, Michael* 2005, Diss. Heidelberg [ThLZ 130,886] [Mt 6,9-13].

3941 *Harmon, Kathleen* The role of the psalms in shaping faith, part 1: how the psalms interpret Israel's story. Liturgical ministry 14/4 (2005) 223-227.

3942 *Helberg, J.L.* Kyk, beleef of luister?: spiritualiteit in die Psalms in die lig van Psalms 1 en 2. In die Skriflig 39 (2005) 273-292 [OTA 29, 156].

3943 *Hicks, John M.* Preaching community laments: responding to disillusionment with God and injustice in the world. Performing the Psalms. 2005 ⇒354. 67-81.

3944 [T]**Hill, Robert C.** John CHRYSOSTOM: spiritual gems from the book of Psalms. 2004 ⇒20,3722. [R]Logos 46/1-2 (2005) 248-250 (*Kuc, Danylo*).

3945 **Hopkins, Denise D.** Journey through the Psalms. 2002 ⇒18,3572. Rev. ed. [R]RBLit (2005)* (*Williams, Tyler F.*).

3946 *Juhre, Arnim* Wenn wir nur wollen. zeitzeichen 6/7 (2005) 57.

3947 **Kizhakkeyil, Sebastian** The Psalms: the prayer book of the bible. Ujjain 2005, Ruhalaya 492 pp. Rs350. [R]ETJ 9 (2005) 189-190 (*John, Michael C.*).

3948 *Lameri, Angelo* I salmi: preghiera di Cristo e della chiesa: la rilettura cristiana del salterio. PaVi 50/1 (2005) 53-55;

3949 I salmi: preghiera di Cristo e della chiesa: l'uso dei salmi nella liturgia delle ore: note storiche. PaVi 50/2 (2005) 52-54;

3950 I salmi: preghiera di Cristo e della chiesa: l'uso dei salmi nella liturgia delle ore: il breviario attuale. PaVi 50/3 (2005) 56-58;

3951 I salmi: preghiera di Cristo e della chiesa: il salmo responsoriale. PaVi 50/4 (2005) 52-54;

3952 I salmi: preghiera di Cristo e della chiesa: il canto dei salmi. PaVi 50/5 (2005) 53-55;

3953 I salmi: preghiera di Cristo e della chiesa: il problema dei salmi 'imprecatori'. PaVi 50/6 (2005) 50-52.

3954 *Lohfink, Norbert* Psalmengebet und Psalterredaktion. Liturgie und Bibel. ÖBS 28: 2005 <1992> ⇒360. 437-459.

3955 *MacEwen, Alastair* Reading and applying the Psalms today. VR 70 (2005) 3-34.

3956 *Mazzinghi, Luca* I salmi: la poesia della preghiera. PaVi 50/1 (2005) 4-10.
3957 **McCabe, Maureen F.** Inside the Psalms: reflections for novices. Monastic wisdom 3: Kalamazoo, MICH 2005, Cistercian x; 137 pp. 0-87907-009-9. Foreword by *Bernardo Bonowitz*.
3958 *McCann, J. Clinton, Jr.* Greed, grace, and gratitude: an approach to preaching the Psalms. Performing the Psalms. 2005 ⇒354. 51-65.
3959 **Merton, Thomas** Orar los salmos. Bilbao 2005, Desclée de B. 64 pp. 84-330-2009-9.
3960 *Miguel González, José María de* La oración de la tarde: salmos de Vísperas de la IV semana. EstTrin 39 (2005) 23-92.
3961 **Seerveld, Calvin** Voicing God's psalms. GR 2005, Eerdmans 188 pp. $20. 0-8028-2806-X. Audio CD incl. [BiTod 44,58–D. Bergant].
3962 **Sire, James W.** Learning to pray through the psalms. DG 2005, Intervarsity 240 pp. $15.
3963 **Swenson, Kristin M.** Living through pain: Psalms & the search for wholeness. Waco 2005, Baylor Univ. Pr. 273 pp. $20. 1-932-792-155. Bibl. 259-269.
3964 *Thomson, Robert W.* Saint NERSES Lambronac'i on the Psalms. Saint Nersess theological review 10 (2005) 23-38.
3965 **Wallace, Howard Neil** Words to God, word from God: the Psalms in the prayer and preaching of the church. Aldershot 2005, Ashgate ix; 197 pp. €17/$30. 0-7546-3691-7. Bibl. 189-190.
3966 *Wilson, Paul Scott* Reading the Psalms for preaching: fictive plot. Performing the Psalms. 2005 ⇒354. 105-120.
3967 **Zevini, Giorgio** Lectio divina per la vita quotidiana, 3: i salmi e i cantici di Lodi e Vespri: prima settimana. 2004 ⇒20,3753. [R]Ter. 56 (2005) 324-326 (*Pasquetto, Virgilio*).
3968 *Zundel, Maurice* L'âme de la psalmodie. VS 85 (2005) 497-501.

## E6.7 *Psalmi: versiculi*—**Psalms by number and verse**

3969 *Botha, Phil J.* Intertextuality and the interpretation of Psalm 1. OTEs 18 (2005) 503-520 [Jer 17; Ezek 47; Josh 1; 1 Chr 22; Ps 52; 92].
3970 *Collins, C. John* Psalm 1: structure and rhetoric. Presbyterion 31 (2005) 37-48 [OTA 28,312].
3971 *Russell, Brian* Psalm 1 as an interpreter of scripture. IBSt 26 (2005) 170-193.
3972 *Tyrol, Anton* Salmo 1—il portale introduttivo al salterio. FolTh 15 (2005) 173-179 [OTA 29,156].
3973 *Helberg, J.L.* Wat het van die land geword?: die psalms (veral Psalms 1 en 2) oor die land, gelees teen die agtergrond van Josua 1. OTEs 18 (2005) 616-628.
3974 *Scaiola, Donatella* La 'porta' del salterio: lettura dei salmi 1 e 2. PaVi 50/1 (2005) 11-17.
3975 *Usue, E.O.* Theological-mythological viewpoints on divine sonship in Genesis 6 and Psalm 2. VeE 26 (2005) 810-825.
3976 **García Ureña, Lourdes** La metáfora de la gestación y del parto al servicio de la analogia: una lectura de Sl 2,1-7. 2003 ⇒19,3896. [R]EstB 63 (2005) 584-587 (*Moreno, Abdón*).
3977 *Fidler, Ruth* A touch of support: Ps 3,6 and the psalmist's experience. Bib. 86 (2005) 192-212.

3978 *Mazzinghi, Luca* Salmo 6: preghiera di un malato. PaVi 50/2 (2005) 11-16.

3979 *Hieke, Thomas* Psalm 7. [F]IRSIGLER, H.: ATSAT 76: 2005 ⇒67. 37-60.

3980 *Grohmann, Marianne* Ambivalent images of birth in Psalm vii 15. VT 55 (2005) 439-449.

3981 *Scalabrini, Patrizio Rota* I salmi e il Nuovo Testamento: il salmo 8. PaVi 50/2 (2005) 49-51.

3982 *Weber, Beat* Zum sogenannten 'Stimmungsumschwung' in Psalm 13. The book of Psalms. VT.S 99: 2005 ⇒390. 116-138.

3983 **Liess, Kathrin** Der Weg des Lebens: Psalm 16 und das Lebens- und Todesverständnis der Individualpsalmen. FAT 2/5: 2004 ⇒20,3777. [R]JETh 19 (2005) 231-233 (*Weber, Beat*); UF 37 (2005) 831-832 (*Loretz, Oswald*); RBLit (2005)* (*De Vos, Christiane*).

3984 *Scalabrini, Patrizio Rota* I salmi e il Nuovo Testamento: il salmo 16. PaVi 50/3 (2005) 54-56.

3985 *Weber, Beat* Notizen zu Form, Pragmatik und Struktur von Psalm 16. BN 125 (2005) 25-38.

3986 *Basson, A.* "Hide me in the shadow of your wings": an image-schematic notion in Psalm 17:8b. JSem 14/1 (2005) 95-111.

3987 *Sigurvinsson, Jón Á.* Ps 17,14c-e: Vorwurf an JHWH oder Fluch über die Feinde?: die Deutung von *ṣapun=ka* als eine sprechaktliche *crux interpretum*. [F]IRSIGLER, H.: ATSAT 76: 2005 ⇒67. 61-79.

3988 *Young, Theron* Psalm 18 and 2 Samuel 22: two versions of the same song. [F]FOX, M. 2005 ⇒43. 53-69.

3989 *Blockman, Noga; Guillaume, Philippe* Bull-leaping in ancient Israel. UF 37 (2005) 5-8 [Ps 18,30].

3990 *Wyatt, Nicolas* The liturgical context of Psalm 19 and its mythical and ritual origins. 'There's...divinity'. 2005 <1995> ⇒329. 103-131.

3991 *Nigro, Giovanni* L'esegesi del Salmo 21 in GIUSTINO. VetChr 42 (2005) 73-102.

3992 **Bauks, Michaela** Die Feinde des Psalmisten und die Freunde Ijobs: Untersuchungen zur Freund-Klage im Alten Testament am Beispiel von Ps 22. SBS 203: 2004 ⇒20,3784. [R]RHPhR 85 (2005) 318-320 (*Heintz, J.-G.*).

3993 *Nel, Philip J.* I am a worm: metaphor in Psalm 22. JSem 14/1 (2005) 40-54.

3994 Animal imagery in Psalm 22. JNSL 31/1 (2005) 75-88.

3995 *Scalabrini, Patrizio Rota* I salmi e il Nuovo Testamento: il salmo 22: il racconto della crocifissione di Gesù. PaVi 50/4 (2005) 50-52.

3996 *Lescow, Theodor* Psalm 22,2-22 und Psalm 88: Komposition und Dramaturgie. ZAW 117 (2005) 217-231.

3997 *Gren, Conrad R.* Piercing the ambiguities of Psalm 22:16 and the Messiah's mission. JETS 48 (2005) 283-299 [OTA 30,390].

3998 *Linville, James* Psalm 22:17b: a new guess. JBL 124 (2005) 733-744.

3999 *Auffret, Pierre* Ma coupe est comble: étude structurelle du psaume 23. BN 126 (2005) 37-43.

4000 **Boff, Leonardo** Der Herr ist mein Hirte: Psalm 23. Dü 2005, Patmos 159 pp. 3-491-70388-3.

4001 *Diller, Carmen* "Du füllst mir reichlich den Becher...": der Becher als Zeichen der Gastfreundschaft am Beispiel von Ps 23. [F]IRSIGLER, H.: ATSAT 76: 2005 ⇒67. 81-104.

4002 *Nel, Philip J.* Yahweh is a shepherd: conceptual metaphor in Psalm 23. HBT 27/2 (2005) 79-103.

4003 *Pellegrini, Rita* Salmo 23: il Signore mio pastore e mio ospite. PaVi 50/2 (2005) 17-24.

4004 *deClaissé-Walford, Nancy L.* An intertextual reading of Psalms 22, 23, and 24. The book of Psalms. VT.S 99: 2005 ⇒390. 139-152.

4005 *Paul, Shalom M.* Psalm 27:10 and the Babylonian theodicy. Divrei Shalom. CHANE 23: 2005 <1982> ⇒273. 121-123.

4006 *Dell'Orto, Giuseppe* Salmo 29: la gloria di YHWH, Signore del mondo. PaVi 50/2 (2005) 25-31.

4007 *Pardee, D.* On Psalm 29: structure and meaning. The book of Psalms. VT.S 99: 2005 ⇒390. 153-183.

4008 *Pietersma, Albert* The seven voices of the Lord: a commentary on Septuagint Psalm 28. LUST, J.: BEThL 192: 2005 ⇒92. 311-329.

4009 *Zenger, Erich* Theophanien des Königsgottes JHWH: Transformationen von Psalm 29 in den Teilkompositionen Ps 28-30 und Ps 93-100. The book of Psalms. VT.S 99: 2005 ⇒390. 407-442.

4010 *Trabacchin, Gianni* Salmo 30: verso una lode per sempre. PaVi 50/2 (2005) 32-39.

4011 *Basson, Alec* "You are my rock and fortress": refuge metaphors in Psalm 31: a perspective from cognitive metaphor theory. AcTh(B) 25/2 (2005) 1-17.

4012 *Colomo, Daniela; Scholl, Reinhold* Psalmen und Rechnungen: P. Bonn. Inv. 147 + P.Lips. I 97. ZPE 153 (2005) 163-167 [Ps 31].

4013 *Bons, Eberhard* Comment le psaume 32[LXX] parle-t-il de la création?. [F]LUST, J.: BEThL 192: 2005 ⇒92. 55-64.

4014 *Bazyliński, Stanislaw* Elementi poetici nel Salmo 34. Il bello della bibbia. 2005 ⇒357. 317-344;

4015 'I will bless Yhwh in every time': the composition of Psalm 34. W nurcie franciszkánskim 14 (2005) 5-16.

4016 *Basson, Alec* Divine metaphors in Psalm 35 explored from a cognitive anthropological perspective. OTEs 18 (2005) 9-21.

4017 *Kronemeijer, Matthijs* A struggle with God: poetics and theology of Psalm 35. [M]VAN TILBORG, S.: BiblInterp 71: 2005 ⇒155. 97-113.

4018 *Gosse, Bernard* Le Psaume 40 et le livre de Jérémie. ZAW 117 (2005) 395-404.

4019 *Human, D.J.; Steenkamp, Y.; Styger, P.* Psalm 40 as a Torah psalm. In die Skriflig 39 (2005) 133-153 [OTA 29,56].

4020 *Scaiola, Donatella* Salmo 40: 'ho sperato, ho sperato nel Signore'. PaVi 50/2 (2005) 40-46.

4021 *Auffret, Pierre* Vers la montagne de ton lieu-saint: étude structurelle du Psaume 42-43. StEeL 22 (2005) 19-33.

4022 *Oloffson, Staffan* "Som hjorten längtar bäckens vatten": en studie av Ps 42-43 med fokus på metaforspråk och teologi. SEÅ 70 (2005) 229-245.

4023 **Strola, Germana** Il desiderio di Dio: studio dei Sal 42-43. 2003 ⇒ 19,3938; 20,3806. [R]ZKTh 127 (2005) 133-134 (*Paganini, Simone*).

4024 *Mazzi, Rita Torto* Salmo 44: supplica nazionale in un momento tragico. PaVi 50/3 (2005) 12-20.

4025 *Benzi, Guido* Salmo 45: le nozze del re Messia. PaVi 50/3 (2005) 21-27.

4026 *Grandy, Andreas; Uehlinger, Christoph* Vom Toben des Meeres zum Jubel der Völker: psalterexegetische Beobachtungen zu Psalm 46. [F]SCHENKER, A.: OBO 214: 2005 ⇒134. 372-393.

4027 *Zucker, David J.* The riddle of Psalm 49. JBQ 33 (2005) 143-152.
4028 [T]**Caruso, Antonio** Flavio Magno Aurelio CASSIODORO: la penitenza con goia: commento al Salmo 50. Spirito e Vita 29: R 2005, Vivere In 72 pp. €5.
4029 *Human, D.J.* God accepts a broken spirit and a contrite heart—thoughts on penitence, forgiveness and reconciliation in Psalm 51. VeE 26 (2005) 114-132.
4030 *Mazzinghi, Luca* Salmo 51: 'pietà di me, o Dio'. PaVi 50/3 (2005) 28-34.
4031 *Tagliacarne, Pierfelice* Beobachtungen zur Struktur und zum Kontext von Psalm 51. [F]SEIDL, T.: ATSAT 75: 2005 ⇒137. 155-182.
4032 *Postell, Seth* Psalm 53: the fool, the wise man, and the messianic motif. Faith & Mission 22/3 (2005) 87-103.
4033 *Doyle, Brian* God as a dog: metaphorical allusions in Psalm 59. Metaphor in the Hebrew Bible. BEThL 187: 2005 ⇒799. 41-53.
4034 *Kselman, John S.* Double entendre in Psalm 59. The book of Psalms. VT.S 99: 2005 ⇒390. 184 -189.
4035 *Strola, Germana* Salmo 63: il canto del desiderio. PaVi 50/3 (2005) 35-42.
4036 *Reemts, Christiana* Psalm 68 (67). EuA 81 (2005) 39-56.
4037 *Müller, Hans-Peter* Zur Grammatik und zum religionsgeschichtlichen Hintergrund von Ps 68,5. ZAW 117 (2005) 206-216.
4038 *Kot, Tomasz* Bóg powiedział raz, dwa razy usłyszałem (Ps 68,12) [Dieu a parlé une fois, deux fois j'ai entendu ceci (Ps 68,12)]. PrzPow 122 (2005) 64-68, 459-463. **P**.
4039 *Groenewald, Alphonso* Psalm 69: a composition-critical contribution. [M]VAN TILBORG, S.: BiblInterp 71: 2005 ⇒155. 77-96.
4040 *Groenewald, Alphonso* Post-exilic conflict as 'possible' historical background to Psalm 69:10ab. HTS 61 (2005) 131-141 [OTA 29, 160].
4041 *Scaiola, Donatella* Salmo 72: 'Dio, dà al re il tuo giudizio. PaVi 50/3 (2005) 43-50.
4042 *Bazylinski, Stanislaw* La crux del Sal 72,5. LASBF 55 (2005) 41-58.
4043 *Paul, Shalom M.* Psalm 72:5—a traditional blessing for the long life of the king. Divrei Shalom. CHANE 23: 2005 <1972> ⇒273. 51-58.
4044 *Lorenzin, Tiziano* Salmo 73: il cammino de fede di una comunità israelitica in difficoltà. PaVi 50/4 (2005) 8-15.
4045 **Mukarantin, Eric-Etom** Das Glück der Gottlosen: eine Untersuchung zum Ps 73. EHS.T 801: Fra 2005, Lang 228 pp. 363153633X.
4046 *Holtmann, Stefan* Die Asafpsalmen als Spiegel der Geschichte Israels: Überlegungen zur Komposition von Ps 73-83, Teil 1. BN 122 (2005) 45-79;
4047 Teil 2. BN 123 (2005) 49-63.
4048 *Auffret, Pierre* Toi le Dieu faisant merveille: étude structurelle du Psaume 77. BeO 47 (2005) 123-138.
4049 *Kim, Yeol; Van Rooy, H.F.* Reading Psalm 78 multidimensionally: the dimension of the reader. Scriptura 88 (2005) 101-117 [OTA 29, 58].
4050 *Gosse, Bernard* Le Psaume 80 dans le cadre du psautier et Ezéchiel 17. SJOT 19 (2005) 48-60.
4051 *Mosser, Carl* The earliest patristic interpretations of Psalm 82, Jewish antecedents, and the origin of christian deification. JThS 56 (2005) 30-74.

4052 *Hutchinson, James Hely* Citoyens de Sion: méditation sur le psaume 87. ThEv(VS) 4/2 (2005) 23-28.
4053 **Schlegel, Juliane** Psalm 88 als Prüfstein der Exegese: zu Sinn und Bedeutung eines beispiellosen Psalms. BThSt 72: Neuk 2005, Neuk 101 pp. 3-7887-2110-3. Bibl. 93-101.
4054 *Schiller, Johannes* "Für die Toten wirst du ein Wunder tun?": Randbemerkungen zur Interpretation von Ps 88,11-13. PzB 14 (2005) 61-66.
4055 *Creach, Jerome F.D.* The mortality of the king in Psalm 89 and Israel's postexilic identity. [F]MCBRIDE, D. 2005 ⇒98. 237-249.
4056 *Mitchell, Matthew* Genre disputes and communal accusatory laments: reflections on the genre of Psalm lxxxix. VT 55 (2005) 511-527.
4057 *Scaiola, Donatella* Salmo 89: 'canterò senza fine le grazie del Signore. PaVi 50/4 (2005) 16-22.
4058 **Steymans, Hans** Ulrich Psalm 89 und der Davidbund: eine strukturale und redaktionsgeschichtliche Untersuchung. ÖBS 27: Fra 2005, Lang 492 pp. €70. 3-631-51253-8. Bibl. 457-488.
4059 *Venter, Pieter M.* The translation of Psalm 89:13 and its implications. HTS 61 (2005) 531-544 [OTA 29,160].
4060 *Clifford, Richard J.* Psalm 90: wisdom meditation or communal lament?. The book of Psalms. VT.S 99: 2005 ⇒390. 190-205.
4061 *Mazzinghi, Luca* Salmo 90: 'Signore, tu sei stato per noi un refugio'. PaVi 50/4 (2005) 26-31.
4062 *Gaiser, Frederick J.* "It shall not reach you": talisman or vocation?: reading Psalm 91 in time of war. Word and world 25 (2005) 191-202.
4063 *Kraus, Thomas J.* Septuaginta-Psalm 90 in apotropäischer Verwendung: Vorüberlegungen für eine kritische Edition und (bisheriges) Datenmaterial. BN 125 (2005) 39-73.
4064 *Sembrano, Lucio* Salmo 95: 'venite, applaudiamo al Signore'. PaVi 50/4 (2005) 32-39.
4065 *Leuchter, Mark* The literary strata and narrative sources of Psalm xcix. VT 55 (2005) 20-38.
4066 *Barré, Michael L.* The shifting focus of Psalm 101. The book of Psalms. VT.S 99: 2005 ⇒390. 206-223.
4067 *Maré, Leonard P.* Psalm 103: lofprysing word gebore uit de swaarkry van die lewe. HTS 61 (2005) 1273-1284 [OTA 29,291].
4068 *Berlin, Adele* The wisdom of creation in Psalm 104. [F]FOX, M. 2005 ⇒43. 71-83.
4069 *Tucker, W. Dennis* Revisiting the plagues in Psalm cv. VT 55 (2005) 401-411.
4070 *Auffret, Pierre* Il est seigneur sur les nations: étude structurelle du psaume 110. BN 123 (2005) 65-73.
4071 *Scalabrini, Patrizio Rota* Salmo 110: la guerra del Messia sacerdote;
4072 I salmi e il Nuovo Testamento: il salmo 110: il Messia: re e sacerdote. PaVi 50/5 (2005) 11-17/51-53.
4073 *Scaiola, Donatella* Salmo 111-112: due salmi gemelli;
4074 *Mazzi, Rita Torti* Salmi 113-118: l'*hallel* egiziano. PaVi 50/5 (2005) 18-24/25-32.
4075 *Scalabrini, Patrizio Rota* I salmi e il Nuovo Testamento: il salmo 118: un inno per il 'séder' pasquale. PaVi 50/6 (2005) 48-50.
4076 *Strola, Germana* Salmo 118: 'ti rendo grazie perché sei stato la mia salvezza'. PaVi 50/5 (2005) 33-39.

4077 **Leonhard, Clemens** ISHODAD of Merw's exegesis of the Psalms 119 and 139-147: a study of his interpretation in the light of the Syriac translation of THEODORE of Mopsuestia's commentary. CSCO.Sub 107: 2001 ⇒17,3355; 18,3698. [R]JSSt 50 (2005) 222-23 (*Lane, D.J.*).

4078 *Mazzinghi, Luca* Salmo 119: meditazione sulla legge del Signore. PaVi 50/5 (2005) 40-47.

4079 *Whybray, Norman* Psalm 119: profile of a psalmist. Wisdom. MSSOTS: 2005 <1997> ⇒324. 299-311.

4080 *Scaiola, Donatella* Salmi 120-134: i canti delle ascensioni. PaVi 50/6 (2005) 12-17.

4081 *Rose, Martin* Je lève les yeux vers les montagnes, vers nos alpes de neige, que Dieu les protège!. [F]SCHENKER, A.: OBO 214: 2005 ⇒134. 295-309 [Ps 121].

4082 *Zenger, Erich* Der Hüter Israels: die Theopoesie von Psalm 121. [F]STENDEBACH, F. 2005 ⇒141. 163-178.

4083 *Prinsloo, Gert T.M.* Historical reality and mythological metaphor in Psalm 124. OTEs 18 (2005) 790-810.

4084 *Hossfeld, Frank-Lothar* Ps 130 und die Gnadenrede vom Sinai in Ex 34. [F]STENDEBACH, F. 2005 ⇒141. 48-56.

4085 *Scaiola, Donatella* Salmo 130: 'dal profondo a te grido, o Signore'. PaVi 50/6 (2005) 18-23.

4086 *Auffret, Pierre* Ton nom pour toujours: nouvelle étude structurelle du Psaume 135. ScEs 57 (2005) 229-241.

4087 *Human, Dirk J.* Psalm 136: 'n liturgie as herinnering en herbelewenis van God se krag in die skepping en in die geskiedenis. HTS 61 (2005) 1209-1226 [OTA 29,291].

4088 *Salvesen, Alison* Psalm 135(136):25 in a Jewish Greek inscription from Nicaea. [F]ULLENDORFF, E.: SStLL 47: 2005 ⇒154. 212-221.

4089 *Bellinger, Jr., William H.* Psalm 137: memory and poetry. HBT 27/2 (2005) 5-20.

4090 *Hays, Christopher B.* How shall we sing?: Psalm 137 in historical and canonical context. HBT 27/2 (2005) 35-55.

4091 *Mazzinghi, Luca* Salmo 137: 'se ti dimentico, Gerusalemme!'. PaVi 50/6 (2005) 24-30.

4092 *Schaefer, Konrad* Salmo 137, canto de amor y oración violenta. Qol 39 (2005) 3-18.

4093 *Sessa, Salvatore Maurizio* Sal 137: il ruggito della fede: per una riconsiderazione del genere letterario imprecatorio come chiave di lettura fondamentale. RivBib 53 (2005) 129-172.

4094 *Auffret, Pierre* Tu me feras vivre: étude structurelle du psaume 138. OTEs 18 (2005) 472-481.

4095 *Seybold, Klaus D.* Zur Geschichte des vierten Davidspsalters (Pss 138 - 145). The book of Psalms. VT.S 99: 2005 ⇒390. 368-390.

4096 *Mosetto, Francesco* Salmo 139: 'Signore, tu mi scruti e mi conosci': una lettura cristiana. PaVi 50/6 (2005) 31-36.

4097 *Booij, Thijs* Psalm 141: a prayer for discipline and protection. Bib. 86 (2005) 97-106;

4098 Psalm 145: een lofzang van David. [F]HOOGEWOUD, F. 2005 ⇒63. 35-42 [OTA 29,59].

4099 *Auffret, Pierre* YHWH aimant les justes: étude structurelle du psaume 146. ScEs 57 (2005) 49-57.

4100 *Bovone, Maria Rita Marenco* Salmo 148: la splendida lode al Dio creatore. PaVi 50/6 (2005) 37-43.

4101 *Scaiola, Donatella* La 'chiusura' del salterio: lettura dei salmi 149 e 150. PaVi 50/1 (2005) 18-24.

### E7.1 **Job**, *textus, commentarii*

4102 [ET]**Gómez Aranda, Mariano** El comentario de Abraham IBN EZRA al libro de Job. 2004 ⇒20,3875. [R]EstB 63 (2005) 342-344 (*Pérez Fernández, Miguel*); EstB 63 (2005) 346-348 (*Ribera-Florit, Josep*).

4103 **Hester, David Charles** Job. Interpretation Bible Studies: LVL 2005, Westminster vi; 122 pp. $10. 0-664-22633-7.

4104 **Japhet, Sara** The commentary of Rabbi Samuel Ben Meir (RASHBAM) on the book of Job. 2000 ⇒16,3341; 17,3380. [R]JQR 95 (2005) 163-181 (*Harris, Robert A.*).

4105 *Kutz, Karl V.* Characterization in the Old Greek of Job. [F]FOX, M. 2005 ⇒43. 345-355.

4106 *Newsome, Carol* The book of Job. OT survey. 2005 ⇒413. 182-196.

4107 *Ntreh, Benjamin A.* Job. Global bible commentary. 2005 ⇒2443. 141-150.

4108 **Ravasi, Gianfranco** Giobbe: traduzione e commento. Roma 2005 <1991>, Borla 854 pp. Ristampa della 3a ed.

4109 *Rechenmacher, Hans* Repetition und Variation von Präpositionen im Parallelismus membrorum, untersucht am Beispiel der Ijob-Poesie. [F]IRSIGLER, H.: ATSAT 76: 2005 ⇒67. 1-14.

4110 *Schwienhorst-Schönberger, Ludger* Il libro di Giobbe. Introduzione AT. 2005 ⇒1159. 507-526.

4111 **Terrien, Samuel** Job. Commentaire de l'Ancien Testament 13: Genève [2]2005 <1963>, Labor et F. 324 pp. €41. 2-8309-1167-9. Avant-propos de *Thomas Römer*; étude d'*Ernst Axel Knauf*.

4112 [E]**Van Wolde, Ellen** De God van Job. Zoetermeer 2005, Meinema 114 pp. €11.50. 9021140527. Articles published in Conc(E) 4, 2004.

4113 **Wharton, James A.** Job. 1999 ⇒15,3188... 17,3386. [R]VJTR 69 (2005) 790-791 (*Meagher, P.M.*).

### E7.2 *Job: themata*, **Topics**... *Versiculi*, **Verse numbers**

4114 *Branch, Robin G.* Space for joy: another look at the book of Job and Job himself in light of some principles of wisdom literature. JSem 14/2 (2005) 384-412.

4115 **Cappelletto, Gianni** Giobbe: l'uomo e Dio si incontrano nella sofferenza. Quaderni del noce: Padova 2005, Messagero 173 pp. €9.50.

4116 *Carreira das Neves, Joaquim* A actualidade da pergunta de Job. Itin. 51 (2005) 363-370.

4117 *Cavalcanti, Elena* Interiorità e identità personale nel commento a Giobbe ("Moralia") di GREGORIO Magno. ASEs 22/1 (2005) 11-35.

4118 *Cebulj, Christian* Warum?—Ijob zwischen Händel und Brahms. KatBl 130 (2005) 427-435.

4119 **Chirpaz, François** Job: la force d'espérance. 2001 ⇒17,3391. [R]RTL 36 (2005) 103-104 (*Lichtert, Cl.*).

4120 *Cohen, Mordechai Z.* A philosopher's peshaṭ exegesis: MAIMONIDES' literary approach to the book of Job and its place in the history of biblical interpretation. Shnaton 15 (2005) 213-264. **H.**

4121 *Cox, Claude* Tying it all together: the use of particles in Old Greek Job. BIOSCS 38 (2005) 41-54.

4122 **David, Pascal** Job ou l'authentique théodicée. P 2005, Bayard 126 pp. €15.90. 22274-70283.

4123 *Dietrich, Luiz J.* Masculinidades em Jó. Estudos bíblicos 86 (2005) 42-50.

4124 **Eisen, Robert** The book of Job in medieval Jewish philosophy. 2004 ⇒20,3892. [R]RRT 12 (2005) 351-353 (*Hamilton, Mark W.*).

4125 **Engljähringer, Klaudia** Theologie im Streitgespräch: Studien zur Dynamik der Dialoge des Buches Ijob. SBS 198: 2003 ⇒19,4041; 20,3894. [R]BZ 49 (2005) 301-303 (*Schwienhorst-Schönberger, Ludger*); JETh 19 (2005) 228-231 (*Wenzel, Heiko*).

4126 **Fokkelman, Johannes Petrus** Major poems of the Hebrew Bible: at the interface of hermeneutics and structural analysis, 4: Job 15-42. SSN 47: 2004 ⇒20,3895. [R]JHScr 5 (2005)* (*Hu, Wesley*).

4127 **Formosinho, Sebastião J.; Branco, J. Oliveira** A pergunta de Job: o homem e o mistério do mal. 2003 ⇒19,4046. [R]REB 65 (2005) 756-758 (*Lepargneur, Hubert*).

4128 *Granados Temes, José M.* Sólo el amor salva: una parábola sobre el rescate de la soledad. VyV 63/242 (2005) 151-175.

4129 **Greschat, Katharina** Die Moralia in Job GREGORs des Großen: ein christologisch-ekklesiologischer Kommentar. [D]*May, Gerhard*: STAC 31: Tü 2005, Mohr S. ix; 298 pp. €54. 31614-86188. Diss.-Habil. Mainz.

4130 *Grimm, Markus* "Dein Auftritt, Ijob!" oder: wie Ijob aus seinem Buch spaziert und sich auf die Bühne stellt. [F]SEIDL, T.: ATSAT 75: 2005 ⇒137. 211-223.

4131 *Heuser, August* Hiob—eine Auseinandersetzung im Bild. [F]STENDEBACH, F. 2005 ⇒141. 43-47.

4132 *Heymel, Michael* Hiob und die Musik: zur Bedeutung der Hiobgestalt für eine musikalische Seelsorge. Das AT und die Kunst. ATM 15: 2005 ⇒711. 129-163.

4133 **Iwanski, Dariusz A.** The dynamics of Job's intercession. [D]*Gilbert, Maurice* 2005, Diss. Gregoriana [RTL 37,609].

4134 *Knauf, Ernst A.* La patrie de Job. Job. 2005 ⇒4111. 12-27.

4135 *Magary, Dennis R.* Answering questions, questioning answers: the rhetoric of interrogatives in the speeches of Job and his friends. [F]FOX, M. 2005 ⇒43. 283-298.

4136 [E]**Marconi, Gilberto; Termini, Cristina** I volti di Giobbe: percorsi interdisciplinari. 2003 ⇒19,694. [R]Ang. 82 (2005) 229-230 (*Garuti, Paolo*).

4137 *Matadi, Ghislain T.* De l'epreuve à la sagesse: une lecture du livre de Job dans le contexte africain. Telema 123/4 (2005) 7-24.

4138 **McKibben, Bill** The comforting whirlwind: God, Job and the scale of creation. CM 2005, Cowley 73 pp. $14.

4139 **Newsom, Carol Ann** The book of Job: a contest of moral imaginations. 2003 ⇒19,4073; 20,3914. [R]AThR 87 (2005) 158, 160 (*Floyd, Michael H.*).

4140 *Nicole, Émile* La théologie des amis de Job. ThEv(VS) 4/1 (2005) 3-17.

4141 *Painter, Rick* Cycle theory and the dialogue cycle of Job. ProcGLM 25 (2005) 59-68.

4142 *Patrick, James E.* The fourfold structure of Job: variations on a theme. VT 55 (2005) 185-206.
4143 **Pfeffer, Jeremy I.** Providence in the book of Job: the search for God's mind. Brighton 2005, Sussex Academic ix; 212 pp. $69.50. 1-8451-9064-5. Bibl. 205.
4144 **Pieri, Fabrizio** Giobbe e il suo Dio. Mi 2005, Paoline 80 pp. €7.50 [CiVi 61/1,99].
4145 **Pyeon, Yohan** You have not spoken what is right about me: intertextuality and the book of Job. Studies in Biblical Literature 45: 2003 ⇒19,4079. [R]HebStud 46 (2005) 427-430 (*Fox, Michael V.*).
4146 **Ravasi, Gianfranco** Hiob: der Mensch im Leid. Mü 2005, Neue Stadt 128 pp. €15. 3-87996-6478 [ThPQ 153,611s–Franz Hubmann].
4147 **Rohde, Michael** Der Knecht Hiob im Gespräch mit Mose. [D]*Van Oorschot, J.* 2005, Diss. Marburg [ThLZ 130,888].
4148 *Roper, L.A.* The social context of the book of Job. VeE 26/3 (2005) 756-772.
4149 **Rossi, Luiz Alexandre S.** A falsa religião e a amizade enganadora: o livro de Jó. Biblia e cotidiano: São Paulo 2005, Paulus 213 pp.
4150 *Sanz Giménez-Rico, Enrique* Escapar del que habla, hablar al que escapa: Dios, esa absoluta angustia. SalTer 93 (2005) 161-170 [Gen 4].
4151 **Syring, Wolf-Dieter** Hiob und sein Anwalt: die Prosatexte des Hiobbuches und ihre Rolle in seiner Redaktions- und Rezeptionsgeschichte. BZAW 336: 2004 ⇒20,3927. [R]Afrika Yetu 8 (2005) 63-66 (*Orji, Chukwuemeka*); ZKTh 127 (2005) 124-125 (*Engljähringer, Klaudia*); ETR 80 (2005) 281-282 (*Römer, Thomas*).
4152 *Szpek, Heidi M.* On the influence of Job on Jewish Hellenistic literature. [F]FOX, M. 2005 ⇒43. 357-370.
4153 **Ticciati, Susannah** Job and the disruption of identity: reading beyond BARTH. L 2005, Clark 240 pp. £45.
4154 *Vincent, Jean M.* Édouard REUSS, traducteur et interprète du livre de Job: à l'occasion du bicentenaire de la naissance de l'exégète strasbourgeois. RHPhR 85 (2005) 337-364.
4155 *White, Ronan* 'Why should innocent people suffer?': Job, suffering and the Aids pandemic in South Africa. MillSt 55 (2005) 48-64.
4156 *Whybray, Norman* Wisdom, suffering and the freedom of God in the book of Job. Wisdom. MSSOTS: 2005 <1999> ⇒324. 194-208.
4157 *Wilson, Gerald* Preknowledge, anticipation, and the poetics of Job. JSOT 30 (2005) 243-256.

4158 *Hoop, Raymond de* The frame story of the book of Job: prose or verse?: Job 1:1-5 as a test case. Layout markers. Pericope 5: 2005 ⇒ 422. 40-77.
4159 *Ticciati, Susannah* Does Job fear God for naught?. MoTh 21 (2005) 353-366 [Job 1,1-9].
4160 *Shepherd, David* Rendering "flesh and bones": pair reversal and the Peshitta of Job 2.5. AramSt 3 (2005) 205-213.
4161 **Ha, Kyung-Taek** Frage und Antwort: Studien zu Hiob 3 im Kontext des Hiob-Buches. Herders biblische Studien 46: FrB 2005, Herder x; 235 pp. €50. 3-451-28535-5. Bibl. 209-235.
4162 *Scherer, Andreas* Hoffnung für den Hilflosen?: die erste Rede des Eliphas in Hiob Kap. 4f. ThZ 61 (2005) 281-300.
4163 *Harding, James E.* A spirit of deception in Job 4:15?: interpretive indeterminacy and Eliphaz's vision. BiblInterp 13 (2005) 137-166.

4164 *Paul, Shalom M.* Job 4:15—a hair-raising encounter <1982>;

4165 A *double entendre* in Job 15:32 in the light of Akkadian <2003>. Divrei Shalom. CHANE 23: 2005 ⇒273. 129-131/315-317.

4166 *Ólason, Kristinn* "Wenn ihr an meiner Stelle wärt": die dialogische Handlungsstruktur im Proömium der fünften Rede Ijobs (Ijob 16,2-6). [F]IRSIGLER, H.: ATSAT 76: 2005 ⇒67. 15-35.

4167 *Kummerow, David* Job, hopeful or hopeless?: the significance of גם in Job 16:19 and Job's changing conceptions of death. JHScr 5/14 (2005)*.

4168 **Grenzer, Matthias** Análise poética da sociedade: um estudo de Jó 24. Exegese: São Paulo 2005, Paulinas 95 pp.

4169 **Lo, Alison** Job 28 as rhetoric: an analysis of Job 28 in the context of Job 22-31. VT.S 97: 2003 ⇒19,4120; 20,3944. [R]Bib. 86 (2005) 427-431 (*Hartley, John E.*).

4170 *Clines, David J.A.* Putting Elihu in his place: a proposal for the relocation of Job 32-37. JSOT 29 (2005) 243-253.

4171 *Fontaine, Carole R.* The proof of the pudding: proverbs and gender in the performance arena. JSOT 29 (2005) 179-203 [Job 32,6-10].

4172 *Rad, Gerhard von* Job 38 and ancient Egyptian wisdom. From Genesis. 2005 <1955> ⇒283. 223-231.

4173 **Schifferdecker, Kathryn** Out of the whirlwind: creation theology in the book of Job. 2005, Diss. Harvard [HThR 98,501] [Job 38-41].

4174 *Walker-Jones, Arthur* The so-called ostrich in the God speeches of the book of Job (Job 39,13-18). Bib. 86 (2005) 494-510.

4175 *Maher, Seán* The answer of Job to God. PIBA 28 (2005) 48-65 [Job 42,1-6].

4176 *Fox, Michael V.* Job the pious. ZAW 117 (2005) 351-366 [Job 42,6].

4177 **Ngwa, Kenneth N.** The hermeneutics of the "happy" ending in Job 42:7-17. BZAW 354: B 2005, De Gruyter xi; 179 pp. 3-11-018412-5. Diss. Princeton, Sem.; Bibl. 147-168.

### E7.3 *Canticum Canticorum*, **Song of Songs, Hohelied,** *textus, comm.*

[E]**Auwers, J.** Regards croisés sur le Cantique 2005 ⇒338.

4178 *Auwers, J.-M.; Wénin, André* Problèmes herméneutiques dans l'interprétation du Cantique des cantiques. RTL 36 (2005) 344-373.

4179 [ET]**Barbára, Maria A.** ORIGENE: commentario al Cantico dei cantici. BPat 42: Bo 2005, EDB 615 pp. €56.20. 88-10-42052-7. Bibl. 7-57.

4180 **Barbiero, Gianni** Cantico dei Cantici 2004 ⇒20,3955. [R]ZKTh 127 (2005) 125-127 (*Paganini, Simone*).

4181 *Barton, John* The canonicity of the Song of Songs. Perspectives on the Song of Songs. 2005 ⇒401. 1-7.

4182 *Bohnenkamp, Anne* "Lieber stark als rein": das Hohelied Salomos in den Übersetzungen Johann Georg HAMANNs, Martin BUBERs und der *Einheitsübersetzung der Heiligen Schrift* von 1974. Gegenwärtigkeit Johann Georg Hamanns. 2005 ⇒830. 335-355.

4183 **Costa, Candido** Commento al Cantico dei Cantici. [T]*Cingano, Ettore*: R 2005, CIPI 1072 pp. Introd. *Max Anselmi*; Trad. italiana con testo latino a fronte; Contiene anche i commenti al Cantico dei Cantici di *Haimo d'Auxerre* (pp 643-817) e di *Egidio Romano* (pp 819-1013).

4184 [T]**Deutz, Helmut; Deutz, Ilse** RUPERT von Deutz: Commentaria in Canticum Canticorum. FC 70/1-2: Turnhout 2005, Brepols 2 vols; 341 + 343-653 pp. €35.42 + 32.63. 2-503-52144-4/6-0.

4185 *Dobbs-Allsop, F.W.* Late linguistic features in the Song of Songs. Perspectives on the Song of Songs. 2005 ⇒401. 27-77.

4186 **Ena, Jean Emmanuel de** Sens et interprétations du Cantique des Cantiques: sens textuel, sens directionnels et cadre du texte. LeDiv 194: 2004 ⇒20,3958. [R]ETR 80 (2005) 127-129 (*Lys, Daniel*); EThL 81 (2005) 225-227 (*Auwers, J.-M.*).

4187 **Exum, J. Cheryl** Song of Songs: a commentary. OTL: LVL 2005, Westminster xxiii; 263 pp. $40. 0-664-22190-4. Bibl. xi-xxiii.

4188 [T]**Falchini, Cecilia** RUPERTO di Deutz: Commento al Cantico dei Cantici; De incarnazione Domini. Padri occidentali: Magnano 2005, Qiqajon 344 pp.

4189 *Flint, Peter W.* The book of Canticles (Song of Songs) in the Dead Sea scrolls. Perspectives on the Song of Songs. 2005 ⇒401. 96-104.

4190 **Fraisse, Otfried** MOSES ibn Tibbons Kommentar zum Hohelied. SJ 25: 2004 ⇒20,3959. [R]Jud. 61 (2005) 275-79 (*Hasselhoff, Görge K.*).

4191 **Hess, Richard S.** Song of Songs. Wisdom and Psalms: GR 2005, Baker 285 pp. $30. 08010-27128. Bibl. 253-269.

4192 **Jenson, Robert W.** Song of Songs. Interpretation: LVL 2005, Westminster x; 106 pp. $25. 0-8042-3117-6. Bibl. 105-106.

4193 **Longman, Tremper** Song of Songs. NIC: 2001 ⇒17,3441 ... 20, 3964. [R]VJTR 69 (2005) 638-639 (*Meagher, P.M.*).

4194 **Luzárraga Fradua, Jesús** Cantar de los Cantares: sendas del amor. Nueva Biblia Española: Estella (Navarra) 2005, Verbo Divino 650, (5*) pp. €38. 84-8169-695-1. Bibl. 607-650.

4195 (a) *Mazzinghi, Luca* Traduzione del Cantico dei Cantici. De sexto. Sussidi biblici 94: 2005 ⇒8836. 47-66.
(b) *Melanchthon, Monica J.* Song of Songs. Global bible commentary. 2005 ⇒2443. 180-185.

4196 **Mitchell, Christopher W.** The Song of Songs. 2003 ⇒20,3965. [R]Faith & Mission 23/1 (2005) 94-96 (*Jones, David W.*).

4197 **Morla Asensio, Víctor** Poemas de amor y de deseo: Cantar de los Cantares. 2004 ⇒20,3967. [R]SalTer 93 (2005) 71-72 (*Sanz Giménez-Rico, Enrique*).

4198 [E]**Norris, Richard** The Song of Songs: interpreted by early christian and medieval commentators. 2003 ⇒19,4142; 20,3968. [R]BiblInterp 13 (2005) 446-448 (*Elliott, Mark W.*); VJTR 69 (2005) 639-640 (*Meagher, P.M.*); RBLit 7 (2005) 472-474 (*Brenner, Athalya*).

4199 *Pasternak, Nurit* The Judeo-Italian translation of the *Song of Songs*_ and Ya'aqov da Corinaldo. Materia giudaica 10/2 (2005) 267-282.

4200 [E]**Rosenbaum, Hans-Udo** NILUS von Ancyra, Schriften, 1: Kommentar zum Hohenlied. PTS 57: 2004 ⇒20,3971. [R]EThL 81 (2005) 534-536 (*Auwers, Jean-Marie*).

4201 *Schwienhorst-Schönberger, Ludger* Il Cantico dei cantici. Introduzione AT. 2005 ⇒1159. 587-597.

4202 **Simoens, Yves** Le Cantique des Cantiques: livre de la plénitude: une lecture anthropologique et théologique. 2004 ⇒20,3973. [R]RSR 93 (2005) 590-591 (*Abadie, Philippe*);

4203 Il libro della pienezza: il Cantico dei Cantici: una lettura antropologica e teologica. Collana biblica: Bo 2005, Dehoniane 208 pp. €15.50. 88-10-22126-5.

4204 **Stoop-van Paridon, Petronella** The Song of Songs: a philological analysis of the Hebrew book שִׁיר הַשִּׁירִים. [D]*Muraoka, Takamitsu*:

ANESt.S 17: Lv 2005, Peeters xvi; 539 pp. €90. 90-429-1638-9. Diss. Leiden; Bibl. 509-522.

4205 *Weems, Renita J.* Song of Songs. OT survey. 2005 ⇒413. 262-269.

4206 [E]**Wright, J. Robert** Proverbs, Ecclesiastes, Song of Solomon. ACCS OT 9: DG 2005, InterVarsity xxix; 434 pp. €32.86. 0-8308-1479-5.

4207 **Zakovitch, Yair** Das Hohelied. HThK.AT: 2004 ⇒20,3977. [R]JETh 19 (2005) 238-240 (*Fischer, Stefan*).

## E7.4 **Canticum**, *themata, versiculi*

4208 The Song of Songs: the honeybee in the garden. Ph 2005, Jewish Publication Society 144 pp. $75. 0-8276-0811-X. Illuminations, commentary by *Debra Band*; Bible translations by the Jewish Publication Society and *David Band.*

4209 *Auwers, Jean-Marie; Gallas, William* Les pères devant le Cantiques des cantiques. Regards croisés. 2005 ⇒338. 9-29.

4210 *Bahar, Shlomo* Perfume in the Song of Songs: an erotic motive and sign of social class. Shnaton 15 (2005) 39-52. **H.**

4211 **Bosatra, Cesare** Pregare con il Cantico dei Cantici. R 2005, ADP 191 pp. 88-7357-368-1.

4212 *Burton, Joan B.* Themes of female desire and self-assertion in the Song of Songs and Hellenistic poetry. Perspectives on the Song of Songs. 2005 ⇒401. 180-205.

4213 **Chrétien, Jean-Louis** Symbolique du corps: la tradition chrétienne du Cantique des cantiques. Épiméthée: P 2005, Presses Universitaires de France 310 pp. 21305-49861.

4214 *Davidson, Richard M.* Is God present in the Song of Songs?. JATS 16 (2005) 143-154 [OTA 29,296].

4215 *Dell, Katharine J.* Does the Song of Songs have any connections to wisdom?. Perspectives on the Song of Songs. 2005 ⇒401. 8-26.

4216 *Delville, Jean-Pierre* Le Cantiques des cantiques au XVIe siècle: vers l'unité du sens. Regards croisés. 2005 ⇒338. 30-59.

4217 *Ena, Jean Emmanuel de* Quel est le sens du Cantique des cantiques?: un 'cas limite d'herméneutique biblique'. Regards croisés. 2005 ⇒ 338. 109-129.

4218 **Ernst, Judith** Song of Songs: erotic poetry. 2003 ⇒19,4155. [R]Faith & Mission 22/2 (2005) 121-122 (*Rooker, Mark F.*); OTEs 18 (2005) 141-143 (*Branch, Robin G.*).

4219 *Exum, J. Cheryl* "Seeing" the Song of Songs: some artistic visions of the bible's love lyrics. Das AT und die Kunst. ATM 15: 2005 ⇒711. 91-127;

4220 The poetic genius of the Song of Songs. Perspectives on the Song of Songs. 2005 ⇒401. 78-95.

4221 *Fischer, Stefan* "Er küsse mich!"—sehnsüchtige Phantasien: assoziatives Lesen als Annäherung an Hoheslied. OTEs 18 (2005) 204-222.

4222 (a) *Gaier, Ulrich* Lieder der Liebe: HERDERS Hohelied-Interpretation. Perspectives on the Song of Songs. 2005 ⇒401. 317-337.
(b) *Gelabert, Martín* Que me bese con el beso de su boca!: la exégesis de San BERNARDO al exordio del mejor Cantar. CTom 132 (2005) 209-223.

4223 *Görg, Manfred* Der Granatapfel in der Bildsprache des Hohenliedes: ein Beitrag zur schöpfungs- und lebensnahen Bibelauslegung. [F]LAUB, F.: Bibel-Schule-Leben 6: 2005 ⇒87. 25-31.

4224 *Grossberg, Daniel* Nature, humanity, and love in Song of Songs. Interp. 59 (2005) 229-242.

4225 [E]**Guglielmetti, Rossana** GILBERTUS Stanfordensis: tractatus super Cantica Canticorum. Per verba 16: 2002 ⇒18,3851. [R]StMed 46 (2005) 205-207 (*Catalani, Luigi*).

4226 *Güthenke, Constanze* 'Do not awaken love until it is ready': George Seferis' *Asma Asmaton* and the translation of intimacy;

4227 *Hagedorn, Anselm C.* Jealousy and desire at night: *Fragmentum Grenfellianum* and Song of Songs. Perspectives on the Song of Songs. 2005 ⇒401. 338-356/206-227.

4228 *Hess, Richard S.* Song of Songs: not just a dirty book. BiRe 21/5 (2005) 30-40 [OTA 29,164].

4229 *Hunter, Richard* 'Sweet talk': Song of Songs and the traditions of Greek poetry. Perspectives on the Song. 2005 ⇒401. 228-244.

4230 *Jericke, Detlef* Toponyme im Hohenlied. ZDPV 121 (2005) 39-58.

4231 *Jung, Franz* 'Die Zeit zum Singen ist da' (Hld 2,12): das Hohelied Salomos und seine Bedeutung in Geschichte und Gegenwart. IKaZ 34 (2005) 341-356;

4232 Le *Cantique des cantiques* et sa signification. Com(F) 30/5-6 (2005) 47-58.

4233 **King, J. Christopher** ORIGEN on the Song of Songs as the spirit of scripture: the bridegroom's perfect marriage-song. Oxford Theological Monographs: Oxf 2005, OUP 292 pp.

4234 *Linafelt, Tod* The arithmetic of Eros. Interp. 59 (2005) 244-258.

4235 *Loprieno, Antonio* Searching for a common background: Egyptian love poetry and the biblical Song of Songs. Perspectives on the Song of Songs. 2005 ⇒401. 105-135.

4236 *Mies, Françoise* Du lien entre le Cantique des cantiques et sa postérité. Regards croisés. 2005 ⇒338. 151-173.

4237 *Moyn, Samuel* Divine and human love: Franz ROSENZWEIG's history of the Song of Songs. JSQ 12 (2005) 194-212.

4238 *Müller, Hans-Peter*† Zum Werden des Lyrischen:am Beispiel des Hohenliedes und frühgriechischer Lyrik. Perspectives on the Song of Songs. 2005 ⇒401. 245-259.

4239 *Paul, Shalom M.* The 'plural of ecstasy' in Mesopotamian and biblical love poetry <1995>;

4240 A lover's garden of verse: literal and metaphorical imagery in ancient Near Eastern love poetry <1997>. Divrei Shalom. CHANE 23: 2005 ⇒273. 239-252/271-284.

4241 *Pelletier, Anne-Marie* Petit bilan herméneutique de l'histoire du Cantique des cantiques. Regards croisés. 2005 ⇒338. 130-147.

4242 *Salvesen, Alison* Pigs in the camps and the breasts of my lambs: Song of Songs in the Syriac tradition. Perspectives on the Song of Songs. 2005 ⇒401. 260-273.

4243 *Scheffler, Eben* In praise of Canticles: a (male) reaction to the second feminist companion to the Song of Songs. OTEs 18 (2005) 309-322.

4244 *Schnabl Schweitzer, Carol L.* Song of Songs: a metaphorical vision for pastoral care. Interp. 59 (2005) 278-289.

4245 *Schwienhorst-Schönberger, Ludger* Das Hohelied und die Kontextualität des Verstehens. Studien zum AT. SBAB 40: 2005 <2001> ⇒ 298. 259-270.

4246 *Scordato, Cosimo Il Cantico dei Cantici*: per una *trans*-apparentia. Ho Theológos 23 (2005) 471-478.

4247 *Sonnet, Jean-Pierre* Du chant érotique au chant mystique: le ressort poétique du Cantique des cantiques. Regards croisés. 2005 ⇒338. 79-105.

4248 *Vernus, Pascal* Le *Cantique des Cantiques* et l'Egypte pharaonique: état de la question. Perspectives on the Song of Songs. 2005 ⇒401. 150-162.

4249 *Virgili dal Prà, Rosanna* Il Cantico dei Cantici: struttura letterario poetica e accostamenti con la poesia greca. Il bello della bibbia. 2005 ⇒357. 79-104.

4250 *Volfing, Annette* Middle High German appropriations of the Song of Songs: allegorical interpretation and narrative extrapolation. Perspectives on the Song of Songs. 2005 ⇒401. 294-316.

4251 *Wénin, André* Interpréter?: un exégète face au Cantique. Regards croisés. 2005 ⇒338. 60-76.

4252 **Meis, Anneliese; Castellano, Antonio; Pinilla, Juan** El dinamismo del encuentro entre Dios y el hombre en los comentarios al 'Cantar' de ORÍGENES, GREGORIO de Nisa y JUAN de la Cruz. 1999 ⇒19, 4168. [R]RTL 36 (2005) 109-110 (*Fabry, G.*) [Cant 1,2-16; 2,3-5,9].

4253 *Dobbs-Allsopp, Fred W.* The delight of beauty and Song of Songs 4:1-7. Interp. 59 (2005) 260-277.

4254 *Paul, Shalom* An unrecognized medical idiom in Song of Songs 6:12 and Job 9:21. Divrei Shalom. 2005 <1978> ⇒273. 91-93.

4255 *Pinto, Sebastiano* La natura teologica dell'amore umano: Cantico dei Cantici 8,5-7. Rivista di science religiose 19/1 (2005) 5-31.

4256 *Jarschel, Haidi; Schmidt, Flávio* O corpo expropriado—uma ameaça para a paz. Espaços 13 (2005) 167-177 [OTA 29,164] [Cant 8,5-14].

4257 *Exum, J. Cheryl* The little sister and Solomon's vineyard: Song of Songs 8:8-12 as a lovers' dialogue. [F]FOX, M. 2005 ⇒43. 269-282.

## E7.5 *Libri sapientiales*—**Wisdom literature**

4258 [T]**Alster, Bendt** Wisdom of ancient Sumer. Bethesda, MD 2005, CDL 426 pp. 1-88305-392-7. 72 pages of pl.; Bibl. 9-15.

4259 **Backes, Burkhard** Das altägyptische "Zweiwegebuch": Studien zu den Sargtext-Sprüchen 1029-1130. ÄA 69: Wsb 2005, Harrassowitz 466 pp. €98. 3-477-05237-6. Bibl. 439-445.

4260 *Calduch-Benages, Nuria* Il lavoro in Proverbi e Siracide. PSV 52 (2005) 21-37.

4261 *Clifford, Richard J.* Introduction to wisdom literature. OT survey. 2005 ⇒413. 222-238.

4262 *Collins, John J.* The biblical precedent for natural theology. Encounters. 2005 <1977> ⇒200. 91-104.

4263 *Contini, Riccardo* Bibliografia ahiqariana. Il saggio Ahiqar. StBi 148: 2005 ⇒52. 275-325.

4264 *Dijkstra, Meindert* Opvoeding in de Levant. Phoe. 51 (2005) 55-74.

4265 *Ego, Beate* Zwischen Aufgabe und Gabe: theologische Implikationen des Lernens in der alttestamentlichen und antik-jüdischen Überlieferung. Religiöses Lernen. WUNT 180: 2005 ⇒384. 1-26.

4266 **Estes, Daniel J.** Handbook on the Wisdom books and Psalms: Job, Psalms, Proverbs, Ecclesiastes, Song of Songs. GR 2005, Baker 448 pp. $35. 0-8010-2699-7. Bibl.

4267 **Fontaine, Carole R.** Smooth words: women, proverbs and performance in biblical wisdom. JSOT.S 356: 2002 ⇒18,3896... 20,4011. [R]HeyJ 46 (2005) 216-217 (*Hill, Robert C.*); BiblInterp 13 (2005) 69-71 (*McKinlay, Judith E.*).

4268 **Freuling, Georg** 'Wer eine Grube gräbt...': der Tun-Ergehen-Zusammenhang und sein Wandel in der alttestamentlichen Weisheitsliteratur. WMANT 102: 2004 ⇒20,4012. [R]OLZ 100 (2005) 274-278 (*Scherer, Andreas*); JETh 19 (2005) 233-235 (*Steinberg, Julius*).

4269 *Garmus, Ludovico* Educação dos filhos nos livros sapienciais. Estudos Bíblicos 85 (2005) 30-43.

4270 **Gilbert, Maurice** La sapienza del cielo: Proverbi, Giobbe, Qohèlet, Siracide, Sapienza. CinB 2005, San Paolo 286 pp. 88-215-5357-4. Bibl. 251-252.

4271 *Greenspoon, Leonard* Translating biblical words of wisdom into the modern world. [F]FOX, M. 2005 ⇒43. 389-405.

4272 *Hagen, Fredrik The prohibitions*: a New Kingdom didactic text. JEA 91 (2005) 125-164.

4273 **Junge, Friedrich** Die Lehre Ptahhoteps und die Tugenden der ägyptischen Welt. OBO 193: 2003 ⇒19,4201; 20,4023. [R]WO 35 (2005) 7-21 (*Quack, Joachim F.*); GGA 257 (2005) 2-9 (*Lippert, Sandra*).

4274 *Loose, Jana* Kind en opvoeding in het oude Egypte. Phoe. 51 (2005) 75-88.

4275 *MacLelland, Joseph C.* The end of wisdom. Arc 33 (2005) 519-525.

4276 *Marböck, Johannes* Zwischen Erfahrung, Systematik und Bekenntnis –zu Eigenart und Bedeutung der alttestamentlichen Weisheitsliteratur. Weisheit...Frömmigkeit. ÖBS 29: 2005 <1999> ⇒254. 201-214;

4277 Lohn–Verdienst–umsonst?: Stationen eines Gesprächs im Alten Testament. Weisheit...Frömmigkeit. 2005 <2002> ⇒254. 227-236 [Exod 34,6-7].

4278 *Merlos Arroyo, Francisco* De la sabiduría bíblica a la sabiduría pastoral: un esbozo del ministerio pastoral en clave sapiencial. [F]JUNCO GARZA, C.: Estudios Bíblicos Mexicanos 4: 2005 ⇒74. 79-101.

4279 *Milani, Marcello* Una reazione biblica: sapienza e rivelazione. StPat 52 (2005) 441-445.

4280 **Morgan, Donn** The making of sages: biblical wisdom and contemporary culture. 2002 ⇒18,3906; 20,4028. [R]RBLit (2005)* (*Washington, Harold C.*).

4281 **Morla Asensio, Victor** Libros Sapienciales y otros escritos. Introducción al estudio de la Biblia 5: 1994 ⇒10,3214... 15,154. [R]RB 112 (2005) 294-297 (*Loza Vera, J.*).

4282 **Müllner, I.** Das hörende Herz: Weisheit in der hebräischen Bibel. Stu 2005, Kohlhammer 159 pp. €16.80. 3-17-018287-0.

4283 *Parpola, Simo* Il retroterra assiro di Ahiqar. Il saggio Ahiqar. StBi 148: 2005 ⇒52. 91-112.

4284 *Raineri, Osvaldo* I detti di Achicar in alcuni codici etiopici della Vaticana. Miscellanea Bibliothecae Apostolicae Vaticanae 12. Studi e Testi 430: Città del Vaticano 2005, Biblioteca Apostolica Vaticana. 483-499.

4285 *Roccati, Alessandro* Note letterarie-II: imparare a memoria nell'età menfita. ZÄS 132/2 (2005) 161-165.

4286 *Roos, J. de* Kinderen en opvoeding bij de Hettieten. Phoe. 51 (2005) 89-98.
4287 *Sanders, Jack T.* Wisdom, theodicy, death and the evolution of intellectual traditions. JSJ 36 (2005) 263-277.
4288 *Sánchez, Jorge Piedad* Algunos aspectos generales de la sabduría bíblica. Qol 39 (2005) 19-39.
4289 *Schwienhorst-Schönberger, Ludger* Den Ruf der Weisheit hören: Lernkonzepte in der alttestamentlichen Weisheitsliteratur. Religiöses Lernen. WUNT 180: 2005 ⇒384. 69-82.
4290 **Shapiro, Rami** The divine feminine in biblical wisdom literature: selections annotated & explained. Woodstock, VT 2005, Skylight P. xxxix; 184 pp. 1-594-73109-8. Foreword by *Cynthia Bourgeault*; Bibl. 183-184.
4291 **Sinnott, Alice M.** The personification of wisdom. MSSOTS: Aldershot 2005, Ashgate x; 208 pp. £45/$100.
4292 *Terrinoni, Ubaldo* La sapienza del cuore. CoSe 54/4 (2005) 40-49.
4293 *Veenhof, K.R.* Kind en opvoeding in het oude Mesopotamië. Phoe. 51 (2005) 99-124.
4294 *Verboom, Wim* La catechesi nella scrittura. SdT 17 (2005) 2-22.
4295 *Wénin, André* Un'arte di vivere... la speranza. Dalla violenza. 2005 <1998> ⇒323. 179-210.
4296 *Whybray, Norman* Slippery words: IV: wisdom <1977-1978>. 6-9;
4297 Wisdom literature. <1990>. 12-15;
4298 Two Jewish theologies: Job and Ecclesiastes. <1980>. 179-193;
4299 Wisdom literature in the reigns of David and Solomon <1982>. 223-236;
4300 The social world of the wisdom writers <1989>. 237-260;
4301 The sage in the Israelite royal court <1990>. 261-267;
4302 Prophecy and wisdom <1982>. Wisdom . MSSOTS: 2005 ⇒324. 271-289.
4303 **Wilke, Alexa Friederike** Kronerben der Weisheit: Gott, König und Frommer in der didaktischen Literatur Ägyptens und Israels. [D]*Spieckermann, Hermann* 2005, Diss. Göttingen [ThLZ 130,884].
4304 *Zenger, Erich* Peculiarità e significato della sapienza di Israele. Introduzione AT. 2005 ⇒1159. 497-506.

## E7.6 **Proverbiorum liber,** *themata, versiculi*

4305 **Alster, Bendt** Proverbs of ancient Sumer. 1997 ⇒13,3153. [R]RA 99 (2005) 13-38 (*Taylor, Jon*).
4306 *Beauchamp, Paul* Le proverbe et le répons. Pages exégétiques. LeDiv 202: 2005 <1993> ⇒183. 241-260.
4307 *Brenner, Athalya* Proverbs. Global bible commentary. 2005 ⇒2443. 163-174.
4308 *Brown, William P.* The didactic power of metaphor in the aphoristic sayings of Proverbs. JSOT 29 (2005) 133-154;
4309 The law and the sages: a reexamination of *tôrâ* in Proverbs. [F]MCBRIDE, D. 2005 ⇒98. 251-280.
4310 *Clifford, Richard J.* Your attention please!: heeding the proverbs. JSOT 29 (2005) 155-163;
4311 The community of the book of Proverbs. [F]MCBRIDE, D. 2005 ⇒98. 281-293.

4312 *Collins, John J.* Proverbial wisdom and the Yahwist vision. Encounters. 2005 <1980> ⇒200. 105-116.

4313 *Cook, Johann* 'Theological/ideological' *Tendenz* in the Septuagint–LXX Proverbs: a case study. [F]LUST, J.: BEThL 192: 2005 ⇒92. 65-79;

4314 The text-critical value of the Septuagint of Proverbs;

4315 *Cook, John A.* Genericity, tense, and verbal patterns in the sentence literature of Proverbs. [F]FOX, M. 2005 ⇒43. 407-419/117-133.

4316 *Crenshaw, James L.* A proverb in the mouth of a fool. [F]FOX, M. 2005 ⇒43. 103-115.

4317 *Fox, Michael V.* The rhetoric of disjointed proverbs. JSOT 29 (2005) 165-177;

4318 LXX-Proverbs as a text-critical resource. Textus 22 (2005) 95-128.

4319 *Häusl, Maria* Zuraten, zurechtweisen und sich zurückhalten: Sprüche zur Sprache aus der älteren Weisheit (Spr 10-22 und 25-29). BZ 49 (2005) 26-45.

4320 *Holmstedt, Robert D.* Word order in the book of Proverbs. [F]FOX, M. 2005 ⇒43. 135-154.

4321 *Jenni, Ernst* Epistemische Modalitäten im Proverbienbuch. Studien II. 2005 <1999> ⇒232. 36-47.

4322 **Kayandakazi, Lucie** La traduction du livre des Proverbes en Kirundi: enjeux d'exégèse et d'inculturation. Città del Vaticano 2005, Urbaniana University Pr. 294 pp. 88401-80893. Préface *Bujo Bénézet.*

4323 **Koptak, Paul E.** Proverbs. NIV Application Comm.: 2003 ⇒19, 4243. [R]BS 162 (2005) 500-501 (*Zuck, Roy B.*).

4324 *Marböck, Johannes* Erfahrungen mit dem Menschsein—am Beispiel der alttestamentlichen Spruchliteratur. Weisheit und Frömmigkeit. ÖBS 29: 2005 <1997> ⇒254. 215-226.

4325 *Mazzinghi, Luca* Il libro dei Proverbi: voce umana e voce divina. Il bello della bibbia. 2005 ⇒357. 105-127.

4326 *Miller, Cynthia L.* Translating biblical proverbs in African cultures: between form and meaning. BiTr 56 (2005) 129-144.

4327 **Miller, John Wolf** Proverbs. Believers church bible commentary: 2004 ⇒20,4061. [R]RBLit (2005)* (*Glazov, Gregory*).

4328 *Schwienhorst-Schönberger, Ludger* Il libro dei Proverbi. Introduzione AT. 2005 ⇒1159. 561-573.

4329 *Strola, Germana* Il desiderare autentico descritto attraverso un antonimo ovvero: le massime sul pigro del libro dei Proverbi. RivBib 53 (2005) 3-30.

4330 *Szlos, M. Beth* Body parts as metaphor and the value of a cognitive approach: a study of the female figures in Proverbs via metaphor. Metaphor in the Hebrew Bible. BEThL 187: 2005 ⇒799. 187-195.

4331 **Tauberschmidt, Gerhard** Secondary parallelism: a study of translation technique in LXX Proverbs. SBL.Academia Biblica 15: 2004 ⇒ 20,4066. [R]CBQ 67 (2005) 328-329 (*McLay, R. Timothy*); BiOr 62 (2005) 578-579 (*Van der Louw, T.A.W.*).

4332 [ET]**Thomson, Robert W.** Hamam: commentary on the book of Proverbs. Hebrew University Armenian Studies 5: Lv 2005, Peeters viii; 307 pp. €40. Edition of the Armenian text, translation, notes, introd.

4333 *Van Leeuwen, Raymond C.* The book of Proverbs. OT survey. 2005 ⇒413. 239-248.

4334 *Waard, Jan de* Indices phonétiques hébreux dans et derrière le grec de la Septante de Proverbes. L'apport de la Septante. LeDiv 203: 2005 ⇒764. 105-117.

4335 **Waltke, Bruce K.** The book of Proverbs: chapters 1-15. NICOT: 2004 ⇒20,4067. [R]RSR 93 (2005) 591 (*Abadie, Philippe*); RBLit (2005)* (*Ortlund, Eric*);

4336 chap. 16-31. NICOT: GR 2005, Eerdmans 623 pp. $50. 0802827764.

4337 *Wegner, Paul D.* Discipline in the book of Proverbs: 'to spank or not to spank?'. JETS 48 (2005) 715-732 [OTA 30,48].

4338 *Whybray, Norman* Proverbs, book of <1976>. 3-5;

4339 Poverty, wealth, and point of view in Proverbs. <1988-1989>. 58-62;

4340 Thoughts on the composition of Proverbs 10-29. Wisdom. MSSOTS: 2005 <1992> ⇒324. 63-75.

[E]**Wright, J. Robert** Proverbs, Eccl., Song 2005 ⇒4206.

4341 *Yoder, Christine R.* Forming 'fearers of Yahweh': repetition and contradiction as pedagogy in Proverbs. [F]FOX, M. 2005 ⇒43. 167-183.

4342 *Yona, Shamir* Exegetical and stylistic analysis of a number of aphorisms in the book of Proverbs: mitigation of monotony in repetitions in parallel texts. [F]FOX, M. 2005 ⇒43. 155-165.

4343 *Høyland Lavik, Marta* Forholdet mellom den framande kvinna, Fru Visdom og Fru D[a- Kreis]rskap i Proverbia 1-9. NTT 106/4 (2005) 253-269.

4344 **Müller, Achim** Proverbien 1-9: der Weisheit neue Kleider. BZAW 291: 2000 ⇒16,3543... 18,3963. [R]ThRv 101 (2005) 30-32 (*Schwienhorst-Schönberger, Ludger*).

4345 *Pemberton, Glenn D.* The rhetoric of the father in Proverbs 1-9. JSOT 30 (2005) 63-82.

4346 *Vermeylen, Jacques* Les sept colonnes de la sagesse: une 'maison de paroles' en Pr 1-9. [F]MALAISE, M. 2005 ⇒95. 111-136.

4347 *Viviers, Hennie* The 'body' and Lady Wisdom (Proverbs 1-9). OTEs 18 (2005) 879-890.

4348 *Whybray, Norman* Some literary problems in Proverbs I-IX. Wisdom. MSSOTS: 2005 <1966> ⇒324. 30-44.

4349 *Yoder, Christine R.* The objects of our affections: emotions and the moral life in Proverbs 1-9. [F]BRUEGGEMANN, W.—COUSAR, C.. 2005 ⇒16. 73-88.

4350 *Fuhs, Hans F.* Das Bildungsprogramm des Sprüche-Buches: Beobachtungen zu Spr 1,1-6 und 2,1-22. ThGl 95 (2005) 147-163.

4351 *Weinfeld, Moshe* 'You will find favour ... in the sight of God and man' (Proverbs 3.4): the history of an idea. Normative and sectarian Judaism. Library of Second Temple Studies 54: 2005 ⇒2732. 239-250.

4352 *Fontaine, Carole R.* Visual metaphors and Proverbs 5:15-20: some archaeological reflections on gendered iconography. [F]FOX, M. 2005 ⇒43. 185-202.

4353 *Floor, Sebastian J.* Poetic fronting in a wisdom poetry text: the information structure of Proverbs 7. JNSL 31/1 (2005) 23-58.

4354 *Forti, Tova; Talshir, Zipora* Proverbs 7 in MT and LXX: form and content. Textus 22 (2005) 129-167.

4355 *Whybray, Norman* Proverbs VIII 22-31 and its supposed prototypes. Wisdom. MSSOTS: 2005 <1965> ⇒324. 19-29.

4356 *Kuntz, J. Kenneth* Affirming less as more: scholarly engagements with aphoristic rhetoric. JSOT 29 (2005) 205-242 [Prov 10-29].

4357 **Heim, Knut Martin** Like grapes of gold set in silver: an interpretation of proverbial clusters in Proverbs 10:1-22:16. BZAW 273: 2001 ⇒17,3550... 20,4074. [R]TrinJ 26 (2005) 325-327 (*Lyu, Sunmyung*).

4358 *Whybray, Norman* Yahweh-sayings and their contexts in Proverbs, 10,1-22,16. Wisdom. MSSOTS: 2005 <1979> ⇒324. 45-57.

4359 **Witek, Bernard** Dio e i suoi figli: analisi retorica della prima raccolta salomonica (Pr 10,1-22,16). [D]*Meynet, Roland*: TGr.T 117: R 2005, E.P.U.G. 412 pp. €23. 88-7839-020-8. Diss. Gregoriana; Bibl. 379-392 [R]RBLit (2005)* (*West, James*).

4360 *Schipper, Bernd U.* Die Lehre des Amenemope und Prov 22,17-24, 22: eine Neubestimmung des literarischen Verhältnisses. ZAW 117 (2005) 53-72, 232-248.

4361 *Shupak, Nili* The Instruction of Amenemope and Proverbs 22:17-24:22 from the perspective of contemporary research. [F]FOX, M. 2005 ⇒43. 203-220.

4362 *Whybray, Norman* The structure and composition of Proverbs 22:17-24:22. Wisdom. MSSOTS: 2005 <1994> ⇒324. 76-89.

4363 *Melero Gracia, Mª Luisa* 'Para que esté en YHWH tu confianza [...]': estudio sobre Pr 22,17-21. La bíblia i els immigrants. 2005 ⇒ 471. 93-119.

4364 **Nguyen, Dinh Anh-Nhue** Figlio mio, se il tuo cuore è saggio... studio esegetico-teologico del discorso paterno in Pro 23,15-28. [D]*Calduch Benages, Núria* 2005, Diss. Gregoriana [RTL 37,610].

4365 *Ribeiro, Osvaldo L.* Como que pellos chifres: o vento na crição, segundo Pr 30,4. Fragmenta de Cultura [Goías] 15 (2005) 1371-1383 [OTA 29,63].

4366 *Fischer, Irmtraud* Gotteslehrerin: ein Streifzug durch Spr 31,10-31 auf den Pfaden unterschiedlicher Methodik. BZ 49 (2005) 237-253.

4367 *Hurowitz, Victor A.* The woman of valor and a woman large of head: matchmaking in the ancient Near East. [F]FOX, M. 2005 ⇒43. 221-234 [Prov 31,10-31].

4368 *Nwaoru, Emmanuel O.* Image of the woman of substance in Proverbs 31:10-31 and African context. BN 127 (2005) 41-66.

4369 *Scaiola, Donatella* Una donna perfetta?: a proposito di Proverbi 31, 10-31. AnStR 6 (2005) 321-333.

## E7.7 *Ecclesiastes*—**Qohelet**; *textus, themata, versiculi*

4370 Kohelet. Entdecken: Stu 2005, Kathol. Bibelwerk 144 pp. 3-460-20063-4. Katholisches Bibelwerk.

4371 *Aitken, James K.* Rhetoric and poetry in Greek Ecclesiastes. BIOSCS 38 (2005) 55-78.

4372 **Anaya Luengo, Pedro** El hombre, destinatario de los dones de Dios en Qohélet. [D]*Calduch Benages, Núria*: R 2005, Diss. Gregoriana.

4373 [T]**Boira Sales, José** San JERÓNIMO: comentario al Eclesiastés. 2004 ⇒20,4088. [R]Studium 45 (2005) 495-496 (*López, L.*); Burg. 46 (2005) 613-615 (*Sánchez, Manuel Diego*).

4374 *Bolin, Thomas* Rivalry and resignation: GIRARD and Qoheleth on the divine-human relationship. Bib. 86 (2005) 245-259.

4375 *Christianson, Eric S.* VOLTAIRE's précis of Ecclesiastes: a case study in the bible's afterlife. JSOT 29 (2005) 455-484.

4376 **Delkurt, Holger** "Der Mensch ist dem Vieh gleich, das vertilgt wird": Tod und Hoffnung gegen den Tod in Ps 49 und bei Kohelet. BThSt 50: Neuk 2005, Neuk 117 pp. €18. 3-7887-1891-9. Bibl. 107-113 [R]UF 37 (2005) 821-822 (*Loretz, Oswald*).

4377 *Duarte, Samuel de Jesus* Qohélet: resistência ao helenismo?. AtT 9 (2005) 353-362.

4378 *Forti, Tova* The fly and the dog: observations on ideational polarity in the book of Qoheleth. [F]FOX, M. 2005 ⇒43. 235-255.

4379 **Fox, Michael V.** Ecclesiastes. 2004 ⇒20,4095. [R]Interp. 59 (2005) 192-194 (*Crenshaw, James L.*).

4380 **Johnston, Robert K.** Useless beauty: Ecclesiastes through the lens of contemporary film. 2004 ⇒20,4099. [R]OTEs 18 (2005) 145-146 (*Maré, L.P.*); RBLit (2005)* (*Shepherd, David*); BTB 35 (2005) 112 (*Crook, Zeba A.*).

4381 *Koosed, Jennifer L.; Seesengood, Robert P.* Constructions and collusions: the making and unmaking of identity in Qoheleth and Hebrews. Hebrews. BiblInterp 75: 2005 ⇒395. 265-280.

4382 **Krüger, Thomas** Qoheleth: a commentary. [T]*Dean, O.C., Jr.*: Hermeneia: 2004 ⇒20,4102. [R]BiTr 56 (2005) 218-19 (*Ogden, Graham S.*).

4384 *Laurent, Françoise* Le livre de Qohéleth ou la retenue de l'écriture. RevSR 79 (2005) 5-22.

4385 **Lee, Eunny P.** The vitality of enjoyment in Qohelet's theological rhetoric. BZAW 353: B 2005, De Gruyter xiii; 168 pp. €68. 3-11-01-8441-9. Diss. Princeton Sem.; Bibl. 141-158.

4386 (a) **Lohfink, Norbert** Qoheleth: a continental commentary. [T]*McEvenue, Sean*: Continental commentaries: 2003 ⇒19,4292; 20,4106. [R]BiTr 56 (2005) 216-218 (*Ogden, Graham S.*);
(b) *Marti, Kurt* Wieso heute noch Kohelet?: ein Schlusswort. Kohelet. entdecken: 2005 ⇒4370. 136-139.

4387 *Maussion, Marie* El libro del Eclesiastés: el despertar de la conciencia creyenye. SelTeol 44 (2005) 119-124 <Christus 200 (2003) 427-434.

4388 **Maussion, Marie** Le mal, le bien et le jugement de Dieu dans le livre de Qohélet. OBO 190: 2003 ⇒19,4296; 20,4108. [R]BiOr 62 (2005) 112-116 (*Schoors, Antoon*); Bib. 86 (2005) 272-275 (*Gilbert, Maurice*).

4389 *Mazzinghi, Luca* Il lavoro umano tra illusione e realtà nel libro del Qohelet. PSV 52 (2005) 39-55.

4390 **Miller, Douglas B.** Symbol and rhetoric in Ecclesiastes: the place of 'Hebel' in Qohelet's work. Academia Biblica 2: 2002 ⇒18,4014; 19, 4299. [R]JR 85 (2005) 112-114 (*Christianson, Eric S.*).

4391 **Mills, Mary E.** Reading Ecclesiastes: a literary and cultural exegesis. 2003 ⇒19,4300. [R]Anton. 80 (2005) 167-168 (*Nobile, Marco*).

4392 [T]**Murray, Campion; Karris, Robert J.** Works of BONAVENTURE, 7: commentary on Ecclesiastes. Saint Bonaventure, NY 2005, Franciscan Institute 461 pp. $40. 1-57659-197-2. Introd., notes. [R]ATOR 36 (2005) 797-798.

4393 *Prior, John M.* Ecclesiastes. Global bible commentary. 2005 ⇒2443. 175-179.

4394 [E]**Schoors, Antoon** Qohelet in the context of wisdom. BEThL 136: 1998 ⇒14,266... 17,3575. Colloque International 1995 Leuven. [R]OLZ 100 (2005) 285-291 (*Lux, Rüdiger*).

4395 *Schultz, Richard L.* A sense of timing: a neglected aspect of Qoheleth's wisdom. [F]FOX, M. 2005 ⇒43. 257-267.

4396 *Schulz-Flügel, Eva* Ecclesiastes. BVLI 49 (2005) 31-33.

4397 *Schwienhorst-Schönberger, Ludger* Kohelet: Stand und Perspektiven der Forschung. Studien zum AT. SBAB 40: 2005 <1997> ⇒298. 123-156;

4398 Das Buch Kohelet: eine philosophische Erörterung im Gewand einer Erzählung. Kohelet. entdecken: 2005 ⇒4370. 8-15;

4399 Il libro del Qoèlet. Introduzione AT. 2005 ⇒1159. 574-586.

4400 **Schwienhorst-Schönberger, Ludger** Kohelet. HThK.AT: 2004 ⇒ 20,4119. [R]JETh 19 (2005) 237-238 (*Steinberg, Julius*).

4401 *Sneed, Mark* Qohelet and his 'vulgar' critics: a Jamesonian reading. BiCT 1/1 2004*.

4402 *Towner, W. Sibley* The book of Ecclesiastes. OT survey. 2005 ⇒413. 249-261.

4403 [T]**Vinel, Françoise** L'Ecclésiaste: traduction de la Septante. La Bible d'Alexandrie 18: 2002 ⇒18,4027... 20,4124. [R]CBQ 67 (2005) 130-131 (*Bolin, Thomas M.*); RSR 93 (2005) 608-609 (*Berthelot, Katell*).

4404 **Violante, Luciano** Secondo Qoèlet: dialogo fra gli uomini e Dio. 2004 ⇒20,4125. [R]Il Tetto 246-7 (2005) 147-149 (*Fabrocile, Mario*).

4405 *Whybray, Norman* Ecclesiastes <1990>;

4406 Conservatisme et radicalism [!] dans Qohelet <1979>;

4407 The identification and use of quotations in Ecclesiastes <1981>;

4408 Qoheleth, preacher of joy <1982>. Wisdom. MSSOTS: 2005 ⇒324. 10-11/107-123/124-140/141-152.

[E]**Wright, J. Robert** Proverbs, Ecclesiastes... 2005 ⇒4206.

4409 *Baur, Wolfgang* Viel Wind um nichts?: Kohelet 1,1-11. Kohelet. entdecken: 2005 ⇒4370. 18-27.

4410 **Spaller, Christina** 'Die Geschichte des Buches ist die Geschichte seiner Auslöschung...': die Lektüre von Koh 1,3-11 in vier ausgewählten Kommentaren. 2001 ⇒17,3616; 19,4318. [R]BiblInterp 13 (2005) 72-74 (*Schroer, Silvia*).

4411 *Whybray, Norman* Ecclesiastes 1.5-7 and the wonders of nature. Wisdom. MSSOTS: 2005 <1988> ⇒324. 153-160.

4412 *Leicht, Barbara D.* Jeder ist seines Glückes Schmied?: Kohelet 1,12; 2,4-24. Kohelet. entdecken: 2005 ⇒4370. 30-39.

4413 *Vonach, Andreas* Lebensabschnitte als ständige Chance: Reflexionen über die Zeit (Kohelet 3,1-15). Kohelet. entdecken: 2005 ⇒4370. 42-51.

4414 *Whybray, Norman* 'A time to be born and a time to die': some observations on Ecclesiastes 3.2-8. Wisdom. MSSOTS: 2005 <1991> ⇒ 324. 161-175.

4415 *Remmert, Hans-J.* Für wen doch mühe ich mich ... Kohelet 4,7-12;

4416 *Bauer, Dieter* Vom Recht, sein Leben zu genießen: der rechte Umgang mit dem Geld (Kohelet 5,9-6,9). Kohelet. entdecken: 2005 ⇒ 4370. 54-63/66-75.

4417 *Maussion, Marie* Qohélet vi 1-2: 'Dieu ne permet pas...'. VT 55 (2005) 501-510.

4418 *Laurent, Jean-Paul* Qohélet (ou Ecclésiaste) 7,1-10: mieux vaut la fin que le début. LeD 63 (2005) 7-17.

4419 *Schwienhorst-Schönberger, Ludger* Via media: Koh 7,15-18 und die griechisch-hellenistische Philosophie. Studien zum AT. SBAB 40: 2005 <1998> ⇒298. 157-179.

4420 *Wellmann, Bettina* Wer Gott fürchtet, entgeht den Extremen: Kohelet 7,15-20. Kohelet. entdecken: 2005 ⇒4370. 78-85.

4421 *Whybray, Norman* Qoheleth the immoralist? (Qoh. 7:16-17). Wisdom. MSSOTS: 2005 <1978>⇒324. 93-106.

4422 *Eltrop, Bettina* Frauenfeindliches im Buch Kohelet?: der Mensch allein—ohne Frau (Kohelet 7,23-29). Kohelet. entdecken: 2005 ⇒ 4370. 88-97.

4423 *Schwienhorst-Schönberger, Ludger* 'Bitterer als der Tod ist die Frau' (Koh 7,26): zum Argumentationsgang von Koh 7,25-29. Studien zum AT. SBAB 40: 2005 <2003> ⇒298. 181-193.

4424 *López Garcia, Francisco M.* La imposible interpretación de un mundo trastocado: Qoh 8,9-17. [F]JUNCO GARZA, C. 2005 ⇒74. 177-207.

4425 *Schwienhorst-Schönberger, Ludger* Vertritt Kohelet die Lehre vom absoluten Tod?: zum Argumentationsgang von Koh 9,1-6. Studien zum AT. SBAB 40: 2005 <2003> ⇒298. 195-207.

4426 *Kaiser, Helga* "Carpe diem"—unerträgliche Leichtigkeit?: Kohelet 9, 1-10. Kohelet. entdecken: 2005 ⇒4370. 100-111.

4427 **Raju, Mendem Ananda** A vanity or a well-being according to Qoheleth: an exegetical and critical study of Eccl. 9:1-12. [D]*Boschi, B.G.*: R 2005, Diss. Angelicum [RTL 37,611].

4428 **López Garcia, Francisco Manuel** El desprecio al hombre pobre y sabio: sabiduría, pobreza y poder en el libro de Qohélet a partir de Qoh 9,13-16. Bibliotheca mexicana 19: Mexico 2005, Univ. Pontificia de Mexico 313 pp. 968-5448-22-1.

4429 *Wiegard, Jesaja M.* Nicht warten, sondern leben!: Kohelet 11,1-6. Kohelet. entdecken: 2005 ⇒4370. 114-121.

4430 *Fries, Hans-Joachim* "Freue dich doch, bedenke..."—letzte Worte eines Weisen: Überlegungen zu Koh 11,9-12,7. [F]SEIDL, T.: ATSAT 75: 2005 ⇒137. 101-120.

4431 *Miranda, Juan P.* Lebe jetzt, bevor es zu spät ist!: ein grandioses Finale (Kohelet 11,9-12,7). Kohelet. entdecken: 2005 ⇒4370. 124-33.

4432 *Schwienhorst-Schönberger, Ludger* Buch der Natur: Koh 12,5 und die Rückkehr des Lebens. Studien zum AT. SBAB 40: 2005 <2004> ⇒298. 209-222.

4433 *Blokker, Dries* De wijze die stimuleert, de koning en de landbouwer: RASHBAM's commentaar op Kohelet en de SHA-vertaling. [F]HOOGEWOUD, F. 2005 ⇒63. 11-16 [OTA 29,64] [Qoh 12,11].

### E7.8 *Liber Sapientiae*—**Wisdom of Solomon**

4434 *Baslez, Marie-Françoise* The author of Wisdom and the cultured environment of Alexandria. The book of Wisdom. 2005 ⇒713. 33-52.

4435 *Beauchamp, Paul* Epouser la sagesse—ou n'épouser qu'elle?: une énigme du livre de la Sagesse. Pages exégétiques. LeDiv 202: 2005 <1979, 1991> ⇒183. 299-327.

4436 *Bellia, Giuseppe; Passaro, Angelo* Infinite passion for justice. The book of Wisdom. 2005 ⇒713. 307-328.

4437 [E]**Bellia, Giuseppe; Passaro, Angelo** Il libro della Sapienza: tradizione, redazione, teologia. 2004 ⇒20,655. [R]JSJ 36 (2005) 326-328 (*Berthelot, Katell*); CBQ 67 (2005) 164-165 (*Ceresko, Anthony R.*); SR 34 (2005) 123-124 (*Lavoie, Jean-Jacques*).

4438 *Bellia, Giuseppe* Historical and anthropological reading of the book of Wisdom. The book of Wisdom. 2005 ⇒713. 83-115.
4439 *Collins, John J.* The reinterpretation of apocalyptic traditions in the Wisdom of Solomon. The book of Wisdom. 2005 ⇒713. 143-157.
4440 **Doré, Daniel** O livro da Sabedoria. Cadernos Bíblicos 91: Lisboa 2005, Difusora Bíblica 68 pp.
4441 *Gilbert, Maurice* Potenza e mitezza nella Sapienza di Salomone. PSV 51 (2005) 81-92;
4442 The literary structure of the book of Wisdom: a study of various views. The book of Wisdom. 2005 ⇒713. 19-32.
4443 *Kolarcik, Michael* The book of Wisdom. OT survey. 2005 ⇒413. 494-502.
4444 *Lietaert Peerbolte, Bert J.* The Wisdom of Solomon and the gnostic sophia. [F]LUTTIKHUIZEN, G.: AGJU 59: 2005 ⇒93. 97-114.
4445 **Neher, Martin** Wesen und Wirken der Weisheit in der Sapientia Salomonis. BZAW 333: 2004 ⇒20,4156. [R]ThLZ 130 (2005) 762-764 (*Marböck, Johannes*); CBQ 67 (2005) 503-504 (*Goff, Matthew*); ZKTh 127 (2005) 121-122 (*Premstaller, Volkmar*).
4446 *Puech, Emile* The book of Wisdom and the Dead Sea scrolls: an overview. The book of Wisdom. 2005 ⇒713. 117-141.
4447 *Rizzi, Giovanni* Hermeneutic phenomena in the translation of the Peshitta Wisdom. The book of Wisdom. 2005 ⇒713. 219-253.
4448 *Schroer, Silvia* Il libro della Sapienza. Introduzione AT. 2005 ⇒ 1159. 598-615.
4449 *Winston, David* A century of research on the book of Wisdom. The book of Wisdom. 2005 ⇒713. 1-18.

4450 *Manfredi, Silvana* The trial of the righteous in Wis 5:1-14 (1-7) and in the prophetic traditions. Book of Wisdom. 2005 ⇒713. 159-178.
4451 **Corona, Mary** 'Sophia' God's associate in his works: an exegetical and theological study of Wis 8:1-6. [D]*Juric, S.*: R 2005, Diss. Angelicum [RTL 37,608].
4452 *Vignolo, Roberto* Wisdom, prayer and kingly pattern: theology, anthropology, spirituality of Wis 9;
4453 *Passaro, Angelo* The serpent and the manna or the saving word: exegesis of Wis 16. The book of Wisdom. 2005 ⇒713. 255-82/179-93.
4454 *Beauchamp, Paul* Le salut corporel des justes et la conclusion du livre de la Sagesse. Pages exégétiques. 2005 <1964>⇒183. 261-298.
4455 *Pistone, Rosario* The lyre and the creation: music theory and persuasive strategy in Wisdom 19;
4456 *Mazzinghi, Luca* Wis 19:13-17 and the civil rights of the Jews of Alexandria. The book of Wisdom. 2005 ⇒713. 195-217/53-82.

## E7.9 *Ecclesiasticus, Siracides*; **Wisdom of Jesus Sirach**

4457 *Auwers, Jean-Marie* L'apport du texte long du Siracide au lexique du grec biblique. [F]LUST, J.: BEThL 192: 2005 ⇒92. 33-44.
4458 **Auwers, Jean-Marie** Concordance du Siracide (Grec II et Sacra Parallela). CRB 58: P 2005, Gabalda 93 pp. €25. 2-85021-159-X. Collab. *Églantine Proksch-Strajtmann*.

4459 *Beentjes, Pancratius C.* In search of parallels: Ben Sira and the book of Kings. [F]DI LELLA, A.: CBQ.MS 38: 2005 ⇒35. 118-131;

4460 Some major topics in Ben Sira research. Bijdr. 66 (2005) 131-144.

4461 *Böhmisch, Franz* Die Blattvertauschung (Lage 12 und 13) im griechischen Sirachbuch. PzB 14 (2005) 17-22.

4462 [E]**Calduch Benages, Nuria; Ferrer, Joan; Liesen, Jan** La sabiduría del escriba—Wisdom of the scribe. Biblioteca Midrásica 26: 2003 ⇒ 19,4355; 20,4174. Edición diplomática de la versión siriaca del libro de Ben Sira según el Códice Ambrosiano... [R]JSJ 36 (2005) 94-101 (*Van Peursen, Wido*); HeyJ 46 (2005) 355-356 (*Corley, Jeremy*).

4463 *Camp, Claudia V.* Becoming canon: women, texts, and scribes in Proverbs and Sirach. [F]FOX, M. 2005 ⇒43. 371-387 [Prov 1-9].

4464 *Corley, Jeremy* An intertextual study of Proverbs and Ben Sira. [F]DI LELLA, A.: CBQ.MS 38: 2005 ⇒35. 155-182.

4465 *Crenshaw, James L.* The book of Sirach. OT survey. 2005 ⇒413. 503-530.

4466 *Duggan, Michael W.* Ezra, scribe and priest, and the concerns of Ben Sira. [F]DI LELLA, A.: CBQ.MS 38: 2005 ⇒35. 201-210.

4467 *Egger-Wenzel, Renate* "Faith in God" rather than "fear of God" in Ben Sira and Job: a necessary adjustment in terminology and understanding. [F]DI LELLA, A.: CBQ.MS 38: 2005 ⇒35. 211-226.

4468 *Fabry, Heinz-Josef* Fehler, die es eigentlich nicht geben sollte: Anmerkungen zum Text des griechischen Sirach. [F]LUST, J.: BEThL 192: 2005 ⇒92. 139-149.

4469 *Gilbert, Maurice* Ben Sira, reader of Genesis 1-11. [F]DI LELLA, A.: CBQ.MS 38: 2005 ⇒35. 89-99.

4470 **Harrington, Daniel J.** Jesus Ben Sira of Jerusalem: a biblical guide to living wisely. Interfaces: ColMn 2005, Liturgical ix; 141 pp. $15. 0-8146-5212-3. Bibl. 133-135.

4471 **Kaiser, Otto** Weisheit für das Leben: das Buch JESUS SIRACH. Stu 2005, Radius 195 pp. €19. 3-87173-313-X.

4472 *Marböck, Johannes* Il libro del Siracide. Introduzione AT. 2005 ⇒ 1159. 616-629;

4473 Zur Einführung: neuere Studien und Hilfsmittel zur Arbeit am Sirachbuch. Weisheit und Frömmigkeit. ÖBS 29: 2005 ⇒254. 11-13;

4474 Sirach / Sirachbuch <2000> 15-29;

4475 Structure and redaction history of the book of Ben Sira —review and prospects <1997> 31-45;

4476 Text und Übersetzung—Horizonte einer Auslegung im Prolog zum griechischen Sirachbuch <2003> 47-63;

4477 Ein Weiser an einer Wende–Jesus Sirach–Buch, Person und Botschaft: Versuch einer Gesamtschau <2004> 65-78;

4478 Gerechtigkeit Gottes und Leben nach dem Sirachbuch–ein Antwortversuch in seinem Kontext <2000>. Weisheit und Frömmigkeit. ÖBS 29: 2005 ⇒254. 173-197.

4479 *Owens, J. Edward* "Come, let us be wise": Qoheleth and Ben Sira on true wisdom, with an ear to Pharao's folly;

4480 *Perdue, Leo G.* Ben Sira and the prophets;

4481 *Reiterer, Friedrich* The influence of the book of Exodus on Ben Sira. [F]DI LELLA, A.: CBQ.MS 38: 2005 ⇒35. 227-240/132-154/100-117;

4482 Der Pentateuch in der spätbiblischen Weisheit Ben Siras. Critical study. ATM 20: 2005 ⇒457. 160-183.

4483 [E]**Reiterer, Friedrich V.; Egger-Wenzel, Renate** Zählsynopse zum Buch Ben Sira. FoSub 1: 2003 ⇒19,4374; 20,4188. [R]Gr. 86 (2005) 405-406 (*Calduch-Benages, Nuria*).

4484 **Reymond, Eric D.** Innovations in Hebrew poetry: parallelism and the poems of Sirach. Studies in Biblical Literature 9: 2004 ⇒20, 4189. [R]RBLit 7 (2005) 200-202 (*Beentjes, Pancratius*).

4485 **Seger, Nicolas** L'utilisation de la polysémie des racines hébraïques chez Ben Sira. [D]*Joosten, J.* 2005, 267 pp. Diss. Strasbourg [RTL 37, 612].

4486 *Thiele, Walter* Sirach/Ecclesiasticus. BVLI 49 (2005) 33.

4487 **Thiele, Walter** Sirach (Ecclesiasticus): 9. Lief.: Sir 23,7-24,47; Register. BVLI 11/2: FrB 2005, Herder 641-726 pp. 3-451-00473-9.

4488 **Van Peursen, W.Th.** The verbal system in the Hebrew text of Ben Sira. SStLL 41: 2004 ⇒20,4192. [R]Materia giudaica 10/1 (2005) 188-190 (*Di Giulio, Marco*).

4489 *Whybray, Norman* Ben Sira and history. Wisdom. MSSOTS: 2005 <1999> ⇒324. 211-219.

4490 **Wicke-Reuter, Ursel** Göttliche Providenz und menschliche Verantwortung bei Ben Sira und in der frühen Stoa. BZAW 298: 2000 ⇒ 16,3670... 20,4194. [R]JSJ 36 (2005) 387-388 (*Lange, Armin*).

4491 **Włosiński, Marian** Przesłanie katechetyczne księgi Syracha [Messaggio catechetico del libro del Siracide]. Włocławek 2005, PWSZ 256 pp. [R]Ang. 82 (2005) 931-932 (*Mirri, Luciana Maria*). **P.**

4492 *Wright, Benjamin G.* Ben Sira and the Book of the Watchers on the legitimate priesthood. [F]DI LELLA, A.: 2005 ⇒35. 241-54;

4493 Putting the puzzle together: some suggestions concerning the social location of the wisdom of Ben Sira. Conflicted boundaries. SBL. Symp. 35: 2005 ⇒495. 89-112.

4494 *Calduch-Benages, Núria* Amid trials: Ben Sira 2:1 and James 1:2. [F]DI LELLA, A.: 2005 ⇒35. 255-263.

4495 *Marböck, Johannes* Apokalyptische Traditionen im Sirachbuch?. Weisheit und Frömmigkeit. ÖBS 29: 2005 <2004> ⇒254. 137-153 [Sir 3,17-25].

4496 *Rossetti, Marco* Le aggiunte ebraiche, greche e latine a Sir 15,11-20. Sal. 67 (2005) 233-254.

4497 *Schäfer, Hermann* "Der Tor lacht mit lauter Stimme, der Kluge aber lächelt kaum leise" (Jesus Sirach 21,29). Kanzelreden. 2005 ⇒376. 59-72.

4498 *Marböck, Johannes* Gefährdung und Bewährung—Kontexte zur Freundschaftsperikope Sir 22,19-26. Weisheit und Frömmigkeit. ÖBS 29: 2005 <1995> ⇒254. 105-120.

4499 *Agosti, Gianfranco* LXX, *Siracides* 29.13-26 (MS 2633). Greek Papyri, Volume I. 2005 ⇒682. 45-48.

4500 **Chávez Jiménez, Hugo Alberto** La misericordia en el libro del Sirácida: estudio exégetico de Sir 35,11-24; 36,1-17; 18,1-14. México 2005, Pont. Univ. Mexicana xii; 424 pp. Diss.; Bibl. 349-380.

4501 *Marböck, Johannes* Kohelet und Sirach—eine vielschichtige Beziehung. Weisheit und Frömmigkeit. ÖBS 29: 2005 <1997> ⇒254. 79-103 [Sir 39,12-35; Qoh 3,11].

4502 **Piwowar, Andrzej** La vergogna come criterio della fama perpetua: studio esegetico-teologico di Sir 40,1-42,14 come unità letteraria. [D]*Gilbert, Maurice* 2005, Diss. Gregoriana [RTL 37,611].

4503 *Limongi, Donatella* LXX, *Siracides* 40.25-41.10 (MS 44). Greek Papyri, Volume I. 2005 ⇒682. 49-54.

4504 *Beauchamp, Paul* Sur deux mots de l'Ecclésiastique (Si 43,27b). Pages exégétiques. LeDiv 202: 2005 <1993> ⇒183. 329-342.

4505 *Marböck, Johannes* Jesaja in Sirach 48,15-25—zum Prophetenverständnis in der späten Weisheit. Weisheit und Frömmigkeit. ÖBS 29: 2005 <2000> ⇒254. 121-135.

4506 *Hayward, C.T. Robert* Multum in parvo: Ben Sira's portrayal of the patriarch Joseph. [F]DI LELLA, A.: 2005 ⇒35. 185-200 [Sir 49,14-16; 50,1-24].

4507 *Marböck, Johannes* Der Hohepriester Simon in Sir 50—ein Beitrag zur Bedeutung von Priestertum und Kult im Sirachbuch. Weisheit und Frömmigkeit. ÖBS 29: 2005 <1999> ⇒254. 155-168.

4508 **Mulder, Otto** Simon the High Priest in Sirach 50. JSJ.S 78: 2003 ⇒ 19,4393. [R]Bib. 86 (2005) 276-279 [=Weisheit und Frömmigkeit 169-172 ⇒254] (*Marböck, Johannes*).

4509 *Gurtner, Daniel M.* The 'house of the veil' in Sirach 50. JSPE 14/3 (2005) 187-200 [Exod 26,33; Lev 16,2-12; Num 18,7; Sir 50,5].

4510 *Chávez, Hugo* En el centro del peligro, la memoria en el Dios de la misericordia: anotaciones exegéticas a Sir 51,1-12. [F]JUNCO GARZA, C.: Estudios Bíblicos Mexicanos 4: 2005 ⇒74. 209-221.

4511 *Mies, Françoise* "De la brûlure d'un feu ..."—Ben Sira 51,5a (hébreu). Bib. 86 (2005) 260-268.

## VII. Libri prophetici VT

### E8.1 Prophetismus

4512 *Barstad, Hans M.* Mari and the Hebrew Bible: some parallels. SEÅ 70 (2005) 21-32.

4513 *Barton, John* The prophets and the cult. Temple and worship. LHBOTS 422: 2005 ⇒731. 111-122.

4514 **Baumann, Gerlinde** Love and violence: marriage as metaphor for the relationship between YHWH and Israel in the prophetic books. [T]*Maloney, Linda M.* 2003 ⇒19,4406; 20,4215. [R]HebStud 46 (2005) 407-409 (*Fuchs, Esther*).

4515 **Behrens, Achim** Prophetische Visionsschilderungen im Alten Testament: sprachliche Eigenarten, Funktion und Geschichte einer Gattung. AOAT 292: 2002 ⇒18,4123; 20,4217. [R]ThLZ 130 (2005) 150-153 (*Delkurt, Holger*); RBLit 7 (2005) 222-225 (*Schmid, Konrad*).

4516 *Block, Daniel I.* What has Delphi to do with Samaria?: ambiguity and delusion in Israelite prophecy. [F]MILLARD, A.: LHBOTS 426: 2005 ⇒102. 189-216.

4517 *Cándido, Fernando* O êxtase profético em Mari e Israel: uma leitura socio-antropológica. Fragmenta de Cultura [Goías] 15 (2005) 1401-1414 [OTA 29,65].

4518 **Chapman, Cynthia R.** The gendered language of warfare in the Israelite-Assyrian encounter. HSM 62: 2004 ⇒20,9197. [R]JANER 5 (2005) 239-244 (*Richardson, Seth*).

4519 **Conrad, Edgar W.** Reading the latter prophets: toward a new canonical criticism. JSOT.S 376: 2003 ⇒19,4419; 20,4226. [R]CBQ 67 (2005) 112-13 (*Vogels, Walter A.*); HeyJ 46 (2005) 531-532 (*Briggs, Richard S.*); RBLit (2005)* (*Boda, Mark; Vermeylen, Jacques*); BiCT 1/2 (2005)* (*Miscall, Peter D.*).

4520 *Constandse, Coen* Een ontzagwekkend oordeel ten leven: pathos en oordeel bij de profeten volgens Abraham Joshua HESCHEL. ITBT 13/3 (2005) 10-12.

4521 **Doan, William; Giles, Terry** Prophets, performance, and power: performance criticism of the Hebrew Bible. L 2005, Clark xi; 194 pp. $32. 0-567-02951-4. Bibl. 177-187.

4522 **Garelli, Claude; Gilbert, Maurice** Les livres des prophètes: pastels; exégèse des textes bibliques. Bibliothèque Universitaire Moretus Plantin, Publications 10: Namur 2005, Bibliothèque Universitaire Moretus Plantin 168 pp. 2-87235-015-2.

4523 **Gärtner, Judith** Jesaja 66 und Sacharja 14 als Summe der Prophetie: eine traditions- und redaktionsgeschichtliche Untersuchung zum Abschluss des Jesaja- und Zwölfprophetenbuches. [D]*Jeremias, Jörg* 2005, Diss. Marburg [RTL 37,609].

4524 **Geyer, John B.** Mythology and lament: studies in the oracles about the nations. 2004 ⇒20,4235. [R]ScrB 35 (2005) 46-47 (*Mills, Mary*).

4525 *Hardmeier, Christof* Die judäische Unheilsprophetie: Antwort auf einen Gesellschafts- und Normenwandel im Israel des 8. Jahrhunderts vor Christus. Erzähldiskurs. FAT 46: 2005 <1983> ⇒222. 243-271;

4526 Die Propheten Micha und Jesaja im Spiegel von Jeremia 26 und II Regum 18-20: zur Prophetie-Rezeption in der nachjoschijanischen Zeit. Erzähldiskurs. FAT 46: 2005 <1991> ⇒222. 273-289.

4527 *Holmgren, Fredrick C.* Priests and prophets: spirituality and social conscience. Worship 79 (2005) 304-316.

4528 *Hubmann, Franz D.* Prophetie und Öffentlichkeit. ThPQ 153 (2005) 35-46.

4529 *Huh, Do-Hwa* A new understanding of prophetic preaching. Evangel 23 (2005) 39-47.

4530 **Hutton, Rodney R.** Fortress introduction to the prophets. 2004 ⇒ 20,4246. [R]RBLit (2005)* (*Camp, Phillip; Himbaza, Innocent; Polaski, Donald*).

4531 *Jong, M.J. de* 'Fear not, O King!': the Assyrian prophecies as a case for a comparative approach. JEOL 38 (2003-2004) 113-121.

4532 *Kalluveettil, Paul* The mystical dimensions of biblical prophetism. ThirdM 8/3 (2005) 19-48.

4533 *Kirova, Milena* Why should the harlot be a woman?: gender identity as allegorical strategy of representation in prophetic texts. BiCT 1/4 2005*.

4534 [E]**Köckert, Matthias; Nissinen, Martti** Propheten in Mari, Assyrien und Israel. FRLANT 201: 2003 ⇒19,756; 20,4251. [R]ThLZ 130 (2005) 637-638 (*Schart, Aaron*).

4535 **Lange, Armin** Vom prophetischen Wort zur prophetischen Tradition: Studien zur Traditions- und Redaktionsgeschichte innerprophetischer Konflikte in der Hebräischen Bibel. FAT 34: 2002 ⇒18,4149 ... 20,4258. [R]RBLit (2005)* (*Becker, Uwe*).

4536 **Lee, Young-Ho** Einflüsse der Weisheit auf Worte der Propheten des 8. Jahrhundert—Amos und Jesaja—ein Forschungsbericht. [D]*Schmidt, W.H.* 2005, Diss. Bonn [ThLZ 130,882].

4537 **Lehnart, Bernhard** Prophet und König im Nordreich Israel: Studien zur sogenannten vorklassischen Prophetie im Nordreich Israel anhand der Samuel-, Elija- und Elischa-Überlieferungen. VT.S 96: 2003 ⇒19,4449. [R]RBLit (2005)* (*Nocquet, Dany*).

4538 *Lujic, Bozo* Shvacanje obracenja kod Ezekiela i Deuteroizaije;

4539 Shvacanje obracenja u predsuzanjskih proroka. BoSm 75 (2005) 519-539/487-518. **Croatian**.

4540 *Mays, James L.* Justice: perspectives from the prophetic tradition. [F]MCBRIDE, D. 2005 <1983> ⇒98. 57-71.

4541 **McLaughlin, John** The marzeah in the prophetic literature: references and allusions in light of extra-biblical evidence. VT.S 39: 2001 ⇒17,3725... 19,4455. [R]OLZ 100 (2005) 95-99 (*Fabry, Heinz-Josef*).

4542 **Mowinckel, Sigmund O.P.** The Spirit and the word: prophecy and tradition in Ancient Israel. [E]*Hanson, Kenneth C.* 2002 ⇒18,4160... 20,4269. [R]JQR 95 (2005) 328-330 (*Brettler, Marc Zvi*); JSSt 50 (2005) 214-216 (*Tomes, Roger*).

4543 The Navarre bible: major prophets: the books of Isaiah, Jeremiah, Lamentations, Baruch, Ezekiel and Daniel in the Revised Standard Version and New Vulgate with a commentary by members of the Faculty of Theology of the University of Navarre. Dublin 2005, Four Courts 896 pp. 1-85182-872-9. Bibl. 357-358.

4544 *Nissinen, Martti* How prophecy became literature. SJOT 19 (2005) 153-172.

4545 **Nissinen, Martti** Prophets and prophecy in the ancient Near East. 2003 ⇒19,4464; 20,4272. [R]JSSt 50 (2005) 359-361 (*Floyd, Michael H.*); RBLit 7 (2005) 69-72 (*Sweeney, Marvin*).

4546 **Nurmi, Janne J.** Die Ethik unter dem Druck des Alltags: die Impulse der gesellschaftlichen Änderungen und Situation zu der sozialkritischen Prophetie in Juda im 8. Jahrhundert v.Chr. 2004 ⇒20,4273. [R]ZAR 11 (2005) 380-382 (*Otto, Eckart*).

4547 *O'Kennedy, D.F.* God as healer in the prophetic books of the Hebrew Bible. HBT 27/1 (2005) 87-113.

4548 *Paul, Shalom M.* Prophets and prophecy. Divrei Shalom. CHANE 23: 2005 <2001> ⇒273. 363-398.

4549 *Petersen, David L.* Introduction to prophetic literature. OT survey. 2005 ⇒413. 270-294.

4550 *Pretorius, S.P.* Word volgelinge van sommige hedendaagse "profete" mislei en van hulle regte ontneem die dekmantel van profesie?. VeE 26 (2005) 507-526.

4551 *Rad, Gerhard von* The city on the hill. From Genesis. 2005 <1949> ⇒283. 115-122 [Isa 60].

4552 **Renaud, Bernard** Nouvelle où éternelle alliance?: le message des prophètes. LeDiv 189: 2002 ⇒18,4173... 20,4277. [R]Brot. 161 (2005) 298-299 (*Silva, Isidro Ribeiro da*).

4553 **Sandy, D. Brent** Plowshares and pruning hooks: rethinking the language of biblical prophecy and apocalyptic literature. 2002 ⇒18, 1251. [R]BS 162 (2005) 119-120 (*Johnson, Elliott E.*).

4554 *Sankarathil, John* Called to be prophets of holiness: challenges and dynamics of prophetic witness in the Indian context. VJTR 69 (2005) 42-56.

4555 *Schaper, Joachim* Exilic and post-exilic prophecy and the orality/literacy problem. VT 55 (2005) 324-342.

4556 *Schmid, Konrad; Steck, Odil H.* Heilserwartungen in den Prophetenbüchern des Alten Testaments. Prophetische Heils- und Herrschererwartungen. SBS 194: 2005 ⇒479. 1-36.
4557 *Solà, Teresa* L'home, 'imatge de Déu': raons d'una absència de els profetes. RCatT 30/1 (2005) 17-35 [Gen 1,26].
4558 *Strydom, Gerrie* Israel and South Africa in unity: the same old di-(ve)r(si)ty (of) tricks, as narrated by the prophets. OTEs 18 (2005) 356-370.
4559 *Sweeney, Marvin A.* The truth in true and false prophecy. Form and intertextuality. FAT 45: 2005 ⇒313. 78-93.
4560 **Sweeney, Marvin A.** The prophetic literature. Interpreting biblical texts: Nv 2005, Abingdon 240 pp. £11. 0687-008441. Bibl. 221-232.
4561 *Tiemeyer, Lena-Sofia* Prophecy as a way of cancelling prophecy—the strategic uses of foreknowledge. ZAW 117 (2005) 329-350 [1 Sam 23,9-13; 1 Kgs 22; 2 Kgs 3; 6,8-23; 8,7-15].
4562 *Titus, P. Joseph* Prophets and prayer. ITS 42/1 (2005) 15-37.
4563 *Virgili dal Prà, Rosanna* Per un lavoro secondo giustizia: i richiami dei profeti. PSV 52 (2005) 81-99.
4564 *Voth, Esteban* Orality and writtenness in ancient Near Eastern prophecy: its effect on translation as communication in Latin America. BiTr 56 (2005) 114-127 [Isa 13];
4565 Lo oral y lo escrito en la profecía del Antiguo Cercano Oriente. Cuadernos de teología 24 (2005) 47-66.
4566 **Weisman, Zeev** Saviours and prophets—two aspects of biblical charisma. Heilal Ben-Haim Library: TA 2003, Hakibbutz Hameuchad 222 pp.
4567 *Wessels, W.J.* 'Return to the Lord your God, for he is gracious and compassionate...' (Jl 2:13): a prophetic perspective on reconciliation and restoration. VeE 26 (2005) 308-325.
4568 *Zenger, Erich* Peculiarità e significato della profezia di Israele. Introduzione AT. 2005 ⇒1159. 633-647.

## E8.2 **Proto-Isaias,** *textus, commentarii*

4569 **Beuken, Willem A.M.** Jesaja 1-12. [T]*Berges, Ulrich*: HThK.AT: 2003 ⇒19,4501; 20,4302. [R]RivBib 53 (2005) 227-231 (*Paganini, Simone*); Bib. 86 (2005) 419-424 (*Sweeney, Marvin A.*).
4570 **Butler, Trent C.** Isaiah. Holman OT Comm.: 2002 ⇒20,4304. [R]JRTI 7/1 (2005) 90-91 (*Beard, Craig W.*).
4571 **Childs, Brevard S.** Isaiah: a commentary. OTL: 2000 ⇒16,3776... 20,4305. [R]EstB 63 (2005) 576-577 (*Ramis Darder, Francesc*);
4572 Isaia. Brescia 2005, Queriniana 613 pp. 88-399-1135-9. Bibl. 600-3.
4573 *Croatto, J. Severino* Fourth Isaiah. Global bible commentary. 2005 ⇒2443. 207-211.
4574 *Cronauer, Patrick T.* Reading First Isaiah in context. BiTod 43 (2005) 241-347.
4575 *Duhaime, Jean* Les manuscrits de Qumrân dans trois traductions du livre d'Isaïe. Traduire la Bible hébraïque. 2005 ⇒728. 319-349.
4576 **Harman, Allan** Isaiah: a covenant to be kept for the sake of the church. Fearn 2005, Christian Focus 472 pp.
4577 **Hollerich, Michael J.** EUSEBIUS of Caesarea's commentary on Isaiah: christian exegesis in the age of Constantine. 1999 ⇒15,3611 ... 19,4506. [R]VigChr 59 (2005) 460-462 (*Inowlocki, Sabrina*).

4578 **Höffken, Peter** Jesaja: der Stand der theologischen Diskussion. 2004 ⇒20,4308. [R]RBLit 7 (2005) 171-173 (*Vermeylen, Jacques*).

4579 *Jüngling, Hans-Winfried* Il libro di Isaia. Introduzione AT. 2005 ⇒ 1159. 648-683.

4580 *Le Moigne, Philippe* οὐχ ὡς dans Ésaïe-LXX. L'apport de la Septante. 2005 ⇒764. 71-104 [Isa 8,14; 8,20; 29,16; 54,6. 16].

4581 **Lohfink, Norbert; Zenger, Erich** Der Gott Israels und die Völker: Untersuchungen zum Jesajabuch und...Pss. SBS 154: 1994 ⇒10, 3402...13,3447. [R]ThR 70 (2005) 285-87 (*Reventlow, Henning Graf*).

4582 *Munnich, Olivier* Le texte lucianique d'*Isaïe*-Septante. [F]LUST, J.: BEThL 192: 2005 ⇒92. 269-299.

4583 **Oswalt, John** Isaiah. GR 2003, Zondervan 736 pp. 978-03102-0613-8. Bibl. 67-69.

4584 [E]**Reggi, Roberto** ישעיהו Isaia: traduzione interlineare in italiano. Bo 2005, EDB 144 pp. €11.40. 8810-82018-5.

4585 *Troxel, Ronald L.* What's in a name?: contemporization and toponyms in LXX-Isaiah. [F]FOX, M. 2005 ⇒43. 327-344.

4586 *Tucker, Gene M.* The book of Isaiah 1-39. OT survey. 2005 ⇒413. 295-305.

4587 *Van der Kooij, Arie* La Septante d'Isaïe et la critique textuelle de l'Ancien Testament. L'enfance de la Bible hébraïque. MoBi 52: 2005 ⇒477. 185-198.

4588 **Watts, John D.W.** Isaiah 34-66. [E]*Hubbard, David A.*: WBC 25: Waco, Tex. [2]2005, Word Books xvii; 504-956 pp. 0-7852-5011-5.

4589 **Wildberger, Hans** Isaiah, vol. 3: chapters 28-39. A Continental Commentary: 2003 ⇒19,4513. [R]RBLit (2005)* (*Engle, John; Mutombo, Jean*).

4590 *Zinkuratire, Victor* Isaiah 1-39. Global bible commentary. 2005 ⇒ 2443. 186-194.

## E8.3 **Isaias 1-39**, *themata, versiculi*

4591 **Chieregatti, Arrigo** Isaia: se non avete fede. Bo 2005, EDB 136 pp. €11.50. 88107-0987X [OTA 28,231].

4592 **Childs, Brevard S.** The struggle to understand Isaiah as christian scripture. 2004 ⇒20,4322. [R]Augustinus 50 (2005) 231-232 (*Silva, Álvaro*); ETR 80 (2005) 558-561 (*Vincent, Jean Marcel*); TJT 21 (2005) 230-231 (*Dunn, Matthew W.I.*); JETh 19 (2005) 242-44 (*Klement, Herbert H.*); OTEs 18 (2005) 135-136 (*Maré, L.P.*) RBLit (2005)* (*Melugin, Roy; Williamson, H.G.M.*); RBLit 7 (2005) 162-165 (*Melugin, Roy*); PIBA 28 (2005) 129-131 (*O'Leary, Anthony*); HBT 27/1 (2005) 116-117 (*Roberts, J.J.M.*).

4593 *Garzón Moreno, Miguel Ángel* Biblia y alegría: campo semántico de la alegría en el libro de Isaías. Isidorianum 28 (2005) 485-517.

4594 **Goulder, Michael D.** Isaiah as liturgy. 2004 ⇒20,4325. [R]ScrB 35 (2005) 47-49 (*Robinson, Bernard P.*); JThS 56 (2005) 501-503 (*Sawyer, John F.A.*).

4595 *Hanson, Paul D.* Covenant and politics. [F]MCBRIDE, D. 2005 ⇒98. 205-233.

4596 **Janthial, Dominique** L'oracle de Nathan et l'unité du livre d'Isaïe. BZAW 343: 2004 ⇒20,4327. [R]Vies consacrées 77 (2005) 201-202

(*Luciani, Didier*); CBQ 67 (2005) 496-497 (*Miscall, Peter D.*); ThLZ 130 (2005) 936-937 (*Höffken, Peter*) [2 Sam 7].

4597 *Leclerc, Thomas L.* Isaiah and the God of justice. BiTod 43 (2005) 359-364.

4598 **Leclerc, Thomas L.** Yahweh is exalted in justice: solidarity and conflict in Isaiah. 2001 ⇒17,3780... 20,4328. [R]HeyJ 46 (2005) 354-355 (*Briggs, Richard S.*).

4599 *Machinist, Peter* Hosea and the ambiguity of kingship in ancient Israel. [F]MCBRIDE, D. 2005 ⇒98. 153-181.

4600 **Ortlund, Raymond C., Jr.** Isaiah: God saves sinners. Wheaton, IL 2005, Crossway 495 pp. $28. 1-58134-727-8.

4601 *Patella, Michael* Seers' Corner: Isaiah the prophet: geography and imagery. BiTod 43 (2005) 365-370.

4602 *Roberts, J.J.M.* Bearers of the polity: Isaiah of Jerusalem's view of the eighth-century Judean society. [F]MCBRIDE, D. 2005 ⇒98. 145-52.

4603 *Schmid, Konrad* Herrschererwartungen und -aussagen im Jesajabuch: Überlegungen zu ihrer synchronen Logik und zu ihren diachronen Transformationen. Prophetische Heils- und Herrschererwartungen. SBS 194: 2005 ⇒479. 37-74.

4604 *Sweeney, Marvin A.* The book of Isaiah as prophetic Torah. Form and intertextuality. FAT 45: 2005 ⇒313. 13-27.

4605 **Vlková, Gabriela** Cambiare la luce in tenebre e le tenebre in luce: studio...dell'alternarsi tra la luce e le tenebre nel libro di Isaia. TGr.T 107: 2004 ⇒20,4336. [R]CBQ 67 (2005) 517-8 (*Ceresko, Anthony R.*).

4606 *Williamson, Hugh G.M.* Isaiah, Micah and Qumran. [F]ULLENDORFF, E.: SStLL 47: 2005 ⇒154. 203-211 [Isa 2,2-4; Mic 4,1-3].

4607 *Croatto, José S.* The 'nations' in the salvific oracles of Isaiah. VT 55 (2005) 143-161 [Isa 2,2-5].

4608 **Lemana, Emmanuel** Qu'avez-vous à opprimer mon peuple (Is 3,15): étude linguistique et exégétique d'Isaïe 3,1-4,1. FzB 108: Wü 2005, Echter xi; 435 pp. 3-429-02742-X. Diss. Würzburg; Bibl. 404-435.

4609 *Landy, Francis* The parable of the vineyard (Isaiah 5:1-7), or what is a love song doing among the prophets?. SR 34 (2005) 147-164.

4610 *Lemana, Emmanuel* Le chant de la vigne chez Isaie 5,1-7: entre parabole, poésie et autres genres littéraires du texte: question éternellement ouverte?: essai de recherche et de précision d'un genre littéraire. [F]SEIDL, T.: ATSAT 75: 2005 ⇒137. 139-153.

4611 *Gosse, Bernard* Isaïe 6, la mort des rois de Juda dans le livre d'Isaïe et la royauté de Yahvé. BN 125 (2005) 5-10 [Isa 6; 1 Kgs 22,19-20; 2 Kgs 15,5].

4612 *Hardmeier, Christof* Jesaja's Verkündigungsabsicht und Jahwes Verstockungsauftrag in Jes 6. Erzähldiskurs. FAT 46: 2005 <1981> ⇒ 222. 211-228.

4613 *Polan, Gregory J.* The call and commission of Isaiah. BiTod 43 (2005) 348-352 [Isa 6].

4614 *Williamson, H.G.M.* Temple and worship in Isaiah 6. Temple and worship. LHBOTS 422: 2005 ⇒731. 123-144.

4615 *Hardmeier, Christof* Verkündigung und Schrift bei Jesaja: zur Entstehung der Schriftprophetie als Oppositionsliteratur im alten Israel. Erzähldiskurs. FAT 46: 2005 <1983> ⇒222. 229-242 [Isa 6-8].

4616 **Wagner, Thomas** Gottes Herrschaft: eine Analyse der Denkschrift Jes 6,1-9,6. [D]*Kreuzer, S.* 2005, Diss. Wuppertal [ThLZ 131,343].

4617 *Weinfeld, Moshe* The heavenly praise in unison. Normative and sectarian Judaism. Library of Second Temple Studies 54: 2005 ⇒2732. 45-52 [Isa 6,3].

4618 **Lehnert, Volker A.** Die Provokation Israels: die paradoxe Funktion von Jes 6,9-10 bei Markus und Lukas. 1999 ⇒15,3673... 18,4232. [R]ThLZ 130 (2005) 654-56 (*Hübner, Hans*) [Mk 4,10-13; Lk 8,9-10].

4619 *Wagner, Thomas* Ein Zeichen für den Herrscher—Gottes Zeichen für Ahas in Jesaja 7,10-17. SJOT 19 (2005) 74-83.

4620 *Couturier, Guy* Ésaïe 7,14: étude philologique du terme עַלְמָה. [F]GENEST, O. 2005 ⇒46. 323-340.

4621 *Blocher, Henri* Dieu-avec, Dieu-contre. ThEv(VS) 4/1 (2005) 89-94 [Isa 8].

4622 *Sweeney, Marvin A.* On umeśoś in Isaiah 8:6. Form and intertextuality. FAT 45: 2005 ⇒313. 36-45.

4623 *Nagel, Elizabeth M.* The ideal leader in the kingdom of God. BiTod 43 (2005) 353-358 [Isa 8,23-9,6; 11,1-9].

4624 *Sweeney, Marvin A.* On multiple settings in the book of Isaiah. Form and intertextuality. FAT 45: 2005 ⇒313. 28-35 [Isa 9,1-6].

4625 **Shipp, R. Mark** Of dead kings and dirges: myth and meaning in Isaiah 14:4b-21. Academia Biblica 11: 2002 ⇒18,4241... 20,4356. [R]EThL 81 (2005) 221-224 (*Scatolini, S.S.*).

4626 *Hagelia, Hallvard* A crescendo of universalism: an exegesis of Isa 19:16-25. SEÅ 70 (2005) 73-88.

4627 *Beuken, Willem A.M.* Obdurate short-sightedness in the valley of vision: how atonement of iniquity is forfeited (Isa 22:1-14). [M]VAN TILBORG, S.: BiblInterp 71: 2005 ⇒155. 45-63.

4628 *Höffken, Peter* Ein Hochgrab in Jerusalem und in Akragas: eine Anmerkung zu Jes 22,16. BN 126 (2005) 29-35.

4629 **Lessing, Robert Reed** Interpreting discontinuity: Isaiah's Tyre oracle. 2004 ⇒20,4362. [R]RBLit (2005)* (*Beuken, W.A.M.; Engle, John*) [Isa 23].

4630 *Oswalt, John N.* Isaiah 24-27: songs in the night. CTJ 40 (2005) 76-84.

4631 *Hibbard, J. Todd* Isaiah xxvii 7 and intertextual discourse about "striking" in the book of Isaiah. VT 55 (2005) 461-476.

4632 *Zanetti, Paolo S.* Et mussitatores discent legem (Is. 29,24 Vulg.). Imitatori di Gesù Cristo. 2005 <1989> ⇒330. 459-463.

4633 *Gosse, Bernard* L'écriture d'Is 34 dans le livre d'Isaïe. BN 124 (2005) 9-17.

4634 *Dan, Doron* The myriad of meanings of ''k' (and the directives of the verbs 'bqʿ 'dgr') in Isaiah 34:14-15. BetM 183 (2005) 345-361 Sum. 391. **H**.

4635 *Mashiah, Rachel* wtgl ʿrbh wtprḥ kḥbṣlt: the biblical accentuation and exegesis of Isaiah 35:1-2. Textus 22 (2005) 65-75.

4636 **Barré, Michael L.** The Lord has saved me: a study of the Psalm of Hezekiah (Isaiah 38:9-20). CBQ.MS 39: Wsh 2005, Catholic Biblical Association of America x; 294 pp. $12. 0-915170-388.

## E8.4 **Deutero-Isaias 40-52**: *commentarii, themata, versiculi*

4637 **Baltzer, Klaus** Deutero-Isaiah: a commentary on Isaiah 40-55. [T]*Kohl, Margaret;* [E]*Machinist, Peter*: Hermeneia: 2001 ⇒17,3832...

20,4371. [R]EstB 63 (2005) 575-576 (*Ramis Darder, Francesc*); RBLit (2005)* (*Baltzer, Klaus*); RBLit 7 (2005) 20-35 (*Sommer, Benjamin D.; Kratz, Reinhard G.; Baltzer, Klaus*).

4638 **Blenkinsopp, Joseph** Isaiah 40-55. AncB 19A: 2002 ⇒18,4254... 20,4373. [R]HeyJ 46 (2005) 529-530 (*Briggs, Richard S.*); RBLit 7 (2005) 173-176 (*Landy, Francis*).

4639 *Croatto, J. Severino* Isaiah 40-55. Global bible commentary. 2005 ⇒ 2443. 195-200.

4640 **Dille, Sarah J.** Mixing metaphors: God as mother and father in Deutero-Isaiah. JSOT.S 398: 2004 ⇒20,4375. [R]JHScr 5 (2004-2005)* (*Mitchell, Mary L.*); RBLit (2005)* (*Korpel, Marjo*).

4641 **Goldingay, John** The message of Isaiah 40-55: a literary-theological commentary. L 2005, Clark 578 pp. £45. 0-567-03038-5.

4642 *Hardmeier, Christof* Erzählen–Erzählung–Erzählgemeinschaft: zur Rezeption von Abrahamserzählungen in der Exilsprophetie. Erzähldiskurs. FAT 46: 2005 <1981> ⇒222. 35-55.

4643 **Heintz, Jean-Georges**, *al.* Le livre prophétique du Deutéro-Esaïe: texto-bibliographie du XXème siècle. 2004 ⇒20,4378. [R]ThLZ 130 (2005) 1053-1054 (*Hermisson, Hans-Jürgen*).

4644 *Höffken, Peter* Zur Mardukinterpretation in Babylonien mit besonderer Hinsicht auf Deuterojesaja. BN 125 (2005) 11-23;

4645 Xerxes und (k)eine Marduk-Statue: Überlegungen zu einem Randthema alttestamentlicher Prophetenexegese. Ment. *Herodotus*: VT 55 (2005) 477-485.

4646 *Keiser, Thomas A.* The Song of Moses: a basis for Isaiah's prophecy. VT 55 (2005) 486-500 [Deut 32].

4647 **Kim, Hyun Chul Paul** Ambiguity, tension, and multiplicity in Deutero-Isaiah. Studies in Biblical Literature 52: 2003 ⇒19,4579; 20, 4380. [R]OLZ 100 (2005) 601-609 (*Hermisson, Hans-Jürgen*).

4648 *Paul, Shalom M.* Deutero-Isaiah and cuneiform royal inscriptions. Divrei Shalom. CHANE 23: 2005 <1968> ⇒273. 11-22;

4649 Literary and ideological echoes of Jeremiah in Deutero-Isaiah. Divrei Shalom. CHANE 23: 2005 <1972> ⇒273. 399-416.

4650 **Scheuer, Blaženka** The return of Yhwh: the tension between deliverance and repentance in Isaiah 40-55. Lund 2005, Univ. of Lund 211 pp. Diss. Lund.

4651 *Seitz, Christopher R.* The book of Isaiah 40-66. OT survey. 2005 ⇒ 413. 306-315.

4652 *Ska, Jean Louis* Espiritualidad del Adviento: lecturas del Deuteroisaías. El camino. 2005 <1996> ⇒302. 103-126.

4653 *Van der Woude, Annemarieke* "Hearing voices while reading": Isaiah 40-55 as a drama. [M]VAN TILBORG, S.: BiblInterp 71: 2005 ⇒155. 149-173.

4654 *Colli, Gelci A.* O prólogo de Déutero-Isaías: Isaías 40,1-11: dinâmica profética através da memôria do Êxodo. Via Teológia (2005) 73-92 [OTA 31,97].

4655 **Van der Woude, A.** Geschiedenis van de terugkeer: de rol van Jesaja 40,1-11 in het drama van Jesaja 40-55. [D]*Van der Wall, E.G.E.*: Maastricht 2005, Shaker 267 pp. 90-423-0268-2. Diss. Nijmegen.

4656 *Van Wieringen, Archibald L.H.M.* Isaiah's roles: the unity of a bible book from the perspective of the sender-role. [M]VAN TILBORG, S.: BiblInterp 71: 2005 ⇒155. 115-124 [Isa 40,1-11].

4657 **Akpunonu, Peter Damian** The overture of the Book of Consolations (Isaiah 40:1-11). 2004 ⇒20,4388. [R]BOTSA 19 (2005) 20 (*Holter, Knut*); RBLit (2005)* (*Kennedy, James*).

4658 **Ramis Darder, Francesc** El triunfo de Yahvé sobre los ídolos (Is 40,12-44, 23): "en vez de zarzas crecerá el ciprés". Sant Pacià 75: 2002 ⇒18,4269, 20,4389. [R]Ang. 82 (2005) 479-481 (*Garuti, Paolo*).

4659 *Zanetti, Paolo S.* Poesia per ritrovare forza (Is. 40,27-31). Imitatori di Gesù Cristo. 2005 <1988> ⇒330. 427-436.

4660 *Hardmeier, Christof* 'Geschwiegen habe ich seit langem... wie die Gebärende schreie ich jetzt': zur Komposition und Geschichtstheologie von Jes 42,14-44,23. Erzähldiskurs. FAT 46: 2005 <1989> ⇒ 222. 291-313.

4661 *Achenbach, Reinhard* Das Kyros-Orakel in Jesaja 44,24-45,7 im Lichte altorientalischer Parallelen. ZAR 11 (2005) 155-194.

4662 *Baumgart, Norbert C.* "JHWH ... erschafft Unheil": Jes 45,7 in seinem unmittelbaren Kontext. BZ 49 (2005) 202-236.

4663 *Ogden, Graham S.* A note on the translation of Isaiah 49.23. BiTr 56 (2005) 110-111.

4664 **Borghino, Angelo** La "nuova alleanza" in Is 54: analisi esegetico-teologica. [D]*Bovati, Pietro*: TGr.T 118: R 2005, E.P.U.G. 475 pp. €25. 88-7839-024-0. Diss. Gregoriana; Bibl. 423-461.

4665 *Paganini, Simone* Who speaks in Isaiah 55.1?: notes on the communicative structure in Isaiah 55. JSOT 30 (2005) 83-92.

### E8.5 *Isaiae 53ss. Carmina Servi YHWH*: **Servant Songs**

4666 *Elgvin, T.* The individual interpretation of the Servant. Mishkan [J] 43 (2005) 25-33 [NTAb 50,114].

4667 *Wilks, John G.F.* The suffering servant and personhood. EvQ 77 (2005) 195-210.

4668 *Smillie, Gene R.* Isaiah 42:1-4 in its rhetorical context. BS 162/645 (2005) 50-65.

4669 *Zehnder, Markus* Phonological subtext: a short note on Isa 42,1-9. BN 123 (2005) 35-40.

4670 *Kummerow, David* Re-examining the Referent(s) of Isaiah 49:1-13. HIPHIL 2 (2005)*.

4671 [TE]**Alobaidi, Joseph** The messiah in Isaiah 53: the commentaries of SAADIA Gaon, SALMON ben Yeruham and YEFET ben Eli on Is 52,13-53,12. La Bible dans l'histoire, textes et études 2: 1998 ⇒14,3427; 17,3856. [R]JThS 56 (2005) 191-195 (*Polliack, Meira*).

4672 *Beauchamp, Paul* Lecture et relectures du quatrième chant du Serviteur: d'Isaïe à Jean. Pages exégétiques. LeDiv 202: 2005 <1989> ⇒183. 183-220 [John 12,38-41].

4673 *Colautti, Federico* The triumphant Messiah and the exalted Christ. Henoch 27/1-2 (2005) 183-213 [Isa 52,13-53,12].

4674 *Niccacci, Alviero* Quarto carme del Servo del Signore (Is 52,13-53, 12): composizione, dinamiche e prospettive. LASBF 55 (2005) 9-26.

4675 *Oswalt, John N.* Isaiah 52:13-53:12: servant of all. CTJ 40 (2005) 85-94.

4676 *Wénin, André* La strategia divina della salvezza. Dalla violenza. 2005 <2002> ⇒323. 125-143 [Isa 52,13-53,12].

4677 *Santala, R.* The despised Messiah and his despised people. Mishkan [J] 43 (2005) 16-24 [NTAb 50,121] [Isa 53].
[E]**Stuhlmacher, P.** The suffering servant: Isaiah 53 2004 ⇒490.

## E8.6 [Trito]Isaias 56-66

4679 **Blenkinsopp, Joseph** Isaiah 56-66. AncB 19B: 2003 ⇒19,4615; 20, 4420. [R]JSSt 50 (2005) 381-383 (*Barstad, Hans M.*); RBLit 7 (2005) 176-179 (*Schramm, Brooks*).
4680 *Croatto, J. Severino* Isaiah 56-66. Global bible commentary. 2005 ⇒ 2443. 201-206.
4681 **Grant-Henderson, Anna L.** Inclusive voices in post-exilic Judah. 2002 ⇒18,4297. [R]ACR 82 (2005) 246-247 (*Boyle, Brian*).
4682 *Middlemas, Jill* Divine reversal and the role of the temple in Trito-Isaiah. Temple and worship. LHBOTS 422: 2005 ⇒731. 164-187.
4683 *Tiemeyer, Lena-Sofia* The watchman metaphor in Isaiah lvi-lxvi. VT 55 (2005) 378-400.

4684 **Park, Kyung-Chul** Die Gerechtigkeit Israels und das Heil der Völker: Kultus, Tempel, Eschatologie und die Gerechtigkeit in der Endgestalt des Jesajabuches (Jes 56,1-8; 58,1-14; 65,17-66; 24). BEAT 52: 2003 ⇒19,4621; 20,4424. [R]ThG 48 (2005) 229-230 (*Hentschel, Georg*); ThLZ 130 (2005) 260-262 (*Gärtner, Judith*).
4685 *Staubli, Thomas* Die Darbringung der *näfäsch* in Jes 58,3-12. [F]SCHENKER, A.: OBO 214: 2005 ⇒134. 310-324 [Lev 16,29-31].
4686 *Oswalt, John N.* Isaiah 60-62: the glory of the Lord. CTJ 40 (2005) 95-103.
4687 **Goldenstein, Johannes** Das Gebet der Gottesknechte: Jesaja 63,7 - 64,11 im Jesajabuch. WMANT 92: 2001 ⇒17,3885... 20,4428. [R]ThRv 101 (2005) 128-130 (*Zapff, Burkard M.*).
4688 *Sweeney, Marvin A.* Prophetic exegesis in Isaiah 65-66. Form and intertextuality. FAT 45: 2005 ⇒313. 46-62.
4689 *Gardner, A.* Isaiah 65,20: centenarians or millenarians?. Bib. 86 (2005) 88-96 [Job 24,18].

## E8.7 Jeremias

4690 *Backhaus, Franz-Josef; Meyer, Ivo* Il libro di Geremia. Introduzione AT. 2005 ⇒1159. 684-722.
4691 *Baxla, Zephyrinus* The shepherd figure in Jeremiah. [M]JOHN PAUL II. 2005 ⇒72. 120-132.
4692 **Davidson, Steed Vernyl** Finding a place: a postcolonial examination of the ideology of place in the book of Jeremiah. [D]*Carr, D.*: NY 2004-2005, Diss. Union [RTL 37,608].
4693 *Diamond, A.R. Pete* Playing God: "polytheizing" *YHWH-alone* in Jeremiah's metaphorical spaces. Metaphor in the Hebrew Bible. BEThL 187: 2005 ⇒799. 119-132.
4694 [E]**Feder, Frank** Biblia Sahidica: Ieremias, Lamentationes (Threni), Epistula Ieremiae et Baruch. TU 147: 2002 ⇒18,4319; 20,4445. [R]JNES 64 (2005) 230-231 (*Förster, Hans*).

4695 *Fischer, Georg* Zur Relativierung des Tempels im Jeremiabuch. [F]SCHENKER, A.: OBO 214: 2005 ⇒134. 87-99;

4696 Jeremia—ein Prophet im Streit mit Allen. Querdenker: Visionäre und Außenseiter in Philosophie und Theologie. [E]**Knapp, Markus; Kobusch, Theo**: Da:Wiss 2005. 14-23. 3-534-18385-1.

4697 **Fischer, Georg** Jeremia 1-25. HThK.AT: FrB 2005, Herder 764 pp. €100. 34512-68388. [R]RivBib 53 (2005) 484-89 (*Paganini, Simone*);

4698 Jeremia 26-52. HThK.AT: FrB 2005, Herder 744 pp. €100. 34512-6-8397.

4699 **Fretheim, Terence** Jeremiah. 2002 ⇒18,4323; 20,4447. [R]CBQ 67 (2005) 113-114 (*Lessing, Reed*).

4700 *Gonçalves, Francolino J.* Baruc e Jeremias nas duas edições mais antigas do livro de Jeremias conhecidas. Did(L) 35 (2005) 85-115.

4701 *Gosse, Bernard* L'influence du livre d'Ezechiel et du Psautier sur la rédaction du livre de Jérémie. OTEs 18 (2005) 603-615 [Jer 1,10; Ezek 18; Ps 9,7; 58,7; 79; 83].

4702 *Holt, Else K.* The fountain of living water and the deceitful brook: the pool of water metaphors in the book of Jeremiah (MT). Metaphor in the Hebrew Bible. BEThL 187: 2005 ⇒799. 99-117.

4703 [E]**Kessler, Martin** Reading the book of Jeremiah: a search for coherence. 2004 ⇒20,376. [R]CTJ 40 (2005) 336-339 (*Williams, Michael J.*); RBLit (2005)* (*Glatt-Gilad, David; Holt, Else*).

4704 *Laberge, Léo* Nabuchodonosor, Jérusalem et Dieu dans le texte de Jérémie. Traduire la Bible hébraïque. 2005 ⇒728. 173-196.

4705 *Lundbom, Jack R.* Haplography in the Hebrew *Vorlage* of LXX Jeremiah. HebStud 46 (2005) 301-320.

4706 **Lundbom, Jack R.** Jeremiah 21-36. AncB 21B: 2004 ⇒20,4460. [R]CBQ 67 (2005) 499-500 (*Hayes, Katherine M.*); OTEs 18 (2005) 946-8 (*Branch, Robin*); RBLit 7 (2005) 179-183 (*Sharp, Carolyn J.*);

4707 Jeremiah 21-36; 37-52. AncB 21B-C: 2004 ⇒20,4460-1. [R]Interp. 59 (2005) 412-414 (*O'Connor, Kathleen M.*);

4708 Jeremiah 37-52. AncB 21C: 2004 ⇒20,4461. [R]RBLit (2005)* (*Engle, John*).

4709 **Maier, Christl** Jeremia als Lehrer der Tora. FRLANT 196: 2002 ⇒ 18,4335; 19,4653. [R]OLZ 100 (2005) 88-95 (*Graupner, A.*).

4710 *Miller, Patrick D.* The book of Jeremiah. OT survey. 2005 ⇒413. 316-327.

4711 *O'Connor, Kathleen M.* The prophet Jeremiah and exclusive loyalty to God. Interp. 59 (2005) 130-140;

4712 Jeremiah's "prophetic imagination": pastoral intervention for a shattered world. [F]BRUEGGEMANN, W.—COUSAR, C. 2005 ⇒16. 59-71.

4713 **Roncace, Mark** Jeremiah, Zedekiah, and the fall of Jerusalem. JSOT.S 423; LHBOTS 423: NY 2005, Clark ix; 193 pp. $95. 0-567-02671-X. Diss. Emory; Bibl. 174-182.

4714 *Stulman, Louis* Conflicting paths to hope in Jeremiah. [F]BRUEGGEMANN, W.—COUSAR, C. 2005 ⇒16. 43-57.

4715 **Stulman, Louis** Jeremiah. Abingdon OT Comm.: Nv 2005, Abingdon xxi; 400 pp. $39. 0-687-05796-5. Bibl. 395-400. [R]TJT 21 (2005) 277-278 (*Kessler, Martin*); RBLit (2005)* (*Holt, Else; Sharp, Carolyn*); HBT 27/1 (2005) 122-124 (*Dearman, J. Andrew*).

4716 *Sweeney, Marvin A.* The Masoretic and Septuagint versions of the book of Jeremiah in synchronic and diachronic perspective. Form and intertextuality. FAT 45: 2005 ⇒313. 65-77.

4717 **Vonach, Andreas** Die Jer-LXX als Dokument des alexandrinischen Judentums. [D]*Bons, Eberhard* 2005, Diss.-Habil. Innsbruck [ThRv 102,xv].

4718 **Waard, Jan de** A handbook on Jeremiah. 2003 ⇒19,4666; 20,4487. [R]CBQ 67 (2005) 519-520 (*Silver, Edward*); BiTr 56 (2005) 220-222 (*Weis, Richard D.*); RBLit 7 (2005) 193-196 (*Weis, Richard D.*).

4719 **Wanke, Gunther** Jeremia, Teilbd. 1-2. ZBK.AT 20,1-2: 1995-2003 ⇒19,4667. [R]ThLZ 130 (2005) 158-160 (*Haag, Ernst*).

4720 *Weems, Renita J.* Jeremiah. Global bible commentary. 2005 ⇒2443. 212-225.

4721 *Yates, Gary E.* Narrative parallelism and the 'Jehoiakim frame': a reading strategy for Jeremiah 26-45. JETS 48 (2005) 263-281 [OTA 30,360].

4722 *Strawn, Brent A.* Jeremiah's in/effective plea: another look at נער in Jeremiah i 6. VT 55 (2005) 366-377.

4723 *Sweeney, Marvin A.* Structure and redaction in Jeremiah 2-6. Form and intertextuality. FAT 45: 2005 ⇒313. 94-108.

4724 *Shields, Mary E.* Circumscribing the prostitute: the rhetorics of intertextuality, metaphor and gender in Jeremiah 3.1-4.4. JSOT.S 387: 2004 ⇒20,4494. [R]JBL 124 (2005) 538-541 (*Stulman, Louis*); RBLit (2005)* (*Biddle, Mark*); BiCT 1/4 (2005)* (*Fuchs, Esther*).

4725 **Manfredi, Silvana** Geremia in dialogo: nessi con le tradizioni profetiche e originalità in Ger 4,5-6,30. 2002 ⇒18,4358... 20,4496. [R]RB 112 (2005) 299-300 (*Mies, Françoise*).

4726 *Van Ruiten, Jacques* Back to chaos: the relationship between Jeremiah 4:23-26 and Genesis 1. Creation of heaven and earth. Themes in biblical narrative 8: 2005 ⇒492. 21-30.

4727 *Gosse, Bernard* Le prophète Jérémie selon le psautier et selon le livre d'Ézéchiel. RB 112 (2005) 511-20 [Jer 6,27-29; Ezek 14,9; Ps 26,2].

4728 *Leuchter, Mark* The temple sermon and the term mqwm in the Jeremianic corpus. JSOT 30 (2005) 93-109 [Jer 7,1-15].

4729 *Paul, Shalom M.* Cuneiform light on Jer 9:20. Divrei Shalom. CHANE 23: 2005 <1968> ⇒273. 23-26.

4730 *Cohen, Chaim* Two misunderstood verses in the latter prophets: Jer 9:24, Amos 1:13. [F]KLEIN, J. 2005 ⇒79. 685-706.

4731 *Avioz, Michael* The call for revenge in Jeremiah's complaints (Jer xi-xx). VT 55 (2005) 429-438.

4732 *Goldman, Yohanan A.P.* Le Seigneur est fidèle à son alliance: continuité et rupture dans l'histoire d'Israël d'après la forme longue du livre de Jérémie (TM Jr 31,31-37; 17,1-4; 11,7-8). L'enfance de la Bible hébraïque. MoBi 52: 2005 ⇒477. 199-219.

4733 *Rom-Shiloni, Dalit* Facing destruction and exile: inner-biblical exegesis in Jeremiah and Ezekiel. ZAW 117 (2005) 189-205 [Jer 21,1-7; Ezek 20,1-38].

4734 *Torreblanca, Jorge* Continuidad para el futuro del pueblo de Dios: análisis exegético-estructural de Jeremías 52, 24 y 29. Cuadernos de teología 24 (2005) 17-35.

4735 *Bogaert, Pierre-Maurice* La datation par souscription dans les rédactions courte (LXX) et longue (TM) du livre de Jérémie. L'apport de la Septante. LeDiv 203: 2005 ⇒764. 137-159 [Jer 25,1-13];

4736 La liste des nations dans l'oracle de la coupe (Jr 25,16-26): Juda, les peuples voisins et les grandes puissances. [F]SCHENKER, A.: OBO 214: 2005 ⇒134. 1-14.

4737 *Aejmelaeus, Anneli* 'Nebuchadnezzar, my servant': redaction history and textual development in Jer 27. FLUST, J.: BEThL 192: 2005 ⇒ 92. 1-18.

4738 *Osuji, Anthony* Jer. 28 (MT) and the question of prophetic authenticity: from the ideological to the narratological. EstB 63 (2005) 175-193.

4739 *Hadey, Jean* Jérémie 29: demain n'est pas hier... LeD 64 (2005) 3-12.

4740 **Willi, Regina** Les pensées de bonheur de Dieu pour son peuple selon JR 29: un temoignage de l'ésperance au temps de l'éxil: étude critique, littéraire et théologique. D*Paximadi, G.*: Lugano 2005, Fac. de Théologie 366 pp. Diss. Lugano; Bibl. 337-366.

4741 *Sweeney, Marvin A.* Jeremiah 30-31 and King Josiah's program of national restoration and religious reform. Form and intertextuality. FAT 45: 2005 ⇒313. 109-122.

4742 *Ognibeni, Bruno* La ronde des jeunes filles: à propos de Jr 31,22. FSCHENKER, A.: OBO 214: 2005 ⇒134. 266-272.

4743 *Carillo Alday, Salvador* Dos cumbres del mensaje profético. FJUNCO GARZA, C.: Estudios Bíblicos Mexicanos 4: 2005 ⇒74. 165-175 [Jer 31,31-34; Ezek 36,16-32].

4744 *Rhymer, David* Jeremiah 31:31-34. Interp. 59 (2005) 294-296.

4745 *Finsterbusch, Karin* "Ich habe meine Tora in ihre Mitte gegeben": Bemerkungen zu Jer 31,33. BZ 49 (2005) 86-92.

4746 *Di Pede, Elena* Jer 32, exergue du récit des chapitres 32-45?. ZAW 117 (2005) 559-573.

4747 **Pardo Izal, José J.** Pasión por un futuro imposible: estudio literario-teológico de Jeremías 32. TGr.T 76: 2001 ⇒17,3936... 19,4697. RRevBib 67 (2005) 249-250 (*Albistur, Fernando*).

4748 **Shead, Andrew G.** The open book and the sealed book: Jeremiah 32 in its Hebrew and Greek recensions. JSOT.S 347: 2002 ⇒18,4384; 20,4514. RBZ 49 (2005) 107-109 (*Fischer, Georg*); CBQ 67 (2005) 126-128 (*Sweeney, Marvin A.*).

4749 **Di Pede, Elena** Au-delà du refus: l'espoir: recherches sur la cohérence narrative de Jr 32-45 (TM). D*Wénin, A.*: BZAW 357: B 2005, De Gruyter xvii; 404 pp. €118. 3-11-018846-5. Diss. Louvain.la-Neuve; Bibl. 357-386.

4750 *Herrmann, Wolfram* Zu Jer 33,11. BN 123 (2005) 41-44.

4751 *Yates, Gary E.* Ishmael's assassination of Gedaliah: echoes of the Saul-David story in Jeremiah 40:7-41:18. WThJ 67 (2005) 103-112 [2 Kgs 25,22-26].

4752 *Bogaert, Pierre-Maurice* Heshbon entre Moab et Ammon: la finale ajoutée à l'oracle sur Moab en Jr 48,45-47TM. FLUST, J.: BEThL 192: 2005 ⇒92. 45-54.

4753 **Jua, Lukas** The oracle concerning Babylon: a literary and theological investigation of Jeremiah 50:1-51:64. D*Conroy, Charles*: R 2005, 110 pp. Extr. Diss. Gregoriana; Bibl. 93-110.

4754 **Kessler, Martin** Battle of the Gods: the God of Israel versus Marduk of Babylon: a literary/theological interpretation of Jeremiah 50-51. SSN 42: 2003 ⇒19,4704; 20,4526. RThLZ 130 (2005) 635-636 (*Höffken, Peter*); BZ 49 (2005) 109-111 (*Fischer, Georg*); HebStud 46 (2005) 413-416 (*Sharp, Carolyn J.*); RBLit (2005)* (*Biddle, Mark E.*).

4755 *Köszeghy, Miklós* Zur šešek-Frage. ZAW 117 (2005) 616-620 [Jer 51,41].

## E8.8 **Lamentations**, *Threni*; **Baruch**; *Ep. Jer.*

4756 [ET]**Andrée, Alexander** GILBERTUS Universalis, glossa ordinaria in Lamentationes Ieremie Prophete: prothemata et liber 1: a critical edition. AUS 52: Sto 2005, Almqvist & W. xiv; 323 pp [RBen 116,142 —P.-M. Bogaert].

4757 [T]**Assan-Dhôte, Isabelle; Moatti-Fine, Jacqueline** Baruch, Lamentations, Lettre de Jérémie. La bible d'Alexandrie 25/2: P 2005, Cerf 342 pp. €45. 2-204-07730-5. [R]Igreja e Missão 58 (2005) 154-155 (*Couto, A.*); RSR 93 (2005) 585-587 (*Abadie, Philippe*); Carthaginensia 21 (2005) 502-503 (*Sanz Valdivieso, R.*); REG 118 (2005) 317-318 (*Pouderon, Bernard*).

4758 *Bergant, Dianne* Why does the city suffer?. BiTod 43 (2005) 73-78.

4759 *Berges, Ulrich* The violence of God in the book of Lamentations. [M]VAN TILBORG, S.: BiblInterp 71: 2005 ⇒155. 21-44.

4760 **Berges, Ulrich** Klagelieder. HThK.AT: 2002 ⇒18,4395. [R]ThLZ 130 (2005) 256-258 (*Kaiser, Otto*).

4761 **Berlin, Adele** Lamentations: a commentary. OTL: 2002 ⇒18,4396... 20,4529. [R]BS 162 (2005) 121-2 (*McCarty, Jake; Chisholm, Robert* ).

4762 *Chi Chung Lee, Archie* Mothers bewailing: reading Lamentations. Her master's tools?. 2005 ⇒493. 195-210.

4763 *Cody, Aelred* The forms and genres of the book of Lamentations. BiTod 43 (2005) 79-82.

4764 *Day, Linda* Despair and hope in the book of Lamentations. BiTod 43 (2005) 83-89.

[E]**Feder, F.** Biblia Sahidica: Ier., Lam., Ep. Ier., Bar. 2002 ⇒4694.

4765 *Houk, Cornelius* Multiple poets in Lamentations. JSOT 30 (2005) 111-125.

4766 *Keel, Othmar* Das je verschiedene theologische Profil der Klagelieder und der Volksklagen. [F]SCHENKER, A.: OBO 214: 2005 ⇒134. 128-142.

4767 *Labahn, Antje* Wild animals and chasing shadows: animal metaphors in Lamentations as indicator for individual threat. Metaphor in the Hebrew Bible. BEThL 187: 2005 ⇒799. 67-97.

4768 *Lee, Archie C.C.* Lamentations. Global bible commentary. 2005 ⇒ 2443. 226-233.

4769 **Lee, Nancy C.** The singers of Lamentations: cities under siege, from Ur to Jerusalem to Sarajevo.... BiblInterp 60: 2002 ⇒18,4402; 20, 4535. [R]BiblInterp 13 (2005) 197-200 (*Berlin, Adele*).

4770 *Martin, Seán* Lamentations during Holy Week Liturgy. BiTod 43 (2005) 90-95.

4771 *Meyer, Ivo* Lamentazioni. Introduzione AT. 2005 ⇒1159. 723-732.

4772 *Middlemas, Jill* The violent storm in Lamentations. JSOT 29 (2005) 81-97.

4773 **Morla Asensio, Víctor** Lamentaciones. Nueva Biblia Española: 2004 ⇒20,4538. [R]SalTer 93 (2005) 253-254 (*Sanz Giménez-Rico, Enrique*).

4774 *O'Connor, Kathleen M.* The book of Lamentations. OT survey. 2005 ⇒413. 328-335.

4775 **O'Connor, Kathleen** Lamentations and the tears of the world. 2002 ⇒18,4405. [R]BiblInterp 13 (2005) 201-203 (*Joyce, Paul M.*).

4776 *Pakala, James C.* A librarian's comments on commentaries: 20 (Lamentations and 2 Peter). Presbyterion 31 (2005) 107-111 [OTA 29,168].

4777 *Eidevall, Göran* Spatial metaphors in Lamentations 3,1-9;
4778 *Labahn, Antje* Bitterkeit und Asche als Speise—das Leiden Jeremias am Schicksal Jerusalems: Metaphern und Metaphervariationen in Thr 3,1-21 LXX;
4779 *Baumann, Gerlinde* "Er hat mir den Weg mit Quadersteinen vermauert" (Thr 3,9): ein Vorschlag zur Auslegung einer ungewöhnlichen Metapher. Metaphor in the Hebrew Bible. BEThL 187: 2005 ⇒ 799. 133-137/147-183/139-145.
4780 *Berlin, Adele* Poetry and theology in Lamentations 3:43-44 and 5:7. [F]KLEIN, J. 2005 ⇒79. 670-677.
4781 *Gous, Ignatius G.P.* Lamentations 4 in the light of poetry therapy. OTEs 18 (2005) 223-239.
4782 *Urbanz, Werner* Das Ende der Klagelieder: Notizen zu Klgl 5. PzB 14 (2005) 49-60.

4783 *Bogaert, Pierre-Maurice* Le livre de Baruch dans les manuscrits de la bible latine: disparition et réintégration. RBen 115 (2005) 286-342.
4784 *Meyer, Ivo* Il libro di Baruc e la lettera di Geremia. Introduzione AT. 2005 ⇒1159. 733-740.
4785 *Saldarini, Anthony J.* The book of Baruch. OT survey. 2005 ⇒413. 531-536.
4786 *Venter, P.M.* Penitential prayers in the books of Baruch and Daniel. OTEs 18 (2005) 406-425 [Dan 9,4-19].
4787 **Wright, J. Edward** Baruch ben Neriah: from biblical scribe to apocalyptic seer. Studies on personalities of the OT: 2003 ⇒19,4726; 20,4548. [R]JSJ 36 (2005) 135-136 (*De Troyer, Kristin*).

4788 [ET]**Herzer, Jens** 4 Baruch (Paraleipomena Jeremiou). SBL.Writings from the Ancient World 22: Atlanta, GA 2005, SBL xlii; 212 pp. $30. 1-58983-173-X.
4789 *Leuenberger, Martin* Ort und Funktion der Wolkenvision und ihrer Deutung in der syrischen Baruchapokalypse: eine These zu deren thematischer Entfaltung. JSJ 36 (2005) 206-246.
4790 **Nir, Rivka** The destruction of Jerusalem and the idea of redemption in the Syriac Apocalypse of Baruch. Early Judaism and its literature 20: 2003 ⇒19,4728; 20,4550. [R]JR 85 (2005) 155-157 (*Anderson, Gary A.*); JSSt 50 (2005) 403-405 (*Lied, Liv Ingeborg*); CrSt 26 (2005) 553-557 (*Ruzer, Serge*).
4791 *Wolff, Christian* Die Paralipomena Jeremiae und das Neue Testament. NTS 51 (2005) 123-136.

4792 *Saldarini, Anthony J.* The letter of Jeremiah. OT survey. 2005 ⇒413. 537-541.

## E8.9 **Ezekiel**: *textus, commentarii; themata, versiculi*

4793 San JERÓNIMO: obras completas: edición bilingüe, 5: comentario a Ezequiel (libros I-VIII). M 2005, BAC 599 pp.

4794 *Almada, Samuel E.* Ezekiel 1-39. Global bible commentary. 2005 ⇒ 2443. 234-245.

4795 **Betts, Terry J.** Ezekiel the priest: a custodian of tôrâ. Studies in biblical literature 74: NY 2005, Lang xv; 191 pp. $65/€54.10. 0-8204-7425-8. Bibl. 145-169. [R]RBLit (2005)* (*Fredenburg, Brandon*).

4796 [E]**Cohen, Menachem** Mikra'ot Gedolot 'Haketer': Ezekiel. 2000 ⇒ 16,4019; 20,4558. [R]REJ 164 (2005) 359-361 (*Kogel, Judith*).

4797 [E]**Cook, Stephen L.; Patton, Corrine L.** Ezekiel's hierarchical world: wrestling with a tiered reality. Symposium series 31: 2004 ⇒ 20,329. [R]RBLit (2005)* (*Konkel, Michael*).

4798 *Darr, Katheryn P.* The book of Ezekiel. OT survey. 2005 ⇒413. 336-354.

4799 *Dohmen, Christoph* "In weiter Ferne, so nah!": Ezechiel—Prophet für das Exil. WUB 37 (2005) 43-47.

4800 *Dreyer, Leonid* The temple of Ezekiel: why are some data lacking?. [M]DIAKONOFF, M. 2005 ⇒36. 727-730.

4801 *Fernández Marcos, Natalio* On Symmachus and Lucian in Ezekiel. [F]LUST, J.: BEThL 192: 2005 ⇒92. 151-161.

4802 *Ferrari, Michele C.* Before the glossa ordinaria: the Ezekiel fragment in Irish Minuscule Zürich, Staatsarchiv W3.19.XII, and other experiments towards a 'Bible commentée' in the early Middle Ages. Biblical studies. 2005 ⇒773. 283-307 [Scr. 60/1,49*—G. Michiels].

4803 *Ferry, Joëlle* Prophétie et apocalyptique chez Ezéchiel. Graphè 14 (2005) 13-28.

4804 *Gallazzi, Alessandro* Ezekiel 40-48. Global bible commentary. 2005 ⇒2443. 246-252.

4805 *García Martínez, Florentino* The apocalyptic interpretation of Ezekiel in the Dead Sea scrolls. [F]LUST, J.: BEThL 192: 2005 ⇒92. 163-176.

4806 *Gillmayr-Bucher, Susanne* Inanspruchnahme mit "Haut und Haar". BiKi 60 (2005) 136-138.

4807 *Gluska, Isaac* Akkadian influence on the book of Ezekiel. [F]KLEIN, J. 2005 ⇒79. 718-737.

4808 *Goff, Matthew J.* Hellenistic instruction in Palestine and Egypt: Ben Sira and Papyrus Insinger. JSJ 36 (2005) 147-172.

4809 **Greenberg, Moshe** Ezechiel 21-37. HThK.AT: FrB 2005, Herder 488 pp. 3-451-26843-4.

4810 *Haran, Menahem* Observations on Ezekiel as a book prophet. [F]FOX, M. 2005 ⇒43. 3-19.

4811 *Hauspie, Katrin* ἀκούω dans le livre d'Ezéchiel: étude sémantique en vue d'une traduction française et anglaise. [F]LUST, J.: BEThL 192: 2005 ⇒92. 177-192.

4812 *Hossfeld, Frank-Lothar* Ezechiel und sein Buch. BiKi 60 (2005) 148-152;

4813 Il libro di Ezechiele. Introduzione AT. 2005 ⇒1159. 741-766.

4814 **Hummel, Horace D.** Ezekiel 1-20. St. Louis 2005, Concordia xxiv; 614 pp. $43.

4815 *Kizhakkeyil, Sebastian* Ezekiel, a prophet in exile. JJSS 4 (2004) 78-93.

4816 *Knibb, Michael A.* Two notes on the Ethiopic text of Ezekiel. [F]ULLENDORFF, E.: SStLL 47: 2005 ⇒154. 236-244.

4817 **Kohn, Risa Levitt** A new heart and a new soul: Ezekiel, the exile and the torah. JSOT.S 358: 2002 ⇒18,4431... 20,4572. [R]BiblInterp

13 (2005) 85-88 (*Kaminsky, Joel S.*); JSSt 50 (2005) 217-218 (*Boadt, Lawrence*).

4818 *Lang, Bernhard* Ezechiel: Ort, Zeit und Botschaft des Propheten. BiKi 60 (2005) 130-135.

4819 *Lapsley, Jacqueline* Doors thrown open and waters gushing forth: Mark, Ezekiel, and the architecture of hope. [M]JUEL, D. 2005 ⇒73. 139-153.

4820 *Leicht, Barbara D.* Ich bin ein Mahnzeichen für euch: Priester, Prophet, Performance-Künstler. BiKi 60 (2005) 145-147.

4821 **Manning, Gary T.** Echoes of a prophet: the use of Ezekiel in the gospel of John and in literature of the second temple period. JSNT.S 270: 2004 ⇒20,4575. [R]RBLit (2005)* (*Miller, David*).

4822 **Odell, Margaret S.** Ezekiel. Macon, GA 2005, Smyth & H. 565 pp. $60. 1-57312-0731.

4823 *Poser, Ruth* "In der ruach liegt die Kraft": zur Bedeutung der Geistkraft im Buch Ezechiel. BiKi 60 (2005) 162-166.

4824 **Premstaller, Volkmar** Fremdvölkersprüche des Ezechielbuches. [D]*Block, Daniel*: FzB 104: Wü 2005, Echter xii; 292 pp. €30. 3-429-02687-3. Diss.-Habil. Innsbruck; Bibl. 268-279 [ThRv 102,xv].

4825 *Rom-Shiloni, Dalit* Ezekiel as the voice of the exiles and constructor of exilic ideology. HUCA 76 (2005) 1-45.

4826 *Schöpflin, Karin* The composition of metaphorical oracles within the book of Ezekiel. VT 55 (2005) 101-120.

4827 **Schöpflin, Karin** Theologie als Biographie im Ezechielbuch: ein Beitrag zur Konzeption alttestamentlicher Prophetie. FAT 36: 2002 ⇒18,4438. [R]Bib. 86 (2005) 424-427 (*Simian-Yofre, Horacio*); RBLit (2005)* (*Engle, John*).

4828 **Sedlmeier, Franz** Das Buch Ezechiel: Kapitel 1-24. Neuer Stuttgarter Kommentar, AT 21/1: 2002 ⇒18,4421; 19,4756. [R]CBQ 67 (2005) 512-513 (*Fechter, Friedrich*).

4829 *Sedlmeier, Franz Xaver* Fremdvölker unter JHWHs Gericht (Ez 25-32). BiKi 60 (2005) 158-161.

4830 **Stiebert, Johanna** The exile and the prophet's wife: historic events and marginal perspectives. Interfaces: ColMn 2005, Liturgical xxv; 130 pp. $15. 0-8146-5177-1. Bibl. 117-120.

4831 [E]**Talmon, Shemaryahu; Goshen-Gottstein, Moshe Henry** The book of Ezekiel. 2004 ⇒20,4594. [R]JSJ 36 (2005) 351-352 (*Tigchelaar, Eibert*); CBQ 67 (2005) 316-317 (*Marcus, David*); Sef. 65 (2005) 439-440 (*Fernández Tejero, E.*).

4832 *Terblanche, Marius* A sign to the reader: the proper name עֵדֶן in the book of Ezekiel. OTEs 18 (2005) 124-134.

4833 *Tigchelaar, Eibert* Notes on the Ezekiel scroll from Masada (Masezek). RdQ 22 (2005) 269-275.

4834 *Van der Kooij, Arie* The Septuagint of Ezekiel and Hasmonaean leadership. [F]LUST, J.: BEThL 192: 2005 ⇒92. 437-446.

4835 **Christman, Angela Russell** "What did Ezekiel see?": christian exegesis of Ezekiel's vision of the chariot from IRENAEUS to GREGORY the Great. The Bible in ancient Christianity 4: Lei 2005, Brill 195 pp. 90-04-14537-0. Bibl. 175-185 [Ezek 1].

4836 *Van Rooy, H.F.* The Peshitta of Ezekiel and the Septuagint: a study of the two traditions in Ezekiel 1. OTEs 18 (2005) 394-405.

4837 *Koch, Christiane* Von göttlichen und menschlichen Versicherungen .... BiKi 60 (2005) 186 [Ezek 1; 10].
4838 *Keel, Othmar* Merkwürdige Geschöpfe. BiKi 60 (2005) 139-144 [Ezek 1,4-28; 10].
4839 *Phinney, D. Nathan* The prophetic objection in Ezekiel iv 14 and its relation to Ezekiel's call. VT 55 (2005) 75-88.
4840 *Sweeney, Marvin A.* The destruction of Jerusalem as purification in Ezekiel 8-11. Form and intertextuality. FAT 45: 2005 ⇒313. 144-55.
4841 *Langer, Gerhard* Ein blutiges Bundesdrama: der Text Ezechiel 16 in Bibel und rabbinischer Auslegung. BiKi 60 (2005) 153-157.
4842 **Kamionkowski, S. Tamar** Gender reversal and cosmic chaos: a study in the book of Ezekiel. JSOT.S 368: 2003 ⇒19,4738; 20,4601. [R]CBQ 67 (2005) 320-321 (*Odell, Margaret S.*) [Ezek 16; 23].
4843 *Rosen-Zvi, Ishay* Another look at the adulteress' punishment in Ezekiel 16 and 23. BetM 181 (2005) 163-193. Sum 197. **H.**
4844 **Dus, Ramón A.** Las parábolas del reino de Judá: lingüística textual y comunicación (Ez 17; 19 y 21). 2003 ⇒19,4771. [R]EE 80 (2005) 183-4 (*Yebra, Carme*); RevBib 67 (2005) 108-112 (*Nápole, Gabriel M.*).
4845 **Alaribe, Gilbert N.** Ezekiel 18 and the ethics of responsibility: a study in biblical interpretations and christian ethics. [D]*Irsigler, Hubert* 2005, Diss. Freiburg [ThRv 102,v].
4846 *Friebel, Kelvin G.* The decrees of Yahweh that are 'not good': Ezekiel 20:25-26. [F]FOX, M. 2005 ⇒43. 21-36.
4847 *Davidovich, Tal* A new approach to Ezekiel 23,20. SJOT 19 (2005) 193-202.
4848 *Setodzo, Frédéric* Ezéchiel 24,15-27: demain ne meurt jamais. LeD 64 (2005) 13-22.
4849 *Udd, Kris J.* Prediction and foreknowledge in Ezekiel's prophecy against Tyre. TynB 56/1 (2005) 25-41 [Ezek 26].
4850 *Stager, Lawrence E.* Phoenician shipwrecks and the ship Tyre (Ezekiel 27). [F]MCCANN, A. 2005 ⇒99. 238-254.
4851 *Arbel, Daphna* "Seal of resemblance, full of wisdom, and perfect in beauty": the Enoch/Metatron narrative of 3 Enoch and Ezekiel 28. HThR 98 (2005) 121-142.
4852 *Wong, Ka Leung* The Prince of Tyre in the Masoretic and Septuagint texts of Ezekiel 28,1-10. [F]LUST, J.: BEThL 192: 2005 ⇒92. 447-461.
4853 *Virgili dal Prà, Rosanna* Il re di Tiro-Lucifero (Ez 28,1-19). PSV 51 (2005) 93-111.
4854 *Arbel, Daphna* Questions about Eve's iniquity, beauty, and fall: the "primal figure" in Ezekiel 28:11-19 and Genesis Rabbah traditions of Eve. JBL 124 (2005) 641-655.
4855 **Minj, Sudhir K.** Egypt: the lower kingdom: an exegetical study of God's dealing with Egypt in Ezekiel's oracles of judgment against Egypt in Ezek. 29,1-30,19. [D]*Jüngling, Hans-Winfried* 2005, 365 pp. Diss. Sankt Georgen [ThRv 102,v].
4856 *Sweeney, Marvin A.* The assertion of divine power in Ezekiel 33:21-39:29. Form and intertextuality. FAT 45: 2005 ⇒313. 156-172.
4857 *Varickasseril, Jose* The shepherds and the sheep in Ezekiel 34:1-31. [M]JOHN PAUL II. 2005 ⇒72. 133-142.
4858 *Scatolini Apóstolo, Silvio S.* Ezek 36, 37, 38 and 39 in Papyrus 967 as pre-text for re-reading Ezekiel. [F]LUST, J.: BEThL 192: 2005 ⇒92. 331-357.

4859 *Spronk, Klaas* Wie het weet mag het zeggen: opstanding der doden volgens Ezechiël 37. ITBT 13/3 (2005) 4-6.

4860 *Wendland, Ernst* Translating Ezekiel's vision of the dry bones—visually. BiTr 56 (2005) 76-87 [Ezek 37].

4861 **Fitzpatrick, Paul E.** The disarmament of God: Ezekiel 38-39 in its mythic context. CBQ.MS 37: 2004 ⇒20,4614. [R]ATG 68 (2005) 308-309 (*Vílchez, José*); HebStud 46 (2005) 417-419 (*Tooman, William A.*); JThS 56 (2005) 503-507 (*Murray, Robert*).

4862 *Joyce, Paul M.* Temple and worship in Ezekiel 40-48. Temple and worship. LHBOTS 422: 2005 ⇒731. 145-163.

4863 *Konkel, Michael* Paradies mit strengen Regeln: die Schlussvision des Ezechielbuches (Ez 40-48). BiKi 60 (2005) 167-172.

4864 *Schenker, Adrian* Das Allerheiligste in Ezechiels Tempel war ein Hof: die Tragweite der ursprünglichen Septuaginta in Ez 41,1-4. [F]LUST, J.: BEThL 192: 2005 ⇒92. 359-369.

## E9.1 Apocalyptica VT

4865 *Allison, Dale C., Jr.* The problem of apocalyptic: from polemic to apologetics;

4866 *Allison, Dale C.; Arnal, William* Responses. Apocalypticism, anti-Semitism. JSNT.S 275; JSHJ.S: 2005 ⇒767. 98-110/122-130.

4867 *Aspinen, Mika* Apocalyptic traditions in the bible. [F]AEJMELAEUS, L.: SESJ 89: 2005 ⇒1. 40-61.

4868 **Beyerle, Stefan** Die Gottesvorstellungen in der antik-jüdischen Apokalyptik. JSJ.S 103: Lei 2005, Brill xii; 547 pp. €129/$184. 90-04-13116-7. Bibl. 413-500.

4869 **Carey, G.** Ultimate things: an introduction to Jewish and christian apocalyptic literature. St. Louis, MO 2005, Chalice xiii; 280 pp. $25. 08272-38037. Bibl. [NTAb 50,431].

4870 *Collins, John J.* Some issues in the study of apocalyptic literature. Henoch 27/1-2 (2005) 21-26;

4871 Temporality and politics in Jewish apocalyptic literature <2002>;

4872 The legacy of apocalypticism <2001>. Encounters. 2005 ⇒200. 129-141/155-166.

4873 *Gruenwald, Ithamar* Apocalypticism and the religion and ritual of the "pre-Sinaitic" narratives. Enoch and Qumran origins. 2005 ⇒ 921. 148-151.

4874 **Jonaitis, D.** Unmasking apocalyptic texts: a guide to preaching and teaching. NY 2005, Paulist xvi; 198 pp. $19. 08091-43569. Bibl. [NTAb 50,614].

4875 *Lange, Armin* Dream visions and apocalyptic milieus;

4876 *Lim, Timothy H.* The Enochic circles, the Hasidim, and the Qumran community. Enoch and Qumran origins. 2005 ⇒921. 27-34/204-206.

4877 *Marshall, John W.* Apocalypticism and anti-Semitism: inner-group resources for inter-group conflicts. Apocalypticism, anti-Semitism. JSNT.S 275; JSHJ.S: 2005 ⇒767. 68-82.

4878 *McGinn, Bernard* Apocalypticism and violence: aspects of their relation in antiquity and the middle ages. Scripture and pluralism. 2005 ⇒757. 209-229.

4879 *Murphy, Frederick J.* Introduction to apocalyptic literature. OT survey. 2005 ⇒413. 355-370.

4880 *Muthunayagom, Daniel J.* Bible and the state: a view from the apocalyptic literature. BiBh 31 (2005) 27-37.
4881 *Nel, M.* Versoening in Joodse apokaliptiese literatuur. VeE 26 (2005) 186-204.
4882 *Sweeney, Marvin A.* The priesthood and the proto-apocalyptical reading of prophetic and pentateuchal texts. Form and intertextuality. FAT 45: 2005 ⇒313. 239-247.
4883 *Towner, Wayne S.* The dangers of dualism and the kerygma of Old Testament apocalyptic. Word and world 25 (2005) 264-273.
4884 *Valentin, Joachim* Endkampf–Hölle–Paradies: die Wirkungsgeschichte der Apokalyptik in den monotheistischen Religionen. StZ 223 (2005) 843-856.
4885 *Vonach, Andreas* Biblische Ursprünge apokalyptischen Denkens. Wenn alles aus ist—christliche Hoffnung angesichts von Tod und Weltende: Vorträge der fünften Innsbrucker Theologischen Sommertage 2004. [E]**Böhm, Thomas H.; Wandinger, Nikolaus**: theologische trends 14: Fra 2005, Lang 71-87. 3-631-54382-4.

## E9.2 **Daniel**: *textus, commentarii: themata, versiculi*

4886 *Boccaccini, Gabriele* The covenantal theology of the apocalyptic book of Daniel. Enoch and Qumran origins. 2005 ⇒921. 39-44.
4887 *Collins, Adela Yarbro; Collins, John J.* The book of Truth: Daniel as reliable witness to past and future in the United States of America. Encounters. 2005 <2003> ⇒200. 142-154.
4888 *Collins, John J.* Response: the apocalyptic worldview of Daniel;
4889 *Davila, James R.* The animal apocalypse and Daniel. Enoch and Qumran origins. 2005 ⇒921. 59-66/35-38.
4890 *DiTommaso, Lorenzo* 4QPseudo-Daniel A-B (4Q243-4Q244) and the book of Daniel. DSD 12 (2005) 101-133.
4891 **DiTommaso, Lorenzo** The book of Daniel and the apocryphal Daniel literature. SVTP 20: Lei 2005, Brill xx; 547 pp. €125. 90-04-14-4-129.
4892 *García Martínez, Florentino* Comparing the groups behind dream visions and Daniel: a brief note;
4893 *Henze, Matthias* Enoch's dream visions and the visions of Daniel reexamined. Enoch and Qumran origins. 2005 ⇒921. 45-46/17-22.
4894 **Kim, Sung Ik** Proclamation in cross-cultural context: missiological implications of the book of Daniel. [D]*Bauer, Bruce L.* 2005, Diss. Andrews 2005 [AUSS 43,332].
4895 **Koch, Klaus** Daniel 1-4. BK.AT 22/1: Neuk 2005, Neuk'er viii; 463 pp. €109.
4896 *LaCocque, André* Daniel. Global bible commentary. 2005 ⇒2443. 253-261.
4897 *Lemcio, Eugene E.* "Son of man", "pitiable man", "rejected man" equivalent expressions in the Old Greek of Daniel. TynB 56/1 (2005) 43-60.
4898 **Marconcini, Benito** Daniele. 2004 ⇒20,4631. [R]StPat 52 (2005) 651-652 (*Lorenzin, Tiziano*); ZKTh 127 (2005) 130-131 (*Paganini, Simone*); RivBib 53 (2005) 354-357 (*Cimosa, Mario*); PaVi 50/3 (2005) 63 (*Cirignano, Giulio*).

4899 *McLay, R. Timothy* Double translations in the Greek versions of Daniel. [F]LUST, J.: BEThL 192: 2005 ⇒92. 255-267.

4900 *Munnich, Olivier* La Peshitta de Daniel et ses relations textuelles avec la Septante. [F]SCHENKER, A.: OBO 214: 2005 ⇒134. 229-247;

4901 Le cadrage dynastique et l'ordre des chapitres dans le livre de Daniel. L'apport de la Septante. LeDiv 203: 2005 ⇒764. 161-195.

4902 *Nel, Marius* Huidige Danielnavorsing, en die pad vorentoe. OTEs 18 (2005) 777-789;

4903 Pentateugtradisies en -temas in Daniël. HTS 61 (2005) 1321-1337 [OTA 29,311] [Ps 69,10].

4904 *Niehr, Herbert* Il libro di Daniele. Introduzione AT. 2005 ⇒1159. 767-782.

4905 **Niskanen, Paul** The human and the divine in history: HERODOTUS and the book of Daniel. JSOT.S 396: 2004 ⇒20,4636. [R]RBLit (2005)* (*Venter, Pieter*).

4906 *Paul, Shalom M.* From Mari to Daniel: instructions for the acceptance of servants into the royal court. Divrei Shalom. CHANE 23: 2005 <1993> ⇒273. 205-211.

4907 *Pyper, Hugh S.* Reading in the dark: Zechariah, Daniel and the difficulty of scripture. JSOT 29 (2005) 485-504.

4908 *Roberto, Umberto* Das Buch des Propheten Daniel als Grundlage der christlichen Weltchronistik. Welt-Zeit. 2005 ⇒597. 59-62.

4909 *Smith-Christopher, Daniel L.* The additions to Daniel;

4910 The book of Daniel. OT survey. 2005 ⇒413. 542-543/371-383.

4911 *Sweeney, Marvin A.* The end of eschatology in Daniel?: theological and socio-political ramifications of the changing contexts of interpretation. Form and intertextuality. FAT 45: 2005 ⇒313. 248-261.

4912 *Thomas, Madathilparampil M.* The book of Daniel: the apocalypse with a distinct charter for liberative praxis and theological vision. AJTh 19/2 (2005) 284-308.

4913 *Tiller, Patrick* The sociological context of the dream visions of Daniel and 1 Enoch. Enoch and Qumran origins. 2005 ⇒921. 23-26.

4914 *Van Deventer, Hans* The bold, the beautiful and the beasts in the book of Daniel. Scriptura 90 (2005) 722-730 [OTA 30,61].

4915 *Wesselius, Jan W.* The literary nature of the book of Daniel and the linguistic character of its Aramaic. AramSt 3 (2005) 241-283.

4916 *Holm, Tawny L.* Daniel 1-6: a biblical story-collection. Ancient fiction. SBL.Symp. 32: 2005 ⇒721. 149-166.

4917 **Kirkpatrick, Shane** Competing for honor: a social-scientific reading of Daniel 1-6. [D]*Ulrich, Eugene*: BiblInterp 74: Lei 2005, Brill xvii; 196 pp. 90-04-14487-0. Diss. Notre Dame; Bibl. 174-186.

4918 *Paul, Shalom M.* The Mesopotamian background of Daniel 1-6. Divrei Shalom. CHANE 23: 2005 <2001> ⇒273. 285-297.

4919 *Valeta, David M.* Court or jester tales?: resistance and social reality in Daniel 1-6. Ment. *Bakhtin, M.*: PRSt 32/3 (2005) 309-324.

4920 *Van Deventer, H.J.M.* Testing-testing, do we have a translated text in Daniel 1 and Daniel 7?. JNSL 31/2 (2005) 91-106.

4921 *Regalado, Ferdinand O.* The meaning of אַזְדָּא in Daniel 2:5,8 and its implications for Nebuchadnezzar's dream. DavarLogos 4/1 (2005) 17-37.

4922 *Xeravits, Géza G.* Poetic passages in the Aramaic part of the book of Daniel. BN 124 (2005) 29-40 [Dan 2,20-3; 3,31-3; 4,31-2; 6,26-28].

4923 *Barkhuizen, Jan H.* ROMANOS Melodos: Kontakion 8 "on the three children". APB 16 (2005) 1-28 [Dan 3].

4924 *Botha, Phil J.* The interpretation of Daniel 3 in the Syriac commentary ascribed to EPHREM the Syrian. APB 16 (2005) 29-53.

4925 *Kritzinger, J.P.* St JEROME's commentary on Daniel 3;

4926 *Prinsloo, Gert T.* Daniel 3: intratextual perspectives and intertextual tradition. APB 16 (2005) 54-69/70-90.

4927 *Stander, Hendrik F.* CHRYSOSTOM's interpretation of the narrative of the three confessors in the fiery furnace [Dan 3];

4928 *Swart, G.J.* Divergences between the OG and Th versions of Daniel 3: evidence of early Hellenistic interpretation of the narrative of the three young men in the furnace?. APB 16 (2005) 91-105/106-120.

4929 *Silva, Rafael R. da* Ironizando a violência do poder: uma leitura dos contos de Daniel. Espaços 13 (2005) 193-205 [OTA 29,171] [Dan 3; 6].

4930 *Paul, Shalom M.* Daniel 3:29: a case study of 'neglected' blasphemy. Divrei Shalom. CHANE 23: 2005 <1983> ⇒273. 133-137.

4931 *Neef, Heinz-Dieter* Menschliche Hybris und göttliche Macht: Dan 4 LXX und Dan 4 Th im Vergleich. JNSL 31/2 (2005) 59-89.

4932 *McLay, R. Timothy* The Old Greek translation of Daniel iv-vi and the formation of the book of Daniel. VT 55 (2005) 304-323.

4933 *Paul, Shalom M.* Decoding a 'joint' expression in Daniel 5:6, 16. Divrei Shalom. CHANE 23: 2005 <1993> ⇒273. 195-203.

4934 *Martin de Viviés, Pierre de* Les séjours de Daniel dans la fosse aux lions: regard narratif synoptique. Analyse narrative. BEThL 191: 2005 ⇒742. 131-143 [Dan 6; 14].

4935 *Paul, Shalom M.* Dan 6:8: an Aramaic reflex of Assyrian legal terminology <1984>;

4936 Daniel 6:20: an Aramaic calque on an Akkadian expression <2004>. Divrei Shalom. CHANE 23: 2005 ⇒273. 139-144/329-331.

4937 **Keel, Othmar; Staub, Urs** Hellenismus und Judentum: vier Studien zu Daniel 7 und zur Religionsnot unter Antiochus IV. OBO 178: 2000 ⇒16,280...20,4653. [R]BiOr 62 (2005) 580-82 (*Grabbe, Lester*).

4938 *Kvanvig, Helge S.* Throne visions and monsters: the encounter between Danielic and Enochic traditions. ZAW 117 (2005) 249-272 [Dan 7].

4939 *Scalabrini, Patrizio Rota* Il Figlio dell'uomo e la bestia. PSV 51 (2005) 113-131 [Dan 7].

4940 *Olivares, Carlos* El león con alas de águila en Daniel 7:4: un resumen de la locura y restauración de Nabucodonosor (Dn 4). DavarLogos 4/2 (2005) 149-158.

4941 *Albani, Matthias* The "One like a son of man" (Dan 7:13) and the royal ideology. Enoch and Qumran origins. 2005 ⇒921. 47-53.

4942 *Beyerle, Stefan* "One like a son of man": innuendoes of a heavenly individual. Enoch & Qumran origins. 2005 ⇒921. 54-58 [Dan 7,13].

4943 *Hofius, Otfried* Der Septuaginta-Text von Daniel 7,13-14: Erwägungen zu seiner Gestalt und seiner Aussage. ZAW 117 (2005) 73-90 [Mark 14,62].

4944 **Gzella, Holger** Cosmic battle and political conflict: studies in verbal syntax and contextual interpretation of Daniel 8. BibOr 47: 2003 ⇒19,4852; 20,4658. [R]JSSt 50 (2005) 385-386 (*Meadowcroft, Tim*).

4945 *Meadowcroft, Tim* Who are the princes of Persia and Greece (Daniel 10)?: pointers towards the Danielic vision of earth and heaven. JSOT 29 (2005) 99-113.

4946 *Toepel, Alexander* Planetary demons in early Jewish literature. JSPE 14/3 (2005) 231-238 [Dan 10,13-21].

4947 *Steinmann, Andrew E.* Is the antichrist in Daniel 11?. BS 162/646 (2005) 195-209.

4948 *McGarry, Eugene* The ambidextrous angel (Daniel 12:7 and Deuteronomy 32:40): inner-biblical exegesis and textual criticism in counterpoint. JBL 124 (2005) 211-228 [Rev 10; 15,3-4].

4949 *Paul, Shalom M.* Daniel 12:9: a technical Mesopotamian scribal term. Divrei Shalom. CHANE 23: 2005 <2003> ⇒273. 319-321.

## E9.3 *Prophetae Minores*, **Dōdekaprophetōn...Hosea, Joel**

4950 The Navarre bible: minor prophets: the books of Hosea, Joel, Amos, Obadiah, Jonah, Micah, Nahum, Habakkuk, Zephaniah, Haggai, Zechariah and Malachi in the Revised Standard Version and New Vulgate...commentary by members of the Fac. of Theol. Univ. of Navarre. Dublin 2005, Four Courts 362 pp. 1851829717. Bibl. 357-358.

4951 **Achtemeier, Elizabeth** I Dodici Profeti parte seconda: Naum, Abacuc, Sofonia, Aggeo, Zaccaria, Malachia. [E]*Ferri, Corrado*: Strumenti Commentari 31: T 2004, Claudiana 441 pp. 978-88-7016-665-1. Bibl. 281-284.

4952 **Barco del Barco, Francisco J. del** Profecía y sintaxis: el uso de las formas verbales en los Profetas Menores preexílicos. TECC 69: 2003 ⇒19,4864; 20,4668. [R]RB 112 (2005) 139-42 (*Steymans, Hans U.*).

4953 **Beck, Martin** Der "Tag YHWH's" im Dodekapropheton: Studien im Spannungsfeld von Traditions- und Redaktionsgeschichte. [D]*Schmitt, H.-C.*: BZAW 356: B 2005, De Gruyter xi; 350 pp. €98. 3-11-01857-5-X. Diss.-Habil. Erlangen-Nürnberg; Bibl. 325-346.

4954 **Boda, Mark J.** Haggai, Zechariah. GR 2004, Zondervan 576 pp. 978-0-310-20615-6. Bibl. 73-84.

4955 **Bruckner, James K.** Jonah, Nahum, Habakkuk, Zephaniah. GR 2004, Zondervan 356 pp. 0-310-20637-5.

4956 [T]**Hill, Robert C.** THEODORE of Mopsuestia: commentary on the Twelve Prophets. *Theodorus M <author>* FaCh 103: 2004 ⇒20, 4676. [R]EThL 81 (2005) 237 (*Auwers, J.-M.*).

4957 *Joosten, Jan* A Septuagintal translation technique in the Minor Prophets: the elimination of verbal repetitions. [F]LUST, J.: BEThL 192: 2005 ⇒92. 217-223.

4958 *Leuenberger, Martin* Herrschaftsverheißungen im Zwölfprophetenbuch: ein Beitrag zu seiner thematischen Kohärenz und Anlage. Prophetische Heils- und Herrschererwartungen. 2005 ⇒479. 75-111.

4959 **Limburg, James** I dodici profeti, parte prima: Osea, Gioele, Amos, Abdia, Giona, Michea. [T]*Ferri, Corrado*: Strumenti 23: T 2005, Claudiana 300 pp. €24.50. 88701-65914.

4960 *Lux, Rüdiger* "Still alles Fleisch vor JHWH ...": das Schweigegebot im Dodekapropheton und sein besonderer Ort im Zyklus der Nachtgesichte des Sacharja. leqach 6 (2005) 99-113.

4961 **Masini, Mario** Profeti minori. Dabar: Padova 2005, EMP 252 pp. €12.50. [R]CredOg 25/5 (2005) 150-151 (*Cappelletto, Gianni*).

4962 **Mason, Rex** Micah, Nahum and Obadiah. Study Guides: L 2004, Clark 116 pp. $18. [R]RBLit (2005)* (*O'Brien, Julia*).

4963 **Nobile, Marco** Amos e Osea. Padova 2005, EMP 180 pp.

4964 **O'Brien, Julia M.** Nahum, Habakkuk, Zephaniah, Haggai, Zechariah, Malachi. 2004 ⇒20,4682. [R]CBQ 67 (2005) 504-505 (*Jones, Barry A.*); RBLit 7 (2005) 168-170 (*Becking, Bob*).

4965 **Parmentier, Roger** Les prophètes Amos et Osée (VIIIe siècle avant l'ère chrétienne) actualisées. P 2005, L'Harmattan 94 pp. €11. 978-27475-99993.

4966 **Perlitt, Lothar** Die Propheten Nahum, Habakuk, Zephanja. ATD 25/1: 2004 ⇒20,4684. [R]JETh 19 (2005) 244-246 (*Renz, Thomas*).

4967 [E]**Redditt, Paul L.; Schart, Aaron** Thematic threads in the book of the Twelve. BZAW 325: 2003 ⇒19,633; 20,4685. [R]BZ 49 (2005) 111-114 (*Scoralick, Ruth*).

4968 [E]**Reggi, Roberto** שנים עשר: Profeti minori: traduzione interlineare in italiano. Bo 2005, EDB xii; 119 pp. €9. 88-10-82015-0.

4969 **Roth, Martin** Israel und die Völker im Zwölfprophetenbuch: eine Untersuchung zu den Büchern Joel, Jona, Micha und Nahum. FRLANT 210: Gö 2005, Vandenhoeck & R. 316 pp. 3-525-53074-9. Bibl. 303-313.

4970 *Scherer, Andreas* Vom Sinn prophetischer Gerichtsverkündigung bei Amos und Hosea. Bib. 86 (2005) 1-19.

4971 **Simundson, Daniel J.** Hosea, Joel, Amos, Obadiah, Jonah, Micah. Nv 2005, Abingdon ix; 350 pp. $39. 0-687-34244-9. Bibl. 348-350 [R]RBLit (2005)* (*Cathey, Joseph*).

4972 **Smith, Gary V.** Hosea, Amos, Micah. GR 2001, Zondervan 596 pp. 978-0-310-20614-9.

4973 *Sweeney, Marvin A.* Sequence and interpretation in the book of the Twelve. Form and intertextuality. FAT 45: 2005 ⇒313. 175-188.

4974 *Sykes, Seth* Time and space in Haggai-Zechariah 1-8: a Bakhtinian analysis of a prophetic chronicle. Studies in Biblical Literature 24: 2002 ⇒18,4532. [R]BiblInterp 13 (2005) 203-06 (*Mandolfo, Carleen*).

4975 **Szmajdzinski, Mariusz** 'Ogień pożerający' (esz + 'akal) w Zbiorze Dwunastu Prorków ['Le feu dévorant' ('ech + 'akal) dans la Collection des Douze Prophètes]. [D]*Tronina, A.* 2005, 282 pp. Diss. Lublin [RTL 37,612]. **P.**

4976 *Zenger, Erich* Il libro dei Dodici profeti. Introduzione AT. 2005 ⇒1159. 783-882.

4977 [E]**Zenger, Erich** "Wort JHWHs, das geschah ..." (Hos 1,1): Studien zum Zwölfprophetenbuch. Herders biblische Studien 35: 2002 ⇒18,4115. [R]ThLZ 130 (2005) 1316-1318 (*Schart, Aaron*).

4978 **Ben Zvi, Ehud** Hosea. FOTL 21A/1: GR 2005, Eerdmans xiii; 321 pp. $55. 0-8028-0795-X.

4979 **Keefe, Alice A.** Woman's body and the social body in Hosea. JSOT.S 338; Gender, Culture, Theory 10: 2001 ⇒17,4131. [R]CBQ 67 (2005) 498-499 (*Seeman, Chris*); RBLit (2005)* (*Hunziker-Rodewald, Regine*); BiCT 1/4 (2005)* (*Fuchs, Esther*).

4980 *Lima, María de L.C.* A volta de Deus e a volta de Israel: o tema da conversão no livro do profeta Oséias. Colectânea (2005) 267-282.

4981 *Moreira, Gilvander* Oséias, o profeta das relações de amor e da anti-idolatria: 'Quero misericórdia; sacrificio, não!' (Os 6,6); 'Eu vou, eu mesmo, persuadir o povo, conduzi-lo ao deserto e convencê-lo' (Os 2,16). Convergência 40 (2005) 219-239.

4982 **Pentiuc, Eugen J.** Long-suffering love: a commentary on Hosea with patristic annotations. 2002 ⇒18,4542... 20,4697. [R]JThS 56 (2005) 507-509 (*Macintosh, A.A.*).

4983 **Pfeiffer, Henrik** Das Heiligtum von Bethel im Spiegel des Hoseabuches. FRLANT 183: 1999 ⇒15,4023... 18,4543. [R]OLZ 100 (2005) 633-636 (*Crüsemann, Frank*).

4984 *Šporčić, Ivan* Flora u svijetu simbola drugog dijela Hošejine knjige: metaforički izrazi za narod. BoSm 75 (2005) 61-78. **Croatian**;

4985 "Kad je Efrajim svoju bolest vidio, a Judeja ranu svoju ...": o bolesti u knjizi proroka Hošeje. BoSm 75 (2005) 79-95. **Croatian**.

4986 *Puykunnel, Shaji J.* The shepherd and the beast: pastoral imagery for Yahweh in the book of Hosea. [M]JOHN PAUL II. 2005 ⇒72. 108-119.

4987 **Rudnig-Zelt, Susanne** Hoseastudien: redaktionskritische Untersuchungen zur Genese des Hoseabuches. [D]*Pohlmann, Karl-Friedrich* 2005, Diss. Münster [ThLZ 130,889].

4988 *Sampaio, Tânia M.* Hosea. Global bible commentary. 2005 ⇒2443. 262-271.

4989 [E]**Siebert-Hommes, J.** Hosea 1-3. Kampen 2000, Kok 120 pp. f30. 90-242-6239-9.

4990 **Trotter, James M.** Reading Hosea in Achaemenid Yehud. JSOT.S 328: 2001 ⇒17,4140. [R]HebStud 46 (2005) 419-422 (*Hill, John*).

4991 *Yee, Gale A.* The book of Hosea. OT survey. 2005 ⇒413. 384-395.

4992 *Mitchell, Matthew W.* Hosea 1-2 and the search for unity. JSOT 29 (2005) 115-127.

4993 **Kelle, Brad E.** Hosea 2: metaphor and rhetoric in historical perspective. SBL.Academia Biblica 20: Lei 2005, Brill xiv; 355 pp. 90-04-14669-5. Bibl. 299-324; also Atlanta: SBL $46; 158983-1896.

4994 *Lima, Maria de Lourdes Corrêa* A fidelidade de Yhwh diante da infidelidade do povo: o anúncio de Os 2,18-25 no contexto de Os 1-3. AtT 9 (2005) 295-306.

4995 *Tsukimoto, Akio* Peace in the book of Hosea: Hos 2:20a in the biblical context. AJBI 30-31 (2004-2005) 22-29.

4996 *Hoffmeyer, Jeffrey H.* Covenant and creation: Hosea 4:1-3. RExp 102 (2005) 143-151.

4997 *Marques, Maria A.; Nakanose, Shigeyuki* Sangue derramado soma-se ao sangue derramado: uma leitura de Oséias 4,1-3. Espaços 13 (2005) 133-144 [OTA 29,173].

4998 *Bons, Eberhard* Une vache folle dans la bible?: la comparaison ὡς δάμαλις παροιστρῶσα παροίστρησεν Ισραηλ· (Os 4,16LXX) et son arrière-fond littéraire. [F]SCHENKER, A.: OBO 214: 2005 ⇒134. 30-7.

4999 *Johansen, Merete B.* "Jeg fandt Israel som druer i ørkenen, jeg s[a-Kreis] jeres faedre som tidlige figner i den første høst". Om brugen af metaforer i Hoseas' Bog med saerligt fokus p[a- Kreis] Hos 5,8-15 og 6,1-3. DTT 68/2 (2005) 81-96.

5000 *Paul, Shalom M.* The image of the oven and the cake in Hosea 7:4-10 <1968>;

5001 Hosea 7:16: gibberish jabber <1995>;

5002 משא מלך שרים: Hosea 8:8-10 and ancient Near Eastern royal epithets <1986>. Divrei Shalom. 2005 ⇒273. 3-9/257-262/145-154.

5003 *Wehrle, Josef* "Als Israel jung war, gewann ich ihn lieb [...]": Jahwes Liebe und Erbarmen als konstitutive Komponenten für das alttestamentliche Gottesverständnis nach der Botschaft des Propheten Hosea. [F]LAUB, F.: Bibel-Schule-Leben 6: 2005 ⇒87. 9-24 [Hos 11,1-9].

5004 **Kakkanattu, Joy Philip** A hymn of the enduring love of God: a synchronic and diachronic analysis of Hosea 11,1-11. [D]*Conroy, Charles*: R 2005, xiii; 89 pp. Extr. Diss. Gregoriana; Bibl. 59-85.

5005 *Chalmers, R. Scott* Who is the real El? a reconstruction of the prophet's polemic in Hosea 12:5a. ProcGLM 25 (2005) 97-106.
5006 *Boshoff, Willem* 'Who is wise?': interpretations of the postscript of the book Hosea (14:10 [English 14:9]). OTEs 18 (2005) 172-88 [Ps 1-2].
5007 *Achtemeier, Elizabeth* The book of Joel. OT survey. 2005 ⇒413. 396-397.
5008 *Andiñach, Pablo R.* Joel. Global bible commentary. 2005 ⇒2443. 272-276.
5009 *Godoy, Daniel* Os Persas chegaram: a violência permanesceu!. Espaços 13 (2005) 179-192 [OTA 29,173].
5010 *Sweeney, Marvin A.* The place and function of Joel in the book of the Twelve. Form and intertextuality. FAT 45: 2005 ⇒313. 189-209.
5011 *Linville, James R.* Letting the "Bi-word" "rule" in Joel 2:17. JHScr 5/2 (2004)*.

## E9.4 Amos

5012 **Auld, A. Graeme** Amos. Study Guides: L 2004, Clark 93 pp. $14. RRBLit (2005)* (*Roesel, Nahum*).
5013 *Ausín Olmos, Santiago* El pasado de Israel: la evocación del Éxodo. ResB 48 (2005) 23-34.
5014 *Ábrego de Lacy, José María* Amós el profeta. ResB 48 (2005) 5-12.
5015 *Barriocanal Gómez, José Luis* El libro: su entramado y su estructura. ResB 48 (2005) 13-22.
5016 *Berthoud, Pierre* The covenant and the social message of Amos. EurJT 14/2 (2005) 99-109.
5017 **Bulkeley, Tim** Amos: hypertext bible commentary. Auckland 2005, Hypertext Bible. $25 (pers. use); $40 (instit.). CD-ROM.
5018 **Carroll R., M. Daniel** Amos—the prophet and his oracles: research on the book of Amos. 2002 ⇒18,4559... 20,4730. RRBLit 7 (2005) 188-190 (*McEntire, Mark*).
5019 *Carroll Rodas, M. Daniel* Can the prophets shed light on our worship wars?: how Amos evaluates religious ritual. Stone-Campbell Journal [Joplin, MO] 8 (2005) 215-227 [OTA 29,174].
5020 *Dijkstra, Meindert* Unit delimitation and interpretation in the book of Amos. Layout markers. Pericope 5: 2005 ⇒422. 114-140.
5021 *Gowan, Donald E.* The book of Amos. OT survey. 2005 ⇒413. 398-405.
5022 **Möller, Karl** A prophet in debate: the rhetoric of persuasion in the book of Amos. JSOT.S 372: 2003 ⇒19,4929; 20,4732. RKerux 20/1 (2005) 64-65 (*Dennison, James T. Jr.*); RBLit 7 (2005) 190-193 (*Garber, David G.*).
5023 *Ngan, Lai L.* Amos. Global bible commentary. 2005 ⇒2443. 277-85.
5024 **Pierri, Rosario** Parole del profeta Amos: il libro di Amos secondo i LXX. SBFA 59: 2002 ⇒18,4566... 20,4733. REstTrin 39 (2005) 587-589 (*Vázquez Allegue, Jaime*).
5025 *Ramis Darder, Francesc* El futuro de Israel: 'el día de Yahvé'. ResB 48 (2005) 45-53.
5026 *Sevilla Jiménez, Cristóbal* El presente de Israel: '¡buscad a Yahvé y vivréis!': culto, derecho, justicia y vida. ResB 48 (2005) 35-44.

5027 *Snyman, S.D.* The land as a Leitmotiv in the book of Amos. VeE 26 (2005) 527-542.

5028 **Steiner, Richard C.** Stockmen from Tekoa, sycomores from Sheba: a study of Amos' occupations. CBQ.MS 36: 2003 ⇒19,4935; 20,4736. [R]JThS 56 (2005) 135-137 (*Gillingham, Susan*) [Amos 1,1; 7,14-15].

5029 *Paul, Shalom M.* A literary reinvestigation of the authenticity of the oracles against the nations of Amos <1981> [Amos 1,3-2,3];

5030 Amos 1:3-2:3: a concatenous literary pattern <1971>. Divrei Shalom. CHANE 23: 2005 ⇒273. 417-437/353-362.

5031 *Steins, Georg* Das Chaos kehrt zurück!: Aufbau und Theologie von Amos 3-6. BN 122 (2005) 35-43 [Gen 6-8; Exod 20; 32-34].

5032 *Barriocanal Gómez, José Luis* La singularidad de Israel: 'solamente a vosotros os he conocido' (Am 3,2). ResB 48 (2005) 55-59.

5033 *Paul, Shalom M.* Amos 3:3-8: the irresistible sequence of cause and effect. Divrei Shalom. CHANE 23: 2005 <1983> ⇒273. 439-455;

5034 Amos 3:15—winter and summer mansions <1978>;

5035 Fishing imagery in Amos 4:2 <1978>. Divrei Shalom. CHANE 23: 2005 ⇒273. 77-79/81-89.

5036 *Lombaard, Christo* What is Isaac doing in Amos 7?. Critical study. ATM 20: 2005 ⇒457. 152-159.

5037 *Ramis Darder, Francesc* Amós: el clam per la pau que brolla de la justícia social. Comunicació [Palma de Mallorca] 113 (2005) 9-21 [OTA 29,78] [Amos 7,10-17].

5038 *Paul, Shalom M.* Two cosmographical terms in Amos 9:6. Divrei Shalom. CHANE 23: 2005 ⇒273. 343-349.

## E9.5 Jonas

5039 **Cardona Ramírez, Hernán** Jonás salvado por los paganos: algunos matices en el texto hebreo. Colección Religión: Medellín 2005, Univ. Pont. Bolivariana 153 pp. 958-696-431-0. Bibl. 139-151.

5040 *Carreira, José Nunes* Motivos egípcios no livro de Jonas. Did(L) 35 (2005) 35-47.

5041 *Chen, Nan J.* Jonah. Global bible commentary. 2005 ⇒2443. 291-4.

5042 *Coetzee, Johan H.* Jonah from the perspective of Jonah: embodied theology illustrated. Scriptura 90 (2005) 850-858 [OTA 30,63].

5043 *Eynikel, Erik* The book of Jonah and the parable of the Prodigal Son. [F]LUST, J.: BEThL 192: 2005 ⇒92. 121-138 [Luke 15,11-32].

5044 **Gaines, Janet H.** Forgiveness in a wounded world: Jonah's dilemma. SBL.Studies in Biblical Literature 5: 2003 ⇒19,4961. [R]CBQ 67 (2005) 491-492 (*Craig, Kenneth*); RBLit (2005)* (*Bolin, Thomas*).

5045 **Green, Barbara** Jonah's journeys. Interfaces: ColMn 2005, Liturgical xix; 172 pp. $15. 0-8146-5038-4. Bibl. 159-164.

5046 *Handy, Lowell K.* Joining Leviathan, Behemoth and the dragons: Jonah's fish as monster. ProcGLM 25 (2005) 77-85.

5047 *Lichtert, Claude* Un siècle de recherche à propos de Jonas. RB 112 (2005) 192-214, 330-354.

5048 *Lietaert Peerbolte, Bert J.* Het teken van Jona als christologische typologie. ACEBT 22 (2005) 139-150 [OTA 30,392].

**Mosis, R.** Welterfahrung und Gottesglaube 2004 ⇒3661.

5049 ETRisse, S. HIERONYMUS: Commentarius in Ionam prophetam: Kommentar zu dem Propheten Jona. FC 60: 2003 ⇒19,4972; 20,4770. RJThS 56 (2005) 681-682 (*Hayward, C.T.R.*).

5050 **Sherwood, Yvonne** A biblical text and its afterlives: the survival of Jonah in western culture. 2000 ⇒16,4221... 20,4773. RRBLit 7 (2005) 476-478 (*Linafelt, Tod*); BiCT 1/2 (2005)* (*Aichele, George*).

5051 *Siebert-Hommes, Jopie* Een kikajonstruik om Jona te redden... (Jona 4:6): compositie en interpretatie van het boek Jona. ACEBT 22 (2005) 47-58 [OTA 30,368].

5052 *Smelik, Klaas A.D.* Mens en dier in zak en as: de bijfiguren in het boek Jona. ACEBT 22 (2005) 101-111 [OTA 30,369].

5053 *Solà, Teresa* Llibertat de Jahvè per a ser bo amb els estrangers en Jonàs. La bíblia i els immigrants. 2005 ⇒471. 73-92.

5054 *Spronk, Klaas* Het boek Jona: een overzicht van het recente onderzoek. ACEBT 22 (2005) 1-22 [OTA 30,369].

5055 *Talstra, Eep* Tussen structuur en strategie: tekstanalyse van Jona 1-4. ACEBT 22 (2005) 23-45 [OTA 30,369].

5056 *Trible, Phyllis* The book of Jonah. OT survey. 2005 ⇒413. 412-432.

5057 *Wilt, Timothy L.* PIGEON: a translation of *Yonah*. BiTr 56 (2005) 45-57.

5058 *Wimmer, Joseph F.* Jonah's lessons on conversion. BiTod 43 (2005) 377-381.

5059 *Wit, Hans de* Lezen met Jona: Jona in intercultureel perspectief. ACEBT 22 (2005) 151-166 [OTA 30,369].

5060 *Yuen, Royan S.C.* Yahweh loves Jonah and he loves Nineveh: some thoughts on the rhetorical intention of the book of Jonah. ThLi 28 (2005) 91-96.

5061 *Van Dorp, Jaap* Enkele aantekeningen bij de vertaling van Jona 1:1. ACEBT 22 (2005) 71-80 [OTA 30,369].

5062 *Lichtert, Claude* La prière de Jonas (Jon 2,3-10) comme élément narratif. Analyse narrative. BEThL 191: 2005 ⇒742. 407-414.

5063 *Mulzer, Martin* Syntax, Sprechakte und Metaphorik im Jonapsalm (Jona 2,3b-10). FIRSIGLER, H.: ATSAT 76: 2005 ⇒67. 105-126.

5064 *Tadiello, Roberto* La strana preghiera di un profeta in fuga: Gio 2,3b-10. BeO 47 (2005) 139-162.

5065 *Van Midden, Piet* Zingen met Jona. ACEBT 22 (2005) 81-89 [OTA 30,370] [Jonah 2,3-10].

5066 *Paul, Shalom M.* An overlooked *double entendre* in Jonah 2:5. Divrei Shalom. CHANE 23: 2005 <2001> ⇒273. 485-487.

5067 *Spronk, Klaas* Hoe Jona de vis uitkwam: Jona 2:11 in de beeldende kunst. ACEBT 22 (2005) 91-100 [OTA 30,371].

5068 *Eynikel, Erik* One day, three days, and forty days in the book of Jonah. MVAN TILBORG, S.: BiblInterp 71: 2005 ⇒155. 65-76 [Jonah 3,3-4].

5069 *Kamp, Albert* De dynamiek van verandering: over de consequenties van een dynamisch godsbeeld in Jona 3:10 [OTA 30,371];

5070 *Keurloo, Karel* 'Was dit niet mijn word?...': Jona 4:2 [OTA 30,371];

5071 *Dyk, Janet W.* Als God twee keer vraagt: overwegingen bij Jona 4:4-11 [OTA 30,372]. ACEBT 22 (2005) 113-123/125-129/131-139.

### E9.6 *Micheas*, **Micah**

5072 *Ho, Huang P.* Micah. Global bible commentary. 2005 ⇒2443. 295-300.

5073 *Pazzini, Massimo; Pierri, Rosario* Il libro di Michea secondo la versione siriaca (Peshitto). LASBF 55 (2005) 27-39.

5074 *Simundson, Daniel J.* The book of Micah. OT survey. 2005 ⇒413. 433-437.

5075 **Utzschneider, Helmut** Micha. ZBK.AT 24,3: Z 2005, Theol. Verl. 175 pp. €25. 3-290-17368-2.

5076 **Mladen, Horvat** I destinatari di Mic 3,1-4 come chiave per l'interpretazione anche del suo contesto immediato. R 2005, n.p. 174 pp. Bibl. 162-169.

5077 *Schwienhorst-Schönberger, Ludger* Zion–Ort der Tora: Überlegungen zu Mi 4,1-3. Studien zum AT. 2005 <1993> ⇒298. 61-76.

5078 *Sweeney, Marvin A.* Micah's debate with Isaiah. Form and intertextuality. FAT 45: 2005 ⇒313. 210-221 [Isa 2,2-4; Mic 4,1-5].

5079 *Leroy, Marc* 'Ô petite ville de Bethléem...'. VS 85 (2005) 486-494 [Mic 5,1-5].

5080 *Moor, Johannes C. de* The structure of Micah 6 in the light of ancient delimitations. Layout markers. Pericope 5: 2005 ⇒422. 78-113.

5081 *Lauber, Stephan* "Es ist dir gesagt, Mensch, was gut ist...": illokutionärer Textverlauf in Mi 6,2-8. [F]IRSIGLER, H.: ATSAT 76: 2005 ⇒67. 127-145.

5082 *Hyman, Ronald T.* Questions and response in Micah 6:6-8. JBQ 33 (2005) 157-165.

5083 *Loretz, Oswald* Ugaritisch-kanaanäische Poetik in den Nichtigkeitsflüchen des Micha-Buches 6,14-15. UF 37 (2005) 405-409.

### E9.7 *Abdias, Sophonias*...**Obadiah, Zephaniah, Nahum**

5084 *Dick, Michael B.* The poetics of the book of Obadiah. JNSL 31/2 (2005) 1-32.

5085 *Pagán, Samuel* The book of Obadiah. OT survey. 2005 ⇒413. 406-411.

5086 *Torreblanca, Jorge* Obadiah. Global bible commentary. 2005 ⇒ 2443. 286-290.

5087 *Bennett, Robert A.* The book of Zephaniah. OT survey. 2005 ⇒413. 446-452.

5088 *Doren, Fernando; Nakanose, Shigeyuki; Pedro, Enilda de P.* Zephaniah. Global bible commentary. 2005 ⇒2443. 310-314.

5089 **Sweeney, Marvin A.** Zephaniah. Hermeneia: 2003 ⇒19,5018; 20, 4797. [R]Interp. 59 (2005) 428-429 (*Ryou, Daniel Hojoon*); Bib. 86 (2005) 123-126 (*Spreafico, Ambrogio*); RBLit 7 (2005) 160-162 (*Hamilton, Mark W.*).

5090 **Baumann, Gerlinde** Gottes Gewalt im Wandel: traditionsgeschichtliche und intertextuelle Studien zu Nahum 1,2-8. WMANT 107:

Neuk 2005, Neuk x; 285 pp. €39.90. 3-7887-2107-3. Diss.; Bibl. 249-280.

5091 *Becking, Bob* Is God good for his people?: critical remarks on a recently proposed emendation of Nahum 1,7. ZAW 117 (2005) 621-623.

5092 *Garcia-Treto, Francisco O.* The book of Nahum. OT survey. 2005 ⇒413. 438-441.

5093 *Pinker, Aron* Nahum—the prophet and his message. JBQ 33 (2005) 81-90;

5094 Smoking out the fire in Nahum II 14. BN 123 (2005) 45-48;

5095 Descent of the goddess Ishtar to the netherworld and Nahum ii 8. VT 55 (2005) 89-100;

5096 Nahum 2,4 revisited. ZAW 117 (2005) 411-419;

5097 The hard "sell" in Nah 3:4. JHScr 5/7 (2004)*.

5098 *Silva, Valmor da* Nahum. Global bible commentary. 2005 ⇒2443. 301-305.

5099 *Wessels, W.J.* Yahweh, the awesome God: perspectives from Nahum 1. JSem 14/1 (2005) 55-73.

## E9.8 *Habacuc*, **Habakkuk**

5100 *Ahirika, Edwin* The problemof theodecy [!]: if God why then evil?: application of the book of Habakkuk (1-3). BiBh 31 (2005) 87-105.

5101 **Andersen, Francis I.** Habakkuk. AncB 25: 2001 ⇒17,4214... 20, 4806. [R]JJS 56 (2005) 139-141 (*Williamson, H.G.M.*).

5102 *Hiebert, Theodore* The book of Habakkuk. OT survey. 2005 ⇒413. 442-445.

5103 *Himbaza, Innocent* Habakkuk. Global bible commentary. 2005 ⇒ 2443. 306-309.

5104 *Pereira, Nancy C.* Olho por olho deixa o mundo cego!: um estudo sobre violência, império e teologia na profecia de Habacuqe. Espaços 13 (2005) 145-153 [OTA 29,175].

5105 *Álvarez Barredo, Miguel* Queja de Habacuc ante Dios por la violencia de su entorno: perfiles literarios y teológicos de Hab 1,1-4. Cart. 21 (2005) 1-32.

5106 *Gnandt, Georg* Der Steppenwolf: zu Hab 1,8 und Zef 3,3. [F]IRSIGLER, H.: ATSAT 76: 2005 ⇒67. 147-157.

5107 *Behrens, Achim* Habakuk 2,1-4 und die Treue zur Offenbarung. [F]STOLLE, V. 2005 ⇒2721. 173-187.

5108 *Pinker, Aron* "Captors" for "years" in Habakkuk 3:2. RB 112 (2005) 20-26 [Ps 138].

5109 *Passoni Dell'Acqua, Anna* 'Yhwh si adira contro *Neharayim*': il mitema della lotta cosmogonica in Abacuc 3,8-15. Materia giudaica 10/1 (2005) 33-56.

5110 *Pinker, Aron* On the meaning of מטיו in Habakkuk 3,14a. Bib. 86 (2005) 376-386 [Ps 23,5-6].

## E9.9 *Aggaeus*, **Haggai**—*Zacharias*, **Zechariah**—*Malachias*, **Malachi**

5111 **Taylor, Richard A.; Clendenen, E. Ray** Haggai, Malachi. NAC 21A: 2004 ⇒20,4817. [R]CBQ 67 (2005) 515-516 (*Redditt, Paul L.*); RBLit (2005)* (*Cathey, Joseph*).

5112 *Dogniez, Cécile* Aggée et ses suppléments (TM et LXX) ou le développement littéraire d'un livre biblique. L'apport de la Septante. LeDiv 203: 2005 ⇒764. 197-218.

5113 *Kalluveettil, Paul* Haggai. Global bible commentary. 2005 ⇒2443. 315-317.

5114 **Kessler, John** The book of Haggai: prophecy and society in early Persian Yehud. VT.S 91: 2002 ⇒18,4641... 20,4818. [R]RBLit 7 (2005) 185-187 (*Jacobs, Mignon*).

5115 *Lewis, Theodore J.* The mysterious disappearance of Zerubbabel. [F]FOX, M. 2005 ⇒43. 301-314 [Hag 2,20-23].

5116 *March, W. Eugene* The book of Haggai. OT survey. 2005 ⇒413. 453-456.

5117 *Wendland, E.R.* The structure, style, sense, and significance of Haggai's prophecy concerning the 'house of the LORD'—with special reference to bible interpretation and translation in Africa (Part One);

5118 *Wessels, Willie* Bridging the gap: Haggai's use of tradition to secure the future. OTEs 18 (2005) 907-926/426-443.

5119 **Blum, Sandra** Zur Rezeption von Sach 9-14 im Neuen Testament. [D]*Beutler, Johannes* 2005, 300 pp. Diss. St. Georgen, Frankfurt [RTL 37,613].

5120 *Boda, Mark J.* Terrifying the horns: Persia and Babylon in Zechariah 1:7-6:15. CBQ 67 (2005) 22-41.

5121 *Dogniez, Cécile* L'intertextualité dans la LXX de Zacharie 9-14. [F]LUST, J.: BEThL 192: 2005 ⇒92. 81-96.

5122 *Frolov, Serge* Is the narrator also among the prophets?: reading Zechariah without presuppositions. BiblInterp 13 (2005) 13-40.

5123 *Ollenburger, Ben C.* The book of Zechariah. OT survey. 2005 ⇒413. 457-463.

5124 *Paul, Shalom M.* A technical expression from archery in Zechariah 9: 13a. Divrei Shalom. CHANE 23: 2005 <1989> ⇒273. 155-157.

5125 **Pola, Thomas** Das Priestertum bei Sacharja: historische und traditionsgeschichtliche Untersuchungen zur frühnachexilischen Herrschererwartung. FAT 35: 2003 ⇒19,5068; 20,4826. [R]RBLit 7 (2005) 183-185 (*Reventlow, Henning Graf*).

*Pyper, Hugh S.* Reading in the dark 2005 ⇒4907.

5126 *Sosa, Carlos R.* La influencia de Isaias II en Zacarias II. Kairós 37 (2005) 39-57 [OTA 29,80].

5127 *Swarup, Paul* Zechariah. Global bible commentary. 2005 ⇒2443. 318-324.

5128 *Sweeney, Marvin A.* Zechariah's debate with Isaiah. Form and intertextuality. FAT 45: 2005 ⇒313. 222-235.

5129 *Van Amerongen, Marianne* The structure of Zechariah 4: a comparison between the divisions in the Masoretic text, ancient translations, and modern commentaries. Layout markers. Pericope 5: 2005 ⇒422. 191-208.

5130 *Van Nie, Mirjam* Wie is de bode?. ITBT 13/2 (2005) 11-12.

5131 *Hennig, Gerhard* Maleachi 3,13-20. ThBeitr 36 (2005) 113-116.

5132 *Mendoza, Claudia* Malachi. Global bible commentary. 2005 ⇒2443. 325-328.

5133 *Schuller, Eileen M.* The book of Malachi. OT survey. 2005 ⇒413. 464-468.

5134 *Snyman, S.D.* Maleagi 1:9—'n crux interpretum. AcTh(B) 25/2 (2005) 90-103.

5135 *Tiemeyer, Lena-Sofia* 'Giving a voice to Malachi's interlocutors'. SJOT 19 (2005) 173-192.

## VIII. NT Exegesis generalis

### F1.1 New Testament introduction

5136 **Achtemeier, Paul J.; Green, Joel B.; Thompson, Marianne M.** Introducing the New Testament: its literature and theology. 2001 ⇒17, 4235...20,4840. [R]BZ 49 (2005) 275-7 (*Untergaßmair, Franz Georg*).

5137 **Berger, Klaus** Formen und Gattungen im Neuen Testament. Uni-Taschenbücher 2532: Tü 2005, Francke xii; 483 pp. 3-7720-3009-2.

5138 *Berry, W.* The burden of the gospels. CCen 122/19 (2005) 22-27 [NTAb 50,23].

5139 **Burkett, Delbert Royce** An introduction to the New Testament and the origins of christianity. 2002 ⇒18,4663... 20,4847. [R]SBET 23 (2005) 96-97 (*MacLeod, John A.*).

5140 **Burnet, Régis** Le Nouveau Testament. QSJ: 2004 ⇒20,4848. [R]REJ 164 (2005) 344-347 (*Couteau, Élisabeth*).

5141 **Carson, D.A.; Moo, Douglas J.** An introduction to the New Testament. Leicester [2]2005 <1992>, Apollos 781 pp. £25. 1-84474-0895.

5142 **da Silva, David** An introduction to the NT. 2004 ⇒20,4852. [R]SNTU 30 (2005) 262-264 (*Fuchs, Albert*); MissTod 7 (2005) 283-284 (*Varickasseril, Jose*); Faith & Mission 23/1 (2005) 90-92 (*Kellum, Scott*); RBLit 7 (2005) 286-288 (*Anderson, Kevin L.*).

5143 **Di Nuccio, Luisa** Guida alla lettura del Nuovo Testamento. R 2005, ADP 125 pp. €8. 88-7357-385-1. Bibl. 121-125.

5144 **Elwell, Walter A.; Yarbrough, Robert W.** Encountering the New Testament: a historical and theological survey. GR [2]2005 <1998>, Baker 448 pp. $45. 0-8010-2806X.

5145 [E]**Gass, Ildo Bohn** Uma introdução à bíblia: as comunidades cristãs a partir da segunda geração. São Paulo 2005, Paulus 171 pp.

5146 **Holladay, Carl R.** A critical introduction to the New Testament: interpreting the message and meaning of Jesus Christ. Nv 2005, Abingdon xxiii; 609 pp. £28. 0-687-08569-1. Incl. CD.

5147 **Kee, Howard Clark** The beginnings of christianity: an introduction to the New Testament. NY 2005, Clark vii; 502 pp. £50/19. 0-567-02731-7.

5148 [E]**Marguerat, Daniel** Introduzione al Nuovo Testamento. 2004 ⇒20, 4860. [R]Ter. 56 (2005) 600-601 (*Pasquetto, Virgilio*);

5149 Introduction au Nouveau Testament. MoBi 41: [3]2004 <2000> ⇒20, 4861. [R]RBLit (2005)* (*Kealy, Sean*).

5150 **Piñero, Antonio; Peláez del Rosal, Jesús** The study of the New Testament: a comprehensive introduction. [T]*Orton, David E.; Ellingworth, Paul*: 2003 ⇒19,5134; 20,4862. [R]ThLZ 130 (2005) 660-663 (*Smit, Peter-Ben*); JETh 19 (2005) 261-263 (*Stenschke, Christoph*).

5151 **Rolland, Philippe** Et le Verbe s'est fait chair: introduction au Nouveau Testament. Biblik: P 2005, Renaissance 350 pp. €18.50. 2-750-9-00816.

5152 **Theissen, Gerd** Das Neue Testament. Wissen 2192: 2002, 2004 ⇒18,4682; 19,5143. [R]FrRu 12 (2005) 224-226 (*Renker, Alwin*);

5153 Fortress Press introduction to the New Testament. [T]*Bowden, John* 2003 ⇒19,5144; 20,4865. [R]RBLit 7 (2005) 281-4 (*Lockett, Darian*);

5154 The New Testament: history, literature, religion. 2003 ⇒19,5145. [R]RBLit (2005)* (*Van der Watt, Jan G.*).

5155 **Tofană, Stelian** Einleitung in das Studium des Neuen Testaments. 2000-2002 ⇒19,5147. [R]OrthFor 19 (2005) 315-6 (*Basarab, Mircea*).

5156 **Van Voorst, R.E.** Reading the New Testament today. Belmont, CA 2005, Wadsworth xx; 604 pp. $52. 05345-41801. Bibl. [NTAb 49, 388].

5157 **Weißenborn, Thomas** Apostel, Lehrer und Propheten, 3: Petrusbrief bis Offenbarung. Marburg 2005, Francke 217 pp. €13.50;

5158 Apostel, Lehrer und Propheten, 1-3. 2004-2005 ⇒20,4869s. [R]JETh 19 (2005) 263-265 (*Schröder, Michael*).

### F1.2 *Origo Evangeliorum*, **the origin of the Gospels**

5159 *Bird, Michael F.* The formation of the gospels in the setting of early christianity: the Jesus tradition as corporate memory. WThJ 67 (2005) 113-134.

5160 *Bockmuehl, Markus* The making of gospel commentaries;

5161 *Burridge, Richard A.* Who writes, why, and for whom?. [F]STANTON, G. 2005 ⇒138. 274-295/99-115.

5162 **Burridge, Richard A.** What are the gospels?: a comparison with Graeco-Roman biography. Biblical resource: [2]2004 <1992> ⇒20,4873. [R]SNTU 30 (2005) 265-266 (*Hintermaier, Johann*); TJT 21 (2005) 228-230 (*Hamilton, Catherine Sider*);

5163 Four gospels, one Jesus?: a symbolic reading. GR [2]2005 <1994>, Eerdmans xviii; 198 pp. $16. 0-8028-2980-5.

5164 *Carleton Paget, James* The Four among Jews. [F]STANTON, G. 2005 ⇒138. 205-221.

5165 *Ceruti-Cendrier, M.-C.* The gospels—direct testimonies or late writings?. HPR 105/4 (2005) 46-52 [NTAb 49,254].

5166 *Chilton, Bruce* James, Peter, Paul and the formation of the gospels. The missions of James. NT.S 115: 2005 ⇒369. 3-28.

5167 *Gundry, Robert* The symbiosis of theology and genre criticism of the canonical gospels. The old is better. WUNT 178: 2005 ⇒220. 18-48.

5168 *Holmås, G.O.* Er evangeliene koherente fortellinger?: om et hermeneutisk premiss i den litteraert-narrative eksegese. TTK 76 (2005) 242-261.

5169 *Hooker, Morna D.* Beginnings and endings. [F]STANTON, G. 2005 ⇒138. 184-202.

5170 Introduzione ai vangeli. I vangeli. 2005 ⇒432. 341-358.

5171 *Kister, Menahem* Words and formulae in the gospels in the light of Hebrew and Aramaic sources. The Sermon on the Mount. CRB 60: 2005 ⇒350. 117-147.

5172 *Mitchell, Margaret M.* Patristic counter-evidence to the claim that 'the gospels were written for all christians'. NTS 51 (2005) 36-79.

5173 *Tannehill, Robert C.* The gospels and narrative literature. NT survey. 2005 ⇒3144. 1-16.
5174 **Trocmé, Étienne** Anajeel arba'at wa Iman Wahed [Quatre évangiles, une seule foi]. 2004 ⇒20,4891. [R]ThRev 26 (2005) 82-86 (*Awwad, Johnny*).

## F1.3 Historicitas, *chronologia* Evangeliorum

5175 *Hengel, Martin* Eye-witness memory and the writing of the gospels: form criticism, community tradition and the authority of the authors. [F]STANTON, G. 2005 ⇒138. 70-96.
5176 *Kealey, Séan P.* Change and the gospels. BTB 35 (2005) 13-19.
5177 *Tuckett, Christopher M.* Jesus and the gospels. NT survey. 2005 ⇒3144. 17-33.

## F1.4 *Jesus historicus*—The human Jesus

5178 *Abesamis, Carlos H.* Jesus: an Asian perspective. Global bible commentary. 2005 ⇒2443. 333-336.
5179 *Alexander, Philip S.* Jesus and the golden rule [Mt 7,12];
5180 *Allison, Dale C.* The allusive Jesus. The historical Jesus in recent research. 2005 ⇒379. 489-508/238-247.
5181 **Atwill, Joseph** Caesar's messiah: the Roman conspiracy to invent Jesus. Berkeley 2005, Ulysses (6), 354 pp. 15697-54578. Bibl. 354.
5182 *Batten, A.* Studying the historical Jesus through service. Teaching Theology & Religion [Oxf] 8/2 (2005) 107-113 ]NTAb 49,481].
5183 *Bellia, Giuseppe* La Third Quest: antiche questioni e prospettive storico-teologiche. RStB 17/2 (2005) 217-248.
5184 **Benazzi, N.** 10 domande a Gesù: un esercizio di speranza. CasM 2005, Piemme 204 pp.
5185 **Bennett, Clinton** In search of Jesus: insider and outsider images. 2001 ⇒17,4295; 19,5175. [R]JRH 29 (2005) 312-314 (*Strelan, Rick*).
5186 **Berger, Klaus** Jesus. 2004 ⇒20,4903. [R]ThRv 101 (2005) 130-132 (*Eckstein, Hans-Joachim*).
5187 *Bermejo, Fernando* Historiografía, exégesis e ideología: la ficción contemporánea de las 'tres búsquedas' del Jesús histórico. RCatT 30 (2005) 349-406.
5188 *Bird, Michael F.* The purpose and preservation of the Jesus tradition: moderate evidence for a conserving force in its transmission. BBR 15/2 (2005) 161-185;
5189 Jesus and the gentiles after Jeremias: patterns and prospects. CuBR 4 (2005) 83-108;
5190 **Blomberg, Craig L.** Contagious holiness: Jesus' meals with sinners. New Studies in Biblical Theology 19: DG 2005, InterVarsity 216 pp. $20. 0-8308-2620-3. Bibl. 181-202.
5191 **Bloom, Harold** Jesus and Yahweh: the names divine. NY 2005, Penguin xi; 238 pp. $25. 15372-23220 [NTAb 50,189].
5192 **Bock, Darrell L.** Jesus according to scripture: restoring the portrait from the gospels. 2002 ⇒18,4717... 20,4905. [R]HeyJ 46 (2005) 534-536 (*Hill, Robert C.*).

5193 *Borg, Marcus J.* The spirit-filled experience of Jesus. The historical Jesus in recent research. 2005 ⇒379. 302-314;
5194 The search begins: the fathers of historical Jesus scholarship. BiRe 21/3 (2005) 17-19 [NTAb 50,25].
5195 **Boscione, Franco** Los gestos de Jesús: la comunicación no verbal en los evangelios. T*Ballester, Carolina* 2004 ⇒20,4907. RVyV 63/1 (2005) 251-252.
5196 *Botha, Pieter J. J.; Craffert, Pieter F.* Why Jesus could walk on the sea but he could not read and write: reflections on historicity and interpretation in Historical Jesus research. Neotest. 39 (2005) 5-38 [Mt 14,22-33; Mk 6,45-52; Lk 4,16-30; John 6,16-21; 7,15; 8,6].
5197 **Boyer, Chrystian** Jésus contre le temple?: analyse socio-historique des textes. Héritage et projet 68: Saint-Laurent (Québec) 2005, Fides 163 pp. €27. 2-7621-2563-4.
5198 *Braun, Willi* 'Wir haben doch den amerikanischen Jesus': das amerikanische Jesus-Seminar: eine Standortbestimmung. ZNT 8/16 (2005) 30-39.
5199 **Bridge, Steven L.** Getting the gospels: understanding the New Testament accounts of Jesus' life. 2004 ⇒20,4911. RRBLit (2005)* (*Peterson, Dwight*).
5200 *Bultmann, Rudolf* View-point and method;
5201 "I"-sayings. The historical Jesus in recent research;
5202 The message of Jesus and the problem of mythology;
5203 *Cadbury, Henry J.* The cause and cure of modernization;
5204 *Caird, George B.* Jesus and the Jewish nation. The historical Jesus in recent research. 2005 ⇒379. 50-55/90-106/531-542/56-66/275-287.
5205 *Campbell, K.M.* What was Jesus' occupation?. JETS 48 (2005) 501-519 [NTAb 50,254].
5206 *Cardona Ramírez, Hernán* El servicio del martirio. El grano. 2005 ⇒197. 161-173.
5207 *Charlesworth, James H.* The historical Jesus and christian origins: reflections on methodologies for future Jesus research. Henoch 27/1-2 (2005) 35-51.
5208 *Craffert, P.F.* How historiography creates (some) body: Jesus, the Son of David—royal stock or social construct?. Scriptura 90 (2005) 608-620 [NTAb 51,249].
5209 **Crossan, John Dominic; Reed, Jonathan L.** Jesus ausgraben: zwischen den Steinen—hinter den Texten. T*Krülls-Hepermann, Claudia* 2003 ⇒19,5198; 20,4922. RFKTh 21 (2005) 60-61 (*Kreiml, Josef*).
5210 *Dart, J.* Up against Caesar: Jesus and Paul versus the empire. CCen 122/3 (2005) 20-24 [NTAb 49,256].
5211 **De Martino, Gianni** L'uomo che Gesù amava. 2004 ⇒20,4927. RIl tetto 246-247 (2005) 135-139 (*Pignata, Ausilia Riggi*).
5212 **Denton, Donald L.** Historiography and hermeneutics in Jesus studies: an examination of the work of J. Crossan and B. Meyer. JSNT.S 262; JSHS.S: 2004 ⇒20,4928. RRBLit (2005)* (*Licona, Michael*).
5213 *Dunn, James D.G.* The tradition;
5214 Introduction;
5215 Pharisees, sinners, and Jesus. The historical Jesus in recent research. 2005 ⇒379. 167-184/187-189/463-488.
5216 **Dunn, James D.G.** Jesus remembered. Christianity in the making 1: 2003 ⇒19,5206; 20,4935. RThTo 62 (2005) 100, 102, 104 (*Hurtado, L.W.*); JThS 56 (2005) 140-149 (*Bockmuehl, M.*); NewTR 18/2

(2005) 93-94 (*Caponi, Francis J.*); ThLZ 130 (2005) 37-40 (*Schröter, Jens*); HeyJ 46 (2005) 388-390 (*Jung, Ken Alan*); SBET 23 (2005) 222-224 (*Balla, Peter*); CTJ 40 (2005) 335-336 (*Deppe, Dean*); WThJ 67 (2005) 429-434 (*McCartney, Dan*; RBLit 7 (2005) 317-322 (*Painter, John*); JSHJ 3 (2005) 109-110 (*Webb, Robert L.*).

5217 **Dunn, James D.G.** The new perspective on Jesus: what the quest for the historical Jesus missed. GR 2005, Baker 136 pp. $13. 0-8010-27-10-1. [R]RBLit (2005)* (*Pokorny, Petr*); HBT 27/1 (2005) 106-108 (*Karlson, William*).

5218 *Duran, Nicole W.* Jesus: a Western perspective. Global bible commentary. 2005 ⇒2443. 346-349.

5219 **Ebner, Martin** Jesus von Nazaret in seiner Zeit. SBS 196: 2003 ⇒ 19,5208; 20,4936. [R]ThPh 80 (2005) 272-273 (*Diefenbach, M.*).

5220 **Edwards, James R.** Is Jesus the only savior?. GR 2005, Eerdmans 250 pp. $13. 0-8028-0981-2.

5221 *Elizondo, Miguel* Jesus and prayer. Way 44/3 (2005) 9-20.

5222 *Espinosa G., Sergio César; Sánchez I., Sergio* Prácticas simbólicas de Jesús de Nazaret. ThX 55 (2005) 73-90.

5223 *Eve, Eric* Meier, miracle and multiple attestation. JSHJ 3 (2005) 23-45.

5224 *Fiedler, Peter* Die Tora bei Jesus und in der Jesusüberlieferung. Studien zur biblischen Grundlegung. 2005 <1986> ⇒209. 103-119.

5225 **Fiorenza, Elisabeth Schüssler** Jesus e a política da interpretação. [T]*Sobral, Adail*: São Paulo 2005, Loyola 169 pp.

5226 **Flusser, David** Jésus. [T]*Veyret, Gabriel R.*: P 2005, l'Éclat 283 pp. 2-84162-1014.

5227 **Fogliata, Giovanni Matteo** Siz im Leben wypowiedzi Jezusa o żniwie i formy jej recepcji [Sitz im Leben of the Jesus saying on the harvest and forms of its reception]. [D]*Mędala, S.*: 2005, Diss. Warsaw [RTL 37,614]. **P.**

5228 **Freyne, Seán** Jesus, a Jewish Galilean: a new reading of the Jesus-story. 2004 ⇒20,4941. [R]Studies 94 (2005) 311-313 (*King, Nicholas*); ThLZ 130 (2005) 1187-1189 (*Schröter, Jens*); RBLit (2005)* (*Burns, Joshua*); PIBA 28 (2005) 124-125 (*O'Brien, Mary T.*); JThS 56 (2005) 526-531 (*Bockmuehl, M.*).

5229 **Fricker, Denis** Quand Jésus parle au masculin-féminin: étude contextuelle et exégétique d'une forme littéraire originale. EtB 53: 2004 ⇒20,4942. [R]RevSR 79 (2005) 420-421 (*Deneken, Michel*); ETR 80 (2005) 562-563 (*Cuvillier, Elian*); Ang. 82 (2005) 233-235 (*Jurič, Stipe*) [Mt 2,21-22; Lk 11,31-32; 12,22-31].

5230 **Galston, D.** Postmodernism, the historical Jesus, and the church. The Fourth R [Santa Rosa, CA] 18/5 (2005) 11, 14-18 [NTAb 50,255].

5231 *Gamberini, Paolo* Gesù di Nazaret, chi sei?. RdT 46 (2005) 325-337.

5232 *García Cordero, Maximiliano* Hipérboles y paradojas en la predicación de Jesús (IIa parte). CTom 132 (2005) 237-263.

5233 **García, José Miguel** La vita di Gesù nel testo aramaico dei vangeli. I libri dello spirito cristiano: Mi 2005, BUR-Rizzoli 324 pp. €9.50.

5234 *Georgi, Dieter* The hour of the gospel: Jesus and Caesar;

5235 The interest in Life-of-Jesus theology as a paradigm for the social history of biblical criticism. The city in the valley. Studies in biblical literature 7: 2005 ⇒214. 69-92/221-254.

5236 *Gerhardsson, Birger* The secret of the transmission of the unwritten Jesus tradition. NTS 51 (2005) 1-18.

5237 *Grech, Prosper* I limiti del metodo storico di fronte a Gesù. Il messaggio biblico. SRivBib 44: 2005 ⇒216. 203-214.

5238 **Gronchi, Maurizio; Ilunga Muya, Juvénal** Gesù di Nazaret: un personaggio storico. Diaconia alla verità 3: Mi 2005, Paoline 234 pp. €12.

5239 *Gruson, Philippe, al.* Une géo-théologie des évangiles. MoBi (printemps 2005) 54-64.

5240 **Grün, Anselm** Jesus—Wege zum Leben: die Evangelien des Matthäus, Markus, Lukas und Johannes. Stu 2005, Kreuz 589 pp. 3-7831-2107-8.

5241 *Guijarro Oporto, Santiago* La aportación del "Documento Q" al estudio del Jesús histórico. RStB 17/2 (2005) 55-82.

5242 *Hammes, Érico João* Pietre trasformate in pane: perché no?: eucharistia—koinonia—diaconia. Conc(I) 41 (2005) 201-213; Conc(D) 41,137-146; Conc(US) 2,25-35.

5243 **Harpur, Tom** Le Christ païen: retrouver la lumière perdue. [T]*Bellefeuille, Elise de; Saint-Germain, Michel*: Montréal 2005, Boréal 294 pp. Préf. *Jacques Languirand.*

5244 *Hasitschka, Martin* "Wer ist dieser?" (Mk 4,41): Gottes Wirken in der Welt: der Mensch Jesus. Wie wirkt Gott. Forum St. Stephan 15: 2005 ⇒555. 93-103.

5245 **Herzog, William R., II** Prophet and teacher: an introduction to the historical Jesus. LVL 2005, Westminster 243 pp. $25. 0-664-22528-4 [BiTod 44,61—Donald Senior].

5246 **Hirschberg, Peter** Jesus von Nazareth: eine historische Spurensuche. 2004 ⇒20,4954. [R]ThRv 101 (2005) 40-41 (*Beinert, Wolfgang*).

5247 *Horsley, R.A.* Jesus and empire. USQR 59/3-4 (2005) 44-74 [NTAb 50,256];

5248 Mission to Israel. Secrets of the bible. 2005 ⇒482. 130-134;

5249 Abandoning the unhistorical quest for an apolitical Jesus. The historical Jesus in recent research. 2005 ⇒379. 288-301.

5250 *Hurtado, Larry W.* Homage to the historical Jesus and early christian devotion. How on earth. 2005 <2003> ⇒227. 134-151.

5251 **Jang, Ho-Koang** Die Bedeutung der Leben-Jesu-Forschung für die systematische Theologie. Ment. *Pannenberg, Wolfhart; Marquardt, Friedrich-Wilhelm*: EHS.T 798: Fra 2005, Lang 298 pp. 3-631-517-91-2.

5252 **Jensen, Peter** The future of Jesus: Boyer lectures 2005. Sydney 2005, ABC 128 pp. $23 [ACR 84/1,115—Neil Ormerod].

5253 *Jeremias, Joachim* Characteristics of the ipsissima vox;

5254 'Abba as an address to God. The historical Jesus in recent research. 2005 ⇒379. 107-114/201-206.

5255 *Jossa, Giorgio* Il quadro storico, sociale, archeologico. RStB 17/2 (2005) 9-25.

5256 **Kazen, Thomas** Jesus and purity halakhah: was Jesus indifferent to impurity?. CB.NT 38: 2002 ⇒18,4784; 20,4967. [R]JSJ 36 (2005) 117-121 (*Koet, Bart J.*); EstB 63 (2005) 581-584 (*Bernabé, Carmen*); Bib. 86 (2005) 432-434 (*Paul, André*); JThS 56 (2005) 540-543 (*Stettler, Hanna*); Bijdr. 66 (2005) 459-460 (*Lammers, Hans*).

5257 *Kähler, Martin* Against the Life-of-Jesus movement. The historical Jesus in recent research. 2005 ⇒379. 67-84.

5258 *Kea, P.V.* The road to the Jesus Seminar. The Fourth R [Santa Rosa, CA] 18/1 (2005) 9-11, 14-16 [NTAb 49,483].

5259 *Keizer, G.* Slow to answer: the reticence of Jesus. CCen 122/7 (2005) 26-27 [NTAb 49,484].

5260 *Kirk, Alan; Thatcher, Tom* Jesus tradition as social memory. Memory, tradition, and text. SBL.Semeia Studies 52: 2005 ⇒416. 25-42.

5261 **Klinghoffer, David** Why the Jews rejected Jesus. 2004 ⇒20,4971. [R]First Things 150 (2005) 58-60 (*Neuhaus, Richard John*).

5262 *Kloppenborg, John S.* As one unknown, without a name?: co-opting the apocalyptic Jesus. Apocalypticism, anti-Semitism. JSNT.S 275; JSHJ.S: 2005 ⇒767. 1-23.

5263 *Kümmel, W.G.* The pressing imminence of the end. The historical Jesus in recent research. 2005 ⇒379. 190-200.

5264 *Laiti, Giuseppe* Gesù e lo scandalo. Presbyteri 39 (2005) 181-189.

5265 *Landgrave G., Daniel R.* Jesús, los pobres, los ricos y el reino de Dios, segunda parte. EfMex 23 (2005) 155-189.

5266 *Lemcio, Eugene E.* The past of Jesus in the gospels. The historical Jesus in recent research. 2005 ⇒379. 145-166.

5267 *Lessard, Sylvie P.* La liberté de Jésus: un modèle pour une vie chrétienne authentique. Scriptura(M) 7/1 (2005) 13-25.

5268 *Levine, Amy-Jill* The earth moved: Jesus, sex, and eschatology. Apocalypticism, anti-Semitism. 2005 ⇒767. 83-97.

5269 The word becomes flesh: Jesus, gender, and sexuality. The historical Jesus in recent research. 2005 ⇒379. 509-523.

5270 *Léon-Dufour, Xavier* I vangeli e la storia di Gesù. Un biblista cerca Dio. Collana biblica: 2005 <1963> ⇒245. 61-78.

5271 **Loader, William** Jesus' attitude towards the law. [3]2002 ⇒18,4795... 20,4977. [R]TJT 21 (2005) 249-50 (*Smith, Daniel A.*).

5272 *Luciani, Rafael* El Jesús histórico como norma hermenéutica para la teología y criterio para ser testigos en el seguimiento. Iter 16/37-38 (2005) 17-116.

5273 **Maggioni, Bruno** Cet homme qui était Dieu: revisiter le visage de Jésus dans les évangiles. [T]*Courteille, Bernard*: P 2005, L'Atelier 174 pp. €20.

5274 *Manicardi, Ermenegildo* Criteri di storicità e storia di Gesù oggi. RStB 17/2 (2005) 27-54;

5275 Gesù di Nazaret, le scritture e lo Spirito <2000>;

5276 Criteri di storicità e storia di Gesù oggi. Gesù la cristologia. 2005 <2003> ⇒253. 85-117/187-214.

5277 **Marsh, Clive; Moyise, Steve** Jesus and the gospels. Approaches to biblical studies: NY 2005, Clark 127 pp. $22. 0-567-04372-X [ThD 52,379—W. Charles Heiser].

5278 *Marshall, Mary J.* Jesus: glutton and drunkard?. JSHJ 3 (2005) 47-60 [Mt 11,19; Mk 2,14-17; Lk 6,27-36; 7,34; 15,1-2; 19,1-10].

5279 **Martínez Fresneda, Francisco** Jesús de Nazaret. Textos 1: Murcia 2005, Espigas 829 pp. €19.80. 84860-42631.

5280 *Mattam, Joseph* Jesus source and model of evangelisation. VJTR 69 (2005) 585-591.

5281 **McClymond, Michael J.ames** Familiar stranger: an introduction to Jesus of Nazareth. 2004 ⇒20,4983. [R]Theol. 108 (2005) 208-209 (*Morgan, Robert*).

5282 *McKnight, Scot* Introduction. The historical Jesus in recent research. 2005 ⇒379. 271-274, 347-349, 423-425.

5283 *McMahon, Christopher* Stories, hypotheses, and Jesus: N.T. Wright, John Meier, and historical Jesus research. NBl 86 (2005) 537-545.

5284 *Meier, John P.* Criteria: how do we decide what comes from Jesus?. The historical Jesus in recent research. 2005 ⇒379. 123-144.

5285 **Meier, John P.** A marginal Jew: rethinking the historical Jesus, 3: companions and competitors. 2001 ⇒17,4387... 20,4988. [R]AsbTJ 60/2 (2005) 124-126 (*Greathouse, Mattie*);

5286 Un ebreo marginale: ripensare il Gesù storico, 1-3. [T]*De Santis, Luca; Ferrari, Laura*: BTCon 117, 120, 125: 2001-2003 ⇒17,4388... 20, 4987. [R]Asp. 52 (2005) 259-262 (*Di Palma, Gaetano*);

5287 Un certain juif Jésus: les données de l'histoire, 1: les sources, les origines, les dates. [T]*Degorce, Jean-Bernard; Ehlinger, Charles; Lucas, Noël*: P 2005, Cerf 496 pp. €35. [R]LASBF 55 (2005) 547-551 (*Manns, Frédéric*);

5288 2. les parole et les gestes. [T]*Degorce, Jean-B.; Ehlinger, Charles; Lucas, Noël*: P 2005, Cerf 1,329 pp. €80. 2-204-07037-8. [R]Cart. 21 (2005) 234-236 (*Martínez Fresneda, F.*); CEv 134 (2005) 60-61 (*Runacher, Caroline*); RBLit (2005)* (*Kraus, Thomas*);

5289 3: attachements, affrontements, ruptures. [T]*Ehlinger, Charles; Lucas, Noël*: P 2005, Cerf 739 pp. €50. 2-204-07038-6.

5290 **Men, Alexander** Jesús, el Maestro de Nazaret. [T]*Conejo López-Lago, M.*: 2002 ⇒18,4815... 20,4989. [R]Eccl(R) 19/1 (2005) 122-123 (*Ortega, Verónica*).

5291 *Meyer, Ben F.* The judgment and salvation of Israel. The historical Jesus in recent research. 2005 ⇒379. 426-443.

5292 *Milazzo, Maisa* Culto dei morti o speranza di risurrezione?: l'atteggiamento di Gesù verso le onoranze funebri. RivBib 53 (2005) 71-90.

5293 *Miller, Robert J.* Theological stakes in the apocalyptic Jesus debate. Apocalypticism, anti-Semitism. 2005 ⇒767. 111-121.

5294 *Moda, Aldo* Gesù e le donne: qualche pista metodologica. [F]GHIBERTI, G.: SRivBib 46: 2005 ⇒47. 341-351.

5295 *Morgan, Robert* Christian faith and historical Jesus research: a reply to James Dunn. ET 116 (2005) 217-223;

5296 The historical Jesus and the theology of the New Testament. The historical Jesus in recent research. 2005 ⇒379. 567-584.

5297 **Moschetta, Jean-Marc** Jésus, fils de Joseph: comment comprendre aujourd'hui la conception virginale de Jésus?. 2002 ⇒18,4826; 20, 4996. [R]RTL 36 (2005) 236-237 (*Focant, C.*).

5298 **Moxnes, Halvor** Putting Jesus in his place: a radical vision of household and kingdom. 2003 ⇒19,5272; 20,4997. [R]JR 85 (2005) 302-303 (*Osiek, Carolyn*); ThLZ 130 (2005) 1186-1187 (*Schröter, Jens*).

5299 *Mulloor, A.* Inculturation in the gospels. Jeevadhara 35 (2005) 151-160 [NTAb 50,253].

5300 **Murphy, Frederick James** An introduction to Jesus and the gospels. Nv 2005, Abingdon xvi; 394 pp. $29. 0-687-49692-6.

5301 *Müller, Wolfgang W.* Vom Wissen Jesu: ein Lehrstück zum Zusammenspiel von Exegese und Dogmatik. FZPhTh 52 (2005) 568-585.

5302 *Neville, Graham* Sinlessness and uncertainty in Jesus. ET 116 (2005) 361-365.

5303 **Nodet, Etienne** Histoire de Jésus?: nécessité et limites d'une enquête. LiBi 135: 2003 ⇒19,5278; 20,5000. [R]LTP 61 (2005) 178-179 (*Dîncă, Lucian*).

5304 *Norelli, Enrico* La presenza di Gesù nella letteratura gentile dei primi due secoli. RStB 17/2 (2005) 175-215.

5305 *Oshri, Aviram* Where was Jesus born?. Arch. 58/6 (2005) 42-45.
5306 **Palackal, Jose** Interpreting Jesus: history and faith in the quest for the historical Jesus—1985-2000. [D]*Merrigan, T.*: 2005, Diss. Leuven [TTh 46,78].
5307 *Parappally, Jacob* Jesus' vision of a new world order and his stand against society and religion of his day. JPJRS 8 (2005) 143-163.
5308 *Patterson, S.J.* Jesus lives!: looking back on 20 years of Jesus scholarship. BiRe 21/3 (2005) 14-16, 20-26, 48, 50.
5309 *Pearson, B.A.* Did Jesus marry?. BiRe 21/2 (2005) 32-39, 47 [NTAb 49,464].
5310 *Pesce, Mauro* I detti extracanonici di Gesù e la loro rilevanza per la ricerca sul Gesù storico. RStB 17/2 (2005) 109-136.
5311 *Piovanelli, Pierluigi* Jesus' charismatic authority: on the historical applicability of a sociological model. JAAR 73 (2005) 395-427.
5312 *Pitta, Antonio* Il Gesù storico nelle fonti del I-II secolo: introduzione. RStB 17/2 (2005) 5-7.
5313 **Puig i Tàrrech, Armand** Jesús: una biografía. [T]*Salas Mezquita, David*: Imago mundi 83: Barc 2005, Destino 662 pp. 84-233-3752-9. Bibl. 621-628.
5314 **Quesnel, Michel** Jésus, l'homme et le Fils de Dieu. 2004 ⇒20,5011. [R]ETR 80 (2005) 283-284 (*Campbell, Gordon*);
5315 Jesus—o homem e o filho de Deus. Lisboa 2005, Gradiva 220 pp.
5316 *Ramelli, Ilaria* Gesù tra i sapienti greci perseguitati ingiustamente in un antico documento filosofico pagano di lingua siriaca. RFNS 97/4 (2005) 545-570.
5317 *Reinstorf, D.H.* Jesus in new contexts. HTSTS 61/1-2 (2005) 385-399 [NTAb 50,257].
5318 *Reiser, Marius* Drei Präfigurationen Jesu: Jesajas Gottesknecht, PLATONs Gerechter und der Gottessohn im Buch der Weisheit. EuA 81 (2005) 438-456.
5319 *Riaudel, Olivier* L'influence d'une étude du Jésus de l'histoire sur la théologie: l'exemple de Johannes WEISS. RSPhTh 89 (2005) 501-21.
5320 *Richard, Pablo* Jesus: a Latin American perspective. Global bible commentary. 2005⇒2443. 337-341.
5321 *Riesen, R.* 'Jesus the logician': a (very) modest proposal. CScR 34 (2005) 341-351 [NTAb 49,485].
5322 *Rivas, Luis Heriberto* La investigación sobre el Jesús histórico ('third quest'). La palabra viva. 2005 ⇒746. 113-149.
5323 *Robinson, James M.* Jesus as *Sophos* and *Sophia*: wisdom tradition and the gospels <1975>;
5324 Early collections of Jesus' sayings <1982>;
5325 The study of the historical Jesus after Nag Hammadi <1988>;
5326 Der wahre Jesus: der historische Jesus im Spruchevangelium Q <1997>;
5327 What Jesus had to say <2002>. The sayings gospel Q. BEThL 189: 2005 ⇒ 289. 119-130/169-175/275-284/519-534/887-889.
5328 *Robinson, John A.T.* The last tabu?: the self-consciousness of Jesus. The historical Jesus in recent research. 2005 ⇒379. 553-566.
5329 *Sanders, Ed Parish* Jesus and the first table of the Jewish law;
5330 Jesus and the temple. The historical Jesus in recent research. Sources for biblical and theological study 10: 2005 ⇒379. 225-237/361-381.
5331 **Schlosser, Jacques** Gesù di Nazaret. Nuove vie dell'esegesi: 2002 ⇒18,4853; 20,5022. [R]ATT 11 (2005) 191-193 (*Marenco, Maria Rita*); PaVi 50/1 (2005) 62-63 (*Marenco, Maria Rita*);

5332 Jesús, el profeta de Galilea. S 2005, Sígueme 333 pp. [R]Cart. 21 (2005) 236-237 (*Martínez Fresneda, F.*); EstTrin 39 (2005) 579-580 (*Vázquez Allegue, Jaime*).

5333 *Schnabel, E.J.* 'As the Father has sent me, so I send you' (John 20:21): the mission of Jesus and the mission of the church. Missionalia 33 (2005) 263-286 [NTAb 50,325].

5334 *Schottroff, Luise* Der Hunger Jesu: Mk 11,11-25; Mt 21,10-22. [F]STEGEMANN, W. 2005 ⇒139. 150-160 [Rev 8,7-9].

5335 *Schröter, Jens* Jesus und der Kanon: die frühe Jesusüberlieferung im Kontext der Entstehung des neutestamentlichen Kanons. BThZ 22 (2005) 181-201.

5336 *Schweitzer, Albert* The solution of thoroughgoing eschatology. The historical Jesus in recent research. 2005 ⇒379. 6-49.

5337 **Schweitzer, Albert** The quest of the historical Jesus. [T]*Montgomery, W.*: Mineola, NY 2005 <1911>, Dover vi; 410 pp. $17. 0-486-4402-7-3 [ThD 52,388—W. Charles Heiser].

5338 *Ska, Jean Louis* Moisés–Josué–Jesús. El camino. 2005 <2001> ⇒ 302. 193-220.

5339 *Söding, Thomas* Jesu Güte—Jesu Zorn—Jesu Liebe. IKaZ 34 (2005) 322-332.

5340 **Spencer, F. Scott** What did Jesus do?: gospel profiles of Jesus' personal conduct. 2003 ⇒19,5300; 20,5030. [R]ThTo 62 (2005) 130, 132 (*Downs, David J.*); CBQ 67 (2005) 158-160 (*Lux, Richard C.*).

5341 *Stanton, Graham N.* The gospel traditions and early christological reflection. The historical Jesus in recent research. Sources for biblical and theological study 10: 2005 ⇒379. 543-552.

5342 *Stock, Klemens* Poznanie osoby Jezusa jako cel egzegezy biblijnej. Interpretacja (w) dialogu. 2005 ⇒2043. 28-39 [AcBib 11,149]. **P.**

5343 *Stuhlmacher, Peter* Jesus' readiness to suffer and his understanding of his death. The historical Jesus in recent research. Sources for biblical and theological study 10: 2005 ⇒379. 392-412.

5344 **Taylor, Brian C.** Becoming human: core teachings of Jesus. CM 2005, Cowley 208 pp. 1-561-01257-2.

5345 *Thacker, A.* Jesus—'mad, bad or God?'—revisited. EpRe 32/4 (2005) 51-56 [NTAb 50,258].

5346 **Theissen, Gerd; Winter, Dagmar** The quest for the plausible Jesus: the question of criteria. 2002 ⇒18,4871... 20,5037. [R]RBLit 7 (2005) 304-306 (*Byron, John*);

5347 *Theißen, Gerd* The historical intention of primitive christian miracle stories. The historical Jesus in recent research. 2005 ⇒379. 350-360.

5348 **Theißen, Gerd** Die Jesusbewegung: Sozialgeschichte einer Revolution der Werte. [2]2004 <1977> ⇒20,5036. [R]SNTU 30 (2005) 281-282 (*Fuchs, Albert*).

5349 **Thiede, Carsten Peter** Jesus: der Glaube; die Fakten. 2003 ⇒19, 5317. [R]Aevum 79 (2005) 181-186 (*Ramelli, Ilaria*).

5350 *Tilliette, Xavier* Unverwundete Natur?: über die Keuschheit Jesu. IKaZ 34 (2005) 90-94.

5351 **Van Aarde, Andries** Fatherless in Galilee: Jesus as child of God. 2001 ⇒17,4454...20,5039. [R]RBLit 7 (2005) 322-24 (*Batten, Alicia*).

5352 *Vegge, Tor* The literacy of Jesus the carpenter's son: on the literary style in the words of Jesus. StTh 59 (2005) 19-37.

5353 **Vicent Cernuda, Antonio** Jesús perseguido a muerte: estudios exegéticos sobre las personas y los hechos. Monografias 82: 2002 ⇒18, 4882. [R]Cart. 21 (2005) 239-240 (*Martínez Fresneda, F.*).

5354 **Vidal, Senén** Los tres proyectos de Jesús y el cristianismo naciente. 2003 ⇒19,5323; 20,5041. [R]EstAg 40 (2005) 176-177 (*Cineira, D.*).
5355 *Ware, Kallistos* Jesus from a christian perspective. Abraham's children. 2005 ⇒544. 72-86.
5356 *Wasike, Anne N.* Jesus: an African perspective. Global bible commentary. 2005 ⇒2443. 329-332.
5357 **Weaver, W.P.** Jesus and his biographers. North Richland Hills, TX 2005, BIBAL xiii; 96 pp. $13. 09305-6614X. Foreword by *J.H. Charlesworth*; Bibl. [NTAb 50,601].
5358 *White, Thomas J.* The voluntary action of the earthly Christ and the necessity of the beatific vision. Ment. *Aquinas*: Thom. 69/4 (2005) 497-534.
5359 **Wilckens, Ulrich** Theologie des Neuen Testaments, 1: Geschichte der urchristlichen Theologie, 1: Geschichte des Wirkens Jesu in Galiläa. 2002 ⇒18,4888; 19,5328. [R]JThS 56 (2005) 598-601 (*Morgan, Robert*).
5360 *Willitts, Joel* Presuppositions and procedures in the study of the 'historical Jesus': or, why I decided not to be a 'historical Jesus' scholar. JSHJ 3 (2005) 61-108.
5361 **Winter, D.** In the footsteps of Jesus: explorations and reflections in the land of the Holy One. L 2005, Epworth x; 130 pp. £8/$11. 07162-05815. Bibl. [NTAb 50,410].
5362 *Witmer, S.E.* The lost message of *The lost message of Jesus*. Themelios 31/1 (2005) 60-67. Cf. S. Chalke & A. Mann, *The lost message of Jesus* (2003) [NTAb 50,259].

## F1.5 *Jesus et Israel*—Jesus the Jew

5363 *Arnal, William* The cipher 'Judaism' in contemporary historical Jesus scholarship. Apocalypticism, anti-Semitism. 2005 ⇒767. 24-54.
5364 **Arnal, William Edward** The symbolic Jesus: historical scholarship, Judaism and the construction of contemporary identity. L 2005, Equinox viii; 98 pp. 1-84553-007-1. Bibl. 88-93.
5365 **Baeck, Leo** Les evangiles, une source juive. [T]*Hayoun, Maurice-Ruben* 2002 ⇒18,4897. [R]ETR 80 (2005) 133-134 (*Couteau, Elisabeth*).
5366 **Baldet, Jacques** Jesus the rabbi prophet: a new light on the gospel message. [T]*Rowe, Joseph*: Rochester, Vt 2005, Inner Traditions xi; 260 pp. 1-594-77070-0. Bibl. 247-252.
5367 **Barbaglio, Giuseppe** Gesù ebreo di Galilea: indagine storica. La Bibbia nella storia 11: 2002 ⇒18,4898... 20,5049. [R]RelCult 51 (2005) 225-226 (*Moral, Alejandro*); Asp. 52 (2005) 257-259 (*Castello, Gaetano*);
5368 Jesús, hebreo de Galilea: investigación histórica. Ágape 34: 2003 ⇒ 19,5335; 20,5048. [R]CDios 218 (2005) 561-562 (*Gutiérrez, J.*); Cart. 21 (2005) 237-39 (*Martínez Fresneda, F.*).
5369 *Barnett, Paul W.* The Jewish sign prophets. The historical Jesus in recent research. 2005 ⇒379. 444-462.
5370 *Baumbach, Günther* Randbemerkungen zu Jesu Judaizität <1989>;
5371 Fragen der modernen jüdischen Jesusforschung an die christliche Theologie <1977>;
5372 Das Problem einer nichtantijüdischen Christologie. Josephus–Jesusbewegung–Judentum. 2005 ⇒182. 107-117/191-205/249-260.

5373 **Ben-Chorin, Schalom** Brother Jesus: the Nazarene through Jewish eyes. [TE]*Klein, Jared S.; Reinhart, Max* 2001 ⇒17,4469. [R]JAAR 73 (2005) 222-224 (*Levine, Amy-Jill*);

5374 Werke, 4: Bruder Jesus: der Nazarener in jüdischer Sicht. [E]*Lenzen, Verena; Ben-Chorin, Avital*: Gü 2005, Gü xvii; 193 pp. 3-579-0534-3-4.

5375 *Brackman, H.* Jesus, SPINOZA, and Jewish modernity. Midstream [NY] 51/1 (2005) 8-15.

5376 [E]**Bruteau, Beatrice** Jesus through Jewish eyes. 2001 ⇒17,4467... 20,5050. [R]Horizons 32 (2005) 167-168 (*Boisclair, Regina A.*).

5377 [E]**Charlesworth, J.H.** L'ebraicità di Gesù. Piccola biblioteca teologica 56: 2002 ⇒18,4903; 19,5339. [R]CDios 218 (2005) 559-561 (*Gutiérrez, J.*).

5378 **Fenske, Wolfgang** Wie Jesus zum 'Arier' wurde: Auswirkungen der Entjudaisierung Christi im 19 und zu Beginn des 20. Jahrhunderts. Da:Wiss 2005, 288 pp. €59.90. 3-534-18928-0.

5379 *Frankemölle, Hubert* Der Jude Jesus und der christliche Glaube. Studien zum jüdischen Kontext. SBAB 37: 2005 <1999> ⇒210. 137-160.

5380 *Fredriksen, Paula* Compassion is to purity as fish is to bicycle and other reflections on constructions of 'Judaism' in current work on the historical Jesus. Apocalypticism, anti-Semitism. JSNT.S 275; JSHJ.S: 2005 ⇒767. 55-67.

5381 *Freyne, Sean* Jesus a Jewish Galilean: a new reading of the Jesus story. PIBA 28 (2005) 106-123.

5382 *Garber, Z.* The Jewish Jesus: a partisan's imagination. Shofar [West Lafayette, IN] 23/3 (2005) 137-143 [NTAb 50,25].

5383 *Herweg, Rachel* Jesus aus jüdischer Sicht: zur Begründung einer Trennungsgeschichte. WUB 38 (2005) 16-23.

5384 *Instone Brewer, David* The historical Jesus among the rabbis: prayer, divorce and earthly rewards. Anvil 22/3 (2005) 173-182.

5385 *Levine, Amy-Jill* Jesus and Judaism: why the connection still matters. Ethical dimensions. 2005 ⇒739. 54-75.

5386 **Maccoby, Hyam** Jesus the pharisee. 2003 ⇒19,5347; 20,5057. [R]CoTh 75/2 (2005) 243-246 (*Skierkowski, Marek*).

5387 *Pilch, John J.* The Middle Eastern Jesus. BiTod 43 (2005) 119-122.

5388 *Quarles, Charles L.* Jesus as Merkabah mystic. JSHJ 3 (2005) 5-22.

5389 *Reitsma, Bernard* The Jewishness of Jesus: relevant or essential?. ThRev 26/1 (2005) 55-69.

5390 **Sanders, E.P.** Jesús y el judaísmo. 2004 ⇒20,5060. [R]CDios 218 (2005) 563-564 (*Gutiérrez, J.*); ActBib 42 (2005) 214-215 (*Boada, Josep*).

5391 *Schlosser, Jacques* Jésus de Nazareth, un juif enraciné et libre. EeV 115/120 (2005) 1-8.

5392 *Sheridan, Sybil* Jesus from a Jewish perspective. Abraham's children. 2005 ⇒544. 87-98.

5393 *Silver, Matthew* A Jew's view of Jesus: Stephen Wise, Joseph Klausner, and discourse about the Jewish Jesus in the inter-war period. Zion 70 (2005) 31-62. **H**.

5394 *Skierkowski, M.* Jezus Gezy Vermesa: prezentacja i krytyka. CoTh 75/2 (2005) 97-132 [NTAb 51,28]. **P**.

5395 **Tomson, Peter J.** 'If this be from heaven...': Jesus and the New Testament authors in their relationship to Judaism. BiSe 76: 2001 ⇒ 17,4509... 20,5065. [R]RBLit 7 (2005) 246-251 (*Murray, Michele*);

5396 Jésus et les auteurs du Nouveau Testament dans leur relation au judaïsme. [T]*Duponcheele, Joseph*: Initiations bibliques: 2003, [R]RTL 36 (2005) 234-235 (*Focant, C.*); EstB 63 (2005) 353-355 (*Sen, Felipe*).

5397 *Tyson, Joseph B.* Jesus-a faithful Jew. Seeing Judaism anew. 2005 ⇒ 618. 29-37.

5398 **Van 't Riets, Peter** Lukas versus Matteüs: de treugkeer van de midrasj bij de uitleg van de evangeliën. Kampen 2005, Kok 300 pp. €21.50. 9-435-1074-2. ITBT 13/7,32s—Reedijk, Wim.

5399 **Varo, Francisco** Rabí Jesús de Nazaret. M 2005, BAC xxii; 224 pp. €13.46. 84-7914-786-5.

5400 **Vermes, Geza** Jesus in his Jewish context. 2003 ⇒19,5361; 20, 5066. [R]JSJ 36 (2005) 385-387 (*Tomson, Peter J.*);

5401 L'évangile des origines. [T]*Billoteau, Emmanuelle* 2004 ⇒20,5067. [R]PastSC 24/2 (2005) 127-128 (*Marleau, Diane*).

## F1.6 *Jesus in Ecclesia*—The Church Jesus

5402 *Bazarra, Carlos* Jesús, evangelio para hoy. Iter 16/37-38 (2005) 307-332.

5403 **Doni, Rodolfo** Storia di Gesù. Mi 2005, Paoline 336 pp. €18 [CiVi 61/1,97].

5404 **Fox, R.W.** Jesus in America: personal savior, cultural hero, national obsession. SF 2005 <2004>, HarperSanFrancisco viii; 488 pp. $17. 00606-2874X. 24 pl. [NTAb 49,595].

5405 **Guardini, Romano** Il Signore: riflessioni sulla persona e sulla vita di Gesù Cristo. [T]*Colombi, Giulio*: Brescia 2005, Morcelliana 756 pp. 88-372-2083-9. Introduzione di *Giacomo Canobbio*.

5406 **Holmgren, Frederick C.** The Old Testament and the significance of Jesus. 1999 ⇒15, 4474...17,4521. [R]ThR 70 (2005) 299-301 (*Reventlow, Henning Graf*).

5407 **Koch, Traugott** Jesus von Nazareth, der Mensch Gottes: eine gegenwärtige Besinnung. 2004 ⇒20,5071. [R]ThLZ 130 (2005) 1060-1061 (*Schröter, Jens*).

5408 **López-Dóriga, Enríque** ¿Quién eres, Jesús de Nazaret?. Barc [2]2005, Balmes 302 pp [RevAg 41,202s—G. Tejerina Arias].

5409 *Manzi, Franco* Memoria, identità e tradizione della chiesa nell'attestazione narrativa dei vangeli. ScC 133 (2005) 445-499.

5410 **Marini, M.** Gesù di Nazareth, il Signore. CinB 2005, Itaca 64 pp. €7.50. [R]Sacrum Ministerium 11 (2005) 165 (*Ouellet, Marc Card.*).

5411 *Milhoc, Vasile* Jesus: an Orthodox perspective. Global bible commentary. 2005 ⇒2443. 342-345.

5412 *Pagazzi, Giovanni Cesare* 'Vogliamo vedere Gesù': un volto da contemplare (NMI 16-28): i sensi spirituali e i sensi di Gesù. Path 4/1 (2005) 27-56.

5413 *Poupard, Card. Paul* Cristo e la scienza: un profilo inedito. VP 88 (2005) 87-94.

5414 *Schwartz, Barry* Jesus in first-century memory—a response. Memory, tradition, and text. SBL.Semeia Studies 52: 2005 ⇒416. 249-261.

5415 **Snyder, Graydon F.** Irish Jesus, Roman Jesus: the formation of early Irish christianity. 2002 ⇒18,4952; 20,5075. [R]HeyJ 46 (2005) 247-249 (*McNamara, Martin*).

5416 **Varak, Florent** Le mariage de Jésus. Lyon 2005, Clé 102 pp [ThEv (VS) 5/1,77—Henri Blocher].
**Zanetti, P.**, *al.* Imitatori di Gesù Cristo 2005 ⇒330.

### F1.7 *Jesus 'annormalis'*: **to atheists, psychoanalysts, romance...** Dan Brown, *Da Vinci code*; Mel Gibson *The Passion of the Christ*

5418 **Borrmans, Maurice** Jésus et les musulmans d'aujourd'hui. CJJC 69: P $^{2}$2005 <1996>, Desclée 315 pp. €28.50. 2-7189-0981-1.
5419 **Carotta, Francesco** Jesus was Caesar: on the Julian origin of christianity: an investigative report. $^{T}$*Hendriks, Tommie, al.*: Soesterberg 2005, Aspekt 512 pp. $35. 90-5911-369-9. Foreword *Fotis Kavoukopoulos*; afterword *Erika Simon* [ThD 52,48—W. Charles Heiser].
5420 *Charette, B.B.* Messiah without anointing: a missing element in cinematic portrayals of Jesus. Pneuma [Lei] 27/2 (2005) 355-365 [NTAb 50,254].
5421 *Counet, Patrick Chatelion* 'Vergeef het hun, ze weten niet wat ze doen': antisemitisme in hedendaagse Jezusfilms en de evangeliën. Str. 72 (2005) 229-237.
5422 *Despotis, Sotirios* He eikona tu Iesu ston kinematographo. DBM 23/2 (2005) 185-207. **G.**
5423 **Dumas, Alexandre** Isaac Laquedem ou le roman du juif errant. P 2005 <1852>, Belles Lettres 452 pp. €25 [MoBi 170,44–S. Laurant].
5424 **Gibran, Khalil** Jesus, Filho do Homem. $^{T}$*Tornquist, Brunilde Arndt*: São Leopoldo 2005, Sinodal 166 pp.
5425 **Marx, Friedhelm** 'Ich aber sage ihnen...': Christusfigurationen im Werk Thomas MANNs. Thomas-Mann-Studien 25: 2002 ⇒19,5391. $^{R}$ThLZ 130 (2005) 676-678 (*Albrecht, Christian*).
5426 *Mustafa, Basil* Jesus from a Muslim perspective. Abraham's children. 2005 ⇒544. 99-107.
5427 *Patterson, James Alan* Revolution and the eschaton: images of Jesus in the Jesus movement. TrinJ 26 (2005) 267-277.
5428 **Prothero, Stephen** American Jesus: how the Son of God became a national icon. 2003 ⇒19,5392. $^{R}$JR 85 (2005) 129-30 (*Pals, Daniel*).
5429 **Teklak, Ceslaw** Le ricerche marxiste su Gesù di Nazareth. SPAA 39: R 2005, Antonianum 552 pp. €33. 88-7257-067-0.
5430 *Trevi, Mario* Il non credente di fronte al vangelo. Il Mulino 54 (2005) 793-798.

5431 **Bock, Darrell L.** Il Codice da Vinci: verità e menzogne. CinB 2005, San Paolo 252 pp. €14. $^{R}$Cultura & libri 151 (2005) 136-140 (*Averna, Laura*);
5432 Un vistazo a *El Código Da Vinci*: tres errores mayores y unos cuantos más. Kairós 37 (2005) 111-120 [NTAb 50,136].
5433 *Brett, Stephen F.* "The Da Vinci code": conspiracy or communion?. HPR 106/2 (2005) 46-50.
5434 **Brown, Dan** Il codice da Vinci. $^{T}$*Valla, R.*: 2003 ⇒19,5379. $^{R}$Itin(M) 13 (2005) 245-265 (*Savagnone, Giuseppe*);
5435 O Código da Vinci. $^{T}$*Cavalcante, Celina*: 2004 ⇒20,5116. $^{R}$PerTeol 37 (2005) 419-436 (*Filho, Carlos R. Caldas*); REB 65 (2005) 762-763 (*Galvão, Carmen*).

5436 *Hughes, Louis* Theology fiction (1)—behind the *Da Vinci Code*. Furrow 56 (2005) 522-530.
5437 **Price, Robert M.** The Da Vinci fraud: why the truth is stranger than fiction. Amherst, NY 2005, Prometheus 296 pp. $18. 1-59102-388-3.
5438 **Ullate Fabio, José Antonio** Contro il 'Codice da Vinci'. Mi 2005, Sperling & K. 212 pp. [R]Cultura & libri 151 (2005) 141-152 (*Livi, Antonio*).
5439 ¿Verdad o ficción?: los especialistas responden acerca del Código da Vinci. M 2004, Lumen 216 pp. [R]RelCult 51 (2005) 213-220 (*Olmo Veros, Rafael del*).
5440 **Welborn, Amy** Desconfiando a Da Vinci: los hechos reales ocultos en El Código Da Vinci. 2004 ⇒20,5097. [R]RelCult 51 (2005) 220-223 (*Olmo Veros, Rafael del*).

5441 *Aitken, Tom, al.* Table talk: reflections on The Passion of the Christ (Mel Gibson, 2004). Cinéma divinité. 2005 ⇒520. 311-330.
5442 *Backhaus, Knut* Die Passion Christi und ihr Publikum: ein Film, vier Evangelien und das Schauspiel eines Sterbenden. MThZ 56 (2005) 98-112.
5443 *Ballabio, Fabio* Spiritualità sul grande schermo. Ambrosius 81/4 (2005) 819-823.
5444 *Boomershine, T.E.* Mel, go to seminary, please: a biblical storyteller's reflections on 'The Passion of the Christ'. JTh 109 (2005) 17-30 [NTAb 50,27].
5445 *Cardona Ramírez, Hernán* La pasión de Cristo, según Mel Gibson—¿una película fiel al relato bíblico?. El grano. 2005 ⇒197. 19-38.
5446 [E]**Corley, Kathleen E.; Webb, Robert L.** Jesus and Mel Gibson's The Passion of the Christ: the film, the gospels and the claims of history. 2004 ⇒20,330. [R]Theol. 108 (2005) 390-391 (*Lawrence, Louise*); TJT 21 (2005) 231-232 (*Beavis, Mary Ann*); RBLit (2005)* (*Denzey, Nicola*).
5447 *Deutschmann, Anton* Die Grausamkeit der Bilder: Anmerkungen zur Diskussion um M. Gibsons "Passion of Christ". [F]LAUB, F.: Bibel-Schule-Leben 6: 2005 ⇒87. 165-173.
5448 *Eberhart, Christian A.* 'The Passion' of Gibson: evaluating a recent interpretation of Christ's suffering and death in light of the New Testament. Consensus [Saskatoon, SK] 30/1 (2005) 37-74 [NTAb 50,28].
5449 *Fitzgerald, Benedict; Fulco, William J.; Shepherd, David* From gospel to Gibson: an interview with the writers behind Mel Gibson's "The passion of the Christ". Religion and the arts 9/3 (2005) 321-31.
5450 *Gilmour, Peter* Text and context: "The passion of the Christ" and other Jesus films. RelEd 100/3 (2005) 311-325.
5451 *Holderness, G.* 'Animated icons': narrative and liturgy in *The Passion of the Christ*. JLT 19 (2005) 384-401 [NTAb 50,259].
5452 *Lawrence, Louise J.* "The passion of the Christ": gospel world-making and real presence. Theol. 108/842 (2005) 83-90.
5453 **Miller, Monica M.** The theology of *The Passion of the Christ*. NY 2005, Alba xxix; 170 pp. $15 [BiTod 43,202—Donald Senior].
5454 *Petit Sulla, José* La 'nueva' Pasión de Cristo, de Mel Gibson. Cristiandad 62/884 (2005) 3-5.
5455 *Reuter, Ingo* Mel Gibsons Passion Christi: Anmerkungen zu Ästhetik und Inhalt. rhs 48 (2005) 62-65.

5456 *Scham, Sandra* Holywood Holy Land. Secrets of the bible. 2005 ⇒ 482. 201-205.
5457 *Young, G.D.* History, archaeology, and Mel Gibson's Passion. Shofar [West Lafayette, IN] 23/3 (2005) 74-79 [NTAb 50,29]

### F2.2 *Unitas VT-NT*: **The Unity of OT-NT**; Unity of NT

5458 *Baslez, Marie-Françoise* "L'autre Écriture": la culture biblique des premiers chrétiens (Ier-IIIe siècles). $^{F}$THELAMON, F. 2005 ⇒148. 33-47.
5459 *Beauchamp, Paul* Accomplir les écritures: un chemin de théologie biblique. Pages exégétiques. LeDiv 202: 2005 <1992> ⇒183. 413-446.
5460 *Blanchard, Yves-Marie* 'Je ne suis pas venu abolir mais accomplir': la relation aux écritures, selon les évangiles. EeV 129 (2005) 1-9 [NTAb 50,23] [Mt 5,17].
5461 *Bos, Rein* Van wie zegt de profeet die?: een een-voudige vraag en een meer-voudig antwoord. HTS 61 (2005) 1049-1069 [OTA 29, 302] [Isa 53; Acts 8,26-39].
5462 *Calloud, Jean* Ces écritures qui devaient s'accomplir. $^{F}$GENEST, O. 2005 ⇒46. 107-125.
5463 **Cantera Ortiz de Urbina, Jesús** La bíblia commentada por ella misma. M 2005, EDIBESA 366 pp.
5464 *Christoph, Markus* "Novum in Vetere latet in ambobus natura patet": der innere Zusammenhang von AT, NT und Schöpfungsgeschichte. Theologisches 35 (2005) 569-586 [Gen 1-3].
5465 *Ferry, Brenton C.* Cross-examining Moses' defense: an answer to Ramsey's critique of Kline and Karlberg. WThJ 67 (2005) 163-168.
5466 *Frankemölle, Hubert* Die heiligen Schriften der Juden und die Christologie <2003>;
5467 'Biblische' Theologie: semantisch-historische Anmerkungen und Thesen <2002>;
5468 Das Neue Testament als Kommentar?: Möglichkeiten und Grenzen einer hermeneutischen These aus der Sicht eines Neutestamentlers <2001>. Studien zum jüdischen Kontext. SBAB 37: 2005 ⇒210. 123-136/1-22/28-90.
5469 *Harrelson, Walter* Contemporary christians and Israel's ancient scriptures. Seeing Judaism anew. 2005 ⇒618. 115-123.
5470 *Hensell, Eugene* Death and resurrection: patterns of loss and hope. RfR 64 (2005) 89-93.
5471 *Hentschel, Georg* Ist die jüdische Bibel ein christliches Buch?. Heilige Schriften. 2005 ⇒362. 31-40, 232-235.
5472 *Jinbachian, Manuel* L'Ancien Testament dans le Nouveau. Traduire la Bible hébraïque. 2005 ⇒728. 199-213.
5473 **Kirsch, Anne** Das Verhältnis von Altem und Neuem Testament im Spiegel romanischer Kirchenportale Frankreichs (das Südportal von Saint-Pierre in Moissac, das Westportal von Saint-Trophime in Arles, das Westportal von Sainte-Madeleine in Vézelay). $^{D}$*Frankemölle, Hubert* 2005, Diss. Paderborn [ThRv 102,x].
5474 **Lierman, John** The New Testament Moses: christian perceptions of Moses and Israel in the setting of Jewish religion. WUNT 2/173:

2004 ⇒20,5217. RTrinJ 26 (2005) 145-147 (*Grindheim, Sigurd*); Sal. 67 (2005) 183-184 (*Vicent, Rafael*).

5475 *Manzi, Franco* Identità e memoria di Gesù nell'attestazione narrativa di Lc 24,1-49 e 4,16-30. ScC 133 (2005) 351-382.

5476 *März, Claus-Peter* Eine Bibel in zwei Testamenten: zur Entstehung der christlichen Bibel: ein Plakat. Heilige Schriften. 2005 ⇒362. 17-30, 231-232.

5477 E**Menken, Maarten J.J.; Moyise, Steve** The Psalms in the New Testament. 2004 ⇒20,3627. RTheol. 108 (2005) 443-444 (*Downing, F. Gerald*).

5478 *Meynet, Roland* La citation au centre. MUSJ 58 (2005) 29-65.

5479 *Moyise, Steve* Intertextuality and historical approaches to the use of scripture in the New Testament. VeE 26 (2005) 447-458 [Isa 8,12-13; 1 Pet 3,14-15];

5480 Intertextualität und historische Zugänge zum Schriftgebrauch im Neuen Testament. Die Bibel im Dialog. NET 10: 2005 ⇒333. 23-34 [Isa 8,12-13; 1 Pet 3,14-15; Rev 5,5-6; 20-22].

5481 **Moyise, Steve** The Old Testament in the New: an introduction. 2001 ⇒17,4567. RRBLit (2005)* (*Gosnell, Peter*).

5482 *Pickering, Wilbur N.* Repopulating after the flood: was Cainan or Shelah the son of Arphaxad?. Journal of the Grace Evangelical Society 18/34 (2005) 45-48 [Gen 11,12-13; Lk 3,35-36].

5483 *Puig, Armand* La importancia del Antiguo Testamento. Phase 45 (2005) 405-413.

5484 **Sals, Ulrike** Die Biographie der "Hure Babylon": Studien zur Intertextualität der Babylon-Texte in der Bibel. FAT 2/6: 2004 ⇒20, 5229. ROLZ 100 (2005) 621-625 (*Höffken, Peter*); ThZ 61 (2005) 371-373 (*Raguse, Hartmut*) [Rev 17-19].

5485 *Schwank, Benedikt* Von der Einheit der heiligen Schriften. EuA 81 (2005) 72-74 [Isa 7,14; Mt 1,22].

5486 *Steins, Georg* Die Einheit der Heiligen Schrift—ein "aufgegebenes" Thema der Bibelexegese. rhs 48 (2005) 140-150.

5487 *Voorwinde, Stephen* The Psalms—key to the New Testament?. VR 70 (2005) 56-83.

## F2.5 *Commentarii*—Commentaries on the whole NT

5488 **Boring, M. Eugene; Craddock, Fred B.** The people's New Testament commentary. 2004 ⇒20,5239. RRBLit (2005)* (*Kealy, Sean; Lamp, Jeffrey; Nicklas, Tobias*).

5489 E**Bray, Gerald** Giacomo, 1-2 Pietro, 1-3 Giovanni, Giuda: la bibbia commentata dai padri, NT 11. T*Genovese, Armando*: R 2005, Città Nuova 325 pp. €34. 88-311-9376-7.

5490 E**Edwards, Mark J.** Galati, Efesini, Filippesi: la bibbia commentata dai padri, NT 8. E*Dell'Osso, Carlo*: R 2005, Città Nuova 331 pp. €37. 88-311-9377-5. Introd.generale *Angelo di Berardino*. RAsp. 52 (2005) 422-424 (*Longobardo, Luigi*).

5491 **Fallon, Michael** Saints James, Peter, John, Jude & Hebrews: an introductory commentary . New Testament Letters 2: Kensington, NSW 2004, Chevalier 289 pp. 0-86940-304-4.

E**Levoratti, Armando J.** I vangeli. 2005 ⇒432.

5492 The Navarre bible: the letters of Saint Paul, in the Revised Standard Version and New Vulgate with a commentary by members of the Faculty of Theology of the University of Navarre. Dublin 2005, Four Courts 671 pp. 1-85182-912-1. Reader's edition.

5493 **Smiles, Vincent M.** First Thessalonians, Philippians, Second Thessalonians, Colossians, Ephesians. New Collegeville Bible Commentary: ColMn 2005, Liturgical 125 pp. $7. 978-0-8146-2867-6 [BiTod 44,128—Donald Senior].

5494 **Stern, David H.** Komentarz żydowski do Nowego Testamentu [Commentaire juif au Nouveau Testament]. 2004 ⇒20,5243. [R]PrzPow 122 (2005) 283-295 (*Baraniak, Marek*). **P**.

# IX. Evangelia

## F2.6 Evangelia Synoptica: *textus, synopses, commentarii*

5495 **Bartnicki, R.** Ewangelie synoptyczne, geneza i interpretacja. 2003 ⇒19,5451. [R]StBob (2005/1) 175-184 (*Kasiłowski, Piotr*). **P**.

5496 *Huprelle, Anne-Cécile* Selon Marc, Matthieu et Luc. Le monde des religions 14 (2005) 30-33.

5497 **Meynet, Roland** A new introduction to the synoptic gospels. [T]*Muthiah, Arul Jesu Robin*: R 2005, Claretian 366 pp. Bibl. 347-353.

5498 *Miler, Jean* Bulletin d'exégèse des synoptiques. RSR 93 (2005) 83-106.

5499 **Stein, Robert H.** Studying the synoptic gospels: origin and interpretation. [2]2001 ⇒17,4601... 19,5456. [R]SNTU 30 (2005) 193-214 (*Fuchs, Albert*).

## F2.7 *Problema synopticum*: The Synoptic Problem

5500 *Asgeirsson, Jon Ma.* Complex and community: from the prophets of Q to the scribe(s) of St. Matthew or vice versa. The formation of the early church. WUNT 183: 2005 ⇒708. 93-122.

5501 **Bergemann, Thomas** Q auf dem Prüfstand: die Zuordnung des Mt/Lk-Stoffes zu Q am Beispiel der Bergpredigt. FRLANT 158: 1993 ⇒ 9,4572. [R]ThR 70 (2005) 374-376 (*Lindemann, Andreas*).

5502 *Caballero Cuesta, José María* La fuente 'Q': el documento escrito más antiguo sobre Jesús. Burg. 46 (2005) 535-565.

5503 *Coulot, C.* Synoptique (le problème). DBS 13/75. 2005 ⇒970. 785-828.

5504 *Day, Matthew* Reading the fossils of faith: Thomas Henry HUXLEY and the evolutionary subtext of the synoptic problem. ChH 74 (2005) 534-556.

5505 **Derrenbacker, R.A., Jr.** Ancient compositional practices and the synoptic problem. Lv 2005, Peeters xxviii; 290 pp. €80. 90-429-1637-0. Bibl. xv-xxviii.

5506 *Dunn, James D.G.* Q[1] as oral tradition. [F]STANTON, G. 2005 ⇒138. 45-69.

5507 **Fleddermann, Harry T.** Q: a reconstruction and commentary. Biblical Tools and Studies 1: Lv 2005, Peeters 13; 995 pp. €105. 90-429-1656-7. Bibl. 941-969.

5508 *Fricker, Denis* La femme, la famille et la communauté dans la source des Logia. RevSR 79 (2005) 97-116.

5509 *Fuchs, Albert* Zum Stand der Synoptischen Frage–J.S. Kloppenborg;

5510 Zum Stand der Synoptischen Frage—Ch. Münch;

5511 Zum Stand der Synoptischen Frage—D.A. de Silva;

5512 Zum Stand der Synoptischen Frage—L.W. Hurtado;

5513 Zum Stand der Synoptischen Frage—R.H. Stein;

5514 Zum Stand der Synoptischen Frage—M. Goodacre. SNTU.A 30 (2005) 123-143/146-172/173-184/185-192/193-214/215-223;

5515 Probleme der Zweiquellentheorie anhand der Perikope vom obersten Gebot: Mk 12,28-34 par Mt 22,34-40 par Lk 10,25-28. [F]ZMIJEWSKI, J.: BBB 151: 2005 ⇒172. 73-102.

5516 *Goff, Matthew J.* Discerning trajectories: 4QInstruction and sapiential background of the sayings source Q. JBL 124 (2005) 657-673.

5517 **Goodacre, Mark** The case against Q: studies in Markan priority and the synoptic problem. 2002 ⇒18,5028... 20,5288. [R]SNTU 30 (2005) 215-223 (*Fuchs, Albert*); ET 117 (2005) 124-125 (*Brash, Damon*);

5518 The synoptic problem: a way through the maze. BiSe 80: 2001 ⇒17, 4623; 20,5289. [R]RBLit 7 (2005) 324-326 (*Matson, Mark A.*).

5519 [E]**Goodacre, Mark; Perrin, Nicholas** Questioning Q: a multidimensional critique. 2004 ⇒20,5290. [R]RBLit (2005)* (*Verheyden, Joseph*); ET 116 (2005) 354-355 (*Foster, Paul*).

5520 **Head, Peter M.** Christology and the synoptic problem: an argument for Markan priority. MSSNTS 94: C 2005 <=1997>, CUP xviii; 337 pp. £29/$50. 05210-18897. [R]SNTU 30 (2005) 286-7 (*Fuchs, Albert*).

5521 **Heil, Christoph** Lukas und Q; Studien zur lukanischen Redaktion des Sprachevangeliums Q. BZNT 111: 2003 ⇒19,5475; 20,5296. [R]ThPh 80 (2005) 446-447 (*Diefenbach, M.*).

5522 **Hultgren, Stephen** Narrative elements in the double tradition: a study of their place within the framework of the gospel narrative. BZNW 113: 2002 ⇒18,5034; 19,5478. [R]RBLit (2005)* (*Baldwin, Matthew C.*).

5523 *Kahl, Werner* Vom Ende der Zweiquellentheorie oder Zur Klärung des synoptischen Problems. [F]STEGEMANN, W.: 2005 ⇒139. 404-442.

5524 *Keylock, Leslie Robert* The sayings of Jesus: source (Q) in recent research: a review article. TrinJ 26 (2005) 119-130.

5525 **Kloppenborg, J.** The formation of Q. 1999 <1987> ⇒15,4587. [R]SNTU 30 (2005) 123-143 (*Fuchs, Albert*);

5526 Q: el evangelio desconocido. S 2005, Sígueme 432 pp. 84301-15684. [R]EstB 63 (2005) 131-134 (*Gil Arbiol, C.*).

5527 *Michaud, Jean-Paul* Effervescence in Q Studies. SNTU.A 30 (2005) 61-103.

5528 **Mournet, Terence C.** Oral tradition and literary dependency: variability and stability in the synoptic tradition and Q. [D]*Dunn, James D. G.*: WUNT 2/195: Tü 2005, Mohr S. xv; 327 pp. €64. 31614-84541. Diss. Durham; Bibl. 294-306.

5529 *Mußner, Franz* Johannes und die Synoptiker: gibt es eine Grundgemeinsamkeit?. [F]ZMIJEWSKI, J.: BBB 151: 2005 ⇒172. 199-210.

5530 **Parmentier, Roger** Paroles de Jesus (appelées aussi 'logia', source Q) actualisées (transpositions en notre temps, réécritures). P 2005, L'Harmattan 62 pp. €10. 978-27475-96084.

5531 *Robinson, James M.* Λόγοι σοφῶν: on the *Gattung* of Q. The sayings gospel Q. BEThL 189: 2005 <1964>⇒289. 37-74;
5532 The sayings of Jesus: Q <1983> 177-192;
5533 The Q trajectory between John and Matthew via Jesus <1991> 285-307;
5534 A critical text of the sayings gospel Q <1992> 309-317;
5535 The sayings gospel Q <1992> 319-348;
5536 Die Logienquelle: Weisheit oder Prophetie: Anfragen an Migaku Sato, Q und Prophetie <1993> 349-374;
5537 The Jesus of the sayings gospel Q <1993> 375-388;
5538 The Son of Man in the sayings gospel Q <1994> 405-425;
5539 The history-of-religions taxonomy of Q: the Cynic hypothesis <1994> 427-448;
5540 The Jesus of Q as liberation theologian <1995> 449-463;
5541 The *incipit* of the sayings gospel Q <1995> 465-492;
5542 Building blocks in the social history of Q <1996> 493-517;
5543 Galilean upstarts: a sot's Cynical disciples? <1997> 535-557;
5544 The sequence of Q: the lament over Jerusalem <1998> 559-598 [Lk 13,34-35];
5545 The Matthean trajectory from Q to Mark <1998> 599-627;
5546 From safe house to house church: from Q to Matthew <1999> 629-644;
5547 The image of Jesus in Q <2001> 645-662;
5548 The critical edition of Q and the study of Jesus <2001> 663-688;
5549 Jesus' theology in the sayings gospel Q <2003> 689-709;
5550 Zeugnisse eines schriftlichen, griechischen vorkanonischen Textes Mt 6,28b א*, P.Oxy. 655 I,1-17 (EvTh 36) und Q 12,27 <1998> 713-728;
5551 A written Greek sayings cluster older than Q: a vestige <1999> 777-794 [Lk 12,27];
5552 Noch einmal: der Schreibfehler in Q 12,27 <2001> 795-808;
5553 The lilies of the field: saying 36 of the Gospel of Thomas and secondary accretions in Q 12.22b-31 <2001> 809-834;
5554 P.Oxy. 655 und Q: zum Diskussionsbeitrag von Stanley E. Porter <2002>. The sayings gospel Q. BEThL 189: 2005 ⇒289. 835-844.
5555 [E]**Robinson, James M.; Hoffmann, Paul; Kloppenborg, John S.** The critical edition of Q: synopsis including the gospels of Matthew and Luke, Mark and Thomas. 2000 ⇒16,4698... 20,5319. [R]RBLit 7 (2005) 333-334 (*Gurtner, Daniel M.*).
5556 **Robinson, James M.** The gospel of Jesus: in search of the original good news. SF 2005, HarperSanFrancisco xiv; 238 pp. 00607-62179;
5557 I detti di Gesù: il 'proto-vangelo' dei detti Q in italiano. Giornale di teologia 310: Brescia 2005, Queriniana 53 pp. 88-399-0810-2.
5558 **Rondez, Pascale** Alltägliche Weisheit?: Untersuchungen zum Erfahrungsbezug von Weisheitslogien in der Q-Tradition. [D]*Weder, H.* 2005, Diss. Zürich.
5559 *Sisson, Russell B.* Who is John's audience in Q?: the rhetorical unity of John's preaching and Q. ProcGLM 25 (2005) 135-141 [Lk 7].
5560 *Thomas, R.L.* Discerning synoptic gospel origins: an inductive approach (part 2). MastJ 16/1 (2005) 7-47 [NTAb 50,30].
5561 **Valantasis, Richard** The new Q: a fresh translation with commentary. L 2005, Continuum x; 238 pp. £17. 978-05670-25616.

## F2.8 *Synoptica*: **themata**

5562 *Byrskog, Samuel* Das Lernen der Jesusgeschichte nach den synoptischen Evangelien. Religiöses Lernen. 2005 ⇒384. 191-209.

5563 **Fihavango, George Mark** Jesus and leadership: analysis of rank, status, power and authority as reflected in the synoptic gospels from a perspective of the Evangelical Lutheran Church in Tanzania. [D]*Stegemann, Wolfgang*: 2005, Diss. Neuendettelsau [ThRv 102,x].

5564 *Gardner, A.E.* Reading between the texts: minor characters who prepare the way for Jesus. Encounter 66/1 (2005) 45-66 [NTAb 49, 498].

5565 *Grappe, Christian* Marc et Luc, deux évangiles aux "stratégies catéchétiques" bien distinctes. PosLuth 53/4 (2005) 343-353.

5566 *Gundry, Robert H.* The apostolically Johannine pre-Papian tradition concerning the gospels of Mark and Matthew. The old is better. WUNT 178: 2005 ⇒220. 49-73.

5567 **Hochholzer, Martin** Feindes- und Bruderliebe im Widerstreit?: eine vergleichende Studie zur synoptischen und johanneischen Ausprägung des Liebesgebots. [D]*Schwankl, Otto* 2005, Diss. Passau [ThRv 102,x] [Mk 12,30-31].

5568 **Karkowski, Annerose** Konfliktmanagement im Matthäusevangelium: destruktive und konstruktive Gruppendynamik in der Gemeinde. [D]*Stegemann, Wolfgang* 2005, Diss. Neuendettelsau [ThRv 102,x].

5569 *Klumbies, Paul-Gerhard* Rivalisierende Rationalitäten im Markus- und Lukasevangelium. ThZ 61 (2005) 320-333.

5570 **Laaksonen, Jari** Jesus und das Land: das Gelobte Land in der Verkündigung Jesu. 2002 ⇒18,5066; 19,5497. [R]JSJ 36 (2005) 358-360 (*Vos, J. Cornelis de*).

5571 *Lupieri, Edmondo* Dodici, sette, undici, ventiquattro: numeri, chiese e fine del mondo. ASEs 22/2 (2005) 355-369.

5572 *Maggioni, Bruno* Servizio, autorità e regalità secondo i vangeli. PSV 51 (2005) 169-175 [John 18,33-38; 19,8-11].

5573 *Malina, Bruce J.* From the Jesus faction to the synoptic gospels: the synoptic gospels as third generation phenomena. [F]STEGEMANN, W. 2005 ⇒139. 61-74.

5574 *Manicardi, Ermenegildo* La parola di Gesù sulla croce del discepolo nella comprensione dei vangeli <1988>;

5575 Gesù e gli stranieri <1996>. Gesù la cristologia. 2005 ⇒253. 29-47/ 49-84;

5576 Le guarigioni come opera del sabato (sinottici). PSV 52 (2005) 149-174.

5577 *Philip, Abraham* Jesus and the state: a synopitc [sic] perspective. BiBh 31 (2005) 68-76.

5578 *Reimer, Ivoni R.* The forgiveness of debts in Matthew and Luke: for an economy without exclusions. God's economy. 2005 <1999> ⇒ 415. 152-168.

5579 *Rudman, D.* The significance of the phrase 'fishers of men' in the synoptic gospels. IBSt 26 (2005) 106-118.

5580 *Spencer, F. Scott* "Follow me": the imperious call of Jesus in the synoptic gospels. Interp. 59 (2005) 142-153.

5581 **Sullivan, Kevin P.** Wrestling with angels: a study of the relationship between angels and humans in ancient Jewish literature and the New

Testament. AGJU 55: 2004 ⇒20,2589. [R]RdQ 22 (2005) 291-294 (*Puech, Émile*).

5582 **Tiwald, Markus** Wanderradikalismus: Jesu erste Jünger–ein Anfang und was davon bleibt. ÖBS 20: 2002 ⇒18,5078... 20,5344. [R]ThLZ 130 (2005) 168-169 (*Niederwimmer, Kurt*); BZ 49 (2005) 129-134 (*Hoffmann, Paul*).

5583 *Tuckett, Christopher* Isaiah in Q. Isaiah in the NT. 2005 ⇒443. 51-61.

5584 **Wahlen, Clinton** Jesus and the impurity of spirits in the synoptic gospels. WUNT 2/185: 2004 ⇒20,5347. [R]SNTU 30 (2005) 259 (*Fuchs, Albert*).

5585 **Wilk, Florian** Jesus und die Völker in der Sicht der Synoptiker. BZNT 109: 2002 ⇒18,5079... 20,5348. [R]ThG 48 (2005) 232-233 (*März, Claus-Peter*).

### F3.1 **Matthaei evangelium**: *textus, commentarii*

5586 *Allison, Dale C.* Reading Matthew through the church fathers. Studies in Matthew: interpretation. 2005 ⇒5587. 117-131.

5587 **Allison, Dale C.** Studies in Matthew: interpretation past and present. GR 2005, Baker 282 pp. $35. 0-8010-2791-8.

5588 **Barbaglio, Giuseppe** I vangeli: Matteo. [2]2004 <1975> ⇒20,5352. [R]SapDom 58 (2005) 233-234 (*Miele, Michele*).

5589 *Beaton, Richard C.* How Matthew writes. [F]STANTON, G. 2005 ⇒138. 116-134.

5590 *Boring, M. Eugene* The gospel of Matthew. NT survey. 2005 ⇒ 3144. 34-61.

5591 **Bruner, Frederick D.** Matthew: a commentary. [2]2004 <1987/1990> ⇒20,5355. [R]RRT 12/1 (2005) 179 (*Seddon, Philip*); RBLit (2005)* (*Bredin, Mark*).

5592 **Carter, Warren C.** Matthew and the margins: a socio-political and religious reading. JSNT.S 204: 2000 ⇒16,4723... 19,5515. [R]ThR 70 (2005) 352-354 (*Lindemann, Andreas*);

5593 Matthew: storyteller, interpreter, evangelist. [2]2004 <1994-1995> ⇒ 20,5356. [R]RBLit (2005)* (*Gurtner, Daniel*).

5594 **Davies, W.D.; Allison, Dale C.** The gospel according to Saint Matthew III: XIX-XXVIII. ICC: 1997 ⇒4,4439...9,4446. [R]ThR 70 (2005) 179-182 (*Lindemann, Andreas*).

5595 *Duarte, Alejandro* Matthew. Global bible commentary. 2005 ⇒2443. 350-360.

5596 **Fortna, Robert T.** The gospel of Matthew: the Scholars Version annotated with introduction and Greek text. Scholars Bible 3: Santa Rosa, CA 2005, Polebridge 269 pp. $22. 09443-44607. Bibl. 259-260.

5597 **Francis, Leslie J.; Atkins, Peter** Exploring Matthew's gospel: a guide to the gospel readings in the Revised Common Lectionary. Personality type and scripture: L 2005 <2001>, Morehouse x; 224 pp. £19/$38. 08192-81336. Bibl. [NTAb 50,393].

5598 **Frankemölle, Hubert** Matthäus Kommentar, 1-2. 1997 ⇒10,4277... 17,4704. [R]ThR 70 (2005) 186-190 (*Lindemann, Andreas*).

5599 [F]FRANKEMÖLLE, Hubert 'Dies ist das Buch...': das Matthäusevangelium: Interpretation—Rezeption—Rezeptionsgeschichte. [E]**Kampling, Rainer** 2004 ⇒20,42. [R]Str. 72 (2005) 180-181 (*Faseur, Geert*).

5600 **Galizzi, Mario** Evangelio según Mateo: comentario exegético-espiritual. [T]*Vázquez, Lourdes*: Sicar 2: M 2005, San Pablo 580 pp. €23. 84-285-2805-5.

5601 **Hare, Douglas R.A.** Matthew. 1993 ⇒9,4453... 13,4471. [R]ThR 70 (2005) 184-185 (*Lindemann, Andreas*).

5602 **Harrington, Daniel J.** Il vangelo di Matteo. [T]*Vischioni, G.*: Sacra Pagina 1: Leumann 2005, Elledici 384 pp. €30. 88-01-02195-X.

5603 **Heras Oliver, Gloria** Jesús según San Mateo: análisis narrativo del primer evangelio. Teológica 105: 2001 ⇒17,4705... 19,5519. [R]RSR 93 (2005) 89-91 (*Miler, Jean*).

5604 **Keener, Craig S.** A commentary on the gospel of Matthew. 1999 ⇒ 15,4652... 18,5087. [R]ThR 70 (2005) 192-194 (*Lindemann, Andreas*).

5605 **Kubski, Grzegorz** L'exégèse, la rhétorique et les idées: les commentaires des prêtres W. Serwatowski et W. Szczepanski sur la traduction de l'évangile selon saint Matthieu de Wujek. 2005, Diss.-Habil. Lublin [RTL 37,616]. **P.**

5606 *Levoratti, Armando J.* Vangelo secondo san Matteo. I vangeli. 2005 ⇒432. 359-556.

5607 *Lindemann, Andreas* Literatur zu den Synoptischen Evangelien 1992-2000 (V): das Matthäusevangelium (Teil 1). ThR 70 (2005) 174-216;

5608 (Teil 2). ThR 70 (2005) 338-382;

5609 *Luz, Ulrich* Matthew the evangelist: a Jewish christian at the crossroads. Studies in Matthew. 2005 ⇒252. 3-17

5610 The gospel of Matthew: a new story of Jesus or a rewritten one?. Studies in Matthew. 2005 <2001> ⇒252 18-36;

5611 Matthew and Q. Studies in Matthew. 2005 <1998> ⇒252. 39-53.

5612 **Luz, Ulrich** Das Evangelium nach Matthäus: 3. Teilband: Mt 18-25. Evangelisch-katholischer Komm. zum NT 1/3: 1997 ⇒13,4476; 17, 4711. [R]ThR 70 (2005) 176-179 (*Lindemann, Andreas*);

5613 4: Mt 26-28. Evangelisch-katholischer Komm. zum NT 1/4: 2002 ⇒ 18,5092... 20,5362. [R]SNTU 30 (2005) 225-227 (*Fuchs, Albert*);

5614 Das Evangelium nach Matthäus. Evangelisch-katholischer Komm. zum NT 1/1-4: 1997-2002 ⇒13,4476...20,5362. [R]Choisir 551 (2005) 10-12 (*Hug, Joseph*); EvTh 65 (2005) 398-408 (*Ritter, Adolf M.*);

5615 Matthew 21-28: a commentary. [T]*Crouch, James E.*; [E]*Köster, Helmut* Hermeneia: Mp 2005, Fortress xliv; 681 pp. $90. 0-8006-3770-4. Bibl. xxvii-xliv.

5616 **Madigan, Kevin** OLIVI and the interpretation of Matthew in the High Middle Ages. 2003 ⇒19,5526; 20,5363. [R]SCJ 36 (2005) 308-309 (*Pak, G. Sujin*); JEH 56 (2005) 582-583 (*Ocker, Christopher*).

5617 **Min, Kyoung Shik** Die früheste Überlieferung des Matthäusevangeliums (bis zum 3./4. Jh.). Edition und Untersuchung. [D]*Aland, Barbara*: ANTT 34: B 2005, De Gruyter x; 357 pp. 3-11-018281-5. Diss. Münster; Bibl. 326-343.

5618 **Morris, Leon** The gospel according to Matthew. Pillar: 1992 ⇒8, 4588... 11/1,2830. [R]ThR 70 (2005) 182-184 (*Lindemann, Andreas*).

5619 **Neyrey, Jerome H.** Honor y vergüenza: lectura cultural del evangelio de Mateo. BEB 114: S 2005, Sígueme 398 pp [EstAg 40,379—Cineira, D.A.].

5620 **Nolland, John** The gospel of Matthew: a commentary on the Greek text. International Greek Testament Commentary: GR 2005, Eerdmans xcviii; 1481 pp. $80. 0-8028-2389-0. Bibl. 1273-1468.

5621 **Osculati, Roberto** Il vangelo di Matteo. Mi 2004, IPL 277 pp. €14. 90. Collab. *Arianna Rotondo.* RHo Theológos 23 (2005) 305-308 (*Nicolaci, Maria A.*); Orph. 27 (2005) 256-58 (*Corsaro, Francesco*).

5622 **Paciorek, Antoni** Ewangelia wedlug świętego Mateusza: wstęp—przeklad z oryginalu—komentarz [Evangelium nach dem hl. Matthäus: Einführung—Übersetzung vom Original—Kommentar], Kap. 1-13. NKB NT I/1: Częstochowa 2005, Święty Pawel 608 pp. 83-72-68-752-6. Bibl. RBiLi 78 (2005) 152-154 (*Flis, Jan*); STV 43/2 (2005) 191-202 (*Łach, Jan*); CoTh 75/3 (2005) 231-234 (*Wojciechowski, Michał*). **P.**

5623 **Patte, Daniel** The gospel of Matthew: a contextual introduction for group study. 2003 ⇒19,5527; 20,5367. RRBLit 7 (2005) 493-496 (*Yoshikawa, Scott T.*).

5624 **Paul, Dagmar J.** "Untypische" Texte im Matthäusevangelium: Studien zu Charakter, Funktion und Bedeutung einer Textgruppe des matthäischen Sonderguts. D*Schmeller, Thomas*: NTA 50: Müns 2005, Aschendorff viii; 364 pp. €49. 3-402-04798-5. Diss. Technische Univ., Dresden; Bibl. 339-358.

5625 **Poucouta, Paulin** Du neuf et de l'ancien: l'évangile de Matthieu en dix étapes. 2004 ⇒20,5368. RSpiritus 179 (2005) 249-250 (*Guillaume, Jean-Marie*).

5626 **Pregeant, Russell** Matthew. 2004 ⇒20,5369. RRBLit (2005)* (*Combrink, H.J.*).

5627 **Racine, Jean-François** The text of Matthew in the writings of BASIL of Caesarea. SBL.NT in the Greek Fathers 5: 2004 ⇒20, 5370. RNT 47 (2005) 386-97 (*Guthrie, Sally*); TJT 21 (2005) 298-299 (*Keough, Shawn W.J.*); RBLit (2005)* (*Cousland, Robert; Jongkind, Dirk*).

5628 **Reid, Barbara E.** The gospel according to Matthew. New Collegeville Bible Commentary.NT 1: ColMn 2005, Liturgical 160 pp. $7. 0-8146-2860-5 [BiTod 44,128—Donald Senior].

5629 E**Rittmueller, J.** Liber questionum in Evangeliis. CChr.SL 108 F; Scriptores Celtigenae 5: 2003 ⇒19,5528; 20,5371. RRBen 115 (2005) 221-222 (*Bogaert, Pierre-Maurice*).

5630 E**Simonetti, Manlio** La biblia comentada por los padres le la iglesia: Nuevo Testamento, 1a: evangelio según San Mateo (1-13). T*Merino Rodríguez, Marcelo*: 2004 ⇒20,5379. REstTrin 39 (2005) 575-577 (*Miguel, José María de*).

5631 **Ska, Jean-Louis** Cose nuove e cose antiche (Mt 13,52): pagine scelte del vangelo di Matteo. Lettura pastorale della bibbia, bibbia e spiritualità 22: 2004 ⇒20,278. REfMex 23 (2005) 276-278 (*Landgrave G., Daniel R.*).

5632 MTHOMPSON, William G.: The gospel of Matthew in current study. E*Aune, David E.* 2001 ⇒17,108... 19,144. RRSR 93 (2005) 91-92 (*Miler, Jean*).

5633 **Toussaint, S.D.** Behold the king: a study of Matthew. GR 2005 <1980>, Kregel 399 pp. $20. 08254-38454. Bibl. [NTAb 50,173].

5634 **Wiefel, Wolfgang** Das Evangelium nach Matthäus. ThHK 1: 1998 ⇒14,4203.. 16,4744. RThR 70 (2005) 190-92 (*Lindemann, Andreas*).

5635 **Wilkins, Michael J.** Matthew. GR 2004, Zondervan 1003 pp. 0-310-49310-2. Bibl.

5636 **Zuurmond, Rochus** Novum Testamentum Aethiopice: part III: the gospel of Matthew. ÄthF 55: 2001 ⇒17,4727... 20,5382. RNT 47 (2005) 403-406 (*Baarda, Tjitze*).

## F3.2 **Themata** *de Matthaeo*

5637 *Ăbel, František* The interpretation of the term 'battalogein' in the context of the gospel according to Matthew. ITE 14 (2005) 27-41.
5638 *Aitken, James K.* Sanctus Matthaeus, magister sapientiae, summa cum laude. FDi Lella, A.: CBQ.MS 38: 2005 ⇒35. 264-279.
5639 **Allison, Dale C.** The new Moses: a Matthean typology. 1993 ⇒9, 4470... 12,4291. RThR 70 (2005) 356-357 (*Lindemann, Andreas*).
5640 *Allison, Dale C.* Structure, biographical impulse, and the Imitatio Christi. Studies in Matthew: interpretation. 2005 ⇒5587. 135-155;
5641 Deconstructing Matthew. Studies in Matthew. 2005 ⇒5587. 237-49.
5642 *Antony, Abraham M.* Jesus the shepherd in the gospel of Matthew. MJohn Paul II. 2005 ⇒72. 143-185 [Ps 23].
5643 **Barnet, John A.** Not the righteous but sinners: M.M. Bakhtin's theory of aesthetics and the problem of reader-character interaction in Matthew's gospel. JSNT.S 246: 2003 ⇒19,5537; 20,5386. RThLZ 130 (2005) 769-770 (*Schenk, Wolfgang*); RBLit (2005)* (*Kennedy, Joel; Spencer, Patrick*); JThS 56 (2005) 149-152 (*Jones, Ivor H.*).
5644 E**Bauer, David R.; Powell, Mark Allan** Treasures new and old: recent contributions to Matthean studies. SBL.Symposium 1: 1996 ⇒ 12,4265; 13,4461. RThR 70 (2005) 343-344 (*Lindemann, Andreas*).
5645 *Beaton, Richard* Isaiah in Matthew's gospel. Isaiah in the NT. 2005 ⇒443. 63-78.
5646 **Beaton, Richard** Isaiah's Christ in Matthew's gospel. MSSNTS 123: 2002 ⇒18,5106... 20,5387. RBiblInterp 13 (2005) 94-96 (*Nolland, John*); NT 47 (2005) 167-169 (*Menken, M.J.J.*); ScrB 35 (2005) 57-58 (*Docherty, Susan*); Neotest. 39 (2005) 440-442 (*Eloff, Mervyn*).
5647 *Beauchamp, Paul* L'évangile de Matthieu et l'héritage d'Israël. Pages exégétiques. LeDiv 202: 2005 <1988> ⇒183. 345-383.
5648 **Bianco, Enzo** Meditare con Matteo: materiali per la lectio divina. Leumann 2005, LDC 126 pp. €6.50.
5649 **Blickenstaff, Marianne** 'While the bridegroom is with them': marriage, family, gender and violence in the gospel of Matthew. JSNT.S 292: L 2005, Clark vii; 244 pp. $120. 0-567-04112-3. Bibl. 185-213.
5650 *Brown, Jeannine K.* Direct engagement of the reader in Matthew's discourses: rhetorical techniques and scholarly consensus. NTS 51 (2005) 19-35.
5651 **Byrne, Brendan** Lifting the burden: reading Matthew's gospel in the church today. 2004 ⇒20,5391. RRBLit (2005)* (*Carter, Warren*).
5652 **Cairoli, Marco** La "poca fede" nel vangelo di Matteo: uno studio esegetico-teologico. D*Stock, Klemens*: AnBib 156: R 2005, E.P.I.B. 302 pp. €20. 88-7653-156-4. Diss. Gregoriana; Bibl. 271-290.
5653 *Carter, Warren* Matthew and empire. USQR 59/3-4 (2005) 86-91 [NTAb 50,263].
5654 **Carter, Warren** Matthew: storyteller, interpreter, evangelist. 1996 ⇒12,4299...20,5356. RThR 70 (2005) 344-45 (*Lindemann, Andreas*).
5655 *Carter, Warren* Constructions of violence and identities in Matthew's gospel. Violence in the NT. 2005 ⇒439. 81-108;
5656 Matthew's people. Christian origins. 2005 ⇒550. 138-161.
5657 **Charette, Blaine B.** Restoring presence: the Spirit in Matthew's gospel. JPentec.S 18: 2000 ⇒16,4749... 18,5117. RThR 70 (2005) 369-370 (*Lindemann, Andreas*).

5658 *Claudel, Gérard* À la recherche du disciple modèle de Matthieu. RevSR 79 (2005) 77-95 [Mt 27-28].

5659 **Cousland, J.R.C.** The crowds in the gospel of Matthew. NT.S 102: 2002 ⇒18,5118; 19,5543. [R]RBLit (2005)* (*Jackson-Mccabe, Matt*).

5660 *Cuvillier, Élian* Mission vers Israël ou mission vers les païens?: à propos d'une tension féconde dans le premier évangile. Analyse narrative. BEThL 191: 2005 ⇒742. 251-258 [Mt 10; 15,24].

5661 **Deutsch, Celia M.** Lady Wisdom, Jesus, and the sages: metaphor and social context in Matthew's gospel. 1996 ⇒12,4303; 13,4502. [R]ThR 70 (2005) 370-372 (*Lindemann, Andreas*).

5662 *Donaldson, Terence L.* The vindicated Son: a narrative approach to Matthean christology. Contours of christology. McMaster NT Studies 7: 2005 ⇒775. 100-121.

5663 *Draper, Jonathan A.* Do the Didache and Matthew reflect an 'irrevocable parting of the ways' with Judaism?. Matthew and the Didache. 2005 ⇒797. 217-241.

5664 *Duling, Dennis C.* Ethnicity, ethnocentrism, and the Matthean *ethnos*. BTB 35 (2005) 125-143 [Mt 21,43].

5665 **Edwards, R.A.** Matthew's narrative portrait of disciples: how the text-connoted reader is informed. 1997 ⇒16,4753. [R]ThR 70 (2005) 201-202 (*Lindemann, Andreas*).

5666 *Eltrop, Bettina* "Euch muss es zuerst um seine Gerechtigkeit gehen": Heiligkeit im Alltag nach dem Matthäusevangelium. BiHe 41/164 (2005) 17.

5667 *Fabris, Rinaldo* 'Fate mie discepole tutte le nazioni' (Mt 28,19). RTE 9/1 (2005) 207-218.

5668 *Fiedler, Peter* Das Matthäusevangelium und 'die' Pharisäer. Studien zur biblischen Grundlegung. SBAB 35: 2005 <1994> ⇒209. 209-31.

5669 **Foster, Paul** Community, law and mission in Matthew's gospel. WUNT 2/177: 2004 ⇒20,5400. [R]em 21 (2005) 117-118 (*Stenschke, Christoph*); ATG 68 (2005) 309-311 (*Rodríguez Carmona, A.*) [Mt 5,21-48].

5670 *Frankemölle, Hubert* Von der Wurzel getragen (Röm 11,18): das Neue Testament im 'Alten' verwurzelt lesen—am Beispiel des Matthäusevangeliums <2000>;

5671 Antijudaismus im Matthäusevangelium?: Reflexionen zu einer angemessenen Auslegung. Studien zum jüdischen Kontext <1999>. SBAB 37: 2005 ⇒210. 161-167/168-198.

5672 **Gale, Aaron M.** Redefining ancient borders: the Jewish scribal framework of Matthew's gospel. NY 2005, Clark x; 197 pp. $55. 0-567-02511-X. Bibl. 168-186.

5673 **Garbe, Gernot** Der Hirte Israels: eine Untersuchung zur Israeltheologie des Matthäusevangeliums. [D]*Roloff, Jürgen*: WMANT 106: Neuk 2005, Neuk xii; 242 pp. €40. 3-7887-2086-7. Diss. Erlangen-Nürnberg; Bibl. 215-238.

5674 **Garrow, Alan J.P.** The gospel of Matthew's dependence on the *Didache*. JSNT.S 254: 2004 ⇒20,5403. [R]CBQ 67 (2005) 146-147 (*Milavec, Aaron*); Neotest. 39 (2005) 196-99 (*Draper, Jonathan A.*); Bib. 86 (2005) 438-41 (*Kloppenborg, John S.*); RBLit (2005)* (*Sim, David; Sweeney, James*); JThS 56 (2005) 152-154 (*Jones, Ivor H.*).

5675 *Gundry, Robert H.* Matthew: Jewish-Christian or Christian-Jewish?: at an intersection of sociology and theology;

5676 Salvation in Matthew. The old is better. WUNT 178: 2005 ⇒220. 111-119/120-128.

5677 **Ham, Clay Alan** The coming king and the rejected shepherd: Matthew's reading of Zechariah's messianic hope. NTMon 4: Shf 2005, Phoenix xvi; 176 pp. $47.50. 1-905048-017. Bibl. 127-154. [R]ASEs 22 (2005) 518-519 (*Nicklas, Tobias*).

5678 *Hamilton, Janet* The Bogomil commentary on St Matthew's gospel. Byz. 75 (2005) 171-198.

5679 *Hays, R.B.* The gospel of Matthew: reconfigured torah. HTSTS 61/1-2 (2005) 165-190 [NTAb 50,264].

5680 **Häfner, Gerd** Der verheißene Vorläufer: redaktionskritische Untersuchung zur Darstellung Johannes des Täufers im Matthäus-Evangelium. SBB 27: 1994 ⇒10,4387; 15,4754. [R]ThR 70 (2005) 198-199 (*Lindemann, Andreas*).

5681 *Huizenga, Leroy A.* Der Jesus des Matthäusevangeliums und der Isaak der antiken jüdischen Enzyklopädie: Akedah-Überlieferungen und das Matthäusevangelium. Die Bibel im Dialog. NET 10: 2005 ⇒ 333. 71-91 [Gen 22].

5682 *Huizenga, Leroy A.; Schneider, Michael* Das Matthäusevangelium in intertextueller Perspektive. ZNT 8/16 (2005) 20-29.

5683 *Jefford, Clayton N.* The milieu of Matthew, the Didache, and IGNATIUS of Antioch: agreements and differences. Matthew and the Didache. 2005 ⇒797. 35-47.

5684 *Keener, Craig S.* 'Brood of vipers' (Matthew 3.7; 12.34; 23.33). JSNT 28 (2005) 3-11.

5685 *Keerankeri, George* Listen to the Spirit: the gospel of Matthew: Jesus in Matthew: christology in the first gospel. VJTR 69 (2005) 921-934;

5686 Listen to the Spirit: The gospel of Matthew: the love commandments;

5687 Listen to the Spirit: the gospel of Matthew: Jesus' counter-cultural community: the church in Matthew. VJTR 69 2005, 535-543/461-473 [NTAb 50,264].

5688 *Kelly, C.* The Messiah: whose son is he?: another look at the Son of David and Son of God titles in Matthew. Trinity Seminary Review [Columbus, OH] 26/1 (2005) 17-28 [NTAb 49,493].

5689 **Kim, Jeong Rae** "... Perché io sono mite e umile di cuore" (Mt 11, 29): studio esegetico-teologico sull'umiltà del Messia secondo Matteo: dimensione cristologica e risvolti ecclesiologici. [D]*Grilli, Massimo*: TGr.T 120: R 2005, E.P.U.G. 334 pp. €22. 88-7839-031-3. Diss. Gregoriana; Bibl. 275-295.

5690 **Knowles, Michael** Jeremiah in Matthew's gospel: the rejected-prophet motif in Matthean redaction. JSNT.S 68: 1993 ⇒9,4487; 10, 4313. [R]ThR 70 (2005) 365-366 (*Lindemann, Andreas*).

5691 **LaGrand, James** The earliest Christian mission to "all nations": in the light of Matthew's gospel. 1995 ⇒11/1,2870... 17,4748. [R]ThR 70 (2005) 358-359 (*Lindemann, Andreas*).

5692 **Luomanen, Petri** Entering the kingdom of heaven: a study on the structure of Matthew's view of salvation. WUNT 2/101: 1998 ⇒14, 4237... 17,4751. [R]ThR 70 (2005) 363-364 (*Lindemann, Andreas*).

5693 **Luz, Ulrich** Die Jesusgeschichte des Matthäus. 1993 ⇒9,4490... 11/1,2872. [R]ThR 70 (2005) 174-176 (*Lindemann, Andreas*).

5694 *Luz, Ulrich* Fictionality and loyalty to tradition in Matthew's gospel in the light of Greek literature <1993>;

5695 Matthean christology outlined in theses <1991>;

5696 The Son of Man in Matthew: heavenly judge or human Christ? <1992>;
5697 The disciples in the gospel according to Matthew <1995>;
5698 Discipleship: a Matthean manifesto for a dynamic ecclesiology <1989>;
5699 Anti-Judaism in the gospel of Matthew as a historical and theological problem: an outline <1993>;
5700 The significance of Matthew's Jesus story for today. Studies in Matthew. 2005 ⇒252. 54-79/83-96/97-112/115-142/143-164/243-261/370-379.
5701 *Marissen, Michael* Blood, people, and crowds in Matthew, LUTHER, and BACH. LuthQ 19/1 (2005) 1-22.
5702 *McDonald, Patricia M.* 'I am with you always, to the end of the age': presence in the gospel according to Matthew. PIBA 28 (2005) 66-86.
5703 **Miler, Jean** Les citations d'accomplissement dans l'évangile de Matthieu: quand Dieu se rend présent en toute humanité. AnBib 140: 1999 ⇒15,4697... 20,5428. RThR 70 (2005) 367-369 (*Lindemann, Andreas*); SNTU 30 (2005) 228-230 (*Müller, Paul-Gerhard*).
5704 **Neyrey, Jerome H.** Honor and shame in the gospel of Matthew. 1998 ⇒14,4244... 17,4762. RThR 70 (2005) 351-352 (*Lindemann, Andreas*).
5705 **Nkhoma, Jonathan S.** The use of fulfilment quotations in the gospel according to Matthew. Kachere theses 4: Zomba 2005, 306 pp. 978-99908-76093. Bibl. 289-297.
5706 *Noble, Ivana* Keine Familie, die in sich gespalten ist, wird Bestand haben: eine ökumenische Interpretation der matthäischen Symbole von Sünde und Umkehr. ÖR 54/4 (2005) 446-461.
5707 *Räisänen, Heikki* Matthäus und die Hölle: von Wirkungsgeschichte zu ethischer Kritik. FLUZ, U.: SBS 199: 2005 ⇒94. 103-124 [Mt 25].
5708 **Repschinski, Boris** The controversy stories in the gospel of Matthew: their redaction, form and relevance for the relationship between the Matthean community and formative Judaism. FRLANT 189: 2000 ⇒16,4784... 20,5434. RThR 70 (2005) 205-208 (*Lindemann, Andreas*); RBLit (2005)* (*Cousland, J.R.C.*).
5709 *Riches, John* Matthew's missionary strategy in colonial perspective. Gospel of Matthew. JSNT.S 276: 2005 ⇒484. 128-142.
5710 **Riley, Harold** The first gospel. 1992 ⇒8,4629... 10,4333. RThR 70 (2005) 338-340 (*Lindemann, Andreas*).
5711 *Runyon, P.W.* The gospel of Matthew: the unfoldinng of missions. Caribbean Journal of Evangelical Theology [Kingston, Jamaica] 9 (2005) 21-53 [NTAb 50,31].
5712 **Saldarini, Anthony J.** Matthew's Christian-Jewish community. 1994 ⇒10,4335... 12,4337. RThR 70 (2005) 341-3 (*Lindemann, Andreas*).
5713 **Sánchez Navarro, Luis** "Venid a mí" (Mt 11,28-30): el discipulado, fundamento de la ética en Mateo. Studia Theologica Matritensia 4: 2004 ⇒20,5437. RAnVal 31 (2005) 181-183 (*Villota, Salvador*); EstTrin 39 (2005) 598-600 (*Pikaza, X.*); ATG 68 (2005) 325-326 (*Rodríguez Carmona, A.*).
5714 **Scheuermann, Georg** Gemeinde im Umbruch: eine sozialgeschichtliche Studie zum Matthäusevangelium. FzB 77: 1996 ⇒12, 4339... 16,4787. RThR 70 (2005) 349-351 (*Lindemann, Andreas*).
5715 *Shin, L.-C.; Van Aarde, A.* Matthew's and Paul's inclusive tendencies: a comparison. HTSTS 61 (2005) 1353-1372 [NTAb 51,32].

5716 *Siker, Judy Y.* Unmasking the enemy: deconstructing the "other" in the gospel of Matthew. PRSt 32/2 (2005) 109-123.
5717 **Sim, David C.** Apocalyptic eschatology in the gospel of Matthew. MSSNTS 88: 1996 ⇒12,4344; 14,4252. [R]ThR 70 (2005) 360-362 (*Lindemann, Andreas*).
5718 *Sim, David C.* Rome in Matthew's eschatology. Gospel of Matthew. JSNT.S 276: 2005 ⇒484. 91-106.
5719 **Slee, Michelle** The church in Antioch in the first century CE.: communion and conflict. JSNT.S 244: 2003 ⇒19,5569; 20,5439. [R]Neotest. 39 (2005) 207-210 (*Draper, Jonathan A.*).
5720 *Sonnet, Jean-Pierre* De la généalogie au "faites disciples" (Mt 28, 19): le livre de la génération de Jésus. Analyse narrative. BEThL 191: 2005 ⇒742. 199-209 [Mt 1-2; 28].
5721 **Stanton, Graham** A gospel for a new people: studies in Matthew. 1992 ⇒8,313... 11/1,2891. [R]ThR 70 (2005) 340-341 (*Lindemann, Andreas*).
5722 *Szymik, Stefan* Mateuszowa metaforyka swiatla (Mt 4,15-16; 5,14-16; 6,22-23). CoTh 75/4 (2005) 35-47. **P.**
5723 *Tuilier, André* Les charismatiques itinérants dans la Didachè et dans l'évangile de Matthieu. Matthew and the Didache. 2005 ⇒797. 157-172.
5724 *Van Aarde, Andries G.* Ἰησοῦς, the Davidic messiah, as political saviour in Matthew's history. Salvation in the New Testament. NT.S 121: 2005 ⇒798. 7-31.
5725 **Wainwright, Elaine Mary** Towards a feminist critical reading of the gospel according to Matthew. BZNW 60: 1991 ⇒7,3879... 11/1, 2901. [R]ThR 70 (2005) 346-349 (*Lindemann, Andreas*).
5726 *Weaver, Dorothy J.* 'Thus you will know them by their fruits': the Roman characters of the gospel of Matthew. Gospel of Matthew. JSNT.S 276: 2005 ⇒484. 107-127.
5727 *Weren, Wim* The history and social setting of the Matthean community. Matthew and the Didache. 2005 ⇒797. 51-62.
5728 **Wouters, Armin** '...wer den Willen meines Vaters tut': eine Untersuchung zum Verständnis vom Handeln im Matthäusevangelium. BU 23: 1992 ⇒8,4644... 12,4354. [R]ThR 70 (2005) 354-356 (*Lindemann, Andreas*).
5729 **Yieh, John Yueh-Han** One teacher: Jesus' teaching role in Matthew's gospel report. BZNW 124: 2004 ⇒20,5447. [R]RBLit (2005)* (*Macaskill, Grant*).

## F3.3 *Mt 1s (Lc 1s⇒F7.5) Infantia Jesu*—**Infancy Gospels**

5730 *Alvarez Valdés, Ariel* ¿Dónde nació Jesús?. Qol 38 (2005) 81-90.
5731 **Benassi, Giovanni** Dal presepe al vangelo. Assisi 2005, Cittadella 160 pp. €9.80.
5732 **Cuvillier, Elian** Naissance et enfance d'un Dieu: Jésus Christ dans l'évangile de Matthieu. Paris 2005, Bayard 236 pp. €19.80. 2-227-47-520-X. Bibl. 217-226.
5733 [T]**Homann, Frederick A.** Jerome NADAL, S.J.: Annotations and meditations on the gospels, 1: the infancy narratives. 2003 ⇒19,5581; 20, 5455. [R]BHR 67 (2005) 515-516 (*Engammare, Max*).

5734 *Keerankeri, George* Listen to the Spirit: the gospel of Matthew: the infancy story. VJTR 69 (2005) 64-70.

5735 **Kelly, Joseph F.** The origins of Christmas. 2004 ⇒20,5456. RWorship 79 (2005) 283-85 (*Roll, Susan K.*); RBLit (2005)* (*Clark, Ronald; Nadella, Raj*); RBLit 7 (2005) 536-537 (*Clark, Ronald*).

5736 **Llamas, R.** El evangelio de San José. Logos 84: M 2005, Espiritualidad 318 pp. 84-7068-301-2.

5737 **Mayordomo-Marín, Moisés** Den Anfang hören: leserorientierte Evangelienexegese am Beispiel von Matthäus 1-2. FRLANT 180: 1998 ⇒14,4276... 17,4806. RThR 70 (2005) 195-198 (*Lindemann, Andreas*).

5738 **Miller, Robert J.** Born divine: the births of Jesus and other sons of God. Santa Rosa, CA 2003, Polebridge xviii; 337 pp. $22.

5739 **Mittmann-Richert, Ulrike** Magnifikat und Benediktus: die ältesten Zeugnisse der judenchristlichen Tradition von der Geburt des Messias. WUNT 2/90: 1996 ⇒14,4277... 17,4807. RThR 70 (2005) 67-70 (*Lindemann, Andreas*).

5740 *Myre, A.* Christmas and the confrontation of empire. Way 44/1 (2005) 21-32 [NTAb 49,265].

5741 **Perry, Paul** Jesus in Egypt: discovering the secrets of Christ's childhood years. NY 2005, Ballatine xv; 277 pp. 0345-45146-5.

5742 *Peterson, Erik* Zur Herkunft Jesu. Peterson: Lukasevangelium und Synoptica. 2005 ⇒277. 415-416.

5743 *Puig i Tàrrech, Armand* El naixement de Jesús. RCatT 30 (2005) 289-329.

5744 *Reilly, Frank* Jane Schaberg, Raymond E. Brown, and the problem of the illegitimacy of Jesus. JFSR 21/1 (2005) 57-80.

5745 *Ricker Parks, Aaron G.* A sign of contradiction: Jesus traditions as an axis for dialogue. Scriptura(M) 7/1 (2005) 103-111 [Virgin birth tradition].

5746 *Schaberg, Jane* Feminist interpretations of the infancy narrative of Matthew <1997>;

5747 Virgin mother or bastard child? <2003>. A feminist companion to mariology. 2005 ⇒431. 15-36/37-55.

5748 **Stuhlmacher, Peter** Die Geburt des Immanuel: die Weihnachtsgeschichten aus dem Lukas- und Matthäusevangelium. Gö 2005, Vandenhoeck & R. 105 pp. €14.90. 3-525-53535-X.

5749 *Welser, Maria von* Joseph als Vorbild. zeitzeichen 6/4 (2005) 55.

5750 *Alkier, S.* From text to intertext: intertextuality as a paradigm for reading Matthew. HTSTS 61/1-2 (2005) 1-18 [NTAb 50,265] [Mt 1].

5751 **Capshaw, Jeffery L.** A textlinguistic analysis of selected Old Testament texts in Matthew 1-4. Studies in biblical literature 62: 2004 ⇒ 20,5453. RRBLit (2005)* (*Keith, Pierre*).

5752 *Allison, Dale C.* Matthew's first two words (Matt. 1:1). Studies in Matthew: interpretation. 2005 ⇒5587. 157-162.

5753 *Carter, Warren* Matthean christology in Roman imperial key: Matthew 1:1. Gospel of Matthew. JSNT.S 276: 2005 ⇒484. 143-165.

5754 *Warner, Megan* Uncertain women: sexual irregularity and the greater righteousness in Matthew 1. Pacifica 18 (2005) 18-32 [Mt 1,1-17].

5755 *Allison, Dale C.* Divorce, celibacy, and Joseph (Matt. 1:18-25). Studies in Matthew: interpretation. 2005 ⇒5587. 163-172.

5756 *Tonini, Hermes* Silêncios, sonhos, prodígios e nomeações: uma hermenêutica de gênero de Mateus 1,18-25. Estudos bíblicos 86 (2005) 66-86.
5757 *Moschetta, Jean-Marc* Concebido del Espíritu Santo. SelTeol 44 (2005) 99-109 <NRTh 125 (2003) 555-573 [Mt 1,20].
5758 *Aveni, Anthony F.* A star in the east: the star of Bethlehem;
5759 A star in the east: dialogue with the firmament. Secrets of the bible. 2005 ⇒482. 66-70/71-75 [Mt 2,1-12].
5760 *Charbel, Antonio* Were the Magi Nabateans?. Holy Land (Winter 2005) 32-39, 49-51 [Mt 2,1-12].
5761 **Neumann, Johannes** Der Stern von Bethlehem aus Sicht der Astronomie, der Geschichtswissenschaft und der antiken Astrologie. Radebeul 2005, Neumann 40 pp. €9.90. 3-9801-2643-9 [Mt 2,1-12].
5762 *Pettem, Michael* Identifying the star of Bethlehem. Arc 33 (2005) 281-301 [Mt 2,1-12].
5763 *Allison, Dale C.* The magi's angel (Matt. 2:2, 9-10). Studies in Matthew: interpretation. 2005 ⇒5587. 17-41.
5764 *Dalla Torre, Giuseppe* Scienza e fede: una lettura della visita dei Magi (Mt 2,12). Studium 101 (2005) 5-14.
5765 *Prema, Sr.* When the protector turns perpetrator... (Matthew 2:16): a Christmas meditation. ITS 42 (2005) 351-359 [NTAb 50,266] [Mt 2, 13-23].
5766 *Menken, Maarten J.J.* 'Out of Egypt I have called my son': some observations on the quotation from Hosea 11.1 in Matthew 2.15. [F]LUTTIKHUIZEN, G.: AGJU 59: 2005 ⇒93. 143-152.
5767 *Allison, Dale C.* Slaughtered infants. Studies in Matthew: interpretation. 2005 ⇒5587. 251-264 [Mt 2,17; 27,9].

## F3.4 *Mt 3...Baptismus Jesu*, Beginnings of the Public Life

5768 *Batut, Jean-Pierre* Pour une lecture théologique du baptême de Jésus. Com(F) 30/1 (2005) 7-19; Com(US) 32/1,6-18.
5769 *Bertalotto, Pierpaolo* Immersion and expiation: water and spirit from Qumran to John the Baptist. Henoch 27/1-2 (2005) 163-181.
5770 **Briend, Jacques**, *al.*, Les tentations du Christ au désert (Mt 4,1-11; Mc 1,12-13; Lc 4,1-13). CEv.S 134: P 2005, Cerf 132 pp. 02229714.
5771 *Congourdeau, Marie-Hélène* L'icône du baptême du Seigneur: une lecture liturgique. Com(F) 30/1 (2005) 51-59.
5772 **Dapaah, Daniel S.** The relationship between John the Baptist and Jesus of Nazareth: a critical study. Lanham 2005, University Press of America xiv; 205 pp. $31. 0-7618-3109-6. Bibl. 157-184.
5773 *Fedalto, Giorgio* Il battesimo di Gesù nei padri. Com(I) 199 (2005) 38-48.
5774 *Figura, Michaël* Le baptême de Jésus comme révélation du Dieu trinitaire. Com(F) 30/1 (2005) 35-50; IKaZ 34,33-46.
5775 *Fisichella, Rino* Dimensione trinitaria del battesimo di Gesù. Com(I) 199 (2005) 9-18.
5776 **Gibson, Shimon** The cave of John the Baptist: the first archaeological evidence of the truth of the gospel story. 2004 ⇒20,5482. [R]PEQ 137 (2005) 175-181 (*Taylor, Joan E.*);
5777 The cave of John the Baptist: the stunning archaeological discovery that has redefined christian history. NY 2005, Doubleday 304 pp.

$26. 03855-03474. RAmerica 192/7 (2005) 19-20 (*Murphy, Frederick*).

5778 *Gibson, Shimon; Tabor, James* John the Baptist's cave: the case in favor. BArR 31/3 (2005) 36-41, 58.

5779 *Granados, J.* The ages of the life of Jesus: the mystery of the baptism in the Jordan. Com(US) 32/1 (2005) 19-51.

5780 *Häkkinen, Sakari* The baptism of Jesus. FAEJMELAEUS, L.: SESJ 89: 2005 ⇒1. 73-91.

5781 *Keerankeri, George* Listen to the Spirit: the gospel of Matthew: fulfilling all righteousness: the baptism of Jesus. VJTR 69 (2005) 144-151.

5782 *Machan, Richard* L'accomplissement du baptême de Jésus-Christ. Com(F) 30/1 (2005) 61-67.

5783 *Malone, Richard* 'You are my beloved Son': the baptism of the Lord as a trinitarian event. Com(US) 32/1 (2005) 52-75.

5784 *Murphy-O'Connor, Jerome* Sites associated with John the Baptist. RB 112 (2005) 253-266.

5785 **Quaglia, R.** Giovanni figlio di grazia: il vangelo di Giovanni Battista. Bo 2005, Dehoniane 152 pp. €10. 88108-08126 [NTAb 49, 603].

5786 *Rigger, Hansjörg* Johannes der Täufer und die Frucht der Umkehr. IKaZ 34 (2005) 23-32.

5787 **Rothschild, Clarke K.** Baptist traditions and Q. WUNT 190: Tü 2005, Mohr S. xvii; 309 pp. €74. 3-16-148791-5. Bibl. 241-270.

5788 **Ryu, Ho-Seung** Johannes der Täufer im Matthäusevangelium: eine sozio-rhetorische Untersuchung zur Darstellung Johannes des Täufers und Jesu im Matthäusevangelium. D*Theißen, Gerd* 2005, Diss. Heidelberg [ThLZ 131,338].

5789 *Welker, Michael* Baptism as change of lordship. MJUEL, D. 2005 ⇒ 73. 107-114.

5790 **Yamasaki, Gary** John the Baptist in life and death: audience-oriented criticism of Matthew's narrative. JSNT.S 167: 1998 ⇒14,4302; 17,4846. RThR 70 (2005) 199-201 (*Lindemann, Andreas*).

5791 **Kelhoffer, James A.** The diet of John the Baptist: "locusts and wild honey" in synoptic and patristic interpretation. WUNT 176: Tü 2005, Mohr S. xxiii; 256 pp. €69. 3-16-148460-6. Bibl. 207-234 [Mt 3,4].

5792 **Tavardon, Paul** Les métamorphoses de l'Esprit: une exégèse du logion des deux baptêmes: Mt 3,10-12 et parallèles. D*Schlosser, J.*: EtB 48: P 2002, Gabalda 545 pp. €75. 28502-11427. Préface *M.-E. Boismard*; Diss. Strasbourg; Bibl. 469-516.

5793 *Rubio, Miguel* La búsqueda de identidad en el horizonte de la fe cristiana. Moralia 28 (2005) 443-473 [Mt 4,1-11].

5794 *Blumenthal, Christian* Zur "Zinne des Tempels". ZNW 96 (2005) 274-283 [Mt 4,5; Lk 4,9].

### F3.5 Mt 5...Sermon on the Mount [...plain, Lk 6,17]

5795 *Allison, Dale C.* The configuration of the Sermon on the Mount and its meaning. Studies in Matthew. 2005 ⇒5587. 173-215.

E**Becker, H.**, *al.*, The Sermon on the Mount 2005 ⇒350.

5796 *Becker, Hans-Jürgen* Matthew, the rabbis and Billerbeck on the kingdom of heaven. Sermon on the Mount. CRB 60: 2005 ⇒350. 57-69.

5797 **Bergemann, Thomas** Q auf dem Prüfstand: die Zuordnung des Mt/Lk-Stoffes zu Q am Beispiel der Bergpredigt. FRLANT 158: 1993 ⇒ 9,4572. RThR 70 (2005) 374-376 (*Lindemann, Andreas*).

5798 **Betz, Hans Dieter** The sermon on the mount: a commentary on the sermon on the mount, including the sermon on the plain (Matthew 5: 3-7:27 and Luke 6:20-49). E*Collins, Adela*: Hermeneia: 1995 ⇒11/1, 2966...16,4840. RThR 70 (2005) 376-380 (*Lindemann, Andreas*).

5799 *Charry, Ellen T.* The law of Christ all the way down. IJST 7/2 (2005) 155-168.

5800 *Gundry, Robert H.* The Sermon on the Mount according to H.D. Betz. The old is better. WUNT 178: 2005 ⇒220. 129-148.

5801 *Hoestermann, Marita* "Den Alten wurde gesagt ..."—"Ich aber sage euch ...": Dekalog und Bergpredigt—Gegensatz oder Erfüllung?. Katholische Bildung 106/1 (2005) 34-36 [Exod 20,1-17].

5802 *Käsemann, Ernst* Bergpredigt—eine Privatsache?. In der Nachfolge. 2005 ⇒236. 117-129.

5803 *Keerankeri, George* Listen to the Spirit: the gospel of Matthew: the sermon on the mount: task of discipleship and project of mission. VJTR 69 (2005) 206-216 [Mt 28,16-20].

5804 *Kos, Elmar* "Liebt eure Feinde ..." (Mt 5,44): die Bergpredigt als Herausforderung der Moraltheologie. Das Buch. 2005 ⇒487. 181-192.

5805 **Köhnlein, M.** Die Bergpredigt. Stu 2005, Kohlhammer 192 pp. €20. 31701-88798. Ill. [NTAb 50,166].

5806 **Lapide, Pinchas** Il discorso della montagna: utopia o programma?. StBi 138: 2003 ⇒19,5620; 20,5505. RAsp. 52 (2005) 445-446 (*Di Palma, Gaetano*).

5807 **Patte, Daniel** Discipleship according to the Sermon on the Mount. 1996 ⇒12,4427; 14,4327. RThR 70 (2005) 380-382 (*Lindemann, Andreas*).

5808 *Pawłowski, Zdzisław* Kazanie na Górze a przemoc: utopia czy większa sprawiedliwość? [The Sermon on the Mount and violence: utopia or surpassing righteousness?]. StBob 2 (2005) 61-100. **P.**

5809 **Petersen, Walter** Zur Eigenart des Matthäus: Untersuchung zur Rhetorik in der Bergpredigt. 2001 ⇒17,4856; 18,5219. RThRv 101 (2005) 381-382 (*Deines, Roland*).

5810 *Peterson, Erik* Bergpredigt—biblisch. Peterson: Lukasevangelium und Synoptica. 2005 ⇒277. 432-436.

5811 **Royster, Dmitri** Il regno di Dio: il sermone della montagna. Ecumene 17: 2000 ⇒18,5220. RRSEc 23 (2005) 155-157 (*Syty, J.*).

5812 *Sánchez Navarro, Luis* El Padre en la Enseñanza de la montaña (Mt 5-7): estructura y teología. RET 65 (2005) 197-210.

5813 **Sánchez Navarro, Luis** La enseñanza de la montaña: comentario contextual a Mateo 5-7. Estella (Navarra) 2005, Verbo Divino 214 pp. 84-8169-656-0. Bibl. 183-186.

5814 **Stiewe, Martin; Vouga, François** Le Sermon sur la Montagne: un abrégé de l'évangile dans le miroitement de ses interprétations. 2002 ⇒18,5221. RRSR 93 (2005) 92-94 (*Miler, Jean*).

5815 *Sugirtharajah, R.S.* Matthew 5-7: the Sermon on the Mount and India. Global bible commentary. 2005 ⇒2443. 361-366.

5816 **Talbert, Charles H.** Reading the Sermon on the Mount: character formation and decision making in Matthew 5-7. 2004 ⇒20,5512.

[R]RBLit (2005)* (*Bryant, Robert*); CR&T 3/2 (2005) 119-122 (*Houlden, L.*).

5817 **Tremolada, Pierantonio** La regola di vita della comunità de Gesù:: un commento al Discorso della montagna (Mt 5-7). Uomini e parola 2: Mi 2005, In dialogo 136 pp. €12.

5818 *Cárdenas Pallares, José* Destino de los discípulos de Jesús (Mt 5,13-14). Qol 37 (2005) 103 -107.

5819 **Deines, Roland** Die Gerechtigkeit der Tora im Reich des Messias: Mt 5,13-20 als Schlüsseltext der matthäischen Theologie. WUNT 2/ 177: 2004 ⇒20,5515. [R]FZPhTh 52 (2005) 790-4 (*Viviano, Benedict T.*); JETh 19 (2005) 277-280 (*Gäckle, Volker*).

5820 *Luz, Ulrich* The fulfillment of the law in Matthew (Matt. 5:17-20). Studies in Matthew. 2005 <1978> ⇒252. 185-218.

5821 *Zawadzki, Ryszard* L'abbondare della giustizia in vista del Regno dei cieli (Mt 5,20). Anton. 80 (2005) 453-484.

5822 *Allison, Dale C.* Murder and anger, Cain and Abel (Matt. 5:21-25). Studies in Matthew. 2005 ⇒5587. 65-78 [Gen 4,1-16; 1 John 3].

5823 *Ruzer, Serge* Antitheses in Matthew 5: midrashic aspects of exegetical techniques [Mt 5,21-48];

5824 *Schaller, Bernd* The character and function of the antitheses in Matt 5:21-48 in the light of rabbinical exegetic disputes;

5825 *Frey, Jörg* The character and background of Matt 5:25-26: on the value of Qumran literature in New Testament interpretation. The Sermon on the Mount. CRB 60: 2005 ⇒350. 89-116/70-88/3-39.

5826 **Davis, James F.** Lex talionis in early Judaism and the exhortation of Jesus in Matthew 5.38-42. JSNT.S 281: L 2005, Clark xv; 192 pp. $115. 0-567-04150-6. Bibl. 173-182.

5827 *Ordon, Hubert* Prawo odwetu a przykazanie miłości nieprzyjaciól [The law of talion versus the commandment: love your enemies]. Ethos 18/3-4 (2005) 202-209 [Mt 5,38-48].

5828 *Ginsburskaya, Mila; Ruzer, Serge* Matt 6:1-18: collation of two avenues to God's forgiveness. The Sermon on the Mount. CRB 60: 2005 ⇒350. 151-242.

5829 *Macaskill, Grant* Matthew 6:19-34: the kingdom, the world and the ethics of anxiety. SBET 23 (2005) 18-29.

5830 **Sihombing, Batara** Wealth and wisdom in Matthew 6:19-34. 2005, Diss.Trinity, Singapore; Sum. TynB 57/1,155s.

5831 *Hendriks, Wim M.A.* Brevior lectio praeferenda est verbosiori. RB 112 (2005) 567-595 [Mt 6,33].

5832 *Stelter, Bernd* "... denn wer bittet, der empfängt" (Matthäus 7,7-11). Kanzelreden. 2005 ⇒376. 73-77.

5833 *Stanglin, Keith D.* The historical connection between the golden rule and the second greatest love command. JRE 33 (2005) 357-371 [Mt 7,12].

5834 *Cárdenas P., José* Hay que vivir la verdad (Mt 7,13-29). Qol 38 (2005) 35-40.

### F3.6 **Mt 5,3-11** (Lc 6,20-22) **Beatitudines**; *Divorce*

5835 [E]**Pesch, Otto H.; Van Cangh, Jean-Marie** Béatitude eschatologique et bonheur humain. Bru 2005, Académie Internationale des Sciences Religieuses 260 pp. 2204-07874-3.

5836 [E]**Berry, Wendell** Blessed are the peacemakers: Christ's teachings of love, compassion, and forgiveness. Emeryville, CA 2005, Shoemaker & H. 68 pp. 1-593-76100-7.

5837 **Bird, David** The royal road to joy: the Beatitudes and the Eucharist. 2003 ⇒19,5650. [R]HPR 105/8 (2005) 74-75 (*Kalpakgian, Mitchell*).

5838 **Crosby, Michael H.** Spirituality of the beatitudes: Matthew's vision for the church in an unjust world. Mkn [2]2005 <1981>, Orbis xviii; 221 pp. $20. 1-57075-549-3 [ThD 52,156—W. Charles Heiser].

5839 **Fernández Márquez, M.J.** En ti vivimos, Señor: dimensión contemplativa de las bienaventuranzas. 2004 ⇒20,5531. [R]SalTer 93 (2005) 873-875 (*Gómez-Limón, M. Ángeles*).

5840 **Green, H. Benedict** Matthew, poet of the beatitudes. JSNT.S 203: 2001 ⇒17,4877... 20,5532. [R]RSR 93 (2005) 85-86 (*Miler, Jean*); HeyJ 46 (2005) 361-363 (*Loubser, J.A.*).

5841 *Hall, Stuart G.* St GREGORY of Nyssa on the Beatitudes of Jesus. Béatitude eschatologique. 2005 ⇒5835. 95-106.

5842 *Lichtenberger, Hermann* Makarisms in Matthew 5:3ff. in their Jewish context. The Sermon on the Mount. CRB 60: 2005 ⇒350. 40-56.

5843 *Mangan, Charles M.* The beatitudes of Jesus as manifested in the life of his mother and as a pattern for consecrated persons: some pastoral indications. Clar. 45 (2005) 357-392.

5844 **Oliveira, Ivone** Brandão de Caminhar para o reino com as bemaventuraças. Teologia bíblica: São Paulo 2005, Paulinas 311 pp.

5845 *Söding, Thomas* "Selig, ihr Armen": die Seligpreisungen im Zentrum der Verkündigung Jesu;

5846 *Van Cangh, Jean-Marie* Les béatitudes de Matthieu et des manuscrits de la mer Morte. Béatitude eschatologique. 2005 ⇒5835. 37-75/77-91.

5847 **Zhdan, Volodymyr** Les huit béatitudes (Mt 5,1-12) dans la prédication polonaise postconciliaire: étude biblique et homilétique. [D]*Bielecki, S.* 2005, 271 pp. Diss. Lublin [RTL 37,619].

5848 *Manzi, Franco* Memoria, imitazione e testimonianza della beatitudine sulla povertà. EL 119/1 (2005) 53-82 [Mt 5,3].

5849 *Vampa, Enrico* L'interpretazione patristica di Mt 5,3: 'Beati i poveri di spirito, perché di essi è il regno dei cieli'. Ter. 56/115 (2005) 499-529.

5850 *Rukundwa, L.S.; Van Aarde, A.G.* Revisiting justice in the first four beatitudes in Matthew (5:3-6) and the story of the Canaanite woman (Mt 15:21-28): a postcolonial reading. HTSTS 61 (2005) 927-951 [NTAb 50,482].

5851 **Talbot, Michel** "Heureux les doux, car ils héritont la terre": (Mt 5,4 [5]). [D]*Gourgues, M.*: EtB 46: P 2002, Gabalda 454 pp. ⇒18,5245... 20,5537. €62. 2-85021-139-7. Diss. Collège dominican Ottawa; Bibl. 382-414. [R]RSR 93 (2005) 83-85 (*Miler, Jean*) [Mt 5,4-5; 11,29; 21, 5; 1 Pet 3,4].

5852 *Calderón, C.* ¿Qué significa 'justicia' en Mateo 5:6: 'beati i poveri di spirito, perché di essi è il regno dei cieli. Kairós 37 (2005) 59-80 [NTAb 50,33].

5853 *Käsemann, Ernst* Die vierte Seligpreisung (Matthäus 5,6). In der Nachfolge. 2005 ⇒236. 139-149.

5854 *Allison, Dale C.* Seeing God (Matt. 5:8). Studies in Matthew: interpretation. 2005 ⇒5587. 43-63.

5855 *Day, Charles R.* Those who are persecuted because of righteousness, are those who pursue righteousness: an examination of the origin and meaning of the eighth beatitude. APB 16 (2005) 157-165 [Dt 16,20; Isa 51,1; Mt 5,10].

5856 *Wróbel, Miroslaw S.* Błogosławieństwo prześladowanych (Mt 5,10). Roczniki Teologiczne 52/1 (2005) 55-66 [NTAb 50,483]. **P.**

5857 **Dingemans, Louis** Jésus face au divorce. 2004 ⇒20,5542. [R]NRTh 127 (2005) 512-514 (*Radermakers, J.*).

5858 *Garuti, Paolo* Scripsit vobis praeceptum istud: Gesù, il ripudio e la scrittura fallace. Ang. 82 (2005) 335-354 [Lev 21,14; Dt 24,1-4; Mt 5,32; Mk10,11-12; Lk 16,18; 1 Cor 7,10-11].

5859 **Instone-Brewer, David** Divorce and remarriage in the bible: the social and literary context. 2002 ⇒18,5248... 20,5543. [R]JSSt 50 (2005) 379-381 (*Osiek, Carolyn*); JThS 56 (2005) 591-594 (*Williams, Catrin H.*).

F3.7 *Mt 6,9-13 (Lc 11,2-4)* **Oratio Jesu**, *Pater Noster*, **Lord's Prayer**; Mt 8

5860 **Baudoz, Jean-François; Dahan, Gilbert; Guinot, Jean-Noël**, *al.*, La Prière du Seigneur (MT 6,9-13; Lc 11,2-4). CEv.S 132: P 2005, Cerf 136 pp. 0222-9714.

5861 **Brown, Michael Joseph** The Lord's prayer through North African eyes: a window into early christianity. Ment. *Clemens Alexandrinus; Tertullian* 2004 ⇒20,5546. [R]RBLit (2005)* (*West, Gerald*).

5862 **Hallikainen, Olli** The Lord's Prayer in the sayings gospel Q. Helsinki 2005, Univ. of Helsinki 201 pp. Diss. Helsinki [StTh 60,113].

5863 **John, Frère** Das Vaterunser beten. [E]*Kunzendorf, Gerda; Hanisch, Patricia*: Lp [3]2005, Evang. Verl.-Anst. 91 pp. 3-374-01509-3.

5864 *Lohfink, Norbert* Das Vaterunser, intertextuell gebetet. Liturgie und Bibel. ÖBS 28: 2005 <1999> ⇒360. 343-365;

5865 [F]STENDEBACH, F. 2005 ⇒141. 73-96.

5866 **Martini, Carlo Maria** Non sprecate parole: esercizi spirituali con il Padre Nostro. CasM 2005, Portalupi 182 pp. €18.

5867 **Mathias, Philip** The perfect prayer: search for the kingdom through the Lord's Prayer. Mp 2005, Augsburg xiii; 159 pp. $17. 0-8066-51-56-3.

5868 **Stevenson, Kenneth W.** The Lord's Prayer: a text in tradition. 2004 ⇒20,5559. [R]RRT 12/1 (2005) 50-53 (*Atkins, Peter*).

5869 **Vílchez, J.** Vosotros, cuando oréis, decid: Padre Nuestro. Estella 2005, Verbo Divino 288 pp.

5870 **Wiggermann, Karl-Friedrich** Das Vaterunser. Studienbrief: A, Missionarische Dienste A74: Stu 2005, Arb.-Gem. Missionar 15 pp.

5871 [E]**Zappella, Marco** Le origini degli anni giubilari: dalle tavolette in cuneiforme dei sumeri ai manoscritti arabi del mille dopo Cristo. [T]*Pahk, James Yeong-Sik*: Seoul 1999, St Pauls 415 pp. 898015-3740.

5872 *Gébara, Joseph C.* Sied-il à Dieu, quand il pardonne, de prendre l'homme comme modèle?: lecture patristique de la cinquième demande du 'Notre Père'. Al-Machriq 79 (2005) 159-76 [Mt 6,12]. **A.**

5873 *Apecechea Perurena, Juan* Comentario del padrenuestro de Joaquín Lizarraga, Vicario de Elcano (1748-1835): sexta petición, IX. Scriptorium Victoriense 52 (2005) 185-213 [Mt 6,13; Lk 11,4].

5874 **Gourvil, Jean-Marie** Ne nous laisse pas entrer dans l'épreuve. 2004 ⇒20,5565. [R]Contacts 57 (2005) 186-87 (*Minet, Jacques*) [Mt 6,13].
5875 *Lohfink, Norbert* Die Bitte um Bewahrung und Erlösung: Sinndimension der letzten Vaterunser-Bitte im Alten Testament. Liturgie und Bibel. ÖBS 28: 2005 <1999> ⇒360. 339-342 [Mt 6,13]
5876 *Stramare, Tarcisio* Non ci indurre in tentazione. BeO 47 (2005) 163-167 [Mt 6,13].

## F4.1 *Mt 9-12: Miracula Jesu*—The Gospel miracles

5877 *Anderwald, Andrzej* Wunder im Zeitalter der Naturwissenschaften: Kritik an den Kritikern. ThGl 95 (2005) 439-450.
5878 *Aune, David E.* Magic in early christianity. Apocalypticism, prophecy. WUNT 199: 2005 <1980> ⇒177. 368-420.
5879 *Fernández, Victor M.* ¿Mover montañas en el mundo de hoy?: el mensaje bíblico ante el desencanto posmoderno. La palabra viva. 2005 ⇒746. 59-97.
5880 *Freund, Annegret* Die Rezeption von Wundergeschichten-empirisch erforscht. EvTh 65 (2005) 155-158.
5881 **John, Jeffrey** The meaning in the miracles. 2004 ⇒20,5582. [R]RBLit (2005)* (*Larsen, Kevin*).
5882 *Kahl, Werner* Wunder und Mission in ethnologischer Perspektive. ZNT 8/15 (2005) 35-43.
5883 **Kollmann, Bernd** Storia dei miracoli nel Nuovo Testamento. [T]*Bologna, Anna*: Giornale di teologia 307: Brescia 2005, Queriniana 245 pp. €20.50. 88-399-0807-2 [StPat 52,956s—Giuseppe Segalla].
5884 *Korte, Anne-Marie* Verbeelding van het wonder(lijke) in hedendaagse wonderverhalen. TTh 45 (2005) 397-413.
5885 *Mach, Michael* Jesus' miracles in context. Beginnings of christianity. 2005 ⇒786. 173-201.
5886 *Manicardi, Ermenegildo* I miracoli di Gesù. Gesù la cristologia. 2005 <2002> ⇒253. 119-132.
5887 *Milani, Marcello* Vuoi guarire?: Gesù guarisce e salva. CredOg 25/1 (2005) 43-62.
5888 **Montefiore, H.** The miracles of Jesus. L 2005, SCPK v; 120 pp. 02810-57052 [NTAb 49,400].
5889 *Morrill, Bruce T.* Christ the healer: a critical investigation of liturgical, pastoral, and biblical sources. Worship 79 (2005) 482-504.
5890 *Palermo, Carlo* John LOCKE e la stuttura [!] testimoniale del miracolo. ConAss 7/1 (2005) 53-77.
5891 **Sorensen, Eric** Possession and exorcism in the New Testament and early christianity. WUNT 2/157: 2002 ⇒18,5294... 20,5588. [R]ThLZ 130 (2005) 282-284 (*Busch, Peter*).
5892 **Trunk, Dieter** Der messianische Heiler: eine redaktions- und religionsgeschichtliche Studie zu den Exorzismen im Matthäusevangelium. Herders Biblische Studien 3: 1994 ⇒10,4487... 17,4932. [R]ThR 70 (2005) 208-211 (*Lindemann, Andreas*).

5893 **Park, Eung Chun** The mission discourse in Matthew's interpretation. WUNT 2/81: 1995 ⇒11/1,3072... 14,4415. [R]ThR 70 (2005) 211-212 (*Lindemann, Andreas*) [Mt 9,35-11,1].

5894 *Keerankeri, George* Listen to the Spirit: the gospel of Matthew: the mighty deeds of Jesus. VJTR 69 (2005) 298-308 [Mt 8-9].

5895 *Luz, Ulrich* The miracle stories of Matthew 8-9. Studies in Matthew. 2005 <1987> ⇒252. 221-240.

5896 **Vledder, Evert-Jan** Conflict in the miracle stories: a socio-exegetical study of Matthew 8 and 9. JSNT.S 152: 1997 ⇒13,4717... 17, 4939. RThR 70 (2005) 202-205 (*Lindemann, Andreas*).

5897 **Landmesser, Christof** Jüngerberufung und Zuwendung zu Gott: ein exegetischer Beitrag zum Konzept der matthäischen Soteriologie im Anschluß an Mt 9,9-13. WUNT 133: 2001 ⇒17,4940... 19,5706. RRSR 93 (2005) 86-89 (*Miler, Jean*).

5898 *Bromley, Donald H.* The healing of the hemorrhaging woman: miracle or magic?. JBSt 5/1 (2005) 1-20 [Mt 9,20-22].

5899 **LeMarquand, Grant** An issue of relevance: a comparative study of the story of the bleeding woman (Mk 5:25-34; Mt 9:20-22; Lk 8:43-48) in North Atlantic and African contexts. 2004 ⇒20,5595. RRBLit (2005)* (*Bergen, Wes; Jacobs, Mignon*).

5900 *Keith, Pierre* L'envoi en mission selon Mt 10,5-15: à propos de quelques affirmations contraires. FSCHENKER, A.: OBO 214: 2005 ⇒134. 143-151.

5901 *Zell, P.E.* Matthew 10:23—which coming of the Son of Man?. WLQ 102/3 (2005) 210-212 [NTAb 50,34].

5902 *Stander, H.F.* The sparrow's fall (Mt 10:29). HTSTS 61 (2005) 1071-1083 [NTAb 51,34].

5903 **Laansma, Jon** I will give you rest: the rest motif in the New Testament with special reference to Mt 11 and Heb 3-4. WUNT 2/98: 1997 ⇒13,4733... 17,4945. RThR 70 (2005) 372-374 (*Lindemann, Andreas*).

5904 *Boerman, Daniel* The chiastic structure of Matthew 11-12. CTJ 40 (2005) 313-325.

5905 **Di Paolo, Roberto** Il servo di Dio porta il diritto alle nazioni: analisi retorica di Matteo 11-12. D*Meynet, Roland*: TGr.T 128: R 2005, E.P.U.G. 282 pp. €17. 88-7839-045-3. Bibl. 255-270 REstB 63 (2005) 341-342 (*Sánchez Navarro, Luis*).

5906 **Lybaek, Lena** New and old in Matthew 11-13: normativity in the development of three theological themes. FRLANT 198: 2002 ⇒18, 5304; 20,5597. RFZPhTh 52 (2005) 794-796 (*Viviano, Benedict T.*).

5907 *Manicardi, Ermenegildo* Gesù, la sapienza e la legge nel vangelo secondo Matteo: un sondaggio in Mt 11-13. Gesù la cristologia. 2005 <1987> ⇒253. 231-259.

5908 *Castaño Fonseca, Adolfo M.* Juan, Jesús y esta generación: a propósito de Mt 11,16-19. FJUNCO GARZA, C.: Estudios Bíblicos Mexicanos 4: 2005 ⇒74. 243-258.

5909 *Sánchez Navarro, Luis* Ser discípulo (Mt 11,29). EstB 63 (2005) 235-250.

5910 *Fiedler, Peter* 'Der Gottesknecht': Israel (Jes 42,1-4) und Jesus (Mt 12,18-21). Studien zur biblischen Grundlegung. SBAB 35: 2005 <1997> ⇒209. 193-208.

### F4.3 Mt 13...*Parabolae Jesu*—The Parables

5911 **Blomberg, Craig L.** Preaching the parables: from responsible interpretation to powerful proclamation. 2004 ⇒20,5611. RCTJ 40 (2005) 151-153 (*Deppe, Dean*); TrinJ 26 (2005) 158-160 (*Scharf, Greg R.*).

5912 **Cànopi, Anna Maria** ¿Has dicho esto por nosotros?: las parábolas de la misericordia. [T]*Ballester, Carolina*: Espiritualidad: M 2005, Narcea 84 pp.

5913 **Duke, P.S.** The parables: a preaching commentary. Nv 2005, Abingdon vii; 127 pp. $18. 06870-90490 [NTAb 50,589].

5914 *Giroud, Jean-Claude* Qu'est-ce que "parler en paraboles"?. SémBib 118 (2005) 4-20;

5915 Qu'est-ce que parler en parabole?. Analyse narrative. BEThL 191: 2005 ⇒742. 417-423.

5916 *Girón Blanc, Luis* Parábolas rabínicas y Nuevo Testamento. ResB 47 (2005) 13-22.

5917 **Hedrick, Charles W.** Many things in parables: Jesus and his modern critics. 2004 ⇒20,5614. [R]CBQ 67 (2005) 345-346 (*LaHurd, Carol Schersten*); RBLit (2005)* (*Hood, Renate V.; Metzger, James; Skinner, Christopher*); ET 117 (2005) 123-124 (*Doering, Lutz*).

5918 *Hensell, Eugene* Encountering the parables of Jesus. RfR 64 (2005) 316-320 [NTAb 50,30].

5919 *Herget, Ferdinand* Gleichnisse verstehen: Erwägungen zur Struktur von Gleichnissen aus denkpsychologischer Sicht. [F]LAUB, F.: Bibel-Schule-Leben 6: 2005 ⇒87. 101-113 [Lk 15,11-32].

5920 *Jódar-Estrella, Carlos* Parábolas y protestas: alegoría, historia y lectura del texto. AnnTh 19/1 (2005) 57-97 [Mt 20,10-16; Lk 19,25].

5921 *Keerankeri, George* Listen to the Spirit: the gospel of Matthew: Jesus' parable discourse. VJTR 69 (2005) 370-386.

5922 *Kistemaker, S.J.* Jesus as story teller: literary perspectives on the parables. MastJ 16/1 (2005) 49-55 [NTAb 50,30].

5923 [E]**Longenecker, Richard N.** The challenge of Jesus' parables. 2000 ⇒16,4929... 18,5328. [R]RExp 102 (2005) 157-158 (*May, David M.*).

5924 **Meynet, Roland** Jezyk Przypowieschi Biblijnych. [T]*Walecki, Andrzej*: Mysl Teologiczna 51: Kraków 2005, WAM 194 pp. 83-7318-485-6.

5925 **Münch, Christian** Die Gleichnisse Jesu im Matthäusevangelium. WMANT 104: 2004 ⇒20, 5619. [R]SNTU 30 (2005) 145-172 (*Fuchs, Albert*); ThPh 80 (2005) 444-446 (*Wucherpfennig, Ansgar*); ThRv 101 (2005) 482-484 (*Häfner, Gerd*).

5926 *Neubrand, Maria* Und Jesus sprach in Gleichnissen .... [F]LAUB, F.: Bibel-Schule-Leben 6: 2005 ⇒87. 89-99.

5927 **Oldenhage, Tania** Parables for our time: rereading New Testament scholarship after the Holocaust. AAR.Cultural Criticism: 2002 ⇒18, 5330; 19,5722. [R]RBLit (2005)* (*Schottroff, Luise*).

5928 *Ramírez Fueyo, Francisco* Ayer y hoy de las parábolas. SalTer 93 (2005) 189-200.

5929 *Ricoeur, Paul* Le "Royaume" dans les paraboles de Jésus. ETR 80/4 (2005) 31-35.

5930 **Schottroff, Luise** Die Gleichnisse Jesu. Gü 2005, Gü 320 pp. €20. 3-579-05200-4;

5931 The parables of Jesus. [T]*Maloney, Linda M.*: Mp 2005, Fortress viii; 288 pp. $18 [BiTod 44,332—Donald Senior].

5932 *Snodgrass, Klyne R.* From allegorizing to allegorizing: a history of the interpretation of the parables of Jesus. The historical Jesus in recent research. 2005 ⇒379. 248-268.

5933 **Stiller, Brian** Preaching parables to postmoderns. Fortress resources for preaching: Mp 2005, Fortress viii; 200 pp. $17. 0-8006-3713-5. [R]AcTh(B) 25 (2005) 202-204 (*Van den Berg, Jan-Albert*).

5934 *Tabuyo, María* La difícil sencillez de las parábolas. SalTer 93 (2005) 201-211.

5935 **Wierzbicka, Anna** What did Jesus mean?: explaining the Sermon on the Mount and the parables in simple and universal human concepts. 2001 ⇒17,4973... 20,5627. [R]JOT 1/3 (2005) 69-75 (*Franklin, Karl J.*) [Mt 5-7].

5936 *Wojciechowski, Michał* Przypowieści o elitach [Parabole sur les élites]. AtK 145 (2005) 434-449. **P**.

5937 *Irigoin, Jean* La parabole de l'ivraie, la parabole du semeur et les béatitudes: études de syllabation. RHPhR 85 (2005) 517-527 [Mt 5,3-10; 13,24-30; 13,36-43; Mk 4; Lk 8].

5938 *Rimoldi, Monica* L'interpretazione delle parabole evangeliche negli scritti hegeliani di Tubinga e Berna. Ment. *Hegel, F; Ricoeur, P.*: FilTeo 19 (2005) 384-399 [Mt 13].

5939 **Roloff, Jürgen** Jesu Gleichnisse im Matthäusevangelium: ein Kommentar zu Mt 13,1-52. [E]*Kreller, Helmut; Oechslen, Rainer*: BThSt 73: Neuk 2005, Neuk 105 pp. €16.90. 3-7887-2109-X.

5940 *Bettiolo, Paolo* Predizione delle eresie, esortazione alla conversione, illustrazione della condotta cristiana: appunti sulla recezione di Mt 13,24-30 nelle chiese della Siria. CrSt 26 (2005) 173-188.

5941 *Fatti, Federico* Il seme del diavolo: la parabola della zizzania e i conflitti politico-dottrinali a Bisanzio (IV-V sec.);

5942 *Köhn, Andreas* Zum "Gleichnis vom Unkraut des Ackers" und seiner Deutung in der theologischen Reflexion des 20. Jahrhunderts;

5943 *Lettieri, Gaetano* Tollerare o sradicare?: il dilemma del discerniment: la parabola della zizzania nell'Occidente latino da AMBROGIO a LEONE Magno;

5944 *Ruggieri, Giuseppe* Il male nel mondo e nella chiesa: il destino di una parabola;

5945 *Visonà, Giuseppe* La parabola della zizzania nei primi tre secoli. CrSt 26 (2005) 123-172/321-348/65-121/5-23/25-64 [Mt 13,24-30].

5946 *Bühler, Pierre* Le blé et l'ivraie: réception de la parabole dans la période de la Réforme. RHPhR 85 (2005) 89-101 [Mt 13,24-30; 13,36-43].

5947 *Cepeda Salazar, Antonino* Parábola de la levadura: Mt 13,33//Lc 13, 20-21. Qol 38 (2005) 61-79.

5948 *Miller, R.J.* The pearl, the treasure, the fool, and the cross. The Fourth R [Santa Rosa, CA] 18/6 (2005) 3-10 [NTAb 50,268] [Mt 13, 44-46].

5949 *Summers, Charles A.* Matthew 14:13-21. Interp. 59 (2005) 298-299.

5950 *Panier, Louis* Discours et figures dans le récit: dispositifs parboliques et énonciatifs dans des séquences narratives. SémBib 118 (2005) 21-41 [Mt 15; Lk 13].

5951 *Bradley, M.* Jesus' dialectical-hypocritical act: Matthew 15:1-11. JHiC 11/2 (2005) 39-49[NTAb 50,484].

5952 *LeMarquand, Grant* The Canaanite conquest of Jesus (Mt 15:21-28). Arc 33 (2005) 237-247.

5953 **Usarski, Christa** Jesus und die Kanaanäerin (Matthäus 15,21-28): eine predigtgeschichtliche Recherche. PTHe 69: Stu 2005, Kohlhammer 239 pp. €25. 3-17-018533-0.

### F4.5 Mt 16...*Primatus promissus*—The promise to Peter

5954 *Agua, Agustín del* Los fundamentos bíblicos del primado en la exégesis actual del NT: a modo de estado de la cuestión. EstB 63 (2005) 195-234.

5955 *Cunningham, W.P.* Literary evidence for Peter's primacy. HPR 105/10 (2005) 65-69.

5956 **Gibert, Pierre** Simon Pietro. Sintesi: Brescia 2005, Queriniana 128 pp. €10.50.

5957 **Gnilka, Joachim** Pietro a Roma: la figura di Pietro nei primi due secoli. Introduzione allo studio della bibbia, suppl. 12: 2003 ⇒19, 5744; 20,5642. [R]Asp. 52 (2005) 576-577 (*Di Palma, Gaetano*).

5958 *Grech, Prosper* Il Simone della storia e il Pietro della fede. Il messaggio biblico. SRivBib 44: 2005 <2001> ⇒216. 227-235.

5959 **Mazzeo, Michele** Pietro: roccia della chiesa. 2004 ⇒20,5646. [R]Asp. 52 (2005) 577-578 (*Di Palma, Gaetano*).

5960 **Schmidt, Joël** Saint Pierre. P 2005, Presses de la Renaissance 370 pp. €21. 2-7509-00344.

5961 *Stylianopoulos, Theodore* Ἡ βιβλικε βασε του πρoτειου. DBM 23/1 (2005) 7-32. **G**.

5962 *Goodwin, Mark J.* Hosea and "the Son of the living God" in Matthew 16:16b. CBQ 67 (2005) 265-283 [Mt 14,33; Mk 8,29].

5963 *Kvalbein, Hans* The authorization of Peter in Matthew 16:17-19: a reconsideration of the power to bind and loose. The formation of the early church. WUNT 183: 2005 ⇒708. 145-174.

5964 *Luz, Ulrich* The primacy saying of Matthew 16:17-19 from the perspective of its effective history. Studies in Matthew. 2005 <1991> ⇒ 252. 165-182.

5965 *Divry, Edouard* La montagna della trasfigurazione, luogo teologico di dialogo. RTLu 10 (2005) 235-252 [Mt 16,27-17,9; Mk 9,1-10; Lk 9,26-36].

5966 *Gispert-Sauch, G.* The Transfiguration, the Christ-Messiah, the Avatara. VJTR 69 (2005) 786-787 [Mt 17,1-8].

5967 **Cerbelaud, Dominique** Sainte montagne. P 2005, Lethielleux 125 pp. €16. 22836-12403 [Mt 17,1-9].

5968 *Divry, Edouard* La Montagna della Trasfigurazione, luogo teologico di dialogo. RTLu 10 (2005) 235-252 [Mt 17,1-9].

5969 **Hubaut, Michel** La trasfigurazione. Brescia 2005, Queriniana 143 pp. 88-399-2902-9. Bibl. 139-140 [Mt 17,1-9].

5970 *Steenberg, M.C.* Two-natured man: an anthropology of transfiguration. ProEc 14 (2005) 413-432 [Mt 17,1-9].

5971 *Stevenson, Kenneth* "Rooted in detachment": Transfiguration as narrative, worship and community of faith. Ecclesiology 1/3 (2005) 13-26 [Mt 17,1-9].

5972 *Mangoni, Maria B.D.* L'episodio del 'tributo al tempio' (Mt 17,24-27): continuità e rottura nel vangelo di Matteo. Giudei o cristiani?. 2005 ⇒833. 157-165.

5973 *Langner, Cordula* "... sei Er dir wie der Heide und der Zöllner": das pragmatische Potential von Mt 18,17 in seinem Kontext (Mt 18,15-20). BN 126 (2005) 83-101;

5974 '...sea para ti como el gentil y el publicano': el potencial pragmático de Mt 18,17 en su contexto (Mt 18,15-20). FJUNCO GARZA, C.: Estudios Bíblicos Mexicanos 4: 2005 ⇒74. 259-283.

5975 *Sievers, Joseph* 'Wo zwei oder drei...': der rabbinische Begriff der Schechina und Matthäus 18,20. Das Prisma [Mü] 17/1 (2005) 18-29 [AcBib 11,147].

5976 **Carter, Warren** Households and discipleship: a study of Matthew 19-20. JSNT.S 103: 1994 ⇒10,4565; 12,4580. RThR 70 (2005) 212-215 (*Lindemann, Andreas*).

5977 *Hester, J. David* Eunuchs and the postgender Jesus: Matthew 19.12 and transgressive sexualities. JSNT 28 (2005) 13-40.

### F4.8 Mt 20...*Regnum eschatologicum*—Kingdom eschatology

5978 *Seidel, Johannes* Von der Gerechtigkeit Gottes: das Gleichnis von den Arbeitern im Weinberg (Mt 20,1-16). FLAUB, F.: Bibel-Schule-Leben 6: 2005 ⇒87. 115-124.

5979 *Rudman, Dominic* Whose kingdom is it anyway?: the sons of Zebedee as antitypes for Adonijah in Matthew 20. BN 125 (2005) 97-104 [1 Kgs 2,19; Mt 20,20-23; Mk 10,35-40].

5980 *Safrai, Chana* The mother of the Zebedee brothers (Matthew 20:20-28). Beginnings of christianity. 2005 ⇒786. 151-159.

5981 *Kinman, Brent* Jesus' royal entry into Jerusalem. BBR 15/2 (2005) 223-260 [Mt 21].

5982 **Wilson, Alistair I.** When will these things happen?: a study of Jesus as judge in Matthew 21-25. 2004 ⇒20,5673. RSBET 23 (2005) 238-239 (*Macaskill, Grant*).

5983 *Basser, H.W.* Planting christian trees in Jewish soil. RRJ 8 (2005) 91-112 [NTAb 50,269] [Mt 21,1-11].

5984 *Kinman, Brent* Jesus' royal entry in Jerusalem;

5985 *Klingbeil, Gerald A.* Jesus' royal entry into Jerusalem: Brent Kinman cultural criticism and biblical hermeneutics: definition, origins, benefits, and challenges. BBR 15 (2005) 223-260/261-277 [Mt 21,1-17].

5986 **Mullooparambil, Sebastian** Jesus in the temple: a redaction critical study of Matthew 21:12-17. D*Juric, S.*: R 2005, n.p. 127 pp. Extr. Diss. Angelicum; Bibl. 79-120.

5987 *Smillie, Gene R.* Jesus' response to the question of his authority in Matthew 21. BS 162/648 (2005) 459-469 [Mt 21,23-27].

5988 **Olmstead, Wesley G.** Matthew's trilogy of parables: the nation, the nations and the reader in Matthew 21:28-22:14. MSSNTS 127: 2003 ⇒19,5767; 20,5683. RSR 34 (2005) 287-288 (*Cousland, J.R.C.*); JR 85 (2005) 656-657 (*Reid, Barbara E.*).

5989 **Savarimuthu, Stanislas** A community in search of its identity: Mt 21:28-22:14 in a subaltern perspective. D*Baudoz, J.F.* 2005, Diss. Leuven.

5990 *Terrinoni, Ubaldo* La parabola dei due figli o dell'obedienza fattiva (Mt 21,28-32), 1. Presbyteri 39 (2005) 701-706.

5991 *Brooke, George J.* 4Q500 1 and the use of scripture in the parable of the vineyard. Dead Sea scrolls and the NT. 2005 <1995> ⇒194. 235-260 [Mt 21,33-45].

5992 *Olson, Daniel C.* Matthew 22:1-14 as midrash. CBQ 67 (2005) 435-453 [Zeph 1].

5993 *Bérubé, Béatrice* La loi: le commandement de l'amour de Dieu et du prochain. Scriptura(M) 7/1 (2005) 81-101 [Mt 22,37-40; Lk 10,30-37].

5994 *Keerankeri, George* Listen to the Spirit: the gospel of Matthew: 'Woe to you, scribes and pharisees...': Jesus' prophetic denunciation of inauthentic religious leadership. VJTR 69 (2005) 613-624 [Mt 23].

5995 *Miler, Jean* L'apostrophe aux scribes et aux Pharisiens (Mt 23) et le commandement de l'amour des ennemis. Analyse narrative. BEThL 191: 2005 ⇒742. 259-272.

5996 **Newport, Kenneth G.** The sources and Sitz im Leben of Matthew 23. JSNT.S 117: 1995 ⇒11/1,3174... 16,5005. [R]ThR 70 (2005) 215-216 (*Lindemann, Andreas*).

5997 *Weinfeld, Moshe* The charge of hypocrisy in Matthew 23 and in Jewish sources. Normative and sectarian Judaism. Library of Second Temple Studies 54: 2005 ⇒2732. 279-285.

5998 **Sakr, Michel** Le sévère Sauveur: lecture pragmatique des sept 'Οὐαί' dans Mt 23,13-36. [D]*Grilli, Massimo*: EHS.T 808: Bern 2005, Lang xx; 370 pp. 3-03910-775-5. Diss. Gregoriana; Bibl. 321-344.

5999 *Keerankeri, George* Listen to the Spirit: the gospel of Matthew: the eschatological discourse: Jesus as the end-time judge. VJTR 69 (2005) 687-697 [Mt 24-25].

6000 *Eliav, Yaron Z.* A new/old reading of the '*Lithos epi lithon*' prophecy and the role of the Temple Mount in the Jesus movement. Beginnings of christianity. 2005 ⇒786. 325-347 [Mt 24,2].

6001 *Chenoweth, Ben* Identifying the talents: contextual clues for the interpretation of the parable of the talents (Matthew 25:14-30). TynB 56/1 (2005) 61-72.

6002 *Frankemölle, Hubert* Das Gleichnis von den Zentnern/Talenten (Mt 25,14-30): zwei Leseweisen: Jesus und Matthäus. Orien. 69/1 (2005) 10-12.

6003 *Locker, Markus* Reading and re-reading Matthew's parable of the talents in context. BZ 49 (2005) 161-173 [Mt 25,14-30].

6004 *Pesch, Wilhelm* Ein Versuch über Matthäus 25,31-46. [F]STENDEBACH, F.: 2005 ⇒141. 128-140.

6005 *Müntefering, Franz* Die Gerechten und die Barmherzigkeit (Matthäus 25,31-40). Kanzelreden. 2005 ⇒376. 79-87.

6006 *Vouga, François* Gratuité et poétique du jugement dans l'évangile de Matthieu (Mt 25,31-46). Analyse narrative. BEThL 191: 2005 ⇒ 742. 273-278.

## F5.1 *Redemptio*, **Mt 26,** *Ultima coena*; **The Eucharist** [⇒H7.4]

6007 *Arens, Eduardo* El cuerpo de Cristo: el significado primigenio de la eucaristia. Páginas 30/194 (2005) 36-49 [NTAb 50,529].

6008 *Athikalam, James* The Eucharist in the New Testament. JJSS 5 (2005) 147-167.

6009 *Blocker, D.* The traditional translation and interpretation of the Last Supper: the betrayal of the original text. JHiC 11/1 (2005) 35-54 [NTAb 50,27].

6010 *Boschi, Bernardo Gianluigi* L'eucaristia: il sacramento dell'amore: per una fondazione biblica del rapporto eucaristia e agápe. Vivar(C) 13 (2005) 151-173.

6011 **Bradshaw, Paul F.** Eucharistic origins. ACC 80: L 2004, SPCK x; 166 pp. $20.

6012 *Bradshaw, Paul F.* The eucharistic sayings of Jesus. StLi 35 (2005) 1-11 [Mk 14,17-25; Lk 22,14-22; John 6].

6013 *Bueno de la Fuente, Eloy* La Eucaristía: Pascua de la nueva alianza. MisEx(M) 206 (2005) 272-287.

6014 *Castellano Cervera, Jesús* Il mistero eucaristico fonte di verità e di vita: spunti di catechesi biblica.. RVS 59/1 (2005) 61-84.

6015 *Cervantes Gabarrón, José* El dinamismo eucarístico del cuerpo de Cristo. ResB 47 (2005) 50-62.

6016 *Chempakassery, P.* The sacrificial aspect of the eucharist and the family. Indian Journal of Family Studies [Thuruthy, Kerala] 3/1 (2005) 17-39 [NTAb 49,542].

6017 *Chung-mo Koo, Mark* The New Testament in the eucharistic vision: a meditative and experiential reflection on the New Testament. KaKe 74 (2005) 33-62 Sum. ii. **J.**

6018 **Dabic, Goran** La condivisione di tavola di Gesù con i peccatori e nel cenacolo e la grazia eucaristica quale stimolo all'umanizzazione del mondo negli scritti di Edward SCHILLEBEECKX. R 2005, Pont. Univ. Gregoriana 152 pp. Exc. Diss.; Bibl. 126-145.

6019 *Daly, Robert J.* Eucharistic origins: from the New Testament to the liturgies of the Golden Age. TS 66 (2005) 3-22.

6020 *Di Palma, Gaetano* "Venite a mangiare" (Gv 21,12): l'eucaristia sulla riva del mare di Tiberiade. Asp. 52 (2005) 41-58 [John 21,1-14].

6021 *Dulles, Avery* Eucharistie: das lebendige Geschenk Jesu. IKaZ 34 (2005) 391-400.

6022 *Fendrich, Herbert* Hartes Brot—kaltes Büfett!: Klaus Staeck, Abendmahl, Pax-Christi-Kirche Krefeld, 1982. BiHe 41/164 (2005) 20-21.

6023 *Fernando, L.* The eucharist in the writings of the fathers of the church. JPJRS 8/2 (2005) 22-33 [NTAb 50,139].

6024 *Ferrer Arellano, Joaquín* Palabra bíblica, palabra sacramental y protopalabra eucarística. StLeg 46 (2005) 113-152.

6025 *Fiedler, Peter* Probleme der Abendmahlforschung. Studien zur biblischen Grundlegung. SBAB 35: 2005 <1982> ⇒209. 22-69.

6026 *Hahn, Ferdinand* Zwei Auffassungen vom Herrenmahl: neutestamentliche Theologie zwischen vorösterlicher und nachösterlicher Tradition. Zeitzeichen 6/2 (2005) 52-54 [Lk 14,1-24].

6027 *Hainz, Josef* Christus—"Brot für das Leben der Welt": zur Feier der Eucharistie im NT und heute: Brücken zu einem "ökumenischen Herrenmahl". TThZ 114 (2005) 171-187.

6028 *Horbury, William Cena pura* and the Lord's Supper. Beginnings of christianity. 2005 ⇒786. 219-265.

6029 **Jeremias, Joachim** La última cena: palabras de Jesús. $^{T}$*Mínguez, Dionisio*: Sagrada Escritura: $^{2}$2003 <1980> ⇒19,5792; 20,5764. $^{R}$RTLi 39/1 (2005) 127-130 (*Zárate, Nilton*).

6030 *Joachim, Thomas* Eucharistie et temporalité. Aletheia 27 (2005) 85-96.

6031 **Kereszty, Roch A.** Wedding feast of the Lamb: eucharistic theology from a historical, biblical, and systematic perspective. 2004 ⇒20, 5767. $^{R}$Worship 80/1 (2005) 87-88 (*Daly, Robert J.*).

6032 *Kizhakkeyil, Sebastian* The Jewish celebration of the Passover and the christian Eucharist. JJSS 5 (2005) 126-146.

6033 *Lang, Uwe M.* Zum Einsetzungsbericht bei ostsyrischen Liturgiekommentatoren. OrChr 89 (2005) 63-76.

6034 *Lang, Walter* Paschaopfer und Ostermahl als Vorbild der Eucharistie. Una Voce-Korrespondenz 35 (2005) 79-84.

6035 **Levering, Matthew** Sacrifice and community: Jewish offering and christian eucharist. Illuminations: Oxf 2005, Blackwell 210 pp. £50/20; $85/30. 1-4051-3689-8/90-1.

6036 *Léon-Dufour, Xavier* 'Fate questo in memoria di me' <1981>;

6037 Presenza reale, presenza simbolica <1983>. Un biblista cerca Dio. Collana biblica: 2005 ⇒245. 139-151/201-206.

6038 *Linton, G.* House church meetings in the New Testament era. Stone-Campbell Journal [Joplin, MS] 8 (2005) 229-244 [NTAb 51,316].

6039 *Martin, Pierre* Le christ autophage. RHPhR 85 (2005) 365-400.

6040 *Mayemba Kubuta, Bienvenu* Pain eucharistique et paix fraternelle: la dimension socio-anthropologique de l'eucharistie. Telema 120 (2005) 7-19.

6041 *Mazza, Enrico* De la última cena al siglo XXI: comprensión e incomprensiones sobre la eucaristía y su celebración. Phase 268 (2005) 237-261.

6042 *McGowan, Andrew* Food, ritual, and power. Late ancient christianity. 2005 ⇒517. 145-164.

6043 **Miglietta, Carlo** L'eucaristia secondo la bibbia: itinerario biblico-spirituale. 2004 ⇒20,5781. RItin. 31 (2005) 255-56 (*Conte, Nunzio*).

6044 *Mukasa, Edoth* La foi qui fleurit en oeuvres de justice: l'eucharistie et la faim dans le monde: une reconsidération. Telema 120 (2005) 20-7.

6045 *Perroni, Marinella* La cena di Gesù: tra addio e presenza. Centro pro unione 68 (2005) 15-19.

6046 *Peterson, Erik* Herrenmahlfeier und Opfervorstellung. Peterson: Lukasevangelium und Synoptica. 2005 ⇒277. 418-420.

6047 *Rapp, Francis* Notes sur l'eucharistie à la veille de la Réformation: ce que nous apprennent quelques documents sur la communion. RHPhR 85 (2005) 5-16.

6048 *Rizzo, Francesco P.* Il "Simposio" greco e l'"Ultima Cena". CivCatt 156/3 (2005) 262-270.

6049 *Roth, Diethardt* Das Heilige Abendmahl im kirchlichen Unterricht: ein Beitrag zum Unterrichtsmodell "Das heilige Abendmahl" (1997). FSTOLLE, V. 2005 ⇒143. 501-510.

6050 **Sayés, J.A.** El misterio eucarístico. 2003 ⇒19,5801. REstTrin 39 (2005) 130-133 (*Miguel, José María de*).

6051 **Smith, Gordon T.** A holy meal. GR 2005, Baker 121 pp.

6052 *Theobald, Michael* "Tut dies zu meinem Gedächtnis!": die Eucharistie in der frühen Kirche. Orien. 69/7 (2005) 76-80.

6053 *Tremblay, Réal* L'eucaristia, l'amore dei nemici e l'essere cristiano. RdT 46 (2005) 377-384.

6054 *Trummer, Peter* Frühchristliche Eucharistie: Texte und Ikonographie. FNIEDERWIMMER, K.: Gutachten und Studien 2: 2005 ⇒112. 97-112.

6055 **Trummer, Peter** "Das ist mein Leib": neue Perspektiven zu Eucharistie und Abendmahl. Dü 2005, Patmos 200 pp. €18. 3-491-70383-2.

6056 *Vanhoye, Albert* La eucaristia, fuente y cumbre de la vida consagrada. Manresa 77 (2005) 289-304 [NTAb 50,101].

6057 *Vassiliadis, Petros* Πεγε τον λογιον και εὐχαριστια. DBM 23/1 (2005) 33-51. **G.**

6058 *Wolfinger, Franz* Opfer und Gebet im Katholizismus. Opfer und Gebet. 2005 ⇒506. 80-86.

### F5.3 Mt 26,30...//*Passio Christi*; Passion narrative

6059 *Aejmelaeus, Anneli* The Suffering Servant: Isaiah 53 as an intertext of the New Testament. FAEJMELAEUS, L.: SESJ 89: 2005 ⇒1. 475-494 [Rom 4,25; 1 Cor 15,3-5].

6060 **Aitken, Ellen Bradshaw** Jesus' death in early christian memory: the poetics of the passion. NTOA 53: 2004 ⇒20,5817. RBTB 35 (2005) 155-156 (*Kloppenborg, John S.*); RBLit (2005)* (*Heen, Erik*) [1 Cor 15,3-5; 1 Pet 2,22-25].

6061 *Allison, Dale C.* Foreshadowing the passion. Studies in Matthew: interpretation. 2005 ⇒5587. 217-235.

6062 *Banchini, Francesca* Giuda Iscariota: tra condanna e assoluzione: testimonianze letterarie ed epigrafiche dei primi tre secoli di cristianesimo. Vivens Homo 16 (2005) 141-155.

6063 *Boda, Mark J.; Porter, Stanley E.* Literature to the third degree: prophecy in Zechariah 9-14 and the passion of Christ. Traduire la Bible hébraïque. 2005 ⇒728. 215-254.

6064 **Bond, Helen K.** Caiaphas: friend of Rome and judge of Jesus?. 2004 ⇒20,5823. RTheol. 108 (2005) 214-215 (*Lyons, W.J.*); TJT 21 (2005) 222-224 (*Spilsbury, Paul*); RBLit (2005)* (*Byron, John; Gillman, Florence; Tilly, Michael*).

6065 **Bovon, François** Les derniers jours de Jésus: textes et évènements. Essais bibliques 34: 22004 <1974> ⇒20,4908. RRB 112 (2005) 458-459 (*Devillers, Luc*); CrSt 26 (2005) 551-553 (*Nilsen, Tina Dykesteen*); Theoforum 36 (2005) 205-210 (*Mathieu, Yvan*).

6066 **Brown, Raymond** La mort du Messie: encyclopédie de la passion du Christ: de Gethsémané au tombeau: un commentaire des récits de la passion dans les quatre évangiles. T*Mignon, Jacques*: P 2005, Bayard 1696 pp. €59. 2-227-35025-3. RVS 85 (2005) 555-556 (*Haudebert, Pierre*); ETR 80 (2005) 563-565 (*Cuvillier, Elian*); CEv 133 (2005) 85-86 (*Haudebert, Pierre*);

6067 La muerte del Mesías: desde Getsemaní hasta el sepulcro, 1: comentario a los relatos de la pasión de los cuatro evangelios. Estella 2005, Verbo Divino 1032 pp.

6068 *Carrier, Richard C.* The burial of Jesus in light of Jewish law. The empty tomb. 2005 ⇒435. 369-392.

6069 *Cousland, J.R.C.* The choral crowds in the tragedy according to St. Matthew. Ancient fiction. SBL.Symp. 32: 2005 ⇒721. 255-273.

6070 *Culpepper, Richard A.* Designs for the church in the gospel accounts of Jesus' death. NTS 51 (2005) 376-392.

6071 *Dewey, Arthur J.* The locus for death: social memory and the passion narrative. Memory, tradition, and text. 2005 ⇒416. 119-128.

6072 *Fiedler, Peter* '... gekreuzigt durch Pontius Pilatus': Erwägungen zum Problem der Verantwortung für den Tod Jesu. Studien zur biblischen Grundlegung. SBAB 35: 2005 <2000> ⇒209. 232-255.

6073 *Frey, Jörg* Probleme der Deutung des Todes Jesu in der neutestamentlichen Wissenschaft: Streiflichter zur exegetischen Diskussion. Deutungen. WUNT 181: 2005 ⇒392. 3-50.

6074 *Guerrero Ramos, Daniel* Qué podemos saber de la muerte de Jesús?: las fuentes y los datos históricos. Proyección 52 (2005) 175-205.

6075 *Hafner, Johann Ev.* War der Prozess Jesu Lynchjustiz?: Kritik an der Reduktion von Gewalt auf Mimesis in René Girards "Violence and Religion". Das Gewaltpotential. QD 216: 2005 ⇒863. 191-210.

6076 *Hinkle, Mary E.* People like us: minor characters in Matthew's passion. Word and world 25 (2005) 76-83.

6077 **Jossa, Giorgio** Il processo di Gesù. StBi 133: 2002 ⇒18,5432; 20, 5834. [R]Filosofia Oggi 28 (2005) 496-498 (*Tugnoli, Claudio*).

6078 *Keerankeri, George* Listen to the Spirit: the gospel of Matthew: the passion narrative. VJTR 69 (2005) 763-774.

6079 *Kilgallen, John J.* Pontius Pilate and the 'Jews'. BiTod 43 (2005) 102-110.

6080 **Klassen, William** Judas: betrayer or friend of Jesus?. Mp 2005, Fortress xiv; 238 pp. $25.

6081 **Lambiasi, Francesco** Fu crocifisso: perché?: sette domande sulla morte di Gesù. R 2005, AVE 96 pp. Pref. di *Luigi Accattoli.*

6082 **Légasse, Simon** Le procès de Jésus, 1: histoire. 2004 ⇒20,5838. [R]Brot. 160 (2005) 89-90 (*Silva, I. Ribeiro da*).

6083 *Léon-Dufour, Xavier* L'ultimo grido di Gesù. Un biblista cerca Dio. Collana biblica: 2005 <1978> ⇒245. 91-108 [Mk 15,34; Lk 23,46].

6084 **Loupan, Victor; Noël, Alain** Enquête sur la mort de Jésus. P 2005, Presses de la Renaissance 384 pp. €22. 27509-00883.

6085 *Magness, Jodi* Ossuaries and the burials of Jesus and James. JBL 124 (2005) 121-154.

6086 **McKnight, Scot** Jesus and his death: historiography, the historical Jesus, and atonement theory. Waco, TX 2005, Baylor Univ. Pr. 451 pp. $60. 1932-792-295.

6087 **Nodet, Étienne** Le Fils de Dieu: procès de Jésus et évangiles. Josèphe et son temps 4: 2002 ⇒18,5436; 19,5833. [R]CDios 218 (2005) 564-565 (*Gutiérrez, J.*).

6088 **Paffenroth, Kim** Judas: images of the lost disciple. 2001 ⇒17,5071; 19,5834. [R]CBQ 67 (2005) 535-536 (*Reinhartz, Adele*); HeyJ 46 (2005) 227-229 (*McNamara, Martin*).

6089 *Panier, Louis* Figures et discours sur la mort de Jésus: contributions sémiotiques à une réflexion théologique. [F]GENEST, O.: 2005 ⇒46. 61-84.

6090 **Patterson, Stephen J.** Beyond the passion: rethinking the death and life of Jesus. 2004 ⇒20,5844. [R]CBQ 67 (2005) 356-357 (*Doran, Robert*); RBLit (2005)* (*Mcmahon, Christopher; Smith, Daniel*).

6091 *Retief, François P.; Cilliers, Louise* Christ's crucifixion as a medico-historical event. Health and healing. AcTh(B).S 7: 2005 <2004> ⇒ 686. 294-309.

6092 *Szczurowski, Rafał* Postać Judasza społecznie użyteczna [Le personnage de Judas socialement utile]. PrzPow 122 (2005) 259-275. **P.**

6093 [T]**Tomàs, Assumpta** Tomàs MORE: L'agonia de Crist: cartes des de la Torre. Clàssics del cristianisme 92: 2002 ⇒18,5444; 19,5839. [R]RCatT 30/1 (2005) 217-228 (*Grau i Arau, Andreu*).

6094 **Tomson, Peter J.** Presumed guilty: how the Jews were blamed for the death of Jesus. [T]*Dyk, Janet*: Mp 2005, Fortress xiv; 146 pp. $15. 08006-3707-0. [R]RBLit (2005)* (*Montonini, Matthew; Punt, Jeremy*).

6095 *Tyson, Joseph B.* The death of Jesus. Seeing Judaism anew. 2005 ⇒ 618. 38-45.

6096 **Untergaßmair, Franz Georg** Leiden, Tod und Auferstehung: eine exegetisch-homiletische Handreichung. Vechtaer Beiträge zur Theologie 12: Müns 2005, LIT 229 pp. 3-8258-8014-1.
6097 *Van Henten, Jan W.* Jewish martyrdom and Jesus' death. Deutungen. WUNT 181: 2005 ⇒392. 139-168.
6098 **Vermes, Geza** The Passion. L 2005, Penguin 130 pp. €12.24. 978-014-102132-4.
6099 **Vos, Johan** De betekenis van de dood van Jezus: tussen seculiere exegese en christelijke dogmatiek. Zoetermeer 2005, Meinema 150 pp. €14.90. 90-211-4049-7.

6100 *Reed, David A.* "Saving Judas"—a social scientific approach to Judas's suicide in Matthew 27:3-10. BTB 35 (2005) 51-59.
6101 **Rigato, Maria-Luisa** Il titolo della croce di Gesù: confronto tra i vangeli e la tavoletta-reliquia della Basilica Eleniana a Roma. TGr.T 100: 2003 ⇒19,5852; 20,5864. [R]FKTh 21 (2005) 58-60 (*Heid, Stefan*); Ho Theológos 23 (2005) 301-303 (*Iovino, Paolo*) [Mt 27,37];
6102 [2]2005 <2003>, E.P.U.G. 392 pp. 88-7652-969-1. [R]RivCC 81 (2005) 343-346 (*Heid, Stefan*) [Mt 27,37].
6103 *Allison, Dale C.* Darkness at noon (Matt. 27:45). Studies in Matthew: interpretation. 2005 ⇒5587. 79-105 [Amos 8,9-10].
6104 **Bigaouette, Francine** Le cri de déreliction de Jésus en croix: densité existentielle et salvifique. 2004 ⇒20,5865. [R]Theoforum 36 (2005) 238-241 (*Peelman, Achiel*) [Mt 27,46].
6105 **Gurtner, Daniel M.** The *velum scissum*: Matthew's exposition of the death of Jesus. [D]*Bauckham, Richard J.* 2005, Diss. St Andrews 2005; Sum. TynB 56,147-150 [Mt 27,51].
6106 **Scaglioni, Germano** I prodigi alla morte di croce in Mt 27,51b-53: elementi biblici per una teologia della morte di Gesù nel vangelo di Matteo. R 2005, n.p. 93 pp. Bibl. 75-93.

### F5.6 Mt 28//: Resurrectio

6107 La résurrection chez les Pères. CaBiP 7: 2003 ⇒19,5854. [R]VetChr 42 (2005) 174-175 (*Valentini, Angela*); RBLit (2005)* (*Kraus, Thomas J.*).
6108 *Agua, Agustín del* El testimonio narrativo de la resurreción de Cristo. Qol 37 (2005) <2002> 3-41 ⇒18,5471.
6109 *Allison, Dale C.* Explaining the resurrection: conflicting convictions. JSHJ 3 (2005) 117-133.
6110 **Binz, Stephen J.** The resurrection and the life. Threshold Bible Study: New London, CT 2005, Twenty-Third 120 pp. $13 [BiTod 44,198 —Donald Senior].
6111 *Bryan, David J.* The Jewish background to The resurrection of the Son of God by N.T. Wright. JSHJ 3 (2005) 155-169.
6112 *Bubel, Grzegorz* Zmartwychwstał trzeciego dnia [Ressuscité le troisième jour]. PrzPow 122 (2005) 407-419. **P**.
6113 *Buglass, A.E.; Viljoen, F.P.* The resurrection of Jesus: do extra-canonical sources change the landscape?. VeE 26 (2005) 851-866.
6114 *Cardellino, Lodovico* Fede e resurrezione (Mt 22,23-33; Mc 12,18-27; Lc 20,27-38). BeO 47 (2005) 71-87.

6115 *Carrier, Richard C.* The plausibility of theft. The empty tomb. 2005 ⇒435. 349-368.

6116 **Castellucci, Erio** Davvero il Signore è risorto: indagine teologico-fondamentale sugli avvenimenti e le origini della fede pasquale. Assisi 2005, Cittadella 420 pp. €28.50. [R]ScC 133 (2005) 735-737 (*Brambilla, Franco Giulio*).

6117 *Cavin, Robert G.* Is there sufficient historical evidence to establish the resurrection of Jesus?. The empty tomb. 2005 ⇒435. 19-41.

6118 *Cranfield, C.E.B.* The resurrection of Jesus Christ. The historical Jesus in recent research. 2005 ⇒379. 382-391.

6119 *Crossley, James G.* Against the historical plausibility of the empty tomb story and bodily resurrection of Jesus: a response to N.T. Wright. JSHJ 3 (2005) 171-186.

6120 *Derrett, J. Duncan M.* Financial aspects of the resurrection;

6121 *Drange, Theodore M.* Why resurrect Jesus?. The empty tomb. 2005 ⇒435. 393-409/55-67.

6122 *Evans, Craig A.* Jewish burial traditions and the resurrection of Jesus. JSHJ 3 (2005) 233-248 [Dt 21,22-23].

6123 *Fales, Evan* Reformed epistemology and biblical hermeneutics;

6124 Taming the tehom: the sign of Jonah in Matthew [Mt 12,39-40]. The empty tomb. 2005 ⇒435. 469-489/307-348.

6125 *Filser, Hubert* "Er hat ihn wirklich auferweckt!": die aktuelle Diskussion um die Wirklichkeit der Auferweckung Jesu. [F]LAUB, F.: Bibel-Schule-Leben 6: 2005 ⇒87. 175-194.

6126 **Flew, A.G.N.; Habermas, G.R.** Resurrected?: an atheist and theist dialogue. [E]*Ankerberg, J.F.*: Lanham, MD 2005, Rowman & L. ix; 112 pp. $45/16. 07425-42254/62 [NTAb 49,596].

6127 *Flint, J.* The resurrection of Jesus: our eucatastrophe. HPR 106/3 (2005) 8-13 [NTAb 50,260].

6128 *Goulder, Michael* Jesus' resurrection and christian origins: a response to N.T. Wright. JSHJ 3 (2005) 187-195.

6129 *Gundry, Robert H.* The essential physicality of Jesus' resurrection according to the New Testament. The old is better. WUNT 178: 2005 ⇒220. 171-194.

6130 *Habermas, Gary R.* Resurrection research from 1975 to the present: what are critical scholars saying?. JSHJ 3 (2005) 135-153.

6131 [T]**Homann, Frederick A.** Jerome NADAL, S.J.: annotations and meditations on the gospels, 3: the resurrection narratives. Ph 2005, Saint Joseph's xv; 181 pp. $40. 0-916-101-479. CD-ROM, incl. 153 images; introd. *Walter Melion* [ThD 52,144—W. Charles Heiser].

6132 *Hurtado, Larry W.* Jesus' resurrection in the early christian texts: an engagement with N.T. Wright. JSHJ 3 (2005) 197-208.

6133 *Keating, J.F.* N.T. Wright and the necessity of a historical apologetic of the resurrection. Josephinum Journal of Theology [Columbus, OH] 12/1 (2005) 43-56 [NTAb 49,489].

6134 *Keerankeri, George* Listen to the Spirit: the gospel of Matthew: God's victory over death and the turning point of history: the resurrection of Jesus in Matthew. VJTR 69 (2005) 844-854.

6135 *Kline, J.B.* The Day of the Lord in the death and resurrection of Christ. JETS 48 (2005) 757-770 [NTAb 50,328].

6136 *Léon-Dufour, Xavier* Quale linguaggio su Gesù trionfatore della morte?. Un biblista cerca Dio. 2005 <1973> ⇒245. 185-198.

6137 *Lowder, Jeffery J.* Historical evidence and the empty tomb story: a reply to William Lane Craig. The empty tomb. 2005 ⇒435. 261-306.

6138 *Luedemann, Gerd* The history and nature of the earliest christian belief in the resurrection. The historical Jesus in recent research. Sources for biblical and theological study 10: 2005 ⇒379. 413-419.

6139 *Martin, Michael* The resurrection as initially improbable;

6140 SWINBURNE on the resurrection. The empty tomb. 2005 ⇒435. 43-54/453-468.

6141 *Martuccelli, Paolo* Gesù risorto, risurrezione dell'uomo: riflessioni teologiche a partire dal Nuovo Testamento. Theologia Viatorum 9-10 (2005) 13-57.

6142 *Meacham, J.* From Jesus to Christ. Newsweek [NY] (March 28 2005) 40-48.

6143 *Moingt, Joseph* S'éveiller à la résurrection. Etudes (Juin 2005) 771-781.

6144 *Parsons, Keith* Peter Kreeft and Ronald Tacelli on the hallucination theory. The empty tomb. 2005 ⇒435. 433-451.

6145 **Pitstick, Alyssa Helene** Lux in tenebris: the traditional Catholic doctrine of Christ's descent into Hell and the theological opinion of Hans Urs VON BALTHASAR. R 2005, s.n. xv; 478 pp. Bibl. 451-478.

6146 *Price, Robert M.* The empty tomb: introduction: the second life of Jesus. The empty tomb. 2005 ⇒435. 9-18.

6147 *Price, Robert M.* By this time he stinketh: the attempts of William Lane Craig to exhume Jesus. The empty tomb. 2005 ⇒435. 411-431.

6148 **Pritchard, J.** Living Easter through the year: making the most of the resurrection. ColMn 2005, Liturgical xiii; 133 pp. $13. 08146-31525. Bibl. [NTAb 50,403].

6149 *Reimer, Andy M.* A biography of a motif: the empty tomb in the gospels, the Greek novels, and SHAKESPEARE's Romeo and Juliet. Ancient fiction. SBL.Symp. 32: 2005 ⇒721. 297-316.

6150 *Ridruejo Alonso, Pedro* La resurrección de Cristo. CDios 218 (2005) 301-334.

6151 **Schlier, Heinrich** Sulla risurrezione di Gesù Cristo. Brescia [5]2005, Morcelliana 81 pp. €8. 88-372-2029-4. Pref. card. *Joseph Ratzinger*.

6152 **Sesboüé, Bernard** La résurrection et la vie. 2004 ⇒20,5885. [R]Théologie évangélique(VS) 4/2 (2005) 90-93 (*Jaeger, Lydia*).

6153 *Souletie, Jean-Louis* De la résurrection à l'histoire de Jésus. EeV 137 (2005) 1-11.

6154 **Swinburne, Richard** The resurrection of God incarnate. 2003 ⇒19, 5882; 20,5887. [R]HeyJ 46 (2005) 360-361 (*Madigan, Patrick*).

6155 **Thiede, Carsten Peter** The Emmaus mystery: discovering evidence for the risen Christ. L 2005, Continuum viii; 205 pp. £20. 0-8264-67-97-0. Introd. *Matthew d'Ancona*.

6156 *Trigo, Pedro* La resurrección de Jesús. Iter 16/37-38 (2005) 231-306.

6157 *Trudinger, Paul The* Christ, *the* resurrection, Jesus and christianity. ET 116 (2005) 190-192.

6158 *Valdés, Ariel Alvarez* ¿Quiénes descubrieron la tumba vacía de Jesús?. Theologica 40 (2005) 175-182.

6159 *Wright, N.T.* Resurrecting old arguments: responding to four essays. JSHJ 3 (2005) 209-231.

6160 **Wright, Nicholas T.** The resurrection of the Son of God. Christian origins and the question of God 3: 2003 ⇒19,5890; 20,5894. [R]CThMi 32 (2005) 95-98 (*Tietjen, John H.*); TS 66 (2005) 184-186

(*Smith, Daniel A.*); TrinJ 26 (2005) 140-143 (*Hamilton, James M., Jr.*); RBLit 7 (2005) 300-304 (*Licona, Michael R.*); ET 116 (2005) 229-233 (*Newman, Carey C.*).

6161 *Waters, Kenneth L.* Matthew 28:1-6 as temporally conflated text: temporal-spatial collapse in the gospel of Matthew. ET 116 (2005) 295-301.

6162 *Allison, Dale C.* Touching Jesus' feet (Matt. 28:9). Studies in Matthew: interpretation. 2005 ⇒5587. 105-116.

6163 *Friedrichsen, Timothy A.* The commissioning of women disciples: Matthew 28:9-10. [F]MOLONEY, F.: BSRel 187: 2005 ⇒104. 265-279.

6164 *Wilk, Florian* Eingliederung von "Heiden" in die Gemeinschaft der Kinder Abrahams: die Aufgabe der Jünger Jesu unter "allen Weltvölkern" nach Mt 28,16-20. ZNT 8/15 (2005) 52-59.

6165 *Dobbeler, Axel von* Richtet sich der Missionsauftrag in Mt 28,19 auch an Israel?: eine Einführung zur Kontroverse. ZNT 8/15 (2005) 44.

6166 *Frankemölle, Hubert* Die Sendung der Jünger Jesu "zu allen Völkern" (Mt 28,19). ZNT 8/15 (2005) 45-51.

## F6.1 Evangelium Marci—*Textus, commentarii*

6167 **Aliquò, Pietro** La bella notizia del regno: commento al vangelo di Marco. Mi 2005, Paoline 280 pp. €9.50. 88-315-2948-X.

6168 *Amphoux, Christian B.* Marc 1,1-11: la tradition manuscrite grecque. MSR 62/2 (2005) 5-15.

6169 *Arbache, Samir; Roisse, Philippe* Marc 1,1-11 arabe: versions anciennes de Syrie-Palestine et d'al-Andalus. MSR 62/2 (2005) 65-78.

6170 **Bloom, Antoine** La rencontre avec le Dieu vivant: lecture spirituelle de l'évangile selon saint Marc. Epiphanie: 2004 ⇒20,5901. [R]Contacts 57/1 (2005) 81-83 (*Minet, Jacques*).

6171 **Bolchi, Carlo M.M.** Satana, le fiere e gli angeli: il vangelo secondo Marco. 2004 ⇒20,5903. [R]Hum(B) 60 (2005) 629-631 (*Asciutto, Liborio*).

6172 *Boud'hors, Anne; Torallas Tovar, Sofía* Mc 1,1-11: la tradition manuscrite copte. MSR 62/2 (2005) 37-49.

6173 *Briglia, Sergio* Vangelo secondo san Marco. I vangeli. 2005 ⇒432. 557-671.

6174 **Burkett, Delbert R.** Rethinking the gospel sources: from proto-Mark to Mark. 2004 ⇒20,5905. [R]RBLit (2005)* (*Geyer, Douglas; Peabody, David*).

6175 *Cairoli, Marco* Il vangelo di Marco. Orientamenti bibliografici [Brescia] 26 (2005) 25-28.

6176 **Cardona Ramírez, Hernán** Jesús de Nazareth en el evangelio de San Marcos: comentarios bíblicos al ciclo litúrgico B. Medellín 2005, Univ. Pont. Bolivariana 320 pp. 958-696-4639. Bibl. [NTAb 50,390].

6177 **Carlson, Stephen C.** The gospel hoax: Morton Smith's invention of Secret Mark. Ment. *Clemens Alexandrinus*: Waco 2005, Baylor Univ. Pr. xix; 151 pp. $20. 1-932792-48-1. Bibl. 131-141. [R]ET 117 (2005) 66-68 (*Foster, Paul*).

6178 **Casalini, Nello** Introduzione a Marco. J 2005, Franciscan Printing Press 303 pp. 965-516-068-8;

6179 Lettura di Marco: narrativa, esegetica, teologica. ASBF 67: J 2005, Franciscan Printing Press 381 pp. 965-516-068-8.

6180 **Christ, Jennifer** Journeying with Mark: five minute preparation for each Sunday liturgy. NY 2005, Paulist iii; 76 pp. $8. 0-8091-4354-2.

6181 **Costa, G.** Il vangelo dei dodici: introduzione e teologia: lectio su brani scelti del vangelo di Marco. Messina 2005, Cooperativa S. Tommaso 166 pp.

6182 **Couture, André; Vouga, François** La présence du royaume: une nouvelle lecture de l'évangile de Marc. Genève 2005, Labor et F. 199 pp. €20. 2-8309-1155-5. [R]ASEs 22 (2005) 260-262 (*Mazza, Roberta*).

6183 **Crossley, James G.** The date of Mark's gospel: insight from the law in earliest christianity. JSNT.S 266: 2004 ⇒20,5906. [R]CBQ 67 (2005) 526-527 (*Maloney, Elliott C.*); JR 85 (2005) 649-650 (*Harrington, Daniel J.*) [Mk 7,1-23].

6184 **Dal Covolo, Enrico** 'E voi, chi dite che io sia?: il vangelo di Marco: per essere 'discepoli del Maestro?'. Quaderni di pastorale universitaria 1: R 2005, Lateran 64 pp. 88-465-0504-2.

6185 *Debié, Muriel* Marc 1,1-11: la tradition manuscrite syriaque. MSR 62/2 (2005) 27-35.

6186 **Donahue, John R.; Harrington, Daniel** The gospel of Mark. Sacra Pagina 2: 2002 ⇒18,5533... 20,5910. [R]RBLit 7 (2005) 328-331 (*Peterson, Dwight N.*);

6187 ColMn [2]2005 <2002>, Liturgical xv; 481 pp. Suppl. bibl.

6188 **Dormeyer, Detlev** Das Markusevangelium. Da:Wiss. 2005, 239 pp. €59.90. 3-534-15613-7.

6189 *Evans, Craig A.* How Mark writes. [F]STANTON, G. 2005 ⇒138. 135-148.

6190 **Fabris, Rinaldo** Marco. Assisi 2005, Citadella 390 pp.

6191 **Fallon, Michael** The gospel according to Saint Mark, an introductory commentary. 2002 ⇒19,5912. [R]ThirdM 8/3 (2005) 127-128 = 8/4 (2005) 101-102 (*Mattam, Joseph*).

6192 **Focant, Camille** L'évangile selon Marc. Comm. biblique, NT: 2004 ⇒20,5915. [R]RSR 93 (2005) 96-98 (*Miler, Jean*); RTL 36 (2005) 527-531 (*Lémonon, Jean-Pierre*); RB 112 (2005) 426-427 (*Poffet, J.-M.*); RBLit 7 (2005) 331-332 (*Kealy, Sean*).

6193 **France, Richard Thomas** The gospel of Mark: a commentary on the Greek text. NIGTC: 2002 ⇒18,5537... 20,5196. [R]RSR 93 (2005) 95-96 (*Miler, Jean*); RBLit 7 (2005) 326-328 (*Patton, Steve*).

6194 **Gauger, Hans-Martin** Vom Lesen und Wundern: das Markus-Evangelium. Fra 2005, Suhrkamp 134 pp. €15. 3-518-41729-0.

6195 **Graffy, Adrian** Take and read: the gospel of Mark. L 2005, Matthew James 150 pp. £9. 1-899-481-29X.

6196 **Greeven, Heinrich; Güting, Eberhard** Textkritik des Markusevangeliums. Theologie Forschung und Wissenschaft 11: Hamburg 2005, LIT (8); 768 pp. €100. 3-8258-6878-8. Bibl. 746-768.

6197 **Grün, Anselm** Gesù via alla libertà: il vangelo di Marco. Commento spirituale ai vangeli: Brescia 2005, Queriniana 176 pp. €11;

6198 Jesús, maestro de salvación: el evangelio de Marco. Teologia y espiritualidad: Estella 2005, Verbo Divino 139 pp.

6199 *Haelewyck, Jean C.* Marc 1,1-11: la tradition latine (Vetus Latina et Vulgate). MSR 62/2 (2005) 17-26.

6200 **Harrington, Daniel J.** What are they saying about Mark?. Mahwah, NJ 2005, Paulist vi; 94 pp. $13. 0-8091-4263-5. Bibl. [ThD 52,165 —W. Charles Heiser].

6201 *Kinukawa, Hisako* Mark. Global bible commentary. 2005 ⇒2443. 367-378.

6202 **Lavatori, Renzo; Sole, Luciano** Marco, I: interrogativi e sorprese su Gesù. Lettura pastorale della Bibbia, Bibbia e spiritualità 24: Bo 2005, Dehoniane 263 pp. €18.50. 88-1020161-2. Bibl. 257-260.

6203 [E]**Levine, Amy-Jill** A feminist companion to Mark. 2001 ⇒17,5147... 20,5921. [R]RBLit (2005)* (*Omerzu, Heike*).

6204 *Léonard, Philippe* Évangile de Jésus Christ selon saint Marc. CEv 133 (2005) 3-78.

6205 *Malevez, Marc* La tradition manuscrite éthiopienne de Marc 1,1-11. MSR 62/2 (2005) 79-89.

6206 **Margheri, F.; Noceti, S.; Sartor, P.** Le domande della fede: Marco il vangelo del catecumeno. Bo 2005, EDB 250 pp. €18. 8810502574.

6207 **Martin, George** The gospel according to Mark: message and meaning. Opening the scriptures: Ch 2005, Loyola xvii; 477 pp. $23. 0-82-94-1970-5. Bibl. 467-471 [BiTod 44,63—Donald Senior].

6208 **Moloney, Francis** The gospel of Mark: a commentary. 2002 ⇒18, 5544...20,5923. [R]Interp. 59 (2005) 416-18 (*Black, C. Clifton*); PIBA 28 (2005) 131-134 (*Harrington, Wilfrid J.*);

6209 Mark: storyteller, interpreter, evangelist. 2004 ⇒20,5924. [R]CBQ 67 (2005) 154-155 (*Rhoads, David*); CoTh 75/4 (2005) 225-228 (*Pawłowski, Zdisław*).

6210 **Mullins, Michael** The gospel of Mark: a commentary. Dublin 2005, Columba 506 pp. €20/£14. 1-85607-489-7. Bibl. 478-496 [R]IThQ 70 (2005) 375-376 (*Harrington, Wilfrid*).

6211 *Nightingale, J.R.* Practices in the composition of certain christian documents, and the purposes to which they were directed. JHiC 11/1 (2005) 95-117 [NTAb 50,43] [Mk 14,1-16,20].

6212 *Noceti, Serena* All'inizio la parola: leggere il vangelo di Marco con i catecumeni. Ambrosius 81/4 (2005) 731-742.

6213 **Osculati, Roberto** L'evangelo di Marco. Mi 2005, IPL 206 pp.

6214 *Outtier, Bernard* La tradition géorgienne de Marc 1,1-11 et 1,40-45. MSR 62/2 (2005) 51-63.

6215 *Perkins, Pheme* The gospel of Mark. NT survey. 2005 ⇒3144. 62-72.

6216 **Rhoads, David** Reading Mark, engaging the gospel. 2004 ⇒20,264. [R]RBLit (2005)* (*Driggers, Ira B.; Kealy, Sean; Verheyden, Joseph*).

6217 **Rodd, Cyril Stanley** The gospel of Mark. Peterborough 2005, Epworth xvii; 199 pp. 0-7162-0594-7. Bibl. xi-xii.

6218 **Roskam, Hendrika N.** The purpose of the gospel of Mark in its historical and social context. NT.S 114: 2004 ⇒20,5928. [R]JBL 124 (2005) 553-558 (*Crook, Zeba A.*); ET 117 (2005) 124 (*Foster, Paul*).

6219 **Sabin, Marie Noonan** Reopening the word: reading Mark as theology in the context of early Judaism. 2002 ⇒18,5555... 20,5929. [R]RBLit (2005)* (*Morrison, Gregg S.*).

6220 **Schenke, Ludger** Das Markusevangelium: literarische Eigenart—Text und Kommentierung. Stu 2005, Kohlhammer 357 pp. €32. 3-17-018938-7.

6221 *Scholtissek, Klaus* Grunderzählung des Heils: zum aktuellen Stand der Markusforschung. ThLZ 130 (2005) 858-880.

6222 **Stock, Klemens** Vangelo secondo Marco: introduzione e commento. Dabar: Padova [2]2005, Messagero 227 pp [AcBib 11,148].

6223 **Story, Cullen I.K.** The beginning of the gospel of Jesus Christ according to Mark: introduction and commentary. 2004 ⇒20,5932. [R]PSB 26 (2005) 248-250 (*Mauser, Ulrich*).

6224 **Thurston, Bonnie B.** Preaching Mark. 2001 ⇒17,5156... 20,5933. [R]RExp 102 (2005) 745-746 (*Sinner, Christopher W.*).

6225 **Van Cangh, Jean-Marie; Toumpsin, Alphonse** L'évangile de Marc: un original hébreu?. Langues et cultures anciennes 4: Bru 2005, Safran 460 pp. €60. 2-9600469-8-6.

6226 **Van Oyen, Geert** De Marcus code. Kampen 2005, Averbode 204 pp. €14.50. 90-435-1184-6.

6227 **Venetz, Hermann-Josef** Er geht euch voraus nach Galiläa: mit dem Markusevangelium auf dem Weg. FrS 2005, Paulus 230 pp. €18. 3-7228-0668-2 [BiKi 61,115—Dieter Bauer].

6228 *Verhelst, Stéphane* Les capitules du Codex Vaticanus et les péricopes liturgiques de Jérusalem: le cas de l'évangile selon Saint Marc. QLP 86 (2005) 273-283. Les notes se trouvent dans QLP 87, 220-225.

6229 *Voelz, James W.* The Greek of Codex Vaticanus in the second gospel and Marcan Greek. NT 47 (2005) 209-249;

6230 Textual criticism of the gospel of Mark: trying to make progress. ConJ 31/1 (2005) 2-11 [NTAb 49,270].

6231 **Witherington, Ben** The gospel of Mark: a socio-rhetorical commentary. 2001 ⇒17,5160... 20,5935. [R]BZ 49 (2005) 135-137 (*Feneberg, Rupert*); AsbTJ 60/2 (2005) 126-127 (*Carey, Greg*).

## F6.2 *Evangelium Marci*, **Themata**

6232 *Adams, Edward* The coming of the Son of Man in Mark's gospel. TynB 56/2 (2005) 39-61.

6233 *Aletti, Jean-Noël* La construction du personnage Jésus dans les récits évangeliques: le cas de Marc. Analyse narrative. BEThL 191: 2005 ⇒742. 19-42.

6234 **Babut, Jean-Marc** Pour lire Marc: mots et thèmes. 2004 ⇒20,5939. [R]CBQ 67 (2005) 521-523 (*Coloe, Mary L.*).

6235 *Becker, Eve-Marie* Der jüdisch-römische Krieg (66-70 n. Chr.) und das Markus-Evangelium: zu den 'Anfängen' frühchristlicher Historiographie. Antike Historiographie. BZNW 129: 2005 ⇒348. 213-236.

6236 **Becker, Eve-Marie** Das Markus-Evangelium im Rahmen antiker Historiographie: ein Beitrag zur Erforschung von Quellen, Redaktion und Gattung des frühesten Evangeliums. [D]*Wischmeyer, O.* 2005, Diss.-Habil. Erlangen-Nürnberg [ThLZ 130,882].

6237 *Bird, Michael* "Jesus is the Christ": messianic apologetics in the gospel of Mark. RTR 64/1 (2005) 1-14.

6238 *Black, C. Clifton* The face is familiar—I just can't place it. [M]JUEL, D. 2005 ⇒73. 33-49.

6239 **Bolt, Peter G.** Jesus' defeat of death: persuading Mark's early readers. MSSNTS 125: 2003 ⇒19,5939; 20,5941. [R]CBQ 67 (2005) 132-134 (*Beavis, Mary Ann*); SR 34 (2005) 127-129 (*Tuzlak, Ayse*); JBL

124 (2005) 560-562 (*Campbell, William Sanger*); JThS 56 (2005) 154-157 (*Upton, Bridget G.*).

6240 **Bonneau, Guy** Stratégies rédactionelles et fonctions communautaires de l'évangile de Marc. ÉtB 44: 2001 ⇒17,5170; 19,5940. [R]RSR 93 (2005) 103-105 (*Miler, Jean*).

6241 **Bourquin, Yvan** Marc, une théologie de la fragilité: obscure clarté d'une narration. MoBi 55: Genève 2005, Labor et F. 466 pp. €32. 2-8309-1174-1. Diss. Lausanne; Bibl. 443-463.

6242 **Carbullanca Núñez, César** Análisis del género pesher en el evangelio de Marcos: normas y motivos. [D]*Trebolle Barrera, J.* 2005, 660 pp. Diss. Madrid [RTL 37,614].

6243 **Casey, Maurice** Aramaic sources of Mark's gospel. MSSNTS 102: 1998 ⇒14,4688... 19,5943. [R]JSSt 50 (2005) 223-225 (*Klutz, Todd*).

6244 *Castro Sánchez, Secundino* Jesús, misionero, en Marcos. Biblia y nueva evangelización. 2005 ⇒491. 13-78.

6245 **Castro Sánchez, Secundino** El sorprendente Jesús de Marcos: el evangelio de Marcos por dentro. Bilbao 2005, Univ. Comillas 508 pp. 84-8468-169-6.

6246 *Chronis, Harry L.* To reveal and to conceal: a literary-critical perspective on 'the Son of Man' in Mark. NTS 51 (2005) 459-481.

6247 *Combrink, H.J. Bernard* Salvation in Mark. Salvation in the New Testament. NT.S 121: 2005 ⇒798. 33-66.

6248 *Crocker, Cornelia C.* Emotions as loopholes for answerability in the unfinalized gospel according to Mark. Ment. *Bakhtin, M.*: PRSt 32/3 (2005) 281-294.

6249 **Danove, Paul L.** Linguistics and exegesis in the gospel of Mark: applications of a case frame analysis. JSNT.S 218: 2001 ⇒17,5176... 20,5948. [R]BiblInterp 13 (2005) 209-211 (*Telford, W.R.*);

6250 The rhetoric of the characterization of God, Jesus, and Jesus' disciples in the gospel of Mark. JSNT.S 290: NY 2005, Clark xii; 190 pp. $55. 0-567-02810-0. Bibl. 174-183.

6251 **Di Palma, Gaetano** Sei tu il Cristo?: tra gesuologia e messianicità. Collana di cristologia 10: R 2005, Herder 323 pp. 88-87931-44-5. Bibl. 289-319.

6252 *Dube, Musa W.* Mark's healing stories in an AIDS context. Global bible commentary. 2005 ⇒2443. 379-384.

6253 *Elliott, Scott S.* "Witless in your own cause": divine plots and fractured characters in the "Life of Aesop" and the gospel of Mark. R&T 12 (2005) 397-418.

6254 *Fortin, Anne* Dalla profondità della fame. Conc(I) 41 2005, 225-234; Conc(D) 41,155-162.

6255 **Geyer, Douglas W.** Fear, anomaly, and uncertainty in the gospel of Mark. ATLA.MS 47: 2002 ⇒18,5580... 20,5955. [R]BiblInterp 13 (2005) 206-208 (*Wright, Stephen I.*).

6256 **Guttenberger, Gudrun** Die Gottesvorstellung im Markusevangelium. BZNW 123: 2004 ⇒20,5956. [R]CBQ 67 (2005) 342-343 (*Davids, Peter H.*).

6257 *Hensell, Eugene* Mark's gospel and Jesus' radical humanity. RfR 64 (2005) 424-428.

6258 *Holmås, Geir O.* Markusevangeliets renessanse som fortelling i resepsjonsteoretisk perspektiv. Ung teologi 38/3 (2005) 61-74.

6259 *Hooker, Morna D.* Isaiah in Mark's gospel. Isaiah in the NT. 2005 ⇒ 443. 35-49;

6260 "Who can this be?": the christology of Mark's gospel. Contours of christology. McMaster NT Studies 7: 2005 ⇒775. 79-99.

6261 **Horsley, Richard A.** Hearing the whole story: the politics of plot in Mark's gospel. 2001 ⇒17,5192... 20,5959. [R]BZ 49 (2005) 134-135 (*Feneberg, Rupert*).

6262 **Incigneri, Brian J.** The gospel to the Romans: the setting and rhetoric of Mark's gospel. BiblInterp 65: 2003 ⇒19,5961; 20,5960. [R]JBL 124 (2005) 553-558 (*Crook, Zeba A.*); RBLit (2005)* (*Bird, Michael; Peterson, Dwight N.*).

6263 **Iverson, Kelly** 'Even the dogs under the table eat the children's crumbs': a literary and theological study of the gentiles in the gospel of Mark. [D]**Moloney, Francis J.** 2005, 334 pp. Diss. Catholic Univ. of America [RTL 37,615].

6264 *Joynes, Christine E.* The returned Elijah?: John the Baptist's angelic identity in the gospel of Mark. SJTh 58 (2005) 455-467.

6265 *Kealey, Séan P.* Recent reflections on the gospel according to Mark. BTB 35 (2005) 82-88.

6266 *Kloppenborg, John S.* Evocatio deorum and the date of Mark. JBL 124 (2005) 419-450 [Mk 13,1-2; 13,14].

6267 **Knijpenga, Siegwart** Nietsis verborgen: kosmische dimensies in het Marcus-evangelie. 2004 ⇒20,5963. [R]ITBT 13/7 (2005) 31-32 (*Hanhart, Karel*).

6268 *Léon-Dufour, Xavier* Dal presente alla presenza secondo il vangelo. Un biblista cerca Dio. 2005 <1989> ⇒245. 259-273.

6269 *MacDonald, Dennis R.* Hyperche he Maria Magdalene prin ten epinoesei ho Markos?. DBM 23/1 (2005) 97-113. **G.**

6270 **Malina, Artur** Gli scribi nel vangelo di Marco: studio del loro ruolo nella sua narrazione e teologia. 2002 ⇒18,5604... 20,5970. [R]RCatT 30/1 (2005) 229-231 (*Borrell, Agustí*).

6271 **Maloney, Elliott C.** Jesus' urgent message for today: the kingdom of God in Mark's gospel. 2004 ⇒20,5971. [R]NewTR 18/2 (2005) 84-85 (*Cavanaugh, Ellen*).

6272 **Miller, Susan** Women in Mark's gospel. JSNT.S 259: 2004 ⇒20, 5974. [R]RBLit (2005)* (*Bauman-Martin, Betsy*).

6273 **Mrakovcic, Bozidar** La triplice chiamata di Pietro nel vangelo di Marco. [D]*Stock, Klemens* 2005, Diss. Gregoriana [RTL 37,616].

6274 *Murchison, D. Cameron* Unsettling generosity: fearful disciples on this side of the text. [M]JUEL, D. 2005 ⇒73. 51-64.

6275 **Naluparayil, Jacob C.** The identity of Jesus in Mark: an essay on narrative christology. SBFA 49: 2000 ⇒16,5191... 20,5980. [R]RSR 93 (2005) 98-99 (*Miler, Jean*).

6276 *Niedner, Frederick* Precious, inevitable scandal: theology of the cross in Mark. CThMi 32 (2005) 417-425.

6277 *Nouis, Antoine* Proposition de plan de l'évangile de Marc. Ḥokhma 87 (2005) 32-60.

6278 *Nowell, Irene* Peter in the gospels of Mark and Matthew. BiTod 43 (2005) 216-221.

6279 *O'Loughlin, T.* Proclaiming Christ in the year of Mark. PaRe 1/6 (2005) 24-28 [NTAb 50,272].

6280 *Osculati, Roberto* Rito ed etica: per una lettura dell'evangelo di Marco. Synaxis 23/1 (2005) 19-28.

6281 *Pickett, Raymond* Following Jesus in Galilee: resurrection as empowerment in the gospel of Mark. CThMi 32 (2005) 434-444.

6282 *Riches, John* Introduction to John J. Vincent's 'outworkings'. ET 116 (2005) 153-154.
6283 *Rosik, Mariusz* Chrzest Jezusa jako zapowiedź i figura jego śmierci: analiza narracji Markowych [Baptême de Jésus comme annonce et figure de sa mort: analyse des narrations de saint Marc]. AtK 145 (2005) 95-110. **P**.
6284 *Salvatore, Emilio* Il mistero del messia nel vangelo di Marco: per una nuova formulazione del segreto messianico. RdT 46 (2005) 485-517.
6285 *Senior, Donald* Preaching Mark. NewTR 18/3 (2005) 85-87.
6286 **Shiner, Whitney** Proclaiming the gospel: first century performance of Mark. 2003 ⇒19,5994. [R]CBQ 67 (2005) 157-158 (*Kelber, Werner, H.*); RBLit (2005)* (*Morrison, Gregg*).
6287 **Stewart, Eric** Gathered around Jesus: an alternative spatial practice in the gospel of Mark. [D]*Neyrey, Jerome* 2005, 324 pp. Diss. Notre Dame [RTL 37,618].
6288 *Vaage, Leif E.* En otra casa: el discipulado en Marcos como ascetismo doméstico. EstB 63 (2005) 21-42.
6289 *Vignolo, Roberto* La recherche de Jésus comme forme du récit évangélique: un exemple à partir de l'évangile de Marc. Analyse narrative. BEThL 191: 2005 ⇒742. 537-546.
6290 *Vincent, John J.* Outworkings: the practice of disciples. ET 116 (2005) 155-159;
6291 Outworkings: next steps. ET 116 (2005) 334-335.
6292 **Vines, Michael E.** The problem of Markan genre: the gospel of Mark and the Jewish novel. Academia biblica 3: 2002 ⇒18,5631... 20,6002. [R]BiblInterp 13 (2005) 96-99 (*Cummins, S.A.*).
6293 *Wainwright, Elaine M.* Telling stories of healing in a broken world. [F]MOLONEY, F.: BSRel 187: 2005 ⇒104. 231-247.
6294 **Watson, David F.** Honor among christians: a reassessment of the 'Messianic Secret'. [D]*Bassler, J.M.* 2005, 266 pp. Diss. Dallas, Southern Methodist [RTL 37,619].
6295 **Weihs, Alexander** Die Deutung des Todes Jesu im Markusevangelium: eine exegetische Studie zu den Leidens- und Auferstehungsansagen. FzB 99: 2003 ⇒19,6004; 20,6004. [R]RBLit 7 (2005) 335-338 (*Geyer, Douglas W.*); BiLi 79 (2006) 73-75 (*Bruners, Wilhelm*) [Mk 8,31; 9,31; 10,33-34].
6296 *West, Audrey* Preaching the mysteries of the reign of God. CThMi 32 (2005) 406-416.
6297 *Winter, Martin* Jesu Weg und der Weg der Jünger: zur literarischen und theologischen Bedeutung des Weges im Markusevangelium. WuD 28 (2005) 73-88.

## F6.3 **Evangelii Marci versiculi**

6298 *Kilgallen, John* Life in Jesus Christ: two exegetical reflections. ChiSt 44 (2005) 273-283 [NTAb 50,274] [Mk 1,1; Lk 22,39-46].
6299 *Lobo, A.* Are the words 'Son of God' in Mark 1,1 original or an omission?. BiBh 31 (2005) 183-199.
6300 *Miller, Susan* Mark 1:1-8. ET 117 (2005) 70-72.
6301 *Moyise, Steve* The wilderness quotation in Mark 1.2-3. [F]YOUNG, F.: JSNT.S 295: 2005 ⇒168. 78-87.

6302 *Kelhoffer, James A.* Early christian studies among the academic disciplines: reflections on John the Baptist's 'Locusts and wild honey'. BR 50 (2005) 5-17 [Mk 1,6];

6303 John the Baptist's 'wild honey' and 'honey' in antiquity. GRBS 45/1 (2005) 59-73 [Mk 1,6].

6304 *Pérez Herrero, Francisco* Conversión y fe: respuesta del hombre al evangelio de Dios (Mc 1,14-15). Burg. 46 (2005) 333-346.

6305 *Käsemann, Ernst* Markus 1,16-20: von der Nachfolge des Kommenden. In der Nachfolge. 2005 ⇒236. 315-321.

6306 **Peron, Gian Paolo** Seguitemi!: vi farò diventare pescatori di uomini (Mc 1,17): gli imperativi ed esortativi di Gesù ai discepoli come elementi di un loro cammino formativo. 2000 ⇒16,5226... 18,5644. [R]Anton. 80 (2005) 390-391 (*Stamm, Heinz-Meinolf*).

6307 *Jodoin, Danielle* Jésus impose le silence, les démons crient: étude narratologique d'une toute-puissance controversée: Mc 1,21-28. Scriptura(M) 7/1 (2005) 27-38.

6308 *Hipólito, Isaías* Jesus 'perseguido' pelos discípulos e 'procurado' por 'todos': uma leitura narrativa de Mc 1,35-39 à luz de 1 Sam 23,15-28. Did(L) 35 (2005) 149-174.

6309 *Selvarajah, M.* The truth of the gospel and christian leadership: a human rights perspective: biblical reflections on Mark 1:40-45. SLJTR 1/1 (2005) 32-35 [NTAb 50,274].

6310 *Ehrman, Bart D.* Did Jesus get angry or agonize?: a test critic pursues the original Jesus story. BiRe 21/5 (2005) 17-26, 49-50 [NTAb 50,275] [Mk 1,41; Lk 22,43-44].

6311 *Koskenniemi, Erkki Iannes redivivus* and the help from Beelzebub (Mark 3:22). [F]AEJMELAEUS, L.: SESJ 89: 2005 ⇒1. 62-70.

6312 *Alkier, Stefan* Die Bibel im Dialog der Schriften und das Problem der Verstockung in Mk 4: Intertextualität im Rahmen einer kategorialen Semiotik biblischer Texte. Die Bibel im Dialog. NET 10: 2005 ⇒333. 1-22.

6313 *Leandro, José C.* A linguagem corporale e as parábolas: uma análise a partir de Mc 4,1-9. Estudos bíblicos 87 (2005) 80-89.

6314 *Frangi, Abdallah* Die Saat des Friedens (Markus 4,1-9.13-20). Kanzelreden. 2005 ⇒376. 89-93.

6315 *Beauchamp, Paul* Paraboles de Jésus, vie de Jésus: l'encadrement évangélique et scripturaire des paraboles (Mc 4,1-34). Pages exégétiques. LeDiv 202: 2005 <1989> ⇒183. 385-404.

6316 *Niemand, Christoph* Das Geheimnis der Gottesherrschaft und die Verhärtung der Herzen: Markus 4,11-12 und Jesaja 6,9-10. PzB 14 (2005) 35-47.

6317 *Cardona Ramírez, Hernán* La parábola del grano de mostaza–hacia una prospectiva de Mc 4,30-32. El grano. 2005 <2004> ⇒197. 39-53.

6318 *Käsemann, Ernst* Die Heilung der Besessenen: neutestamentliche Gesichtspunkte zur Heilung der Krankheit unserer Zeit. In der Nachfolge. 2005⇒236. 191-201 [Mk 5].

6319 **Aus, Roger D.** My name Is "Legion": Palestinian Judaic traditions in Mark 5:1-20 and other gospel texts. Studies in Judaism: Lanham, Md. 2003, University Press of America 364 pp. $39. [R]RBLit (2005)* (*Evans, Craig*).

6320 *Joy, C.I.D.* Mark 5:1-20: a postcolonial subaltern reading. BTF 37/2 (2005) 26-39 [NTAb 50,488].

6321 **Newheart, Michael Willett** "My name is legion": the story and soul of the Gerasene demoniac. Interfaces: 2004 ⇒20,6035. [R]Furrow 56 (2005) 638-640 (*O'Connell, Séamus*); IThQ 70 (2005) 183-4 (*Lynch, Fiona*); RBLit (2005)* (*Kille, D.; Blessing, Kamila*) [Mk 5,1-20].

6322 *Bonneau, Normand* Suspense in Mark 5:21-43: a narrative study of two healing stories. Theoforum 36/2 (2005) 131-154 [Mt 9,18-26].

6323 *Bromley, Donald Howard* The healing of the hemorrhaging woman: miracle or magic?. ProcGLM 25 (2005) 15-27 [Mk 5,24-34].

6324 **Estévez López, Elisa** El poder de una mujer creyente: cuerpo, identidad y discipulado en Mc 5,24b-34. 2003 ⇒19,6037; 20,6039. [R]Bib. 86 (2005) 565-568 (*Bonifacio, Gianattilio*).

6325 *Powell, Charles E.* The "passivity" of Jesus in Mark 5:25-34. BS 162/645 (2005) 66-75.

6326 *Hoffeditz, David M.; Yates, Gary E.* Femme fatale redux: intertextual connection to the Elijah/Jezebel narratives in Mark 6:14-29. BBR 15 (2005) 199-221.

6327 *Metzdorf, Justina* Väterexegese als ein Schlüssel zum Bibelverständnis: ein Beitrag am Beispiel des Brotwunders (Mk 6,33-44 parr). rhs 48 (2005) 170-177.

6328 *Ballhorn, Egbert* Zu neuen Ufern: Bibel lesen schrittweise. BiHe 41/162 (2005) 4-7 [Mk 6,45-52].

6329 *Riedl, Hermann J.* Der Seewandel Jesu Mk 6,45-52 parr.: eine Epiphanieerzählung und ihre textpragmatische Intention. SNTU.A 30 (2005) 5-17.

6330 *Elliott, J.H.* Jesus, Mark, and the evil eye. LTJ 39/2-3 (2005) 157-168 [NTAb 50,41] [Mk 7,1-23].

6331 *Guida, Annalisa* 'Cosí dichiarava puri tutti i cibi...' (Mc 7,19c): Marco interprete di Gesù alla luce di Paolo?: ipotesi sulla ricezione di un–presunto–*dictum Iesu*. Giudei o cristiani?. 2005 ⇒833. 123-133.

6332 *Alonso, Pablo* La mujer sirofenicia en la interpretación patrística. EE 80 (2005) 455-483 [Mk 7,24-30].

6333 *Chadwallader, A.H.* What's in a name?: the tenacity of a tradition of interpretation. LTJ 39/2-3 (2005) 218-234 [NTAb 50,14] [Mk 7,24-30].

6334 *Delorme, Jean* Passage de frontière: Jesus et une Syrophénicienne (7, 24-30). SémBib 119 (2005) 10-31.

6335 **Muthiah, Arul Jesu Robin** Jesus—Giver of life: composition and interpretation of Mark 7:31-9:50. [D]*Meynet, Roland*: Chennai 2005, Claretian 400 pp. Diss.Gregoriana; Bibl. 345-364.

6336 **Larsen, Kevin W.** Seeing and understanding Jesus: a literary and theological commentary on Mark 8:22-9:13. [D]*Moloney, Francis J.*: Lanham 2005, University Press of America xx; 218 pp. 0-7618-3209-2. Diss. Catholic Univ. of America; Bibl. 173-194.

6337 *Larsen, Kevin W.* A focused christological reading of Mark 8:22-9:13. TrinJ 26 (2005) 33-46.

6338 *Kwan, Lai Man* The meaning of discipleship according to Mk 8,22-10,52. ThLi 28 (2005) 173-185 Sum. 184s. C.

6339 **Salvatore, Emilio** "E vedeva a distanza ogni cosa": il racconto della guarigione del cieco di Betsaida (Mc 8,22-26). Aloisiana 32: 2003 ⇒ 19,6041; 20,6054. [R]LASBF 55 (2005) 551-554 (*Bissoli, Giovanni*).

6340 **Traore, Côme** L'aveugle de Bethsaïde (Mc 8,22-26): les disciples entre 'sequela' et incompréhension. R 2005, Diss. Lateranum [RTL 37,619].

6341 **St. Clair, Raquel Annette** Call and consequences: a sociolinguistic reading through a womanist cultural lens of Mark 8:31-38. 2005, Diss. Princeton, Sem. [RTL 37,618].

6342 *Hatina, Thomas R.* Who will see "the kingdom of God coming with power" in Mark 9,1—protagonists or antagonists?. Bib. 86 (2005) 20-34 [Mk 8,38; 13,26; 14,62].

6343 **Sesadima, Silvadima** The theological significance of Mark 9,1 in the context of discipleship. R 2005, n.p. 134 pp. Bibl. 107-131.

6344 **Schreiber, Hannes** Die Metamorphosis Jesu und die Wolkenstimme: Mk 9,2-8 par; 2 Petr 2,16-18 und deren Wirkungsgeschichte in der Ostkirche. D*Kühschelm, Roman* 2005, Diss. Wien [ThRv 102,xii].

6345 **Brandt, Pierre-Yves** L'identité de Jésus et l'identité de son disciple: le récit de la transfiguration comme clef de lecture de l'Évangile de Marc. NTOA 50: 2002 ⇒18,5682; 20,6061. RRSR 93 (2005) 100-102 (*Miler, Jean*) [Mk 9,2-10].

6346 *Tuor-Kurth, Christina* Nochmals: "Wer eines solcher Kinder aufnimmt": ein Beitrag zur sozialgeschichtlichen Auslegung von Mk 9, 35-37. FSTEGEMANN, E. 2005 ⇒139. 87-99.

6347 **Progorowicz, Magdalena** Le voyage de Jésus à Jérusalem (Mc 10, 2-30. 35-52) dans les commentaires aux lectures des messes dominicales publiés dans des sélections hebdomadaires catholiques postconciliaires: étude biblique et pastorale. D*Bielecki, S.* 2005, 282 pp. Diss. Lublin [RTL 37,617]. **P.**

6348 *Ebner, Martin* "Lasst die Kinder zu mir kommen ...": das "Kinderevangelium" des Markus. BiHe 41/163 (2005) 14-16 [Mk 10,10-16].

6349 *Schavan, Annette* Der Stachel der Freiheit (Markus 10,17-27). Kanzelreden. 2005 ⇒376. 95-101.

6350 *Crossley, James G.* The damned rich (Mark 10:17-31). ET 116 (2005) 397-401.

6351 **Landgrave Gándara, Daniel R.** El proyecto de Jesús: una familia nueva: ricos y pobres en Mc 10,17-31: estudio exegético-teológico. Biblicos estudios 17: México 1997, Dabar 237 pp. Diss. REfMex 67 (2005) 128-131 (*Díaz, Carlos*).

6352 **Kaminouchi, Alberto de Mingo** "But it is not so among you": echoes of power in Mark 10.32-45. JSNT.S 249: 2003 ⇒19,6061; 20,6073. RJBL 124 (2005) 558-560 (*Campbell, William Sanger*).

6353 *Pitre, Brant* The 'ransom for many,' the new exodus, and the end of the exile: redemption as the restoration of all Israel (Mark 10:35-45). L&S 1 (2005) 41-68.

6354 *Landgrave G., Daniel R.* Glorias y patologías del poder en la iglesia: meditación teológica en torno a Mc 10,35-45. FJUNCO GARZA, C.: Estudios Bíblicos Mexicanos 4: 2005 ⇒74. 285-326.

6355 **Uzowulu, C. Cosmas** Ambition and rivalry among the chosen: an exegetico-theological study of Mark 10,35-45 and its centrality in the gospel of Mark. D*Juric, S.*: R 2005, xiv; 204 pp. Diss. Angelicum; Bibl. 179-204.

6356 *Aichele, George* The politics of sacrifice. BiCT 1/2 (2005)* [Mk 10, 45].

6357 *Menken, M.J.J.* The call of blind Bartimaeus (Mark 10:46-52). HTSTS 61/1-2 (2005) 273-290 [NTAb 50,276].

6358 *Esler, Philip F.* The incident of the withered fig tree in Mark 11: a new source and redactional explanation. JSNT 28 (2005) 41-67 [Mk 14,1-17].

6359 *Vledder, E.-J.* Was Jezus' optreden in de tempel een reiniging?. HTSTS 61/1-2 (2005) 593-617 [NTAb 50,277] [Mk 11,12-18].

6360 **Peguero Pérez, Javier** La figura de Dios en los diálogos de Jesús con las autoridades en el templo: lectura de Mc 11,27-12,23 a partir de su instancia comunicativa. TGr.T 113: 2004 ⇒20,6081. [R]CBQ 67 (2005) 537-539 (*Swetnam, James*); RevBib 67 (2005) 245-247 (*Doldán, Felipe Luis*).

6361 *Mikołajczak, Mieczysław* Działalność Jezusa w świątyni jerozolimskiej-teologia HIERON (Mk 12). CoTh 75/1 (2005) 5-45. **P**.

6362 *Fast, Lesley* Rejection and reinstatement (Mark 12:1-11): the rhetoric of represented speech in Mark. Neotest. 39 (2005) 111-126.

6363 *Brandt, Pierre-Yves* Erzählung und Identitätsbildung: die Spiegelfunktion von Mk 12,1-12 in der Konstruktion der Identität Jesu. EvTh 65 (2005) 135-147.

6364 *Aguilar, Mario I.* The archaeology of memory and the issue of colonialism: mimesis and the controversial tribute to Caesar in Mark 12:13-17. BTB 35 (2005) 60-66.

6365 *McDaniel, Karl J.* Tax evasion honour intact: rendering Caesar his due. Scriptura(M) 7/1 (2005) 49-62 [Mk 12,13-17].

6366 *Wegner, Uwe* Jesus und die kaiserlichen Steuern: Mk 12,13-17. [F]STEGEMANN, W. 2005 ⇒139. 161-170.

6367 **Keerankeri, George** The love commandment in Mark: an exegetico-theological study of Mk 12,28-34. AnBib 150: 2003 ⇒19,6078. [R]RSR 93 (2005) 105-106 (*Miler, Jean*); Neotest. 39 (2005) 452-454 (*Nel, Marius*).

6368 *Jossa, Giorgio* La domanda di Gesú sul figlio di David: Mc 12,35-37. [F]GHIBERTI, G.: SRivBib 46: 2005 ⇒47. 231-239.

6369 *Kern, Karl* Jesus und die arme Witwe. GuL 78 (2005) 470-473 [Mk 12,41-44].

6370 *West, Gerald* Structural sin: a South African perspective. Ung teologi 38/1 (2005) 15-26 [Mk 12,41-44].

6371 *Mikołajczak, Mieczysław* Mowa eschatologiczna Jezusa—teologia ἱερόν (Mk 13) [Die eschatologische Rede Jesu—Theologie von ἱερόν (Mk 13)]. RBL 58 (2005) 119-132. **P**.

6372 *Verbaas, Frans Willem* 'Leven in de breedte': een literaire illustratie bij Marcus 13. ITBT 13/3 (2005) 16-18.

6373 *Zuurmond, Rochus* Marcus 13 en de 'De laatste dingen'. ITBT 13/3 (2005) 13-16.

## F6.8 **Passio secundum Marcum**, 14,1...[⇒F5.3]

6374 *Doi, Yumi* Zur Forschung über die Passionsgeschichte des Markusevangeliums. AJBI 30-31 (2004-2005) 125-136.

6375 *Fander, Monika* "Mein Gott, mein Gott, warum hast du mich verlassen?" (Mk 15,34): (Kriegs-)Traumatisierung als Thema des Markusevangeliums. Christologie im Lebensbezug. 2005 ⇒577. 116-156.

6376 *Focant, Camille* Finale suspendue et prolepses de l'au-delà du récit: l'exemple de Marc. Analyse narrative. BEThL 191: 2005 ⇒742. 211-222 [[Mk 13; 14; 16].

6377 *Guijarro, Santiago* El relato pre-marcano de la pasión como fuente para el estudio de la generación apostólica. ASEs 22/2 (2005) 305-335.

6378 *Lescow, Theodor* Die Markuspassion: eine antike Tragödie. BN 127 (2005) 91-104.

6379 *Reid, Barbara E.* Telling Mark's story of the passion. CThMi 32 (2005) 426-433.

6380 *Hearon, Holly* The art of biblical interpretation: re-membering the past into the present. Encounter 66/3 (2005) 189-197 [NTAb 50,43] [Mk 14,3-9];

6381 The story of 'the woman who anointed Jesus' as social memory: a methodological proposal for the study of tradition as memory. Memory, tradition, and text. 2005 ⇒416. 99-118 [Mk 14,3-9].

6382 *La Barge, Karen Fitz* Who prepared the feast?: women disciples prepare the passover in Mark 14,12-17. ProcGLM 25 (2005) 121-34.

6383 *Schenk, Wolfgang* Die Rezeption der paulinischen Herrenmahlworte bei Markus. [F]STOLLE, V.: Theologie: Forschung und Wissenschaft 12: 2005 ⇒143. 261-270 [Mk 14,22-25; 1 Cor 11,23-26].

6384 *Edmonds, Peter* The 'history' in Ignatian contemplation: from the Last Supper to the garden. Way 44/2 (2005) 21-36 [Mk 14,26-52].

6385 *Thériault, Jean Y.* L'acceptation de la coupe quand passe l'heure en Mc 14,26-52. [F]GENEST, O. 2005 ⇒46. 417-433.

6386 *Manicardi, Ermenegildo* La paura di Gesù al Getsemani nel racconto secondo Marco. Gesù la cristologia. 2005 <1996> ⇒253. 133-146 [Mk 14,32-42].

6387 *Gundry, Robert H.* Jesus' blasphemy according to Mark 14:61b-64 and *Mishnah Sanhedrin* 7:5. The old is better. WUNT 178: 2005 ⇒ 220. 98-110.

6388 *Piskorski, Dariusz* Vedere il Cristo stabilire il suo regno (Mc 14, 62b). Ricerche teologiche 16/1 (2005) 59-69.

6389 *Štrba, Blažej* Čo urobil Peter, ked' kohút druhýkrát zaspieval?: filologická poznámka k slovesu ἐπιβάλλω v Mk 14,72 [What has Peter done, when the cock crowed a second time?: a philological note on the verb ἐπιβάλλω in Mk 14,72]. SBSl (2005) 60-72. **Slovak**.

6390 **Louder, David K.** Mark's poem of the passion (15:16-26): a study in poetics and biblical interpretation. 2005, Diss. Princeton, Sem.

6391 *Koskenniemi, Erkki; Nisula, Kirsi; Toppari, Jorma* Wine mixed with myrrh (Mark 15.23) and crurifragium (John 9.31-32): two details of the passion narratives. JSNT 27 (2005) 379-391.

6392 *Manicardi, Ermenegildo* Gesù e la sua morte secondo Mc 15,33-37. Gesù la cristologia. 2005 <1984> ⇒253. 147-163.

6393 *Lupo, Maria* Il 'forte grido' della parola (Mc 15,37). LSDC 20 (2005) 255-272.

6394 *Byrne, Brendan* Paul and Mark before the cross: common echoes of the day of atonement ritual. [F]MOLONEY, F.: BSRel 187: 2005 ⇒104. 217-229 [Exod 25-26; Lev 16; Mk 15,37-39; Rom 3,25].

6395 *Catalano, Rosann M.* A matter of perspective: an alternative reading of Mark 15:38. Seeing Judaism anew. 2005 ⇒618. 187-199.

6396 *Kirby, Peter* The case against the empty tomb. The empty tomb. 2005 ⇒435. 233-260 [Mk 16].

6397 *Trainor, Michael* Intertextuality, the hermeneutics of "other", and Mark 16:6-7: a new but not new challenge for biblical interpreters. BTB 35 (2005) 144-150.

6398 *Brossier, François* 'Il vous précède en Galilée...' (Mc 16,7). RICP 96 (2005) 187-191.

6399 *Blount, Brian K.* Is the joke on us?: Mark's irony, Mark's God, and Mark's ending. [M]JUEL, D. 2005 ⇒73. 15-32 [Mk 16,8].

6400 *Juel, Donald H.* A disquieting silence: the matter of the ending. [M]JUEL, D. 2005 <1994> ⇒73. 1-13 [Mk 16,8].

6401 **Kelhoffer, James A.** Miracle and mission: the authentication of missionaries and their message in the longer ending of Mark. WUNT 2/ 112: 2000, ⇒16,5316... 19,6117. [R]ZNT 8/1 (2005) 69-71 (*Dronsch, Kristina*) [Mk 16,9-20].

6402 *Kuske, D.P.* Mark 16:9-20. WLQ 102/1 (2005) 58-59 [NTAb 50,43].

6403 *Zamagni, Claudio* L'état canonique du texte face à ses variantes: EUSÈBE et Mc 16,9-20. Adamantius 11 (2005) 133-142.

## X. Opus Lucanum

### F7.1 *Opus Lucanum*—Luke-Acts

6404 *Alexander, Loveday Septuaginta, Fachprosa, imitatio*: Albert Wifstrand and the language of Luke-Acts. Acts in its ancient literary context. LNTS 298: 2005 <2004> ⇒174. 231-252.

6405 *Bartholomew, Craig G.; Holt, Robby* Prayer in/and the drama of redemption in Luke: prayer and exegetical performance. Reading Luke. 2005 ⇒710. 350-375.

6406 *Berder, Michel* Quelques traits d'humour dans la présentation du personnage de Jésus en Luc-Actes. Analyse narrative. BEThL 191: 2005 ⇒742. 547-58 [Lk 2,40-52; 10,29-37; 24,13-35; Acts 19,15; 25,19].

6407 *Borse, Udo* Gedanken zur Entstehung des lukanischen Doppelwerks. [F]ZMIJEWSKI, J.: BBB 151: 2005 ⇒172. 1-6.

6408 *Bovon, François* La mort de Jésus en Luc-Actes: la perspective sotériologique. [F]GENEST, O. 2005 ⇒46. 359-374.

6409 *Brooke, George J.* Luke-Acts and the Qumran scrolls: the case of MMT. Dead Sea scrolls and the NT. 2005 <1995> ⇒194. 158-176.

6410 *Castillo Chouza, Ana L.* La mujer en la iglesia doméstica lucana. [F]JUNCO GARZA, C.: 2005 ⇒74. 327-352 [Acts 16,11-15].

6411 *Catto, Stephen* A critical analysis of the present state of synagogue research and its implications for the study of Luke-Acts. [D]*Gathercole, Simon J.*: 2005, Diss. Aberdeen [TynB 57,313-315].

6412 *Collins, Raymond F.* "The man who came to dinner". [F]DENAUX, A.: BEThL 182: 2005 ⇒34. 151-172.

6413 *Croatto, José Severino* Jesus, prophet like Elijah, and prophet-teacher like Moses in Luke-Acts. JBL 124 (2005) 451-465.

6414 **Franklin, Eric** Luke: interpreter of Paul, critic of Matthew. JSNT.S 92: 1994, ⇒10,4882. [R]ThR 70 (2005) 46-47 (*Lindemann, Andreas*).

6415 **Fusco, Vittorio** Da Paolo a Luca: studi su Luca-Atti, 2. StBi 139: 2003 ⇒19,6131; 20,6132. [R]RivBib 53 (2005) 246-248 (*Rossé, Gérard*); VivH 16 (2005) 431-433 (*Tarocchi, Stefano*).

6416 **Garrison, Roman** The significance of Theophilus as Luke's reader . SBEC 62: Lewiston (N.Y.) 2004, Mellen iv; 117 pp. 0-7734-6384-4. Bibl. 99-110.

6417 *Giesen, Heinz* "Noch heute wirst du mit mir im Paradies sein" (Lk 23,43): zur individuellen Eschatologie im lukanischen Doppelwerk. [F]ZMIJEWSKI, J.: BBB 151: 2005 ⇒172. 151-177 [Lk 23,33-43].

6418 *Goheen, Michael* A critical examination of David Bosch's missional reading of Luke. Reading Luke. 2005 ⇒710. 229-264.

6419 **Gradl, Hans-Georg** Zwischen Arm und Reich: das lukanische Doppelwerk in leserorientierter und textpragmatischer Perspektive. [D]*Beutler, Johannes*: FzB 107: Wü 2005, Echter 500 pp. 3-429-0274-1-1. Diss. Gregoriana; Bibl. 461-490.

6420 *Grappe, Christian* De Zacharie à Jésus ressuscité, la construction de la figure du prêtre de part et d'autre de l'évangile selon Luc et au début des Actes. Analyse narrative. BEThL 191: 2005 ⇒742. 297-308 [Lk 1; 24].

6421 *Green, Joel B.* Learning theological interpretation from Luke. Reading Luke. 2005 ⇒710. 55-78.

6422 **Gregory, Andrew** The reception of Luke and Acts in the period before IRENAEUS: looking for Luke in the second century. WUNT 2/169: 2003 ⇒19,6134; 20,6138. [R]ThLZ 130 (2005) 387-388 (*Buschmann, Gerd*).

6423 **Hagene, Sylvia** Zeiten der Wiederherstellung: Studien zur lukanischen Geschichtstheologie als Soteriologie. NTA 42: 2003 ⇒19, 6135; 20,6139. [R]ThLZ 130 (2005) 770-773 (*Böttrich, Christfried*); BZ 49 (2005) 286-288 (*Neubrand, Maria*); CBQ 67 (2005) 148-150 (*Stenschke, Christoph*) [Acts 3].

6424 *Hahn, Scott W.* Kingdom and church in Luke-Acts: from Davidic christology to kingdom ecclesiology. Reading Luke. 2005 ⇒710. 294-326.

6425 *Hays, Richard B.* Die Befreiung Israels im lukanischen Doppelwerk: intertextuelle Narration als kulturkritische Praxis. Die Bibel im Dialog. NET 10: 2005 ⇒333. 117-136.

6426 *Hedrick, Pamela* The Good Samaritan, Cornelius, and the just use of force. Acts and ethics. 2005 ⇒464. 123-134 [Lk 10,25-37; Acts 10].

6427 *Heil, Christoph; Klampfl, Thomas* Theophilos (Lk 1,3; Apg 1,1). [F]ZMIJEWSKI, J.: BBB 151: 2005 ⇒172. 7-28.

6428 **Heusler, Erika** Kapitalprozesse im Lukanischen Doppelwerk: die Verfahren gegen Jesus und Paulus in exegetischer und rechtshistorischer Analyse. NTA 38: 2000 ⇒16,5341... 19,6138. [R]ThR 70 (2005) 76-78 (*Lindemann, Andreas*).

6429 *Johnson, Luke T.* Literary criticism of Luke-Acts: is reception-history pertinent?. JSNT 28 (2005) 159-162.

6430 *Kalervo, Salo* Luke's story of the Old Testament. [F]AEJMELAEUS, L.: SESJ 89: 2005 ⇒1. 116-139.

6431 *Klein, Hans* Der soziale Stand des Lukas;

6432 Die Bildung des Lukas;

6433 Rechtfertigung aus Glauben als Ergänzung der Rechtfertigung durch das Gesetz <1998> [Acts 13,38-39]. Lukasstudien. FRLANT 209: 2005 ⇒239. 26-32/32-40/140-148.

6434 **Klutz, Todd E.** The exorcism stories in Luke-Acts: a sociostylistic reading. MSSNTS 129: 2004 ⇒20,6144. [R]ScrB 35 (2005) 115-117 (*Docherty, Susan*); JR 85 (2005) 653-654 (*Brawley, Robert L.*); RBLit (2005)* (*Kealy, Sean*); JThS 56 (2005) 543-548 (*Twelftree, Graham H.*).

6435 *Koet, Bart J.* Isaiah in Luke-Acts. Isaiah in the NT. 2005 ⇒443. 79-100.

6436 *Koperski, Veronika* Is "Luke" a feminist or not?: female-male parallels in Luke-Acts. [F]DENAUX, A.: BEThL 182: 2005 ⇒34. 25-48.

6437 *Kraus, Wolfgang* Lukas: urchristlicher Schriftsteller zwischen Judentum und Hellenismus. [F]STOLLE, V. 2005 ⇒143. 227-244.

6438 [E]**Levine, Amy-Jill** A feminist companion to Luke. FCNT 2: 2002 ⇒ 18,5732; 20,6146. [R]JBL 124 (2005) 562-565 (*Lopez, Davina C.*); RBLit (2005)* (*Lopez, Davina C.*).

6439 **Litwak, Kenneth Duncan** Echoes of scripture in Luke-Acts: telling the history of God's people intertextually. JSNT.S 282: E 2005, Clark x; 234 pp. $130. 0-567-03025-3. Diss.; Bibl. 209-222.

6440 *MacKenzie, Robert* Ideology in Luke-Acts: a firmer grasp of the obvious. Ment. *Sternberg, Meir*: Arc 33 (2005) 318-327.

6441 *Manicardi, Ermenegildo* La ultima parola di Gesù secondo Luca e il racconto della morte di Stefano in Atti. Gesù la cristologia. 2005 <1998> ⇒253. 165-186 [Lk 23,46; Acts 7,58-8,1].

6442 *Marshall, I. Howard* The christology of Luke's gospel and Acts. Contours of christology. 2005 ⇒775. 122-147.

6443 **Mathieu, Yvan** La figure de Pierre dans l'oeuvre de Luc (évangile et Actes des Apôtres): une approche synchronique. EtB 52: 2004 ⇒20, 6154. [R]CBQ 67 (2005) 532-533 (*Patella, Michael*); TS 66 (2005) 664-6 (*Heil, John P.*); Theoforum 36 (2005) 210-215 (*Gourgues, Michel*); TJT 21 (2005) 255-256 (*Racine, Jean-François*); ScEs 57 (2005) 288-291 (*Gourgues, Michel*).

6444 **Mineshige, Kiyoshi** Besitzverzicht und Almosen bei Lukas: Wesen und Forderung des lukanischen Vermögensethos. WUNT 2/163: 2003 ⇒19,6149; 20,6157. [R]OrdKor 46 (2005) 370-371 (*Giesen, Heinz*).

6445 *Moessner, David P.* "Managing" the audience: DIODORUS Siculus and Luke the evangelist on designing authorial intent. [F]DENAUX, A.: BEThL 182: 2005 ⇒34. 61-80.

6446 [E]**Moessner, David P.** Jesus and the heritage of Israel: Luke's narrative claim upon Israel's legacy. 1999 ⇒15,5312; 17,5352. [R]NT 47 (2005) 78-80 (*Stenschke, Christoph*).

6447 **Nave, Guy D.** The role and function of repentance in Luke Acts. Academia biblica 4: 2002 ⇒18,5770; 19,6154. [R]BZ 49 (2005) 137-139 (*Bendemann, Reinhard von*).

6448 **Pokorny, Petr** Theologie der lukanischen Schriften. FRLANT 174: 1998 ⇒14,4849... 17,5358. [R]ThR 70 (2005) 48-50 (*Lindemann, Andreas*).

6449 *Preusler, Burghard* Die zeitlichen Güter—eine menschenwissenschaftliche Skizze zu einem theologischen Thema. [F]ZMIJEWSKI, J.: BBB 151: 2005 ⇒172. 321-337.

6450 *Puig i Tàrrech, Armand* La finale de Luc: une synthèse ouverte. Analyse narrative. BEThL 191: 2005 ⇒742. 223-239 [Lk 24; Acts 1].

6451 **Ratamales, Santiago S.** Discípulo de Jesus e discipulo segundo a obra de São Lucas. São Paulo 2005, Paulinas/Paulus 107 pp. 85-349-2443-0.

6452 *Rius-Camps, Josep* Confrontación en la iglesia primitiva: los círculos hebreos y helenistas en la obra de Lucas (evangelio y Hechos des los apóstoles). FgNT 18 (2005) 45-84.

6453 *Robertson, Charles K.* The limits of leadership: challenges to apostolic homeostasis in Luke-Acts. AThR 87/2 (2005) 273-290.

6454 *Rowe, C. Kavin* Luke-Acts and the imperial cult: a way through the conundrum?. JSNT 27 (2005) 279-300 [Acts 10,36];

6455 History, hermeneutics and the unity of Luke-Acts. JSNT 28 (2005) 131-157.
6456 **Rusam, Dietrich** Das Alte Testament bei Lukas. BZNW 112: 2003 ⇒19,6161; 20,6168. [R]NT 47 (2005) 309-312 (*Stenschke, Christoph*).
6457 *Schröter, Jens* Lukas als Historiograph: das lukanische Doppelwerk und die Entdeckung der christlichen Heilsgeschichte. Antike Historiographie. BZNW 129: 2005 ⇒348. 237-262.
6458 *Scobie, Charles H.H.* A canonical approach to interpreting Luke: the journey motif as a hermeneutical key;
6459 *Spencer, F. Scott* Preparing the way of the Lord: introducing and interpreting Luke's narrative: a response to David Wenham. Reading Luke. 2005 ⇒710. 327-349/104-124.
6460 **Stettberger, Herbert** Nichts haben—alles geben?: eine kognitiv-linguistisch orientierte Studie zur Besitzethik im lukanischen Doppelwerk. [D]*Laub, F.*: Herders Biblische Studien 45: FrB 2005, Herder 568 pp. €55. 3-451-28532-0. Diss. München; Bibl. 533-549.
6461 **Talbert, Charles H.** Reading Luke-Acts in its Mediterranean milieu. NT.S 107: 2003 ⇒19,6164; 20,6173. [R]RBLit (2005)* (*Tannehill, Robert*).
6462 *Tannehill, Robert C.* Israel in Luke-Acts: a tragic story. The shape of Luke's story. 2005 <1985> ⇒315. 105-124.
6463 *Thiselton, Anthony C.* The hermeneutical dynamics of 'Reading Luke' as interpretation, reflection and formation;
6464 *Turner, Max* Luke and the Spirit: renewing theological interpretation of biblical pneumatology. Reading Luke. 2005 ⇒710. 3-52/267-293.
6465 *Upchurch, Cackie* Luke's lessons about Peter. BiTod 43 (2005) 222-227.
6466 *Wenham, David* The purpose of Luke-Acts: Israel's story in the context of the Roman Empire. Reading Luke. 2005 ⇒710. 79-103.
6467 *Wifstrand, Albert* Luke and Greek classicism <1940>;
6468 Luke and the Septuagint. Epochs and styles <1940>. WUNT 179: 2005 ⇒325. 17-27/28-45.
6469 **Zampieri, Girolamo** La tomba di San Luca evangelista: la cassa di piombo e l'area funeraria della basilica di Santa Giustina in Padova. 2003 ⇒19,6169. [R]RQ 100 (2005) 334-336 (*Dresken-Weiland, Jutta*); RivCC 81 (2005) 387-388 (*Warburg, Inés*).

## F7.3 *Evangelium Lucae*—**Textus, commentarii**

6470 **Bovon, F.** Luca, 1: introduzione: commento a 1,1-9,50. [E]*Ianovitz, O.*: Comm. Paideia, NT 3/1: Brescia 2005, Paideia 611 pp. €62.50;
6471 L'évangile selon saint Luc, 2 (9,51-14,35). Commentaire du NT 3B: 1996 ⇒12,5032... 14,4865. [R]ThR 70 (2005) 51-52 (*Lindemann, Andreas*);
6472 3 (Lk 15,1-19,27). Commentaire du NT 3C: 2001 ⇒17,5375... 20, 6180. [R]RBLit (2005)* (*Kraus, Thomas*).
6473 **Costa, Giuseppe** Il vangelo della gioia: introduzione e teologia: lectio su brani scelti del vangelo di Luca. Messina 2005, Ist. Teologico 'S. Tommaso' 190 pp. 88862-12364.
6474 *Culpepper, R. Alan* The gospel of Luke. NT survey. 2005 ⇒3144. 73-94.

6475 [T]**Eijkenboom, Peter; Pijnenborg, Fried; Van Reisen, Hans** AMBROSIUS van Milaan: Zingen met mijn geest en ook met mijn verstand: uitleg van het evangelie volgens Lucas [Expositio evangelii secundum Lucam]. Budel 2005, Damon 590 pp. €39.90. 90557-36449.

6476 **Fitzmyer, Joseph A.** El evangelio según Lucas IV: capitulos 18,15-24,53. [T]*Mínguez, Dionisio*: Sagrada Escritura: M 2005, Cristiandad 713 pp. 84-7057-477-9. Bibl. 633-639.

6477 **Green, Joel B.** The gospel of Luke. NICNT: 1997 ⇒13,5269... 17, 5378. [R]ThR 70 (2005) 52-53 (*Lindemann, Andreas*).

6478 **Kealy, Seán** The interpretation of the gospel of Luke, 1: From apostolic times through the nineteenth century, 2: In the twentieth century. Studies in the Bible and Early Christianity: Lewiston 2005, Mellen 618+633 pp. $150+150. 0-7734-6104-3/06-X.

6479 *Klein, Hans* Die Jesusüberlieferung kommt nach Europa: Lukas und sein Evangelium. Lukasstudien. FRLANT 209: 2005 ⇒239. 11-26;

6480 Zum Text des Lukasevangeliums. Lukasstudien. FRLANT 209: 2005 ⇒239. 198-201 [Lk 6,1].

6481 *Levoratti, Armando J.; Mora Paz, César* Vangelo secondo san Luca. I vangeli. 2005 ⇒432. 673-873.

6482 *Lindemann, Andreas* Literatur zu den Synoptischen Evangelien 1992-2000 (IV): das Lukasevangelium. ThR 70(2005) 44-80.

6483 **López Vergara, Juan** De camino con Jesús: lectura histórico-critica de un trayecto del viaje, guiados por San Lucas. Guadalajara 1999, Fototecnia 284 pp [EfMex 19,129—Castillo Torres, Roberto].

6484 **Meynet, Roland** Il vangelo secondo Luca. [2]2003 <1994> ⇒19, 6185; 20,6187. [R]Asp. 52 (2005) 417-419 (*Di Palma, Gaetano*);

6485 L'évangile de Luc. Rhétorique sémitique 1: P 2005, Lethielleux 1037 pp. €50. 2-283-61239-X. Bibl. 1003-1012. [R]CEv 133 (2005) 84-85 (*Berder, Michel*).

6486 *Moessner, David P.* How Luke writes. [F]STANTON, G. 2005 ⇒138. 149-170.

6487 *Monferrer Sala, Juan P.* Descripción lingüística de la columna árabe del BnF Suppl. grec. 911 (año 1043). CCO 2 (2005) 93-139.

6488 *Monferrer-Sala, J.P.; Urban, Á.* Some remarks on textual criticism in a Greek-Arabic MS. BnF Suppl. grec 911 (A.D. 1043). ParOr 30/1 (2005) 79-102 [NTAb 51,43].

6489 **Patella, Michael F.** The gospel according to Luke. New Collegeville Bible Commentary.NT 3: ColMn 2005, Liturgical 168 pp. $7. 0-814-6-2862-1 [BiTod 44,128—Donald Senior].

6490 *Peterson, Erik* Auslegung des Lukasevangeliums: Kap. 1,1-9,48 (1925/26 und 1928). Peterson: Lukasevangelium und Synoptica. 2005 ⇒277. 1-400.

6491 **Radl, Walter** Das Evangelium nach Lukas: Kommentar, Bd. 1. Kap. 1,1-9,50. 2003 ⇒19,6192; 20,6190. [R]ThLZ 130 (2005) 663-665 (*Böttrich, Christfried*); OrdKor 46 (2005) 508-509 (*Giesen, Heinz*); ThGl 95 (2005) 496-498 (*Kowalski, Beate*); Bib. 86 (2005) 126-129 (*Tannehill, Robert C.*).

6492 **Shellard, Barbara** New light on Luke: its purpose, sources and literary context. JSNT.S 215: 2002 ⇒18,5806... 20,6192. [R]BZ 49 (2005) 284-285 (*Jeska, Joachim*).

6493 *Ukpong, Justin* Luke. Global bible commentary. 2005 ⇒2443. 385-394.

6494 *Urbán, Angel* Los intercambios vocálicos en un manuscrito greco-árabe inédito del Evangelio de Lucas. (BnF, Suppl. gr. 911, s. XI). CCO 2 (2005) 245-272.

6495 **Vaz, Eurides Divino** O Evangelho de Lucas: a infancia, preparçao para o ministério e ministério publico de Jesus: comentários pastoral, parte 1. Goiania, Brasil 2005, GEV 203 pp. 85-905663-3-1.

6496 **Walker, Thomas W.** Luke. Interpretation Bible Studies: LVL 2000, Geneva 114 pp. $10.

6497 *Weren, Wim* Lucas in de Nieuwe Bijbelvertaling: een beoordeling van de gekozen vertaalprincipes en hun toepassing. TTh 45 (2005) 75-87.

## F7.4 *Lucae themata*—Luke's Gospel, topics

6498 *Ayuch, Daniel Alberto* Jesús y el templo de Jerusalén en Lucas: entre narración e historia. RevBib 67 (2005) 179-192.

6499 **Bieberstein, Sabine** Verschwiegene Jüngerinnen—vergessene Zeuginnen: gebrochene Konzepte im Lukasevangelium. NTOA 38: 1998 ⇒14,4885... 17,3854. [R]ThR 70 (2005) 62-64 (*Lindemann, Andreas*).

6500 *Bovon, François* The reception and use of the gospel of Luke in the second century. Reading Luke. 2005 ⇒710. 379-400.

6501 **Böhlemann, Peter** Jesus und der Täufer: Schlüssel zur Theologie und Ethik des Lukas . MSSNTS 99: 1997 ⇒13,5283; 15,5438. [R]ThR 70 (2005) 59-61 (*Lindemann, Andreas*).

6502 *Campbell, W. Gordon* Le récit du Royaume de Dieu dans l'évangile selon saint Luc: 'son règne sera sans fin' (Lc 1,33). RRef 56/233 (2005) 24-43 [NTAb 50,44].

6503 *Denaux, Adelbert* Een vreemdeling in de stad: Lucas' narratieve christologie in perspectief. Coll. 35/4 (2005) 373-386;

6504 A stranger in the city: a contribution to the study of the narrative christology in Luke's gospel. LouvSt 30/4 (2005) 255-275.

6505 **Elvey, Anne F.** An ecological feminist reading of the gospel of Luke: a gestational paradigm. Lewiston, NY 2005, Mellen xxiii; 388 pp. 0-7734-5974-X. Bibl. 301-362.

6506 **Gourgues, Michel** As parábolas de Lucas–do contexto às ressonáncias. Bíblica 47: São Paulo 2005, Loyola 212 pp. 85-15-03117-5.

6507 **Grassi, Joseph** Peace on earth: roots and practices from Luke's gospel. 2004 ⇒20,6202. [R]CBQ 67 (2005) 147-148 (*Mercer, Calvin*).

6508 *Gregory, Andrew* Prior or posterior?: the gospel of the Ebionites and the gospel of Luke. NTS 51 (2005) 344-360;

6509 Looking for Luke in the second century: a dialogue with François Bovon. Reading Luke. 2005 ⇒710. 401-415.

6510 *Hornik, Heidi J.; Parsons, Mikeal C.* Illuminating Luke: the third gospel in Italian Renaissance and Baroque painting. Reading Luke. 2005 ⇒710. 416-436.

6511 **Hotze, Gerhard** Jesus als Gast: Studien zu einem christologischen Leitmotiv im Lukasevangelium. [D]*Untergaßmair, Franz Georg* 2005, Diss.-Habil. Osnabrück [ThRv 102,xvi].

6512 *Ibita, M. Marilou* Dining with Jesus in the third gospel: celebrating eucharist in the third world. EAPR 42 (2005) 249-261.

6513 **Kimball, Charles A.** Jesus' exposition of the Old Testament in Luke's gospel. JSNT.S 94: 1994 ⇒10,4945... 17,5403. [R]ThR 70 (2005) 56-57 (*Lindemann, Andreas*).

6514 *Klein, Hans* Zur Redaktionsarbeit des Lukas am Beispiel der verba dicendi. Lukasstudien. FRLANT 209: 2005 ⇒239. 41-48;
6515 Der Weg des Heils: das theologische Konzept des Lukas. 105-119;
6516 Erzählte Welt und reale Welt im Lukasevangelium. 174-185;
6517 Zur Möglichkeit der Rekonstruktion von Texten des lukanischen Sondergutes. Lukasstudien. FRLANT 209: 2005 ⇒239. 48-58;
6518 Die mündlichen Überlieferungen bei Lukas. 59-64;
6519 Lukas und die Schriften. 119-127;
6520 Weltanschauung und Lebensgestaltung bei Lukas. 127-140;
6521 Der Missionar Jesus als Gast im Lukasevangelium. 186-197;
6522 Das dritte Evangelium und sein Verfasser. 11-40;
6523 Lukas und seine Quellen. 41-84;
6524 Lukas als Theologe. 105-173 [Lk 14,15-35];
6525 Lukas als Erzähler. Lukasstudien. FRLANT 209: 2005 ⇒239. 174-197.
6526 *Krüger, René* Conversion of the pocketbook: the economic project of Luke's gospel. God's economy. 2005 <1998> ⇒415. 169-201;
6527 Luke's God and mammon, a Latin American perspective. Global bible commentary. 2005 ⇒2443. 395-400.
6528 **Kügler, Joachim** Pharao und Christus?: religionsgeschichtliche Untersuchung zur Frage einer Verbindung zwischen altägyptischer Königstheologie und neutestamentlicher: Christologie im Lukasevangelium. BBB 113: 1997 ⇒13,5304... 15,5454. [R]ThR 70 (2005) 57-59 (*Lindemann, Andreas*) [Acts 13,32-33].
6529 **Kwong, Ivan Shing Chung** The word order of the gospel of Luke: its foregrounded messages. Studies in NT Greek 12; Library of NT Studies 298: L 2005, Clark xi; 251 pp. 0-567-03051-2. Bibl. 216-34.
6530 **Łabuda, Piotr** Specyfika eschatologii indywidualnej w ewangelii św. Łukasza [La spécificité de l'eschatologie individuelle dans l'évangile de saint Luc]. [D]*Paciorek, A.* 2005, 290 pp. Diss. Lublin [RTL 37, 616].
6531 **LaVerdière, Eugène** Comer en el reino de Dios: los orígenes de la eucaristía en el evangelio de Lucas. [T]*Tosaus Abadía, José Pedro* 2002 ⇒18,5820; 19,6217. [R]ResB 46 (2005) 68-69 (*Tosaus Abadía, José Pedro*).
6532 *Loney, Alexander C.* Narrative structure and verbal aspect choice in Luke. FgNT 18 (2005) 3-31.
6533 *López Mauleón, J.M.* To Πνεῦνα (το) ἅγιον en San Lucas. Mayéutica 31/72 (2005) 273-370 [NTAb 51,42].
6534 *Manicardi, Ermenegildo* Il servizio della parola e la problematica dell'ascolto nella tradizione del Nuovo Testamento: la testimonianza di Luca. Gesù la cristologia. 2005 <2001> ⇒253. 393-408.
6535 *Marconi, Gilberto* Il bello da vedere: il rapporto dell'uomo con Dio nel terzo vangelo. Il bello della bibbia. 2005 ⇒357. 35-48.
6536 *Marguerat, Daniel* Luc, metteur en scène des personnages. Analyse narrative. BEThL 191: 2005 ⇒742. 281-295.
6537 *Marshall, I. Howard* Political and eschatological language in Luke. Reading Luke. 2005 ⇒710. 157-177.
6538 *März, Claus-Peter* Zur lukanischen Rezeption der Gerichtspredigt Jesu in Q. [F]DENAUX, A.: BEThL 182: 2005 ⇒34. 1-24.
6539 **McComiskey, Douglas S.** Lukan theology in the light of the gospel's literary structure. Milton Keynes 2004, Paternoster xvii; 388 pp. 1-8422-7148-2. Bibl. 356-368.

6540 *Moessner, David P.* Reading Luke's gospel as ancient Hellenistic narrative: Luke's narrative plan of Israel's suffering messiah as God's saving 'plan' for the world. Reading Luke. 2005 ⇒710. 125-154.
6541 **Neale, David A.** None but the sinners: religious categories in the gospel of Luke. JSNT.S 58: 1991 ⇒7,4473... 11/1,3638. [R]ThR 70 (2005) 54-55 (*Lindemann, Andreas*).
6542 **Orsatti, M.** Un Padre con corazón de madre. M 2005, San Pablo 150 pp. 84-285-2731-8.
6543 **Resseguie, James** Spiritual landscape: images of the spiritual life in the gospel of Luke. 2004 ⇒20,6216. [R]Theoforum 36 (2005) 215-216 (*Perrin, David B.*); TJT 21 (2005) 310-311 (*Di Giovanni, Andrea*).
6544 *Rius-Camps, Josep* L'home i la dona, 'afaiçonats segons la imatge de Déu', en el primer volum de l'obra de Lluc. RCatT 30 (2005) 267-288.
6545 **Robertson, A.T.** Word pictures in the New Testament: Luke. GR 2005 <1930>, Kregel 320 pp. [E]*Perschbacher, Wesley J.*
6546 *Scaer, P.J.* Lukan christology: Jesus as beautiful savior. CTQ 69/1 (2005) 63-74 [NTAb 51,268].
6547 *Scheffler, Eben* Ordinary fickle, suffering people: the disciples in Luke's gospel. APB 16 (2005) 274-288.
6548 *Serra, Aristide* Maria di Nazaret nel vangelo di Luca. Maria di Nazaret. DSBP 40: 2005 ⇒579. 237-351.
6549 *Steyn, Gert J.* Soteriological perspectives in Luke's gospel. Salvation in the New Testament. NT.S 121: 2005 ⇒798. 67-99.
6550 *Tannehill, Robert C.* 'Cornelius' and 'Tabitha' encounter Luke's Jesus. The shape of Luke's story. 2005 <1994> ⇒315. 286-297;
6551 Freedom and responsibility in scripture interpretation <1998>;
6552 Repentance in the context of Lukan soteriology <2004>;
6553 Should we love Simon the Pharisee?: reflections on the Pharisees in Luke <1994>;
6554 The story of Israel within the Lukan narrative <1999> [Lk 1-2]. The shape of Luke's story. 2005 ⇒315. 272-85/84-101/257-270/125-144.
6555 *Williams, M.C.* Teologia de Lucas. Kairós 37 (2005) 81-95 [NTAb 50,45].
6556 *Wojciechowski, Michał* Wady jako zalety: trzy trudne przypowieści Jezusa [Défauts en tant que bonnes qualités: trois paraboles difficiles de Jésus]. AtK 145 (2005) 111-119 [Lk 11,5-8; 16,1-8; 18,1-8]. **P.**

### F7.5 *Infantia, cantica*—Magnificat, Benedictus: Luc. 1-3

6557 *Coyle, K.* Towards a scriptural foundation for a theology of Mary: a Lukan perspective. Landas 19/1 (2005) 1-18 [NTAb 50,280].
6558 *Dennison, James T., Jr.* Tiberius Caesar. Kerux 20/3 (2005) 26-38.
6559 *Flichy, Odile* Quand le récit se fait poésie: les hymnes de Luc 1-2. Analyse narrative. BEThL 191: 2005 ⇒742. 389-406.
6560 **Hornik, Heidi J.; Parsons, Mikeal C.** Illuminating Luke: the Infancy Narrative in Italian Renaissance painting. 2003 ⇒20,12420. [R]ThTo 61 (2005) 562, 564 (*Dietrich, R.S.*).
6561 *Klein, Hans* Die Legitimation der Täufer- und der Jesusbewegung nach den Kindheitsgeschichten des Lukas <1998>;
6562 Zur Kindheitsgeschichte des Lukas. Lukasstudien. FRLANT 209: 2005 ⇒239. 85-93/85-104.

6563 *Lohfink, Norbert* Psalmen im Neuen Testament: die Lieder in der Kindheitsgeschichte bei Lukas. Liturgie und Bibel. ÖBS 28: 2005 <1994> ⇒360. 461-480.

6564 *Manicardi, Ermenegildo* Il racconto lucano dell'infanzia di Gesù e la cristologia. Gesù la cristologia. 2005 <2000> ⇒253. 261-284.

6565 *Pemsel-Maier, Sabine* Vom Erhoffen und Verheißen: die Geburt des Messias: die Weihnachtsgeschichte im Lukasevangelium—ein Rückblick auf die Verheißung des Ersten Testaments. AnzSS 114/12 (2005) 11-14.

6566 **Radl, Walter** Der Ursprung Jesu: traditionsgeschichtliche Untersuchungen zu Lukas 1-2. 1996 ⇒12,5081; 13,5342. [R]ThR 70 (2005) 65-7 (*Lindemann, Andreas*); CV 39/1 (1997) 60-94 (*Kaut, Thomas*).

6567 *Robbins, Vernon* Bodies and politics in Luke 1-2 and Sirach 44-50: men, women, and boys. Scriptura 90 (2005) 824-838 [OTA 30,51].

6568 **Syiemlieh, B.H.** God's favourites: a socio-narrative analysis of the characters in the Lukan infancy narratives (Luke 1:5-2:52). Diss. Serampore 2003. [D]*Mathews, John*: Delhi 2005, JRTS xvi; 403 pp. Rs 300/$18/£13. 81-7214-8739..

6569 *Tannehill, Robert C.* What kind of king?: what kind of kingdom?. The shape of Luke's story. 2005 <1992> ⇒315. 48-55.

6570 *Witherington, Ben* Mary, Simeon or Anna: who first recognized Jesus as Messiah?. BiRe 21/5 (2005) 12, 14, 51 [NTAb 50,280].

6571 *Siffer-Wiederhold, Nathalie* Le projet littéraire de Luc d'après le prologue de l'évangile (Lc 1,1-4). RevSR 79 (2005) 39-54 [Lk 1,1-4].

6572 *Kasiłowski, Piotr* Zapowiedź narodzenia Jana Chrzciciela (Łk 1,5-25) [The announcement of the birth of John the Baptist (Lk 1:5-25]. StBob 1 (2005) 95-119. **P**.

6573 *Sutter Rehmann, Luzia* Der Glanz der Schekhinah und Elisabeths Verhüllung (Lukas 1,24). LecDif 1 (2005)*.

6574 *Wenell, Karen* Luke 1:26-38. ET 117 (2005) 72-73.

6575 *Seidel, K.* Letting go of power: searching for an erotic reading of Luke 1:26-56. Women Church [Sydney] 37 (2005) 41-47 [NTAb 50, 45].

6576 *Simons, R.* La pregunta de María (Lucas 1:34). Kairós 36 (2005) 51-64 [NTAb 50,45].

6577 *Tannehill, Robert C.* The Magnificat as poem. The shape of Luke's story. 2005 <1974> ⇒315. 31-47.

6578 *Klein, Hans* Das Magnifikat als jüdisches Frauengebet. Lukasstudien. FRLANT 209: 2005 <1997> ⇒239. 94-104 [Lk 1,46-55].

6579 *Valentini, Alberto* Il Magnificat (Lc 1,46b-55). Maria di Nazaret. DSBP 40: 2005 ⇒579. 211-236.

6580 **Wüthrich, Serge** Le Magnificat, témoin d'un pacte socio-politique de Luc-Actes. Christianismes anciens 2: 2003 ⇒19,6253. [R]ThLZ 130 (2005) 514-515 (*Herren, Luc*) [Lk 1,46-55].

6581 *Ernst, Josef* Überlegungen zu den jüdischen Wurzeln christlicher Gesänge in der Kindheitsgeschichte des Lukasevangeliums. [F]ZMIJEWSKI, J.: BBB 151: 2005 ⇒172. 29-47 [Lk 1,46-55.68-79].

6582 *Lambrecht, Jan* "But you too": a note on Luke 1,76. EThL 81 (2005) 487-490.

6583 *Gathercole, Simon* The heavenly ἀνατολή (Luke 1:78-9). JThS 56 (2005) 471-488.

6584 *Delobel, Joël* In defence of the belief in the virginal conception?: textual variants in Lk 2. [F]DENAUX, A.: BEThL 182: 2005 ⇒34. 81-91.
6585 *McLaren, James S.* The census in Judea. Ment. *Josephus*: ABR 53 (2005) 70-75 [Lk 2,2].
6586 *Rist, John M.* Luke 2:2: making sense of the date of Jesus' birth. JThS 56 (2005) 489-491.
6587 *Marucci, Corrado* "Pace agli uomini di buona volontà"?: la traduzione di εὐδοκία in Lc 2,14: 1, storia dell'esegesi. RdT 46 (2005) 845-872.
6588 *Olsson, Birger* Gloria in a multitude of voices. ET 117 (2005) 89-94 [Lk 2,14].
6589 *Tronina, Antoni* Matka jego zachowywała wszystkie te słowa w sercu (Łk 2,51b). Roczniki Teologiczne 52/1 (2005) 67-79 [NTAb 50, 492]. **P.**
6590 *Koehne, Mark* An exegesis of *The Presentation* (Luke 2:22-35). ScrB 35 (2005) 5-17.
6591 *Jacques, André* Luc 2,22-38: présentation de Jésus au temple (Syméon et Anne). LeD 63 (2005) 18-27.
6592 *McCord Adams, Marilyn* Housing the holiness. Luke 2:22-40. ET 117 (2005) 112-113.
6593 **Serra, Aristide M.** "Una spada trafiggerà la tua vita" (Lc 2,35a): quale spada?: bibbia e tradizione giudaico-cristiana a confronto. 2003 ⇒19,6263; 20,6238. [R]Ter. 56 (2005) 586-589 (*Fornara, Roberto*); Asp. 52 (2005) 452-453 (*Langella, Alfonso*); Ang. 82 (2005) 240-242 (*Garuti, Paolo*); Gr. 86 (2005) 676-678 (*Kapusta, Paweł*).
6594 *Cardona Ramírez, Hernán* Hacia un nuevo paradigma familiar—pistas de evangelio. El grano. 2005 <2004> ⇒197. 211-5 [Lk 2,41-52].
6595 *Heininger, Bernhard* Familienkonflikte: der zwölfjährige Jesus im Tempel (Lk 2,41-52). [F]ZMIJEWSKI, J.: BBB 151: 2005 ⇒172. 49-72.
6596 **Mahfouz, Hady** La fonction littéraire et théologique de Lc 3,1-20 dans Luc-Actes. 2003 ⇒19,6267. [R]CBQ 67 (2005) 151-152 (*Bridge, Steven L.*); ThRev 26 (2005) 147-153 (*Schoeni, Marc*).

## F7.6 Evangelium Lucae 4,1...

6597 *Mendonça, José Tolentino* Identidade e enigma: a interacção dos personagens na secção galilaica de Lucas. Did(L) 35 (2005) 175-200.
6598 *Morandi, Giacomo* 'Ti darò tutta questa potenza': le tentazioni di Gesù (Lc 4,1-13). PSV 51 (2005) 135-167 [Lk 4,1-13].
6599 *Pyper, Hugh S.* Jesus reads the scriptures. Those outside. 2005 ⇒ 332. 1-16 [Lk 4,14-30].
6600 *Barr, George K.* Jesus in Nazareth. IBSt 26 (2005) 93-104 [Lk 4,16-30].
6601 *Tannehill, Robert C.* The mission of Jesus according to Luke 4:16-30. The shape of Luke's story. 2005 <1972> ⇒315. 3-30.
6602 **Vaz, Eurides Divino** O ministério de Jesus no evangelho de Lucas: como fazer um estudo teológico-bíblico a partir de Lc 4,16-30. Salvador 2005, A Partilha 64 pp;
6603 Como fazer uma análise narrativa e pragmática de Lc 4,16-30: teologia e literatura. Salvador 2005, A Partilha 80 pp. Bibl. 62-64;
6604 Quem é Jesus no evangelho de Lucas?: como fazer um estudo teologico-bíblico a partir de Lc 4,16-30. Goiania, Brasil 2005, Ed. da UCG 100 pp. 85-7103-248-3. Bibl. 97-100.

6605 *Busse, Ulrich* Begegnung mit dem Wort nach Lk 5,1-11. [F]DENAUX, A.: BEThL 182: 2005 ⇒34. 113-129.

6606 *Manzi, Franco* I segni della chiamata: la vocazione di Pietro in *Lc* 5, 1-11. RCI 86 (2005) 121-132.

6607 *Maleparambil, Joseph* The call of Levi, the great feast and Jesus' table fellowship with the marginalized (Luke 5,27-39). LivWo 111 (2005) 73-84 .

6608 *Meynet, Roland* Le vin de la nouvelle alliance: la parabole du vieux et du neuf (Lc 5,36-39) dans son contexte. Gr. 86 (2005) 5-27.

6609 *Flebbe, Jochen* Alter und neuer Wein bei Lukas: zum Verständnis der sogenannten "Weinregel" Lk 5,39. ZNW 96 (2005) 171-187.

6610 *Klein, Hans* Am ersten Sabbat: eine Konjektur zu Lk 6,1. Lukasstudien. FRLANT 209: 2005 <1996> ⇒239. 198-201.

6611 *Stasiak, Slawomir* Gesù è Signore del sabato: studio diacronico di Lc 6,1-5. Anton. 80 (2005) 245-276.

6612 *Klein, Hans* Gerichtsankündigung und Liebesforderung: Lk 6,24-26.27 innerhalb der Botschaft des frühen Christentums. Lukasstudien. FRLANT 209: 2005 <1996> ⇒239. 148-159;

6613 Annahme der Andersartigen: Lk 6,36-46 im Verständnis des Lk und seiner Leser. [F]DENAUX, A.: BEThL 182: 2005 ⇒34. 131-149 [Mt 7,1-5].

6614 *Alegre i Santamaria, Xavier* Un estranger, model de creient a l'evangeli de Lluc: el centurió de Cafarnaüm (Lc 7,1-10). La bíblia i els immigrants. 2005 ⇒471. 143-167.

6615 *Cosgrove, Charles H.* A woman's unbound hair in the Greco-Roman world, with special references to the story of the "sinful woman" in Luke 7:36-50. JBL 124 (2005) 675-692.

6616 *Kilgallen, John J.* What does it mean to say that there are additions in Luke 7,36-50?. Bib. 86 (2005) 529-535;

6617 Faith and forgiveness: Luke 7,36-50. RB 112 (2005) 372-384 [Mk 2, 1-12].

6618 **Mendonça, José Tolentino** A construçao de Jesus: uma leitura narrativa de Lc 7,36-50. Fundamenta 26: 2004 ⇒20,6253. [R]Brot. 160 (2005) 279-284 (*Sena-Lino, Pedro*).

6619 **Mullen, J. Patrick** Dining with Pharisees. 2004 ⇒20,6254. [R]RBLit (2005)* (*Smit, Peter*) [Lk 7,36-50].

6620 *Pillay, M.N.* Luke 7:36-50: see this woman?: towards a theology of gender equality in the context of HIV and AIDS. Scriptura 89 (2005) 441-455 [NTAb 50,493].

### F7.7 *Iter hierosolymitanum—Lc 9,51...*—**Jerusalem journey**

6621 **Mayer, Edgar** Die Reiseerzählung des Lukas (Lk 9,51 - 19,10): Entscheidung in der Wüste. EHS.T 554: 1996 ⇒12,5114. [R]ThR 70 (2005) 70-71 (*Lindemann, Andreas*).

6622 **Noël, Filip** The travel narrative in the gospel of Luke: interpretation of Lk 9,51-19,28. CBRA 5: 2004 ⇒20,6257. [R]ETR 80 (2005) 435-436 (*Singer, Christophe*); TJT 21 (2005) 258-259 (*Trites, Allison*).

6623 *Radl, Walter* Zu Umfang, Form und Funktion des sogenannten Lukanischen Reiseberichts. [F]DENAUX, A.: BEThL 182: 2005 ⇒34. 173-191.

6624 *Peterson, Erik* Von der Nachfolge (Lk 9,56-62). Peterson: Lukasevangelium und Synoptica. 2005 ⇒277. 403-410.

6625 *Busse, U.* A study of Luke 10 in context. HTSTS 61/1-2 (2005) 81-91 [NTAb 50,282].

6626 *Verheyden, Joseph* How many were sent according to Lk 10,1?. ^F^DENAUX, A.: BEThL 182: 2005 ⇒34. 193-238.

6627 *Theobald, Michael* "Ich sah den Satan aus dem Himmel stürzen ...": überlieferungskritische Beobachtungen zu Lk 10,18-20. BZ 49 (2005) 174-190.

6628 *Gardascia [Cardascia], Guillaume* "Trahisons" bibliques: Nb 5,31 & Lc 10,25-37. RB 112 (2005) 369-371.

6629 *Mbuyi, Beda Kaji-Ngulu* Hatred, war and division in the Democratic Republic of Congo: Lucan hermeneutics (10,25-37) as a way forward. Afrika Yetu 9 (2005) 8-22.

6630 *Silva R., Santiago* Evangelizar como Jesús, buen samaritano (Lc 10, 25-37). Revista católica 105/1 (2005) 13-24.

6631 *Van Cangh, Jean-Marie* Le Bon Samaritan: une création de Jésus ou de Luc?. ^F^DENAUX, A.: BEThL 182: 2005 ⇒34. 239-263 [Lk 10, 25-37].

6632 *Grey, Mary* Rescuing Martha from the dishes: a challenge of retrieval and proclamation. PaRe 1/5 (2005) 12-18 [NTAb 50,282] [Lk 10,38-42].

6633 *Penrose, M.E.* Martha and Mary: the everlasting saga. ChiSt 44 (2005) 250-262 [NTAb 50,282] [Lk 10,38-42].

6634 *Rentrop, Norman* Lebensmitte als geistliche Herausforderung (Lukas 10,38-42). Kanzelreden. 2005 ⇒376. 103-116.

6635 *Fleddermann, Harry T.* Three friends at midnight (Luke 11,5-8). ^F^DENAUX, A.: BEThL 182: 2005 ⇒34. 265-282.

6636 *North, J. Lionel* Praying for a good spirit: text, context and meaning of Luke 11.13. JSNT 28 (2005) 167-188.

6637 *Baraniak, Marek* The return of an unclean spirit: Luke 11,24-26. StBob 4 (2005) 109-182.

6638 *Rakocy, W.* The sense of the *logion* about the sign of Jonah in the gospel according to St Luke (11:29b-30). Roczniki Teologiczne 52/1 (2005) 81-94 [NTAb 50,494].

6639 *Johnson-DeBaufre, Melanie* The blood required of this generation: interpreting communal blame in a colonial context. Violence in the NT. 2005 ⇒439. 22-34 [Lk 11,49-51].

6640 *Radl, Walter* Von der Habsucht und dem törichten Reichen (Lk 12, 13-21). ^F^ZMIJEWSKI, J.: BBB 151: 2005 ⇒172. 103-114.

6641 *Gundry, Robert H.* Spinning the lilies and unraveling the ravens: an alternative reading of Q 12:22b-31 and P. Oxy. 655. The old is better. WUNT 178: 2005 ⇒220. 149-170 [Mt 6,25-33].

6642 *Van Aarde, Andries* Resolving communication disturbances in Luke 12:35-48 through narratology. ^M^VAN TILBORG, S.: BiblInterp 71: 2005 ⇒155. 177-195.

6643 *Bruce, Patricia* "A daughter of Abraham": Luke 13:10-17 and the inclusion of people with disabilities. Journal of constructive theology 11/1 (2005) 3-27.

6644 *Panier, Louis* Des figures dans le récit: la guérison de la femme courbée en Lc 13,10-17. Analyse narrative. BEThL 191: 2005 ⇒742. 425-430.

6645 *Torgerson, Heidi* The healing of the bent woman: a narrative interpretation of Luke 13:10-17. CThMi 32 (2005) 176-186.

6646 **Braun, Willi** Feasting and social rhetoric in Luke 14. MSSNTS 85: 1995 ⇒11/1,3741... 16,5512. [R]ThR 70 (2005) 71-72 (*Lindemann, Andreas*).

6647 *Venetz, Hermann-Josef* "Und du wirst selig sein...": kritische Beobachtungen zu Lk 14,14. [F]SCHENKER, A.: OBO 214: 2005 ⇒134. 394-409.

6648 *Tannehill, Robert C.* The Lukan discourse on invitations. The shape of Luke's story. 2005 <1992> ⇒315. 56-72 [Lk 14,7-24].

6649 *Krüger, René* La inclusión de las personas excluidas: la propuesta contracultural de Lucas 14:12-14. Cuadernos de teología 24 (2005) 67-88.

6650 *Michel, Karl-Heinz* Eine Frage der Prioritäten: das große Festmahl (Lukas 14,15-24). ThBeitr 36 (2005) 169-172.

6651 *Klein, Hans* Botschaft für viele—Nachfolge von wenigen?: Überlegungen zu Lk 14,15-35. Lukasstudien. FRLANT 209: 2005 <1997> ⇒239. 159-173.

6652 *Hoppe, Rudolf* Tischgespräche und Nachfolgebedingungen: Überlegungen zum Gleichnis vom großen Mahl Lk 14,16-24 im Kontext von Lk 14,1-35. [F]ZMIJEWSKI, J.: BBB 151: 2005 ⇒172. 115-130.

6653 *Van den Eynde, Sabine* Come and hate?: on the interpretation of Luke 14,26. [F]DENAUX, A.: BEThL 182: 2005 ⇒34. 283-297 [Mt 10, 37].

6654 *Vaz, Armindo dos Santos* Lectio divina da parábola do pai misericordioso. Did(L) 35 (2005) 201-224 [Lk 15,1-32].

6655 *Peterson, Erik* Das Gleichnis vom verlorenen Sohn (Lk 15,11-20). Peterson: Lukasevangelium und Synoptica. 2005 ⇒277. 411-414.

6656 **Bailey, Kenneth E.** Jacob and the prodigal: how Jesus retold Israel's story. 2003 ⇒19,6325; 20,6281. [R]SJTh 58 (2005) 354-356 (*Moxnes, Halvor*) [Lk 15,11-32];

6657 The cross & the prodigal: Luke 15 through the eyes of Middle Eastern peasants. DG [2]2005, InterVarsity 151 pp. 0-8308-3281-5. Bibl. 149-151.

6658 *Dirschauer, Johannes* Meditation über den verlorenen Sohn. Deutsches Pfarrerblatt 105/8 (2005) 407-409 [Lk 15,11-32].

6659 *Kitoko Mfinyi, Gaston* De la liberté à tout prix à la sagesse de la patience: crises et salut des relations sociales dans la parabole du fils prodigue. Telema 123/4 (2005) 25-44 [Lk 15,11-32].

6660 *Lambrecht, Jan* A note on Luke 15,11-32. [F]DENAUX, A.: BEThL 182: 2005 ⇒34. 299-306.

6661 *Landgrave G., Daniel R.* Los dos hijos que no conocían a su padre, o el hijo pródigo: Lc 15,11-32. Qol 38 (2005) 41-59;

6662 Lc 15,11-32 (II). Qol 39 (2005) 61-86.

6663 **Luneau, René** L'enfant prodigue. Evangiles: P 2005, Bayard 166 pp. €19.90 [Lk 15,11-32].

6664 *Nolland, John* The role of money and possessions in the parable of the Prodigal Son (Luke 15:11-32). Reading Luke. 2005 ⇒710. 178-209.

6665 *Oliveira, Josemar M. de* No discurso bíblico descentramento do sujeito. Hermenêutica 5 (2005) 1-20 [Lk 15,11-32].

6666 *Wright, Stephen I.* Reading Luke, hearing Jesus and understanding God: reflections on some hermeneutical issues: a response to John Nolland. Reading Luke. 2005 ⇒710. 210-228 [Lk 15,11-32].

6667 *Reinmuth, Eckart* Alles muss raus: die Parabel Lk 16,1-8 ist moralischer als ihre Auslegungen. FSTEGEMANN, W. 2005 ⇒139. 223-231.
6668 *Deichmann, Heinz-Horst* Mammon: Segen oder Götze—Mittel zum Zweck oder Selbstzweck (Lukas 16,9). Kanzelreden. 2005 ⇒376. 117-124.
6669 *Dagron, Alain* La parabole du riche et du pauvre Lazare (Luc 16,19-31). SémBib 117 (2005) 46-55.
6670 *Gowler, David B.* "At his gate lay a poor man": a dialogic reading of Luke 16:19-31. PRSt 32/3 (2005) 249-265.
6671 *Gradl, Hans-Georg* Von den Kosten des Reichtums: die Beispielerzählung vom reichen Mann und armen Lazarus (Lk 16,19-31) textpragmatisch gelesen. MThZ 56 (2005) 305-317.
6672 *Igboin, Benson O.* An African understanding of the parable of the rich man and Lazarus: problems and possibilities. AJTh 19/2 (2005) 256-269 [Lk 16,19-31].
6673 **Sievers, Kai Detlev** Die Parabel vom reichen Mann und armen Lazarus im Spiegel bildlicher Überlieferung. Kiel 2005, Ludwig 176 pp. 3-937719-13-X [Lk 16,19-31].
6674 *Cotter, Wendy J.* The parable of the feisty widow and the threatened judge (Luke 18.1-8). NTS 51 (2005) 328-343.
6675 *Reid, Barbara E.* La viuda y el juez (Lc 18,1-8) desde la perspectiva de una hermenéutica feminista. Qol 37 (2005) 69-82.
6676 **Tomasevic, Darko** The parable about the widow and the judge (Lk 18:1-8): exegetical theological study. D*Juric, S.*: R 2005, 275 pp. Diss. Angelicum [RTL 37,619].
6677 *Cifrak, Mario* Slika o Bogu ili etika (Lk 18,9-14)!?. BoSm 75 (2005) 541-555. **Croatian**.
6678 *Harrison, Stephanie* The case of the pharisee and the tax collector: justification and social location in Luke's gospel. CThMi 32 (2005) 99-111 [Lk 18,9-14].
6679 *Friedrichsen, Timothy A.* The temple, a pharisee, a tax collector, and the kingdom of God: rereading a Jesus parable (Luke 18:10-14a). JBL 124 (2005) 89-119.
6680 *Panier, Louis* Récit et figure dans la paraboles des mines (Luc 19): un modèle pour une sémiotique du discours. SémBib 117 (2005) 30-45.
6681 **Rathnasamy, Charles** Jesus encounters Zacchaeus: an exegetical-theological study of Luke 19,1-10: toward the function of house/household in Luke-Acts. D*Jurić, Stipe*: R 2005, x; 202 pp. Diss. Angelicum; Bibl. 179-202.

### F7.8 **Passio**—Lc 22...

6682 *Böttrich, Christfried* Proexistenz im Leben und Sterben: Jesu Tod bei Lukas. Deutungen. WUNT 181: 2005 ⇒392. 413-436.
6683 *Gourgues, Michel* Mort de Jésus et universalisme: deux types de référence au Deutéro-Ésaïe dans la représentation lucanienne du salut. FGENEST, O. 2005 ⇒46. 397-415.
6684 *Klein, Hans* Zur Frage einer Lukas und Johannes zu Grunde liegenden Passions- und Osterüberlieferung. Lukasstudien. FRLANT 209: 2005 ⇒239. 65-84.

6685 **Mittmann-Richert, Ulrike** Der Sühnetod des Gottesknechts: die lukanische Interpretation von Jes 53. [D]**Hengel, Martin** 2005, Diss.-Habil. Tübingen [ThLZ 130,890].

6686 **Scaer, Peter J.** The Lukan passion and the praiseworthy death. New Testament Monographs 10: Shf 2005, Sheffield Academic viii; 155 pp. $60. 1-905048-24-6. Bibl. 135-143.

6687 *Van Henten, Jan W.* Jewish martyrs and the Lukan passion narrative revisited. [F]DENAUX, A.: BEThL 182: 2005 ⇒34. 325-344.

6688 *Leppä, Heikki* Luke's account of the Lord's Supper [Lk 22,14-20];

6689 *Luomanen, Petri* Sacrifices abolished: the Last Supper in Luke (Codex Bezae) and in the *Gospel of the Ebionites* [Lk 22,15-19]. [F]AEJMELAEUS, L.: SESJ 89: 2005 ⇒1. 364-373/186-208.

6690 **Nelson, Peter K.** Leadership and discipleship: a study of Luke 22: 24-30. SBL.DS 138: 1994 ⇒10,5042... 13,5483. [R]ThR 70 (2005) 74-75 (*Lindemann, Andreas*).

6691 *Zani, Lorenzo* 'Simone, Simone, io ho pregato per te'. Presbyteri 39 (2005) 60-65 [Lk 22,31].

6692 *Weissenrieder, Annette; Wendt, Friederike* "Warum schlaft ihr?" (Lk 22,46): Überlegungen zum Jüngerbild in Lk 22,39-46 im Lichte ikonographischer und medizinhistorischer Quellen. Picturing the New Testament. WUNT 2/193: 2005 ⇒396. 96-126.

6693 *Clivaz, Claire* The angel and the sweat like "drops of blood" (Lk 22:43-44): P69 and f13. HThR 98 (2005) 419-440.

6694 *Giesen, Heinz* Auf dem Weg zur Richtstätte (Lk 23,26-32). ThG 48 (2005) 64-74.

6695 *MacDonald, Dennis R.* The breasts of Hecuba and those of the daughters of Jerusalem: Luke's transvaluation of a famous Iliadic scene. Ancient fiction. SBL.Symp. 32: 2005 ⇒721. 239-254 [Lk 23, 27-31].

6696 *Lewis, Carrie L.* Narrative insights into the crucifixion of Jesus in Luke (23:33-43). CThMi 32 (2005) 355-365.

6697 **Blum, Matthias** "...denn sie wissen nicht, was sie tun": zur Rezeption der Fürbitte Jesu am Kreuz (Lk 23,34a) in der antiken jüdisch-christlichen Kontroverse. NTA 46: 2004 ⇒20,6311. [R]CBQ 67 (2005) 131-132 (*Tyson, Joseph B.*); ThLZ 130 (2005) 944-946 (*Maier, Johann*); Sal. 67 (2005) 180-181 (*Vicent, Rafael*); JThS 56 (2005) 221-222 (*Wickham, L.R.*).

6698 *Torchia, Joseph* The death of a righteous man: redactional elements in Luke's passion narrative (23:44-56). IBSt 26 (2005) 60-92.

6699 *Müller, Christoph G.* Josef von Arimathäa und die Grablegung Jesu (Lk 23,50-56). [F]ZMIJEWSKI, J.: BBB 151: 2005 ⇒172. 179-198.

6700 *Mainville, Odette* De Jésus à l'église: étude rédactionnelle de Luc 24. NTS 51 (2005) 192-211.

6701 *Manns, Frédéric* Quelques variantes du codex Bezae de Luc 24. LASBF 55 (2005) 131-139.

6702 **Prince, Deborah** Visions of the risen Jesus: the rhetoric of certainty in Luke 24 and Acts 1. [D]*D'Angelo, M.R.* 2005, Diss. Notre Dame [RTL 37,617].

6703 **Van Tilborg, Sjef; Counet, Patrick C.** Jesus' appearances and disappearances in Luke 24. Bibl.Interp. 45: 2000 ⇒16,5554. [R]ThR 70 (2005) 79-80 (*Lindemann, Andreas*).

6704 **Chenu, Bruno** I discepoli di Emmaus. Brescia 2005, Queriniana 127 pp. 88-399-2901-0. Bibl. 125-126 [Lk 24,13-35].

6705 **Gilliéron, Bernard** Un dimanche à Emmaüs: quand le Vivant nous fait revivre. Poliez-le-grand 2005, Moulin 90 pp. €11. 2-88469-019-0 [Lk 24,13-35].

6706 **Korbacher, Joachim** Die Emmaus Geschichte—etwas anders gelesen. Glauben und Leben 24: Müns 2005, LIT (4) i; 67 pp. 3-8258-81-51-2. Bibl. 63-67 [Lk 24,13-35].

6707 *Maxey, James* The road to Emmaus: changing expectations: a narrative critical study. CThMi 32 (2005) 112-123 [Lk 24,13-35].

6708 *Myllykoski, Matti* On the way to Emmaus (Luke 24:13-35): narrative and ideological aspects of fiction. [F]AEJMELAEUS, L.: SESJ 89: 2005 ⇒1. 92-115.

6709 *Schipani, D.* A la manera de Jesús: inspiración para el proceso de enseñanza-aprendizaje según Lucas 24:13-35. Kairós 36 (2005) 65-72 [NTAb 50,49].

6710 *Trautmann, Franz; Trautmann, Maria* Die Emmaus-Erzählung und ihre Weg-Theologie. BiHe 41/161 (2005) 10-13 [Lk 24,13-35].

6711 *Manicardi, Ermenegildo* La terza apparizione del Risorto nel vangelo secondo Luca. Gesù la cristologia. 2005 <1997> ⇒253. 285-309 [Lk 24,36-53].

6712 *Kapic, Kelly M.* Receiving Christ's priestly benediction: a biblical, historical, and theological exploration of Luke 24:50-53. WThJ 67 (2005) 247-260.

## F8.1 *Actus Apostolorum*, **Acts**—*text, commentary, topics*

6713 *Alexander, Loveday* 'Acts and ancient intellectual biography'. Acts in its ancient literary context. LNTS 298: 2005 <1993> ⇒174. 43-68;

6714 'In journeyings often': voyaging in the Acts of the Apostles and in Greek romance <1995> 69-96;

6715 Narrative maps: reflections on the toponomy of Acts <1995> 97-131;

6716 Fact, fiction and the genre of Acts <1998> 133-163;

6717 New Testament narrative and ancient epic <2003-2004> 165-182;

6718 The Acts of the Apostles as an apologetic text. Acts in its ancient literary context <1999>. LNTS 298: 2005 ⇒174. 183-206.

6719 **Avemarie, Friedrich** Die Tauferzählungen der Apostelgeschichte: Theologie und Geschichte. WUNT 139: 2002 ⇒18,5962... 20,6324. [R]ZRGG 57 (2005) 87-88 (*Horn, Friedrich W.*).

6720 **Barnard, W.** Tot in Athene: Handelingen 1-17: leesoefeningen bij het tweede boek van Lukas. Zoetermeer 2005, Meinema 272 pp. €22. 50. 90-211-3767-4.

6721 **Barrett, Charles K.** Atti degli apostoli, volume primo: prolegomeni, commento ai capitoli 1-14. [E]*Zoroddu, D.*: Comm. NT 5.1: 2003 ⇒ 19,6384; 20,6325. [R]VivH 16 (2005) 433-434 (*Tarocchi, Stefano*);

6722 2: introduzione, commento ai capitoli 15-28. [E]*Zoroddu, D.*: Commentario Paideia, NT 5.2: Brescia 2005, Paideia 742-1501 pp. €80;

6723 1-2. 2003-2005. [R]Asp. 52 (2005) 569-572 (*Palinuro, Massimiliano*).

6724 *Baslez, Marie-Françoise* Le monde des Actes des Apôtres: approches littéraires et études documentaires. Actes des Apôtres. LeDiv 199: 2005 ⇒715. 63-84.

6725 *Bauckham, Richard* James, Peter, and the gentiles. The missions of James. NT.S 115: 2005 ⇒369. 93-142 [Acts 15].

6726 *Berder, Michel* Lire les Actes des Apôtres aujourd'hui: ouvertures. Les Actes des Apôtres. LeDiv 199: 2005 ⇒715. 243-251.

6727 [E]**Blickenstaff, Marianne; Levine, Amy-Jill** A feminist companion to the Acts of the Apostles. The feminist companion to the NT 9: 2004 ⇒20,6329. [R]RBLit (2005)* (*Stratton, Kimberly*).

6728 *Blümer, Wilhelm* Apostelgeschichte. BVLI 49 (2005) 35-37.

6729 *Bockmuehl, Markus* Why not let Acts be Acts?: in conversation with C. Kavin Rowe. JSNT 28 (2005) 163-166.

6730 *Bonneau, Guy* Le fils du réconfort: la construction du personnage de Barnabas dans les Actes. Analyse narrative. BEThL 191: 2005 ⇒ 742. 309-317.

6731 **Casalegno, Alberto** Ler os Atos des Apóstolos: estudo da teologia lucana da missão. São Paulo 2005, Loyola 468 pp. 85-15-03059-4. Bibl. 15-17.

6732 **Chocheyras, J.** Les Actes des apôtres Pierre et Paul: histoire, tradition et légende. Religion et sciences humaines: 2003 ⇒19,6390. [R]NRTh 127 (2005) 123-124 (*Radermakers, J.*).

6733 **Cortés, José Luis** Tus amigos no te olvidan: Hechos de los Apóstolos. 2004 ⇒20,6334. [R]SalTer 93 (2005) 692-693 (*Gill, Fátima*).

6734 **Dibelius, Martin** The book of Acts: form, style, and theology. [E]*Hanson, Kenneth C.* 2004 ⇒20,6336. [R]RBLit (2005)* (*Blomberg, Craig; Toney, Carl*).

6735 **Dionne, Christian** La bonne nouvelle de Dieu dans les Actes des Apôtres. LeDiv 195: 2004 ⇒20,6337. [R]EeV 120 (2005) 19-20 (*Cothenet, Édouard*); Theoforum 36 (2005) 121-24 (*Michaud, Jean-P.*).

6736 **Dirnbeck, Josef; Moser, Franziska; Olivera Perz, Manuel** Der Weg der ersten Christen: Bausteine zu einem geschichtlichen Verständnis der Apostelgeschichte. W 2005, Va Bene 255 pp. 3-85167-180-5.

6737 **Dormeyer, Detlev; Galindo, Florencio** Die Apostelgeschichte: ein Kommentar für die Praxis. 2003 ⇒19,6394. [R]ThRv 101 (2005) 379-381 (*Müller, Christoph G.*).

6738 *Dormeyer, Detlev* Bakchos in der Apostelgeschichte. Griechische Mythologie. 2005 ⇒542. 153-172.

6739 *Dupont-Roc, Roselyne* La tradition textuelle des Actes des Apôtres. Les Actes des Apôtres. LeDiv 199: 2005 ⇒715. 43-62.

6740 *Eckert, Jost* "Durch viele Drangsale müssen wir in das Reich Gottes hineingehen" (Apg 14,22b): zum Paulusbild der Apostelgeschichte. [F]ZMIJEWSKI, J.: BBB 151: 2005 ⇒172. 259-276.

6741 *Epp, Eldon J.* Anti-judaic tendencies in the D-Text of Acts: forty years of conversation <2003>;

6742 The 'ignorance motif' in Acts and anti-Judaic tendencies in Codex Bezae <1962>;

6743 Coptic manuscript G67 and the role of Codex Bezae as a western witness in Acts <1966>. Perspectives on NT textual criticism. NT.S 116: 2005 ⇒207. 699-739/ 1-13/15-39.

6744 **Fallon, Michael** The Acts of the Apostles: an introductory commentary. Kensington, NSW 2003, Chevalier 264 pp. 0-86940-288-9.

6745 *Faure, Patrick* Le mystère d'Israël selon les textes Alexandrin et Occidental des Actes des Apôtres. NRTh 127 (2005) 3-17;

6746 L'émergence du christianisme dans la bible. Bible et sciences des religions. 2005 ⇒445. 41-69.

6747 **Fitzmyer, Joseph A.** Gli Atti degli Apostoli. 2003 ⇒19,6399; 20, 6339. [R]RelCult 51 (2005) 794-795 (*Moral, Alejandro*).

6748 *Flichy, Odile* État des recherches actuelles sur les Actes des Apôtres. Les Actes des Apôtres. LeDiv 199: 2005 ⇒715. 13-42.

6749 *Garribba, Dario* Il ruolo dei *timorati di Dio* nel conflitto tra giudei e cristiani nelle sinagoghe della diaspora. Giudei o cristiani?. 2005 ⇒ 833. 83-91.

6750 **Gaventa, Beverly Roberts** The Acts of the Apostles. Abingdon NT Commentaries: 2003 ⇒19,6403; 20,6342. [R]Interp. 59 (2005) 304-306 (*Walaskay, Paul W.*); RBLit (2005)* (*Keener, Craig*).

6751 *Giovannini, Adalberto* Il contesto culturale dell'evangelista Luca. La cultura storica. 2005 ⇒893. 189-197.

6752 **Green, Chris** The word of his grace: a guide to teaching and preaching from Acts. Leicester 2005, IVP 189 pp. £9. 1-84474-0757.

6753 **Hamm, Dennis** The Acts of the Apostles. New Collegeville Bible Commentary: ColMn 2005, Liturgical 135 pp. $7. 0-8146-2864-8 [BiTod 44,128—Donald Senior].

6754 *Hensell, Eugene* Reading the Acts of the Apostles. RfR 64 (2005) 201-205.

6755 **Hintermaier, Johann** Die Befreiungswunder in der Apostelgeschichte. BBB 143: 2003 ⇒19,6408; 20,6347. [R]ThLZ 130 (2005) 644-6 (*Kollmann, Bernd*); Bib. 86 (2005) 568-71 (*Talbert, Charles*).

6756 *Holmås, Geir O.* 'My house shall be a house of prayer': regarding the temple as a place of prayer in Acts within the context of Luke's apologetical objective. JSNT 27 (2005) 393-416.

6757 *Howes, L.* Handelinge se uitbeelding van die rol van vroue in die vroeë kerk. HTSTS 61 (2005) 1183-1208 [NTAb 51,58].

6758 **Hupe, Henning** Lukas' Schweigen: dekonstruktive Relektüren der 'Wir-Stücke' in Acta. [D]*Lampe, Peter*: 2005, Diss. Heidelberg [ThLZ 131,338].

6759 **Jeong, Chang-Kyo** Die Auferstehung in der Apostelgeschichte. [D]*Berger, Klaus*: 2005, Diss. Heidelberg [ThLZ 131,338].

6760 **Kollmann, Bernd** Joseph Barnabas: his life and legacy. [T]*Henry, Miranda*: 2004 ⇒20,6357. [R]CBQ 67 (2005) 351-2 (*Mitchell, Alan*).

6761 *Kyrychenko, Alexander* The Old Slavonic Acts in apparatus critici of the Greek NT: observations and suggestions. NT 47 (2005) 69-74.

6762 **Langevin, Paul-Émile** Les Actes des Apôtres. 2003 ⇒19,6415. [R]ScEs 57 (2005) 190-193 (*Gourgues, Michel*).

6763 **Le Cornu, Hilary; Shulam, Joseph** A commentary on the Jewish roots of Acts. 2003 ⇒19,6418. [R]Evangel 23/1 (2005) 23 (*Marshall, I. Howard*).

6764 *Liew, Benny T.* Acts. Global bible commentary. 2005 ⇒2443. 419-428.

6765 **Lüdemann, Gerd** The Acts of the Apostles: what really happened in the earliest days of the church. Amherst, NY 2005, Prometheus 419 pp. $28. 1-59102-301-7. Bibl. 403-408.

6766 **MacDonald, Dennis R.** Does the New Testament imitate HOMER?: four cases from the Acts of the Apostles. 2003 ⇒19,6422. [R]RBLit (2005)* (*Harstine, Stan*).

6767 *Marguerat, Daniel* L'image de Paul dans les Actes des Apôtres. Les Actes des Apôtres. LeDiv 199: 2005 ⇒715. 121-154.

6768 **Marguerat, Daniel** The first christian historian: writing the 'Acts of the Apostles'. T*McKinney, Ken; Laughery, Gregory J.; Bauckham, Richard*: MSSNTS 121: 2002 ⇒18,5990... 20,6366. RTrinJ 26 (2005) 143-145 (*Pao, David W.*); RBLit 7 (2005) 360-363 (*Moreland, Milton*).
6769 **Mena Salas, Enrique** También a los Griegos (Hch 11,20): factores del inicio de la misión a los gentiles en Antioquia de Siria. D*Trevijano Etcheverría, R.*: 2005, 558 pp. Diss. Salamanca [RTL 37,616].
6770 *Najda, Andrzej J.* Prophetie und Propheten in der Apostelgeschichte. FZMIJEWSKI, J.: BBB 151: 2005 ⇒172. 211-226.
6771 **Neuberth, Ralph** Demokratie im Volk Gottes: Untersuchungen zur Apostelgeschichte. SBB 46: 2001 ⇒17,5571; 19,6433. RSNTU 30 (2005) 235-237 (*Fuchs, Albert*) [Acts 6,1-7; 13,1-3; 15; 20,17-38].
6772 E**Nicklas, Tobias; Tilly, Michael** The book of Acts as church history. BZNW 120: 2003 ⇒19,388. RThLZ 130 (2005) 409-411 (*Schmid, Ulrich*); CBQ 67 (2005) 189-191 (*Phillips, Thomas E.*); NT 47 (2005) 170-183 (*Güting, Eberhard*);.
6773 **Öhler, Markus** Barnabas: die historische Person und ihre Rezeption in der Apostelgeschichte. WUNT 156: 2003 ⇒19,6439; 20,6373. Rem 21/1 (2005) 36-37 (*Drews, Alexander*); OrdKor 46 (2005) 372-373 (*Giesen, Heinz*); NT 47 (2005) 305-308 (*Stenschke, Christoph*) [1 Cor 9,6; Gal 2,1-14].
6774 **Öhler, Markus** Barnabas: der Mann in der Mitte. Biblische Gestalten 12: Lp 2005, Evang. Verl.-Anst. 205 pp. €14.80. 3-374-02308-8. Bibl. 197-202.
6775 *Patella, Michael* Seers' Corner: Peter's paths. BiTod 43 (2005) 250-255.
6776 **Pelikan, Jaroslav Jan** Acts: Brazos theological commentary on the bible. GR 2005, Brazos 320 pp. $30. 1-587-43094-0. Bibl. 298-304.
6777 *Vander Stichele, Caroline* "All the world's a stage": the rhetoric of gender in Acts. FDENAUX, A.: BEThL 182: 2005 ⇒34. 373-396.
6778 E**Penner, Todd C.; Vander Stichele, Caroline** Contextualizing Acts: Lukan narrative and Greco-Roman discourse. SBL.Symposium 20: 2003 ⇒19,628. RTJT 21 (2005) 261-262 (*Henderson, Ian H.*); RBLit (2005)* (*Elbert, Paul*).
6779 *Pervo, R.I.* The gates have been closed (Acts 21:30): the Jews in Acts. JHiC 11/2 (2005) 128-149 [NTAb 50,503].
6780 **Pesch, Rudolf** Atti degli Apostoli. Assisi ²2005 <1992>, Cittadella 1120 pp. €62. 88-308-0508-4.
6781 *Pérez-Aradros, Carmelo* El paradigma de la inculturación en la misión de hoy, según los Hechos de los Apóstoles. MisEx(M) 208 (2005) 506-522.
6782 **Pilch, John J.** Visions and healing in the Acts of the Apostles: how the early believers experienced God. 2004 ⇒20,6376. RRBLit (2005)* (*Clark, Ronald; Nicklas, Tobias; Walton, Steve*); RBLit 7 (2005) 357-360 (*Walton, Steve*).
6783 *Porter, Stanley E.* The genre of Acts and the ethics of discourse. Acts and ethics. 2005 ⇒464. 1-15.
6784 **Prime, Derek** Active evangelism. 2003 ⇒19,6448. RSBET 23 (2005) 220-224 (*Macleod, Malcolm*).
6785 *Racine, Jean-François* L'hybridité des personnages: une stratégie d'inclusion des gentils dans les Actes des Apôtres. Analyse narrative. BEThL 191: 2005 ⇒742. 559-566.

6786 *Read-Heimerdinger, Jenny; Rius-Camps, Josep* The variant readings of the Western Text of the Acts of the Apostles (XVII) (Acts 11:19-12:25). FgNT 18 (2005) 135-165.

6787 **Reimer, Andy M.** Miracle and magic: a study in the Acts of the Apostles and the Life of APOLLONIUS of Tyana. JSNT.S 235: 2002 ⇒18,6004... 20,6384. [R]BZ 49 (2005) 298-300 (*Kollmann, Bernd*); TJT 21 (2005) 264-265 (*Muir, Steven C.*).

6788 *Rius-Camps, Josep* Le mesianismo de Jesús investigado por el rabino Lucas a partir de sus fuentes judías y cristianas: un escrito a modo de 'demostración' (ἐπίδειξις) dirigido al sumo sacerdote Teófilo. EstB 63 (2005) 527-557.

6789 **Rius-Camps, Josep; Read-Heimerdinger, Jenny** The message of Acts in Codex Bezae: a comparison with the Alexandrian tradition, 1: Acts 1.1-5.42: Jerusalem. JSNT.S 257: 2004 ⇒20,6388. [R]CBQ 67 (2005) 539-540 (*Mullen, Roderic L.*); RCatT 30/1 (2005) 231-234 (*Borrell, Agustí*); RBLit (2005)* (*Dupertuis, Ruben*); JThS 56 (2005) 610-613 (*Elliott, J.K.*).

6790 *Rowe, C. Kavin* Authority and community: Lukan *dominium* in Acts. Acts and ethics. 2005 ⇒464. 96-108.

6791 *Schwartz, Joshua J.* Temple and Temple Mount in the book of Acts: early christian activity, topography, and *halakhah*. Beginnings of christianity. 2005 ⇒786. 279-295.

6792 *Sembrano, Lucio* Tra Gerusalemme e Roma: Antiochia alle origini del cristianesimo. Giudei o cristiani?. 2005 ⇒833. 135-145.

6793 **Shipp, Blake** Paul the reluctant witness: power and weakness in Luke's portrayal. Eugene, OR 2005, Cascade xiv; 174 pp. $22.

6794 **Sicre Díaz, José Luis** Hasta los confines de la tierra, 1: la fuerza del Espíritu. Estella (Navarra) 2005, Verbo Divino 310 pp. 8481696862.

6795 *Spencer, F. Scott* Wise up, young man: the moral vision of Saul and other νεανίσκοι in Acts. Acts and ethics. 2005 ⇒464. 34-48.

6796 **Spencer, Franklin Scott** Journeying through Acts: a literary-cultural reading. 2004 ⇒20,6392. [R]TJT 21 (2005) 276-7 (*Miller, David M.*).

6797 *Tannehill, Robert C.* Do the ethics of Acts include the ethical teaching in Luke?. Acts and ethics. NTMon 9: 2005 ⇒464. 109-122;

6798 The function of Peter's mission speeches in the narrative of Acts. The shape of Luke's story. 2005<1991> ⇒315. 169-184.

6799 **Taylor, Justin** Les Actes des deux apôtres, 4: commentaire historique (Act. 1,1-8,40). EtB 41: 2000 ⇒16,5584; 18,6015. [R]RivBib 53 (2005) 240-243 (*Fabris, Rinaldo*).

6800 *Tucker, J. Brian* God-Fearers: literary foil or historical reality in the book of Acts. JBSt 5/1 (2005) 21-39.

6801 *Tyson, J.B.* Why dates matter: the case of the Acts of the Apostles. The Fourth R [Santa Rosa, CA] 18/2 (2005) 8-11, 14, 17-18 [NTAb 50,56].

6802 *Van Zyl, Hermie C.* The soteriology of Acts: restoration to life. Salvation in the New Testament. NT.S 121: 2005 ⇒798. 133-160.

6803 *Varickasseril, Jose* The Lukan portrait of the early church: a study of the major summaries in the Acts of the Apostles. MissTod 7 (2005) 40-50;

6804 Shepherding through teaching: pastoral reflections on the Acts of the Apostles. [M]JOHN PAUL II. 2005 ⇒72. 195-208.

6805 *Wall, Robert W.* The Acts of the Apostles. NT survey. 2005 ⇒3144. 113-133.

6806 *Wendland, Heinz-Dietrich* Schriftgebundenheit und Geistesleitung in der urchristlichen Mission. em 21 (2005) 140-144.

6807 **Willimon, William H.** Atti degli Apostoli. [E]*Comba, Fernanda Jourdan*: Strumenti—Commentari 13: 2003 ⇒19,6475; 20,6408. [R]Eccl(R) 19 (2005) 537-539 (*Izquierdo, Antonio*).

## F8.3 *Ecclesia primaeva Actuum*—**Die Urgemeinde**

6808 *Bilde, Per* Kognitive Dissonanzreduktion in der Jesusbewegung: ein sozialpsychologischer Beitrag zum Verständnis neutestamentlicher Texte. EvTh 65 (2005) 118-135 [Mt 13,9-17; Mk 8,14-21; Lk 24,13-32; Rom 11,25-27; 1 Cor 1,8-25].

6809 **Borragán Maia, Vicente** En los orígenes del cristianismo: así vivian nuestros primeros hermanos. M 2005, San Pablo 256 pp. €10.35. 84-285-2769-5.

6810 *Boschi, Bernardo Gianluigi* I luoghi di culto e i calendari nelle origini cristiane. RivBib 53 (2005) 325-332.

6811 **Boschi, Bernardo G.** Le origini della chiesa: una rilettura prospettica. CSB 48: Bo 2005, EDB 208 pp. €18. 88-10-40749-0.

6812 *Chilton, Bruce* Conclusions and questions. The missions of James. NT.S 115: 2005 ⇒369. 487-494.

6813 *Deines, Roland* Appendix 2: are there good reasons for studying early christian literature at Ben-Gurion University?. How on earth. 2005 ⇒227. 215-216.

6814 *Gnilka, Joachim* Die urchristliche Hausgemeinde. [F]LAUB, F.: Bibel-Schule-Leben 6: 2005 ⇒87. 125-137.

6815 *Guijarro Oporto, Santiago; Miquel Pericás, Esther* El cristianismo naciente: delimitación, fuentes y metodología. Salm. 52 (2005) 5-37.

6816 *Henry, Martin* Christianity and Hellenism. IThQ 70/4 (2005) 366.

6817 *Klostergaard Petersen, Anders* At the end of the road—reflections on a popular scholarly metaphor. The formation of the early church. WUNT 183: 2005 ⇒708. 45-72.

6818 *Koch, Dietrich-Alex* Crossing the border: the "Hellenists" and their way to the gentiles. Neotest. 39/2 (2005) 289-312 [Acts 6,11-14; Rom 3,25-26; Gal 3,26-28].

6819 **Lüdemann, Gerd** Das Urchristentum: eine kritische Bilanz seiner Erforschung. ARGU 12: 2002 ⇒18,6026. [R]Aevum 79 (2005) 186-189 (*Ramelli, Ilaria*).

6820 *Öhler, Markus* Die Jerusalemer Urgemeinde im Spiegel des antiken Vereinswesens. NTS 51 (2005) 393-415 [Acts 2,42-47; 4,32-35; 5, 12-16].

6821 **Penn, Michael Philip** Kissing christians: ritual and community in the late ancient church. Ph 2005, Univ. of Pennsylvania Pr. 186 pp. 0-81-22-3880-X. Bibl. 163-176.

6822 *Richard, Pablo* Experiencias pluralistas de las primeras comunidades christianas según los Hechos de los Apóstoles. Qol 38 (2005) 3-22.

6823 *Stenström, Hanna* New voices in biblical exegesis—new views on the formation of the church;

6824 *Tellbe, Mikael* The temple tax as a pre-70CE identity marker [Mt 17, 24-27; Rom 13,1-10; 1 Pet 2,4-17]. The formation of the early church. WUNT 183: 2005 ⇒708. 73-90/19-44 .

6825 **Theissen, Gerd** La religione dei primi cristiani: una teoria sul cristianesimo delle origini. Strumenti 16: 2004 ⇒20,6451. [R]Ter. 56 (2005) 321-324 (*Pasquetto, Virgilio*).

6826 *Vitelli, Marco* Quando nasce il cristianesimo?: il contributo di una pubblicazione recente al dibattito sulle origini cristiane. RdT 46 (2005) 757-780.

6827 *Wengst, Klaus* Der "neue Weg": wann begann das Christentum?. WUB 38 (2005) 11-15.

### F8.5 Ascensio, Pentecostes; ministerium Petri—*Act 1...*

6828 **Biffi, Giacomo** Alla destra del Padre. 2004 ⇒20,6457. [R]DT 40 (2005) 261-263 (*Barzaghi, Giuseppe*).

6829 **Dawson, Gerritt Scott** Jesus ascended: the meaning of Christ's continuing incarnation. 2004 ⇒20,6458. [R]RRT 12 (2005) 504-507 (*McCosker, Philip*).

6830 *DeGruchy, Steve* Mission in Acts 1-11: an experiment in bible study. IRM 94 (2005) 228-234.

6831 *Gubler, Marie-Louise* Pfingsten: Geburtstag der Kirche. Diak. 36 (2005) -81 [NTAb 51,02].

6832 **Estrada, Nelson P.** From followers to leaders: the apostles in the ritual of status transformation in Acts 1-2. JSNT.S 255: 2004 ⇒20, 6459. [R]JR 85 (2005) 651-653 (*Rothschild, Clare K.*).

6833 *Alexander, Loveday* The preface to Acts and the historians. Acts in its ancient literary context. LNTS 298: 2005 <1993> ⇒174. 21-42.

6834 *Epp, Eldon J.* The Ascension in the textual tradition of Luke-Acts. Perspectives on NT textual criticism. NT.S 116: 2005 <1981> ⇒ 207. 211-225 [Lk 24,50-51; Acts 1,1-11].

6835 *Pilch, John J.* The ascension of Jesus: a social scientific perspective. [F]STEGEMANN, W. 2005 ⇒139. 75-82 [Lk 24,50-51; Acts 1,1-11].

6836 **Faure, Patrick** Pentecôte et parousie Ac 1,6-3,26: l'église et le mystère d'Israël entre les textes alexandrin et occidental des Actes des Apôtres. EtB 50: 2003 ⇒19,6498; 20,6463. [R]ThRv 101 (2005) 206-207 (*Dormeyer, Detlev*); NRTh 127 (2005) 118-9 (*Radermakers, J.*).

6837 *Melbourne, B.L.* Acts 1:8 re-examined: is Acts 8 its fulfillment?. JRT 58/1-2 (2005) 1-18 [NTAb 50,504].

6838 **Cifrak, Mario** Die Beziehung zwischen Jesus und Gott nach den Petrusreden der Apostelgeschichte: ein exegetischer Beitrag zur Christologie der Apostelgeschichte. FzB 101: 2003 ⇒19,6391. [R]ThLZ 130 (2005) 508-509 (*Krauter, Stefan*); ATG 68 (2005) 305-306 (*Rodríguez Carmona, A.*).

6839 *Beale, Gregory K.* The descent of the eschatological temple in the form of the Spirit at Pentecost, part 1: the clearest evidence. TynB 56/1 (2005) 73-102 [Acts 2].

6840 *Brawley, Robert L.* Social identity and the aim of accomplished life in Acts 2. Acts and ethics. 2005 ⇒464. 16-33.

6841 *Forrester, Duncan B.* The perennial Pentecost. ET 116 (2005) 224-227 [Acts 2].

6842 *Weinfeld, Moshe* Pentecost as festival of the giving of the law. Normative and sectarian Judaism. 2005 ⇒2732. 268-278 [Acts 2].

6843 *Willmes, Bernd* Lukas als Interpret von Joël 3,1-5 in Apg 2. [F]ZMIJEWSKI, J.: BBB 151: 2005 ⇒172. 227-258 [Acts 2].

6844 *Dupertuis, Rubén R.* The summaries of Acts 2, 4, and 5 and PLATO's Republic. Ancient fiction. SBL.Symp. 32: 2005 ⇒721. 275-295.

6845 *Beale, Gregory K.* The descent of the eschatological temple in the form of the Spirit at Pentecost, part 2: corroborating evidence. TynB 56/2 (2005) 63-90 [Acts 2,1-41].

6846 *Charette, Blaine* "Tongues as of fire": judgment as a function of glossolalia in Luke's thought. JPentec 13/2 (2005) 173-186 [Acts 2,3].

6847 *Drewes, Barend* Een pinksterpreek verklaart wie Jezus is. ITBT 13/3 (2005) 21-24 [Acts 2,14-40].

6848 *Riemersma, Nico* Petrus met Pinksteren over Pasen. ITBT 13/3 (2005) 24-26 [Acts 2,14-40].

6849 *Parsons, Mikeal C.* The character of the lame man in Acts 3-4. JBL 124 (2005) 295-312.

6850 *Tannehill, Robert C.* The composition of Acts 3-5: narrative development and echo effect. The shape of Luke's story. 2005 <1984> ⇒ 315. 185-219.

6851 *Cervera, Jordi* A l'encalç d'un lloc de repòs: una aproximació a He 3,7-4,13. La bíblia i els immigrants. 2005 ⇒471. 185-196.

6852 *Abela, Anthony* Acts 4,25a: recognizing a concentric arrangement. MTh 56/1 (2005) 93-100.

6853 *Combet-Galland, Corina* L'expulsion du mal: un acte de naissance de l'église: pourquoi Satan a-t-il rempli ton coeur?. FV 104/1 (2005) 43-61 [Acts 5,1-11].

6854 *Ntumba, V.K.* Ac 5,1-11: Ananie et Saphire: lecture exégétique et réflexions théologiques. Hekima Review 34 (2005) 43-55[NTAb 50, 504].

6855 *Hamidovic, David* La remarque énigmatique d'Ac 5,4 dans la légende d'Ananias et Saphira. Bib. 86 (2005) 407-415.

6856 *Tasca, Francesca* La pia disobbedienza: l'esegesi di Atti 5,29 dalla patristica latina ai "libelli de lite". ASEs 22/1 (2005) 223-254.

6857 *Nagel, N.* The Twelve and the Seven in Acts 6 and the needy. ConJ 31/2 (2005) 113-126 [NTAb 49,514].

6858 *Mainville, Odette* Étienne face à la mort: le disciple à l'image du Maître. [F]GENEST, O. 2005 ⇒46. 375-395 [Acts 6-7].

6859 *Penner, Todd* Early christian heroes and Lukan narrative: Stephen and the Hellenists in ancient historiographical perspective. Rhetoric and reality. SCJud 16: 2005 ⇒515. 75-97 [Acts 6-7].

6860 *Bovon, F.* Beyond the book of Acts: Stephen, the first christian martyr, in traditions outside the New Testament canon of scripture. PRSt 32/2 (2005) 93-107 [Acts 6-8].

6861 *Penner, Todd* In praise of christian origins: Stephen and the Hellenists in Lukan apologetic historiography. 2004 ⇒20,6478. [R]Theol. 108 (2005) 441-442 (*Downing, F. Gerald*); TJT 21 (2005) 259-260 (*Alary, Laura D.*); RBLit (2005)* (*Malas, William; Seland, Torrey*) [Acts 6,1-8,3].

6862 *Matthews, Shelly* The need for the stoning of Stephen. Violence in the NT. 2005 ⇒439. 124-139 [Acts 6,8-8,1].

6863 *Kilgallen, John J.* Stephen's lesson. BiTod 43 (2005) 371-6 [Acts 7].

6864 **Jeska, Joachim** Die Geschichte Israels in der Sicht des Lukas: Apg 7,2b-53 und 13,17-25 im Kontext antik-jüdischer Summarien der Geschichte Israels. FRLANT 195: 2001 ⇒17,5636... 20,6483. ᴿRBLit (2005)* (*Litwak, Kenneth*).

6865 *Hilhorst, Ton* 'And Moses was instructed in all the wisdom of the Egyptians' (Acts 7.22). ᶠLUTTIKHUIZEN, G.: AGJU 59: 2005 ⇒93. 153-176.

6866 *Cartlidge, D.R.* The fall and rise of Simon Magus. BiRe 21/4 (2005) 24-36 [NTAb 50,58] [Acts 8,9-24].

6867 **Ferreiro, Alberto** Simon Magus in patristic, medieval and early modern traditions. Studies in the history of christian traditions 125: Lei 2005, Brill xi; 371 pp. €89/$115. 90-04-14495-1 [Acts 8,9-24].

6868 **Haar, Stephen** Simon Magus: the first gnostic?. BZNW 119: 2003 ⇒19,6519; 20,6488. ᴿThLZ 130 (2005) 1330-1332 (*Zangenberg, Jürgen*) [Acts 8,9-24].

6869 *Bos, R.* Van wie zegt de profeet dit?; een een-voudige vraag en een meervoudig antwoord. HTSTS 61(2005) 1183-1208 [NTAb 51,60] [Acts 8,26-40].

6870 *Rendón Leal, Ruy* El bautismo del eunuco etíope (Hech 8,26-40). ᶠJUNCO GARZA, C. 2005 ⇒74. 377-403.

6871 *Erichsen-Wendt, Friederike* Tabitha—Leben an der Grenze. BN 127 (2005) 67-90 [Acts 9,36-43].

6872 *Lawson, Veronica* Tabitha of Joppa: disciple, prophet and biblical prototype for contemporary religious life. ᶠMOLONEY, F.: BSRel 187: 2005 ⇒104. 281-292 [Acts 9,36-43].

6873 *Steffek, Emmanuelle* Quand juifs et païens se mettent à table (Ac 10). ETR 80 (2005) 103-111.

6874 *Wahlen, Clinton* Peter's vision and conflicting definitions of purity. NTS 51 (2005) 505-518 [Acts 10-11].

6875 *Shea, Chris* Imitating imitation: VERGIL, HOMER, and Acts 10:1-11: 18. Ancient fiction. SBL.Symp. 32: 2005 ⇒721. 37-59.

6876 *Djomhoué, Priscille* Une histoire de rapprochement: Actes 10-11,18. FV 104/4 (2005) 71-82.

## F8.7 Act 13...*Itinera Pauli*; Paul's journeys

6877 *Goodman, Martin* The persecution of Paul by Diaspora Jews. Beginnings of christianity. 2005 ⇒786. 379-387.

6878 *Heininger, Bernhard* Im Dunstkreis der Magie: Paulus als Wundertäter nach der Apostelgeschichte. Biographie...des Paulus. WUNT 187: 2005 ⇒349. 271-291.

6879 *Phillips, Thomas E.* Paul as a role model in Acts: the 'we'-passages in Acts 16 and beyond. Acts and ethics. 2005 ⇒464. 49-63.

6880 **Porter, Stanley E.** Paul in Acts. 2001 ⇒17,5656. ᴿJBSt 5/1 (2005) 40-44 (*Cooke, Robert*).

6881 *Skinner, Matthew L.* Unchained ministry: Paul's Roman custody (Acts 21-28) and the sociopolitical outlook of the book of Acts. Acts and ethics. 2005 ⇒464. 79-95.

6882 *Tannehill, Robert C.* Paul outside the christian ghetto: intercultural conflict and cooperation in Acts. The shape of Luke's story. 2005 <1990> ⇒315. 220-237;

6883 Rejection by Jews and turning to gentiles: the pattern of Paul's mission in Acts. The shape of Luke's story. 2005 <1986> ⇒315. 145-65.

6884 *Thompson, Richard P.* 'What do you think you are doing, Paul?': synagogues, accusations, and ethics in Paul's ministry in Acts 16-21. Acts and ethics. 2005 ⇒464. 64-78.

6885 *Fitzmyer, Joseph A.* Pauline justification as presented by Luke in Acts 13. [F]MOLONEY, F.: BSRel 187: 2005 ⇒104. 249-263.

6886 *Kuberski, Jürgen* Wer sandte die ersten Missionare?. em 21/1 (2005) 13-16 [Acts 13,1-4].

6887 *Dionne, Christian* L'épisode de Lystre (Ac 14,7-20a): une analyse narrative. ScEs 57 (2005) 5-33;

6888 La figure narrative de Dieu dans le discours à Lystre (Ac 14,15-17). ScEs 57 (2005) 101-124.

6889 *Casalegno, Alberto* A ação do Espírito Santo na assembléia de Jerusalém (At 15). PerTeol 37 (2005) 367-380.

6890 **Neubrand, Maria** Israel, die Völker und die Kirche—eine exegetische Studie zu Apg 15. [D]*Mayer, Bernhard* 2005, Diss.-Habil. Eichstätt [ThRv 102,xiii].

6891 **Taylor, Justin** The "Council" of Jerusalem in Acts 15. Synod and synodality: theology, history, canon law and ecumenism in new contact: international colloquium, Bruges 2003. [E]*Melloni, Alberto*: Christianity and history 1: Müns 2005, LIT 107-113 978-3-8258-74-37-7.

6892 *Hoet, Hendrik* ἐξ ἐθνῶν λαὸν (Ac 15,14);

6893 *Koet, Bart J.* Im Schatten des Aeneas: Paulus in Troas (Apg 16,8-10). [F]DENAUX, A.: BEThL 182: 2005 ⇒34. 397-413/415-439.

6894 *Isaak, Jon M.* Lydia's story: christian conversion as relational, collaborative, and invitational (Acts 16:11- 15). Arc 33 (2005) 229-236.

6895 *Suazo, D.* El poder de la verdad para transformar culturas: el evangelio transforma a individuos, estruturas y sociedades (Hechos 16:11-40). Kairós 37 (2005) 97-110 [NTAb 50,58].

6896 *Winter, B.W.* Introducing the Athenians to God: Paul's failed apologetic in Acts 17. Themelios 30/1 (2005) 38-59 [NTAb 50,295].

6897 *Gaventa, Beverly R.* "Turning the world upside down": a reflection on the Acts of the Apostles. [F]BRUEGGEMANN, W.—COUSAR, C. 2005 ⇒16. 105-116 [Acts 17,1-9].

6898 **Gunn, Têtê Délali** Prosopopée idéologique de Paul: une lecture socio-rhétorique du discours de Paul à Athènes (Actes 17,15-18,1). [D]*Bloomquist, G.* 2005, Diss. Ottawa [RTL 37,607].

6899 *Charles, J. Daryl* Paul before the Areopagus: reflections on the apostle's encounter with cultured paganism. Philosophia Christi 7/1 (2005) 125-140 [Acts 17,16-34].

6900 *Torkki, Juhana* Paul in Athens (Acts 17:16-34): a dramatic episode. [F]AEJMELAEUS, L.: SESJ 89: 2005 ⇒1. 337-363.

6901 *Gray, Patrick* Athenian curiosity (Acts 17:21). NT 47 (2005) 109-16.

6902 *Schnabel, Eckhard J.* Contextualising Paul in Athens: the proclamation of the gospel before pagan audiences in the Graeco-Roman world. R&T 12 (2005) 172-190 [Acts 17,22-31].

6903 *Clivaz, Claire* L'analyse narrative signale-t-elle l'arrivée du muthos en exégèse?: histoire et poétique autour d'Ac 17,28. Analyse narrative. BEThL 191: 2005 ⇒742. 483-495.

6904 **Shauf, Scott** Theology as history, history as theology: Paul in Ephesus in Acts 19. [D]*Holladay, C.R.*: BZNW 133: B 2005, De Gruyter x; 377 pp. €98. 3-11-018395-1. Diss. Emory; Bibl. 333-357.

6905 *Weren, Wim* The riot of the Ephesian silversmiths (Acts 19,23-40): Luke's advice to his readers. [F]DENAUX, A.: BEThL 182: 2005 ⇒34. 441-456.

6906 *Kowalski, Beate* Der Fenstersturz in Troas (Apg 20,7-12). SNTU.A 30 (2005) 19-37.

6907 *Haraguchi, Takaaki* A tragic farewell discourse?: in search of a new understanding of Paul's Miletus speech (Acts 20:18-35). AJBI 30-31 (2004-2005) 137-153.

6908 **Skinner, Matthew L.** Locating Paul: places of custody as narrative settings in Acts 21-28. Academia Biblica 13: 2003 ⇒19,6566; 20, 6529. [R]RBLit (2005)* (*Nicklas, Tobias; Omerzu, Heike*).

6909 *Quesnel, Michel* Analyse rhétorique des discours d'apologie de Paul: Ac 22 et 26. Les Actes des Apôtres. LeDiv 199: 2005 ⇒715. 155-76.

6910 *Tannehill, Robert C.* The narrator's strategy in the scenes of Paul's defense. The shape of Luke's story. 2005 <1992> ⇒315. 238-253 [Acts 24-26].

6911 *Gangloff, Frédéric* Actes 26,4-23: retour vers le futur. LeD 64 (2005) 23-33.

6912 **Mendonca, Dominik** Shipwreck and providence: the mission programme of Acts 27-28. [D]*Klauck, Hans-Josef* 2005, Diss. München [ThRv 102,ix].

6913 **Seul, Peter** 'Rettung für alle': die Romreise des Paulus nach Apg 27, 1-28,16. BBB 146: 2003 ⇒19,6571. [R]ThLZ 130 (2005) 959-961 (*Labahn, Michael*).

6914 *Clabeaux, John* The story of the Maltese viper and Luke's apology for Paul. CBQ 67 (2005) 604-610 [Acts 28,1-6].

6915 *Weissenrieder, Annette* "He is a god!": Acts 28:1-9 in the light of iconographical and textual sources related to medicine. Picturing the New Testament. WUNT 2/193: 2005 ⇒396. 127-156.

6916 *Kilgallen, John* '...and I will heal them' (Acts 28:27). PIBA 28 (2005) 87-105.

## XI. Johannes

### G1.1 *Corpus johanneum*: John and his community

6917 **Becker, Jürgen** Johanneisches Christentum: seine Geschichte und Theologie im Überblick. 2004 ⇒20,6536. [R]Cart. 21 (2005) 244-245 (*Alvarez Barredo, M.*); RHPhR 85 (2005) 450-451 (*Grappe, Ch.*): ThQ 185 (2005) 152-153=234-235 (*Theobald, Michael*); RB 112 (2005) 427-436 (*Devillers, Luc*); BiLi 78 (2005) 59-61 (*Scholtissek, Klaus*).

6918 **Brown, Tricia Gates** Spirit in the writings of John: Johannine pneumatology in social-scientific perspectives. JSNT.S 253: 2003 ⇒19, 6575. [R]CBQ 67 (2005) 134-135 (*Montague, George T.*); BiblInterp 13 (2005) 435-438 (*North, Wendy E.S.*); RBLit (2005)* (*Fay, Ron; Hunt, Steven A.*); RBLit 7 (2005) 341-345 (*Hunt, Steven A.*); JThS 56 (2005) 551-555 (*Edwards, Ruth B.*).

6919 **Callahan, Allen Dwight** A love supreme: a history of the Johannine tradition. Mp 2005, Fortress x; 128 pp. $20. 0-8006-3708-9. Bibl. 115-119 [ThD 52,150—W. Charles Heiser].

6920 **Fernández Ramos, Felipe** Diccionario del mundo joánico: Evangelio-Cartas-Apocalipsis. 2004 ⇒20,6539. [R]StLeg 46 (2005) 263-264 (*Robles García, Constantino*); ATG 68 (2005) 306-307 (*Contreras Molina, Francisco*).

6921 *Fitzmyer, Joseph A.* Qumran literature and the Johannine writings. [M]BROWN, R. 2005 ⇒15. 117-133.

6922 [E]**Fortna, Robert T.; Thatcher, Tom** Jesus in Johannine tradition. 2001 ⇒17,5694... 20,6540. [R]BiblInterp 13 (2005) 74-77 (*North, Wendy S.*).

6923 *Frey, Jörg* Eschatology in the Johannine circle. Theology and christology. BEThL 184: 2005 ⇒796. 47-82.

6924 **Ghiberti, Giuseppe**, al., Opera giovannea. Logos 7: 2003 ⇒19, 6579; 20,6541. [R]EeV 127 (2005) 19-20 (*Cothenet, Édouard*); RivBib 53 (2005) 108-113 (*Fabris, Rinaldo*); Asp. 52 (2005) 419-422 (*Castello, Gaetano*).

6925 *Grech, Prosper* Il kerigma della comunità giovannea. Atti del X Simposio di Efeso. Turchia 19: 2005 ⇒785. 7-16 [John 3,11-21; 12,42-50; 1 John 4,7-10];

6926 =Il messaggio biblico. SRivBib 44: 2005 ⇒216. 343-349;

6927 L'escatologia degli scritti giovannei (quarto vangelo e lettere). Il messaggio biblico. SRivBib 44: 2005 <1999> ⇒216. 319-332.

6928 *Gregory, Andrew* On rescuing John from scholarly orthodoxy. ET 116 (2005) 263-266.

6929 *Harrington, Daniel J.* Response to Joseph A. Fitzmyer, S.J. "Qumran literature and the Johannine writings". [M]BROWN, R. 2005 ⇒15. 134-137.

6930 *Heiligenthal, Roman* Der johanneische Gemeindekonflikt: Hintergründe der Konfliktparänese im johanneischen Schrifttum. [F]BÜMLEIN, K. 2005 ⇒18. 31-42.

6931 **Hill, Charles E.** The Johannine corpus in the early church. 2004 ⇒ 20,6544. [R]CBQ 67 (2005) 346-348 (*Culpepper, R. Alan*); ThLZ 130 (2005) 1321-1323 (*Heckel, Theo K.*); JR 85 (2005) 657-659 (*Attridge, Harold W.*); ASEs 22 (2005) 519-522 (*Kraus, Thomas J.*); RBLit (2005)* (*Keefer, Kyle*); JThS 56 (2005) 202-207 (*Edwards, M.J.*); ET 116 (2005) 263-266 (*Gregory, Andrew*).

6932 **Kinlaw, Pamela E.** The Christ is Jesus: metamorphosis, possession, and Johannine christology. Academia biblica 18: Lei 2005, Brill xii; 206 pp. 90-04-13767-X. Also Atlanta: SBL $33; 15898-31659. [R]RBLit (2005)* (*Carson, Donald; Nicklas, Tobias*).

6933 *Klauck, Hans-Josef* Community, history, and text(s): a response to Robert Kysar. [M]BROWN, R. 2005 ⇒15. 82-90.

6934 *Kysar, Robert* The whence and whither of the Johannine community. [M]BROWN, R. 2005 ⇒15. 65-81.

6935 [E]**Levine, Amy-Jill; Blickenstaff, Marianne** A feminist companion to John, 1-2. FCNT 4-5: 2003 ⇒19,372. [R]Faith & Mission 22/2 (2005) 107-111 (*Köstenberger, Andreas J.*).

6936 **Lupo, Angela Maria** La sete, l'acqua, lo spirito: studio esegetico e teologico sulla connessione die termini negli scritti giovannei. AnGr 289: 2003 ⇒19,6583. [R]RivBib 53 (2005) 233-238 (*Marino, Marcello*) [John 7,37-39; 4; 19,28-30; Rev 7,14-17; 21-22].

6937 **Marino, Marcello** Custodire la parola: tra ascolto e prassi. [D]*Vanni, Ugo*: Commenti e studi biblici: Assisi 2005, Cittadella 352 pp. €29. 90. Diss. Gregoriana [PaVi 51/2,63—Michelangelo Priotto].

6938 *Morgen, Michèle* Les écrits johanniques. RSR 93 (2005) 291-324.
6939 *Müller, Ekkehardt* The Jews and the Messianic community in Johannine literature. DavarLogos 4/2 (2005) 159-180.
6940 *Nalewaj, Aleksandra* Janowe wyznania wiary w ujęciu Prospera Grecha [John's confessions of faith according to Prosper Grech]. RBL 58 (2005) 191-196. **P.**
6941 **Pasquetto, Virgilio** In comunione con Cristo e con i fratelli: lessico antropologico del vangelo e delle lettere di Giovanni. 2001 ⇒17, 5706; 18,6125. [R]CDios 218 (2005) 249-250 (*Gutiérrez, J.*).
6942 *Pastorelli, David* Le participe adverbial dans le corpus johannique. REA 107 (2005) 713-726.
6943 **Popkes, Enno Edzard** Die Theologie der Liebe Gottes in den johanneischen Schriften: Studien zur Semantik der Liebe und zum Motivkreis des Dualismus. [D]*Frey, Jörg*: WUNT 2/197: Tü 2005, Mohr S. xviii; 466 pp. €74. 3-16-148669-2. Diss. München; Bibl. 363-423.
6944 **Scholtissek, Klaus** In ihm sein und bleiben: die Sprache der Immanenz in den Johanneischen Schriften. Herders biblische Studien 21: 2000 ⇒16,5757...19,6591. [R]RB 112 (2005) 113-19 (*Devillers, Luc*); RBLit (2005)* (*Labahn, Michael*) [John 13,31-14,31; 6; 15-17; 10].
6945 *Segalla, Giuseppe* Gesù Cristo, ho logos: un socioletto della comunità giovannea. [F]VANNI, U. 2005 ⇒156. 245-255.
6946 *Tepedino, Ana Maria* A importância do Espírito Santo/Paráclito na tradição joanina. AtT 9 (2005) 156-175.
6947 **Thomas, John Christopher** The spirit of the New Testament. Lei 2005, Deo xiii; 283 pp. £20. 90-5854-029-4.
6948 *Turner, John D.* Sethian gnosticism and Johannine christianity. Theology and christology. BEThL 184: 2005 ⇒796. 399-433.
6949 *Untergassmair, Franz G.* "Du bist der Lehrer Israels und verstehst das nicht?" (Joh 2,10b)—Lernen bei Johannes. Religiöses Lernen. WUNT 180: 2005 ⇒384. 211-233.

## G1.2 Evangelium Johannis: *textus, commentarii*

6950 [E]**Aland, Kurt; Aland, Barbara; Wachtel, Klaus** Text und Textwert der griechischen Handschriften des Neuen Testaments, 5: das Johannesevangelium, 1: Textstellenkollation der Kapitel 1-10, T. 1: Handschriftenliste und vergleichende Beschreibung; 2: Resultate der Kollation und Hauptliste. ANTT 35-36: B 2005, De Gruyter viii; 648 +695+82* pp. 311-018673-X. Plus inserted booklet *Ergänzungsliste.*
6951 **Bennema, Cornelis** Excavating John's gospel: a commentary for today. Delhi 2005, ISPCK xiii; 238 pp [MissTod 9,278–Jose Varickasseril].
6952 **Borghesi, Fabio** La libertà del Verbo incarnato: i commentari al vangelo di Giovanni, di TEODORO di Mopsuestia, CIRILLO di Alessandria e AGOSTINO di Ippona. R 2000, Lateranum 187 pp. Diss.; Bibl. 179-183.
6953 **Burge, Gary M.** John. NIV Application Comm.: GR 2000, Zondervan 618 pp. $30. 0-310-49750-7. Bibl. 47-50.
6954 *Burton, Philip* Johannes. BVLI 49 (2005) 33-35.
6955 **Dietzfelbinger, Christian** Das Evangelium nach Johannes, 1: Johannes 1-12; 2: 13-21. Zürcher Bibelkommentare 4,1-2: 2001 ⇒17, 5722; 19,6605. [R]CDios 218 (2005) 246-247 (*Gutiérrez, J.*).

6956 **Edwards, Mark** John. Blackwell Bible Commentaries: 2004 ⇒20, 6560. [R]RRT 12/1 (2005) 143-144 (*Armson, John*); EThL 81 (2005) 229-230 (*Van Belle, G.*).

6957 *Head, Peter M.* P. Bodmer II (P66): three fragments identified. NT 47 (2005) 105-108 [John 18,31; 18,36; 19,10; 19,14; 21,5; 21,7-8].

6958 **Keener, Craig S.** The gospel of John, a commentary. 2003 ⇒19, 6608; 20,6566. [R]RSR 93 (2005) 303-304 (*Morgen, Michèle*); ScrB 35 (2005) 111-115 (*Corley, Jeremy*); EThL 81 (2005) 231-235 (*Dennis, John*); JETh 19 (2005) 267-270 (*Stenschke, Christoph*); RBLit 7 (2005) 345-347 (*Klink, Edward W., III*); PIBA 28 (2005) 125-127 (*Goan, Seán*); JThS 56 (2005) 548-551 (*Edwards, Ruth B.*).

6959 **Köstenberger, Andreas J.** John. Exeg. Comm. on the NT: 2004 ⇒ 20,6568. [R]Faith & Mission 22/3 (2005) 109-111 (*Keener, Craig*); RBLit (2005)* (*Van der Watt, Jan*).

6960 **Kruse, Colin G.** The gospel according to John: an introduction and commentary. TNTC: 2003 ⇒19,6609; 20,6569. [R]RBLit (2005)* (*Van Der Merwe, Dirk*).

6961 **Lewis, Scott M.** The gospel according to John and the Johannine letters. New Collegeville Bible Commentary: ColMn 2005, Liturgical 142 pp. $7 [BiTod 44,128—Donald Senior].

6962 **Lincoln, Andrew T.** The gospel according to Saint John. Black's New Testament Commentaries 4: L 2005, Hendrickson ix; 584 pp. $30. 1-56563-401-2. Bibl. 537-547.

6963 **Moloney, Francis** El evangelio de Juan. [T]*Pérez Escobar, José*: Estella 2005, Verbo Divino 597 pp. 84-816-9680-3. Bibl. 49-54 [RevAg 46,626s—Antonio Salas];

6964 The gospel of John: text and context. BiblInterp 72: Lei 2005, Brill xvi; 389 pp. 0-391-04246-7. Bibl. 348-369.

6965 **Mullins, Michael** The gospel of John: a commentary. 2003 ⇒19, 6611; 20,6572. [R]IThQ 70 (2005) 375-376 (*Harrington, Wilfrid*).

6966 *Muñoz León, Domingo* Vangelo secondo san Giovanni. I vangeli. 2005 ⇒432. 875-1026.

6967 *Nongbri, Brent* The use and abuse of P52: papyrological pitfalls in the dating of the fourth gospel. HThR 98 (2005) 23-48.

6968 **Patier, Claire** Maître, où demeures-tu?: commentaire de l'évangile de Jean. Biblik: P 2005, Renaissance 168 pp. €15.

6969 *Pintaudi, Rosario* NT, *Johannes* 17.1-14 (MS 1367). Greek Papyri, Volume I. 2005 ⇒682. 55-56.

6970 **Rivas, Luis Heriberto** El evangelio de Juan: introducción, teología, comentario. BA 2005, San Benito 576 pp. $43. 98711-77186. Teol. 42,491.

6971 **Schnelle, Udo** Das Evangelium nach Johannes. ThHK 4: [3]2004 <1998> ⇒20,6575. [R]BiLi 78 (2005) 62-63 (*Scholtissek, Klaus*).

6972 **Thyen, Hartwig** Das Johannesevangelium. HNT 6: Tü 2005, Mohr S. xii; 796 pp. €49. 3-16-147485-1. [R]EstAg 40 (2005) 584 (*Cineira, D.A.*); StPat 52 (2005) 912-922 (*Segalla, Giuseppe*); ThGl 95 (2005) 500-501 (*Kowalski, Beate*).

6973 **Van Tilborg, Sjef** Das Johannes-Evangelium: ein Kommentar für die Praxis. [E]*Dillmann, Rainer; Dormeyer, Detlev* Stu 2005, Kath. Bibelwerk xiv; 320 pp. €24.90. 3-460-33128-3;

6974 Comentario al evangelio de Juan. Evangelio y cultura: Estella 2005, Verbo Divino 452 pp.

6975 **Vanier, Jean** Drawn into the mystery of Jesus through the gospel of John. 2004 ⇒20,6579. [R]NBl 86 (2005) 557-559 (*Cargin, Jim*).

6976 *Veerkamp, Ton* Das Evangelium nach Johannes in kolometrischer Übersetzung. TeKo 28/2 (2005) 3-111.

6977 [E]**Wechsler, Michael G.** Evangelium Iohannis Aethiopicum. CSCO. Ae 109; CSCO 617: Lv 2005, Peeters xliv; 210 pp. €79. 90-429-164-8-6. Bibl. xlii-xliv.

6978 **Wengst, Klaus** Das Johannesevangelium, 1. Teilband: Kapitel 1-10. TKNT 4/1: [2]2004 <2000> ⇒20,6581. [R]EvTh 65 (2005) 73-78 (*Karrer, Martin*);

6979 Das Johannesevangelium, 1-2. TKNT 4/1-2: 2001 ⇒18,6152... 20, 6583. [R]EvTh 65 (2005) 73-78 (*Karrer, Martin*);

6980 Il vangelo di Giovanni. Brescia 2005, Queriniana 843 pp. 88-339-11-34-0. [R]StPat 52 (2005) 905-911 (*Segalla, Giuseppe*).

6981 **Wojciechowski, Michal** Pochodzenie swiata, czlowieka, zla: odpowiedz biblii. Czestochowa 2005, Swiety Pawel 126 pp. 83-7168-960-8. **P.**

## G1.3 **Introductio** *in Evangelium Johannis*

6982 **Brown, Raymond E.** An introduction to the gospel of John. [E]*Moloney, Francis J.*: AncB Reference Library: 2003 ⇒19,6623; 20,6586. [R]RB 112 (2005) 273-277 (*Devillers, Luc*); RevBib 67 (2005) 112-114 (*Rivas, Luis H.*); JThS 56 (2005) 158-160 (*Griffith-Jones, R.*).

6983 *Cardellino, Lodovico* Priorità di Giovanni. BeO 47 (2005) 187-276.

6984 *Culpepper, R. Alan* The legacy of Raymond E. Brown and beyond: a response to Francis J. Moloney. [M]BROWN, R. 2005 ⇒15. 40-51.

6985 *Harrington, Daniel J.* John's gospel revisited. America 193/9 (2005) 25-26.

6986 *Lieu, Judith* How John writes. [F]STANTON, G. 2005 ⇒138. 171-183.

6987 *Magri, Annarita* Notes sur la réception de l'évangile de Jean au IIe siècle: l'idée gnostique de canon. Le canon du NT. MoBi 54: 2005 ⇒ 334. 117-140.

6988 *Merlin, Benoît* Jean le mystique. Le monde des religions 14 (2005) 34-35.

6989 *Moloney, Francis J.* The gospel of John: the legacy of Raymond E. Brown and beyond. [M]BROWN, R. 2005 ⇒15. 19-39;

6990 =The gospel of John. BiblInterp 72: 2005 ⇒6964. 112-136;

6991 Where does one look?: reflections on some recent Johannine scholarship. The gospel of John. BiblInterp 72: 2005 ⇒6964. 137-166.

6992 *Naffziger, A.* Meeting Jesus again. America 192/8 (2005) 14-17 [NTAb 49,481].

6993 **Nagel, Titus** Die Rezeption des Johannesevangeliums im 2. Jahrhundert. ABiG 2: 2000 ⇒16,5799... 18,6169. [R]ThLZ 130 (2005) 749-752 (*Markschies, Christoph*).

6994 *O'Day, Gail R.* The gospel of John. NT survey. 2005 ⇒3144. 95-112.

6995 **Ricca, Paolo** Evangelo di Giovanni. [E]*Caramore, G.*: Brescia 2005, Morcelliana 302 pp. Conversazione con Gabriella Caramore.

6996 *Smith, D. Moody* Future directions of Johannine studies. [M]BROWN, R. 2005 ⇒15. 52-62.

6997 **Smith, Dwight Moody** John among the gospels. [2]2001 <1992> ⇒ 17,5746...20,6604. [R]RBLit 7 (2005) 348-351 (*Boring, M. Eugene*).

6998 *Thatcher, Tom* Why John wrote a gospel: memory and history in an early christian community. Memory, tradition, and text. SBL.Semeia Studies 52: 2005 ⇒416. 79-97.

6999 **Waetjen, Herman C.** The gospel of the beloved disciple: a work in two editions. NY 2005, Clark xx; 468 pp. $40. 0-567-02781-3. Bibl. 428-450.

## G1.4 *Themata de evangelio Johannis*—John's Gospel, topics

7000 *Alvarez, Francisco* 'Vita e vita in abbondanza' nel vangelo di Giovanni. Camillianum 14 (2005) 219-247.

7001 **Asiedu-Peprah, Martin** Johannine sabbath conflicts as juridical controversy. WUNT 2/132: 2001 ⇒17,5751... 19,6634. [R]RSR 93 (2005) 292-294 (*Morgen, Michèle*).

7002 *Baddeley, Jennifer* Two witnesses and a discourse: the gospel of John on christian joy. RTR 64/1 (2005) 35-47.

7003 *Barnett, Paul* Indications of earliness in the gospel of John. RTR 64/2 (2005) 61-75.

7004 **Barreiro, Álvaro** Vimos a sua glória. Sede de Deus: São Paulo 2005, Paulinas 199 pp.

7005 *Bauckham, Richard* Monotheism and christology in the gospel of John. Contours of christology. 2005 ⇒775. 148-166.

7006 **Bennema, Cornelis** The power of saving wisdom: an investigation of spirit and wisdom in relation to the soteriology of the fourth gospel. WUNT 2/148: 2002 ⇒18,6184... 20,6609. [R]BZ 49 (2005) 140-142 (*Löning, Karl*); RSR 93 (2005) 294-295 (*Morgen, Michèle*).

7007 *Bennema, Cornelis* The sword of the messiah and the concept of liberation in the fourth gospel. Bib. 86 (2005) 35-58.

7008 [E]**Bieringer, Reimund; Pollefeyt, D.; Vandecasteele-Vanneuville, F.** Anti-Judaism and the fourth gospel: Leuven Colloq. 2000. 2001 ⇒17,5747...20,6614. [R]ScEs 57 (2005) 71-76 (*Gourgues, Michel*).

7009 *Biguzzi, Giancarlo* I "segni" giovannei. [F]GHIBERTI, G.: SRivBib 46: 2005 ⇒47. 25-33.

7010 *Blanchard, Yves-Marie* Le quatrième évangile, au feu de l'analyse narrative: relecture et perspectives. Raconter. CRB 61: 2005 ⇒717. 69-81;

7011 La fonction régulatrice et inspirante de la référence scripturaire en mariologie. Ist. 50/3 (2005) 261-272 [NTAb 50,285].

7012 *Boer, Martinus de* Jesus' departure to the father in John: death or resurrection?. Theology & christology. BEThL 184: 2005 ⇒796. 1-19.

7013 *Borgonovo, Gianantonio* Calendario e feste nel quarto vangelo: un tentativo di spiegazione.[F]GHIBERTI, G.: 2005 ⇒47. 35-41.

7014 *Boyarin, Daniel* What kind of a Jew is an evangelist?. Those outside. 2005 ⇒332. 109-153 [John 1,1-18].

7015 **Brant, Jo-Ann A.** Dialogue and drama: elements of Greek tragedy in the fourth gospel. 2004 ⇒20,6619. [R]RBLit (2005)* (*Matson, Mark*).

7016 **Brunson, Andrew C.** Psalm 118 in the gospel of John: an intertextual study on the New Exodus pattern in the theology of John. WUNT 2/158: 2003 ⇒19,6655; 20,6621. [R]NT 47 (2005) 297-299 (*Doble, Peter*).

7017 *Buchhold, Jacques* L'évangile de Jean: une 'traduction' des synoptiques. ThEv(VS) 4/1 (2005) 19-30.

7018 **Busse, Ulrich** Das Johannesevangelium: Bildlichkeit, Diskurs und Ritual...Bibliographie 1986-1998. BEThL 162: 2002 ⇒18,6195; 20, 6622. [R]RSR 93 (2005) 296-298 (*Morgen, Michèle*).

7019 *Byron, Brian* Non-explicit allusions to the pentateuch in the gospel of John: catchwords for catechesis on Jewish basics?. ACR 82 (2005) 335-345.

7020 *Callahan, Allen D.* The gospel of John as people's history. Christian origins. A people's history of christianity 1: 2005 ⇒550. 162-176.

7021 **Campbell, Joan C.** Divided family and fictive family: an investigation of kinship relations in the fourth gospel. [D]*Donaldson, T.* 2005, 330 pp. Diss. Toronto, St. Michael [RTL 37,613].

7022 **Cothenet, Édouard** La chaîne des témoins dans l'évangile de Jean: de Jean-Baptiste au disciple bien-aimé. LiBi 142: P 2005, Cerf 151 pp. €20. 2-204-07865-4. Bibl. 145-147.

7023 *Destro, Adriana; Pesce, Mauro* Conflitti e soluzione dei conflitti nel vangelo di Giovanni. Atti del X Simposio di Efeso. Turchia 19: 2005 ⇒785. 91-117.

7024 *Devillers, L.* Dieu le Père dans le quatrième évangile. Roczniki Teologiczne 52/1 (2005) 95-116 [NTAb 50,496].

7025 **Diefenbach, Manfred** Der Konflikt Jesu mit den "Juden". NTA 41: 2002 ⇒18,6211... 20,6633. [R]CDios 218 (2005) 248-249 (*Gutiérrez, J.*); RSR 93 (2005) 299-301 (*Morgen, Michèle*).

7026 *Du Rand, Jan A.* The creation motif in the fourth gospel: perspectives on its narratological function within a Judaistic background. Theology and christology. BEThL 184: 2005 ⇒796. 21-46.

7027 *Dugandžić, Ivan* Majka, žena, učenica: mjesto i uloga Isusove majke u Ivanovu evandelju. BoSm 75 (2005) 97-116 [John 1,14; 2,1-11; 19, 25-27]. **Croatian**.

7028 **Dumm, Demetrius R.** A mystical portrait of Jesus: new perspectives on John's gospel. 2001 ⇒17,5794... 19,6676. [R]RBLit (2005)* (*Matson, Mark*).

7029 *Erlemann, Kurt* Beobachtungen zur Feinstruktur von Joh 1-12. [F]STEGEMANN, W.: 2005 ⇒139. 390-403.

7030 *Farelly, N.* 'Je suis la vérité' dans l'évangile de Jean. RRef 56/235 (2005) 1-20 [NTAb 50,286].

7031 *Fossati, Matteo; Vignolo, Roberto* 'Mio padre lavora sempre' (Gv 5, 17): l'opera/le opere come tratto della missione cristologica nel vangelo di Giovanni. PSV 52 (2005) 117-148.

7032 [E]**Frey, Jörg; Schnelle, Udo** Kontexte des Johannesevangeliums. WUNT 175: 2004 ⇒20,674. [R]ThRv 101 (2005) 207-209 (*Nicklas, Tobias*); RHPhR 85 (2005) 449 (*Grappe, Ch.*); EstAg 40 (2005) 585-586 (*Cineira, D.A.*); ThLZ 130 (2005) 1318-1321 (*Frenschkowski, Marco*); ActBib 42 (2005) 199-200 (*Boada, Josep*).

7033 **Fuglseth, Kåre Sigvald** Johannine sectarianism in perspective: a sociological, historical, and comparative analysis of temple and social relationships in the gospel of John, PHILO and Qumran. NT.S 118: Lei 2005, Brill xiv; 448 pp. €97/$139. 90-04-14411-0. Diss. Trondheim 2002; Bibl. 379-409.

7034 *Gemünden, Petra von* Weisheitliche Bilderkonstellationen im Johannesevangelium?: einige strukturelle Überlegungen. Picturing the New Testament. WUNT 2/193: 2005 ⇒396. 159-182.

7035 **Gennaro, Giuseppe de; Salzer, Elisabetta C.** Literatura mística: el evangelista místico. Burgos 2003, Monte Carmelo 286 pp.

7036 *Getty, Mary Ann* Peter and the gospel of John. BiTod 43 (2005) 228-232.

7037 *Gignac, Francis T.* The use of verbal variety in the fourth gospel. [F]MOLONEY, F.: BSRel 187: 2005 ⇒104. 191-200.

7038 *Gourgues, Michel* Le paraclet, l'esprit de vérité: deux désignations, deux fonctions. Theology and christology. BEThL 184: 2005 ⇒796. 83-108.

7039 *Grech, Prosper* Ebrei e cristiani ad Efeso: riflessi nel vangelo di Giovanni <1994>;

7040 Le confessioni di fede in Giovanni <1996>. Il messaggio biblico. SRivBib 44: 2005 ⇒216. 311-318/333-341.

7041 **Grün, Anselm** Jésus, la porte vers la vie: l'évangile de Jean. 2004 ⇒ 20,6647. [R]RTL 36 (2005) 238-239 (*Kaefer, J.-Ph.*).

7042 *Gundry, Robert H.* Is John's gospel sectarian?. The old is better. WUNT 178: 2005 ⇒220. 315-323.

7043 **Gusa, Alexsandar** Excentriske venner: om venskabet i Johannes-evangeliet [Excentric friends: on friendship in the gospel of John]. [D]*Engberg-Pedersen, T.* 2005, 340 pp. Diss. Copenhagen [RTL 37, 615].

7044 *Günther, Hartmut* "... dass die Schrift endgültige Erfüllung finde ..." (Joh 19,28): eine Weise, das Evangelium nach Johannes zu lesen. [F]STOLLE, V. 2005 ⇒143. 193-207.

7045 *Haaland, Gunnar* Mer om antisemittisme og bibeloversettelse. Ung teologi 38/1 (2005) 61-75.

7046 **Hakola, Raimo** Identity matters: John, the Jews and Jewishness. NT.S 118: Lei 2005, Brill vii; 291 pp. €105. 90-04-14324-6. Diss. Helsinki; Bibl. 243-274.

7047 *Hartenstein, Judith* Women in John's gospel. ThD 52 (2005) 127-131 <'Frauen im Johannesevangelium', BiKi 59 (2004) 131-136.

7048 *Hedrick, Charles W.* Vestigial scenes in John: settings without dramatization. NT 47 (2005) 354-366.

7049 *Hong, Emiliano* El análisis narrativo en la exégesis del cuarto evangelio. RevBib 67 (2005) 193-224.

7050 *Hübner, Hans* ἐν ἀρχῇ ἐγώ εἰμι. <2004>;

7051 Wahrheit und Wort: HEIDEGGERS 'Vom Wesen der Wahrheit' und Wahrheit im Johannes-Evangelium. Wahrheit und Wirklichkeit. 2005 <2004> ⇒229. 65-81/139-161.

7052 **Hübner, Hans** Evangelium secundum Iohannem. Vetus Testamentum in Novo 1/2: 2003 ⇒19,6697; 20,6658. [R]ZRGG 57 (2005) 188-189 (*Horn, Friedrich W.*).

7053 *Jayachitra, L.* A postcolonial exploration of *water* in the fourth gospel. BTF 37/2 (2005) 114-129 [NTAb 50,497].

7054 *Jean, Etienne* "Qui me mange vivra par moi": recherche sur le corps du Christ en saint Jean. Aletheia 27 (2005) 63-73.

7055 *Kangas, B.* Word, breath, flesh: the processed God in the gospel of John. Affirmation & Critique [Anaheim, CA] 10/1 (2005) 3-13 [NTAb 49,506].

7056 *Kelly, Anthony J.* Dimensions of meaning: theology and exegesis. [F]MOLONEY, F.: BSRel 187: 2005 ⇒104. 41-55.

7057 **Kelly, Anthony J.; Moloney, Francis J.** Experiencing God in the gospel of John. 2003 ⇒19,6701; 20,6660. [R]ACR 82 (2005) 377-378 (*Turner, Marie*); RB 112 (2005) 459-462 (*Devillers, Luc*).

7058 **Kerber, Daniel** "No me eligieron ustedes a mí, sino que yo los elegí a ustedes": estudio exegético teológico sobre el verbo ἐκλέγομαι en el cuarto evangelio. 2002 ⇒18,6237. [R]RevBib 67 (2005) 114-117 (*Castellarín, Tomás*).

7059 **Kerr, Alan R.** The temple of Jesus' body: the temple theme in the gospel of John. JSNT.S 220: 2002 ⇒18,6238... 20,6661. [R]RBL 58 (2005) 311-313 (*Maciejewski, Andrzej*).

7060 *Koester, Craig* The death of Jesus and the human condition: exploring the theology of John's gospel. [M]BROWN, R.. 2005 ⇒15. 141-157.

7061 **Koester, Craig R.** Symbolism in the fourth gospel: meaning, mystery, community. [2]2003 ⇒19,6705; 20,6665. [R]RBLit (2005)* (*Maritz, Petrus*).

7062 *Köstenberger, Andreas* The destruction of the second temple and the composition of the fourth gospel. TrinJ 26 (2005) 205-242.

7063 *Kusmirek, Anna* Posrednik objawienia w pismach qumranskich i w czwartej Ewangelii. CoTh 75/3 (2005) 63-83. **P**.

7064 *Kvalbein, Hans* "Jødene" i Johannesevangeliet: en sluttkommentar. Ung teologi 38/2 (2005) 65-69.

7065 **Kysar, Robert** Voyages with John: charting the fourth gospel. Waco, Tex. 2005, Baylor Univ. Pr. x; 339 pp. $30. 1-932792-43-0. Bibl. 293-326.

7066 **L'Epine, T. de** Dieu a planté sa tente parmi nous: les sacrements et le mystère pascal dans l'évangile de Jean. Cahiers de l'Ecole cathédrale 71: P 2005, Parole et Silence 122 pp. €14. 28457-33321.

7067 *Labbé, Yves* Symbole et dialogue: une double structure d'accueil de l'évangile. RSPhTh 89 (2005) 295-314.

7068 **Lafon, Guy** La parole et la vie: lectures de l'évangile selon saint Jean. Ecritures: Bru 2005, Lumen Vitae 144 pp. €18. 2-87324-2647.

7069 *Latour, Élie* La fonction narrative de l'articulation entre récit et discours dans le quatrième évangile. Raconter. CRB 61: 2005 ⇒717. 33-47.

7070 *Lee, Dorothy* Friendship, love and abiding in the gospel of John. [F]MOLONEY, F.: BSRel 187: 2005 ⇒104. 57-74.

7071 **Lee, Dorothy A.** Flesh and glory: symbol, gender, and theology in the gospel of John. 2002 ⇒18,6248; 19,6714. [R]EAPR 42 (2005) 303-310 (*Salazar, Merle*); RBLit (2005)* (*Skinner, Christopher*).

7072 **Leinhäupl-Wilke, Andreas** Rettendes Wissen im Johannesevangelium: ein Zugang über die narrativen Rahmenteile (Joh 1,19-2,12-20,1-21,25). NTA 45: 2003 ⇒19,6716; 20,6677. [R]ThLZ 130 (2005) 269-271 (*Cebulj, Christian*); RBLit (2005)* (*Nicklas, Tobias*).

7073 *Léon-Dufour, Xavier* Per una lettura simbolica del IV vangelo. Un biblista cerca Dio. Collana biblica: 2005 <1983> ⇒245. 207-217;

7074 Ascoltare incessantemente il vangelo <1981>;

7075 Le due memorie del cristiano <1991> [Lk 22,19; John 13,15];

7076 Prospettive giovannee sulla mistica <1994>. Un biblista cerca Dio. Collana biblica: 2005 ⇒245. 245-256/219-235/275-285.

7077 *Loader, William R.G.* Jesus and the law in John. Theology and christology. BEThL 184: 2005 ⇒796. 135-154.

7078 *Loza Vera, José* Pedro en el evangelio de Juan. Qol 37 (2005) 43-67.

7079 *Maggioni, Bruno* Il Cristo *Logos* nel vangelo di Giovanni. Il messia. 2005 ⇒719. 125-136.

7080 **Makambu, Mulopo Apollinaire** La conception de l'esprit dans l'évangile de Jean en dehors des verset sur le paraclet. [D]*Heininger, Bernard* 2005, Diss. Würzburg [ThRv 102,xiii].

7081 **Maniparampil, Jose** Why are you speaking with a woman?. 2004 ⇒ 20,6688 [missiology of the gospel of John]. [R]ETJ 9 (2005) 190-191 (*Ottapurackal, Joseph*) [John 4,31-38].

7082 **Manns, Frédéric** L'évangile de Jean et la sagesse. SBFA 62: 2003 ⇒19,236; 20,6689. [R]CDios 218 (2005) 247-248 (*Gutiérrez, J.*); JSJ 36 (2005) 360-363 (*Daly-Denton, Margaret*).

7083 **Marchadour, Alain** Les personnages dans l'évangile de Jean: miroir pour une christologie narrative. LiBi 139: 2004 ⇒20,6690. [R]RTL 36 (2005) 239-240 (*Kaefer, J.-Ph.*).

7084 *Marcheselli, Maurizio* 'Il figlio vi farà liberi' (Gv 8,36): da Gesù uomo libero alla libertà del discepolo. Libertà va cercando. Sussidi biblici 87: 2005 ⇒353. 83-103 [John 8,31-36; 9].

7085 **McGrath, James Frank** John's apologetic christology: legitimation and development in Johannine christology. MSSNTS 111: 2001 ⇒ 17,5849... 19,6732. [R]ScEs 57 (2005) 82-85 (*Létourneau, Pierre*).

7086 *McIlhone, J.P.* Jesus as God's agent in the fourth gospel: implications for christology, ecclesiology, and mission. ChiSt 44 (2005) 295-315 [NTAb 50,237].

7087 *Meessen, Yves* Un monde sépare tout cela d'HÉRACLITE. RSR 93 (2005) 331-353.

7088 *Menken, Maarten J.J.* Observations on the significance of the Old Testament in the fourth gospel. Theology and christology. BEThL 184: 2005 ⇒796. 155-175.

7089 **Metzner, Rainer** Das Verständnis der Sünde im Johannesevangelium. WUNT 122: 2000 ⇒16,5878... 19,6736. [R]RSR 93 (2005) 305-307 (*Morgen, Michèle*).

7090 **Meyer, Annegret** Kommt und seht: Mystagogie im Johannesevangelium ausgehend von Joh 1,35-51. [D]*Backhaus, Knut*: FzB 103: Wü 2005, Echter viii; 395 pp. €35. 3-429-02657-1. Diss. Paderborn; Bibl. 353-380. [R]Cart. 21 (2005) 243-244 (*Sanz Valdivieso, R.*); ATG 68 (2005) 318-319 (*Contreras Molina, Francisco*).

7091 *Mirguet, Françoise* La mise en scène de l'écriture et de la lecture dans le quatrième évangile: comment le texte construit son herméneutique. Raconter. CRB 61: 2005 ⇒717. 13-31.

7092 **Mlakuzhyil, George** Path to abundant life in the gospel of John: a guide to study, prayer, preaching and retreat. Delhi 2005, Media House 381 pp. Rs200/$20. 81-7495-214-4. Bibl. 379-381. [R]VJTR 69 (2005) 513, 551 (*Thomas, K.T.*).

7093 **Molath, Mathew** The obedience of Jesus and of the believers according to the fourth gospel in the light of the Johannine community hypothesis. [D]*Taylor, Richard* 2005, Diss. Angelicum [RTL 37,616].

7094 *Moloney, Francis J.* The gospel of John as scripture. CBQ 67 (2005) 454-468;

7095 The gospel of John and evangelization 4-19;

7096 'The Jews' in the fourth gospel: another perspective 20-44;

7097 The fourth gospel and the Jesus of history 45-65;

7098 The Johannine Son of Man revisited 66-92;

7099 Telling God's story: the fourth gospel 93-111;

7100 The gospel of John: a story of two paracletes 241-259;

7101 The gospel of John as scripture. The gospel of John. BiblInterp 72: 2005 ⇒6964. 333-347;

7102 The Johannine Son of Man revisited. Theology and christology. BEThL 184: 2005 ⇒796. 177-202.

7103 *Morfino, Mauro M.* Tradizioni targumico-midrashiche e middot rabbiniche nel quarto vangelo. FGHIBERTI, G.: SRivBib 46: 2005 ⇒47. 43-59.

7104 *Morrison, Craig E.* The "hour of distress" in Targum Neofiti and the "hour" in the gospel of John. CBQ 67 (2005) 590-603.

7105 *Müller, Philipp* "Der Jünger, den Jesus liebte": ideale Nachfolge im Johannesevangelium. GuL 78 (2005) 81-91.

7106 **Newheart, Michael Willett** Word and soul: a psychological, literary, and cultural reading of the fourth gospel. 2001 ⇒17,5859... 19,6745. RStBob (2005/1) 189-192 (*Górka, Bogusław*).

7107 **Ng, Wai-yee** Water symbolism in John: an eschatological interpretation. Studies in Biblical Literature 15: 2001 ⇒17,5860... 19,6747. RRBLit (2005)* (*Fay, Ron*).

7108 **Nicklas, Tobias** Ablösung und Verstrickung: "Juden" und Jüngergestalten als Charaktere der erzählten Welt des Johannesevangeliums. RSTh 60: 2001 ⇒17, 5861... 20,6703. RRSR 93 (2005) 307-308 (*Morgen, Michèle*); RBLit 7 (2005) 355-357 (*Seim, Turid K.*).

7109 *Nobile, Marco* Le citazioni di Zaccaria nel vangelo di Giovanni. FGHIBERTI, G.: SRivBib 46: 2005 ⇒47. 61-69.

7110 *O'Day, Gail R.* Jesus as friend in the gospel of John. FMOLONEY, F.: BSRel 187: 2005 ⇒104. 75-92;

7111 The love of God incarnate: the life of Jesus in the gospel of John. MBROWN, R. 2005 ⇒15. 158-167.

7112 *Olsson, Birger* "All my teaching was done in synagogues ..." (John 18,20). Theology and christology. BEThL 184: 2005 ⇒796. 203-24.

7113 *Painter, John* Monotheism and dualism: John and Qumran. Theology and christology. BEThL 184: 2005 ⇒796. 225-243.

7114 *Park, Kyung-mi* John. Global bible commentary. 2005 ⇒2443. 401-411.

7115 **Parmentier, Roger** L'évangile selon Jean actualisé et demythisé. P 2005, L'Harmattan 202 pp. €17.50. 978-22960-00029.

7116 *Parsenios, George L.* "No longer in the world" (John 17:11): the transformation of the tragic in the fourth gospel. HThR 98 (2005) 1-21 [John 17].

7117 **Pesch, Rudolf** Antisemitismus in der Bibel?: das Johannesevangelium auf dem Prüfstand. Augsburg 2005, Sankt Ulrich 157 pp. €14.90. 3-936484-44-9.

**Peterson, E.** Ausgewählte Schriften, 3: Johannesevangelium und Kanonstudien. E*Nichtweiß, Barbara* 2003 ⇒275.

7118 *Philippe, Marie D.* Commentaire de l'évangile de saint Jean: vivre de la présence de Jésus. Aletheia 27 (2005) 125-143;

7119 La femme: Marie, au coeur du gouvernement du Père. Aletheia 28 (2005) 75-85.

7120 **Philippe, Marie-Dominique** Suivre l'Agneau, lumière du monde, 3. P 2005, Médiaspaul 224 pp. €18 [Carmel(T) 117,123];

7121 Seguir al Cordero: dondequiera que vaya: retiro sobre el evangelio de San Juan (II). Cuadernos Palabra 148: M 2005, Palabra 492 pp. 84-8239-902-0 [John 2-5].

7122 *Pratscher, Wilhelm* Tiefenpsychologische Erwägungen zur negativen Rede von "den Juden" im Johannesevangelium. Theology and christology. BEThL 184: 2005 ⇒796. 277-290.

[E]**Prinzivalli, E.** Il commento a Giovanni di ORIGENE 2005 ⇒789.

7123 *Proctor, M.A.* 'Nothing good from Nazareth': John and the problem of Jesus' natural origins. JHiC 11/2 (2005) 108-127 [NTAb 50,498].

7124 **Pudło, Wiesław** Jésus-Prophète dans le quatrième évangile: étude exégétique et théologique. [D]*Witczyk, H.* 2005, 233 pp. Diss. Lublin [RTL 37,617]. **P.**

7125 **Ramos Pérez, Fernando** Ver a Jesús y sus signos, y creer en él: estudio exegético-teológico de la relación 'ver y creer' en el evangelio según san Juan. 2004 ⇒20,6717. [R]ATG 68 (2005) 323 (*Contreras Molina, Francisco*); RBLit (2005)* (*Morrow, Jeffrey*); LASBF 55 (2005) 542-543 (*Manns, Frédéric*).

7126 *Reim, Günter* Die Sondersprache des Evangelisten Johannes—oder: warum spricht er so, wie er spricht?: Antworten in Kommentaren. BZ 49 (2005) 93-102.

7127 *Reinhartz, Adele* John and Judaism: a response to Burton Visotzky. [M]BROWN, R. 2005 ⇒15. 108-116;

7128 John, gender and Judaism: a feminist's dilemma. [F]STEGEMANN, E. 2005 ⇒139. 182-195;

7129 Love, hate, and violence in the gospel of John. Violence in the NT. 2005 <2003> ⇒439. 109-123.

7130 **Reinhartz, Adele** Befriending the beloved disciple: a Jewish reading of the gospel of John. 2001 ⇒17,5874... 20,6724. [R]Teol(M) 30/1 (2005) 105-107 (*Vignolo, Roberto*); RBLit 7 (2005) 352-355 (*Siker, Jeffrey S.*);

7131 Freundschaft mit dem Geliebten Jünger: eine jüdische Lektüre des Johannesevangeliums. [T]*Kobel, Esther*: Z 2005, Theologischer 245 pp. €22.50. 3-290-17358-5. Nachwort *Ekkehard W. Stegemann.*

7132 *Remaud, Michel* Jean et les traditions juives anciennes sur l'Exode: dépendances et oppositions. NRTh 127 (2005) 557-570.

7133 **Ripley, Jason John** Behold the Lamb of God: Johannine christology and the martyrdoms of Isaac. 2005, Diss. Princeton, Sem. [RTL 37, 618].

7134 *Romanowsky, J.W.* 'When the Son of Man is lifted up': the redemptive power of the crucifixion in the gospel of John. Horizons 32 (2005) 100-116 [NTAb 49,507].

7135 *Rotondo, Arianna* Volti di donna nel quarto vangelo. AnStR 6 (2005) 287-305;

7136 *Rusam, Dietrich* Das Johannesevangelium—eine "Relecture" der synoptischen Evangelien?: intertextuelle Beobachtungen zu den "Ich-bin-Worten" des Johannesevangeliums. [F]STEGEMANN, W. 2005 ⇒ 139. 377-389;

7137 Das "Lamm Gottes" (Joh 1,29.36) und die Deutung des Todes Jesu im Johannesevangelium. BZ 49 (2005) 60-80.

7138 **Ruschmann, Susanne** Maria von Magdala im Johannesevangelium: Jüngerin—Zeugin—Lebensbotin. NTA 40: 2002 ⇒18,6287... 20,6726. [R]BiblInterp 13 (2005) 212-214 (*Frey, Jörg*); NT 47 (2005) 80-82 (*Brock, Ann Graham*) [John 19,25; 20].

7139 **Sadananda, Daniel Rathnakara** The Johannine exegesis of God. BZNW 121: 2004 ⇒20,6727. [R]CBQ 67 (2005) 540-541 (*Blomberg, Craig L.*); Faith & Mission 22/3 (2005) 116-117 (*Köstenberger, Andreas J.*); LuThK 29 (2005) 210-211 (*Stolle, Volker*).

7140 **Salier, Willis Hedley** The rhetorical impact of the semeia in the gospel of John. WUNT 2/186: 2004 ⇒20,6728. [R]TrinJ 26 (2005) 137-140 (*Köstenberger, Andreas J.*).

7141 *Sánchez Navarro, Luis* Estructura testimonial del evangelio de Juan. Bib. 86 (2005) 511-528.

7142 **Scheiring, Peter-Paul** Freunde oder Konkurrenten?: Simon Petrus und der geliebte Jünger im Johannesevangelium. D*Hasitschka, Martin* 2005, Diss. Innsbruck [ThRv 102,vii].

7143 **Schlund, Christine** 'Kein Knochen soll gebrochen werden': Studien zu Bedeutung und Funktion des Pesachfests in Texten des frühen Judentums und im Johannesevangelium. D*Breytenbach, Cilliers*; Ment. *Melito Sardis*: WMANT 107: Neuk 2005, Neuk xiii; 254 pp. €39.90. 3-7887-2087-5. Diss. Humboldt; Bibl. 229-244 [1 Cor 5,7].

7144 *Schnelle, Udo* Das Johannesevangelium als neue Sinnbildung;

7145 *Scholtissek, Klaus* "Ich und der Vater, wir sind eins" (Joh 10,30): zum theologischen Potential und zur hermeneutischen Kompetenz der johanneischen Christologie;

7146 *Schwankl, Otto* Aspekte der johanneischen Christologie. Theology and christology. BEThL 184: 2005 ⇒796. 291-313/315-45/347-375.

7147 *Segalla, Giuseppe* Gesù di Nazaret fondamento storico del racconto evangelico giovanneo. RStB 17/2 (2005) 83-107;

7148 Luoghi della memoria del discepolo amato (Gv 1,28; 3,23; 10,40-42). FGHIBERTI, G.: SRivBib 46: 2005 ⇒47. 85-98.

7149 *Seim, Turid Karlsen* Descent and divine paternity in the gospel of John: does the mother matter?. NTS 51 (2005) 361-375.

7150 **Smith, Kym** The amazing structure of the gospel of John. Blackwood, South Aust. 2005, Sherwood xiv; 314 pp. 0-646-37447-8.

7151 *Spencer, P.E.* Eucharistic reconciliation in the gospel of John: theological appropriation for today. Stone-Campbell Journal [Joplin, M0] 8 (2005) 73-83 [NTAb 49,507] [John 6].

7152 **Spijkerboer, Anne Marijke** Wij hebben ongelofelijke dingen gezien: Johannes vanuit de kunst gelezen. 2004 ⇒20,6737. RStr. 72 (2005) 277-278 (*Beentjes, Panc*).

7153 **Straub, Esther** Kritische Theologie ohne ein Wort vom Kreuz: zum Verhältnis von Joh 1-12 und 13-20. FRLANT 203: 2003 ⇒19,6773. RThLZ 130 (2005) 511-512 (*Leonhardt-Balzer, Jutta*).

7154 **Stuckey, Tom** Beyond the box: mission challenges from John's gospel. Peterborough 2005, Inspire 128 pp. £7. 9781-818585-22852.

7155 **Theobald, Michael** Herrenworte im Johannesevangelium. Herders Biblische Studien 34: 2002 ⇒18,6300; 19,6779. RThLZ 130 (2005) 284-87 (*Schröter, Jens*); RSR 93 (2005) 308-311 (*Morgen, Michèle*).

7156 *Thomas, John C.* Healing in the atonement: a Johannine perspective. JPentec 14/1 (2005) 23-39.

7157 *Thompson, Marianne M.* When the ending is not the end. MJUEL, D. 2005 ⇒73. 65-75.

7158 **Thompson, Marianne M.** The God of the gospel of John. 2001 ⇒17,5898... 19,6780. RRSR 93 (2005) 311-314 (*Morgen, Michèle*); BiblInterp 13 (2005) 77-79 (*Williams, John Tudno*); ScEs 57 (2005) 96-98 (*Létourneau, Pierre*).

7159 *Tolmie, D. Francois* The IOUDAIOI in the fourth gospel. A narratological perspective. Theology and christology. BEThL 184: 2005 ⇒796. 377-397.

7160 **Tukasi, Emmanuel** Determinism and petitionary prayer in the gospel of John and the Rule of the Community (IQS). D*Lieu, J.* 2005, Diss. London [RTL 37,619].

7161 **Urban, Christina** Das Menschenbild nach dem Johannesevangelium: Grundlagen johanneischer Anthropologie. WUNT 137: 2001 ⇒ 17,5905... 20,6742. [R]RSR 93 (2005) 314-316 (*Morgen, Michèle*).
7162 **Urbanek, Beata** Le rôle de la voix de Jésus dans l'oeuvre de la révélation: étude de théologie johannique. [D]*Witczyk, H.* 2005, 308 pp. Diss. Lublin [RTL 37,619]. **P**.
7163 *Van Belle, Gilbert* Lukan style in the fourth gospel. [F]DENAUX, A.: BEThL 182: 2005 ⇒34. 351-372 [Lk 24,36-49; John 20,19-29];
7164 Style criticism and the fourth gospel. [M]VAN TILBORG, S.: BiblInterp 71: 2005 ⇒155. 291-316.
7165 *Van der Watt, Jan G.* Salvation in the gospel according to John. Salvation in the New Testament. NT.S 121: 2005 ⇒798. 101-131;
7166 Double entendre in the gospel according to John. Theology and christology. BEThL 184: 2005 ⇒796. 463-481.
7167 *Van Tilborg, Sjef* Cosmological implications of Johannine christology. Theology and christology. BEThL 184: 2005 ⇒796. 483-502.
7168 **Vanier, Jean** Acceder al misterio de Jesús: a través del evangelio de Juan. [T]*Díez Aragón, Ramón Alfonso*: El Pozo de Siquem 170: Sdr 2005, Sal Terrae 365 pp. 84-293-1579-9;
7169 Entrer dans le mystère de Jésus: une lecture de l'évangile de Jean. [T]*Miribel, C. de*: Montréal 2005, Novalis 384 pp. €19.80. 2-895-075-476.
7170 *Vassiliadis, Petros* John in an Orthodox perspective. Global bible commentary. 2005 ⇒2443. 412-418.
7171 **Verdezoto, Walter** El tema del pecado en el cuarto evangelio: estudio exegético-teológico de los términos ἁμαρτία, ἁμαρτάνω y ἁμαρτωλός en el cuarto evangelio. [D]*Pastor, Félix*: R 2005, 116 pp. Extr. Diss. Gregoriana; Bibl. 97-110.
7172 **Vettikuzhiyil, George** Πέμπω and ἀποστέλλω as designations of the mission of the disciples in the gospel of John: an exegetical theological study of Jn 4:31-38; 17:17-19; 20:19-23. [D]*Caba, José* R 2005, viii; 112 pp. Extr. Diss. Gregoriana; Bibl. 69-106.
7173 *Vignolo, Roberto* Il quarto vangelo in due parole: in margine ai macarismi giovannei (Gv 13,17; 20,29). [F]GHIBERTI, G.: SRivBib 46: 2005 ⇒47. 119-132.
7174 *Visotzky, Burton L.* Methodological considerations in the study of John's interaction with first-century Judaism. [M]BROWN, R. 2005 ⇒15. 91-107.
7175 *Volf, M.* Johannine dualism and contemporary pluralism. MoTh 21 (2005) 189-217 [NTAb 49,507].
7176 **Voorwinde, Stephen** Jesus' emotions in the fourth gospel: human or divine?. LNTS 284: E 2005, Clark xiii; 344 pp. £65. 0-567-03026-1. Diss. Australian College of Theology 2003; Bibl. 304-322.
7177 **Webster, Jane S.** Ingesting Jesus: eating and drinking in the gospel of John. Academia biblica 6: 2003 ⇒19,6787; 20,6749. [R]Interp. 59 (2005) 430, 432 (*Anderson, Paul N.*); TJT 21 (2005) 282-283 (*Froese, Dan*); RBLit (2005)* (*Baker, Robert; Smit, Peter-Ben*).
7178 *Willams, Catrin H.* Isaiah in John's gospel. Isaiah in the NT. 2005 ⇒ 443. 101-116.
7179 **Wróbel, Mirosław Stanisław** Antyjudaizm a ewangelia według św. Jana: nowe spojrzenie na relację czwartej ewangelii do judaizmu. Lublin 2005, KUL 351 pp. 83-7363-247-6. Diss.-Habil. Lublin. [R]CoTh 75/3 (2005) 235-242 (*Chrostowski, Waldemar*). **P**.

7180 *Wróbel, Miroslaw S.* Pisma qumranskie e Ewangelia Janowa. CoTh 75/3 (2005) 55-61.**P**.

7181 *Wyatt, Nicolas* 'Supposing him to be the gardener' (John 20:15): a study of the paradise motif in John. 'There's such divinity'. 2005 <1990> ⇒329. 61-76 [John 19,41-20,17].

7182 **Yamaguchi, Satoko** Mary and Martha: women in the world of Jesus. 2002 ⇒18,6313. [R]ThirdM 8/2 (2005) 104-105 (*Mattam, Joseph*).

7183 **Zimmermann, Ruben** Christologie der Bilder im Johannesevangelium...Joh 10. WUNT 171: 2004 ⇒20,6753. [R]SNTU 30 (2005) 232-233 (*Grohmann, Marianne*); RHPhR 85 (2005) 452-453 (*Grappe, Ch.*); ActBib 42 (2005) 197-199 (*Boada, Josep*).

7184 **Zingg, Edith** Das Sprechen von Gott als 'Vater' im Johannesevangelium. [D]*Kirchschläger, Walter* 2005, Diss. Luzern [ThRv 102,viii ].

### G1.5 Johannis Prologus 1,1...

7185 *Sterling, Gregory E.* 'Day one': platonizing exegetical traditions of Genesis 1:1-5 in John and Jewish authors. Ment. *Philo*: StPhiloA 17 (2005) 118-140.

7186 *Attridge, Harold W.* PHILO and John: two riffs on one Logos. StPhiloA 17 (2005) 103-117 [John 1,1-18].

7187 *Böhler, Dieter* Abraham und seine Kinder im Johannesprolog: zur Vielgestaltigkeit des alttestamentlichen Textes bei Johannes. [F]SCHENKER, A.: OBO 214: 2005 ⇒134. 15-29 [John 1,1-18].

7188 **Endo, Masanobu** Creation and christology: a study on the Johannine Prologue in the light of early Jewish creation accounts. WUNT 2/149: 2002 ⇒18,6323; 19,6808. [R]ThLZ 130 (2005) 162-164 (*Leonhardt-Balzer, Jutta*) [John 1,1-18].

7189 *Gundry, Robert H.* How the Word in John's prologue pervades the rest of the fourth gospel. The old is better. WUNT 178: 2005 ⇒220. 324-362 [John 1,1-18].

7190 **Lioy, Dan** The search for ultimate reality: intertextuality between the Genesis and Johannine prologues. Studies in Biblical literature 93: NY 2005, Lang xi; 223 pp. 0-820-481-21-1. Bibl. 177-214 [John 1,1-18].

7191 *Murphy, Austin G.* Re-reading the Johannine prologue. ProEc 14 (2005) 306-323 [John 1,1-18].

7192 *Niccacci, Alviero* Logos e sapienza nel prologo di Giovanni. [F]GHIBERTI, G.: SRivBib 46: 2005 ⇒47. 71-83 [John 1,1-18].

7193 *Nobile, Marco* Ancora sul Logos in rapporto alla tradizione giudaica del secondo tempio. Atti del X Simposio di Efeso. Turchia 19: 2005 ⇒785. 17-27 [John 1,1-18].

7194 [T]**Sellés, Juan Fernando** TOMÁS de Aquino: sobre el Verbo: comentario al prólogo del evangelio de San Juan. Pensamiento Medieval y Renacentista 73: Pamplona 2005, EUNSA 172 pp. 84-313-2329-9. [John 1,1-18].

7195 *Walter, Norbert* Gottesbezug und Menschenwürde—"und nichts ist geworden ohne das Wort" (Johannes 1,3). Kanzelreden. 2005 ⇒376. 125-129 [John 1,1-18].

7196 *McCord Adams, Marilyn* Imaginative faith, surprising hope! Advent III—John 1:6-8, 19-28. ET 117 (2005) 74-75.

7197 *Van Kooten, George H.* The 'true light which enlightens everyone' (John 1:9): John, Genesis, the Platonic notion of the 'true, noetic light,' and the allegory of the cave in PLATO's Republic. Creation of heaven and earth. Themes...biblical narrative 8: 2005 ⇒492. 149-94.

7198 **Uhrig, Christian** 'Und das Wort ist Fleisch geworden': zur Rezeption von Joh 1,14a und zur Theologie der Fleischwerdung in der griechischen vornizänischen Patristik. MBTh 63: 2004 ⇒20,6767. [R]ThRv 101 (2005) 141-142 (*Beinert, Wolfgang*); Gr. 86 (2005) 678-680 (*Hercsik, Donath*).

7199 *Belano, Alessandro* χάριν ἀντὶ χάριτος· (Gv 1,16): "grazia su grazia"?. RivBib 53 (2005) 479-482.

7200 *Devillers, Luc* Le sein du père: la finale du prologue de Jean. RB 112 (2005) 63-79 [Exod 3,14; John 1,18].

7201 *Häfner, Gerd* Die Jesuserzählung des Johannes—ein intertextuelles Spiel mit den Synoptikern?. [F]LAUB, F.: Bibel-Schule-Leben 6: 2005 ⇒87. 41-52 [John 1,21; 1,29-34].

7202 *López Rosas, Ricardo* 'He ahí el cordero de Dios...': anotaciones en torno a Jn 1,29. [F]JUNCO GARZA, C.: Estudios Bíblicos Mexicanos 4: 2005 ⇒74. 353-376.

7203 *Flink, Timo* Son and chosen: a text-critical study of John 1,34. FgNT 18 (2005) 85-109.

7204 *Baumann, Rolf* Schritte zum eigenen Glauben: Bibelarbeit zu Joh 1,38-51. BiHe 41/161 (2005) I-IV.

7205 *King, Rosemary* Narrative sermon on John 1:43-51: call of Philip and Nathaniel. ET 117 (2005) 114-115.

7206 *Blanchard, Yves-Marie* Le fils de l'homme et l'échelle de Jacob: réflexion sur l'intertextualité scripturaire et relecture de Jean 1,51, à la lumière de la bible juive. Analyse narrative. BEThL 191: 2005 ⇒ 742. 181-195.

7207 *Ellens, Harold* A christian pesher: John 1:51. ProcGLM 25 (2005) 143-155.

7208 *Schwank, Benedikt* Jakobstraum (Gen 28,12) und christologische Erfüllung (Joh 1,51). EuA 81/5 (2005) 386-397.

7209 *Berliet, Gérard* Les noces de Cana: Dieu tient compte de nos désirs. Vie Chrétienne 509 (2005) 4-8 [John 2,1-11].

7210 *Klink, Edward W.* What concern is that to you and to me?: John 2:1-11 and the Elisha narratives. Neotest. 39 (2005) 273-287 [2 Kgs 3-4].

7211 *Welker, Michael* Weinwunder–Weinstock–lebendiges Wasser–Geist: die anstößige Botschaft auf der Hochzeit zu Kana. [F]BÜMLEIN, K. 2005 ⇒18. 201-205 [John 2,1-11].

7212 *Girard, Marc* Cana ou l'"heure" de la vrai noce (Jean 2,1-12): structure stylistique et processus de symbolisation. [F]GHIBERTI, G.: SRivBib 46: 2005 ⇒47. 99-109.

7213 *Savasta, Carmelo* Le nozze di Cana (Gv 2,1-12). BeO 47 (2005) 100-122.

7214 *Nicklas, Tobias* Die johanneische "Tempelreinigung" (Joh 2,12-22) für Leser der Synoptiker. ThPh 80 (2005) 1-16.

7215 **López Rosas, Ricardo** La señal del templo: Jn 2,13-22: redefinición cristológica de lo sacro. 2001 ⇒17,5955... 20,6787. [R]EstB 63 (2005) 134-136 (*Rodríguez Ruiz, M.*).

## G1.6 Jn 3ss... Nicodemus, Samaritana

7216 *Safrai, Zeev* Nakdimon b. Guryon: a Galilean aristocrat in Jerusalem. Beginnings of christianity. 2005 ⇒786. 297-314 [John 3].

7217 *Borg, Marcus J.* Reclaiming a metaphor: 'born again'. Search 28/1 (2005) 13-26 [NTAb 49,508] {John 3,1-10].

7218 *Sandnes, Karl O.* Whence and whither: a narrative perspective on birth ἄνωθεν (John 3,3-8). Bib. 86 (2005) 153-173 [John 3,3-8].

7219 *Gundry, Robert H.* The sense and syntax of John 3:14-17 with special reference to the use of οὕτως... ὥστε in John 3:16. The old is better. WUNT 178: 2005 ⇒220. 363-376.

7220 *Botha, J.E.; Rousseau, P.A.* For God did not so love the whole world —only Israel!: John 3:16 revisited. HTSTS 61 (2005) 1149-1168 [NTAb 51,54].

7221 *Towne, E.A.* Reason and the 'more excellent' spirit: a reformed reflection on John 3:16. Encounter 66/3 (2005) 233-253 [NTAb 50, 53].

7222 *Cuvillier, Elian* La femme samaritaine et les disciples de Jésus: histoire de rencontres et de malentendus: une lecture de l'évangile de Jean 4,1-43. Ḥokhma 88 (2005) 62-75.

7223 *Davidson, Jo A.* John 4: another look at the Samaritan woman. AUSS 43 (2005) 159-168.

7224 [E]**Jonker, Louis**, *al.*, Through the eyes of another: intercultural reading of the bible. Amst 2005, Institute of Mennonite Studies, Vrije Univ. 532 pp. €26.90 [John 4].

7225 *John de Taizé* À beira da fonte—Jesus e a Samaritana. Braga 2005, A.O. 126 pp. [John 4,5-42].

7226 *Kemdirim, Protus O.* The Samaritan woman: an apostle of ancestorhood. VFTW 28/2 (2005) 169-176 [John 4,1-42].

7227 **Malzoni, Cláudio Vianney** Jesus: Messias e vivificador do mundo: Jo 4,1-42 na antiga tradição siríaca. CRB 59: P 2005, Gabalda 546 pp. €75. 2-85021-162-X. Bibl. 507-533. [R]LASBF 55 (2005) 539-541 (*Pazzini, Massimo*).

7228 *Misset-van de Weg, Magda* 'Samaritaanse vrouw, geef mij te drinken'. ITBT 13/2 (2005) 15-18 [John 4].

7229 *Sánchez Campos, Ángel* Otro discipulado es posible o el cuestionamiento a un discipulado establecido: Juan 4,1-42. Christus(M) (2005) 27-31.

7230 *Ska, Jean Louis* Jesús y la samaritana (Jn 4): utilidad del Antiguo Testamento. El camino. 2005 <1996> ⇒302. 221-235 [John 4].

7231 *Snoek, Hans* Wie zeggen de mensen dat wij zijn?: identificatiepatronen in Johannes 4. Theologisch debat 2/2 (2005) 56-62.

7232 *Wahlde, Urban C. von* The Samaritan woman episode, synoptic form-criticism, and the Johannine miracles: a question of criteria. Theology & christology. BEThL 184: 2005 ⇒796. 503-518 [John 4].

7233 *Wyckoff, Eric J.* Jesus in Samaria (John 4:4-42): a model for cross-cultural ministry. BTB 35 (2005) 89-98.

7234 **Kutschera, Rudolf** Das Heil kommt von den Juden (Joh 4,22): Untersuchungen zur Heilsbedeutung Israels. 2003 ⇒19,6852; 20,6809. [R]ThRv 101 (2005) 210-212 (*Theobald, Michael*).

7235 *Bruce, Patricia* John 5:1-18 the healing at the pool: some narrative, socio-historical and ethical issues. Neotest. 39 (2005) 39-56.
7236 *Baarda, Tjitze* The text of John 5,7 in the Liège Harmony: two studies on the thesis of Daniël Plooij. EThL 81 (2005) 491-502.
7237 **Andrzejewski, Janusz Maria** La cristologia di Gv 5,16-30: studio di teologia biblica. [D]*Marcato, G.*: R 2005, 144 pp. Diss. Angelicum; Bibl. 137-141.
7238 *Johnson, K.L.* Just as the Father, so the Son: the implications of John 5:16-30 in the gender-role debate. Priscilla Papers [Mp] 19/1 (2005) 13-17 [NTAb 51,278].
7239 *Asiedu-Peprah, Martin* The use of 'internal analepsis': a new look at John 5:36-37a. [F]MOLONEY, F.: BSRel 187: 2005 ⇒104. 93-103.

### G1.7 Panis Vitae—*Jn 6...*

7240 *Brouns-Wewerinke, Door* Eeuwig leven smaken: nieuw licht op Johannes 6,51-58. KeTh 56/1 (2005) 23-37.
7241 *Dennis, John* The presence and function of Second Exodus-Restoration imagery in John 6. SNTU.A 30 (2005) 105-121.
7242 **Hylen, Susan** Allusion and meaning in John 6. BZNW 137: B 2005, De Gruyter ix; 237 pp. 3-11-018577-6. Bibl. 197-223.
7243 **Léon-Dufour, Xavier** Le pain de la vie. Parole de Dieu: P 2005, Seuil 177 pp. €18. 2-02-084482-6 [John 6,35-48].
7244 **Mackay, Ian D.** John's relationship with Mark: an analysis of John 6 in the light of Mark 6-8. WUNT 2/182: 2004 ⇒20,6816. [R]ET 116 (2005) 427-428 (*Foster, Paul*).
7245 *Moloney, Francis J.* The function of prolepsis for the interpretation of John 6. The gospel of John. BiblInterp 72: 2005 ⇒6964. 169-192.
7246 *Scaer, David P.* "Werdet ihr nicht essen das Fleisch des Menschensohnes ...": ein Versuch über Johannes 6. LuthBei 10/3 (2005) 139-156 [John 6].
7247 **Stare, Mira** Durch ihn leben: die Lebensthematik in Joh 6. NTA 49: 2004 ⇒20,6818. [R]Bogoslovni Vestnik 65 (2005) 308-311 (*Matjaž, Maksimilijan*).
7248 *Ternynck, Marie J.* Le discours du pain de vie: festin de la sagesse et sacrement eucharistique. Aletheia 27 (2005) 99-123 [John 6].
7249 *Vicent Cernuda, Antonio* El histórico origen joaneo de la fe apostólica en la eucaristía. EstB 63 (2005) 251-281 [John 6,51-58].
7250 *Zumstein, Jean* La réception de l'écriture en Jean 6. Analyse narrative. BEThL 191: 2005 ⇒742. 147-166.
7251 *Grech, Prosper* La comunità giovannea nei cc. 7 e 8 del vangelo di Giovanni. Il messaggio biblico. SRivBib 44: 2005 <1991> ⇒216. 301-310.
7252 *Riesner, Rainer* Joh 7,1: fehlender Wille oder fehlende Vollmacht Jesu?. ZNW 96 (2005) 259-262.
7253 *Moloney, Francis J.* Narrative and discourse at the feast of tabernacles: John 7:1-8:59. The gospel of John. BiblInterp 72: 2005 ⇒6964. 193-213.
7254 **Devillers, Luc** La fête de l'Envoyé: la section johannique de la Fête des Tentes (Jean 7,1-10,21) et la christologie. ÉtB 49: 2002 ⇒18, 6376... 20,6825. [R]RSR 93 (2005) 298-299 (*Morgen, Michèle*);

7255 La saga de Siloé: Jésus et la fête des Tentes (Jean 7,1-10,21). LiBi 143: P 2005, Cerf 223 pp. €17. 2-204-07932-4.

7256 *Balabanski, V.* 'Let anyone who is thirsty come to me': John 7:37-38 in dialogue with JOSEPHUS and the archaeology of aqueducts. LTJ 39/2-3 (2005) 132-139 [NTAb 50,53].

7257 *Counet, Patrick C.* No anti-Judaism in the fourth gospel: a deconstruction of readings of John 8. [M]VAN TILBORG, S.: BiblInterp 71: 2005 ⇒155. 197-225.

7258 *Geddert, T.; Schellenberg, R.* Phinehas and the Pharisees: identity and tolerance in biblical perspective. Direction 34 (2005) 170-180 [NTAb 50,290] [Num 25,1-18; John 8,2-11].

7259 *Combet-Galland, Corina* Venir en lumière: une violence?: évangile de Jean 8,12-59. Revue d'éthique et de théologie morale–le supplément [P] 236 (2005) 113-128 [NTAb 50,290].

7260 *Hasitschka, Martin* Joh 8,44 im Kontext des Gesprächsverlaufes von Joh 8,21-59. Theology and christology. BEThL 184: 2005 ⇒796. 109-116.

7261 *Rico, Christophe* Jn 8,25 au risque de la philologie: l'histoire d'une expression grecque. RB 112 (2005) 596-627.

7262 *Puech, Émile* Le diable, homicide, menteur et père du mensonge en Jean 8,44. RB 112 (2005) 215-252.

7263 **Sarasa Gallego, Luis Guillermo** Para ser hijos de Dios: un estudio exegético de Juan 8,44. Teología hoy 50: Bogotá 2005, Pontificia Universidad Javeriana 91 pp. 958-683-805-6. Bibl. 87-91.

7264 **Wróbel, Miroslaw Stanislaw** Who are the father and his children in Jn 8:44?: a literary, historical and theological analysis of Jn 8:44 and its context. CRB 63: P 2005, Gabalda 309 pp. 2-85021-168-0.

7265 *Syreeni, Kari* Working in the daylight: John 9:4-5 and the question of Johannine "literary archaeology". SEÅ 70 (2005) 265-279.

7266 *Shafer, Grant R.* The divinization of the blind man: 'Εγώ εἰμι in John 9:9. ProcGLM 25 (2005) 157-167.

7267 *Van Belle, G.* L'usage proleptique du pronom αὐτὸς en Jn 9:13, 18. NT 47 (2005) 1-18.

7268 *Beutler, Johannes* El discurso del Buen Pastor en Juan 10. CuesTF 32/78 (2005) 243-270 [AcBib 11,144].

7269 *Puykunnel, Shaji J.* Communicating abundant life: the identity and mission of Jesus in the light of the shepherd imagery in John 10. [M]JOHN PAUL II. 2005 ⇒72. 186-194.

7270 *Grech, Prosper* Il significato della citazione del Sal 82,6 in Gv 10,34. Il messaggio biblico. SRivBib 44: 2005 <2003> ⇒216. 351-356.

7271 *Beutler, Johannes* 'Ich habe gesagt, ihr seid Götter': zur Argumentation mit Ps 82,6 in Joh 10,34-36. Hören–Glauben–Denken: Festschrift für Peter Knauer S.J. [E]**Gäde, Gerhard**: Münst 2005, LIT 101-113. €25. 978-38258-71420 [AcBib 11,30].

7272 *Athanasopoulou, Eleftheria N.* Το θέμα της ανάστασης στην κλασσική λογοτεχνία και στη χριστιανική παράδοση: το παράδειγμα της 'Αλκηστης και του Λαζάρου [The theme of resurrection according to classical literature and according to the christian tradition: the example of Alcestis and of Lararus]. APB 16 (2005) 121-131 [John 11,1-45].

7273 *Hofius, Otfried* Die Auferweckung des Lazarus: Joh 11,1-44 als Zeugnis narrativer Christologie. ZThK 102 (2005) 17-34.

7274 *Kiessel, Marie-É.* Intertextualité et hypertextualité en Jn 11,1-12,11. EThL 81 (2005) 29-56 [Mk 5,21-43; 14,3-9: Lk 7,11-17; 10,38-42; 16,19-31].

7275 *Manzi, Franco* Resa credente o resistenza incredula al segno della risurrezione di Lazzaro. [F]GHIBERTI, G.: SRivBib 46: 2005 ⇒47. 111-118 [John 11].

7276 *Moloney, Francis J.* Can everyone be wrong?: a reading of John 11: 1-12:8. The gospel of John. BiblInterp 72: 2005 ⇒6964. 214-240.

7277 **North, Wendy E.S.** The Lazarus story within the Johannine tradition. JSNT.S 212: 2001 ⇒17,6004; 18,6395. [R]RB 112 (2005) 119-121 (*Devillers, Luc*) [John 11].

7278 *Rogit, Sr.* Faith confession of Martha: an exegetical survey (John 11, 17-27). BiBh 31 (2005) 200-214.

7279 *Theobald, Michael* Trauer um Lazarus: womit die Juden Martha und Maria zu trösten suchten (Joh 11,19). TThZ 114 (2005) 243-256.

7280 *Dennis, John* Restoration in John 11,47-52: reading the key motifs in their Jewish context. EThL 81 (2005) 57-86.

7281 *Hakola, Raimo* The counsel of Caiaphas and the social identity of the Johannine community (John 11:47-53). [F]AEJMELAEUS, L.: SESJ 89: 2005 ⇒1. 140-163.

7282 *Coloe, Mary L.* Anointing the temple of God: John 12,1-8. [F]MOLONEY, F.: BSRel 187: 2005 ⇒104. 105-118.

7283 *Häfner, Gerd; Pettinger, Diana; Witetschek, Stephan* Die Salbung Jesu durch Maria (Joh 12,1-8): zwei Rätsel und drei Lösungen. BN 122 (2005) 81-104.

7284 *Philippe, Marie D.* Commentaire de l'évangile de saint Jean: la dernière semaine: de Béthanie à Jérusalem. Aletheia 28 (2005) 121-139 [John 12,1-19].

7285 *Gemünden, Petra von* Die Palmzweige in der johanneischen Einzugsgeschichte (Joh 12,13): ein Hinweis auf eine symbolische Uminterpretation im Johannesevangelium?. Picturing the New Testament. WUNT 2/193: 2005 ⇒396. 207-227.

7286 **Lee, Hye Ja** (Induk Maria) "Signore, vogliamo vedere Gesù": la conclusione dell'attività pubblica di Gesù secondo Gv 12,30-36. [D]*Beutler, Johannes*: TGr.T 124: R 2005, E.P.U.G. 298 pp. €17. 8878-390-399. Bibl. 265-86 [R]EstB 63 (2005) 344-45 (*Sánchez Navarro, Luis*).

7287 *Moka, W.* Jesus' hour in the fourth gospel: a reading of John 12:20-36. Hekima Review 34 (2005) 56-65 [NTAb 50,502].

7288 *Manns, Frédéric* Une tradition synoptique reprise en Jn 12,26. Atti del X Simposio di Efeso. Turchia 19: 2005 ⇒785. 29-44.

7289 *Painter, John* Monotheism and dualism: reconsidering predestination in John 12:40. [F]MOLONEY, F.: BSRel 187: 2005 ⇒104. 118-139.

## G1.8 Jn 13... Sermo sacerdotalis et Passio

7290 **Franco Martínez, César Augusto** La pasión de Jesús según San Juan: escenas con cuestiones disputadas. Studia Semitica NT 14: M 2005, Encuentro 262 pp. [R]LASBF 55 (2005) 543-547 (*Chrupcała, Lesław D.*).

7291 *Glancy, Jennifer A.* Torture: flesh, truth, and the fourth gospel. BiblInterp 13 (2005) 107-136.

7292 *Hearon, Holly E.* Discipleship as journey. BiTod 43 (2005) 288-292 [Mary Magdalene].

7293 *Syreeni, Kari* The witness of blood: the narrative and ideological function of the 'beloved disciple' in John 13-21. [F]AEJMELAEUS, L.: SESJ 89: 2005 ⇒1. 164-185.

7294 *Abramowski, Luise* Die Geschichte von der Fußwaschung (Joh 13). ZThK 102 (2005) 176-203.

7295 *Spitaler, Peter* "Ich habe euch ein Beispiel gegeben": zeichenhaftes Handeln in Joh 13. [F]LAUB, F. 2005 ⇒87. 53-66.

7296 **Brouwer, Wayne** The literary development of John 13-17: a chiastic reading. SBL.DS 182: 2000 ⇒16,6006; 18,6407. [R]RB 112 (2005) 462-463 (*Devillers, Luc*).

7297 *Holloway, Paul A.* Left behind: Jesus' consolation of his disciples in John 13,31-17,26. ZNW 96 (2005) 1-34.

7298 *Moloney, Francis J.* The function of John 13-17 within the Johannine narrative. The gospel of John. BiblInterp 72: 2005 ⇒6964. 260-283.

7299 **Parsenios, George L.** Departure and consolation: the Johannine farewell discourses in light of Greco-Roman literature. [D]*Attridge, Harold*: NT.S 117: Lei 2005, Brill xi; 174 pp. €75. 90-04-14278-9. Diss. Yale; Bibl. 155-164 [John 13-17].

7300 **Pillai, Vijay** Being in God: spatial language in the Johannine farewell discourse. [D]*Watson, Francis* 2005, Diss. Aberdeen [RTL 37, 617] [John 13-17].

7301 *García-Moreno, Antonio* La otra cara de la pasión de Cristo. ScrTh 37 (2005) 161-177.

7302 **Weidemann, Hans-Ulrich** Der Tod Jesu im Johannesevangelium: die erste Abschiedsrede (Joh 13,31-14,31) als Schlüsseltext für den johanneischen Passions- und Osterbericht (Joh 18-20). BZNW 122: 2004 ⇒20,6874. [R]ThGl 95 (2005) 498-500 (*Kowalski, Beate*); BiKi 60 (2005) 122-123 (*Beutler, Johannes*).

7303 **Kellum, L. Scott** The unity of the farewell discourse: the literary integrity of John 13:31-16:33. JSNT.S 256: 2004 ⇒20,6875. [R]RBLit (2005)* (*Matos, Joseph*).

7304 *Bryan, Steven M.* The eschatological temple in John 14. BBR 15/2 (2005) 187-198.

7305 *Vogel, Hans-Jochen* "Herr, wir wissen nicht, wo du hingehst" (Johannes 14,5). Kanzelreden. 2005 ⇒376. 131-137.

7306 *Baumann, Rolf* Die vielen Wege und der eine Weg. BiHe 41/161 (2005) 21-24 [John 14,6].

7307 *Koester, Craig R.* Jesus as the way to the father in Johannine theology (John 14,6). Theology and christology. BEThL 184: 2005 ⇒796. 117-133.

7308 *Buchhold, Jacques* De plus grandes oeuvres que celles de Jésus!: Jean 14.12-13. ThEv(VS) 4/3 (2005) 3-22.

7309 *Beutler, Johannes* "Levatevi, partiamo di qui" (Gv 14,31): un invito a un itinerario spirituale?. [F]GHIBERTI, G. 2005 ⇒47. 133-143.

7310 *Chennattu, Rekha M.* The covenant motif: a key to the interpretation of John 15-16. [F]MOLONEY, F.: BSRel 187: 2005 ⇒104. 141-159.

7311 *Derickson, Gary W.* Viticulture and John 15:1-6. Journal of the Grace Evangelical Society 18/34 (2005) 23-43.

7312 *Elsen-Novák, Gabriele; Novák, Mirko* "Ich bin der wahre Weinstock und mein Vater ist der Weingärtner": zur Semiotik des Weinstocks in

Joh 15,1-8 aus Sicht der Altorientalistik. Picturing the New Testament. WUNT 2/193: 2005 ⇒396. 183-206.

7313 *Giurisato, Giorgio* Il comandamento di Gesù e l'odio del mondo (Gv 15,9-17.18-25). [F]GHIBERTI, G. 2005 ⇒47. 145-161.

7314 **Mputu Mokuba, Evariste** 'Comme je vous ai aimés': analyse exégétique et théologique de Jn 15,12-17 dans le contexte de Jn 13-17. [D]*Boschi, B.G.* 2005, Diss. Angelicum [RTL 37,616].

7315 *Stefan, C.* The Paraclete and prophecy in the Johannine community. Pneuma [Lei] 27/2 (2005) 273-296 [NTAb 50,291] [John 16,12-15].

7316 *Moloney, Francis J.* To make God known: a reading of John 17:1-26;

7317 John 18:15-27: a Johannine view of the church. The gospel of John. BiblInterp 72: 2005 ⇒6964. 284-312/313-329.

7318 *Köstenberger, J.A.* 'What is truth?': Pilate's question in its Johannine and larger biblical context. JETS 48 (2005) 33-62 [NTAb 49,510] [{John 18,28-19,16].

7319 *Zimmermann, Ruben* 'Deuten' heißt erzählen und übertragen: Narrativität und Metaphorik als zentrale Sprachformen historischer Sinnbildung zum Tod Jesu. Deutungen. WUNT 181: 2005 ⇒392. 315-373 [John 18,28-19,16].

7320 *Mazzucco, Clementina* "Allora lo consegnò a loro perché fosse crocifisso" (Gv 19,16a). [F]GHIBERTI, G. 2005 ⇒47. 163-174.

7321 *Przyszychowska, Marta* J 15,25-27 w interpretacji łacińskich ojców kościoła [Jn 19,25-27 in the interpretation of the Latin fathers of the church]. STV 43/1 (2005) 55-78. **P.**

7322 *Kysar, Robert* 'He gave up the spirit': a reader's reflection on John 19:30b. [F]MOLONEY, F.: BSRel 187: 2005 ⇒104. 161-172.

7323 *O'Brien, Kelli S.* Written that you may believe: John 20 and narrative rhetoric. CBQ 67 (2005) 284-302.

7324 *Oiry, Béatrice* De ce qui est en passage dans le récit pascal du quatrième évangile. Raconter. CRB 61: 2005 ⇒717. 49-68 [John 20].

7325 *Schneiders, Sandra M.* The resurrection (of the body) in the fourth gospel: a key to Johannine spirituality. [M]BROWN, R. 2005 ⇒15. 168-198 [John 20];

7326 Touching the risen Jesus: Mary Magdalene and Thomas the Twin in John 20. PCTSA 60 (2005) 13-35 [NTAb 50,291].

7327 *Senior, Donald* The resurrection (of the body) in the fourth gospel as a key to Johannine spirituality: a response to Sandra M. Schneiders, I.H.M. [M]BROWN, R. 2005 ⇒15. 199-203 [John 20].

7328 *Denaux, Adelbert; Mardaga, Hellen* Johannes' verrijzenisverhaal (Joh 20-21). Coll. 35/1 (2005) 5-39.

7329 **Korniak, Maria** Les événements pascaux (Jn 20,1-9.19-21,19) dans les commentaires aux lectures des messes dominicales publiés dans des sélections hebdomadaires catholiques postconciliaires. [D]*Bielecki, S.* 2005, 246 pp. Diss. Lublin [RTL 37,615]. **P.**

7330 *Chardonnens, Denis* Marie se tenait près du tombeau, au-dehors, tout en pleurs: la lecture de Maître ECKHART sur Jn 20,11. Carmel(T) 115 (2005) 109-117.

7331 *Bieringer, R.* 'Nader mij niet': de betekenis van μή μου ἅπτου in Johannes 20:17. HTSTS 61/1-2 (2005) 19-43 [NTAb 50,292].

7332 *Pretlove, J.* John 20:22—help from dry bones?. Criswell Theological Review [Dallas] 3/1 (2005) 93-101 [NTAb 50,292].

7333 **Most, Glenn W.** Doubting Thomas. CM 2005, Harvard University Pr. xv; [2], 267 pp. £19. 0674019148. Bibl. 229-56 [John 20,24-29].

7334 *Johnson, Brian D.* Thomas and *marturia*: John 20:24-31. ProcGLM 25 (2005) 169-178.

7335 *Collins, Raymond F.* 'Blessed are those who have not seen': John 20: 29. [F]MOLONEY, F.: BSRel 187: 2005 ⇒104. 173-190.

7336 *Carson, D.A.* Syntactical and text-critical observations on John 20: 30-31: one more round on the purpose of the fourth gospel. JBL 124 (2005) 693-714.

7337 *Van Belle, Gilbert* Christology and soteriology in the fourth gospel: the conclusion to the gospel of John revisited. Theology and christology. BEThL 184: 2005 ⇒796. 435-461 [John 20,30-31].

7338 *Sevrin, Jean-Marie* Les deux finales du quatrième évangile. Analyse narrative. BEThL 191: 2005 ⇒742. 241-7 [John 20,30-31; 21,24-5].

7339 *Brooke, George J.* 4Q252 and the 153 fish of John 21.11. Dead Sea scrolls and the NT. 2005 <1999> ⇒194. 282-297.

7340 *Greenlee, J. Harold* "More than these?" John 21:15. JOT 1/2 (2005) 19-20.

## G2.1 Epistulae Johannis

7341 **Beutler, Johannes** Die Johannesbriefe. Regensburger Neues Testament: 2000 ⇒16,6049...18,6452. [R]BZ 49 (2005) 149-152 (*Hasitschka, Martin*); RSR 93 (2005) 316-317 (*Morgen, Michèle*).

7342 *Beutler, Johannes* 1, 2 and 3 John. Global bible commentary. 2005 ⇒2443. 553-558.

7343 *Black, C. Clifton* The first, second and third letters of John. NT survey. 2005 ⇒3144. 321-331.

7344 *Bryant, Michael* Annotated bibliography: the Johannine epistles, 2000-2005. Faith & Mission 23/1 (2005) 83-89.

**Lewis, S.** The gospel...John and Johannine letters 2005 ⇒6961.

7345 **Morgen, Michèle** Les épîtres de Jean. Commentaire biblique: NT 19: P 2005, Cerf 264 pp. €26. 2-204-07643-0. Bibl. 13-19.

7346 **Painter, John** 1, 2, and 3 John. Sacra Pagina 18: 2002 ⇒18,6455... 20,6923. [R]BZ 49 (2005) 150-152 (*Hasitschka, Martin*); RSR 93 (2005) 317-318 (*Morgen, Michèle*); Bib. 86 (2005) 130-133 (*Beutler, Johannes*).

7347 **Thomas, John Christopher** The Pentecostal commentary on 1 John, 2 John, 3 John. 2004 ⇒20,6925. [R]RBLit (2005)* (*Bostock, David; Dunn, Matthew*).

7348 **Uebele, Wolfram** "Viele Verführer sind in die Welt ausgegangen": die Gegner in den Briefen des IGNATIUS von Antiochien und in den Johannesbriefen. BWANT 151: 2001 ⇒17,6053; 18,6457. [R]SCI 24 (2005) 213-215 (*Lehner, Thomas*).

7349 *Van der Merwe, Dirk J.* Understanding 'sin' in the Johannine epistles. VeE 26 (2005) 543-570;

7350 Salvation in the Johannine epistles. Salvation in the New Testament. NT.S 121: 2005 ⇒798. 437-464.

7351 **Armogathe, Jean-R.** L'Antichrist à l'âge classique: exégèse et politique. P 2005, Mille et une nuits 301 pp. €13.50. 2842-05925. Bibl.

7352 *Bottini, Giovanni* Peccato e intercessione in 1Gv 5,16-17: dalla struttura al messaggio. [F]GHIBERTI, G.: SRivBib 46: 2005 ⇒47. 175-184.
7353 **Ferro, A.** Teologia ed ecclesiologia di 1 Gv 5,1-13. Caltanissetta 2004, Pont. Fac. Teol. di Sicilia 289 pp. Dissertazioni 3.
7354 **Griffith, Terry** Keep yourselves from idols: a new look at 1 John. JSNT.S 233: 2002 ⇒18,6460... 20,6932. [R]BiblInterp 13 (2005) 330-333 (*North, Wendy Sproston*); RB 112 (2005) 121-126 (*Devillers, Luc*); RBLit 7 (2005) 422-424 (*Van der Watt, Jan*).
7355 *Keener, Craig* Transformation through divine vision in 1 John 3:2-6. Faith & Mission 23/1 (2005) 13-22.
7356 *Kellum, L. Scott* On the semantic structure of 1 John: a modest proposal. Faith & Mission 23/1 (2005) 34-82.
7357 *Kim, Jintae* The concept of atonement in Hellenistic thought and 1 John. JGRChJ 2 (2005) 100-116.
7358 *Kruse, Colin G.* Sin and perfection in 1 John. Faith & Mission 23/1 (2005) 23-33.
7359 **López Barrio, Mario** El tema del ágape en la primera carta de san Juan: estudio de 1 Jn 4,7-21: una perspectiva antropológico-social. TGr.T 114: 2004 ⇒20,6936. [R]ThX 55 (2005) 107-108 (*Ortiz V., Pedro*); ATG 68 (2005) 316-317 (*Contreras Molina, Francisco*).
7360 *Mazzarolo, Isidoro* A pedagogia na família segundo 1Jo 2,12-14. Estudos Bíblicos 85 (2005) 90-102.
7361 *Morgen, Michèle* Le prologue de la première épître de Jean: sa structure et sa visée. RevSR 79 (2005) 55-75.
7362 *Perkins, Pheme* Gnostic revelation and Johannine sectarianism: reading 1 John from the perspective of Nag Hammadi. Theology and christology. BEThL 184: 2005 ⇒796. 245-276.
7363 *Renkema, Marcus J.* Biblical theology and counseling: I John 4:7-21. Kerux 20/3 (2005) 15-24.
7364 **Scarano, Angelo** Storia dell'interpretazione ed esegesi di 1 Gv 3,18-22. [D]*Beutler, Johannes*: AnBib 157: R 2005, E.P.I.B. 303 pp. €20. 88-7653-157-2. Bibl. 281-293.
7365 **Schmid, Hans-Jörg** Gegner im 1. Johannesbrief?: zur Konstruktion und Selbstreferenz im johanneischen Sinnsystem. BWANT 159: 2002 ⇒18,6462... 20,6942. [R]BZ 49 (2005) 293-295 (*Frey, Jörg*).
7366 *Smith, W.T.* Authentic morality: the living values in First John. Journal of Biblical Counseling [Glenside, PA] 23/4 (2005) 44-53 [NTAb 50,318].
7367 *Velde, Herman te* Looking at the condemning heart of 1 John 3.18-20 through the eyes of an ancient Egyptian. [F]LUTTIKHUIZEN, G.: AGJU 59: 2005 ⇒93. 217-225.

7368 *Akin, Daniel L.* Truth or consequences: 2 John 1-13. Faith & Mission 23/1 (2005) 3-12.
7369 *Campbell, Barth L.* Honor, hospitality and haughtiness: the contention for leadership in 3 John. EvQ 77 (2005) 321-341.
7370 Novum Testamentum Graecum: editio critica maior, 4: die Katholischen Briefe, Lfg. 4: der zweite und dritte Johannesbrief; der Judasbrief, Teil 1: Text. [E]**Aland, Barbara**, *al.*: Stu 2005, Deutsche Bibelgesellschaft xvii; xviii; 31*-38*; 369-346 pp. €18.50. 3-438-05603-8;
7371 Teil 2: Begleitende Materialien. [E]**Aland, Barbara**, *al.*,: Stu 2005, Deutsche Bibelgesellschaft vi; B 127-155.

7372 *Smit, Peter-Ben* A note on the relationship between II and III John. BN 123 (2005) 93-101.

### G2.3 *Apocalypsis Johannis*—Revelation: text, commentaries

7373 [E]**Barr, David L.** Reading the book of Revelation: a resource for students. Resources for biblical study 44: 2003 ⇒19,6979; 20,6949. [R]RBLit 7 (2005) 444-447 (*Bredin, Mark*).

7374 **Bianchi, Enzo** Le monde sauvé: commentaire de l'Apocalypse de Jean. 2004 ⇒20,6950. [R]Contacts 57 (2005) 184-86 (*Minet, Jacques*).

7375 **Biguzzi, Giancarlo** L'Apocalisse e i suoi enigmi. StBi 143: 2004 ⇒ 20,6951. [R]RBLit (2005)* (*West, James*);

7376 Apocalisse. I libri biblici.NT 20: Mi 2005, Paoline 476 pp. €28. 88-315-2875-0.

7377 **Blanchard, Yves-Marie** L'Apocalypse. La bible tout simplement: 2004 ⇒20,6952. [R]EeV 128 (2005) 25-26 (*Poucouta, Paulin*); RICP 95 (2005) 252-253 = 96 (2005) 213-214 (*Nabert, Nathalie*); RB 112 (2005) 301-302 (*Grelot, Pierre*).

7378 **Bock, Emil** The Apocalypse of St. John. EX 2005 <1957>, Floris 208 pp. 0-86315-539-1. Rev. ed.

7379 **Doglio, Claudio** Apocalisse di Giovanni. Padova 2005, Messaggero 239 pp. €10.50. 88-250-1344-2. Bibl. 229-231.

7380 **Durham, James** A commentary on Revelation. Willow Street, Pa. 2000 <1658>, Old Paths xii; 1024 pp. $50. Introd. *David C. Lachman* [CTJ 36,383s—Muller, Richard A].

7381 **Fallon, Michael** The Apocalypse: a call to embrace the love that is stronger than death. Kensington, NSW 2002, Chevalier 129 pp. 1-87-5463-00-3;

7382 = Bangalore 2005 [1990], Asia Trading ii; 131 pp. Rs100. 81-7086-346-5.

7383 **Farmer, Ronald L.** Revelation. Chalice commentaries for today: St. Louis, MO 2005, Chalice xiii; 146 pp. $23. 0-8272-0528-7. Bibl. 143-146.

7384 *Gryson, Roger* Le commentaire de TYCONIUS sur l'Apocalypse. BVLI 49 (2005) 41-47.

7385 [E]**Gryson, Roger** Apocalypsis Johannis, Lfg. 7-10. VL 26/2: 2003 ⇒19,6985-8. [R]REAug 51 (2005) 195-197 (*Milhau, Marc*);

7386 Apocalypsis Johannis. VL 26/2: 2000-2003 ⇒19,6982. [R]RTL 36 (2005) 96-100 (*Parker, D.C.*);

7387 Commentaria minora in Apocalypsin Johannis. CChr.SM 107: 2003 ⇒19,6989. [R]ThLZ 130 (2005) 494-496 (*Karrer, Martin*); RevSR 79 (2005) 422-423 (*Vinel, Françoise*); JThS 56 (2005) 247-248 (*Ward, Benedicta*).

7388 **Knorr von Rosenroth, Christian** Apokalypse-Kommentar. [E]*Battafarano, Italo M.*: IRIS 22: Bern 2004, Lang 209 pp. 3-03910-401-2.

7389 **Kovacs, Judith; Rowland, Christopher** Revelation: the Apocalypse of Jesus Christ. Blackwell Bible Commentaries: 2004 ⇒20,6961. [R]JThS 56 (2005) 578-581 (*Boxall, Ian*).

7390 **Marshall, John William** Parables of war: reading John's Jewish Apocalypse. 2001 ⇒17,6078; 19,6996. [R]SR 34 (2005) 592-593 (*Broadhurst, Lawrence*); RBLit (2005)* (*Royalty, Robert*).

7391 **Men, Alexandre** Au fil de l'Apocalypse. $^{T}$*Lhoest, Françoise* 2003 ⇒19,6997. $^{R}$Contacts 57 (2005) 181-182 (*Minet, Jacques*).

7392 **Mesters, Carlos; Orofino, Francisco** Apocalipse de São João: a teimosia da fé dos pequenos. Comentário Bíblico: 2003 ⇒19,6998; 20, 6963. $^{R}$REB 65 (2005) 747-750 (*Correia, João Luiz, Júnior*).

7393 **Orlando, Luigi** L'Apocalisse di San Giovanni: lettura teologica. Taranto 2005, Puntopace 206 pp. €20. Bibl. 12-15.

7394 *Rowland, Christopher C.* The book of Revelation. NT survey. 2005 ⇒3144. 339-384;

7395 Revelation. Global bible commentary. 2005 ⇒2443. 559-570.

7396 **Schmidt, Frederick W.** Conversations with scripture: Revelation. Harrisburg, PA 2005, Morehouse xix; 119 pp. $13 [BiTod 45,266—Donald Senior].

7397 **Smalley, Stephen S.** The Revelation to John: a commentary on the Greek text of the Apocalypse. DG 2005, InterVarsity xvii; 633 pp. $65. 0-8308-2800-1. Bibl. 588-597.

7398 **Stock, Klemens** La última palabra es de Dios: el Apocalipsis como buena noticia. Sicar 3: M 2005, San Pablo 207 pp. 84-285-2818-7.

7399 **Trafton, Joseph L.** Reading Revelation: a literary and theological commentary. Macon, GA 2005, Smyth & H. vii; 224 pp. $21. 1-573-12-289-0. $^{R}$RBLit (2005)* (*Barr, David*).

7400 $^{E}$**Weinrich, William C.** Revelation. ACCS.NT 12: DG 2005, Inter-Varsity xxxii; 454 pp. $40. 0-8308-1497-3. Bibl. 432-438.

7401 **Witherington, Ben, III** Revelation. New Cambridge Bible Commentary: 2003 ⇒19,7007; 20,6969. $^{R}$Faith & Mission 22/2 (2005) 117-119 (*Owens, Mark D.*); SNTU 30 (2005) 243-245 (*Kowalski, Beate*); RBLit 7 (2005) 441-444 (*Hieke, Thomas*).

## G2.4 *Apocalypsis, themata*—**Revelation, topics**

7402 *Abir, Peter* Bible and the state: a view from the Apocalypse of John. BiBh 31 (2005) 38-67.

7403 *Arcari, Luca* I rapporti tra Apocalisse e 'apocalittica giudaica': lineamenti essenziali del dibattito scientifico da Bousset alle più recenti acquisizioni sulla cosiddetta 'apocalittica giudaica'. Giudei o cristiani?. 2005 ⇒833. 147-156.

7404 **Attinger, Daniel** Apocalypse de Jean: à la rencontre du Christ dévoilé. Le Mont-sur-Lausanne 2005, Ouverture 124 pp.

7405 *Aune, David E.* The Apocalypse of John and the problem of genre. Apocalypticism, prophecy. WUNT 199: 2005 <1986> ⇒177. 39-65;

7406 Following the Lamb: discipleship in the Apocalypse. Apocalypticism, prophecy. WUNT 199: 2005 <1996> ⇒177. 66-78;

7407 Qumran and the book of Revelation <1999> 79-98;

7408 The influence of Roman Imperial court ceremonial on the Apocalypse of John <1983> 99-119;

7409 An intertextual reading of the Apocalypse of John 120-149;

7410 The Apocalypse of John and Palestinian Jewish apocalyptic 150-174;

7411 The social matrix of the Apocalypse of John <1981> 175-189;

7412 Stories of Jesus in the Apocalypse of John 190-211 [= Contours of christology ⇒775. 292-319];

7413 God and time in the Apocalypse of John <2002> 261-279;

7414 The Apocalypse of John and Graeco-Roman revelatory magic <1987> 347-367;

7415 Understanding Jewish and christian apocalyptic. Apocalypticism, prophecy. WUNT 199: 2005 ⇒177. 1-12.

7416 *Awad Hanna, Kamal F.* La passione di Cristo e dei cristiani nell'Apocalisse. [F]VANNI, U. 2005 ⇒156. 501-511.

7417 *Álvarez Valdés, Ariel* El libro del Apocalipsis: historia de su interpretación. EstB 63 (2005) 283-311.

7418 *Bachmann, Michael* Apocalypse now, Apocalypse once: der Film Francis Ford Coppolas auf dem Hintergrund der Johannesoffenbarung. [F]BÖCHER, O. 2005 ⇒14. 381-401.

7419 *Baumeister, Theofried* Der Brief der Gemeinden von Vienne und Lyon und die Offenbarung des Johannes;

7420 *Beisser, Friedrich* Trinitätsaussagen in der Offenbarung des Johannes.[F]BÖCHER, O. 2005 ⇒14. 339-355/120-135.

7421 *Bendemann, Reinhard von* "Lebensgeist kam in sie ...": der Ezechielzyklus von Dura Europos und die Rezeption von Ez 37 in der Apk des Johannes: ein Beitrag zum Verhältnisproblem von Ikonizität und Narrativität. Picturing the New Testament. WUNT 2/193: 2005 ⇒ 396. 253-286.

7422 *Biguzzi, Giancarlo* Giovanni di Patmos e la cultura ellenistica. [F]VANNI, U. 2005 ⇒156. 93-126;

7423 Il potere della bestia e il demoniaco nell'Apocalisse. PSV 51 (2005) 197-214.

7424 **Binz, Stephen J.** The Lamb and the beasts. Threshold Bible Study: New London, CT 2005, Twenty-Third 131 pp. $13 [BiTod 44,198—Donald Senior].

7425 *Blount, Brian K.* The witness of active resistance: the ethics of *Revelation* in African American perspective. From every people. 2005 ⇒472. 28-46.

7426 **Blount, Brian K.** Can I get a witness?: reading Revelation through African American culture. LVL 2005, Westminster 155 pp. $17. 0-6-6422-8690. [R]JBL 124 (2005) 578-581 (*Sigler, Danielle Brune*); RBLit (2005)* (*Sigler, Danielle Brune*).

7427 *Bosetti, Elena* L'agnello pastore in 1Pietro e Apocalisse: quando la liturgia interpella la vita. [F]VANNI, U. 2005 ⇒156. 277-307.

7428 *Botha, N.A.* Mission as prophecy: reading the Apocalypse as forthtelling rather than foretelling. Missionalia 33 (2005) 315-328 [NTAb 50,318].

7429 *Böcher, Otto* Aspekte einer Hermeneutik der Johannes-Offenbarung. [F]NIEDERWIMMER, K.: Gutachten und Studien 2: 2005 ⇒112. 23-33.

7430 **Bredin, Mark R.** Jesus, revolutionary of peace: a nonviolent christology in the book of Revelation. Paternoster biblical and theological monographs: 2003 ⇒19,7017. [R]RBLit (2005)* (*Nicklas, Tobias*).

7431 [E]**Burgos, Jean** L'imaginaire des apocalypses. Bibliothèque Circé 4: 2003 ⇒19,579. [R]ETR 80 (2005) 148-149 (*Cottin, Jérôme*).

7432 *Bümlein, Klaus* Ein Speyerer Apokalypse-Ausleger von 1654: Johann Heinrich Ursinus und sein Richtiges Zeigerhändlein. [F]BÖCHER, O. 2005 ⇒14. 356-367.

7433 *Campbell, W. Gordon* La royauté de Dieu, de l'agneau et des siens dans l'Apocalypse de Jean: 'le vainqueur, je lui donnerai de s'asseoir avec moi sur mon trône...' (Ap 3.21). RRef 56/233 (2005) 44-61 [NTAb 50,82].

7434 *Carvalho, José Carlos* A 'mulher' hebraica do Apocalipse. HumTeo 26/1 (2005) 3-19;

7435 *Cimosa, Mario* L'autore dell'Apocalisse ha usato la bibbia greca?. FVANNI, U. 2005 ⇒156. 63-92.

7436 *Cipriani, Settimio* Apocalittica e Apocalisse: spunti di riflessione per un libro "misterioso". Asp. 52 (2005) 323-338.

7437 *Colacrai, Angelo* Attività dello scrivere: un confronto tra Paolo e Apocalisse. FVANNI, U. 2005 ⇒156. 203-223.

7438 *Collins, Adela Y.* Integrating apocalypticism into modern theology. Reflections [NHv] 92/1 (2005) 10-15 [NTAb 50,84].

7439 *Corsini, Eugenio* I numeri nell'Apocalisse. FVANNI, U. 2005 ⇒156. 391-416.

7440 *Cowan, Martyn* New world, new temple, new worship: the book of Revelation in the theology and practice of christian worship, part 1. ChM 119/4 (2005) 297-312.

7441 *Delorme, Jean* Mondes figuratifs, parole et position du lecteur dans l'Apocalypse de Jean. FGENEST, O. 2005 ⇒46. 127-155.

7442 *deSilva, David A.* The Revelation of John and the practice of christian counseling. AsbTJ 60/1 (2005) 67-87.

7443 *Doglio, Claudio* L'annuncio del kairós escatologico: il senso del tempo nell'Apocalisse di Giovanni. RTLu 10 (2005) 23-40.

7444 **Doglio, Claudio** Il primogenito dei morti: la risurrezione di Cristo e dei cristiani nell'Apocalisse di Giovanni. RivBib.S 45: Bo 2005, EDB 357 pp. €32. 88-10-30232-X. Bibl. 331-346.

7445 **Doukhan, Jacques B.** Secrets of Revelation: the Apocalypse through Hebrew eyes. 2002 ⇒19,7028. RAUSS 43 (2005) 218-219 (*Stefanovic, Ranko*).

7446 **D'Souza, Jerome** The book of Revelation: power, violence and suffering: a contextual reading. Bangalore 2005, Asian Trading xx; 296 pp. 81-7086-356-2. Bibl. 239-296.

7447 *Du Rand, Jan A.* Soteriology in the Apocalypse of John. Salvation in the New Testament. NT.S 121: 2005 ⇒798. 465-504.

7448 **Fanzaga, L.** Dies irae: los días del anticristo. Cristianismo y sociedad 73: Bilbao 2005, Desclée de B. 220 pp. 84-330-1972-4.

7449 *Franco, Ettore* Profeti e profezia nell'Apocalisse. FVANNI, U. 2005 ⇒156. 335-369.

7450 *Frenschkowski, Marco* Die Johannesoffenbarung zwischen Vision, astralmythologischer Imagination und Literatur: Perspektiven und Desiderate der Apokalypse-Forschung. FBÖCHER, O. 2005 ⇒14. 20-45.

7451 *Friesen, Steven J.* Satan's throne, imperial cults and the social settings of Revelation. JSNT 27 (2005) 351-373.

7452 **Frilingos, Christopher A.** Spectacles of empire: monsters, martyrs, and the book of Revelation. Divinations: 2004 ⇒20,6998. RJBL 124 (2005) 573-575 (*Royalty, Robert M., Jr.*); RBLit 7 (2005) 438-440 (*Van Henten, Jan*).

7453 **Gentry, Kenneth L., Jr.** The beast of Revelation. 2002 ⇒19,7036. RBS 162 (2005) 382-383 (*Larsen, James M.; Kreider, Glenn R.*).

7454 *Georgi, Dieter* Who is the true prophet?. The city in the valley. Ment. *Horatius*: Studies in biblical literature 7: 2005 ⇒214. 25-51.

7455 *Gerwing, Manfred* Heinrich Bitterfeld als Reformer: Anmerkungen zum Gottesbild der Apokalypse. ThGl 95 (2005) 409-422.

7456 *Giesen, Heinz* Lasterkataloge und Kaiserkult in der Offenbarung des Johannes. FBÖCHER, O. 2005 ⇒14. 210-231 [Rev 9,20-21; 21,7-8; 22,14-15].

7457 **Gilbertson, Michael** God and history in the book of Revelation: New Testament studies in dialogue with PANNENBERG and MOLTMANN. MSSNTS 124: 2003 ⇒19,7040; 20,7000. RJThS 56 (2005) 584-585 (*Rowland, Christopher C.*).

7458 *González, Justo L. Revelation*: clarity and ambivalence, a Hispanic/ Cuban American perspective. From every people. 2005 ⇒472. 47-61.

7459 *Grech, Prosper* Lo splendore della gloria celeste: estetica teologica. PATH 4 (2005) 337-346.

7460 *Groote, Marc de* Die Johannesapokalypse und die Kanonbildung im Osten. ZKG 116 (2005) 147-160.

7461 *Guerra Suarez, Luis M.* Il cavallo bianco: la forza trasformante della risurrezione (Ap 6,1-2; 19,11-16). FVANNI, U. 2005 ⇒156. 513-534 [Rev 6,1-2; 19,11-16].

7462 **Guerra Suárez, Luis María** El caballo blanco en el Apocalipsis (Ap 6,1-2/9,11-16) y la presencia de Cristo resucitado en la historia: investigación teológico-bíblica. 2004 ⇒20,7001. REstTrin 39 (2005) 593-595 (*Vázquez Allegue, Jaime*) [Rev 6,1-2; 6,11-16].

7463 *Gundry, Robert H.* Angelomorphic christology in the book of Revelation. The old is better. WUNT 178: 2005 ⇒220. 377-398.

7464 *Hahn, Ferdinand* Die Offenbarung des Johannes als Geschichtsdeutung und Trostbuch. KuD 51/1 (2005) 55-70;

7465 Das Geistverständnis in der Johannesoffenbarung. FBÖCHER, O. 2005 ⇒14. 3-9.

7466 **Hanna, Kamal F.A.** La passione di Cristo nell'Apocalisse. TGr.T 77: 2001 ⇒17,6130. RRivBib 53 (2005) 248-251 (*Fabris, Rinaldo*).

7467 *Hasitschka, Martin* Offenbarung des Johannes und Archäologie. PzB 14 (2005) 149-158 [Rev 2,12-17];

7468 Was sagen uns biblisch-apokalyptische Bilder heute?: Christusbilder in der Offenbarung des Johannes. Wenn alles aus ist: christliche Hoffnung angesichts von Tod und Weltende. E**Böhm, Thomas H.; Wandinger, Nikolaus**: theologische trends 14: Fra 2005, Lang. 978-3-631-54382-5. 89-110 [Rev 1,9-20; 4-5; 21,9-22,5].

7469 **Herghelegiu, Monica-Elena** Siehe, er kommt mit den Wolken!: Studien zur Christologie der Johannesoffenbarung. EHS.T 785: 2004 ⇒ 20,7003. RThLZ 130 (2005) 391-393 (*Karrer, Martin*).

7470 **Hoffmann, Matthias R.** The destroyer and the lamb: the relationship between angelomorphic and lamb christology in the book of Relevation [i.e. Revelation]. D*Stuckenbruck, L.T.*: WUNT 2/203: Tü 2005, Mohr S. xvi; 311 pp. €59. 3-16-148778-8. Diss. Durham; Bibl. 255-79.

7471 *Holtz, Traugott* Sprache als Metapher: Erwägungen zur Sprache der Johannesapokalypse. FBÖCHER, O.: 2005 ⇒14. 10-19.

7472 *Horn, Friedrich W.* Johannes auf Patmos. FBÖCHER, O. 2005 ⇒14. 139-159 [Rev 1,9].

7473 **Jauhiainen, Marko** The use of Zechariah in Revelation. D*Carleton Paget, James*: WUNT 2/199: Tü 2005, Mohr S. x; 200 pp. €39. 3-16-148663-3. Diss. Cambridge; Bibl. 169-182 [TynB 56/1,157-160].

7474 *Johns, L.L.* Conceiving violence: the Apocalypse of John and the Left Behind series. Direction 34 (2005) 194-214 [NTAb 50,319].

7475 **Johns, Loren L.** The lamb christology of the Apocalypse of John. WUNT 2/167: 2003 ⇒19,7052; 20,7009. [R]ThLZ 130 (2005) 393-94 (*Karrer, Martin*); JBL 124 (2005) 571-573 (*Royalty, Robert M., Jr.*); RBLit (2005)* (*Heyman, George; Nicklas, Tobias*) [Rev 5].

7476 *Johnson, Galen K.* The tribulation in Revelation and its literary-theological milieu. JGRChJ 2 (2005) 52-75.

7477 **Kaithakottil, Ice Joice** The conversion of the church and the conversion of the world: a biblical theological study of μετανοέω in the book of Revelation. [D]*Vanni, Ugo* 2005, Diss. Gregoriana [RTL 37, 615].

7478 *Karrer, Martin* Himmel, Millennium und neuer Himmel in der Apokalypse. JBTh 20 (2005) 225-259;

7479 Ein optisches Instrument in der Hand der Leser: Wirkungsgeschichte und Auslegung der Johannesoffenbarung. [F]BÖCHER, O. 2005 ⇒14. 402-432.

7480 *Karrer, Martin; Wahl, Heribert* Apocalisse e psicanalisi. [F]VANNI, U. 2005 ⇒156. 753-795.

7481 [E]**Kitterick, David**, *al.*, The Trinity Apocalypse (Trinity College Cambridge, Ms. R.16.2): commentary on the facsimile edition. British Library Studies in Medieval Culture: L 2005, British Library xv; 173 pp. £20. 0-7123-0690-0. CD-ROM [Scr. 60/1,123*–A. Dubois].

7482 *Klingbeil, Gerald A.* 'Eating' and 'drinking' in the book of Revelation. JATS 16 (2005) 75-92 [NTAb 50,523].

7483 *Knöppler, Thomas* Das Blut des Lammes: zur soteriologischen Relevanz des Todes Jesu nach der Johannesapokalypse. Deutungen. WUNT 181: 2005 ⇒392. 477-511.

7484 *Koester, Craig R.* Revelation and the "Left behind" novels;

7485 *Kovacs, Judith L.* The Revelation to John: lessons from the history of the book's reception. Word and world 25 (2005) 274-282/255-263.

7486 **Kowalski, Beate** Die Rezeption des Propheten Ezechiel in der Offenbarung des Johannes. SBB 52: 2004 ⇒20,7011. [R]RRT 12 (2005) 609-610 (*Moyise, Steve*).

7487 **Kundert, Lukas Jost** Die große Wende—Theologie im Neuen Testament angesichts von Apokalypse und Erlösung. 2005, Diss.-Habil. Basel [ThRv 102,xiii].

7488 **Lioy, Dan** The book of Revelation in christological focus. Studies in Biblical Literature 58: 2003 ⇒19,7058; 20,7016. [R]ThLZ 130 (2005) 392 (*Karrer, Martin*); Faith & Mission 23/1 (2005) 92-94 (*Owens, Mark D.*).

7489 *Maier, Harry O.* The President's revelation: the Apocalypse, American providence, and the war on terror. Word and world 25 (2005) 294-307;

7490 Coming out of Babylon: a first-world reading of *Revelation* among immigrants. From every people. 2005 ⇒472. 62-81.

7491 **Maier, Harry O.** Apocalypse recalled: the book of Revelation after christendom. 2002 ⇒18,6536... 20,7019. [R]TJT 21 (2005) 253-254 (*Marshall, John W.*).

7492 *Manns, Frédéric* Apocalisse e apocalissi. [F]VANNI, U. 2005 ⇒156. 19-48.

7493 *Marcato, Giorgio* L'Apocalisse di Giovanni: libro o lettera?. Ang. 82 (2005) 7-18.

7494 *Marconi, Gilberto* Contributo a un catalogo sull'iconografia dell'Apocalisse nella seconda metà del sec. XX;

7495 *Marino, Marcello* Custodire il libro dell'Apocalisse [Rev 1,3; 22,7-9]. FVANNI, U. 2005 ⇒156. 797-820/371-389.

7496 **Marino, Marcello** Custodire la parola: il verbo τηρεῖν nell'Apocalisse alla luce della tradizione giovannea. SRivBib 40: 2003 ⇒19,7063; 20,7021. RGr. 86 (2005) 185-186 (*Ferraro, Giuseppe*).

7497 *Marshall, John W.* Collateral damage: Jesus and Jezebel in the Jewish war. Violence in the NT. 2005 ⇒439. 35-50.

7498 *Marucci, Corrado* La canonicità dell'Apocalisse nel primo millennio. FVANNI, U. 2005 ⇒156. 649-676.

7499 *Mathewson, David* Isaiah in Revelation. Isaiah in the NT. 2005 ⇒ 443. 189-210.

7500 **Mazzanti, Giorgio** Ultimo avvento. Bo 2005, EDB 93 pp. €8. 88-10-80813-4.

7501 *Mazzinghi, Luca* I "misteri di Dio" dal libro della Sapienza all'Apocalisse. FVANNI, U. 2005 ⇒156. 147-181.

7502 *Moyise, Steve* Word frequencies in the book of Revelation. AUSS 43 (2005) 285-299.

7503 *Möllendorff, Peter von* Christliche Apokalypsen und ihr mimetisches Potential in der paganen Bildungskultur: ein Beitrag zu LUKIANs Wahren Geschichten. Die Bibel im Dialog. NET 10: 2005 ⇒333. 179-194.

7504 *Murray, James S.* The urban earthquake imagery and divine judgment in John's Apocalypse. NT 47 (2005) 142-161.

7505 *Müller, Christoph G.* Gott wird alle Tränen abwischen—Offb 21,4: Anmerkungen zum Gottesbild der Apokalypse. ThGl 95 (2005) 275-297.

7506 *Müller, Peter* Das Buch und die Bücher in der Johannesoffenbarung. FBÖCHER, O. 2005 ⇒14. 293-309.

7507 *Neufeld, Dietmar* Under the cover of clothing: scripted clothing performances in the Apocalypse of John. BTB 35 (2005) 67-76.

7508 *Niclós Albarracín, Josep-Vicent* Menahem el consolador y el vidente de Patmos?: contemporaneidad del Apocalipsis de Zorobabel y el de Juan?. Ment. *Domitian*; EstB 63 (2005) 65-99.

7509 *Nobile, Marco* "Sarò per essi un tempio per poco tempo": da Ezechiele all'Apocalisse: il tragitto di un'idea. FVANNI, U. 2005 ⇒156. 127-146.

7510 E**Nogueira, Paulo Augusto de S.** Religião de visionários: apocalíptica e misticismo no cristianismo primitivo. Bíblica Loyola 48: São Paulo 2005, Loyola 340 pp.

7511 *Nusca, A. Robert* Liturgia e Apocalisse: alcuni aspetti della questione. FVANNI, U. 2005 ⇒156. 459-478.

7512 **Nwachukwu, Oliver O.** Beyond vengeance and protest: a reflection on the macarisms in Revelation. Studies in Biblical Literature 71: NY 2005, Lang xix; 292 pp. 0-8204-7131-3. Bibl. 249-267 RRBLit (2005)* (*Giesen, Heinz*).

7513 *O'Day, Gail R.* Teaching and preaching the book of Revelation. Word and world 25 (2005) 246-254.

7514 *Okoye, James C.* Power and worship: *Revelation* in African perspective. From every people. 2005 ⇒472. 110-126.

7515 *Omerzu, Heike* "Wer ist dieser?": Wilhelm Boussets Beitrag zur Erforschung des Antichrist-Mythos. FBÖCHER, O. 2005 ⇒14. 93-119.

7516 *Paluku, J.M.V.* War and victory of the Lamb in the book of Revelation: its relevance in African peace building. Hekima Review 34 (2005) 66-82 [NTAb 50,524].

7517 *Parchem, Marek* Wybrane motywy wspólne dla Ksiegi Apokalipsy i literatury qumranskiej. CoTh 75/3 (2005) 85-123.

7518 **Parmentier, Roger** L'Apocalypse de Jean actualisée. P 2005, L'Harmattan 74 pp. €11. 978-22960-00001.

7519 **Pattemore, Stephen** The people of God in the Apocalypse: discourse, structure, and exegesis. MSSNTS 128: 2004 ⇒20,7033. [R]RBLit (2005)* (*Barr, David*) JThS 56 (2005) 581-84 (*Boxall, Ian*).

7520 **Pellistrandi, Christine; Villefranche, Henry de** Contempler l'Apocalypse. P 2005, Parole et S. 160 pp. €35. Préf. Card. *Lustiger, Jean-Marie*; Miniatures de *Béatus de Liebana*.

7521 *Penna, Romano* Il caso degli "idolotiti": un test sulla sorte del cristianesimo da Paolo all'Apocalisse. [F]VANNI, U. 2005 ⇒156. 225-244.

7522 **Peters, Olutola K.** The mandate of the church in the Apocalypse of John. Studies in Biblical literature 77: NY 2005, Lang xiv; 167 pp. 0-8204-7461-4. Bibl. 147-163.

7523 **Peterson, Erik** Ausgewählte Schriften, 4: Offenbarung des Johannes und politisch-theologische Texte. [E]*Nichtweiß, Barbara; Löser, Werner* 2004 ⇒20,256. [R]ThLZ 130 (2005) 396-398 (*Lohse, Eduard*).

7524 *Pippin, Tina* The heroine and the whore: the *Apocalypse of John* in feminist perspective. From every people. 2005 ⇒472. 127-145.

7525 **Rambourg, M.** L'Apocalypse de saint Jean, message d'espérance. P 2004, Thélès 146 pp. €14.90.

7526 *Reiser, Marius* Das Buch in der Apokalypse. Kirchliches Buch- und Bibliothekswesen: Jahrbuch 2004 [Trier]. 2005, 69-83;

7527 Das christliche Geschichtsbild: seine Herkunft und seine moderne Rezeption. [F]BÖCHER, O. 2005 ⇒14. 46-70.

7528 *Richard, Pablo* Reading the *Apocalypse*: resistance, hope, and liberation in Central America. From every people. 2005 ⇒472. 146-164.

7529 *Rossing, Barbara R.* City visions, feminine figures, and economic critique: a sapiental topos in the Apocalypse. Conflicted boundaries. SBL.Symp. 35: 2005 ⇒495. 181-196;

7530 For the healing of the world: reading *Revelation* ecologically. From every people. 2005 ⇒472. 165-182;

7531 Apocalyptic violence and politics: end-times fiction for Jews and christians. Reflections [NHv] 92/1 (2005) 16-22 [NTAb 50,84].

7532 **Rossing, Barbara R.** The rapture exposed: the message of hope in the book of Revelation. 2004 ⇒20,7045. [R]RBLit (2005)* (*De Villiers, Pieter; Mathewson, David*); CR&T 3/1 (2005) 54-60 (*Landau, Y.*); Reflections [NHv] 92/1 (2005) 46-49 (*Ziegler, V.*).

7533 *Rowland, Christopher* Imagining the Apocalypse. NTS 51 (2005) 303-327;

7534 English radicals and the exegesis of the Apocalypse. [F]LUZ, U.: SBS 199: 2005 ⇒94. 160-177.

7535 *Royalty, Robert M.* The dangers of the Apocalypse. Word and world 25 (2005) 283-293.

7536 *Saunders, Stanley P.* Between blessing and curse: reading, hearing, and performing the Apocalypse in a world of terror. [F]BRUEGGEMANN, W.—COUSAR, C. 2005 ⇒16. 141-155.

7537 *Sänger, Dieter* "Amen, komm, Herr Jesus!" (Apk 22,20): Anmerkungen zur Christologie der Johannes-Apokalypse. [F]BÖCHER, O. 2005 ⇒14. 71-92 [Mt 1].

7538 *Snyder, L.* Argument as intervention in the Revelation of John: a rhetorical analysis. Stone-Campbell Journal [Joplin, MS] 8 (2005) 245-259 [NTAb 51,311].

7539 *Spatafora, Andrea* Il tempio nell'Apocalisse;

7540 *Tagliabue, Carlo* Apocalisse e cinema: per una storia senza fine. [F]VANNI, U. 2005 ⇒156. 535-557/821-840.

7541 *Tavo, Felise* The structure of the Apocalypse: re-examining a perennial problem. NT 47 (2005) 47-68.

7542 **Tavo, Felise** Woman, mother and bride: an exegetical investigation into the ecclesial notions of the Apocalypse. [D]*Denaux, A.* 2005, lxxiii; 349 pp. Diss. Leuven.

7543 *Theunissen, H.* Defining the situation in Revelation: John's intention and action-lines. HTSTS 61/1-2 (2005) 441-460 [NTAb 50,319].

7544 *Toribio Cuadrado, José F.* Stilizzazione liturgica della venuta di Cristo nell'Apocalisse. [F]VANNI, U. 2005 ⇒156. 479-500.

7545 **Tóth, Franz** Kult als Wirklichkeitskonstruktion: motiv- und religionsgeschichtliche Untersuchungen zur Kultsprache und zum Kultkonzept in der Johannesoffenbarung. [D]*Schnelle, Udo* 2005, Diss. Halle-Wittenberg [ThLZ 130,885].

7546 *Vanhoye, Albert* L'Apocalisse e la lettera agli Ebrei. [F]VANNI, U. 2005 ⇒156. 257-275.

7547 *Vanni, Ugo* L'attesa della venuta di Cristo nell'Apocalisse come motivazione morale. [F]GHIBERTI, G.: SRivBib 46: 2005 ⇒47. 185-91;

7548 La dimensione letteraria dell'Apocalisse. Il bello della bibbia. 2005 ⇒357. 49-78.

7549 **Vanni, Ugo** Lecturas del Apocalipsis: hermenéutica, exégesis, teología. Estella (Navarra) 2005, Verbo Divino 454 pp. 84-8169-633-1. Bibl. 423-435. [R]RelCult 51 (2005) 1037-1047 (*Olmo Veros, Rafael del*).

7550 *Weiss, Wolfgang* Aufbruch und Bewährung: Hebräerbrief und Apokalypse im Vergleich. [F]BÖCHER, O. 2005 ⇒14. 248-262.

7551 **Whiteley, Iwan** A search for cohesion in the book of Revelation, with specific reference to chapter one. [D]*O'Kane, Martin* 2005, Diss. Wales, Lampeter [TynB 57,309-312].

7552 *Wilson, Mark* The early christians in Ephesus and the date of Revelation, again. Neotest. 39 (2005) 163-193.

7553 *Witulski, Thomas* Ein neuer Ansatz zur Datierung der neutestamentlichen Johannesapokalypse. SNTU.A 30 (2005) 39-60 [Rev 2,12-17; 13].

7554 *Wolter, Michael* Apokalyptik als Redeform im Neuen Testament. NTS 51 (2005) 171-191 [Mk 13; Rom 11,25-26; 1 Cor 15,51-52; 1 Thess 4,13-18; Rev 4,1-2];

7555 Christliches Ethos nach der Offenbarung des Johannes. [F]BÖCHER, O. 2005 ⇒14. 189-209.

7556 **Worth, Roland H.** The seven cities of the Apocalypse & Roman culture. 1999 ⇒15,6268; 16,6203. [R]VJTR 69 (2005) 238-239 (*Menezes, Albert M.*).

7557 *Yeo, Khiok-khng* Hope for the persecuted, cooperation with the state, and meaning for the dissatisfied: three readings of *Revelation* from a Chinese context. From every people. 2005 ⇒472. 200-221.

7558 *Zager, Werner* Gericht Gottes in der Johannesapokalypse. [F]BÖCHER, O. 2005 ⇒14. 310-327.

7559 *Zbroja, Bogdan* Osobiste doznania św. Jana opisane w Apokalipsie [Personal experiences of Saint John portrayed in the book of Revelation]. RBL 58 (2005) 181-187. **P**.

G2.5 *Apocalypsis*, **Revelation 1,1...**

7560 *Kiejza, A.* Ἐκκλησία w księdze Apokalipsy św. Jana—kościół powszechny czy lokalny?. Roczniki Teologiczne 52/1 (2005) 135-149 [NTAb 50,524] [Rev 1-3]. **P**.
7561 *Smidt, Kobus de* The human freedom to find meaning: a logophilosophical reading of Revelation 1:3. Missionalia 33 (2005) 510-531 [NTAb 51,83];
7562 The acts of God and the spirit in the church(es) and in the world: a meta-theology of ho theos and ho [!] Pneuma in Revelations [!] 1:4. APB 16 (2005) 166-195.
7563 *Haraguchi, Takaaki* Effective use of duality: an epistolographical study of Revelation 1:4-3:22. AJTh 19/2 (2005) 270-283.
7564 *Doglio, Claudio* Il Cristo risorto "principe" dei re della terra: il titolo cristologico di Ap 1,5a. [F]GHIBERTI, G.: SRivBib 46: 2005 ⇒47. 193-201.
7565 *Santos García, Carlos A.* ¿Qué celebramos?: Ap 1,10 en perspectiva: pasado y presente del culto cristiano. [F]JUNCO GARZA, C.: Estudios Bíblicos Mexicanos 4: 2005 ⇒74. 499-516.
7566 *Aune, David E.* The form and function of the proclamations to the seven churches (Revelation 2-3). Apocalypticism, prophecy. WUNT 199: 2005 <1990> ⇒177. 212-232.
7567 *Luongo, Gennaro* "Antipa, il mio fedele testimone" (Apoc 2,13): il dossier agiografico di S. Antipa di Pergamo;
7568 *Penna, Romano* Il caso degli "idolotiti" in Ap 2,14.20: un test sulla sorte del cristianesimo dall'apostolo Paolo al veggente Giovanni [Acts 15; 1 Cor 8-10]. Atti del X Simposio di Efeso. Turchia 19: 2005 ⇒785. 183-203/75-90 .
7569 *Guttenberger, Gudrun* Johannes von Thyateira: zur Perspektive des Sehers. [F]BÖCHER, O. 2005 ⇒14. 160-188 [Rev 2,18-29].
7570 *Royalty, Robert M.* Etched or sketched?: inscriptions and erasures in the messages to Sardis and Philadelphia (Rev. 3.1-13). JSNT 27 (2005) 447-463.
7571 **Schimanowski, Gottfried** Die himmlische Liturgie in der Apokalypse des Johannes: die frühjüdischen Traditionen in Offenbarung 4-5 unter Einschluß der Hekhalotliteratur. WUNT 2/154: 2002 ⇒ 18, 6599... 20,7061. [R]ThG 48 (2005) 236-237 (*Giesen, Heinz*) RSR 93 (2005) 322-323 (*Morgen, Michèle*).
7572 *Sieg, F.* The introductory formula of Rev 4:1-2a in the context of traditions. FgNT 18 (2005) 33-43.
7573 *Aune, David E.* Revelation 5 as an ancient Egyptian enthronement scene?: the origin and development of a scholarly myth. Apocalypticism, prophecy. WUNT 199: 2005 <2000> ⇒177. 233-239.
7574 *Thoma, Clemens* Das endzeitliche Zusammenkommen Israels und der Weltvölker. FrRu 12 (2005) 168-174 [Rev 7].
7575 *Dalrymple, Rob* These are the ones ... (Rev 7). Bib. 86 (2005) 398-406 [Rev 11,03-13].

7576 *Rigato, Maria-Luisa* Vesti "rese bianche nel sangue dell'Agnellino" (Ap 7,14g): un possibile rapporto tra questa strana immagine e la vasca di Betsaida (Gv 5,2.7): agnellino/agnello: evocazione dell'olocausto templare. Atti del X Simposio di Efeso. 2005 ⇒785. 45-73.

7577 *Mora Paz, César A.* Ap 11,1-13 desde una perspectiva pragmática. FJUNCO GARZA, C.: 2005 ⇒74. 517-541.

7578 *Frenschkowski, Marco* Die Entrückung der zwei Zeugen zum Himmel (Apk 11,11-14). JBTh 20 (2005) 261-290.

7579 **Collins, Adela Y.** The combat myth in the book of Revelation. Eugene, Or. 2001, Wipf & S. xvi; 292 pp. 1-57910-716-8 [Rev 12].

7580 *Georgi, Dieter* The wrath of the dragon: patriarchy's last stand. The city in the valley. 2005 ⇒214. 187-193 [Rev 12].

7581 *Häfner, Gerd* Die "Sonnenfrau" im Himmel und ihr Kind (Offb 12): ein altes Rätsel neu bedacht. MThZ 56 (2005) 113-133.

7582 **Monighan-Schäfer, Johanna** Offenbarung 12 im Spiegel der Zeit: eine Untersuchung theologischer und künstlerischer Entwicklung anhand der apokalyptischen Frau. D*Schwebel, Horst* 2005, Diss. Marburg [ThLZ 131,340].

7583 *Sánchez, D.A.* Recontextualizing resistance: the revelation to John. USQR 59/3-4 (2005) 113-121 [NTAb 50,320] [Rev 12].

7584 *Treacy-Cole, Diane* Women in the wilderness: rereading Revelation 12. FYOUNG, F.: JSNT.S 295: 2005 ⇒168. 45-58.

7585 *Valentini, Alberto* Apocalisse 12 e il simbolismo della "donna". FVANNI, U. 2005 ⇒156. 417-442.

7586 *Vetrali, Tecle* La madre del Messia in Ap 12. Maria di Nazaret. DSBP 40: 2005 ⇒579. 352-395.

7587 *MacPherson, Anthony* The mark of the beast as a 'sign commandment' and 'anti-Sabbath' in the worship crisis of Revelation 12-14. AUSS 43 (2005) 267-283.

7588 *Westhelle, Vitor Revelation*_13: between the colonial and the postcolonial, a reading from Brazil. From every people. 2005 ⇒472. 183-199.

7589 *López, Javier* La bestia dell'Apocalisse nell'esegesi moderna. FVANNI, U. 2005 ⇒156. 443-458 [Rev 13; 17].

7590 *Binni, Walther* Le applicazioni storiche del 666 di Ap 13,18 nella storia dell'esegesi in Volgare italiano. RivBib 53 (2005) 423-462.

7591 *Chapa, Juan* Il papiro 115: qualcosa in più del numero della bestia. FVANNI, U. 2005 ⇒156. 311-333 [Rev 13,18].

7592 *DeVilliers, Pieter G.* The septet of bowls in Revelation 15:1-16:21 in the light of its composition. APB 16 (2005) 196-222.

7593 *Doglio, Claudio* Il cantico di Mosè e il cantico dell'agnello: rilettura apocalittica di Dt 32. FVANNI, U. 2005 ⇒156. 559-583 [Rev 15,3-4].

7594 *Jauhiainen, Marko* The OT background to Armaggedon (Rev. 16:16) revisited. NT 47 (2005) 381-393 [Ezek 38-39; Zech 12,11].

7595 *Aune, David E.* Revelation 17: a lesson in remedial reading. Apocalypticism, prophecy. WUNT 199: 2005 ⇒177. 240-249.

7596 *Bedriñán, Claudio* Contro quelli che rovinarono la terra: saggio di teologia politica. FVANNI, U. 2005 ⇒156. 597-619 [Rev 17-18].

7597 *Biguzzi, Giancarlo* Il lavoro maledetto in Ap 18. PSV 52 (2005) 197-210.

7598 *Roose, Hanna* The fall of the "great harlot" and the fate of the aging prostitute: an iconographic approach to Revelation 18. Picturing the New Testament. WUNT 2/193: 2005 ⇒396. 228-252.

7599 *Martin, Clarice J.* Polishing the unclouded mirror: a womanist reading of *Revelation* 18:13. From every people. 2005 ⇒472. 82-109.
7600 *Meynet, Roland* La dossologia dell'alleluia (Ap 19,1-8). [F]VANNI, U. 2005 ⇒156. 585-596.
7601 *Tanner, J. Paul* The 'marriage supper of the Lamb' in Rev 19:6-10: implications for the judgment seat of Christ. TrinJ 26 (2005) 47-68.

## G2.7 **Millenniarismus,** *Apc 20...*

7602 *Alvarez Valdés, Ariel* El lago de fuego y la muerte segunda en el libro del Apocalipsis. RevBib 67 (2005) 225-243.
7603 *Aune, David E.* Understanding Jewish and Christian apocalyptic. Word and world 25 (2005) 233-245 [= Apocalypticism, prophecy ⇒ 177. 1-12].
7604 *Aune, David E.; Stewart, Eric* From the idealized past to the imaginary future: eschatological restoration in Jewish apocalyptic literature. Apocalypticism, prophecy. WUNT 199: 2005 <2001> ⇒177. 13-38.
7605 *Dearman, J.A.* Reading the bible with dispensationalists. Insights [Austin, TX] 120/2 (2005) 4-12 [Ezek 38-48; 1 Thess 4,13-18].
7606 **Fenn, Richard K.** Dreams of glory: the sources of apocalyptic terror. Aldershot 2005, Ashgate vii; 157 pp. £37.50. 0-7546-54508 [JSSt 52,433—Crawford Gribben].
7607 *Gundry, Robert H.* The new Jerusalem: people as place, not place for people. The old is better. WUNT 178: 2005 ⇒220. 399-411.
7608 [E]**Hunt, Stephen** Christian millenarianism: from the early church to Waco. 2001 ⇒17,6236; 20,7088. [R]JRH 29/1 (2005) 78-79 (*Tovías, Blanca*).
7609 *Leclercq, Jean* La Jérusalem céleste au regard de la philosophie. Ment. *Ladrière, Jean*: Graphè 14 (2005) 155-173.
7610 *Martyn, J. Louis* World without end or twice-invaded world?. [F]BRUEGGEMANN, W.—COUSAR, C. 2005 ⇒16. 117-132.
[E]**McGhee, G.** War in heaven 2005 ⇒569.
7611 *Neall, Beatrice S.* Amillennialism reconsidered. AUSS 43 (2005) 185-210.
7612 **Riddlebarger, Kim** A case of amillennialism: understanding the end times. GR 2003, Baker 271 pp. $17.

7613 *Kellerman, J.A.* Why one thousand years?. ConJ 31/2 (2005) 140-49 [NTAb 49,536] [Rev 20].
7614 *Bergier, Eric* Apocalypse 20,11-15: devant le tribunal de Dieu. LeD 63 (2005) 36-46.
7615 **Lee, Pilchan** The New Jerusalem in the book of Revelation: a study of Revelation 21-22 in the light of its background in Jewish tradition. WUNT 2/129: 2001 ⇒17,6255... 19,7137. [R]RSR 93 (2005) 319-321 (*Morgen, Michèle*).
7616 *Beale, G.K.* Eden, the temple, and the church's mission in the new creation. JETS 48 (2005) 5-31 [NTAb 49,539] [Rev 21,1-22,5].
7617 *Contreras Molina, Francisco* La nuova Gerusalemme, città aperta. [F]VANNI, U. 2005 ⇒156. 621-645 [Rev 21,1-22,5].
7618 *Georgi, Dieter* John's "heavenly" Jerusalem. The city in the valley. Studies in biblical literature 7: 2005 ⇒214. 161-186 [Rev 21,1-22,5].

7619 *Gundry, Robert H.* The New Jerusalem: people as place, not place for people. The old is better. WUNT 178: 2005 ⇒220. 399-411 [Rev 21,1-22,5].

7620 **Mathewson, David** A new heaven and a new earth: the meaning and function of the Old Testament in Revelation 21.1-22.5. JSNT.S 238: 2003 ⇒19,7138; 20,7098. [R]RBLit 7 (2005) 447-450 (*Sweeney, James P.*).

7621 **Müller-Fieberg, Rita** Das "neue Jerusalem"—Vision für alle Herzen und alle Zeiten?: eine Auslegugng von Offb 21,1-22,5 im Kontext von alttestamentlich-frühjüdischer Tradition und literarischer Rezeption. BBB 144: 2003 ⇒19,7141. [R]ThLZ 130 (2005) 274-276 (*Reichelt, Hansgünter*).

7622 *Pisano, Ombretta* "E abiterà con loro" (Ap 21,3): la Gerusalemme nuova e la Shekinah. [F]VANNI, U. 2005 ⇒156. 183-201 [Rev 21,1-22,5].

7623 *Prigent, Pierre* L'ultime prophétie (Ap 21,1-22,5). Graphè 14 (2005) 29-40.

7624 *Rowland, Christopher* Wilderness, Revelation and the New Jerusalem in radical christian writings. [F]YOUNG, F.: JSNT.S 295: 2005 ⇒ 168. 134-142 [Rev 21,1-22,5].

7625 *Stanley, John E.* The new creation as a people and city in Revelation 21:1-22:5: an alternative to despair. AsbTJ 60/2 (2005) 25-38.

7626 *Haacker, Klaus* Neuer Himmel, neue Erde, neues Jerusalem: zur Bedeutung von Apk 21,1-4. [F]BÖCHER, O. 2005 ⇒14. 328-338.

7627 **Hieke, Thomas; Nicklas, Tobias** "Die Worte der Prophetie dieses Buches": Offenbarung 22,6-21 als Schlussstein der christlichen Bibel Alten und Neuen Testaments gelesen. BThSt 62: 2003 ⇒19,7146; 20,7102. [R]OrdKor 46 (2005) 111-112 (*Giesen, Heinz*).

7628 *Aune, David E.* The prophetic circle of John of Patmos and the exegesis of Revelation 22:16. Apocalypticism, prophecy. WUNT 199: 2005 <1989, 1995> ⇒177. 250-260.

7629 *Tilly, Michael* Textsicherung und Prophetie: Beobachtungen zur Septuaginta-Rezeption in Apk 22,18f. [F]BÖCHER, O. 2005 ⇒14. 232-247.

## XII. Paulus

### G3.1 Pauli biographia

7630 *Becker, Eve-Marie* Biographie und Person des Paulus;

7631 Autobiographisches bei Paulus: Aspekte und Aufgaben. Biographie ...des Paulus. WUNT 187: 2005 ⇒349. 1-6/67-87.

7632 **Berger, Klaus** Paulus. Wissen 2197: 2002 ⇒18,6641; 19,7151. [R]RBLit 7 (2005) 363-368 (*Scott, Ian*).

7633 *Bormann, Lukas* Autobiographische Fiktionalität bei Paulus;

7634 *Brennecke, Hanns C.* Die Anfänge einer Paulusverehrung. Biographie...des Paulus. WUNT 187: 2005 ⇒349. 106-124/295-305.

7635 **Chilton, Bruce** Rabbi Paul: an intellectual biography. 2004 ⇒20, 7108. [R]CBQ 67 (2005) 524-526 (*Taylor, Nicholas H.*); RSR 93 (2005) 386-387 (*Aletti, Jean-Noël*); EstB 63 (2005) 578-580 (*Pérez

*Fernández, Miguel*); RBLit (2005)* (*Garber, Zev; Reed, David*); RBLit 7 (2005) 377-379 (*Reed, David*).

7636 **Crossan, John Dominic; Reed, Jonathan L.** In search of Paul: how Jesus's apostle opposed Rome's empire with God's kingdom. 2004 ⇒20,7111. [R]ThLi 28 (2005) 217-227 (*Zimmerman, Ted*).

7637 *Demling, Joachim H.; Göttel-Leypold, Monika* Die Persönlichkeitsstruktur des Paulus nach seinen Selbstzeugnissen. Biographie...des Paulus. WUNT 187: 2005 ⇒349. 125-148.

7638 **Dunn, James D.G.** The new perspective on Paul: collected essays. WUNT 185: Tü 2005, Mohr S. xii; 539 pp. 3-16-148677-3.

7639 *Dunn, James D.G.* Paul's conversion: a light to twentieth century disputes. New perspective. WUNT 185: 2005 <1997> ⇒7638. 341-359 [Gal 1,13-16].

7640 [E]**Fenske, Wolfgang** Paulus lesen und verstehen: ein Leitfaden zur Biographie und Theologie des Apostels. 2003 ⇒19,7155; 20,7116. [R]ThLZ 130 (2005) 268-269 (*Rein, Matthias*); SNTU 30 (2005) 267-268 (*Huber, Konrad*).

7641 *Frey, Jörg* Paulus und die Apostel: zur Entwicklung des paulinischen Apostelbegriffs und zum Verhältnis des Heidenapostels zu seinen "Kollegen". Biographie... Paulus. WUNT 187: 2005 ⇒349. 192-227.

7642 *Haacker, Klaus* Rettender Glaube und Abrahams Rechtfertigung; zum Verhältnis zwischen Paulus und Jakobus (und Petrus?). [F]STOLLE, V. 2005 ⇒143. 209-225.

7643 *Jäggi, Carola* Archäologische Zeugnisse für die Anfänge der Paulus-Verehrung. Biographie... Paulus. WUNT 187: 2005 ⇒349. 306-322.

7644 *Langton, Daniel R.* The myth of the 'traditional view of Paul' and the role of the apostle in modern Jewish-Christian polemics. JSNT 28 (2005) 69-104.

7645 **Lüdemann, Gerd** Paul: the founder of christianity. 2002 ⇒18,6661; 20,7120. [R]RBLit 7 (2005) 372-377 (*Kaler, Michael*).

7646 **Marguerat, Daniel** Paolo di Tarso. 2004 ⇒20,7121. [R]Protest. 60 (2005) 78-79 (*Noffke, Eric*).

7647 *Merk, Otto* Die Persönlichkeit des Paulus in der Religionsgeschichtlichen Schule. Biographie... Paulus. WUNT 187: 2005 ⇒349. 29-45.

7648 **Murphy-O'Connor, Jerome** Paul. 2004 ⇒20,7123. [R]Interp. 59 (2005) 420-2 (*Carlson, Richard*); RBLit (2005)* (*Gombis, Timothy*);

7649 Histoire de Paul de Tarse. [T]*Barrios-Delgado, Dominique*: 2004 ⇒ 20,7125. [R]EeV 126 (2005) 9-12 (*Bony, Paul*); EstB 63 (2005) 117-8 (*Pastor-Ramos, F.*); RBLit 7 (2005) 371-372 (*Stoutenburg, Dennis*).

7650 *Pilch, John J.* Paul the apostle in cultural context. BiTod 43 (2005) 317-322.

7651 **Riesner, Rainer** Paul's early period: chronology, mission strategy, and theology. 1998 ⇒14,5740... 17,6280. [R]VJTR 69 (2005) 311-313 (*Menezes, Albert M.*).

7652 *Rowe, C. Kavin* New Testament iconography?: situating Paul in the absence of material evidence. Picturing the New Testament. WUNT 2/193: 2005 ⇒396. 289-312.

7653 **Schäfer, Ruth** Paulus bis zum Apostelkonzil: ein Beitrag zur Einleitung in den Galaterbrief, zur Geschichte der Jesusbewegung und zur Pauluschronologie. WUNT 2/179: 2004 ⇒20,7128. [R]ThRv 101 (2005) 41-43 (*Schreiber, Stefan*); RSR 93 (2005) 385-386 (*Aletti, Jean-Noël*); RB 112 (2005) 468-470 (*Murphy-O'Connor, Jerome*); ThLZ 130 (2005) 1069-1072 (*Broer, Ingo*).

7654 *Schnelle, Udo* Paulus und das Gesetz: Biographisches und Konstruktives. Biographie...des Paulus. WUNT 187: 2005 ⇒349. 245-270.

7655 **Schnelle, Udo** Paulus: Leben und Denken. 2003 ⇒19,7173; 20, 7129. [R]ThRv 101 (2005) 133-135 (*Schmeller, Thomas*);

7656 Apostle Paul: his life and theology. [T]*Boring, M. Eugene*: GR 2005, Baker 695 pp. $50. 0-8010-2796-9. Bibl. 605-641.

7657 *Sparn, Walter* Einführung in die Thematik "Biographie und Persönlichkeit des Paulus". Biographie...des Paulus. WUNT 187: 2005 ⇒ 349. 9-28.

7658 *Stemberger, Günther* The pre-christian Paul. Beginnings of christianity. 2005 ⇒786. 65-81.

7659 **Stourton, Edward** Paul of Tarsus: a visionary life. Mahwah, NJ 2005, HiddenSpring vii; 215 pp. $24. 1-587-68032-7. Bibl. 200-203.

7660 **Trocmé, Eitenne** San Paolo. Sintesi: Brescia 2005, Queriniana 136 pp. €10.50.

7661 **Van Bruggen, Jakob** Paul: pioneer for Israel's Messiah. [T]*Van der Maas, E M.*: Phillipsburg, NJ 2005, P&R xix; 411 pp. £12. 0-87552-648-9.

7662 *Vouga, François* Personalität und Identität bei Paulus: die theologische Entdeckung des Humors;

7663 *Wedderburn, Alexander J.M.* Eine neue Paulusperspektive?;

7664 *Wischmeyer, Oda* Paulus als Ich-Erzähler: ein Beitrag zu seiner Person, seiner Biographie und seiner Theologie;

7665 *Wischmeyer, Wolfgang* Paulus und AUGUSTIN. Biographie...des Paulus. WUNT 187: 2005 ⇒349. 149-165/46-64/88-105/323-343.

## G3.2 **Corpus paulinum**; *generalia, technica epistularis*

7666 *Alcock, Susan E.* Searching for Paul. Secrets of the bible. 2005 ⇒ 482. 135-138.

7667 **Barr, George K.** Scalometry and the Pauline epistles. JSNT.S 261: 2004 ⇒20,7135. [R]CBQ 67 (2005) 523-524 (*Ruiz, Jean-Pierre*).

7668 **Buchegger, Jürg** Erneuerung des Menschen: exegetische Studien zu Paulus. TANZ 40: 2003 ⇒19,7188. [R]JETh 19 (2005) 282-285 (*Gebauer, Roland*).

7669 **Burnet, Régis** Épîtres et lettres Ier-IIer siècle: de Paul de Tarse à POLYCARPE de Smyrne. LeDiv 192: 2003 ⇒19,7190. [R]RTL 36 (2005) 242-243 (*Auwers. J.-M.*); RSR 93 (2005) 400-401 (*Aletti, Jean-Noël*); ETR 80 (2005) 565-566 (*Cuvillier, Elian*).

7670 *Campbell, Douglas A.* Possible inscriptional attestation to Sergius Paul[l]us (Acts 13:6-12), and the implications for Pauline chronology. JThS 56 (2005) 1-29.

7671 [E]**Dettwiler, Andreas; Kaestli, Jean-Daniel; Marguerat, Daniel L.** Paul, une théologie en construction. MoBi 51: 2004 ⇒20,337. [R]ETR 80 (2005) 437-438 (*Singer, Christophe*); RBLit (2005)* (*Nicklas, Tobias*).

7672 [E]**Dunn, James D.G.** The Cambridge companion to St. Paul. 2003 ⇒ 19,336; 20,7145. [R]SBET 23 (2005) 99-101 (*Bayes, Jonathan*); ScrB 35 (2005) 53-56 (*McDonald, Patricia M.*); RBLit 7 (2005) 411-414 (*Sumney, Jerry L.*).

7673 *Ellingworth, Paul* 'We' in Paul. BiTr 56 (2005) 226-232.

7674 *Elliott, Neil* Lecture politique: le cas mystérieux de l'apôtre Paul. Guide des nouvelles lectures. 2005 ⇒426. 306-315.

7675 [E]**Engberg-Pedersen, Troels** Paul beyond the Judaism/Hellenism divide. 2001 ⇒17,262... 20,343. [R]BiblInterp 13 (2005) 80-83 (*Gerdmar, Anders*).

7676 *Féghall, P.* Les épîtres de saint Paul dans une des premières traductions en arabe. ParOr 30/1 (2005) 103-129 [NTAb 51,63].

7677 **Freed, Edwin D.** The apostle Paul and his letters. L 2005, Equinox xix; 182 pp. $27. 1-84553-003-9. Bibl. 171-182.

7678 *Gaston, Lloyd* The impact of new perspectives on Judaism and improved Jewish-Christian relations on the study of Paul. BiblInterp 13 (2005) 250-254.

7679 **Gorman, Michael J.** Apostle of the crucified Lord: a theological introduction to Paul and his letters. 2004 ⇒20,7150. [R]MissTod 7 (2005) 91-92 (*Kaippananickal, Joy M.*); ThLZ 130 (2005) 948-950 (*Habermann, Jürgen*); VeE 26 (2005) 648-650 (*Steyn, Gert J.*).

7680 *Grieb, A. Katherine* "The one who called you...": vocation and leadership in the Pauline literature. Interp. 59 (2005) 154-165.

7681 **Horrell, David G.** An introduction to the study of St. Paul. 2000 ⇒ 16,6338. [R]BS 162 (2005) 246-247 (*Fantin, Joe*).

7682 **Jankowski, Gerhard** Brandstifter: auf den Spuren des Paulus in Rom: eine Erzählung. 2004 ⇒20,7156. [R]FrRu 12 (2005) 304-305 (*Schoenborn, Paul Gerhard*).

7683 *Keck, Leander E.* What if Paul was right?. BRUEGGEMANN, W.—COUSAR, C. 2005 ⇒16. 133-139.

7684 **Kim, Byung-Mo** Die paulinische Kollekte. TANZ 38: 2002 ⇒18, 6687. [R]BZ 49 (2005) 288-290 (*Börschel, Regina*).

[E]**Levine, A.** A feminist companion to Paul 2004 ⇒430.

7685 *Longenecker, Bruce W.* On critiquing the 'new perspective' on Paul: a case study. ZNW 96 (2005) 263-271.

7686 [E]**Longenecker, Bruce W.** Narrative dynamics in Paul: a critical assessment. 2002 ⇒18,351... 20,395. [R]RRT 12/1 (2005) 28-30 (*Barram, Michael*); BiblInterp 13 (2005) 441-443 (*Fowl, Stephen*).

7687 [E]**Maggioni, Bruno; Manzi, Franco** Le lettere di Paolo. Assisi 2005, Cittadella 1717 pp [SdT 18,220—Martinengo, Emanuele].

7688 *Meyers, Eric M.; White, L. Michael* Jews and christians in a Roman world. Secrets of the bible. 2005 ⇒482. 118-129.

7689 *Mimouni, Simon C.* Les Judéens et les Grecs chez Paul de Tarse à partir d'une lecture de Giorgio Agamben: à la recherche de "l'homme messianique". ASEs 22/2 (2005) 291-303.

7690 *Oakes, Peter* Re-mapping the universe: Paul and the emperor in 1 Thessalonians and Philippians. JSNT 27 (2005) 301-322 [Phil 2,9-11; 1 Thess 4,15-17; 5,3].

7691 **Pastor, Federico** Corpus paulino II: Efesios, Filipenses, Colosenses, 1-2 Tesalonicenses, Filemón, 1-2 Timoteo, Tito. Comentarios a la Nueva Biblia de Jerusalén: Bilbao 2005, Desclée de B. 300 pp. 84-330-1953-8.

7692 *Patte, Daniel* Lecture globaliste: l'épître aux Romains. Guide des nouvelles lectures. 2005 ⇒426. 338-362.

7693 *Peterson, Jeffrey* The extent of christian theological diversity: Pauline evidence. RestQ 47/1 (2005) 1-12.

7694 **Polaski, Sandra Hack** A feminist introduction to Paul. St. Louis 2005, Chalice 159 pp. $20. 0-827210-37-X.

7695 *Porter, Stanley E.* Introduction to the study of Paul's opponents. Paul and his opponents. Pauline studies 2: 2005 ⇒469. 1-5.

7696 [E]**Porter, Stanley E.** The Pauline canon. Pauline Studies 1: 2004 ⇒ 20,420. [R]RB 112 (2005) 465-6 (*Murphy-O'Connor, Jerome*); NT 47 (2005) 400-3 (*Nicklas, Tobias*); JBL 124 (2005) 569-571 (*Fay, Ron*).

7697 **Quesnel, Michel** Paul et les commencements du christianisme. 2001 ⇒17,6321; 18,6701. [R]ScEs 57 (2005) 266-267 (*Doutre, Jean*).

7698 **Reicke, Bo Ivar** Re-examining Paul's letters: the history of the Pauline correspondence. [E]*Moessner, David P.; Reicke, Ingalisa*: 2001 ⇒17,6257; 19,7221. [R]NT 47 (2005) 85-88 (*Hays, Richard B.*).

7699 **Richards, E. Randolph** Paul and first-century letter writing: secretaries, composition and collection. 2004 ⇒20,7168. [R]WThJ 67 (2005) 170-172 (*Berding, Kenneth*); RB 112 (2005) 628-633 (*Murphy-O'Connor, Jerome*).

7700 [E]**Scilironi, C.** San Paolo e la filosofia del novecento. 2004 ⇒20,723. [R]Dialoghi 5/2 (2005) 94-99 (*Sansonetti, Giuliano*).

7701 *Silberman, Neil Asher* The world of Paul. Secrets of the bible. 2005 ⇒482. 111-117.

7702 **Son, Sang-Won** (Aaron) Corporate elements in Pauline anthropology: a study of selected terms, idioms, and concepts in the light of Paul's usage and background. AnBib 148: 2001 ⇒17,6329; 19,7224. [R]HumTeo 26/1 (2005) 142-144 (*Carvalho, José Carlos*).

7703 **Stanley, Christopher D.** Arguing with scripture: the rhetoric of quotations in the letters of Paul. 2004 ⇒20,7174. [R]RBLit (2005)* (*Williams, H.H. Drake, III*); ET 117 (2005) 37 (*Allen, David*).

7704 *Sumney, Jerry L.* Studying Paul's opponents: advances and challenges. Paul and his opponents. Pauline studies 2: 2005 ⇒469. 7-58.

7705 **Tellbe, Mikael** Paul between synagogue and state: christians, Jews, and civic authorities in 1 Thess., Romans, and Philippians. CB.NT 34: 2001 ⇒17,6332... 20,7176. [R]RBLit (2005)* (*Ascough, Richard*).

7706 *Ullern-Weité, Isabelle* Les "relectures de Paul" et la question du contemporain: questionnements à partir d'un séminaire. ASEs 22/2 (2005) 501-509.

7707 *Verhoef, E.* Determining the authenticity of the Paulines. JHiC 11/2 (2005) 83-95 [NTAb 50,510].

7708 **Vos, Johan S.** Die Kunst der Argumentation bei Paulus: Studien zur antiken Rhetorik. WUNT 149: 2002 ⇒18,6712; 19,7230. [R]ThLZ 130 (2005) 512-514 (*Betz, Hans Dieter*).

7709 *Wall, Robert W.* Introduction to epistolary literature. NT survey. 2005 ⇒413. 137-158.

7710 *Wilk, Florian* Paulus als Nutzer, Interpret und Leser des Jesajabuches. Die Bibel im Dialog. NET 10: 2005 ⇒333. 93-116.

7711 **Wright, Tom** Paul for everyone: Galatians and Thessalonians. 2004 ⇒20,7188. [R]Kerux 20/1 (2005) 68-75 (*Sanborn, Scott F.*).

7712 *Zavalloni, Marisa* Effets identitaires des lettres pauliniennes: une lecture ego-écologique. [F]GENEST, O. 2005 ⇒46. 297-322.

## G3.3 **Pauli theologia**

7713 **Aasgaard, Reidar** "My beloved brothers and sisters!": christian siblingship in Paul. JSNT.S 265: 2004 ⇒20,7189. [R]JBL 124 (2005)

565-569 (*Mitchell, Matthew W.*); RBLit (2005)* (*Mitchell, Matthew; Seid, Timothy; Williams, H. Drake, III*).

7714 **Adams, Edward** Constructing the world: a study in Paul's cosmological language. 1999 ⇒15,6428; 16,6313. [R]RBLit (2005)* (*Jones, F. Stanley*).

7715 *Aletti, Jean-Noël* Retribución y juicio de Dios en Rm 1-3: los pro y los contra del problema y propuesta de interpretación. CuesTF 32/77 (2005) 25-42 [AcBib 11,143].

7716 **Ashton, John** La religione dell'apostolo Paolo. StBi 136: 2002 ⇒ 18,6717... 20,7193. [R]Alpha Omega 8/1 (2005) 129-131 (*Izquierdo, Antonio*).

7717 *Avemarie, Friedrich* Die Wiederkehr der Werke: neuere Verschiebungen im Umkreis der New Perspective on Paul. JETh 19 (2005) 123-138.

7718 *Bachmann, Michael* Von den Schwierigkeiten des exegetischen Verstehens: Erwägungen am Beispiel der Interpretation des paulinischen Ausdrucks "'Werke' des Gesetzes". [F]STEGEMANN, E. 2005 ⇒139. 49-59.

7719 *Baker, Murray* Paul and the salvation of Israel: Paul's ministry, the motif of jealousy, and Israel's Yes. CBQ 67 (2005) 469-484.

7720 **Barbaglio, Giuseppe** Il pensare dell'Apostolo Paolo. La Bibbia nella storia 9bis: 2004 ⇒20,7197. [R]RivBib 53 (2005) 357-361 (*Sacchi, Alessandro*); EfMex 23 (2005) 427-8 (*Landgrave Gándara, Daniel*);

7721 La teología de San Pablo. [T]*Torres Antoñazas, Fernando*: Ágape 42: Trinitario 2005, 487 pp. €26.92. 84964-88047.

7722 *Barnbrock, Christoph* Mimesis: praktisch-theologische Überlegungen. [F]STOLLE, V. 2005 ⇒143. 467-483.

7723 *Baumbach, Günther* 'Glaubensgerechtigkeit' contra 'Gesetzesgerechtigkeit': die Auseinandersetzung des Paulus mit seiner pharisäischen Vergangenheit. Josephus–Jesusbewegung–Judentum. ANTZ 9: 2005 <1999> ⇒182. 134-147.

7724 **Baumert, Norbert** Der Dativ bei Paulus: eine syntaktische Studie mit neuen Interpretationen. Estudios de filologia neotestamentaria 6: Córdoba 2005, Almendro 536 pp. 84-8005-085-3.

7725 **Beattie, Gillian** Women and marriage in Paul and his early interpreters. JSNT.S 296: L 2005, Clark xii; 181 pp. $120. 0-567-03050-4. Bibl. 162-173.

7726 *Bird, M.F.* When the dust finally settles: coming to a post-new perspective perspective. Criswell Theological Review [Dallas] 2/2 (2005) 57-69 [NTAb 50,60].

7727 **Bond, Gilbert I.** Paul and the religious experience of reconciliation: diasporic community and Creole consciousness. LVL 2005, Westminster x: 179 pp. $40. 0-664-22271-4. Bibl. 149-165.

7728 *Bony, Paul* La place de Paul dans le développement du christianisme. EeV 126 (2005) 1-8.

7729 **Brändl, Martin** Der Agon bei Paulus. [D]*Stuhlmacher, Peter* 2005, Diss. Tübingen [ThLZ 131,342].

7730 *Breytenbach, Cilliers* Der einzige Gott-Vater der Barmherzigkeit: Thoratexte als Grundlage des paulinischen Redens von Gott. BThZ 22 (2005) 37-54;

7731 The "for us" phrases in Pauline soteriology: considering their background and use [Rom 5; 2 Cor 5];

7732 Salvation of the reconciled (with a note on the background of Paul's metaphor of reconciliation) [Rom 5,10-11; 2 Cor 5,18-20]. Salvation in the New Testament. NT.S 121: 2005 ⇒798. 163-185/271-286.

7733 *Busenitz, I.A.* The Reformers' understanding of Paul and the law. MastJ 16/2 (2005) 245-259 [NTAb 50,297].

7734 **Calvert-Koyzis, Nancy** Paul, monotheism and the people of God: the significance of Abraham traditions for early Judaism and christianity. JSNT.S 273: 2004 ⇒20,7204. $^{R}$RBLit (2005)* (*Nanos, Mark; Smith, Chris*).

7735 *Campbell, William S.* Perceptions of compatibility between Christianity and Judaism in Pauline interpretation. BiblInterp 13 (2005) 298-316.

7736 **Cassidy, Richard J.** Pablo encadenado: cartas desde la prisión romana. 2004 ⇒20,7209. $^{R}$EstTrin 39 (2005) 127-129 (*Villalón Villalón, David*).

7737 *Chester, T.* Justification, ecclesiology and the new perspective. Themelios 30/2 (2005) 5-20 [NTAb 49,517].

7738 *Chilton, Bruce; Neusner, Jacob* Paul and Gamaliel. RRJ 8 (2005) 113-162 [NTAb 50,297] [Acts 22,3].

7739 *Dognin, Paul Dominique* La foi du Christ dans la théologie de saint Paul. RSPhTh 89 (2005) 713-728.

7740 *Dunn, James D.G.* The new perspective on Paul <1983> 89-110;

7741 The new perspective on Paul: Paul and the law <1988> 131-141;

7742 What was the issue between Paul and "those of the circumcision"? <1991> 143-165;

7743 The justice of God: a renewed perspective on justification by faith <1991> 187-205;

7744 Yet once more-'the works of the law': a response <1992> 207-220;

7745 How new was Paul's gospel?: the problem of continuity and discontinuity <1994> 241-258;

7746 Was Paul against the law?: the law in Galatians and Romans: a test-case of text in context <1995> 259-277;

7747 In search of common ground <2001> 279-305;

7748 Paul and justification by faith <1997> 361-374;

7749 Whatever happened to 'works of the law'? <1998> 375-388;

7750 Jesus the judge: further thoughts of Paul's christology and soteriology <2001> 389-405;

7751 Noch einmal 'works of the law': the dialogue continues <2002> 407-422;

7752 Paul and the Torah: the role and function of the law in the theology of Paul the apostle <2004>. New perspective. WUNT 185: 2005 ⇒ 7638. 441-461.

7753 **Dunn, James D.G.** The theology of Paul the apostle. 1998 ⇒14, 5800... 19,7250. $^{R}$AThJ 37 (2005) 91-98 (*Bevere, A.R.*);

7754 A teologia do apóstolo Paulo. $^{T}$*Royer, Edwino* 2003 ⇒19,7251. $^{R}$REB 65 (2005) 741-747 (*Marques, Valdir*).

7755 *Ehrensperger, Käthy* Paulus und die Gnade: zu Fragen von Macht, Dominanz und Ermächtigung. $^{F}$STEGEMANN, E. 2005 ⇒139. 60-73.

7756 *Eisenbaum, Pamela* Paul, polemics, and the problem of essentialism. BiblInterp 13 (2005) 224-238.

7757 *Engberg-Pedersen, Troels* The relationship with others: similarities and differences between Paul and stoicism. ZNW 96 (2005) 35-60 [Rom 12].

7758 *Esler, Philip F.* Paul and the *agon*: understanding a Pauline motif in its cultural and visual context. Picturing the New Testament. WUNT 2/193: 2005 ⇒396. 356-384.

7759 *Evans, Craig A.* Paul and "works of law" language in late antiquity. Paul and his opponents. Pauline studies 2: 2005 ⇒469. 201-226.

7760 *Fabris, Rinaldo* Il Cristo *Kyrios* nella tradizione paolina. Il messia. 2005 ⇒719. 111-123.

7761 *Farnell, F.D.* The new perspective on Paul: its basic tenets, history, and presuppositions. MastJ 16/2 (2005) 189-243 [NTAb 50,298].

7762 **Finlan, Stephen** The background and content of Paul's cultic atonement metaphors. Academia Biblica 19: 2004 ⇒20,7231. [R]RBLit (2005)* (*Haber, Susan; McMahon, Christopher*).

7763 *Frankemölle, Hubert* "Apokalyptische Weisheit" bei Paulus?: hermeneutische Prolegomena <2003>;

7764 Die paulinische Theologie im Kontext der heiligen Schriften Israels: 'so viele Verheißungen Gottes, in ihm das Ja' (2 Kor 1,20) <2002>;

7765 'Wie geschrieben steht': ist die paulinische Christologie schriftgemäß?. Studien zum jüdischen Kontext. SBAB 37: 2005 ⇒210. 226-254/199-225/255-291.

7766 *Fredriksen, Paula* Paul, purity, and the *ekklēsia* of the gentiles. Beginnings of christianity. 2005 ⇒786. 205-217.

7767 *Garlington, D.B.* The new perspective on Paul: an appraisal two decades later. Criswell Theological Review [Dallas] 2/2 (2005) 17-38 [NTAb 50,62].

7768 *Gawlina, Manfred* Paulus und PLATO: *prosopon* gegen *idea*. ThPh 80 (2005) 17-30.

7769 *Georgi, Dieter* On Paul's image of the human. The city in the valley. Studies in biblical literature 7: 2005 ⇒214. 93-101.

7770 *Gräbe, Petrus J.* Salvation in Colossians and Ephesians. Salvation in the New Testament. NT.S 121: 2005 ⇒798. 287-304 [Eph 1,13-14; 2,1-10; Col 1,12-23].

7771 *Grech, Prosper* Formule trinitarie in san Paolo. Il messaggio biblico. SRivBib 44: 2005 <1996> ⇒216. 357-361.

7772 *Grieb, A.K.* People of God, body of Christ, koinonia of Spirit: the role of ethical ecclesiology in Paul's "trinitarian" language. AThR 87/2 (2005) 225-252.

7773 **Griffith-Jones, Robin** The gospel according to Paul: the creative genius who brought Jesus to the world. 2004 ⇒20,7239. [R]RB 112 (2005) 466-468 (*Murphy-O'Connor, Jerome*).

7774 *Gundry, Robert H.* The inferiority of the new perspective on Paul;

7775 The nonimputation of Christ's righteousness. The old is better. WUNT 178: 2005 ⇒220. 195-224/225-251.

7776 *Haacker, Klaus* Verdienste und Grenzen der "neuen Perspektive" der Paulus-Auslegung. Lutherische und neue Pauluspersperspektive. WUNT 182: 2005 ⇒339. 1-15.

7777 *Hagopian, R.* 'To be right with God': an exploration of the new perspective view on Paul. AThJ 37 (2005) 19-37 [NTAb 50,298].

7778 **Harink, Douglas** Paul among the postliberals: Pauline theology beyond christianity and modernity. 2003 ⇒19,7265; 20,7241. [R]MoTh 21/1 (2005) 178-180 (*Fowl, Stephen*); TS 66 (2005) 666-667 (*Reumann, John*); SJTh 58 (2005) 353-354 (*Gombis, Timothy G.*).

7779 *Harrill, J. Albert* Paul and the slave self. Religion and the self in antiquity. 2005 ⇒818. 51-69 [Rom 7].

7780 *Hays, Richard B.* 'Who has believed our message?' <2002>;

7781 Apocalyptic hermeneutics: Habakkuk proclaims 'the righteous one' <1988>. The conversion. 2005 ⇒223. 25-49/119-142;

7782 On the rebound: a response to critiques of *Echoes of scripture in the letters of Paul* <1993>. The conversion. 2005 ⇒223. 163-189.

7783 *Hebart, F.* The logic of justification in the theology of Paul: some ecclesiological and ethical implications. LTJ 39/2-3 (2005) 140-156 [NTAb 50,62].

7784 **Hubbard, Moyer V.** New creation in Paul's letters and thought. MSSNTS 119: 2002 ⇒18,6751... 20,7247. $^{R}$CBQ 67 (2005) 150-151 (*Paffenroth, Kim*); BiblInterp 13 (2005) 214-216 (*Carter, Tim*) [Rom 6,1-11; 7,1-6; 2 Cor 5,17; 2,19-20; Gal 6,15].

7785 *Hughes, J.* The new perspective's view of Paul and the law. MastJ 16/2 (2005) 261-276 [NTAb 50,298].

7786 *Hübner, Hans* Die paulinische Rechtfertigungstheologie als ökumenisch-hermeneutisches Problem. Wahrheit und Wirklichkeit. 2005 <1999> ⇒229. 38-64.

7787 *Jeal, Roy R.* Clothes make the (wo)man. Scriptura 90 (2005) 685-699 [NTAb 51,288].

7788 *Joubert, Stephan J.* χάρις in Paul: an investigation into the apostle's "performative" application of the language of grace within the framework of his theological reflection on the event/process of salvation. Salvation in the New Testament. NT.S 121: 2005 ⇒798. 187-211.

7789 *Kamphuis, Barend* Alles in alles: rehabilitatie van het panentheïsme?. ThRef 48 (2005) 194-206.

7790 *Käsemann, Ernst* Gottes Gerechtigkeit bei Paulus;

7791 Leiblichkeit bei Paulus;

7792 Rechtfertigung und Freiheit. In der Nachfolge. 2005 ⇒236. 15-24/36-49/50-57.

7793 *Keightley, Georgia* Christian collective memory and Paul's knowledge of Jesus. Memory, tradition, and text. SBL.Semeia Studies 52: 2005 ⇒416. 129-150.

7794 *Kelly, D.* Nouvelles approches à la théologie biblique de la justification. Résister et Construire [Lausanne] 55-56 (2005) 9-21 [NTAb 50, 63].

7795 **Kim, Jung Hoon** The significance of clothing imagery in the Pauline corpus. JSNT.S 268: 2004 ⇒20,7250. $^{R}$RBLit (2005)* (*Huber, Lynn; Jeal, Roy*); BTB 35 (2005) 114 (*Neufeld, Dietmar I.*).

7796 *Kraus, Wolfgang* Gottes Gerechtigkeit und Gottes Volk: ökumenisch-ekklesiologische Aspekte der New Perspective on Paul. Lutherische und neue Paulusperspektive. WUNT 182: 2005 ⇒339. 329-347.

7797 *Langton, Daniel R.* Modern Jewish identity and the apostle Paul: Pauline studies as an intra-Jewish ideological battleground. JSNT 28 (2005) 217-258.

7798 *Manicardi, Ermenegildo* L'antitesi tra Adamo e Gesù nelle lettere paoline. Gesù la cristologia. 2005 <1997> ⇒253. 311-328.

7799 *Martin, Ralph P.* The christology of the prison epistles. Contours of christology. McMaster NT Studies 7: 2005 ⇒775. 193-218.

7800 *Miller, Ed. L.* More Pauline references to homosexuality?. EvQ 77 (2005) 129-134.

7801 *Moo, Douglas J.* The christology of the early Pauline letters. Contours of christology. McMaster NT Studies 7: 2005 ⇒775. 169-192.

7802 *Moreiras, Alberto* Children of light: neo-Paulinism and the cathexis of difference (part I). BiCT 1/1 (2004)*;

7803 Children of light: neo-Paulinism and the cathexis of difference (part II). BiCT 1/2 (2005)*.

7804 *Nanos, Mark D.* Introduction. BiblInterp 13 (2005) 221-223;

7805 How inter-christian approaches to Paul's rhetoric can perpetuate negative valuations of Jewishness—although proposing to avoid that outcome. BiblInterp 13 (2005) 255-269.

7806 *Oegema, Gerbern S.* Biblical interpretation in the letters of Paul. Traduire la Bible hébraïque. 2005 ⇒728. 255-272 [Gal 3,6-14].

7807 **Park, E.C.** Either Jew or gentile: Paul's unfolding theology of inclusivity. 2003 ⇒19,7293; 20,7271. [R]RB 112 (2005) 151-152 (*Murphy-O'Connor, Jerome*).

7808 **Philip, Finny** The origins of Pauline pneumatology: the eschatological bestowal of the Spirit upon gentiles in Judaism and in the early development of Paul's theology. [D]*Dunn, James*: WUNT 2/194: Tü 2005, Mohr S. xi; 307 pp. €54. 3-16-148598-X. Diss. Durham; Bibl. 229-263.

7809 *Pilch, J.J.* Paul's call to be a holy man (apostle): in his own words and in other words. HTSTS 61/1-2 (2005) 371-383 [NTAb 50,299] [Gal 1,15-16].

7810 **Plietzsch, Susanne** Kontexte der Freiheit: Konzepte der Befreiung bei Paulus und im rabbinischen Judentum. Judentum und Christentum 16: Stu 2005, Kohlhammer 208 pp. €20. 3-17-018743-0. Diss. Leipzig 1999.

7811 *Poirier, John C.* Three early christian views on ritual purity: a historical note contributing to an understanding of Paul's position. EThL 81 (2005) 424-434.

7812 *Prostmeier, Ferdinand R.* Was bedeutet die Autorität der Schrift bei Paulus?. Die Bedeutung. QD 215: 2005 ⇒363. 97-130.

7813 *Punt, Jeremy* Paul, body theology, and morality: parameters for a discussion. Neotest. 39/2 (2005) 359-388.

7814 *Quarles, C.L.* The new perspective and the means of atonement in Jewish literature of the second temple period. Criswell Theological Review [Dallas] 2/2 (2005) 39-56 [NTAb 50,120].

7815 **Reinmuth, Eckart** Paulus: Gott neu denken. Biblische Gestalten 9: 2004 ⇒20,7276. [R]BiKi 60 (2005) 184-185 (*Beck, Reinhold*).

7816 *Reuter, Rainer* Paul's terminology describing time, periods of time and history. [F]AEJMELAEUS, L.: SESJ 89: 2005 ⇒1. 247-267.

7817 *Roose, Hanna* Die Hierarchisierung der Leib-Metapher im Kolosser- und Epheserbrief als "Paulinisierung": ein Beitrag zur Rezeption paulinischer Tradition in pseudo-paulinischen Briefen. NT 47 (2005) 117-141.

7818 *Rose, Martin* "Wie denn geschrieben steht: Da ist nicht, der rechtfertig sei, auch nicht einer" (Römer 3,10)—ein Alttestamentler sieht Paulus auf die Finger. WuD 28 (2005) 345-359.

7819 *Ruhstorfer, Karlheinz* 'Du sollst ein Segen sein': das paulinische Wort vom Kreuz im Widerstreit. IKaZ 34 (2005) 512-527.

7820 **Sandnes, Karl O.** Belly and body in the Pauline epistles. MSSNTS 120: 2002 ⇒18,6790...20,7278. [R]NT 47 (2005) 97-8 (*Fox, Kenneth*).

7821 *Saunders, Ross* Paul and the imperial cult. Paul and his opponents. Pauline studies 2: 2005 ⇒469. 227-238.

7822 *Schmidt, D.D.* Translating Paul's faith. The Fourth R [Santa Rosa, CA] 18/3 (2005) 17-19 [NTAb 50,65].

7823 *Schrage, Wolfgang* Schöpfung und Neuschöpfung in Kontinuität und Diskontinuität bei Paulus. EvTh 65 (2005) 245-259.

7824 *Setzer, Claudia* Does Paul need to be saved?. BiblInterp 13 (2005) 289-297.

7825 *Sprinkle, P.M.* The old perspective on the new perspective: a review of some 'pre-Sanders' thinkers. Themelios 30/2 (2005) 21-31 [NTAb 49,520].

7826 *Stegemann, Wolfgang* Gerechtigkeit bei Paulus: gesehen aus einer "neuen Perspektive" auf die paulinische Theologie. BiHe 41/164 (2005) 14-16.

7827 *Strecker, Christian* Fides–Pistis–Glaube: Kontexte und Konturen einer Theologie der "Annahme" bei Paulus. Lutherische und neue Pauluspersperspektive. WUNT 182: 2005 ⇒339. 223-250.

7828 *Streett, R.A.* An interview with Martin HENGEL.;

7829 An interview with N.T. WRIGHT. Criswell Theological Review [Dallas] 2/2 (2005) 13-15/5-11[ NTAb 50,65].

7830 *Stünkel, Knut M.* Metaschematismus und formale Anzeige—über ein biblisch-paulinisches Rüstzeug des Denkens bei Johann Georg Hamann und Martin HEIDEGGER. NZSTh 47/3 (2005) 259-287.

7831 *Swanson, D.M.* Bibliography of works on the new perspective on Paul. MastJ 16/2 (2005) 259-287 [NTAb 50,300].

7832 **Sztuk, Dariusz** 'Vivre pour Dieu' selon saint Paul: étude exégétique des formules de préexistence du chrétien. [D]*Chrostowski, W.* 2005, 251 pp. Diss. Warsaw [RTL 37,618].

7833 *Tang Abomo, P.-E.* Church tradition dilemma on the worth of the human body: St Paul or PLATO?. Hekima Review 33 (2005) 45-55 [NTAb 50,509] [John 12,20-36].

7834 *Thomas, R.L.* Hermeneutics of the new perspective on Paul. MastJ 16/2 (2005) 293-316 [NTAb 50,301].

7835 *Thurén, Lauri* Paul had no antagonists. [F]AEJMELAEUS, L.: SESJ 89: 2005 ⇒1. 268-288.

7836 **Thurén, Lauri** Derhetorizing Paul: a dynamic perspective on Pauline theology and the law. WUNT 124: 2000 ⇒16,6434... 20,7297. [R]ScEs 57 (2005) 267-272 (*Doutre, Jean*).

7837 *Tolmie, D. Francois* Salvation as redemption: the use of "redemption" metaphors in Pauline literature. Salvation in the New Testament. NT.S 121: 2005 ⇒798. 247-269.

7838 *Van Aarde, A.G.* Geloof as antwoord op versoening—'n Pauliniese perspektief. VeE 26 (2005) 222-243.

7839 *Van Kooten, George H.* Kort antwoord aan Barend Kamphuis. ThRef 48 (2005) 207-211.

7840 **Van Spanje, Teunis E.** Inconsistency in Paul?: a critique of the work of Heikki Räisänen. WUNT 2/110: 1999 ⇒15,6499... 18,6804. [R]ThLZ 130 (2005) 1328-1330 (*Hübner, Hans*).

7841 **Vidal, Senén** El proyecto mesiánico de Pablo. Biblioteca de estudios bíblicos 116: S 2005, Sígueme 366 pp.

7842 *Vironda, Marco* Paolo prigioniero di Cristo: la libertà in Paolo. Libertà va cercando. Sussidi biblici 87: 2005 ⇒353. 105-124.

7843 *Vollenweider, Samuel* Paulus zwischen Exegese und Wirkungsgeschichte. [F]LUZ, U.: SBS 199: 2005 ⇒94. 142-159;

7844 Der Apostel Paulus im Spiegel seiner Rezeption. [F]NIEDERWIMMER, K.: Gutachten und Studien 2: 2005 ⇒112. 5-22.

7845 *Vouga, François* Die politische Relevanz des Evangeliums: Rezeption des Paulus in der philosophischen Diskussion. [F]STEGEMANN, W. 2005 ⇒139. 192-208.

7846 **Vouga, François** Moi, Paul!. P 2005, Bayard 311 pp. €20. 2-227-47-539-0.

7847 *Wagner, J. Ross* Isaiah in Romans and Galatians. Isaiah in the NT. 2005 ⇒443. 117-132.

7848 **Waters, Guy Prentiss** Justification and the new perspective on Paul: a review and a response. 2004 ⇒20,7302. [R]Kerux 20/3 (2005) 52-61 (*Sanborn, Scott F.*); Faith & Mission 23/1 (2005) 96-8 (*Lytle, Matt*).

7849 **Watson, Francis** Paul and the hermeneutics of faith. 2004 ⇒20, 7303. [R]RBLit (2005)* (*Gignilliat, Mark*); JThS 56 (2005) 555-558 (*Houlden, Leslie*).

7850 *Wedderburn, A.J.M.* Paul and the mysteries revisited. [F]STEGEMANN, W. 2005 ⇒139. 260-269.

7851 **Wendt, Friederike** Gerichtshandeln Gottes: eine komparative Motivstudie zum *Corpus paulinum* und zu PLUTARCHs Dialog *De sera numinis vindicta*. [D]*Theißen, Gerd*: Heid 2005, Universität 3 Mikrofiches. Diss. Heidelberg [ThLZ 131,338].

7852 **Westerholm, Stephen** Perspectives old and new on Paul: the "Lutheran" Paul and his critics. 2004 ⇒20,7307. [R]Cart. 21 (2005) 241-242 (*Sanz Valdivieso, R.*); CBQ 67 (2005) 553-554 (*Reumann, John*); RSR 93 (2005) 402-403 (*Aletti, Jean-Noël*); SR 34 (2005) 599-600 (*Jervis, L. Ann*); TJT 21 (2005) 283-284 (*Wettlaufer, Ryan*).

7853 **Williams, David J.** Paul's metaphors: their context and character. 1999 ⇒15,6504... 18,6812. [R]RBLit (2005)* (*Nicklas, Tobias*).

7854 *Wolter, Michael* Escatologia paolina. Protest. 60 (2005) 91-106, 199-221.

7855 **Woyke, Johannes** Götter, "Götzen", Götterbilder: Aspekte einer paulinischen "Theologie der Religionen". BZNW 132: B 2005, De Gruyter xvi; 570 pp. €138. 3-11-018396-X. Diss. Tübingen. [R]Afrika Yetu 9 (2005) 65-68 (*Orji, Chukwuemeka*).

7856 **Wright, Nicholas T.** Paul in fresh perspective. Mp 2005, Augsburg xii; 195 pp. $25. 0-8006-3766-6. Bibl. 182-184.

### G3.4 *Pauli stylus et modus operandi*—**Paul's image**

7857 *Crook, Zeba* The divine benefactions of Paul the client. JGRChJ 2 (2005) 9-26.

7858 *Gager, John G.; Gibson, E. Leigh* Violent acts and violent language in the apostle Paul. Violence in the NT. 2005 ⇒439. 13-21.

7859 **Walsh, Richard** Finding St. Paul in film. NY 2005, Clark 218 pp. $22. 9780-567-028501 [BiTod 44,132—Donald Senior].

7860 **Wright, Nicholas T.** What Saint Paul really said. 1997 ⇒13,6205... 16,6455. [R]ScEs 57 (2005) 265-267 (*Doutre, Jean*).

### G3.5 **Apostolus Gentium** [⇒G4.6, Israel et Lex/Jews & Law]

7861 **Badiou, Alain** Saint Paul: the foundation of universalism. Stanford, CA 2005, Stanford Univ. Pr. 111 pp. $16.

7862 *Combet-Galland, Corina* Paul l'apôtre: un voyage contrarié pour bagage. ETR 80 (2005) 361-374 [Acts 9].

7863 **Das, A. Andrew** Paul and the Jews. 2003 ⇒19,7334; 20,7327. RCBQ 67 (2005) 138-139 (*Gillman, Florence Morgan*); HeyJ 46 (2005) 221-223 (*Madigan, Patrick*); AUSS 43 (2005) 213-217 (*Choi, P. Richard*).

7864 *García Mateo, Rogelio S.* Francisco JAVIER y S. Pablo. StMiss 54 (2005) 1-26.

7865 *Grams, R.G.* Paul among the mission theologians. Missionalia 33 (2005) 459-479 [NTAb 51,64] [Heb 11,39-12,3].

7866 *Hodge, Caroline Johnson* Apostle and the gentiles: constructions of Paul's identity. BiblInterp 13 (2005) 270-288 [Gal 2,7-9].

7867 *Horn, Friedrich W.* Juden und Heiden: Aspekte der Verhältnisbestimmung in den paulinischen Briefen: ein Gespräch mit Krister STENDAHL. Lutherische und neue Paulusperspektive. WUNT 182: 2005 ⇒339. 17-39.

7868 **Jones, Peter R.** Capturing the pagan mind: Paul's blueprint for thinking and living in the new global culture. 2003 ⇒19,7337; 20, 7329. RFaith & Mission 22/3 (2005) 120-121 (*Solc, Josef*).

7869 *Judge, Edwin A.* The Roman base of Paul's mission. TynB 56/1 (2005) 103-117.

7870 **Little, Christopher R.** Mission in the way of Paul: biblical mission for the church in the twenty-first century. Studies in biblical literature 80: NY 2005, Lang xii; 345 pp. €68.60. 0-8204-7635-8.

7871 *Marguerat, Daniel* Jüdischer Sektierer oder authentischer Apostel?: Paulus als Interpret Jesu. WUB 38 (2005) 26-30.

7872 *Matera, Frank J.* Preaching in a different key: preaching the gospel according to Paul. NewTR 18/3 (2005) 52-65.

7873 *Nápole, Gabriel M.* Evangelizar en las culturas: aporte desde el Nuevo Testamento. Teol. 42 (2005) 141-162.

7874 *Park, Heon-Wook* Israel and the nations in Pauline theology. AJBI 30-31 (2004-2005) 181-194.

7875 **Quesnel, Michel** Paolo e gli inizi del cristianesimo. 2004 ⇒20,7333. RVetChr 42 (2005) 173-174 (*Bertalotto, Pierpaolo*).

7876 *Ramírez Fueyo, Francisco* San Pablo, gigante de la comunicación. SalTer 93 (2005) 701-710.

7877 *Schwemer, Anna M.* Verfolger und Verfolgte bei Paulus: die Auswirkungen der Verfolgung durch Agrippa I. auf die paulinische Mission. Biographie...des Paulus. WUNT 187: 2005 ⇒349. 169-191.

7878 *Taylor, N.H.* Apostolic identity and the conflicts in Corinth and Galatia. Paul and his opponents. Pauline studies 2: 2005 ⇒469. 99-127.

7879 *Turner, G.* Paul and the globalisation of christianity. NBl 86 (2005) 165-171 [NTAb 49,521].

7880 *Wehr, Lothar* Paulus der Völkerapostel–zur Strategie der paulinischen Mission. Grosse Gestalten. 2005 ⇒623. 123-135.

### G3.6 *Pauli fundamentum* philosophicum [⇒G4.3] *et* morale

7881 **Badiou, Alain** Saint Paul: the foundation of universalism. T*Brassier, Ray* 2003 ⇒19,7349. RJR 85 (2005) 304-305 (*Betz, Hans Dieter*).

7882 **Borghi, Ernesto** Giustizia e amore nelle lettere di Paolo: dall'esegesi alla cultura contemporanea. 2004 ⇒20,7342. RASEs 22 (2005) 516-518 (*Manini, Filippo*).

7883 **Bosman, Philip** Conscience in PHILO and Paul: a conceptual history of the Synoida word group. WUNT 2/166: 2003 ⇒19,7352; 20,7343. RJSJ 36 (2005) 90-93 (*Runia, David T.*).

7884 *Crossan, J. Dominic* Paul and Rome: the challenge of a just world order. USQR 59/3-4 (2005) 6-20 [NTAb 50,297].

7885 **Fenske, Wolfgang** Die Argumentation des Paulus in ethischen Herausforderungen. Gö 2004, Vandenhoeck & R. 341 pp. €36. 3-89-97-11645.

7886 **Gaca, Kathy L.** The making of fornication: eros, ethics, and poltical reform in Greek philosophy and early christianity. 2003 ⇒19,7359; 20,7346. RAJP 126 (2005) 138-142 (*Buell, Denise Kimber*).

7887 *Georgi, Dieter* Living with chaos: meditations on Paul's ethics. The city in the valley. Studies in biblical literature 7: 2005 ⇒214. 135-45.

7888 **Giustozzi, Gianfilippo** La riabilitazione del 'ciarlatano': HEIDEGGER lettore di San Paolo. Firmana.S 4: Fermo 2005, Istituto Teologico Marchigiano 116 pp. €12. Bibl. 103-112.

7889 *Hays, Richard B.* The role of scripture in Paul's ethics. The conversion. 2005 <1996> ⇒223. 143-162.

7890 *Horrell, David G.* Paul among liberals and communitarians: models for christian ethics. Ment. *Habermas, Jürgen*: Pacifica 18 (2005) 33-52.

7891 **Horrell, David G.** Solidarity and difference: a contemporary reading of Paul's ethics. L 2005, Clark 339 pp. $50. 0-567-04322-3. Bibl. 292-319.

7892 *Kroeker, P. Travis* Whither Messianic ethics?: Paul as political theorist. Journal of the Society of Christian Ethics [Wsh] 25/2 (2005) 37-58 [NTAb 50,299].

7893 **Lewis, John G.** Looking for life: the role of 'theo-ethical' reasoning in Paul's religion. D*Morgan, R.*: NY 2005, Clark x; 297 pp. $130. 97-80-5670-42729. Diss. Oxford.

7894 *Loubser, G.M.H.* Pauls's ethic of freedom: no flash in the Galatian pan. Neotest. 39/2 (2005) 313-337.

7895 **Mayordomo, Moisés** Argumentiert Paulus logisch?: eine Analyse vor dem Hintergrund antiker Logik. D*Luz, Ulrich*: WUNT 188: Tü 2005, Mohr S. xiii; 302 pp. €79. 3-16-148793-1. Diss.-Habil. Bern; Bibl. 243-274.

7896 **Pani, Giancarlo** Paolo, AGOSTINO, LUTERO: alle origini del mondo moderno. Ermeneutica: Soveria Mannelli (Catanzaro) 2005, Rubbettino 209 pp. €18. 88-498-1175-6. Bibl. 235-270.

7897 *Peng, Wang Koinonia* and ethical thought in Paul's epistles. CTR 19 (2005) 69-84.

7898 *Rehmann, J.* NIETZSCHE, Paul, and the subversion of empire. USQR 59/3-4 (2005) 147-161 [NTAb 50,300].

## G3.7 *Pauli* communitates *et* spiritualitas

7899 **Ascough, Richard S.** Paul's Macedonian associations: the social context of Philippians and 1 Thessalonians. WUNT 2/161: 2003 ⇒ 19,7372; 20,7367. RTrinJ 26 (2005) 334-337 (*Schnabel, Eckhard*).

7900 **Biser, Eugen** Paulus: Zeugnis—Begegnung—Wirkung. 2003 ⇒19, 7376; 20,7371. RThLZ 130 (2005) 1184-1186 (*Rein, Matthias*).

7901 **Brovelli, F.** En el corazón del apóstel: a la escucha de san Pablo. 2004 ⇒20,7373. [R]Seminarios 51 (2005) 132-133 (*Morata, A.*).

7902 *Byrne, Brendan* Paul and the diaspora: re-imagining church with the aid of RAHNER and Harink. ABR 53 (2005) 1-12.

7903 **Canopi, Anna Maria** Costruire la casa sulla roccia: lectio divina sulle parabole delle scelte decisive. Mi 2005, Paoline 120 pp. €8.30.

7904 **Carson, Donald** La prière renouvelée. Sel & Lumière: Cléon d'Andran 2005, Excelsis 268 pp.

7905 **Cosgrove, Charles H.; Yeo, Khiok-Khng; Weiss, Herold** Cross-cultural Paul: journeys to others, journeys to ourselves. GR 2005, Eerdmans vii; 293 pp. $25. 0-8028-2843-4.

7906 **Crossan, John D.; Reed, Jonathan** In search of Paul: how Jesus' apostle opposed Rome's empire with God's kingdom: a new vision of Paul's words & world. L 2005, SCPK xiv; 450 pp. £20. 0281057273.

7907 *Downing, Francis G.* The nature(s) of christian women and men. Theol. 108/843 (2005) 178-184.

7908 **Fassnacht, Martin R.M.** Kyriotop: personale Formation von Religion bei Paulus. [D]*Löning, Karl* 2005, Diss. Münster [ThRv 102,i].

7909 *Fellows, Richard G.* Renaming in Paul's churches: the case of Crispus-Sosthenes revisited. TynB 56/2 (2005) 111-130 [Acts 18,8; 18,17; 1 Cor 1,1].

7910 **Freed, Edwin D.** The morality of Paul's converts. L 2005, Equinox xxii; 335 pp. 1-845530-23-3. Bibl. 283-312.

7911 **Gerber, Christine** Paulus und seine Kinder: Studien zur Beziehungsmetaphorik der paulinischen Briefe. [D]*Breytenbach, Cilliers*: BZNW 136: B 2005, De Gruyter xvii; 576 pp. €148. 3-11-018478-8. Diss.-Habil. Humboldt; Bibl. 537-576.

7912 *Gil Arbiol, Carlos* Extranjero y hermano: el otro en las comunidades paulinas. ResB 46 (2005) 29-36.

7913 **Gilchrist, John J.** Alter Christus: St Paul speaks to priests. Notre Dame, IN 2005, Ave Maria 282 pp. $15 [BiTod 44,61: D. Senior].

7914 *Hvalvik, Reidar* All those who in every place call on the name of our Lord Jesus Christ: the unity of the Pauline churches. The formation of the early church. WUNT 183: 2005 ⇒708. 123-143.

7915 *Keay, Robert D.* Paul the spiritual guide: a social identity perspective on Paul's apostolic self- identity. TynB 56/1 (2005) 151-155.

7916 **Konradt, Matthias** Gericht und Gemeinde: eine Studie zur Bedeutung und Funktion von Gerichtsaussagen im Rahmen der paulinischen Ekklesiologie und Ethik im 1 Thess und 1 Kor. BZNW 117: 2003 ⇒19,7388; 20,7386. [R]ThLZ 130 (2005) 950-952 (*Aejmelaeus, Lars*); RBLit 7 (2005) 388-392 (*Nicklas, Tobias*).

7917 *Martinez, Ernest R.* "In Christ Jesus": spiritual experience in St. Paul. [F]BERNARD, C. 2005 ⇒8. 45-62.

7918 *Neubrand, Maria* Im Dienst lebendiger christlicher Gemeinden: Paulus und seine Mit-Wirkenden. "Lebendige Gemeinde". ESt 54: 2005 ⇒578. 47-68.

7919 *O'Mahony, K.J.* Paul as pastor. DoLi 55/5 (2005) 45-59 [NTAb 49, 520].

7920 **Pieri, Fabrizio** Pablo e IGNACIO: testigos y maestros del discernimiento espiritual. Sdr 2005, Sal Terrae 214 pp.

7921 **Pitta, Antonio** Trasformati dallo Spirito: lectio divina sulle lettere di Paolo. Mi 2005, Paoline 212 pp. €11.

7922 **Schluep, Christoph** Der Ort des Christus: soteriologische Metaphern bei Paulus als Lebensregeln. [D]*Weder, H.*: Z 2005, Theologischer 453 pp. €25. 3-290-17355-0. Diss. Zürich.

7923 *Taylor, W.F.* Reciprocity, siblings, and Paul: why act ethically?. LTJ 39/2-3 (2005) 181-195 [NTAb 50,66].

7924 *Theißen, Gerd* Paulus—der Unglücksstifter: Paulus und die Verfolgung der Gemeinden in Jerusalem und Rom. Biographie...des Paulus. WUNT 187: 2005 ⇒349. 228-244.

7925 **Winter, Bruce** Roman wives, Roman widows: the appearance of new women and the Pauline communities. 2003 ⇒19,7400; 20,7404. [R]RRT 12/1 (2005) 141-2 (*McNary-Zak, Bernadette*); RBLit 7 (2005) 417-9 (*Knust, Jennifer*); JR 85 (2005) 480-1 (*D'Angelo, Mary*); JThS 56 (2005) 558-61 (*Dixon, Suzanne*); CBQ 67 (2005) 162-3 (*Matthews, Shelly*); ChM 119/3 (2005) 262-6 (*James, S.*); SNTU 30 (2005) 273-5 (*Pratscher, W.*); INTAMS.R 11 (2005) 285-6 (*Kowalski, Beate*); RB 112 (2005) 147-149 (*Murphy-O'Connor, Jerome*); REJ 164 (2005) 565-568 (*Cillières, Hélène*); ScrB 35 (2005) 56-57 (*Docherty, Susan*); TJT 21 (2005) 285-286 (*Crook, Zeba A.*).

## G3.8 *Pauli receptio*, history of research

7926 *Aletti, Jean-Noël* Bulletin paulinien. RSR 93 (2005) 381-405.

7927 *Bony, Paul* L'ecclésiologie paulinienne dans la recherche récente. EeV 130-133 (2005) 18-23, 12-16, 16-21, 14-21 [NTAb 50,60].

7928 **Ehrensperger, Kathy** That we may be mutually encouraged: feminism and the new perspective in Pauline studies. Biblical studies: 2004 ⇒20,7406. [R]RBLit 7 (2005) 508-510 (*Omerzu, Heike*); ET 117 (2005) 36-37 (*Lawrence, Louise*).

7929 *Elliott, Neil* An American "myth of innocence" and contemporary Pauline studies. BiblInterp 13 (2005) 239-249.

7930 *Georgi, Dieter* BULTMANN was not first: Josiah Royce as interpreter of Paul. The city in the valley. Studies in biblical literature 7: 2005 ⇒214. 309-322.

7931 **Holland, Thomas A.** Contours of Pauline theology: a radical new survey of the influences on Paul's biblical writings. 2004 ⇒20,7407. [R]Evangel 23 (2005) 62 (*Dray, Stephen*); SBET 23 (2005) 120-122 (*Roberts, Mostyn*); RBLit (2005)* (*Bird, Michael*); ET 116 (2005) 425-426 (*Thiselton, Anthony C.*).

7932 *Horrell, D.G.* Recent Pauline studies. EpRe 32/3 (2005) 65-74 [NTAb 50,62].

7933 *Merkel, Helmut* Der Lehrer Paulus und seine Schüler: forschungsgeschichtliche Schlaglichter. Religiöses Lernen. WUNT 180: 2005 ⇒ 384. 235-252.

7934 *Murphy-O'Connor, Jerome* Pauline studies. RB 112 (2005) 147-152, 465-470 [NTAb 50,508].

## G4.1 **Ad Romanos** *Textus, commentarii*

7935 **Agamben, Giorgio** The time that remains: a commentary on the letter to the Romans. [T]*Dailey, Patricia*: Stanford, CA 2005, Stanford Univ. Pr. x; 197 pp. 0-8047-4382-7. Bibl. 187-193.

7936 **Cobb, John B.; Lull, David John** Romans. St. Louis, MO 2005, Chalice viii; 200 pp. 0-8272-0529-5. Bibl. 191-194.

7937 [E]**Díaz Rodelas, J.M.** Carta aos Romanos. [T]*Balancin, Euclides Martins*: Resenha bíblica: São Paulo 2005, Paulinas 110 pp.

7938 **Dumbrell, William J.** Romans: a new commentary. Eugene, Ore. 2005, Wipf & S. 147 pp. €19.

[E]**Gaca, K.** Early patristic readings of Romans 2005 ⇒393.

7939 [E]**Grenholm, C.; Patte, D.** Gender, tradition and Romans: shared ground, uncertain borders. Romans through history and culture: L 2005, Clark vi; 297 pp. $40. 05670-29115. Bibl. [NTAb 50,414].

7940 **Grieb, A. Katherine** The story of Romans: a narrative defense of God's righteousness. 2002 ⇒18,6913... 20,7423. [R]AThR 87 (2005) 340-341 (*Reed, David A.*).

7941 **Karris, Robert J.** Galatians and Romans. New Collegeville Bible Commentary.NT 6: ColMn 2005, Liturgical 107 pp. $7. 0-8146-286-5-6. Bibl. 97-98 [BiTod 44,128—Donald Senior].

7942 **Keck, Leander E.** Romans. Nv 2005, Abingdon 400 pp. $30. 0-687-05705-1. Bibl. 387-397.

7943 **Keener, Craig S.** Romans unlocked. Springfield 2005, 21st Century 319 pp. $15.

7944 **Légasse, Simon** L'épître de Paul aux Romains. LeDiv 10: 2002 ⇒18, 6915... 20,7424. [R]RSR 93 (2005) 394-395 (*Aletti, Jean-Noël*); ScEs 57 (2005) 273-275 (*Doutre, Jean*).

7945 *Limongi, Donatella* NT, *Epistula ad Romanos* 4.23-5.3; 5.8-13 (MS 113). Greek Papyri, Volume I. 2005 ⇒682. 65-68.

7946 **Lohse, Eduard** Der Brief an die Römer. KEK 4: [15]2003 ⇒19,7413; 20,7426. [R]OrdKor 46 (2005) 369-370 (*Giesen, Heinz*); ThLZ 130 (2005) 776-778 (*Holtz, Traugott*); Bib. 86 (2005) 287-289 (*Aletti, Jean-Noël*); RBLit 7 (2005) 394-397 (*Frenschkowski, Marco*).

7947 [T]**Mondin, Battista** Lettera ai Romani. S.TOMMASO d'Aquino, Commento al Corpus Paulinum 1: Bo 2005, Studio Domenicano 1024 pp. €140. 88-7094-562-6.

7948 **Moo, Douglas J.** Romans. NIV Application Comm.: GR 2000, Zondervan 532 pp. $28. 978-0-310-49400-3. Bibl.

7949 *Patte, Daniel* Romans. Global bible commentary. 2005 ⇒2443. 429-443.

7950 **Penna, Romano** Lettera ai Romani I, Rm 1-5. Scritti delle origini cristiane 6: 2004 ⇒20,7429. [R]Gr. 86 (2005) 447-448; CBQ 67 (2005) 536-537 (*Bernas, Casimir*); ASEs 22 (2005) 514-516 (*Walt, Luigi*).

7951 [E]**Peppermüller, Rolf** Anonymi auctoris saeculi XII: expositio in epistolas Pauli (Ad Romanos - II Ad Corinthios 12). BGPhMA 68: Müns 2005, Aschendorff xx; 450 pp. 3-402-04019-0.

7952 **Reasoner, Mark** Romans in full circle: a history of interpretation. LVL 2005, Westminster xxvii; 194 pp. $25. 0-664-22873-9. Bibl. 151-177.

7953 **Seemuth, David** Romans. Nv 2005, Nelson x; 240 pp. 07852-49427.

7954 [E]**Swanson, Reuben J.** New Testament Greek manuscripts: variant readings arranged...against Codex Vaticanus: Romans. 2001 ⇒17, 6507; 19,7423. [R]RBLit (2005)* (*Nicklas, Tobias*).

7955 **Toews, John E.** Romans. Believers church bible commentary: 2004 ⇒20,7432. [R]RBLit (2005)* (*Gombis, Timothy*).

7956 **Tosolini, Fabrizio** The letter to the Romans and St. Paul's grace and apostleship: towards a new interpretation. Taipei Hsien 2005, Fu Jen Catholic University Press xiv; 493 pp. 986-7587-67-7. Bibl. 459-474.

7957 **Witherington, Ben, III** Paul's letter to the Romans: a socio-rhetorical commentary. 2004 ⇒20,7433. [R]RRT 12/1 (2005) 30-33 (*Bury, Benjamin*) SBET 23 (2005) 89-91 (*Bird, Mike*); AThR 87 (2005) 719, 722 (*Kittredge, Cynthia*); RBLit 7 (2005) 398-400 (*Rich, Fred*).

7958 *Wright, N.T.* The letter to the Romans. NT survey. 2005 ⇒3144. 159-168.

## G4.2 *Ad Romans: themata*, **topics**

7959 *Armenteros, Victor M.* Una propuesta semítica a la estructura de la epístola a los Romanos. Hermenêutica 5 (2005) 95-103.

7960 *Baldanza, G.* Il linguaggio cultuale nella lettera ai Romani e le sue caratteristiche. EL 119/3 (2005) 265-287 [NTAb 50,301].

7961 **Bond, Lee** Renewing the mind: Paul's theological and ethical use of φρόνημα and cognates in Romans and Philippians. [D]*Clarke, A.* 2005, Diss. Aberdeen [TynB 58,317-320].

7962 **Campbell, Douglas Atchison** The quest for Paul's gospel: a suggested strategy. JSNT.S 274: L 2005, Clark xi; 290 pp. $115. 0-567-08332-2 [Gal 3].

7963 *Castelli, Elizabeth A.* Gender and ideology critique in the study of Paul's letter to the Romans: a response to Pamela Eisenbaum and Teresa J. Hornsby. Gender, tradition & Romans. 2005 ⇒7939. 167-77.

7964 *Du Toit, Andrie B.* Forensic metaphors in Romans and their soteriological significance. Salvation in the New Testament. NT.S 121: 2005 ⇒798. 213-246 [Rom 1,16-32: 2,1-16; 3,21-31; 8,31-34].

7965 *Ehrensperger, Kathy* New perspectives on Paul: new perspectives on Romans in feminist theology?;

7966 *Eisenbaum, Pamela* A remedy for having been born of woman: Jesus, gentiles, and genealogy in Romans. Gender, tradition and Romans. 2005 ⇒7939. 227-255/101-142.

7967 *Ely, P.B.* The Adamic myth in the christian idea of salvation: an exploration. URM 28/2 (2005) 127-148 [NTAb 50,94].

7968 **Esler, Philip Francis** Conflict and identity in Romans: the social setting of Paul's letter. 2003 ⇒19,7434; 20,7444. [R]ThTo 62 (2005) 248-249 (*Gaventa, Beverly Roberts*); CBQ 67 (2005) 141-143 (*Hodge, Caroline Johnson*); Neotest. 39 (2005) 442-443 (*Loubser, J.A.*); RBLit (2005)* (*Aymer, Margaret; Lockett, Darian*).

7969 *Gaventa, Beverly R.* The God who will not be taken for granted: reflections on Paul's letter to the Romans. [M]JUEL, D. 2005 ⇒73. 77-89.

7970 *Georgi, Dieter* Why was Paul killed?: the epistle to the Romans as a document of resistance. The city in the valley. 2005 ⇒214. 147-160.

7971 *Grenholm, Cristina* Feminism and the ambiguities of texts and reality: a response to Sheila McGinn and Yak-hwee Tan;

7972 *Grenholm, Cristina; Patte, Daniel* Choices of interpretations: regarding gender and the authority of Romans. Gender, tradition and Romans. 2005 ⇒7939. 81-98/181-194.

7973 **Guerra, Anthony J.** Romans and the apologetic tradition: the purpose, genre and audience of Paul's letter. MSSNTS 81: C 2005 <1995>, CUP xiii; 200 pp. $33.

7974 *Haacker, K.* One gospel, different people, manifold preaching: Paul's missionary strategy. Missionalia 33 (2005) 249-262 [NTAb 50,302].

7975 **Haacker, Klaus** The theology of Paul's letter to the Romans. New Testament theology: 2003 ⇒19,7439; 20,7448. [R]ThTo 61 (2005) 558, 560, 562 (*Westerholm, Stephen*); CBQ 67 (2005) 343-344 (*Johnson, E. Elizabeth*); RBLit (2005)* (*Lindsay, Dennis R.*); RBLit 7 (2005) 380-383 (*Kirk, James R.D.*).

7976 *Hays, Richard B.* A hermeneutic of trust. The conversion. 2005 <2002> ⇒223. 190-201.

7977 *Hornsby, Teresa J.* The gendered sinner in Romans 1-7. Gender, tradition and Romans. 2005 ⇒7939. 143-166.

7978 *Iovino, Paolo* 'The only wise God' in the letter to the Romans: connections with the book of Wisdom. The book of Wisdom. 2005 ⇒ 713. 283-305 [Rom 11,33-36; 16,25-27].

7979 *Jorgenson, A.G.* RAHNER, Romans and suffering hope. TJT 21/2 (2005) 183-197 [NTAb 50,510].

7980 *Khiok-khng, Yeo* Cross-tradition and cross-gender hermeneutics: a Confucian reading of Romans and a critical reading of Confucian ethics. Gender, tradition and Romans. 2005 ⇒7939. 63-79.

7981 *Kittredge, Cynthia B.* Scriptural criticism and feminist interpretation of Romans. Gender, tradition and Romans. 2005 ⇒7939. 259-270.

7982 *Mustakallio, Antti* The continuing problem of the audience of Romans. [F]AEJMELAEUS, L.: SESJ 89: 2005 ⇒1. 289-310.

7983 *Penna, Romano* La chiesa di Roma come *test* del rapporto tra giudaismo e cristianesimo alla metà del I secolo d.C.. Giudei o cristiani?. 2005 ⇒833. 105-121.

7984 *Porter, Stanley E.* Did Paul have opponents in Rome and what were they opposing?. Paul and his opponents. Pauline studies 2: 2005 ⇒ 469. 149-168 [Rom 1; 15].

7985 **Reichert, Angelika** Der Römerbrief als Gratwanderung: eine Untersuchung zur Abfassungsproblematik. FRLANT 194: 2001 ⇒17,6523 ... 20,7459. [R]RBLit (2005)* (*Omerzu, Heike*).

7986 **Starnitzke, Dierk** Die Struktur paulinischen Denkens im Römerbrief: eine linguistisch-logische Untersuchung. BWANT 163: 2004 ⇒20,7464. [R]EstAg 40 (2005) 376-377 (*Cineira, D.A.*).

7987 **Stendahl, Krister** Das Vermächtnis des Paulus: eine neue Sicht auf den Römerbrief. 2001 ⇒18,6951. [R]LuThK 29 (2005) 154-155 (*Stolle, Volker*); JETh 19 (2005) 280-282 (*Gebauer, Roland*).

7988 *Tan Yak-hwee* Judging and community in Romans: an action within the boundaries. Gender, tradition and Romans. 2005 ⇒7939. 39-62.

7989 *Tasmuth, Randar* Paul's *Gospel* to the Romans. [F]AEJMELAEUS, L.: SESJ 89: 2005 ⇒1. 311-323.

7990 **Tobin, Thomas H.** Paul's rhetoric in its contexts: the argument of Romans. 2004 ⇒20,7466. [R]RBLit (2005)* (*Burnett,, Gary*).

7991 *Tomson, Peter* "Die Täter des Gesetzes werden gerechtfertigt werden" (Röm 2,13): zu einer adäquaten Perspektive für den Römerbrief. Lutherische und neue Paulusperspektive. WUNT 182: 2005 ⇒339. 183-221.

7992 *Vining, P.* Comparing SENECA's ethics in *Epistulae Morales* to those of Paul in Romans. RestQ 47/2 (2005) 83-104.

7993 **Wagner, J. Ross** Heralds of the good news: Isaiah and Paul "in concert" in the letter to the Romans. NT.S 101: 2002 ⇒18,6956; 20,

7467. [R]ThLZ 130 (2005) 49-51 (*Wilk, Florian*); Bib. 86 (2005) 571-575 (*Belli, Filippo*).

### G4.3 *Naturalis cognitio Dei*, **Rom 1-4**

7994 *Doutre, Jean* Cohérence narrative en Rm 1-4?: un point de vue sémiotique. Analyse narrative. BEThL 191: 2005 ⇒742. 449-461.

7995 **Gathercole, Simon J.** Where is boasting?: early Jewish soteriology and Paul's response in Romans 1-5. 2002 ⇒18,6961... 20,7472. [R]SNTU 30 (2005) 256-258 (*Labahn, Michael*); BiblInterp 13 (2005) 99-103 (*Stowers, Stanley*); WThJ 67 (2005) 434-437 (*Waters, Guy Prentiss*); JThS 55 (2004) 646-649 (*Hooker, Morna D.*); JQR 95 (2005) 700-704 (*Westerholm, Stephen*).

7996 *Clark, Elizabeth A.* History, theology, and context: the analysis of Romans in Bernadette Brooten's *Love between women* and Francis Watson's *Agape, eros, gender*. Gender, tradition and Romans. 2005 ⇒7939. 195-207 [Rom 1; 7].

7997 *MacLeod, David J.* Eternal Son, Davidic Son, Messianic Son: an exposition of Romans 1:1-7. BS 162/645 (2005) 76-94.

7998 *Lambrecht, Jan* Het evangelie over Gods zoon: Romeinen 1,3-4 en De Nieuwe Bijbelvertaling. Coll. 35/2 (2005) 135-138.

7999 *Swart, Gerhard* Why without excuse?: an inquiry into the syntactic and semantic relations of Romans 1:18-21. Neotest. 39/2 (2005) 389-407.

8000 *Reinmuth, Eckart* Allegorese und Intertextualität: narrative Abbreviaturen der Adam-Geschichte bei Paulus (Röm 1,18-28). Die Bibel im Dialog. NET 10: 2005 ⇒333. 57-69.

8001 *Gaca, Kathy L.* Paul's uncommon declaration in Romans 1:18-32 and its problematic legacy for pagan and christian relations. Early patristic readings. 2005 ⇒393. 1-33.

8002 *Gaventa, Beverly* God handed them over: reading Romans 1:18-32 apocalyptically. ABR 53 (2005) 42-53.

8003 *Winterer, Angelika* Ein Konflikt zwischen "Starken" und "Schwachen": Anlass für die Gestaltung und Gewichtung von Röm 1,18-32. [F]LAUB, F.: Bibel-Schule-Leben 6: 2005 ⇒87. 139-149.

8004 *Sennett, James F.* Bare bones inclusivism and the implications of Romans 1:20. EvQ 77 (2005) 309-319.

8005 *Horn, Friedrich W.* Die Herrlichkeit des unvergänglichen Gottes und die vergänglichen Bilder der Menschen: Überlegungen im Anschluss an Röm 1,23. [F]BÜMLEIN, K.: 2005 ⇒18. 43-57.

8006 *Odell-Scott, David W.* Patriarchy and heterosexual eroticism: the question in Romans and Corinthians. Gender, tradition and Romans. 2005 ⇒7939. 209-226 [Rom 1,26-27; 1 Cor 7; 11,3-16].

8007 **Winterer, Angelika** Verkehrte Sexualität—ein umstrittenes Pauluswort: eine exegetische Studie zu Röm 1,26f. in der Argumentationsstruktur des Römerbriefes und im kulturhistorisch-sozialgeschichtlichen Kontext. EHS.T 810: Fra 2005, Lang 355 pp. 3-631-53766-2.

8008 **Thorsteinsson, Runar M.** Paul's interlocutor in Romans 2: function and identity in the context of ancient epistolography. CB.NT 40: 2003 ⇒19,7476; 20,7490. [R]CDios 218 (2005) 567-569 (*Gutiérrez, J.*); Gr. 86 (2005) 439 (*Farahian, Edmond*); ThLZ 130 (2005) 786-

789 (*Horn, Friedrich W.*); RBLit (2005)* (*Lee, Bryan*); JThS 56 (2005) 561-565 (*Stowers, Stanley*).

8009 *Hodges, Zane C.* The moralistic wrath-dodger Romans 2:1-5. Journal of the Grace Evangelical Society 18/34 (2005) 15-21.

8010 *Cornaz, Jean-Patrice* Romains 2,1-16: jugera bien qui jugera le dernier. LeD 65 (2005) 3-17.

8011 *Hays, Richard B.* Psalm 143 as testimony to the righteousness of God. The conversion. 2005 <1980> ⇒223. 50-60 [Rom 3];

8012 Three dramatic roles: the law in Romans 3-4. The conversion. 2005 <1996> ⇒223. 85-100.

8013 *Gignac, Alain* Procès de l'humain ou procès de Dieu?: le jeu intertextuel entre Rm 3,1-9 et Ps 50 (LXX). RB 112 (2005) 46-62.

8014 *Dumbrell, William J.* Remarks on the interpreting of Paul and the function of Romans 3:20 in its context. RTR 64/3 (2005) 135-146.

8015 *Patte, Daniel* Pluralité des lectures du "Christ de la Passion" de Rm 3,21-26: exégèse herméneutique dans une perspective structurale. [F]GENEST, O. 2005 ⇒46. 179-214.

8016 *Penna, Romano* The meaning of πάρεσις in Romans 3:25c and the Pauline thought on the divine acquittal. Lutherische und neue Paulusperspektive. WUNT 182: 2005 ⇒339. 251-274.

8017 *Söding, Thomas* Sühne durch Stellvertretung: zur zentralen Deutung des Todes Jesu im Römerbrief. Deutungen. WUNT 181: 2005 ⇒392. 375-396 [Rom 3,21-26].

8018 *Genuyt, François* La justice d'Abraham selon saint Paul: épître aux Romains, chapitre 4. LV(L) 54/2 (2005) 33-42.

8019 *Hays, Richard B.* Abraham as father of Jews and gentiles. The conversion. 2005 <1985> ⇒223. 61-84 [Rom 4].

8020 **López Sojo, Dagoberto** Abraham, padre de todos nosotros ... análisis estilístico-argumentativo de Rm 4,1-25: Abraham, paradigma de fe monoteísta. [D]*Garuti, P.*: CRB 64: P 2005, Gabalda 384 pp. 2-850-21-170-9. Diss. Angelicum, Roma; Bibl. 353-379.

### G4.4 *Redemptio cosmica*: **Rom 5-8**

8021 *Lamp, Jeffrey S.* The rhetoric of righteousness: an overview of Paul's argument in Romans 5-8. AsbTJ 60/2 (2005) 55-66.

8022 *Ricoeur, Paul* Romains 5. ETR 80/4 (2005) 79-84.

8023 *Charrière, Nicolas* Romains 5,1-11: "Je suis en paix avec Dieu ... même quand je souffre!". LeD 65 (2005) 18-28.

8024 *Collins, Nina L.* The Jewish source of Rom 5:17,16,10 and 9: the verses of Paul in relation to a comment in the Mishnah at M. Makk 3. 15. RB 112 (2005) 27-45.

8025 *Anguiano García, Alberto* El pecado original: ¿defecto hereditario o defecto gramatical en una traducción latina de Rom. 5,12-21?: reflexiones en torno al método histórico-crítico y la ruptura entre dogma y escritura. [F]JUNCO GARZA, C.: 2005 ⇒74. 7-26.

8026 *Venema, C.P.* N.T. Wright on Romans 5:12-21 and justification: a case study in exegesis, theological method, and the 'new perspective on Paul'. Mid-America Journal of theology [Dyer, IN] 16 (2005) 29-81 [NTAb 50,303].

8027 **Sabou, Sorin** Between horror and hope: Paul's metaphorical language of death in Romans 6:1-11. Milton Keynes 2005, Paternoster xi; 159 pp. 1-84227-322-1. Bibl. 145-156.

8028 **Karakolis, Christos** Sin–baptism–grace (Rom 6:1-14): a contribution to Pauline soteriology. Thessalonici 2002, Pournaras 436 pp. €25. 96024-22696.

8029 *Bohnenblust-Pidoux, Laurence* Romains 6,15-23: vivre en accord. LeD 65 (2005) 29-37.

8030 *Giesen, Heinz* Das heilige Gesetz—missbraucht durch die Sünde (Röm 7). TThZ 114 (2005) 202-221.

8031 *Huttunen, Niko* The human contradiction: EPICTETUS and Romans 7. [F]AEJMELAEUS, L.: SESJ 89: 2005 ⇒1. 324-333.

8032 *Thyen, Hartwig* Zwei verfehlte Alternativen in der Auslegung von Römer 7. [F]STEGEMANN, W. 2005 ⇒139. 270-288. [Phil 3,4-6].

8033 *Rollins, Wayne G.* Lecture psychologique: l'expérience de la foi chez Paul. Guide des nouvelles lectures. 2005 ⇒426. 168-198 [Rom 7-8].

8034 *Lee, C.W.* Understanding the law in Rom. 7:1-6: an enthymemic analysis. Scriptura 88 (2005) 126-138 [NTAb 50,68].

8035 *Viard, Jean-Sébastien* Loi, chair et libération: une solution structurelle au problème de Romains 7,1-6. Theoforum 36/2 (2005) 155-73.

8036 *Nicolet, Christine* Romains 7,7-8,2: un homme qui s'appelait "Désiré". LeD 65 (2005) 38-48.

8037 *Gundry, Robert H.* The moral frustration of Paul before his conversion: sexual lusts in Romans 7:7-25. The old is better. WUNT 178: 2005 ⇒220. 252-271.

8038 **Bertone, John A.** "The law of the Spirit": experience of the Spirit and displacement of the law in Romans 8:1-16. Studies in Biblical literature 86: NY 2005, Lang xxii, 351 pp. 08204-78539. Bibl. 319-39.

8039 **Christoph, Monika** Das Integrationspotential des Begriffes Pneuma nach Röm 8,1-30: Studien zur Semantik und Pragmatik der Rede von Pneuma im Römerbrief. [D]*Frey, Jörg* 2005, Diss. München [ThLZ 131,340].

8040 **Meißner, Joachim** Das Kommen der Herrlichkeit: eine Neuinterpretation von Röm 8,14-30. FzB 100: 2003 ⇒19,7498. [R]ThLZ 130 (2005) 784-785 (*Horn, Friedrich W.*); ATG 68 (2005) 317-318 (*Rodríguez Carmona, A.*).

8041 *McGinn, Sheila E.* Feminists and Paul in Romans 8:18-23. Gender, tradition and Romans. 2005 ⇒7939. 21-37.

8042 *Bieberstein, Sabine* Die Schöpfung in Geburtswehen: Röm 8,18-25, das Leben unter der Pax Romana und die Ideologien des goldenen Zeitalters. BiKi 60 (2005) 38-44.

8043 *Braaten, Laurie J.* The groaning creation: the biblical background for Romans 8:22. BR 50 (2005) 19-39.

8044 **Bénétreau, S.** La prière par l'Esprit: la prière de demande et l'intercession de l'Esprit selon Romains 8,26-27. P 2004, Excelsis 138 pp. €12. 29044-07375.

8045 *McCall, Tom; Stanglin, Keith D.* S.M. Baugh and the meaning of foreknowledge: another look. TrinJ 26 (2005) 19-31 [Rom 8,29].

## G4.6 *Israel et Lex*; **The Law and the Jews**, *Rom 9-11*

8046 *Bachmann, Michael* Keil oder Mikroskop?: zur jüngeren Diskussion um den Ausdruck "'Werke' des Gesetzes". Lutherische und neue Paulusperspektive. WUNT 182: 2005 ⇒339. 69-134.

8047 *Beißer, Friedrich* Was heißt bei Paulus "Jesus Christus ist das Ende des Gesetzes"?—eine Anfrage an Mogens Müller. KuD 51/1 (2005) 52-54.

8048 **Bell, Richard H.** The irrevocable call of God: an inquiry into Paul's theology of Israel. WUNT 184: Tü 2005, Mohr S. xxv; 550 pp. $175. 3-16-148009-0. Bibl. 423-489 [Gal 3-4; 1 Thess 2,13-16].

8049 *Bergmeier, Roland* Vom Tun der Tora. Lutherische und neue Paulusperspektive. WUNT 182: 2005 ⇒339. 161-181.

8050 [E]**Carson, Donald A.; O'Brien, Peter T.; Seifrid, Mark A.** Justification and variegated nomism, 2: the paradoxes of Paul. WUNT 2/181: 2004 ⇒20,327. [R]JETh 19 (2005) 297-300 (*Stenschke, Christoph*); RBLit (2005)* (*Nicklas, Tobias*).

8051 *Diefenbach, Manfred* "Gott erbarmt sich aller": literaranalytische Interpretation von Röm 9,1-11,36 als Beitrag zum jüdisch-christlichen Dialog. KuI 20 (2005) 9-18.

8052 *Dunn, James D.G.* The dialogue progresses. Lutherische und neue Paulusperspektive. WUNT 182: 2005 ⇒339. 389-430.

8053 *Gillespie, Thomas W.* Prophetic surprise in Romans 9-11. [M]JUEL, D. 2005 ⇒73. 91-105.

8054 **Grindheim, Sigurd** The crux of election: Paul's critique of the Jewish confidence in the election of Israel. [D]*Carson, D.A.*: WUNT 2/202: Tü 2005, Mohr S. xi; 282 pp. €49. 3-16-148690-0. Diss. Trinity Evang. Divinity; Bibl. 201-243.

8055 **Kuula, Kari** The law, the covenant and God's plan, 2: Paul's treatment of the law and Israel in Romans. SESJ 85: 2003 ⇒19,7516. [R]RBLit (2005)* (*Yakiyama, Mariko*).

8056 **Rapa, Robert Keith** The meaning of "works of the law" in Galatians and Romans. 2001 ⇒17,6580. [R]RBLit (2005)* (*Waters, Guy*).

8057 *Steinmetz, Devora* Justification by deed: the conclusion of Sanhedrin-Makkot and Paul's rejection of law. HUCA 76 (2005) 133-187 [Hab 2,4].

8058 **Sanguinetti, Corrado** La funzione retorica e teologica di Romani 9 nel contesto della sezione Rm 9-11. [D]*Estrada, B.*: R 2005, Pont. Univ. Sanctae Crucis 390 pp. 88-8333-1524. Diss. Santa Croce; Bibl. 363-388.

8059 **Abasciano, Brian J.** Paul's use of the Old Testament in Romans 9.1-9 : an intertextual and theological exegesis. JSNT.S 301; LNTS 301: L 2005, Clark xi; 265 pp. 0-567-03073-3. Bibl. 236-248.

8060 *Dunn, James D.G.* Did Paul have a covenant theology?: reflections on Romans 9.4 and 11.27. New perspective. WUNT 185: 2005 <2004> ⇒7638. 423-439.

8061 *Tanner, James P.* The new covenant and Paul's quotations from Hosea in Romans 9:25-26. BS 162/645 (2005) 95-110.

8062 *Avemarie, Friedrich* Paul and the claim of the law according to the scripture: Leviticus 18:5 in Galatians 3:12 and Romans 10:5. Beginnings of christianity. 2005 ⇒786. 125-148.

8063 *Grech, Prosper* Il retroscena di Rm 10,5-13 e il discorso ad Antiochia. Il messaggio biblico. SRivBib 44: 2005 <1998> ⇒216. 363-371.

8064 *Mohrmann, Douglas C.* Boast not in your righteousness from the law: a new reading of Romans 10.6-8. JGRChJ 2 (2005) 76-99.

8065 *Gignac, Alain* Ἀκοὴ πίστεως (Ga 3,1.5) et ῥῆμα τῆς πίστεως (Rm 10, 8). [F]GENEST, O. 2005 ⇒46. 435-460.

8066 **Panjikaran, Joy Gervasis** "The word of faith which we proclaim": Paul's concept of mission: an exegetical and theological study of Rom 10:8-17. [D]*Viejo, J.M.*: R 2005, xii; 97 pp. Extr. Diss. Angelicum; Bibl. 84-92.

8067 *Beauchamp, Paul* Un parallèle problématique: Rm 11 et Ez 16. Pages exégétiques. LeDiv 202: 2005 <1995> ⇒183. 221-238.

8068 *Chrostowski, Waldemar* "Czyz Bóg odrzucił lud swój?" (Rz 11,1): refleksja biblijno-teologiczna. CoTh 75/2 (2005) 39-56. **P.**

8069 *Cohen, Jeremy* The mystery of Israel's salvation: Romans 11:25-26 in patristic and medieval exegesis. HThR 98 (2005) 247-281.

8070 *Waymeyer, M.* The dual status of Israel in Romans 11:28. MastJ 16/1 (2005) 57-71 [NTAb 50,69].

### G4.8 Rom 12...

8071 *Olree, A.G.* Government as God's agent: a reconsideration of Romans 12 and 13. Stone-Campbell Journal [Joplin, MO] 8 (2005) 181-197 [NTAb 51,292].

8072 *Schreiber, Stefan* Imperium Romanum und römische Gemeinden: Dimensionen politischer Sprechweise in Röm 13. Die Bedeutung. QD 215: 2005 ⇒363. 131.

8073 *Mathew, Regi* Bible and the state: a Pauline perspective. BiBh 31 (2005) 77-83 [Rom 13,1-7].

8074 *Romanello, Stefano* Il rispetto dell'autorità nella lettera ai Romani (13,1-7): sue ragioni prospettive per l'oggi. PSV 51 (2005) 177-195.

8075 *McCruden, Kevin B.* Judgment and life for the Lord: occasion and theology of Romans 14,1-15,13. Bib. 86 (2005) 229-244.

8076 *Marjanen, Antti* Phoebe, a letter courier. [F]AEJMELAEUS, L.: SESJ 89: 2005 ⇒1. 495-508 [Rom 16,1-2].

8077 *Belleville, Linda* Ἰουνιᾶν... ἐπίσημοι ἐν τοῖς ἀποστόλοις: a re-examination of Romans 16.7 in light of primary source materials. NTS 51 (2005) 231-249.

### G5.1 Epistulae ad Corinthios I (vel I-II), *textus, commentarii*

8078 [E]**Adams, Edward; Horrell, David G.** Christianity at Corinth: the quest for the Pauline church. 2004 ⇒20,306. [R]RRT 12 (2005) 507-510 (*Bash, Anthony*); RBLit (2005)* (*Johnson, Alan; Verbrugge, Verlyn*).

8079 **Collins, Raymond F.** First Corinthians. Sacra Pagina 7: 1999 ⇒15, 6705... 19,7559. [R]PhilipSac 40 (2005) 491-492 (*Ofilada, Macario*).

8080 **Garland, David E.** 1 Corinthians. 2003 ⇒19,7562; 20,7566. [R]CBQ 67 (2005) 144-146 (*Gillman, John*).

8081 **Johnson, Alan F.** 1 Corinthians. IVP NT Comm.: 2004 ⇒20,7568. [R]MissTod 7 (2005) 95-96 (*Varickasseril, Jose*).

8082 **Keener, Craig S.** 1-2 Corinthians. New Cambridge Bible Commentary: C 2005, CUP xii; 299 pp. £13. 0-521-54243-X.

8083 *Kloha, Jeff* Epistula ad Corinthios I. BVLI 49 (2005) 37-41.

8084 [TE]**Kovacs, Judith L.** 1 Corinthians: interpreted by early christian commentators. The church's bible: GR 2005, Eerdmans xxix; 340 pp. $35. 0-8028-2577-X. Bibl. 317-319.

8085 **Lang, F.** Le lettere ai Corinzi. 2004 ⇒20,7569. REstTrin 39 (2005) 592-593 (*Vázquez Allegue, Jaime*).

8086 **Lindemann, Andreas** Der erste Korintherbrief. HNT 9/1: 2000 ⇒ 16,6683... 19,7564. RThLZ 130 (2005) 46-49 (*Bieringer, Reimund*).

8087 **Marangon, Antonio** Prima lettera ai Corinzi. Dabar-Logos-Parola: Padova 2005, EMP 187 pp. €10.50. RCredOg 25/6 (2005) 143-144 (*Cappelletto, Gianni*).

8088 **Merklein, Helmut; Gielen, Marlis** Der erste Brief an die Korinther, 3: Kapitel 11,2-16,24. ÖTBK 7/3: Gü 2005, Gü 470 pp. €50. 3-579-00551-0.

8089 T**Mondin, Battista** Prima Lettera ai Corinzi. S.TOMMASO d'Aquino, Commento al Corpus Paulinum 2: Bo 2005, Studio Domenicano 924 pp. €140. 88-7094-563-4.

8090 **Pascuzzi, Maria A.** First and Second Corinthians. New Collegeville Bible Commentary.NT 7: ColMn 2005, Liturgical 152 pp. $7. 0-814-6-2866-4 [BiTod 44,128—Donald Senior].

8091 *Pathrapankal, Joseph* 1 Corinthians. Global bible commentary. 2005 ⇒2443. 444-450.

E**Peppermüller, R.** Expositio in epistolas Pauli 2005 ⇒7951.

8092 *Sampley, J. Paul* The first letter to the Corinthians. NT survey. 2005 ⇒3144. 169-181.

8093 E**Schowalter, Daniel N.; Friesen, Steven J.** Urban religion in Roman Corinth: interdisciplinary approaches. HThS 53: CM 2005, Harvard University Press xiv; 523 pp. $50. 0674-016599. Bibl. 459-498.

8094 **Somerville, Robert** La première épître de Paul aux Corinthiens, 2. Commentaires évangéliques de la bible: Vaux-sur-Seine 2005, Edifac 234 pp. €22. 2-904407-308. RAng. 82 (2005) 931-2 (*Mirri, Luciana*).

8095 **Thiselton, Anthony C.** The first epistle to the Corinthians. NIGTC: 2000 ⇒16,6689... 20,7572. RNV 80/4 (2005) 103-104 (*Borel, Jean*).

## G5.2 *1 & 1-2 ad Corinthios*—**themata, topics**

8096 **Badley, Karen Jo-Ann** Paul's use of creation narratives in 1 Corinthians: indication for a Pauline theology of creation. D*Lincoln, A.* 2005, 221 pp. Diss. Toronto, St. Michael [RTL 37,613].

8097 **Carter, Christopher** The synoptic sermon tradition as a fiscal framework in 1 Corinthians: towards a Pauline theology of possessions. D*Clarke, A.* 2005, 660 pp. Diss. Aberdeen [RTL 37,614].

8098 **Chester, Stephen J.** Conversion at Corinth: perspectives on conversion in Paul's theology and the Corinthian church. SNTW: L 2005 <2003>, Clark 393 pp. £25/$50. 05670-40534. Bibl. 343-374.

8099 **Chester, Stephen J.** Conversion at Corinth: perspectives on conversion in Paul's theology and the Corinthian church. SNTW: 2003 ⇒ 19,7576; 20,7579. RCBQ 67 (2005) 135-6 (*Anderson, Garwood P.*).

8100 **Crocker, Cornelia Cyss** Reading 1 Corinthians in the twenty-first century. Biblical studies: 2004 ⇒20,7580. RRBLit (2005)* (*Donahoe, Kate*).

8101 **Dutch, Robert S.** The educated elite in 1 Corinthians: education and community conflict in Graeco-Roman context. JSNT.S 217: L 2005, Clark xvii; 343 pp. $125. 0-8264-70882-2.

8102 **Ebel, Eva** Die Attraktivität früher christlicher Gemeinden: die Gemeinde von Korinth im Spiegel griechisch-römischer Vereine.

WUNT 2/178: 2004 ⇒20,7583. RSNTU 30 (2005) 252-253 (*Gmainer-Pranzl, Franz*); RHPhR 85 (2005) 458-460 (*Grappe, Ch.*).

8103 *Finney, Mark T.* Christ crucified and the inversion of Roman imperial ideology in 1 Corinthians. BTB 35 (2005) 20-33.

8104 *Friesen, Steven J.* Prospects for a demography of the Pauline mission: Corinth among the churches. Urban religion in Roman Corinth. HThS 53: 2005 ⇒8093. 351-370.

8105 *Gil Arbiol, Carlos* La casa amenazada: conflicto de modelos familiares en 1 Co. EstB 63 (2005) 43-63.

8106 *Grech, Prosper* Aspetti eucaristici nella prima lettera ai Corinzi. Il messaggio biblico. SRivBib 44: 2005 ⇒216. 249-258.

8107 **Hall, David R.** The unity of the Corinthian correspondence. JSNT.S 251: 2003 ⇒19,7583. RBiblInterp 13 (2005) 443-446 (*Chester, Stephen J.*); RBLit (2005)* (*Sisson, Russell; Verbrugge, Verlyn*); JThS 56 (2005) 566-568 (*Thiselton, Anthony C.*).

8108 *Hays, Richard B.* The conversion of the imagination: scripture and eschatology in 1 Corinthians. The conversion. 2005 <1999> ⇒223. 1-24.

8109 **Heil, John Paul** The rhetorical role of Scripture in 1 Corinthians. SBL.Studies in Biblical Literature 15: Lei 2005, Brill xiii; 309 pp. €153.56. 90-04-13769-6. Bibl. 263-285; also Atlanta: SBL $36; 158-983-1675.

8110 *Hogeterp, Albert L.A.* Paul's Judaism reconsidered: the issue of cultic imagery in the Corinthian correspondence. EThL 81 (2005) 87-108.

8111 *Horsley, Richard A.* Paul's assembly in Corinth: an alternative society;

8112 *Koester, Helmut* The silence of the apostle. Urban religion in Roman Corinth. HThS 53: 2005 ⇒8093. 371-395/339-349.

8113 *Liese, Andreas* "... nicht viele Vornehme ...": eine sozialhistorische Annäherung an den ersten Brief an die Korinther. Zeitschrift für Theologie und Gemeinde 10 (2005) 269-285.

8114 *Malan, F.S.* Vaderskap in die pauliniese korpus volgens 1 Korintiërs. HTSTS 61/1-2 (2005) 253-271 [NTAb 50,304].

8115 *Mitchell, Margaret M.* Paul's letters to Corinth: the interpretive intertwining of literary and historical reconstruction. Urban religion in Roman Corinth. HThS 53: 2005 ⇒8093. 306-338.

8116 **Monsengwo Pasinya, Laurent** La notion de nomos dans le pentateuque grec. AnBib 52; Recherches Africaines de Théologie 5: R 2005 <1973>, E.P.I.B. 246 pp. €18. 88-7653-052-5.

8117 *Njoroge Wa Ngugi, Joseph* Method in inculturated evangelization: a challenge from 1st Corinthians. African christian studies 21/3 (2005) 5-34.

8118 **Odell-Scott, David W.** Paul's critique of theocracy: a/theocracy in Corinthians and Galatians. JSNT.S 250; Playing the Texts 8: 2003 ⇒ 19,7589. RThLZ 130 (2005) 280-281 (*Schenk, Wolfgang*); BiblInterp 13 (2005) 438-441 (*Nanos, Mark D.*).

8119 *Pickett, Ray* Conflicts at Corinth. Christian origins. A people's history of christianity 1: 2005 ⇒550. 113-137.

8120 *Schnabel, Eckhard J.* The objectives of change: factors of transformation, and the causes of results: the evidence of Paul's Corinthian correspondence. TrinJ 26 (2005) 179-204.

8121 **Voss, Florian** Das Wort vom Kreuz und die menschliche Vernunft: eine Untersuchung zur Soteriologie des 1. Korintherbriefes.

FRLANT 199: 2002 ⇒18,7089; 19,7594. $^{R}$ThLZ 130 (2005) 398-400 (*Knöppler, Thomas*).

8122 *Walters, James* Civic identity in Roman Corinth and its impact on early christians. Urban religion in Roman Corinth. HThS 53: 2005 ⇒ 8093. 397-417.

8123 *Wilk, Florian* Isaiah in 1 and 2 Corinthians. Isaiah in the NT. 2005 ⇒ 443. 133-158.

8124 **Winter, Bruce W.** PHILO and Paul among the Sophists: Alexandrian and Corinthian responses to a Julio-Claudian movement. $^{2}$2002 <1997> ⇒18,9705... 20,7607. $^{R}$NT 47 (2005) 83-85 (*Burke, T.J.*).

### G5.3 1 Cor 1-7: *sapientia crucis... abusus matrimonii*

8125 **Strüder, Christof W.** Paulus und die Gesinnung Christi: Identität und Entscheidungsfindung aus der Mitte von 1 Kor 1-4. $^{D}$*Bieringer, R.*: BEThL 190: Lv 2005, Peeters lii; 545 pp. €80. 90-429-1653-2. Diss. Leuven; Bibl. xxiii-lii.

8126 **Welborn, Laurence L.** Paul, the fool of Christ: a study of 1 Corinthians 1-4 in the comic-philosophic tradition. JSNT.S 293: L 2005, Clark xiv; 322 pp. 0-567-03041-5. Bibl. 254-285.

8127 *Wanamaker, Charles A.* Metaphor and morality: examples of Paul's moral thinking in 1 Corinthians 1-5. Neotest. 39/2 (2005) 409-433.

8128 **Kammler, Hans-Christian** Kreuz und Weisheit: eine exegetische Untersuchung zu 1 Kor 1,10-3,4. WUNT 159: 2003 ⇒19,7609; 20, 7619. $^{R}$ThLZ 130 (2005) 650-652 (*Sellin, Gerhard*); TThZ 114 (2005) 262-263 (*Schwindt, Rainer*).

8129 *Adam, A.K.M.* Lecture postmoderne: un exercice d'interprétation paulinienne. Guide des nouvelles lectures. 2005 ⇒426. 319-337 [1 Cor 1,12-17].

8130 *George, T.* Is Christ divided?. ChrTo 49/7 (2005) 30-33 [NTAb 50, 69] [1 Cor 1,13].

8131 **Poggemeyer, Joseph** The dialectic of knowing God in the cross and the creation: an exegetico-theological study of 1 Corinthians 1,18-25 and Romans 1,18-23. $^{D}$*Brodeur, Scott*: TGr.T 127: R 2005, E.P.U.G. 340 pp. €25. 88-7839-044-5. Diss. Gregoriana; Bibl. 317-330.

8132 *McDonough, Sean M.* Competent to judge: the Old Testament connection between 1 Corinthians 5 and 6. JThS 56 (2005) 99-102.

8133 **May, Alistair Scott** 'The body for the Lord': sex and identity in 1 Corinthians 5-7. JSNT.S 278: 2004 ⇒20,7628. $^{R}$RBLit (2005)* (*Ivarsson, Fredrik*).

8134 *Eapen, J.* 'Malakoi' will not inherit the kingdom (1 Cor 6,9). BiBh 31 (2005) 141-147 [NTAb 50,305].

8135 *Moka, W.* Paul's view of the human body. Hekima Review 33 (2005) 37-44 [NTAb 50,513] [1 Cor 6,12-20].

8136 *Welch, E.T.* The apostle Paul: on sex. Journal of Biblical Counseling [Glenside, PA] 23/4 (2005) 13-20 [NTAb 50,305] [1 Cor 6,12-20].

8137 *Amici, Roberto* Bontà del matrimonio e carisma della verginità in 1 Cor 7. Vivar(C) 13 (2005) 265-275.

8138 *Caruso, Giuseppe* L'esegesi di 1 Cor 7 nell'epistola pelagiana *De castitate*. Aug. 45 (2005) 467-499.

8139 **Deming, Will** Paul on marriage and celibacy: the Hellenistic background of 1 Corinthians 7. $^{2}$2004 <1995> ⇒20,7635. $^{R}$SNTU 30

(2005) 249-250 (*Gmainer-Pranzl, Franz*); ScrB 35 (2005) 51-53 (*Boxall, Ian*); Pacifica 19/1 (2006) 97-99 (*Watson, Nigel M.*).

8140 *Girardi, Mario* 1 Cor 7 nell'esegesi di BASILIO e GREGORIO di Nazianzo: l'economia salvifica fra matrimonio e verginità. VetChr 42 (2005) 59-72.

8141 *Zeller, Dieter* Der Vorrang der Ehelosigkeit in 1 Kor 7. ZNW 96 (2005) 61-77.

8142 *Wanamaker, Charles A.* Connubial sex and the avoidance of πορνεια: Paul's rhetorical argument in 1 Corinthians 7:1-5. Scriptura 90 (2005) 839-849 [NTAb 51,294].

8143 *Felber, Anneliese* Königinnen unter missionarischem Erfolgszwang: Salvabitur vir infideli—eine frühmittelalterliche Aktualisierung von 1Kor 7,14a. PzB 14 (2005) 133-139.

8144 *Tábet, Michelangelo* La situazione ordinaria di vita come "chiamata" in 1 Cor 7,17-24. RivBib 53 (2005) 277-312.

8145 *Pelser, G.M.M.* The relation between church and world/culture in view of the Pauline 'as if not' (ὡς μή). HTSTS 61 (2005) 709-727 [NTAb 50,513] [1 Cor 7,29-31].

8146 **Choo, Myung Sung** (Marie-Joseph) La verginità nell'insegnamento di San Paolo in 1 Cor 7,32-35. R 2005, Urbaniana 58 pp. Extr. Diss.; Bibl. 41-55.

## G5.4 *Idolothyta... Eucharistia*: 1 Cor 8-11

8147 *Fotopoulos, John* Τροφε, οίνος και σεχυαλικες σχεσεις: ή ηελλενορρομαικε παραθησε δειρνυ ηοπος διαφαινεται μεσα απο τις όδεγιες του Πηαυλου σχετικα μη τα είδολοθυτα (1 Kor 8,1-11,1). DBM 23/1 (2005) 53-75.

8148 **Fotopoulos, John** Food offered to idols in Roman Corinth: a social-rhetorical reconsideration of 1 Corinthians 8:1-11:1. WUNT 2/151: 2003 ⇒19,7632. [R]BZ 49 (2005) 142-144 (*Poplutz, Uta*); CBQ 67 (2005) 339-340 (*Coutsoumpos, P.*); RB 112 (2005) 149-151 (*Murphy-O'Connor, Jerome*).

8149 *Garland, D.E.* 'Becoming all things to all people': mission in a context of idolatry: accommodation or fidelity?. Missionalia 33/2 (2005) 287-302 [NTAb 50,305].

8150 **Gäckle, Volker** Die Starken und die Schwachen in Korinth und Rom. zur Herkunft und Funktion der Antithese in 1Kor 8,1-11,1 und Röm 14,1-15,13. [D]*Frey, Jörg*: WUNT 2/200: Tü 2005, Mohr S. 636 pp. €79. 3-16-1486-781. Diss. München.

8151 *Kraml, Martina* Ein Abendmahl unter Freunden?: Überlegungen aus eucharistiekatechetischer Sicht. Diak. 36 (2005) 38-45.

8152 **Phua, Richard Liong-Seng** Idolatry and authority: a study of 1 Corinthians 8.1-11.1 in the light of the Jewish diaspora. Library of NT studies 299: L 2005, Clark xi; 236 pp. 0-567-03060-1. Bibl. 209-221.

8153 *Sandelin, Karl-Gustav* PHILO and Paul on alien religion: a comparison. [F]AEJMELAEUS, L.: SESJ 89: 2005 ⇒1. 211-246.

8154 **Smith, Dennis E.** From symposium to eucharist: the banquet in the early christian world. 2002 ⇒18,7125;... 20,7652. [R]TS 66 (2005) 186-187 (*Perkins, Pheme*); RB 112 (2005) 144-147 (*Nodet, Etienne*); Neotest. 39 (2005) 457-461 (*Wanamaker, Charles A.*).

8155 **Smit, Joop F.M.** "About the idol offerings": rhetoric, social context and theology of Paul's discourse in First Corinthians 8:1-11:1. CBET 27: 2000 ⇒16,6734. [R]ThLZ 130 (2005) 786 (*Kraus, Wolfgang*).

8156 *Alarcón Mota, José Alberto* Estudio de 1 Cor 8,1-6. Qol 38 (2005) 91-114.

8157 **Waaler, Erik** One God and one Lord: Paul's christological re-reading of Shema in 1 Cor 8:1-6. Oslo 2005, Norwegian Lutheran School of Theology. Diss. Norwegian Lutheran School of Theology [StTh 60,115].

8158 *Fotopoulos, John* Arguments concerning food offered to idols: Corinthian quotations and Pauline refutations in a rhetorical partitio (1 Corinthians 8:1-9). CBQ 67 (2005) 611-631.

8159 **Coutsoumpos, Panayotis** Paul and the Lord's Supper: a socio-historical investigation. [D]*Martin, R.P.*: Studies in Biblical literature 84: NY 2005, Lang xi; 198 pp. $33.30. 0-8204-7843-1. Diss. Sheffield; Bibl. 179-191 [1 Cor 8,10-20].

8160 *Phua, R.L.-S.* Authority and example: 1 Corinthians 9 in the context of debates on idolatry. Trinity Theological Journal [Singapore] 13 (2005) 52-74 [NTAb 50,305].

8161 *Untergaßmair, Franz G.* "Bin ich nicht frei?" (1 Kor 9,1a): die paulinische Rede vom "gesetzesfreien Evangelium". Das Buch. Vechtaer Beiträge zur Theologie 11: 2005 ⇒487. 35-48.

8162 *Leyrer, D.P.* All things to all people: an exegetical study of 1 Corinthians 9:19-23 with application to North American outreach. WLQ 102/2 (2005) 89-100 [NTAb 50,71].

8163 *Schneider, Michael* Wie handelt Gott?: intertextuelle Lektüren zu 1Kor 10. Die Bibel im Dialog. NET 10: 2005 ⇒333. 35-55.

8164 *Bénétreau, Samuel* Liberté, vigilance et confiance: 1 Corinthiens 10. 1-13. ThEv(VS) 4/1-2 (2005) 81-87, 57-62.

8165 *Williams-Tinajero, L.M.* Christian unity: the communal participation in Christ's body and blood. OiC 40/2 (2005) 46-61 [NTAb 49,525] [1 Cor 10,16].

8166 *Rigato, Maria-Luisa* Una rilettura di 1Cor 10,32-33 + 11,1-16. RivBib 53 (2005) 31-70.

8167 **De Virgilio, Giuseppe** Condividere la cena del Signore: una lettura vocazionale di 1Cor 11. R 2005, Rogate 86 pp. €8.

8168 *Demirer, Derya K.; Duran, Nicole W.* 1 Corinthians 11 in christian and Muslim dialogue. Global bible commentary. 2005 ⇒2443. 451-454.

8169 *Panier, Louis* Il pane e il calice: parola data per un tempo di assenza. Conc(I) 41 (2005) 235-246; Conc(D) 41,162-171; Conc(US) 2,54-63 [1 Cor 11].

8170 *Bearden, A.* On whether 1 Corinthians 11:2-16 allows an egalitarian exegesis. Priscilla Papers [Mp] 19/4 (2005) 16-21 [NTAb 51,295].

8171 *Brown, Sherri* The dialectic of relationship: Paul and the veiling of women in 1 Corinthians 11:2-16. Sal. 67 (2005) 457-477.

8172 *Fee, Gordon D.* Praying and prophesying in the assemblies: 1 Corinthians 11:2-16. Discovering biblical equality. 2005 ⇒387. 142-160.

8173 *Nothaas, Johannes R.* Die Stellung der Frau in der Kirche nach 1 Kor 11,2-16. FKTh 21/3 (2005) 161-181.

8174 **Økland, Jorunn** Women in their place: Paul and the Corinthian discourse of gender and sanctuary space. JSNT.S 269: 2004 ⇒20,7667.

RRBLit (2005)* (*Lopez, Davina; Marchal, Joseph; Wire, Antoinette*) [1 Cor 11,2-16; 14,33-36].

8175 *Bolt, Peter G.* Three heads in the divine order: the early church fathers and 1 Corinthians 11:3. RTR 64/3 (2005) 147-161.

8176 *Mount, Christopher* 1 Corinthians 11:3-16: Spirit possession and authority in a non-Pauline interpolation. JBL 124 (2005) 313-340.

8177 *Keener, Craig* 'Let the wife have authority over her husband' (1 Corinthians 11:10). JGRChJ 2 (2005) 146-152.

8178 **Inziku, John** Overcoming divisive behaviour in the assembly—ἀλλήλους ἐκδέχεσθε: an attempt to interpret 1 Cor 11:17-34 from another perspective. D*Baumert, N.* 2005, 318 pp. Diss. Sankt Georgen [ThRv 102,v].

8179 *Escalona Sánchez, Abel I.* El Señor Jesús la noche en que iba a ser entregado. EfMex 23 (2005) 105-121 [1 Cor 11,23].

## G5.5 1 Cor 12s... Glossolalia, charismata

8180 *Montagnini, Felice* Appunti sui carismi. FGHIBERTI, G.: SRivBib 46: 2005 ⇒47. 323-330.

8181 *Rossing, Barbara R.* Prophets, prophetic movements, and the voices of women. Christian origins. A people's history of christianity 1: 2005 ⇒550. 261-286.

8182 *Rowe, Arthur J.* 1 Corinthians 12-14: the use of a text for christian worship. EvQ 77 (2005) 119-128.

8183 *Shogren, Gary S.* The "ultracharismatics" of Corinth and the Pentecostals of Latin America as the religion of the disaffected. TynB 56/2 (2005) 91-110.

8184 **Tibbs, Eugene** 'Now concerning spiritism': communication with the spirit world as religious experience in First Corinthians 12 and 14. D*Collins, R.F.* 2005, 441 pp. Diss. Catholic Univ. of America [RTL 37,618].

8185 *Viviano, Benedict T.* The dogma of the prophetless time in Judaism: does prophecy cease with Christ for christians?: some explorations. FSCHENKER, A.: OBO 214: 2005 ⇒134. 418-431.

8186 *Locker, Markus* A church of lesser members: 1 Cor 12 as a model of Paul's vision of building the Corinthian church. Ethical dimensions. 2005 ⇒739. 131-139.

8187 *Käsemann, Ernst* Was meint Solidarität nach 1. Korinther 12,12-27?. In der Nachfolge. 2005 ⇒236. 231-241.

8188 *Biguzzi, Giancarlo* La bellezza della carità in 1Cor 13. Il bello della bibbia. 2005 ⇒357. 131-158.

8189 *Portier-Young, Anathea* Tongues and cymbals: contextualizing 1 Corinthians 13:1. BTB 35 (2005) 99-105.

8190 *Perera, Claude* Burn or boast?: a text critical analysis of 1 Cor 13:3. FgNT 18 (2005) 111-128.

8191 *Kritzer, Ruth E.* Zum Wechsel von Simplex und Kompositum in 1Kor 13,12. BN 124 (2005) 103-104.

8192 **Choi, Sung Bok** Glossolalie und christliche Existenz: das Glossolalieverständnis des Paulus im ersten Korintherbrief (1 Kor 14). D*Lindemann, Andreas* 2005, 356 pp. Diss. Bethel [RTL 37,614] [1 Cor 14].

8193 *Chester, Stephen J.* Divine madness?: speaking in tongues in 1 Corinthians 14.23. JSNT 27 (2005) 417-446.

8194 *Keener, Craig S.* Learning in the assemblies: 1 Corinthians 14:34-35. Discovering biblical equality. 2005 ⇒387. 161-171.

8195 *Kontzi-Méresse, Nicola* Le silence des femmes dans l'assemblée: réflexion autour de 1 Corinthiens 14,34-35. ETR 80 (2005) 273-278.

8196 *Rasimus, Tuomas* Ophite myth of Adam and the Corinthian situation. [F]AEJMELAEUS, L.: SESJ 89: 2005 ⇒1. 391-414 [1 Cor 15,45-47].

### G5.6 **Resurrectio**; *1 Cor 15*...[⇒F5.6]

8197 *Craffert, Pieter F.* What on earth (or in heaven) is a resurrected body?: the outline of a historical-anthropological answer. [M]VAN TILBORG, S.: BiblInterp 71: 2005 ⇒155. 227-253.

8198 **Frost, Samuel M.** Exegetical essays on the resurrection of the dead. Xenia, Ohio 2004, Truth Voice 181 pp. $18. [R]RBLit (2005)* (*Licona, Michael*).

8199 *Gundry, Robert H.* The essential physicality of Jesus' resurrection according to the New Testament. The old is better. WUNT 178: 2005 ⇒220. 171-194.

8200 *Moltmann, J.; Moltmann-Wendel, E.* To believe with all your senses: the resurrection of the body. PCTSA 60 (2005) 1-12 [NTAb 50,261].

8201 *Setzer, Claudia* "Talking their way into empire": Jews, christians, and pagans debate resurrection of the body. Ancient Judaism. JSJ.S 95: 2005 ⇒626. 155-175.

8202 **Setzer, Claudia** Resurrection of the body in early Judaism and early christianity: doctrine, community, and self-definition. 2004 ⇒20, 7697. [R]CoTh 75/3 (2005) 246-249 (*Dańczak, Andrzej*); RBLit (2005)* (*Noffke, Eric*).

8203 *Carrier, Richard C.* The spiritual body of Christ and the legend of the empty tomb. The empty tomb. 2005 ⇒435. 105-231 [1 Cor 15].

8204 **Janssen, Claudia** Anders ist die Schönheit der Körper: Paulus und die Auferstehung in 1 Kor 15. [D]*Standhartinger, A.*: Gü 2005, Gü 358 pp. €35. 3-579-05210-1. Diss.-Habil. Marburg.

8205 *Pester, J.* Living under the divine administration through the divine dispensing of the processed Christ as the last Adam and life-giving Spirit: the gospel presented in 1 Corinthians 15. Affirmation & Critique [Anaheim, CA] 10/1 (2005) 26-40 [NTAb 49,526].

8206 **Schneider, Sebastian** Auferstehen: eine Deutung von 1 Kor 15. FzB 105: Wü 2005, Echter 252 pp. €25. 3-429-02696-2. Diss.-Habil. Vallendar; Bibl. 244-249. [R]SNTU 30 (2005) 237-239 (*Giesen, Heinz*).

8207 *Price, Robert M.* Apocryphal apparitions: 1 Corinthians 15:3-11 as a post-Pauline interpolation. The empty tomb. 2005 ⇒435. 69-104.

8208 *Derrett, J. Duncan* 'Over five hundred at one time' (1 Cor 15:6). JHiC 11/2 (2005) 50-54 [NTAb 50,514].

8209 **Chirayath, Babu** Paul's exceptional easter-experience: an exegetical-theological study of 1 Cor 15,8 in relation to Acts 9,3-19; 22,6-21; 26,12-18. 2002 ⇒19,7685. [R]VJTR 69 (2005) 797-798 (*Meagher, P.M.*).

8210 **Hull, Michael F.** Baptism on account of the dead (1 Cor 15:29): an act of faith in the resurrection. Academia biblica 22: Atlanta, Ga. 2005, SBL xv; 327 pp. $43. 1-58983-177-2. Bibl. 257-301.

8211 *Szymik, Stefan* Textkritische und exegetisch-theologische Untersuchung zu 1 Kor 15,49. Roczniki Teologiczne 52/1 (2005) 117-133 [NTAb 50,514].

### G5.9 Secunda epistula ad Corinthios

8212 **Becker, Eve-Marie** Schreiben und Verstehen: paulinische Briefhermeneutik im zweiten Korintherbrief. NET 4: 2002 ⇒19,7695. RBZ 49 (2005) 144-146 (*Schmeller, Thomas*).

8213 **Goulder, Michael D.** Paul and the competing mission in Corinth. Library of Pauline Studies: 2001 ⇒17,6728; 20,7710. RHeyJ 46 (2005) 365-6 (*Madigan, Patrick*); RSR 93 (2005) 382-3 (*Aletti, Jean-Noël*).

8214 **Gräßer, Erich** Der zweite Brief an die Korinther, 2: Kapitel 8,1-13, 13. ÖTBK 8/2; GTBS 514: Gü 2005, Gü 277 pp. €29.90. 3-579-005-14-6.

8215 **Hafemann, Scott J.** 2 Corinthians. NIV Application Comm.: GR 2000, Zondervan 536 pp. $28. 978-0-310-49420-1.

8216 **Harris, Murray J.** The second epistle to the Corinthians: a commentary on the Greek text. NIGTC: GR 2005, Eerdmans cxxviii; 989 pp. $75. 0-8028-2393-3. Bibl. xxvi-cxxviii. RJETh 19 (2005) 270-272 (*Schnabel, Eckhard*); RBLit (2005)* (*Nicklas, Tobias*).

8217 **Kapkin, David** 2 Corintios: del llanto a la alegría. Medellín 2005, Departamento de Publicaciones FUNLAM 340 pp. 958-97524-4-6.

8218 **Long, Fredrick J.** Ancient rhetoric and Paul's apology: the compositional unity of 2 Corinthians. MSSNTS 131: 2004 ⇒20,7712. RRRT 12 (2005) 531-533 (*Bash, Anthony*); RBLit (2005)* (*Silva, Moises*).

8219 *Manus, Ukachukwu C.* 2 Corinthians. Global bible commentary. 2005 ⇒2443. 455-462.

8220 **Martini, Carlo Maria** Paul et son ministère: deuxième lettre aux Corinthiens. T*Ispérian, G.*: Saint-Maurice 2005, Saint-Augustin 100 pp. €18.

8221 *Matera, F.J.* Paul and the renewal of the ministerial priesthood: a reflection on 2 Cor 2:14-7:4. LouvSt 30/1-2 (2005) 49-69 [NTAb 50, 72].

8222 **Matera, Frank J.** II Corinthians: a commentary. NTLi: 2003 ⇒19, 7699; 20,7713. RRB 112 (2005) 634-6 (*Murphy-O'Connor, Jerome*); RBLit 7 (2005) 383-385 (*Nicklas, Tobias*).

8223 *Moreno García, Abdón* Sintaxis trinitaria y pascual del ministerio de la nueva alianza en 2Co 1-7. EstTrin 39 (2005) 309-345.

8224 *Sampley, J. Paul* The second letter to the Corinthians. NT survey. 2005 ⇒3144. 182-205.

8225 **Stegman, Thomas** The character of Jesus: the linchpin to Paul's argument in 2 Corinthians. AnBib 158: R 2005, E.P.I.B. xi; 470 pp. €30. 88-7653-158-0. Bibl. 382-411.

8226 T**Stroobant de Saint-Eloy, Jean-Eric** THOMAS d'Aquin: commentaire de la deuxième épître aux Corinthiens. P 2005, Cerf xlviii; 371 pp. €64. Introd. *G. Dahan*; annot. *Borella, J.* et *Stroobant de S.-Eloy, J.-E.* RSedes Sapientiae 92 (2005) 77-79 (*Elders, Léon*); Studium 45 (2005) 315-317 (*López, L.*); NV 80/3 (2005) 101-102 (*Elders, Léon*).

8227 E**Swanson, Reuben J.** New Testament Greek manuscripts: variant readings arranged in horizontal lines against Codex Vaticanus: 2 Corinthians. Wheaton, IL 2005, Tyndale xli; 347 pp. $41. 0-86585-073-9. Foreword *Bruce Metzger*.

8228 **Thrall, Margaret E.** A critical and exegetical commentary on the second epistle to the Corinthians, 2: commentary on II Corinthians VIII-XIII. ICC: 2000 ⇒16,6810; 17,6733. [R]SJTh 58 (2005) 372-373 (*Horrell, David G.*).

8229 **Young, Frances; Ford, David F.** Meaning and truth in 2 Corinthians. 1987 ⇒3,5999... 8,6453. [R]VJTR 69 (2005) 313-316 (*Menezes, Albert M.*).

8230 **Aus, Roger D.** Imagery of triumph and rebellion in 2 Corinthians 2: 14-17 and elsewhere in the epistle: an example of the combination of Greco-Roman and Judaic traditions in the Apostle Paul. Lanham 2005, Univ. Pr. of America viii; 94 pp. 07618-33218. Bibl. 85-92.

8231 **Hafemann, Scott** Paul, Moses, and the history of Israel: the letter/ spirit contrast and the arguments from scripture in 2 Corinthians 3. Paternoster Biblical Monogr.: Milton Keynes 2005 <1995>, Paternoster xii; 497 pp. £30. 18422-73175 [NTAb 50,178] [1 Cor 3,7-18].

8232 *Pretorius, M.* The key to the present fulfillment of the eschatological inclusion of the gentiles into the people of God. HTSTS 61 (2005) 1339-1352 [NTAb 51,71] [2 Cor 3].

8233 *Weissenrieder, Annette* Der Blick in den Spiegel: II Kor 3,18 vor dem Hintergrund antiker Spiegeltheorien und ikonographischer Abbildungen. Picturing the New Testament. WUNT 2/193: 2005 ⇒396. 313-343.

8234 *Cole, V.B.* The message and messenger of the gospel. ERT 29/2 (2005) 178-184 [2 Cor 4-5].

8235 *Zanetti, Paolo S.* Una nota su *2 Cor*. 4,8b. Imitatori di Gesù Cristo. 2005 <1995> ⇒330. 517-522.

8236 **Lindgård, Fredrik** Paul's line of thought in 2 Corinthians 4:16-5:10. [D]*Aejmelaeus, Lars*: WUNT 2/189: Tü 2005, Mohr S. xi; 282 pp. €59. 3-16-148444-4. Diss. Helsinki; Bibl. 227-254.

8237 **Vogel, Manuel** Commentatio mortis—2. Kor. 5,1-10 auf dem Hintergrund antiker ars moriendi. [D]*Taeger, Jens-W.* 2005, Diss.-Habil. Univ. Frankfurt/M [ThRv 102,xiv].

8238 *Dewey, A.J.* Reminting Paul. The Fourth R [Santa Rosa, CA] 18/2 (2005) 15-17 [NTAb 50,73].

8239 *Gignilliat, Mark* 2 Corinthians 6:2: Paul's eschatological "now" and hermeneutical invitation. WThJ 67 (2005) 147-161.

8240 *Leppä, Outi* Believers and unbelievers in 2 Corinthians 6:14-15. [F]AEJMELAEUS, L.: SESJ 89: 2005 ⇒1. 374-390.

8241 **Wodka, Andrzej** Una teologia biblica del dare nel contesto della colletta paolina (2Cor 8-9). TGr.T 68: 2000 ⇒16,6824; 17,6753. [R]HumTeo 26/1 (2005) 144-145 (*Menezes, Ramiro D.B. de*).

8242 *Zanetti, Paolo S.* Consenso al vangelo e gloria di Dio: in margine a *2 Cor*. 9,11-13. Imitatori di Gesù Cristo. 2005 <1996> ⇒330. 543-53.

8243 *Guttenberger, Gudrun* Klugheit, Besonnenheit, Gerechtigkeit und Tapferkeit: zum Hintergrund der Vorwürfe gegen Paulus nach 2Kor 10-13. ZNW 96 (2005) 78-98.

8244 *Gerber, Christine* Krieg und Hochzeit in Korinth: das metaphorische Werben des Paulus um die Gemeinde in 2 Kor 10,1-6 und 11,1-4. ZNW 96 (2005) 99-125.

8245 *Brink, Laurie* A general's exhortation to his troops: Paul's military rhetoric in 2 Cor 10:1-11. BZ 49 (2005) 191-201.

8246 *Beaude, Pierre-Marie* Narrateur éclairé et mise en discours du "je". Analyse narrative. BEThL 191: 2005 ⇒742. 431-434 [2 Cor 12].

8247 *Barrier, Jeremy* Visions of weakness: apocalyptic genre and the identification of Paul's opponents in 2 Corinthians 12:1-6. RestQ 47/1 (2005) 33-42.

8248 *Roukema, Riemer* Paul's rapture to paradise in early christian literature. [F]LUTTIKHUIZEN, G.: 2005 ⇒93. 267-283 [2 Cor 12, 1-10].

8249 *Lambrecht, Jan* Zwakheid en kracht (2 Korintiërs 12,1-13): kritische beschouwingen bij de Nieuwe Bijbel Vertaling. Bijdr. 66 (2005) 326-340.

8250 *Nicdao, Victor* The paradox of power and weakness in 2 Cor 12:9-10 and the Pauline indicative-imperative. Ethical dimensions. 2005 ⇒ 739. 11-50.

8251 *Bartchy, S. Scott* "When I'm weak, I'm strong": a Pauline paradox in cultural context. [F]STEGEMANN, W.: 2005 ⇒139. 49-60 [2 Cor 12,10].

## G6.1 Ad Galatas

8252 *Arnold, Clinton E.* 'I am astonished that you are so quickly turning away!' (Gal 1.6): Paul and Anatolian folk belief. NTS 51 (2005) 429-449.

8253 **Asano, Atsuhiro** Community-identity construction in Galatians: exegetical, social-anthropological and socio-historical studies. [D]*Rowland, Christopher*: JSNT.S 285: L 2005, Clark x; 272 pp. $125. 0-567-03027-X. Diss. Oxford; Bibl. 230-253. [R]RBLit (2005)* (*Vouga, François*).

8254 **Bachmann, Michael** Antijudaismus im Galaterbrief?. NTOA 40: 1999 ⇒15,6862... 20,7736. [R]JThS 56 (2005) 573-575 (*Stanton, Graham*).

8255 *Brawley, Robert L.* Meta-ethics and the role of works of law in Galatians. Lutherische und neue Paulusperspektive. WUNT 182: 2005 ⇒339. 135-159.

8256 **Bryant, Robert A.** The risen crucified Christ in Galatians. SBL.DS 185: 2001 ⇒17,6776... 20,7738. [R]RBLit (2005)* (*Harmon, Matthew*).

8257 [T]**Cooper, Stephen Andrew** MARIUS Victorinus' Commentary on Galatians: introduction, translation, and notes. Oxf 2005, OUP xvi; 414 pp. $160. 0-19-827027-5. Bibl. 370-403.

8258 *Dianzon, Bernardita* Polemic against the law in Galatians: perspectives then and now. Ethical dimensions. 2005 ⇒739. 117-130.

8259 *Dunn, James D.G.* The theology of Galatians: the issue of covenantal nomism <1991>;

8260 Echoes of intra-Jewish polemic in Paul's letter to the Galatians <1993>;

8261 4QMMT and Galatians <1997>. New perspective. WUNT 185: 2005 ⇒7638. 167-186/221-239/333-339.

8262 **Edwards, Mark J.** Galatians, Ephesians, Philippians. ACCS.NT 8: DG [2]2005 <1999>, InterVarsity xxv; 322 pp.

8263 **Elliott, Susan** Cutting too close for comfort: Paul's letter to the Galatians in its Anatolian cultic context. JSNT.S 248: 2003 ⇒19, 7726; 20,7745. [R]ThLZ 130 (2005) 946-948 (*Witulski, Thomas*); RBLit (2005)* (*Hunt, Steven A.; Rich, Fred*).

8264 **Ferreira, Joel A.** Gálatas: a epístola da abertura de fronteiras. Comentário Bíblico Latino-Americano: São Paulo 2005, Loyola 212 pp.

8265 *Fiedler, Peter* Antijudaismus als Argumentationsfigur: gegen die Verabsolutierung von Kampfesäußerungen des Paulus im Galaterbrief. Studien zur biblischen Grundlegung. SBAB 35: 2005 <1999> ⇒209. 145-176.

8266 *Hays, Richard B.* The letter to the Galatians. NT survey. 2005 ⇒ 3144. 206-216.

8267 *Hurd, John C.* Reflections concerning Paul's "opponents" in Galatia. Paul and his opponents. Pauline studies 2: 2005 ⇒469. 129-148.

8268 *Kahl, Brigitte* Reading Galatians and empire at the great altar of Pergamon. USQR 59/3-4 (2005) 21-43 [NTAb 50,308];

8269 Galaterlektüre am Großen Altar von Pergamon. TeKo 28/4 (2005) 3-25.

8270 **Karris, Robert J.** Galatians and Romans. New Collegeville Bible Commentary.NT 6: ColMn 2005, Liturgical 107 pp. $7. 0-8146-2865-6. Bibl. 97-98 [BiTod 44,128—Donald Senior].

8271 *Konradt, Matthias* "Die aus Glauben, diese sind Kinder Abrahams" (Gal 3,7): Erwägungen zum galatischen Konflikt im Lichte frühjüdischer Abrahamtraditionen. [F]STEGEMANN, E. 2005 ⇒139. 25-48.

8272 **Kremendahl, Dieter** Die Botschaft der Form: zum Verhältnis von antiker Epistolographie und Rhetorik im Galaterbrief. NTOA 46: 2000 ⇒16,6856... 20,7748. [R]ThRv 101 (2005) 209-210 (*Jürgens, Burkhard*).

8273 *Lattke, Michael* Conflict and peace in Paul's letter to the Galatians. AJBI 30-31 (2004-2005) 155-180.

8274 *Lopez, D.C.* Paul, Gentiles, and gender paradigms. USQR 59/3-4 (2005) 92-106 [NTAb 50,299].

8275 *Míguez, Néstor O.* Galatians. Global bible commentary. 2005 ⇒ 2443. 463-472.

8276 **Nanos, Mark D.** The irony of Galatians: Paul's Letter in first-century context. 2001 ⇒17,6787... 20,7754. [R]ThLZ 130 (2005) 1192-1194 (*Sänger, Dieter*); LouvSt 30 (2005) 233-234 (*Koperski, Veronica*); RBLit (2005)* (*Nicklas, Tobias*); JThS 56 (2005) 568-572 (*Stanton, Graham*).

8277 [E]**Nanos, Mark** The Galatians debate: contemporary issues in rhetorical and historical interpretation. 2002 ⇒18,6668... 20,7755. [R]HeyJ 46 (2005) 537-538 (*Hill, Robert C.*).

8278 **Odell-Scott, David W.** Paul's critique of theocracy: a/theocracy in Corinthians and Galatians. JSNT.S 250; Playing the Texts 8: 2003 ⇒ 19,7589. [R]ThLZ 130 (2005) 280-281 (*Schenk, Wolfgang*); BiblInterp 13 (2005) 438-441 (*Nanos, Mark D.*).

8279 [ET]**Plummer, Eric** AUGUSTINE's commentary on Galatians: introduction, text, translation and notes. Oxford Early Christian Studies: 2003 ⇒19,7735; 20,7756. [R]JRS 95 (2005) 295-296 (*Fuhrer, Therese*).

**Rapa, R.** "Works of the law" in Gal. & Rom 2001 ⇒8056.

8280 **Romanello, Stefano** Lettera ai Galati. Dabar: Padova 2005, Messagero 137 pp. €9.50.

8281 **Ryken, P.G.** Galatians. Reformed Expository Commentary: Phillipsburg, NJ 2005, P&R xiv; 290 pp. $25. 08755-27825 [NTAb 50,183].

8282 *Sicre, José Luis* La carta de Pablo a los Gálatas (una introducción narrativa). Proyección 52 (2005) 401-416.

8283 **Silva, Moisés** Interpreting Galatians: explorations in exegetical method. 2001 ⇒17,6795...20,7763. ᴿRBLit 7 (2005) 386-388 (*Fay, Ron*).

8284 **Tolmie, D. François** Persuading the Galatians: a text-centred rhetorical analysis of a Pauline letter. WUNT 2/190: Tü 2005, Mohr S. xii; 287 pp. $76. 3-16-148455-X. Diss. Bloemfontein; Bibl. 257-274.

8285 **Tsang, Sam** From slaves to sons: a new rhetoric analysis on Paul's slave metaphors in his letter to the Galatians. Studies in Biblical Theology 81: NY 2005, Lang xii; 235 pp. 0-8204-7636-6. Bibl. 207-232. ᴿRBLit (2005)* (*Lucas, Roy*).

8286 **Wiley, Tatha** Paul and the Gentile women: reframing Galatians. NY 2005, Continuum 168 pp. £17. 0-8264-1707-8. ᴿRBLit (2005)* (*Kraus, Thomas*).

8287 *Wilson, Todd A.* 'Under law' in Galatians: a Pauline theological abbreviation. JThS 56 (2005) 362-392.

8288 *Yeo, Khiok K.* "Li" and law in the Analects and Galatians: a Chinese christian understanding of ritual and propriety. AJTh 19/2 (2005) 309-332.

8289 *Aletti, Jean-Noël* Galates 1-2: quelle fonction et quelle démonstration?. Bib. 86 (2005) 305-323.

8290 *Martínez, Salvador* El uso paulino de la retórica en Gá 1-2. ᶠJUNCO GARZA, C.: 2005 ⇒74. 437-459.

8291 *Käsemann, Ernst* Galater 1,1-2,10: die Freiheit des Apostels. In der Nachfolge. 2005 ⇒236. 69-80.

8292 *Tolmie, D. Francois* The rhetorical analysis of Galatians: is there another way?. ᴹVAN TILBORG, S.: BiblInterp 71: 2005 ⇒155. 275-289 [Gal 1,1-10].

8293 *Gathercole, Simon J.* The Petrine and Pauline Sola Fide in Galatians 2. Lutherische und neue Paulusperspektive. WUNT 182: 2005 ⇒ 339. 309-327.

8294 *Lindemann, Andreas* Die Jerusalem-Kollekte des Paulus als "diakonisches Unternehmen". WuD 28 (2005) 99-116 [Rom 15,25-31; 1 Cor 16,1-4; 2 Cor 8-9; Gal 2].

8295 *Neusner, Jacob* What, exactly, is Israel's gentile problem?: rabbinic perspectives on Galatians 2. The missions of James. NT.S 115: 2005 ⇒369. 275-306.

8296 *Nanos, Mark D.* Intruding "spies" and "pseudo-brethren": the Jewish intra-group politics of Paul's Jerusalem meeting (Gal 2:1-10). Paul and his opponents. Pauline studies 2: 2005 ⇒469. 59-97.

8297 **Zeigan, Holger** Aposteltreffen in Jerusalem: eine forschungsgeschichtliche Studie zu Galater 2,1-10 und den möglichen lukanischen Parallelen. ABIG 18: Lp 2005, Evangelische 592 pp. €84. 3-374-02315-0. Bibl. 499-539.

8298 *Na, Kang-Yup* The conversion of Izates and Galatians 2:11-14: the significance of a Jewish dispute for the christian church. HBT 27/2 (2005) 56-78.

8299 *Käsemann, Ernst* Galater 2,11-21: Gesetz und Evangelium. In der Nachfolge. 2005 ⇒236. 81-92.

8300 *Melczewski, Pawel* Niewłaściwe postępowanie Piotra w Antiochii (Ga 2,14) [The improper behavior of Peter in Antioch (Gal 2,14)]. RBL 58 (2005) 263-277. **P.**

8301 *Boer, Martinus C. de* Paul's use and interpretation of a justification tradition in Galatians 2.15-21. JSNT 28 (2005) 189-216.

8302 **Mendoza Magallón, Pedro** "Estar crucificado juntamente con Cristo": el nuevo status del creyente en Cristo: estudio exegético-teológico de Gal 2,15-21 y Roma 6.5-11. TGr.T 122: R 2005, E.P.U.G. 324 pp. €22. 88-7839-037-2. Bibl. 293-316.

8303 **Núñez Regodón, Jacinto** El evangelio en Antioquía: Gál 2,15-21 entre el incidente Antioqueno y la crisis Gálata. 2002 ⇒18,7329... 20,7778. RCDios 218 (2005) 569-570 (*Gutiérrez, J.*).

8304 *Barrick, W.D.* The new perspective and 'works of the law' (Gal 2:16 and Rom 3:20). MastJ 16/2 (2005) 277-292 [NTAb 50,309].

8305 *Ellingworth, Paul* A note on Galatians 2.16. BiTr 56 (2005) 109-110.

8306 **Hietanen, Mika** Paul's argumentation in Galatians: a pragma-dialectical analysis of Gal. 3.1-5.12. Helsinki 2005, M. Hietanen Diss. Åbo Akademi Univ. [StTh 60,112].

8307 *Käsemann, Ernst* Galater 3,1-9.26-29: des Geistes Kinder. In der Nachfolge. 2005 ⇒236. 93-104.

8308 **Davis, Basil S.** Christ as devotio: the argument of Galatians 3:1-14. 2002 ⇒18,7333. RCBQ 67 (2005) 335-337 (*Nanos, Mark D.*).

8309 **Wakefield, Andrew H.** Where to live: the hermeneutical significance of Paul's citations from scripture in Galatians 3:1-14. Academia biblica 14: 2003 ⇒19,7761; 20,7784. RBib. 86 (2005) 575-577 (*Rastoin, Marc*); RBLit (2005)* (*Harmon, Matthew; Sprinkle, Preston*); JThS 56 (2005) 165-168 (*Hooker, Morna D.*).

8310 **Rastoin, Marc** Tarse et Jérusalem: la double culture de l'Apôtre Paul en Galates 3,6-4,7. AnBib 152: 2003 ⇒19,7762. RRHPhR 85 (2005) 461-3 (*Grappe, Ch.*); RTL 36 (2005) 92-96 (*Lémonon, Jean-Pierre*); RivBib 53 (2005) 496-502 (*Pitta, Antonio*); ATG 68 (2005) 324-325 (*Rodríguez Carmona, A.*); RBLit (2005)* (*Witetschek, Stephan*).

8311 *Dunn, James D.G.* Works of the law and the curse of the law (Galatians 3.10-14). New perspective. WUNT 185: 2005 <1985> ⇒7638. 111-130.

8312 *Hahn, Scott W.* Covenant, oath, and the Aqedah: διαθήκη in Galatians 3:15-18. CBQ 67 (2005) 79-100.

8313 *Fee, Gordon D.* Male and female in the new creation: Galatians 3:26-29. Discovering biblical equality. 2005 ⇒387. 172-185.

8314 *Heidebrecht, D.* Distinction and function in the church: reading Galatians 3:28 in context. Direction 34 (2005) 181-193 [NTAb 50,309].

8315 *Moxnes, Halvor* A response: reading Paul in a frontier context: moral criticism and Paul's picture of 'gentiles'. Early patristic readings. 2005 ⇒393. 34-41 [⇒8001] [Gal 3,28].

8316 *Aguilar Chiu, José Enrique* Gál 3,29: descendencia de Abraham y herederos según la promesa. Qol 37 (2005) 83-101.

8317 *Beltrán Flores, Agustin* Análisis de Gál 4,1-7: elaboración de un método exegético pastoral. Qol 41 (2005) 83-116.

8318 **Santos, Nilson Faria dos** Adoção filial e plenitude do tempo/plenitude dos tempos: estudo exegético-teológico de Gl 4,1-7 e Ef 1,3-10. Rio de Janeiro 2005, n.p. 2 vols. Bibl. 288-307.

8319 *Vidović, Marinko* 'Pujnina vremena' (Gal 4,4)—iskaz prisutnosti eshatona u povijesti (1.) ['The fullness of time' (Gal 4,4)—the enunciation of the eschaton's presence in history]. Crkva u svijetu 40/1 (2005) 7-28. **Croatian**.

8320 **Ossa, Leonor** Das obere Jerusalem ist eine Freie: Demokratie und Urbanität im Galater-Brief. Ment. *Philo Alexandrinus*: EHS.T 783: Fra 2004, Lang 156 pp. 3-631-51854-4 [Gal 4,21].

8321 *Gignac, Alain* Lorsque Paul "raconte" Abraham, Agar et l'autre femme: narrativité et intertextualité en Ga 4,21-5,1. Analyse narrative. BEThL 191: 2005 ⇒742. 463-480.

8322 *Willitts, Joel* Isa 54,1 in Gal 4,24b-27: reading Genesis in light of Isaiah. ZNW 96 (2005) 188-210.

8323 **Schewe, Susanne** Die Galater zurückgewinnen: paulinische Strategien in Galater 5 und 6. [D]*Taeger, Jens-W.*: FRLANT 208: Gö 2005, Vandenhoeck & R. 215 pp. €62. 3-525-53072-2. Diss. Münster; Bibl. 203-215.

8324 *Dunn, James D.G.* 'Neither circumcision nor uncircumcision, but ...' (Gal. 5.1-12; 6.12-16; cf. 1 Cor. 7,17-20). New perspective. WUNT 185: 2005 <1996> ⇒7638. 307-331.

8325 **Wilson, Todd A.** The leading of the Spirit and the curse of the law: reassessing Paul's response to the Galatian crisis. [D]*Stanton, Graham N.* 2005, Diss. Cambridge; Sum. TynB 57/1,157-160 [Gal 5,13-6,10].

8326 *Beale, G.K.* The Old Testament background of Paul's reference to 'the fruit of the Spirit' in Galatians 5:22. BBR 15 (2005) 1-38 [Isa 32; 57].

## G6.2 Ad Ephesios

8327 *Bolewski, Jacek* Mądrość i misterium *Listu do Efezjan* [The wisdom and the mystery of the letter to the Ephesians]. StBob 1 (2005) 15-35. **P.**

8328 *Díaz Rodelas, Juan Miguel* La espiritualidad de la carta a los Efesios. ResB 45 (2005) 47-55.

**Edwards, M.** Galatians, Ephesians, Philippians 2005 ⇒8262.

8329 *Foster, Paul* Insights into Ephesian christianity. ET 116 (2005) 412-414.

8330 *Gombis, G.T.* A radically new humanity: the function of the *Haustafel* in Ephesians. JETS 48 (2005) 317-330 [NTAb 50,75].

8331 **Gombis, Timothy G.** The triumph of God in Christ: divine warfare in the argument of Ephesians. [D]*Longenecker, Bruce W.* 2005, Diss. St. Andrews [TynB 56,157-160].

8332 **Hayford, Jack W.; Seemuth, David P.** Ephesians & Colossians. Nv 2005, Nelson xii; 231 pp. 0-7852-4943-5.

8333 **Hoehner, Harold W.** Ephesians: an exegetical commentary. 2002 ⇒ 18,7349; 20,7804. [R]SBET 23 (2005) 236-237 (*Campbell, Iain D.*).

8334 **Kohlgraf, Peter** Die Ekklesiologie des Epheserbriefes in der Auslegung durch Johannes CHRYSOSTOMUS: eine Untersuchung zur Wirkungsgeschichte paulinischer Theologie. Hereditas 19: 2001 ⇒17, 6850... 19,7792. [R]ZKG 116 (2005) 95-96 (*Bracht, Katharina*).

8335 *Lémonon, Jean-Pierre* Les christianismes à Éphèse au Ier siècle. Les Actes des Apôtres. LeDiv 199: 2005 ⇒715. 85-119.

8336 *Manicardi, Ermenegildo* Teologia della creazione nella lettera agli Efesini. Gesù la cristologia. 2005 <2002> ⇒253. 329-359.

8337 **Martin, Aldo** La tipologia adamica nella lettera agli Efesini. [D]*Aletti, Jean-Noël*: AnBib 159: R 2005, E.P.I.B. 408 pp. €25. 88-7653-159-9. Diss. Pont. Ist. Biblico; Bibl. 357-378.

8338 *Muddiman, John* The church in Ephesians, *2 Clement*, and the *Shepherd of Hermas*. Trajectories. 2005 ⇒753. 107-121.

8339 **Muddiman, John** The epistle to the Ephesians. Black's NT commentaries: 2001 ⇒17,6842... 20,7810. [R]RB 112 (2005) 436-441 (*Murphy-O'Connor, Jerome*);

8340 2004 ⇒20,7810. [R]RBLit (2005)* (*Gombis, Timothy*).

8341 *Otero Lázaro, Tomás* La relación entre Colosenses y Efesios. ResB 45 (2005) 15-24.

8342 *Perkins, Pheme* The letter to the Ephesians. NT survey. 2005 ⇒ 3144. 217-231.

8343 *Ramírez Fueyo, Francisco* Claves para una relectura actual de la teología de Efesios. ResB 45 (2005) 37-46.

8344 **Ravasi, Gianfranco** L'altro nella scrittura: Paolo agli Efesini (2,19). Conversazioni bibliche: 2003 ⇒19,262. [R]EfMex 67 (2005) 123-125 (*Landgrave G., Daniel R.*).

8345 *Redalié, Yann* L'epistola agli Efesini oggi. Ethik als angewandte Ekklesiologie. SMBen.BE 17: 2005 ⇒498. 211-227.

8346 *Riches, John* Ephesians. Global bible commentary. 2005 ⇒2443. 473-481.

8347 **Schwindt, Rainer** Das Weltbild des Epheserbriefes: eine religionsgeschichtlich-exegetische Studie. WUNT 2/148: 2002 ⇒18,7366... 20,7812. [R]ThLZ 130 (2005) 165-167 (*Heckel, Theo K.*).

8348 *Tosaus Abadía, José Pedro* La carta a los Efesios ante la crítica. ResB 45 (2005) 4-14.

8349 **Van Kooten, George H.** Cosmic christology in Paul and the Pauline school: Colossians and Ephesians in the context of Graeco-Roman cosmology. WUNT 2/171: 2003 ⇒19,7809. [R]ThLZ 130 (2005) 652-654 (*Du Toit, David*); RSR 93 (2005) 398-399 (*Aletti, Jean-Noël*); Bib. 86 (2005) 441-445 (*Bockmuehl, Markus*).

8350 **Van Leeuwen, J.H.** Brief uit de kerker: verklaring van de brief van de heilige apostel Paulus aan de christenen van Efeze. Tegelen 2005, St. Petrus Canisiusstichting 258 pp. €19. 90-7439545-7.

8351 *Wolter, Michael* Der Epheserbrief als nachpaulinischer Paulusbrief: Zusammenfassung. Ethik als angewandte Ekklesiologie. SMBen.BE 17: 2005 ⇒498. 189-210.

[E]**Wolter, M.** Ethik...der Brief an die Epheser 2005 ⇒498.

8352 **Yee, Tet-Lim N.** Jews, gentiles and ethnic reconciliation: Paul's Jewish identity and Ephesians. [D]*Dunn, James D.G.*: MSSNTS 130: C 2005, CUP xxi; 302 pp. $75. 0-521-83831-2. Diss. Durham; Bibl. 229-260.

8353 *Zanetti, Paolo S.* Sul commento all'*Epistola agli Efesini* di Heinrich Schlier. Imitatori di Gesù Cristo. 2005 <1967> ⇒330. 257-266.

8354 *Saltarelli, Maria* La "Lettera agli Efesini" al capitolo 1: un esempio scritturistico di teologia mistagogica. DT(P) 108/41 (2005) 118-134.

8355 *Karakolis, Christos* 'A mystery hidden to be revealed?': philological and theological correlations betwen Eph 3 and 1. Ethik als angewandte Ekklesiologie. SMBen.BE 17: 2005 ⇒498. 65-108.

8356 *Tosaus Abadía, José Pedro* El himno de Ef 1,3-14. ResB 45 (2005) 25-36.

8357 *Lambrecht, Jan* Efeziërs 1,7-10 in De Nieuwe Bijbelvertaling. AcTh (B) 25/2 (2005) 196-200.

8358 *Bieringer, Reimund* '...was die Welt im Innersten zusammenhält': eine exegetische Untersuchung zu ἀνακεφαλαιώσασθαι in Eph 1,10;

8359 *Quesnel, Michel* Valoriser ses destinataires: Ephésiens 2. Ethik als angewandte Ekklesiologie. SMBen.BE 17: 2005 ⇒498. 3-35/37-64.

8360 *Borrell, Agustí* 'Ja no sou estrangers no forasters': la simbologia del temple en Ef 2,11-22. La bíblia i els immigrants. 2005 ⇒471. 169-183.

8361 *Pauw, A.P.* Theological meditations on Ephesians 2:11.22. ThTo 62/1 (2005) 78-83 [NTAb 51,73].

8362 *Melbourne, B.L.* Ephesians 2:13-16: are the barriers still broken down?. JRT 58/1-2 (2005) 107-119 [NTAb 50,517].

8363 *Kreitzer, Larry J.* The messianic man of peace as temple builder: Solomonic imagery in Ephesians 2.13-22. Temple and worship. LHBOTS 422: 2005 ⇒731. 484-512.

8364 *Joosten, Jan* Christ a-t-il aboli la loi pour réconcilier juifs et païens?. ETR 80 (2005) 95-102 [Eph 2,15].

8365 *Bartolomé, Juan José* 'Que Cristo habite en vuestros corazones por medio de la fe' (Ef 3,17): la oración de un apóstol por su comunidad. EstB 63 (2005) 559-574.

8366 *Byrskog, Samuel* Ephesians 4:1-16—paraenesis and identity formation. Ethik als angewandte Ekklesiologie. 2005 ⇒498. 109-138.

8367 *Scholtus, Silvia C.* Crecimiento en Cristo: una introducción a la eclesiología de la epístola a los Efesios. DavarLogos 4/2 (2005) 181-195 [Eph 4,1-16].

8368 *Käsemann, Ernst* Befreiung der Gefangenen (Epheser 4,7-10). In der Nachfolge. 2005 ⇒236. 270-275.

8369 *Gombis, Timothy G.* Cosmic lordship and divine gift-giving: Psalm 68 in Ephesians 4:8. NT 47 (2005) 367-380.

8370 *Page, Sydney H.T.* Whose ministry?: a re-appraisal of Ephesians 4:12. NT 47 (2005) 26-46.

8371 *Nortjé-Meyer, L.* Qestioning the 'perfect male body': a critical reading of Ephesians 4:13. Scriptura 90 (2005) 731-739 [NTAb 51,301].

8372 *Hoppe, Rudolf* Ekklesiologie und Paränese im Epheserbrief (Eph 4,17-5,20). Ethik als angewandte Ekklesiologie. SMBen.BE 17: 2005 ⇒498. 139-162.

8373 *Walden, Wayne* Translating Ephesians 5:21. RestQ 47/3 (2005) 179-182.

8374 *Hooker, Morna D.* 'Submit to one another': the transformation of relationships in Christ (Eph 5:21-6:9). Ethik als angewandte Ekklesiologie. SMBen.BE 17: 2005, 163-188.

8375 *Marshall, I. Howard* Mutual love and submission in marriage: Colossians 3:18-19 and Ephesians 5:21-33. Discovering biblical equality. 2005 ⇒387. 186-204.

8376 *Pénicaud, Anne* Éphésiens 5,21-33: asservissement ou libération?: proposition de lecture sémiotique. FGENEST, O. 2005 ⇒46. 267-295.

8377 *Sumner, S.* Bridging the Ephesians 5 divide. ChrTo 49/11 (2005) 59-61 [NTAb 50,311] [Eph 5,22-33].

8378 *Reinhard, D.R.* Ephesians 6:10-18: a call to personal piety or another way of describing union with Christ?. JETS 48 (2005) 521-532 [NTAb 50,311].

8379 *McVay, John K.* "Our struggle": "ecclesia militans" in Ephesians 6: 10-20. AUSS 43 (2005) 91-100.

### G6.3 Ad Philippenses

8380 **Aletti, Jean-Noël** Saint Paul épître aux Philippiens. EtB 55: P 2005, Gabalda vii; 359 pp. €65. 2-85021-171-0. Bibl. 331-357.

8381 **Bittasi, Stefano** Gli esempi necessari per discernere: il significato argomentativo della struttura della lettera di Paolo ai Filippesi. AnBib 153: 2003 ⇒19,7826; 20,7825. [R]ATG 68 (2005) 303-304 (*Rodríguez Carmona, A.*).

8382 **Edart, Jean-Baptiste** L'Épître aux Philippiens, rhétorique et composition stylistique. ÉtB 45: 2002 ⇒18,7385; 19,7827. [R]RSR 93 (2005) 390-394 (*Aletti, Jean-Noël*).

**Edwards, M.** Galatians, Ephesians, Philippians 2005 ⇒8262.

8383 **Fee, Gordon D.** Comentario de la epístola a los Filipenses. Col. Teológica Contemporánea 19: Barc 2004, Clie 594 pp.

8384 **Fowl, Stephen E.** Philippians. Two Horizons NT Comm.: GR 2005, Eerdmans x; 254 pp. $20. 0-8028-2551-6. Bibl. 236-243.

8385 *Franco, Ettore* Ciò che vale di più: una lettura di Filippesi originale e coinvolgente. RdT 46 (2005) 133-140.

8386 *Hooker, Morna D.* The letter to the Philippians. NT survey. 2005 ⇒ 3144. 232-237.

8387 *Marchal, Joseph A.* Mutuality rhetorics and feminist interpretation: examining Philippians and arguing for our lives. BiCT 1/3 (2005)*.

8388 *Oakes, Peter* Leadership and suffering in the letters of POLYCARP and Paul to the Philippians. Trajectories. 2005 ⇒753. 353-373.

8389 **Oakes, Peter** Philippians: from people to letter. MSSNTS 110: 2001 ⇒17,6871... 19,7832. [R]BTB 35 (2005) 151 (*Ascough, Richard S.*).

8390 **Reymond, Sophie** Connaissance du Christ et élan de la foi: la course spirituelle dans l'épître aux Philippiens. ConBib 39: Bru 2005, Lumen V. 80 pp. €9.

8391 *Richards, William* Reading Philippians: strategies for unfolding a story. SR 34 (2005) 69-79.

8392 **Silva, Moisés** Philippians. Baker Exegetical Comm. on NT: GR [2]2005 <1988>, Baker 213 pp.

8393 **Smith, James A.** Marks of an apostle: deconstruction, Philippians, and problematizing Pauline theology. SBL.Semeia Studies 53: Atlanta, GA 2005, SBL xiii; 185 pp. 1-58983-172-1. Bibl. 159-173.

8394 *Theobald, Michael* Paulus und POLYKARP an die Philipper: Schlaglichter auf die frühe Rezeption des Basissatzes von der Rechtfertigung. Lutherische und neue Paulusperspektive. WUNT 182: 2005 ⇒ 339. 349-388.

8395 **Thurston, Bonnie Bowman; Ryan, Judith M.** Philippians and Philemon. Sacra Pagina 10; ColMn 2005, Liturgical xiv; 290 pp. $40. 0-8146-58202. Bibl. 39-43, 198-207 [R]RBLit (2005)* (*Nicklas, Tobias*).

8396 **Ware, James Patrick** The mission of the church in Paul's letter to the Philippians in the context of ancient Judaism. NT.S 120: Lei 2005, Brill xv; 380 pp. 90-04-14641-5. Bibl. 293-335.

8397 *Williams, Demetrius K.* Philippians. Global bible commentary. 2005 ⇒2443. 482-489.

8398 *Marchal, Joseph A.* Military images in Philippians 1-2: a feminist analysis of the rhetorics of scholarship, Philippians, and current contexts. Her master's tools?. 2005 ⇒493. 265-286.

8399 *Rham, Raymond de* Philippiens 1,12-26: pour moi, vivre c'est Christ, et mourir c'est un gain. LeD 63 (2005) 28-35.

8400 *Snyman, A.H.* A rhetorical analysis of Philippians 1:27-2:18. VeE 26 (2005) 783-809.

8401 **Williams, Demetrius** Enemies of the cross of Christ: a rhetorical analysis of the terminology of the cross and conflict in Philippians. JSNT.S 223: 2002 ⇒18,7397. [R]NT 47 (2005) 88-91 (*Doble, Peter*) [Phil 2-3].

8402 *Asaju, D.F.* Philippians 2:5-11: an African reading of Paul's christological hymn of exaltation. BTF 37/1 (2005) 198-207 [NTAb 50, 517].

8403 *Gundry, Robert H.* Style and substance in Philippians 2:6-11. The old is better. WUNT 178: 2005 ⇒220. 272-291.

8404 **Hellerman, Joseph H.** Reconstructing honor in Roman Philippi: Carmen Christi as cursus pudorum. MSSNTS 132: C 2005, CUP xii; 239 pp. £48/$80. 0-521-84909-8. Bibl. 214-225 [Phil 2,6-11].

8405 *Hurtado, Larry W.* A "case study" in early christian devotion to Jesus: Philippians 2:6-11. How on earth. 2005 ⇒227. 83-107.

8406 *Snyman, Andreas H.* Philippians 2:19-30 from a rhetorical perspective. APB 16 (2005) 289-307.

8407 **Jané i Coca, José M.** 'Ser hallado en él': la reciprocidad intersubjetiva entre Pablo y Cristo: un estudio exegético-teológico de Flp 3. [D]*Vanni, Ugo*: R 2005, 185 pp. Extr. Diss. Gregoriana; Bibl. 147-178.

8408 *Hoover, R.W.* Translating Paul's jargon: a pair of puzzles in Philippians. The Fourth R [Santa Rosa, CA] 18/1 (2005) 17-19 [NTAb 49, 528] [Phil 3,3-4; 3,9].

## G6.4 **Ad Colossenses**

8409 **Dübbers, Michael** Christologie und Existenz im Kolosserbrief: exegetische und semantische Untersuchungen zur Intention des Kolosserbriefes. WUNT 2/191: Tü 2005, Mohr S. xii; 377 pp. 3-16-14860-8-0. Bibl. 317-336.

**Hayford, J.** Ephesians & Colossians 2005 ⇒8332.

8410 *Johnson, J.F.* The apostolic tradition in Colossae: christology in action. ConJ 31/2 (2005) 127-131 [NTAb 49,528].

8411 **Leppä, Outi** The making of Colossians: a study on the formation and purpose of a Deutero-Pauline letter. SESJ 86: 2003 ⇒19,7864. [R]RBLit 7 (2005) 404-407 (*Sanders, E.P.*).

8412 *Lincoln, Andrew T.* The letter to the Colossians. NT survey. 2005 ⇒ 3144. 238-262.

8413 *MacDonald, Margaret Y.* Can Nympha rule this house?: the rhetoric of domesticity in Colossians. Rhetoric and reality. SCJud 16: 2005 ⇒ 515. 99-120.

8414 *Maier, Harry O.* A sly civility: Colossians and Empire. JSNT 27 (2005) 323-349.

8415 **Maisch, Ingrid** Der Brief an die Gemeinde in Kolossä. Theologischer Komm. zum NT 12: 2003 ⇒19,7866. [R]FrRu 12 (2005) 63-64 (*Scholtissek, Klaus*) ThLZ 130 (2005) 952-55 (*Lindemann, Andreas*).

8416 *Okure, Teresa* Colossians. Global bible commentary. 2005 ⇒2443. 490-499.

8417 *Stettler, Christian* The opponents at Colossae. Paul and his opponents. Pauline studies 2: 2005 ⇒469. 169-200.

8418 **Thompson, Marianne Meye** Colossians and Philemon. Two Horizons NT Comm.: GR 2005, Eerdmans x; 287 pp. $20. 0-8028-2715-2. Bibl. 267-273.

**Van Kooten, G.** Cosmic christology...Col. and Eph. 2003 ⇒8349.

8419 **Walsh, Brian J.; Keesmaat, Sylvia C.** Colossians remixed: subverting the empire. 2004 ⇒20,7852. [R]SdT 17 (2005) 194-195 (*Lazisi, Pier Paolo*); TJT 21 (2005) 280-281 (*Black, Steve D.*).

8420 **Wilson, Robert M.** A critical and exegetical commentary on Colossians and Philemon. L 2005, Clark xxxvi; 380 pp. $100. 0-567-0447-1-8. Bibl. xviii-xxxvi.

8421 *Hepner, M.* Waiting table in God's household: a personal theology of ministry. AThJ 37 (2005) 51-64 [NTAb 50,311] [Col 1].

8422 *Gruber, Margareta* Zwischen Bilderverbot und "Vera Icon" oder: wie viel Bild ist von Christus erlaubt?. LebZeug 60 (2005) 100-115 [Col 1,15-20].

8423 *Romanello, Stefano Col* 1,15-20: la posta in gioco di una cristologia singolarmente pregnante. Teol(Br) 30 (2005) 13-48.

8424 *Trainor, Michael* The cosmic christology of Colossians 1:15-20 in the light of contemporary ecological issues. ABR 53 (2005) 54-69.

8425 *Luttenberger, Joram* Der gekreuzigte Schuldschein: ein Aspekt der Deutung des Todes Jesu im Kolosserbrief. NTS 51 (2005) 80-95 [Col 2,14].

8426 *Maier, Harry O.* Barbarians, Scythians and imperial iconography in the epistle to the Colossians. Picturing the New Testament. WUNT 2/193: 2005 ⇒396. 385-406 [Col 3,11].

8427 *Müller-Gerbes, Geert* "... und ertrage einer den anderen" (Kolosser 3, 12-15). Kanzelreden. 2005 ⇒376. 139-144.

### G6.6 Ad Thessalonicenses

8428 **Brocke, Christoph vom** Thessaloniki—Stadt des Kassander und Gemeinde des Paulus: eine frühe christliche Gemeinde in ihrer heidnischen Umwelt. WUNT 2/125: 2001 ⇒17,6903... 19,7894. [R]ThRv 101 (2005) 34-36 (*Witulski, Thomas*).

8429 [E]**Donfried, Karl P.; Beutler, Johannes** The Thessalonians debate: methodological discord or methodological synthesis?. 2000 ⇒16,255 ... 19,7895. [R]STV 43 (2005) 201-207 (*Kręcidło, Janusz*).

8430 **Donfried, Karl Paul** Paul, Thessalonica, and early christianity. 2002 ⇒18,7427... 20,7864. [R]BS 162 (2005) 502-503 (*Fantin, Joseph D.*); RBLit 7 (2005) 400-404 (*Peerbolte, Bert J.L.*).

8431 *Gundry, Robert* The hellenization of dominical tradition and christianization of Jewish tradition in the eschatology of 1-2 Thessalonians. The old is better. WUNT 178: 2005 ⇒220. 292-314.

8432 **Jones, Ivor H.** The epistles to the Thessalonians. L 2005, Epworth xxxix; 130 pp. 0-7162-0595-5. Bibl. 125-130.

8433 **Malherbe, Abraham J.** The letters to the Thessalonians. AncB 32 B: 2000 ⇒16,7006... 20,7860. [R]RivBib 53 (2005) 243-245 (*Fabris, Rinaldo*).

8434 **Nicholl, Colin R.** From hope to despair in Thessalonica: situating 1 and 2 Thessalonians. MSSNTS 126: 2004 ⇒20,7861. [R]SNTU 30 (2005) 239-241 (*Giesen, Heinz*); JR 85 (2005) 654-656 (*Mitchell, Alan C.*).

8435 **Phillips, John** Exploring 1 and 2 Thessalonians. GR 2005, Kregel 233 pp.

8436 *Roose, Hanna* Polyvalenz durch Intertextualität im Spiegel der aktuellen Forschung zu den Thessalonicherbriefen. NTS 51 (2005) 250-269.

8437 *Bonneau, Normand* Explorations du fait narratif et son effet théologique dans 1 Thessaloniciens. Analyse narrative. BEThL 191: 2005 ⇒742. 437-448.

8438 **Burke, Trevor J.** Family matters: a socio-historical study of kinship metaphors in 1 Thessalonians. JSNT.S 247: 2003 ⇒19,7903. [R]TS 66 (2005) 447-449 (*Donfried, Karl Paul*).

8439 *Carson, M.* For now we live: a study of Paul's pastoral leadership in 1 Thessalonians. Themelios 30/3 (2005) 23-41 [NTAb 50,76].

8440 **Manini, Filippo** L'itinerario dei credenti nella prima Lettera ai Tessalonicesi: la composizione della lettera. [D]*Aletti, Jean-Noël*: Sussidi biblici 89: Reggio Emilia 2005, San Lorenzo 144 pp. 88-8071-167-9. Estr. Diss. Pont. Ist. Biblico; Bibl. 111-131.

8441 *Müller, Paul-Gerhard* Entschränkung des Judentums im 1. Tessalonicherbrief [sic]. [F]STENDEBACH, F. 2005 ⇒141. 107-127.

8442 **Paddison, Angus** Theological hermeneutics and 1 Thessalonians. Ment. *Aquinas*: MSSNTS 133: C 2005, CUP xvi; 230 pp. $80. 0-52-1-84983-7. Bibl. 197-222.

8443 **Parmentier, Roger** L'épître de Jacques et la première épître de Paul aux Thessaloniciens actualisées. P 2005, L'Harmattan 41 pp. €8. 978-22960-00018.

8444 *Roure, Damià* Elecció i identitat cristiana en la primera carta als Tessalonicencs. RCatT 30/1 (2005) 37-47.

8445 *Smith, Abraham* The first letter to the Thessalonians. NT survey. 2005 ⇒3144. 263-271.

8446 *Villiers, Pieter G.R. de* Safe in the family of God: soteriological perspectives in 1 Thessalonians. Salvation in the New Testament. NT.S 121: 2005 ⇒798. 305-330.

8447 *Yeo, Khiok-khng* 1 Thessalonians. Global bible commentary. 2005 ⇒2443. 500-503.

8448 *Kim, Seyoon* Paul's entry (εἴσοδος) and the Thessalonians' faith (1 Thessalonians 1-3). NTS 51 (2005) 519-542.

8449 *Blumenthal, Christian* Was sagt 1 Thess 1.9b-10 über die Adressaten des 1 Thess?: literarische und historische Erwägungen. NTS 51 (2005) 96-105.

8450 *Burchard, Christoph* Satzbau und Übersetzung von 1Thess 1,10. ZNW 96 (2005) 272-273.

8451 *Varickasseril, Jose* Establishing in the faith through personal presence: a study with special reference to 1 Thessalonians 3:1-13. MissTod 7 (2005) 362-369 [NTAb 50,76].

8452 *Hurd, John C.* 1 Thessalonians 3:11-13: the pivotal importance of prayer in the structure of Paul's letters. Arc 33 (2005) 257-280.

8453 **Córdova González, Eduardo** El mensaje escatológico de 1 Tes 4, 13-5,11 a partir de un análisis histórico-critico, retórico y sociológico. 2005, Diss. México [RTL 37,614].

8454 *Seitz, Manfred* Die Grundhaltung des Mönchtums: "Betet ohne Unterlass!" (1. Thessalonicher 5,17): ein Beitrag zur Wirkungsgeschichte. ThBeitr 36 (2005) 80-91.

8455 **Ernst, Michael** Distanzierte Unpersönlichkeit: Analyse von Sprache und Stil des Zweiten Thessalonicherbriefes im Vergleich mit paulinischen Texten. Salzburg 1998, Institut für Neutestamentliche Bibelwissenschaft 181 pp. 3-901636-04-8.

8456 *Smith, Abraham* The second letter to the Thessalonians. NT survey. 2005 ⇒3144. 272-273.

8457 *Yeo, Khiok-khng* 2 Thessalonians. Global bible commentary. 2005 ⇒ 2443. 504-507.

8458 *Van Kooten, George H.* 'Wrath will drip in the plains of Macedonia': expectations of NERO's return in the Egyptian Sibylline Oracles (book 5), 2 Thessalonians, and ancient historical writings. [F]LUTTIKHUIZEN, G.: AGJU 59: 2005 ⇒93. 177-215 [2 Thess 2].

8459 **Metzger, Paul** Katechon: II Thess 2,1-12 im Horizont apokalyptischen Denkens. [D]*Böcher, Otto*: BZNW 135: B 2005, De Gruyter xi; 368 pp. €98. 3-11-018460-5. Diss. Mainz; Bibl. 297-343. [R]EstAg 40 (2005) 587-588 (*Cineira, D.A.*).

8460 *Harris, G.H.* Does God deceive?: the 'deluding influence' of Second Thessalonians 2:11. MastJ 16/1 (2005) 73-93 [NTAb 50,77].

## G7.0 Epistulae pastorales

8461 *Aageson, James* The Pastoral Epistles and the Acts of Paul: a multiplex approach to authority in Paul's legacy. LexTQ 40 (2005) 237-248.

8462 *Betz, Monika* Die "Einehe" der Pastoralbriefe im Spiegel frühkaiserzeitlicher Ehemoral. [F]LAUB, F.: Bibel-Schule-Leben 6: 2005 ⇒87. 151-164;

8463 *Betz, Monika* Thekla und die jüngeren Witwen der Pastoralbriefe: ein Beispiel für die Situationsgebundenheit paulinischer Tradition. AnStR 6 (2005) 335-356.

8464 *Bjelland Kartzow, Marianne* Female gossipers and their reputation in the pastoral epistles. Neotest. 39/2 (2005) 255-272 [1 Tim 5].

8465 **Collins, Raymond F.** 1 & 2 Timothy and Titus: a commentary. The New Testament Library: 2002 ⇒18,7457... 20,7878. [R]Interp. 59 (2005) 74, 76 (*Krause, Deborah*); BS 162 (2005) 247-249 (*Waters, Larry J.*); RBLit 7 (2005) 392-394 (*Arichea, Daniel C., Jr.*).

8466 *Cothenet, Édouard* Les ministères dans les pastorales. [F]RIES, J. 2005 ⇒127. 189-201.

8467 *Downs, David J.* "Early catholicism" and apocalypticism in the Pastoral Epistles. CBQ 67 (2005) 641-661.

8468 *Dunn, James D.G.* The first and second letters to Timothy and the letter to Titus. NT survey. 2005 ⇒3144. 274-282.

8469 *Fatum, Lone* Christ domesticated: the household theology of the Pastorals as political strategy. The formation of the early church. WUNT 183: 2005 ⇒708. 175-207.

8470 *Häfner, Gerd* Schriftauslegung und "gesunde Lehre" in den Pastoralbriefen: von der Problematik eines spannungsfreien Verhältnisses. Die Bedeutung. QD 215: 2005 ⇒363. 171-198 [2 Tim 3,15-16].

8471 **Häfner, Gerd** "Nützlich zur Belehrung" (2 Tim 3,16): die Rolle der Schrift in den Pastoralbriefen im Rahmen der Paulusrezeption. Herders Biblische Studien 25: 2000 ⇒16,7055; 18,7460. [R]ThLZ 130 (2005) 389-391 (*Herzer, Jens*).

8472 **Iovino, Paolo** Lettere a Timoteo; lettera a Tito. I libri biblici, NT 15: Mi 2005, Paoline 307 pp. €28. 88-315-2907-2. Bibl. 282-289.

8473 **Kincannon, Karla** God's commitment our response. Great Themes of the Bible: Nv 2005, Abingdon 92 pp.

8474 *Malherbe, Abraham J.* "Christ Jesus came into the world to save sinners": soteriology in the Pastoral Epistles. Salvation in the New Testament. NT.S 121: 2005 ⇒798. 331-358.

8475 **Merz, Annette** Die fiktive Selbstauslegung des Paulus: intertextuelle Studien zur Intention und Rezeption der Pastoralbriefe. NTOA 52; StUNT 52: 2004 ⇒20,7887. [R]ThLZ 130 (2005) 509-511 (*Janßen, Martina*); BiLi 78 (2005) 276-277 (*Nicklas, Tobias*); RBLit 7 (2005) 407-411 (*Sturcke, Henry*).

8476 *Penna, Romano* La funzione ecclesiale dell'episkopos nel Nuovo Testamento (Lettere Pastorali). Lat. 71/2-3 (2005) 299-309.

8477 **Pietersen, Lloyd K.** The polemic of the pastorals: a sociological examination of the development of Pauline christianity. JSNT.S 264: 2004 ⇒20,7890. [R]RBLit (2005)* (*Downs, David*); JThS 56 (2005) 594-596 (*Marshall, I. Howard*).

8478 *Polaski, Sandra H.* "Let no one despise your youth": the deconstruction of traditional authority in the Pastoral Epistles. LexTQ 40 (2005) 249-263.

8479 **Richards, William A.** Difference and distance in post-Pauline christianity: an epistolary analysis of the Pastorals. Studies in Biblical Literature 44: 2002 ⇒18,7466; 19,7933. [R]TJT 21 (2005) 267-268 (*LaFosse, Mona Tokarek*).

8480 **Stepp, Perry Leon** Leadership succession in the world of the Pauline circle. NTMon 5: Shf 2005, Phoenix xvi; 227 pp. $85/£50. 1-905-04-810-6. Bibl. 208-217.

8481 *Towner, Philip* Christology in the letters to Timothy and Titus. Contours of christology. McMaster NT Studies 7: 2005 ⇒775. 219-244.

8482 **Van Neste, Ray** Cohesion and structure in the Pastoral Epistles. JSNT.S 280: L 2005, Clark xii; 354 pp. 0-567-08337-3. Bibl. 316-346 [R]RBLit (2005)* (*Hutson, Christopher; Nicklas, Tobias*).

8483 *Weiser, Alfons* Die heiligen Schriften Israels und die Pastoralbriefe: einige Aspekte der neueren Forschung. [F]STENDEBACH, F. 2005 ⇒ 141. 149-162.

## G7.2 1-2 ad Timotheum, ad Titum

8484 **Barcley, William Bayless** A study commentary on 1 and 2 Timothy. Webster, NY 2005, Evangelical 315 pp. $30.

8485 **Johnson, Luke Timothy** The First and Second Letters to Timothy. AncB 35A: 2001 ⇒17,6948... 20,7896. [R]RExp 102 (2005) 155-156 (*Skinner, Christopher W.*).

8486 *Neyrey, Jerome H.* "First", "only", "one of a few", and "no one else": the rhetoric of uniqueness and the doxologies in 1 Timothy. Bib. 86 (2005) 59-87.
8487 *Tamez, Elsa* 1 Timothy. Global bible commentary. 2005 ⇒2443. 508-515.
8488 **Támez, Elsa** Luchas de poder en los orígenes del cristianismo: un estudio de la primera carta a Timoteo. Presencia teológica 141: Sdr 2005, Sal Terrae 206 pp. 84-293-1605-1.
8489 *Nadar, S.* Paradigm shifts in mission: from an ethic of domination to an ethic of justice and love: the case of 1 Tim 2:8-15. Missionalia 33/2 (2005) 303-314 [NTAb 50,313].
8490 *Jacobs, M.M.* On 1 Timothy 2:9-15: why still interpret 'irredeemable' biblical texts?. Scriptura 88 (2005) 85-100 [NTAb 50,77].
8491 [E]**Köstenberger, Andreas J.; Schreiner, Thomas R.** Women in the church: a fresh analysis of 1 Timothy 2:9-15. GR [2]2005 <1995>, Baker 287 pp. $22. 0-8010-2904X.
8492 *Belleville, Linda L.* Teaching and usurping authority: 1 Timothy 2: 11-15. Discovering biblical equality. 2005 ⇒387. 205-223.
8493 *Owens, Mark D.* Should churches ordain the divorced and remarried?: an examination of μιᾶς γυναικὸς ἀνήρ in the Pastoral Epistles. Faith & Mission 22/3 (2005) 42-50 [1 Tim 3,2].
8494 *Dehandschutter, Boudewijn* The history-of-religions background of 1 Timothy 4:4: 'Everything that God has created is good'. Creation of heaven and earth. 2005 ⇒492. 211-221.
8495 *Elengabeka, Elvis* Une médiation pastorale entre le livre et la communauté: l'anagnôsis en 1 Tm 4,13. RevSR 79 (2005) 117-126.

8496 *Arichea, Daniel C., Jr.* 2 Timothy and Titus. Global bible commentary. 2005 ⇒2443. 516-521.
8497 *Dalrymple, R.* A preaching strategy for 2nd Timothy. Ministry [Franklin, TN] 10/1 (2005) 55-62 [NTAb 51,304].
8498 *Mourlam, Claude* 2 Timothée 4,1-8: demain, petit-fils d'hier. LeD 64 (2005) 34-44.
8499 **Smith, Craig A.** A study of 2 Timothy 4:1-8: the contribution of epistolary analysis and rhetorical criticism. [D]*Nolland, John* 2005, Diss. Bristol; Sum. TynB 57/1,151-154.

8500 [E]**Bucchi, Federica** S. HIERONYMI Presbyeri: Commentarii in epistulas Pauli Apostoli ad Titum et ad Philemonem. CChr.SL 77C, Pars I, Opera exegetica; S. Hieronymi Presbyteri Opera 1.8: 2003 ⇒19, 14754. [R]JThS 56 (2005) 682-684 (*Winterbottom, Michael*).
8501 *Grubbs, Norris C.* The truth about elders and their children: believing or behaving in Titus 1:6?. Faith & Mission 22/2 (2005) 3-15.
8502 *Faber, Riemer* "Evil beasts, lazy gluttons": a neglected theme in the epistle to Titus. WThJ 67 (2005) 135-145 [Titus 1,10-16].

## G7.3 Ad Philemonem

8503 *Adamczewski, Bartosz* Współczesne kierunki badań nad listem do Filemona [Contemporary trends in the research of the letter to Philemon]. RBL 58 (2005) 45-55. **P**.

8504 **Artz-Grabner, Peter** Philemon. PKNT 1: 2003 ⇒19,7946; 20,7915. [R]ThLZ 130 (2005) 160-162 (*Chapa, Juan*).

[E]**Bucchi, F**. S. HIERONYMI Comm. in...Philemonem 2003 ⇒8500.

8505 *Buchhold, Jacques* Paul et l'esclavage. ThEv(VS) 4/2 (2005) 29-38.

8506 *Caballero, Juan Luis* Retórica y teología: la carta a Filemón. ScrTh 37 (2005) 441-474.

8507 *Felder, Cain H.* The letter to Philemon. NT survey. 2005 ⇒3144. 283-286.

8508 *Kim, Jean* Philemon. Global bible commentary. 2005 ⇒2443. 522-526.

8509 **Kumitz, Christopher** Der Brief als Medium der ἀγάπη: eine Untersuchung zur rhetorischen und epistolographischen Gestalt des Philemonbriefes. EHS.T 787: Fra 2004, Lang 255 pp. 3-631-52504-4.

8510 *Lyons, Kirk D., Sr.* Paul's confrontation with class: the letter to Philemon as counter-hegemonic discourse. CrossCur 55 (2005) 322-339.

8511 *Pereira, Daniel S.* Além dos limites impostos pela cultura e pelos preconceitos: pistas para uma releitura da Carta a Filêmon, Apia e Arquipo na perspectiva das masculinidades. Estudos bíblicos 86 (2005) 37-41.

8512 *Still, Todd D.* Pauline theology and ancient slavery: does the former support or subvert the latter?. HBT 27/2 (2005) 21-34;

8513 Philemon among the letters of Paul: theological and canonical considerations. RestQ 47/3 (2005) 113-142 [NTAb 50,78].

**Thompson, M**. Colossians and Philemon 2005 ⇒8418.

**Thurston, B**. Philippians and Philemon 2005 ⇒8395.

8514 **Wengst, Klaus** Der Brief an Philemon. TKNT 16: Stu 2005, Kohlhammer 120 pp. €23. 3-17-018675-2.

**Wilson, R**. A critical...comm. on Col...Philemon 2005 ⇒8420.

8515 *Zmijewski, Josef* Der Philemonbrief: ein Plädoyer für die christliche Brüderlichkeit. TThZ 114 (2005) 222-242.

8516 *Bentoglio, Gabriele* Il ministero di Paolo in catene (Fm 9). RivBib 53 (2005) 173-189.

## G8 Epistula ad Hebraeos

8517 *Aitken, Ellen B.* Reading Hebrews in Flavian Rome. USQR 59/3-4 (2005) 82-85 [NTAb 50,314];

8518 Portraying the temple in stone and text: the arch of Titus and the epistle to the Hebrews. Hebrews. 2005 ⇒395. 131-148.

8519 *Backhaus, Knut* Auf Ehre und Gewissen!: die Ethik des Hebräerbriefes. Ausharren. SBS 204: 2005 ⇒412. 111-134;

8520 How to entertain angels: ethics in the epistle to the Hebrews. Hebrews. BiblInterp 75: 2005 ⇒395. 149-175.

8521 *Benjamin, David E.* Commentaries on Hebrews for pastors and teachers. RExp 102 (2005) 303-321.

8522 *Canoy, Robert W.* Insights for preaching and teaching Hebrews. RExp 102 (2005) 281-301.

8523 **Ciccarelli, Michele** La sofferenza di Cristo nell'epistola agli Ebrei: analisi di una duplice dimensione della sofferenza: soffrire-consoffrire con gli uomini e soffrire-offrire a Dio. [D]*Vanhoye, Albert*: 2005, Diss. Pont. Ist. Biblico [AcBib 11,213ss].

8524 *Craddock, Fred B.* The letter to the Hebrews. NT survey. 2005 ⇒ 3144. 287-296.

8525 **Crocetti, Giuseppe** La lettera agli Ebrei: meditazione e preghiera. Bibbia e spiritualità 23: Bo 2005, EDB 197 pp. 88-10-21116-2.

8526 *Deselaers, Paul; Sattler, Dorothea* Jesus hat 'die Himmel durchschritten' (Hebr 4,14): der christologisch-soteriologische Kontext der Rede vom Himmel im Hebräerbrief. JBTh 20 (2005) 293-312.

8527 *Dunning, Benjamin* The intersection of alien status and cultic discourse in the epistle to the Hebrews;

8528 *Eberhart, Christian A.* Characteristics of sacrificial metaphors in Hebrews. Hebrews. BiblInterp 75: 2005 ⇒395. 177-198/37-64.

8529 **Eisele, Wilfried** Ein unerschütterliches Reich: die mittelplatonische Umformung des Parusiegedankens im Hebräerbrief. Ment. *Philo; Plutarch; Seneca*: BZNW 116: 2003 ⇒19,723; 20,7938. [R]ThRv 101 (2005) 38-40 (*Backhaus, Knut*); BZ 49 (2005) 290-292 (*Karrer, Martin*); CBQ 67 (2005) 140-41 (*Schenck, Kenneth*); RBLit (2005)* (*Gray, C. Patrick*).

8530 *Eisenbaum, Pamela M.* Locating Hebrews within the literary landscape of christian origins. Hebrews. 2005 ⇒395. 213-237.

8531 **Gäbel, Georg** Wir haben einen Hohenpriester im Himmel: Untersuchungen zur Kulttheologie des Hebräerbriefes und ihren religionsgeschichtlichen Kontexten. [D]*Haacker, Klaus*: 2005, Diss. Wuppertal [ThLZ 131,343].

8532 *Gelardini, Gabriella* Introduction;

8533 Hebrews, an ancient synagogue homily for Tisha Be-Av: its function, its basis, its theological interpretation;

8534 *Georgi, Dieter* Hebrews and the heritage of Paul. Hebrews. 2005 ⇒ 395. 1-9/107-127/239-244.

8535 **Gray, Patrick** Godly fear: the epistle to Hebrews and Greco-Roman critiques of superstition. SBL.Academia Biblica 16: 2003 ⇒19,7965; 20,7940. [R]CBQ 67 (2005) 340-342 (*Mitchell, Alan C.*); ThLZ 130 (2005) 1190-1192 (*Karrer, Martin*); RBLit 7 (2005) 432-434 (*Bertone, John A.*).

8536 *Griffith, Sheila* The Epistle to the Hebrews in modern interpretation. RExp 102 (2005) 235-254.

8537 *Haber, Susan* From priestly torah to Christ cultus: the re-vision of covenant and cult in Hebrews. JSNT 28 (2005) 105-124.

8538 *Hagner, Donald A.* The Son of God as unique high priest: the christol‹ gy of the epistle to the Hebrews. Contours of christology. McMaster NT Studies 7: 2005 ⇒775. 247-267.

8539 **Hagner, Donald Alfred** Encountering the book of Hebrews: an exposition. Encountering biblical studies: 2002 ⇒18,7497; 20,7925. [R]HeyJ 46 (2005) 538-539 (*Hill, Robert C.*).

8540 *Hampson, P.* Persons and places in sacred spaces: a psychologist reads Hebrews. EpRe 32/3 (2005) 51-63 [NTAb 50,79].

8541 *Harmon, Steven R.* Hebrews in patristic perspective. RExp 102 (2005) 215-233.

8542 **Harrington, Daniel J.** What are they saying about the letter to the Hebrews?. Mahwah, NJ 2005, Paulist v; 96 pp. $13. 978-08091-432-07. Bibl.

8543 [E]**Heen, Erik M.; Krey, Philip D.W.** Hebrews. ACCS.NT 10: DG 2005, InterVarsity xxvi; 292 pp. €33. 0-8308-1495-7. Bibl. 267-280.

8544 **Jang, Seung-Ik** Das Gottesvolk im Hebräerbrief: ein Beitrag zur Theologie und Ekklesiologie des Hebräerbriefes. [D]*Lichtenberger, H.* 2005, Diss. Tübingen [ThLZ 131,342].

8545 *Just, A.A.* Entering holiness: christology and eucharist in Hebrews. CTQ 69/1 (2005) 75-95 [NTAb 51,305].

8546 *Kampling, Rainer* Sich dem Rätsel nähern: Fragen zu den Einleitungsfragen des Hebräerbriefes. Ausharren. 2005 ⇒412. 11-34.

8547 **Karrer, Martin** Der Brief an die Hebräer: Kapitel 1,1-5,10. ÖTBK 20/1: 2002 ⇒18,7498; 20,7927. [R]ThLZ 130 (2005) 394-396 (*März, Claus-Peter*); BZ 49 (2005) 146-148 (*Backhaus, Knut*).

8548 *Koester, Craig R.* Conversion, persecution, and malaise: life in th community for which Hebrews was written. HTSTS 61/1-2 (2005) 231-251 [NTAb 50,314];

8549 God's purposes and Christ's saving work according to Hebrews. Salvation in the New Testament. NT.S 121: 2005 ⇒798. 361-387.

8550 **Koester, Craig R.** Hebrews. AncB 36: 2001 ⇒17,6985... 20,7928. [R]ScC 133 (2005) 730-732 (*Manzi, Franco*); RivBib 53 (2005) 469-477 (*Manzi, Franco*).

8551 *Koosed, Jennifer L.; Seesengood, Robert P.* Constructions and collusions: the making and unmaking of identity in Qoheleth and Hebrews. Hebrews. BiblInterp 75: 2005 ⇒395. 265-280.

8552 **Lewicki, Tomasz** "Weist nicht ab den Sprechenden!": Wort Gottes und Paraklese im Hebräerbrief. PaThSt 41: 2004 ⇒20,7944. [R]SNTU 30 (2005) 242-243 (*Gmainer-Pranzl, Franz*).

8553 *Löhr, Hermut* Wahrnehmung und Bedeutung des Todes Jesu nach dem Hebräerbrief: ein Versuch. Deutungen. WUNT 181: 2005 ⇒ 392. 455-476;

8554 Reflections of rhetorical terminology in Hebrews. Hebrews. 2005 ⇒ 395. 199-210.

8555 *MacKnight, Edgar V.* Literary and rhetorical form and structure in the "Epistle to the Hebrews". RExp 102 (2005) 255-279.

[E]**Maggioni, B.** Le lettere di Paolo 2005 ⇒7687.

8556 *Manzi, Franco* 'Antiquum documentum novo cedat ritui': compimento cristologico del sacrificio dell'Antico Testamento. EL 119 (2005) 289-336.

8557 **Manzi, Franco** Carta a los hebreos. Comentarios a la Nueva Biblia de Jerusalén: Bilbao 2005, Desclée de B. 213 pp. 84-330-2010-2.

8558 **Marchaselli-Casale, Cesare** Lettera agli Ebrei: nuova versione, introduzione e commento. I libri biblici,.NT 16: Mi 2005, Paoline 832 pp. €38. 88-315-2741-X. Bibl. 770-807. [R]StPat 52 (2005) 954-956 (*Lorenzin,Tiziano*).

8559 **Mason, Eric** The concept of the priestly Messiah in Hebrews and second temple Judaism. [D]*VanderKam, James* 2005, 206 pp. Diss. Notre Dame [RTL 37,613].

8560 *März, Claus-Peter* Zur Aktualität des Hebräerbriefes. Studien zum Hebräerbrief. 2005 <1993> ⇒8568. 13-23;

8561 Vom Trost der Theologie: zur Pragmatik der christologisch-soteriologischen Reflexion im Hebräerbrief <1992> 25-46;

8562 'Wir haben einen Hohenpriester...': Anmerkungen zur kulttheologischen Argumentation des Hebräerbriefes <2003> 47-64;

8563 'Geschenkte und ergriffene Zuversicht': der Hebräerbrief im Bemühen um Gewissheit des Glaubens <1994> 67-80;

8564 'Der neue lebendige Weg durch den Vorhang hindurch...': zur Soteriologie des Hebräerbriefes <1998> 141-158;

8565 Melchisedek: bibeltheologische Überlegungen zu den Melchisedek-Bezügen im Hebräerbrief <1998> 159-175;

8566 Das 'Wort vom Kult' und der 'Kult des Wortes': der Hebräerbrief und die rechte Feier des Gottesdienstes <2002> 177-192;

8567 Den Hebräerbrief predigen: exegetische Hinweise zur homiletischen Praxis. Studien zum Hebräerbrief. SBAB 39: 2005 ⇒8568. 195-204.

8568 **März, Claus-Peter** Studien zum Hebräerbrief. SBAB 39: Stu 2005, Kath. Bibelwerk x; 241 pp. 3-460-06391-2.

8569 *McCullough, J. Cecil* Isaiah in Hebrews. Isaiah in the NT. 2005 ⇒ 443. 159-173.

8570 **McKnight, Edgar; Church, Christopher** Hebrews-James. 2004 ⇒ 20,7929. [R]RBLit (2005)* (*Bauer, David*).

8571 *Miller, James C.* Paul and Hebrews: a comparison of narrative worlds. Hebrews. BiblInterp 75: 2005 ⇒395. 245-264.

8572 **Molinaro, Italo** "Ha parlato nel Figlio": progettualità di Dio e risposta del Cristo nella lettera agli Ebrei. SBFA 55: 2001 ⇒17,7002... 19,7976. [R]EstTrin 39 (2005) 566-567 (*Pikaza, X.*).

8573 *Motyer, Steve* 'Not apart from us' (Hebrews 11:40): physical community in the letter to the Hebrews. EvQ 77 (2005) 235-247.

8574 *Nkutziudes, Moschos* He ennoia tes hamartias sten Pros Hebraius. DBM 23/2 (2005) 249-264. **G**.

8575 *Nyende, Peter* Why bother with Hebrews?: an African perspective. HeyJ 46 (2005) 512-524.

8576 *Okure, Teresa* Hebrews: sacrifice in an African perspective. Global bible commentary. 2005 ⇒2443. 535-538.

8577 **Portalatin, Antonio** Temporal oppositions as hermeneutical categories in the epistle to the Hebrews. [D]*Beutler, Johannes* 2005, Diss. Pont. Ist. Biblico [AcBib 11,103].

8578 **Salevao, Lutisone** Legitimation in the letter to the Hebrews: the construction and maintenance of a symbolic universe. JSNT.S 219: 2002 ⇒18,7527; 19,7983. [R]BiblInterp 13 (2005) 217-9 (*Young, Norman*).

8579 **Sanches, Sidney de Moraes** 'Tão grande salvação!'—o discurso de salvação na 'epístola' aos hebreus. [D]*Konings, Johan*: Belo Horizonte 2005, Faculdade Jesuíta Diss. [REB 263,762].

8580 **Schenck, Kenneth** Understanding the book of Hebrews: the story behind the sermon. 2003 ⇒19,7984; 20,7951. [R]CBQ 67 (2005) 357-359 (*Croy, N. Clayton*); AUSS 43 (2005) 371-372 (*Gallos, Erhard*).

8581 *Söding, Thomas* "Hoherpriester nach der Ordnung des Melchisedek" (Hebr 5,10): zur Christologie des Hebräerbriefes. Ausharren. SBS 204: 2005 ⇒412. 63-109.

8582 *Stegemann, Ekkehard W.; Stegemann, Wolfgang* Does the cultic language in Hebrews represent sacrificial metaphors?: reflections on some basic problems. Hebrews. BiblInterp 75: 2005 ⇒395. 13-23.

8583 *Thompson, J.W.* The epistle to the Hebrews and the Pauline legacy. RestQ 47/4 (2005) 197-206 [NTAb 50,315].

8584 *Tofană, Stelian* Hebrews. Global bible commentary. 2005 ⇒2443. 527-534.

8585 *Tönges, Elke* The epistle to the Hebrews as a "Jesus-Midrash". Hebrews. BiblInterp 75: 2005⇒395. 89-105.

8586 **Urso, Filippo** "Imparò l'obbedienza dalle cose che patì" (Eb 5,8): il valore educativo della sofferenza in Gesù e nei cristiani nella lettera agli Ebrei. [D]*Vanhoye, Albert*: TGr.T 119: R 2005, E.P.U.G. 509 pp. €28. 88-7839-026-7. Bibl. 425-458. [R]Camillianum 15 (2005) 535-540 (*Cinà, Giuseppe*).

8587 *Valério, Paulo F.* A oferenda do corpo: solidariedade de Cristo conosco e entre nós na Carta aos Hebreus. Estudos bíblicos 87 (2005) 65-79.

8588 *Vander Beek, W.L.* Hebrews: a 'doxology' of the Word. Mid-America Journal of theology [Dyer, IN] 16 (2005) 13-28 [NTAb 50,315].

8589 *Vanhoye, Albert* Il mistero del Verbo incarnato: Cristo e l'uomo a partire dalla lettera agli Ebrei. Mistero di Cristo. 2005 ⇒525. 17-46.

8590 **Westfall, Cynthia Long** A discourse analysis of the letter to the Hebrews: the relationship between form and meaning. LNTS 297: L 2005, Clark xii; 339 pp.

8591 *Willi-Plein, Ina* Some remarks on Hebrews from the viewpoint of Old Testament exegesis. Hebrews. BiblInterp 75: 2005 ⇒395. 25-35.

8592 *Zesati Estrada, Carlos* Cristo, mediador de la nueva alianza. [F]JUNCO GARZA, C.: Estudios Bíblicos Mexicanos 4: 2005 ⇒74. 461-479.

8593 *Smillie, Gene R.* Contrast or continuity in Hebrews 1.1-2?. NTS 51 2005, 543-560.

8594 *Dognin, Paul D.* Épître aux hébreux, traduction inédite du prologue (He 1,1-4). RB 112 (2005) 80-100.

8595 *MacLeod, David J.* The finality of Christ: an exposition of Hebrews 1:1-4. BS 162/646 (2005) 210-230.

8596 *März, Claus-Peter* Predigtmeditationen zu Hebr 1,1-6; 9,1-14; 10,19-25. Studien zum Hebräerbrief. SBAB 39: 2005 ⇒8568. 205-222.

8597 *Sanches, Sidney de M.* Narrative e discursividade: um teste de leitura em Hebreus 1:3b. Via Teológica [Paraná, Brazil] 1/11 (2005) 23-35.

8598 *Hohnjec, Nikola* Die Interpretation von Ps 2 in Hebr 1,5a; 5,5b: zur Christologie des Sohnes Gottes und des Hohenpriesters. AUPO 6 (2005) 17-28.

8599 *März, Claus-Peter* '...nur für kurze Zeit unter die Engel gestellt' (Hebr 2,7): Anthropologie und Christologie in Hebr 2,5-9 <1996>;

8600 "Herrenworte" im Hebräerbrief: zum Verständnis und zur Funktion von Hebr 2,12f und 10,5-7. Studien zum Hebräerbrief. SBAB 39: 2005 ⇒8568. 81-96/97-139.

8601 *Swetnam, James* Abraham's seed and Isaac as promise: a study of Hebrews 2,16 and 11,11 in the context of Hebrews 11,18-19. MTh 56/1 (2005) 53-60.

8602 *Scholtissek, Klaus* Den Unsichtbaren vor Augen (Hebr 11,27): die Ecclesia ab Abel im Israelkapitel des Hebräerbriefes. Ausharren. SBS 204: 2005 ⇒412. 135-164 [Heb 3,7-4,11; 11,4-38].

8603 *Kowalski, Beate* Die Rezeption alttestamentlicher Theologie im Hebräerbrief. Ausharren. SBS 204: 2005 ⇒412. 35-62 [Ps 95; Heb 3,7-4,13; 11,1-40].

8604 *Garuti, Paolo* Il coltello sacrificale, il λόγος τοῦ θεοῦ e l'isonomia eucaristica in Eb 4,12-13. Ang. 82 (2005) 783-802.

8605 *Swetnam, James* Another note on Λόγος as Christ in Hebrews 4,12-13. FgNT 18 (2005) 129-133.

8606 *Smillie, Gene R.* "The other λόγος" at the end of Heb. 4:13. NT 47 (2005) 19-25.

8607 *Mason, Eric F.* Hebrews 7:3 and the relationship between Melchizedek and Jesus. BR 50 (2005) 41-62.

8608 *MacLeod, David J.* Christ, the believer's high pries: an exposition of Hebrews 7:26-28. BS 162/647 (2005) 331-343.

8609 *Bogaert, Pierre-Maurice* La construction de la tente (Ex 36-40) dans le *Monacensis* de la plus ancienne version latine: l'autel d'or et Hébreux 9,4. L'enfance de la Bible hébraïque. 2005 ⇒477. 62-76 [RBen 116,147—P.-M. Bogaert].

8610 *Hahn, Scott W.* Covenant, cult, and the curse-of-death: διαθήκη in Heb 9:15-22. Hebrews. BiblInterp 75: 2005 ⇒395. 65-88.

8611 *Wedderburn, Alexander* Sawing off the branches: theologizing dangerously *Ad Hebraeos*. JThS 56 (2005) 393-414 [Heb 10,5-9; 10,19-20].

8612 **Gheorghita, Radu** The role of the Septuagint in Hebrews: an investigation of its influence with special consideration to the use of Hab 2:3-4 in Heb 10:37-38. WUNT 2/160: 2003 ⇒19,8009; 20,7971. [R]Alpha Omega 8/1 (2005) 138-142 (*Kranz, Dirk Kurt*); CBQ 67 (2005) 492-494 (*Wooden, R. Glenn*) [Hab 2,3-4].

8613 *Esler, Philip F.* Collective memory and Hebrews 11: outlining a new investigative framework. Memory, tradition, and text. SBL.Semeia Studies 52: 2005 ⇒416. 151-171.

8614 *Van der Merwe, D.* Perseverance through suffering: a spirituality for mission. Missionalia 33/2 (2005) 329-354 [NTAb 50,316] [Heb 11,39-12,3].

8615 *Sisson, R.B.* Overcoming the fear of death: physical body and community in Hebrews. Scriptura 90 (2005) 670-678 [NTAb 51,233] [Heb 12,1-13].

8616 **Son, K.** Zion symbolism in Hebrews: Hebrews 12:18-24 as a hermeneutical key to the epistle. [D]*Motyer, S.*: Paternoster Biblical Monographs: Milton Keynes 2005, Paternoster xviii; 248 pp. £20. 18422-7368X. Diss. London School of Theology; Bibl. [NTAb 50,610].

8617 *Cepeda Salazar, Antonino* El Dios de la paz: Heb 13,20-21. Qol 39 (2005) 111-125.

8618 *Clement, Wolfgang* Woher nimmt Politik ihre Zuversicht? (Hebräer 13,20-21). Kanzelreden. 2005 ⇒376. 145-158.

### G9.1 **1 Petri** (vel I-II)

8619 *Aizpurúa, Fidel* El inmigrante/extranjero en las cartas católicas y en escritos posteriores. ResB 46 (2005) 37-45.

8620 *Bockmuehl, Markus* Simon Peter and Bethsaida. The missions of James. NT.S 115: 2005 ⇒369. 53-91.

8621 **Lapham, Fred** Peter: the myth, the man and the writings: a study of early Petrine text and tradition. JSNT.S 239: 2003 ⇒19,8029; 20, 7983. [R]TS 66 (2005) 449-451 (*Elliott, John H.*).

8622 [E]**Lazzari, Loredana; Valente Bacci, Anna M.** La figura di san Pietro nelle fonti del Medioevo. 2001 ⇒17,7031; 19,8030. [R]CrSt 26 (2005) 547-550 (*Barcellona, Francesco S.*).

8623 *Ringe, Sharon* 1 and 2 Peter, Jude. Global bible commentary. 2005 ⇒2443. 545-552.

8624 [E]**Schmitz, Franz-J.** Das Verhältnis der koptischen zur griechischen Überlieferung des NT: ...zum Jakobusbrief und den beiden Petrusbriefen. ANTT 33: 2003 ⇒19,8034; 20,7987. [R]NT 47 (2005) 163-166 (*Boud'hors, Anne*); BiOr 62 (2005) 523-526 (*Rogl, Christine*).

8625 *Senior, Donald* The Petrine letters and the Petrine ministry. BiTod 43 (2005) 233-237.

8626 **Senior, Donald P.; Harrington, Daniel J.** 1 Peter, Jude, and 2 Peter. Sacra Pagina 15: 2003 ⇒19,8021; 20,7988. [R]TS 66 (2005) 181-182 (*Campbell, Barth L.*); Interp. 59 (2005) 196-198 (*Elliott, John H.*).

8627 **Skaggs, Rebecca** The Pentecostal commentary on 1 Peter, 2 Peter, Jude. 2004 ⇒20,7989. [R]RBLit (2005)* (*Lamp, Jeffrey; Seland, Torrey*).

8628 *Wifstrand, Albert* Stylistic problems in the epistles of James and Peter. Epochs and styles. WUNT 179: 2005 <1947> ⇒325. 46-58.

8629 **Achtemeier, Paul** 1 Peter: a commentary on First Peter. Hermeneia: 1996 ⇒12,6577...14,6426. [R]NV 80/4 (2005) 104-6 (*Borel, Jean*).

8630 *Bartlett, David L.* The first letter of Peter. NT survey. 2005 ⇒3144. 303-314.

8631 **Bony, Paul** La première épître de Pierre: chrétiens en diaspora. LiBi 137: 2004 ⇒20,7992. [R]EeV 123 (2005) 22 (*Cothenet, Édouard*); EstB 63 (2005) 119-120 (*Sánchez Navarro, L.*).

8632 *Breytenbach, Cilliers* "Christus litt euretwegen": zur Rezeption von Jesaja 53 LXX und anderen frühjüdischen Traditionen im 1. Petrusbrief. Deutungen. WUNT 181: 2005 ⇒392. 437-454.

8633 *Cervantes Gabarrón, José* La disponibilidad como actitud cristiana. ResB 45 (2005) 56-64.

8634 *Feldmeier, Reinhard* Wiedergeburt im 1. Petrusbrief. Wiedergeburt. BTSP 25: 2005 ⇒533. 75-99.

8635 **Feldmeier, Reinhard** Der erste Brief des Petrus. ThHK.NT 15/1: Lp 2005, Evangelische xxxv; 172 pp. €34. 33740-23231. Bibl. xix-xxxv.

8636 *Iovino, Paolo* La 'speranza viva' nella *Prima lettera di Pietro*. Ho Theológos 23 (2005) 459-470.

8637 **Jobes, Karen H.** 1 Peter. Baker Exegetical Commentary on the NT: GR 2005, Baker xvii; 364 pp. $40. 0-8010-2674-1. Bibl. 339-351.

8638 *Moyise, Steve* Isaiah in 1 Peter. Isaiah in the NT. 2005 ⇒443. 175-188.

8639 *Nisus, Alain* L'église et la cité dans la première épître de Pierre. ThEv(VS) 4/2 (2005) 3-11.

8640 *Obermann, Andreas* Fremd im eigenen Land: die Heimatkonzeption frühchristlicher Gemeinden nach dem 1. Petrusbrief und ihre praktischen Implikationen heute. KuD 51/4 (2005) 263-289.

8641 *Pakala, James C.* A librarian's comments on commentaries: 19 (1 Peter). Presbyterion 31 (2005) 49-53 [NTAb 49,532].

8642 *Puig i Tàrrech, Armand* Els cristians com a forasters en la primera carta de Pere. La bíblia i els immigrants. 2005 ⇒471. 197-242.

8643 *Seland, Torrey* Strangers in the light;

8644 The making of 1 Peter in light of ancient Graeco-Roman letterwriting and distribution;

8645 "Conduct yourselves honorably among the gentiles" (1 Peter 2:12): acculturation and assimilation in 1 Peter;

8646 Paroikos kai parepidemos: proselyte characterizations in 1 Peter? <2001>. Strangers in the light. BiblInterp 76: 2005 ⇒301. 1-8/9-37/ 147-189/39-78.

8647 *Soon, D.K.K.* Resident aliens and alienated residents. Trinity Theological Journal [Singapore] 13 (2005) 103-124 [NTAb 50,325].

8648 *Van Rensburg, Fika J.J.* Metaphors in the soteriology in 1 Peter: identifying and interpreting the salvific imageries. Salvation in the New Testament. NT.S 121: 2005 ⇒798. 409-435.

8649 *Wolff, Christian* Die Auferstehung Jesu Christi im Ersten Petrusbrief. FS Ghiberti, G.. SRivBib 46: 2005, 257-266.

8650 *Lugo Rodríguez, Raúl H.* Cristo, la piedra viva. [F]JUNCO GARZA, C.: Estudios Bíblicos Mexicanos 4: 2005 ⇒74. 481-498 [1 Pet 2,1-10].

8651 *Seland, Torrey* The 'common priesthood' of PHILO and 1 Peter: a Philonic reading of 1 Peter 2:5 & 9 <1995> [Exod 19,6];

8652 The moderate life of Christian paroikoi: a Philonic reading of 1 Peter 2:11 <2004>. Strangers in the light. BiblInterp 76: 2005 ⇒301. 79-115/117-145.

8653 *Vouga, François* Christ, le Serviteur souffrant (1 Pierre 2,21-25). Analyse narrative. BEThL 191: 2005 ⇒742.

8654 *Davids, Peter H.* A silent witness in marriage: 1 Peter 3:1-7. Discovering biblical equality. 2005 ⇒387. 224-238.

8655 *Forbes, Greg* Becoming children of Sarah: interpreting 1 Peter 3:6b. BBR 15 (2005) 105-109.

8656 *Gounelle, Rémi* I Pierre 3,18-20 et la descente du Christ en enfer. PosLuth 53/4 (2005) 381-398.

8657 *Christudhas, M.* Shepherd the flock of God: an exegetical study of 1 Pet 5:1-5. [M]JOHN PAUL II. 2005 ⇒72. 209-253.

8658 *Mancilla Sánchez, Juan Manuel* Inclinaos bajo la poderosa mano de Dios. [F]JUNCO GARZA, C. 2005 ⇒74. 73-77 [1 Pet 5,6].

## G9.2 2 Petri

8659 *Charles, J. Daryl* The angels under reserve in 2 Peter and Jude. BBR 15 (2005) 39-48.

8660 **Grasso, Santi** Lettera di Giacomo; seconda lettera di Pietro; lettera di Giuda. Dabar: Padova 2005, Messagero 192 pp. €10.50.

8661 **Kraus, Thomas J.** Sprache, Stil und historischer Ort des zweiten Petrusbriefes. WUNT 2/136: 2001 ⇒17,7055... 20,8043. [R]Cart. 21 (2005) 248 (*Sanz Valdivieso, R.*).

8662 **Marconi, Gilberto** Lettera di Giuda; seconda lettera di Pietro. Scritti delle origini cristiane 19: Bo 2005, EDB 229 pp. €19.60. 88-10-206-24-X. Bibl. 203-220.

*Pakala, J.* A librarian's comments (Lam...2 Peter) 2005 ⇒4776.

8663 **Riedl, Hermann Josef** Anamnese und Apostolizität: der Zweite Petrusbrief und das theologische Problem neutestamentlicher Pseudepigraphie. RSTh 64: Fra 2005, Lang 297 pp. €51.50. 3-631-54557-6.

8664 *Watson, Duane F.* The second letter of Peter. NT survey. 2005 ⇒ 3144. 315-320.

8665 *Callan, Terrance* The syntax of 2 Peter 1:1-7. CBQ 67 (2005) 632-640.

8666 *Hübner, Hans* 2 Petr 1,4—eine Blasphemie, die keineswegs gotteslästerlich ist. [F]NIEDERWIMMER, K. 2005 ⇒112. 67-79.
8667 *Bénétreau, Samuel* Évangile et prophétie: un texte original (1 P 1,10-12) peut-il éclairer un texte difficile (2 P 1,16-21)?. Bib. 86 (2005) 174-191.
8668 *Marconi, Gilberto* La rappresentazione della falsità (2Pt 2,10b-22). [F]GHIBERTI, G.: SRivBib 46: 2005 ⇒47. 267-273.
8669 *Adams, Edward* 'Where is the promise of His coming?': the complaint of the scoffers in 2 Peter 3.4. NTS 51 (2005) 106-122;
8670 Creation 'out of' and 'through' water in 2 Peter 3:5. Creation of heaven and earth. 2005 ⇒492. 195-210.

## G9.4 **Epistula Jacobi**..data on both apostles James

8671 *Botha, J. Eugene* Simple salvation, but not of straw.... Jacobean soteriology. Salvation in the NT. NT.S 121: 2005 ⇒798. 389-408.
8672 **Brosend, William F.** James and Jude. 2004 ⇒20,8049. [R]ScrB 35 (2005) 119-121 (*Boxall, Ian*); RBLit (2005)* (*Wasserman, Tommy*).
8673 **Cheung, Luke Leuk** The genre, composition and hermeneutics of the epistle of James. 2003 ⇒19,8067; 20,8082. [R]JThS 56 (2005) 170-172 (*Isaacs, Marie E.*).
8674 *Chilton, Bruce* Wisdom and grace. The missions of James. NT.S 115: 2005 ⇒369. 307-322.
8675 *Cirillo, Luigi* Jacques de Jérusalem d'après le roman du pseudo-Clément. [F]RIES, J. 2005 ⇒127. 177-188.
8676 *Conti, Cristina* James. Global bible commentary. 2005 ⇒2443. 539-544.
8677 *Davids, Peter H.* James and Peter: the literary evidence;
8678 Why do we suffer?: suffering in James and Paul. The missions of James. NT.S 115: 2005 ⇒369. 29-52/435-466.
8679 **Edgar, David Hutchinson** Has God not chosen the poor?: the social setting of the epistle of James. JSNT.S 206: 2001 ⇒17,7067; 19, 8068. [R]RBLit (2005)* (*Konradt, Matthias*).
8680 *Fabris, Rinaldo* La lettera di Giacomo nella tradizione sapienziale e apocalittica. [F]GHIBERTI, G.: SRivBib 46: 2005 ⇒47. 241-256.
8681 **Fabris, Rinaldo** Lettera di Giacomo: introduzione, versione, commento. 2004 ⇒20,8054. [R]Cart. 21 (2005) 246-247 (*Alvarez Barredo, M.*); CBQ 67 (2005) 143-144 (*Chávez, Emilio G.*).
8682 *Franz, G.* The synagogue on the island of Delos and the epistle of James. Bible and Spade [Akron, PA] 18/3 (2005) 83-94 [NTAb 50, 335].
**Grasso, S.** Lettera di Giacomo... 2005 ⇒8660.
8683 *Gruenwald, Ithamar* Ritualizing death in James and Paul in light of Jewish apocalypticism. The missions of James. NT.S 115: 2005 ⇒ 369. 467-486.
8684 *Hartin, Patrick J.* "Who is wise and understanding among you?" (James 3:13): an analysis of wisdom, eschatology, and apocalypticism in the letter of James. Conflicted boundaries. SBL.Symp. 35: 2005 ⇒495. 149-168.
8685 **Hartin, Patrick J.** A spirituality of perfection: faith in action in the letter of James. 1999 ⇒15,7231... 20,8085. [R]RBLit (2005)* (*Bowman, Christopher; Konradt, Matthias*);

8686 James. Sacra pagina 14: 2003 ⇒19,8060; 20,8056. [R]RBLit 7 (2005) 428-432 (*Nicklas, Tobias*);

8687 James of Jerusalem: heir to Jesus of Nazareth. 2004 ⇒20,8057. [R]RBLit (2005)* (*Davids, Peter; Johnson, Luke T.; Lockett, Darian*).

8688 *Hoppe, Rudolf* Von der Ambivalenz des Menschen und der Wahrheit Gottes: der Jakobusbrief und seine Botschaft. WuA(M) 46/4 (2005) 186-188.

8689 **Jackson-McCabe, Matt A.** Logos & law in the letter of James: the law of nature, the law of Moses, & the law of freedom. NT.S 100: 2001⇒17,7075... 20,8087. [R]RBLit (2005)* (*Konradt, Matthias*).

8690 *Johnson, Luke T.* The letter of James. NT survey. 2005 ⇒3144. 297-302.

8691 **Johnson, Luke Timothy** Brother of Jesus, friend of God: studies in the letter of James. 2004 ⇒20,217. [R]CThMi 32 (2005) 139-140 (*Linss, Wilhelm C.*); RBLit (2005)* (*Patton, Steve*); RBLit 7 (2005) 427-428 (*Oehler, Markus*); JThS 56 (2005) 575-578 (*Painter, John*).

8692 **Keenan, John P.** The wisdom of James: parallels with Mahayana Buddhism. NY 2005, Newman viii; 266 pp. $25. 0-8091-4168-X. Bibl. 245-261.

8693 **Kot, Tomasz** La fede, via della vita: composizione e interpretazione della lettera di Giacomo. Retorica biblica 6: 2002 ⇒18,7592; 19, 8080. [R]RivBib 53 (2005) 361-364 (*Fabris, Rinaldo*); Ang. 82 (2005) 235-237 (*Garuti, Paolo*).

8694 **Krüger, René** Der Jakobusbrief als prophetische Kritik der Reichen: eine exegetische Untersuchung aus lateinamerikanischer Perspektive. Beiträge zum Verstehen der Bibel 12: Müns 2005, LIT 304 pp. €30. 3-8258-8786-3.

8695 *Lockett, Darian* The spectrum of wisdom and eschatology in the epistle of James and 4QInstruction. TynB 56/2 (2005) 131-148.

8696 **Maier, Gerhard** Der Brief des Jakobus. 2004 ⇒20,8067. [R]JETh 19 (2005) 274-277 (*Buchegger, Jürg*).

8697 [E]*Mantovani, Piera Arata* Compostela: sulle tracce di san Giacomo. Il mondo della bibbia 3 (2005) 1-42.

**McKnight, E.** Hebrews-James 2004 ⇒8570.

8698 **Nienhuis, David** The letter of James in the formation of the New Testament catholic epistle collection. [D]*Watson, Francis* 2005, Diss. Aberdeen [RTL 37,617].

8699 *Painter, John* James and Peter: models of leadership and mission;

8700 The power of words: rhetoric in James and Paul. The missions of James. NT.S 115: 2005 ⇒369. 143-209/235-273.

8701 **Painter, John** Just James: the brother of Jesus in history and tradition. [2]2004 ⇒20,8069. [R]RBLit 7 (2005) 424-26 (*Wilson, William R.*).

**Parmentier, R.** L'épître de Jacques... 2005 ⇒8443.

8702 *Pilhofer, Peter* Von Jakobus zu JUSTIN: Lernen in den Spätschriften des Neuen Testaments und bei den Apologeten. Religiöses Lernen. WUNT 180: 2005 ⇒384. 253-269.

8703 *Popkes, Wiard* Leadership: James, Paul, and their contemporary background. The missions of James. NT.S 115: 2005 ⇒369. 323-54.

8704 **Popkes, Wiard** Der Brief des Jakobus. ThHK 14: 2001 ⇒17,7083; 20,8070. [R]ThRv 101 (2005) 212-215 (*Wischmeyer, Oda*); RBLit 7 (2005) 435-438 (*Konradt, Matthias*).

8705 *Porter, Virgil V.* The Sermon on the Mount in the book of James. BS 162 (2005) 344-360, 470-482.

8706 *Sawicki, Marianne* Person or practice?: judging in James and in Paul. The missions of James. NT.S 115: 2005 ⇒369. 385-408.

[E]**Schmitz, F.** Das Verhältnis der koptischen zur griechischen Überlieferung des NT... Jakobusbrief 2003 ⇒8624.

8707 *Tiller, Patrick* The rich and the poor in James: an apocalyptic ethic. Conflicted boundaries. SBL.Symp. 35: 2005 ⇒495. 169-179.

*Wifstrand, A.* Stylistic problems in...James...Peter 2005 ⇒8628.

8708 **Yates, Jonathan** In epistula alterius apostoli: the presence and use of the epistle of James in the writings of AUGUSTINE of Hippo (354-430). [D]*Lamberigts, M.*: 2005, xxx; 494 pp. Diss. Leuven.

8709 *Neusner, Jacob* Sin, repentance, atonement and resurrection: the perspective of rabbinic theology on the views of James 1-2 and Paul in Romans 3-4. The missions of James. NT.S 115: 2005 ⇒369. 409-34.

8710 *Miller, J.D.* Can the 'Father of lights' give birth?. Priscilla Papers [Mp] 19/1 (2005) 5-7 [NTAb 51,307] [James 1,17-18].

8711 **Musengamana, Papias** 'θρησκεία καθαρὰ καὶ ἀμίαντος...' (Jas 1: 27): the emergence and the problem of church and christian identity in the epistle of James: exegetical study on Jas 1:19-27. [D]*Oberlinner, Lorenz* 2005, Diss. Freiburg [ThRv 102,v].

8712 *Palmer, D.V.* James 2:14-26: justification as orthopraxy. Caribbean Journal of Evangelical Theology [Kingston, Jamaica] 9 (2005) 54-78 [NTAb 50,81].

8713 *Abela, Anthony* Exegeting and translating Jas 4,5b. MTh 56/2 (2005) 59-69.

8714 *Kuske, D.P.* James 5:14—'anoint him with oil'. WLQ 102/2 (2005) 125-127 ]NTAb 50,81].

## G9.6 Epistula Judae

**Brosend, W.** James and Jude 2004 ⇒8672.

**Grasso, S.** Lettera di... Giuda 2005⇒8660.

**Marconi, G.** Lettera di Giuda 2005 ⇒8662.

8715 *Nicklas, Tobias* Der "lebendige Text" des Neuen Testaments: der Judasbrief in P 72 (P. Bodmer VII). ASEs 22/1 (2005) 203-222.

*Ringe, S.* 1 and 2 Peter, Jude 2005 ⇒2443.

**Senior, D.** 1 Peter, Jude, and 2 Peter 2003 ⇒8626.

**Skaggs, R.** Pentecostal commentary on...Jude 2004 ⇒8627.

8716 *Watson, Duane* The letter of Jude. NT survey. 2005 ⇒3144. 332-36.

8717 *Witherington, Ben* Jude: another brother of Jesus. BiRe 21/4 (2005) 15-16, 50 [NTAb 50,82].

# XIII. Theologia Biblica

## H1.1 Biblical Theology [OT] God

8718 *Ashmon, S.A.* The wrath of God: a biblical overview. ConJ 31 (2005) 348-358 [NTAb 50,325].

8719 *Astell, Ann W.* Biblical images of God and the reader's "I" as imago dei: the contribution of Edith STEIN. Interp. 59 (2005) 382-391.

8720 *Batthyany, Alexander* Gottsuche und Sinnfrage: über dieses Buch. Gottsuche. 2005 ⇒536. 33-45.

8721 BENEDICTUS XVI 'Chi ha visto me ha visto il Padre' (Gv 14,9): il volto di Cristo nella santa scrittura. Volto dei volti 8/1 (2005) 11-19.

8722 *Burnett, Joel S.* The question of divine absence in Israelite and West Semitic religion. CBQ 67 (2005) 215-235 [Jer 2,6].

8723 *Cardellini, Innocenzo* La metafora del "pastore" nell'Antico Testamento alla luce del retroterra culturale mesopotamico. Lat. 71 (2005) 249-278.

8724 **Coulange, Pierre** Dieu, ami des pauvres: une étude sur la connivence entre le Très-Haut et les petits. [D]*Schenker, Adrian* 2005, Diss. Fribourg [ThRv 102,v].

8725 **Crenshaw, James L.** Defending God: biblical responses to the problem of evil. Oxf 2005, OUP 275 pp. $35. 0-1951-1400-2. Bibl. [R]America 193/6 (2005) 21-23 (*Harrington, Daniel J.*).

8726 *Del Signore, Gabriella* ... e Tu non rispondi. Horeb 14/1 (2005) 28-34 [Ps 22; 42].

8727 *Ehrlich, Carl S.* Gott der Geschichte und der Weisheit: Response auf Christoph Schwöbel. Biblische Theologie. 2005 ⇒756. 155-159.

8728 **Fornara, Roberto** La visione contradetta: la dialettica fra visibilità e non-visibilità divina nella Bibbia ebraica. AnBib 155: 2004 ⇒20, 8134. [R]ZKTh 127 (2005) 127-128 (*Paganini, Simone*); EE 80 (2005) 609-611 (*Sanz Giménez-Rico, Enrique*); Ter. 56 (2005) 285-303 (*Pasquetto, Virgilio*).

8729 *Frankl, Viktor E.; Lapide, Pinchas* Gottsuche und Sinnfrage. Gottsuche. 2005 ⇒536. 47-144.

8730 **Freedmann, Amelia** God as an absent character in Biblical Hebrew narrative: a literary-theoretical study. Studies in Biblical literature 82: NY 2005, Lang xvi; 229 pp. $67. 08204-78288. Diss.; Bibl. 215-223.

8731 *García Bachmann, Mercedes L.* "And YHWH saw and was displeased": mediation as human responsibility (Isaiah 59). LecDif 1 (2005)*.

8732 *Gericke, J.W.* YHWH and the God of philosophical theology. VeE 26 (2005) 677-699;

8733 YHWH unlimited: realist and non-realist ontological perspectives on theo-mythology in the Old Testament. ZAR 11 (2005) 274-295;

8734 Sounds of silence: an anti-realist perspective on YHWH's ipsissima verba in the Old Testament. OTEs 18 (2005) 61-81.

8735 *Gordon, Robert P.* 'Comparativism' and the God of Israel. The OT in its world. OTS 52: 2005 ⇒749. 45-67.

8736 *Groenewald, Alphonso* "And please, do not hide your face from your servant!" (Ps 69:18a): the image of the "Hidden God". [F]SEIDL, T.: ATSAT 75: 2005 ⇒137. 121-138.

8737 *Hamilton, James* God with men in the Prophets and the Writings: an examination of the nature of God's presence. SBET 23 (2005) 166-193.

8738 *Heckl, Raik* Die persönliche Gottesbeziehung als "Urerlebnis" auf dem Weg zum biblischen Monotheismus. leqach 6 (2005) 57-98.

8739 *House, P.R.* God's character and the wholeness of scripture. SBET 23 (2005) 4-17 [Exod 34,6-7].

8740 **Hunziker-Rodewald, Regine** Hirt und Herde: ein Beitrag zum alttestamentlichen Gottesverständnis. BWANT 155: 2001 ⇒17,7122... 19,8129. [R]ThR 70 (2005) 447-449 (*Reventlow, Henning Graf*).

8741 **Hübner, Hans** Wer ist der biblische Gott?: Fluch und Segen der monotheistischen Religionen. BThSt 64: 2004 ⇒20,8143. [R]ThRv 101 (2005) 201-203 (*Ruster, Thomas*).

8742 *Jacobson, Howard* God as consuming fire. HThR 98 (2005) 219-22.

8743 **Jeremias, Jörg** Die Reue Gottes: Aspekte alttestamentlicher Gottesvorstellung. Biblisch-theologische Studien 31: [2]1997 ⇒13,6880. [R]ThR 70 (2005) 453-454 (*Reventlow, Henning Graf*).

8744 *Kaiser, Gerhard* Theodizee als biblisch erzählte Geschichte. ZThK 102 (2005) 115-142.

8745 **Kaiser, Otto** Der Gott des Alten Testaments, 1-3. 1993-2003 ⇒9, 7019... 19,8131. [R]ThR 70 (2005) 5-6 (*Reventlow, Henning Graf*).

8746 *Kellenberger, James* God's goodness and God's evil. Ment. *Dostoevsky, Fedor*: RelSt 41/1 (2005) 23-37.

8747 *Kotecki, Dariusz* "On Bogiem wiernym, a nie zwodniczym" (Pwt 32, 4): refleksja biblijno-teologiczna nad wiernościa Boga w Starym Testamencie. CoTh 75/2 (2005) 13-38. **P**.

8748 *Köckert, Matthias* Wandlungen Gottes im antiken Israel. BThZ 22 (2005) 3-36.

8749 **Kugel, James L.** The God of old: inside the lost world of the bible. 2003 ⇒19,8133. [R]Interp. 59 (2005) 64-66 (*Brueggemann, Walter*).

8750 **Lang, Bernhard** Jahwe der biblische Gott: ein Portrait. 2002 ⇒18, 7641... 20,8147. [R]ThR 70 (2005) 425-27 (*Reventlow, Henning Graf*);

8751 The Hebrew God: portrait of an ancient deity. 2002 ⇒18,7640... 20, 8146. [R]BiblInterp 13 (2005) 64-66 (*Brueggemann, Walter*); BiOr 62 (2005) 557-559 (*Spronk, Klaas*); AsbTJ 60/2 (2005) 123-124 (*Arnold, Bill T.*).

8752 *Limbeck, Meinrad* Spuren im Sand?. [F]STENDEBACH, F. 2005 ⇒141. 97-106.

8753 *MacDonald, N.* Whose monotheism?: which rationality?: reflections on Israelite monotheism in Erhard Gerstenberger's Theologies in the Old Testament. The OT in its world. OTS 52: 2005 ⇒749. 158-167.

8754 **March, W. Eugene** The wide, wide circle of divine love: a biblical case for religious diversity. LVL 2005, Westminster $15 [BiTod 44, 56—Dianne Bergant].

8755 *Miggelbrink, Ralf* Vom Zorn Gottes: warum wir das biblische Zeugnis nicht unterschlagen dürfen. Christ in der Gegenwart Extra-Heft/2005 (2005) 24-27.

8756 **Mills, Mary E.** Images of God in the Old Testament. 1998 ⇒14, 6527; 16,7272. [R]ThR 70 (2005) 449-451 (*Reventlow, Henning Graf*).

8757 *Muffs, Yochanan* Theological anthropomorphism. Personhood of God. 2005 ⇒265. 29-33;

8758 The gods and the law. 35-44;

8759 Biblical anthropomorphism. 55-60;

8760 The living machine. 61-64;

8761 Divine aspirations: four aspects of kingship. 65-81;

8762 Power, love, and justice: the positive expression of the divine will. 83-88;

8763 On the uses of divine power. 89-94;

8764 God and the world <1974>. Personhood of God. 2005 ⇒265. 159-170.

8765 *Navone, John* Shepherding in the Hebrew Bible. BiTod 43 (2005) 111-118.

8766 *Proja, Giovanni Battista* 'Signore, rivelaci il tuo volto'. Volto dei volti 8/1 (2005) 31-36.

8767 *Reimer, Haroldo* Corporeidade de Deus na Bíblia Hebraica. Fragmenta de Cultura [Goías] 15/1 (2005) 13-22 [OTA 28,352].

8768 *Schenker, Adrian* L'institution des dieux et des religions: l'unicité du Dieu de la bible. Bible et sciences des religions. 2005 ⇒445. 17-40.

8769 *Schmid, Konrad* Himmelsgott, Weltgott und Schöpfer: 'Gott' und der 'Himmel' in der Literatur der Zeit des zweiten Tempels. JBTh 20 (2005) 111-148.

8770 **Schrage, Wolfgang** Vorsehung Gottes?: zur Rede von der providentia Dei in der Antike und im Neuen Testament. Neuk 2005, Neuk 280 pp. €24.90. 3-7887-2088-3.

8771 *Schwienhorst-Schönberger, Ludger* Gottesbilder des Alten Testaments. Studien zum AT. SBAB 40: 2005 <2000> ⇒298. 99-112.

8772 *Schwöbel, Christoph* Der Gott der Geschichte und der Gott der Weisheit: systematisch-theologische Erwägungen im Anschluss an Gerhard VON RAD. Biblische Theologie. ATM 14: 2005 ⇒756. 139-153.

8773 **Smith, Mark S.** The memoirs of God: history, memory, and the experience of the divine in ancient Israel. 2004 ⇒20,8166. [R]TJT 21 (2005) 274-276 (*Oeste, Gordon*); JHScr 5 (2004-5)* (*White, Ellen*); RBLit (2005)* (*Barmash, Pamela; Lang, Bernhard*).

8774 **Spong, John Shelby** The sins of scripture: exposing the bible's texts of hate to reveal the God of love. SF 2005, HarperSanFrancisco xvii; 315 pp. 0-06-076205-5. Bibl. 305-310.

8775 **Stolz, Fritz** Einführung in den biblischen Monotheismus. 1996 ⇒12, 6661; 16,7286. [R]ThR 70 (2005) 420-423 (*Reventlow, Henning Graf*).

8776 *Šimiç, Krešimir* Književno-biblijski pristup teodicejskoj problematici. BoSm 75 (2005) 31-59. **Croatian**.

8777 *Thiel, Winfried* Jahwe, der Gott Israels. Gedeutete Geschichte. BThSt 71: 2005<1974> ⇒316. 1-14.

8778 *Toni, Roberto* La parola che rigenera. Horeb 14/2 (2005) 21-27.

8779 *Tronina, Antoni* Jahwe—wojownik czy Bóg pokoju? [Yahweh: warrior or God of peace?]. Ethos 18/3-4 (2005) 193-201. **P**.

8780 Il volto di Cristo nelle lezioni dell'VIII congresso internazionale (2004). Volto dei volti 8/1 (2005) 37-60.

8781 *Wagner, Andreas* Alttestamentlicher Monotheismus und seine Bindung an das Wort. [F]BÜMLEIN, K. 2005 ⇒18. 1-22.

8782 *Whybray, Norman* 'Shall not the judge of all the earth do what is just?': God's oppression of the innocent in the Old Testament. Wisdom. MSSOTS: 2005 <2000> ⇒324. 315-333.

### H1.4 *Femininum in Deo*—**God as father and mother**

8783 **Böckler, Annette** Gott als Vater im Alten Testament: traditionsgeschichtliche Untersuchungen zur Entstehung und Entwicklung eines Gottesbildes, Jes 63,16. 2000 ⇒16,7298... 19,8164. [R]ThR 70 (2005) 443-444 (*Reventlow, Henning Graf*).

8784 *Cunha, Evandro L* A face feminina de Deus. Hermenêutica 5 (2005) 33-57.

8785 *Miles, Jack* Israel as foundling: abandonment, adoption, and the fatherhood of God. HebStud 46 (2005) 7-24.

8786 **Schäfer, Peter** Mirror of His beauty: feminine images of God from the bible to the early kabbalah. 2002 ⇒18,7686... 20,8178. [R]JQR 95 (2005) 715-720 (*Hollywood, Amy*).

8787 *Wright, R.K.M.* God, metaphor and gender: is the God of the bible a male deity?. Discovering biblical equality. 2005 ⇒387. 287-300.

## H1.7 **Revelatio**

8788 *Fiorenza, Francis S.* Changes in culture and society and the interdisciplinarity of theology. Reconsidering the boundaries. 2005 ⇒ 598. 201-216.

8789 **Gaburro, Sergio** La voce della rivelazione: fenomenologia della voce per una teologia della rivelazione. CinB 2005, San Paolo 397 pp. Bibl. 363-391.

8790 *Herms, Eilert* The rationality of theological disciplines and their interdisciplinarity. Reconsidering the boundaries. 2005 ⇒598. 123-32.

8791 *Junttila, Maria* Prekenrefleksjon. Ung teologi 38/3 (2005) 75-78 [1 Cor 1,17-25].

8792 *Manicardi, Ermenegildo* Bibbia e inculturazione della fede. Gesù la cristologia. 2005 <1996> ⇒253. 363-369.

8793 *Osmer, Richard* The rationality of the theological disciplines: response to Eilert Herms. Reconsidering the boundaries. 2005 ⇒598. 133-135.

8794 **Pizzuto, Pietro** La teologia della rivelazione di Jean DANIÉLOU: influsso su Dei Verbum e valore attuale. TGr.T 96: 2003 ⇒19,8187. [R]RSR 93 (2005) 445-447 (*Holzer, Vincent*).

8795 *Rüpke, Jörg* Heilige Schriften und Buchreligionen: Überlegungen zu Begriffen und Methoden. Heilige Schriften. 2005 ⇒362. 191-204, 250-251.

8796 **Saldanha, Peter Paul** Revelation as 'self-communication of God': a study of the influences of Karl BARTH and Karl RAHNER on the concept of revelation in the documents of the Second Vatican Council. Vatican 2005, Urbaniana Univ. Pr. 469 pp. €24.

8797 **Samuelson, Norbert Max** Revelation and the God of Israel. 2002 ⇒ 18,7714... 20,8193. [R]JQR 95 (2005) 768-770 (*Braiterman, Zachary*).

8798 *Schwienhorst-Schönberger, Ludger* Theologie und Mystik—eine Integrationsaufgabe. Studien zum AT. SBAB 40: 2005 <2001> ⇒298. 281-285.

8799 *Stramare, Tarcisio* 'Historia salutis' e 'mysterium' nell'economia della rivelazione. BeO 47 (2005) 55-69.

8800 *Theobald, Christoph* La scrittura e la fede: la rivelazione nel nostro tempo. Il Regno 7 (2005) 22-27;

8801 La révélation: quarante ans après "Dei Verbum". RTL 36 (2005) 145-165.

8802 **Wenz, G.** Offenbarung: Problemhorizonte moderner evangelischer Theologie. Gö 2005, Vandenhoeck & R. 285 pp. €29.90.

8803 **Zielinski, V.** A la découverte de la parole. P 2004, Parole et S. 187 pp. €22. 28457-32228.

## H1.8 Theologia fundamentalis

8804 **Biser, Eugen; Heinzmann, Richard** Theologie der Zukunft: Eugen Biser im Gespräch mit Richard Heinzmann. Da:Wiss 2005, 150 pp. €24.90. 3-534-18387-8. [R]ActBib 42 (2005) 169-170 (*Boada, Josep*).

8805 **Bongardt, Michael** Einführung in die Theologie der Offenbarung. Einführung, Theologie: Da:Wiss 2005, 206 pp. €19.90. 3534159969.

8806 **Caviglia, Giovanni** Gesù Cristo via, verità e vita: linee di teologia fondamentale. R 2005, LAS 549 pp. €28. 889-788821-305955.

8807 *Grech, Prosper* 'Quid est veritas?': rivelazione e ispirazione: nuove prospettive. Il messaggio biblico. SRivBib 44: 2005 <1995> ⇒216. 277-285.

8808 **Hercsik, Donath** Die Grundlagen unseres Glaubens: eine theologische Prinzipienlehre. Theologie, Forschung und Wissenschaft 15: Müns 2005, LIT iii; 192 pp. €19.90. 3-8258-8427-9 [ThGl 95,510—Dieter Hattrup].

8809 **Hübner, Hans** Evangelische Fundamentaltheologie: Theologie der Bibel. Gö 2005, Vandenhoeck & R. 255 pp. €74.90. 3-525-53563-5.

8810 **Kessler, Hans** Sucht den Lebenden nicht bei den Toten: die Auferstehung Jesu Christi in biblischer, fundamentaltheologischer und systematischer Sicht. Topos plus Taschenbücher 419: [2]2002 <1985> ⇒ 19,8194. [R]ThPQ 153 (2005) 329-330 (*Gmainer-Pranzl, Franz*).

8811 *Krautter, Bernhard* Die Doppelgestalt des biblischen Glaubens. [F]STENDEBACH, F. 2005 ⇒141. 57-72.

8812 *Martens, Elmer A.* Moving from scripture to doctrine. BBR 15 (2005) 77-103.

8813 **Patrick, Dale A.** The rhetoric of revelation in the Hebrew Bible. 1999 ⇒15,7382... 18,7723. [R]ThR 70 (2005) 335-337 (*Reventlow, Henning Graf*).

8814 *Raske, Michael* Entdeckungen alttestamentlicher Glaubenszeugnisse mit Frankfurter Studierenden. [F]STENDEBACH, F. 2005 ⇒141. 141-48.

8815 *Treziak, Heinrich* Wort * Schweigen * Anfang—philosophische Überlegungen. [F]STENDEBACH, F. 2005 ⇒141. 317-325.

8816 *Valentin, Joachim* Relative Gotteskrise: fundamentaltheologische Anmerkungen zur Diskussion um Theologie nach Auschwitz. Streitfall Christologie. QD 214: 2005 ⇒549. 13-40.

8817 **Vanhoozer, Kevin J.** The drama of doctrine: a canonical-linguistic approach to christian theology. LVL 2005, Westminster 488 pp. $40.

8818 **Ward, Keith** What the bible really teaches: a challenge to fundamentalists. 2004 ⇒20,1351. [R]Theol. 108 (2005) 358-359 (*Goldingay, John*).

8819 **Webster, John** Holy scripture: a dogmatic sketch. Current issues in theology: 2003 ⇒19,8199; 20,8204. [R]AThR 87 (2005) 170, 172-173 (*Brittain, Christopher C.*); SBET 23 (2005) 108-109 (*Williams, P.J.*).

## H2.1 Anthropologia theologica—VT & NT

8820 *Aichelburg, Peter C.* Das anthropische Prinzip—über die Stellung des Menschen im Kosmos. Wie wirkt Gott. Forum St. Stephan 15: 2005 ⇒555. 15-27.

8821 *Angelini, Anna* Batoni, scettri e rami nell'Antico Testamento: materiali per un'analisi linguistica e antropologica. Acme 58/3 (2005) 3-26.

8822 **Arterbury, Andrew E.** Entertaining angels: early christian hospitality in its Mediterranean setting. NTMon 8: Shf 2005, Shf Academic ix; 227 pp. $90. 1-905048-21-1. Diss.; Bibl. 192-207.

8823 *Ashwin-Siejkowski, Piotr* Theological integrity questioned: a hermeneutical glossa to the debate on the issue of homosexuality. Theol. 108/842 (2005) 100-109.

8824 *Aveline, Jean-Marc* L'énigme de l'humain et le désir de Dieu: hommage théologique à Paul RICOEUR. ChDial 26 (2005) 145-162.

8825 **Babik, Marek** Współżycie seksualne w nauczaniu biblijnym [Sexual relationship in biblical teaching]. Studia Pedagogiczne 12: 2003 ⇒ 20,8209. [R]SRATK 9/1 (2005) 181-182 (*Najda, Andrzej J.*). **P**.

8826 **Bakke, O.M.** When children became people: the birth of childhood in early christianity. [T]*McNeil, Brian*: Mp 2005, Fortress 348 pp. $18. 0-8006-3725-9. [R]RBLit (2005)* (*Osiek, Carolyn*).

8827 **Bar, Shaul** A letter that has not been read: dreams in the Hebrew Bible. [T]*Schramm, Lenn J.*: MHUC 25: 2001 ⇒17,7205... 20,8210. [R]JNES 64 (2005) 137-139 (*Sweek, Joel*).

8828 **Basset, Lytta** Sainte colère: Jacob, Job, Jésus. Genève 2002, Labor et F. 358 pp. 978-22274-76095. Bibl. 351-355 [Gen 32,23-33].

8829 *Battaglia, Oscar* La comunicazione nella bibbia. ConAss 7 (2005) 51-68.

8830 *Báez, Silvio José* La gioia nell'Antico Testamento. RVS 59/1 (2005) 8-24.

8831 **Beck, James R.; Demarest, Bruce** The human person in theology and psychology: a biblical anthropology for the twenty-first century. GR 2005, Kregel 428 pp.

8832 *Bellah, Robert N.* God and king. God, truth, and witness. 2005 ⇒ 532. 112-130.

8833 *Berger, Klaus* Biblisches Christentum als Heilungsreligion. Heilung. BTSP 26: 2005 ⇒585. 226-246.

8834 **Berger, Klaus** Identity and experience in the New Testament. [T]*Muenchow, Charles*: 2003 ⇒19,8206; 20,8213. [R]TS 66 (2005) 182-184 (*Pilch, John J.*).

8835 *Berlejung, Angelika* Physiognomik im Alten Testament, den Apokryphen und Qumran. leqach 6 (2005) 7-25.

8836 [E]**Bigarelli, Alberto; Peri, Aldo** De Sexto: la sessualità nelle scritture sacre. Sussidi biblici 94: Reggio Emilia 2005., San Lorenzo 129 pp. 88-8071-175-X.

8837 **Bouyer, Louis** Gnosis: la connaissance de Dieu dans l'Écriture. 2004 ⇒20,8219. [R]Brot. 160 (2005) 307-308 (*Silva, Isidro Ribeiro da*).

8838 *Boyle, Marjorie O.* Broken hearts: the violation of biblical law. JAAR 73 (2005) 731-757.

8839 *Brandy, Hans C.* Vom Leiden des Menschen und vom Leiden Gottes. KuD 51/4 (2005) 33-51.

8840 **Brin, Gershon A.** The concept of time in the bible and the Dead Sea scrolls. StTDJ 39: 2001 ⇒17,7215... 20,8220. [R]JSJ 36 (2005) 93-94 (*Martone, Corrado*).

8841 *Brueggemann, Walter* Holy intrusion: the power of dreams in the bible. CCen 122/13 (2005) 28-29, 31 [NTAb 50,93].

8842 **Burrus, Virginia** The sex lives of Saints: an erotics of ancient hagiography. Ph 2004, Univ. of Pennsylvania Pr. vi; 216 pp. 0-8122-3745-5. Bibl. 199-208.

8843 *Butting, Klara* Unsere Vorfahren haben gesündigt, wir aber tragen ihre Schuld. JK 66/3 (2005) 19-22 [Lam 5,7].
8844 *Bülow, Vicco von* Verordnete Toleranz: ein kurzer Durchgang durch die Geschichte religiöser Duldungsedikte. WuD 28 (2005) 183-191.
8845 *Cameron, Charles* An introduction to 'theological anthropology'. Evangel 23 (2005) 53-61.
8846 *Campbell, W. Gordon* Vivre et mourir devant Dieu: esquisse de théologie biblique. RRef 56/234 (2005) 5-20 [NTAb 50,93].
8847 *Caro, Luciano* 'Non commettere adulterio': la visione della Bibbia ebraica sul matrimonio. De sexto. Sussidi biblici 94: 2005⇒8836. 69-89.
8848 **Carr, David McClain** The erotic word: sexuality, spirituality, and the bible. 2003 ⇒19,8223. [R]Interp. 59 (2005) 300-302 (*Yoder, Christine Roy*); INTAMS.R 11 (2005) 298-299 (*Villegas, Diana L.*).
8849 **Carson, Donald** Jusqu'à quand?: réflexions sur le mal et la souffrance. Sel & Lumière: Cléon d'Andran 2005, Excelsis 318 pp.
8850 *Cimosa, Mario* Dov'è tuo fratello?: riflessioni sulla famiglia nell'Antico Testamento. Il matrimonio. DSBP 42: 2005 ⇒459. 84-138.
8851 **Cipriani, Settimio** Uomini e donne nella bibbia: Antico Testamento. Pompei 2005, Santuario di Pompei 200 pp. €8.
8852 **Claassens, L. Juliana** The God who provides: biblical images of divine nourishment. 2004 ⇒20,8226. [R]BTB 35 (2005) 157 (*Craghan, John F.*); RBLit (2005)* (*Sanders, Paul*).
8853 *Coetzee, Johan* Silence, ye women! God is at work with the womb: Psalm 139 as illustration of Israel's embodied patriarchal theology of containment. OTEs 18 (2005) 521-530.
8854 *Cohen, Jeffrey M.* God's voice: from creation to the sanctuary. JBQ 33 (2005) 184-186.
8855 *Combet-Galland, Corina* Mythes et vérité métaphorique: pour une lecture anthropologique des évangiles. FV 104/4 (2005) 56-70.
8856 *Comblin, José* Corporeidade e bíblia;
8857 *Correia Júnior, João L.* A dimensão do corpo na Bíblia. Estudos bíblicos 87 (2005) 57-64/10-23.
8858 *Cothenet, Edouard* La parole de Dieu comme dialogue entre Dieu et les hommes. EeV 135 (2005) 18-25.
8859 *Crüsemann, Frank* Gen 1-4 als Einführung in das biblische Reden von Gott: ein Beitrag zu Verständnis und Übersetzung. Die Bibel—übersetzt. 2005 ⇒423. 165-172.
8860 **Dawson, Audrey** Perspectives on healing in the New Testament: a comparative study of Mark, Luke and Paul. [D]*Clarke, A.*: 2005 Diss. Aberdeen [RTL 37,614].
8861 *Dayler, G.B.* Beyond the biblical impasse: homosexuality through the lens of theological anthropology. Dialog 44/1 (2005) 81-89.
8862 *Ebach, Jürgen* Auf Dauer-zum Zeugnis: biblische Erinnerungen zum Thema "Erinnerung". JK 66/3 (2005) 1-5.
8863 *Facioni, Silvano* Lontano dall'astro: uno sguardo dalla tradizione ebraica sull'amore divino. Com(I) 201 (2005) 31-41.
8864 **Flannery-Dailey, Frances** Dreamers, scribes, and priests: Jewish dreams in the Hellenistic and Roman eras. JSJ.S 90: 2004 ⇒20,8238. [R]JSJ 36 (2005) 108-111 (*Nicklas, Tobias*).
8865 *Frey, Christofer* Konvergenz und Divergenz der Interessen von Ethik und Praktischer Theologie. Reconsidering the boundaries. 2005 ⇒ 598. 113-122.

8866 *Friedrich, Marcus A.* Spielstätte Gottes: wer sehen will, muss die Augen schließen: biblische Perspektiven auf das Reich der Träume. zeitzeichen 6/8 (2005) 26-30.

8867 *Gagnon, Robert A.* Scriptural perspectives on homosexuality and sexual identity. JPsC 24/4 (2005) 293-303.

8868 *Galpaz-Feller, Pnina* Hair in the bible and in ancient Egyptian culture: cultural and private connotations. BN 125 (2005) 75-94.

8869 **García Trapiello, Jesús** El hombre según la biblia: pensamiento antropológico del Antiguo Testamento. Glosas 33: 2002 ⇒18,7769; 19, 8251. [R]CDios 218 (2005) 556-557 (*Gutiérrez, J.*).

8870 *Gonçalves, Joaquim* A bíblia e a cultura. Did(L) 35 (2005) 735-750.

8871 *Hardmeier, Christof* 'Stark wie der Tod ist die Liebe': der Mensch und sein Tod in den Schriften des Alten Testaments. Erzähldiskurs. 2005 <2001> ⇒222. 77-94 [2 Sam 12,15-25; Ps 90,10-12; Cant 8,6];

8872 'Denn im Tod ist kein Gedenken an dich...' (Psalm 6,6): der Tod des Menschen–Gottes Tod?. Erzähldiskurs. 2005 <1988> ⇒222. 315-35.

8873 **Heckel, Ulrich** Der Segen im Neuen Testament: Begriff, Formeln, Gesten: mit einem praktisch-theologischen Ausblick. WUNT 150: 2002 ⇒18,7776... 20,8251. [R]TThZ 114 (2005) 258-260 (*Schwindt, Rainer*).

8874 *Hieke, Thomas* Echos des Exils—Babylon als Szenerie und "große Hure": Babylon in alttestamentlichen Spätschriften und im Neuen Testament. WUB 37 (2005) 40-42;

8875 Ein Symbol für Strafe und Hoffnung: Babylon in der Bibel. WUB 37 (2005) 32-38.

8876 *Hoping, Helmut* Gottes Ebenbild: theologische Anthropologie und säkulare Vernunft. ThQ 185 (2005) 127-149.

8877 **Hughes, Richard A.** Lament, death, and destiny. 2004 ⇒20,8257. [R]RBLit (2005)* (*Brandt, Pierre-Yves; Schearing, Linda*).

8878 *Human, Dirk* Homoseksualiteit—perspektiewe uit die antieke Nabye Ooste. OTEs 18 (2005) 629-636 [Gen 19; Lev 18; 20; Judg 19].

8879 **Hummel, Pascale** La maison et le chemin: petit essai de philologie théologique. 2004 ⇒20,8258. [R]REJ 164 (2005) 400-402.

8880 **Hutchison, John C.** Thinking right when things go wrong: biblical wisdom for surviving tough times. GR 2005, Kregel 256 pp. 0-8254-2810-6.

8881 *Janowski, Bernd* Der Mensch im alten Israel: Grundfragen alttestamentlicher Anthropologie. ZThK 102 (2005) 143-175 [Gen 1].

8882 *Jean Hilaire, Frère* Homme et femme, il les créa: les catéchèses de JEAN-PAUL II sur la Genèse. Aletheia 28 (2005) 65-72 [Gen 1-3].

8883 *Jenson, Robert W.* Male and female he created them. I am the Lord your God. 2005 ⇒816. 175-188 [OTA 28,350].

8884 *Jobsen, Aarnoud* Bijbelse beelden bij een natuurramp. ITBT 13/3 (2005) 27-29.

8885 *Johnston, P.S.* Death in Egypt and Israel: a theological reflection. The OT in its world. OTS 52: 2005 ⇒749. 94-116.

8886 *Käsemann, Ernst* Gottes Ebenbild und Sünder. In der Nachfolge. 2005 ⇒236. 105-116.

8887 *Kirwan, Michael* Easter light: the insights of René Girard. PaRe 1/2 (2005) 11-15 [NTAb 50,235].

8888 *Kotzé, Zacharias* Metaphors and metonymies for anger in the Old Testament: a cognitive linguistic approach. Scriptura 88 (2005) 118-125 [OTA 29,3].

8889 *Kruger, Paul* The inverse world of mourning in the Hebrew Bible. BN 124 (2005) 41-49;
8890 Depression in the Hebrew Bible: an update. JNES 64 (2005) 187-92;
8891 The face and emotions in the Hebrew Bible. OTEs 18 (2005) 651-63.
8892 **Lawrence, Louise J.** Reading with anthropology: exhibiting aspects of New Testament religion. Milton Keynes 2005, Paternoster viii; 212 pp. $35. 1-84227-375-2. Bibl. 193-212.
8893 *Leuenberger, Martin* "Deine Gnade ist besser als Leben" (Ps 63,4): Ausformungen der Grundkonstellation von Leben und Tod im alten Israel. Bib. 86 (2005) 343-368 [Ps 63; Prov 3; Qoh 3,16-22].
8894 **Limbeck, Meinrad** Alles Leid ist gottlos: Ijobs Hoffnung contra Jesu Todesschrei. Stu 2005, Kathol. Bibelwerk 116 pp. 3-460-33174-7.
8895 *Loader, James A.* Emptied life—death as the reverse of life in ancient Israel. OTEs 18 (2005) 681-702;
8896 Text and co-text in the sphere of theologising with the Old Testament: on the status of biblical archaeology in theology. OTEs 18 (2005) 703-721.
8897 **Loader, William R.G.** Sexuality and the Jesus tradition. GR 2005, Eerdmans viii; 288 pp. $30. 0-8028-2862-0. Bibl. 253-274 RRBLit (2005)* (*Stander, Hennie*).
8898 *Loughlin, Gerard* Biblical bodies. Theology and sexuality 12/1 (2005) 9-27.
8899 *Lucas, Ernest C.* A statue, a fiery furnace and a dismal swamp: a reflection on some issues in biblical hermeneutics. EvQ 77 (2005) 291-307 [Dan 2; 3,17; 9,24-27].
8900 *Lüsebrink, Hans-Jürgen* Fremdem begegnen. Zwischen Bibel und Wissenschaft. Glauben und Leben 31: 2005 ⇒407. 79-87.
8901 *Maire, C.-D.* La parole de Dieu au risque de la culture des hommes. RRef 56/231 (2005) 19-43 [NTAb 49,238].
8902 *Manicardi, Ermenegildo* 'Così che maschio e femmina non sono più due, ma una sola carne': l'insegnamento di Gesù e del Nuovo Testamento. De sexto. Sussidi biblici 94: 2005 ⇒8836. 91-128.
8903 *Manicardi, Luciano* Visitare i malati: approccio biblico. Firmana 38-39 (2005) 79-88.
8904 *Manns, Frédéric* Il matrimonio nell'Antico Testamento. Il matrimonio. DSBP 42: 2005 ⇒459. 14-83.
8905 *Manolopoulos, Mark* About gifts: Derrida, scripture, earth. BiCT 1/4 (2005)*.
8906 **Margron, Véronique** La douceur inespérée: quand la bible raconte nos histoires d'amour. 2004 ⇒20,8279. RRTL 36 (2005) 104-105 (*Lichtert, Cl.*).
8907 *Maurie, B.* Dynamics of inculturation: a theologico-scriptural perspective. MissTod 7 (2005) 123-136 [NTAb 49,545].
8908 *Mazzinghi, Luca* 'Quanto sono soavi le tue carezze, sorella mia sposa': il Cantico dei Cantici: la sessualità come incontro. De sexto. Sussidi biblici 94: 2005 ⇒8836. 17-45.
8909 *McArdle, Patrick* Called by name: contemporary christian anthropology. SJTh 58 (2005) 219-236.
8910 **McWilliams, Warren** Where is the God of justice?: biblical perspectives on suffering. Peabody, MA 2005, Hendrickson xi; 259 pp. $17. 1-565-63571-X. Bibl. 225-249.
8911 *Merlo, Paolo* L'immagine di Dio: maschio e femmina in Gn 1,26-27 e nella figura di Dio. Anthropotes 21 (2005) 105-119.

8912 *Murken, Todd* Hath God said...?. CThMi 32 (2005) 195-203.
8913 *Nadeau, Jean-Guy* La souffrance rédemptrice: légitimation ou subversion religieuse de la violence?. Théologiques 13 (2005) 5-19.
8914 **Neumann-Gorsolke, Ute** Herrschen in den Grenzen der Schöpfung: ein Beitrag zur alttestamentlichen Anthropologie. WMANT 101: 2004 ⇒20,8291. [R]ZAR 11 (2005) 374-380 (*Otto, Eckart*); ThLZ 130 (2005) 938-940 (*Witte, Markus*) [Gen 1; Ps 8].
8915 *Ohlig, Karl-Heinz* Christologie ist Anthropologie. Wie wirkt Gott. Forum St. Stephan 15: 2005 ⇒555. 119-149.
8916 *Oliva, José R.* Corpos terrestres e corpos celestes: Jesus de Nazaré e o Cristo. Estudos bíblicos 87 (2005) 90-101.
8917 *Olyan, Saul M.* The search for the elusive self in texts of the Hebrew Bible. Religion and the self in antiquity. 2005 ⇒818. 40-50.
8918 **Olyan, Saul M.** Biblical mourning: ritual and social dimensions. 2004 ⇒20,8293. [R]RBLit (2005)* (*Lawrence, Louise*); RBLit 7 (2005) 47-49 (*Becking, Bob*).
8919 *Panimolle, Salvatore A.* Così sarà benedetto chi teme il Signore!. Il matrimonio. DSBP 42: 2005 ⇒459. 7-13.
8920 *Parker, Kim I.* Adam: the postmodernist bourgeois liberal?. JSOT 29 (2005) 439-453.
8921 *Paul, Shalom M.* Euphemistically 'speaking' and a covetous eye. Divrei Shalom. CHANE 23: 2005 <1994> ⇒273. 213-222;
8922 Untimely death in the Semitic languages <1994>;
8923 The shared legacy of sexual metaphors and euphemisms in Mesopotamian and biblical literature <2002>. Divrei Shalom. CHANE 23: 2005 ⇒273. 223-238/299-314.
8924 *Pelletier, Anne-Marie* La révélation au risque d'éros. Com(F) 30/5-6 (2005) 35-46.
8925 *Peregrino, Artur* O corpo revalorizado na religião. Estudos bíblicos 87 (2005) 102-112.
8926 *Peterson, Erik* Gottesfreunde. Peterson: Lukasevangelium und Synoptica. 2005 ⇒277. 436-437.
8927 *Pfeiffer, Henrik* "Ein reines Herz schaffe mir, Gott!": zum Verständnis des Menschen nach Ps 51. ZThK 102 (2005) 293-311.
8928 *Pilch, John J.* Status by gender and age. BiTod 43 (2005) 188-192;
8929 Jesus' ascent to the sky. BiTod 43 (2005) 389-393.
8930 *Poli, Felice* Il volto sorridente di Cristo ad Auschwitz. Volto dei volti 8/1 (2005) 78-84.
8931 **Quesnel, Michel** La sagesse chrétienne: un art de vivre. P 2005, Desclée de B. 184 pp. €19. 2-220-05566-3 [EeV 147,21—E. Cothenet].
8932 *Ravasi, Gianfranco* Umiltà e sublimità della parola di Dio. Il bello della bibbia. 2005 ⇒357. 307-316.
8933 *Räisänen, Heikki* Sold under sin?: early christian notions of the human condition. [F]STEGEMANN, W. 2005 ⇒139. 289-300.
8934 *Riemer, Ulrike* Der fremde Bruder: Gastfreundschaft im Neuen Testament. Xenophobie. 2005 ⇒687. 241-261.
8935 **Rizzini, Ilaria** L'occhio parlante: per una semiotica dello sguardo nel mondo antico. Memorie, Classe di scienze morali lettere ed arti, Istituto Veneto di scienze lettere ed arti 77: Venezia 1998, Istituto Veneto di Scienze, Lettere ed Arti viii; 204 pp. 88-86166-62-1. Bibl.
8936 **Sawyer, Deborah F.** God, gender and the bible. 2002 ⇒18,7824; 19,8328. [R]ScrB 35 (2005) 42-43 (*Mills, Mary*).

8937 *Schneider-Flume, Gunda* Zur Frage nach dem christlichen Menschenbild. Biographie..des Paulus. WUNT 187: 2005 ⇒349. 347-65.

8938 *Schorch, Stefan* "Du bist ein verschlossener Garten": Theologie, Anthropologie und Geschlechterverhältnis im Alten Testament. WuD 28 (2005) 11-25.

8939 *Schroer, Silvia* Das Image der Frauenbrüste im alten Israel. WuA(M) 46/2 (2005) 90-92.

8940 *Schwienhorst-Schönberger, Ludger* Inkubation im Alten Testament?. Studien zum AT. SBAB 40: 2005 <2003> ⇒298. 113-119.

8941 *Séguin, Michaël* René Girard et le Jésus révélateur de la violence humaine. Scriptura(M) 7/1 (2005) 113-128.

8942 *Sheriffs, Deryck* 'Personhood' in the Old Testament?: who's asking?. EvQ 77 (2005) 13-34.

8943 *Shin, Samuel S.* Homosexual hermeneutics and its deadly implications: a pastoral reflection. TrinJ 26 (2005) 91-117.

8944 **Simian-Yofre, Horacio** Sofferenza dell'uomo e silenzio di Dio: nell' Antico Testamento e nella letteratura del Vicino Oriente Antico. Studia Biblica 2: R 2005, Città N. 326 pp. 88-311-362-59. Bibl. 287-303.

8945 **Smelik, Klaas A.D.** Zij doet hem goed en geen kwaad: man en vrouw in de bijbel. Zoetermeer 2005, Boekencentrum 204 pp. €18.90. 90-239-1066-4 [ITBT 14/7,33—Van Wieringen, Willien].

8946 *Söding, Thomas* Eros and agape. ThD 52 (2005) 210-216. Cf. GuL (2004) 248-260.

8947 *Stackhouse, Max L.* Christian ethics, practical theology, and public theology in a global era. Reconsidering the boundaries. 2005 ⇒598. 99-111.

8948 **Stone, Ken** Practicing safer texts: food, sex and bible in queer perspective. L 2005, Clark vi; 185 pp. £30/$30. 0-567-08172-9. Bibl. 150-175.

8949 **Temple, Gray** Gay unions in the light of scripture, tradition, and reason. 2004 ⇒20,8322. [R]RRT 12 (2005) 575-578 (*Woodard, Randall*).

8950 **Terrien, Samuel L.** Till the heart sings: a biblical theology of manhood and womanhood. Biblical resource: 2004 <1985> ⇒20,8324. [R]RBLit (2005)* (*Brenner, Athalya*).

8951 *Terrinoni, Ubaldo* Le ultime realtà dell'uomo: la morte. RVS 59/1 (2005) 25-60.

8952 *Turner, Max* Approaching 'personhood' in the New Testament, with special reference to Ephesians. EvQ 77 (2005) 211-233.

8953 *Utzschneider, Helmut* Der friedvolle und der bittere Tod: Einstellungen und Horizonte gegenüber Tod und Sterben im Alten Testament. [F]STEGEMANN, W. 2005 ⇒139. 37-48.

8954 *Van Leeuwen, Mary S.* Gender relations and the biblical drama. JPsT 33/2 (2005) 122-126.

8955 **Van Sevenant, Ann** Sexual intercourse: a philosophy of lovemaking. Lv 2005, Peeters 249 pp. 90-429-1617-6.

8956 *Vorster, N.* Human dignity and sexual behavious—a theological perspective. VeE 26/3 (2005) 891-911.

8957 *Vorster, V.* The rhetoric of Graeco-Roman erotic love versus early christian rhetoric. Scriptura 90 (2005) 740-764 [NTAb 51,326].

8958 **Warrington, Keith** Healing and suffering: biblical and pastoral reflections. Milton Keynes 2005, Paternoster 219 pp. £9. 1-85234-593-8. Bibl. 205-207.

8959 *Webb, William J.* Gender equality and homosexuality. Discovering biblical equality. 2005 ⇒387. 401-413.
8960 *Weiler, Lúcia* Encontro entre homem e mulher como espaço de mútuo enriquecimento—resgate de encontros numa perspectiva bíblica de gênero. Convergência 40 (2005) 240-253.
8961 *Wernik, Uri* Will the real homosexual in the bible please stand up?. Theology and sexuality 11/3 (2005) 47-64.
8962 *Wénin, André* Personnages humains et anthropologie dans le récit biblique. Analyse narrative. BEThL 191: 2005 ⇒742. 43-71 [Gen 37-39; 1 Kgs 21,1-16];
8963 Le 'origini' del lavoro umano secondo Gen 1-11. PSV 52 (2005) 9-19;
8964 La felicità raccontata nella bibbia <2003>;
8965 Nascita, morte, resurrezione <2003>;
8966 Tra Giardino dell'Eden e Gerusalemme celeste <2002>. Dalla violenza. 2005 ⇒323. 145-178/211-225/227-249.
8967 **Wénin, André** Non di solo pane: violenza e alleanza nella bibbia. 2004 ⇒20,8333. [R]Cart. 21 (2005) 233-234 (*Alvarez Barredo, M.*).
8968 *Wifstrand, Albert* Focus on the child. Epochs and styles. WUNT 179: 2005 <1943, 1961> ⇒325. 171-196.
8969 **Womack, Mari** Symbols and meaning: a concise introduction. Walnut Creek, CA 2005, Alta Mira 159 pp. $69.12. 0-7591-0321-6. Bibl. 141-146.
8970 *Wyatt, Nicolas* Marriage, mayhem and murder: an everyday story of royal folk. 'There's such divinity'. 2005 ⇒329. 231-251.
8971 *Younker, Randall W.* A look at biblical and ancient extra-biblical perspectives on death. JATS 16 (2005) 30-42 [OTA 29,328] [Gen 3].
8972 *Zbroja, Bogdan* Biblijne 'szemranie' [Biblical 'grumble']. RBL 58 (2005) 29-42. **P**.

## H2.8 **œcologia VT & NT**—*saecularitas*

8973 *Adam, Hella* Gras und Ufer. [F]STOLLE, V. 2005 ⇒143. 465-466.
8974 *Baudin, F.* Bible et écologie: protection de l'environnement et responsabilité chrétienne. RRef 56/232 (2005) 61-77 [NTAb 49,541].
8975 **Bernstein, Ellen** The splendor of creation: a biblical ecology. Cleveland 2005, Pilgrim 145 pp. $16 [BiTod 44,121—Dianne Bergant].
8976 *Brueggemann, Walter* A disaster of 'biblical' proportions. CCen 122/20 (2005) 23 [NTAb 50,92].
8977 *Florio, Lucio* Il messaggio biblico sulla natura: una nuova visione dell'ecologia. I vangeli. 2005 ⇒432. 141-147.
8978 [E]**Goren-Inbar, Naama; Speth, John D.** Human paleoecology in the Levantine Corridor. Oxf 2004, Oxbow xviii, 220 pp. 1-8421-7155-0.
8979 *Johnson, L.T.* Caring for the earth: why environmentalism needs theology. Commonweal 132/13 (2005) 16-20 [NTAb 50,95].
8980 *Levoratti, Armando J.* Dinanzi alla crisi dell'ecologia. I vangeli. 2005 ⇒432. 148-151.
8981 **MacDonald, Ivor** Land of the living: christian reflections on the countryside. College Station 2005, Virtualbookworm.com 249 pp. $14. 1-58939-782-7.
8982 **McDonagh, Seán** The death of life: the horror of extinction. Dublin 2004, Columba 152 pp. €10. 1-85607-4641. [R]PIBA 28 (2005) 128-129 (*Mangan, Céline*).

8983 **Pikaza, Xabier** El desafío ecológico: creación bíblica y bomba atómica. 2004 ⇒20,8342. [R]SalTer 93 (2005) 872-3 (*Pascual, Pablo J.*).
8984 *Schravesande, Hans* Natuur en geschiedenis: klimaatverandering in de bijbelse theologie. ITBT 13/2 (2005) 24-26.
8985 **Wagner, Volker** Profanität und Sakralisierung im Alten Testament. BZAW 351: B 2005, De Gruyter ix; 358 pp. €98. 3-11-018463-X. Bibl. 332-352. [R]ZAR 11 (2005) 351-360 (*Otto, Eckart*).

### H3.1 *Foedus*—**The Covenant**; *the Chosen People, Providence*

8986 *Barbaglia, Silvio* Il campo lessicale, il campo associativo e il campo semantico dell'"elezione d'Israele" nel TaNaK e nella Bibbia: dalla linguistica all'ermeneutica della tradizione. RStB 17/1 (2005) 13-71.
8987 **Bergjan, Silke-Petra** Der fürsorgende Gott: der Begriff ΠΡΟΝΟΙΑ in der apologetischen Literatur der Alten Kirche. AKG 81: 2002 ⇒ 19,7858; 20,8343. [R]JThS 56 (2005) 213-215 (*Meredith, Anthony*).
8988 *Braulik, Georg* Gott für Israel preisen: zur Heilsprärogative Israels und zum 4. Hochgebet. Liturgie und Bibel. ÖBS 28: 2005 ⇒360. 301-329.
8989 *Davis, J.P.* Who are the heirs of the Abrahamic covenant?. ERT 29/2 (2005) 149-163 [Mt 28,19-20].
8990 *Dulles, Avery Cardinal* The covenant with Israel. First Things 157 (2005) 16-21.
8991 *Fesko, J.V.* N.T. Wright and the sign of the covenant. SBET 23 (2005) 30-39 [Mt 6,19-34].
8992 *Fiedler, Peter* 'Geh ins Land Israel!' (Mt 2,20): die Landverheißung an das jüdische Volk im Licht des Neuen Testaments. Studien zur biblischen Grundlegung. SBAB 35: 2005 <1995> ⇒209. 177-192.
8993 **Forthomme, Bernard** La jalousie: élection divine, secret de l'être, force naturelle et passions humaines. Donner raison 16: Bru 2005, Lessius 815 pp. 28729-91379. Préf. *Jacques Le Brun*; Bibl. 797-800.
8994 *Garbini, Giovanni* L'eponimia di Israele. RStB 17/1 (2005) 75-88.
8995 *Hahn, Scott* Covenant in the Old and New Testaments: some current research (1994-2004). CuBR 3 (2005) 263-292.
8996 **Harless, Hal** How firm a foundation: the dispensations in the light of the divine covenants. Studies in biblical literature 63: 2004 ⇒20, 8346. [R]RBLit (2005)* (*Graves, David*).
8997 *Hoping, Helmut* Das Mysterium Israels und die Messianität Jesu: Israeltheologie als Aufgabe der Christologie. Streitfall Christologie. QD 214: 2005 ⇒549. 159-181.
8998 **Horton, Michael S.** Covenant and eschatology: the divine drama. 2002 ⇒18,7868; 19,8379. [R]SdT 17 (2005) 197-198 (*De Chirico, Leonardo*).
8999 *Leithart, P.J.* Old covenant and new in sacramental theology new and old. ProEc 14 (2005) 174-190 [NTAb 49,544].
9000 *Maggi, Lidia* Uno sguardo cristiano sulla singolarità di Israele. Studi Fatti Ricerche 110 (2005) 3-5.
9001 *Martone, Corrado* L'idea di elezione e le sue potenzialità ermeneutiche nelle diverse correnti giudaiche. RStB 17/1 (2005) 227-237.
9002 *McMichael, Steven J.* The covenant in patristic and medieval christian theology. Two faiths. 2005 ⇒844. 45-64.

9003 *McNamara, Martin* Some reflections on covenant and towards a theology of the absurd. MillSt 55 (2005) 65-81.

9004 *Menke, Karl-Heinz* Jesus Christus: Wiederholung oder Bestimmung der Heilsgeschichte Israels?: zwei Grundgestalten jüdisch perspektivierter Christologie. Streitfall Christologie. QD 214: 2005 ⇒549. 125-158.

9005 *Moggi, Mauro* Il *barbaros* fra ideologia e realtà (dalla fine del V secolo a.C. all'epoca ellenistica). RStB 17/1 (2005) 203-223.

9006 *Niccacci, Alviero* La separazione di Israele nello spazio e del tempo: gli spostamenti geografici con particolare riferimento ai motivi esodici. RStB 17/1 (2005) 113-134.

9007 **Novak, David** The election of Israel: the idea of the chosen people. 1995 ⇒11/2,3145... 15,7479. RThR 70 (2005) 301-305 (*Reventlow, Henning Graf*).

9008 *Rendtorff, Rolf* Die "Erwählung" Israels in der Hebräischen Bibel: exegetische Bemerkungen. FSTEGEMANN, E. 2005 ⇒139. 319-327.

9009 *Rizzi, Armido* L'elezione: funzione e ambiguità. RStB 17/1 (2005) 285-295.

9010 **Souzenelle, Annick de; Lenoir, Frédéric** L'alliance oubliée: la bible revisitée. Spiritualité: P 2005, Michel 268 pp. €18.50. 2-226-165428-0.

9011 *Termini, Cristina* L'elezione di Israele: la problematica e le traiettorie del Convegno: introduzione. RStB 17/1 (2005) 7-11.

9012 *Thoma, Clemens* Der göttliche Weggefährte des Volkes Israel. FrRu 12 (2005) 2-18.

9013 *Vignolo, Roberto* Domanda antropologica e modello regale: fortune alterne di una cifra universale dell'elezione. RStB 17/1 (2005) 239-283.

9014 **Wells, Jo B.** God's holy people: a theme in biblical theology. JSOT.S 305: 2000 ⇒16,7489... 20,8355. RThR 70 (2005) 166-167 (*Reventlow, Henning Graf*).

9015 **Williams, Michael D.** Far as the curse is found: the covenant story of redemption. Phillipsburg, NJ 2005, P&R xv; 315 pp. £10. 0-87552-5-10-5.

9016 *Zappella, Marco* L'immagine dell'elezione come strumento dell'esaltazione apologetica di Israele secondo quattro testi ebraici in lingua greca (Tobia, Ben Sira, Giuditta, Ester). RStB 17/1 (2005) 167-201.

## H3.5 *Liturgia, spiritualitas VT*—**OT prayer**

9017 *Bartolini, Elena* La proclamazione della scrittura nell'Antico Testamento. RPLi 43/3 (2005) 3-10.

9018 *Braulik, Georg* Das Volk, das Fest, die Liebe: alttestamentliche Spiritualität. Liturgie und Bibel. ÖBS 28: 2005 <2004> ⇒360. 29-49.

9019 **Brueggemann, Walter** Worship in ancient Israel: an essential guide. Nv 2005, Abingdon (12); 104 pp. $14. 0687343364. RRBLit (2005)* (*Gupta, Nijay; Hieke, Thomas; Kraus, Thomas; Levine, Baruch A.*).

9020 *Dohmen, Christoph* Gott sei's geklagt ... vom Verlust einer biblischen Gebetsform. Ren. 61/1 (2005) 53-63.

9021 *Lefebvre, Philippe* 'Allons chez Celui-qui-voit' (1 Samuel 9,9): des racines à l'accompagnement spirituel dans l'Ancien Testament?. LV(L) 54/3 (2005) 5-17.

9022 *Lohfink, Norbert* Die richtige Gesellschaft <1982>;

9023 Altes Testament und Liturgie: unsere Schwierigkeiten und unsere Chancen <1988>;

9024 Alttestamentliche Exegese und Liturgiewissenschaft <1999>;

9025 Freizeit <1977>. Liturgie und Bibel. ÖBS 28: 2005 ⇒360. 13-28/65-83/85-90/93-108.

9026 *Regev, Eyal* Temple prayer as the origin of the fixed prayer: on the evolution of prayer during the period of the second temple. Zion 70 (2005) 5-29. **H.**

9027 *Scalabrini, Patrizio R.* Le convocazioni d'Israele nel Primo Testamento. RPLi 248 (2005) 3-10.

9028 **Secondin, Bruno** La lettura orante della Parola: "Lectio divina" in comunità e in parrocchia. 2001 ⇒17,7347; 20,8369. [R]PaVi 50/4 (2005) 59-60 (*Doglio, Claudio*).

9029 *Ska, Jean Louis* Percorsi di riconciliazione: 'Io sono Giuseppe vostro fratello'. CoSe 7-8 (2005) 78-90 [Gen 37-50].

9030 *Watts, James W.* Biblical psalms outside the Psalter. The book of Psalms. VT.S 99: 2005 ⇒390. 288-309.

### H3.7 *Theologia moralis*—**OT moral theology**

9031 **Barton, John** Understanding Old Testament ethics: approaches and explorations. 2003 ⇒19,167; 20,8374. [R]NBl 86 (2005) 116-118 (*Ounsworth, Richard*); Interp. 59 (2005) 70, 72 (*Carroll R., M. Daniel*); Faith & Mission 22/3 (2005) 112-113 (*Tarwater, John*).

9032 **Biddle, Mark E.** Missing the mark: sin and its consequences in biblical theology. Nv 2005, Abingdon 190 pp. $19. 978-0687-494620.

9033 *Chinitz, Jacob* Four biblical options of moral choice. JBQ 33 (2005) 153-156.

9034 *Collins, John J.* Faith without works: biblical ethics and the sacrifice of Isaac. Encounters. 2005 <1999> ⇒200. 47-58 [Gen 22];

9035 The biblical vision of the common good. Encounters. 2005 <1987> ⇒200. 78-88.

9036 *Davies, Eryl W.* The morally dubious passages of the Hebrew Bible: an examination of some proposed solutions. CuBR 3 (2005) 197-228 [Josh 6-11].

9037 *Fabry, Heinz J.* Der Generationenvertrag und das biblische Gebot der Elternehrung. [F]STENDEBACH, F. 2005 ⇒141. 14-29 [Exod 20,12; 21, 15].

9038 *Fischer, Stefan* Mein Vater ein Aramäer: vom Umgang mit Fremden. ZMiss 31/4 (2005) 288-292.

9039 *Gagnon, Robert A.* The Old Testament and homosexuality: a critical review of the case made by Phyllis Bird. ZAW 117 (2005) 367-394.

9040 *Garrone, Daniele* Antico Testamento e diritti umani: alcune riflessioni. Protest. 60 (2005) 283-292.

9041 *Granados García, Carlos* La justicia en el Antiguo Testamento: dimensiones esenciales y perspectivas. Burgense 46/1 (2005) 95-105.

9042 **Hoppe, Leslie J.** There shall be no poor among you: poverty in the bible. 2004 ⇒20,8381. [R]CBQ 67 (2005) 495-496 (*McCann, J. Clinton, Jr.*); Theoforum 36 (2005) 216-220 (*Vogels, Walter*); RBLit (2005)* (*Latvus, Kari; Shemesh, Yael*).

9043 **Janzen, Waldemar** Old Testament ethics. 1994 ⇒10,7324... 12, 6801. [R]ThR 70 (2005) 169-171 (*Reventlow, Henning Graf*).
9044 *Katz, Claire E.* Raising Cain: the problem of evil and the question of responsibility. CrossCur 55/2 (2005) 215-233 [Gen 4,1-16].
9045 *Kegler, Jürgen* Sünde im Alten Testament. GlLern 20 (2005) 108-18.
9046 **Kleine, Michael** Hilfe für Schwache im Alten Testament: Motivation und Formen der Hilfe im Kontext von Familie und Staat. [D]*Gerstenberger, Erhard* 2005, Diss. Marburg [ThLZ 131,340].
9047 **Krahe, Susanne** Aug' um Auge, Zahn um Zahn?: Beispiele biblischer Streitkultur. Wü 2005, Echter 136 pp. 3-429-02669-5.
9048 *Lindström, Fredrik* Slavmoral: teologiska perspektiv på Mose lag. SEÅ 70 (2005) 177-192 [Exod 20,2-17; 21-23 [Deut 5,6-21].
9049 **Mills, Mary E.** Biblical morality: moral perspectives in Old Testament narratives. 2001 ⇒17,7364... 20,8386. [R]HeyJ 46 (2005) 359-360 (*Hill, Robert C.*).
9050 *Pehlke, Helmuth* Glauben und Handeln im Alten Testament. JETh 19 (2005) 73-91.
9051 **Rodd, Cyril S.** Glimpses of a strange land: studies in Old Testament ethics. Old Testament Studies: 2001 ⇒17,7371... 19,8426. [R]JThS 56 (2005) 130-134 (*Barton, John*).
9052 **Rogerson, John W.** Theory and practice in Old Testament ethics. [E]*Carroll R., M. Daniel*: JSOT.S 405: 2004 ⇒20,267. [R]ZAR 11 (2005) 386-388 (*Becking, Bob*); RBLit (2005)* (*Otto, Eckart; Reed, Stephen; Shemesh, Yael*).
9053 **Sekine, Seizo** A comparative study of the origins of ethical thought: Hellenism and Hebraism. [T]*Wakabayashi, Judy*: Lanham 2005, Rowman & L. xviii; 281 pp. 0-7425-3239-9.
9054 *Spreafico, Ambrogio* Giustizia e misericordia: un contributo a partire dall'Antico Testamento. Iustitia in caritate: miscellanea in onore di Velasio DE PAOLIS. [E]**Conn, James J.** Studi giuridici 72: Città del Vaticano 2005, Urbaniana Univ. Press. 105-112. 88-401-4015-8.
9055 **Van Meegen, Sven** Alttestamentliche Ethik als Grundlage einer heutigen Lebensethik: ein Beitrag zum interreligiösen Dialog. Bibel und Ethik 3: Müns 2005, Lit 440 pp. 3-8258-8316-7.
9056 **Weber, Max** Die Wirtschaftsethik der Weltreligionen: das antike Judentum: Schriften und Reden 1911-1920. [E]*Otto, Eckart; Offermann, Julia*: Max Weber Gesamtausgabe 21/1-2: Tü 2005, Mohr S. 2 vols; xxix; 606 + xxi; 607-1157 pp. €214 + 189. 3-16-148487-8/529-7. Bibl. vol. II 995-1012.
9057 **Wenham, Gordon J.** Story as torah: reading the Old Testament ethically. Old Testament Studies: 2000 ⇒16,7534... 19,8430. [R]ThR 70 (2005) 171-173 (*Reventlow, Henning Graf*).
9058 **Wright, Christopher J.H.** Old Testament ethics for the people of God. 2004 ⇒20,8409. [R]JETh 19 (2005) 249-251 (*Klement, Herbert*).
9059 *Zenger, Erich* Gott und Mensch—Zwillinge der Gerechtigkeit: das Programm der Psalmen 111 und 112. BiHe 41/164 (2005) 8-10.

### H3.8 *Bellum et pax VT-NT*—War and peace in the whole Bible

9060 **Abécassis, Armand** Puits de guerre, sources de paix: affrontements monothéistes. P 2003, Seuil 240 pp. €18. 978-20205-73238.

9061 *Alinsangan, Gil A.* Jesus our peace: the biblical dimension of peace. Ethical dimensions. 2005 ⇒739. 76-90 [Eph 2,13-18].

9062 *Andrade, William C. de* Shalom como resposta a toda violência. Fragmenta de Cultura [Goías] 15/1 (2005) 47-68 [OTA 28,347].

9063 *Aono, Tashio* Christian belief and violent conflict. AJBI 30-31 (2004-2005) 117-123.

9064 *Assmann, Jan* Monotheismus und die Sprache der Gewalt. Das Gewaltpotential. QD 216: 2005 ⇒863. 18-38.

9065 **Avalos, Hector** Fighting words: the origins of religious violence. NY 2005, Prometheus 444 pp. $16.38.

9066 **Batsch, Christophe** La guerre et les rites de guerre dans le judaïsme du deuxième temple. JSJ.S 93: Lei 2005, Brill xvi; 491 pp. €159/ $214. 90-04-13897-8. Bibl. 463-476.

9067 **Beauchamp, Paul; Vasse, Denis** A violência na bíblia. Cadernos Bíblicos 90: Lisboa 2005, Difusora Bíblica 72 pp.

9068 *Bechmann, Ulrike* Die kriegsgefangene Frau (Dtn 21,10-14). BiKi 60 (2005) 200-204 [Deut 21,10-14].

9069 *Britt, Brian* Death, social conflict, and the barley harvest in the Hebrew Bible. JHScr 5/15 (2005) [Ruth 1; 2 Sam 21].

9070 *Cardona Ramírez, Hernán* La no-violencia, nido de paz. El grano. 2005 <2004> ⇒197. 83-97.

9071 *Chennattu, Rekha M.* A creative approach to violence: a biblical perspective. JPJRS 8/1 (2005) 5-19 [Mt 5,38-42].

9072 **Dietrich, Walter; Mayordomo, Moisés**, *al.*, Gewalt und Gewaltüberwindung in der Bibel. Z 2005, Theologischer 392 pp. €34.50. 3-290-17340-2.

9073 *Emcke, Carolin* Kriegsgebiete—von Tod und Normalität. BiKi 60 (2005) 232-233.

9074 *Giles, Terry* Why biblical studies?: EGLBS presidential address 2005. ProcGLM 25 (2005) 1-13.

9075 *Grünenfelder, Regula* Stell' dir vor, niemand lernt mehr für den Krieg!. BiKi 60 (2005) 194-199.

9076 **Guilaine, Jean; Zammit, Jean** The origins of war: violence in prehistory. T*Hersey, Melanie*: Oxf 2005, Blackwell xi, 282 pp. 1-405-1-1259-X. Bibl. 257-273.

9077 *Hoeren, Jürgen* Kultur basiert auf Frieden. BiKi 60 (2005) 250-251.

9078 *Hofheinz, Marco* Friedenstiften: biblisch-theologische Perspektiven einer kirchlichen Friedensethik. PTh 94 (2005) 378-395.

9079 *Kamphaus, Franz* "Wo ist dein Bruder Abel?" (Gen 4,9): zur biblischen Kultur der Gewaltlosigkeit. GuL 78 (2005) 321-331.

9080 **Kashemwa Kabso, Johannes** Fondement biblique de la paix: défi aux églises des pays des grands lacs: une approche pragmatique du 'shâlôm'. D*Feldtkeller, Andreas*: 2005, Diss. Humboldt [ThRv 102, ii].

9081 *Kirk, Alan* The memory of violence and the death of Jesus in Q. Memory, tradition, and text. SBL.Semeia Studies 52: 2005 ⇒416. 191-206 [Lk 11,47-51].

9082 *Krüger, Thomas* Der Weg zu einer Konzeption von Frieden ohne Kriegführung in der hebräischen Bibel. Krieg–Gesellschaft–Institutionen. 2005 ⇒672. 117-133.

9083 *Lefevre, Frans* Geweld in de bijbel. Coll. 35/4 (2005) 341-371.

9084 *Lohfink, Norbert* Gewalt und Monotheismus: Beispiel Altes Testament. ThPQ 153 (2005) 149-162;

9085 Wie wird in der Eucharistiefeier um den Frieden gebetet?. Liturgie und Bibel. ÖBS 28: 2005 <1994> ⇒360. 333-338.

[E]**Matthews, S.** Violence in the New Testament 2005 ⇒439.

9086 **McDonald, Patricia M.** God and violence: biblical resources for living in a small world. 2004 ⇒20,8433. [R]ScrB 35 (2005) 97-99 (*Corley, Jeremy*); OTEs 18 (2005) 950-952 (*Branch, Robin G.*).

9087 *Michel, Andreas* Gott und Gewalt gegen Kinder. BiHe 41/163 (2005) 10-11.

9088 *Milner, Anthony* The bible and conflict. ScrB 35 (2005) 85-94.

9089 *Müller, Klaus* Gewalt und Wahrheit: zu Jan Assmanns Monotheismuskritik. Das Gewaltpotential. QD 216: 2005 ⇒863. 74-82.

9090 **Nelson-Pallmeyer, Jack** Is religion killing us? violence in the bible and the Qur'an. NY 2005, Continuum 169 pp. $15 [BiTod 45,193—Dianne Bergant].

9091 **Neri, Umberto** Guerra, sterminio e pace nella bibbia: catechesi biblica. Sussidi biblici 88: Reggio Emilia 2005, San Lorenzo 166 pp. 88-8071-167-9.

[E]**Sherwood, Y.** Sanctified aggression 2003 ⇒483.

9092 *Simon, Fritz B.* Lust am Krieg?. BiKi 60 (2005) 227-231.

9093 **Smelik, Klaas A.D.** Een tijd van oorlog, een tijd van vrede: bezetting en bevrijding in de bijbel. Zoetermeer 2005, Boekencentrum 220 p. €19.90. 90-239-1887-8 [ITBT 13/7,31—Snoek, Hans].

9094 *Stadelmann, Luis I.J.* Antítese da violência na bíblia. Convergência 40 (2005) 84-98.

9095 *Thiel, Winfried* Aspekte des Friedens im Alten Testament. Gedeutete Geschichte. BThSt 71: 2005 <1983> ⇒316. 107-120.

9096 *Tolbert, Mary Ann* The reproduction of domination. USQR 59/1-2 (2005) 9-14 [OTA 28,353].

9097 *Van Meenen, Bernard* Biblia y violencia. SelTeol 44/1 (2005) 39-47 <Etudes 3995 (2003) 495-506.

9098 *Warrior, Robert A.* Canaanites, cowboys, and Indians. USQR 59/1-2 (2005 <1980>) 1-8 [OTA 28,353];

9099 Response to special issue on religion and narratives of conquest. USQR 59/1-2 (2005) 125-130 [OTA 28,354].

9100 *Wénin, André* L'essere umano e Dio di fronte alla violenza <2004>;

9101 Al di là della violenza quale giustizia?<2003>. Dalla violenza. 2005 ⇒323. 77-87/89-123.

9102 **Wink, Walter** Jesus and nonviolence: a third way. Facets: 2003 ⇒ 19,8491; 20,8446. [R]CBQ 67 (2005) 359-360 (*Berquist, Jon L.*).

9103 *Zenger, Erich* Der Mosaische Monotheismus im Spannungsfeld von Gewalttätigkeit und Gewaltverzicht: eine Replik auf Jan Assmann. Das Gewaltpotential. QD 216: 2005 ⇒863. 39-73.

9104 *Zwick, Reinhold* Apokalyptisches Inferno und Sehnsucht nach Eden: biblische Koordinaten im Kriegsfilm. BiKi 60 (2005) 212-220.

## H4.1 Messianismus

9105 *Banon, David* Messianismi o messianismo?: il dibattito Idel-Scholem. Hum(B) 60 (2005) 111-121.

9106 *Boccaccini, Gabriele* Uomo, angelo o Dio?: alle radici del messianismo ebraico e cristiano. Il messia. 2005 ⇒719. 15-48.

9107 *Bonola, Gianfranco* Taubes contro Scholem: una diatriba sul messianismo ebraico. Hum(B) 60 (2005) 122-152.
9108 *Camera, Francesco* I 'giorni del messia' in BUBER e LEVINAS;
9109 *Capelli, Piero* Come i rabbini della tarda antichità attendevano il messia. Hum(B) 60 (2005) 328-359/28-56.
9110 *Caruso, Sergio* Messianismo e politica. Il messia. 2005 ⇒719. 149-168.
9111 **Condra, Ed** Salvation for the righteous revealed: Jesus amid covenantal and messianic expectations in second temple Judaism. AGJU 51: 2002 ⇒18,7945; 19,8501. [R]ThLZ 130 (2005) 384-386 (*Schimanowski, Gottfried*).
9112 *Cunico, Gerardo* Ripensare il messianismo: introduzione;
9113 Il messianismo polacco: Hoene Wroński, Mickiewicz, Cieszkowski;
9114 *Czajka, Anna* Il dialaogo messianico tra Ernst Bloch e Margarete Susman. Hum(B) 60 (2005) 5-27/200-220/246-266.
9115 [E]**Day, John** Rei e messias em Israel e no antigo Oriente Próximo. [T]*Lambert, Barbara Theoto*: Biblia e história: São Paulo 2005, Paulinas 527 pp.
9116 *De Benedetti, Paolo; Luzzatto, Amos* Il messia è ancora un nome per le nostre speranze?. Il messia. 2005 ⇒719. 169-179.
9117 *Desideri, Fabrizio* Il messia di Benjamin. Hum(B) 60 (2005) 278-302.
9118 *Déroche, Vincent* Muhammad—Messias der Juden?: jüdisches Leben im byzantinischen Reich. WUB 35 (2005) 18-19.
9119 *Eckert, Michael* Messianismo e cultura ebraica: l'autocomprensione culturale di Ernst Bloch. Hum(B) 60 (2005) 267-277.
9120 *Ehrlich, Ernst L.* Messianismus und Zionismus: pseudomessianische Bewegungen im Judentum. [F]STEGEMANN, E. 2005 ⇒139. 391-402.
9121 *Ferraris, Maurizio* La fenomenologia e il messia: rileggendo HUSSERL con DERRIDA. Hum(B) 60 (2005) 360-377.
9122 *Fiorato, Pierfrancesco* Un confronto tra il messianismo di Cohen e ROSENZWEIG. Hum(B) 60 (2005) 221-245.
9123 *Gatti, Roberto* Messianismo ed escatologia nell'ebraismo filosofico medioevale: MAIMONIDE e CRESCAS. Hum(B) 60 (2005) 57-75.
9124 *Giuliani, Massimo* L'ortodossia ebraica e la questione messianica. Hum(B) 60 (2005) 153-168.
9125 *Gruenwald, Ithamar* Messianismo ebraico e messianismo cristiano: un approccio psicoanalitico. Il messia. 2005 ⇒719. 137-147.
9126 *Hengel, Martin* The beginnings of christianity as a Jewish-Messianic and universalistic movement. Beginnings of christianity. 2005 ⇒786. 85-100.
9127 **Horbury, William** Messianism among Jews and Christians: twelve biblical and historical studies. 2003 ⇒19,210; 20,8452. [R]JQR 95 (2005) 336-340 (*Meeks, Wayne A.*).
9128 *Idel, Moshe* 'Il tempo della fine': la spiritualizzazione dell'apocalittica in Abraham ABULAFIA. Hum(B) 60 (2005) 76-110.
9129 *Janse, S.* De wapens van de Messias. ThRef 48 (2005) 41-64.
9130 *Jewett, Robert* Die biblischen Wurzeln des amerikanischen Messianismus. ZNT 8/15 (2005) 60-68.
9131 **Kavka, Martin** Jewish messianism and the history of philosophy. 2004 ⇒20,8455. [R]JHP 43 (2005) 370-371 (*Reinhard, Kenneth*); RBLit (2005)* (*Levy, Gabriel*).

9132 **Kinzer, Mark S.** Post-missionary Messianic Judaism: redefining christian engagement with the Jewish people. GR 2005, Baker 320 pp. $25. 1-587-43152-1.
9133 **Mack, Burton** Wer schrieb das Neue Testament?: die Erfindung des christlichen Mythos. 2000 ⇒16,7585. [R]SNTU 30 (2005) 266-267 (*Fuchs, Albert*).
9134 *Mack, Hananel* From Qumran to Provence: the notion of a Manassite Messiah. Meghillot III. 2005 ⇒608. 85-100. **H.**
9135 *Mitchell, David* The fourth deliverer: a Josephite Messiah in 4QTestimonia. Bib. 86 (2005) 545-553.
9136 *Moltmann, Jürgen* Il futuro della cristianità come popolo messianico. Hum(B) 60 (2005) 178-199.
9137 **Mowinckel, Sigmund** He that cometh: the Messiah concept in the Old Testament and later Judaism. [T]*Anderson, G.W.*: Biblical resource: GR 2005 <1956>, Eerdmans xxxii; 528 pp. $40/£25. 0-8028-2850-7. Foreword *John J. Collins*; Bibl. xxix-xxxii; 473-498. [R]RBLit (2005)* (*Fabry, Heinz-Josef; West, James*).
9138 *Oppenheimer, Aharon* Messianismus in römischer Zeit: zur Pluralität eines Begriffes bei Juden und Christen. Between Rome and Babylon. TSAJ 108: 2005 <1998> ⇒272. 263-282.
9139 *Petzel, Paul* Sabbatai Zwi—ein Bruder des Messias Jesus?: Anmerkungen und Fragen zu einer schwierigen Verwandtschaft. ZKTh 127 (2005) 415-448.
9140 *Sacchi, Paolo* Le figure messianiche superumane del secondo tempio e il figlio dell'uomo. Il messia. 2005 ⇒719. 69-85.
9141 *Schiller, Hans-Ernst* Nella spanna di un attimo: motivi messianici in Adorno e Horkheimer. Hum(B) 60 (2005) 303-327.
9142 *Schoon, Simon* Messiaanse koorts bij joden en christenen. Theologisch debat 2/1 (2005) 35-39.
9143 *Stefani, Piero* Il nascondimento messianico. Hum(B) 60 (2005) 169-177.
9144 *Sweeney, Marvin* The democratization of messianism in modern Jewish thought. Biblical interpretation. 2005 ⇒758. 87-101.
9145 **Thompson, T.L.** The Messiah myth: the Near Eastern roots of Jesus and David. NY 2005, Basic xiii; 414 pp. $35. 04650-85776.
9146 *Trudinger, Paul* Real messianism. DR 123 (2005) 295-299.
9147 *Vaiss, Paul* L'interprétation juive des prophéties messianiques de l'Ancien Testament de l'époque hellénistique aux *talmuds* et aux premiers *midrashim*. RICP 96 (2005) 105-138.
9148 **Worth, Roland H.** Messiahs and Messianic movements through 1899. Jefferson, N.C. 2005, McFarland vii; 255 pp. 0-7864-2311-0. Bibl. 236-248.
9149 *Yangarber-Hicks, Natalia* Messianic believers: reflections on identity of a largely misunderstood group. JPsT 33 (2005) 127-139.

## H4.3 *Eschatologia VT*—**OT hope of future life**

9150 **Dim, Emmanuel Uchenna** The eschatological implications of Isa 65 and 66 as the conclusion of the book of Isaiah. Bern 2005, Lang xviii; 409 pp. €62.80. 3-03910-596-5. Bibl. 381-409.
9151 **Fischer, Alexander A.** Tod und Jenseits im alten Orient und Alten Testament. Neuk 2005, Neuk 271 pp. €24.90. 3-7887-2104-9.

9152 **Gowan, Donald E.** Eschatology in the OT. $^{2}$2000 <1986> ⇒16, 7608; 17,7438. $^{R}$JETh 19 (2005) 251-252 (*Pehlke, Helmuth*).

9153 *Grosby, Steven* The biblical 'nation' as a problem for philosophy. HPolS 1/1 (2005) 7-23.

9154 *Jindo, Job Y.* On myth and history in prophetic and apocalyptic eschatology. VT 55 (2005) 412-415.

9155 *Kruger, Paul A.* Symbolic inversion in death: some examples from the Old Testament and the ancient Near Eastern world. VeE 26 (2005) 398-411.

9156 *Römer, Thomas* La mort et les morts dans le Proche-Orient ancien et dans la Bible hébraïque. ETR 80 (2005) 347-358 [Isa 26; Ezek 37].

9157 *Ska, Jean Louis* 'Il sepolcro sarà loro casa per sempre' (Sal 49,12): l'aldilà nell'Antico Testamento. L'aldilà. 2005 ⇒507. 17-47.

9158 *Van Wieringen, Willien* De dood en de één na laatste dingen. ITBT 13/3 (2005) 6-9.

9159 *Weinfeld, Moshe* The day of the Lord: aspirations for the kingdom of God in the bible and the Jewish liturgy;

9160 Expectations of the divine kingdom in biblical and postbiblical literature. Normative and sectarian Judaism. Library of Second Temple Studies 54: 2005 ⇒2732. 68-89/294-304.

### H4.5 *Theologia totius VT*—**General Old Testament theology**

9161 **Anderson, Bernhard Word** Contours of Old Testament Theology. 1999 ⇒15,7610... 17,7447. $^{R}$ThR 70 (2005) 14-15 (*Reventlow, Henning Graf*).

9162 **Barr, James** The concept of biblical theology: an Old Testament perspective. 1999 ⇒15,7611... 18,7968. $^{R}$ThR 70 (2005) 3 (*Reventlow, Henning Graf*).

9163 **Brueggemann, Walter** Theology of the Old Testament: testimony, dispute, advocacy. 1997 ⇒13,7170... 18,7970. $^{R}$ThR 70 (2005) 9-11 (*Reventlow, Henning Graf*);

9164 Mp 2005 <1997>, Augsburg 777 pp. $32. 0-8006-3765-8. Incl. CD-ROM [BiTod 44,122—Dianne Bergant].

9165 $^{E}$**Dohmen, Christoph; Söding, Thomas** Eine Bibel—zwei Testamente: Positionen biblischer Theologie. UTB 1893: 1995 ⇒11/2, 3372. $^{R}$ThR 70 (2005) 145-154 (*Reventlow, Henning Graf*).

9166 **Gerstenberger, Erhard** Theologien im Alten Testament. 2001 ⇒17, 7455...19,8545. $^{R}$ThR 70 (2005) 19-21 (*Reventlow, Henning Graf*);

9167 Theologies of the Old Testament. $^{T}$*Bowden, John*: 2002 ⇒18,7976... 20,8487. $^{R}$HeyJ 46 (2005) 211-213 (*McNamara, Martin*); BiblInterp 13 (2005) 191-194 (*MacDonald, Nathan*); OTEs 18 (2005) 143-145 (*Wessels, W.J.*);

9168 Teologie nell'Antico Testamento: pluralità e sincretismo della fede veterotestamentaria. Introduzione allo studio della bibbia, Suppl. 25: Brescia 2005, Paideia 343 pp. €33. 88-394-0708-1. Bibl. 323-327.

9169 *Gesundheit, Shimon* Gibt es eine jüdische Theologie in der Hebräischen Bibel?. Biblische Theologie. ATM 14: 2005 ⇒756. 53-64.

9170 **Goldingay, John** Old Testament theology, 1: Israel's gospel. 2003 ⇒19,8547; 20,8488. $^{R}$CBQ 67 (2005) 314-316 (*Hawkins, Ralph K.*); JETh 19 (2005) 247-249 (*Klement, Herbert H.*); JThS 56 (2005) 517-520 (*Clements, Ronald E.*).

9171 **Gunneweg, Antonius H.J.** Teologia bíblica do Antigo Testamento. T*Fuchs, Werner*; E*Reimer, Haroldo*: Biblioteca de estudos do Antigo Testamento: São Paulo 2005, Loyola 368 pp. 85-89067-23-8.
9172 *Hardmeier, Christof* Systematische Elemente der Theo-logie in der Hebräischen Bibel: das Loben Gottes—ein Kristallisationsmoment biblischer Theo-logie. Erzähldiskurs. 2005 <1995> ⇒222. 339-354;
9173 New relations between systematic theology and exegesis and the perspectives on practical theology and ethics. Erzähldiskurs. FAT 46: 2005 ⇒222. 371-381.
9174 **Hermisson, Hans-Jürgen** Alttestamentliche Theologie und Religionsgeschichte Israels. Forum Theologische Literaturzeitung 3: 2000 ⇒16,7630. RThR 70 (2005) 414-416 (*Reventlow, Henning Graf*).
9175 **Herrmann, Wolfram** Theologie des Alten Testaments: Geschichte und Bedeutung des israelitisch-jüdischen Glaubens. 2004 ⇒20,8489. RThR 70 (2005) 21-23 (*Reventlow, Henning Graf*).
9176 *Janowski, Bernd* Theologie des Alten Testaments: Zwischenbilanz und Zukunftsperspektiven;
9177 *Jeremias, Jörg* Neuere Entwürfe zu einer "Theologie des Alten Testaments". Theologie und Exegese. 2005 ⇒410. 87-124/125-158.
9178 *Klein, Stephanie* Die Erinnerung an Lernerfahrungen im Exil als eine Perspektive für die Pastoral heute. ThQ 185 (2005) 196-203.
9179 **Knierim, Rolf** The task of Old Testament theology. 1995 ⇒11/2, 3381... 13,7177. RThR 70 (2005) 23-30 (*Reventlow, Henning Graf*).
9180 **Marchand, Jacques** Sagesses: enquête historique sur la recherche de l'autonomie et du bonheur. L'idéologie biblique: aux sources du fondamentalisme occidental, 3. Montréal 2005, Liber 612 pp.
9181 **Motte, Jochen** Biblische Theologie nach Walther ZIMMERLI: Darstellung und Würdigung der alttestamentlichen Theologie Walther Zimmerlis und der sich aus ihr ergebenden Perspektive zum Neuen Testament in systematisch-theologischer Sicht. EHS.T 521: 1995 ⇒ 11/2,3385. RThR 70 (2005) 37-39 (*Reventlow, Henning Graf*).
9182 *Nielsen, Kirsten* Jeg er som en love for Efraim: overvejelser over dyrebilleder og gammeltestamentlig teologi. SEÅ 70 (2005) 215-227.
9183 **Nobile, Marco** Teologia dell'Antico Testamento. 1998 ⇒15,7620... 20,8492. RThR 70 (2005) 17-19 (*Reventlow, Henning Graf*).
9184 **Oden, Robert A., Jr.** The bible without theology. 1987 ⇒3,269... 7,983. RThR 70 (2005) 39-41 (*Reventlow, Henning Graf*).
9185 **Perdue, Leo G.** Reconstructing Old Testament theology: after the collapse of history. Overtures to biblical theology: Mp 2005, Fortress 399 pp. $20. 0-8006-3716-X [BiTod 44,124—Dianne Bergant].
9186 Religionsgeschichte Israels oder Theologie des Alten Testaments?. JBTh 10 (1995). RThR 70 (2005) 408-14 (*Reventlow, Henning Graf*).
9187 **Rendtorff, Rolf** Theologie des Alten Testaments: ein kanonischer Entwurf. 2001 ⇒15,7625... 19,8557. RThR 70 (2005) 8-9 (*Reventlow, Henning Graf*);
9188 The canonical Hebrew Bible: a theology of the Old Testament. T*Orton., David E.*: Tools for biblical study 7: Lei 2005, Deo xiv; 813 pp. $62. 90-5854-020-0. Bibl. 757-781.
9189 *Schmidt, Werner H.* Elemente einer "Theologie des Alten Testaments": zur Frage nach seiner Eigenart. VF 50/1/2 (2005) 25-34.
9190 *Schöttler, Heinz-Günther* Die Anklage Gottes als Krisenintervention: eine erlittene Exilstheologie Israels. ThQ 185 (2005) 158-181.

9191 **Schroven, Brigitte** Theologie des Alten Testaments zwischen Anpassung und Widerspruch: christologische Auslegung zwischen den Weltkriegen. 1996 ⇒12,6901; 13,7191. [R]ThR 70 (2005) 4 (*Reventlow, Henning Graf*).

9192 *Schwienhorst-Schönberger, Ludger* Einheit und Vielheit: gibt es eine sinnvolle Suche nach der Mitte des Alten Testaments?. Studien zum AT. SBAB 40: 2005 <2001> ⇒298. 225-258.

9193 *Schwöbel, Christoph* Erwartungen an eine Theologie des Alten Testaments aus der Sicht der Systematischen Theologie. Theologie und Exegese. SBS 200: 2005 ⇒410. 159-185.

9194 **Smith-Christopher, Daniel L.** A biblical theology of exile. Overtures to Biblical Theology: 2002 ⇒18,7993... 20,8497. [R]HeyJ 46 (2005) 213-214 (*McNamara, Martin*); BiblInterp 13 (2005) 324-327 (*Linville, James R.*); JSSt 50 (2005) 218-222 (*Scott, James M.*).

9195 *Wénin, André* L'idolâtrie comme prostitution dans la bible. L'idole dans l'imaginaire occidental. 2005 ⇒524. 57-66.

9196 **Woungly-Massaga, Ebénézer M.** À travers l'Ancien Testament: perspective théologique. Yaoundé 2005, CLÉ 91 pp. 99560-90263.

9197 *Zenger, Erich* Ist das Projekt "Theologie der Hebräischen Bibel/des Alten Testaments" überhaupt bibelgemäß?: response auf den Vortrag von Shimon Gesundheit. Biblische Theologie. 2005 ⇒756. 65-68;

9198 Was sind Essentials eines theologischen Kommentars zum Alten Testament?. Theologie und Exegese. SBS 200: 2005 ⇒410. 213-238.

## H5.1 *Deus*—**NT—God** [as Father ⇒H1.4]

9199 **Bachmann, Michael** Göttliche Allmacht und theologische Vorsicht: zu Rezeption, Funktion und Konnotationen des biblisch-frühchristlichen Gottesepithetons pantokrator. SBS 188: 2002 ⇒18,7996... 20, 8501. [R]ThLZ 130 (2005) 144-145 (*Frenschkowski, Marco*).

9200 *Charry, Ellen T.* Following an unfollowable God. [M]JUEL, D. 2005 ⇒ 73. 155-163.

9201 *Collins, John J.* Jewish monotheism and christian theology. Encounters. 2005 <1997> ⇒200. 179-189.

9202 *Enuwosa, J.* Exploring the nature of God in the New Testament for meaningful development in Nigeria. BiBh 31 (2005) 106-122.

9203 *Foschia, Laurence* ΘΕΟΣ ΓΕΝΝΗΤΩΡ ΠΑΝΤΩΝ: divinité païenne et/ou chrétienne?. Nommer les dieux. 2005 ⇒504. 453-466.

9204 *Hübner, Hans* Martin HEIDEGGERs Götter und der christliche Gott: theologische Besinnung über Heideggers 'Besinnung' (Band 66). Wahrheit und Wirklichkeit. 2005 <1999> ⇒229. 82-108.

9205 *Käsemann, Ernst* Der Eine und die Vielen. In der Nachfolge. 2005 ⇒236. 202-211.

9206 *Kessler, Hans* Wie wirkt Gott in der Welt und an der Welt?: die Auferstehung Jesu als Paradigma. Wie wirkt Gott. Forum St. Stephan 15: 2005 ⇒555. 53-92.

9207 **Kinlaw, D.F.** Let's start with Jesus: a new way of doing theology. GR 2005, Zondervan $16. 03102-62615 [NTAb 50,427].

9208 *Krause, Deborah* Keeping it real: the image of God in the New Testament. Interp. 59 (2005) 358-368.

9209 *Pardo, José Javier* Dios justo y misericordioso. SalTer 93 (2005) 849-859.

9210 *Schwankl, Otto* Monotheismus im Neuen Testament. FolTh 16 (2005) 153-176.

## H5.2 **Christologia ipsius NT**

9211 **Armstrong Cox, Sergio** Jesús de Nazaret: síntesis de cristología bíblica. Talca [2]2005, Univ. Católica 128 pp [Mensaje 55/1,61—César Lambert].
9212 *Brug, J.F.* Could Jesus have sinned?. WLQ 102/2 (2005) 128-131 [NTAb 50,87] [Mt 10,23].
9213 **Cane, Anthony** The place of Judas Iscariot in christology. Aldershot 2005, Ashgate vi; 211 pp. $95. 0-7546-5284-X.
9214 *Creegan, N. Hoggard* Jesus in the land of spirits and *Utu*. Pacifica 18 (2005) 141-153 [NTAb 50,87].
9215 *Edwards, D.J.* The Davidic priesthood—Jesus as priest. JHiC 11/1 (2005) 118-127 [NTAb 50,87].
9216 *Gieschen, C.A.* Confronting current christological controversy. CTQ 69/1 (2005) 3-32 [NTAb 51,314].
9217 *Golding, Carole; Rochon, Claude* Jésus, figure de controverse pour les victimes d'abus sexuels. Scriptura(M) 7/1 (2005) 39-48.
9218 *Hays, Richard B.* Christ prays the psalms: Israel's psalter as matrix of early christology. The conversion. 2005 <1993> ⇒223. 101-118.
9219 *Horbury, William* Jewish messianism and early christology. Contours of christology. McMaster NT Studies 7: 2005 ⇒775. 3-24.
9220 **Horton, Michael S.** Lord and servant: a covenant christology. LVL 2005, Westminster 282 pp. £17. 0-664-22863-1.
9221 *Hurtado, Larry W.* Introduction;
9222 How on earth did Jesus become a God?: approaches to Jesus-devotion in earliest christianity;
9223 Devotion to Jesus and second-temple Jewish monotheistic piety;
9224 Epilogue. How on earth. 2005 ⇒227. 1-9/13-30/31-55/205-206.
9225 **Hurtado, Larry W.** Lord Jesus Christ: devotion to Jesus in earliest christianity. 2003 ⇒19,8590; 20,8529. [R]JEH 56 (2005) 118-120 (*Crossley, James G.*); RBLit 7 (2005) 307-309 (*Goutzioudis, Moschos*); ET 116 (2005) 193-196 (*Dunn, James D.G.*); KaKe 74 (2005) 129-141 (*Iwashima, T.*); JThS 56 (2005) 531-539 (*Horbury, William*); ThTo 62 (2005) 262, 264 (*Dunn, James D.G.*); ET 116 (2005) 193-196 (*Dunn, James D.G.*); ChH 74 (2005) 345-347 (*Weinrich, William C.*); BZ 49 (2005) 254-261 (*Dautzenberg, G.*); JR 85 (2005) 486-488 (*Guttenberger, Gudrun*); ThLZ 130 (2005) 646-650 (*Löhr, Hermut*); Gr. 86 (2005) 206-208 (*Janssens, Jos*); VJTR 69 (2005) 559-560 (*Meagher, P.M.*); Bib. 86 (2005) 283-7 (*O'Collins, Gerald*);
9226 GR 2005 <2003>, Eerdmans 764 pp. $35£20. 0802-831672. Bibl. 655-702 [NTAb 50,427].
9227 *Keck, Leander* The task of New Testament christology. PSB 26 (2005) 266-276.
9228 *Kirby, Jeffrey* The ecclesial priesthood of Jesus Christ. HPR 105/10 (2005) 24-28.
9229 *Laughlin, P.A.* The once and future Christ of faith: promising options beyond the history-faith dichotomy. The Fourth R [Santa Rosa, CA] 18/2 (2005) 2-7, 18 [NTAb 50,88].

9230 *Lieu, Judith* Reading Jesus in the wilderness. [F]YOUNG, F. JSNT.S 295: 2005 ⇒168. 88-100 [Mt 4,1-11; Lk 4,1-13].

9231 *Longenecker, Richard N.* Christological materials in the early christian communities. Contours of christology. 2005 ⇒775. 47-76.

9232 *Manicardi, Ermenegildo* La scoperta di Cristo verità di Dio e verità dell'uomo: il percorso neotestamentario. Gesù la cristologia. 2005 <1997> ⇒253. 217-230.

9233 **Matera, Frank J.** New Testament christology. 1999 ⇒15,7681... 17,7511. [R]VJTR 69 (2005) 558-559 (*Meagher, P.M.*).

9234 **Medina Estévez, Jorge Cardinal** Lord, who are you?: the names of Christ. 2004 ⇒20,8537. [R]HPR 105/4 (2005) 77-78 (*Anger, Matthew M.*); Spiritual Life (Winter 2005) 248-250 (*Looney, Thomas P.*).

9235 *Michaels, J. Ramsey* Catholic christologies in the catholic epistles. Contours of christology. 2005 ⇒775. 268-291.

9236 *Mies, F.* Le Fils et Serviteur humilié. Christus 52 (2005) 429-438 [NTAb 50,323].

9237 *Pagliara, Cosimo* Il ritorno di Elia: dalle attese escatologiche giudaiche del I secolo a.C. al *novum* della primitiva cristologia. Giudei o cristiani?. 2005 ⇒833. 93-103.

9238 *Robinson, James M.* Very goddess and very man: Jesus' better self. The sayings gospel Q. BEThL 189: 2005 <1988> ⇒289. 259-273.

9239 *Siegwalt, G.* Le Christ, unique fondement de l'église: exclusivité et inclusivité du Christ. Irén. 78/1-2 (2005) 5-23 [NTAb 50,325] [1 Cor 3].

9240 *St-Arnaud, Guy-Robert* Le travail fait de langage en christologie. [F]GENEST, O. 2005 ⇒46. 85-106.

9241 *Theißen, Gerd* Monotheistische Dynamik im Neuen Testament: der Glaube an den einen und einzigen Gott und die neutestamentliche Christologie. KuI 20 (2005) 130-143.

9242 *Varghese, R.A.* Your Christ is too small. HPR 106/2 (2005) 8-16 [NTAb 50,323].

9243 *Witherington, Ben, III* Jesus as the alpha and omega of New Testament thought. Contours of christology. 2005 ⇒775. 25-46.

9244 **Wright, Nicholas Thomas** Christian origins and the question of God. Jesus and the victory of God, 2. 1996 ⇒12,6939... 16,7696. [R]ET 116 (2005) 228-229 (*Newman, Carey C.*).

### H5.3 *Christologia praemoderna*—**Patristic to Reformation**

9245 *Andrist, Patrick* Les protagonistes égyptiens du débat apollinaristes: le *Dialogue d'Athanase et Zachée* et les dialogues pseudoathanasiens —intertextualité et polémique religieuse en Égypte vers la fin du IVe siècle. RechAug 34 (2005) 63-141.

9246 **Bathrellos, Demetrios** The Byzantine Christ: person, nature, and will in the christology of Saint MAXIMUS the Confessor. 2004 ⇒20, 8550. [R]RRT 12 (2005) 372-375 (*McCosker, Philip*).

9247 *Bishoy, Metropolitan* The shaping of christian thought: the councils of Ephesus and Chalcedon: the christological controversies of the 4th and 5th centuries. Christianity. 2005 ⇒607. 191-217.

9248 *Bourgine, Benoît* Que faire des premiers conciles?. RTL 36 (2005) 449-475.

9249 *Brandt, Sigrid* Jeus Christus—Gottes Bild und Bild des Bildes: auf dem Weg zu einer "imagologischen" Näherbestimmung der christologischen Zweinaturenlehre. Picturing the New Testament. WUNT 2/ 193: 2005 ⇒396. 344-355.

9250 *Buhagiar, Joseph* The shaping of christian thought: the councils of Nicaea and Constantinople. Christianity. 2005 ⇒607. 161-189.

9251 **Deme, Daniel** The christology of ANSELM of Canterbury. 2003 ⇒19, 8621. [R]RRT 12/1 (2005) 43-45 (*McCosker, Philip*); AThR 87 (2005) 139, 141 (*Hefling, Charles*).

9252 **Edmondson, Stephen** CALVIN's christology. 2004 ⇒20,8551. [R]RRT 12 (2005) 460-462 (*Holder, R. Ward*).

9253 *Fédou, Michel* Le verbe de Dieu et l'universel chrétien: l'héritage de la tradition patristique. Théophilyon 10 (2005) 309-323.

9254 [T]**Fraïsse-Bétoulières, Anne** FACUNDUS d'Hermiane: Défense des Trois Chapitres (à Justinien), 2/1-2/2 (livres 3-7). [E]**Clément, J.-M.; Vander Plaetse, R.** SC 478-479: 2003 ⇒19,8623-4. [R]REAug 51 (2005) 210-212 (*Weiss, Jean-Pierre*);

9255 3 (livres 8-10). SC 484: 2004 ⇒20,8553. [R]REAug 51 (2005) 212-214 (*Weiss, Jean-Pierre*).

9256 *Freyer, Johannes B.* 'Das wahre Licht, unseren Herrn Jesus Christus sehen'—die Christologie des heiligen FRANZISKUS nach seinen Schriften. AFH 98 (2005) 9-40.

9257 *Gray, Patrick* The legacy of Chalcedon: christological problems and their significance. Cambridge companion to the age of Justinian. 2005 ⇒667. 215-238.

9258 **Grillmeier, Alois** Jesus der Christus im Glauben der Kirche, 2/3: die Kirchen von Jerusalem und Antiochien. [E]*Hainthaler, Theresia* 2002 ⇒18,8057; 19,8628. [R]ThLZ 130 (2005) 53-56 (*Pinggéra, Karl*);

9259 Le Christ dans la tradition chrétienne: de l'âge apostolique au concile de Chalcédoine (451). [T]*Pascale-Dominique, Soeur*: CFi 230: 2003 <1973> ⇒19,8629; 20,8554. [R]RelCult 51 (2005) 229-230 (*Langa, Pedro*); LTP 61 (2005) 181-182 (*Dîncă, Lucian*); Gr. 86 (2005) 934-935 (*Farahian, Edmond*).

9260 [T]**Guidi, Patrizia** VIGIULIUS Thapsensis: Contro gli Ariani. CTePa 184: R 2005, Città N. 216 pp. 88-311-3184-2. Bibl. 45-47.

9261 *McLynn, Neil* 'Genere Hispanus': THEODOSIUS, Spain and Nicene orthodoxy. Hispania. 2005 ⇒617. 77-120.

9262 *Mostert, Walter* Bemerkungen zum Verständnis der altkirchlichen Christologie. ZThK 102 (2005) 73- 92.

9263 *Röwekamp, Georg* "Für wen aber haltet ihr mich"?: die christologischen Streitigkeiten der frühen Kirchen und ihr Einfluss auf die Begegnung von Islam und Christentum. WUB 35 (2005) 16-17.

9264 **Thumpanirappel, George** Christ in the East Syriac tradition: a study of the christology of the Assyrian Church of the East and the Common Christological Declaration of 1994. 2003 ⇒19,8638; 20,8560. [R]JJSS 4 (2004) [2005] 99-101 (*Kurikilamkatt, James*).

## H5.4 *(Commentationes de) Christologia* **moderna**

9265 **Amaladoss, Michael** The Asian Jesus. Delhi 2005, ISPCK x; 206 pp. Rs150/$9/£7. 81-7214-884-4. [R]VJTR 69 (2005) 936-937 (*Gispert-Sauch, G.*).

9266 **Bagot, Jean-Pierre** Jésus, un homme... et puis?. P 2005, Cerf 106 pp. €17.

9267 **Burridge, Richard A.; Gould, Graham** Jesus now and then. 2004 ⇒20,8563. RRBLit (2005)* (*Bird, Michael; Pahl, Michael*).

9268 *Chapman, J.H.* Engaging Neville's *Symbols of Jesus*. AJTP 26/1-2 (2005) 60-76 ⇒17,7583 [NTAb 49,313].

9269 Cristología y sociedad. Caracas 2005, Publicaciones ITER-UCAB 332 pp. 0798-1236. Bibl.

9270 **Duquoc, Christian** El único Cristo: la sinfonía diferida. 2004 ⇒20, 8567. RRF 251 (2005) 263-264 (*Irazabal, Juan Antonio*).

9271 *Echlin, Edward P.* Jesus and the earth, walking our christology. NBl 86 (2005) 493-504.

9272 **Gamberini, Paolo** Questo Gesù (At 2,32): pensare la singolarità di Gesù. Manuali 24: Bo 2005, Dehoniane 272 pp. €22. 88-10-43009-3.

9273 **Gesché, A.** Chrystus. T*Kuryś, A.*: Poznań 2005, W drodze 278 pp. RStBob 2 (2005) 236-247 (*Gardocki, Dariusz*). **P.**;

9274 Dieu pour penser, 6: le Christ. 2001 ⇒17,7563; 19,8655. RCom(F) 30/1 (2005) 89-97 (*Espezel, Alberto*).

9275 **Greene, Colin J.D.** Christology in cultural perspective: marking out the horizons. 2004 ⇒20,8570. RFaith & Mission 22/2 (2005) 125-127 (*Bush, L. Russ, III*).

9276 **Haight, Roger** Jesus, símbolo de Deus. 2003 ⇒19,8658. RREB 65 (2005) 293-314 (*Teixeira, Fustino*).

9277 **Hoping, Helmut** Einführung in die Christologie. 2004 ⇒20,8573. ROrdKor 46 (2005) 375-377 (*Eckholt, Margit*).

E**Hoping, H.** Streitfall Christologie 2005 ⇒549.

9278 **Lobo, Joseph** Encountering Jesus Christ in India: an alternative way of doing christology in a cry-for-life situation based on the writings of George M. Soares-Prabhu. Bangalore 2005, Asian Trading xvi; 522 pp. Diss. Innsbruck.

E**Malek, R.** The Chinese face of Jesus Christ, 3a 2005 ⇒564.

9279 **Marchesi, Giovanni** Gesù di Nazaret chi sei?: lineamenti di cristologia. 2004 ⇒20,8580. RConAss 7 (2005) 108-110 (*Testaferri, Francesco*).

9280 **McCready, Douglas** He came down from heaven: the preexistence of Christ and the christian faith. DG 2005, InterVarsity 341 pp. $26. 08308-27749.

9281 **Moingt, Joseph** Dieu qui vient à l'homme, II-1: de l'apparition à la naissance de Dieu–1: apparition. CFi 245: 2/1 P 2005, Cerf 480 pp. €38.90. 978-22040-79020.

9282 *Morujão, Carlos* A cristologia de SCHELLING. Did(L) 35 (2005) 285-303.

9283 **Pottakkal, Joshy Poulose** The Incarnation according to Karl RAHNER (1904-1984). R 2005, n.p. x; 126 pp. Bibl. 79-120.

9284 *Rausch, T.P.* Postmodern Jesus: the Vatican's quarrel with Roger Haight. CCen 122/9 (2005) 28-31 [NTAb 49,538].

9285 **Rovira Belloso, Josep M.** Qui és Jesús de Natzaret: una teologia per unir coneixement i vida. Barc 2005, Ed. 62. 382 pp. 84-297-5610-8.

9286 **Schoenborn, Christoph Card.** My Jesus: encountering Christ in the gospel. T*Shea, Robert J.*: SF 2005, Ignatius 225 pp. 0-89870-987-3.

9287 **Schwarz, Hans** Christology. 1998 ⇒14,7000... 19,8681. RAsbTJ 60/2 (2005) 139-140 (*Carey, Greg*).

9288 **Simonis, Walter** Jesus Christus, wahrer Mensch und unser Herr: Christologie. 2004 ⇒20,8588. [R]ActBib 42 (2005) 225-226 (*Boada, Josep*).

9289 **Souletie, Jean-Louis** Les grands chantiers de la christologie. CJJC 90: P 2005, Desclée 252 pp. €24. 2-7189-0980-3. [R]EeV 136 (2005) 25-27 (*Roure, P. David*).

9290 *Striet, Magnus* Christologie nach der Shoah?: Horizontverschiebungen. Streitfall Christologie. QD 214: 2005 ⇒549. 182-215.

9291 **Tilliette, Xavier** Jésus romantique. CJJC 85: 2002 ⇒18,8110... 20, 8592. [R]RTL 36 (2005) 250-252 (*Brito, E.*).

9292 [E]**Virgoulay, René** Le Christ de Maurice BLONDEL. CJJC 86: 2003 ⇒ 19,8686; 20,8594. [R]Gr. 86 (2005) 411-412 (*D'Agostino, Simone*).

9293 *Wright, T.J.* How is Christ present to the world. IJST 7/3 (2005) 300-315 [NTAb 50,89].

9294 **Yoder, John H.** Preface to theology: christology and theological method. 2002 ⇒18,8116...20,8597. [R]MoTh 21 (2005) 519-21 (*Stassen, Glenn H.*).

## H5.5 *Spiritus Sanctus: pneumatologia*—**The Holy Spirit**

9295 *Athikalam, James* The Holy Spirit in the christian sacred scripture. JJSS 5 (2005) 68-91.

9296 **Cho, Y.** Spirit and kingdom in the writings of Luke and Paul: an attempt to reconcile these concepts. [D]*Clarke, A.*: Milton Keynes 2005, Paternoster xviii; 227 pp. £20. 18422-73167. Diss. Aberdeen; Bibl. [NTAb 50,391].

9297 **Coffey, David** 'Did you receive the Holy Spirit when you believed?': some basic questions for pneumatology. Pere Marquette Lecture in Theology: Milwaukee 2005, Marquette Univ. Pr. 125 pp. $15. 0-874-62-585-8 [ThD 52,251—W. Charles Heiser] [Acts 19].

9298 **Hauschild, Wolf-Dieter; Drecoll, Volker H.** Pneumatologie in der Alten Kirche. TC 12: 2004 ⇒20,8604. [R]ThLZ 130 (2005) 411-412 (*Staats, Reinhart*); ThGl 95 (2005) 251-252 (*Fuchs, Gotthard*);

9299 Le Saint-Esprit dans l'église ancienne. [T]*Poupon, Gérard*: TC 12: 2004 ⇒20,8603. [R]POC 55 (2005) 206-207 (*Attinger, D.*).

9300 **Kaniyamparampil, Emmanuel** The Spirit of life: a study of the Holy Spirit in the early Syriac tradtion. 2003 ⇒19,8696. [R]VJTR 69 (2005) 715-716 (*Gispert-Sauch, G.*).

9301 *Käsemann, Ernst* "Wo der Geist des Herrn ist, da ist Freiheit": was ist fällig in der Kirche?. In der Nachfolge. 2005 ⇒236. 258-269.

9302 **Kimutai Rono, Daniel** The Holy Spirit and the sacraments in the international bilateral ecumenical dialogues: Roman Catholic and Orthodox, Anglican, Lutheran, Methodist, Reformed dialogues. R 2005, Pont. Univ. Sanctae Crucis Fac. Theol. xx; 464 pp. Bibl. 423-463.

9303 **Romerowski, Sylvain** L'oeuvre du Saint-Esprit dans l'histoire du salut. Charols 2005, Excelsis 399 pp.

9304 *Schütz, Christian* Der Heilige Geist—Liebe in Person. IKaZ 34 (2005) 333-340.

9305 **Warrington, Keith** Discovering the Holy Spirit in the New Testament. Peabody 2005, Hendrickson x; 230 pp. $17. 1-56563-871-9.

### H5.6 *Spiritus et Filius*; 'Spirit-Christology'

9306 *Gronchi, Maurizio* La presenza dello Spirito nell'evento cristologico. Rivista di science religiose 19/1 (2005) 63-75.

9307 **Madonia, N.** Cristo sempre vivente nello Spirito: per una cristologia pneumatologica. CNST 66: Bo 2005, EDB 307 pp. €23.50. 88-1040-5-773.

9308 *Navone, John* The sending of the Spirit. MillSt 55 (2005) 11-34.

### H5.7 *Ssma Trinitas*—The Holy Trinity

9309 **Berger, Klaus** Ist Gott Person?: ein Weg zum Verstehen des christlichen Gottesbildes. 2004 ⇒20,8617. [R]ThGl 95 (2005) 395-6 (*Gerwing, Manfred*).

9310 *Bosman, Hendrik J.* Monotheism and Trinity beyond arithmetic: response to Samuel Vollenweider. Biblische Theologie. ATM 14: 2005 ⇒756. 135-138.

9311 *Böhnke, Michael* Gott ist Liebe: ein Beitrag zur trinitätstheologischen Debatte. ThPh 80 (2005) 249-256.

9312 *Carpenter, Mark* A synopsis of the development of trinitarian thought from the first century church fathers to the second century apologists. TrinJ 26 (2005) 293-319.

9313 *Di Bianco, Nicola* La Trinità nel vangelo secondo Matteo. Asp. 52 (2005) 163-178 [Mt 28,19].

9314 **Douglass, Scot** Theology of the gap: Cappadocian language theory and the trinitarian controversy. AmUSt.TR 235: NY 2005, Lang x; 289 pp. 0-8204-7463-0. Bibl. 277-285.

9315 **Kärkkäinen, Veli-Matti** The doctrine of God: a global introduction: a biblical, historical and contemporary survey. 2004 ⇒20,8622. [R]TJT 21 (2005) 328-329 (*Skira, Jaroslav Z.*).

9316 *Lachner, Raimund* Zur Schriftargumentation in der Dogmatik des 20. Jahrhunderts: dargestellt am Beispiel der Trinitätstheologie. Das Buch. Vechtaer Beiträge zur Theologie 11: 2005 ⇒487. 114-129.

9317 **Lopes, Steven J.** From the Trinity to the Eucharist: towards a trinitarian theology of the sacrifice of Christ and its representation in the eucharist of the church. R 2005, Pontificia Universitas Gregoriana (12), 292 pp. Diss. Bibl. 263-292.

9318 *Marks, E.* The revelation and experience of the 'journeying' triune God. Affirmation & Critique [Anaheim, CA] 10/1 (2005) 14-25 [NTAb 49,506].

9319 **Mazza, Giuseppe** La liminalità come dinamica di passaggio: la rivelazione come struttura osmotico-performativa dell'inter-esse trinitario. TGr.T 125: Roma 2005, E.P.U.G. 782 pp. 88-7839-040-2. Bibl. 711-761.

9320 *Ohst, Martin* Theaterdonner: kritische Notizen zu R. Slenczkas Aufsatz "Die Heilige Schrift, das Wort des dreieinigen Gottes". Ment. *Luther*. KuD 51/3 (2005) 192-196.

9321 *Slenczka, Reinhard* Die Heilige Schrift, das Wort des dreieinigen Gottes. Ment. *Luther*. KuD 51/3 (2005) 174-191.

9322 **Ware, Bruce A.** Father, Son, and Holy Spirit: relationship, roles, and relevance. Wheaton, IL 2005, Crossway 173 pp. 1-58134-668-9.

9323 **Witherington, Ben; Ice, Laura M.** The Shadow of the Almighty: Father, Son and Spirit in biblical perspective. 2002 ⇒18,8145... 20, 8630. [R]STV 43 (2005) 207-209 (*Kręcidło, Janusz*); RBLit 7 (2005) 43-44 (*Clark, Ron*).

## H5.8 *Regnum messianicum, Filius hominis*—Messianic kingdom Son of Man

9324 *Aune, David* Christian prophecy and the messianic status of Jesus. Apocalypticism, prophecy. WUNT 199: 2005 <1992> ⇒177. 300-19.

9325 *Bergey, R.* Le royaume de Dieu: l'attente et la venue du Messie dans la foi d'Abraham. RRef 56/233 (2005) 1-8 [NTAb 50,87].

9326 *Boshoff, H.J.; Van Aarde, A.G.* Grieks-romeinse apokaliptiek en die christelike kerugma. HTSTS 61 (2005) 1131-1148 [NTAb 51,129].

9327 *Casey, P. Maurice* Son of man. The historical Jesus in recent research. 2005 ⇒379. 315-324.

9328 *Charlesworth, James H.* Il figlio dell'uomo, il primo giudaismo, Gesù e la cristologia delle origini. Il messia. 2005 ⇒719. 87-110.

9329 *Chilton, Bruce* Regnum Dei Deus est. The historical Jesus in recent research. 2005 ⇒379. 115-122.

9330 *Collins, John J.* Jesus and the messiahs of Israel. Encounters. 2005 <1996> ⇒200. 169-178.

9331 *David, Pablo S.* Who did Jesus say the Son of Man was?. Ethical dimensions. 2005 ⇒739. 91-116.

9332 *Evans, Craig A.* Inaugurating the kingdom of God and defeating the kingdom of Satan. BBR 15 (2005) 49-75.

9333 *Frades Gaspar, Eduardo* El mesias Jesús y los 'bienes mesiánicos'. Iter 16/37-38 (2005) 157-209.

9334 *Grelot, Pierre* Jésus, Fils de l'homme. RThom 105 (2005) 89-102.

9335 **Hengel, Martin; Schwemer, Anna Maria** Der messianische Anspruch Jesu und die Anfänge der Christologie: vier Studien. WUNT 138: 2001 ⇒17,276... 20,362. [R]TS 66 (2005) 446-447 (*Perkins, Pheme*); SvTK 81 (2005) 137-139 (*Kazen, Thomas*).

9336 **Kavanagh, Preston** Secrets of the Jewish exile: the bible's codes, Messiah, and Suffering Servant. Tarentum, Pennsylvania 2005, Word (8) 454 pp. $25. 1-59571-030-2.

9337 *Käsemann, Ernst* Der Anfang des Evangeliums: die Botschaft vom Reiche Gottes. In der Nachfolge. 2005 ⇒236. 1-12.

9338 *Leandro, Francisco Javier* Jesucristo, el Hijo del hombre: la alternativa humana de Dios a la historia. Iter 16/37-38 (2005) 211-230.

9339 **Lee, Aquila** From Messiah to preexistent Son: Jesus' self-consciousness and early christian exegesis of Messianic psalms. WUNT 2/192: Tü 2005, Mohr S. xii; 375 pp. €69. 3-16-148616-1. Diss. Aberdeen; Bibl. 323-352. [R]StPat 52 (2005) 952-954 (*Segalla, Giuseppe*).

9340 *Matera, Frank J.* Transcending messianic expectations: Mark and John. [F]MOLONEY, F.: BSRel 187: 2005 ⇒104. 201-216.

9341 *Mimouni, Simon C.* Comment les chrétiens d'origine juive au Ier siècle ont-ils désigné leur messie Jésus?. Nommer les dieux. 2005 ⇒ 504. 201-208.

9342 *Moloney, Francis J.* The Son of Man and christian discipleship. LTJ 39/2-3 (2005) 110-121 [NTAb 50,88].

9343 *Neusner, Jacob* The Kingdom of Heaven in kindred systems, Judaic and Christian. BBR 15/2 (2005) 279-305.
9344 *Orlando, Luigi* Il Figlio dell'uomo: percorso teologico. Anton. 80 (2005) 207-244.
9345 **Petersen, Claus** Die Botschaft Jesu vom Reich Gottes: Aufruf zum Neubeginn. Stu 2005, Kreuz 156 pp. 3-7831-2591-X.
9346 *Snodgrass, Klyne* The gospel of Jesus. [F]STANTON, G. 2005 ⇒138. 31-44.
9347 *Stuhlmacher, Peter* The messianic Son of man: Jesus' claim to deity. The historical Jesus in recent research. 2005 ⇒379. 325-344.
9348 **Vanoni, Gottfried; Heininger, Bernhard** Das Reich Gottes: Perspektiven des Alten und Neuen Testaments. Die neue Echter-Bibel, Themen 4: 2002 ⇒18,8159... 20,8644. [R]FrRu 12 (2005) 147-149 (*Thoma, Clemens*); BiLi 78 (2005) 150-152 (*Braulik, Georg*).
9349 **Weder, Hans** Tempo presente a signoria di Dio: la concezione del tempo in Gesù e nel cristianesimo delle origini. StBi 147: Brescia 2005, Paideia 86 pp. €10.50. 88-394-07073. Bibl. 81-84.
9350 *Wright, N.T.* Kingdom redefined: the announcement. The historical Jesus in recent research. 2005 ⇒379. 207-224.
9351 *Zanetti, Paolo S.* Per una comprensione neotestamentaria dell'annuncio del regno di Dio. Imitatori di Gesù Cristo. 2005 <1971> ⇒330. 267-290.

## H6.1 *Creatio, sabbatum NT*; **The Creation** [⇒E1.6]

9352 *Bass, Dorothy C.* Christian formation in and for Sabbath rest. Interp. 59 (2005) 25-37.
9353 *Bianchi, Enzo* Qu'est-ce que le dimanche?. RSR 93 (2005) 27-51.
9354 *Klostergaard Petersen, Anders* Skabelse og frelse i det Nye Testamente. Kritisk forum for praktisk teologi 25/102 (2005) 31-44.
9355 *Krygier, Rivon* Le chabbat de Jésus. RSR 93 (2005) 9-25.
9356 **Löning, Karl; Zenger, Erich** To begin with, God created... biblical theologies of creation. 2000 ⇒16,1889; 17,7656. [R]RivBib 53 (2005) 106-108 (*Nobile, Marco*).
9357 **Mayer-Haas, Andrea J.** "Geschenk aus Gottes Schatzkammer" (bSchab 10b): Jesus und der Sabbat im Spiegel der neutestamentlichen Schriften. NTA 43: 2003 ⇒19,8734; 20,8648. [R]ThLZ 130 (2005) 781-784 (*Becker, Michael*); Bib. 86 (2005) 434-438 (*Weiss, Herold*); RBLit 7 (2005) 314-316 (*Morton, Russell*).
9358 *Mohn, Jürgen* Dimensionen weiterer zentraler religiöser Vorstellungen: Schöpfungsvorstellungen. Handbuch Religionswissenschaft. 2005 ⇒1016. 612-627.
9359 *Pié-Ninot, Salvador* El acto de creer: algunos aspectos bíblicos y teológico-fundamentales. Burg. 46 (2005) 445-450.
9360 *Ringe, Sharon H.* "Holy, as the Lord your God commanded you": Sabbath in the New Testament. Interp. 59 (2005) 17-24.
9361 *Sherman, Robert* Reclaimed by Sabbath rest. Interp. 59 (2005) 38-50.
9362 **Sturcke, H.** Encountering the rest of God: how Jesus came to personify the sabbath. [D]*Zumstein, Jean*: TVZ Dissertationen: Z 2005, Theologischer 393 pp. €34.50. 32901-73518. Diss. Zurich; Bibl. [NTAb 50,172].

9363 *Welker, Michael* Schöpfung des Himmels und der Erde, des Sichtbaren und des Unsichtbaren. JBTh 20 (2005) 313-323.

## H6.3 *Fides, veritas in NT*—**Faith and truth**

9364 *Burfeind, Carsten* "Die Wahrheit des Evangeliums". FSTOLLE, V.: Theologie: Forschung und Wissenschaft 12: 2005 ⇒143. 189-191.
9365 *Deavel, David P.* Faith and works: a biblical language of salvation. HPR 105/8 (2005) 8-18.
9366 *Grelot, Pierre* Croire en Dieu par Jésus-Christ. EeV 137 (2005) 24-7.
9367 *Grindheim, Sigurd* 'Everything is possible for one who believes': faith and healing in the NT. TrinJ 26 (2005) 11-17.
9368 *Käsemann, Ernst* Evangelische Wahrheit in den Umbrüchen christlicher Theologie. In der Nachfolge. 2005 ⇒236. 25-35.
9369 *Léon-Dufour, Xavier* Credere in Dio. Un biblista cerca Dio. Collana biblica: 2005 <1958> ⇒245. 31-47.
9370 *Robbins, John W.* The biblical view of truth. Journal of the Grace Evangelical Society 18/34 (2005) 49-69.
9371 *Vollenweider, Samuel* Vom israelitischen zum christologischen Monotheismus: Überlegungen zum Verhältnis zwischen dem Glauben an den einen Gott und dem Glauben an Jesus Christus. Biblische Theologie. ATM 14: 2005 ⇒756. 123-133.
9372 **Yeung, Maureen W.** Faith in Jesus and Paul: a comparison with special reference to 'Faith that can remove mountains' and 'Your faith has healed/saved you'. WUNT 2/147: 2002 ⇒18,8185; 20,8660. RRBLit (2005)* (*Heen, Erik*).

## H6.6 *Peccatum NT*—**Sin, evil** [⇒E1.9]

9373 *Baumbach, Günther* Die Funktion des Bösen in neutestamentlichen Schriften. Josephus–Jesusbewegung–Judentum. ANTZ 9: 2005 <1992> ⇒182. 148-167.
9374 *Cunningham, W.P.* The books of lists. HPR 106/2 (2005) 58-61.
9375 *Doutre, Jean* Le "moi" dominé par le péché et le "nous" libéré dans le Christ: deux paradigmes simultanés pour penser le sujet en Rm 7, 7-8,30. FGENEST, O. 2005 ⇒46. 157-177.
9376 *Fiedler, Peter* Sünde und Sündenvergebung in der Jesustradition. Studien zur biblischen Grundlegung. 2005 <1996> ⇒209. 70-87.
9377 *Gieschen, C.A.* Original sin in the New Testament. ConJ 31 (2005) 359-375 [NTAb 50,328].
9378 *Henriksen, Jan O.* Synd. Eller: åå stenge Den andre ute. Ung teologi 38/1 (2005) 5-13.
9379 *Maurer, Ernstpeter* Kennwort "Sünde". GlLern 20 (2005) 97-107.
9380 *Panimolle, Salvatore A.* Padre, custodisci i miei discepoli dal Maligno. Male. DSBP 39: 2005 ⇒580. 7-26.
9381 *Pella-Grin, Gérard* Gémissements et espérance: démarche biblique basée sur Romains 8,18-39. Ḥokhma 88 (2005) 76-87.
9382 *Röhser, Günter* Vom Gewicht der Sünde und des Redens davon: biblische Aspekte für eine heutige Vermittlung. ÖR 54 (2005) 427-445.
9383 *Weaver, D.J.* Resistance and nonresistance: New Testament perspectives on confronting the powers. HTSTS 61/1-2 (2005) 619-638 [NTAb 50,331].

9384 *Wolter, Michael* Sünde: Neutestamentliche Aspekte. GlLern 20 (2005) 119-130.

## H7.0 **Soteriologia NT**

9385 *Anatolios, Khaled; Clifford, Richard J.* Christian salvation: biblical and theological perspectives. TS 66 (2005) 739-769.
9386 **Anikuzhikattil, Thomas** Jesus Christ the Saviour: soteriology according to East Syriac tradition. 2002 ⇒18,8192; 19,8764. [R]LouvSt 30 (2005) 239-42 (*Palackal, Jose*); JJSS 4 (2004) 97-9 (*Kudiyiruppil, John*).
9387 *Barentsen, Jack* Redemption has a price: a case study of Jewish influence on Greek words from a cognitive semantic perspective. AnBru 10 (2005) 70-88.
9388 *Baumert, Norbert* Werke des Gesetzes oder "Werke-Gesetz"?. STOLLE, V. 2005 ⇒143. 153-172.
9389 **Bengel, Johann Albrecht** Der Gnomon: lateinisch-deutsche Teilausgabe der Hauptschriften zur Rechtfertigung: Römer-, Galater-, Jakobusbrief und Bergpredigt nach dem Druck von 1835/36. [E]*Gaese, Heino* 2003 ⇒19,8766. [R]ZKG 116 (2005) 123 (*Jung, Martin H.*).
9390 *Bergèse, D.* La bible: une parole en prise avec le réel. RRef 56/231 (2005) 45-58 [NTAb 49,233].
9391 **Boersma, Hans** Violence, hospitality, and the cross: reappropriating the atonement tradition. 2004 ⇒20,8671. [R]RBLit (2005)* (*Finlan, Stephen*).
9392 *Danaher, James* A phenomenal understanding of law and the nature of sin. AsbTJ 60/2 (2005) 39-54.
9393 **Finlan, Stephen** Problems with atonement: the origins of, and controversy about, the atonement doctrine. ColMn 2005, Liturgical 144 pp. $16. 0-8146-5220-4.
9394 *Fletcher, J.* The meaning of the death of Jesus: a violent means to a nonviolent end, part 2. JRadRef 12/2 (2005) 2-16 [NTAb 50,28].
9395 *Gauthier, Jean-Marc* Violence, souffrance, mort et croix... rédemptrices?: questions de sens et de foi. Théologiques 13 (2005) 21-44.
9396 *Georgi, Dieter* Is there justification in money?: a historical and theological meditation on the financial aspects of justification by Christ. The city in the valley. 2005 ⇒214. 283-307.
9397 *Gray, D.* What does scripture say about universal salvation. Unitarian Universalist Christian [Turley, OK] 60 (2005) 63-80 [NTAb 51,91] [Lk 16,19-31].
9398 **Green, Joel B.; Baker, Mark D.** Recovering the scandal of the cross: atonement in the New Testament and contemporary contexts. 2003 <2000> ⇒19,8772. [R]SBET 23 (2005) 111-3 (*Campbell, Iain*).
9399 **Grün, Anselm** Nuestro Dios cercano: imágenes bíblicas de la redención. M 2005, Nancea 108 pp. [R]Studium 45 (2005) 326-328 (*López, L.*); VyV 63/1 (2005) 250-251; REsp 64 (2005) 320-321 (*Husillos Tamarit, Ignacio*);
9400 *Gundry, Robert H.* The nonimputation of Christ's righteousenss. The old is better. WUNT 178: 2005 ⇒220. 225-251.
9401 *Härle, Wilfried* Allein aus Glauben!: und was ist mit den guten Werken?. Ment. *Luther; Wesley. J.*: ThFPr 31/1 (2005) 32-43.

9402 *Heim, S.M.* Cross purposes: rethinking the death of Jesus. CCen 122/ 6 (2005) 20-25 [NTAb 49,488].

9403 **Jones, J.** Jesus and the earth. L 2005, SPCK ix; 102 pp. £7/$13. 028-10-56234. Bibl. [NTAb 50,192].

9404 *Käsemann, Ernst* Gottes Gerechtigkeit in einer ungerechten Welt;

9405 Gottes Ja zu allen Menschen;

9406 Recht für Rechtlose. In der Nachfolge. 2005 ⇒236. 177-190/212-221/222-230.

9407 *Kim, Jintae* The concept of atonement in early rabbinic thought and the New Testament writings. JGRChJ 2 (2005) 117-145.

9408 *Klaiber, Walter* Rechtfertigung und Kirche: exegetische Anmerkungen zum aktuellen ökumenischen Gespräch: Ernst Käsemann zum 90. [F]KLAIBER, W.: emk Studien 7: 2005 ⇒77. 58-114;

9409 Wahrheit oder Einheit: zur ökumenischen Hermeneutik der Rechtfertigungslehre. [F]KLAIBER, W.: emk Studien 7: 2005 ⇒77. 115-138.

9410 **Knöppler, Thomas** Sühne im Neuen Testament: Studien zum urchristlichen Verständnis der Heilsbedeutung des Todes Jesu. WMANT 88: 2001 ⇒17,7695; 19,8778. [R]ThLZ 130 (2005) 773-776 (*Stettler, Christian*).

9411 *Marshall, I. Howard* Some thoughts on penal substitution. IBSt 26 (2005) 119-151.

9412 *McDade, John* A promise fulfilled, a ransom paid. Tablet (October 8 2005) 6-7 [NTAb 50,97].

9413 **McGrath, Alister E.** Iustitia Dei: a history of the christian doctrine of justification. NY [3]2005 <1986>, CUP xiv; 448 pp. $75. 0-521-53-389-9 [ThD 52,379—W. Charles Heiser].

9414 *Míguez, Néstor O.* Crisis en el pueblo de Dios en tiempos bíblicos: ¿lecciones para hoy?. Conc(E) 311 (2005) 385-392; Conc(I) 3/2005, 119-128; Conc(GB) 3/2005,89-96; Conc(D) 41,296-303.

9415 *Nüssel, Friederike* Die Sühnevorstellung in der klassischen Dogmatik und ihre neuzeitliche Problematisierung. Deutungen. WUNT 181: 2005 ⇒392. 73-94.

9416 **Nwachukwu, Mary Sylvia Chinyere** Creation-covenant scheme and justification by faith: a canonical study of the God-human drama in the pentateuch and the letter to the Romans. TGr.T 89: 2002 ⇒18, 8211; 19,8781. [R]JThS 56 (2005) 160-162 (*Gathercole, Simon*).

9417 **Picca, Salvatore** La discesa agli inferi e la salvezza dei non cristiani: linee teologiche per una soluzione del problema. R 2005, Pont. Univ. Sanctae Crucis 458 pp. Diss.; Bibl. 425-458 [1 Pet 3,19-20].

9418 *Popkes, Wiard* Two interpretations of 'justification' in the New Testament: reflections on Galatians 2:15-21 and James 2:21-25. StTh 59 (2005) 129-146.

9419 **Rainbow, Paul A.** The way of salvation: the role of christian obedience in justification. Milton Keynes 2005, Paternoster xxi; 329 pp. $30. 1-84227-352-3. Bibl. 271-300.

9420 *Schröter, Jens* Sühne, Stellvertretung und Opfer: zur Verwendung analytischer Kategorien zur Deutung des Todes Jesu. Deutungen. WUNT 181: 2005 ⇒392. 51-71.

9421 **Schwager, Raymund** Jesus in the drama of salvation: towards a biblical doctrine of redemption. 1999 ⇒15,7850; 16,7823. [R]HeyJ 46 (2005) 539-541 (*Madigan, Patrick*).

9422 **Stevenson, Peter K.; Wright, Stephen I.** Preaching the atonement. L 2005, Clark 224 pp. £55/15.

9423 *Stoellger, Philipp* Deutung der Passion als Passion der Deutung: zur Dialektik und Rhetorik der Deutungen des Todes Jesu. Deutungen. WUNT 181: 2005 ⇒392. 577-607.

9424 *Van der Watt, Jan G.* Soteriology of the New Testament: some tentative remarks. Salvation in the New Testament. NT.S 121: 2005 ⇒ 798. 505-522.

9425 *Vouga, François* Le discours du Nouveau Testament sur la mort de Jésus. [F]GENEST, O. 2005 ⇒46. 341-357.

9426 *Wilkin, Robert N.* Justification by faith alone is an essential part of the gospel. Journal of the Grace Evangelical Society 18/35 (2005) 3-14.

9427 *Yarnell, M.* Christian justification: a Reformation and Baptist view. Criswell Theological Review [Dallas] 2/2 (2005) 71-89 [NTAb 50, 102].

H7.2 *Crux, sacrificium*; **The Cross, the nature of sacrifice** [⇒E3.4]

9428 **Benson, George W.** The cross, its history and symbolism. Mineola, NY 2005 <1934>, Dover 224 pp. $13. 0486440540 [ThD 52,246—W. Charles Heiser].

9429 **Berger, Klaus** Po co Jezus umarł na krzyżu?. 2004 ⇒20,8688. [R]StBob 2 (2005) 230-235 (*Gardocki, Dariusz*). **P**.

9430 **Binz, Stephen J.** The tragic and triumphant cross. Threshold bible study: New London, CT 2005, Twenty-Third ix; 119 pp. $13 [BiTod 43,200—Donald Senior].

9431 **Ciholas, Paul** The omphalos and the cross: pagans and christians in search of a divine center. 2003 ⇒19,8799. [R]AsbTJ 60/2 (2005) 141-143 (*Harstad, Michael*).

9432 **D'Ancona, M.; Thiede, Carsten P.** Das Jesus Fragment: was wirklich über dem Kreuz Jesu stand: das Abenteuer einer archäologischen Entdeckung. Giessen 2004, Brunnen 363 pp.

9433 *De Mingo, Alberto* Sacrificio y expiación: un estudio bíblico. Moralia 28 (2005) 389-411.

9434 [E]**Dettwiler, Andreas; Zumstein, Jean** Kreuzestheologie im NT. WUNT 151: 2002 ⇒18,298; 19,332. [R]NT 47 (2005) 200-202 (*Stenschke, Christoph*); ThRv 101 (2005) 377-79 (*Labahn, Michael*).

9435 *Flasche, Rainer* Opfer und Gebet in der Religionswissenschaft: eine Einführung. Opfer und Gebet. 2005 ⇒506. 11-19.

9436 *Girard, René* La pierre rejetée par les bâtisseurs. Théologiques 13 (2005) 165-179.

9437 **Hall, Douglas J.** The cross in our context: Jesus and the suffering world. Mp 2004, Fortress x; 274 pp. $17. [R]RBLit (2005)* (*Heen, Erik; Morishima-Nelson, Judy*).

9438 **Heid, Stefan** Kreuz Jerusalem Kosmos: Aspekte frühchristlicher Staurologie. JAC.E 31: 2001 ⇒17,7714; 20,8704. [R]ZKTh 127 (2005) 339-341 (*Lies, Lothar*).

9439 *Iammarrone, Giovanni* Le teologie della croce di S. Paolo, Martin LUTERO e Jürgen MOLTMANN: loro contestualità e precomprensioni: questione della precomprensione di quella di s. BONAVENTURA. Doctor Seraphicus 52 (2005) 15-53.

9440 *Janowski, Bernd* Das Leben für andere hingeben: alttestamentliche Voraussetzungen für die Deutung des Todes Jesu. Deutungen.

WUNT 181: 2005 ⇒392. 97-118 [Mk 14,34; John 10,11; Rom 3, 25].

9441 *Käsemann, Ernst* Opfer und Anpassung. In der Nachfolge. 2005 ⇒ 236. 242-257.

9442 *Kelsey, D.H.* Redeeming Sam: the difference Jesus makes. CCen 122/ 13 (2005) 22-27 [NTAb 50,95].

9443 *Michaud, Jean-Paul* Figures de la mort de Jésus: dans les lettres de Paul, l'évangile de Jean et l'épître aux Hébreux. [F]GENEST, O. 2005 ⇒ 46. 461-487.

9444 *Schlund, Christine* Deutungen des Todes Jesu im Rahmen der Pesach-Tradition. Deutungen. WUNT 181: 2005 ⇒392. 397-411 [1 Cor 5,7].

9445 *Servais, Jacques* L'epreuve de la croix, fondement de l'expérience chrétienne. [F]BERNARD, C. 2005 ⇒8. 257-278.

9446 **Trojan, Jakub S.** Ježišův příběh—výzva pro nás [Vom Kreuz Jesu zu seiner Lebensgeschichte]. Praha 2005, Oikoymenh 413 pp. 80-72-98-136-6. **Czech.**

9447 **Vanhoye, Albert** Tanto amò Dios al mundo: lectio sobre el sacrificio de Cristo. [T]*Maio, Maria Teresa*: M 2005, San Pablo 119 pp. 84-285-2730-X. [R]Seminarios 51 (2005) 452-453.

9448 *Versnel, Henk S.* Making sense of Jesus' death: the pagan contribution. Deutungen. WUNT 181: 2005 ⇒392. 213-294.

9449 *Voss, Gerhard* Die kosmische Bedeutung des Kreuzes Christi in der Frühen Kirche. US 60 (2005) 311-326.

9450 *Wolter, Michael* Der Heilstod Jesu als theologisches Argument. Deutungen. WUNT 181: 2005 ⇒392. 297-313.

9451 **Zani, Lorenzo** La vittoria dell'amore, meditazioni bibliche sulla croce. Mi 2005, Ancora 175 pp. €12. [R]LSDC 20/1 (2005) 109-110 (*Maximus a S.R.P.Cp.*).

9452 *Zimmermann, Ruben* Die neutestamentliche Deutung des Todes Jesu als Opfer: zur christologischen Koinzidenz von Opfertheologie und Opferkritik. KuD 51/2 (2005) 72-99.

## H7.4 *Sacramenta, gratia*

9453 *Back, Frances* Wiedergeburt in der religiösen Welt der hellenistisch-römischen Zeit. Wiedergeburt. BTSP 25: 2005 ⇒533. 45-73.

9454 *Braulik, Georg* Gibt es "sacramenta veteris legis"?. Liturgie und Bibel. ÖBS 28: 2005 <2000> ⇒360. 369-401.

9455 *Buchinger, Harald* Towards the origins of paschal baptism: the contribution of ORIGEN. StLi 35 (2005) 12-31.

9456 **Castanho, Amaury** O casal humano na sagrada escritura. Cachoeira Paulista 2005, Canção Nova 164 pp.

9457 *Cheriampanatt, J.* Sacraments in the christian sacred scripture. JJSS 4 (2004) 19-39.

9458 **Coleman, Peter** Christian attitudes to marriage: from ancient times to the third millennium. 2004 ⇒20,8726. [R]RRT 12 (2005) 472-473 (*Woodard, Randall Jay*).

9459 *Combs, W.W.* Does the bible teach prevenient grace?. Detroit Baptist Seminary Journal [Allen Park, MI] 10 (2005) 3-18 [NTAb 50,327].

9460 **Dannecker, Klaus Peter** Taufe, Firmung und Erstkommunion in der ehemaligen Diözese Konstanz: eine liturgiegeschichtliche Untersuchung der Initiationssakramente. LWQF 92: Müns 2005, Aschendorff 585 pp. 3-402-04072-7.

9461 **Diaz Mateos, Manuel** O sacramento do pão. 2004 ⇒20,8728. [R]REB 65 (2005) 758-759 (*Silva, Rogério Augusto da*).

9462 *Dünzl, Franz* Rigorismus oder pastorales Entgegenkommen?: zur Entstehung des kirchlichen Bußverfahrens im 2. Jahrhundert. ZKTh 127 (2005) 77-97.

9463 **Fortin, A.** L'annonce de la bonne nouvelle aux pauvres: une théologie de la grâce et du Verbe fait chair. Montréal 2005, Médiaspaul 309 pp. 289420-6631 [NRTh 129,305—Radermakers, J].

9464 **Frettlöh, Magdalene L.** Theologie des Segens: biblische und dogmatische Wahrnehmungen. Gü 2005 <1998>, Gü 436 pp. €30. 3579-052179. Bibl. [NTAb 50,190].

9465 *Grech, Prosper* La practica del battesimo ai tempi di Gesù. Il messaggio biblico. SRivBib 44: 2005 <1991> ⇒216. 215-225.

9466 *Gros, Miquel S.* Fragment d'une ancienne bénédiction nord-africaine de l'eau baptismale. EO 22/1 (2005) 7-12.

9467 *Hailer, Martin* Wie viel Weltfremdheit gehört zur Wiedergeburt?: ein Vesuch, NIETZSCHEs "Fluch auf das Christentum" ein wenig Segen abzugewinnen. Wiedergeburt. BTSP 25: 2005 ⇒533. 101-148.

9468 *Hainz, Josef* Fußwaschung als Sakrament?. [F]STENDEBACH, F. 2005 ⇒141. 30-42 [John 13,1-20].

9469 **Infante, Lorenzo** Lo sposo e la sposa: percorsi di analisi simbolica tra sacra scrittura e cristianesimo delle origini. 2004 ⇒20,8732. [R]SMSR 29 (2005) 203-207 (*Walt, Luigi*).

9470 *Jensen, Robin M.* Baptismal rites and architecture. Late ancient christianity. 2005 ⇒517. 117-144.

9471 *Kapellari, Egon* Die Heiligung des Wassers. IKaZ 34 (2005) 47-54.

9472 *Koch, Kurt* Die christliche Taufe. IKaZ 34 (2005) 5-22;

9473 Il battesimo cristiano. Com(I) 199 (2005) 19-37.

9474 *Labbé, Yves* L'économie symbolique du baptême. NRTh 127 (2005) 200-225.

9475 *Lenchak, Timothy* What's biblical about holy water?. BiTod 43 (2005) 123-124.

9476 *Liperi, Bastianina* Il matrimonio nel Nuovo Testamento. Il matrimonio. DSBP 42: 2005 ⇒459. 213-299.

9477 *Lohfink, Norbert* Wasser, Öl und Licht—Symbole der christlichen Taufe. Liturgie und Bibel. ÖBS 28: 2005 ⇒360. 403-408.

9478 *Pastwa, Andrzej* Instytucjonalne cele małżeństwa w optyce biblijnej hermeneutyki Papieża Jana Pawła II [Institutionelle Zwecke der Ehe in der Optik der biblischen Hermeneutik von Papst Johannes Paul II]. PraKan 48 (2005) 85-100. **P.**

9479 *Schoberth, Wolfgang* Zur neuen Welt kommen: Überlegungen zur theologischen Logik der Metapher "Wiedergeburt". Wiedergeburt. BTSP 25: 2005 ⇒533. 149-164.

9480 *Serra, Dominic E.* Baptism: birth in the Spirit or dying with Christ. EO 22/3 (2005) 295-314.

9481 **Siffer-Wiederhold, Nathalie** La présence divine à l'individu d'après le Nouveau Testament. LeDiv 203: P 2005, Cerf 437 pp. €45. 2-204-07545-0. Bibl. 411-419.

9482 *Van den Heever, G.A.* Making body politic: the rhetoric of early christian baptismal discourse. Scriptura 90 (2005) 709-721 [NTAb 51,323].

## H7.6 *Ecclesiologia, Theologia missionis, laici*—**The Church**

9483 **Akpunonu, Peter Damian** The vine, Israel and the church. Studies in Biblical Literature 51: 2004 ⇒20,8740. [R]RBLit (2005)* (*Dempsey, Carol J.*).

9484 *Alves, Herculano* A bíblia nas missões portuguesas (séculos XVII-XVIII). Did(L) 35 (2005) 701-720.

9485 *Arulsamy, S.* Money and mission from the perspective of the evangelizer and the evangelized. MissTod 7 (2005) 293-311 [NTAb 50,89].

9486 **Bauckham, Richard** Bible and mission: christian witness in a postmodern world. 2003 ⇒19,8864. [R]SBET 23 (2005) 253-254 (*Macdonald, Fergus*).

9487 *Cobb, D.* Jésus le Messie et l'église: *Verus Israel*?. RRef 56/233 (2005) 62-80 [NTAb 50,90].

9488 *Coleman, R.E.* The Jesus way to win the world. ERT 29/1 (2005) 77-81 [Mt 28,19-20].

9489 **Collins, Raymond F.** The many faces of the church: a study in New Testament ecclesiology. Companions to the NT: 2003 ⇒19,8869. [R]LouvSt 30 (2005) 230-232 (*Koperski, Veronica*).

9490 *Collinson, S.W.* Making disciples and the christian faith. ERT 29/3 (2005) 240-250 [NTAb 50,90] [2 Cor 4-5].

9491 *Conradie, Ernst M.* Mission as evangelism and as development?: some perspectives from the Lord's Prayer. IRM 94 (2005) 557-575 [Mt 6,9-13].

9492 *da Silva, Gilberto* Gottes Gerechtigkeit als Missionsmotiv. [F]STOLLE, V.: Theologie: Forschung und Wissenschaft 12: 2005 ⇒143. 401-13.

9493 **Fleming, Dean** Contextualization in the New Testament: patterns for theology and mission. DG 2005, InterVarsity 344 pp. $26 [BiTod 45, 128—Donald Senior].

9494 *Fürst, Alfons* Gestaltungsräume: gemeindliche Strukturen in altchristlichen Kirchenordnungen. LS 56 (2005) 112-119.

9495 **Gehring, Roger W.** House church and mission: the importance of household structures in early christianity. 2004 ⇒20,8754. [R]TJT 21 (2005) 239-240 (*Trites, Allison A.*); RBLit (2005)* (*Coloe, Mary*).

9496 *Georgi, Dieter* The urban adventure of the early church. The city in the valley. Studies in biblical literature 7: 2005 ⇒214. 53-68.

9497 **Glasser, Arthur F.**, *al.*, Announcing the kingdom: the story of God's mission in the bible. 2003 ⇒19,8879. [R]em 21/1 (2005) 35-36 (*Kasdorf, Hans*).

9498 *Good, R.* God's building. Affirmation & Critique [Anaheim, CA] 10/2 (2005) 66-73.

9499 **Haight, Roger** Christian community in history, 1: historical ecclesiology. 2004 ⇒20,8757. [R]EE 80 (2005) 613-615 (*Madrigal, S.*); Commonweal [NY] 132/2 (2005) 34-36 (*Johnson, L.T.*);

9500 Christian community in history, 2: comparative ecclesiology. NY 2005, Continuum ix; 518 pp. $35. 08264-16314. [NTAb 49,619].

9501 *Harrison, Peter* "Fill the earth and subdue it": biblical warrants for colonization in seventeenth century England. JRH 29/1 (2005) 3-24.

9502 *Henkel, Willi* Der Katechismus von Lima (1584): eine missionarische Einführung in den christlichen Glauben. [F]STENDEBACH, F. 2005 ⇒ 141. 213-224.

9503 *Kampling, Rainer* "... Sorgt euch nicht um eure Seelen!" (Mt 6,25): auf dem Weg zur Selbstwerdung-Gemeindewerden in frühchristlicher Zeit. ThPQ 153 (2005) 286-296.

9504 *Kasselouri-Hatzivassiliadi, Eleni* Oikos kai protochristianikes koinotetes. DBM 23/2 (2005) 209-221. **G.**

9505 *Käsemann, Ernst* Volkskirche und Christusleib;

9506 Prophetische Aufgabe und Volkskirche. In der Nachfolge. 2005 ⇒236. 276-286/287-301.

9507 *Klaiber, Walter* Proexistenz und Kontrastverhalten: Beobachtungen zu einer Grundstruktur neutestamentlicher Ekklesiologie;

9508 Biblische Perspektiven einer heutigen Lehre von der Heiligung. $^F$KLAIBER, W.: emk Studien 7: 2005 ⇒77. 15-39/40-57.

9509 *Klauck, Hans-Josef* Nicht durch das Wort allein—neutestamentliche Paradigmen indirekter Verkündigung. MThZ 56 (2005) 194-211 [Acts 27-28; Heb 2,10-15; 13,11-14; Rev 14,6-7].

9510 *Klosterkamp, Thomas* Bischof Ovide Charlebois (1862-1933): "Relecture" eines Missionarslebens im Licht von Redemptoris missio. $^F$STENDEBACH, F. 2005 ⇒141. 270-287.

9511 *Koch, D.-A.* The origin, function, and disappearance of the 'Twelve': continuity from Jesus to the post-Easter community. HTSTS 61/1-2 (2005) 211-229 [NTAb 50,324] [1 Cor 15,3-5].

9512 *Koppelin, Frank; Schirrmacher, Thomas* Die Evangelien als Beweis für die Notwendigkeit der kulturellen Anpassung der missionarischen Verkündigung. em 21/2 (2005) 57-61.

9513 **Kraft, Charles H.; Kraft, Marguerite G.** Christianity in culture: a study in biblical theologizing in cross-cultural perspective. Mkn $^2$2005 <1979>, Orbis xxxii; 344 pp. $30. 1-57075-588-4 [ThD 52, 273—W. Charles Heiser].

9514 *Kyrtatas, Dimitris J.* The significance of leadership and organisation in the spread of christianity. Spread of christianity. 2005 ⇒545. 53-68.

9515 *Legrand, L.* Missionary communication: a biblical perspective. ITS 42/2 (2005) 139-146.

9516 *Lugo Rodríguez, Raúl H.* De movimiento a institución: las iglesias cristianas primitivas. Qol 39 (2005) 87-110.

9517 *Maciel del Río, Carlos* La misión cristiana universal: ¿un imperialismo cristiano?. $^F$JUNCO GARZA, C.: Estudios Bíblicos Mexicanos 4: 2005 ⇒74. 405-415.

9518 *Manicardi, Ermenegildo* La bibbia nell'evento dell'evangelizzazione. Gesù la cristologia. 2005 <1998> ⇒253. 371-391;

9519 Chiesa e *missio ad gentes* nelle scritture neotestamentarie. Gesù la cristologia. 2005 <2004> ⇒253. 447-468.

9520 *Manjaly, T.* The role of the laity in the early church. MissTod 7 (2005) 242-258 = BiBh 31 (2005) 123-140 [NTAb 50,91].

9521 *Martini, Carlo M.* La bibbia e le tradizioni indigene: introduzione. I vangeli. 2005 ⇒432. 111-116.

9522 *März, Claus-Peter* Neutestamentliche und patristische Anmerkungen zum kirchlichen Sprachgebrauch vom 'Laien'. Studien zum Hebräerbrief. SBAB 39: 2005 <1989> ⇒8568. 223-233.

9523 *Medina, Richard W.* Paradigma divino para la evangelización mundial en los sucesos del éxodo de Egipto. Misión y contextualización. SMEBT 2: 2005 ⇒766. 135-155 [OTA 28,276].

9524 **Moreau, A. Scott; Corwin, Gary R.; McGee, Gary B.** Introducing world missions: a biblical, historical, and practical survey. 2003 ⇒ 19,8898; 20,8774. [R]Faith & Mission 23/1 (2005) 127-8 (*Solc, Josef*).

9525 *Pathrapankal, Joseph* 'Making disciples' (Mt 28:16-20) and 'being witnesses of Christ' (Acts 1:8): a re-reading of the theology of mission. VJTR 69 (2005) 566-584.

9526 **Philibert, Paul J.** The priesthood of the faithful: key to a living church. ColMn 2005, Liturgical viii; 173 pp. 0-8146-3023-5.

9527 *Prasad, Jacob* Models of inter-culturation in the early christian period. Jeevadhara 35 (2005) 161-176 [NTAb 50,330] [Gal 3,26-29].

9528 *Quiroga, Raúl* ¿Qué hacer cuando no se ha prescrito qué se deber hacer?: el caso paradigmático de las hijas de Zelofehad en Números 27: 1-11. Misión y contextualización. SMEBT 2: 2005 ⇒766. 157-171 [OTA 28,287].

9529 **Radner, Ephraim** Hope among the fragments: the broken church and its engagement of scripture. 2004 ⇒20,8784. [R]ThTo 62 (2005) 272, 274, 276.

9530 **Rodríguez Mansur, Carlos** Uma avaliaçao crítica do estudo missiológico da bíblis na igreja evangélica brasileira no período de 1983 a 1994. Tesis 26: S 2005, Universidad Pontificia de Salamanca, Facultad de Teología 103 pp. 84-7299-652-2. Extr. Diss.

9531 *Rudolph, D.J.* Messianic Jews and christian theology: restoring an historical voice to the contemporary discussion. ProEc 14 (2005) 58-84 [NTAb 49,540].

9532 **Ryken, Philip Graham** City on a hill: reclaiming the biblical pattern for the church in the 21st century. 2003 ⇒19,8911. [R]SBET 23 (2005) 240-242 (*Black, William B.*).

9533 *Saayman, W.A.* New Testament studies and missiology in South Africa: uneasy bedfellows?. Missionalia 33/1 (2005) 35-45 [NTAb 50, 239].

9534 *Schmeller, Thomas* Mission im Urchristentum: Definition–Motivation–Konkretion. ZNT 8/15 (2005) 2-11.

9535 **Simonnot, Philippe** Les papes, l'église et l'argent: histoire économique du christianisme des origines à nos jours. P 2005, Bayard 810 pp. 2227-13901-3.

9536 *Smith, Susan* 'Biblical interpretation: a power for good or evil?'. IRM 94 (2005) 524-534.

9537 *Stenschke, C.* New Testament studies and missiology in South Africa: comfortable bedfellows!. Missionalia 33 (2005) 214-233 [NTAb 50, 241].

9538 **Thompson, Michael B.** When should we divide?: schism and discipline in the New Testament. Grove Biblical Series: 2004 ⇒20, 8793. [R]SBET 23 (2005) 233-234 (*Watson, Ian*).

9539 *Titus, P. Joseph* A shining community: a mission model: an exegetical comparative study of Is 60:1-9 and Mt 2:1-12. ITS 42 (2005) 307-335.

9540 *Wendland, Heinz D.* Schriftgebundenheit und Geistesleitung in der urchristlichen Mission. em 21/4 (2005) 140-144.

## H7.7 *Oecumenismus*—The ecumenical movement

9541 *Aletti, Jean-Noël* Bible et dialogue oecuménique. Bible et sciences des religions. 2005 ⇒445. 123-144.

9542 **Burgwald, Christopher T.** The sinfulness of the justified in Lutheran-Catholic dialogue in the United States of America. Siouxormen 2005, n.p. iv; 169 pp. Bibl. 152-169.

9543 **Burkhard, John J.** Apostolicity then and now: an ecumenical church in a postmodern world. ColMn 2004, Liturgical xiv; 250 pp. 0-8146-5121-6.

9544 *Cottini, Valentino* La casa della sapienza luogo di incontro delle religioni?: III: ordine creaturale. RSEc 23 (2005) 613-623.

9545 [E]**Denaux, Adelbert; Donnelly, Doris; Famerée, Joseph** The Holy Spirit, the church, and christian unity: proceedings of the consultation held at the Monastery of Bose, Italy, 14-20 October, 2002. BEThL 181: Lv 2005, Peeters xii; 417 pp. 90-429-1560-9.

9546 *Eißler, Friedmann* Abrahamische Ökumene—eine Option?. ThBeitr 36 (2005) 173-187.

9547 **Feiler, B.** Where God was born: a journey by land to the roots of religion. NY 2005, Morrow x; 405 pp. $27. 00605-74879. Bibl.; [NTAb 50,207].

9548 **Foucher, Daniel** Père unique, tous frères. Réponses aux questions 48: Nantes 2005, Espérance et bonne nouvelle 147 pp. 29525-49508.

9549 *Hintersteiner, Norbert* Gesellschaftliche und rechtliche Dimensionen. Dialog der Religionen. Handbuch Religionswissenschaft. 2005 ⇒1016. 834-852.

9550 *Jorgensen, Janyce C.* The bible and ecumenism: 'That they may all be one' (John 17:21). Scripture. 2005 ⇒398. 253-264.

9551 *Keel, Othmar* Was ist unter vertikaler Ökumene zu verstehen?. Vertikale Ökumene. 2005 ⇒590. 7-10.

9552 *LaHurd, Carol Schersten* Holding together the gospel and interfaith relations in a lifelong journey. CThMi 32 (2005) 245-255.

9553 *Lienemann, Wolfgang* Grenzüberschreitungen: kurze Beobachtungen zu Gleichzeitigkeiten des Ungleichzeitigen im Religionskontakt. Vertikale Ökumene. 2005 ⇒590. 57-65.

9554 *Menn, Esther M.* The gospel and interfaith understanding: how do we hold them together?. CThMi 32 (2005) 256-263.

9555 *Mullins, Patrick* The ecumenical movement and the transmission of the Word of God in Vatican II's Dei Verbum. ER 57/4 (2005) 406-432.

9556 **Noceti, Serena** La chiesa segno del regno: l'ecclesiologia ecumenica di Wolfhart PANNENBERG. F 2005, Facultatis Theologica Italiae Centralis 294; ii pp. Exc. Diss.; Bibl. 163-289.

9557 *Polan, Gregory J.* JOHN PAUL II: in the footsteps of Saints Peter and Paul. BiTod 43 (2005) 210-215.

9558 *Segalla, Giuseppe* La bibbia, strumento di unione?: quarant'anni dalla *Dei Verbum*, 22. Rivista di science religiose 19/1 (2005) 203-224.

9559 **Sell, Alan P.F.** Enlightenment, ecumenism, evangel: theological themes and thinkers, 1550-2000. Milton Keynes 2005, Paternoster xviii; 421 pp. 978-1-84227-330-2.

9560 *Silva, Carlos H. do C.* Jesus oriental—para um diálogo cristão místico ecuménico. Did(L) 35 (2005) 225-284.

9561 *Tamez, E.* Living ecumenically: an absolute necessity: reflections from academic experience. ER 57/1 (2005) 12-18 [NTAb 50,22].

9562 *Untergassmair, Franz Georg* Ökumene und Kirche: Bibelauslegung als Promotor der Ökumene. TThZ 114 (2005) 188-201.

9563 *Witherup, Ronald D.* The biblical foundations of interreligious dialogue. Pro Dialogo 120 (2005) 282-294.

## H7.8 Amt—*Ministerium ecclesiasticum*

9564 The ancient fathers on the office and work of the priesthood in the Church of Christ: being an English translation of a principal portion of a work published under the title of "Du Sacerdoce", by "A director of the seminary" in Latin and French. [T]**Male, Edward**: Piscataway (N.J.) 2005 <1891>, Gorgias xi; 172 pp. 1-59333-043-X. Facsimile.

9565 *Bakke, Odd M.* The episcopal ministry and the unity of the church from the Apostolic Fathers to CYPRIAN. The formation of the early church. WUNT 183: 2005 ⇒708. 379-408.

9566 **Beckwith, Roger** Elders in every city: the origin and role of the ordained ministry. 2003 ⇒19,8940. [R]AThR 87 (2005) 487-488 (*Koenig, John*).

9567 *Brown, Raymond E.* The challenge of New Testament priesthood. Emmanuel 111/3 2005 <1980>, 252-263 [NTAb 49,539].

9568 *Capper, Brian J.* To keep silent, ask husbands at home, and not to have authority over men (1 Corinthians 14:33-36 and 1 Timothy 2:11-12): the transformation from gathering in private to meeting in public space in second generation christianity and the exclusion of women from leadership of the public assembly. ThZ 61 (2005) 113-131, 301-319.

9569 *Dziadosz, D.* Kapłaństwo przestrzenią, w której człowiek spotyka boga. Roczniki Teologiczne 52/1 (2005) 151-174 [NTAb 50,527]. **P.**

9570 *Fee, Gordon D.* The priority of Spirit gifting for church ministry;

9571 *Grenz, Stanley J.* Biblical priesthood and women in ministry. Discovering biblical equality. 2005 ⇒387. 241-254/272-286.

9572 Hermeneutics and the ordination of women. LTJ 39/1 (2005) 5-22 [NTAb 49,539].

9573 *Hélou, Clémence* The deaconess in the Syriac church. Christianity. 2005 ⇒607. 413-433.

9574 *Kretschmar, Georg* Vom Dienst des Bischofs. KuD 51/3 (2005) 217-227.

9575 *Lamirande, Émilien* L'interdiction faite aux femmes d'enseigner dans l'église ancienne. StCan 39/1-2 (2005) 5-39 [1 Cor 11].

9576 *Liefeld, Walter L.* The nature of authority in the New Testament. Discovering biblical equality. 2005 ⇒387. 255-271.

9577 *Martens, Gottfried* Gibt es das "eine, von Christus gestiftete Amt der Wortverkündigung und Sakramentsverwaltung"?: Beobachtungen zur Frage von Amt und Ämtern im Neuen Testament unter besonderer Berücksichtigung der Pastoralbriefe. LuthBei 10/1 (2005) 3-20.

9578 *Methuen, Charlotte* Vidua–presbytera–episcopa: women with oversight in the early church. Theol. 108/843 (2005) 163-177.

9579 *Odasso, Giovanni* Il ministero pastorale nella chiesa primitiva: la categoria del "Pastore" applicata al vescovo. Lat. 71 (2005) 279-298.

9580 Il prete e la sua immagine. Oggi e domani II/40: Bo 2005, EDB 110 pp. 88-10-14024-9. Servizio nazionale per il progetto culturale della Conferenza Episcopale Italiana.

9581 **Schmelz, Georg** Kirchliche Amtsträger im spätantiken Ägypten. 2002 ⇒18,8387. [R]BiOr 62 (2005) 526-530 (*Wilfong, T.G.*).

9582 *Schneider, Theodor* Das Amt in der frühen Kirche: Versuch einer Zusammenschau. ThG 48 (2005) 49-63.
9583 *Starnitzke, Dierk* Diakonie als Außenbezug der Kirche: neutestamentliche Beobachtungen. WuD 28 (2005) 89-98.
9584 *Steichele, Hanneliese* "Bei euch aber soll es nicht so sein ..." (Mk 10, 43): Bilder und Figuren von Leitung in der Bibel. AnzSS 114/3 (2005) 5-9.
9585 *Vaahtoranta, Martti* Dies Geheimnis ist groß—der Sinn von "des Herrn Gebot" (1. Kor. 14,37): einige sehr persönliche Überlegungen. LuthBei 10/1 (2005) 35-42.
9586 *Vanhoye, Albert* Aspectos fundamentales del sacerdocio en el Nuevo Testamento. SelTeol 44/1 (2005) 29-38 <CuesTF 30 (2003) 277-98.
9587 *Virgili, Rosanna* La presenza della donna nell'annuncio del regno e della parola. Ad Gentes 9/1 (2005) 32-44.
9588 **Winston, George; Winston, Dora** Recovering biblical ministry by women: an exegetical response to traditionalism and feminism. 2003 ⇒19,8967. [R]BS 162 (2005) 505-506 (*Waters, Larry J.*).

## H8.0 **Oratio**, *spiritualitas personalis NT*

9589 *Amato, Angelo Lectio divina* e aspetti teologici. Lectio divina. 2005 ⇒437. 67-96.
9590 **Baker, Robert J.; Groeschel, Benedict J.** When did we see you, Lord?. Huntington, IN 2005, Our Sunday Visitor 175 pp. $15. 1-592-76-068-6 [ThD 52,366—W. Charles Heiser] [Mt 25,31-46].
9591 **Bastianel, Sergio** Figure di preghiera nella bibbia. R 2005, ADP 152 pp. €8. 88-7357-371-1.
9592 *Bissoli, Cesare* 'Dove va la *lectio divina*?': una lettura della prassi. Lectio divina. 2005 ⇒437. 17-35.
9593 **Bowe, Barbara E.** Biblical foundations of spirituality: touching a finger to the flame. 2003 ⇒19,8980; 20,8832. [R]HeyJ 46 (2005) 386-387 (*Hardy, Richard P.*).
9594 **Boyer, Mark G.** Reflections on the mysteries of the rosary. ColMn 2005, Liturgical 55 pp. $5.
9595 **Buetow, Harold A.** Life out of death. Staten Island 2005, Alba xxxvi; 139 pp. $13.
9596 *Buzzetti, Carlo; Cimosa, Mario* Lectio divina e scuola della parola: i rapporti. Ripartire da Cristo. 2005 ⇒800. 141-166.
9597 **Cannato, Judy** Quantum grace: the Sunday readings: lenten reflections on creation and connectedness. ND 2005, Ave Maria 125 pp. $10. 1-59471-024-4 [ThD 52,151—W. Charles Heiser].
9598 *Cardona Ramírez, Hernán* La oración de Jesús: dejar crear al Abbá. El grano. 2005 ⇒197. 201-209.
9599 *Carlotti, Paolo Lectio divina* ed esperienza morale. Lectio divina. 2005 ⇒437. 113-133.
9600 *Ciardi, Fabio* La parabola dei tre comandamenti: il cammino storico verso la 'spiritualità della comunione'. Nuova Umanità 27 (2005) 309-334.
9601 **Dell'Agli, Nello** Lectio divina e lectio humana: un nuovo modello di accompagnamento spirituale. 2004 ⇒20,8837. [R]Clar. 45 (2005) 411-413 (*La Volpe, Benedict M.*).

9602 **Domek, Johanna** Respuestas que liberan—veinticuatro preguntas a la biblia. Espiritualidad: M 2005, Narcea 124 pp.

9603 **Dumm, Demetrius** Praying the scriptures. 2003 ⇒19,8994. $^{R}$NewTR 18/3 (2005) 94-95 (*Wimmer, Joseph*).

9604 **Duranti, Samuele** Gesù modello e maestro di preghiera. Assisi 2005, Porziuncola 188 pp. €15. $^{R}$ATOR 36 (2005) 813-814.

9605 **Ekblad, Bob** Reading the bible with the damned. LVL 2005, Westminster xviii; 203 pp. $18. 0-664-22917-4.

9606 *Endean, Philip* IGNATIUS Loyola, prayer and scripture. Bible in pastoral practice. 2005 ⇒341. 275-285.

9607 *Engberg-Pedersen, Troels* Sjaelens tilbagekomst til kristendommen?: det Nye Testamente som eksempel. Kritisk forum for praktisk teologi 25/99 (2005) 29-44.

9608 *Fortin, Anne* Lire et brûler: l'interprétation théologique à partir de la sémiotique. $^{F}$GENEST, O. 2005 ⇒46. 503-522.

9609 *Fosarelli, Patricia D.; Gorman, Michael J.* The bible and spiritual growth. Scripture. 2005 ⇒398. 229-238.

9610 **Foster, David** Reading with God, lectio divina. L 2005, Continuum vii; 161 pp. £10. 0-8254-6984-4.

9611 **Foucauld, Jean-Baptiste de** L'Esprit de Jésus, tome VIII: méditations et explications de l'évangile (1896-1915). P 2005, Nouvelle Cité 350 pp. €25.

9612 *Frey, Christofer* Sünde und Buße: das Thema der Lebenswende. GlLern 20 (2005) 131-141.

9613 *García, Jesús M.* Dalla '*lectio mundi*' alla '*lectio divina*': per una educazione dei giovani alla lettura orante della parola;

9614 *Genre, Ermanno Lectio divina*: itinerari di spiritualità ecumenica. Lectio divina. 2005 ⇒437. 177-196/37-50.

9615 **Gianto, Agustinus** Langkah-Nya...langkah-ku!. Yogykarta 2005, Kanisius xiv; 236 pp. Bibl. 189-190. **Indonesian**.

9616 **Gray, Tim** The luminous mysteries: biblical reflections on the life of Christ. Steubenville, OH 2005, Emmaus R. 34 pp. $12 [HPR 106/ 1,79 Rawley Myers].

9617 **Grenz, Stanley J.** Prayer: the cry for the kingdom. GR $^{2}$2005 <1988>, Eerdmans xii; 131 pp. $14. 0-8028-2847-7.

9618 **Gross, Francis** The gospels with salt: Jesus wildman—Jesus woman: meditations on the gospels. Lanham 2005, Hamilton xiv; 279 pp. 0-7-618-3174-6.

9619 **Hauerwas, Stanley** Cross-shattered Christ: meditations on the seven last words. GR 2005, Brazos 108 pp. $15. 1-58743-131-9 [ThD 52, 166—W. Charles Heiser].

9620 *Hensell, Eugene* The role of scripture on the spiritual journey. RfR 64 (2005) 51-64.

9621 **Howard, Katherine** Daily reflections for Advent & Christmas. ColMn 2005, Liturgical 107 pp. $2.

9622 *Hurtado, Larry W.* Early Jewish opposition to Jesus-devotion. How on earth. 2005 <1999> ⇒227. 152-178.

9623 **Kiechle, Stefan** Größer als unser Herz: biblische Meditationen: Exerzitien im Alltag. 2003 ⇒19,9011. $^{R}$GuL 78/1 (2005) 78-79 (*Köster, Peter*).

9624 *Kollmann, Roland* Spiritualität des dritten Lebens. LS 56 (2005) 289-295.

9625 *Kurichianil, John* Walking through the desert: a study on the desert ideal in the bible. BiBh 31 (2005) 149-167.

9626 *Lambiasi, Francesco* Sulla bellezza e bontà della *lectio divina*: lettera aperta del vescovo Guido alla sorella Cristiana. Lectio divina. 2005 ⇒437. 161-175.

9627 **Lambiasi, Francesco** Vorrei pregare con la bibbia: lettera a Cristiana sulla *lectio divina*. Bo 2005, EDB 46 pp.

9628 *Lefebvre, Philippe* Peut-on suivre un accompagnement spirituel auprès de Jésus-Christ?. LV(L) 54/3 (2005) 18-26.

9629 *Levoratti, Armando J.* La *lectio divina*. I vangeli. 2005 ⇒432. 62-64.

9630 *Léon-Dufour, Xavier* Il buon uso di questo mondo <1973>;

9631 Perdere la propria vita secondo il vangelo <1979>. Un biblista cerca Dio. Collana biblica: 2005 ⇒245. 131-138/167-183.

9632 *Lombaard, C.* Four South Africans' proposals for a central theme to 'scriptural spirituality'. Scriptura 88 (2005) 139-150 [NTAb 50,96].

9633 **Loosen, Loed** Het derde testament: de bijbel verder schrijven. 's-Hertogenbosch 2005, Katholieke Bijbelstichting 103 pp. 90-6173-798-2.

9634 **MacArthur, John** The heart of the bible: explore the power of key bible passages. Nv 2005, Nelson vi; 143 pp. 0-7852-5064-6.

9635 *Manicardi, Ermenegildo* Esperienze ed esempi di *fractio verbi* nella tradizione biblica. Gesù la cristologia. 2005 <2002> ⇒253. 409-429;

9636 Spiritualità cristiana e bisogno odierno di spiritualità. Gesù la cristologia. 2005 <2003> ⇒253. 431-445;

9637 La vie spirituelle chrétienne aujourd'hui: repenser l'unité entre le corps et l'esprit. Ḥokhma 88 (2005) 3-21.

9638 **Marcovits, Paul-Dominique** Maître, explique-nous!: questions des disciples à Jésus. Epiphanie: P 2005, Cerf 184 pp. €16.

9639 *Martini, Carlo M.* La pratica della *lectio divina* nella pastorale biblica. I vangeli. 2005 ⇒432. 54-61.

9640 *Mickiewicz, Franciszeck* Mystère de la vie publique de Jésus mystère de la lumière de Dieu. Com(F) 30/1 (2005) 21-33.

9641 *Musskopf, André S.; Schinelo, Edmilson* Atençao: homens conversando!. Estudos bíblicos 86 (2005) 51-56.

9642 *Navone, John* Carlo Martini and the gospel matrix for christian formation in the light of Lonergan's conversion theology. [F]BERNARD, C. 2005 ⇒8. 29-43.

9643 *Neuman, Matthias* The role of scripture on the spiritual journey. RfR 64 (2005) 51-64.

9644 **Newell, J. Philip** Celtic treasure. GR 2005, Eerdmans xi; 244 pp. $20 [BiTod 44,201—Donald Senior].

9645 Orientamenti per leggere la bibbia in gruppi. I vangeli. 2005 ⇒432. 65-70. La Casa della Bibbia (Spagna).

9646 *Pasqualetti, Fabio* Tra '*lectio divina*' e vita: sussidi e riflessioni fuori campo. Lectio divina. 2005 ⇒437. 197-207.

9647 **Pasquetto, Virgilio** Chiamati a vita nuova: temi di spiritualità biblica, 1: Antico Testamento, 2: Nuovo Testamento. 2002 ⇒18,8435... 20,8876. [R]ATT 11 (2005) 457-460 (*Ghiberti, Giuseppe*).

9648 *Passaro, Angelo* La direzione spirituale: un profilo biblico: vita nello Spirito come 'respons-abilità' credente. Sacrum Ministerium 11 (2005) 134-147.

9649 *Pastore, Corrado* La lectio divina oggi: la lettura orante nella pastorale della chiesa. Ripartire da Cristo. 2005 ⇒800. 115-140;

9650 Modelli di lectio divina. Ripartire da Cristo. 2005 ⇒800. 231-248.
9651 *Paul, Claudio* 'Pura e perene fonte da vida espiritual': a palavra de Deus como alimento da nossa vida no Espirito a partir da *Dei Verbum*. Convergência 40 (2005) 599-616.
9652 **Peterson, Eugene H.** Christ plays in ten thousand places: a conversation in spiritual theology. GR 2005, Eerdmans xii; 368 pp.
9653 **Prabhu, R. Rajendra** Understanding Jesus. Bangalore 2005, Asian Trading xii; 239 pp. Rs150. 81-7086-374-0 [VJTR 70,938—Gispert-Sauch, G.].
9654 **Reeves, Shawn Christopher** A journey in Exodus. NY 2005, St Paul's 115 pp. $7 [BiTod 44,196—Dianne Bergant].
9655 *Reid, Barbara E.* What's biblical about... the rosary?. BiTod 43 (2005) 182-187.
9656 **Rivas Rebaque, Fernando** La experiencia espiritual de Jesús: materiales para reflexionar personalmente y en grupo. M 2005, San Pablo 294 pp.
9657 **Rossi de Gasperis, Francesco** Sentieri di vita: la dinamica degli esercizi ignaziani nell'itinerario delle scritture, 1: principio e fondamento e prima settimana. Mi 2005, Paoline 504 pp. €23.75. 88-315-2902-1.
9658 **Schlegel, Helmut** Mit dem Feuer des Geistes: biblische Meditationen zum Werden und Wachsen des inneren Menschen. Wü 2005, Echter 136 pp. €9.90. 3-429-02708-X.
9659 *Schneiders, Sandra M.* Biblical foundations of spirituality. Scripture as the soul of theology. 2005 ⇒776. 1-22.
9660 *Schoon, Simon* De bijbel als bron van spiritualiteit;
9661 De bijbel als bron van levenskunst. ITBT 13/1 (2005) 16-18/19-21.
9662 *Schwienhorst-Schönberger, Ludger* Erleuchtungserfahrung und Schriftverständnis. Studien zum AT. SBAB 40: 2005 <2001> ⇒298. 287-296 = Mystik—Spiritualität der Zukunft: Erfahrung des Ewigen, [F]Willigis JÄGER, ed. **Peter Lengsfeld**, FrB: Herder (2005) 251-264.
9663 *Sebastiani, Lilia* Riflettere con la parola: con la fraternità Anawim. VM 59/232 (2005) 101-104.
9664 *Secondin, Bruno* "Lectio divina" e spiritualità: un itinerario urbano. VM 59/232 (2005) 97-100;
9665 Lectio divina: natura e prassi: la parola di Dio fonte privilegiata di esperienza spirituale. [F]BERNARD, C. 2005 ⇒8. 63-91;
9666 Lectio divina e ascolto della parola di Dio: testi–discorsi–percorsi. Ripartire da Cristo. 2005 ⇒800. 11-32.
9667 *Shea, John* Persevering in the perfect law of liberty: scriptural resources for pastoral care. Scripture as the soul of theology. 2005 ⇒ 776. 60-83.
9668 [E]**Silvano, Renu Rita; Mascarenhas, Fio** Inspiring teaching of Jesus Christ: (from the Holy Bible). Mumbai 2005, Catholic Bible Institute 213 pp.
9669 **Spidlik, Tomas** El evangelio dominical y festivo: reflexiones para los ciclos A, B y C. 2004 ⇒20,8889. [R]VyV 63/1 (2005) 240-241.
9670 *Spielberg, Bernhard* Das Meer in mir—Mar Adentro. LS 56 (2005) 300-302.
9671 **Standaert, Benoît** L'espace Jésus: la foi pascale dans l'espace des religions. L'autre et les autres 7: Bru 2005, Lessius 350 pp. €26. 287-299-1387 [Études (jan. 2005) 141—Marc Rastoin].

9672 **Stock, Klemens** Vivir en la fe la comunión con Jesús. Onda, Castellón 2005, Carmelitanas 90 pp [AcBib 11,149].
9673 *Thekkekara, Matthew* La lectio divina: significato e metodo. Ripartire da Cristo. 2005 ⇒800. 87-96.
9674 *Thurston, Bonnie* Words and the Word: reflections on scripture, prayer and poetry. Way 44/2 (2005) 7-20.
9675 *Tidball, Derek* The bible in evangelical spirituality. Bible in pastoral practice. 2005 ⇒341. 258-274.
9676 **Treitler, Wolfgang** Auf Wanderschaft: Betrachtungen zum biblischen Glauben. Kirchstetten [2]2005, Achinoam 286 pp.
9677 *Tremolada, Pierantonio* Itinerari di lettura biblica: una proposta. RCI 86 (2005) 700-715.
9678 *Uro, Risto* Explaining early christian asceticism: methodological considerations. [F]AEJMELAEUS, L. SESJ 89: 2005 ⇒1. 458-474.
9679 **Vanhoye, Albert** Le don du Christ: lecture spirituelle. P 2005, Bayard 243 pp. 2-227-47468-8;
9680 Il sacerdozio di Cristo e dei cristiani: esercizi spirituali. Siena 2005, Basilica S. Francesco 126 pp [AcBib 11,35].
9681 *Vasciaveo, Chiara* "Chi ha orecchi ascolti ciò che lo Spirito dice alle chiese". Horeb 14/3 (2005) 54-62 [Rev 2-3].
9682 *Venturi, Gianfranco Lectio divina* e liturgia della parola: per una corretta prassi pastorale. Lectio divina. 2005 ⇒437. 135-159.
9683 *Vicent, Rafael Lectio* della parola nel giudaismo antico. Ripartire da Cristo. 2005 ⇒800. 33-60.
9684 **Vogels, Walter** Becoming fully human: living the bible with God, each other and the environment. 2003 ⇒19,9062; 20,8897. [R]Spiritual Life 51/1 (2005) 59-60 (*Flynn, D.M.*).
9685 *Volný, Vladislav* "Jesus Christus spricht: 'Ich aber habe für dich gebeten, daß dein Glaube nicht aufhöre; und wenn du dereinst dich bekehrst, so stärke deine Brüder.'" (Lukas 22,32): zur Jahreslosung für 2005. LKW 52 (2005) 11-13.
9686 *Witczyk, Henryk* 'Apparve la misericordia di Dio: la fonte della trasformazione dell'uomo': lectio divina della lettera a Tito (3,3-8). Ripartire da Cristo. 2005 ⇒800. 97-112.
9687 *Wolfram, Gernot* Der gerechte Zuhörer: warum ich die Bibel nicht ohne den Mann Eutychus lesen kann. zeitzeichen 6/11 (2005) 36-38 [Acts 20,09-12].
9688 *Zevini, Giorgio* La *lectio divina* fonte di esperienza ecclesiale e spirituale. Lectio divina. 2005 ⇒437. 51-65;
9689 Bibliografia sulla *lectio divina*. Lectio divina. 2005 ⇒437. 209-217;
9690 La *lectio* della parola nel Nuovo Testamento. Ripartire da Cristo. 2005 ⇒800. 61-71.
9691 [E]**Zevini, Giorgio; Cabra, Pier Giordano** Lectio divina para la vida diaria, 2: los textos bíblicos de la vida consagrada. [T]*Montes, Miguel*: Estella (Navarra) 2005, Verbo Divino 310 pp. 84-8169-438-X.

## H8.1 *Spiritualitas publica*: **Liturgia, Via communitatis, Sancti**

9692 **Alphonso, Herbert** Tu m'as appelé par nom: la vocation personelle du croyant. R 2005, E.P.U.G. 80 pp. 88-7839-028-3.
9693 *Baumann, Arnulf H.* Gottesdienst bei Juden und Christen. [F]STOLLE, V.: Theologie: Forschung und Wissenschaft 12: 2005 ⇒143. 21-28.

9694 *Beckwith, Roger T.* The three cycles of the christian year;

9695 Daily and weekly worship: from Jewish to christian;

9696 Worship on special occasions: from Jewish to christian;

9697 Introduction: the relationship of calendar, chronology and worship. Calendar, chronology. 2005 ⇒184. 91-98/171-212/213-235/1-4.

9698 *Bexell, Oloph* När Gamla testamentet lyftes ur balansen: en episod i den svenska evangeliebokens historia. SEÅ 70 (2005) 33-42.

9699 [E]**Bohác, Voijtech; Kunzler, Michael,** *al.*, Die biblischen Lesungen, Troparien und Konkadien, Antiphonen und alle anderen liturgischen Texte für die Feier der göttlichen Liturgie und des Stundengebets in den heiligen Kirchen des byzantinischen Ritus nach den Tagen des Kirchenjahres. Pd 2005, Bonifatius 880 pp. €69.90. 3-89710-325-7. [EuA 82,117—Theodor Hogg].

9700 *Bonaccorso, Giorgio* L'atto del leggere e dell'ascoltare. RPLi 43/3 (2005) 15-21.

9701 *Braulik, Georg* Pentateuch-Bahnlesung an den Sonntagen im Jahreskreis: Bemerkungen zur Kritik an der Wiener Perikopenordnung;

9702 Die Tora als Bahnlesung: zur Hermeneutik einer zukünftigen Auswahl der Sonntagsperikopen <1995>;

9703 Das göttliche Bundesangebot an die Menschheit: zum 4. Hochgebet <1997>;

9704 Gott für Israel preisen: zur Heilsprärogative Israels und zum 4. Hochgebet <2004>. Liturgie und Bibel. ÖBS 28: 2005 ⇒360. 225-266/125-149/269-281/301-329.

9705 *Brufani, Stefano* Le citazioni evangeliche della 'scoperta' del vangelo nella *Regula non bullata*. Franciscana [Spoleto] 7 (2005) 1-31.

9706 *Buchinger, Harald* Neues Testament und Liturgie. ALW 47/2 (2005) 288-306.

9707 [E]**Buzzetti, Carlo** La nostra voce per la sua parola: la lettura orale: come leggere meglio in chiesa. Leumann (Torino) 2005, Elle Di Ci 95 pp. €9. 88-01-03105-X.

9708 [E]**Casarin, Giuseppe** Lezionario commentato feriale: rigenerati dalla parola di Dio, 1. Avvento—Natale. Ascoltare, celebrare, vivere: Padova 2005, EMP 256 pp. €14.80. [R]CredOg 25/6 (2005) 142 (*Cappelletto, Gianni*).

9709 **Castelli, Elizabeth A.** Martyrdom and memory: early christian culture making. Gender, theory, and religion: 2004 ⇒20,8917. [R]BTB 35 (2005) 153-154 (*Stratton, Kimberly B.*).

9710 *Cavalletti, Sofia* Memorial and typology in Jewish and christian liturgy. L&S 1 (2005) 69-86.

9711 **Ceresko, Anthony Raymond** St FRANCIS de Sales and the bible. Bangalore 2005, S.F.S. 192 pp. Rs140/$10. 81-85376-689. [R]ITS 42 (2005) 341-342 (*Legrand, Lucien*).

9712 **Clements-Jewery, Philip** Intercessory prayer: modern theology, biblical teaching and philosophical thought. Aldershot 2005, Ashgate viii;158 pp. $20. 07546-38286 [Worship 80/1,76s: David N. Power].

9713 *Correia, João Alberto Sousa* Figuras bíblicas da vocação. Theologica 40 (2005) 265-292.

9714 **Costa, M.G.** Le mani della misericordia: formazione umana attraverso le figure bibliche. R 2005, OCD 272+282 pp. €18+18.

9715 **Dagron, A.** A l'épreuve des évangiles: lectures des dimanches, année B. P 2005, Bayard 247 pp. €20.50. 22274-75199. Préf. *J.-P. Ricard*.

9716 *David, Robert* Du but initial au but subjectif: la réponse des appelés dans les textes de la première alliance. SR 34 (2005) 197-211.
9717 *Dozeman, Thomas* The priestly vocation. Interp. 59 (2005) 117-128.
9718 *Driscoll, Jeremy* The word of God in the liturgy of the new covenant. L&S 1 (2005) 87-100.
9719 *Ducruet, Bernard* La quête des premiers disciples. Christus 52/1 (2005) 10-18.
9720 **Due, Noel** Created for worship: from Genesis to Revelation. Fearn, Ross-shire 2005, CFP Mentor 310 pp. £11. 1-84550-0261.
9721 *Fiedler, Peter* Kultkritik im Neuen Testament?. Studien zur biblischen Grundlegung. SBAB 35: 2005 <2002> ⇒209. 256-291.
9722 Fioriti, Luigi L'Evangeliario bizantino dell'Eparchia di Lungro degli Italo-Albanesi dell'Italia continentale. RivLi 92 (2005) 511-515.
9723 *Fowler, James W.* God's praxis and our callings: reclaiming providence and vocation. Reconsidering the boundaries. 2005 ⇒598. 187-196.
9724 *Franz, Ansgar* Kirchenlied und Heilige Schrift. ThG 48 (2005) 275-280.
9725 *Frøyshov, Stig R.* Bønnens praksis i den egyptiske [skand- oe]rkenmonastisismen: en innledende studie. NTT 106/3 (2005) 147-169.
9726 *Galadza, Paul* Principles applied in the compilation and translation of The Divine Liturgy: an anthology for worship. StLi 35 (2005) 81-99.
9727 *García Rojo, Jesús* Itinerario espiritual del hombre sanjuanista. Salm. 52 (2005) 39-67.
9728 *Gerhards, Albert* Abbilden und Einbilden—von der Ambivalenz biblischer Bilder im liturgischen Feierraum. ThG 48 (2005) 281-289.
9729 *Giorda, Mariachiara* Il dossier egiziano nel "Prato Spirituale" di Giovanni Mosco: alcune riflessioni. AnStR 6 (2005) 67-83.
9730 *González de la Bandera Romero, Ginés* Martirio: entrega, vida, testimonio y sacramento. Isidorianum 28 (2005) 519-553.
9731 **González Oña, Juan María** Una lectura de la vida y escritos de FRANCISCO de Asís en clave Joánica: presencia e influencia de la teología del cuarto evangelio. Burgos 2005, Facultad de Teologia del Norte de España 99 pp.
9732 [E]**González Silva, Santiago** La palabra de Dios en la comunidad religiosa. 2004 ⇒20,8933. [R]SalTer 93 (2005) 876-878 (*González Bejarano, Óscar*).
9733 *Gruber, Margareta* Eunucos por el reino de Dios. SelTeol 44/1 (2005) 74-80 <GuL 76 (2003) 263-271 [Mt 9,12].
9734 **Haag, Ulrich** Du sollst dir kein Bildnis machen?: Gemeindegottesdienste mit Bildern gestalten. Gü 2005, Gü 138 pp. 3-579-02742-5.
9735 **Hahn, Scott** Letter and spirit: from written text to living word in the liturgy. NY 2005, Doubleday xvi; 238 pp. $22. 0-385-50933-2. Bibl. 177-229.
9736 *Hahn, Scott W.* Worship in the word: toward a liturgical hermeneutic. L&S 1 (2005) 101-136.
9737 *Haunerland, Winfried* Gottes Gegenwart in seinem Wort: der liturgische "Mehrwert" der Schriftlesung im Gottesdienst. Gottesdienst 39/11 (2005) 81-83.
9738 *Heinemann, Christoph* Den Machthabern ein Schnippchen schlagen: zur Entstehung der Predigtreihe "Gottes Wort im Kirchenjahr". [F]STENDEBACH, F. 2005 ⇒141. 198-212.

9739 [E]**Heinemann, Christoph** Gottes Wort im Kirchenjahr 2005: Lesejahr A, Band III: die Zeit nach Pfingsten. Wü 2005, Echter 336 pp. €19. CD-ROM €25.

9740 [E]**Hoefelmann, Verner; Silva, João Artur Müller da** Proclamar libertação, 31. Auxílios para o anúncio do evangelho: São Leopoldo 2005, Sinodal 335 pp. Ano B da Liturgia.

9741 **Hooker, Morna D.** Endings: invitations to discipleship. 2003 ⇒19, 9116; 20,8940. [R]RBLit (2005)* (*Coloe, Mary; Harstine, Stan*).

9742 *Hödl, Hans G.* Praxis-Dimensionen (Ritual, religiöse Erfahrung, Ethik): Ritual (Kult, Opfer, Ritus, Zeremonie). Handbuch Religionswissenschaft. 2005 ⇒1016. 664-689.

9743 *Hughes, Tomaz* O diálogo profético na vida religiosa à luz da bíblia. Convergência 40 (2005) 269-278.

9744 *Iotti, Paolo* Proclamare e ascoltare la parola nell'assemblea liturgica. RPLi 43/3 (2005) 23-29.

9745 *Kaschewsky, Rudolf* "Das Rätsel von Addai und Mari"—zu einer neuen vatikanischen Veröffentlichung. Una Voce-Korrespondenz 35 (2005) 36-55.

9746 **Kelly, Joseph F.** El origen de la Navidad. Bilbao 2005, Mensajero 150 pp. 84-271-2731-6.

9747 *Kempiak, Ryszard* Lectio divina e liturgia delle ore. Ripartire da Cristo. 2005 ⇒800. 223-229.

9748 *Kranemann, Benedikt* Biblische Texte–liturgische Kontexte: Intertextualität und Schriftrezeption in der Liturgie. ThG 48 (2005) 254-264;

9749 Biblische Texte als Heilige Schrift in der Liturgie. Heilige Schriften. 2005 ⇒362. 159-171, 246-248.

9750 *Kranemann, Daniela* "Wendet euer Ohr zu den Worten meines Mundes ..." (Ps 78,1): die Liturgie als Schule des Hörens—und Antwortens. BiLi 78 (2005) 15-19.

9751 **Krempa, S. Joseph** Captured fire: the Sunday homilies cycle B. Staten Island 2005, St Paul's vii; 200 pp. $15 [BiTod 44,62–D. Senior].

9752 *Lang, Bernhard* Aspekter af kristen gudsdyrkelse set i lyset af historiske studier og ritualstudier. RVT 47 (2005) 3-18.

9753 Lectionnaire pour chaque jour de l'année, 1. P 2005, Cerf 785 pp. €35 [VS 85,560s–Raffin, Pierre].

9754 *Leder, A.C.* The place of christian worship: gathered round the throne of the Almighty. CTJ 40 (2005) 227-247.

9755 [E]**Legendre, Olivier** Collectaneum exemplorum et visionum Clarevallense: e codice Trecensi 946. CChr.CM 208: Turnhout 2005, Brepols cxiv; 468 pp. 2-503-05089-1.

9756 *Léon-Dufour, Xavier* Chi è un santo?. Un biblista cerca Dio. Collana biblica: 2005 ⇒245. 287-296.

9757 *Lischer, Richard* The called life: an essay on the pastoral vocation. Interp. 59 (2005) 166-175.

9758 *Lohfink, Norbert* Zu Heinz Schürmanns 10 Punkten: geplanter Anhang zu Norbert Lohfink, "Perikopenordnung 'Patmos'" 185-197;

9759 Zwischen "hebraica veritas" und liturgischem Text 563-579;

9760 Die Feier des Sonntags und der Lebensrhythmus einer apostolischen Kommunität <1987> 109-121;

9761 Moses Tod, die Tora und die alttestamentliche Sonntagslesung <1996> 151-164;

9762 Perikopenordnung "Patmos": Gedanken eines Alttestamentlers zu dem Leseordnungsentwurf von Hansjakob Becker <1997> 165-183;

9763 Zur Perikopenordnung für die Sonntage im Jahreskreis <2001> 199-224;

9764 Der Alte Bund im 4. Hochgebet <2000> 283-300;

9765 Liturgische Bibelverdunstung: die Bibel-Intertextualität bei der Verdeutschung der lateinischen Liturgie <2000> 581-593;

9766 Das "Pange Lingua" im "Gotteslob" <2003>. Liturgie und Bibel. ÖBS 28: 2005 ⇒360. 595-607.

9767 **Mangione, Salvatore** La festa dei Giudei e i riti della settimana santa. Messina 2005, San Fratello 143 pp. €15. Collab. *Regina Adelaide*.

9768 *Manicardi, Ermenegildo* La sacra scrittura nella liturgia: operatività ed efficacia. [F]GHIBERTI, G.: SRivBib 46: 2005 ⇒47. 283-296.

9769 *Martini, Carlo M.* Il ruolo centrale della parola di Dio nella vita della chiesa: l'animazione biblica dell'esercizio pastorale. CivCatt 156/4 (2005) 24-35.

9770 **Masseroni, Enrico** La parola come pane: il vangelo della domenica: Anno C. Parola e liturgia 26: CinB 2000, San Paolo 275 pp. 88-215-4281-5.

9771 **McCaffrey, James** Captive flames: a biblical reading of the Carmelite saints. Dublin 2005, Veritas 213 pp. €13. 1-85390-920-3 [IThQ 71,200—Nicholas Madden].

9772 *Mette, Norbert* Hermeneutik göttlicher Praxis und menschlicher Berufung als gemeinsame Aufgabe—Bemerkungen zu Fowlers theologischem Ansatz. Reconsidering the boundaries. 2005 ⇒598. 197-99.

9773 *Mitescu, Adriana Moedim* e le preghiere ebraiche di Gesù quale modello della liturgia delle ore. Ter. 56/115 (2005) 225-284 [John 20, 11].

9774 *Monti, Stefania* Scritture sante e culto: un rapporto controverso. VM 59/232 (2005) 19-32.

9775 *Moorhead, John* Hearing the bible in St BENEDICT. StMon 47/1 (2005) 7-17.

9776 *Ockel, Eberhard* Lektorenprobleme mit der Bibel. Das Buch. Vechtaer Beiträge zur Theologie 11: 2005 ⇒487. 224-236.

9777 **Odenthal, Andreas** Die Ordinatio Cultus Divini et Caeremoniarum des Halberstädter Domes von 1591: Untersuchungen zur Liturgie eines gemischtkonfessionellen Domkapitels nach Einführung der Reformation. LWQF 93: Müns 2005, Aschendorff viii; 318 pp. 3-402-04073-5. Bibl. 281-308.

9778 *Orsatti, Mauro* Spunti di comunione: aspetti di vita comunitaria partendo da due brani biblici. VitaCon 41 (2005) 471-486 [2 Kgs 5,1-19; Acts 2,42-7].

9779 **Pardilla, Angel** Christ's way of life at the centre of formation for religious life: the biblical and theological perspective of formation. R 2005, Rogate 425 pp [CRM 86,203—Andrés, Domingo J.].

9780 *Pardilla, Ángel* Le langage canonique concernant le programme de vie des religieux à la lumière de la bible. CRM 86 (2005) 135-159.

9781 *Perrenchio, Fausto* La parola di Dio negli scritti di Don BOSCO. Ripartire da Cristo. 2005 ⇒800. 167-188.

9782 **Peterson, David** En esprit et en vérité: théologie biblique de l'adoration. Théologie biblique: Cléon d'Andran 2005, Excelsis 341 pp.

9783 *Peterson, Erik* Die Nachfolge Christi. Peterson: Lukasevangelium und Synoptica. 2005 ⇒277. 425-427.

9784 **Poirot, Eliane** Pour chanter le saint prophète Élisée dans la tradition byzantine. Spiritualité orientale 84: 2005, Abbaye de Bellefontaine 174 pp. Préf. *Michel Evdokimov*.

9785 *Popescu, Leontin* La liturgia della parola nella divina liturgia. RPLi 43/3 (2005) 31-37.

9786 *Riches, John* Exegetical reflections on lectionary readings: Johannine prologue. ET 117 (2005) 69-70 [John 1,1-18].

9787 *Rocco Tedesco, Diana* Las vírgenes en la iglesia primitiva. Cuadernos de teología 24 (2005) 257-268.

9788 [E]**Rose, Els** Missale Gothicum e codice Vaticano Reginensi latino 317. CChr.SL 159 D: Turnholti 2005, Brepols 601 pp. 2-503-01599-9. Bibl. 329-348.

9789 *Schätzel, Michael* Von Lukas lernen: gottesdienstliches Fürbittgebet als Gestaltungsaufgabe. [F]STOLLE, V. 2005 ⇒143. 511-530.

9790 **Schirrmacher,Thomas** The persecution of christians concerns us all: towards a theology of martyrdom: 70 biblical-theological theses written for the German Evangelical Alliance. 2001 ⇒19,9164. [R]Missionalia 33/1 (2005) 192-193 (*Van Rooyen, G.W.S.*).

9791 *Schlosser, Jacques* Christologie du Nouveau Testament et liturgie. [F]GHIBERTI, G.: SRivBib 46: 2005 ⇒47. 297-308.

9792 *Secondin, Bruno* De Jérusalem à Antioche: repenser le modèle biblique de la vie consacrée. Vies consacrées 77 (2005) 174-194.

9793 **Shea, John** The spiritual wisdom of the gospels for christian preachers and teachers—Year B: eating with the bridegroom. ColMn 2005, Liturgical xi; 281 pp. $30. 0-8146-2914-8.

9794 **Slattery, J.A.** The challenge of the gospel: reflections on the Sunday gospels: cycle B. Staten Island, NY 2005, St Pauls x; 160 pp. $16. 08189-09676. [NTAb 50,171].

9795 *Sorci, Pietro* Il Lezionario dell'Ordo paenitentiae. RivLi 92 (2005) 837-862.

9796 *Spronk, Klaas* Liever langer lezen: over bijbelleesroosters, tekstcombinaties en systeemdwang. Theologisch debat 2/1 (2005) 46-51.

9797 *Steins, G.* "Wort des lebendigen Gottes": neue Brücken zwischen Bibelauslegung und Liturgie. ThG 48 (2005) 242-253.

9798 **Stock, Klemens** La liturgia de la palabra: comentarios a los evangelios dominicales y festivos: ciclo B (Marcos). Caminos 15: M 2005, San Pablo 463 pp. 84-285-2808-X.

9799 **Swanson, Richard W.** Provoking the gospel: methods to embody biblical storytelling through drama. Cleveland, OH 2004, Pilgrim 136 pp. $18. [R]RBLit (2005)* (*Fowler, Robert*);

9800 Provoking the gospel of Mark: a storyteller's commentary, year B. Cleveland, OH 2005, Pilgrim 349 pp. 0-8298-1690-9. Incl. 1 DVD.

9801 Il tempo della festa: dieci voci per riscoprire la domenica. Dimensioni dello spirito 65: CinB 2005, San Paolo 148 p. 88-215-5297-7. A cura del Servizio Nazionale per il Progetto Culturale.

9802 **Terrinoni, Ubaldo** Parola di Dio e voti religiosi: icone bibliche, 3. povertà. 2003 ⇒19,9174. [R]Clar. 45 (2005) 418-419 (*Rovira, J.*).

9803 [E]**Upchurch, Cackie** A year of Sundays: gospel reflections 2006. Little Rock 2005, Little Rock Scripture Study 80 pp. $2 [BiTod 44, 64—Donald Senior].

9804 *Vanhoomissen, Guy* Une messe sans paroles de consécration?: à propos de la validité de l'anaphore d'Addaï et Mari. NRTh 127 (2005) 36-46.

9805 **Vanhoye, Albert** Le letture bibliche delle domeniche: Anno B. R 2005, ADP 374 pp. €20. 88-7357-378-9.

9806 *Vannier, Marie-Anne* Naissance de la tradition chrétienne [de la Pâque]. MoBi 164 (2005) 30-35.
9807 *Venturi, Gianfranco* 'Oggi la parola si compie per voi': teologia della liturgia della parola. RPLi 43/3 (2005) 11-14.
9808 **Verhelst, Stéphane** Les traditions judéo-chrétiennes dans la liturgie de Jérusalem, spécialement la Liturgie de saint Jacques frère de Dieu. 2003 ⇒19,9184. [R]REJ 164 (2005) 568-570 (*Mimouni, Simon C.*).
9809 *Voisin, Jean-Louis* Prosopographie des morts volontaires chrétiens (en particulier chez EUSÈBE de Césarée). Prosopographie et histoire religieuse. 2005 ⇒810. 351-362.
9810 *Wahle, Stephan* Liturgie als Gedächtnisgeschehen: dargestellt anhand eines Vergleichs von christlicher Sonntags- und jüdischer Sabbatliturgie. ALW 47/2 (2005) 153-180.
9811 *Webster, John* Discipleship and calling. SBET 23 (2005) 133-147.
9812 *Wedon, Athanasius von* "Fervor Novicii": Neubesinnung in der Ordens- und Priesterausbildung. [F]STENDEBACH, F. 2005 ⇒141. 326-41.
9813 **Wick, Peter** Die urchristlichen Gottesdienste: Entstehung und Entwicklung im Rahmen der frühjüdischen Tempel-, Synagogen- und Hausfrömmigkeit. BWANT 150: 2002 ⇒18,8558; 20,8990. [R]CBQ 67 (2005) 160-161 (*Hamm, Dennis*).
9814 *Zell, Anne* La proclamazione della parola nella tradizione protestante. RPLi 43/3 (2005) 39-42.

## H8.2 Theologia moralis NT

9815 *Adam, Albrecht* Gottes Weisungen heute: eine Orientierung in einer multikomplexen Welt. [F]STOLLE, V. 2005 ⇒143. 303-322.
9816 *Barthel, Jörg* Am andern Ufer?: Bibel und Homosexualität. ThFPr 31/1 (2005) 99-113.
9817 *Bedford-Strohm, Heinrich* Theological ethics and the church: reconsidering the boundaries between practical theology and theological ethics in light of the debate on Liberalism and Communitarism. Reconsidering the boundaries. 2005 ⇒598. 175-186.
9818 *Beed, Cara; Beed, Clive* Jesus and equity in material distribution. EvQ 77 (2005) 99-118.
9819 **Bockmuehl, Markus** Jewish law in Gentile churches: halakhah and the beginning of christian public ethics. 2000 ⇒16,8074... 20,9006. [R]RB 112 (2005) 302-304 (*Nodet, Etienne*);
9820 2003 <2000> ⇒19,9203; 20,9005. [R]RBLit 7 (2005) 251-254 (*Doering, Lutz*).
9821 *Brondos, D.A.* Freedom, the 'letter' and the 'Spirit': interpreting scripture with the 'mind of Christ'. Trinity Seminary Review [Columbus, OH] 26/1 (2005) 7-15 [NTAb 49,463].
9822 *Browning, Don* The relation of practical theology to theological ethics. Reconsidering the boundaries. 2005 ⇒598. 161-173.
9823 *Butting, Hermann* Jesus, der Unternehmer. zeitzeichen 6/8 (2005) 59.
9824 *Carter, Warren* Proclaiming (in/against) empire then and now. Word and world 25 (2005) 149-158.
9825 **Cox, Harvey** When Jesus came to Harvard: making moral choices today. 2004 ⇒20,9018. [R]America 192/1 (2005) 24-26 (*Gula, Richard M.*).

9826 *Davids, Peter H.* The test of wealth. The missions of James. NT.S 115: 2005 ⇒369. 355-384.
9827 *Den Hertog, Gerard C.* Een symposium in Apeldoorn over bijbel en ethiek: een lezing van O. O'Donovan en een reactie van H.W. de Knijff. ThRef 48 (2005) 114-120.
9828 **Doldi, M.; Picozzi, M.; Ponte, A.** Bioetica: la parola di Dio e le parole dell'uomo. R 2005, Città N. 270 pp.
9829 *Donahue, John R.* The bible and social justice: 'Learn to do right! Seek justice' (Isa 1:17 NIV). Scripture. 2005 ⇒398. 239-251.
9830 **Douglas, Mark** Confessing Christ in the 21st century. Lanham 2005, Rowman & L 288 pp. $28. 0-7425-1433-1.
9831 *Dreyer, Y.* Vergewe en vergeet: 'n pastorale perspektief. VeE 26 (2005) 16-34.
9832 *Drolshagen, Christoph; Garvert, Christa; Kaul, Alexandra* Selbstbestimmt sterben auch im Krankenhaus: Projekte der Marienhaus GmbH Waldbreitbach zum Umgang mit Sterbenden. LS 56 (2005) 268-273.
9833 *Du Rand, Jan A.* Die doodstraf: 'n teologiese standpunt. VeE 26 (2005) 341-356.
9834 *Dugandzic, Ivan* Biblijska inspiracija solidarnosti danas. BoSm 75 (2005) 971-990. **Croatian.**
9835 *Ebner, Martin* Neutestamentliche Ethik zwischen weisheitlichen alltagsratschlägen und sozialethischen Visionen. Ethik im Brennpunkt. 2005 ⇒855. 57-95.
9836 *Ernst, Stephan* Innere Grenze der Autonomie: ethische Überlegungen zur gesetzlichen Regelung von Patientenverfügungen;
9837 Wider eine grenzenlose Autonomie: Stephan Ernsts Antwort auf "Selbstbestimmt sterben". LS 56 (2005) 248-252/258-260.
9838 *Ettl, Claudio* "Tu ihm nichts zuleide ...": Gott als Anwalt der Kinder. BiHe 41/163 (2005) 7-9.
9839 *Florio, Lucio* I diritti umani nella prospettiva biblica. I vangeli. 2005 ⇒432.152-158.
9840 **Fowl, Stephen E.; Jones, L. Gregory** Reading in communion. 1991 ⇒7,8331... 10,8307. ᴿVJTR 69 (2005) 391-92 (*Menezes, Albert M.*).
9841 **Fuchs, Eric** L'éthique chrétienne: du Nouveau Testament aux défis contemporains. Le champ éthique 40: 2003 ⇒19,9222; 20,9034. ᴿLTP 61 (2005) 395-398 (*Jobin, Guy*).
9842 **Fumagalli, Aristide; Manzi, Franco** Attirerò tutti a me: ermeneutica biblica ed etica cristiana. Trattati di etica teologica: Bo 2005, EDB 482 pp. €39. 88105-0545X.
9843 *Gabriel, Karl* Die Wahrnehmung der Schrift in der Gesellschaft und ihre soziale Relevanz. Die Bedeutung. 2005 ⇒363. 199-226.
9844 *Garhammer, Erich* Ein Gespräch mit Eberhard Schockenhoff. LS 56 (2005) 274-278.
9845 *Georgi, Dieter* Legal dimensions of money and theological consequences. The city in the valley. Studies in biblical literature 7: 2005 ⇒214. 103-134 [Rom 4,1-12; 1 Cor 9; 2 Cor 2,17; 11,7-21; 12,11-18; Gal 2; Phil 4,10-19].
9846 *Gorski, Horst* Liebe ist der Maßstab: warum Homosexualität keine Sünde ist. zeitzeichen 6/10 (2005) 35-36.
9847 **Haan, Roelf** Economie van de eerbied: kanttekeningen bij het bijbelse spreken over geld en goed. Zoetermeer 2005, Meinema 192 pp. €14.50. 90-211-4069-8 [KeTh 58,186—Rein Brouwer].

9848 **Harrington, Daniel J.; Keenan, James F.** Jesus and virtue ethics: building bridges between New Testament studies and moral theology. Lanham, MD 2005 <2002>, Rowman & L. xv; 216 pp. $20. 0-7425-49941. Bibl. [NTAb 50,191].

9849 **Helminiak, Daniel** Ce que la bible dit vraiment de l'homosexualité. P 2005, Empêcheurs 221 pp. €15 [Esprit 322,258—J.-L. Schlegel].

9850 *Hilgendorf, Eric* Selbstbestimmt sterben: offene Fragen zwischen Recht und Religion. LS 56 (2005) 253-257;

9851 Wider die Tabuisierung des Todes: Eric Hilgendorfs Replik auf "Innere Grenzen der Autonomie". LS 56 (2005) 261-263.

9852 *Hoffmann, Johannes* Doppelte Dividende: Ziel der Bewußtseinsbildung für ethische Geldanlagen bei Investoren, Konsumenten und Finanzdienstleistern. [F]STENDEBACH, F. 2005 ⇒141. 225-255.

9853 *Joha, Heribert* Medizin im Wandel der Zeit. LS 56 (2005) 279-283.

9854 *Johnson, Elizabeth* Life together in the household of God. [F]BRUEGGEMANN, W.—COUSAR, C. 2005 ⇒16. 89-103.

9855 **Jung, Patricia Beattie; Coray, Joseph Andrew** Sexual diversity and catholicism: toward the development of moral theology. 2001 ⇒ 17,363... 20,494. [R]RBLit 7 (2005) 537-540 (*Dempsey, Carol J.*).

9856 *Kazen, Thomas* Tidiga Jesusbilder: om erfarenheten bakom och framför kristologin. SvTK 81/2 (2005) 49-66.

9857 *Käsemann, Ernst* Das Evangelium und die Frommen. In der Nachfolge. 2005 ⇒236. 130-138.

9858 *Kizhakkeyil, Sebastian* The biblical concept of repentance. JJSS 4 (2004) 147-160;

9859 Compassion and christian spirituality. JJSS 5 (2005) 31-48.

9860 *Knijff, Henri de* Bijbel en christelijke ethiek: reactie op: O. O'Donovan "Scripture and christian ethics". ThRef 48/2 (2005) 130-37.

9861 **Léon-Dufour, Xavier** Agire secondo il vangelo. CSB 44: 2003 ⇒ 19,9242; 20,9049. [R]RivBib 53 (2005) 113-6 (*De Virgilio, Giuseppe*);

9862 Agir segundo o evangelho. [T]*Endlich, Lúcia Mathilde* 2003 ⇒19, 9241. [R]REB 65 (2005) 493-4 (*Campos, José Benedito de*);

9863 To act according to the gospel. [T]*Smith, Christopher R.*: Peabody, MASS 2005, Hendrickson xviii; 157 pp. £10. 1-565-63201-X.

9864 *Locker, Markus E.* Ethical dimensions in the teaching of Jesus and Paul. Ethical dimensions. 2005 ⇒739. 6-10.

9865 *Lovera, Armando Jesús* Una historia interminable: agar sin Dios, sin ángel y sin pozo alguno.... ResB 46 (2005) 46-51.

9866 *Lüpke, Johannes von* An der Schwelle zum Leben: zur Wahrnehmung der Gottebenbildlichkeit am Ende des Lebens. WuD 28 (2005) 247-264.

9867 **Maguire, Daniel C.** A moral creed for all christians. Mp 2005, Fortress ix; 269 pp. $14. 0-8006-3761-5 [ThD 52,380: W.C. Heiser].

9868 *Masango, M.* Reconciliation: a way of life for the world. VeE 26 (2005) 133-145.

9869 *Matera, Frank J.* New Testament foundations for christian ethics. Scripture as the soul of theology. 2005 ⇒776. 23-39.

9870 **McQuilkin, Robertson** An introduction to biblical ethics. 2002 ⇒ 19,9245. [R]MissTod 7 (2005) 275-276 (*Poonthuruthil, James*).

9871 *Müschenborn, Brian* Selbstbestimmt sterben—auch die Bestattung gehört dazu. LS 56 (2005) 296-299.

9872 *Nadeau, Jean-Guy; Golding, Carole; Rochon, Claude* Les victimes d'abus sexuels confrontées à la souffrance et à la violence de la Passion. Théologiques 13 (2005) 83-107.

9873 **Nardoni, Enrique** Rise up, O Judge: a study of justice in the biblical world. [T]*Martin, Sean C.* 2004 ⇒20,9063. [R]ScrB 35 (2005) 99-101 (*Corley, Jeremy*).

9874 *O'Donovan, Oliver* Scripture and christian ethics. ThRef 48 (2005) 121-129.

9875 *Petersen, David L.* Shaking the world of family values. [F]BRUEGGEMANN, W.—COUSAR, C. 2005 ⇒16. 23-32.

9876 **Piana, Giannino** Vangelo e società: i fondamenti dell'etica sociale cristiana. Assisi 2005, Cittadella 205 pp.

9877 *Raiser, Elisabeth* Die Hütte Gottes bei den Menschen: Visionen einer gerechten Welt und der Ort der Kirche: Vortrag in der Feministischen Basisfakultät beim Kirchentag in Hannover. JK 66/3 (2005) 53-57 [Rev 21].

9878 **Riccioni, Graziano** Il dibattito sull'eutanasia: prospettive bibliche. 2004 ⇒20,9076. [R]SdT 17, Suppl 3 (2005) 76-77 (*Finch, Paul*).

9879 *Schmid, Konrad* Jenseits von Verfügungswissen und Orientierungswissen: evangelische Ethik und das Evangelium. ZEE 49 (2005) 190-197.

9880 *Schmitt, Hanspeter* Schrift und Leben: zur moralpraktischen Bedeutung der Bibel. Orien. 69/9 (2005) 99-104.

9881 *Schneider-Flume, Gunda* Der Realismus der Barmherzigkeit in der Gesellschaft: Überlegungen zur theologischen Debatte um die Bioethik. ThLZ 130 (2005) 727-740.

9882 *Schreijäck, Thomas* "Wen Gott bestrafen will, den macht er zum Erzieher": Janusz Korczacks Option für den Menschen. [F]STENDEBACH, F. 2005 ⇒141. 297-316.

9883 *Schweiker, William* The end of time and the moral texture of reality in early christian ethics. Beginnings of christianity. 2005⇒786. 101-124.

9884 *Schweitzer, Friedrich* Practical theology, ethics, and the challenge of plurality: changing boundaries between practical theology and ethics. Reconsidering the boundaries. 2005 ⇒598. 151-159.

9885 *Söding, Thomas* Umkehr und Versöhnung: Jesu Botschaft und Praxis im Kontext der Heiligen Schrift. HlD 59 (2005) 8-22.

9886 *Spiegel, Egon* Gewaltverzicht Jesu: friedensethische Begründungszusammenhänge als Basis einer christlichen Friedenserziehung. Das Buch. Vechtaer Beiträge zur Theologie 11: 2005 ⇒487. 193-201.

9887 *Stanton, Graham N.* Terrorism and reconciliation. Theol. 108/845 (2005) 331-337 [2 Cor 5,18].

9888 **Stassen, Glen Harold; Gushee, David P.** Kingdom ethics: following Jesus in contemporary context. 2003 ⇒19,9263; 20,9091. [R]CTJ 40 (2005) 378-380 (*Van Til, Kent*).

9889 *Steyn, G.J.* Reconciliation in the general epistles?. VeE 26 (2005) 205-221 [1 Pet 2,4-10].

9890 **Stiewe, Martin; Vouga, François** Das Evangelium im alltäglichen Leben: Beiträge zum ethischen Gespräch. NET 11: Tü 2005, Francke xvi; 413 pp. 3-7720-8134-7.

9891 *Student, Christoph* Was nützt eine Patientenverfügung?—fünf Thesen. LS 56 (2005) 264-267.

9892 *Theißen, Gerd* Urchristliches Ethos: eine Synthese aus biblischer und griechischer Tradition. [F]STEGEMANN, W. 2005 ⇒139. 209-222.

9893 *Thomasset, Alain* Personnages bibliques et "formation" éthique des lecteurs. Analyse narrative. BEThL 191: 2005 ⇒742. 73-94 [2 Kgs 5; Lk 4; 15,11-32].

9894 **Tremblay, Réal** 'Ma io vi dico...': l'agire eccelente, specifico della morale cristiana. ETO 40: Bo 2005, Dehoniane 214 pp.

9895 *Trigo, Jerónimo* Uso da bíblia em teologia moral: o exemplo do debate sobre a pena de morte. Did(L) 35 (2005) 507-537.

9896 *Verhey, A.* What makes christian bioethics christian?: bible, story, and communal discernment. Christian Bioethics [Ph] 11/3 (2005) 297-315 [NTAb 50,534].

9897 **Verhey, Allen** Remembering Jesus: christian community, scripture, and the moral life. 2002 ⇒18,8634... 20,9097. [R]CThMi 32 (2005) 385-386 (*Pilgrim, Walter E.*).

9898 **Via, Dan O.; Gagnon, Robert A.J.** Homosexuality and the bible: two views. 2003 ⇒19,9277; 20,9099. [R]RBLit 7 (2005) 44-47 (*Nissinen, Martti*).

9899 *Vidal, Marciano* El significado bíblico del 'amor al prójimo'. Moralia 28 (2005) 413-441.

9900 *Wetzstein, Verena* Leben in Beziehungen: Grenzen von Patientenverfügungen bei Demenz. LS 56 (2005) 284-288.

9901 **Wolbert, Werner** Was sollen wir tun?: biblische Weisung und ethische Reflexion. SThE 112: FrS 2005, Academic 214 pp. 3-7278-153-4-5.

9902 *Zehnder, Markus* Anstösse aus Dtn 23,2-9 zur Frage nach dem Umgang mit Fremden. FZPhTh 52 (2005) 300-314.

### H8.4 *NT de reformatione sociali*—**Political action in Scripture**

9903 **Bryan, Christopher** Render to Caesar: Jesus, the early church, and the Roman superpower. Oxf 2005, OUP xii; 185 pp. $25. 0-19-5183-34-7.

9904 *Feldmeier, Reinhard* Die zu herrschen scheinen: Gottes Diener und Hure Babylon: weltliche Macht im Neuen Testament. zeitzeichen 6/9 (2005) 26-30.

9905 **Horsley, Richard A.** Jesus and empire: the kingdom of God and the New World disorder. 2003 ⇒19,9287; 20,9103. [R]Interp. 59 (2005) 308-309 (*Nanos, Mark D.*);

9906 Jesus e o império: o reino de Deus e a nova desordem mundial. [T]*Calloni, Euclides Luiz* 2004 ⇒20,9104. [R]PerTeol 37 (2005) 284-286 (*Konings, Johan*).

9907 *Kroeker, P.* Travis Is a messianic political ethic possible?: recent work by and about John Howard Yoder. JRE 33 (2005) 141-174.

9908 **Malina, Bruce J.** O evangelho social de Jesus: o reino de Deus em perspectiva mediterrânea. [T]*Rossi, Luiz Alexandre Solano* 2004 ⇒20, 9105. [R]RRT 12 (2005) 286-288 (*Konings, Johan*).

9909 *Noffke, Eric* Cristo *o* Cesare, Cristo *e* Cesare: il problema del rapporto con la Roma imperiale nel Nuovo Testamento. Protest. 60 (2005) 223-237;

9910 Christ and Caesar, Christ or Caesar: the development of a tension about politics in early christianity—the role of the Roman community. [F]STEGEMANN, E. 2005 ⇒139. 362-372 [Mark 12,13-17; Rom 13; 1 Cor 2].

9911 **Pilgrim, Walter** Uneasy neighbors: church and state in the New Testament. 1999 ⇒15,8145... 18,8652. [R]RBLit (2005)* (*Modica, Joseph B.*).

9912 **Storkey, Alan** Jesus and politics: confronting the powers. GR 2005, Baker 336 pp. $25. 0-8010-2784-5. [R]CTJ 40 (2005) 339-341 (*Deppe, Dean*).
9913 *Ugalde, Luis* Seguimiento de Jesús y política. Iter 16/37-38 (2005) 123-133.
9914 *Vouga, François* La politica e la grazia nel Nuovo Testamento. Protest. 60 (2005) 299-308;
9915 Die politische Relevanz des Evangeliums: Rezeption des Paulus in der philosophischen Diskussion. [F]STEGEMANN, W. 2005 ⇒139. 192-208.
9916 *Wannenwetsch, Bernd* Representing the absent in the city: prolegomena to a negative political theology according to Revelation 21. God, truth, and witness. 2005 ⇒532. 167-192.
9917 *Zangenberg, Jürgen* Beobachtungen zur "politischen Theologie" des Markus anhand von Mk 12,35-37. [F]STEGEMANN, W. 2005 ⇒139. 171-191.

## H8.5 Theologia liberationis latino-americana...

9918 *Costadoat, Jorge* La hermenéutica en las teologías contextuales de la liberación. TyV 46 (2005) 56-74.
9919 **Gonzalez, Antonio** The gospel of faith and justice. [T]*Owens, Joseph*: Mkn 2005, Orbis xii; 179 pp. $24. 1570-756112.
9920 **Huning, Ralf** Bibelwissenschaft im Dienste popularer Bibellektüre: Bausteine einer Theorie der Bibellektüre aus dem Werk von Carlos Mesters. SBB 54: Stu 2005, Kath. Bibelwerk xii; 437 pp. €52. 3-460-00541-6. Diss. Paderborn.
9921 *Martín Salvago, Blanca* Lettura popolare della bibbia. I vangeli. 2005 ⇒432. 71-79.
9922 *Mesters, Carlos* La lecture du livre des Actes des Apôtres dans les communautés ecclésiales de base du Brésil. Les Actes des Apôtres. LeDiv 199: 2005 ⇒715. 231-242.
9923 *Miguez Bonino, José* The economic dimension of biblical hermeneutics. God's economy. 2005 <1998> ⇒415. 34-42.
9924 *Navia Velasco, Carmiña* Women and neoliberalism: contributions for a biblical reading. God's economy. 2005 <2000> ⇒415. 112-123.
9925 *Pimentel Torres, Franklyn* The practice of christian communities at the beginning of a new millennium: a current community reading of Acts 2. God's economy. 2005 <1999> ⇒415. 202-219.
9926 *Pixley, Jorge* The political dimension of biblical hermeneutics. God's economy. 2005 <1999> ⇒415. 18-33.
9927 *Richard, Pablo* Interpretazione latinoamericana della bibbia: realtà, metodo, prospettiva. I vangeli. 2005 ⇒432. 44-53.
9928 **Schüepp, Susann** Bibellektüre und Befreiungsprozesse: eine empirisch-theologische Untersuchung mit Frauen in Brasilien. [D]*Kirchschläger, Walter* 2005, Diss. Luzern [ThRv 102,viii].
9929 **Sobrino, Jon** Jesucristo liberador: lectura histórico-teológica de Jesús de Nazaret. [4]2001 ⇒17,8099; 18,8658. [R]EstTrin 39 (2005) 572-574 (*Gómez, Enrique*).
9930 *Tamez, Elsa* The bible and the five hundred years of conquest. God's economy. 2005 <1993> ⇒415. 3-17;

9931 Leggere la bibbia sotto un cielo senza stelle. I vangeli. 2005 ⇒432. 37-43.
9932 *Vaage, Leif E.* The Sermon on the Mount: an economic proposal. God's economy. 2005 <1998> ⇒415. 127-151.

### H8.6 *Theologiae emergentes*—**Theologies of emergent groups**

9933 *Arulrajah, K.J.* Re-reading the bible in Sri Lanka. SLJTR 1/1 (2005) 36-39 [NTAb 50,229].
9934 *Asaju, Dapo F.* Africentric biblical hermeneutics enroute: a contextual study of chieftaincy institution in post-colonial Nigeria. AJTh 19/1 (2005) 143-165.
9935 **Brown, Michael Joseph** Blackening of the bible: the aims of African American biblical scholarship. 2004 ⇒20,9113. [R]JBL 124 (2005) 575-578 & RBLit (2005)* (*Sigler, Danielle Brune*).
9936 **Ekem, John D.K.** New Testament concepts of atonement in an African pluralistic setting. Accra 2005, SonLife xi; 148 pp. 99886-40331.
9937 *Enis, Larry L.* Biblical interpretation among African-American New Testament scholars. CuBR 4.1 (2005) 57-82.
9938 **Katho, Bungishabaku** The new covenant and the challenge of building a new and transformed community in DR Congo: a contextual reading of Jeremiah 31:31-34. OTEs 18 (2005) 109-123.
9939 **Loba-Mkole, Jean-Claude** Triple heritage: gospels in intercultural mediations. Limete-Kinshasa 2005, Centre de Recherches x; 193 pp. 99951-60900. Bibl. [NTAb 50,167].
9940 *López Hernández, Eleazar* Insorgenza teologica dei popoli indi;
9941 Teologie indie;
9942 La teologia india nell'attuale globalizzazione. I vangeli. 2005 ⇒432. 121-129/130-137/138-140.
9943 *Masenya, Madipoane* HIV/AIDS and African biblical hermeneutics: focus on southern African women. Chakana 3/5 (2005) 21-35;
9944 The optimism of the wise in Israel and in Africa: helpful in the time of HIV/AIDS?. OTEs 18 (2005) 296-308;
9945 An African methodology for South African biblical sciences: revisiting the Bosadi (womanhood) approach. OTEs 18 (2005) 741-751.
9946 *Mbiti, John* Do you understand what you are reading?: the bible in African homes, schools and churches. Missionalia 33/2 (2005) 234-248 [NTAb 50,237].
9947 **Osei-Bonsu, Joseph** The inculturation of christianity in Africa: antecedents and guidelines from the New Testament and the early church. New Testament studies in contextual exegesis 1: Fra 2005, Lang xii; 130 pp. £66. 3-631-53790-5. Bibl. 123-127.
9948 [E]**Sugirtharajah, Rasiah S.** The postcolonial bible. 1998 ⇒15,8166. [R]VJTR 69 (2005) 629 (*Meagher, P.M.*).
9949 **Sugirtharajah, Rasiah S.** The bible and the third world: precolonial, colonial and postcolonial encounters. 2001 ⇒17,8111... 19,9322. [R]RBLit (2005)* (*Roos, Bonnie*);
9950 The bible and empire: postcolonial explorations. C 2005, CUP vi; 247 pp. $75/28. 0-521-82493-1/53191-8. Bibl. 232-241.
9951 *Zerbe, Gordon M.* Constructions of Paul in Filipino theology of struggle. AJTh 19/1 (2005) 188-220.

## H8.7 *Mariologia*—The mother of Jesus in the NT

9952 *Alson, Javier* María signo de contradicción junto con Jesús?: un acercamiento a la mariología neotestamentaria. EphMar 55/1 (2005) 9-18.

9953 **Alvarez, Carlos** Maria discipula de Jesus e mensageira do evangelho. Col. Quinta Conferência: São Paulo 2005, Paulus 101 pp. 85-34-9-2526-7.

9954 **Borgeaud, Philippe** Mother of the gods: from Cybele to the Virgin Mary. [T]*Hochroth, Lysa* 2004 ⇒20,9126. [R]AThR 87 (2005) 676-677 (*Molleur, Joseph*); RBLit (2005)* (*Cueva, Edmund; Schroer, Silvia*).

9955 *Böhler, Dieter* Maria-Tochter Zion: die Bedeutung der Mutter Jesu nach der Heiligen Schrift. GuL 78 (2005) 401-412.

9956 *Budillon, Jean* Signification de quelques expressions bibliques intervenant dans des textes concernant la Vierge Marie. Ist. 50/1 (2005) 78-94.

9957 **Danieli, Silvano M.**, *al.*, Bibliografia mariana, 10, 1994-1998. Scripta Facultatis Marianum 59: R 2005, Marianum xxxvii; 584 pp.

9958 *Díez Marino, L.* Los textos bíblicos y el dogma de la Inmaculada Concepción. EstMar 71 (2005) 17-58.

9959 **Duquesne, Jacques** Maria: die Mutter Jesu. Mü 2005, Dt. Verl.-Anst. 268 pp. €19.90. 3-421-05889-X.

9960 *Ferreira-Martins, J.M.* O segredo de Maria: um estudo sobre os contributos do São Josemaría para a exegese bíblica. HumTeo 26 (2005) 189-211.

9961 **Flusser, D.; Lang, J.; Pelikan, J.** Mary: images of the mother of Jesus in Jewish and christian perspective. Mp 2005 <1986>, Fortress vi; 106 pp. $17. 08006-37062. 48 pl. [NTAb 49,602].

9962 **Foskett, Mary F.** A virgin conceived: Mary and classical representations of virginity. 2002 ⇒18,8698... 20,9134. [R]ThTo 62 (2005) 104, 106, 108 (*Boss, Sarah Jane*).

9963 *Gaventa, Beverly R.* 'All generations will call me blessed': Mary in biblical and ecumenical perspective. A feminist companion to mariology. 2005 <1997> ⇒431. 121-129.

9964 [E]**Gaventa, Beverly R.; Rigby, Cynthia L.** Blessed one: Protestant perspectives on Mary. 2002 ⇒18,311; 20,9135. [R]ThTo 62 (2005) 108, 110 (*Boss, Sarah Jane*).

9965 **Haffner, Paul** The mystery of Mary. 2004 ⇒20,9137. [R]RRT 12 (2005) 533-535 (*Atkins, Peter*).

9966 **Herranz Marco, Mariano** La virginidad perpetua de María. Studia Semitica NT 9: 2002 ⇒18,8703; 20,9138. [R]CDios 218 (2005) 243-244 (*Gutiérrez, J.*).

9967 **Johnson, Elizabeth A.** Truly our sister: a theology of Mary in the communion of saints. 2003 ⇒19,9350. [R]MoTh 21 (2005) 511-513 (*Loades, Ann*).

[E]**Levine, A.** A feminist companion to mariology 2005 ⇒431.

9968 [E]**Longère, Jean** Marie dans les récits apocryphes chrétiens. 2004 ⇒ 20,696. [R]EphMar 55 (2005)158-159 (*Largo Domínguez, Pablo*).

9969 *Magennis, Feidhlimidh* The use of scripture in the ARCIC statement, *Mary: grace and hope in Christ*. MillSt 56 (2005) 114-124.

9970 *Maloney, R.P.* The historical Mary. America 193/20 (2005) 12-15 [NTAb 50,253].

9971 **Manelli, Settimio** Maria corredentrice VI–teologia biblica: 'una spada trapasserà anche la tua stessa anima', Lc 2,35. 2003 ⇒19,9353. [R]Immaculata Mediatrix 5 (2005) 129-142 (*Tábet, Michelangelo*).

9972 **Manelli, Stefano Maria** Mariologia biblica. Frigento [2]2005, Mariana 487 pp. [R]EstJos 59 (2005) 320-321 (*Llamas, Enrique*).

9973 **Manns, F.** 'Heureuse es-tu, toi qui as cru': Marie, une femme juive. Biblik 3: P 2005, Renaissance 222 pp.

9974 [E]**Mantovani, Piera Arata** Maria e la famiglia di Gesù. Mondo della Bibbia 76 (2005) 1-49.

9975 **Manzi, Franco** La bellezza di Maria: riflessioni bibliche. Mi 2005, Ancora 132 pp. €11.

9976 Mary, grace and hope in Christ: fifth agreed statement of the Anglican-Roman Catholic international commission. L 2005, Continuum 86 pp. 0-8192-8132-8. [R]IJSCC 5 (2005) 265-271 (*Warner, Martin*).

9977 **Masini, Mario** Maria di Nazaret nel conflitto delle interpretazioni. Padova 2005, Messagero 297 pp. €18. 88-25016-360;

9978 I silenzi di Maria di Nazaret. Padova 2005, Messagero 313 pp;

9979 Maria di Nazaret: storia, mito, simbolo, interpretazioni. I volti di Maria di Nazaret 2; Bibliotheca Berica 5: Padova 2005, EMP 308 pp. 88-250-1739-1.

9980 *Miguel González, José María de* La relación filial-esponsal de María con Dios Padre: perspectiva bíblica, teológica y litúrgica. Salm. 52 (2005) 529-557.

9981 *Mußner, Franz* Das Jude-Sein der Jüdin Maria. FrRu 12 (2005) 182-188 [Rev 7].

9982 [E]**Naluparayil, Jacob** Mathruteerthangalil. Kalady 2003, Emmas 327 pp. Rs120. [R]JJSS 4 (2004) 217-220 (*Vedikunnel, Joseph*). **Malayalam**.

9983 *Økland, Jorunn* 'The historical Mary' and Dea creatrix: a historical-critical contribution to feminist theological reflection. A feminist companion to mariology. 2005 <1997> ⇒431. 147-163.

9984 *Panimolle, Salvatore A.* Gioisci, piena di grazia!;

9985 Maria vergine nel Nuovo Testamento. Maria di Nazaret. DSBP 40: 2005 ⇒579. 7-14/143-210.

9986 *Puig i Tàrrech, Armand* El entorno de María;

9987 *Rodríguez Carmona, A.* La mujer en tiempos de Maria de Nazaret. EphMar 55/2-3 (2005) 209-221/247-268.

9988 *Salazar, Merle* Miriam of Nazareth: a Jewish Galilean. EAPR 42 (2005) 353-368.

9989 *Serra, Aristide* La presenza e la funzione della madre del Messia nell'Antico Testamento: princìpi per la ricerca e applicazioni. Maria di Nazaret. DSBP 40: 2005 ⇒579. 15-142.

9990 *Shoemaker, Stephen J.* The virgin Mary in the ministry of Jesus and the early church according to the earliest Life of the virgin. HThR 98 (2005) 441-467.

9991 *Sivertsen, Barbara* New Testament genealogies and the families of Mary and Joseph. BTB 35 (2005) 43-50.

9992 **Sri, Edward** Queen Mother: a biblical theology of Mary's queenship. Letter and Spirit: Steubenville, OH 2005, Emmaus R. xvi; 216 pp. $15. 1931018-243. [R]HPR 106/1 (2005) 75-6 (*Grace, Madeleine*).

9993 *Stock, Klemens* María, llamada a ser la madre del Señor: María, la sierva del Señor. Fonte. Revista carmelita de la región ibérica 2 (2005) 11-32 [AcBib 11,149].

9994 *Tavard, George H.* The genesis of mariology. A feminist companion to mariology. 2005 ⇒431. 107-120.

9995 *Tábet, Michelangelo* 'Mariologia biblica': nota sull'opera di padre Stefano M. Manelli. Immaculata Mediatrix 5 (2005) 273-277.

9996 *Van Biema, D.* Hail Mary. Time [NY] (March 21 2005) 60-64, 67-69 [NTAb 49,547].

9997 *Van den Hengel, John* Miriam of Nazareth: between symbol and history. A feminist companion to mariology. 2005 <1985> ⇒431. 130-146.

### H8.8 *Feminae NT*—Women in the NT and church history

9998 *Abrahamsen, Valerie* Human and divine: the Marys in early christian tradition. A feminist companion to mariology. 2005 ⇒431. 164-181.

9999 **Biernath, Andrea** Missverstandene Gleichheit: die Frau in der frühen Kirche zwischen Charisma und Amt. Stu 2005, Steiner 179 pp. 3-515-07754-5.

10000 **Blohm, Uta** Religious traditions and personal stories: women working as priests, ministers and rabbis. Studies in the Intercultural History of Christianity 137: Fra 2005, Lang 469 pp. 3631-53740-9.

10001 **Boer, Esther de** Maria Madalena—a discípula amada. Apelação 2005, Paulus 207 pp [Brot. 163,197—F. Pires Lopes].

10002 **Brock, Ann Graham** Mary Magdalene, the first apostle: the struggle for authority. HThS 51: 2003 ⇒19,9368; 20,9157. [R]SR 34 (2005) 273-274 (*Smith, Daniel*).

10003 **Carbone, Giorgio M.** Maria Maddalena. Bo 2005, Studio Domenicano 175 pp. €10.

10004 *Clark, Elizabeth A.* Thinking with women: the uses of the appeal to 'woman' in pre-Nicene christian propaganda literature. Spread of christianity. 2005 ⇒545. 43-51.

10005 **Corley, Kathleen E.** Women and the historical Jesus: feminist myths of christian origins. 2002 ⇒18,8730; 19,9369. [R]AThR 87 (2005) 334-6 (*Dolan-Henderson, Susan*); CBQ 67 (2005) 334-335 (*Sterling, Gregory E.*); HeyJ 46 (2005) 224-226 (*Corley, Jeremy*).

10006 *Dobrovolny, Mary Kay* Icon of faith in the midst of darkness [Mary Magdalene]. BiTod 43 (2005) 283-287.

10007 **Epp, Eldon Jay** Junia: the first woman apostle. Mp 2005, Fortress xvii; (2), 138 pp. $16. 0-8006-3771-2. Bibl. 110-121; Foreword by *Beverly R. Gaventa* [Rom 16,7].

10008 **Gench, Frances Taylor** Back to the well: women's encounters with Jesus in the gospels. 2004 ⇒20,9162. [R]RBLit (2005)* (*Bauman-Martin, Betsy J.; Hachko, Orysya; Iverson, Kelly;*).

[E]**Good, D.** Mariam, the Magdalen...2005 ⇒397.

10009 **Hureaux, Roland** Jésus et Marie-Madeleine. P 2005, Perrin 170 pp. €16 [MoBi 170,44—Sophie Laurant].

10010 *Ilan, Tal* It's magic: Jewish women in the Jesus movement. Beginnings of christianity. 2005 ⇒786. 161-172.

10011 **Jensen, Anne** Femmes des premiers siècles chrétiens. [T]*Poupon, Gérard*: TC 11: 2002 ⇒18,8737... 20,9170. [R]RSR 93 (2005) 157-8 (*Sesboüé, Bernard*); RevSR 79 (2005) 549-50 (*Faivre, Alexandre*).

10012 **Jensen, Anne** Frauen im frühen Christentum. TC 11: 2002 ⇒18, 8738; 19,9376. [R]ThLZ 130 (2005) 1332-1333 (*Petersen, Silke*).

10013 [E]**Jones, Stanley F.** Which Mary?: the Marys of early christian tradition. Symposium series 19: 2002 ⇒18,8719...20,9171. [R]BiblInterp 13 (2005) 317-319 (*Setzer, Claudia*).

10014 **Lacordaire, Henri-Dominique** Marie-Madeleine. Sagesses chrétiennes: P 2005 <1860>, Cerf 144 pp. €15.

10015 *Lanci, John R.* The post-biblical career of the woman of Magdala. BiTod 43 (2005) 293-299.

10016 *León Martín, Trinidad* El primado evangélico: una reflexión acerca de la memoria olvidada. Proyección 52 (2005) 371-387 [Women in early christianity].

10017 *Livio, Jean-Bernard* De Marie de Magdala à Marie-Madeleine: le 'Da Vinci Code'. Choisir 552 (2005) 21-25.

10018 *Loraschi, Celso* Carta de Aquila. Estudos bíblicos 86 (2005) 26-36.

10019 **López Villanueva, Mariola** Un amor al fondo: mujeres que arriesgan y bendicen. M 2005, San Pablo 124 pp.

10020 *MacDaniel, Karl J.* Transgression, tradition, and transformation: six women of the Matthean genealogy. Arc 33 (2005) 248-256 [Mt 1,1-17].

10021 **MacDonald, Margaret Y.** Las mujeres en el cristianismo primitivo y la opinión pagana. 2004 ⇒20,9173. [R]CTom 133 (2005) 403-404 (*Menéndez, Luis*).

10022 [ET]**Madigan, Kevin; Osiek, Carolyn A.** Ordained women in the early church: a documentary history. Baltimore 2005, Johns Hopkins University xv; 220 pp. $48. 0-8018-7932-9.

10023 **Maggi, Alberto** Le cipolle di Marta. Profili evangelici: Assisi [3]2002, Cittadella 168 pp. 978-88308-06931. Pres. *Adiana Zarri*; Bibl. 154-156.

10024 **Maisch, Ingrid** Between contempt and veneration... Mary Magdalene: the image of a woman through the centuries. [T]*Maloney, Linda M.* 1998 ⇒14,7433. [R]VJTR 69 (2005) 872-873 (*Meagher, P.M.*).

10025 [E]**Miller, Patricia C.** Women in early christianity: translations from Greek texts. Wsh 2005, Catholic Univ. of America Pr. xviii; 340 pp. $30. 0-8132-14173 [ThD 52,394—W. Charles Heiser].

10026 **Mohri, Erika** Maria Magdalena: Frauenbilder in Evangelientexten des 1. bis 3. Jahrhunderts. MThSt 63: 2000 ⇒16,8229. [R]NT 47 (2005) 82-83 (*Brock, Ann G.*).

10027 *Osiek, C. Diakonos* and *prostatis*: women's patronage in early christianity. HTSTS 61/1-2 (2005) 347-370 [NTAb 50,304].

10028 *Osiek, Caroline* The study of women in the early church. BiTod 43 (2005) 277-282.

10029 *Rondou, Katherine* Echos de la Madeleine, figure évangélique, dans la littérature contemporaine. RSLR 41 (2005) 413-432.

10030 **Schaberg, Jane** The resurrection of Mary Magdalene: legends, apocrypha, and the christian Testament. 2002 ⇒18,8750... 20, 9181. [R]NewTR 18/2 (2005) 91-93 (*Reid, Barbara E.*); JR 85 (2005) 478-480 (*Dempsey, Carol J.*); JAAR 73 (2005) 946-948 (*Brock, Ann Graham*).

10031 *Spencer, Aída S.* Jesus' treatment of women in the gospels. Discovering biblical equality. 2005 ⇒387. 126-141.

10032 **Starbird, M.** Mary Magdalene: bride in exile. Rochester, VT 2005, Bear x; 182 pp. $20. 15914-30542. CD; Bibl. [NTAb 50,407].

10033 *Thurston, Bonnie* Women in the New Testament: the example of Romans 16. Scripture as the soul of theology. 2005 ⇒776. 40-59.

10034 *Witherington, Ben* Joanna: apostle of the Lord—or jailbait?. BiRe 21/2 (2005) 12, 14, 46-47.

### H8.9 *Theologia feminae*—**Feminist theology**

10035 *Balseiro, Isabel* Response: a perilous passage from scarlet cord to red ribbon. Feminist NT studies. 2005 ⇒447. 203-208. Resp. to M. Dube.

10036 *Bertrand, Marie-Andrée* Féminisme, perspective épistémologique. [F]GENEST, O. 2005 ⇒46. 215-233.

10037 *Bird, Phyllis A.* Old Testament theology and the God of the fathers: reflections on biblical theology from a North American feminist perspective. Biblische Theologie. ATM 14: 2005 ⇒756. 69-107.

10038 *Brenner, Athalya* Epilogue: babies and bathwater on the road. Her master's tools?. 2005 ⇒493. 333-338.

10039 **Brenner, Athalya** I am... biblical women tell their own stories. 2004 ⇒20,9194. [R]RBLit (2005)* (*Landy, Francis*).

10040 *Byron, Gay L.* The challenge of 'blackness' for rearticulating the meaning of gobal feminist New Testament interpretation;

10041 *Castelli, Elizabeth A.* Globalization, transnational feminisms, and the future of biblical critique;

10042 *Champagne, Noelle; Gomez, Filiberto N.; Van Heest, Katrina* Reflections on conversation three [Africa and the diaspora]. Feminist NT studies. 2005 ⇒447. 85-101/63-84/259-263.

**Chapman, C.** The gendered language of warfare 2005 ⇒4518.

10043 *Conde-Frazier, Elizabeth* Response: a framework toward solidarity and justice. Feminist NT studies. 2005 ⇒447. 131-135 Resp. to *Spencer, Aida S.*

10044 *Couture, Denise* À propos du corpus féministe d'Olivette Genest. [F]GENEST, O. 2005 ⇒46. 235-242.

10045 *Di Matteo, Sabrina* Voix controversées?: perspectives féministes en christologie. Scriptura(M) 7/1 (2005) 63-80.

10046 *Dibo, Graciela* La sapienza di una donna straniera. I vangeli. 2005 ⇒432. 100-110 [Mk 7,24-30].

10047 *Dube, Musa W.* Circle readings of the bible/scriptoratures. [F]OOSTHUIZEN, G.C. 2005 ⇒117. 77-96;

10048 Rahab is hanging out a red ribbon: one African woman's perspective on the future of feminist New Testament scholarship. Feminist NT studies. 2005 ⇒447. 177-202.

10049 *Enzner-Probst, Brigitte* Kreative Erlösung: eine Perspektive auf Schöpfungstheologie und Christologie aus der liturgischen Praxis von Frauen. Christologie im Lebensbezug. 2005 ⇒577. 88-115.

10050 *Erbele-Küster, Dorothea* Der Gott der Väter und Mütter: eine Reaktion aus der Perspektive einer deutschsprachigen Theologin: Response auf Phyllis A. Bird. Biblische Theologie. ATM 14: 2005 ⇒ 756. 109-121.

10051 *Ferrari Schiefer, Valeria* Beheimatet sein—am Baum des Lebens die eigenen Wurzeln finden: der Schwarze Christus und die Symbolik des Baumes in der theologischen Reflexion der Béatrice Kim-pa Vita (1684-1706) (Kongo). Christologie im Lebensbezug. 2005 ⇒577. 157-182.

10052 *Ferretti, Cloe T.* Il molteplice rapporto delle donne con la bibbia. RdT 46 (2005) 917-925.

10053 *Fiorenza, Elisabeth S.* The power of the word: charting critical global feminist biblical studies. Feminist NT studies. 2005 ⇒447. 43-62.

10054 **Fiorenza, Elisabeth Schüssler** Los caminos de la sabiduría: una introducción a la interpretación feminista de la biblia. [T]*Lozano Gotor, José Manuel*: 2004 ⇒20,9205. [R]CTom 133 (2005) 401-403 (*Menéndez, Luis*); EE 80 (2005) 184-186 (*Yebra, Carme*);

10055 Weisheits Wege: eine Einführung in feministische Bibelinterpretation. Stu 2005, Kath. Bibelwerk 323 pp. €24.90. 3-460-25275-8.

10056 *Fischer, Irmtraud* Zwischen Kahlschlag, Durchforstung und neuer Pflanzung: zu einigen Aspekten feministischer Exegese und ihrer Relevanz für eine Theologie des Alten Testaments. Theologie und Exegese. SBS 200: 2005 ⇒410. 41-72.

10057 *Galloway, Lincoln E.* Response: Lucy Bailey, 'Likkle but tallawah'. Feminist NT studies. 2005 ⇒447. 239-244 Resp. to *Miller, Althea S.*

10058 *Geisterfer, Priscilla* Full turns and half turns: engaging the dialogue/dance between Elisabeth Schüssler Fiorenza and Vernon Robbins. Her master's tools?. 2005 ⇒493. 129-144.

10059 *Genest, Olivette* Exégèse d'un itinéraire en herméneutique biblique. [F]GENEST, O. 2005 ⇒46. 41-59.

10060 *Globig, Christine* Von Jüdinnen lernen: feministischer Antijudaismus und die neuere Entwicklung der Christologie. KuI 20 (2005) 43-59.

10061 *Good, Deirdre* Jewish feminist scholars: vibrant voices in New Testament study. Seeing Judaism anew. 2005 ⇒618. 80-92.

10062 *Gössmann, Elisabeth* Malwida von Meysenburg (1816-1903) und Friedrich NIETZSCHE (1844-1900) in ihrer Diskussion um Frauenbild und Christusbild. Christologie im Lebensbezug. 2005 ⇒577. 212-239.

10063 [E]**Gößmann , Elisabeth** Wörterbuch der feministischen Theologie. [2]2002 ⇒18,8773; 20,9206. [R]ThRv 101 (2005) 371-73 (*Koll, Julia*).

10064 *Gravlee, Sonya; Jacklin, Erin; Stephens, Prinny* Reflections on conversation one. Feminist NT studies. 2005 ⇒447. 109-112. Global future of feminist NT studies.

10065 *Grohmann, Marianne* Feministische/Gender-faire Exegese: Geschichte—Hermeneutik—Themen. PzB 14 (2005) 81-92.

10066 **Grudem, Wayne** Evangelical feminism and biblical truth: an analysis of more than one hundred disputed questions. 2004 ⇒20,9210. [R]BS 162 (2005) 491-492 (*Waters, Larry J.*).

10067 **Guest, Deryn** When Deborah met Jael: lesbian biblical hermeneutics. L 2005, SCM viii; 306 pp. £20. 0-334-02958-9. Bibl. 271-295.

10068 *Halter, Marek* Et la femme créa Dieu. Les femmes dans l'histoire: les rendez-vous de l'histoire, Blois 2004. [E]**Halter, Marek**, *al.*, Nantes 2005, Pleins Feux. 57-73. 2-84729-033-8.

10069 *Hight, Holly; Sohn, Lydia* Reflections on conversation two. Feminist NT studies. 2005 ⇒447. 171-173. Asia and Latin America.

10070 **Jobling, J'annine** Feminist biblical interpretation in theological context: restless readings. 2002 ⇒18,8780... 20,9213. [R]BiblInterp 13 (2005) 58-61 (*Parris, David P*).

10071 *Jost, Renate* Ist eine feministische Sozialgeschichte des Ersten Testaments möglich?. [F]STEGEMANN, W. 2005 ⇒139. 132-149.

10072 *Kinukawa, Hisako* Biblical studies in the twenty-first century: a Japanese/Asian feminist glimpse. Feminist NT studies. 2005 ⇒447. 137-150.

10073 *Kirchhoff, Renate* "So soll es bei euch nicht sein!" (Mk 10,43a): vom Konflikt als einem Strukturprinzip christlichen Miteinanders. Christologie im Lebensbezug. 2005 ⇒577. 58-87.

10074 Körperkonzepte im Ersten Testament: Aspekte einer feministischen Anthropologie. 2003 ⇒19,362. Hedwig-Jahnow-Forschungsprojekt. [R]BZ 49 (2005) 123-126 (*Häusl, Maria*).

10075 [E]**Kraemer, Ross Shepard** Women's religions in the Greco-Roman world: a sourcebook. 2004 ⇒20,9215. [R]JJS 56 (2005) 151-153 (*Williams, Margaret H.*).

10076 *Krohn-Hansen, Julianne* Frigjørende fortolkning: en lesning av Elisabeth Schüssler Fiorenzas syn på tekst og fortolkning. NTT 106/2 (2005) 90-110.

10077 *Ladislao, María G.* Una parola propria. I vangeli. 2005 ⇒432. 80-90.

10078 *Lancaster, Sarah H.* Scriptural criticism and religious perception. Gender, tradition and Romans. 2005 ⇒461. 271-283.

10079 **Loewenthal, Elena** Eva e le altre: letture bibliche al femminile. Mi 2005, Bompiani 336 pp. [R]Hum(B) 60 (2005) 1356-1357 (*Ronchi, Anna Teresa*).

10080 *Løland, Hanne* Kvinne og kjønnsforskning i studiefaget det Gamle Testamente med et sideblikk til det Nye Testamente. TTK 76 (2005) 262-283.

10081 *Makuruetsa, Masego M.* "En zij hield hem in haar schoot": een Afrikaans feministische lezing van 1 Koningen 17 tegen de achtergrond van de hiv/aids problematiek. Theologisch debat 2/4 (2005) 49-54.

10082 *McDonnell, Kilian* Feminist mariologies: heteronomy/ subordination and the scandal of christology. TS 66 (2005) 527-567.

10083 *Miller, Althea S.* Feminist pedagogies: implications of a liberative praxis. Feminist NT studies. 2005 ⇒447. 17-40;

10084 Lucy Bailey meets the feminists. Feminist NT studies. 2005 ⇒447. 209-238.

10085 *Moltmann-Wendel, Elisabeth* Antijudaismus in der Feministischen Theologie?. EvTh 65 (2005) 313-316;

10086 Ein anderer Jesus: Befreier-Ganzmacher-Geborener. Christologie im Lebensbezug. 2005 ⇒577. 12-33.

10087 *Müllner, Ilse* Dialogische Autorität: feministisch-theologische Überlegungen zur kanonischen Schriftauslegung. LecDif 2 (2005)*.

10088 *Naurath, Elisabeth* Gott kommt als Kind zu uns: Christologie und Kindertheologie. Christologie im Lebensbezug. 2005 ⇒577. 34-57.

10089 *Navarro Puerto, Mercedes* Amor de sí, amor de Dios, amor del prójimo: una relectura feminista a partir de Mc 12,28-34. AnStR 6 (2005) 385-406.

10090 *Navia Velasco, Carmiña* Ermeneutica biblica femminile, riflessioni e proposte. I vangeli. 2005 ⇒432. 91-99.

10091 *Økland, Jorunn* Why can't the heavenly Miss Jerusalem just shut up?. Her master's tools?. 2005 ⇒493. 311-332 [Rev 7; 14,1-5; 21, 1-22,5].

10092 *Paganini, Simone* Feministische Exegese in der Außenperspektive: Anmerkungen zum Dokument der Päpstlichen Bibelkommission und zum "Tübinger Gutachten". PzB 14 (2005) 93-101.

10093 *Penner, Todd; Vander Stichele, Caroline* Paul and the rhetoric of gender. Her master's tools?. 2005 ⇒493. 287-310 [1 Cor 11].

10094 **Praetorius, Ina** Handeln aus der Fülle: postpatriarchale Ethik in biblischer Tradition. Gü 2005, Gü 224 pp. 3-579-05216-8.

10095 **Reimer, Ivoni Richter** Grava-me somo selo sobre teu coração. Teologia biblica feminista: São Paulo 2005, Paulinas 135 pp.

10096 *Robbins, Vernon K.* The rhetorical full-turn in biblical interpretation and its relevance for feminist hermeneutics. Her master's tools?. 2005 ⇒493. 109-127.

10097 *Ruether, Rosemary R.* Feminist theologies in Latin America. Feminist NT studies. 2005 ⇒447. 159-170.

10098 **Ruether, Rosemary R.** Goddesses and the divine feminine: a western religious history. Univ. of California Pr. 2005, ix; 381 pp. £27. 50. 0-520-23146-5.

10099 **Runions, Erin** How hysterical: identification and resistance in the bible and film. Religion/culture/critique: 2003 ⇒19,9460; 20,9225. RTJT 21 (2005) 269-270 (*Jobling, David*); BiCT 1/1 (2004)* (*Walsh, Richard*).

10100 *Sauvé, Madeleine* Féminisme anonyme ou occulté?: en marge de l'Institut supérieur de sciences religieuses. FGENEST, O. 2005 ⇒46. 243-265.

10101 *Scholz, Susanne* The Christian Right's discourse on gender and the bible. JFSR 21/1 (2005) 81-100.

10102 *Spencer, Aída S.* My journey as a Latin American feminist New Testament scholar. Feminist NT studies. 2005 ⇒447. 115-129.

10103 *Stenström, Hanna* Historical-critical approaches and the emancipation of women: unfulfilled promises and remaining possibilities. Her master's tools?. 2005 ⇒493. 31-45.

10104 *Taschl-Erber, Andrea* "Ich habe den Herrn gesehen" (Joh 20,18): ein geschlechtsspezifisches Apostolatskriterium?. PzB 14 (2005) 103-131 [Mt 28,9-10; Mk 16,9-11; {Lk 24,34; 1 Cor 9,1; 15].

10105 *Toensing, Holly* Women of Sodom and Gomorrah: collateral damage in the war against homosexuality?. JFSR 21/2 (2005) 61-74 [Gen 19,1-29].

10106 *Torjesen, Karen J.* Responses: paradoxes of positionality as the key to feminist New Testament studies;

10107 *Wimbush, Vincent L.* Signifying on scriptures: an African diaspora proposal for radical readings;

10108 *Zhiru* Response: an Asian Buddhist response to a Japanese feminist glimpse of biblical studies in the twenty-first century. Feminist NT studies. 2005 ⇒447. 103-107/245-258/151-158. Resp. to *Kinukawa, Hisako*.

## H9.0 Eschatologia NT, *spes*, hope

10109 **Ancona, Giovanni** Escatologia cristiana. Nuovo corso di teologia sistematica 13: 2003 ⇒20,9243. RAnnTh 19 (2005) 301-304 (*O'Callaghan, P.*).

10110 *Ancona, Giovanni* La parusia come compimento dell'evento Gesù Cristo. RTLu 10 (2005) 41-54.

10111 *Beckwith, Roger T.* The fullness of time in New Testament and Jewish thinking. Calendar, chronology. AGJU 61: 2005 ⇒184. 134-143.

10112 *Bergant, Dianne* To judge the living and the dead. BiTod 43 (2005) 382-386.

10113 **Bloesch, Donald G.** The last things: resurrection, judgment, glory. Christian foundations: 2004 ⇒20,9244. [R]ProEc 14 (2005) 372-373 (*Colyer, Elmer M.*).

10114 [E]**Braaten, Carl E.; Jenson, Robert W.** The last things: biblical and theological perspectives on eschatology. 2002 ⇒18,279; 19, 9484. [R]HeyJ 46 (2005) 541-542 (*Hall, Lindsey E.*).

10115 *Cardona Ramírez, Hernán* Degustar la esperanza—unos rasgos bíblicos. El grano. 2005 ⇒197. 133-144.

10116 *Evans, Craig A.* Inaugurating the kingdom of God and defeating the kingdom of Satan. BBR 15 (2005) 49-75.

10117 *Figl, Johann; Heller, Birgit; Hutter, Manfred* Dimensionen weiterer zentraler religiöser Vorstellungen: Jenseitsvorstellungen. Handbuch Religionswissenschaft. 2005 ⇒1016. 628-650.

10118 *Fuchs, Ottmar* Aspekte einer praktischen Theologie des Himmels. JBTh 20 (2005) 433-457.

10119 *Grünschloss, Andreas* Diskurse um "Wiedergeburt" zwischen Reinkarnation, Transmigration und Transformation der Person: Versuch einer systematisch-religionswissenschaftlichen Orientierung. Wiedergeburt. BTSP 25: 2005 ⇒533. 11-44.

10120 *Hartwig, Paul Bruce* The obedience of the church as a prelude to the Parousia: ecclesial and temporal factors in New Testament eschatology. VeE 26 (2005) 382-397.

10121 *Hauke, Manfred* La riscoperta degli angeli: note sul ricupero di un tratto dimenticato. RTLu 10 (2005) 55-71.

10122 **Hill, Craig C.** In God's time: the bible and the future. 2002 ⇒18, 8824... 20,9251. [R]ThTo 62 (2005) 114, 116 (*Sauter, Gerhard*); Interp. 59 (2005) 310-312 (*Royalty, Robert M.*); VJTR 69 (2005) 870-871 (*Meagher, P.M.*).

10123 *Humphrey, Edith M.* Which way is up?: revival, resurrection, assumption, and ascension in the rhetoric of Paul and John the Seer. Arc 33 (2005) 328-339.

10124 **Keller, Catherine** God and power: counter-apocalyptic journeys. Mp 2005, Fortress 184 pp. $22. 0-8006-3727-5.

10125 **Kim, Kyoung-Shik** God will judge each one according to his works. [D]*Gathercole, S.* 2005, Diss. Aberdeen [RTL 37,615].

10126 **Klaine, Roger** La fin du monde selon les écrits bibliques de notre ère. Le devenir du monde et la bible 3: P 2005, Cerf 320 pp. €35. 2-204-07897-2.

10127 *Klinger, Susanne* Die biblische Hoffnung in der postsäkularen Gesellschaft: die kulturprägende Kraft der Bibel. Das Buch. Vechtaer Beiträge zur Theologie 11: 2005 ⇒487. 237-245.

10128 *Kundert, Lukas* Die Apokalypse ist bereits geschehen: neutestamentliche Eschatologie am Beispiel der Evangelienschlüsse. [F]STEGEMANN, E. 2005 ⇒139. 100-115 [Mk 16].

10129 **Kurz, William** What does the bible say about the end times?: a catholic view. Cincinnati 2005, Servant 199 pp. $12.

10130 **Łanoszka, Miroslaw** L'idée du rétablissement du cosmos dans la doctrine eschtologique de la tradition synoptique et johannique. DPaciorek, A. 2005, 234 pp. Diss. Lublin [RTL 37,616]. **P.**

10131 *Léon-Dufour, Xavier* Oltre la morte. Un biblista cerca Dio. Collana biblica: 2005 <1972> ⇒245. 307-322.

10132 *Manicardi, Ermenegildo* 'Alla risurrezione si è come angeli del cielo' (Mt 22,30): l'aldilà nel Nuovo Testamento. L'aldilà. 2005 ⇒ 507. 49-87.

10133 **Martin de Viviés, Pierre de** Apocalypses et cosmologie du salut. LeDiv 191: 2002 ⇒18,9670... 20,9258. RRSR 93 (2005) 323-324 (*Morgen, Michèle*); RB 112 (2005) 108-113 (*Grelot, Pierre*).

10134 *Merkle, Benjamin L.* Could Jesus return at any moment?: rethinking the imminence of the second coming. TrinJ 26 (2005) 279-292.

10135 *Miggelbrink, Ralf* Die Lebensfülle Gottes: ein systematisch-theologischer Versuch über die biblische Rede vom Himmel. JBTh 20 (2005) 325-356.

10136 *Míguez, Nestor O.* Economics and abundant life in New Testament apocalypticism. God's economy. 2005 <1998> ⇒415. 220-240.

10137 **Nocke, Franz-Josef** Eschatologie. Leitfaden Theologie 6: Dü 2005, Patmos 160 pp. 3-491-69422-1.

10138 **Peres, Imre** Griechische Grabinschriften und neutestamentliche Eschatologie. WUNT 157: 2003 ⇒19,9504; 20,9262. RSNTU 30 (2005) 277-279 (*Zugmann, Michael*); ThLZ 130 (2005) 1063-1065 (*Schnelle, Udo*).

10139 **Perriman, Andrew** The coming of the Son of Man: New Testament eschatology for an emerging church. Milton Keynes 2005, Paternoster vi; 272 pp. $25. 1-84227-299-3. Bibl. 246-252.

10140 **Pitre, Brant** Jesus, the tribulation, and the end of the exile: restoration eschatology and the origin of the atonement. D*Aune, David*: WUNT 2/204: Tü 2005, Mohr S. xiii; 586 pp. €79. 3-16-148751-6. Diss. Notre Dame; Bibl. 519-542; also GR: Baker, $50.

10141 *Räisänen, Heikki* Last things first: 'eschatology' as the first chapter in an overall acount of early christian ideas. Moving beyond NT theology?. SESJ 88: 2005 ⇒463. 444-487.

10142 **Roose, Hanna** Eschatologische Mitherrschaft: Entwicklungslinien einer urchristlichen Erwartung. NTOA 54: 2004 ⇒20,9266. RSNTU 30 (2005) 247-249 (*Giesen, Heinz*) [Mt 19,28].

10143 *Rossi de Gasperis, Francesco* Le nom qui veille sur l'espérance de Jérusalem. Christus 52/1 (2005) 209-216.

10144 **Saward, John** Sweet and blessed country: the christian hope for heaven. Oxf 2005, OUP 195 pp.

10145 **Segal, Alan F.** Life after death: a history of the afterlife in the religions of the West. 2004 ⇒20,9272. RJR 85 (2005) 532-533 (*Sorensen, J. Podemann*); RBLit (2005)* (*Lemche, Niels P.; Levenson, Jon D.; Martone, Corrado*); Materia giudaica 10/1 (2005) 180-183 (*Arcari, Luca*); JThS 56 (2005) 650-652 (*Court, J.M.*); Commonweal 132/6 (2005) 26-27 (*Seltser, B.J.*).

10146 **Smalley, Stephen S.** Hope for ever: the christian view of life and eath. Milton Keynes 2005, Paternoster xii; 94 pp. £8.

10147 *Thiel, John E.* For what may we hope?: thoughts on the eschatological imagination. TS 67 (2005) 517-541.

10148 *Torres Q., Andrés* La estructura de la esperanza bíblica. ThX 55 (2005) 227-252.

10149 **Vaz, Eurides Divino** Uma reflexao sobre céu, inferno e purgatorio. Petrópolis, RJ 2004, Vozes 95 pp. 85-326-3067-7. Bibl. 91-95.

10150 **Vymetalová Hrabáková, Eva** Futuristische und präsente Konzeptionen in der Eschatologie der kanonischen Evangelien. [D]*Sázava, Z.* 2005, 171 pp. Diss. Prague [RTL 37,619]. **Czech.**

10151 *Witulski, Thomas* Gegenwart und Zukunft in den eschatologischen Konzeptionen des Kolosser- und des Epheserbriefes. ZNW 96 (2005) 211-242.

10152 *Woodcock, E.* Images of hell in the tours of hell: are they true?. Criswell Theological Review [Dallas] 3/1 (2005) 11-42 [NTAb 50, 332].

## H9.5 *Theologia totius [VT-]NT*—General [OT-]NT theology

10153 *Balla, Peter* Are we beyond New Testament theology?. Moving beyond NT theology?. Ment. *Räisänen, H.*: SESJ 88: 2005 ⇒463. 32-44.

10154 *Barr, James* Some problems in the search for a pan-biblical theology. Biblische Theologie. Ment. *Rad, G. von*: ATM 14: 2005 ⇒ 756. 31-42.

10155 *Borgonovo, Gianantonio* La "Memoria fondatrice": una funzione che valorizza la proposta di Th. Söding. Teol(Br) 30 (2005) 305-315.

10156 *Brambilla, Franco G.* Teologia biblica e teologia sistematica: per continuare il dialogo. Teol(Br) 30 (2005) 283-296.

10157 *Byrskog, Samuel* Räisänen through Theissen: a program and a theory. Moving beyond NT theology?. SESJ 88: 2005 ⇒463. 197-220.

10158 *Collins, John J.* Is a critical biblical theology possible? <1990>;

10159 Biblical theology and the history of Israelite religion <1989>. Encounters. 2005 ⇒200. 11-23/24-33.

10160 *Crüsemann, Frank* Über die Schrift hinaus?: Response auf James Barr. Biblische Theologie. ATM 14: 2005 ⇒756. 43-51.

10161 *Cummings Neville, Robert* Carrying scripture across imagination. Reconsidering the boundaries. 2005 ⇒598. 65-69.

10162 **Esler, Philip E.** New Testament theology: communion and community. Mp 2005, Fortress xii; 353 pp. $25. 0-281-05758-3. Bibl. 313-334.

10163 *Gundry, Robert H.* The symbiosis of theology and genre criticism of the canonical gospels. The old is better. WUNT 178: 2005 ⇒ 220. 18-48.

10164 **Hahn, Ferdinand** Theologie des Neuen Testaments, 1: Die Vielfalt des NT; 2: Die Einheit des Neuen Testaments. 2002 ⇒18,8875 ... 20,9290. [R]ThLZ 130 (2005) 40-44 (*Lohse, Eduard*); Neotest. 39 (2005) 443-450 (*Stenschke, Christoph*); JThS 56 (2005) 174-179 (*Morgan, Robert*);

10165 Tü [2]2005 <2002>, Mohr S 2 vols; lii; 862 + xlii; 874 pp. €49+49. 9783-1614-87361/7-0.

10166 *Hardmeier, Christof* Unterwegs zu einer performativen Theologie der Bibel. Erzähldiskurs. FAT 46: 2005 ⇒222. 3-31.

10167 *Helmer, Christine* Biblical theology: bridge over many waters. CuBR 3 (2005) 169-196;

10168 Introduction: biblical theology: reality and interpretation across disciplines. Biblical interpretation. SBL.Symp. 26: 2005 ⇒758. 1-13.

10169 [E]**Hossfeld, Frank** Wieviel Systematik erlaubt die Schrift?: auf der Suche nach einer gesamtbiblischen Theologie. QD 185: 2001 ⇒17, 283; 18,331. [R]ThR 70 (2005) 157-160 (*Reventlow, Henning Graf*).

10170 **Hörster, Gerhard** Theologie des Neuen Testaments. 2004 ⇒20, 9292. [R]JETh 19 (2005) 295-296 (*Baumert, Manfred*).

10171 *Hübner, Hans* Neutestamentliche Theologie und Fundamentaltheologie. Wahrheit und Wirklichkeit. 2005 <2004> ⇒229. 162-183.

10172 [E]**Hübner, Hans; Jaspert, Bernd** Biblische Theologie: Entwürfe der Gegenwart. Biblisch-theologische Studien 38: 1999 ⇒15,243; 17,8260. [R]ThR 70 (2005) 154-157 (*Reventlow, Henning Graf*).

10173 *Janowski, Bernd* Biblische Theologie heute: formale und materiale Aspekte. Biblical interpretation. SBL.Sym. 26: 2005 ⇒758. 17-32.

10174 *Juel, Don* The project of a 'Biblical Theology' as a reshaping of the boundaries between systematic and exegetical theology: response to Michael Welker. Reconsidering the boundaries. 2005 ⇒598. 31-4.

10175 *Laffey, Alice L.* Reflections down the road. Moving beyond NT theology?. Ment. *Räisänen, H.*: SESJ 88: 2005 ⇒463. 45-60.

10176 *Lalleman-de Winkel, Hetty* The Old Testament contribution to evangelical models for public theology. EurJT 14/2 (2005) 87-97.

10177 *Legrand, Lucien* Universel biblique et Jésus-Christ: un point de vue biblique indien. Théophilyon 10 (2005) 325-335.

10178 **Marshall, I. Howard** New Testament theology: many witnesses, one gospel. 2004 ⇒20,9298. [R]CBQ 67 (2005) 530-532 (*Witherup, Ronald D.*); JETh 19 (2005) 290-295 (*White, Joel R.*); RBLit (2005)* (*Klink, Edward*).

10179 *Marshall, Ian H.* Biblical patterns for public theology. EurJT 14/2 (2005) 73-86.

10180 *Martens, Elmer A.* Moving from scripture to doctrine. BBR 15 (2005) 77-103.

10181 *Matera, Frank J.* New Testament theology: history, method, and identity. CBQ 67 (2005) 1-21;

10182 Christ in the theologies of Paul and John: a study in the diverse unity of New Testament theology. TS 67 (2005) 237-256.

10183 *Miller, Patrick* Theology from below: the theological interpretation of scripture. Reconsidering the boundaries. 2005 ⇒598. 3-13.

10184 **Niederwimmer, Kurt** Theologie des Neuen Testaments: ein Grundriss. 2004 ⇒20,9303. [R]ThLZ 130 (2005) 276-280 (*Alkier, Stefan*); JThS 56 (2005) 172-174 (*Morgan, Robert*).

10185 **Powell, Mark Allan** Loving Jesus. Mp 2004, Fortress viii; 200 pp. $16. [R]RBLit (2005)* (*McFarlane, Doreen; Williams, Joel*).

10186 *Punt, Jeremy* Decolonising and recolonising New Testament theology: a postcolonial perspective from Africa. Moving beyond NT theology?. Ment. *Räisänen, H.*: SESJ 88: 2005 ⇒463. 133-160.

10187 *Räisänen, Heikki* What's happening in New Testament theology?. [F]AEJMELAEUS, L.: SESJ 89: 2005 ⇒1. 439-457.

10188 *Reeling Brouwer, Rinse* "... maar wij kunnen het niet meer zo zeggen zoals zij het zeiden": weerwoord aan Van der Kooi. Ment. *Breukelman, Frans; Calvin, J.*: KeTh 56/1 (2005) 50-55.

10189 *Romanello, Stefano; Vignolo, Roberto* Sulla teologia della bibbia. Teol(Br) 30 (2005) 92-100 [NTAb 49,546].

10190 *Saebø, Magne* Der Weg der Biblischen Theologie von Gabler zu VON RAD. Biblische Theologie. ATM 14: 2005 ⇒758. 1-25.

10191 *Schweiker, William* Intellectual fences and cultural values: the shifting boundaries between ethics, practical theology, and biblical studies. Reconsidering the boundaries. 2005 ⇒598. 137-150.

10192 **Scobie, Charles H.H.** The ways of our God: an approach to biblical theology. 2003 ⇒19,9559; 20,9309. [R]CThMi 32 (2005) 382-83 (*Giere, Samuel D.*); ThR 70 (2005) 137-140 (*Reventlow, Henning Graf*); BTB 35 (2005) 154-5 (*Dunn, Matthew W.I.*); TJT 21 (2005) 271-273 (*Yeo, John J.*); Bib. 86 (2005) 133-137 (*Conroy, Charles*).

10193 *Sekine, Seizo* Biblische Theologie vs. Dogmatische Theologie?: Response auf den Vortrag von Magne Saebo. Biblische Theologie. Ment. *Gabler, J.; Rad, G. von*: ATM 14: 2005 ⇒758. 27-29.

10194 *Sommer, Benjamin D.* Ein neues Modell für Biblische Theologie. Theologie und Exegese. SBS 200: 2005 ⇒410. 187-211.

10195 *Söding, Thomas* Teologia biblica e teologia sistematica: presupposti e prospettive di un dialogo. Teol(Br) 30 (2005) 257-282.

10196 *Stegemann, Wolfgang* Much ado about nothing?: sceptical inquiries into the alternatives 'theology' or 'religious studies'. Ment. *Räisänen, H.; Theissen, G.*;

10197 *Stenström, Hanna* Fair play?: some questions evoked by Heikki Räisänen's *Beyond New Testament theology*. Moving beyond NT theology?. SESJ 88: 2005 ⇒463. 221-242/105-132.

10198 **Stuhlmacher, Peter** Biblische Theologie des Neuen Testaments, 1: Grundlegung: von Jesus zu Paulus. Gö ³2005 <1992>, Vandenhoeck & R. xi; 418 pp. €46.90. 3-525-53596-1.

10199 *Tarocchi, Stefano* Sapienza e Nuovo Testamento. Vivens Homo 16 (2005) 287-301.

10200 **Thielman, F.** Theology of the New Testament: a canonical and synthetic approach. GR 2005, Zondervan 798 pp. $35. 03102-113-28. Bibl. [NTAb 50,194].

10201 *Van der Kooi, Cornelis* Het goed recht van een voorheretische afwijking: opmerkingen bij Breukelmans beeld van CALVIJN. KeTh 56/1 (2005) 44-49.

10202 **Via, Dan Otto** What is New Testament theology?. Guides to Biblical Scholarship, NT: 2002 ⇒18,8899... 20,9314. [R]BiblInterp 13 (2005) 319-321 (*Morgan, Robert*); RBLit 7 (2005) 450-453 (*Van der Watt, Jan*).

10203 *Vignolo, Roberto* La teologia biblica, al centro di un chiasma. Teol(Br) 30 (2005) 297-304.

10204 **Vos, Gerhardus** †1949 Teologia biblica: Antico e Nuovo Testamento. Caltanissetta 2005, Alfa & Omega 605 pp. Introd. *Richard B. Gaffin, Jr.*

10205 **Watson, Francis** Text and truth: redefining biblical theology. 1997 ⇒13,7993...15,8377. [R]ThR 70 (2005) 140-2 (*Reventlow, Henning*).

10206 **Wilckens, Ulrich** Theologie des Neuen Testaments, Band 1: Geschichte der urchristlichen Theologie: Teilbd. 1-2. 2003 ⇒19,9566; 20,9317. [R]SNTU 30 (2005) 255-256 (*Fuchs, Albert*);

10207 Teilbd. 3: die Briefe des Urchristentums: Paulus und seine Schüler, Theologen aus dem Bereich judenchristlicher Heidenmission. Neuk ²2005, Neuk xviii; 389 pp. €30. 3-7887-1907-9;

10208 Teilbd. 4: die Evangelien, die Apostelgeschichte, die Johannesbriefe, die Offenbarung und die Entstehung des Kanons. Neuk 2005, Neuk xiv; 377 pp. €29.90. 3-7887-2092-1.

10209 *Zimmermann, Markus* Eine katholische Biblische Theologie aus dem geistigen Aufbruch der 20er Jahre: zur Kontextualität, Methodik, Grundstruktur und "Gotteswirklichkeit" der unveröffentlichten Typoskripte von Romano GUARDINIs "Frohe Botschaft". MThZ 56 (2005) 225-237.

# XIV. Philologia biblica

## J1.1 Hebraica *grammatica*

10210 **Arad, Maya** Roots and patterns: Hebrew morpho-syntax. Studies in natural languages and linguistic theory 63: Dordrecht 2005, Springer viii; 286 pp. 1-402-03243-9. Bibl. 275-281.

10211 **Arnold, Bill T.; Choi, John H.** A guide to Biblical Hebrew syntax. 2003 ⇒19,9570; 20,9320. [R]HebStud 46 (2005) 385-387 (*Van der Merwe, Christo H.J.*); RBLit 7 (2005) 96-99 (*Barco del Barco, Francisco del*).

10212 C 2005 <2003>, CUP xii; 228 pp. 0-521-53348-1/82609-8.

10213 *Aspesi, Francesco* Some comparative remarks about the Hebrew stative. 10[th] meeting of Hamito-Semitic linguistics. QuSem 25: 2005, 105-116.

10214 **Bergman, Nava** The Cambridge Biblical Hebrew workbook: introductory level. C 2005, CUP xvi; 375 pp. €18/$32. 0-521-53369-4.

10215 **Brettler, Marc Zvi** Biblical Hebrew for students of modern Israeli Hebrew. 2001 ⇒17,8288...19,9577. [R]RBLit (2005)* (*Clem, H. Eldon*).

10216 *Di Giulio, Marco* I segnali discorsivi: esempi dal *corpus* biblico. Studi afroasiatici. 2005 ⇒885. 253-258.

10217 **Dobson, John H.** Learn Biblical Hebrew. Carlisle [2]2005, Piquant xiv; 392 pp. $30. 0-8010-3102-8. With Audio CD-ROM; Bibl. xiii.

10218 **Doron, Edit** VSO and left-conjunct agreement: Biblical Hebrew vs. Modern Hebrew. Universal grammar. 2005 ⇒664. 239-264.

10219 *Dubovský, Peter; Sova, Milan* Návrh transliterácie a prepisu hebrejských spoluhlások a samohlások do slovenčiny [Proposal for the transcription and transliteration of the Hebrew consonants and vowels into Slovak]. SBSl (2005) 73-76. **Slovak.**

10220 *Eskhult, Mats* Traces of linguistic development in Biblical Hebrew. HebStud 46 (2005) 353-370.

10221 **Ewald, Georg H.** Syntax of the Hebrew language of the Old Testament. [T]*Kennedy, James*: Piscataway (N.J.) 2005 <1881>, Gorgias viii; 323 pp. 1-593-33137-1.

10222 **Furuli, Rolf J.** A new understanding of the verbal system of Classical Hebrew. Oslo 2005, Univ. of Oslo. Diss. [StTh 60,114].

10223 **Garrett, Duane** A modern grammar for Classical Hebrew. 2002 ⇒ 18,8918; 19,9592. [R]BS 162 (2005) 120-121 (*Webster, Brian*).

10224 *Gianto, Agustinus* Some notes on evidentiality in Biblical Hebrew. [M]MORAN, W.: BibOr 48: 2005 ⇒107. 133-153.

10225 **Green, Jennifer S.; Scrivner, Joseph F.; Lester, G. Brooke** Handbook to a grammar for Biblical Hebrew. Nv 2005, Abingdon x; 134 pp. $14/£10. 0-687-00834-4. [R]RBLit (2005)* (*Bonilla-Rios, Daniel; Engle, John*).

10226 *Huehnergard, John* Hebrew verbs I-*w/y* and a proto-Semitic sound rule. [M]DIAKONOFF, M. 2005 ⇒36. 457-474.

10227 *Jenni, Ernst* Vollverb und Hilfsverb mit Infinitiv-Ergänzung im Hebräischen. Studien II. 2005 <1998> ⇒232. 11-35;

10228 Subjektive und objektive Klassifikation im althebräischen Nominalsatz. Studien II. 2005 <1999> ⇒232. 65-76;

10229 Aktionsarten und Stammformen im Althebräischen: das Pi‘el in verbesserter Sicht. Studien II. 2005 <2000> ⇒232. 77-106;

10230 Textinterne Epexegese im Alten Testament <2000> ⇒232. 107-17;

10231 Eine hebräische Abtönungspartikel: *‘l-ken*. <2001> ⇒232. 118-33;

10232 Semantische Gesichtspunkte des Hebräischen und deutscher Übersetzungen am Beispiel von Num 10,29-31. <2001> ⇒232. 134-50;

10233 Presidential address: höfliche Bitte im Alten Testament <2002>;

10234 Untersuchungen zum hebräischen Kohortativ <2003>;

10235 Verwendungen des Imperatifs im Biblisch-Hebräischen. Studien II. 2005 ⇒232. 151-165/166-226/227-315.

10236 *Johnson, Bo* Något om de konsekutiva verbformerna i gammaltestamentlig hebreiska. SEÅ 70 (2005) 119-131.

10237 *Jongeling, Karel* 'And it came to pass' again. [M]DIAKONOFF, M. 2005 ⇒36. 291-329.

10238 *Joosten, Jan* The distinction between Classical and Late Hebrew as reflected in syntax. HebStud 46 (2005) 327-339.

10239 [E]**Kaltner, John; McKenzie, Steven L.** Beyond Babel: a handbook for Biblical Hebrew and related languages. SBL.Resources for Biblical Study 42: 2002 ⇒18,8903... 20,594. [R]JSSt 50 (2005) 366-368 (*Watson, Wilfred G.E.*).

10240 **Khan, Geoffrey** The early Karaite tradition of Hebrew grammatical thought: including a critical edition, translation and analysis of the Diqduq of 'Abu Ya'qub Yusuf ibn Nuh on the Hagiographa. StSLL 32: 2000 ⇒16,8389; 20,9348. [R]OLZ 100 (2005) 191-194 (*Schorch, Stefan*).

10241 *Lambert, Mayer* Mots concrets dont le genre n'est pas constaté dans la bible (Appendice VII). 39-41;

10242 Substantifs à forme masculine et féminine (Appendice VIII). 43;

10243 Substantifs singulier et pluriel dans la bible (Appendice IX). 45-47;

10244 Liste des noms par classes (Appendice X). 49-74;

10245 Liste des verbes unités aux diverses conjugaisons (Appendice XII). 77-88;

10246 Liste des verbes réguliers et irréguliers (Appendice XIII). 89-91;

10247 De la formation des noms propres (Appendice XIV). 93-101;

10248 Particularités de la vocalisation babylonienne (Appendice XV). 103-104. D'après *P. Kahle, Die Masoreten des Ostens*;

10249 Notice sommaire sur l'histoire de la grammaire biblique (Appendice XVII). Termes massorétiques. 2005 ⇒241. 123-130.

10250 **Llamas Vela, Antonio** Instituciones hebraicas. S 2005, n.p. 86 pp. Bibl. 81-84.

10251 **Long, Gary Aland** Grammatical concepts 101 for Biblical Hebrew: learning Biblical Hebrew grammatical concepts through English grammar. 2002 ⇒18,8938; 19,9604. [R]TJT 21 (2005) 252-253 (*Williams, Tyler F.*).

10252 **Luzzatto, Samuele Davide** Prolegomena to a grammar of the Hebrew language. [ET]*Rubin, Aaron D.*: Piscataway, NJ 2005, Gorgias xx; 232 pp. 1-593-33334-X. Bibl. xix-xx.

10253 [ET]*Martínez Delgado, José* El opúsculo sobre la normativa vocálica (Kitāb šurūṭ al-naqṭ) de Ḥayyūŷ (edición y traducción). MEAH 54 (2005) 185-230 [OTA 29,242].

10254 **Matheus, Frank** Einführung in das Biblische Hebräisch: Studienbuch für das Gruppen- und Selbststudium. Münsteraner Einführungen, Theologische Arbeitsbücher 2: Müns 2002, Lit 128 pp. 3-825-8-3172-8;

10255 Einführung in das Biblische Hebräisch: Studiengrammatik. Münsteraner Einführungen, Theologische Arbeitsbücher 1: Müns 2005, Lit 105 pp. 3-8258-3171-x.

10256 *Moomo, David O.* The imperfective meaning of weqatal in Biblical Hebrew. JNSL 31/1(2005) 89-106.

10257 **Moore, Cynthia L.** Grounded Hebrew semantics: a new approach to meaning with special focus on the Hebrew terms 'smeʿim, yarek, and beten'. [D]*Nelson, R.D.* 2005, 331 pp. Diss. Dallas, Southern Methodist [RTL 37,610].

10258 *Olszowy-Schlanger, Judith* A christian tradition of Hebrew vocalisation in medieval England. [F]ULLENDORFF, E.: SStLL 47: 2005 ⇒ 154. 126-146.

10259 *Pazzini, Massimo* Padre Maria da Calasico grammatico e lessicografo (Calasico 1550-Roma 1620). LASBF 55 (2005) 217-238.

10260 *Perry, T.A.* The coordination of *ky / ʿl kn* in Cant. i 1-3 and related texts. VT 55 (2005) 528-541.

10261 *Rechenmacher, Hans; Van der Merwe, Christo H.J.* The contribution of Wolfgang RICHTER to current developments in the study of Biblical Hebrew. JSSt 50 (2005) 59-82.

10262 **Rogland, Max** Alleged non-past uses of qatal in Classical Hebrew. SSN 44: 2003 ⇒19,9623; 20,9358. [R]BZ 49 (2005) 314-316 (*Michel, Andreas*); CBQ 67 (2005) 123-125 (*Miller, Cynthia L.*); JHScr 5 (2004-2005)* (*Gianto, Agustinus*).

10263 **Rubin, Aaron D.** Samuel David LUZZATTO: Prolegomena to a grammar of the Hebrew language. Piscataway, NJ 2005, Gorgias 232 pp. $59. 15933-3334X.

10264 *Schniedewind, William M.* Prolegomena for the sociolinguistics of classical Hebrew. JHScr 5/6 (2004)*.

10265 *Schwartz, Seth* Hebrew and imperialism in Jewish Palestine. Ancient Judaism. JSJ.S 95: 2005 ⇒626. 53-84.

10266 **Silzer, Peter J.; Finley, Thomas J.** How biblical languages work: a student's guide to learning Hebrew and Greek. 2004 ⇒20,9360. [R]CTJ 40 (2005) 122-123 (*Williams, Michael J.*); RBLit 7 (2005) 87-89 (*Rogland, Max*).

10267 *Steiner, Richard C.* *Påṯaḥ* and *Qåmeṣ*: on the etymology and evolution of the names of the Hebrew vowels. Or. 74 (2005) 372-381 Transl. of article in [F]Aaron DOTAN (in press);

On dating of Hebrew sound changes (°Ḫ > Ḥ and °Ġ > ʿ) and Greek translations (2 Esdras and Judith) 2005 ⇒3671.

10268 **Tichit, Agnès** Hébreu biblique: grammaire de base et introduction aux fêtes juives: textes expliqués. Langues et cultures anciennes 3: Bru 2005, Safran 96 pp. 2-87457-000-1.

10269 *Tropper, Josef* Die T-Verbalstämme des Biblisch-Hebräischen. [F]VOIGT, R.: AOAT 317: 2005 ⇒158. 417-424.

10270 **Valla, Danilo** Le basi per lo studio dell'ebraico della bibbia. Pineto (TE) 2002, College 'G.L. Pascale' 256 pp. €30.

10271 **Van der Merwe, Christo H.J.; Naudé, Jackie A.; Kroeze, Jan Hendrik** A Biblical Hebrew reference grammar. 1999 <2002> ⇒ 15,8448... 17,8334. [R]RBLit 7 (2005) 94-96 (*Rogland, Max*).

**Van Peursen, W.** The verbal system in the Hebrew text of Ben Sira 2004 ⇒4488.

10272 **Vance, Donald R.** An introduction to Classical Hebrew. 2004 ⇒ 20,9365. [R]RBLit 7 (2005) 84-87 (*Heider, George*).

10273 **Walker-Jones, Arthur** Hebrew for biblical interpretation. SBL. Resources for Biblical Study 48: 2003 ⇒19,9633; 20,9367. [R]RBLit 7 (2005) 99-103 (*Jefferies, Daryl*).

10274 *Young, Ian* Biblical texts cannot be dated linguistically. HebStud 46 (2005) 341-351.

10275 *Zevit, Ziony* Introductory remarks: historical linguistics and the dating of Hebrew texts ca. 1000-300 B.C.E.;

10276 Symposium discussion session: an edited transcription. HebStud 46 (2005) 321-326/371-376. See Zevit, Introductory remarks.

## J1.2 **Lexica et inscriptiones hebraicae**; *later Hebrew*

10277 *Abramson, Glenda* Modern Hebrew literature. The Oxford handbook of Jewish studies. 2005 ⇒1053. 515-540.

10278 **Aḥituv, Shmuel** HaKetav VeHamiktav: handbook of ancient inscriptions from the land of Israel and the kingdoms beyond the Jordan from the period of the First Commonwealth. Biblical encyclopaedia library 21: J [2]2005 <1992>, Bialik [14], 465 pp. 965-342-9-04-3. Bibl. [R]UF 37 (2005) 817-820 (*Heltzer, Michael*).

10279 *Anstey, Matthew P.* Towards a typological presentation of Tiberian Hebrew. HebStud 46 (2005) 71-128.

10280 *Bar-Aba, Esther Borochovsky* Towards a description of spoken Hebrew. HebStud 46 (2005) 145-167.

10281 *Bohas, Georges; Dat, Mihai* La matrice acoustique {[dorsal], [pharyngal]} en arabe classique et en hébreu biblique: première esquisse. MUSJ 58 (2005) 125-143.

10282 **Bolozky, Shmuel; Coffin, Edna A.** A reference grammar of Modern Hebrew. C 2005, CUP xiv; 447 pp. $90. 0521-527333.

10283 *Cathcart, Kevin J.* Loanwords in Biblical Hebrew and the dating of biblical texts. Studia semitica. JSSt.S 16: 2005 ⇒603. 45-57.

10284 *Chadwick, Jeffrey R.* Discovering Hebron: the city of the patriarchs slowly yields its secrets. BArR 31/5 (2005) 24-33, 70-71.

10285 *Davies, Graham I.* Some uses of writing in ancient Israel in the light of recently published inscriptions. [F]MILLARD, A.: LHBOTS 426: 2005 ⇒102. 155-174.

10286 *De Lumè, Paola* Frammenti del più antico testimone manoscritto (sec. XI) della *Maḥberet* di Menaḥem ben Saruq scoperti a Bologna. Materia giudaica 10/2 (2005) 283-303.

10287 **Dobbs-Allsopp, F.W.**, *al.*, Hebrew inscriptions: texts from the biblical period of the monarchy with concordance. NHv 2005, Yale University Press xxxv; 804 pp. 0-300-10397-2. Bibl. xxvii-xxxv.

10288 [E]**Donner, Herbert** Wilhelm GESENIUS: hebräisches und aramäisches Handwörterbuch über das Alte Testament, 3. Lieferung: מ-כ. [E]*Meyer, Rudolf; Rüterswörden, Udo*: B [18]2005, Springer xii; 519-766 pp. €189. 3-540-23542-6. Collab. *Johannes Renz*.

10289 **Florentin, Moshe** Late Samaritan Hebrew: a linguistic analysis of its different types. SStLL 43: Lei 2005, Brill xxix; 393 pp. 90-04-13841-2. Bibl. 375-378.

10290 **Glinert, Lewis** Modern Hebrew: an essential grammar. L [3]2005, Routledge xx; 300 pp. £17. 0415700825 [JJS 56,362–J. Campbell].

10291 *Goren, Yuval, al.*, A re-examination of the inscribed pomegranate from the Israel Museum. IEJ 55 (2005) 3-20;

10292 Authenticity examination of two Iron Age ostraca from the Moussaieff Collection. IEJ 55 (2005) 21-34.

10293 *Halevi, Pablo-Isaac* The Hebrew language. The Oxford handbook of Jewish studies. 2005 ⇒1053. 491-514.

10294 **Ilan, Tal** Lexicon of Jewish names in late antiquity, 1: Palestine 330 BCE - 200 CE. TSAJ 91: 2002 ⇒18,8977... 20,9384. [R]VDI (2005/1) 233-241 (*Tokhtasiev, S.R.*); RdQ 22 (2005) 285-287 (*Puech, Émile*); BAIAS 23 (2005) 187-188 (*Meyers, Eric M.*); RBLit (2005)* (*Kern-Ulmer, Rivka B.*).

10295 **Jaroš, Karl** Inschriften des Heiligen Landes aus vier Jahrtausenden. 2001 ⇒17,8363. [R]WO 35 (2005) 240-241 (*Röllig, Wolfgang*).

10296 *Kieffer, René* Frimodiga och uthålliga människor i bibeln. SEÅ 70 (2005) 133-144.

10297 **Magen, Yitzhak; Misgav, Haggai; Tsfania, Levana** Mount Gerizim excavations, vol. 1: The Aramaic, Hebrew and Samaritan inscriptions. J 2004, Israel Antiquities Authority xii; 272; 37 [Hebr.] pp. $50. Drawings, photos of 395 inscriptions.

10298 *Mastin, B.A.* A note on some inscriptions and drawings from Kuntillet ʿAjrud. PEQ 137/1 (2005) 31-32.

10299 *Milevski, Ianir* The Hebrew ostraca from site 94/21, Cave A-2, at Ramat Bet Shemesh. ʿAtiqot 50 (2005) 19-25.

10300 *Millard, Alan* Some foreign names in the Hebrew Bible. Studia semitica. JSSt.S 16: 2005 ⇒603. 39-44.

10301 *Modena, Maria L. Mayer* Ispirazione iconografica nella scelta dei nomi femminili in ebraico antico. Acme 58/2 (2005) 28-34.

10302 **Mykytiuk, Lawrence J.** Identifying biblical persons in Northwest Semitic inscriptions of 1200-539 B.C.E. SBL.Academia Biblica 12: 2004 ⇒20,9392. [R]CBQ 67 (2005) 501-503 (*Parker, Simon B.*); RBLit (2005)* (*Sanders, Paul; Cathey, Joseph*).

10303 *Noegel, Scott B.* The 'other' demonstrative pronouns: pejorative colloquialisms in Biblical Hebrew. JBQ 33 (2005) 23-30.

10304 *Norin, Stig* Die sogenannte Joaschinschrift—echt oder falsch?. VT 55 (2005) 61-74.

10305 [E]**Noy, David**, *al.*, Inscriptiones judaicae orientis, 1-3. TSAJ 99, 101, 102: 2004 ⇒20,9817, 9856-7. [R]ThLZ 130 (2005) 629-631 (*Dochhorn, Jan*); REJ 164 (2005) 347-349 (*Mimouni, Simon C.*); Sal. 67 (2005) 176-78 (*Vicent, Rafael*); RSR 93 (2005) 597-9 (*Berthelot, Katell*); JSJ 36 (2005) 65-83 (*Van der Horst, Pieter W.*).

10306 *Perani, Mauro; Stemberger, Günter* A new family tanḥuma manuscript from the Italian genizah: the fragments of Ravenna and their textual tradition. Materia giudaica 10/2 (2005) 241-266.

10307 *Pérez Fernández, Miguel* Sobre las funciones de la partícula še- en Hebreo Misnaico. [F]STEMBERGER, G.: SJ 32: 2005 ⇒140. 183-195.
10308 *Schniedewind, William M.* Problems in the paleographic dating of inscriptions. Bible and radiocarbon dating. 2005 ⇒952. 405-412.
10309 *Sciumbata, M. Patrizia* Diachronic change in Ancient Hebrew: a lexical test-case: *tebuna* and *bina*. Studi afroasiatici. 2005 ⇒885. 259-268.
10310 *Shveka, Avi* Arad ostracon no. 7: in search of the true solution to the riddle. HebStud 46 (2005) 49-70.
10311 **Sirat, Colette** Hebrew manuscripts of the Middle Ages. [ET]*De Lange, Nicholas R.M.* 2002 ⇒18,9005; 20,9399. [R]Medieval Encounters 11 (2005) 126-131 (*Sáenz-Badillos, Angel*).
10312 [E]**Yadin, Yigael; Greenfield, Jonas C.**, *al.*, The documents from the Bar Kokhba period in the Cave of Letters: Hebrew, Aramaic and Nabatean-Aramaic papyri. Judean Desert Studies: 2002 ⇒19, 9011; 20,9401. [R]IEJ 55 (2005) 247-51 (*Qimron, Elisha*).
10313 *Young, Ian* Israelite literacy and inscriptions: a response to Richard Hess. VT 55 (2005) 565-568.
10314 *Zuckermann, Ghil'ad* Dare forma all'identità attraverso la lingua: 'abbinamento fono-semantico' xenofobo in ebraico antico e moderno, yiddish e arabo. Studi afroasiatici. 2005 ⇒885. 269-284.

## J1.3 Voces *ordine alphabetico consonantium* hebraicarum

### *Akkadian*

10315 *ābi*: *Loretz, Oswald* Hurr./akk. *ābi*=ug./he. *ảp/ʾwb* 'Totengeist(er)-Grube' mit Hundeopfer: Archäozoologie und KTU 1.16 I 2-3a. UF 37 (2005) 441-443.
10316 *eṭutu; iṭṭu*: *Malul, Meir* Eṭutu 'darkness' and Iṭṭu 'clay': poetic license or corruption due to etymological similarity?: another interpretation. [F]KLEIN, J. 2005 ⇒79. 548-556.
10317 *ubāru*: *Na'aman, Nadav* Resident-alien or residing foreign delegate?: on the *ubāru* in some Late Bronze Age texts. UF 37 (2005) 475-478.

### *Aramaic*

10318 אנס: *Talshir, David* On the use of אנס in Aramaic and in Hebrew. Meghillot III. 2005 ⇒608. 205-229. **H.**

### *Hebrew*

10319 אבל: *Garr, W. Randall* אבל in Biblical Hebrew and beyond: part I. [M]DIAKONOFF, M. 2005 ⇒36. 265-290.
10320 אהב: *Bosman, Tiana* A critical review of the translation of the Hebrew lexeme ʾhb. OTEs 18 (2005) 22-34.
אוב: *Loretz, O.* Hurr./akk. *ābi*=ug./he. *ảp/ʾwb* 2005 ⇒10315.
10321 איש: *Burke, David* The translation of the Hebrew word *ʾish* in Genesis: a brief historical comparison. Translation and religion. Topics in Translation 28: 2005 ⇒563. 129-140.

10322 אכה: *Hendel, Russell Jay* The meanings of *akh*. JBQ 33 (2005) 100-107.

10323 אלהים: *Slivniak, Dmitri* Our God(s) is one: biblical אלהים and the indeterminacy of meaning. SJOT 19 (2005) 3-23.

10324 אמר: *Jenni, Ernst* Einleitung formeller und famliärer Rede im Alten Testament durch *'mar 'l* und *'mar l*. Studien II 2005 <1999> ⇒232. 48-64.

10325 אמר; דבר: *Ernst, Stephanie; Gathmann, Stephan* Das Unsagbare sagbar machen—das Ungesagte lesbar machen: אמר und דבר als Ausdrucksmöglichkeiten des "Zu-sich-selbst-Redens". [F]SEIDL, T.: ATSAT 75: 2005 ⇒137. 3-41.

10326 אמת: *Krochmalnik, Daniel* Das Siegel Gottes: der Wahrheitsbegriff in Bibel, Talmud, Kabbala, Chassidismus und jüdischer Religionsphilosophie. Jahrbuch für Religionsphilosophie 4 (2005) 71-82.

אנס: *Talshir, D.* On the use of אנס 2005 ⇒10318.

10327 אריוך: *Durant, Jean-Marie* De l'époque amorrite à la bible: le cas d'Arriyuk. [M]DIAKONOFF, M. 2005 ⇒36. 59-69.

10328 אַשְׁרֵי; הִנֵּה; ־י: *Schorch, Stefan* 'Siehe, wohl dem Mann....': die hebräischen Interjektionen אַשְׁרֵי und הִנֵּה und die Partikel *-y*. [F]VOIGT, R.: AOAT 317: 2005 ⇒158. 379-384.

10329 את: *Farina, Margherita* אֶת e אֵת in ebraico biblico: *nota accusativi* e preposizione. EVO 28 (2005) 245-253.

10330 בעל: *Müller, Hans-Peter* Der Gottesname B'l und seine Phraseologien im Hebräischen und im Phönizisch-Punischen. JSSt 50 (2005) 281-296.

10331 ברית: *Linington, Silvia* The term ברית in the Old Testament, part III: an enquiry into the meaning and use of the word in Joshua and Judges. OTEs 18 (2005) 664-680;

10332 **Otte, Marianne** Der Begriff *berit* in der jüngeren alttestamentlichen Forschung: Aspekte der Forschungsgeschichte unter besonderer Berücksichtigung der semantischen Fragestellung bei Ernst Kutsch. [D]*Heinen, Karl*: EHS.T 803: Fra 2005, Lang 290 pp. €51.50. 3-631-53923-1. Diss. Vallendar.

10333 גאל: *Winters, Alicia Goel* in ancient Israel: solidarity and redemption. God's economy. 2005 <1994> ⇒415. 61-70.

10334 גוי; לאום: *Anbar, Moshe* Deux termes amurrites et hébreux. UF 37 (2005) 1-3.

10335 גר; נכרי: *De Benedetti, Paolo* Chi è il mio prossimo?. Studi Fatti Ricerche 109 (2005) 3-5.

10336 גשם: **Dias da Silva, Cássio Murilo** Colui che manda la pioggia sulla faccia della terra. [D]*Simian-Yofre, Horacio*: R 2005, n.p. 128 pp. Extr. Diss. Pont. Ist. Biblico; Bibl. 77-121.

10337 דבר: *Ginsbury, Philip N.* 'Dovér' and 'm'daber'. JBQ 33 (2005) 40-46.

10338 דם: *Hartenstein, Friedhelm* Zur symbolischen Bedeutung des Blutes im Alten Testament. Deutungen. WUNT 181: 2005 ⇒392. 119-137.

10339 הכיר: *Zipor, Moshe A.* The verb הכיר as a literary device. BetM 182 (2005) 241-250. Sum 295. **H.**

10340 הלך: *Green, Dennis* 'Halakhah at Qumran'?: the use of √הלך in the Dead Sea scrolls. RdQ 22 (2005) 235-251.

10341 הלך; עלה: *Paul, Shalom M.* Two cognate Semitic terms for mating and copulation: Gen 31:10, 12 and Amos 2:7. Divrei Shalom. CHANE 23: 2005 <1982> ⇒273. 125-127.

10342 חלל: *Tawil, Hayim* The semantic range of the Biblical Hebrew ḫll; lexicographical note X. ZAW 117 (2005) 91-94.
10343 חרם: *Batsch, Christophe* Le *ḥerem* de guerre dans le Judaïsme du deuxième temple. La cuisine et l'autel. 2005 ⇒539. 101-111;
10344 *Bornapé, Allan* El problema del חֵרֶם en el Pentateuco y su dimensión ritual. DavarLogos 4/1 (2005) 1-16;
10345 *Wiley, Henrietta L.* The war *ḥerem* as martial ritual service and sacrifice. ProcGLM 25 (2005) 69-76.
10346 טף; ילד: *Brenner, Athalya* Regulating 'sons' and 'daughters' in the Torah and in Proverbs: some preliminary insights. JHScr 5/10 (2005)*.
10347 יהוה: *Daams, Nico* Translating YHWH. JOT 1/1 (2005) 47-55;
10348 *Moomo, David O.* Translating יהוה (YHWH) into African languages. Scriptura 88 (2005) 151-160 [OTA 29,21].
10349 יפה: *Piselli, Francesco* Nota sull'idea del bello nella S. Scrittura: yafeh. BeO 47 (2005) 17-22.
10350 ישׂראל: **Hayward, C.T.R.** Interpretations of the name Israel in ancient Judaism and some early christian writings: from victorious athlete to heavenly champion. Oxf 2005, OUP xiii; 397 pp 0-19-92-4237-2. Bibl. 359-369.
10351 לון; תלנה: *Gathmann, Stefan* "Murrende Gemeinde—um Leben ringende Gemeinde": Skizzen zu Semantik, Kontext und Rezeption von *lwn* und *tlnh*. "Lebendige Gemeinde". 2005 ⇒578. 1-46.
10352 מדבר: *Leal, R.B.* Negativity towards wilderness in the biblical record. Ecotheology [L] 10/3 (2005) 364-381 [NTAb 50,532].
10353 מות: **Gulde, Stefanie-Ulrike** 'Der Tod als Figur': eine motiv- und religionsgeschichtliche Untersuchung zum Alten Testament und seiner Umwelt. [D]*Niehr, Herbert* 2005. Diss. Tübingen [ThRv 102, xi].
10354 מכתם: *Ilan, Nahem* SAADIAH Gaon's translation of 'mikhtam'. JJS 56/2 (2005) 298-305.
10355 מנוחה: *Rad, Gerhard von* There remains still a rest for the people of God. From Genesis. 2005 <1933> ⇒283. 82-88.
10356 מנחה: *Weinfeld, Moshe mnḥh* (*Minḥah*). Normative and sectarian Judaism. 2005 ⇒2732. 122-125.
10357 מס: *Na'aman, Nadav* From conscription of forced labor to a symbol of bondage: *Mas* in the biblical literature. [F]KLEIN, J. 2005 ⇒79. 746-758.
10358 מרזח: *Zamora, José-Angel* L'ébriété à Ougarit et la bible: un héritage discuté. [M]CAQUOT, A. 2005 ⇒22. 187-207 [Gen 9,20-25].
10359 משׁל: *Caesar, Lael O.* Studying מָשָׁל without reading Proverbs: an extra-wisdom analysis of the term מָשָׁל. DavarLogos 4/2 (2005) 131-147.
10360 נחשת; קשה: *Pinker, Aron* On the meaning of קשת נחושה. JHScr 5/12 (2005)*.
10361 נצב: *Kerr, Robert M.* North African *centenaria* and Hebrew נְצִיבִים: some remarks relating to the Latino-Punic inscription from Gasr el-Azaiz (*IRT* 893). [M]DIAKONOFF, M. 2005 ⇒36. 475-511.
10362 נקם: **Peels, Hendrik G.L.** The vengeance of God: the meaning of the root NQM. OTS 31: 1995 ⇒11/2,5845... 13,8170. [R]ThR 70 (2005) 451-453 (*Reventlow, Henning Graf*).
10363 נשך; תרבית: *Buch, Joshua* Neshekh and tarbit: usury from bible to modern finance. JBQ 33 (2005) 13-22.

10364 סרים: *Cilliers, J.F.G.; Retief, François P.; Riekert, S.J.P.K.* Eunuchs in the bible. Health and healing. AcTh(B) 7: 2005 <2002> ⇒686. 247-258.

10365 עבד: *Fanuli, Antonio 'Āvad*: schiavitù e servizio. PSV 52 (2005) 57-80.

10366 עם: **Ijezie, Luke Emehielechukwu** The interpretation of the Hebrew word עם (people) in Samuel-Kings. [D]*Pisano, Stephen*: R 2005, 126 pp. Exc. Diss. Gregoriana; Bibl. 83-117.

10367 ענה: *Kogan, Leonid* Comparative notes in the Old Testament (I). [M]DIAKONOFF, M. 2005 ⇒36. 731-737 [Exod 21,10; Judg 5,20].

10368 פינחס: **Thon, Johannes** Pinhas ben Eleasar—der levitische Priester am Ende der Tora: traditions- und literargeschichtliche Untersuchung unter Einbeziehung historisch-geographischer Fragen. [D]*Meinhold, Arndt* 2005, Diss. Halle-Wittenberg [ThLZ 130,884].

10369 צדקה: *Magonet, Jonathan* An der Gerechtigkeit hängt das Überleben der Welt: eine jüdische Betrachtung. BiHe 41/164 (2005) 12-13;

10370 *Pratelli, Simone* '...e il giusto è fondamento eterno' (Pr 10,25): per una definizione di giustizia e rettitudine nell'Antico Testamento. Studi Fatti Ricerche 112 (2005) 10-13;

10371 *Rivas, Luis H.* Justicia y amor: fundamentos bíblicos. RevBib 67 (2005) 5-29;

10372 *Skorka, Abraham* Zedeq y zedaqah en la era postmoderna. Cuadernos de teología 24 (2005) 37-45.

10373 ציר: *Paul, Shalom M.* Hebrew צִיר(ים) and its interdialectal equivalents. Divrei Shalom. CHANE 23: 2005 <2004> ⇒273. 323-327 = [F]KLEIN, J. 2005 ⇒79. 759-763.

10374 צפון: *Wyatt, Nick* The significance of *ṣpn* in West Semitic thought: a contribution to the history of a mythological motif. Mythic mind. 2005 <1995> ⇒328. 102-124.

10375 קדשים: **Stark, Christine** 'Kult Prostitution' im Alten Testament?: die Qedeschen der Hebräischen Bibel und das Motiv der Hurerei. [D]*Krüger, T.* 2005, Diss. Zürich [ThRv 102,xiv].

10376 רגל; רכל: *Zipor, Moshe A.* Talebearers, peddlers, spies, and converts: the adventures of the biblical and post-biblical roots רג"ל and רך"ל. HebStud 46 (2005) 129-144.

10377 רדף: *Riepl, Christian* Jagen, Nachjagen, Hinterherjagen: zur Valenz von G-רדף. [F]SEIDL, T.: ATSAT 75: 2005 ⇒137. 83-98.

10378 רחם: *Farfán Navarro, Enrique* רחם—la compasión que renueva. EstB 63 (2005) 427-450.

10379 רחם; שכן; נחם: *Stefani, Piero* Compassione / misericordia nella tradizione ebraica. Studi Fatti Ricerche 111 (2005) 3-6.

10380 רפאים: *Rouillard-Bonraisin, Hedwige* L'énigme des refa'im bibliques résolue grâce aux rapa'ūma d'Ougarit. [M]CAQUOT, A. 2005 ⇒22. 145-182;

10381 *Williams, P.J.* Are the biblical Rephaim and the Ugaritic RPUM healers?. The OT in its world. OTS 52: 2005 ⇒749. 266-275.

10382 שאול: **Galenieks, Eriks** The nature, function, and purpose of the term שְׁאוֹל in the Torah, Prophets, and Writings. [D]*Davidson, Richard M.*: 2005, Diss. Andrews [AUSS 43,211].

10383 שבט; מתה: **George, Paduthottu G.** The rod in the Old Testament. 2004 ⇒20,9451. [R]TJT 21 (2005) 240-241 (*White, Ellen*).

10384 שׂטן: *Kreuzer, Florian* Der Antagonist: der Satan in der Hebräischen Bibel—eine bekannte Größe? Bib. 86 (2005) 536-544;

10385 *Szuppe, Paweł* Szatan w biblii. CoTh 75/1 (2005) 47-67. **P**.

10386 שׁלום: *Cohen-Solal, Henri* Shalom in Hebrew. Worlds of memory. 2005 ⇒543. 131-139.

10387 שׁלמים: **Modéus, Martin** Sacrifice and symbol: biblical šelamîm in a ritual perspective. [D]*Mettinger, T.*: CB.OT 52: Sto 2005, Almqvist & W. 459 pp. SEK397. 91-22-02120-5. Diss. Lund; Bibl. 394-420.

10388 שׂער: *Galpaz-Feller, Pnina* Hair in the bible and in ancient Egyptian culture: cultural and private connotations. BetM 182 (2005) 221-240. Sum 294. **H**.

10389 שׂרף: *Provençal, Philippe* Regarding the noun śrp in the Hebrew bible. JSOT 29 (2005) 371-379.

10390 שׁררות: **Rasztawicki, Leszek** Funkeja terminu 'szerirut' w Biblii Hebrajskiej [La fonction du terme 'szerirut' dans la Bible hébraïque]. [D]*Rubinkiewicz*, R.: 2005, 218 pp. Diss. Lublin [RTL 37,611]. **P**.

10391 תמים: *Haliwa, Pinhas* On the significance of the term 'tamim' in the torah, midrash and Jewish thought. BetM 181 (2005) 109-124. Sum 199. **H**.

*Syriac*

10392 *rôzô*: *Varghese, Baby* Liturgical use of the word *rôzô*: a preliminary survey. [F]VOIGT, R.: AOAT 317: 2005 ⇒158. 425-432.

*Ugaritic*

*ảp*: *Loretz, O.* Hurr./akk. *ābi*=ug./he. *ảp/'wb* 2005 ⇒10315.

10393 *lb; kbd*: *Loretz, Oswald* Der akkadisch-ugaritisch-hebräische Parallelismus *libbu/lb* ‖ *kabattu/kbd* 'Herz' ‖ 'Leber' in Psalm 16,9: eine lexikalische Studie zu ugaritisch *lb* und *kbd*. UF 37 (2005) 395-404.

*mrzḥ*: *Zamora, J.* L'ébriété à Ougarit et la bible 2005 ⇒10358.

10394 *pgu*: *Watson, Wilfred G.E.* The meaning of Ugaritic **pgu (pga/pgi)*. StEeL 22 (2005) 9-11.

*rpum*: *Rouillard-Bonraisin, H.* L'énigme...refa'im 2005 ⇒10380; *Williams, P.* Are the...Ugaritic RPUM healers? 2005 ⇒10381.

## J1.5 *Phoenicia, ugaritica*—Northwest Semitic [⇒T5.4]

10395 *Amadasi Guzzo, Maria Gulia* Les phases du phénicien: phénicien et punique. 10th meeting of Hamito-Semitic linguistics. QuSem 25: 2005⇒903. 95-103.

10396 *Azize, Joseph* The genre of the Bitnoam inscription. ANES 42 (2005) 318-333.

10397 *Bordreuil, Pierre* Nouvelle inscription phénicienne dédiée à Milqart. V Congresso di studi fenici. 2005 ⇒959. I, 135-137.

10398 **Bordreuil, Pierre; Pardee, Dennis** Manuel d'Ougaritique. 2004 ⇒ 20,9464. [R]BiOr 62 (2005) 309-314 (*Gzella, Holger*).

10399 *Bron, F.* Les stèles votives du *tophet* de Carthage: état de la question. V Congresso di studi fenici. 2005 ⇒959. I, 303-304.

10400 *Cunchillos, J.-L.; Xella, P.; Zamora, J.-A.* Il corpus informatizzato delle iscrizioni fenicie e puniche: un progetto italo-spagnolo. V Congresso di studi fenici. 2005 ⇒959. I, 517-521.

10401 *Dietrich, Manfried; Loretz, Oswald* Vier graphische Besonderheiten im Marziḥu-Text KTU 3.9. UF 37 (2005) 221-226;

10402 'Weihen' (*'ly* Š) von *pgr*, Ochsen und Gegenständen in KTU 6.13, 6.14 und 6.62. UF 37 (2005) 227-239.

10403 [E]**Donner, Herbert; Röllig, Wolfgang** Kanaanäische und aramäische Inschriften Bd.1. [5]2002 ⇒18,9072; 19,9792. [R]OLZ 100 (2005) 472-473 (*Conrad, Joachim*); IEJ 55 (2005) 234-235 (*Aḥituv, Shmuel*).

10404 *Elayi, Josette* Four new inscribed Phoenician arrowheads. StEeL 22 (2005) 35-45.

10405 *Emerton, J.A.* Lines 25-6 of the Moabite Stone and a recently-discovered inscription. VT 55 (2005) 293-303.

10406 *Gross, Andrew D.* A heretofore unrecognized legal formula in *KTU* 3.9. UF 37 (2005) 351-360.

10407 *Hays, Christopher B.* Kirtu and the 'yoke of the poor': a new interpretation of an old crux (KTU 1.16 VI 48). UF 37 (2005) 361-370.

10408 Is the new royal Moabite inscription a forgery?. BArR 31/4 (2005) 55-56.

10409 *James, Peter* The date of the Ekron temple inscription. IEJ 55 (2005) 90-93.

10410 [E]**Jongeling, Karel; Kerr, Robert M.** Late Punic epigraphy: an introduction to the study of Neo-Punic and Latino-Punic inscriptions. Tü 2005, Mohr S. x; 115 pp. €19. 3-16-148728-1. Bibl. 107-114.

10411 *Korpel, Marjo C.A.* Unit delimitation in Ugaritic cultic texts and some Babylonian and Hebrew parallels. Layout markers. 2005 ⇒ 422. 141-160 [Exod 20,1-17; 21-22; Lev 1-7; Num 28,1-30,1].

10412 *Kottsieper, Ingo* Nordwestsemitische Texte (8. Jh. v.Chr.-3. Jh. n.Chr.). Staatsverträge. TUAT N.F. 2: 2005 ⇒661. 307-330.

10413 **Krahmalkov, Charles R.** Phoenician-Punic dictionary. OLA 90; Studia Phoenicia 15: 2000 ⇒16,8568... 20,9471. [R]JNES 64 (2005) 201-202 (*Pardee, Dennis*).

10414 **Lehmann, Reinhard G.** Dynastiesarkophage mit szenischen Reliefs aus Byblos und Zypern, 1.2: die Inschriften des Aḥīrōm-Sarkophags und die Schachtinschrift des Grabes V in Jbeil (Byblos). Forschungen zur phönizisch-punischen und zyprischen Plastik... II.1.2: Mainz 2005, Von Zabern ix; 79 pp. 3-8053-3508-3. 16 pl. [R]UF 37 (2005) 830-831 (*Loretz, Oswald*).

10415 *Lemaire, André* Essai d'interprétation historique d'une nouvelle inscription monumentale moabite. CRAI 1 (2005) 95-108;

10416 Nouveau roi dans une inscription proto-phénicienne?. V Congresso di studi fenici. 2005 ⇒959. I, 43-46.

10417 *LeMon, Joel M.* The power of parallelism in KTU$^2$ 1.119: another 'trial cut'. UF 37 (2005) 375-394.

10418 *Loretz, Oswald* Die 'fetten' Wagenspuren des Wettergottes Baal/YHWH auf den Höhen (KTU 1.4 V 6-9; 1.16 VI 57-58; Psalm 65, 12) und ein Selbstporträt Baals (KTU 1.3 III 20b-28a): die drei Parallelismen *šnt* || *m'gl*, *ṭwbh* || *dšn*, *brq* || *rgm*. UF 37 (2005) 411-440.

10419 *Mosca, Paul G.* The independent object pronoun in Punic. Or. 74 (2005) 65-70.
10420 *Niehr, Herbert* Texte aus Ugarit, 2: Texte in ugaritischer Sprache. Staatsverträge. TUAT N.F. 2: 2005 ⇒661. 178-181.
10421 **Olmo Lete, Gregorio del; Sanmartín Ascaso, Joaquín** A dictionary of the Ugaritic language in the alphabetic tradition, 1: ['(a/i/u-k], 2: [l-z]. [T]*Watson, Wilfred G.E.*: HO 1/67: 2003, 2 vols. ⇒19, 9806. [R]ArOr 73 (2005) 256-257 (*Mynářová, Jana*);
10422 Lei [2]2004 <2003>, Brill xliv; 474+475-1006 pp. 90041-36940.
10423 **Pena, J.C.** Jesús como historia: análisis histórico de las narrativas evangélicas. BA 2005, San Benito 383 pp. $15.50. 98711-77291. Bibl. [NTAb 50,402].
10424 *Prosser, Miller* Detailed epigraphic notes on KTU 1.4 VII 19. UF 37 (2005) 479-489.
10425 *Puech, Emile* Les inscriptions proto-sinaïtiques 346 et 357. V Congresso di studi fenici. 2005 ⇒959. I, 27-41.
10426 *Sasson, Victor* An Edomite Joban text: with a biblical Joban parallel. ZAW 117 (2005) 601-615 [Job 27,10-17].
10427 *Schade, Aaron* New photographs supporting the reading *ryt* in line 12 of the Mesha Inscription. IEJ 55 (2005) 205-208;
10428 A text linguistic approach to the syntax and style of the Phoenician inscription of Azatiwada. JSSt 50 (2005) 35-58.
10429 *Stager, Jennifer M.S.* 'Let no one wonder at this image': a Phoenician funerary stele in Athens. Hesp. 74 (2005) 427-449.
10430 *Wesselius, J.W.* Language play in the Old Testament and in ancient North-West Semitic inscriptions: some notes on the Kilamuwa inscription. The OT in its world. OTS 52: 2005 ⇒749. 253-265.
10431 *Xella, Paolo; Zamora López, J.-Á.* L'inscription phénicienne de Bodashtart *in situ* à *Bustan es-Seh* (Sidon) et son apport à l'histoire du sanctuaire. ZDPV 121 (2005) 119-129.
10432 *Yun, Il-Sung A.* The Transjordanian languages during the Iron Age II. UF 37 (2005) 741-766.

## J1.6 Aramaica

10433 *Aspesi, Francesco* La versione aramaica su papiro dell'iscrizione monumentale trilingue di Dario a Behistun. Acme 58/2 (2005) 15-27.
10434 **Athas, George** The Tel Dan inscription: a reappraisal and a new interpretation. JSOT.S 360; Copenhagen International Seminar 12: 2003 ⇒19,9823; 20,9495. [R]CBQ 67 (2005) 305-306 (*Hess, Richard S.*); RHPhR 85 (2005) 309-310 (*Heintz, J.-G.*); VT 55 (2005) 416 (*Williamson, H.G.M.*); JSSt 50 (2005) 23-34 (*Sasson, Victor*).
10435 *Baarda, Tjitze* Parablepsis in the Christian Palestinian Aramaic lectionary: the case of Matthew 17.26. AramSt 3 (2005) 137-145.
10436 *Borghero, Roberta* The evolution of the verbal system in the north eastern Neo-Aramaic of Ashitha. Studi afroasiatici. 2005 ⇒885. 325-336.
10437 *Burnett, Stephen G.* Christian Aramaism: the birth and growth of Aramaic scholarship in the sixteenth century. [F]FOX, M. 2005 ⇒43. 421-436.

10438 *Coghill, Eleanor* The morphology and distribution of noun plurals in the Neo-Aramaic dialect of Alqosh. Studi afroasiatici. 2005 ⇒885. 337-348.

10439 *Contini, Riccardo* Il testo aramaico di Elefantina. Il saggio Ahiqar. StBi 148: 2005 ⇒52. 113-139.

10440 *Faraj, Ali H.; Moriggi, Marco* Two incantation bowls from the Iraq Museum (Baghdad). Or. 74 (2005) 71-82; Tab. I-II.

10441 **Ferrer, Joan** Esbozo de historia de la lengua aramea. Studia Semitica 3: 2004 ⇒20,9500. [R]Sef. 65/1 (2005) 195-198 (*Ribera-Florit, J.*); LASBF 55 (2005) 534-535 (*Pazzini, Massimo*).

10442 *Fitzmyer, Joseph A.* The James ossuary and its implications. ThD 52 (2005) 321-339.

10443 *Fornberg, Tord* Religion, politics and milestones: two Asokan milestones in Afghanistan. SEÅ 70 (2005) 63-71.

10444 **Gardner, Iain; Lieu, Samuel; Parry, Ken** From Palmyra to Zayton: epigraphy and iconography. Silk Road Studies 10: Turnhout 2005, Brepols 291 pp. 2-503-51883-4.

10445 *Gianto, Agustinus* Variation in the Palmyrene honorific inscriptions. [M]HILLERS, D. 2005 ⇒61. 74-88.

10446 *Gilfo, Manuela E.B.* L'iscrizione aramaica n. 24 di Hatra: benedizione e maledizione. Studi afroasiatici. 2005 ⇒885. 299-308.

10447 **Greenspahn, Frederick E.** An introduction to Aramaic. Resources for biblical study 46: [2]2003 ⇒19,9837; 20,9505. [R]RBLit 7 (2005) 73-75 (*Rogland, Max*).

10448 *Gross, Andrew D.* Three new Palmyrene inscriptions. [M]HILLERS, D.: 2005 ⇒61. 89-102.

10449 *Gzella, Holger* Erscheinungsformen des historischen Präsens im Aramäischen. Or. 74 (2005) 399-408.

10450 **Gzella, Holger** Tempus, Aspekt und Modalität im Reichsaramäischen. VOK 48: 2004 ⇒20,9506. [R]OLZ 100 (2005) 538-42 (*Tropper, Josef*).

10451 *Healey, John F.* The writing on the wall: law in Aramaic epigraphy. [F]MILLARD, A.: LHBOTS 426: 2005 ⇒102. 127-141;

10452 New evidence for the Aramaic legal tradition: from Elephantine to Edessa. Studia semitica. JSSt.S 16: 2005 ⇒603. 115-127.

10453 *Hopkins, Simon* Is Neo-Aramaic a Semitic language?. [F]ULLENDORFF, E. SStLL 47: 2005 ⇒154. 62-83.

10454 Israel: Tel Aviv: Jakobus-Ossuar und kein Ende: Antiquitätenhändler vor Gericht. WUB 36 (2005) 59.

10455 Israeli prosecutor repudiates IAA report on forgery. BArR 31/3 (2005) 46-47. James ossuary [NTAb 49,550].

10456 **Jastrow, Marcus** Dictionary of the targumim, the Talmud Babli, and Yerushalmi, and the midrashic literature. Peabody, PA 2005 <1903>, Hendrickson xvii; 1736 pp. $40. 16556-38603. 2 vols in one [OTA 29,203].

10457 *Jastrow, Otto* Der bestimmte Artikel im Aramäischen: ein Blick auf 3000 Jahre Sprachgeschichte. [F]VOIGT, R.: AOAT 317: 2005 ⇒158. 137-150.

10458 *Johnson, David J.; el-Khouri, Lamia* A new Nabataean inscription from Wadi Mataḥa, Petra. PEQ 137 (2005) 169-174.

10459 *Khan, Geoffrey* Some parallels in linguistic development between Biblical Hebrew and Neo-Aramaic. [F]ULLENDORFF, E.: SStLL 47: 2005 ⇒154. 84-108;

10460 The verbal system of the Jewish Neo-Aramaic dialect of Sulemaniyya. Studi afroasiatici. 2005 ⇒885. 359-370.

10461 **Khan, Geoffrey** The Jewish Neo-Aramaic dialect of Sulemaniyya and Halabja. SStLL 44: 2004 ⇒20,9517. [R]ArOr 73 (2005) 510-513 (*McCollum, Adam C.*); RBLit (2005)* (*Engle, John*).

10462 *Kogan, Leonid* Lexicon of the Old Aramaic inscriptions and the historical unity of Aramaic. [M]DIAKONOFF, M. 2005 ⇒36. 513-566.

10463 *Lambert, Mayer* Grammaire de l'araméen biblique (Appendice XVI). Termes massorétiques. 2005 ⇒241. 105-121.

10464 *Levine, Baruch A.* Lexicographical and grammatical notes on the Palmyrene Aramaic texts. [M]HILLERS, D.: 2005 ⇒61. 103-117.

**Magen, Y**., *al.*, Mount Gerizim... inscriptions 2004 ⇒10297.

10465 **Magnanini, Pietro; Nava, Pier Paolo** Grammatica di Aramaico Biblico. Bo 2005, Studio Domenicano 167 pp. €40. 88-7094-5812. Pres. *Massimo Pazzini*.

10466 **Martínez Borobio, Emiliano** Arameo antiguo: gramática y textos comentados. 2003 ⇒19,9865. [R]Sef. 65/1 (2005) 201-205 (*Alonso de la Fuente, J.A.*).

10467 *Martone, Corrado* Verso un'edizione italiana dell'archivio di Babatha: il papiro Yadin 1: testo e traduzione. [F]STEMBERGER, G.: SJ 32: 2005 ⇒140. 129-138.

10468 *Mengozzi, Alessandro* Extended prepositions in Neo-Aramaic, Kurdish and Italian. Studi afroasiatici. 2005 ⇒885. 371-390.

10469 *Morgenstern, Matthew* Linguistic notes on magic bowls in the Moussaieff Collection. BSOAS 68 (2005) 349-367.

10470 *Moriggi, Marco* Two new incantation bowls from Rome (Italy). AramSt 3 (2005) 43-58;

10471 Peculiarità linguistiche in una coppa magica aramaica inedita. 10th meeting of Hamito-Semitic linguistics. 2005 ⇒903. 257-266.

10472 **Muraoka, Takamitsu; Porten, Besalel** A grammar of Egyptian Aramaic. HO 1/32a: [2]2003 <1998> ⇒19,9869. [R]JSSt 50 (2005) 390-391 (*Morgenstern, Matthew*).

10473 *Mutzafi, Hezy* Etymological notes on North-Eastern Neo-Aramaic. AramSt 3 (2005) 83-107.

10474 **Mutzafi, Hezy** The Jewish Neo-Aramaic dialect of Koy Sanjaq (Iraqi Kurdistan). Semitica Viva 32: 2004 ⇒20,9525. [R]AramSt 3 (2005) 285-287 (*Khan, Geoffrey*).

10475 *Müller-Kessler, Christa* Of Jesus, Darius, Marduk...: Aramaic magic bowls in the Moussaieff Collection. JAOS 125 (2005) 219-240.

10476 **Müller-Kessler, Christa** Die Zauberschalentexte in der Hilprecht-Sammlung, Jena, und weitere Nippur-Texte anderer Sammlungen. Texte und Materialien der Frau Professor Hilprecht Collection of Babylonian Antiquities im Eigentum der Friedrich Schiller-Universität Jena 7: Wsb 2005, Harrassowitz xii; 257 pp. 3-447-05059-4. Bibl. 155-164.

10477 *Parlasca, Klaus* Zu palmyrenischen Inschriften auf Reliefs. [M]HILLERS, D.: 2005 ⇒61. 137-149.

10478 *Pennacchietti, Fabrizio A.*, *al.*, A project for the publication and lexicographic study of christian neo-Aramaic texts. 10th meeting of Hamito-Semitic linguistics. QuSem 25: 2005 ⇒903. 301-313.

10479 *Poizat, Bruno* Un manuscrit retrouvé du P. Jacques Rhétoré. Studi afroasiatici. 2005 ⇒885. 413-423. 'La versification en soureth'.

10480 *Sabar, Yona* Some comparative observations on the lexicons of Nerwa texts in Jewish Neo-Aramaic and the Neo-Syriac poems of Alqosh and Telkepe, both from ca. the 17th century and from Kurdistan, northern Iraq. Studi afroasiatici. 2005 ⇒885. 391-396.

10481 *Saccagno, Rita* The dorekṯā 'On repentance', a Neo-Aramaic poem written in 1607 AD by Hormizd of Alqosh: samples of manuscript variation. Studi afroasiatici. 2005 ⇒885. 407-412.

10482 [E]**Schwiderski, Dirk** Die alt- und reichsaramäischen Inschriften, Band 2: Texte und Bibliographie. FoSub 2: 2004 ⇒20,9532. [R]OLZ 100 (2005) 659-662 (*Gzella, Holger*); ThLZ 130 (2005) 1172-1173 (*Rüterswörden, Udo*); ATG 68 (2005) 446-449 (*Torres, A.*).

10483 **Segal, J.B.** Catalogue of the Aramaic and Mandaic incantation bowls in the British Museum. 2000 ⇒16,8638... 20,9533. [R]IEJ 55 (2005) 121-122 (*Morgenstern, Matthew*); NEA(BA) 68 (2005) 196-197 (*Busch, Peter*).

10484 **Shaked, S.** Le satrape de Bactriane et son gouverneur: documents araméens du IVe s. avant notre ère provenant de Bactriane. Persika 4: P 2004, De Boccard 62 pp.

10485 *Sokoloff, Michael* New Akkadian loanwords in Jewish Babylonian Aramaic. [F]KLEIN, J. 2005 ⇒79. 575-586.

10486 **Sokoloff, Michael** A dictionary of Jewish Babylonian Aramaic of the Talmudic and Geonic periods. 2002 ⇒18,9143; 20,9538. [R]BSOAS 68 (2005) 301-304 (*Geller, M.J.*); JSSt 50 (2005) 394-395 (*Beyer, Klaus*); RBLit 7 (2005) 75-78 (*Schorch, Stefan*); AJS Review 29/1 (2005) 131-144 (*Levine, Baruch A.*);

10487 A dictionary of Jewish Palestinian Aramaic of the Byzantine period. [2]2003 <1990> ⇒19,9887; 20,9536. [R]AJS Review 29/1 (2005) 131-144 (*Levine, Baruch A.*);

10488 A dictionary of Judean Aramaic. 2003 ⇒19,9888; 20,9537. [R]OLZ 100 (2005) 62-63 (*Tilly, Michael*); BSOAS 68 (2005) 304 (*Geller, M.J.*); HebStud 46 (2005) 387-389 (*Rubin, Aaron D.*).

10489 *Strawn, Brent A.* Who's listening to whom?: a syntactical note on the Melqart inscription. UF 37 (2005) 621-641.

10490 *Temerev, A.N.* Regular and occasional payments in later Egypt: on the interpretation of the Aramaic term *mnt*'. VDI 2 (2005) 114-130. **R.**

10491 *Van Reeth, Jan M.F.* L'araméen: la langue du paradis. [F]MALAISE, M. 2005 ⇒95. 137-144.

10492 *Voigt, Rainer* Die Entwicklung der aramäischen zur Kharoṣṭhī- und Brāhmī-Schrift. ZDMG 155 (2005) 25-50.

10493 Was cleanser used to clean the James Ossuary inscription?. BArR 31/1 (2005) 54.

10494 *Yardeni, Ada; Price, Jonathan J.* A new Aramaic dedicatory inscription from Israel. SCI 24 (2005) 125-133.

10495 *Younger, K. Lawson* 'Hazael, son of a nobody': some reflections in light of recent study. [F]MILLARD, A.: LHBOTS 426: 2005 ⇒102. 245-270 [1 Kgs 19,15].

## J1.7 Syriaca

10496 **Al-Kfarnissy, Paul Al-Khoury** Grammar of the Aramaic Syriac language. Piscataway (N.J.) 2005 <1962>, Gorgias 24; 462 pp. 1-593-33031-6. Bibl. 449-451.

10497 [E]**Azar, Boutros** Nos sources: art et littérature Syriaques. Antélias 2005, CERO 600 pp. 9953-0-0370-X.

10498 *Brock, Sebastian P.* Greek and Latin words in Palmyrene inscriptions: a comparison with Syriac. [M]HILLERS, D.: 2005 ⇒61. 11-25.

10499 [E]**Forbes, A. Dean; Taylor, David G.K.** Foundations for Syriac lexicography I: colloquia of the International Syriac Language Project. Perspectives on Syriac linguistics 1: Piscataway, NJ 2005, Gorgias xix; 229 pp. 1-593-33138-X. Bibl.

10500 **Healey, John F.** Leshono suryoyo: first studies in Syriac. Gorgias handbooks 2: Piscataway, NJ 2005, Gorgias xxiii; 220 pp. 1-593-33190-8.

10501 **Moriggi, Marco** La lingua delle coppe magiche siriache. 2004 ⇒ 20,9549. [R]RA 99 (2005) 191 (*Jullien, Christelle*).

10502 *Morrison, Craig* The function of *qtal hwā* in classical Syriac narrative. [M]MORAN, W.: BibOr 48: 2005 ⇒107. 103-131.

10503 **Muraoka, Takamitsu** Classical Syriac: a basic grammar with a chrestomathy. PLO 19: Wsb [2]2005 <1997>, Harrassowitz xxii; 156 pp. €34. 3-47-05021-7. Bibl. by *S.P. Brock*.

10504 **Pazzini, Massimo** Lessico concordanziale del Nuovo Testamento siriaco. ASBF 64: 2004 ⇒20,9550. [R]CDios 218 (2005) 251-252 (*Gutiérrez, J.*); OCP 71 (2005) 245-248 (*Vergani, E.*).

10505 *Pennacchietti, Fabrizio* Il testo siriaco antico di Ahiqar. Il saggio Ahiqar. StBi 148: 2005 ⇒52. 193-225.

10506 **Phenix, Robert R., Jr.** Twelve Syriac sermons on Joseph attributed to Balai: a historical-critical, rhetorical-critical and literary-critical study of poetry from the golden age of Syriac literature. Diss. Tübingen 2005; [D]*Gerö, Stephen*.

10507 **Stoddard, David Tappand** A grammar of the modern Syriac language as spoken in Oroomiah, Persia, and in Koordistan. Piscataway (N.J.) 2004 <1855>, Gorgias 180, 180a-180h pp. 1-593-33-124-X. Facs. reprint.

## J1.8 **Akkadica** (sumerica)

10508 [T]**Black, Jeremy; Cunningham, Graham; Zólyomi, Gábor** The literature of ancient Sumer. 2004 ⇒20,9559. [R]JRAS 15 (2005) 219-20 (*George, A.R.*); Mes. 40 (2005) 182-6 (*Seminara, Stefano*).

10509 **Borger, Riekele** Mesopotamisches Zeichenlexikon. AOAT 305: 2004 ⇒20,9560. [R]BSOAS 68 (2005) 109-11 (*George, Andrew R.*).

10510 **Cochavi-Rainey, Zipora** The Alashia texts from the 14th and 13th centuries BCE: a textual and linguistic study. AOAT 289: 2003 ⇒ 19,9912. [R]ArOr 73 (2005) 144-146 (*Mynářová, Jana*).

10511 *Cohen, Eran* Paronomastic infinitive in Old Babylonian. JEOL 38 (2003-2004) 105-112;

10512 Addenda to non-verbal clauses in Old Babylonian. JSSt 50 (2005) 247-279.

10513 **Cohen, Eran** The modal system of Old Babylonian. Harvard Semitic Studies 56: WL 2005, Eisenbrauns 225 pp. €72. 15750-6921-0. Bibl. 208-217.

10514 *Cohen, Yoram* Feet of clay at Emar: a happy end?. Or. 74 (2005) 165-170.

10515 *Dalley, Stephanie* The language of destruction and its interpretation. BaghM 36 (2005) 275-285.

10516 **Dalley, Stephanie** Old Babylonian texts in the Ashmolean Museum: mainly from Larsa, Sippir, Kish, and Lagaba. Oxford Editions of Cuneiform Texts 15: Oxf 2005, Clarendon 69 pp. 01992-72778. Copies contrib. by *Eleanor Robson, Tina Breckwoldt*; Bibl. vi-viii.

10517 *Dick, Michael B.* A Neo-Sumerian ritual tablet in Philadelphia. JNES 64 (2005) 271-280.

10518 *Dietrich, Manfried; Loretz, Oswald* Alalaḫ-Texte der Schicht VII (II): Schuldtexte, Vermerke und Sonstiges. UF 37 (2005) 241-314.

10519 *Donbaz, Veysel* An Old Assyrian treaty from Kültepe. JCS 57 (2005) 63-68 [OTA 30,4].

10520 **Edzard, Dietz** Sumerian grammar. HO I/71: 2003 ⇒19,9918. [R]RBLit (2005)* (*Gee, John*); BSOAS 68 (2005) 299-301 (*Taylor, Jon*).

10521 **Ellermeier, Friedrich** Sumerisches Glossar: Führer durch die neuere sumerologische Fachliteratur, Bd.3, Teil 2: Sumerisch-Deutsches Kurzglossar in Umschrift und Keilschrift: Lief. 3, Buchstabe G. ThOrAr 4: Hardegsen bei Gö 2005, Ellermeier 203 pp. 3-92174-7295.

10522 **Foster, Benjamin R.** Before the muses: an anthology of Akkadian literature. Bethesda, Md. [3]2005, CDL xx; 1044 pp. $50. [R]RBLit (2005)* (*Lenzi, Alan*).

10523 **Freydank, Helmut; Feller, Barbara** Mittelassyrische Rechtsurkunden und Verwaltungstexte VI. Keilschrifttexte aus mittelassyrischer Zeit 4; Ausgrabungen der Deutschen Orient-Gesellschaft in Assur E: Inschriften 7; WVDOG 109: Saarbrücken 2005, Saarbrücker 88 pp. 3-930843-94-3.

10524 *Gabbay, Uri; Wasserman, Nathan* Literatures in contact: the *BALAĜ ÚRU ÀM-MA-IR-RA-BI* and its Akkadian translation UET 6/2,403. JCS 57 69-84 [OTA 30,9].

10525 *Gehlken, Erlend* Die Adad-Tafeln der Omenserie *Enūma Anu Enlil*, Teil 1: Einführung. BaghM 36 (2005) 235-273.

10526 **Guichard, Michaël** La vaisselle de luxe des rois [de] Mari: matériaux pour le Dictionnaire de Babylonien de Paris, tome II. ARM.T 31: P 2005, Recherches sur les Civilisations ix; 569 pp. €45. 2-865-38-298-2. CD-Rom.

10527 **Hasselbach, Rebecca** Sargonic Akkadian: a historical and comparative study of the syllabic texts. Wsb 2005, Harrassowitz xiii; 292 pp. €78. 3-447-05172-8. Bibl. 237-250.

10528 *Hecker, Karl* Akkadische Texte. Staatsverträge. TUAT N.F. 2: 2005 ⇒661. 27-93.

10529 *Horowitz, W.* An old-new discovery at Hazor. Qad. 38 (2005) 2-13. H.

10530 *Hruška, Blahoslav* Prolegomena zur ältesten mesopotamischen Listenwissenschaft (Uruk, Fāra, Abū Ṣalabīḫ). ArOr 73 (2005) 273-289.

10531 **Huehnergard, John** A grammar of Akkadian. HSM 45: Atlanta [2]2005 <1997>, Scholars xl; 647 pp. $45.

10532 [E]**Hunger, Hermann** Astronomical diaries and related texts from Babylonia, 5: lunar and planetary texts. DÖAW 299: 2001 ⇒17, 8613... 20,9581. [R]BiOr 62 (2005) 546-553 (*Van der Spek, R.J.*).

10533 *Hurowitz, Victor Avigdor* An overlooked allusion to *ludlul* in Urad-Gula's letter to Assurbanipal. SAA Bulletin 14 (2002-5) 129-132.

10534 *Izre'el, Shlomo* The Akkadian verbal system: derivational and inflectional strategies. [F]KLEIN, J. 2005 ⇒79. 533-547.

10535 *Johnson, J. Cale* Internally-headed relative clauses in Akkadian: identifying weak quantification in the construct state. JCS 57 (2005) 85-98 [OTA 30,17].

10536 **Jursa, Michael** Neo-Babylonian legal and administrative documents: typology, contents and archives. Guides to the Mesopotamian Textual Record 1: Müns 2005, Ugarit-Verlag xii; 189 pp. €28. 3-934628-69-9.

10537 *Keetman, Jan* Die altsumerische Vokalharmonie und die Vokale des Sumerischen. JCS 57 (2005) 1-16 [OTA 30,17].

10538 *Kouwenberg, N.J.C.* Initial plene writing and the conjugation of the first weak verbs in Akkadian. JEOL 38 (2003-2004) 83-103.

10539 *Limet, H.* L'inscription d'Antiochos I à Borsippa: un commentaire. TEuph 29 (2005) 117-131.

10540 *Loesov, Sergey* Akkadian sentences about the present time, part one. [M]DIAKONOFF, M. 2005 ⇒36. 101-148;

10541 Additions and corrections to 'T-perfect in Old Babylonian'. [M]DIAKONOFF, M. 2005 ⇒36. 713-717.

10542 **Maidman, Maynard P.** The Nuzi texts of the Oriental Institute: a catalogue raisonné. [E]*Owen, David I.; Wilhelm, Gernot*: Studies on the civilization and culture of Nuzi and the Hurrians 16: Bethesda, MD 2005, CDL xii; 262 pp. 1-883053-900. Bibl. 260-262.

10543 *Mayer, Werner R.* Lexikalische Listen aus Ebla und Uruk. Or. 74 (2005) 157-164; Tab. III-VIII;

10544 Die altbabylonischen Keilschrifttexte in der Sammlung des Päpstlichen Bibelinstituts. Or. 74 (2005) 317-351; Tab. XXVIII-XXXIX.

10545 **Metzler, Kai Alexander** Tempora in altbabylonischen literarischen Texten. AOAT 279: 2002 ⇒18,9192. [R]JAOS 125 (2005) 395-402 (*Cohen, Eran*).

10546 **Mittermayer, Catherine** Die Entwicklung der Tierkopfzeichen: eine Studie zur syro-mesopotamischen Keilschriftpaläographie des 3. und frühen 2. Jahrtausends v. Chr. AOAT 319: Müns 2005, Ugarit-Verlag vii; 161 pp. 3-934628-59-1.

10547 *Neumann, Hans* Keilschriftbibliographie, 63. 2004 (mit Nachträgen aus früheren Jahren). Or. 74 (2005) 1*-119*;

10548 Texte des 3. Jt. v.Chr. in sumerischer, akkadischer und hurritischer Sprache. Staatsverträge. TUAT N.F. 2: 2005 ⇒661. 1-26.

10549 *Oliva, Juan* New collations and remarks on Alalakh VII tablets. JNES 64 (2005) 1-21.

10550 *Paul, Shalom M.* Two proposed Janus parallelisms in Akkadian literature. Divrei Shalom. CHANE 23: 2005 <1995> ⇒273. 253-255.

10551 **Pedersén, Olof** Archive und Bibliotheken in Babylon: die Tontafeln der Grabung Robert Koldeweys 1899 - 1917. ADOG 25: Saarbrücken 2005, SDV xviii; 349 pp. 3-930843-98-6.

10552 **Pruzsinszky, Regine** Die Personennamen der Texte aus Emar. [E]*Wilhelm, Gernot; Owen, David I.* 2003 ⇒19,9940. [R]BiOr 62 (2005) 66-68 (*Tropper, J.*).

10553 [E]**Roth, Martha T.** CAD 12: P: The Assyrian Dictionary of the Oriental Institute of the Univ. of Chicago. Ch 2005, Oriental Institute xxx; 559 pp. 1-885923-35-X.

10554 *Röllig, Wolfgang* Keilschrift versus Alphabetschrift: Überlegungen zu den Epigraphs auf Keilschrifttafeln. [F]MILLARD, A.: LHBOTS 426: 2005 ⇒102. 119-126.

10555 *Römer, W.H.P.* Zur Deutung der Version A der Dichtung 'Bilgameš und Ḫuwawa' unter Berücksichtigung der Zedernwaldproblematik (Z. 9a; 11-12). UF 37 (2005) 517-555.

10556 *Schwemer, Daniel* Texte aus Alalaḫ;

10557 Texte aus Ugarit: Texte in akkadischer Sprache. Staatsverträge. TUAT N.F. 2: 2005 ⇒661. 182-186/163-177.

10558 **Sigrist, René Marcel** Old Babylonian account texts in the Horn Archaeological Museum. 2003 ⇒19,9949. [R]Or. 74 (2005) 409-421 (*Charpin, Dominique*).

10559 [E]**Spar, Ira; Lambert, Wilfred George** Literary and scholastic texts of the first millennium B.C. Cuneiform Texts in the Metropolitan Museum of Art 2: Turnhout 2005, Brepols xlvi; 354 pp. 2-50-3-51740-4. 132 fig.

10560 *Streck, Michael P.* Simply a seller, nothing but gods: the nominal suffix *-ān* in Old Babylonian. [M]DIAKONOFF, M. 2005 ⇒36. 233-43.

10561 *Tropper, Josef; Vita, Juan-Pablo* Der Energikus an Jussiven im Kanaano-Akkadischen der Amarna-Periode. Or. 74 (2005) 57-64.

10562 *Van der Westhuizen, Jasper P.* Morphology and morphosyntax of the adjective as attributive and predicative constructions in the Jerusalem-Amarna letters. [F]KLEIN, J. 2005 ⇒79. 600-623.

10563 [T]**Veenhof, Klaas R.** Letters in the Louvre. ABBU 14: Lei 2005, Brill xxxix; 232 pp. 90-04-15081-1.

10564 **Wasserman, Nathan** Style and form in Old-Babylonian literary texts. Cuneiform Monographs 27: 2003 ⇒19,9969; 20,9607. [R]Or. 74 (2005) 119-121 (*Lambert, W.G.*); ZA 95 (2005) 146-49 (*Streck, Michael P.*); WO 35 (2005) 228-231 (*Groneberg, Brigitte*); JSSt 50 (2005) 198-201 (*Black, Jeremy*).

10565 **Widell, Magnus** The administrative and economic Ur III texts from the city of Ur. 2003 ⇒19,9970. [R]JESHO 48 (2005) 122-124 (*Garfinkle, Steven J.*).

10566 *Zadok, Ran; Zadok, Tikva* Contributions to Neo/Late-Babylonian documentation. [F]KLEIN, J. 2005 ⇒79. 624-669.

### J2.7 Arabica

10567 *al-Farajat, Suleiman; al-Nawafleh, Sami* Kufic inscriptions from ad-Disa and Ramm. ADAJ 49 (2005) *29-*37. **A**.

10568 [E]**Badawi, El-Said; Carter, Michael G.; Gully, Adrian** Modern written Arabic: a comprehensive grammar. L 2005, Routledge xi; 812 pp. 0-415-13084-0. Bibl. 779-780.

10569 [E]**Behnstedt, Peter; Woidich, Manfred** Arabische Dialektgeographie: eine Einführung. HO 1/78: Lei 2005, Brill xviii; 269 pp. 90-04-14130-8. Bibl. 219-237.

10570 [E]**Elgibali, Alaa** Investigating Arabic: current parameters in analysis and learning. SStLL 42: Lei 2005, Brill xi; 223 pp. 90-04-13792-0. Bibl. 209-220.

10571 **Frantsouzoff, Serguei** Raybun: Hadran, Temple de la déesse 'Athtarum/'Astarum. Inventaire des inscriptions sudarabiques 5: 2001 ⇒17,9969. [R]Syria 82 (2005) 381-382 (*Bron, François*).

10572 *Lonnet, Antoine* Emprunts intra-sémitiques: l'exemple des emprunts arabes en sudarabique moderne. AuOr 23 (2005) 199-206.

10573 *Macdonald, Michael C.A.* The Safaitic inscriptions at Dura Europos. MHILLERS, D.: 2005 ⇒61. 118-129.

10574 *Nebes, Norbert* Sabäische Texte. Staatsverträge. TUAT N.F. 2: 2005 ⇒661. 331-367.

10575 *Neuwirth, Angelika* Emblems of exile: Layla and Majnun in Egypt, Palestine, Israel and Lebanon. MUSJ 58 (2005) 163-187.

10576 *Niewöhner-Eberhard, Elke* Schutzstreifen in einem Bremer Evangeliar: zwei Stofffragmente mit arabischer Inschrift aus dem Lüneburger Schatz der Goldenen Tafel. CoMa 52/53 (2005) 47-58.

10577 *Rostagno Giaiero, Paolo* Tre recensioni arabe della Storia di Ḥayqar. Il saggio Ahiqar. StBi 148: 2005 ⇒52. 227-253.

10578 **Ryding, Karin C.** A reference grammar of modern standard Arabic. C 2005, CUP xxv; 708 pp. 0-521-77151-X. Bibl. 691-699.

## J3.0 Aegyptia

10579 **Allen, James P.** The Heqanakht papyri. 2002 ⇒19,9985. RAntiquity 79 (2005) 464-465 (*Tait, John*).

10580 T**Allen, James P.** The ancient Egyptian pyramid texts. E*Der Manuelian, Peter*: SBL.Writings from the Ancient World 23: Atlanta, GA 2005, SBL x; 471 pp. $40. 1-58983-182-9. Bibl. 419-23.

10581 **Altenmüller, Hartwig** Einführung in die Hieroglyphenschrift. Ha 2005, Buske vii; 182 pp. €19.80. 3-87548-373-1. RLingAeg 13 (2005) 273-278 (*Schenkel, Wolfgang*).

10582 **Barbotin, Christophe** La voix des hiéroglyphes: promenade au Département des antiquités égyptiennes du Musée du Louvre. P 2005, Khéops 240 pp. 2-9504368-9-7. Num. ill.; Bibl. 204-215.

10583 **Bárta, Miroslav** Sinuhe, the bible, and the patriarchs. 2003 ⇒20, 9620. RJEA 91 (2005) 219-220 (*Enmarch, Roland*).

10584 *Betrò, Marilina* La tradizione di Ahiqar in Egitto. Il saggio Ahiqar. StBi 148: 2005 ⇒52. 177-191.

10585 **Bresciani, Edda; Menchetti, Angiolo** Nozioni elementari di grammatica demotica: con liste grafiche e letture demotiche di Angiolo Menchetti. Biblioteca di studi egittologici 2: 2002 ⇒18,9239. REnchoria 29 (2004-2005) 187-191 (*Hoffmann, Friedhelm*).

10586 *Breyer, Francis* Ägyptische Texte: die Inschrift des Anchtifi aus Mo'alla. Staatsverträge. TUAT N.F. 2: 2005 ⇒661. 187-196.

10587 *Breyer, Francis, al.*, Ägyptische Texte. Staatsverträge. TUAT N.F. 2: 2005 ⇒661. 187-282.

10588 E**Brinker, A.A. den; Vleeming, Sven P.; Muhs, Brian P.** A berichtigungsliste of demotic documents: Part A: Papyrus editions ; Part B: Ostrakon editions and various publications. Lv 2005, Peeters 2 vols; lii + viii; 861 pp. 90-429-1603-6/4-4.

10589 **Burkard, Günter; Thissen, Heinz J.** Einführung in die ägyptische Literaturgeschichte I–Altes und Mittleres Reich. Einführungen und Quellentexte zur Ägyptologie 1: 2003 ⇒19,9995; 20,9622. ROLZ 100 (2005) 385-387 (*Eyre, Christopher*); JEA 91 (2005) 205-207 (*Enmarch, Roland*).

10590 **Carrier, Claude** *Textes des sarcophages* du Moyen Empire égyptien. Champollion: Monaco 2004, Du Rocher 3 vols; xxix; 2732 pp. 2-2680-5229X. Tome I: spells [1] à [354]; Tome II: spells [355] à [787]; Tome III: spells [788] à [1186].

10591 [E]**Collier, Mark; Quirke, Stephen** The UCL Lahun papyri : religious, literary, legal, mathematical, and medical. BAR Intern. Ser. 1209: Oxf 2004, Archaeopress iii; 160 pp. £34. 18417-15727. Contrib. *Annette Imhausen; Jim Ritter*; CD-ROM.

10592 **Cuvigny, Hélène** Ostraca de Krokodilô: la correspondance militaire et sa circulation, O. Krok. 1-151. FIFAO 51: Cairo 2005, Institut Français d'Archéologie Orientale xii; 283 pp. 2-7247-0370-7.

10593 **Darnell, John Coleman** Theban desert road survey in the Egyptian Western desert: vol. 1: Gebel Tjauti rock inscriptions 1-45 and Wadi el-Hôl rock inscriptions 1-45. UCOIP 119: 2002 ⇒18,9243. [R]Or. 74 (2005) 114-115 (*Roccati, Alessandro*).

10594 *Dias, Geraldo José Amadeu Coelho* O nome de *Israel* na estela do faraó *Merenptah*. Did(L) 35 (2005) 23-34.

10595 **Edel, Elmar; Görg, Manfred** Die Ortsnamenlisten im nördlichen Säulenhof des Totentempels Amenophis' III. ÄA 50: Wsb 2005, Harrassowitz viii; 218 pp. 3-447-05219-8.

10596 **Gabolde, Luc** Monuments décorés en bas relief aux noms de Thoutmosis II et Hatchepsout à Karnak. Mémoires de l'Institut Français d'Archéologie Orientale du Caire 123: Le Caire 2005, Institut Français d'Archéologie Orientale 2 vols. 2-7247-0405-3.

10597 **Gasse, Annie** Ostraca littéraires de Deir al-Médina: Nos. 1775-1873 et 1156. Documents des fouilles 44: 5 Le Caire 2005, Institut Français d'Archéologie Orientale 173 pp. 2-7247-0399-5. Photo. *Alain Lecler*.

10598 *Görg, Manfred* Ionien und Kleinasien in früher ausserbiblischer Bezeugung. BN 127 (2005) 5-10.

10599 [T]**Grandet, Pierre** Contes de l'Egypte ancienne. P 2005 <1998>, Khéops xi; 193 pp. €22. 29504-36889.

10600 **Hannig, Rainer** Ägyptisches Wörterbuch, 1: Altes Reich und Erste Zwischenzeit. 2003 ⇒19,10009. [R]JNES 64 (2005) 312-313 (*Allen, James P.*); LingAeg 13 (2005) 231-263 (*Meeks, Dimitri*).

10601 *Ignatov, Sergei* The name of the serpent in the ancient Egyptian story of the shipwrecked sailor. GöMisz 206 (2005) 33-37.

10602 *Jenni, Hanna* Die pronominalen Erweiterungen beim Imperativ und der Ausdruck verbaler Reflexivität im Ägyptischen. ZÄS 132/2 (2005) 112-122.

10603 **Junge, Friedrich** Late Egyptian grammar: an introduction. [T]*Warburton, David* 2001 ⇒17,8667... 20,9642. [R]JNES 64 (2005) 117-121 (*McClain, J. Brett*).

10604 [E]**Kahl, Jochem**, *al.*, Frühägyptisches Wörterbuch, 3. 2003 ⇒20, 9644. Lief. ḥ-ḫ. [R]ArOr 73 (2005) 373-374 (*Landgráfová, Renata*).

10605 **Kemp, Barry J.** 100 hieroglyphs: think like an Egyptian. L 2005, Macmillan xv; 256 pp. 1-86207-658-8.

10606 *Kuhlmann, Klaus P.* Der "Wasserberg des Djedefe" (Chufu 01/1): ein Lagerplatz mit Expeditionsinschriften der 4. Dynastie im Raum der Oase Dachla. MDAI.K 61 (2005) 243-289.

10607 *Malek, Jaromir* A significant development in hieroglyphic word-processing: the release of the new InScribe 2004 for Mircrosoft® Windows. DiscEg 61 (2005) 61-66.

10608 *Moers, Gerald* Ägyptische Texte: der Palästinafeldzug Scheschonqs I. Staatsverträge. TUAT N.F. 2: 2005 ⇒661. 246-271.

10609 *Morenz, Ludwig D.* Em-habs Feldzugsbericht: bild-textliche Inszenierung von "großer Geschichte" im Spiegel der Elite. Ä&L 15 (2005) 169-180.

10610 **Morenz, Ludwig** Bild-Buchstaben und symbolische Zeichen: die Herausbildung der Schrift in der hohen Kultur Altägyptens. OBO 205: 2004 ⇒20,9654. [R]BiOr 62 (2005) 451-459 (*David, Arlette*); DiscEg 61 (2005) 89-94 (*DuQuesne, Terence*); RBLit (2005)* (*Moore, Michael*).

10611 *Müller, Matthias* Ägyptische Texte: die Krönungsinschrift der Hatschepsut. Staatsverträge. TUAT N.F. 2: 2005 ⇒661. 197-211.

10612 **Obsomer, Claude** Égyptien hiéroglyphique: grammaire pratique du Moyen Égyptien et exercices d'application. Langues et cultures anciennes 1: Bru 2003, Safran 191 pp. 2-9600371-1-1. Bibl. 13-14.

10613 *Peust, Carsten* Ägyptische Texte: aus der Chronik des Prinzen und Hohepriesters Osorkon (Jahr 11 Takeloths II.). Staatsverträge. TUAT N.F. 2: 2005 ⇒661. 272-278.

10614 **Quack, Joachim Friedrich** Einführung in die altägyptische Literaturgeschichte, 3: die demotische und gräko-ägyptische Literatur. Einführungen und Quellentexte zur Ägyptologie 3: Müns 2005, LIT 216 pp. €19.90. 38258-82225. [R]LingAeg 13 (2005) 279-83 (*Schentuleit, Maren*); Enchoria 29 (2004-5) 106-118 (*Stadler, Martin A.*).

10615 **Quirke, Stephen** Egyptian literature 1800 BC: questions and readings. Egyptology 2: 2004 ⇒20,9662. [R]DiscEg 62 (2005) 99-102 (*Enmarch, Roland*).

10616 **Ray, J.D.** Demotic papyri and ostraca from Qasr Ibrim. Texts from Excavations, Memoir 13: L 2005, Egypt Exploration Society xi; 62 pp. £25. 0-85698-158-3.

10617 *Recklinghausen, Daniel von* Ägyptische Quellen zum Judentum. ZÄS 132/2 (2005) 147-160.

10618 **Schipper, Bernd Ulrich** Die Erzählung des Wenamun: ein Literaturwerk im Spannungsfeld von Politik, Geschichte und Religion. OBO 209: FrS 2005, Academic xii; 384 pp. FS118. 3-7278-1504-3. Bibl. 340-375.

10619 **Schweitzer, Simon D.** Schrift und Sprache der 4. Dynastie. MENES 3; Studien zur Kultur und Sprache der ägyptischen Frühzeit und des Alten Reiches 3: Wsb 2005, Harrassowitz xi; 650 pp. €125. 3-447-05137-X. Bibl. 637-650.

10620 *Seidlmayer, Stephan Johannes* Die neue Version des *Thesaurus Linguae Aegyptiae* im Internet. GöMisz 207 (2005) 107-111.

10621 [ET]**Smith, Mark** Papyrus Harkness (MMA 31.9.7). Oxf 2005, Griffith Institute xi; 366 pp. £95. 09004-1684X.

10622 *Sternberg-el Hotabi, Heike* Ägyptische Texte: der Denkstein der Sematauifenacht. Staatsverträge. 2005 ⇒661. 279-282.

10623 **Strudwick, Nigel** Texts from the pyramid age. [E]*Leprohon, Ronald J.*: SBL.Writings from the Ancient World 16: Lei 2005, Brill xxxvii; 522 pp. $40. 90-04-13048-9. Bibl. 465-502.

10624 *Ullmann, Martina* Zur Lesung der Inschrift auf der Säule Antefs II. aus Karnak. ZÄS 132/2 (2005) 166-172.

10625 **Van der Molen, Rami** An analytical concordance of the verb, the negation and the syntax in Egyptian coffin texts. HO 1/77: Lei 2005, Brill 2 vols; xvi; 952; 992 pp. €499/$669. 90-04-14213-4.

10626 **Vleeming, Sven P.** Some coins of Artaxerxes and other short texts in the Demotic script. Studia Demotica 5: 2001 ⇒17,8687. ROLZ 100 (2005) 394-402 (*Stadler, Martin A.*).

10627 *Werning, Daniel A.* Ägyptische Texte: die Beth-Sche'an-Gedenkstele Sethos' I. Staatsverträge. TUAT N.F. 2: 2005 ⇒661. 221-227.

## J3.4 Coptica

10628 **Aufrère, Sydney; Bosson, Nathalie** Guillaume BONJOUR: Elementa linguae copticae: grammaire inédite du XVIIe siècle. COr 24: Genève 2005, Cramer civ; 191 pp. €100. Préf. *Ariel Shisha-Halevy*.

10629 *Boud'hors, Anne; Nakano, Chièmi* Vestiges bibliques en Copte fayoumique. JCoS 7 (2005) 137-139.

10630 E**Boud'Hors, Anne; Nancy, O.** Ostraca grecs et coptes des fouilles de Jean MASPERO à Baouit. BEC 17: 2004 ⇒20,9679. RBiOr 62 (2005) 518-523 (*Richter, Tonio Sebastian*).

10631 **Calament, Florence** La Révélation d'Antinoé par Albert GAYET: histoire, archéologie, muséographie. BEC 18.1-2: Le Caire 2005, Institut Français d'Archéologie Orientale du Caire 2 vols; 616 pp. €58. 978-27247-03665. Bibl. vol. 2, 573-612.

10632 *Choat, Malcolm* Thomas the "wanderer" in a Coptic list of the apostles. Or. 74 (2005) 83-85.

10633 *Hasznos, Andrea* Die Struktur der Konsekutivsätze im koptischen Neuen Testament. Enchoria 29 (2004/2005) 32-43.

10634 *Hedrick, Charles W.* A revelation discourse of Jesus. JCoS 7 (2005) 13-15.

10635 *Joest, Christoph* PACHOMs Gebet für drei Menschengruppen und die Irrtümer moderner Übersetzungen. Muséon 118 (2005) 321-26.

10636 **Layton, Bentley** A Coptic grammar: with chrestomathy and glossary: Sahidic dialect. PLO 20: 22004 <2000> ⇒20,9686. RRBLit 7 (2005) 80-84 (*Snyder, Glenn*).

10637 E**Layton, Bentley** Coptic Gnostic chrestomathy: a selection of Coptic texts with grammatical analysis and glossary. 2004 ⇒20, 9687. RBiOr 62 (2005) 517-518 (*Beltz, Walter*); Muséon 118 (2005) 182-183 (*Brankaer, Joanna*).

10638 *Lucchesi, Enzo* Nouvelles glanures pachômiennes. Or. 74 (2005) 86-90;

10639 Une lettre de SÉVÈRE d'Antioche à Thomas, évêque de Germanice, en version copte. Muséon 118 (2005) 327-331.

10640 *MacCoull, Leslie S.B.* Coptic wisdom poetry: the Solomon complex redux. OrChr 89 (2005) 86-92.

T**Righi, D.** SEVERIANUS Gabalensis: In apostolos 2004 ⇒1686.

10641 *Schroeder, Caroline T.* SHENOUTE of Atripe on the resurrection. Arc 33 (2005) 123-137.

10642 **Störk, Lothar** Koptische Handschriften, 4. VOHD 21/4: 2002 ⇒ 18,9316; 19,10055. ROr. 74 (2005) 145-146 (*Luisier, Philippe*).

10643 *Torallas Tovar, Sofía* Los fragmentos coptos bíblicos del fondo Roca-Puig de la Abadía de Montserrat. CCO 2 (2005) 287-296.

10644 *Wees, Jennifer* Room with a limited view: Coptic clairvoyance in Hellenistic Egypt. LTP 61/2 (2005) 261-272.

10645 *Young, Dwight W.* On a possible relationship between P. Vindob. K 9764 and K 9787. Arc 33 (2005) 138-150.

## J3.8 Aethiopica

10646 **Contenson, Henri de** Antiquités éthiopiennes: d'Axoum á Haoulti. Bibliothéque Peiresc 16: Saint-Maur-des-Fossés 2005, Sepia 226 pp. 2-84280-098-2. Bibl. 215-226.

10647 *Kropp, Manfred* Der äthiopische Satan = saytan und seine koranischen Ausläufer; mit einer Bemerkung über verbales Steinigen. OrChr 89 (2005) 93-102.

10648 *Lucchesi, Enzo* La "Vorlage" arabe du Livre du coq éthiopien. Or. 74 (2005) 91-92.

10649 *Lusini, Gianfrancesco* La Storia di Ahiqar in versione etiopica. Il saggio Ahiqar. StBi 148: 2005 ⇒52. 255-266.

10650 *Menuta, Fekede* Derivation of verbs in Eža. Orient 40 (2005) 172-189.

10651 **Procházka, Stephan** Altäthiopische Studiengrammatik. OBO.Subsidia linguistica 2: Gö 2005, Vandenhoeck & R. xii; 109 pp. €21. 90. 3-525-26409-7.

10652 **Raineri, Osvaldo** Salmi etiopici di Cristo e della Vergine. Preghiere dalla varie tradizioni 1: R 2005, Appunti di Viaggio 191 pp. 88-87164-55-X.

## J4.0 Anatolica; *Phrygian, Lydian, Lycian*; Georgica

10653 *Alaura, Silvia* Fleh- und Unterwerfungsgesten in den hethitischen Texten. AltOrF 32 (2005) 375-385.

10654 *Çelik, Bahattin* A new stele base of the Late Hittite Period from Siverek-Şanliurfa. Anat. 28 (2005) 17-24.

10655 *Dardano, Paola* I costrutti perifrastici con il verbo ḫar(k)- dell'ittito: stato della questione e prospettive di metodo. Or. 74 (2005) 93-113.

10656 *De Martino, Stefano* Hittite letters from the time of Tutḫaliya I/II, Arnuwanda I and Tutḫaliya III. AltOrF 32 (2005) 291-321.

10657 **Francia, Rita** Lineamenti di grammatica ittita. Studia Asiana 4: R 2005, Herder vi; 139 pp. €20. 88-89670-045. Bibl. 130-135.

10658 **García Trabazo, José Virgilio; Groddek, Detlev** Hethitische Texte in Transkription KUB 58. Dresdner Beiträge zur Hethitologie 18: Wsb 2005, Harrassowitz x; 300 pp. 3447-05245-7.

10659 *Haas, Volkert* Die Erzählungen von den zwei Brüdern, vom Fischer und dem Findelkind sowie vom Jäger Keššе. AltOrF 32 (2005) 360-374.

10660 *Hawkins, J. David; Klinger, Jörg* Herrscherinschriften und andere Dokumente zur politischen Geschichte des Hethiterreiches. Staatsverträge. TUAT N.F. 2: 2005 ⇒661. 139-159.

10661 *Kitchen, Kenneth A.* The hieroglyphic inscriptions of the neo-Hittite states (c. 1200-700 BC): a fresh source of background to the Hebrew Bible. The OT in its world. OTS 52: 2005 ⇒749. 117-134.

10662 *Klinger, Jörg; Schwemer, Daniel; Wilhelm, Gernot* Staatsverträge mit dem Hethiterreich. Staatsverträge. TUAT N.F. 2: 2005 ⇒661. 95-138.

10663 **Kosak, Silvin; Müller, Gerfrid** Konkordanz der hethitischen Keilschrifttafeln. Hethitologie Portal Mainz, Materialien 1-5: Wsb 2005, Harrassowitz 5 vols. 3-447-05279-1/80-5/81-3//82-1/83-X.

10664 [E]*Lebrun, René* Syro Anatolica scripta minora VI. Muséon 118 (2005) 209-217.

10665 **Miller, Jared L.** Texte aus dem Bezirk des grossen Tempels V. KBo 53: B 2005, Mann xx; 46 pp. 3-7861-2519-8.

10666 [E]**Otten, Heinrich; Rüster, Christel; Wilhelm, Gernot** Textfunde von Büyükkale aus den Jahren 1955-1959. KBo 46: 2004 ⇒20, 9715. [R]OLZ 100 (2005) 58-61 (*Haas, V.; Wegner, I.*);

10667 Textfunde von Büyükkale aus den Jahren 1957-2002. KBo 47: B 2005, Mann xix pp; 58 Bl. 3-7861-2518-X.

10668 **Parmegiani, Neda** Konkordanzen. Corpus der Hurritischen Sprachdenkmäler 1; die Texte aus Bogazköy 10: R 2005, Istituto di Studi sulle Civiltà dell'Egeo e del Vicino Oriente 127 pp. 88-8734-5-12-0.

10669 **Payne, Annick** Hieroglyphic Luwian. Elementa Linguarum Orientis ELO 3: 2004 ⇒20,9716. [R]RBLit (2005)* (*Gee, John*).

10670 *Richter, Thomas* Kleine Beiträge zum hurritischen Wörterbuch. AltOrF 32 (2005) 23-44.

10671 **Roszkowska-Mutschler, Hanna** Hethitische Texte in Transkription. KBo 45; Dresdner Beiträge zur Hethitologie 16: Wsb 2005, Harrassowitz xiii; 361 pp. €34. 3-447-05192-2. [R]UF 36 (2004) 707-710 (*Müller, G.G.W.; Sakuma, Y.*).

10672 **Trémouille, Marie-Claude** Texte verschiedenen Inhalts. Corpus der Hurritischen Sprachdenkmäler 1,. die Texte aus Bogazköy 8: R 2005, Istituto di Studi sulle Civiltà dell'Egeo e del Vicino Oriente xxviii; 362 pp.

10673 *Van den Hout, Theo* On the nature of the tablet collections of Ḫattuša. SMEA 47 (2005) 277-289.

10674 *Woudhuizen, F.C.* The Luwian hieroglyphic inscription on the stele from Karahöyük-Elbistan. AWE 2 (2003) 211-224.

10675 **Zeilfelder, Susanne** Hittite exercise book. [T]*Wagner, Esther-Miriam:*: Dresdner Beiträge zur Hethitologie 17: Wsb 2005, Harrassowitz 309 pp. €29. 3-447-05206-6. Bibl. 301-309.

10676 **Gérard, Raphaël** Phonétique et morphologie de la langue lydienne. BCILL 114: Lv 2005, Peeters 130 pp. €15. 90-429-1574-9.

10677 **Melchert, H. Craig** A dictionary of the Lycian language. AA 2004, Beech Stave xvii; 138 pp. 0-9747927-0-5. Bibl. xiii-xvii.

10678 **Imnaišvili, V.** Älteste georgische Handschriften in Österreich. 2004 ⇒20,9729. [R]Georgica 28 (2005) 235-237 (*Tschumburidse, Tamar*).

## J5.1 Graeca grammatica

10679 **Adrados, Francisco Rodriguez** A history of the Greek language: from its origins to the present. [T]*Rojas del Canto, Francisca*: Lei 2005, Brill xix; 345 pp. 90-04-12835-2. Bibl. 319-342.

10680 **Allan, Rutger** The middle voice in Ancient Greek: a study of polysemy. 2003 ⇒19,10095. [R]AnCl 74 (2005) 390-91 (*Bile, Monique*).

10681 **Bartonek, Antonin** Handbuch des mykenischen Griechisch. 2003 ⇒19,10097. [R]BSL 100/2 (2005) 186-193 (*Guilleux, Nicole*).

10682 *Braun, Willi* Rhetoric, rhetoricality, and discourse performances. Rhetoric and reality. SCJud 16: 2005 ⇒515. 1-26.

10683 **Buijs, M.** Clause combining in ancient Greek narrative discourse: the distribution of subclauses and participial clauses in XENOPHON's *Hellenica* and *Anabasis*. [D]*Sicking, C.M.J.*: Mn.S 260: Lei 2005, Brill x; 277 pp. €85/$115. 90041-42509. Diss. Leiden [NTAb 49,626].

10684 **Caragounis, Chrys C.** The development of Greek and the New Testament: morphology, syntax, phonology, and textual transmission. WUNT 167: 2004 ⇒20,9734. [R]NT 47 (2005) 394-396 (*Elliott, J.K.*); WThJ 67 (2005) 391-404 [Resp. 405-415] (*Silva, Moisés*); NedThT 59/1 (2005) 21-30 (*Van der Horst, Pieter W.*).

10685 **Coulter, George H.** Expressions of agency in ancient Greek. C 2005, CUP x; 288 pp. 0-521-84789-3. Bibl. 271-276.

10686 **Delgado Jara, I.** Dizionario griego-español del Nuevo Testamento. S 2005, Publ. de la Univ. Pont. de Salamanca 228 pp.

10687 **Dobson, John H.** J'apprends le grec du Nouveau Testament. 2004 ⇒20,9740. [R]Ḥokhma 88 (2005) 88-89 (*Décoppet, Alain*);

10688 Learn New Testament Greek. Carlisle [3]2005 <1988>, Piquant xiii; 384 pp. $30. 0-8010-31060. With Audio CD-ROM.

10689 **Duff, Jeremy** The elements of New Testament Greek. C [3]2005, CUP xiii; 340 pp. €15/$24. 0-521-75551-4.

10690 **Färber, Hans; Lindemann, Hans** Griechische Grammatik, 2: Satzlehre, Dialektgrammatik und Metrik. Sprachwissenschaftliche Studienbücher: Heid 2003 <1957>, Winter 172 pp. €22. 38253-13-719. 2nd unchanged ed.

10691 **George, Coulter H.** Expressions of agency in ancient Greek. C 2005, CUP x; 288 pp. £50. 0521-847893.

10692 *Greenlee, J. Harold* New Testament circumstantial participles. JOT 1/1 (2005) 57-59.

10693 *Hasznos, Andrea* A Greek accusativus cum infinitivo construction and its equivalents in Coptic. ZÄS 132/1 (2005) 92-93.

10694 *Hire, P.* The Cambridge New Greek Lexicon project. ClW 98/2 (2005) 179-185 [NTAb 49,474].

10695 *James, Patrick* Participial complementation in Roman and Byzantine documentary papyri: ἐπίσταμαι, μανθάνω, εὑρίσκω. JGRChJ 2 (2005) 153-167.

10696 *Joosten, Jan* The ingredients of New Testament Greek. AnBru 10 (2005) 56-69.

10697 **Koeker, J.D.** What you need to know about New Testament Greek: teach yourself to read 150 verses in the Greek New Testament. North Richland Hills, TX 2005, BIBAL vii; 124 pp. $20. 19410-3-7908. [NTAb 50,579].

10698 *Koffi, Ettien* Logical subjects, grammatical subjects, and the translation of Greek person and number agreement. JOT 1/2 (2005)* 21-33.

10699 **Lee, John A.L.** A history of New Testament lexicography. Studies in Biblical Greek 8: 2003 ⇒19,10109; 20,9754. [R]ThLZ 130 (2005) 490-492 (*Caragounis, Chrys C.*); EThL 81 (2005) 519-521 (*Van Belle, G.*); ThR 70 (2005) 504-507 (*Du Toit, David S.*); RBLit 7 (2005) 516-521 (*Kraus, Thomas J.*);

10700 Greek accents in eight lessons. Sydney 2005, Macquarie Univ. $A15. 1-741381-541.

10701 **Lindauer, Josef; Hotz, Rudolf; Hotz, Michael** Hellenisti: Grundkurs der hellenistisch-griechischen Bibelsprache. Mü 2005, EOS 168; [16] pp. 3-8306-7231-4.

10702 **Lorente Fernández, Paula** L'aspect verbal en grec ancien: le choix des thèmes verbaux chez ISOCRATE. BCILL 111: 2003 ⇒19, 10110. [R]AnCl 74 (2005) 391-393 (*Donnet, Daniel*).

10703 **Luraghi, Silvia** On the meaning of prepositions and cases: the expression of semantic roles in Ancient Greek. 2003 ⇒20,9756. [R]BSL 100/2 (2005) 198-199 (*Jacquinod, Bernard*).

10704 **Machem, J. Gresham** New Testament Greek for beginners. [E]*McCartney, Dan* Upper Saddle River, N.J. [2]2004, Pearson 399 pp. $54.67. [R]RBLit 7 (2005) 89-94 (*Vance, Laurence*).

10705 **Merritt, Michael A.** New Testament Greek for laymen. 2002 ⇒ 19,10113. [R]RBLit (2005)* (*Walton, Stephen J.*).

10706 *Mitiku, Abera* The use of οὐ μή in the New Testament: emphatic or mild negation?. Faith & Mission 22/2 (2005) 85-104.

10707 **O'Donnell, Matthew Brook** Corpus linguistics and the Greek of the New Testament. New Testament Monographs 6: Shf 2005, Phoenix xxi; 552 pp. $95. 1-905048-11-4. Bibl. 488-533.

10708 *Perdicoyianni-Paléologou, Hélène* Étude pragmatique des pronoms personnels dans le Nouveau Testament. RCCM 47 (2005) 305-320.

10709 *Picirilli, R.E.* The meaning of the tenses in New Testament Greek: where are we?. JETS 48 (2005) 533-555 [NTAb 50,245].

10710 *Reiser, Marius* Die Quellen des neutestamentlichen Griechisch und die Frage des Judengriechischen in der Forschungsgeschichte von 1689-1989. BZ 49 (2005) 46-59.

10711 **Renaud, Jean-Michel; Wathelet, Paul** Autonoos: le grec ancien pour grands débutants. 2003 ⇒19,10119; 20,9766. [R]REG 118 (2005) 318-321 (*Blanc, Alain*).

10712 *Rico, Christophe* L'aspect verbal dans le Nouveau Testament: vers une définition. RB 112 (2005) 385-416.

10713 **Rinaldi, Umberto** Il parlato ignoto: saggio sulla fonologia diacronica del greco. Padova 2005, vi, 280 pp. 88873-00445. Bibl. 257-280.

10714 *Sebesta, J.L.* Textbooks in Greek and Latin: 2005 supplementary survey. ClW 98/3 (2005) 337-341 [NTAb 49,575].

10715 **Siebenthal, Heinrich von** Kurzgrammatik zum griechischen Neuen Testament. Gießen 2005, Brunnen xiv; 172 pp. €19.90.

**Silzer, P.**, *al.*, How biblical languages work 2004 ⇒10266.

10716 *Swart, G.J.* Non-past referring imperfects in the New Testament: a test case for an anti-anti-anti-Porter position. HTSTS 61 (2005) 1085-1099 [NTAb 51,15].

10717 [E]**Trapp, Erich** Lexikon zur byzantinischen Gräzität: besonders des 9.-12. Jahrhunderts, Fasz. 5. (l - paliánthropos). DÖAW.PH 326: W 2005, Verl. d. Österr. Akad. d. Wiss. 907-1178 pp. 3-7001-3344-8.

10718 *Voelz, J.W.* Word order. ConJ 31 (2005) 425-427 [NTAb 50,245].

10719 *Wifstrand, Albert* A problem concerning word order in the New Testament <1949> 59-70;

10720 Language and style of the New Testament <1968> 71-77;

10721 Greek prose style: an historical survey <1952> 81-92;

10722 Greek and modern prose style <1944> 93-110;

10723 The centre <1976>. Epochs and styles. WUNT 179: 2005 ⇒325. 204-212.

10724 **Young, Norman H.** Syntax lists for students of New Testament Greek. 2001 ⇒17,8742; 19,10132. [R]NT 47 (2005) 296-297 (*Black, David A.*).

## J5.2 *Voces ordine alphabetico consonantium* graecarum

10725 ἄνθρωπος: *Barr, James* The etymology of ἄνθρωπος: a suggestion. [F]ULLENDORFF, E.: SStLL 47: 2005 ⇒154. 160-164.

10726 ἀγαπάω; φιλέω: *Voorwinde, Stephen* Agapao and phileo–is there a difference? RTR 64/2 (2005) 76-90.

10727 ἀδελφός:: *Harland, Philip A.* Familial dimensions of group identity: "brothers" (ἀδελφοί) in associations of the Greek east. JBL 124 (2005) 491-513.

10728 ἀποκατάστᾰσις: **Harmon, Steven R.** Every knee should bow: biblical rationales for universal salvation in early christian thought. Ment. *Clemens Alexandrinus; Origenes; Gregorius Nyssa* 2003 ⇒ 19,10138. [R]RExp 102 (2005) 162-164 (*Humphreys, Fisher*).

10729 ἀποκρίννομαι: *Elliott, J. Keith* The aorist middle of ἀποκρίννομαι. ZNW 96 (2005) 126-128.

10730 ἀπορριπτειν: *Weissert, David* ἀπορριπτειν: "to pass over in silence": dmm/dmh versus rmh in LXX of Jeremiah and Minor Prophets. Textus 22 (2005) 77-86 [Jer 8,14; 47,5; 51,6; Hos 10,7-15; Obad 5].

10731 ἀπόστολος: *Ovey, Michael* The authority of apostles. ChM 119/2 (2005) 147-158.

10732 βεβαιόω; στηρίζω: *Otto, Rubén R.* La misión posbautismal de la iglesia expresada en los verbos sterizo y bebaioo. DavarLogos 4/1 (2005) 39-48.

10733 γάρ: *Ito, A.* Reconsideration of the particle γάρ with special reference to its translation in the Shinkaiyaku Seisho (New Japanese Bible). Exegetica [Tokyo] 16 (2005) 55-63 [NTAb 50,247]. **J.**

10734 γίνομαι: *Good, R.* Γίνομαι and Christ's 'becomings'. Affirmation & Critique [Anaheim, CA] 10/1 (2005) 41-46.

10735 δαιμονισθεὶς: *Käsemann, Ernst* Die theologische Relevanz des Wortes "Besessenheit" im Neuen Testament. In der Nachfolge. 2005 ⇒236. 58-68.

10736 διακρίνω: *DeGraaf, D.* Some doubts about doubt: the New Testament use of ΔΙΑΚΡΙΝΩ. JETS 48 (2005) 733-755 [NTAb 50,246].

10737 διακονία: **Hentschel, Anni G.** Diakonia im Neuen Testament: eine Untersuchung der Wortwendung bei Paulus und Lukas unter besonderer Berücksichtigung der Rolle der Frauen. [D]*Wischmeyer, O.*: 2005 Diss. Erlangen-Nürnberg [ThLZ 131,336].

10738 δικαιοσύνη: *Käsemann, Ernst* Die göttliche und die bürgerliche Gerechtigkeit. In der Nachfolge. 2005 ⇒236. 302-314.

10739 δικαιοσύνη: *Limbeck, Meinrad* Was meint die Bibel mit Gerechtigkeit?: ein Überblick. BiHe 41/164 (2005) 4-7.

10740 Ἕλληνες: *Lund, Allan* Hellenentum und Hellenizität: zur Ethnogenese und zur Ethnizität der antiken Hellenen. Hist. 54 (2005) 1-17.

10741 ἔθος: *Woerther, F.* Aux origines de la notion rhétorique de l'*èthos*. REG 118 (2005) 79-116 [NTAb 50,560].

10742 ἐπισκοπη: *Carozza, Gianni* L'*episkopé*_nel Nuovo Testamento. Firmana 38-39 (2005) 47-60.

10743 εὐαγγέλιον: *Dickson, John P.* Gospel as news: εὐαγγελ- from ARISTOPHANES to the apostle Paul. NTS 51 (2005) 212-230 [Rom 1,15];

10744 *Horbury, William* 'Gospel' in Herodian Judaea. [F]STANTON, G. 2005 ⇒138. 7-30.

10745 θυσία: *Pernot, Laurent* Le sacrifice dans la littérature grecque de l'époque impériale. La cuisine et l'autel. BEHE.R 124: 2005 ⇒539. 317-328.

10746 ἰδού: *Uchida, K.* On the translation of ἰδού outside the gospels in the Shinkaiyaku Seisho (New Japanese Bible). Exegetica [Tokyo] 16 (2005) 65-79 [NTAb 50,248].

10747 Ἰουδαῖοι: *Newman, Barclay M.* Those Jews…again...and again. JOT 1/1 (2005)* 1-6.

10748 Ἰσραήλ: *Fiedler, Peter* 'Das Israel Gottes' im Neuen Testament—die Kirche oder das jüdische Volk?. Studien zur biblischen Grundlegung. SBAB 35: 2005 <1990> ⇒209. 120-144;

10749 *Pritz, Ray A.* Remnant theology and the salvation of Israel. Ung teologi 38/2 (2005) 15-23.

10750 καταπέτασμα: *Gurtner, Daniel M.* LXX syntax and the identity of the NT veil. NT 47 (2005) 344-353 [Mt 27,51; Mk 15,38; Lk 23, 45; Heb 6,19; 9,3; 10,20].

10751 κόσμος: *Wyrwa, Dietmar* Kosmos. RAC 165/166. 2005 ⇒973. 614-761;

10752 *Theobald, Michael* 'Welt' bei Paulus und Johannes. IKaZ 34 (2005) 435-447.

10753 κύριος: *Wengst, Klaus* Erwägungen zur Übersetzung von "kyrios" im Neuen Testament. Die Bibel—übersetzt. 2005 ⇒423. 178-183.

10754 Μαριὰμ: *Good, Deirdre* What does it mean to call Mary Mariam?. A feminist companion to mariology. 2005 ⇒431. 99-106.

10755 μαρτυς: *Chrétien, Jean-Louis* Neuf propositions sur le concept chrétien de témoignage. Philosophie 88 (2005) 75-94.

10756 μετά: *Luraghi, Silvia* The history of the Greek preposition μετά: from polysemy to the creation of homonyms. Glotta 81 (2005) 130-159.

10757 μονόκερως: *Hedrick, C.W.* Making oxen out of unicorns. The Fourth R [Santa Rosa, CA] 18/4 (2005) 17 [NTAb 50,14].

10758 οἰκονομία: **Richter, Gerhard** Oikonomia: der Gebrauch des Wortes Oikonomia im Neuen Testament, bei den Kirchenvätern und in der theologischen Literatur bis ins 20. Jahrhundert. AKG 90: B 2005, De Gruyter ix; 753 pp. €178. 3-11-016728-X.

10759 οὐρανός: *Frey, Jörg* 'Himmels-Botschaft': Kerygma und Metaphorizität der neutestamentlichen Rede vom 'Himmel'. JBTh 20 (2005) 189-223.

10760 παιδίον: *Eltrop, Bettina* Kein Kinderspiel: das Leben von Kindern in biblischer Zeit. BiHe 41/163 (2005) 17-18.

10761 παιδίον: *Müller, Peter* "Alle, die sich vom Geist Gottes leiten lassen ...": "Kinder Gottes" in der Bibel. BiHe 41/163 (2005) 12-13.

10762 παιδίον: *Okure, Teresa* Kinder in der Bibel und in afrikanischen Kulturen. BiHe 41/163 (2005) 19-22.

10763 παρθένος: *Barr, James* The most famous word in the Septuagint. Studia semitica. JSSt.S 16: 2005 ⇒603. 59-72 [Isa 7,14].

10764 παρρησία: *Bieringer, Reimund* Open, vrijmoedig, onverschrokken: de betekenis van "parresia" in de Septuaginta en in het Nieuwe Testament. Coll. 35/1 (2005) 59-74.

10765 πίστις: *Choi, Hung-Sik* πίστις in Galatians 5:5-6: neglected evidence for the faithfulness of Christ. JBL 124 (2005) 467-490.

10766 πιστεύω: *Penna, Romano* Le costruzioni del verbo πιστεύω nel Nuovo Testamento. [F]GHIBERTI, G.: 2005 ⇒47. 219-229.

10767 σωφροσύνη: **Rademaker, A.** *Sophrosyne* and the rhetoric of self-restraint: polysemy & persuasive use of an ancient Greek value term. Mn.S 259: Lei 2005, Brill xi; 375 pp. €85/$115. 90041-4251-7. Bibl. [NTAb 49,642].

10768 ὕψιστος: *Belayche, Nicole* De la polysémie des épiclèses: ὕψιστος dans le monde gréco-romain. Nommer les dieux. 2005 ⇒504. 427-442.

10769 υἱοθεσία: *Trumper, Tim J.R.* A fresh exposition of adoption: I, an outline; II, some implications. SBET 23 (2005) 60-80, 194-215 [Mt 6,19-34].

10770 Χριστός: *King, Phil* Translating "Messiah," "Christ," and "Lamb of God". JOT 1/3 (2005)* 1-27.

### J5.4 *Papyri et inscriptiones graecae*—Greek epigraphy

10771 *Attardo, Ezio* Ipotesi sull'origine della scrittura greca e relativa documentazione. Studi afroasiatici. 2005 ⇒885. 285-298.

10772 *Bader, Nabil* Greek funerary inscriptions from northern Jordan. Syria 82 (2005) 189-197.

10773 [E]**Bagnall, Roger S.; Derow, Peter** The Hellenistic period: historical sources in translation. [2]2004 <1981> ⇒20,9818. [R]BiOr 62 (2005) 266-270 (*Rochette, Bruno*).

10774 [E]**Bernabé, Albert** Poetae epici graeci testimonia et fragmenta, 2: orphicorum et orphicis similium testimonia et fragmenta, Fasc. 2. BSGRT: Mü [2]2005, Saur xxv; 553 pp. 3-598-71708-3.

10775 *Bohak, Gideon* Ethnic portraits in Greco-Roman literature. Cultural borrowings. Oriens et Occidens 8: 2005 ⇒652. 207-237.

[E]**Boud'Hors, A.** Ostraca grecs et coptes 2004 ⇒10630.

10776 **Capasso, M.** Introduzione alla papirologia: dalla pianta di papiro all'informatica papirologica. Bo 2005, Mulino 260 pp.

10777 *Chiusi, Tiziana J.* Babatha vs. the guardians of her son: a struggle for guardianship—legal and practical aspects of P.Yadin 12-15, 27. Law in the documents. JSJ.S 96: 2005 ⇒662. 105-132.

10778 *Choat, Malcolm; Nobbs, Alanna* Monotheistic formulae of belief in Greek letters on papyrus from the second to the fourth century. JGRChJ 2 (2005) 36-51.

10779 **Cribiore, Raffaella** Gymnastics of the mind: Greek education in Hellenistic and Roman Egypt. 2001 ⇒17,8774... 19,10175. [R]BiOr 62 (2005) 272-273 (*Legras, Bernard*);

10780 Princeton 2005 <2001>, Princeton Univ. Pr. xiii; 270 pp. $20/£13. 0691-00264-9 [NTAb 50,432].

10781 *Davies, John* The origins of the inscribed Greek stela. [F]MILLARD, A.: LHBOTS 426: 2005 ⇒102. 283-300.

10782 *Dettori, Emanuele; Grottanelli, Cristiano* La Vita AESOPI;

10783 La Storia di Combabo. Il saggio Ahiqar. StBi 148: 2005 ⇒52. 167-175/267-273.

10784 *Di Segni, Leah* An inscription from Khirbet el-Jiljil. BAIAS 23 (2005) 101-105.

10785 **Dubois, Laurent** Inscriptions grecques dialectales de Grande Grèce, 2: colonies achéennes. HEMGR 30: 2002 ⇒20,9830. [R]BSL 100/2 (2005) 196-198 (*Guilleux, Nicole*).

10786 *Ellis Hanson, Ann* The widow Babatha and the poor orphan boy. Law in the documents. JSJ.S 96: 2005 ⇒662. 85-103.

10787 *Epp, Eldon J.* The Oxyrhynchus New Testament papyri: "not without honor except in their hometown"? <2004>;

10788 The codex and literacy in early church christianity and at Oxyrhynchus: issues raised by Harry Y. Gamble's *Books and readers in the early church* <1998>. Perspectives on NT textual criticism. NT.S 116: 2005 ⇒207. 743-801/521-550.

10789 **French, D.H.** The inscriptions of Sinope, 1: inscriptions. Inschriften Griechischer Städte aus Kleinasien 64: 2004 ⇒20,9834. RREA 107 (2005) 851-853 (*Barat, Claire*).

10790 E**Frösén, Jaakko; Arjava, Antti; Lehtinen, Marjo** The Petra papyri, I. 2002 ⇒18,9425... 20,9835. RZSRG.R 120 (2005) 425-426 (*Thür, Gerhard*).

10791 *Gagos, Traianos; Gates, Jennifer E.; Wilburn, Andrew T.* Material culture and texts of Graeco-Roman Egypt: creating context, debating meaning. BASPap 42 (2005) 171-188.

10792 *Gibson, E. Leigh* Jews in the inscriptions of Smyrna. JJS 56 (2005) 66-79 [Rev 2,8-11].

10793 E**Gonis, N.**, *al.*, The Oxyrhynchus papyri, 69 [nos 4705-4758]. PEES.GR 89: L 2005, Egypt Exploration Society xii; 234 pp. 0-85-698-143-5. 16 pl.

10794 *Hock, Ronald F.* The educational curriculum in Chariton's Callirhoe. Ancient fiction. SBL.Symp. 32: 2005 ⇒721. 15-36.

10795 *Hook, B.S.* Oedipus and Thyestes among the philosophers: incest and cannibalism in PLATO, DIOGENES, and ZENO. CP 100/1 (2005) 17-40 [NTAb 49,574].

10796 *Hunter, Richard* Literature and its contexts. Companion to the Hellenistic world. 2005 ⇒642. 477-493.

10797 *Huys, Marc; Schmidt, Thomas* A Toronto ostracon with a list of monosyllables (2718 Pack$^2$): re-edition with commentary. ZPE 152 (2005) 209-217.

10798 **Johnson, William Allen** Bookrolls and scribes in Oxyrhynchus. 2004 ⇒20,9841. RAPF 51 (2005) 166-167 (*Poethke, Günter*).

10799 *Jördens, Andrea* Griechische Texte aus Ägypten. Staatsverträge. TUAT N.F. 2: 2005 ⇒661. 369-389.

10800 E**Jördens, Andrea; Schubert, Paul** Griechische Papyri der Cahiers P. 1 und P. 2 aus der Sammlung des Louvre (P. Louvre II). PTA 44: Bonn 2005, Habelt xvi; 172 pp. 3-7749-3319-7. Num. pl.

10801 *Katzoff, Ranon* On P.Yadin 37 = P.Hever 65. Law in the documents. JSJ.S 96: 2005 ⇒662. 133-144.

10802 *Kraus, Christof* Daten und Tabellen von Herrschern, Bischöfen und biblischen Büchern: die dem Patriarchen Nikephoros I. von Konstantinopel zugeschriebene *Chronographia brevis* im Codex Bose f.1 der Thüringer Universitäts- und Landesbibliothek. CoMa 52/53 (2005) 31-42.

10803 **Kritikakou-Nikolaropoulou, Kalliope I.; Meimaris, Yiannis E.** Inscriptions from Palaestina Tertia, vol. Ia: the Greek inscriptions from Ghor es-Safi (Byzantine Zoora). Athens 2005, Research Centre for Greek and Roman Antiquity xviii; LXXI; XIV; 442 pp. 960-7905-229.

10804 **Lajtar, Adam** Catalogue of the Greek inscriptions in the Sudan National Museum at Khartoum (I. Khartoum Greek). OLA 122: 2003 ⇒19,10192. RBiOr 62 (2005) 273-276 (*Hägg, Tomas*).

10805 *Lajtar, Adam* Four inscriptions from Marina/El-Alamein;
10806 Two Greek christian epitaphs from Egypt in the Princes Czartoryski Museum in Cracow. JJP 35 (2005) 99-108/109-119.
10807 **Lilla, Salvatore** I manoscritti vaticani greci: lineamenti di una storia di fondo. Studi e testi 415: Città del Vaticano 2004, Biblioteca Apostolica Vaticana xii; 251 pp. 88-210-0774-X.
10808 [E]**Llewelyn, S.R.** New documents illustrating early christianity, 9: a review of the Greek inscriptions and papyri published in 1986-1987. 2002 ⇒18,9444... 20,9847. [R]RBLit (2005)* (*Elbert, Paul*).
10809 [E]**Loukopoulou, Louisa** Inscriptions de la Thrace égéenne. Athènes 2005, Centre de Recherche de l'Antiquité grecque et romaine 688 pp. 100 pl.
10810 [E]**Maehler, Herwig** Urkunden aus Hermupolis. APF.B 19: Mü 2005, Saur xvi; 201 pp. 3-598-77594-6. Bibl. xiii-xvi.
10811 [ET]**Merkelbach, Reinhold; Stauber, Josef** Jenseits des Euphrats: griechische Inschriften: ein epigraphisches Lesebuch. Mü 2005, Saur xi; 227 pp. €114. 3598-73025-X. Ill.
10812 **Montiglio, S.** Wandering in ancient Greek culture. Ch 2005, Univ. of Chicago Pr. xi; 290 pp. $50/£35. 02265-34979. Bibl. [NTAb 50, 216].
10813 [ET]**Patillon, Michel** Anonyme de séguier: art du discourse politique. P 2005, Les Belles Lettres ciii; 150 pp. 2-251-00526-9.
10814 *Pervo, Richard I.* Die Entführung in das Serail: Aspasia: a female Aesop?. Ancient fiction. SBL.Symp. 32: 2005 ⇒721. 61-88.
10815 [E]**Pilhofer, P.**, *al.*, LUKIAN: der Tod des Peregrinos: ein Scharlatan auf dem Scheiterhaufen. [T]*Hansen, D.U.*: Sapere 9: Da:Wiss 2005, x; 257 pp. €30. 35341-58202. Bibl. [NTAb 50,220].
10816 *Radzyner, Amihai* P.Yadin 21-22: sale or lease?. Law in the documents. JSJ.S 96: 2005 ⇒662. 145-163.
10817 *Rey-Coqais, J.-P.* Dix ans d'épigraphie libanaise: inscriptions antiques grecques ou latines. Archaeology and History in Lebanon 21 (Spring 2005) 80-98 [UF 36,652—Heltzer, M].
10818 [E]**Rhodes, Peter J.; Osborne, Robin** Greek historical inscriptions: 404-323 BC. 2003 ⇒19,10205; 20,9863. [R]AJA 109 (2005) 314-315 (*Sickinger, James P.*).
10819 *Römer, Cornelia* Christliche Texte VIII (2004-2005). APF 51/1 (2005) 334-340 [Josh 9,27-11,3; Ps 90; 148,2-5; Sir 40,25-41,10; John 17,1-4].
10820 *Scheid, John* Épigraphie ou identité religieuse ou l'art de la traduction. Le monde romain. 2005 ⇒876. 217-229.
10821 *Scibilia, Anna* La dialettica della quantità: interazioni magico-religiose in alcuni papiri magici greci. SMSR 29 (2005) 275-308.
10822 *Tchernetska, Natalie* Cambridge UL Add. 4489, Athens EBE 4079, and the Burdett-Coutts collection of Greek manuscripts. CoMa 52/53 (2005) 21-30.
10823 [ET]**West, Martin L.** Homeric hymns: Homeric apocrypha: lives of Homer. LCL 496: CM 2003, Harvard University Press xii; 467 pp. 0-674-99606-2.
10824 *Wifstrand, Albert* Classical and post-classical Greeks. Epochs and styles. WUNT 179: 2005 <1942, 1961> ⇒325. 135-150.
10825 [E]**Worp, Klaas Anthony** Greek ostraka from Kellis: O. Kellis, Nos. 1-293. Dakhleh Oasis Project, Monograph 13: 2004 ⇒20,9877. [R]DiscEg 61 (2005) 85-88 (*Alcock, A.*).

### J5.5 Cypro-Minoan

10826 *Bendall, Lisa M.* Studies in Mycenaean inscriptions and dialect, 1980-1997. AJA 109 (2005) 91-94.

10827 **Facchetti, Giulio M.; Negri, Mario** Creta minoica: sulle trace delle più antiche scritture d'Europa. BArRom.L 55: 2003 ⇒19, 10230; 20,9880. [R]AnCl 74 (2005) 446-448 (*Duhoux, Yves*); Sal. 67 (2005) 609-610 (*Bracchi, Remo*); StEeL 22 (2005) 130-131 (*Xella, Paolo*).

### J6.5 Latina

10828 [E]**Alföldy, Géza; Panciera, Silvio** Corpus inscriptionum latinarum: volumen sextum: inscriptiones urbis Romae latinae: pars octava: titulos et imagines: fasciculus tertius: titulos magistratuum populi Romani ordinum senatorii equestrisque thesauro schedarum imaginumque ampliato. 2000 ⇒16,8854; 18,9489. [R]Gn. 77 (2005) 470-472 (*Schäfer, Christoph*).

10829 *Benario, H.W.* Recent work on TACITUS: 1994-2003. ClW 98/3 (2005) 251-336 [NTAb 49,573].

10830 [ET]**Bonnet, Guillaume** DOSITHEUS: Grammaire latine. P 2005, Belles Lettres xxxviii; 201 pp. 2-251-01441-1. Bibl. 191-192.

10831 **Citti, Vittorio; Casali, Claudia; Neri, Camillo** Gli autori nella letteratura latina: disegno storico e testi. Bo 2005, Zanichelli xvi; 416 pp. 88-08-07913-9. Bibl. 352-400.

10832 *Eck, Werner; Pangerl, Andreas* Neue Militärdiplome für die Provinzen Syria und Iudaea/Syria Palaestina. SCI 24 (2005) 101-118.

10833 *Eck, Werner; Tepper, Yotam* Ein Soldat der Legio VII Claudia in einer Grabinschrift aus Acco/Ptolemais. SCI 24 (2005) 119-123.

10834 *Fortenbaugh, W.W.* CICERO as a reporter of Aristotelian and Theophrastean rhetorical doctrine. Rhetorica [Berkeley, CA] 23/1 (2005) 37-64 [NTAb 49,574].

10835 **Kaster, Robert A.** Emotion, restraint, and community in ancient Rome. Oxf 2005, OUP ix; 245 pp. £27. 0195140788. Bibl. 207-16.

10836 **Lassère, Jean-Marie** Manuel d'épigraphie romaine. Antiquité/Synthèses 8: P 2005, Picard 2 vol.; viii; 1167 pp. 2-7084-0732-5.

10837 Mittellateinisches Wörterbuch, 3/8: efficientia-enitor. [E]**Antony, Heinz**: Mü 2005, Beck 1121-1280 Sp. €29.90. 978-3406-539-329.

10838 [E]**Moreschini, Claudio** M. Tullius CICERO Scripta quae manserunt omnia: Fasc. 43: De finibus bonorum et malorum. Mü 2005, Saur xviii; 215 pp. 3-598-71280-4. Conspectus editionum xvii-xviii.

10839 **Pernot, Laurent** Rhetoric in antiquity. [T]*Higgins, W.E.*: Wsh 2005, Catholic Univ. of America Pr. xiv; 269 pp. 0-8132-1407-6. Bibl. 237-251.

*Rey-Coqais, J.-P.* Dix ans d'épigraphie libanaise 2005 ⇒10817.

10840 **Schmidt, Manfred G.** Einführung in die lateinische Epigraphik. 2004 ⇒20,9894. [R]AnCl 74 (2005) 453-454 (*Raepsaet-Charlier, Marie-Thérèse*).

10841 Thesavrus lingvae latinae, X/1, Fasc. XV: pius-plenarius. [E]**Vogt, Ernst**, *al.*, Lp 2005, Saur 2241-2400 Sp.. 3-598-77053-7.

10842 *Van Slyke, D.G. Sacramentum* in ancient non-christian authors. Antiphon 9/2 (2005) 167-206 [NTAb 50,559].

### J8.1 General philology and linguistics

10843 **Abler, William L.** Structure of matter, structure of mind: man's place in nature, reconsidered. Ph 2005, Bainbridge xii; 221 pp. 1-89169-619-X. Bibl. 197-212.

10844 **Amor Ruibal, Ángel** Los problemas fundamentales de la filología comparada: su historia, su naturaleza y sus diversas relaciones científicas. Santiago de Compostela 2005 <1904-1905>, Consello da Cultura Galega. Electronic version. $^{R}$AuOr 23 (2005) 233-273 (*Olmo Lete, Gregorio del*).

10845 **Anderson, Stephen R.** Aspects of the theory of clitics. Oxf 2005, OUP 317 pp.

10846 *Boley, Jacqueline* Riflessioni sulla logica e sul modo di pensare antichi. RANT 2 (2005) 41-59.

10847 **Booij, Geert** The grammar of words: an introduction to linguistic morphology. Oxf 2005, OUP xiv; 308 pp. 0-1992-5847-3/8042-8.

10848 **Brown, Steven; Attardo, Salvatore** Understanding language structure, interaction, and variation: an introduction to applied linguistics and sociolonguistics for nonspecialists. AA $^{2}$2005, University of Michigan Press xxiv; 440 pp. 0-472-03038-8. Bibl. 403-424.

10849 *Catagnoti, Amalia* Traditions onomastiques sémitiques dans la documentation du III$^{e}$ millénaire. 10$^{th}$ meeting of Hamito-Semitic linguistics. QuSem 25: 2005 ⇒903. 145-154.

10850 **Collin, Finn; Guldmann, Finn** Meaning, use and truth: introducing the philosophy of language. Aldershot, Hampshire 2005, Ashgate ix; 301 pp. 0-7546-0758-5. Bibl. 291-296.

10851 *Corriente, Federico* The phonemic system of Semitic from the advantage [sic] point of Arabic and its dialectology. AuOr 23 (2005) 169-173.

10852 **Culioli, Antoine; Normand, Claudine** Onze rencontres sur le langage et les langues. L'homme dans la langue: P 2005, Ophrys 300 pp.

10853 $^{E}$**Enjalbert, Patrice** Sémantique et traitement automatique du langage naturel. P 2005, Lavoisier 410 pp.

10854 **Fehr, Johannes** SAUSSURE entre linguistique et sémiologie. $^{T}$*Caussat, Pierre*: Sciences, modernités, philosophies: P 2000, PUF 286 pp. 2-13-049977-5. Bibl. 232-286.

10855 **Finch, Geoffrey** Key concepts in language and linguistics. London $^{2}$2005, Palgrave M. xii; 249 pp. 1-403-93391-X. Bibl. 232-243.

10856 *Fronzaroli, Pelio* Etymologies. AuOr 23 (2005) 35-43;

10857 Structures linguistiques et histoire des langues au III$^{e}$ millénaire av. J.-C. ;

10858 *Goldenberg, Gideon* Word-structure, morphological analysis, the Semitic languages and beyond. 10$^{th}$ meeting of Hamito-Semitic linguistics. QuSem 25: 2005 ⇒903. 155-167/169-193.

10859 *Kogan, Leonid* Observations on Proto-Semitic vocalism. AuOr 23 (2005) 131-167.

10860 **Matthews, Peter Hugoe** The concise Oxford dictionary of linguistics. Oxf 2005, OUP xii; 410 pp. 0-19-861050-5.

10861 *Militarev, Alexander* Root extension and root formation in Semitic and Afrasian. AuOr 23 (2005) 83-129.

10862 **Moreno Cabrera, Juan Carlo** Las lenguas y sus escrituras: tipología, evolución e ideología. M 2005, Síntesis 252 pp. 84-9756-321-2. Bibl. 157-164.

10863 *Olmo Lete, Gregorio del* An etymological and comparative Semitic dictionary: phonology versus semantics: questions of method;

10864 The fundamental problems of comparative linguistics: a forgotten Spanish contribution from the early 20th century. Ment. *Amor Ruibal, Ángel*: AuOr 23 (2005) 185-190/233-273.

10865 **Olmo Lete, Gregorio del** Questions de linguistique sémitique: racine et lexème: histoire de la recherche (1940-2000). Antiq. sémitiques V: 2003 ⇒19,10271. [R]OLZ 100 (2005) 662-66 (*Oelsner, J.*).

10866 *Pasquali, Jacopo* Innovazione e continuità nel lessico dell'artigianato nella Siria del III millennio a.C. 10[th] meeting of Hamito-Semitic linguistics. QuSem 25: 2005 ⇒903. 267-299.

10867 *Rubio, Gonzalo* Chasing the Semitic root: the skeleton in the closet;

10868 *Sanmartín, Joaquín* The semantic potential of bases ('roots') and themes ('patterns'): a cognitive approach;

10869 *Takács, Gábor* Recent problems of Semitic-Egyptian and Semito-Cushitic and -Chadic consonant correspondences. AuOr 23 (2005) 45-63/65-81/207-231.

10870 [E]**Tallerman, Maggie** Language origins: perspectives on evolution. Studies in the evolution of language: Oxf 2005, OUP xx; 426 pp.

10871 *Watson, Wilfred G.E.* Loan words in Semitic. AuOr 23 (2005) 191-198.

## J8.2 Comparative grammar

10872 **Barth, J.** Die Pronominalbildung in den semitischen Sprachen. 2003 <1913> ⇒19,10280. [R]ATG 68 (2005) 430-437 (*Torres, A.*).

10873 **Bres, Jacques** L'imparfait dit *narratif*. Sciences du Langage: P 2005, CNRS 250 pp.

10874 **Brinton, Laurel J.; Traugott, Elizabeth C.** Lexicalization and language change. C 2005, CUP xii; 207 pp. Bibl. 161-184.

10875 [E]**Clairis, Christos,** *al.*, Typologie de la syntaxe connective. Rennes 2005, Presses Universitaires 234 pp.

10876 *Gai, Amikam* The *signifié* of the non-active participle in Semitic languages. ZDMG 155 (2005) 9-23.

10877 *Garr, W. Randall* The comparative method in Semitic linguistics. AuOr 23 (2005) 17-21.

10878 *Goldenberg, Gideon* Semitic triradicalism and the biradical question. [F]ULLENDORFF, E.: SStLL 47: 2005 ⇒154. 7-25;

10879 Pronouns, copulas and a syntactical revolution in Neo-Semitic. Studi afroasiatici. 2005 ⇒885. 239-252.

10880 *Gragg, Gene* Morphology and root structure: a Beja perspective. AuOr 23 (2005) 23-33.

10881 [E]**Haspelmath, Martin,** *al.*, The world atlas of language structures. Oxf 2005, OUP xv; 695 pp. 01992-55911. Bibl. 645-63; CD-ROM.

10882 *Huehnergard, John* Features of Central Semitic. [M]MORAN, W.: BibOr 48: 2005 ⇒107. 155-203.

10883 **Kienast, Burkhart** Historische semitische Sprachwissenschaft. 2001 ⇒17,8858... 20,9913. [RM]DIAKONOFF, M. 2005 ⇒36. 775-782 (*Kogan, Leonid*).

[E]**Kiss, K.** Universal grammar 2005 ⇒664.

10884 *Pennacchietti, Fabrizio A.* Ripercussioni sintattiche in conseguenza dell'introduzione dell'articolo determinativo proclitico in semitico. AuOr 23 (2005) 175-184.

10885 **Rubin, Aaron D.** Studies in Semitic grammaticalization. Harvard Semitic Studies 57: WL 2005, Eisenbrauns xv; 177 pp. $33. 1-575-06923-7. Bibl. 155-173.

10886 *Sanmartín, Joaquín* Notizen zur Komponentenverkettung und -syntax bei den prädikativen Personal pronomina der 1. und 2. Person im Semitischen. [M]DIAKONOFF, M. 2005 ⇒36. 609-622.

10887 *Takahashi, Yona* General linguistic approach for Semitic word-structure. Orient 48/2 (2005) 28-46. **J.**

10888 **Thompson, Ellen** Time in natural language: syntactic interfaces with semantics and discourse. Interface explorations 11: B 2005, De Gruyter xv; 224 pp. 3-11-018414-1. Bibl. 205-219.

10889 *Tonietti, Maria V.* Le système prépositionnel de l'eblaïte. $10^{th}$ meeting of Hamito-Semitic linguistics. QuSem 25: 2005 ⇒903. 315-332.

10890 *Zaborski, Andrzej* Comparative Semitic studies: *status quaestionis*. AuOr 23 (2005) 9-15.

## J8.4 **The origin of writing**

10891 **Glassner, Jean-Jacques** The invention of cueniform: writing in Sumer. [TE]*Bahrani, Zainab; Van De Mieroop, Marc*: 2003 ⇒19, 10306. [R]Or. 74 (2005) 115-116 (*Edzard, Dietz Otto*); BSOAS 68 (2005) 107-109 (*George, A.R.*); BiOr 62 (2005) 57-64 (*Charvát, Petr*); CamArchJ 15 (2005) 279-280 (*Postgate, Nicholas*); NEA (BA) 68 (2005) 135-136 (*McGeough, Kevin*).

10892 *Kitchen, Kenneth A.* Now you see it, now you don't!: the monumental use and non-use of writing in the ancient Near East;

10893 *MacDonald, M.C.A.* Literacy in an oral environment. [F]MILLARD, A.: LHBOTS 426: 2005 ⇒102. 175-187/49-118.

10894 **Mander, Pietro** L'origine del cuneiforme, 1: caratteristiche, lingue e tradizioni., 2: archivi e biblioteche pre-sargoniche. Quaderni napoletani di assiriologia 1; AIO 126/1: R 2005, Aracne 89 pp. 88-5-48-0019-8.

10895 **Sass, Benjamin** The alphabet at the turn of the millennium: the West Semitic alphabet ca. 1150-850 B.C.E.: the antiquity of the Arabian, Greek and Phrygian alphabets. Journal of the Inst. of Archaeology of Tel Aviv Univ., Occasional Publ. 45: TA 2005, Tel Aviv Univ. 195 pp. 965-266-021-3. Ill.; Bibl. 161-182. [R]UF 36 (2004) 711-716 (*Heltzer, M.*).

10896 **Türcke, Christoph** Vom Kainszeichen zum genetischen Code: kritische Theorie der Schrift. Mü 2005, Beck 246 pp. 3-406-53472-4.

10897 **Yardeni, Ada** The book of Hebrew script: history, palaeography, script styles, calligraphy & design. 2002 <1997> ⇒18,9555; 19, 10312. [R]JRTI 7/1 (2005) 75-77 (*Blake, Richard D.*).

### J9.1 *Analyis linguistica loquelae de Deo*—**God talk**

10898 **Neyrey, Jerome H.** Render to God: New Testament understandings of the divine. 2004 ⇒20,9930. [R]JR 85 (2005) 507-8 (*Guttenberger, Gudrun*); CBQ 67 (2005) 533-534 (*Patterson, Stephen J.*); RBLit (2005)* (*Edwards, Richard; Mason, John*).

## XV. Postbiblica

### K1.1 **Pseudepigrapha [=catholicis 'Apocrypha']** *VT generalis*

10899 **Atkinson, Kenneth** I cried to the Lord : a study of the Psalms of Solomon's historical background and social setting. JSJ.S 84: 2004 ⇒20,9932. [R]ThLZ 130 (2005) 1306-1308 (*Kaiser, Otto*).

10900 *Aune, David E.* The *Odes of Solomon* and early christian prophecy. Apocalypticism, prophecy. WUNT 199: 2005 <1982> ⇒177. 320-346.

10901 [TE]**Buitenwerf, Rieuwerd** Book III of the Sibylline oracles and its social setting. SVTP 17: 2003 ⇒19,10320. [R]RSR 93 (2005) 611-612 (*Berthelot, Katell*).

10902 **Charlesworth, James** Die Schrift des Sem. JSHRZ 2: weisheitliche, magische und legendarische Erzählungen 9: Gü 2005, Gü viii; 35 pp. €30. 35790-52411. [R]JSJ 36 (2005) 335-7 (*Nicklas, Tobias*).

10903 *Davila, James R.* The Old Testament pseudepigrapha as background to the New Testament. ET 117 (2005) 53-57;

10904 (How) Can we tell if a Greek Apocryphon or Pseudepigraphon has been translated from Hebrew or Aramaic?. JSPE 15/1 (2005) 3-61.

10905 **Davila, James R.** The provenance of the pseudepigrapha: Jewish, christian, or other?. Lei 2005, Brill vi; 278 pp. €99/$142. 90-04-13-752-1. Bibl. 237-259.

10906 *Delamarter, S.* In the margins of Charlesworth's Old Testament Pseudepigrapha: controlled vocabulary and the challenges of scripture indices. JRTI 7/2 (2005) 91-109 [NTAb 52,112].

10907 **DeSilva, David Arthur** Introducing the Apocrypha: message, context, and significance. 2002 ⇒18,9568... 20,9935. [R]TJT 21 (2005) 232-234 (*Porter, Stanley E.*); JRTI 7/1 (2005) 88-90 (*Gillum, Gary P.*); RBLit (2005)* (*Noffke, Eric*).

10908 *Embry, Bradley J.* Prayer in Psalms of Solomon or The temple, covenant fidelity, and hope. Studies in Jewish prayer. JSSt.S 17: 2005 ⇒828. 89-99.

10909 *Herbst, Adrian J.* Las influencias homéricas en la antigua literatura apócrifa judía y cristiana. Cuadernos de teología 24 (2005) 201-13.

10910 *Hostetter, Edwin C.* Significant noncanonical books. Scripture. 2005 ⇒398. 91-101.

10911 **Kaiser, Otto** The Old Testament apocrypha: an introduction. 2004 ⇒20,9941. [R]CBQ 67 (2005) 319-320 (*Redditt, Paul L.*); TJT 21 (2005) 245-246 (*Humphrey, Edith M.*); RBLit 7 (2005) 198-200 (*Clanton, Dan W.*).

10912 **Lattke, Michael** Oden Salomos: Text, Übersetzung, Kommentar, 3: Oden 29-42. NTOA 41: FrS 2005, Academic xxxvii; 422 pp. €84. 3-7278-1513-2.

10913 **Lorein, Geert Wouter** The antichrist theme in the intertestamental period. JSPE.S 44: 2003 ⇒19,10332; 20,9945. [R]Bib. 86 (2005) 294-297 (*Aranda Pérez, Gonzalo*); CBQ 68 (2006) 154-155 (*Stokes, Ryan E.*).

10914 *Passoni Dell'Acqua, Anna* La Prière de Manassé: une fantaisie linguistique pour chanter la miséricorde de Dieu. L'apport de la Septante. LeDiv 203: 2005 ⇒764. 221-268 [2 Chr 33,1-20].

10915 *Reed, Annette Y.* "Revealed literature" in the second century B.C. E.: Jubilees, 1 Enoch, Qumran, and the prehistory of the biblical canon. Enoch and Qumran origins. 2005 ⇒921. 94-98.

10916 *Suomala, Karla R.* The Colloquy of Moses on Mount Sinai: where Syriac christianity meets Islamic Spain and Africa between the 16th and 19th centuries. Hugoye 8/1 (2005)*.

10917 *Tigchelaar, Eibert* Jubilees and 1 Enoch and the issue of transmission of knowledge. Enoch...Qumran origins. 2005 ⇒921. 99-101.

10918 [T]**Tolmie, Francois; Van der Watt, Jan** Apokriewe Ou en Nuwe Testament: verlore boeke uit die bybelse tyd. Vereeniging, SA 2005, Christelike 791 pp. R200. 1-77000-192-1.

10919 *VanderKam, James C.* Response: Jubilees and Enoch. Enoch and Qumran origins. 2005 ⇒921. 162-170.

10920 *Werline, Rodney A.* The Psalms of Solomon and the ideology of rule. Conflicted boundaries. SBL.Symp. 35: 2005 ⇒495. 69-87.

## κ1.2 Henoch

10921 *Adler, William* Enoch, Moses, and the Essenes. Enoch and Qumran origins. 2005 ⇒921. 384-387.

10922 *Arcari, Luca* Il *Nachleben* del testo greco di *Enoc* in alcuni scritti del cristianesimo antico: è esistita 'una' traduzione greca di *Enoc*?. Materia giudaica 10/1 (2005) 57-72.

10923 **Barker, Margaret** The lost prophet: the book of Enoch and its influence on christianity. Shf 2005, Phoenix xi; 115 pp. 1905048181;

10924 The older testament: the survival of themes from the ancient royal cult in sectarian Judaism and early christianity. Shf 2005 <1987>, Sheffield Phoenix xi; 314 pp. £25/$40. 19050-4819X. Bibl. [NTAb 50,198].

10925 **Bautch, Kelley Coblentz** A study of the geography of 1 Enoch 17-19: "No one has seen what I have seen". JSJ.S 81: 2003 ⇒19, 10340; 20,9952. [R]RBLit (2005)* (*Scott, James; Whitley, John*).

10926 *Beckwith, Roger T.* The earliest Enoch literature and its calendar: marks of their origin, date and motivation. Calendar, chronology. AGJU 61: 2005 ⇒184. 16-53.

10927 *Bedenbender, Andreas* Reflection on ideology and date of the Apocalypse of Weeks. Enoch and Qumran origins. 2005 ⇒921. 200-203.

10928 *Bhayro, Siam* 'and you know everything before it happens...': a complaint against the inaction of the Most High in 1 Enoch 9. Studies in Jewish prayer. JSSt.S 17: 2005 ⇒828. 33-54.

10929 **Bhayro, Siam** The Shemihazah and Asael narrative of 1 Enoch 6-11: introduction, text, translation and commentary with reference to ancient near eastern and biblical antecedents. AOAT 322: Müns 2005, Ugarit-Verlag xii; 295 pp. 3-934628-62-1. Bibl. 261-272.

10930 *Boccaccini, Gabriele* Introduction: from the Enoch literature to Enochic Judaism. Enoch and Qumran origins. 2005 ⇒921. 1-14.

10931 *Boyarin, Daniel* The Parables of Enoch and the foundation of the rabbinic sect: a hypothesis. FSTEMBERGER, G.: SJ 32: 2005 ⇒140. 53-72.

10932 *Dimant, Devorah* The *Book of parables* (1 Enoch 37-71) and the Qumran scrolls. Meghillot III. 2005 ⇒608. 49-67. **H.**

10933 *Ego, Beate* Vergangenheit im Horizont eschatologischer Hoffnung: die Tiervision (1 Hen 85-90) als Beispiel apokalyptischer Geschichtskonzeption. Antike Historiographie. BZNW 129: 2005 ⇒ 348. 171-195.

10934 *Fletcher-Louis, Crispin H.T.* The Aqedah and the Book of Watchers (1 Enoch 1-36). Studies in Jewish prayer. JSSt.S 17: 2005 ⇒ 828. 1-31 [Gen 22,1-19].

10935 *Flint, Peter W.* The Greek fragments of Enoch from Qumran cave 7. Enoch and Qumran origins. 2005 ⇒921. 224-233.

10936 *Henze, Matthias* The Apocalypse of Weeks and the architecture of the end time. Enoch and Qumran origins. 2005 ⇒921. 207-209.

10937 *Hessayon, Ariel* Og, re di Basan, Enoc e i libri di Enoc: testi non canonici e interpretazioni di *Genesi* 6,1-4. RSLR 41 (2005) 249-295 [Gen 6,1-4].

10938 **Jackson, David R.** Enochic Judaism: three defining paradigm exemplars. Library of Second Temple Studies 49: 2004 ⇒20,9956. RRBLit (2005)* (*Noffke, Eric*).

10939 *Knibb, Michael A.* The text-critical value of the quotations from 1 Enoch in Ethiopic writings. FLUST, J.: BEThL 192: 2005 ⇒92. 225-235;

10940 The Apocalypse of Weeks and the Epistle of Enoch. Enoch and Qumran origins. 2005 ⇒921. 213-219.

10941 *Leuenberger, Martin* Die 10-Siebent-Apokalypse im Henochbuch: ihre Stellung im material rekonstruierten Manuskript 4QEng und Implikationen für die Redaktions- und Kompositionsgeschichte der Traumvisionen (83-91) und des paränetischen Briefs (92-105), Teil 1. BN 124 (2005) 57-102;

10942 Teil 2. BN 126 (2005) 45-82.

10943 *Newsom, Carol A.* Genesis 2-3 and 1 Enoch 6-16: two myths of origin. FBRUEGGEMANN, W.—COUSAR, C. 2005 ⇒16. 7-22.

10944 *Nickelsburg, George W.E.* Response: context, text, and social setting of the Apocalypse of Weeks. Enoch and Qumran origins. 2005 ⇒921. 234-241.

10945 **Nickelsburg, George W.E.** 1 Enoch 1: a commentary on the book of 1 Enoch, chapters 1-36; 81-108. Hermeneia: 2001 ⇒17,8901... 20,9959. RRBLit 7 (2005) 1-12 (*Oegema, Gerbern S.; Stuckenbruck, Loren T.; Tiller, Patrick*);

10946 **Nickelsburg, George W.E.; VanderKam, James C.** 1 Enoch: a new translation: based on the Hermeneia commentary. 2004 ⇒20, 9960. RRBLit (2005)* (*Kugel, James*).

10947 **Olson, Daniel C.** Enoch: a new translation. North Richland Hills, TX 2004, BIBAL xi; 320 pp. $30. 09410-37894. In consultation with Archbishop *Melkesedek Workneneh*; Bibl. [R]RBLit (2005)* (*Suter, David W.*).

10948 *Olson, Daniel C.* Historical chronology after the exile according to 1 Enoch 89-90. JSPE 15/1 (2005) 63-74 [Dan 9,24-27].

10949 *Orlov, Andrei* 'Without measure and without analogy': the tradition of the divine body in 2 (Slavonic) Enoch. JJS 56/2 (2005) 224-244.

10950 **Orlov, Andrei A.** The Enoch-Metatron tradition. TSAJ 107: Tü 2005, Mohr S. xii; 383 pp. $175. 31614-85440. Bibl. 337-56. [R]FJB 32 (2005) 210-213 (*Kuyt, Annelies*).

10951 *Reed, Annette Y.* Interrogating "Enochic Judaism": 1 Enoch as evidence for intellectual history, social realities, and literary tradition. Enoch and Qumran origins. 2005 ⇒921. 336-344.

10952 **Reed, Annette Yoshiko** Fallen angels and the history of Judaism and Christianity: the reception of Enochic literature. C 2005, CUP xii; 318 pp. $75. 0-521-85378-8. Bibl. 278-296.

10953 *Sacchi, Paolo* Un tratto della teologia enochica: il peccato di aver rifiutato di guardare Dio. [F]VANNI, U. 2005 ⇒156. 49-61;

10954 History of the earliest Enochic texts;

10955 *Schiffman, Lawrence H.* 3 Enoch and the Enoch tradition;

10956 *Stuckenbruck, Loren T.* The plant metaphor in its inner-Enochic and early Jewish context;

10957 *Tigchelaar, Eibert J.C.* Evaluating the discussions concerning the original order of chapters 91-93 and codicological data pertaining to 4Q212 and Chester Beatty XII Enoch. Enoch and Qumran origins. 2005 ⇒921. 401-407/152-161/210-212/220-223.

10958 *Tiller, Patrick A.* Israel at the mercy of demonic powers: an Enochic interpretation of postexilic imperialism. Conflicted boundaries. SBL.Symp. 35: 2005 ⇒495. 113-121.

10959 *Viviés, Pierre de Martin de* La littérature intertestamentaire, 1: le livre d'Hénoch éthiopien. EeV 119 (2005) 16-23.

## K1.3 Testamenta

10960 **Allison, Dale C.** Testament of Abraham. Commentaries on early Jewish literature: 2003 ⇒19,10368; 20,9968. [R]RSR 93 (2005) 617-618 (*Berthelot, Katell*); RBLit (2005)* (*Vázquez Allegue, Jaime*).

10961 **Jonge, Marinus de** Pseudepigrapha of the Old Testament as part of christian literature: the case of the Testaments of the Twelve Patriarchs and the Greek Life of Adam and Eve. SVTP 18: 2003 ⇒ 19,10372. [R]ThLZ 130 (2005) 502-505 (*Dochhorn, Jan*); JSJ 36 (2005) 341-344 (*Verheyden, Joseph*).

10962 **Klutz, Todd E.** Rewriting the Testament of Solomon: tradition, conflict and identity in a late antique pseudepigraphon. Library of Second Temple studies 53: L 2005, Clark xii; 164 pp. £65. 0-567-04392-4. Bibl. 147-152.

10963 *Loader, William* Sexuality in *The Testaments of the Twelve Patriarchs* and the New Testament. [F]MOLONEY, F.: BSRel 187: 2005 ⇒ 104. 293-309 [1 Cor 7,5].

10964 *Ludlow, Jared W.* Humor and paradox in the characterization of Abraham in the Testament of Abraham. Ancient fiction. SBL. Symp. 32: 2005 ⇒721. 199-214.

10965 **Ludlow, Jared W.** Abraham meets death: narrative humor in the Testament of Abraham. JSPE.S 41: 2002 ⇒18,9633. [R]JQR 95 (2005) 697-699 (*Burkes, Shannon*).

10966 [ET]**Raurell, Frederic** El Testament de Job. [T]*Morelli, Patrizia*: Barc 2005, Facultat de Teologia de Catalunya 128 pp. Bibl. 49-55. [R]RCatT 30/1 (2005) 234-236 (*Solà, Teresa*).

10967 *Viviés, Pierre de Martin* La littérature intertestamentaire, 3: les testaments des douze patriarches. EeV 121 (2005) 11-19.

## K1.6 Adam, Jubilaea, Asenet

10968 *Díaz Araujo, Magdalena* Estudio preliminar sobre el carácter esotérico de la *Vida griega de Adán y Eva*. Epimelia 14 (2005) 23-40.

10969 [T]**González Casado, Pilar** La cueva de los tesoros. Apócrifos cristianos 5: 2004 ⇒20,9990. [R]Studium 45 (2005) 313-314 (*López, L.*); AnVal 31 (2005) 480-481 (*Calatayud Gascô, Rafael*); EstTrin 39 (2005) 597-598 (*Vázquez Allegue, Jaime*).

10970 *Kaestli, Jean-Daniel* La Vie d'Adam et Eve: un enchaînement d'intrigues épisodiques au service d'une intrigue unifiante. Analyse narrative. BEThL 191: 2005 ⇒742. 321-336.

10971 *Meiser, Martin; Merk, Otto* Das Leben Adams und Evas (JSHRZ II/5). Unterweisung in erzählender Form. 2005 ⇒453. 151-194.

10972 *Neufeld, Dietmar* The rhetoric of body, clothing and identity in the *Vita* and Genesis. Scriptura 90 (2005) 679-684 [OTA 30,79] [Gen 2-3].

10973 **Stone, Michael Edward** Adam's contract with Satan: the legend of the cheirograph of Adam. 2002 ⇒18,9650; 19,10392. [R]JAAR 73 (2005) 586-588 (*Murdoch, Brian*).

10974 **Toepel, Alexander** Die Adam- und Sethlegenden in der syrischen Schatzhöhle. Diss. Tübingen 2005, [D]*Gerö, Stephen*.

10975 **Tromp, Johannes** The Life of Adam and Eve in Greek: a critical edition. PVTG 6: Lei 2005, Brill viii; 206 pp. €73/$104. 90-04-14317-3. Bibl. 185-188. [R]ThRv 101 (2005) 375-377 (*Nicklas, Tobias*); RBLit (2005)* (*Dimant, Devorah*).

10976 [E]**Albani, Matthias; Frey, Jörg; Lange, Armin** Studies in the book of Jubilees. TSAJ 65: 1997 ⇒13,8549... 16,8976. [R]HebStud 46 (2005) 440-442 (*Kudan, David B.*).

10977 *Anderson, Jeff S.* Denouncement speech in Jubilees and other Enochic literature. Enoch and Qumran origins. 2005 ⇒921. 132-136.

10978 *Fröhlich, Ida* Enoch and Jubilees. Enoch and Qumran origins. 2005 ⇒921. 141-147.

10979 *Gilders, William K.* Where did Noah place the blood?: a textual note on Jubilees 7:4. JBL 124 (2005) 745-749 [Gen 9,20-21].

10980 *Halpern-Amaru, Betsy* Joy as piety in the 'book of Jubilees'. JJS 56/2 (2005) 185-205;

10981 Burying the fathers: exegetical strategies and source traditions in Jubilees 46. Reworking the bible. StTDJ 58: 2005 ⇒723. 135-152.

10982 *Himmelfarb, Martha* Jubilees and sectarianism;

10983 *Kvanvig, Helge S.* Jubilees—read as a narrative. Enoch and Qumran origins. 2005 ⇒921. 129-131/75-83.

10984 *Landau, David* The Montanists and the Jubilees calendar. OrChr 89 (2005) 103-112.
10985 *Morisada Rietz, Henry W.* Synchronizing worship: Jubilees as a tradition for the Qumran community. Enoch and Qumran origins. 2005 ⇒921. 111-118.
10986 *Oegema, Gerbern S.* Das Buch der Jubiläen. Einführung zu den jüdischen Schriften. JSHRZ 2/3: 2005 ⇒453. 78-96.
10987 *Rosso Ubigli, Liliana* The historical-cultural background of the book of Jubilees. Enoch and Qumran origins. 2005 ⇒921. 137-40.
10988 *Rothstein, David* Why was Shelah not given to Tamar?: Jubilees 41:20. Henoch 27/1-2 (2005) 115-126;
10989 Same-day testimony and same-day punishment in the Damascus Document and Jubilees. ZAR 11 (2005) 4-11.
10990 **Scott, James M.** On earth as in heaven: the restoration of sacred time and sacred space in the book of Jubilees. JSJ.S 91: Lei 2005, Brill xii; 292 pp. €99/$133. 90-04-13796-3. Bibl. 251-268. [R]RBLit (2005)* (*Bar-Ilan, Meir*).
10991 *Segal, Michael* The relationship between the legal and narrative passages in Jubilees. Reworking the bible. StTDJ 58: 2005 ⇒723. 203-228.
10992 *Sulzbach, Carla* The function of the sacred geography in the book of Jubilees. JSem 14/2 (2005) 283-305.
10993 *Van Ruiten, Jacques T.A.G.M.* The birth of Moses in Egypt according to the book of Jubilees (Jub 47.1-9). [F]LUTTIKHUIZEN, G.: AGJU 59: 2005 ⇒93. 43-65 [Exod 1-2];
10994 A literary dependancy of Jubilees on 1 Enoch?. Enoch and Qumran origins. 2005 ⇒921. 90-93.
10995 *Viviés, Pierre de Martin de* La littérature intertestamentaire, 2: le livre de Jubilés. EeV 120 (2005) 12-18.

10996 *Bolyki, János* Egypt as the setting for Joseph and Aseneth: accidental or deliberate?. [F]LUTTIKHUIZEN, G.: 2005 ⇒93. 81-96.
10997 *Braginskaya, N.V.* 'Joseph and Aseneth': a 'midrash' before midrash and a 'novel' before novel. VDI 3 (2005) 73-96. **R.**
10998 *Brooke, George J.* Men and women as angels in Joseph and Aseneth. JSPE 14/2 (2005) 159-177.
10999 *Burchard, Christoph* Küssen in Joseph and Aseneth. JSJ 36 (2005) 316-323;
11000 The text of Joseph and Aseneth reconsidered. JSPE 14/2 (2005) 83-96;
11001 Joseph und Aseneth: eine jüdisch-hellenistische Erzählung von Liebe, Bekehrung und vereitelter Entführung. ThZ 61 (2005) 65-77.
11002 [E]**Burchard, Christoph** Joseph und Aseneth. PVTG 5: 2003 ⇒19, 10416. [R]OLZ 100 (2005) 82-85 (*Böttrich, Christfried*).
11003 *Chesnutt, Randall D.* Perceptions of oil in early Judaism and the meal formula in *Joseph and Aseneth*. JSPE 14/2 (2005) 113-132.
11004 *Collins, John J.* Joseph and Aseneth: Jewish or Christian?. JSPE 14/2 (2005) 97-112.
11005 *Guevara Llaguno, Junkal* José y Asenet: historia de una justificación. MEAH 54 (2005) 3-26 [OTA 29,335].
11006 *Oegema, Gerbern S.* Joseph und Aseneth. Einführung zu den jüdischen Schriften. JSHRZ 2/4: 2005 ⇒453. 97-114.

11007 *Portier-Young, Anathea E.* Sweet mercy metropolis: interpreting Aseneth's honeycomb. JSPE 14/2 (2005) 133-157.

11008 [ET]**Tragan, Pius-Ramon** Josep i Àsenet. [T]*Ros, Montserrat*: Literatura intertestamentària, Suppl. 4: Barc 2005, Alpha 208 pp. 84-72-25-856-4. Introducció, text grec revisat i notes. [R]RCatT 30 (2005) 463-465 (*Borrell, Agustí*).

## K1.7 Apocalypses, ascensiones

11009 **Carlsson, Leif** Round trips to heaven: otherworldly travelers in early Judaism and christianity. 2004 ⇒20,10018. [R]Numen 52 (2005) 500-504 (*Bornet, Philippe*).

11010 **Dochhorn, Jan** Die Apokalypse des Mose: Text, Übersetzung, Kommentar. [D]*Feldmeier, R.*: TSAJ 106: Tü 2005, Mohr S. xiv: 657 pp. €119. 3-16-148255-7. Diss. Göttingen; Bibl. 581-606. [R]JSJ 36 (2005) 344-347 (*Nicklas, Tobias*).

11011 *Hirschfelder, Ulrike* The liturgy of the Messiah: the Apocalypse of David in Hekhalot literature. JSQ 12 (2005) 148-193.

11012 **Kulik, Alexander** Retroverting Slavonic pseudepigrapha: toward the original of the Apocalypse of Abraham. Text-Critical Studies 3: 2004 ⇒20,10020. [R]RBLit (2005)* (*Orlov, Andrei; Vázquez Allegue, Jaime*).

11013 **Laporte, Jean** Les apocalypses et la formation des vérités chrétiennes. Initiations aux Pères de l'Église: P 2005, Cerf 128 pp. €15. 2-204-07536-1.

11014 [T]**Leonhardt-Balzer, Jutta** Apokalypsen und Testamente 1,5: Fragen Esras. JSHRZ N.F. 1: Gü 2005, Gü viii; 28 pp. €30. 3-579-05-240-3.

11015 *Dochhorn, Jan* Die Ascensio Isaiae (JSHRZ II,1: Martyrium Jesajas). Unterweisung in erzählender Form. 2005 ⇒453. 1-48.

11016 **Lusini, Gianfrancesco** Ascensione di Isaia: concordanza della versione etiopica. ÄthF 62: 2003 ⇒19,10441. [R]JSSt 50 (2005) 405-407 (*Knibb, Michael A.*); OrChr 89 (2005) 275-277 (*Wehrle, Josef*).

## K2.1 Philo judaeus alexandrinus

11017 *Berthelot, Katell* "Ils jettent au feu leurs fils et leurs filles pour leurs dieux": une justification humaniste du massacre des Cananéens dans les textes juifs anciens?. RB 112 (2005) 161-191.

11018 **Böhm, Martina** Rezeption und Funktion der Vätererzählungen bei Philo von Alexandria: zum Zusammenhang von Kontext, Hermeneutik und Exegese im frühen Judentum. [D]*Herzer, Jens*: BZNW 128: B 2005, De Gruyter xiii; 502 pp. €128/$179.20. 3-11-018199-1. Diss.-Habil. Leipzig; Bibl. 439-455.

11019 [E]**Calabi, F.** Italian studies on Philo of Alexandria. 2003 ⇒19, 10452. [R]Elenchos 26/1 (2005) 201-206 (*Alesse, Francesca*).

11020 [ET]**Calabi, Francesca** Filone di Alessandria: De Decalogo. Pisa 2005, ETS 151 pp. €14. 884671363X [ASEs 23,566: A. Mazzanti].

[E]**Deines, R.** Philo und das Neue Testament 2004 ⇒734.

11021 *Dillon, John M.* Cosmic gods and primordial chaos in Hellenistic and Roman philosophy: the context of Philo's interpretation of PLATO's Timaeus and the book of Genesis. Creation of heaven and earth. Themes in biblical narrative 8: 2005 ⇒492. 97-107.

11022 *Feldman, Louis H.* Philo's account of the golden calf incident. JJS 56/2 (2005) 245-264 [Exod 32,1-35; Deut 9,12-21].

11023 **Feldman, Louis H.** "Remember Amalek!": vengeance, zealotry, and group destruction in the bible according to Philo, Pseudo-Philo, and JOSEPHUS. MHUC 31: 2004 ⇒20,10043. [R]Zion 70 (2005) 401-403 (*Rappaport, Uriel*) [Deut 25,17-19].

11024 *Goulet, Richard* Allégorisme et anti-allégorisme chez Philon d'Alexandrie. Allégorisme des poètes. 2005 ⇒874. 59-87.

11025 *Hirsch-Luipold, Rainer* Der eine Gott bei Philon von Alexandrien und PLUTARCH. Gott und die Götter. 2005 ⇒880. 141-168.

11026 *Kerkeslager, Allen* The absence of DIONYSIOS, LAMPO, and ISIDOROS from the violence in Alexandria in 38 C.E.. StPhiloA 17 (2005) 49-94.

11027 *Kraft, Robert* Philo's bible revisited: the 'aberrant texts' and their quotations of Moses. [F]LUST, J.: BEThL 192: 2005 ⇒92. 237-253.

11028 *Mach, Michael F.* Lerntraditionen im hellenistischen Judentum unter besonderer Berücksichtigung Philons von Alexandrien. Religiöses Lernen. WUNT 180: 2005 ⇒384. 117-139.

11029 *Marin, Maurizio* La forza di persuasione della logica aristotelica: Filone di Alessandria e l'eternità del mondo. Sal. 67 (2005) 213-32.

11030 **Martens, John** One God, one law: Philo of Alexandria on the Mosaic and Greco-Roman law. 2003 ⇒19,10472; 20,10058. [R]RBLit (2005)* (*Bloch, René*).

11031 *Miralles Maciá, Lorena* Thíasoi y syssítia esenios: la perspectiva helenística de Filón de Alejandría acerca de la organización esenia. MEAH 54 (2005) 27-42 [OTA 29,339].

11032 *Oegema, Gerbern S.* Pseudo-Philo: Antiquitates Biblicae. Einführung zu den jüdischen Schriften. JSHRZ 2/2: 2005 ⇒453. 66-77.

11033 *Radice, Roberto* La funzione teologica del *Logos* nel giudaismo alessandrino e i suoi possibili sviluppi. Hum(B) 60 (2005) 844-858.

11034 [E]**Radice, Roberto** Filone di Alessandria: tutti i trattati del commentario allegorico alla bibbia. Mi 2005, Bompiani clx; 1946 pp. Pres. *Giovanni Reale*; introd. *G. Reale* e *R. Radice*.

11035 *Royse, James R.* Three more spurious fragments of Philo. StPhiloA 17 (2005) 95-98.

11036 *Runia, David T.* A conference on Philo in Germany;

11037 *Runia, David T., al.*, Philo of Alexandria: an annotated bibliography 2002;

11038 Supplement: a provisional bibliography 2003-2005. StPhiloA 17 (2005) 141-152/161-197/198-214.

11039 [T]**Runia, David T.** Philo of Alexandria: on the creation of the cosmos according to Moses: introduction, translation and commentary. Philo of Alexandria Commentary 1: Atlanta 2005 <2001>, SBL xviii; 443 pp. $35. 15898-31608. Bibl. 404-423; [NTAb 49,643].

11040 **Schenck, Kenneth** A brief guide to Philo. LVL 2005, Westminster xi; 172 pp. $25. 0-664-22735-X.. [R]RBLit (2005)* (*Seland, Torrey*).

11041 *Shaw, Frank* The emperor Gaius' employment of the divine name. StPhiloA 17 (2005) 33-48.

11042 *Spuntarelli, Chiara* "Uomo a immagine" in Filone: assimilazione della legge e immortalità dell'Albero dei Virtuosi. Commento a Giovanni di ORIGENE. 2005 ⇒789. 381-411 [Gen 1,26-27; 2,7].

11043 **Taylor, Joan E.** Jewish women philosophers of first-century Alexandria: Philo's 'Therapeutae' reconsidered. 2003 ⇒19,10493; 20, 10083. [R]JSJ 36 (2005) 373-376 (*Richardson, Peter*); DSD 12 (2005) 220-223 (*Collins, John J.*); RBLit 7 (2005) 208-211 (*Okland, Jorunn*).

11044 [T]**Van der Horst, Pieter W.illem** Philo's Flaccus: the first pogrom. Philo of Alexandria Commentary 2: 2003 ⇒19,10496; 20,10089. [R]SCI 24 (2005) 317-318 (*Niehoff, Maren*); JSJ 36 (2005) 376-381 (*Borgen, Peder*); RSR 93 (2005) 612-613 (*Berthelot, Katell*); ThLZ 130 (2005) 1175-1177 (*Noethlichs, Karl Leo*); JThS 56 (2005) 188-191 (*Leonhardt-Balzer, Jutta*);

11045 Atlanta 2005 <2003>, SBL xii; 277 pp. $30. 15898-31888. Bibl. 246-261.

11046 *Wilson, Walter T.* Pious soldiers, gender deviants and the ideology of Actium: courage and warfare in Philo's De Fortitudine. Ment. *Cicero*. StPhiloA 17 (2005) 1-32.

11047 *Wright, Archie T.* Some observations of Philo's De Gigantibus and evil spirits in second temple Judaism. JSJ 36 (2005) 471-488.

### K2.4 *Evangelia apocrypha*—**Apocryphal gospels**

11048 *Bauer, Dieter* Nur was verboten ist, ist interessant!. BiKi 60 (2005) 124.

11049 **Baum, Armin D.** Pseudepigraphie und literarische Fälschung im frühen Christentum: mit ausgewählten Quellentexten samt deutscher Übersetzung. WUNT 2/138: 2001 ⇒17,8975; 19,10503. [R]NT 47 (2005) 91-93 (*Stenschke, Christoph*).

11050 *Bechmann, Ulrike* Apokryphe Evangelientradition im Koran. BiKi 60 (2005) 108-111.

11051 *Beyers, Rita* Dans l'atelier des compilateurs: remarques à propos de la *Compilation latine de l'Enfance*. Apocrypha 16 (2005) 97-135;

11052 Le charme discret de la Compilation latine de l'enfance. Analyse narrative. BEThL 191: 2005 ⇒742. 351-368.

11053 *Bingen, Jean* 'Protévangile' de Jacques, XIII-XV (p. Ashmolean inv. 9). CÉg 80 (2005) 201-214 [Scr. 60/1,23*—M. Wittek].

11054 *Blackhirst, R.* Fra Marino's treasure: a report on new investigations into the origins of the gospel of Barnabas. JHiC 11/2 (2005) 55-66 [NTAb 50,561].

11055 **Boer, Esther A. de** The gospel of Mary: beyond a Gnostic and a biblical Mary Magdalene. JSNT.S 260: 2004 ⇒20,10095. [R]CBQ 67 (2005) 527-528 (*Thimmes, Pamela*); RBLit (2005)* (*Jones, F. Stanley*);

11056 JSNT.S 260: L 2005 <2004>, Clark x; 248 pp. £10/$20. 0-8264-8-0012. Bibl. 209-229.

11057 *Bowe, Barbara E.* Peter in the noncanonical literature. BiTod 43 (2005) 238-243.

11058 *Brown, Scott G.* The secret gospel of Mark: is it real?: and does it identify "Bethany beyond the Jordan"?. BArR 31/1 (2005) 44-49, 60-61.

11059 **Brown, Scott G.** Mark's other gospel: rethinking Morton Smith's controversial discovery. SCJud 15: Waterloo, Ontario 2005, Wilfrid Laurier University Press xxiii; 332 pp. $65. 0-88920-461-6. Bibl. 283-312. $^{R}$ET 117 (2005) 64-66 (*Foster, Paul*).

11060 **Bütz, Jeffrey J.** The brother of Jesus and the lost teachings of christianity. Rochester (Vt.) 2005, Inner Traditions xviii; 220 pp. 1-594-77043-3. Bibl. 204-212.

11061 *Destro, Adriana; Pesce, Mauro* Constellations of texts in early christianity: the "Gospel of the Savior" and Johannist writings. ASEs 22/2 (2005) 337-353.

11062 *Dunderberg, Ismo* Valentinian views about Adam's creation: Valentinus and the gospel of Philip. $^{F}$AEJMELAEUS, L. SESJ 89: 2005 ⇒1. 509-527.

11063 **Ehrman, Bart D.** Lost christianities: the battles for scripture and the faiths we never knew. 2003 ⇒19,10509; 20,10100. $^{R}$CTJ 40 (2005) 119-120 (*Pomykala, Kenneth E.*); ChH 74 (2005) 347-349 (*Salvesen, Alison G.*); JR 85 (2005) 477-478 (*Albertson, David C.*); RBLit 7 (2005) 460-463 (*Kaler, Michael*);

11064 Oxf 2005 <2003>, OUP xv (2); 294 pp. $30. 01951-82499. Bibl. 281-287 [NTAb 50,207];

11065 Lost scriptures: books that did not make it into the New Testament. 2003 ⇒19,10508. $^{R}$CTJ 40 (2005) 120-122 (*Pomykala, Kenneth E.*); RBLit 7 (2005) 463-464 (*Kaler, Michael*);

11066 NY 2005 <2003>, OUP 342 pp. £9/$16. 01951-82502 [NTAb 50, 207];

11067 Cristianos perdidos: los credos proscritos del Nuevo Testamento. 2004 ⇒20,10101. $^{R}$CTom 133 (2005) 399-401 (*Huarte, Juan*);

11068 I cristianesimi perduti: apocrifi, sette ed eretici nella battaglia per le sacre scritture. R 2005, Carocci 356 pp.

11069 **Elliott, J.K.** The apocryphal New Testament: a collection of apocryphal christian literature in an English translation. Oxf 2005 <1993>, Clarendon xxv; 782 pp. 0-19826-1829. Pb.[EThL 81,525 —Van Belle, G.]

11070 *Emmel, Stephen* Ein altes Evangelium der Apostel taucht in Fragmenten aus Ägypten und Nubien auf. ZAC 9 (2005) 85-99.

11071 **Faria, Jacir de Freitas** As origens apócrifas do cristianismo: comentário aos evangelhos de Maria Madalena e Tomé. Bíblia em Comunidade: 2003 ⇒19,10514; 20,10102. $^{R}$REB 65 (2005) 750-753 (*Lepargneur, Hubert*);

11072 O outro Pedro e a outra Madalena segundo os apócrifos: uma leitura de gênero. 2004 ⇒20,10103. $^{R}$REB 65 (2005) 210-211 (*Pixley, Jorge*);

11073 El otro Pedro y la otra Magdalena según los apócrifos. Estella (Navarra) 2005, Verbo Divino 182 pp. 84-8169-682-X.

11074 *Foskett, Mary F.* Virginity as purity in the *Protevangelium of James*. A feminist companion to mariology. 2005 ⇒431. 67-76.

11075 *Foster, Paul* Secret Mark: its discovery and the state of research;

11076 Secret Mark is not secret anymore;

11077 Secret Mark: uncovering a hoax. ET 117 (2005) 46-52/64-6/66-68.

11078 **Fradejas Lebrero, José** Los evangelios apócrifos en la literatura española. M 2005, BAC xxvi; 610 pp. €25.48. 84-7914-771-7.

11079 *Frey, Jörg* Ein Weg zurück zu den Ursprüngen?: die Fragmente judenchristlicher Evangelienüberlieferungen. BiKi 60 (2005) 75-81.

11080 [E]**Geoltrain, Pierre; Kaestli, Jean-Daniel** Écrits apocryphes chrétiens, 2. Bibliothèque de la Pléiade 516: P 2005, Gallimard 156 pp. €79. 207-011388-4. [R]CEv 134 (2005) 61-62 (*Billon, Gérard*).

11081 *Grypeou, Emmanouela* The table from heaven: a note on Qur'an, Surah 5,111 ff.. CCO 2 (2005) 311-316.

11082 *Gundry, Robert H.* On the secret gospel of Mark. The old is better. WUNT 178: 2005 ⇒220. 74-97.

11083 *Hartenstein, Judith* "Was euch verborgen ist, werde ich euch verkündigen": das Evangelium nach Maria (von Magdala). BiKi 60 (2005) 96-101.

11084 *Huber, Konrad* Was das Neue Testament (so) nicht erzählt: Apokryphen im Verhältnis zu den kanonischen Evangelien. BiKi 60 (2005) 82-88.

11085 *Huber, Konrad; Leicht, Barbara* Sind die apokryphen Evangelien "Evangelien"?. BiKi 60 (2005) 66-67.

11086 **Janßen, Martina** Unter falschem Namen: eine kritische Forschungsbilanz frühchristlicher Pseudepigraphie. ARGU 14: 2003 ⇒19,10523. [R]NT 47 (2005) 166-167 (*Baum, A.D.*).

11087 *Kazen, Thomas* Sectarian gospels for some christians?: intention and mirror reading in the light of extra-canonical texts. NTS 51 (2005) 561-578.

11088 [TE]**King, Karen L.** The gospel of Mary of Magdala: Jesus and the first woman apostle. 2003 ⇒19,10527. [R]JR 85 (2005) 495-497 (*Perkins, Pheme*).

11089 **Klauck, Hans-Josef** Apocryphal gospels: an introduction. [T]*McNeil, Brian*: 2003 ⇒19,10529; 20,10108. [R]EThL 81 (2005) 525-528 (*Hogeterp, A.L.A.*).

11090 [E]**Kraus, Thomas J.; Nicklas, Tobias** Neutestamentliche Apokryphen, 1.: das Petrusevangelium und die Petrusapokalypse: die griechischen Fragmente mit deutscher und englischer Übersetzung. GCS 11: 2004 ⇒20,10110. [R]ThR 70 (2005) 242-245 (*Lührmann, Dieter*); SR 34 (2005) 281-283 (*Piovanelli, Pierluigi*).

11091 **Kruger, Michael J.** The Gospel of the Savior: an analysis of P. Oxy 840 and its place in the gospel traditions of early christianity. TENTS 1: Lei 2005, Brill xv; 299 pp. €79. 90-04-14393-9. Bibl. 267-287.

11092 *Laine, Minna* Gnosis, love and resurrection: interpretation of Pauline epistles in the Valentinian gospel of Philip. AEJMELAEUS, L.: SESJ 89: 2005 ⇒1. 415-435.

11093 **Lapham, Fred** An introduction to the New Testament Apocrypha. 2003 ⇒19,10531; 20,10112. [R]JR 85 (2005) 111-112 (*Klauck, Hans-Josef*); RBLit 7 (2005) 464-467 (*Gurtner, Daniel M.*).

11094 [E]**Lenzuni, Anna** Apocrifi del Nuovo Testamento. Letture patristiche 10: 2004 ⇒20,10092. [R]VetChr 42 (2005) 317-318 (*Trabace, Ilaria*); ASEs 22 (2005) 525-526 (*Nicklas, Tobias*).

11095 *Luomanen, Petri* On the fringes of canon: EUSEBIUS' view of the "Gospel of the Hebrews". The formation of the early church. WUNT 183: 2005 ⇒708. 265-281.

11096 *Lührmann, Dieter* Das Petrusbild VAN HAELST 741–eine Replik. ZAC 9 (2005) 424-434. Gospel of Peter.

11097 **Lührmann, Dieter** Die apokryph gewordenen Evangelien: Studien zu neuen Texten und zu neuen Fragen. NT.S 112: 2004 ⇒20,236.

RThLZ 130 (2005) 778-781 (*Schröter, Jens*); RBLit (2005)* (*Kraus, Thomas*).

11098 T**Mara, Maria Grazia** Il vangelo di Pietro. SOCr 30: 2002 ⇒18, 9724. RASEs 22 (2005) 522-525 (*Kraus, Thomas J.*).

11099 E**McNamara, Martin J.**, *al.*, Apocrypha Hiberniae: 1, evangelia infantiae. CChr.SA 13: 2001 ⇒17,8988; 20,10123. RIThQ 70 (2005) 86-89 (*McConvery, Brendan*).

11100 T*Morard, Françoise*: Evangile selon Marie. Écrits apocryphes chrétiens, 2. 2005 ⇒11080. 3-23.

11101 *Nicklas, Tobias* Zwei petrinische Apokryphen im Akhmîm-Codex oder eines?: kritische Anmerkungen und Gedanken. Apocrypha 16 (2005) 75-96.

11102 *Norelli, Enrico* Dévoiler les apocryphes. Choisir 552 (2005) 16-20.

11103 E**Pesce, Mauro** Le parole dimenticate di Gesù. 2004 ⇒20,10131. RIl Regno 50 (2005) 185 (*Ruggiero, Fabio*); ATT 11 (2005) 193-196 (*Marenco, Maria Rita*); Hum(B) 60 (2005) 1348-1356 (*Magris, Aldo*).

11104 *Petersen, Silke* "Selig sind, die dieser Welt entsagt haben ...": Askese, Körperfeindlichkeit und die Aufhebung der Geschlechterdifferenz. BiKi 60 (2005) 102-107.

11105 *Piovanelli, Pierluigi* What is a christian apocryphal text and how does it work?: some observations on apocryphal hermeneutics. NedThT 59/1 (2005) 31-40.

11106 *Plisch, Uwe-Karsten* Zu einigen Einleitungsfragen des unbekannten Berliner Evangeliums (UBE). ZAC 9 (2005) 64-84.

11107 *Rau, Eckhard* Zwischen Gemeindechristentum und christlicher Gnosis: das geheime Markusevangelium und das Geheimnis des Reiches Gottes. NTS 51 (2005) 482-504.

11108 **Rau, Eckhard** Das geheime Markusevangelium: ein Schriftfund voller Rätsel. 2003 ⇒19,10540. RThLZ 130 (2005) 1066-1067 (*Schröter, Jens*).

11109 *Rigo, Antonio* I vangeli dei Bogomili. Apocrypha 16 (2005) 163-197.

11110 *Roig Lanzillotta, F. Lautaro* Devolution and recollection, deficiency and perfection: human degradation and the recovery of the primal condition according to some early christian texts. FLUTTIKHUIZEN, G.: AGJU 59: 2005 ⇒93. 443-459.

11111 **Schmid, Herbert** 'Die Eucharistie ist Jesus': Anfänge einer Theorie des Sakraments im koptischen Philippusevangelium (NHC II 3). D*Hübner, Reinhard* 2005, Diss. München [ThRv 102,ix].

11112 T**Smith, Andrew Phillip** The gospel of Philip: annotated & explained. Woodstock, VT 2005, Skylight Paths xxxiv; 116 pp. 1-594-73111-X. Foreword *Stevan Davies*; Bibl. 115-116.

11113 *Tuckett, Christopher* Forty other gospels. FSTANTON, G. 2005 ⇒ 138. 238-253.

11114 *Van der Horst, Pieter* Sex, birth, purity and asceticism in the *Protevangelium Jacobi*. A feminist companion to mariology. 2005 <1995> ⇒431. 56-66.

11115 *Van der Vliet, Jacques* Fate, magic and astrology in Pistis Sophia, chaps 15-21. FLUTTIKHUIZEN, G.: AGJU 59: 2005 ⇒93. 519-536.

11116 *Van Dijk, Jacobus* Early christian apocrypha and the secret books of ancient Egypt. FLUTTIKHUIZEN, G.: 2005 ⇒93. 419-428.

11117 *Vinson, Éric* Apocryphes, les évangiles de l'ombre. Le monde des religions 14 (2005) 36-39.

11118 *Zervos, George T.* Christmas with Salome. A feminist companion to mariology. 2005 ⇒431. 77-98. Protevangelium Jacobi.

### K2.7 *Alia apocrypha NT*—**Apocryphal acts of apostles**

11119 *Agosti, Gianfranco* Acta Pauli et Theclae 10-11; 13 (MS 2634/1). Greek Papyri, Volume I. 2005 ⇒682. 69-71.

11120 T*Albert, Dominique, al.*, Passion de Matthieu 809-835;

11121 Passion de Jacques frère de Jean 771-788;

11122 Passion de Jacques frère du Seigneur 747-760;

11123 Passion de Barthélemy 789-808;

11124 Passion de Simon et Jude 837-864;

11125 T*Amsler, Frédéric; Bouvier, Bertrand* Martyre de Matthieu. Écrits apocryphes chrétiens, 2. 2005 ⇒11080. 539-564.

11126 *Andrist, P.* Un témoin oublié du *Dialogue de Timothée et Aquila* et des *Anastasiana antiiudaica (Sinaiticus Gr. 399)*. Byz. 75 (2005) 9-24.

11127 *Antonopulos, Athanasios* Ho Apostolos Andreas sten exobiblike grammateia. Prolegomena kritikes hermeneutikes theoreses. DBM 23/2 (2005) 223-248. **G**.

11128 *Aragione, Gabriella* Tecla di Iconio e Ipparchia di Maronea: modelli di conversione al femminile?. RiSCr 2/1 (2005) 133-155.

11129 T*Backus, Irena* Lettre de Paul aux Laodicéens;

11130 Lettre de Jésus-Christ sur le dimanche;

11131 Lettre de Lentulus. Écrits apocryphes chrétiens, 2. 2005 ⇒11080. 1087-1097/1099-1119/1121-1129.

11132 **Baldwin, Matthew C.** Whose Acts of Peter?: text and historical context of the *Actus Vercellenses*. WUNT 2/196: Tü 2005, Mohr S. xvi; 339 pp. €64. 3-16-148408-8. Diss. Chicago; Bibl. 322-329.

11133 T*Bausi, Alessandro* Prédication de Barthélemy dans la ville de l'Oasis et Martyre de Barthélemy 873-899;

11134 T*Besson, Gisèle; Brossard-Dandre, Michèle; Izydorczyk, Zbigniew* Vengeance du Sauveur 369-398;

11135 T*Beylot, Robert; Peres, Jacques-Noël; Piovanelli, Pierluigi* Prédication de Jacques fils de Zébédée et Martyre de Jacques fils de Zébédée 933-957;

11136 Martyre de Luc 959-978;

11137 T*Boud'hors, Anne* Histoire de Joseph le charpentier 25-59;

11138 T*Bovon, François; Callahan, Allen D.* Martyre de Marc l'évangéliste. Écrits apocryphes chrétiens, 2. 2005 ⇒11080. 567-586.

11139 *Bradshaw Aitken, Ellen* "The basileia of Jesus is on the wood": the epistle of Barnabas and the ideology of rule. Conflicted boundaries. SBL.Symp. 35: 2005 ⇒495. 197-213.

11140 T*Calzolari Bouvier, Valentin* Martyre de Thaddée arménien;

11141 T*Cennac, Caroline; Peres, Jacques-Noël* Mort de Pilate. Écrits apocryphes chrétiens, 2. 2005 ⇒11080. 661-696/399-413.

11142 *Chalmet, Philippe* Le pouvoir de guérir: connaissances médicales et action thaumaturge dans les plus anciens Actes apocryphes des Apôtres. Les Pères de l'Église. ThH 117: 2005 ⇒813. 193-215.

11143 [T]*Cirillo, Luigi; Schneider, André* Roman pseudo-clémentin; Reconnaissances. Écrits apocryphes chrétiens, 2. 2005 ⇒11080. 1591-2003.

11144 [ET]**Colin, Gérard** Le livre éthiopien des miracles de Marie: Taamra Mâryâm. Patrimoines christianisme: 2004 ⇒20,10152. [R]AnBoll 123 (2005) 210-211 (*Lequeux, X.*); SR 34 (2005) 276-278 (*Piovanelli, Pierluigi*).

11145 [T]*Cottier, Jean-François* Epître du Pseudo-Tite. Écrits apocryphes chrétiens, 2. 2005 ⇒11080. 1131-1171.

11146 *Czachesz, István* The identity of Lithargoel in the Acts of Peter and the Twelve. [F]LUTTIKHUIZEN, G.: AGJU 59: 2005 ⇒93. 485-502.

11147 *Daguet-Gagey, Anne* Le procès du Christ dans les *Acta Pilati*: étude des termes et *realia* institutionnels juridiques et administratifs. Apocrypha 16 (2005) 9-34.

11148 [T]*Dolbeau, François* Listes d'apôtres et de disciples;

11149 [T]*Dubois, Jean-Daniel; Gounelle, Rémi* Lettre de Pilate à l'empereur Claude. Écrits apocryphes chrétiens, 2. 2005 ⇒11080. 453-480/355-367.

11150 *Ebner, Martin* Sein und Schein auf dem "Königsweg": Figurenaufstellung und "Einspurung" des Lesers (ActThecl 1-4) 52-63;

11151 Paulinische Seligpreisungen à la Thekla: narrative Relecture der Makarismenreihe in ActThecl 5f. 64-79;

11152 Gemeindestrukturen in Exempeln: eine eindeutig frauenfreundliche Kompromisslösung 180-186;

11153 *Ebner, Martin; Lau, Markus* Überlieferung, Gliederung und Komposition 1-11;

11154 Übersetzung der Theklaakten 12-29;

11155 [E]**Ebner, Martin** Aus Liebe zu Paulus?: die Akte Thekla neu aufgerollt. SBS 206: Stu 2005, Kathol. Bibelwerk vii; 197 pp. 3-460-03-064-X. Bibl. 187-193.

11156 *Esch, Elisabeth* Thekla und die Tiere: oder: die Zähmung der Widerspenstigen. Akte Thekla. SBS 206: 2005 ⇒11155. 159-179.

11157 *Esch, Elisabeth; Leinhäupl-Wilke, Andreas* Auf die Spur gekommen: Plädoyer für eine leserorientierte Literarkritik in den ActThecl. Akte Thekla. SBS 206: 2005 ⇒11155. 30-51.

11158 *Faerber, Robert* Les *Acta apocrypha apostolorum* dans le corpus littéraire vieil-anglais: *Acta Andreae*. Apocrypha 16 (2005) 199-227.

11159 **Faria, Jacir de Freitas** A vida secreta dos apóstolos e apóstolas à luz dos Atos apócrifos. Comentários aos Apócrifos: Petrópolis 2005, Vozes 326 pp [REB 65,1005].

11160 *Flores, M.S. Acta Johannis*: apuntes sobre un apócrifo apasionante. Mayéutica 31 (2005) 383-409 [NTAb 51,138].

11161 [T]*Frey, Albert; Outtier, Bernard* Déclaration de Joseph d'Arimathée. Écrits apocryphes chrétiens, 2. 2005 ⇒11080. 329-354.

11162 [T]*Furrer, Christiane; Gounelle, Rémi* Evangile de Nicodème ou Actes de Pilate. Écrits apocryphes chrétiens, 2. 2005 ⇒11080. 249-297.

11163 *Gavrilyuk, Paul* MELITO's influence upon the Anaphora of *Apostolic Constitutions* 8.12. VigChr 59 (2005) 355-376.

11164 *Gounelle, Rémi* Traductions de textes hagiographiques et apocryphes latins en grec. Apocrypha 16 (2005) 35-73;

11165 Les Actes apocryphes des apôtres témoignent-ils de la réception des *Actes des Apôtres* canoniques?. Les Actes des Apôtres. LeDiv 199: 2005 ⇒715. 177-211.

11166 [T]*Gounelle, Rémi* Rapport de Pilate; Réponse de Tibère à Pilate; Comparution de Pilate. Écrits apocryphes chrétiens, 2. 2005 ⇒ 11080. 299-325.

11167 [T]**Harrak, Amir** The Acts of Mar Mari the Apostle. SBL.Writings from the Greco-Roman World 11: Boston 2005, Brill xxxvii; 110 pp. $20. 90-04-13050-0.

11168 **Hartenstein, Judith** Die zweite Lehre: Erscheinungen des Auferstandenen als Rahmenerzählungen frühchristlicher Dialoge. TU 146: 2000 ⇒16,9099; 18,9743. [R]SCI 24 (2005) 211-213 (*Schoenborn, Ulrich*).

11169 **Hovhanessian, Vahan** Third Corinthians: reclaiming Paul for christian orthodoxy. 2000 ⇒16,9126... 18,9744. [R]LTP 61 (2005) 185-186 (*Johnston, Steve*).

11170 *Illert, Martin* Ein Städtegleichnis des Makarios/Symeon. ZAC 9 (2005) 561-565. Abgar-Jesus correspondence.

11171 *Johnston, Steve; Poirier, Paul-Hubert* Nouvelles citations chez ÉPHREM et APHRAATE de la correspondance entre Paul et les Corinthiens. Apocrypha 16 (2005) 137-147.

11172 [T]*Junod, Éric; Kaestli, Jean-Daniel* Actes de Jean à Rome;

11173 [T]*Kaestli, Jean-Daniel; Picard, Jean-Claude* Première Apocalypse apocryphe de Jean. Écrits apocryphes chrétiens, 2. 2005 ⇒11080. 697-708/981-1018.

11174 *Kaler, Michael* Contextualizing the "Apocalypse of Paul". LTP 61/ 2 (2005) 233-246.

11175 **Klauck, Hans-Josef** Apokryphe Apostelakten: eine Einführung. Stu 2005, Kath. Bibelwerk 291 pp. €24. 3-460-33023-6.

11176 *Kochaniewicz, B.* Il *Transitus Mariae* dello Pseudo-Giuseppe da Arimatea—un apocrifo di origine italiana?. Ang. 82 (2005) 99-121 [NTAb 49,578].

11177 *Kötzel, Michael* Thekla und Alexander—oder: Kleider machen Leute: dramatische Ouvertüre des Antiochia-Zyklus;

11178 *Lau, Markus* Enthaltsamkeit und Auferstehung: narrative Auseinandersetzungen in der Paulusschule. Akte Thekla. SBS 206: 2005 ⇒ 11155. 91-109/80-90.

11179 [T]*Le Boulluec, Alain, al.*, Roman pseudo-clémentin; Homélies. Écrits apocryphes chrétiens, 2. 2005 ⇒11080. 1193-1589.

11180 *Leinhäupl-Wilke, Andreas* Vom Einfluss des lebendigen Gottes: zwei Bekenntnisreden gegen den Strich gelesen. Akte Thekla. SBS 206: 2005 ⇒11155. 139-158.

11181 *Loman, Janni* The letter of Barnabas in early second-century Egypt. [F]LUTTIKHUIZEN, G.: AGJU 59: 2005 ⇒93. 247-265.

11182 **MacDonald, Dennis R.** The Acts of Andrew. Early Christian Apocrypha 1: Santa Rosa, CA 2005, Polebridge viii; 125 pp. $18.

11183 [T]*Mimouni, Simon C.* Assomption de Marie ou Transitus grec 'R'. Écrits apocryphes chrétiens, 2. 2005 ⇒11080. 205-239.

11184 [E]**Monferrer Sala, Juan Pedro** Textos apócrifos árabes cristianos. 2003 ⇒19,10571. [R]EstB 63 (2005) 122-123 (*Sen, F.*).

11185 [T]*Morard, Françoise* Homélie sur la vie de Jésus et son amour pour les apôtres. Écrits apocryphes chrétiens, 2. 2005 ⇒11080. 101-134.

11186 *Nieto Ibañez, Jesús M.* Escatologia y universalismo judeo-cristiano en la apología de Pedro y Roma: observaciones sobre algunos apócrifos biblicos. EstB 63 (2005) 101-115.

11187 [T]*Norelli, Enrico* Actes de Barnabé 617-642;

11188 [T]*Nuvolone, Flavio G.* Sur le sacerdoce du Christ ou confession de Théodose 75-99;

11189 [T]*Outtier, Bernard* Dialogue du paralytique avec le Christ 61-74;

11190 [T]*Palmer, Andrew N.* Actes de Thaddée 643-660;

11191 [T]*Peres, Jacques-Noël* Actes de Matthieu dans la ville de Kahnat et Martyre de Matthieu en Parthie. Écrits apocryphes chrétiens, 2. 2005 ⇒11080. 901-932.

11192 *Perkins, Judith* Animal voices. Ment. *Apuleius*. R&T 12 (2005) 385-396;

11193 Fictional narratives and social critique. Late ancient christianity. 2005 ⇒517. 46-69;

11194 Resurrection and social perspectives in the apocryphal Acts of Peter and Acts of John. Ancient fiction. SBL.Symp. 32: 2005 ⇒ 721. 217-237.

11195 [T]*Petit, Madeleine* Vies des prophètes. Écrits apocryphes chrétiens, 2. 2005 ⇒11080. 419-452.

11196 [E]**Piñero, Antonio; Del Cerro, Gonzalo** Hechos apócrifos de los Apóstoles, 2: Hechos de Pablo y Tomás. M 2005, BAC xvii; 685-1598 pp. €30.65. 84-7914-716-4. Ed. bilingüe.

11197 [T]*Piovanelli, Pierluigi* Livre du coq 135-203;

11198 [T]*Poupon, Gérard* Passion de Pierre (dite du Pseudo-Linus) 709-34;

11199 [T]*Prieur, Jean-Marc* Actes d'André et de Matthias 483-519;

11200 Actes de Pierre et André. Écrits apocryphes chrétiens, 2. 2005 ⇒ 11080. 521-538.

11201 **Rhodes, James N.** The epistle of Barnabas and the Deuteronomic tradition: polemics, paraenesis, and the legacy of the golden-calf incident. WUNT 2/188: 2004 ⇒20,10182. [R]VigChr 59 (2005) 457-459 (*Nicklas, Tobias*) [Exod 32].

11202 [T]*Roessli, Jean-Michel* Oracles sibyllins;

11203 [T]*Rordorf, Willy* Actes de Tite. Écrits apocryphes chrétiens, 2. 2005 ⇒11080. 1045-1083/603-615.

11204 [ET]**Rosenstiehl, Jean-Marc** L'Apocalypse de Paul: (NH V,2). BCNH.T 31: Québec 2005, Presses de l'Université Laval xxvii; 326 pp. €70. 90429-16001. Commenté: *Michael Kaler*; Bibl. vii-xxiv.

11205 *Sanchez, Hector* Paulus nachfolgen—aber wie?: die Bedeutung des "Hauses" in den Theklaakten;

11206 *Scherer, Hildegard* Haus-Frauen-Geschichten: die beiden Mutterfiguren in den Theklaakten. Akte Thekla. SBS 206: 2005 ⇒11155. 124-138/110-123.

11207 *Scopello, Madeleine* Histoire de Charitiné;

11208 "Ils leur enseignèrent les charmes et les incantations ..." <1980>. Femme, gnose et manichéisme: de l'espace mythique au territoire du réel. NHMS 53: Lei 2005, Brill. 317-346/29-47;

11209 Images et métaphores de la médecine dans les écrits manichéens coptes. Les Pères de l'Église. ThH 117: 2005 ⇒813. 231-252.

11210 **Shoemaker, Stephen J.** The ancient traditions of the Virgin Mary's Dormition and Assumption. 2002 ⇒18,9762; 20,10187. [R]JR 85 (2005) 498-499 (*Louth, Andrew*).

11211 *Speck, P.* Die Johannes-Akten in der Debatte des Bilderstreits. [F]PRINZING, L. 2005 ⇒124. 127-139.
11212 *Stewart-Sykes, Alistair* Mimesis, typology and the institution narrative: some observations on Traditio Apostolica 4 and its afterlife. [F]YOUNG, F.: JSNT.S 295: 2005 ⇒168. 106-119.
11213 *Streete, Gail P.C.* Authority and authorship: the Acts of Paul and Thecla as a disputed Pauline text. LexTQ 40 (2005) 265-276.
11214 *Sullivan, Kevin P.; Wilfong, T.G.* The reply of Jesus to King Abgar: a Coptic New Testament apocryphon reconsidered (P.Mich. Inv. 6213) (Plates 2-3). BASPap 42 (2005) 107-123.
11215 *Thiering, B.* Authenticity of the Abgar documents and the letter of Jesus. JHiC 11/2 (2005) 67-82 [NTAb 50,567].
11216 **Thomas, Christine** The *Acts of Peter*, gospel literature, and the ancient novel: rewriting the past. 2003 ⇒19,10580; 20,10189. [R]RivCC 81 (2005) 346-347 (*Heid, Stefan*).
11217 *Tubach, Jürgen* Reisewege der Apostel in den Acta Petri aus Nag Hammadi. [F]LUTTIKHUIZEN, G.: AGJU 59: 2005 ⇒93. 461-483.
11218 [ET]**Vinogradov, A.J.** Greceskie predanija o sv. apostole Andree: tom 1: Žitija [S. Andreae Apostoli traditio graeca: tomus I: Vitae]. Biblioteka "Christianskogo vostoka" 3: St. Petersburg 2005, S.-Peterburgskogo Univ. 351 pp. 5288-03825-2. **R**.
11219 [T]*Zamagni, Claudio* Actes de Timothée. Écrits apocryphes chrétiens, 2. 2005 ⇒11080. 587-601.

### K3.1 Qumran—*generalia*

11220 *Anderson, Jeff S.* From "communities of texts" to religious communities: problems and pitfalls. Enoch and Qumran origins. 2005 ⇒921. 351-355.
11221 *Bar-Asher, Moshe* Some unusual spellings in Qumran scrolls. Meghillot III. 2005 ⇒608. 165-176. **H**.
11222 *Brooke, George J.* The scrolls in the British media (1987-2002). DSD 12 (2005) 38-51;
11223 The Qumran Scrolls and the demise of the distinction between higher and lower criticism. New directions. 2005 ⇒928. 26-42.
11224 *Clements, Ruth* On the fringe at the center: close encounters between "popular culture" and the Orion Center for the Study of the Dead Sea Scrolls. DSD 12 (2005) 52-67;
11225 *Clements, Ruth; Sharon, Nadav* The Orion Center bibliography of the Dead Sea scrolls (July 2004-December 2004);
11226 The Orion Center bibliography of the Dead Sea scrolls (January-June 2005). RdQ 22 (2005) 141-162/301-323.
11227 *Donceel, Robert* Khirbet Qumrân (Palestine): le locus 130 et les "ossements sous jarre": mise à jour de la documentation. Qumran Chronicle 13/1 (2005) 7-66.
11228 *Du Toit, Jacqueline S.; Kalman, Jason* Great Scott!: the Dead Sea scrolls, McGill University, and the Canadian media. DSD 12 (2005) 6-23.
11229 **Elledge, Casey D.** The Bible and the Dead Sea scrolls. SBL.Archaeology and biblical studies 14: Atlanta, Ga. 2005, SBL xii; 148 pp. $16. 1-58983-183-7.
[E]**Flint, P.** The bible at Qumran 2001 ⇒391.

11230 **Freund, Richard A.** Secrets of the Cave of Letters: rediscovering a Dead Sea mystery. 2004 ⇒20,10205. RRBLit (2005)* (*Nitzan, Bilha*).

11231 *García Martínez, Florentino* Lo stato attuale degli studi qumranici: cambiamenti e prospettive. Il messia. 2005 ⇒719. 205-211.

11232 *Grossman, Maxine L.; Murphy, Catherine M.* Introduction: the Dead Sea scrolls in the popular imagination. DSD 12 (2005) 1-5.

11233 *Grossman, Maxine L.* Mystery or history: the Dead Sea scrolls as pop phenomenon. DSD 12 (2005) 68-86.

11234 **Hirschfeld, Yizhar** Qumran in context: reassessing the archaeological evidence. 2004 ⇒20,10207. RBASOR 340 (2005) 94-95 (*Roller, Duane W.*); Theoforum 36 (2005) 223-225 (*Laberge, Léo*); TJT 21 (2005) 242-243 (*Wassen, Cecilia*); RBLit (2005)* (*Magness, Jodi*); JAOS 125 (2005) 389-394 (*Eshel, Hanna*).

11235 **Jokiranta, Jutta** Identity on a continuum: constructing and expressing sectarian social identity in Qumran serakhim and pesharim. Helsinki 2005, Univ. of Helsinki Diss. [StTh 60,113].

11236 *Kapera, Zdzisław Jan* Qumranologia polska: dokonania i perspektywy. CoTh 75/3 (2005) 21-54. **P**.

EKatzoff, R. Law in the documents...Judaean Desert 2005 ⇒662.

11237 E**Kiraz, George Anton** Anton Kiraz's Dead Sea scrolls archive. Piscataway, NJ 2005, Gorgias xxxiv; 266 pp. $65. 1-931956-38-3.

11238 **Lim, Timothy H.** The Dead Sea scrolls: a very short introduction. Very short introductions 143: Oxf 2005, OUP 138 pp. £7. 019-280-659-9.

11239 E**Lim, Timothy H.** The Dead Sea scrolls in their historical context. 2000 ⇒16,419... 20,10213. RCDios 218 (2005) 558-559 (*Gutiérrez, J.*).

11240 *Magness, Jodi* Toilet practices at Qumran: a response. RdQ 22 (2005) 277-278.

11241 **Magness, Jodi** The archaeology of Qumran and the Dead Sea scrolls. 2002 ⇒18,9795... 20,10222. RHebStud 46 (2005) 445-447 (*Strange, James F.*); VT 55 (2005) 140-141 (*Gillingham, Sue*); RBLit (2005)* (*Atkinson, Kenneth*);

11242 Debating Qumran: collected essays on its archaeology. 2004 ⇒20, 237. RThLZ 130 (2005) 1177-1178 (*Zangenberg, Jürgen*).

11243 *Mahan, Jeffrey H.* The Dead Sea scrolls in popular culture: "I can give you no idea of the contents". DSD 12 (2005) 87-94.

11244 **Newsom, Carol Ann** The self as symbolic space: constructing identity and community at Qumran. StTDJ 52: 2004 ⇒20,10224. RRBLit (2005)* (*Collins, John*).

11245 ET**Raurell, Frederic** Regla de la Comunitat de Qumran. Literatura qumrànica 3: 2004 ⇒20,10225. REstFr 106 (2005) 415-430 (*Klein, Enrique H.*); EstFr 106 (2005) 438-445 (*Bosch i Veciana, Antoni*).

11246 *Reimer, Andy M.* Probing the possibilities and pitfalls of post-colonial approaches to the Dead Sea scrolls. New directions. 2005 ⇒ 928. 182-209.

11247 E**Schattner-Rieser, Ursula** Textes araméens de la Mer morte: édition bilingue, vocalisée et commentée. Langues et cultures anciennes 5: Bru 2005, Safran 159 pp. €39. 287457-001X. Bibl. 12-14.

11248 *Schiffman, Lawrence H.* Inverting reality: the Dead Sea scrolls in the popular media. DSD 12 (2005) 24-37;

11249 The Dead Sea scrolls and rabbinic Judaism: perspectives and desiderata. Henoch 27/1-2 (2005) 27-33;

11250 Reflections on the deeds of sale from the Judaean desert in light of Rabbinic literature. Law in the documents. 2005 ⇒662. 185-203.

11251 [E]**Schiffman, Lawrence H.; VanderKam, James C.** The Encyclopedia of the Dead Sea Scrolls. 2000 ⇒16,9193... 20,10228. [R]JNES 64 (2005) 290-292 (*Pardee, Dennis*).

11252 *Silberman, Neil Asher* Operation scroll. Secrets of the bible. 2005 ⇒482.170-174.

11253 *Silk, Mark* Why the papers love the scrolls. DSD 12 (2005) 95-100.

11254 *Taylor, Joan E., al.*, Qumran textiles in the Palestine Exploration Fund, London: radiocarbon dating results. PEQ 137 (2005) 159-67.

11255 [E]**Tov, Emanuel**, *al.*, The texts from the Judaean desert: indices and introduction to the Discoveries in the Judaean Desert series. DJD 39: 2002 ⇒18,9767; 20,10234. [R]DSD 12 (2005) 369-371 (*Crawford, Sidnie White*).

11256 **Trever, John C.** The Dead Sea scrolls: a personal account. 2003 <1965> ⇒19,10630. Fascimile reprint. [R]DSD 12 (2005) 364-366 (*Lange, Armin*).

11257 **Vaux, Roland de** The excavations of Khirbet Qumran and Ain Feshkha, 1B: synthesis of R. de Vaux's field notes. [T]*Pfann, Stephen J.;* [E]*Humbert, Jean-Baptiste; Chambon, Alain*: NTOA.archaeologica 1B: 2003 ⇒19,10632; 20,10236. [R]OLZ 100 (2005) 456-462 (*Zangenberg, Jürgen*); RBLit 7 (2005) 112-114 (*Brooke, G.J.*).

[E]**Vazquez Allegue, J.** I manoscritti del Mar Morto 2005 ⇒697.

**Washburn, D.** A Catalog of biblical passages in the Dead Sea scrolls 2002 ⇒11301.

### K3.4 *Qumran*, libri biblici et parabiblici

11260 *Abegg, M.G.* A Messianic high priest in the scrolls?. Mishkan [J] 44 (2005) 43-51 [NTAb 50,110].

11261 [E]**Bar-Asher, Moshe; Dimant, Devorah** Meghillot, volume 2. 2004 ⇒20,449. [R]JSJ 36 (2005) 86-89 (*Doering, Lutz*). **H**.

11262 *Baruchi, Yosi* Reconstruction of the missing sections in the Psalms Scroll (11QPsa): a study of three psalms. Textus 22 (2005) 197; ʾ-yṭ [Ps 105; 122; 146]. **H.**;

11263 Fragmentary biblical scrolls from Bar Kokhba revolt refuge caves;

11264 *Baruchi, Yosi; Eshel, Hanan; Porat, Roi* Fragments of a biblical scroll from the Judean Desert [Lev 23-24]. Meghillot III. 2005 ⇒ 608. 177-190/259-260. **H**.

11265 *Bernstein, Moshe J.* From the Watchers to the Flood: story and exegesis in the early columns of the Genesis Apocryphon. Reworking the bible. StTDJ 58: 2005 ⇒723. 39-63.

11266 *Berrin, Shani* Pesher Nahum, Psalms of Solomon and POMPEY. Reworking the bible. StTDJ 58: 2005 ⇒723. 65-84;

11267 Qumran pesharim;.

11268 *Brady, Monica* Biblical interpretation in the 'Pseudo-Ezekiel' fragments (4Q383-391) from Cave 4. Biblical interpretation at Qumran. 2005 ⇒759. 110-133/88-109.

11269 *Brooke, George J.* The *Apocryphon of Levi*$^b$(?) and the Messianic Servant High Priest. Dead Sea scrolls and the NT. 2005 <1993> ⇒ 194. 140-157 [Isa 52,13-53,12];

11270 The bisection of Isaiah in the scrolls from Qumran. Studia semitica. JSSt.S 16: 2005 ⇒603. 73-94;

11271 Thematic commentaries on prophetic scriptures. Biblical interpretation at Qumran. 2005 ⇒759. 134-157.

11272 *Campbell, Jonathan G.* 'Rewritten bible' and 'parabiblical texts': a terminological and ideological critique. New directions. 2005 ⇒ 928. 43-68.

11273 **Campbell, Jonathan G.** The exegetical texts. CQuS 4: 2004 ⇒20, 10247. [R]RBLit (2005)* (*Sprinkle, Preston*).

11274 **Charlesworth, James Hamilton** The pesharim and Qumran: history chaos or consensus?. 2002 ⇒18,9831... 20,10248. [R]BiblInterp 13 (2005) 432-435 (*Hempel, Charlotte*); DSD 12 (2005) 226-228 (*Lim, Timothy H.*); BiOr 62 (2005) 119-120 (*Van der Kooij, Arie*); RBLit (2005)* (*Atkinson, Kenneth*); RBLit 7 (2005) 234-237 (*Berrin, Shani*).

11275 **Cross, Frank Moore**, *al.*, Qumran Cave 4, XII: 1-2 Samuel. DJD 17: Oxf 2005, Clarendon xix; 271 pp. €65. 0-19-924923-7.

11276 **Dahmen, Ulrich** Psalmen- und Psalter-Rezeption im Frühjudentum: Rekonstruktion, Textbestand, Struktur und Pragmatik der Psalmenrolle 11 QPs[a] aus Qumran. StTDJ 49: 2003 ⇒19,10647. [R]BZ 49 (2005) 120-123 (*Jain, Eva*); OLZ 100 (2005) 85-88 (*Rösel, Martin*); RdQ 22 (2005) 279-281 (*Puech, Émile*).

11277 *Dimant, Devorah* L'Apocryphe de Jérémie C de Qoumrân. RHPhR 85 (2005) 497-515;

11278 *Dimant, Devorah* Between sectarian and non-sectarian: the case of the Apocryphon of Joshua. Reworking the bible. StTDJ 58: 2005 ⇒723. 105-134.

11279 [E]**Ego, Beate**, *al.*, Biblia Qumranica 3B: Minor Prophets. Lei 2005, Brill xxiv; 195 pp. $120. 90-04-14330-0. Bibl.

11280 *Eshel, Esther; Eshel, Hanan* New fragments from Qumran: 4QGen F, 4QIsa B, 4Q226, 8QGen, and XpapEnoch. DSD 12 (2005) 134-157.

11281 *Hacham, N.* An Aramaic translation of Isaiah in the Rule of the Community. Leš. 67/2 (2005) 147-152 [NTAb 50,111]. **H.**

11282 *Heger, Paul* Qumran exegesis: "rewritten Torah" or interpretation?. RdQ 22 (2005) 61-87.

11283 *Henze, Matthias* Psalm 91 in premodern interpretation and at Qumran. Biblical interpretation at Qumran. 2005 ⇒759. 168-193.

11284 [E]**Herbert, Edward; Tov, Emmanuel** The bible as book: the Hebrew Bible and the Judean Desert discoveries. The Bible as Book 4: 2002 ⇒18,9817. [R]JRTI 7/1 (2005) 73-75 (*Siedlecki, Armin*).

11285 *Leuenberger, Martin* Aufbau und Pragmatik des 11QPSa-Psalters. RdQ 22 (2005) 165-211.

11286 *Martone, Corrado* Biblico o non biblico?: alcuni dubbi e domande. Il messia. 2005 ⇒719. 189-193.

11287 [E]**Parry, Donald W.; Tov, Emanuel** The Dead Sea scrolls reader, 1, 2, 4. 2004 ⇒20,10268, 10312-3. [R]DSD 12 (2005) 212-215 (*Reynolds, Bennie H., III*);

11288 The Dead Sea scrolls reader, 3: parabiblical texts. Lei 2005, Brill xxiv; 649, xii pp. €39/$39. 90-04-12647-3.

11289 **Paul, André** La bible avant la bible: la grande révélation des manuscrits de la mer Morte. P 2005, Cerf 266 pp. €28. 2-204-07354-7. Bibl. 22-23 [BCLF 675,12s].

11290 *Philonenko, Marc* Sur les expressions 'élus de vérité', 'élus de justice' et 'élu de justice et de fidélité': contribution à l'étude du sociolecte esséno-qoumrânien. [F]STEMBERGER, G.: SJ 32: 2005 ⇒140. 73-76.

11291 *Pietersen, Lloyd K.* 'False teaching, lying tongues and deceitful lips' (4Q169 Frgs 3-4 2.8): the pesharim and the sociology of deviance. New directions. 2005 ⇒928. 166-181.

11292 *Polliack, Meira* Wherein lies the pesher?: re-questioning the connection between the medieval Karaite and Qumranic modes of biblical interpretation. JSIJ 4 (2005) 151-200.

11293 **Pulikottil, Paulson** Transmission of biblical texts in Qumran: the case of the large Isaiah scroll 1QIsa[a]. JSPE.S 34: 2001 ⇒17,9123... 19,10671. [R]CBQ 67 (2005) 507-508 (*Berquist, Jon L.*).

11294 *Rothstein, David* Gen 24:14 and marital law in 4Q271 3: exegetical aspects and implications. DSD 12 (2005) 189-204;

11295 Joseph as pedagogue: biblical precedents for the depiction of Joseph in Aramaic Levi (4Q213). JSPE 14/3 (2005) 223-229.

11296 *Sahm, Ulrich; Schick, Alexander* Bruchstücke einer neuen Schriftrolle nahe dem Toten Meer entdeckt!: ein Sensationsfund und seine theologische Bedeutung. PJBR 4/2 (2005) 167-174 [Lev 23];

11297 Sensation auf Reh-Pergament: Beduinen entdecken ein neues Textstück der Tote-Meer-Rollen. HlL 137/2 (2005) 14-15.

11298 **Schick, Alexander; Glessmer, Uwe** Auf der Suche nach der Urbibel: die Schriftrollen vom Toten Meer, das Alte Testament und der geheime Bibelcode. 2000 ⇒16,9255. [R]OTEs 18 (2005) 952-953 (*Naudé, J.A.*).

11299 *Schiffman, Lawrence H.* Sacrificial Halakhah in the fragments of the Aramaic Levi document from Qumran, the Cairo genizah, and Mt. Athos monastery. Reworking the bible. StTDJ 58: 2005 ⇒723. 177-202.

11300 *Segal, Michael* Between bible and rewritten bible. Biblical interpretation at Qumran. 2005 ⇒759. 10-28.

11301 **Washburn, David L.** A catalog of biblical passages in the Dead Sea Scrolls. SBL Text-Critical Studies: 2003 <2002> ⇒18,9813; 19,10683; 20,10238, 10281. [R]WThJ 67 (2005) 169-170 (*Gurtner, Daniel M.*); RivBib 53 (2005) 364-366 (*Ibba, Giovanni*); HebStud 46 (2005) 442-445 (*Parry, Donald W.*).

11302 *Wise, Michael O.* 4Q245 (psDan' ar) and the high priesthood of Judas Maccabaeus. DSD 12 (2005) 313-362.

## K3.5 *Qumran*—varii rotuli et fragmenta

11303 [E]**Abegg, Martin G., Jr.**, *al.*, The Dead Sea scrolls concordance I: the non-biblical texts from Qumran. 2003 ⇒19,10686; 20,10282. [R]DSD 12 (2005) 366-369 (*Eshel, Hanan*).

11304 *Alexander, Philip S.* The material reconstruction and genre of 4Q285 (Sefer ha-Milḥamah) reconsidered. Studia semitica. JSSt.S 16: 2005 ⇒603. 95-113.

11305 *Beckwith, Roger T.* The Qumran Temple Scroll and its calendar: their character and purpose. Calendar, chronology. AGJU 61: 2005 ⇒184. 67-90.

11306 *Ben-Dov, Jonathan; Horowitz, Wayne* The Babylonian lunar three in calendrical scrolls from Qumran. ZA 95 (2005) 104-120.

11307 *Brooke, George J.* 4Q341: an exercise for spelling and for spells?. [F]MILLARD, A.: LHBOTS 426: 2005 ⇒102. 271-282.

11308 [E]**Charlesworth, James H.** The Dead Sea scrolls: pseudepigraphic and non-Masoretic psalms and prayers. 1997 ⇒13,8851... 20, 10289. [R]RdQ 22 (2005) 131-134 (*Puech, Émile*);

11309 The Dead Sea scrolls: Hebrew, Aramaic, and Greek texts with English translations: angelic liturgy: songs of the sabbath sacrifice. 1999 ⇒15,9278... 20,10287. [R]RdQ 22 (2005) 134-136 (*Puech, Émile*);

11310 The Dead Sea scrolls: Hebrew, Aramaic, and Greek texts with English translations: pesharim, other commentaries, and related documents: songs of the Sabbath sacrifices. The Princeton Theological Seminary Dead Sea Scrolls Project 6B: 2002 ⇒18,2501... 20, 10288. [R]RdQ 22 (2005) 136-139 (*Puech, Émile*).

11311 *Daise, Michael A.* "The days of Sukkot of the month of Kislev": the festival of dedication and the delay of feasts in 1QS 1:13-15. Enoch and Qumran origins. 2005 ⇒921. 119-128.

11312 **DiTommaso, Lorenzo** The Dead Sea New Jerusalem text: contents and contexts. TSAJ 110: Tü 2005, Mohr S. xv; 228 pp. €79. 3-16-148799-0. Bibl. 195-214.

11313 *Doudna, Greg* Ostraca KhQ1 and KhQ2 from the cemetery of Qumran: a new edition. JHScr 5/5 2004*.

11314 **Duhaime, Jean** The war texts: 1QM and related manuscripts. CQuS 6: 2004 ⇒20,10293. [R]CBQ 67 (2005) 488-489 (*Stone, Michael E.*); JJS 56 (2005) 343-345 (*Campbell, Jonathan G.*); RBLit (2005)* (*Steudel, Annette*).

11315 *Eisenman, R.* MMT as a Jamesian letter to 'the Great King of the peoples beyond the Euphrates'. JHiC 11/1 (2005) 55-68 [NTAb 50, 110].

11316 *Goff, Matthew J.* Wisdom, apocalypticism, and the pedagogical ethos of 4QInstruction. Conflicted boundaries. SBL.Symp. 35: 2005 ⇒495. 57-67;

11317 **Goff, Matthew J.** The worldly and heavenly wisdom of 4QInstruction. StTDJ 50: 2003 ⇒19,10712; 20,10301. [R]CBQ 67 (2005) 117-118 (*VanderKam, James C.*); JBL 124 (2005) 548-553 (*Wright, Benjamin, III*).

11318 *Gordley, Matthew E.* Seeing stars at Qumran: the interpretation of Balaam and his oracle in the Damascus Document and other Qumran texts. ProcGLM 25 (2005) 107-119 [Num 24,17].

11319 **Grossman, Maxine L.** Reading for history in the Damascus Document: a methodological method. StTDJ 45: 2002 ⇒18,9928; 19, 10713. [R]JThS 56 (2005) 138-140 (*Hempel, Catherine*).

11320 *Harkins, Angela K.* Observations on the editorial shaping of the so-called community hymns from 1QHa and 4QHa (4Q427). DSD 12 (2005) 233-256.

11321 **Harrington, Hannah K.** The purity texts. CQuS 5: 2004 ⇒20, 10303. [R]EThL 81 (2005) 515-516 (*Hogeterp, A.L.A.*); JJS 56 (2005) 341-343 (*Campbell, Jonathan G.*); RBLit (2005)* (*Gilders, William; Werrett, Ian*).

11322 *Hultgren, Stephen* A new literary analysis of CD XIX-XX, part II: CD XIX:32b-XX:34: the punctuation of CD XIX:33b-XX:1a and the identity of the "New Covenant". RdQ 22 (2005) 7-32.

11323 **Ibba, Giovanni** Le ideologie del Rotolo della Guerra (1QM): studio sulla genesi e la datazione dell'opera. F 2005, Giuntina 276 pp. 88-8057-237-7.

11324 **Jefferies, Daryl Foy** Wisdom at Qumran: a form-critical analysis of the admonitions in 4QInstruction. Gorgias Diss. Near Eastern Studies 3: 2002 ⇒19,10720; 20,10307. [R]DSD 12 (2005) 372-374 (*Tigchelaar, Eibert*).

11325 *Kister, Menahem* 4Q392 1 and the conception of light in Qumran 'dualism'. Meghillot III. 2005 ⇒608. 125-142. **H.**

11326 *Lawrence, Louise J.* 'Men of perfect holiness' (1QS 7.20): social-scientific thoughts on group identity, asceticism and ethical development in the Rule of the Community. New directions. 2005 ⇒ 928. 83-100.

11327 *Lorein, G.W.; Van Staalduine-Sulman, E.* A song of David for each day: the provenance of the Songs of David. RdQ 22 (2005) 33-59.

11328 *Lyons, William J.* 'An unauthorized version': the Temple Scroll in narratological perspective. New directions. 2005 ⇒928. 126-148.

11329 *Nitzan, Bilha* The ideological and literary unity of 4QInstruction and its authorship. DSD 12 (2005) 257-279;

11330 Key terms in 4QInstruction: implications for its ideological unity. Meghillot III. 2005 ⇒608. 101-124. **H.**

11331 *Økland, Jorunn* The language of gates and entering: on sacred space in the Temple Scroll. New directions. 2005 ⇒928. 149-165.

11332 *Paganini, Simone* Osservazioni sull'uso di Dt 22,6c nel Rotolo del Tempio. Henoch 27/1-2 (2005) 127-135.

11333 [E]**Parry, Donald W.; Tov, Emanuel** The Dead Sea scrolls reader, 5: poetic and liturgical texts. Lei 2005, Brill xxiv; 515, xiii pp. €39/ $39. 90-04-12653-8;

11334 The Dead Sea scrolls reader, 6: additional genres and unclassified texts. Lei 2005, Brill xxiv; 347, xxii pp. €39/$39. 90-04-12646-5.

11335 *Puech, Émile* Les fragments eschatologiques de 4QInstruction (4Q416 1 et 1Q418 69 ii, 81-81a, 127). RdQ 22 (2005) 89-119.

11336 *Qimron, Elisha* Improving the editions of the Dead Sea scrolls (3). Meghillot III. 2005 ⇒608. 239-244. 11QT[a]. **H.**

11337 *Robinson, James M.* The *Hodahyot* formula in prayers and hymns of early christianity. The sayings gospel Q. BEThL 189: 2005 <1964> ⇒289. 75-118.

11338 **Saukkonen, Juhana** The story behind the text: scriptural interpretation in 4Q252. Helsinki 2005, Diss. Helsinki [StTh 60,113].

11339 *Shemesh, Aharon* 4Q251: Midrash Mishpatim. DSD 12 (2005) 280-302.

11340 *Sweeney, Marvin A.* Davidic typology in the forty year war between the sons of light and the sons of darkness. Form and intertextuality. FAT 45: 2005 ⇒313. 262-268.

11341 *Tigchelaar, Eibert* A cave 4 fragment of Divre Mosheh (4QDM and the text of 1Q22 1:7-10 and Jubilees 1:9, 14). DSD 12 (2005) 303-312.

11342 **Tigchelaar, Eibert J.C.** To increase learning for the understanding ones: reading and reconstructing the fragmentary early Jewish sapiential text 4QInstruction. StTDJ 44: 2001 ⇒17,9178... 20,10327. [R]RBLit (2005)* (*Goff, Matthew*).

11343 *VanderKam, James C.* Sinai revisited. Biblical interpretation at Qumran. 2005 ⇒759. 44-60. Community Rule.

11344 *Volgger, David* The feast of the wood offering according to the Temple Scroll. BN 127 (2005) 21-39;

11345 Die Reflexion zum Weihefest in TR 15,3b-17,5. [F]SEIDL, T.: ATSAT 75: 2005 ⇒137. 183-207.

11346 **Wassen, Cecilia** Women in the Damascus document. Academia biblica 21: Lei 2005, Brill xiv; 255 pp. $43. 90-04-13770-X.

11347 *Weinfeld, Moshe* The angelic song over the luminaries in the Qumran texts;

11348 The Temple Scroll or 'The law of the king';

11349 The royal guard according to the Temple Scroll;

11350 God versus Moses in the Temple Scroll: 'I do not speak on my own but on God's authority' (Sifre Deuteronomy, sec. 5; John 12,48f.). Normative and sectarian Judaism. Library of Second Temple Studies 54: 2005 ⇒2732. 90-111/158-185/186-188/189-193.

11351 *Wold, Benjamin G.* Reconstructing and reading 4Q416 2 II 21: comments on Menahem Kister's proposal. DSD 12 (2005) 205-211.

11352 **Wold, Benjamin G.** Women, men, and angels: the Qumran wisdom document Musar le Mevin and its allusions to Genesis creation traditions. [D]*Stuckenbruck, Loren*: WUNT 2/201: Tü 2005, Mohr S. xii; 286 pp. €54. 3-16-148691-9. Diss. Durham; Bibl. 246-261 [Gen 1-3].

11353 *Zahn, Molly M.* New voices, ancient words: the Temple Scroll's reuse of the bible. Temple and worship. 2005 ⇒731. 435-458.

## K3.6 **Qumran et Novum Testamentum**

11354 **Annandale-Potgieter, Joan** Qumran in and around the bible: a new look at the Dead Sea scrolls. 1998 ⇒14,8546. [R]OTEs 18 (2005) 927-928 (*Naudé, J.A.*).

11355 *Boccaccini, Gabriele* I manoscritti del Mar Morto tra ebraismo e cristianesimo. Il messia. 2005 ⇒719. 183-188.

11356 *Brooke, George J.* Jesus, the Dead Sea scrolls and scrolls scholarship. Dead Sea scrolls and the NT. 2005 <2003> ⇒194. 19-27;

11357 Levi and the Levites in the Dead Sea scrolls and the New Testament. Dead Sea scrolls and the NT. 2005 <1993> ⇒194. 115-139;

11358 Qumran: the cradle of the Christ? <2000>;

11359 Shared intertextual interpretations in the Dead Sea scrolls and the New Testament <1998>;

11360 The *Commentary on Genesis A* and the New Testament <1996>;

11361 The Temple Scroll and the New Testament <1989>. Dead Sea scrolls and the NT. 2005 ⇒194. 261-271/70-94/177-194/97-114;

11362 Eschatological bible interpretation in the scrolls and in the New Testament. Mishkan [J] 44 (2005) 18-25 [NTAb 50,110].

11363 **Brooke, George J.** The Dead Sea scrolls and the New Testament. Ph 2005, Fortress xxii; 314 pp. £20. 0-8006-3723-2. Bibl. 298-301. [R]RBLit (2005)* (*Frey, Joerg; Kraus, Thomas*);

11364 Qumran and the Jewish Jesus: reading the New Testament in light of the Scrolls. C 2005, Grove 28 pp. £2.75. 185174-5874.

11365 *Chrostowski, Waldemar* Nowy Testament a Qumran—ponad pól wieku dociekan i dylematów. CoTh 75/3 (2005) 139-158. **P**.

11366 *Elgvin, T.* The scrolls and the Jewish gospel. Mishkan [J] 44 (2005) 4-8 [NTAb 50,110].

11367 *Evans, C.A.* The Dead Sea scrolls and the Jewishness of the gospels. Mishkan [J] 44 (2005) 9-17 [NTAb 50,111].

11368 **Feather, Robert** The secret initiation of Jesus at Qumran: the Essene mysteries of John the Baptist. Rochester, Vt. 2005, Bear xx; 457 pp. 1-591-43044-5.

11369 *Gianotto, Claudio* Essenes, Qumran, and christian origins. Enoch and Qumran origins. 2005 ⇒921. 414-416.

11370 *Harrington, D.J.* Wisdom christology in the light of early Jewish and Qumran texts. Mishkan [J] 44 (2005) 36-42 [NTAb 50,111].

11371 **Ruspoli, Stéphane** Le Christ essénien: l'origine essénienne du christianisme et du Messie de Nazareth. Les carnets spirituels: P 2005, Arfuyen 147 pp. €16. 2-84590-070-8. Bibl. 146-147.

11372 *Ulfgard, H.* The Songs of the Sabbath Sacrifice and the heavenly scene of the book of Revelation. Mishkan [J] 44 (2005) 26-35 [NTAb 50,112].

11373 *VanderKam, James C.* Il contributo dei manoscritti di Qumran allo studio delle origini del cristianesimo. Il messia. 2005 ⇒719. 195-200.

11374 **Vermes, Geza** Scrolls, scriptures and early christianity. Library of Second Temple Studies 56: L 2005, Clark viii; 86 pp. 0-567-0838-7-X. Bibl. vi. [R]RBLit (2005)* (*Kraus, Thomas; Nicklas, Tobias*).

### K3.8 Historia et doctrinae Qumran

11375 *Arnold, Russell C.D.* Qumran prayer as an act of righteousness. JQR 95 (2005) 509-529.

11376 *Baumgarten, Albert I.* Reflections on the Groningen hypothesis. Enoch and Qumran origins. 2005 ⇒921. 256-262.

11377 *Baumgarten, Joseph* The avoidance of the death penalty in Qumran law. Reworking the bible. StTDJ 58: 2005 ⇒723. 31-38.

11378 *Beckwith, Roger T.* The Qumran six-jubilee cycle: a reconsideration. Calendar, chronology. AGJU 61: 2005 ⇒184. 125-133.

11379 *Ben-Dov, Jonathan Dwq* and lunar phases in Qumran calendars: new Mesopotamian evidence. Meghillot III. 2005 ⇒608. 3-28. **H**.

11380 *Bernstein, Moshe J.; Koyfman, Shlomo A.* The interpretation of biblical law in the Dead Sea scrolls: forms and methods. Biblical interpretation at Qumran. 2005 ⇒759. 61-87.

11381 *Boccaccini, Gabriele* Qumran: the headquarters of the Essenes or a marginal splinter group?. Enoch and Qumran origins. 2005 ⇒921. 303-309.

11382 *Bolotnikov, Alexander* The theme of apocalyptic war in the Dead Sea scrolls. AUSS 43 (2005) 261-266.

11383 *Brooke, George J.* The ten temples in the Dead Sea scrolls. Temple and worship. LHBOTS 422: 2005 ⇒731. 417-434.

11384 *Castaño Fonseca, Adolfo M.* Algunos rasgos característicos del maestro de justicia en los himnos de Qumrán: un ejemplo en 1QH 5,5-19. Qol 39 (2005) 41-59.

11385 *Collins, John J.* Il messia 'Figlio di Davide' nel giudaismo del secondo tempio alla luce dei manoscritti di Qumran. Il messia. 2005 ⇒719. 49-67;

11386 Interpretations of the creation of humanity in the Dead Sea scrolls. Biblical interpretation at Qumran. 2005 ⇒759. 29-43 [Gen 1-3].

11387 *Dimant, D.* Babylonian and Iranian traditions in the scrolls from Qumran. Teuph 30 (2005) 184-185.
11388 *Duhaime, Jean* Dualisme et construction de l'identité sectaire à Qumrân. Théologiques 13 (2005) 43-57.
11389 *Elgvin, Torleif* The Yahad is more than Qumran;
11390 *Elliott, Mark A.* Sealing some cracks in the Groningen foundation. Enoch and Qumran origins. 2005 ⇒921. 273-279/263-272.
11391 **Fletcher-Louis, Crispin H.T.** All the glory of Adam: liturgical anthropology in the Dead Sea scrolls. StTDJ 42: 2002 ⇒19,9983; 20, 10342. [R]RdQ 22 (2005) 281-285 (*Puech, Émile*); RBLit (2005)* (*Goff, Matthew*).
11392 *Flint, Peter W.* The prophet David at Qumran. Biblical interpretation at Qumran. 2005 ⇒759. 158-167.
11393 *García Martínez, Florentino* Response: the Groningen hypothesis revisited. Enoch and Qumran origins. 2005 ⇒921. 310-316;
11394 Creation in the Dead Sea scrolls. Creation of heaven and earth. Themes in biblical narrative 8: 2005 ⇒492. 49-70.
11395 *Grabbe, Lester L.* Digging among the roots of the Groningen hypothesis. Enoch and Qumran origins. 2005 ⇒921. 280-285.
11396 *Heger, Paul* Did prayer replace sacrifice at Qumran?. RdQ 22 (2005) 213-233.
11397 *Hempel, Charlotte* The Groningen hypothesis: strengths and weaknesses. Enoch and Qumran origins. 2005⇒921. 249-255.
11398 [E]**Hempel, Charlotte; Lange, Armin; Lichtenberger, Hermann** The wisdom texts from Qumran and the development of sapiential thought. BEThL 159: 2002 ⇒18,482... 20,10343. [R]TS 66 (2005) 444-446 (*VanderKam, James C.*); CBQ 67 (2005) 374-376 (*Ben-Dov, Jonathan*); RivBib 53 (2005) 348-353 (*Prato, Gian Luigi*); JNSL 31/1 (2005) 125-129 (*Cook, Johann*); RBLit 7 (2005) 230-234 (*Goff, Matthew*).
11399 *Kaimakis, Dimitris* He angelike leiturgia tu Kumran. DBM 23/2 (2005) 175-184. **G**.
11400 *Katzoff, Ranon; Schaps, David* Introduction. Law in the documents. JSJ.S 96: 2005 ⇒662. 1-6.
11401 *Lim, Timothy H.* The translation of נדמו and its significance for the Groningen hypothesis;
11402 *Martone, Corrado* Beyond "Beyond the Essene hypothesis": some observations on the Qumran Zadokite priesthood. Enoch and Qumran origins. 2005 ⇒921. 291-293/360-365.
11403 **Murphy, Catherine M.** Wealth in the Dead Sea scrolls and in the Qumran community. StTDJ 40: 2002 ⇒18,9993...20,10349. [R]RdQ 22 (2005) 289-91 (*Puech, Émile*); RBLit (2005)* (*Goff, Matthew*).
11404 *Naudé, Jacobus A.* On the boundaries between the sacred and the profane at the community of Qumran. JSem 14/2 (2005) 261-282.
11405 *Nerel, G.* Qumran, Messianic Jews, and modern self-identity. Mishkan [J] 44 (2005) 52-59 [NTAb 50,111].
11406 *Noam, Vered* Divorce in Qumran in light of early Halakhah. JJS 56/2 (2005) 206-223.
11407 *Paganini, Simone* Qumran, i manoscritti del Mar Morto, gli Esseni: un problema aperto. StPat 52 (2005) 149-170.
11408 *Piovanelli, Pierluigi* Some archaeological, sociological, and cross-cultural afterthoughts on the "Groningen" and the "Enochic/Essene" hypotheses. Enoch and Qumran origins. 2005 ⇒921. 366-372.

11409 *Puech, Émile* The Essenes and Qumran, the teacher and the wicked priest, the origins. Enoch & Qumran origins. 2005 ⇒921. 298-302.

11410 *Rivlin, Yosef* Gift and inheritance law in the Judaean desert documents. Law in the documents. JSJ.S 96: 2005 ⇒662. 165-183.

11411 *Safrai, Ze'ev* Halakhic observance in the Judaean desert documents;

11412 *Satlow, Michael L.* Marriage payments and succession strategies in the documents from the Judaean desert. Law in the documents. JSJ.S 96: 2005 ⇒662. 205-236/51-65.

11413 *Schiffman, Lawrence H.* I manoscritti di Qumran e il giudaismo rabbinico. Il messia. 2005 ⇒719. 201-204.

11414 **Schiffman, Lawrence H.** Les manuscrits de la mer Morte et le judaïsme: l'apport de l'ancienne bibliothèque de Qumrân à l'histoire du judaïsme. T*Duhaime, Jean*: 2003 ⇒19,10810; 20,10354. REstB 63 (2005) 124-129 (*Sen, F.*).

11415 *Shemesh, Aharon* The laws of the firstborn and the cattle tithe in Qumran literature and rabbinic halakhah. Meghillot III. 2005 ⇒ 608. 143-161. **H.**

11416 *Steudel, Annette* "Bereitet den Weg des Herrn": religiöses Lernen in Qumran. Religiöses Lernen. WUNT 180: 2005 ⇒384. 99-116.

11417 *Suter, David W.* Theodicy and the problem of the "intimate enemy". Enoch and Qumran origins. 2005 ⇒921. 329-335.

11418 *Talmon, Shemaryahu* Comments concerning the "Qumran-Essenes" hypothesis. Enoch and Qumran origins. 2005 ⇒921. 294-297;

11419 Anti-lunar-calendar polemic in the covenanters' writings. Meghillot III. 2005 ⇒608. 69-84. **H.**

11420 *VanderKam, James C.* Too far beyond the Essene hypothesis?. Enoch and Qumran origins. 2005 ⇒921. 388-393.

11421 *Weinfeld, Moshe* Prayer and liturgical practice in the Qumran sect;

11422 Grace after meals in Qumran. Normative and sectarian Judaism. Library of Second Temple Studies 54: 2005 ⇒2732. 53-67/112-121.

11423 **Wieder, Naphtali** The Judean scrolls and Karaism. J $^{2}$2005 <1962>, Ben-Zvi Institute xii; 502 pp. Bibl.

11424 *Wright, Archie T.* Prayer and incantation in the Dead Sea scrolls. Studies in Jewish prayer. JSSt.S 17: 2005 ⇒828. 75-88.

11425 *Wright, Benjamin G.* One "methodological assumption" of the Groningen hypothesis of Qumran origins. Enoch and Qumran origins. 2005 ⇒921. 286-290.

11426 **Xeravits, Géza G.** King, priest, prophet: positive eschatological protagonists of the Qumran Library. StTDJ 47: 2003 ⇒19,10820. RDSD 12 (2005) 223-226 (*Oegema, Gerbern*); Materia giudaica 10/1 (2005) 171-175 (*Arcari, Luca*).

11427 *Yiftach-Firanko, Uri* Judaean desert marriage documents and Ekdosis in the Greek law of the Roman period. Law in the documents. JSJ.S 96: 2005 ⇒662. 67-84.

11428 **Zurli, Emanuela** La giustificazione 'solo per grazia' negli scritti di Qumran: analisi dell'inno finale della *Regola della communità* e degli *Inni*. 2003 ⇒19,10823; 20,10361. RGr. 86 (2005) 183-184 (*Vanni, Ugo*); RivBib 53 (2005) 366-372 (*Ibba, Giovanni*); ATT 11 (2005) 465-466 (*Marenco, Maria Rita*); Bib. 86 (2005) 445-448 (*Vázquez Allegue, Jaime*).

## K4.1 Sectae iam extra Qumran notae: Esseni, Zelotae

11429 **Gusella, Laura** Esperienze di communità nel Giudaismo antico: esseni, terapeuti, Qumran. 2003 ⇒19,10829; 20,10367. [R]ATT 11 (2005) 461-462 (*Marenco, Maria Rita*).

11430 **Riesner, Rainer** Esseni e prima comunità cristiana a Gerusalemme: nuove scoperte e fonti. 2001 ⇒17,9233; 19,10833. [R]ATT 11 (2005) 463-465 (*Marenco, Maria Rita*); EstTrin 39 (2005) 590-592 (*Vázquez Allegue, Jaime*).

11431 **Taylor, Justin** Pythagoreans and Essenes: structural parallels. 2004 ⇒20,10369. [R]EThL 81 (2005) 517-518 (*Hogeterp, A.L.A.*).

## K4.3 Samaritani

11432 **Anderson, Robert T.; Giles, Terry** The keepers: an introduction to the history and culture of the Samaritans. 2002 ⇒19,10007; 20, 10372. [R]TJT 21 (2005) 218-219 (*Mirecki, Cathy A.*);

11433 Tradition kept: the literature of the Samaritans. Peabody, MASS 2005, Hendrickson xv; 432 pp. $35. 1-56563-747-X. Bibl. 413-21.

11434 *Arnold, Werner* Zur Geschichte der Samaritaner im 20. Jahrhundert: ein Text im arabischen Dialekt der Samaritaner von Holon (Israel). [F]VOIGT, R.: AOAT 317: 2005 ⇒158. 21-38.

11435 **Crown, Alan David; Pummer, Reinhard** A bibliography of the Samaritans. ATLA.BS 51: Lanham [3]2005, Scarecrow xxii; 598 pp. $100. 0-8108-5659-X.

11436 *Knoppers, Gary N.* Mt. Gerizim and Mt. Zion: a study in the early history of the Samaritans and Jews. BCSBS 64 (2004-2005) 5-32 = SR 34 (2005) 309-338.

11437 *Laurant, Sophie* La Pâque des Samaritains, écho de l'ancien Israel. MoBi 164 (2005) 40-45.

11438 **Pummer, Reinhard** Early christian authors on Samaritans and Samaritanism: texts, translations and commentary. TSAJ 92: 2002 ⇒18,10017; 20,10377. [R]SCI 24 (2005) 329-331 (*Ilan, Tal*); REJ 164 (2005) 349-350 (*Mimouni, Simon C.*).

11439 *Wypych, Stanisław* Samarytanie w ujęciu historycznym, geograficznym i religijnym [I samaritani nel contesto storico, geografico e religioso]. RBL 58 (2005) 165-179. **P**.

## K4.5 *Sadoqitae, Qaraitae*–Cairo Genizah; Zadokites, Karaites

11440 **Astren, Fred** Karaite Judaism and historical understanding. Columbia 2004, Univ. of South Carolina Pr. x; 346 pp.

11441 [E]**Becker, Hans-Jürgen** Geniza-Fragmente zu Avot de-Rabbi Natan. TSAJ 103: 2004 ⇒20,10379. [R]RBLit 7 (2005) 237-241 (*Kern-Ulmer, Rivka*).

11442 *Berti, Silvia* Erudition and religion in the Judeo-Christian encounter: the significance of the Karaite myth in seventeenth-century Europe. HPolS 1/1 (2005) 110-120.

11443 *Charlap, Luba R.* Language and meta-language in the Byzantine Karaite school. JJS 56 (2005) 80-100.

11444 *Cohen, Mark R.* Feeding the poor and clothing the naked: the Cairo Geniza. JIntH 35 (2005) 407-421.

11445 **Frank, Daniel H.** Search scripture well: Karaite exegetes and the origins of the Jewish bible commentary in the Islamic East. EJM 29: 2004 ⇒20,10381. [R]RBLit (2005)* (*Hughes, Aaron*).

11446 *Lied, Liv I.* Another look at the land of Damascus: the spaces of the Damascus Document in the light of Edward W. Soja's thirdspace approach. New directions. 2005 ⇒928. 101-125.

11447 *Polliack, Meira* Medieval Karaism. The Oxford handbook of Jewish studies. 2005 ⇒1053. 295-326.

11448 [E]**Polliack, Meira** Karaite Judaism: a guide to its history and literary sources. HO 1/73: 2003 ⇒19,10856. [R]REJ 164 (2005) 350-352 (*Rothschild, Jean-Pierre*).

11449 [E]**Reif, Stefan C.** The Cambridge Genizah collections: their contents and significance. Genizah series 1: 2002 ⇒18,698... 20, 10387. [R]JJS 56 (2005) 157-160 (*Bhayro, Siam*).

11450 **Schäfer, Peter; Shaked, Shaul** Magische Texte aus der Kairoer Geniza, 3. TSAJ 72: 1999 ⇒15,9459; 17,9257. [R]JSSt 50 (2005) 397-399 (*Levene, Dan*).

11451 *Shivtiel, Avihai* A Judaeo-Armenian and Judaeo-Arabic word-list from the Cairo Genizah. Studia semitica. JSSt.S 16: 2005 ⇒603. 139-143.

## K5 Judaismus prior vel totus

11452 *Anderson, Gary A.* From Israel's burden to Israel's debt: towards a theology of sin in biblical and early second temple sources. Reworking the bible. StTDJ 58: 2005 ⇒723. 1-30.

11453 *Aune, David E.* Charismatic exegesis in early Judaism and early christianity. Apocalypticism, prophecy. WUNT 199: 2005 <1993> ⇒177. 280-299.

11454 *Baker, Cynthia* When Jews were women. HR 45 (2005) 114-134.

11455 **Baker, Cynthia M.** Rebuilding the house of Israel: architectures of gender in Jewish antiquity. 2003 ⇒19,10865; 20,10393. [R]JAAR 73 (2005) 896-898 (*Baskin, Judith R.*).

11456 *Baker, Murray* Who was sitting in the theatre at Miletos?: an epigraphical application of a novel theory. JSJ 36 (2005) 397-416.

11457 [E]**Barclay, John M.G.** Negotiating diaspora: Jewish strategies in the Roman empire. Library of Second Temple Studies 45: 2004 ⇒ 20,548. [R]JJS 56 (2005) 345-347 (*Campbell, Jonathan G.*); RBLit (2005)* (*Kerkeslager, Allen; Torijano Morales, Pablo*).

11458 *Barzilai, Gabriel* 'The wife of one's youth': monogamy as an ideal in wisdom, Qumran, and rabbinic literature. Meghillot III. 2005 ⇒ 608. 29-47.

11459 *Beckwith, Roger T.* A recent approach to the Jewish calendar: Sacha Stern's Calendar and Community;

11460 The early Jewish quest for a patriarchal chronology. Calendar, chronology. AGJU 61: 2005 ⇒184. 7-15/105-124.

11461 *Berlin, Andrea M.* Jewish life before the revolt: the archaeological evidence. JSJ 36 (2005) 417-470.

11462 **Berthelot, Katell** Philanthrôpia judaica: le débat autour de la "misanthropie" des lois juives dans l'antiquité. JSJ.S 76: 2003 ⇒ 19,10869. [R]ThLZ 130 (2005) 924-926 (*Avemarie, Friedrich*).

11463 *Betlyon, John Wilson* A people transformed: Palestine in the Persian period. NEA 68/1-2 (2005) 4-58.

11464 *Bianchi, Francesco* La famiglia nella letteratura giudaica apocrifa e nei manoscritti di Qumran. Il matrimonio. DSBP 42: 2005 ⇒459. 192-212.

11465 *Blenkinsopp, Joseph* The Qumran sect in the context of second temple sectarianism. New directions. 2005 ⇒928. 10-25.

11466 *Boccaccini, Gabriele* Response: texts, intellectual movements, and social groups. Enoch and Qumran origins. 2005 ⇒921. 417-425.

11467 **Boccaccini, Gabriele** Roots of rabbinic Judaism: an intellectual history from Ezekiel to Daniel. 2002 ⇒18,10041... 20,10397. RJNES 64 (2005) 140-141 (*Suter, David W.*).

11468 **Bohrmann, Monette** Valeurs du judaïsme du début de notre ère. 2000 ⇒16,9493; 18,10043. RJSJ 36 (2005) 331-332 (*DiTommaso, Lorenzo*).

11469 *Böckler, Annette* Das Judentum entsteht im Babylonischen Exil: 26 Jahrhunderte jüdisches Leben zwischen Euphrat und Tigris. WUB 37 (2005) 48-53;

11470 Beten als Lernen—Lernen als Mitzwa: das Gebetbuch als Lehrbuch im Judentum. Religiöses Lernen. WUNT 180: 2005 ⇒384. 157-73.

11471 **Bringmann, Klaus** Geschichte der Juden im Altertum: vom babylonischen Exil bis zur arabischen Eroberung. Stu 2005, Klett-Cotta 365 pp. €32.

11472 **Burkes, Shannon** God, self, and death: the shape of religious transformation in the second temple period. JSJ.S 79: 2003 ⇒19, 10878. RThLZ 130 (2005) 497-499 (*Kaiser, Otto*).

11473 *Capelli, Piero* The outer and the inner devil: on representing the evil one in second temple Judaism. FSTEMBERGER, G.: SJ 32: 2005 ⇒140. 139-152.

11474 *Charlesworth, James H.* Summary and conclusions: The books of Enoch or 1 Enoch matters: new paradigms for unterstanding pre-70 Judaism. Enoch and Qumran origins. 2005 ⇒921. 436-454.

11475 **Chepey, Stuart Douglas** Nazirites in late second temple Judaism: a survey of ancient Jewish writings, the New Testament, archaeological evidence, and other writings from late antiquity. AGJU 60; AJEC 60: Lei 2005, Brill xi; 211 pp. €90. 90-04-14465-X. Diss. Oxford; Bibl. 201-206.

11476 *Collins, John J.* Natural theology and biblical tradition: the case of Hellenistic Judaism. Encounters. 2005 <1998> ⇒200. 117-126.

11477 Enoch, the Dead Sea scrolls, and the Essenes: groups and movements in Judaism in the early second century B.C.E.. Enoch and Qumran origins. 2005 ⇒921. 345-350;

11478 The literature of the second temple period;

11479 *Cooper, Alan M.* Biblical studies and Jewish studies. The Oxford handbook of Jewish studies. 2005 ⇒1053. 53-78/14-35.

11480 *Davies, Philip R.* Sects from texts: on the problems of doing a sociology of the Qumran literature. New directions. 2005 ⇒928. 69-82.

11481 *Davila, James R.* Enochians, Essenes, and Qumran Essenes. Enoch and Qumran origins. 2005 ⇒921. 356-359.

11482 *Diner, Dan D.* Imperium und Diaspora: das jüdische Exempel. FSTEGEMANN, E. 2005 ⇒139. 458-463.

11483 *Doering, Lutz* Excerpted texts in second temple Judaism: a survey of the evidence. Selecta colligere, II. 2005 ⇒681. 1-38.

11484 *Ego, Beate* Denkbilder für Gottes Einzigkeit, Herrlichkeit und Richtermacht—Himmelsvorstellungen im antiken Judentum. JBTh 20 (2005) 151-188.

11485 *Eshel, Hanan* 4Q390, the 490-year prophecy, and the calendrical history of the second temple period. Enoch and Qumran origins. 2005 ⇒921. 102-110;

11486 *Megillat Ta'anit* in light of holidays found in *Jubilees* and the *Temple Scroll*. Meghillot III. 2005 ⇒608. 253-257 . **H**.

11487 *Fine, Steven* Between liturgy and social history: priestly power in late antique Palestine synagogues?. JJS 56 (2005) 1-9.

11488 **Fine, Steven** Art and Judaism in the Greco-Roman world: toward a new Jewish archaeology. C 2005, CUP xvii; 267 pp. £45. 0-521-8-4491-6. Bibl. 247-252.

11489 **Fishbane, Michael A.** The exegetical imagination: on Jewish thought and theology. 1998 ⇒14,8666; 16,9508. [R]HeyJ 46 (2005) 231-232 (*McNamara, Martin*).

11490 *Fishbane, Michael* L'allégorie dans la pensée, la littérature et la mentalité juives. Allégorisme des poètes. 2005 ⇒874. 89-112.

11491 *Galley, Susanne* Jüdische und christliche Heilige—ein Vergleich. ZRGG 57/1 (2005) 29-47.

11492 **García Moreno, Luis A.** Los judíos de la España antigua. M 2005, Rialp 284 pp. [R]Augustinus 50 (2005) 235-238 (*Touya Pardo, J.*).

11493 [E]**Gernot, Jonas** Alle Morgen neu: Einführung in die jüdische Gedankenwelt anhand eines der wichtigsten jüdischen Gebete [Schemone Esre]. [T]*Braselmann, Wolfram*: Erev-Rav-Hefte, Israelitisch denken lernen 7: Uelzen, Lüneburger Heide 2005, EREV-RAV xvii; 362 pp. €19.90. 3-932810-29-5.

11494 **Gerstenberger, Erhard** Israel in der Perserzeit: 5. und 4. Jahrhundert v. Chr. Biblische Enzyklopädie 8: Stu 2005, Kohlhammer 416 pp. €36. 3-17-012337-8.

11495 **Goldberg, Sylvie Anne** La Clepsydre II: temps de Jérusalem, temps de Babylone. Bibliothèque Albin Michel idées: 2004 ⇒20, 10420. [R]REJ 164 (2005) 340-344 (*Couteau, Élisabeth*); ASSR 131-132 (2005) 252-253 (*Azria, Régine*).

11496 *Goodman, Martin* Jean Juster and the study of Jews under Roman rule. [F]ULLENDORFF, E.: SStLL 47: 2005 ⇒154. 309-322;

11497 Jews and Judaism in the Mediterranean diaspora in the late-Roman period: the limitations of evidence. Ancient Judaism. JSJ.S 95: 2005 ⇒626. 177-203;

11498 The nature of Jewish studies;

11499 Jews and Judaism in the second temple period. The Oxford handbook of Jewish studies. 2005 ⇒1053. 1-13/36-52.

11500 *Gosse, Bernard* Sabbath, identity and universalism go together after the return from exile. JSOT 29 (2005) <2004> 359-370 [Isa 56,1-2; Ezek 18-20].

11501 *Grabbe, Lester L.* Second Temple Judaism: challenges, controversies, and quibbles in the next decade. Henoch 27/1-2 (2005) 13-19.

11502 **Gruen, Erich S.** Diaspora: Jews amidst Greeks and Romans. 2002 ⇒18,10061...20,10427. [R]Latomus 64 (2005) 216-217 (*Lipiński, Edward*); RSR 93 (2005) 599-601 (*Berthelot, Katell*); RBLit (2005)* (*Bredin, Mark*); RBLit 7 (2005) 259-64 (*Jacobs, Andrew*).

11503 *Hannah, Darrell D.* Isaiah within Judaism of the second temple period. Isaiah in the NT. 2005 ⇒443. 7-33.

11504 **Harrington, Hannah K.** Holiness: rabbinic Judaism in the Graeco-Roman world. 2001 ⇒17,9290. [R]JQR 95 (2005) 344-345 (*Koltun-Fromm, Naomi*).

11505 **Hayoun, Maurice-Ruben** Geschichte der jüdischen Philosophie. 2004 ⇒20,10429. [R]Jud. 61 (2005) 75-76 (*Morgenstern, Matthias*).

11506 **Hezser, Catherine** Jewish literacy in Roman Palestine. TSAJ 81: 2001 ⇒17,9291... 20,10430. [R]JJS 56 (2005) 154-5 (*Rajak, Tessa*).

11507 *Himmelfarb, Martha* The torah between Athens and Jerusalem: Jewish difference in antiquity. Ancient Judaism. JSJ.S 95: 2005 ⇒ 626.113-129.

11508 *Horsley, Richard A.* The politics of cultural production in Second Temple Judea: historical context and political-religious relations of the scribes who produced 1 Enoch, Sirach, and Daniel. Conflicted boundaries. SBL.Symp. 35: 2005 ⇒495. 123-145.

11509 *Hurtado, Larry W.* First-century Jewish monotheism. How on earth. 2005 <1998> ⇒227. 111-133.

11510 *Ilan, Tal* Learned Jewish women in antiquity. Religiöses Lernen. WUNT 180: 2005 ⇒384. 175-190.

11511 *Isaac, E.* The question of Jewish identity and Ethiopian Jewish origins. Midstream [NY] 51/5 (2005) 29-34 [NTAb 50,348].

11512 *Jarrassé, Dominique* Fonctions et formes de la synagogue: refus et tentation de la sacralisation. RHR 222/4 (2005) 393-409.

11513 **Kalimi, Isaac** Early Jewish exegesis and theological controversy. Jewish and Christian Heritage 2: 2002 ⇒18,10067... 20,10435. [R]JSJ 36 (2005) 353-355 (*Tomson, Peter J.*).

11514 **Kiefer, Jörn** Exil und Diaspora: Begrifflichkeit und Deutungen im antiken Judentum und in der Hebräischen Bibel. [D]*Willi, Thomas*: ABIG 19: Lp 2005, Evangelische 760 pp. 3-374-02316-9. Diss. Greifswald; Mit CD; Bibl. 696-752.

11515 *Kister, M.D.* The *Scholia* on *Megillat Ta'anit*. Tarb. 74 (2005) 451-477 [NTAb 51,124]. **H**;

11516 Physical and metaphysical measurements ordained by God in the literature of the second temple period. Reworking the bible. StTDJ 58: 2005 ⇒723. 153-176.

11517 *Knibb, Michael A.* Temple and cult in apocryphal and pseudepigraphical writings from before the common era. Temple and worship. LHBOTS 422: 2005 ⇒731. 401-416.

11518 *Koch, Klaus* History as a battlefield of two antagonistic powers in the Apocalypse of Weeks and in the Rule of the Community. Enoch and Qumran origins. 2005 ⇒921. 185-199.

11519 *Korpel, M.C.A.* Disillusion among Jews in the postexilic period. The OT in its world. OTS 52: 2005 ⇒749. 135-157.

11520 **Koskenniemi, Erkki** The Old Testament miracle-workers in early Judaism. WUNT 2/206: Tü 2005, Mohr S. ix; 356 pp. €69. 3-16-148604-8. Bibl. 301-319.

11521 *Krochmalnik, Daniel* 'Sch'ma Jisrael—Höre, Israel': der jüdische Monotheismus. FrRu 12 (2005) 19-29 [Deut 6,4-8].

11522 *Kulp, Joshua* The origins of the Seder and Haggadah. CuBR 4 (2005) 109-134.

11523 *Laato, Antti* The development of the Jewish calendar. [F]AEJMELAEUS, L.: SESJ 89: 2005 ⇒1. 13-39.

11524 **Levine, Lee I.** La sinagoga antica, 1: lo sviluppo storico, 2: l'istituzione. Introduzione allo studio della Bibbia, Suppl. 20-21: Brescia 2005, Paideia 2 vols; 788 pp. 88-394-0699-9/700-6. Bibl. 659-728.

11525 **Maier, Johann** Entre os dois testamentos—história e religião na época do segundo templo. Bíblica 46: São Paulo 2005, Loyola 335 pp. 85-15-02739-9.

11526 *Manns, Frédéric* Il matrimonio nel giudaismo antico. Il matrimonio. DSBP 42: 2005 ⇒459. 139-191.

11527 *Mélèze Modrzejewski, Joseph* What is Hellenistic law?: the documents of the Judean desert in the light of the papyri from Egypt. Law in the documents. JSJ.S 96: 2005 ⇒662. 7-21.

11528 **Middlemas, Jill Anne** The troubles of templeless Judah. Oxf 2005, OUP xv; 288 pp. 0-19-928386-9. Bibl. 236-272.

11529 **Miranda, Evaristo E. de; Schorr Malca, José** Sages pharisiens: réparer une injustice. Lectures bibliques: P 2005, Lethielleux 383 pp. €25.

11530 *Nadeau, Jean-Guy; Trigano, Shmuel* Souffrance rédemptrice dans le judaïsme?: entrevue avec Shmuel Trigano. Théologiques 13 (2005) 45-67.

11531 **Neusner, Jacob** Transformations in ancient Judaism: textual evidence for creative responses to crisis. 2004 ⇒20,10453. [R]RBLit (2005)* (*Levy, Gabriel*);

11532 Parsing the torah—surveying the history, literature, religion and theology of formative Judaism. Lanham 2005, Univ. Pr. of America lxxiv; 281 pp. $47. 0-7618-3266-1.

11533 [E]**Neusner, Jacob** Dictionary of ancient rabbis: selections from the Jewish Encyclopaedia. 2003 ⇒19,10954; 20,10454. [R]RBLit 7 (2005) 241-244 (*Moss, Joshua L.*).

11534 *Nickelsburg, George W.E.* Wisdom and apocalypticism in early Judaism: some points for discussion;

11535 Response to Sarah Tanzer. Conflicted boundaries. SBL.Symp. 35: 2005 ⇒495. 17-37/51-54.

11536 **Nickelsburg, George W.E.** Jewish literature between the bible and the mishnah: a historical and literary introduction. Mp $^2$2005 <1981>, Fortress xxviii; 445 pp. $29. 0-8006-3779-8. CD-ROM; Bibl. 345-423.

11537 *Niehoff, Maren R.* Response to Daniel S. Schwartz. StPhiloA 17 (2005) 99-101.

11538 **Noam, Vered** מגילת תענית. הנוסחים פשרם. תולדותיהם בצירוף מהדורה ביקורתית [Megillat ta'anit: versions: interpretation: history: with a critical edition]. Between Bible and Mishna: 2003 ⇒19,10958. [R]REJ 164 (2005) 338-340 (*Rothschild, Jean-Pierre*). **H.**

11539 *Oppenheimer, Aharon* L'élaboration de la Halakha après la destruction du second temple. Between Rome and Babylon. TSAJ 108: 2005 <1996> ⇒272. 115-144.

11540 *Paul, André* Bulletin de Judaïsme ancien (I). RSR 93 (2005) 597-618;

11541 A l'écoute de la torah: introduction au judaïsme. 2004 ⇒20,10463. [R]Cath(P) 86 (2004-2005) 162-163 (*Barthe, Claude*).

11542 *Peterson, Erik* Zum Kultus im nachexilischen Judentum und zu späteren kirchengeschichtlichen Entwicklungen;

11543 Der Vater im Frühjudentum. Peterson: Lukasevangelium und Synoptica. 2005 ⇒277. 416-418/423-425.

11544 *Pérez Fernández, Miguel* Trasfondo judío del Nuevo Testamento. ResB 47 (2005) 4-12.

11545 *Pilch, John J.* Holy men and their sky journeys: a cross-cultural model. BTB 35 (2005) 106-111.

11546 *Raspa, Carmelo* Fino a quanto è necessaria la relazione maestro-discepolo per la tradizione ebraica?. Itin(M) 13 (2005) 237-243.

11547 *Reeves, John C.* Complicating the notion of an "Enochic Judaism". Enoch and Qumran origins. 2005 ⇒921. 373-383.

11548 *Regev, Eyal* Were the priests all the same?: Qumranic halakhah in comparison with Sadducean halakhah. DSD 12 (2005) 158-188.

11549 **Regev, Eyal** The Sadducees and their halakah: religion and society in the second temple period. J 2005, Yad Ben-Zvi 457 pp. $29.80. [R]RBLit (2005)* (*Mor, Sagit*).

11550 *Riaud, Jean* Étude critique: la vie communautaire dans le judaïsme ancien. RHPhR 85 (2005) 421-425.

11551 *Ribera i Florit, Josep* El judaisme del segel II aC al segle II dC: entre el rebuig i el proselitisme. La bíblia i els immigrants. 2005 ⇒ 471. 243-255.

11552 *Richter, Hans-Friedemann* יצר הרע: ein Beitrag der jüdischen Theologie zum Problem der Theodizee. [F]VOIGT, R.: AOAT 317: 2005 ⇒158. 351-378 [Gen 6,5; 8,21].

11553 *Robin, Christian* Gottessuche im Wüstensand: Juden und Christen auf der Arabischen Halbinsel. WUB 35 (2005) 11-15.

11554 *Roth, Jonathan P.* Distinguishing Jewishness in antiquity. [F]HARRIS, W. 2005 ⇒57. 37-58.

11555 **Sandgren, Leo Duprée** The shadow of God: stories from early Judaism. 2003 ⇒19,10978; 20,10471. [R]TJT 21 (2005) 270-271 (*Mirecki, Cathy A.*).

11556 [E]**Sarshar, Houman** Esther's children: a portrait of Iranian Jews. 2002 ⇒19,10979. [R]JQR 95 (2005) 384-389 (*Sabar, Shalom*).

11557 **Sasse, Markus** Geschichte Israels in der Zeit des zweiten Tempels. 2004 ⇒20,10472. [R]ThLZ 130 (2005) 1313-1316 (*Tilly, Michael*).

11558 **Satlow, Michael L.** Jewish marriage in antiquity. 2001 ⇒17,9334 ... 20,10473. [R]JAAR 73 (2005) 272-276 (*Boyarin, Daniel*).

11559 *Schiffman, Lawrence H.* Jewish spirituality in the bible and second temple literature. Jewish spirituality. 2005 ⇒575. 37-60.

11560 *Schmidt, Francis* L'espace sacrificiel dans le Judaïsme du second temple. La cuisine et l'autel. BEHE.R 124: 2005 ⇒539. 177-196 [Lev 17; Deut 12].

11561 **Schremer, Adiel** Male and female he created them: Jewish marriage in the late second temple, mishnah and talmud periods. 2003 ⇒19,10984. [R]Zion 70 (2005) 494-513 (*Friedman, Mordechai A.*).

11562 *Schwartz, Daniel R.* Jews, Judaeans and the epoch that disappeared: on H. Graetz's changing view of the second temple period. Zion 70 2005, 293-309. **H.**

11563 **Schwartz, Seth** Imperialism and Jewish society, 200 BCE to 640 CE. 2001 ⇒17,9340... 20,10479. [R]JSJ 36 (2005) 125-127 (*Penner, Jeremy*); JRS 95 (2005) 271-273 (*McGing, Brian*); JQR 95 (2005) 151-162 (*Satlow, M.L.*).

11564 *Shaked, Shaul* Magical bowls and incantation texts: how to get rid of demons and pests. Qad. 38 (2005) 2-13. **H.**

11565 **Shepkaru, Shmuel** Jewish martyrs in the pagan and christian worlds. C 2005, CUP 414pp. $70.

11566 **Sivertsev, Alexei** Households, sects, and the origins of rabbinic Judaism. JSJ.S 102: Lei 2005, Brill viii; 301 pp. €95. 90-04-14447-1. Bibl. 276-289.

11567 **Smith, Barry D.** The tension between God as righteous judge and as merciful in early Judaism. Lanham 2005, University Press of America xv; 385 pp. 0-7618-3088-X. Bibl. 315-342.

11568 *Standhartinger, Angela* Frauen in Mahlgemeinschaften: Diskurs und Wirklichkeit einer antiken, frühjüdischen und frühchristlichen Praxis. LecDif 2 (2005)*.

11569 *Stemberger, Günter* "Schaff dir einen Lehrer, erwirb dir einen Kollegen" (mAV 1,6)—Lernen als Tradition und Gemeinschaft. Religiöses Lernen. WUNT 180: 2005 ⇒384. 141-155.

11570 *Sterling, Gregory E.* "The Jewish philosophy": the presence of Hellenistic philosophy in Jewish exegesis in the second temple period. Ancient Judaism. JSJ.S 95: 2005 ⇒626. 131-153.

11571 **Stern, Sacha** Calendar and community: a history of the Jewish calendar second century BCE-tenth century CE. 2001 ⇒17,9345; 19,10990. [R]JSJ 36 (2005) 372-373 (*Grabbe, Lester L.*); JQR 95 (2005) 710-714 (*Adler, William*);

11572 Time and process in ancient Judaism. 2003 ⇒19,10991. [R]BSOAS 68 (2005) 103-04 (*Lipton, Diana*); JJS 56 (2005) 350-352 (*Hezser, Catherine*); JThS 56 (2005) 628-633 (*De Lange, Nicholas R.M.*).

11573 *Stuckenbruck, Loren T.* Pleas for deliverance from the demonic in early Jewish texts. Studies in Jewish prayer. JSSt.S 17: 2005 ⇒828. 55-73.

11574 *Swartz, Michael D.* The aesthetics of blessing and cursing: literary and iconographic dimensions of Hebrew and Aramaic blessing and curse texts. JANER 5 (2005) 187-211.

11575 [ET]**Swartz, Michael D.; Yahalom, Joseph** Avodah: ancient poems for Yom Kippur. Penn State Library of Jewish Literature: University Park, PA 2005, Penn State Univ. Pr. x; 387 pp. £39. 0-271-02-357-0.

11576 *Talmon, Shemaryahu* What's in a calendar?: calendar conformity, calendar controversy, and calendar reform in ancient and medieval Judaism. [F]FOX, M. 2005 ⇒43. 451-460.

11577 *Tanzer, Sarah J.* Response to George Nickelsburg, "Wisdom and apocalypticism in early Judaism". Conflicted boundaries. SBL.Symp. 35: 2005 ⇒495. 39-49.

11578 *Thoma, Clemens* Deutungen frühjüdischer Martyrien und der Schoah. Streitfall Christologie. QD 214: 2005 ⇒549. 41-72.

11579 *Tigchelaar, Eibert J.C.* 'Lights serving as signs for festivals' (Genesis 1:14b) in Enuma eliş and early Judaism. Creation of heaven and earth. 2005 ⇒492. 31-48.

11580 **Tomasino, Anthony J.** Judaism before Jesus: the events and ideas that shaped the NT world. 2003 ⇒19,10996; 20,10489. [R]VeE 26 (2005) 653-654 (*Venter, P.M.*).

11581 *Tropper, Amram* Yohanan ben Zakkai, amicus Caesaris: a Jewish hero in rabbinic eyes. JSIJ 4 (2005) 133-149.

11582 **VanderKam, James C.** From Joshua to Caiaphas: high priests after the exile. 2004 ⇒20,10493. [R]RBLit (2005)* (*Tilly, Michael*); ET 116 (2005) 385-386 (*Foster, Paul*).

11583 *Villeneuve, Estelle* Wo Juden sich trafen: die Entwicklung der Synagogen. WUB 38 (2005) 45-47.

11584 *Weinfeld, Moshe* The morning prayers (Birkhoth Hashachar) in Qumran and in the conventional Jewish liturgy 126-136;

11585 The biblical origins of the Amidah prayer for Sabbath and holy days 137-156;
11586 The crystallization of the 'congregation of the exile' (qhl hgwlh) and the sectarian nature of post-exilic Judaism 232-238;
11587 Universalistic and particularistic trends during the exile and restoration 251-266;
11588 HILLEL and the misunderstanding of Judaism in modern scholarship. Normative and sectarian Judaism. 2005 ⇒2732. 286-293.
11589 **Weitzman, Steven** Surviving sacrilege: cultural persistence in Jewish antiquity. CM 2005, Harvard University Press ix; 193 pp. $40/ £26. 0-674-01708-0.
11590 *Williams, Margaret* The epigraphy of the Jewish diaspora since the publication of Schürer (revised), vol. III (1986). Bulletin of Judaeo-Greek Studies [C] 35 (2004-5) 26-33 [NTAb 49,568] [2 Mac 4,14];
11591 Jewish festal names in antiquity—a neglected area of onomastic research. JSJ 36 (2005) 21-40.
11592 *Wills, Lawrence M.; Wright, Benjamin G.* Introduction. Conflicted boundaries. SBL.Symp. 35: 2005 ⇒495. 1-14.
11593 **Wilson, Walter T.** The Sentences of PSEUDO-PHOCYLIDES. Commentaries on Early Jewish Literature: B 2005, De Gruyter xiv; 302 pp. €74. 311-018241-6. [R]ASEs 22 (2005) 511-12 (*Nicklas, Tobias*).
11594 *Wire, Antoinette C.* Early Jewish birth prophecy stories and women's social memory. Memory, tradition, and text. SBL.Semeia Studies 52: 2005 ⇒416. 173-189;
11595 Women's history from birth-prophecy stories. Christian origins. A people's history of christianity 1: 2005 ⇒550. 71-93.
11596 **Wire, Antoinette Clark** Holy lives, holy deaths: a close hearing of early Jewish storytellers. Studies in Biblical Literature 1: 2002 ⇒ 18,10129...20,10497. [R]ThLZ 130 (2005) 148-9 (*Tromp, Johannes*).
11597 *Wischmeyer, Wolfgang* θεός ὕψιστος: Neues zu einer alten Debatte. ZAC 9 (2005) 149-168.
11598 **Woschitz, Karl Matthäus** Parabiblica: Studien zur jüdischen Literatur in der hellenistisch-römischen Epoche: Tradierung–Vermittlung–Wandlung. Theologie: Forschung und Wissenschaft 16: Müns 2005, Lit 928 pp. €69. 3-8258-8667-0.
11599 *Wright, Benjamin G.* Some remarks on the parting of the ways. Enoch and Qumran origins. 2005 ⇒921. 394-400.
11600 *Zangenberg, Jürgen* Mission in der Antike und im antiken Judentum. ZNT 8/15 (2005) 12-21.

## K6.0 **Mišna**, *tosepta: Tannaim*

11601 *Ames, Tracy* Fellowship, pharisees and the common people in early rabbinic tradition. SR 34 (2005) 339-356.
11602 *Amit, Aaron* The death of Rabbi Akiva's disciples: a literary history. JJS 56/2 (2005) 265-284.
11603 **Becker, Michael** Wunder und Wundertäter im frührabbinischen Judentum: Studien zum Phänomen und seiner Überlieferung im Horizont von Magie und Dämonismus. WUNT 2/144: 2002 ⇒19, 10133; 20,10506. [R]RBLit (2005)* (*Twelftree, Graham*).
11604 *Cohen, Barak S.* Rav Nahman and Rav Sheshet: conflicting methods of exegesis of tannaitic sources. HUCA 76 (2005) *11-*32. **H**.

11605 *Cohen, M.S.* The child at the edge of the cemetery: portraiture and symbolism in *Seder Tohorot*. Conservative Judaism [NY] 57/2 (2005) 95-107 [NTAb 50,124];

11606 The woman with a mouthful of coins: portraiture and symbolism in *Seder Tohorot*. Conservative Judaism [NY] 58/1 (2005) 66-79 [NTAb 51,531].

11607 [T]**Correns, Dietrich** Die Mischna ins Deutsche übertragen, mit einer Einleitung und Anmerkungen: das grundlegende enzyklopädische Regelwerk rabbinischer Tradition. Wsb 2005, Marix xxiv; 1000 pp. €20. 3-86539-016-1.

11608 *Furstenberg, A.* Restitution of lost property in the Tannaitic and Amoraic *halakhah*: preliminary philosphical study of the forming of a conception. AJS Review [Waltham, MA] 29/1 (2005) א-נא, 129 [NTAb 50,125].

11609 *Gundry, Robert H.* Jesus' blasphemy according to Mark 14:61b-64 and Mishnah Sanhedrin 7:5. The old is better. WUNT 178: 2005 ⇒ 220. 98-110.

11610 *Hauptman, Judith* The Tosefta as a commentary on an early Mishnah. JSIJ 4 (2005) 109-132.

11611 **Hauptman, Judith** Rereading the mishnah: a new approach to ancient Jewish texts. TSAJ 109: Tü 2005, Mohr S. xiii; 285 pp. €84. 3-16-148713-3. Bibl. 265-268.

11612 **Instone-Brewer, David** Prayer and agriculture. TRENT 1: 2004 ⇒ 20,10511. [R]RHPhR 85 (2005) 433-434 (*Grappe, Ch.*); JJS 56 (2005) 347-9 (*Hezser, Catherine*); RBLit (2005)* (*Toews, Casey*); Sewanee Theological Review 48 (2005) 335-40 (*Harrington, D.J.*).

11613 **Korsia, Haïm; Penya, David** para, yadayim. Collection de la Michna traduite en français 19: P 2005, C.L.K.H. 115; 29 pp. 2-90-4068-97-X.

11614 *Neusner, Jacob* Crucifixion in rabbinic context: juridical or theological?. Shofar [West Lafayette, IN] 23/3 (2005) 79-85 [NTAb 50, 128].

11615 **Neusner, Jacob** Making God' word work: a guide to the mishnah. 2004 ⇒20,10521. [R]ASEs 22 (2005) 528-530 (*Tilly, Michael*);

11616 The vitality of rabbinic imagination: the mishnah against the bible and Qumran. Lanham 2005, University Press of America xvii; 226 pp. 0-7618-3118-5.

11617 [E]**Neusner, Jacob** The law of agriculture in the mishnah and the tosefta: translation, commentary, theology. HO 1/79.1-3: Lei 2005, Brill 3 vols; xx; 800; xiii; 801-1775; xiii; 1777-2787. 9004145036;

11618 [T]**Neusner, Jacob** The Tosefta, translated from the Hebrew with a new introduction. Peabody 2002 <1977-1986>, Hendrickson 2 vols; lxxxv + xvii + 1984 pp.

11619 *Novick, Tzvi* The blemished first-born animal: a case study in tannaitic sources. HUCA 76 (2005) 113-132.

11620 *Noy, David* Rabbi Aqiba comes to Rome: a Jewish pilgrimage in reverse?. Pilgrimage. 2005 ⇒958. 373-385.

11621 *Oppenheimer, Aharon* Gedaljahu Alon—zwischen der jüdischen Historiographie des 19. Jahrhunderts und der modernen historischen Forschung <1999>;

11622 Jewish penal authority in Roman Judaea <1998>;

11623 Von Jerusalem nach Babylonien: der Aufstieg der babylonischen Judenheit in der parthisch-sassanidischen Epoche <1999>;

11624 Contacts between Eretz Israel and Babylonia at the turn of the period of the *Tannaim* and the *Amoraim*. Between Rome and Babylon. TSAJ 108: 2005 <2004> ⇒272. 13-29/173-182/374-383/417-432.

11625 *Ruiz-Morell, Olga* Elementos singulares en Tosefta Shabbat. [F]STEMBERGER, G.: SJ 32: 2005 ⇒140. 227-241.

11626 **Samely, Alexander** Rabbinic interpretation of scripture in the mishnah. 2002 ⇒18,10142... 20,10523. [R]RRJ 8 (2005) 301-314 (*Gruber, M.I.*).

11627 *Shoshany, Ronit* Rabbi Elazar ben Shimeon and the thieves—a story of sin and atonement. JSIJ 4 (2005) 1-21.

11628 *Stemberger, Günter* Mischna Avot: frühe Weisheitsschrift, pharisäisches Erbe oder spätrabbinische Bildung?. ZNW 96 (2005) 243-258.

11629 *Sutter Rehmann, Luzia* "Hoch und heilig!"—die Gelübdepraxis als religiöses Konfliktmanagement: sozialgeschichtliche Relektüre von Mischna Nedarim. [F]STEGEMANN, E. 2005 ⇒139. 241-254.

11630 **Tönges, Elke** "Unser Vater im Himmel": die Bezeichnung Gottes als Vater in der tannaitischen Literatur. BWANT 147: 2003 ⇒19, 11029. [R]ThLZ 130 (2005) 145-148 (*Becker, Michael*); OLZ 100 (2005) 75-78 (*Hezser, Catherine*).

11631 **Tropper, Amram** Wisdom, politics, and historiography—Tractate Avot in the context of the Graeco-Roman Near East. OOM: 2004 ⇒20,10528. [R]JSJ 36 (2005) 129-132 (*Stemberger, Günter*); Zion 70 (2005) 237-241 (*Geiger, Joseph*); RBLit (2005)* (*Jefferies, Daryl*); JThS 56 (2005) 633-638 (*De Lange, Nicholas R.M.*).

## K6.5 **Talmud; midraš**

11632 [E]**Rubenstein, Jeffrey L.** Creation and composition: the contribution of the Bavli redactors (Stammaim) to the aggada. TSAJ 114: Tü 2005, Mohr S. viii; 458 pp. €124. 3-16-148692-7.

11633 [E]**Teugels, Lieve M.; Ulmer, Rivka** Recent developments in midrash research: proceedings of the 2002 and 2003 SBL consultation on midrash. Judaism in context 2: Piscataway (N.J.) 2005, Gorgias vii; 171 pp. 1-593-33201-7.

11634 *Angel, Hayyim* A midrashic view of Ruth amidst a sea of ambiguity. JBQ 33 (2005) 91-99.

11635 *Avemarie, Friedrich* Lebenshingabe und heilschaffender Tod in der rabbinischen Literatur. Deutungen. WUNT 181: 2005 ⇒392. 169-211.

11636 *Bar-Ilan, Meir* Major trends in Jewish society in the land of Israel: from the 5th century BCE till the 7th century CE. Trumah 15 (2005) 1-23.

11637 *Bartolini, Elena* Il lavoro nella tradizione ebraica. PSV 52 (2005) 101-113.

11638 **Baskin, Judith R.** Midrashic women: formations of the feminine in rabbinic literature. 2002 ⇒19,11034. [R]JAAR 73 (2005) 898-902 (*Sheres, Ita*).

11639 *Basta, Pasquale* La nascita dell'ermeneutica biblica giudaica nell' esempio di HILLEL. Theologia Viatorum 9-10 (2005) 77-93 = P. Basta, Gezerah Shawah (Roma 2006) 13-29.

11640 ^E**Ben-Yashar, Menahem; Gottlieb, Isaac B.; Penkower, Jordan S.** The bible in rabbinic interpretation: rabbinic derashot on Prophets and Writings in talmudic and midrashic literature Vol. 1: Hosea. 2003 ⇒19,11038; 20,10533. ^RJSJ 36 (2005) 329-331 (*Nikolsky, Ronit*); CBQ 67 (2005) 485-487 (*Kalimi, Isaac*).

11641 *Birch, B.C.* The arts, midrash, and biblical teaching. Teaching Theology & Religion [Oxf] 8/2 (2005) 114-122 [NTAb 49,589].

11642 ^E**Bodendorfer, Gerhard; Millard, Matthias** Bibel und Midrasch. FAT 22: 1998 ⇒14,8766... 17,9389. ^RThR 70 (2005) 322-324 (*Reventlow, Henning Graf*).

11643 **Boyarin, Daniel** Sparks of the logos: essays in rabbinic hermeneutics. Brill Reference Library of Ancient Judaism 11: 2003 ⇒19, 11047. ^RJThS 56 (2005) 642-650 (*Samely, Alexander*).

11644 *Boyarin, Daniel* Archives in the fiction: rabbinic historiography and church history. The cultural turn. 2005 ⇒670. 175-192.

11645 *Börner-Klein, Dagmar* Transforming rabbinic exegesis into folktale. Trumah 15 (2005) 139-148 [Qoh 11,1].

11646 **Bregman, Marc** The Tanhuma-Yelammedenu literature: studies in the evolution of the versions. 2003 ⇒19,11049. ^RJSJ 36 (2005) 333-335 (*Börner-Klein, Dagmar*).

11647 *Bruckstein, Almut Sh.* "Und was wären dann die Bilder?": talmudische und philosophische Notizen zur Bilderfrage. ZNT 8/16 (2005) 54-58.

11648 **Cohen, Irun R.** Regen und Auferstehung: Talmud und Naturwissenschaft im Dialog mit der Welt. ^T*Lohse, Eduard*: Gö 2005, Vandenhoeck & R. 185 pp. €39.90. 3-525-53562-7.

11649 *Costa, José* Nascita del giudaismo rabbinico. Il mondo della bibbia 77 (2005) 12-15.

11650 **Costa, José** La bible racontée par le midrash. P 2004, Bayard 372 pp.

11651 *Dagan, Tal; Graur, Dan; Yorav, Avishai* An exploratory study on the use of a phylogenetic algorithm in the reconstruction of stemmata of halachic texts. HUCA 76 (2005) 273-288.

11652 **Diamond, Eliezer** Holy men and hunger artists: fasting and asceticism in rabbinic culture. 2004 ⇒20,10544. ^RJAAR 73 (2005) 911-913 (*Segal, Eliezer*).

11653 *Dieckmann, Detlef* Rabbinische Schriftauslegung und postmoderne Hermeneutik. TeKo 28/1 (2005) 16-29.

11654 *Elman, Yaakov* Midrash Halakhah in its classic formulation. Recent developments in midrash research. 2005 ⇒11633. 3-15.

11655 Encyclopaedia of midrash: biblical interpretation in formative Judaism. ^E**Neusner, Jacob; Avery-Peck, Alan J.**: Lei 2005, Brill 2 vols; xi + vii; 1077 pp. €299/$299. 90-04-14166-9.

11656 *Fine, Steven* Spirituality and the art of the ancient synagogue. Jewish spirituality. 2005 ⇒575. 189-212.

11657 **Fishbane, Michael A.** Biblical myth and rabbinic mythmaking. 2003 ⇒19,11061; 20,10549. ^RRRT 12/1 (2005) 33-40 (*Gruber, Mayer I.*); ZAR 11 (2005) 370-373 (*Otto, Eckart*); JSSt 50 (2005) 395-397 (*Mills, Mary*); JThS 56 (2005) 624-628 (*Reif, Stefan C.*).

11658 *Friedheim, Emmanuel Timi De-Romi* and *Tyche De-Romi*: a reexamination of the historical significance of a talmudic expression. JSIJ 4 (2005) 23-33. Neziqin: Avodah Zarah.

11659 *Friedman, S.* המהדרין מן המהדרין. Leš. 67/2 (2005) 153-160 [NTAb 50,115]. **H.**

11660 *Gil, Moshe* Siqoriqin: forfeited land. HUCA 76 (2005) 47-62.

11661 **Ginzberg, Louis** Les légendes des Juifs, 4: Moïse dans le désert. T*Sed-Rajna, Gabrielle*: 2003 ⇒19,11065; 20,10553. RJSJ 36 (2005) 349-351 (*Verheyden, Joseph*); Sal. 67 (2005) 182-3 (*Vicent, Rafael*).

11662 *Girón-Blanc, Luis F.* Midraš Qohelet: un fragmento de la genizah de El Cairo (Cambridge T-S C2.161) [Qoh 5,14-6,3];

11663 *Goldenberg, David* What did Ham do to Noah? [Gen 9,20-29]. FSTEMBERGER, G.: SJ 32: 2005 ⇒140. 309-318/257-265.

11664 **Gray, Alyssa M.** A talmud in exile: the influence of Yerushalmi Avodah Zarah on the formation of Bavli Avodah Zarah. BJSt 342: Providence 2005, Brown Univ. xv; 275 pp. 1-930675-230.

11665 ET**Guggenheimer, Heinrich W.** The Jerusalem Talmud: first order: Zeraïm: [tractates Berakhot, Terumot, Ma'aserot, Ma'aser Šeni, Hallah, 'Orlah, Bikkurim]. SJ 18, 21, 23: 2000-2003 ⇒19,11069; 20,10556. RThLZ 130 (2005) 249-252 (*Lehnardt, Andreas*);

11666 The Jerusalem Talmud: third order: Našim: tractate Yebamot. SJ 29: 2004 ⇒20,10558. RJud. 61 (2005) 272-273 (*Morgenstern, Matthias*);

11667 The Jerusalem Talmud: third order: Našim: tractates *Soṭah* and *Nedarim* מסכתות סוטה ונדרים. SJ 31: B 2005, De Gruyter xiii; 761 pp. 3-11-018668-3.

11668 *Halivni, David* Aspects of the formation of the talmud. Creation and composition. TSAJ 114: 2005 ⇒11632. 339-360.

11669 **Hedner Zetterholm, Karin** Portrait of a villain: Laban the Aramean in rabbinic literature. 2002 ⇒18,10190; 20,10563. RJSJ 36 (2005) 136-138 (*Lehnardt, Andreas*); JQR 95 (2005) 705-709 (*Neusner, Jacob*) [Gen 24-31].

11670 **Heger, Paul** The pluralistic halakhah: legal innovations in the late second commonwealth and rabbinic periods. SJ 22: 2003 ⇒19, 11077; 20,10564. RJSJ 36 (2005) 112-116 (*Pérez Fernández, Miguel*).

11671 **Heschel, A.J.** Heavenly torah as refracted through the generations. ET*Tucker, G.*: L 2005, Continuum xxiv; 814 pp. $95. 0-82640-8028. RJdm 53 (2004) 300-309 (*Wolf, Arnold J.*).

11672 *Hezser, Catherine* Classical rabbinic literature. The Oxford handbook of Jewish studies. 2005 ⇒1053. 115-140;

11673 'The slave of a scholar is like a scholar': stories about rabbis and their slaves in the Babylonian talmud. Creation and composition. TSAJ 114: 2005 ⇒11632. 181-200.

11674 *Jackson, Bernard, al.*, Halacha and law. The Oxford handbook of Jewish studies. 2005 ⇒1053. 643-679.

11675 *Jacobson, Howard* Two notes on *Berakhot* 59b. REJ 164 (2005) 249-250.

11676 *Jaffé, Dan* Le statut et la place de la femme dans la pensée talmudique: approche textuelle et anthropologique. Chemins de Dialogue 25 (2005) 163-179.

11677 **Jaffé, Dan** Le judaïsme et l'avènement du christianisme: orthodoxie et hétérodoxie dans la littérature talmudique Ier-IIe siècle. Patrimoines judaïsme: P 2005, Cerf 484 pp. €49. 2-204-07759-3. Préf.

*François Blanchetière*; Bibl. 419-452. [R]Vies consacrées 77 (2005) 208-209 (*Luciani, Didier*).

11678 *Jama, Sophie* L'interprétation des rêves dans le *talmud*: une parole agissante. Le récit de rêve. 2005 ⇒696. 57-73.

11679 **Jerrow, Janet** Arguing with God in the wake of the Golden Calf episode: the rabbis read Exodus 32. [D]*Holbert, J.C.*: 2005, 234 pp. Diss. Dallas, Southern Methodist [RTL 37,609] [Exod 32].

11680 *Kalimi, Isaac* Geboren als ein Beschnittener: eine Betrachtung zum Konzept der Vollkommenheit im historischen Kontext einiger jüdischer Quellen. BN 123 (2005) 75-91.

11681 *Kessler, Gwynn* Let's cross that body when we get to it: gender and ethnicity in rabbinic literature. JAAR 73 (2005) 329-359 [Exod 4,25].

11682 *Kimelman, Reuven* Blessing formulae and divine sovereignty in rabbinic liturgy. Liturgy in the life of the synagogue. Duke Judaic Studies 2: 2005 ⇒848. 1-39.

11683 *Krupp, Michael* Der Anfang der *Ḥisronot ha-Schass*-Literatur: christliche Talmudzensur und ihre jüdische Überwindung. [F]STEMBERGER, G.: SJ 32: 2005 ⇒140. 449-462.

11684 *Krygier, Rivon* Did God command the extermination of the Canaanites?: the rabbis' encounter with genocide. Conservative Judaism [NY] 57/2 (2005) 78-94 [NTAb 50,127];

11685 Bible et judaïsme. Bible et sciences des religions. 2005 ⇒445. 71-94.

11686 *Langer, Gerhard* Bruder Esau: zur Frage nach der jüdischen Identität am Beispiel der Auslegung zu Jakob und Esau in Bereshit Rabba. [F]STEGEMANN, E. 2005 ⇒139. 373-390 [Gen 25];

11687 Der Grenzgänger Esau: zur Frage nach jüdischer Identität am Beispiel der talmudischen Auslegung zu Jakob und Esau. [F]STEGEMANN, W. 2005 ⇒139. 235-249 [Gen 25].

11688 *Lauer, Simon* Biblical wisdom in rabbinic garb. Worlds of memory. 2005 ⇒543. 17-23.

11689 *Lecker, Michael; Oppenheimer, Aharon* The genealogical boundaries of Jewish Babylonia <1985>;

11690 Beisetzung westlich des Euphrat im talmudischen Babylonien <1994>. Between Rome and Babylon. TSAJ 108: 2005 ⇒272. 339-355/402-408.

11691 [E]**Malinowitz, Chaim**, *al.*, The Schottenstein edition Talmud Yerushalmi...: tractate Berachos, vol. 1. Art Scroll Series: NY 2005, Mesorah. $35. 1-422-602-346.

11692 **Malka, Victor** La braise et la flamme: les sages qui ont façonné le judaïsme. 2003 ⇒19,11099. [R]ETR 80 (2005) 134-136 (*Couteau, Elisabeth*).

11693 *Martín Contreras, Elvira* El principio hermenéutico *ʾên kĕṯîḇ kaʾn ʾel·la* en la *Meḵilta de Rabbi Yišmael*. Sef. 65 (2005) 85-102.

11694 *Milikowsky, Chaim* Rabbinic interpretation of the bible in the light of ancient hermeneutical practice: the question of the literal meaning. [F]STEMBERGER, G.: SJ 32: 2005 ⇒140. 7-27;

11695 Midrash as fiction and midrash as history: what did the rabbis mean?. Ancient fiction. SBL.Symp. 32: 2005 ⇒721. 117-127.

11696 *Miralles Maciá, Lorena* Las fuentes de la vida: la sal y el vino en la tradición rabínica y el Nuevo Testamento. ResB 47 (2005) 32-40.

11697 *Mitchell, David C.* Les psaumes dans le judaïsme rabbinique. RTL 36 (2005) 166-191.

11698 *Mondriaan, Marlene E.* Lilith and Eve—the wives of Adam. OTEs 18 (2005) 752-762 [Isa 34,14].

11699 *Moscovitz, Leib* "The Holy One blessed be He... does not permit the righteous to stumble": reflections on the development of a remarkable BT theologoumenon. Creation and composition. TSAJ 114: 2005 ⇒11632. 125-179.

11700 *Muffs, Yochanan* Intent, volition, and the roots of rabbinic prayer;

11701 Theology and poetics <1998>. Personhood of God. 2005 ⇒265. 123-131/103-112.

11702 *Nelson, W. David* Critiquing a critical edition: challenges utilizing the *Mekhilta of Rabbi Shimon b. Yoḥai*. Recent developments in midrash research. Judaism in context 2: 2005 ⇒11633. 97-115;

11703 Oral orthography: early rabbinic oral and written transmission of parallel midrashic tradition in the *Mekhilta* of Rabbi Shimon B. Yoḥai and the *Mekhilta* of Rabbi Ishmael. AJS Review [Waltham, MA] 29/1 (2005) 1-33 [NTAb 50,128].

11704 *Neudecker, Reinhard* Der Lehrer-Gott vom Berg Sinai: ein interreligiöser Zugang. [M]MORAN, W.: BibOr 48: 2005 ⇒107. 79-101 [Exod 20,2];

11705 Once and for all—yet forever unfolding: rabbinic commentaries on the revelation on Mount Sinai in the light of Suni and Zen Buddhist texts. Kiyo 29 (2005) 26-36 Collab. *K. Suzawa* [AcBib 11,147].

11706 *Neusner, Jacob* Modernization as a condition, not a uniform period of time: explaining why religious traditions change, illustrated by Judaism. NBl 86 (2005) 546-553;

11707 The parable (mashal), a documentary approach. JHiC 11/1 (2005) 1-21 [NTAb 50,128];

11708 How important was the destruction of the second temple in the formation of rabbinic Judaism?: some reconsiderations. [F]STEMBERGER, G.: SJ 32: 2005 ⇒140. 77-93;

11709 Rabbinic biography exemplary pattern in place of lives of sages. JHiC 11/2 (2005) 19-23 [NTAb 50,552];

11710 Judaism and the interpretation of scripture: introduction to the rabbinic midrash. 2004 ⇒20,10598. [R]CV 47 (2005) 354-357 (*Šuba, Pavel*); RBLit (2005)* (*Kern-Ulmer, Rivka*).

11711 **Neusner, Jacob** Contours of coherence in rabbinic Judaism. JSJ.S 97: Lei 2005, Brill 2 vols ; xxvi; 438; iv; 508 pp. €225/$320. 90-04-14231-2;

11712 Rabbinic literature: an essential guide. Nv 2005, Abingdon (6) 164 pp. $16. 0-687-35193-6. [R]RExp 102 (2005) 536-538 (*Biddle, Mark E.*); RBLit (2005)* (*Maoz, Daniel; Nicklas, Tobias*);

11713 Rabbinic categories: construction and comparison. Lei 2005, Brill xxiii; 426 pp. 90-04-14578-8;

11714 Is scripture the origin of the halakhah?. Lanham 2005, University Press of America xvi; 217 pp. 0-7618-3117-7;

11715 Performing Israel's faith: narrative and law in rabbinic theology. Waco, Texas 2005, Baylor viii; 230 pp. $30. 1-932792-25-2;

11716 Theological dictionary of rabbinic Judaism, 1: principal theological categories. Lanham 2005, Univ. Pr. of America xxxiv; 273 pp. $42. 0-7618-3029-4;

11717 2: making connections and building constructions. Lanham 2005, Univ. Pr. of America xxxiv; 449 pp. $56. 0-7618-3028-6;

11718 3: models of analysis, explanations, and anticipation. Lanham 2005, Univ. Pr. of America xxxiv; 390 pp. $49. 0-7618-3027-8;

11719 Questions and answers: intellectual foundations of Judaism. Peabody, MASS 2005, Hendrickson xxvi; 254 pp. £12. 1565-63865-4.

11720 [T]**Neusner, Jacob** The Babylonian talmud: a translation and commentary. Tractate Qiddushin 12: Peabody 2005 <1994-1999>, Hendrickson 22 vols. £520. 1-56563-707-0; with CD-ROM.

11721 *Noam, Vered* From philology to history: the sectarian dispute, as portrayed in the scholium to *Megillat Ta'anit*. Recent developments in midrash research. Judaism in context 2: 2005 ⇒11633. 53-95.

11722 *Novak, David* The covenant in rabbinic thought. Two faiths. 2005 ⇒844. 65-80.

11723 *Oberhänsli-Widmer, Gabrielle* Elija als Pate des Bundes, oder die Dynamik rabbinischer Rezeption. [F]STEGEMANN, E. 2005 ⇒139. 126-137 [1 Kgs 18].

11724 *Oppenheimer, Aharon* Rabban Gamaliel of Yavneh and his circuits of Eretz Israel <1989> 145-155;

11725 'Those of the school of Rabbi Yannai' <1978> 156-165;

11726 Ethnic groups and religious contexts in the talmudic literature <1995> 166-172;

11727 Jewish conscripts in the Roman army <2005> 183-191;

11728 The attempt of Hananiah, son of Rabbi Joshua's brother, to intercalate the year in Babylonia: a comparison of the traditions in the Jerusalem and Babylonian talmuds <2000> 384-393;

11729 Babylonian synagogues with historical associations <1995> 394-401;

11730 Beziehungen zwischen Messene und Palästina <1982> 409-416;

11731 'Von Qurtawa nach Aspamia' <1988>. Between Rome and Babylon. TSAJ 108: 2005 ⇒272. 433-441.

11732 *Peetz, Melanie* Rabbinische Schriftauslegung am Beispiel des Estermidrasch im Talmudtraktat Megilla, oder: lebendiges Buch—lebendige Gemeinde. "Lebendige Gemeinde". 2005 ⇒578. 69-92.

11733 **Perani, Mauro; Sagradini, Enrica** Talmudic and midrashic fragments from the 'Italian Genizah': reunification of the manuscripts and catalogue. Quaderni di Materia giudaica 1: 2004 ⇒20,10600. [R]Materia giudaica 10/1 (2005) 176-180 (*Sussmann, Yaakov*).

11734 **Peters, Simi** Learning to read midrash. 2004 ⇒20,10601. [R]JBQ 33 (2005) 200-201 (*Vogel, Dan*).

11735 *Plietzsch, Susanne* Religion der Differenz: eine Lektüre von bBerakhot 57b-58b. [F]STEGEMANN, E. 2005 ⇒139. 138-152.

11736 *Radzyner, Amihai* Talmudic law as religious law: the source of the desire to limit judicial powers. Maarav 12 (2005) 121-153.

11737 *Reeg, Gottfried* Die Ursache für die Bindung Isaaks: wie lasen die Rabbinen die Bibel?. [F]STEMBERGER, G.: SJ 32: 2005 ⇒140. 319-329 [Gen 22].

11738 *Reichman, Ronen* Von vier und mehr Gründen, warum man die Pe'a für die Armen am Feldende stehen lassen soll. Trumah 15 (2005) 79-98 [Lev 19,9; 23,22].

11739 *Robberechts, Édouard* Parole et idolâtrie. FV 104/5 (2005) 37-47.

11740 *Rosen-Zvi, Ishay* Joining the club: Tannaitic legal midrash and ancient Jewish hermeneutics. StPhiloA 17 (2005) 153-160.

11741 *Rosik, Mariusz* Postać Jezusa w pozabiblijnej tradycji żydowskiej do czasów redakcji *talmudu* [Personne de Christ dans la tradition extra biblique juive jusqu'aux temps de la rédaction du *talmud*]. AtK 145 (2005) 421-433. **P**.

11742 *Roth, Pinchas* On some rabbinic fragments from the European genizah. Materia giudaica 10/2 (2005) 305-312.

11743 *Rovner, Jay* "Rav Assi had this old mother": the structure, meaning, and formation of a talmudic story. Creation and composition. TSAJ 114: 2005 ⇒11632. 101-124. Nashim: Qiddushin.

11744 **Rubenstein, Jeffrey L.** The culture of the Babylonian talmud. 2003 ⇒19,11128; 20,10611. [R]CBQ 67 (2005) 125-126 (*Jacobs, Steven Leonard*); RBLit (2005)* (*Bloch, René; Kulp, Joshua*); JThS 56 (2005) 638-642 (*Reif, Stefan C.*);

11745 Baltimore 2005 <2003>, Johns Hopkins Univ. Pr. xii; 232 pp. $19. 08018-82656 [NTAb 50,445].

11746 **Ruiz Morell, Olga; Salvatierra, Aurora** La mujer en el talmud: una antología de textos rabínicos. Barc 2005, Riopiedras 197 pp.

11747 *Satlow, Michael L.* Giving for a return: Jewish votive offerings in late antiquity. Religion and the self in antiquity. 2005 ⇒818. 91-108.

11748 *Scanu, Maria Pina* Quale Gesù nella letteratura rabbinica?. RStB 17/2 (2005) 161-173.

11749 *Schiffman, Lawrence H.* Composition and redaction in Bavli, Pereq Ḥeleq. Creation and composition. TSAJ 114: 2005 ⇒11632. 201-215. Neziqin: Sanhedrin.

11750 *Schofer, Jonathan* The beastly body in rabbinic self-formation. Religion and the self in antiquity. 2005 ⇒818. 197-221.

11751 **Schofer, Jonathan Wyn** The making of a sage: a study in rabbinic ethics. Madison 2005, University of Wisconsin Press xiv; 310 pp. $25. 0-299-20460-X. Bibl. 275-294 [R]RBLit (2005)* (*Sherman, Phillip*).

11752 **Schwartz, Michael D.; Yahalom, Joseph** Avodah: an anthology of ancient poetry for Yom Kippur. University Park, PA 2004, Penn State Univ. Pr. x; 390 pp. £34.50. 02710-23570.

11753 *Segal, Eliezer* Rabbi Eleazar's *peruṭah*. JR 85 (2005) 25-42 [NTAb 49,571].

11754 **Segal, Eliezer** From sermon to commentary: expounding the bible in talmudic Babylonia. SCJud 17: Waterloo, Ontario 2005, Laurier Univ. Pr. vii; 164 pp. 0-88920-482-9. Bibl. 141-152.

11755 **Shemesh, Aharon** Punishment and sins: from scripture to the rabbis. 2003 ⇒19,11141. [R]JQR 95 (2005) 341-343 (*Kulp, Joshua*).

11756 *Shulman, D.G.* Clinical psychoanalysis as midrash. CCAR.J 52/3 (2005) 34-56 [NTAb 51,127].

11757 *Siegel, D.* The Golden Calf episode: when the betrayed is the betrayer and the betrayer the betrayed. Conservative Judaism [NY] 57/3 (2005) 23-32 [NTAb 50,129] [Exod 32,10-13].

11758 *Silverman, I.J.* Lessons from the ancient priesthood. Conservative Judaism [NY] 57/3 (2005) 77-101 [NTAb 50,130].

11759 *Smelik, Willem* Translation as innovation in BT Meg. 3a. Recent developments in midrash research. 2005 ⇒11633. 25-49.

11760 *Steinmetz, Devora* Agada unbound: inter-agadic characterization of sages in the Bavli and implications for reading agada. Creation and composition. TSAJ 114: 2005 ⇒11632. 293-337.

11761 **Steinsaltz, Adin** Le Talmud: l'édition Steinsaltz: תלמוד בבלי: guide et lexiques. P 2005, Bibliophane 290 pp. 2-86970-119-5. Trad. française: Rabbins Jean-Jacques Gugenheim et Jacquot Grunewald.

11762 *Stemberger, Günter* Die Ordination der Rabbinen—Idealbild oder historische Wirklichkeit?. Trumah 15 (2005) 25-52 [Num 27].

11763 *Stratton, Kimberly* Imagining power: magic, miracle, and the social context of rabbinic self-representation. JAAR 73/2 (2005) 361-393.

11764 *Sweeney, Marvin A.* Pardes revisited once again: a reassessment of the rabbinic legend concerning the four who entered Pardes. Form and intertextuality. FAT 45: 2005 ⇒313. 269-282.

11765 *Tal, Abraham* Sam IX, 46 of the St. Petersburg Russian National Library: a witness of a lost source. [F]SCHENKER, A.: OBO 214: 2005 ⇒134. 339-354.

11766 *Townsend, John* The significance of midrash;

11767 *Ulmer, Rivka* Creating rabbinic texts: moving from a synoptic to a critical edition of Pesiqta Rabbati. Recent developments in midrash research. Judaism in context 2: 2005 ⇒11633. 17-24/117-135.

11768 *Valle Rodríguez, Carlos del* Los primeros contactos de la iglesia con el talmud: el significado de la deuterosis. [F]STEMBERGER, G.: SJ 32: 2005 ⇒140. 299-308.

11769 *Van Uchelen, Niek A.* Rabbijnse retorica. [F]HOOGEWOUD, F. 2005 ⇒63. 137-142 [OTA 29,32] [Exod 15,1].

11770 *Veltri, Giuseppe* Magic, sex and politics: the media power of theatre amusements in the mirror of rabbinic literature. [F]STEMBERGER, G.: SJ 32: 2005 ⇒140. 243-256.

11771 *Visotzky, Burton L.* On critical editions of midrash. Recent developments in midrash research. 2005 ⇒11633. 155-161.

11772 *Wajsberg, E.* The Aramaic dialect of the Palestinian traditions in the Baylonian talmud. Leš. 67/3-4 (2005) 301-326 [NTAb 50,358]. **H.**

11773 **Wellmann, Bettina** Von David, Königin Ester und Christus: Psalm 22 im Midrasch Tehillim und bei AUGUSTINUS. [D]*Zenger, Erich* 2005, Diss. Münster [ThRv 102,ii].

11774 **Yadin, Azzan** Scripture as logos: Rabbi Ishmael and the origins of midrash. 2004 ⇒20,10634. [R]JJS 56 (2005) 349-350 (*Hezser, Catherine*); RBLit (2005)* (*Kulp, Joshua; Teugels, Lieve*).

11775 **Zumbroich, Walburga** Mythos und Chaos: die Frage nach dem Leiden und nach dem Bösen in der frührabbinischen Literatur. Judentum und Christentum 12: 2003 ⇒19,11163. [R]ThLZ 130 (2005) 254-256 (*Oberhänsli-Widmer, Gabrielle*).

### K7.1 **Judaismus mediaevalis**, *generalia*

11776 [ET]**Abel, Wolfgang von** YŪSUF AL-BAṢĪR: Das Buch der Unterscheidung: judäo-arabisch–deutsch. Herders Bibliothek der Philosophie des Mittelalters 5: FrB 2005, Herder 384 pp. 34512-86882.

11777 **Becker, Dan** Arabic sources of Isaac BEN BARUN's Book of Comparison between the Hebrew and the Arabic languages. Texts and Studies in the Hebrew Language 12: TA 2005, Tel Aviv University pag. varia. **H.**

11778 *Ben-Shalom, Ram* Medieval Jewry in christendom. The Oxford handbook of Jewish studies. 2005 ⇒1053. 153-192.

11779 *Blank, Debra R.* The medieval French practice of repeating Qaddisch and Barekhu for latecomers to synagogue. Liturgy in the life of the synagogue. Duke Judaic Studies 2: 2005 ⇒848. 73-94.

11780 [ET]**Börner-Klein, Dagmar** Pirke de-Rabbi Elieser: nach der Edition Venedig 1544; unter Berücksichtigung der Edition Warschau 1852. SJ 26: 2004 ⇒20,10638. [R]ThLZ 130 (2005) 1179-1181 (*Dochhorn, Jan*).

11781 *Cohen, Mark R.* Medieval jewry in the world of Islam;

11782 *Dan, Joseph* The narratives of medieval Jewish history. The Oxford handbook of Jewish studies. 2005 ⇒1053. 193-218/141-152.

11783 [TE]**Fenton, Paul B.** Sefer Yetsirah ou Le livre de la création: exposé de cosmogonie hébraïque ancienne. P 2002, Rivages poche/Petite Bibliothèque 135 pp. [R]Materia giudaica 10/1 (2005) 199-200 (*Mancuso, Piergabriele*).

11784 *Gómez-Aranda, Mariano* IBN EZRA and RASHBAM on Qohelet: two perspectives in contrast. HebStud 46 (2005) 235-258.

11785 **Harris, Robert A.** Discerning parallelism: a study in Northern French medieval Jewish biblical exegesis. Providence, RI 2005, Brown Judaic Studies 139 pp. $40. 978-19306-75223.

11786 **Harvey, Steven** L'"Opuscolo della contesa" di Falaquera: introduzione alla filosofia ebraica medioevale. [E]*Gatti, Roberto*: Opuscula 135: Genova 2005, Il Melangolo 262 pp. 88-7018-522-2. Bibl. 245-252.

11787 **Hollender, Elisabeth** Clavis commentariorum of Hebrew liturgical poetry in manuscript. Clavis commentariorum Antiquitatis et Medii Aevi 4: Lei 2005, Brill xi; 979 pp. €225. 90041-46407 [Scr. 60, 193*—M. de Schepper].

11788 *Lasker, Daniel J.* Models of spirituality in medieval Jewish philosophy. Jewish spirituality. 2005 ⇒575. 163-185.

11789 *Mann, Vivian B.* Spirituality and Jewish ceremonial art. Jewish spirituality. 2005 ⇒575. 213-231.

11790 *Melamed, Abraham* Is there a Jewish political thought?: the medieval case reconsidered. HPolS 1/1 (2005) 24-56.

11791 *Ragacs, Ursula* Hoffnung für die Zukunft: Feststellungen und Spekulationen zum jüdischen Verständnis von Dtn 30,3. [F]STEMBERGER, G.: SJ 32: 2005 ⇒140. 385-393.

11792 *Rivlin, Yosef* Jewish contracts of the post-talmudic era: a bridge between the judge and society. Maarav 12 (2005) 155-167.

11793 *Ron, Zvi* Eliasaph ben-Deuel/Reuel: a rabbinic interpretation. JBQ 33 (2005) 191-195 [Num 2,14].

11794 **Rosen, Tova** Unveiling Eve: reading gender in medieval Hebrew literature. 2003 ⇒19,11184. [R]JJS 56 (2005) 160-162 (*Skinner, Patricia*).

11795 *Rosen, Tova; Yassif, Eli* The study of Hebrew literature of the Middle Ages: major trends and goals. The Oxford handbook of Jewish studies. 2005 ⇒1053. 241-294.

11796 *Rothschild, Jean-Pierre* L'état présent de la recherche en philosophie juive médiévale. REJ 164 (2005) 251-268.

11797 **Schwartz, Dov** Studies on astral magic in medieval Jewish thought. Lei 2005, Brill 251 pp. £78. 90-041-4234-7.

11798 *Schwarzwald, Ora R.* Judaeo-Spanish studies. The Oxford handbook of Jewish studies. 2005 ⇒1053. 572-600.

11799 **Sirat, Colette** Hebrew manuscripts of the Middle Ages. [ET]*De Lange, Nicholas R.M.* 2002 ⇒18,9005; 20,9399. [R]Medieval Encounters 11 (2005) 126-131 (*Sáenz-Badillos, Angel*).

11800 *Ta-Shma, Israel* Rabbinic literature in the Middle Ages: 1000-1492. Oxford handbook of Jewish studies. 2005 ⇒1053. 219-240.

11801 **Ta-Shma, Israel M.** כנסת מחקרים. עיונים בספרות הרבנית בימי הביניים. כרך א [Studies in medieval rabbinic literature, 1: Germany]. 2004 ⇒20,10658. [R]REJ 164 (2005) 361-362 (*Rothschild, Jean-Pierre*);

11802 Studies in medieval rabbinic literature, 3: Italy & Byzantium. J 2005, Bialik 360 pp. **H.**

11803 *Teugels, Lieve M.* Textual criticism of a late rabbinic midrash: *Aggadat Bereshit*. Recent developments in midrash research. Judaism in context 2: 2005 ⇒11633. 137-153.

## K7.2 Maimonides

11804 *Birnbaum, Ruth* Maimonides, then and now. Jdm 54 (2005) 66-78.

11805 **Davidson, Herbert A.** Moses Maimonides: the man and his works. NY 2005, OUP x; 567 pp. $45. 0-19-517321-X. [R]JHP 43 (2005) 484-485 (*Ivry, Alfred L.*).

11806 *Goldman, Esther W.* Maimonides' illustration of the temple in Jerusalem as a model for later copies. Manuscripts in transition. 2005 ⇒935. 93-98 [Scr. 60/1,56*—A. Dubois].

11807 **Hasselhoff, Görge** Dicit Rabbi Moyses: Studien zum Bild von Moses Maimonides im lateinischen Westen vom 13. bis 15. Jahrhundert. 2004 ⇒20,10672. [R]REJ 164 (2005) 368-369 (*Rothschild, Jean-Pierre*); FrRu 12 (2005) 298-299 (*Oberforcher, Robert*).

11808 **Heschel, Abraham J.** Maimonides: eine Biographie. 1992 <1935> ⇒9,10808. [R]FrRu 12 (2005) 299-300 (*Oberforcher, Robert*).

11809 *Hyman, Arthur* Maimonides on prayer. Jewish spirituality. 2005 ⇒575. 299-313.

11810 **Nuland, Sherwin B.** Maimonides. NY 2005, Nextbook xv; 233 pp. 0-8052-4200-7. Bibl. 227-234.

11811 [E]**Rosso, Stefano; Segre, Franco; Turco, Emilia** Mosè Maimonide: il tempo, l'opera, l'eredità. T 2005, A.E.C. 98 pp.

11812 *Schreiner, Stefan* Die Tübinger Handschrift von Maimonides' "Führer der Verirrten". Jud. 61/1 (2005) 59-68.

11813 *Schwartz, Michael* Die Bedeutung des Unterschieds zwischen den Wundern Moses und denen der anderen Propheten nach dem "Führer der Verirrten". Jud. 61/1 (2005) 55-58.

11814 [E]**Seeskin, Kenneth** The Cambridge companion to Maimonides. C 2005, CUP xv; 406 pp. $70. 0-521-81974-1. Bibl. 361-389.

11815 *Splett, Jörg* Mit Mose ben Maimon im Gespräch: Gottesbild und Gottesdienst. ThPh 80 (2005) 75-91.

11816 *Stroumsa, Sarah* Maimonides' Auffassung vom jüdischen Kalam: sein Wahrheitsgehalt und seine geschichtliche Wirkung. Jud. 61 (2005) 289-308.

11817 [E]**Tamer, Georges** The trias of Maimonides: Jewish, Arabic, and ancient culture. SJ 30: B 2005, De Gruyter vii; 455 pp. 3-11-0183-99-4.

11818 [TE]**Zonta, Mauro** Maimonide: la guida dei perplessi. 2003 ⇒19, 11195; 20,10688. [R]REJ 164 (2005) 553-558 (*Di Donato, Silvia*).

## K7.3 Alteri magistri Judaismi mediaevalis

11819 *Grossman, Avraham* RASHI's teachings concerning women. Zion 70 (2005) 157-190. **H.**

11820 *Haas, Jair* Abarbanel's stance towards the existence of multi-significant words in scripture. BetM 181 (2005) 146-62. Sum 198. **H.**

11821 *Himmelfarb, Lea* On RASHI's use of the Masorah notes in his commentary to the bible. Shnaton 15 (2005) 167-184. **H.**

11822 *Klein-Braslavy, Sara* The Alexandrian prologue paradigm in GERSONIDES' writings. JQR 95 (2005) 257-289.

11823 *Krochmalnik, Daniel* RASCHI 'Parschandata'—'Erklärer des Gesetzes'. FrRu 12 (2005) 254-264.

11824 *Levine, Michelle J.* The inner world of biblical character explored in NAḤMANIDES' commentary on Genesis. JJS 56/2 (2005) 306-34.

11825 *Litke, Joel* RASHI's view of Genesis. JBQ 33 (2005) 187-190.

11826 [TE]**Lockshin, Martin I.** RASHBAM's commentary on Deuteronomy: an annotated translation. BJSt 340: Providence, RI 2004, Brown Univ. xiii; 329 pp. $33.50. 1-930675-19-4.

11827 [ET]**Loewe, R.** Isaac IBN SAHULA: Meshal haqadmoni—fables from the distant past: a parallel Hebrew-English text. 2004 ⇒20,10696. [R]Jud. 61 (2005) 76-78 (*Schreiner, Stefan*).

11828 *Penkower, Jordan R.* RASHI's correction to his commentary on the prophets. Shnaton 15 (2005) 185-211. **H.**

11829 *Perani, Mauro* Yosef BEN ŠIM'ON KARA's lost commentary on the Psalms: the Imola fragment from the 'Italian Genizah'. [F]STEMBERGER, G.: SJ 32: 2005 ⇒140. 395-428.

11830 *Ratson, Menachem* The political attitude in two commentaries of R. Abraham IBN EZRA's advice (Exodus 18:13-26). BetM 182 (2005) 281-291. Sum 292 [Exod 18,13-26]. **H.**

11831 [E]**Sáenz-Badillos, Ángel** Abraham IBN 'EZRA': Śafah Bĕrurah: la lengua escogida. [T]*Ruiz González, Enrique*: Córdoba 2004, El Almendro 208+*64 pp. €30. 84-8005-0764.

11832 **Schwarfuchs, S.** RACHI de Troyes. Spiritualités vivantes: P 2005, Albin 152 pp. 22261-58995.

11833 [E]**Sirat, Colette; Klein-Braslavy, Sara; Weljers, Olga** Les méthodes de travail de GERSONIDE et le maniement du savoir chez les scolastiques. 2003 ⇒19,823. [R]JQR 95 (2005) 353-356 (*Lasker, Daniel J.*).

11834 *Yahlom, Shalem* Universal sources in NAḤMANIDES' commentary on the Torah. Shnaton 15 (2005) 265-293. **H.**

## K7.4 *Qabbalâ, Zohar, Merkabā*—Jewish mysticism

11835 **Afterman, Allen B.** Kabbalah and consciousness and the poetry of Allen Afterman. Riverdale-on-Hudson 2005, Sheep Meadow xxiii; 5-212 pp. 1-931357-23-4.

11836 *Alexander, Philip S.* Mysticism. The Oxford handbook of Jewish studies. 2005 ⇒1053. 705-732.

11837 **Arab, Max** De tien gedaanten van de hemelwachter. Kampen 2005, Kok 384 pp. €21.50. 90-435-1101-3.

11838 **Arbel, Vita Daphna** Beholders of divine secrets: mysticism and myth in the Hekhalot and Merkavah literature. 2003 ⇒19,11211; 20,10705. [R]RBLit 7 (2005) 244-246 (*Van der Horst, Pieter W.*).

11839 **Bloom, Harold** Kabbalah and criticism. L 2005, Continuum v; 68 pp. 0-8264-1737-X.

11840 **Boustan, Ra'anan S.** From martyr to mystic: rabbinic martyrology and the making of Merkavah mysticism. [D]*Schäfer, Peter*: TSAJ 112: Tü 2005, Mohr S. xxii; 376 pp. €99. 3-16-148753-2. Diss. Princeton; Bibl. 303-335.

11841 *Brill, Alan* Dwelling with kabbalah: meditation, ritual, and study. Jewish spirituality. 2005 ⇒575. 127-162.

11842 [ET]**Busi, Giulio** The great parchment: Flavius Mithridates' Latin translation, the Hebrew text, and an English version. [E]*Campanini, Saverio*: The Kabbalistic Library of Giovanni Pico della Mirandola 1: 2004 ⇒20,10709. [R]Materia giudaica 10 (2005) 415-420 (*Perani, Mauro*).

11843 **Bührer, Tony** Jüdische Zahlenmystik: Entschlüsselung der geheimnisvollen Zahlensprache Gottes. Altendorf/SZ 2005, Kabbala 87 pp. 3-9521097-2-X.

11844 *Campanini, Saverio* Talmud, philosophy, and kabbalah: a passage from PICO DELLA MIRANDOLA's *Apologia* and its source. [F]STEMBERGER, G.: SJ 32: 2005 ⇒140. 429-447.

11845 [E]**Campanini, Saverio** The book of Bahir: Flavius Mithridates' Latin translation, the Hebrew text and an English version. The Kabbalistic Library of Giovanni Pico della Mirandola 2: T 2005, Aragno 564 pp. €60. Foreword *Giulio Busi*. [R]Materia giudaica 10 (2005) 415-422 (*Perani, Mauro*).

11846 **Cohen, Shoshanna** Kabbala, wijsheid en adviezen van de boom des levens. [T]*Keizer, Hans P.*: Hoevelaken 2005, Verba 239 pp. 90-5513-647-6.

11847 **Elior, Rachel** The three temples: on the emergence of Jewish mysticism. [T]*Louvish, David*: 2004 ⇒20,10712. [R]JSJ 36 (2005) 104-8 (*Tigchelaar, Eibert*); Jud. 61 (2005) 70-74 (*Necker, Gerold*).

11848 **Hecker, Joel** Mystical bodies, mystical meals: eating and embodiment in medieval kabbalah. Detroit 2005, Wayne State University Press x; 282 pp. 0-8143-3181-5. Bibl. 257-270.

11849 *Idel, Moshe* On *Še'elat ḥalom* in Ḥasidei Aškenaz: sources and influences. Materia giudaica 10/1 (2005) 99-109.

11850 **Idel, Moshe** Absorbing perfections: Kabbalah and interpretation. 2002 ⇒18,10327. [R]JR 85 (2005) 94-103 (*Fishbane, Eitan P.*);

11851 Kabbalah and eros. NHv 2005, Yale University Press x; 371 pp. 0-300-10832-X. Bibl. 323-343;

11852 La mystique messianique de la kabbale au hassidisme XIII$^{e}$-XIX$^{e}$ siècle. [T]*Aslanov, Cyril*: P 2005, Calmann-Lévy 636 pp. Préf. *Umberto Eco*.

11853 **Israel, Giorgio** La kabbalah. Bo 2005, Mulino 128 pp.

11854 **Krafchow, Dovid** Kabbalistic tarot: Hebraic wisdom in the major and minor arcana. Rochester, Vt 2005 <2002>, Inner Traditions x; 133 pp. 1-594-77064-6. Rev. ed. of: Listening to the soul.

11855 *Maier, Johann* Jüdische Mystik. ZMR 90/1-2 (2005) 28-48;

11856 Christliche Elemente in der jüdischen Kabbala?. Katholizismus und Judentum. 2005 ⇒596. 30-45.

11857 [T]**Matt, Daniel C.** The Zohar, 1-2. 2003 ⇒19,11224; 20,10726. Pritzker edition. [R]JJS 56 (2005) 352-353 (*Freedman, Daphne*);

11858 The Zohar: translation and commentary, vol. 3. Stanford, CA 2005, Stanford Univ. Pr. xii; 586 pp. $50. 0-8047-5210-9. Pritzker edition [ThD 52,295—W. Charles Heiser].

11859 **Pinson, Dov** Toward the infinite: the way of Kabbalistic meditation. Lanham 2005, Rowman & L. xviii; 157 pp. 0-7425-4512-1.

11860 *Pöhlmann, Matthias* Roter Faden für die Seele: Kabbala—die Religion der Superstars: Selbstfindung mit 72 Gottesnamen. zeitzeichen 6/3 (2005) 51-52.

11861 **Rosen, Jeremy** Kabbalah inspirations mystic themes, texts and symbols. L 2005, Duncan Baird 160 pp. €11.71. 1-84483-192-2.

11862 **Rotenberg, Mordechai** Creativity and sexuality: a kabbalistic perspective. New Brunswick, NJ 2005, Transaction xxiv; 184 p. 1-412-80489-2. Bibl. 171-176.

11863 [T]**Schäfer, Klaus; Zemach-Tendler, Shulamit** Rabbi Moses Cordovero von Zefat: Tomer Deborah—der Palmbaum der Deborah: eine mystische Ethik radikalen Erbarmens. 2003 ⇒19,11229. [R]FrRu 12 (2005) 206-207 (*Thoma, Clemens*).

11864 *Schäfer, Peter* Mirror of his beauty: the femininity of God in Jewish mysticism and christianity. IThQ 70 (2005) 45-59.

11865 *Schmidt-Biggemann, Wilhelm* Katholizismus und Kabbala: Athanasius Kircher SJ als Beispiel. Katholizismus und Judentum. 2005 ⇒ 596. 46-72.

11866 **Steinsaltz, Adin** Opening the Tanya: discovering the moral and mystical teachings of a classic work of kabbalah. SF 2005, Jossey-Bass xxiii; 360 pp. 0-7879-7892-2. Hebrew text edited by *Meir Hanegbi*, translated by Rabbi *Yaacov Tauber*.

11867 **Stroumsa, Guy G.** Hidden wisdom: esoteric traditions and the roots of christian mysticism. SHR 70: Lei [2]2005, Brill xviii; 211 pp. 90-04-13635-5. Bibl. 201.

11868 *Troiana, Mariano* La figura de Lilith como punto de contacto entre dos moimientos místico-esotéricos medievales: el catarismo y la cábala. Epimelia 14 (2005) 81-101.

11869 **Vajda, Georges** Le commentaire sur le "Livre de la création" de Dunas ben Tamim de Kairouan (Xe siècle). [E]*Fenton, Paul*: Collection REJ 24: 2002 ⇒18,10333. [R]JQR 95 (2005) 346-52 (*Langermann, Y. Tzvi*); REJ 164 (2005) 352-353 (*Rothschild, Jean-Pierre*).

11870 [E]**Van Heertum, Cis** Philosophia symbolica: Johann REUCHLIN and the Kabbalah: catalogue of an exhibition in the Bibliotheca Philosophica Hermetica commemorating Johann Reuchlin (1455-1522). Amst 2005, Bibliotheca Philosophica Hermetica 107 pp. Bibl. 101-106. 7 Nov. 2005 - 28 April 2006.

11871 **Wehr, Gerhard** Kabbala—joodse mystiek. [T]*Den Buurman, Margreet*: Soesterberg 2005, Aspekt 134 pp. 90-5911-241-5.

## K7.5 **Judaismus saec. 14-18**

11872 [E]**Abate, Emma; De Gese, Simona** I libri ebraici della biblioteca angelica, 1: incunaboli e cinquecentine. R 2005, Istituto Italiano per l'Africa e l'Oriente xxi; 183 pp. €45. 88-85320-32-5. Pres. *Marina Panetta*; Bibl. xix-xxi.

11873 **Bourel, Dominique** Moses MENDELSSOHN: la naissance du judaïsme moderne. 2004 ⇒20,10737. RFrRu 12 (2005) 51-54 (*Fontius, Martin*).

11874 *Carlebach, Elisheva* European Jewry in the early modern period: 1492-1750. The Oxford handbook of Jewish studies. 2005 ⇒1053. 363-375.

11875 *Ceballos Viro, Ignacio* Una nueva copla de Šabu'ot: *Los judios en el Sinaí*. Sef. 65 (2005) 41-64.

11876 **Chajes, Jeffrey Howard** Between worlds: dybbuks, exorcists, and early modern Judaism. Jewish culture and contexts: 2003 ⇒19, 11235; 20,10740. RSCJ 36 (2005) 309-312 (*Shear, Adam*).

11877 **Goldish, Matt** The Sabbatean prophets. 2004 ⇒20,10743. RSCJ 36 (2005) 579-580 (*Walton, Michael T.*); JRH 29 (2005) 326-327 (*Simms, Norman*).

11878 **Heller, Marvin J.** The sixteenth century Hebrew book: an abridged thesaurus. 2004 ⇒20,10744. RBHR 67 (2005) 462-463 (*Engammare, Max*).

11879 *Neuman, Kalman* Political Hebraism and the early modern 'Respublica Hebraeorum': on defining the field. Ment. *Spinoza*. HPolS 1/1 (2005) 57-70.

11880 **Quaglia, Fabrizio** I libri ebraici nei fondi storici della Biblioteca Civica di Alessandria: catalogo dei frammenti ebraici della Biblioteca Civica e dell'Archivio di Stato. E*Perani, Mauro*2004 ⇒20, 10750. RLASBF 55 (2005) 535-537 (*Pazzini, Massimo*).

11881 **Rauschenbach, Sina** Josef ALBO (um 1380-1444): jüdische Philosophie und christliche Kontroverstheologie in der frühen Neuzeit. 2002 ⇒18,10346. RJQR 95 (2005) 724-727 (*Kohler, George*).

11882 *Reif, Stefan C.* From manuscript codex to printed volume: a novel liturgical transition?. Liturgy in the life of the synagogue. Duke Judaic Studies 2: 2005 ⇒848. 95-108.

11883 **Schwarzfuchs, Lyse** Le livre hébreu à Paris au XVIe siècle: inventaire chronologique. 2004 ⇒20,10752. RBHR 67 (2005) 463-467 (*Engammare, Max*); REJ 164 (2005) 583-585 (*Schwarzbach, Bertram Eugene*).

11884 T**Shirley, Samuel** SPINOZA: complete works. E*Morgan, Michael L.* 2002 ⇒19,11239. RJQR 95 (2005) 366-368 (*Sutcliffe, Adam*).

11885 *Starck, Astrid* Frau und religiöse Identität im jüdischen Mayse bukh (1602). FSTEGEMANN, E. 2005 ⇒140. 255-266.

11886 T**Weinberg, Joanna** Azariah DE' ROSSI: The light of the eyes. YJS 31: 2001 ⇒17,9506. RJJS 56 (2005) 162-165 (*Hayward, Robert*).

## K7.7 Hasidismus et Judaismus saeculi XIX

11887 **Asenjo, Rosa** El Meam loez de Cantar de los Cantares (Šir haširim) de Ḥayim Y. ŠAKÍ (Constantinopla, 1899). Fuente clara 6: Barc 2003, Tirocinio 214 pp.

11888 **Crouter, Richard** Friedrich SCHLEIERMACHER: between Enlightenment and Romanticism. C 2005, CUP 277 pp. $80. 0521805902.

11889 **Ehrlich, M. Avrum** The Messiah of Brooklyn: understanding LUBAVITCH Hasidism past and present. Jersey City, NJ 2004, Ktav xxvi; 332 pp. $35. 08812-58369. RET 116 (2005) 392-4 (*Hayman, Peter*).

11890 **Facchini, C.** David CASTELLI: ebraismo e scienze delle religioni tra otto e novecento. Scienza e storia delle religioni 4: Brescia 2005, Morcelliana 345 pp. €26. 88372-20650.

11891 [E]**Friedman, Eli** The great mission: the life and story of Rabbi Yisrael Baal Shem TOV. [T]*Lesches, Elchonon*: Brooklyn, NY 2005, Kehot ix; 248 pp. $20. 0-8266-0681-4 [ThD 52,264: W.C. Heiser].

11892 **Galley, Susanne** Der Gerechte ist das Fundament der Welt: jüdische Heiligenlegenden aus dem Umfeld des Chassidismus. Jüdische Kultur 11: 2003 ⇒19,11250. [R]FrRu 12 (2005) 208-211 (*Franz-Klauser, Olivia*).

11893 **Jacobs, Louis** Their heads in heaven: unfamiliar aspects of Hasidism. L 2005, Mitchell x; 190 pp. $29.

11894 **Kajon, Irene** Il pensiero ebraico del novecento: una introduzione. 2002 ⇒18,10355; 19,11253. [R]RFNS 97 (2005) 172-174 (*Maurizi, Marco*).

11895 **Magid, Shaul** Hasidism on the margin: reconciliation, antinomianism, and messianism in Izbica/Radzin hasidism. Madison 2003, Univ. of Wisconsin Pr. xxvii; 400 pp.

11896 **Margolin, Ron** The human temple: religious interiorization and the structuring of inner life in early Hasidism. J 2005, Magnes 11; 501 pp. **H**.

11897 **Perry, Yaron** British mission to the Jews in nineteenth-century Palestine. [T]*Yodim, Elizabeth* 2003 ⇒19,11256. [R]ZDPV 121 (2005) 184-185 (*Löffler, Roland*).

11898 *Schleicher, Marianne* Three aspects of scripture in Rabbi NAHMAN of Bratslav's use of the Psalms. StSp(K) (2005) 1-17.

11899 *Tichit, Agnès* Quand la modernité romanesque puise à la source biblique... 'ahavat Tsiyyon ('l'amour de Sion') une 'oeuvre-mémoire'. RICP 96 (2005) 95-104.

11900 *Urban, Martina* Hermeneutics of renewal: biblical imagery and tropes of ecstatic experience in BUBER's early interpretation of Hasidism. StSp(K) (2005) 19-53.

11901 **Wiesel, Elie** Somewhere a master: Hasidic portraits and legends. [T]*Wiesel, Marion*: NY 2005 <1982>, Schocken 221 pp. 0-805-21-1-87-X.

## K7.8 Judaismus contemporaneus

11902 *Abramson, Glenda* DANTE and modern Hebrew literature. [F]ULLENDORFF, E.: SStLL 47: 2005 ⇒154. 323-337.

11903 **Askenazi, Léon** La parole et l'écrit, 2: penser la vie juive aujourd'hui. Présences du judaïsme: P 2005, Michel 640 pp. €25.

11904 *Azria, Régine* "Lieux juifs": solitude du Mont, rumeurs du monde. RHR 222/4 (2005) 557-572.

11905 *Bambach, Charles* Athens and Jerusalem: ROSENZWEIG, HEIDEGGER, and the search for an origin. HTh 44 (2005) 271-288.

11906 *Belkin, Ahuva; Kaynar, Gad* Jewish theatre;

11907 *Benz, Wolfgang* Anti-semitism research. The Oxford handbook of Jewish studies. 2005 ⇒1053. 870-910/943-955.

11908 *Bodenheimer, Alfred* Kolonialismus des Wohlmeinens?: Theodor HERZLs Roman Altneuland. KuI 20 (2005) 85-92;

11909 In den Himmel gebissen: zu Samuel Josef AGNON. [F]STEGEMANN, E. Ment. *Benjamin, W.; Scholem, G.* 2005 ⇒139. 431-441.
11910 *Bohlman, Philip V.* Music. The Oxford handbook of Jewish studies. 2005 ⇒1053. 852-869.
11911 *Bombaci, Nunzio* El fecundo converger de dos caminos de pensamiento y de vida: una nueva aproximación al carteo entre Martin BUBER y Franz ROSENZWEIG (1915-1929). RevAg 46 (2005) 43-59.
11912 *Buber, Martin* Referat über jüdische Erziehung <1917> 77-83;
11913 Zion und die Jugend: eine Ansprache. <1918> 84-92;
11914 Jüdisch leben: zwei Gespräche: meinem Sohn Rafael gewidmet. <1918> 93-103;
11915 Verständigungsgemeinschaft: Rede bei der Tagung der jüdischen Jugendorganisationen Deutschlands <1918> 104-108;
11916 Cheruth: eine Rede über Jugend und Religion <1919> 109-127;
11917 Die Aufgabe <1922> 128-129;
11918 Über den deutschen Aufsatz <1922> 130-131;
11919 Universität und Volkshochschule: Brief an die Exekutive der Zionistischen Organisation in London vom 22. Januar 1924. 132-135;
11920 Rede über das Erzieherische: nach einer auf der III. Internationalen Pädagogischen Konferenz in Heidelberg gesprochenen <1926> 136-154;
11921 Volkserziehung als unsere Aufgabe: Referat gehalten auf dem XXI. Delegiertentage <1926> 155-164;
11922 Philosophische und religiöse Weltanschauung <1928> 165-168;
11923 Verantwortung <1929> 169-170;
11924 Die Bildungsnot des Volkes und die Volksnot der Gebildeten <1929> 173-182;
11925 Einige Leitsätze für Arbeitsgemeinschaften <1930> 183-184;
11926 "Wie kann Gemeinschaft werden?" <1930> 185-199;
11927 Die Jugend und der Zeitgeist <1930> 200-218;
11928 Religiöse Erziehung <1931> 219;
11929 Warum gelernt werden soll: aus dem "Arbeitsplan" der Berliner Schule der jüdischen Jugend 1932 <1931> 220-222;
11930 Wann denn? <1932> 223-227;
11931 Bildungsziel und Bildungsmethoden der jüdischen Schule <1933> 228-234;
11932 Die Kinder <1933> 235-237;
11933 Entwürfe und Programme: zwei Vorschläge (Mai 1933) <1933> 238-244;
11934 Unser Bildungsziel <1933> 245-248;
11935 Ein jüdisches Lehrhaus <1933> 249-251;
11936 Aufgaben jüdischer Volkserziehung: aus der ersten Frankfurter Lehrhausrede zur Wiedereröffnung des Jüdischen Lehrhauses am 19. November 1933 <1933> 252-255;
11937 Jüdische Erwachsenenbildung <1934> 256;
11938 Die Lehre und die Tat: Frankfurter Lehrhausrede <1934> 257-264;
11939 Das pädagogische Problem des Zionismus <1934> 265-278;
11940 Bildung und Weltanschauung: Frankfurter Lehrhausrede <1935> 279-286;
11941 Das Haltende: ein Wort an die jüdische Jugend Deutschlands <1935> 287;

11942 Die Vorurteile der Jugend: Ansprache an die jüdische Jugend, gehalten in Prag am 13. Jänner 1937 <1937> 288-298;
11943 Nationale Erziehung: aus dem Vortrag Martin Bubers in Cernauti <1939> 303-309;
11944 Ein waches Herz: zum Gedenktag Schloschim von Jakov Sandbank <1939> 310;
11945 National and pioneer education <1941> 311-321;
11946 Die Bildung des Volkes im Lande und die hebräische Erziehung in der Diaspora <1943> 322-324;
11947 Advice to frequenters of libraries <1941> 325-326;
11948 Über Charaktererziehung <1947> 327-340;
11949 Erwachsenenbildung <1949> 341-344;
11950 Erwachsenenbildung <1950> 345-358;
11951 Über den Kontakt: aus Jerusalemer pädagogischen Radio-Reden <1950> 359;
11952 Adult education in Israel <1952> 360-364;
11953 Über die Zukunft der Universität <1953> 365-369;
11954 Erziehen: zum 90. Geburtstag von Paul Geheeb <1960> 370;
11955 Erwachsenenerziehung: Ziele der Erwachsenenerziehung <1961> 371-383;
11956 Existenzielle Situation und dialogische Existenz <1966>. Schriften zu Jugend. 2005 ⇒196. 384-385.
11957 **Chester, M.A.** Divine pathos and human being: the theology of Abraham Joshua HESCHEL. L 2005, Mitchell xi; 228 pp. £37.50. 0-8530-3569-5.
11958 **Cohen, Shaye J.D.** Why aren't Jewish women circumcised?: gender and covenant in Judaism. Berkeley, CA 2005, University of California xvii; 315 pp. $40. 05202-12509. Bibl. 273-92 [Gen 17].
11959 [E]**De Lange, Nicholas; Freud-Kandel, Miri** Modern Judaism: an Oxford guide. Oxf 2005, OUP ix; 459 pp. £23. 0-19-926287-X. [R]RRT 12 (2005) 525-529 (*Bunta, Silviu*).
11960 *Della Pergola, Sergio* Demography. The Oxford handbook of Jewish studies. 2005 ⇒1053. 797-823.
11961 *Dexinger, Ferdinand* Religionen der Gegenwart: Judentum. Handbuch Religionswissenschaft. 2005 ⇒1016. 395-410.
11962 *Diner, Hasia* American Jewish history. The Oxford handbook of Jewish studies 2005 ⇒1053. 471-490.
11963 *Dohrn, Verena* Die Transformation der Haskala zum Prosveščenie in der Überlieferung. Jud. 61/2 (2005) 110-127.
11964 *Domhardt, Yvonne* Auswahlbibliographie von Werken mit jüdisch-judaistischer Thematik, die seit Sommer 2004 bis Redaktionsschluss 2005 in Schweizer Verlagen erschienen sind bzw. durch Inhalt oder Verfasser/in die Schweiz betreffen. BSGJ 14 (2005) 35-55.
11965 **Ehrlich, Uri** The nonverbal language of prayer: a new approach to Jewish liturgy. [T]*Ordan, Dena*: TSAJ 105: 2004 ⇒20,10786. [R]RdQ 22 (2005) 298-299 (*Elengabeka, Elvis*).
11966 **Eisenberg, Ronald L.** The 613 mitzvot: a contemporary guide to the commandments of Judaism. Rockville, MD 2005, Schreiber xli; 396 pp. 0-88400-303-5. Bibl. 335-351.
11967 *Erlanger, Simon* "Schädlingsbekämpfung"—Schweizer Juden zwischen interner Disziplinierung und Abwehr. BSGJ 14 (2005) 3-19.

11968 [E]**Feinberg, Anat** Moderne hebräische Literatur: ein Handbuch. Text und Kritik: Mü 2005, Boorberg 296 pp.

11969 **Ferziger, Adam S.** Exclusion and hierarchy: orthodoxy, nonobservance, and the emergence of modern Jewish identity. Ph 2005, Univ. of Pennsylvania Pr. x; 303 pp. 08122-38656. Bibl. 263-286.

11970 [E]**Fiehland van der Vegt, Astrid; Kayales, Christina** Was jeder vom Judentum wissen muss. Gü [9]2005, Gü 206 pp. €13. 3-579-06-407-X.

11971 *Friedländer, Saul* The Holocaust. The Oxford handbook of Jewish studies. 2005 ⇒1053. 421-444.

11972 **Garber, Zev; Zuckerman, Bruce** Double takes: thinking and rethinking issues of modern Judaism in ancient context. Studies in the Shoah 26: Lanham, MD 2004, University Press of America xiii; 220 pp. $43. [R]RBLit (2005)* (*Greenspahn, Frederick E.*).

11973 *Gesundheit, Shimon* Gibt es eine jüdische Theologie der Hebräischen Bibel?. Theologie und Exegese. 2005 ⇒410. 73-86.

11974 *Goldberg, Harvey E.* Modern Jewish society and sociology. The Oxford handbook of Jewish studies. 2005 ⇒1053. 975-1001.

11975 [E]**Goldish, Matt** Spirit possession in Judaism: cases and contexts from the Middle Ages to the present. 2003 ⇒19,11281. [R]SCJ 36 (2005) 309-312 (*Shear, Adam*).

11976 *Goodman, Lenn E.* The covenant and religious ethics today. Two faiths. 2005 ⇒844. 125-143.

11977 *Greenspahn, Frederick* Competing commentaries. [F]FOX, M. 2005 ⇒43. 461-480.

11978 *Grossi, Stefano* Apertura e responsabilità: la condizione di mortalità creaturale tra ROSENZWEIG e LÉVINAS. Vivens Homo 16 (2005) 269-284.

11979 **Haas, Peter J.** Human rights and the world's major religions, 1: The Jewish tradition. Westport, CT 2005, Praeger P. xxii; 297 pp.

11980 *Hasan-Rokem, Galit* Jewish folklore and ethnography;

11981 *Hoffman, Lawrence A.* Jewish liturgy and Jewish scholarship: method and cosmology. The Oxford handbook of Jewish studies. 2005 ⇒1053. 956-974/733-755.

11982 *Hoffmann, Daniel* GOETHE—nicht nur Bildungsgut: zum Einfluss Goethes auf jüdische Religionsphilosophen des 20. Jahrhunderts. KuI 20 (2005) 73-84.

11983 *Hoheisel, Karl* Opfer und Gebet im Judentum. Opfer und Gebet. 2005 ⇒506. 71-79.

11984 *Ilan, Tal* Jewish women's studies. The Oxford handbook of Jewish studies. 2005 ⇒1053. 770-796.

11985 *Jonas, Gernot; Petzel, Paul* Homosexualität im Judentum. JK 66/2 (2005) 65-66.

11986 *Keller, Zsolt* Jüdische Bücher und der Schweizerische Israelitische Gemeindebund (1930-1950): Anmerkungen zu einem bislang wenig beachteten Thema. BSGJ 14 (2005) 20-34.

11987 [E]**Kertzer, David I.** Old demons, new debates: anti-Semitism in the West. Teaneck, NJ 2005, Holmes & M. 219 pp. 0-8419-1443-5. Yivo Institute for Jewish Research, May 11-14, 2003.

11988 *Khan, Geoffrey* Judaeo-Arabic and Judaeo-Persian. The Oxford handbook of Jewish studies. 2005 ⇒1053. 601-620.

11989 *Kligman, Mark L.* Prayers in an Arab mode: liturgical performance of Syrian Jews in Brooklyn. Liturgy in the life of the synagogue. Duke Judaic Studies 2: 2005 ⇒848. 177-204.

11990 **Krupp, Michael** Die Geschichte des Zionismus. GTBS 1212: 2001 ⇒17,9552. [R]BiLi 78 (2005) 49-50 (*Schipper, Friedrich*).
11991 *Kuznitz, Cecile E.* Yiddish studies. The Oxford handbook of Jewish studies. 2005 ⇒1053. 541-571.
11992 **Langer, Ruth** Sinai, Zion, and God in the synagogue: celebrating Torah in Ashkenaz. Liturgy in the life of the synagogue. Duke Judaic Studies 2: 2005 ⇒848. 121-159.
11993 Leqach 4: Mitteilungen und Beiträge. 2004 ⇒20,502. Forschungsstelle Judentum. Theologische Fakultät, Leipzig. [R]CBQ 67 (2005) 370-371 (*Garber, Zev*).
11994 *Levine, Lee I.* Art, architecture, and archaeology. The Oxford handbook of Jewish studies. 2005 ⇒1053. 824-851.
11995 **Littman, Robert J.; Pasachoff, Naomi E.** A concise history of the Jewish people. Lanham 2005, Rowman & L. xviii; 347 pp. 0-7425-4365-X. Bibl. 337-341.
11996 **Lötzsch, Frieder** Philosophie der Neuzeit im Spiegel des Judentums. Münsteraner Judaistische Studien 19: Müns 2005, LIT iv; 300 pp. 3-8258-8505-4. Bibl. 285-295.
11997 *Maller, Allen S.* Torah teaches: 'everything is very good'. JDh 30/1 (2005) 93-101 [Gen 1,31].
11998 *Martel, Sasja* Die jüdische Sicht auf Leben und Tod. JK 66/1 (2005) 20-22.
11999 *Mendes-Flohr, Paul* Jewish philosophy and theology. The Oxford handbook of Jewish studies. 2005 ⇒1053. 756-769.
12000 **Milgram, Goldie** Meaning & mitzvah: daily practices for reclaiming Judaism through prayer, God, Torah, Hebrew, mitzvot and peoplehood. Woodstock, VT 2005, Jewish Lights xxi; 300 pp. 1-5-80-23256-6.
12001 *Muffs, Yochanan* Joy in the liturgy. 133-143;
12002 Love and alacrity in other liturgies. 145-149;
12003 A Jewish view of God's relation to the world. 171-178;
12004 Judaism and secular culture. 179-187;
12005 Toward a phenomenology of the senses <1999>. Personhood of God. 2005 ⇒265. 113-119.
12006 **Neumann, Moritz** Shabbat Shalom: Streifzüge durch die jüdische Welt. [E]*Bauerochse, Lothar; Hofmeister, Klaus*: Wü 2005, Echter 229 pp. 3-429-02727-6.
12007 **Neusner, Jacob** Theology of normative Judaism: a source book. Lanham 2005, University Press of America vi; 156 pp. 0-7618-3116-9.
12008 *Oberhänsli-Widmer, Gabrielle* Jakob Wassermann: Die Juden von Zirndorf (1897). KuI 20 (2005) 181-188.
12009 **Orvieto Richetti, Enrica** La sposa e lo sposo: il matrimonio nella tradizione ebraica. Shofar 7: F 2005, Giuntina 91 pp. 88-8057-228-8. Pref. Rav *Achille Simone Viterbo*; Bibl. 83.
12010 **Patterson, David** Hebrew language and Jewish thought. L 2005, Routledge ix; 242 pp. 0-415-34697-5. Bibl. 230-236.
12011 **Pelli, Moshe** In search of genre: Hebrew enlightenment and modernity. Lanham 2005, University Pr. of America 361 pp. 0-7618-3307-2. Bibl. 333-352.
12012 *Perani, Mauro* Gli studi giudaici negli ambienti accademici e scientifici italiani dal novecento ad oggi. Materia giudaica 10/1 (2005) 9-32.

12013 *Pettit, Peter A.; Townsend, John* "In every generation": Judaism as a living faith. Seeing Judaism anew. 2005 ⇒618. 95-112.

12014 *Rechter, David* Western and Central European Jewry in the modern period: 1750-1933. The Oxford handbook of Jewish studies. 2005 ⇒1053. 376-395.

12015 *Rosenthal, Gilbert S. Tikkun ha-olam*: the metamorphosis of a concept. JR 85 (2005) 214-240.

12016 **Rosenzweig, Franz** Le cantique de la révélation. T*Malka, Salomon*: La Nuit surveillée: P 2005, Cerf 133 pp. €17. 2-204-07910;

12017 The star of redemption. T*Galli, Barbara E.*: Madison 2005, Univ. of Wisconsin Pr. 459 pp. Introd. *Elliot R.Wolfson*; Pref. *Michael Oppenheim*.

12018 **Rozenberg, Shimon Gershon** Chance and providence: discourses on the inner meaning of Purim. E*Tzurieli, Odeah*; T*Moses, Naftali*: Efrat 2005, Yeshivat Siach Yitzchak 108 pp. 965-7244-04-8.

12019 **Rynhold, Daniel** Two models of Jewish philosophy: justifying one's practices. Oxf 2005, OUP 262 pp. 0-19-927486-X. Bibl. 246.

12020 **Saban, Mario Javier** La matriz intelectual de judaísmo y la génesis de Europa. BA 2005, Saban 619 pp. 987-43-9774-8.

12021 *Sarna, Jonathan D.* Jewish prayers for the United States government: a study in the liturgy of politics and the politics of liturgy. Liturgy in the life of the synagogue. 2005 ⇒848. 205-224.

12022 *Schäfer, Peter* Judaistik und ihr Ort in der *universitas litterarum* heute: einige Überlegungen zum Fach Judaistik in Deutschland. FSTEMBERGER G.: SJ 32: 2005 ⇒140. 475-491.

12023 **Schlör, Joachim** Das Ich der Stadt: Debatten über Judentum und Urbanität 1822-1938. Jüdische Religion, Geschichte und Kultur 1: Gö 2005, Vandenhoeck & R. 512 pp. 3-525-56990-4.

12024 *Schoeps, Julius H.* "Wenn Ihr wollt, ist es kein Märchen...": Theodor HERZL, der Zionismus und die Vision des Judenstaates im Rückblick eines Jahrhunderts. ZRGG 57/1 (2005) 82-86.

12025 *Schubert, Kurt* Zionismus und jüdische Identität. FSTEMBERGER, G.: SJ 32: 2005 ⇒140. 463-473.

12026 **Scolnic, Benjamin Edidin** Conservative Judaism and the faces of God's words. Lanham 2005, University Press of America 205 pp. 0-7618-3243-2.

12027 *Seeman, Don* Violence, ethics, and divine honor in modern Jewish thought. JAAR 73/ (2005) 1015-1048.

12028 **Seinfeld, Alexander** The art of amazement: Judaism's forgotten spirituality. NY 2005, Penguin xiii; 272 pp. 1-585-42418-8. Bibl. 250-255.

12029 **Soloveitchik, Joseph B.** (Dov) The emergence of ethical man. E*Berger, Michael S.*: MeOtzar HoRav 5: Hoboken, NJ 2005, KTAV xxii; 214 pp. $25. 0-88125-873-3.

12030 *Stanislawski, Michael* Eastern European Jewry in the modern period: 1750-1939;

12031 *Stavans, Ilan* Other diaspora Jewish literatures since 1492;

12032 *Stein, Sara A.* Sephardi and Middle Eastern Jewries since 1492. The Oxford handbook of Jewish studies. 2005 ⇒1053. 396-411/621-642/327-362.

12033 **Steinmetz, Sol** Dictionary of Jewish usage: a guide to the use of Jewish terms. Lanham 2005, Rowman & L. xv; 207 pp. 0-7425-43-87-0. Bibl. 189-194.

12034 **Stimilli, E.** Jacob TAUBES: sovranità e tempo messianico. Maestri del pensiero 17: Brescia 2004, Morcelliana 310 pp. €24. 88372-19-822.

12035 *Tabory, Joseph* The piety of politics: Jewish prayers for the state of Israel. Liturgy in the life of the synagogue. 2005 ⇒848. 225-246.

12036 **Trebolle Barrera, J.** Los judíos hoy. Córdoba 2005, El Almendro 180 pp. 84800-50829.

12037 **Trepp, Leo; Wöbken-Ekert, Gunda** 'Dein Gott ist mein Gott': Wege zum Judentum und zur jüdischen Gemeinschaft. Stu 2005, Kohlhammer 240 pp. €24.80. 3-17-017411-8.

12038 *Troen, S. Ilan* Settlement and state in Eretz Israel. The Oxford handbook of Jewish studies. 2005 ⇒1053. 445-470.

12039 *Wachs, Saul P.* Birkat Naḥem: the politics of liturgy in modern Israel. Liturgy in the life of the synagogue. 2005 ⇒848. 247-258.

12040 **Weinberger, Leon J.** Jewish hymnography: a literary history. Littman library: L 2000, Littman L. xxiii; 492 pp. 978-1-874774-37-2.

12041 **Wylen, Stephen M.** The seventy faces of Torah: the Jewish way of reading the sacred scriptures. Mahwah, NJ 2005, Paulist xii; 238 pp. $20. 0-8091-4179-5. Bibl. [ThD 52,295—W. Charles Heiser].

12042 *Zevit, Ziony* Jewish biblical theology: Whence? Why? And whither?. HUCA 76 (2005) 289-340.

12043 *Zimerman, Moshe* Jewish and Israeli film studies. The Oxford handbook of Jewish studies. 2005 ⇒1053. 911-942.

## K8 *Philosemitismus*—Jewish Christian relations

12044 *Aubert, Jean-Jacques* 'Du lard ou du cochon'?: the *Testamentum Porcelli* as a Jewish anti-christian pamphlet. [F]HARRIS, W. 2005 ⇒ 57. 107-141.

12045 **Banon, David; Gisel, Pierre; Trigano, Shmuel** Judaïsme et christianisme, entre affrontement et reconnaissance. P 2005, Bayard 124 pp. €10.50. 22274-75229 [NRTh 129,330—Radermakers, J.].

12046 **Barcala Muñoz, Andrés** Biblioteca antijudaica de los escritores ecclesiásticos hispanos, vol. 2: s. VI-VII: el reino visigodo de Toledo, parte primera: cuestiones previas. M 2005, Aben Ezra 206 pp;

12047 parte segunda: autores i textos. M 2005, Aben Ezra 678 pp.

12048 *Baumbach, Günther* Das Neue Testament—ein judenfeindliches Buch?: zur Frage nach der Entstehung und Verbreitung antijüdischer Tendenzen im frühen Christentum <1986>;

12049 Der christlich-jüdische Dialog–Herausforderung und neue Erkenntnisse <1981, 1984>;

12050 Bedeutung und Deutung der Heiligen Schrift in deutschen kirchlichen Verlautbarungen zum christlich-jüdischen Gespräch seit 1950 <1993>;

12051 Barmen I und die Israel-Problematik <1994>. Josephus–Jesusbewegung–Judentum. ANTZ 9: 2005 ⇒182. 97-106/171-190/206-220/233-248.

12052 [E]**Bellis, Alice Ogden; Kaminsky, Joel S.** Jews, christians, and the theology of Hebrew scriptures. SBL Symposium 8: 2000 ⇒16,237 ... 18,10431. [R]ThR 70 (2005) 291-299 (*Reventlow, Henning Graf*).

12053 *Ben-Chorin, Avital* Im christlich-jüdischen Dialog. [F]STENDEBACH, F. 2005 ⇒141. 344-346.
12054 *Ben-Hur, Oded* Lo Stato d'Israele e la Santa Sede. Chiesa ed ebraismo oggi. 2005 ⇒843. 233-238.
12055 **Bindemann, Walther** Jünger und Brüder: Studien zum Differenzierungsprozeß von Kirche und Judentum. Bibelstudien 1: Müns 2005, Lit 512 pp. 3-8258-8682-4.
12056 *Bobichon, Philippe* Le thème du "Verus Israel": est-il constitutif de la controverse entre christianisme et judaïsme?. ASEs 22/2 (2005) 421-444.
12057 **Boyarin, Daniel** Border lines: the partition of Judaeo-Christianity. 2004 ⇒20,10874. [R]ETR 80 (2005) 444-446 (*Muller, Marc*); JJS 56 (2005) 338-341 (*Carleton Paget, James*); RBLit (2005)* (*Wyrick, Jed*); Commonweal 132/18 (2005) 31-34 (*Miles, J.*).
12058 *Boyarin, Daniel; Burrus, Virginia* Hybridity as subversion of Orthodoxy? Jews and Christians in late antiquity. SocComp 52 (2005) 431-441.
12059 *Boys, Mary C.* The enduring covenant;
12060 Christian feminism and anti-Judaism. Seeing Judaism anew. 2005 ⇒618. 17-25/70-79.
12061 *Brugues, Jean-Louis* Erinnern und Versöhnen. ZMR 89 (2005) 12-23.
12062 *Brumlik, Micha* "Juden und Christen anerkennen die moralischen Prinzipien der Tora"–haben Juden und Christen dieselbe Ethik?. Juden und Christen. 2005 ⇒535. 215-233.
12063 *Buchholz, René* "Im Bewusstsein des Erbes ...": Christen und Juden 40 Jahre nach "Nostra aetate". LebZeug 60 (2005) 244-260.
12064 **Cahnman, Werner** Jews and gentiles: a historical sociology of their relations. [E]*Marcus, Judith T.; Tarr, Zoltan* 2004 ⇒20,10881. [R]ASSR 130 (2005) 181-182 (*Löwy, Michael*).
12065 **Chalier, Catherine; Faessler, Marc** Judaïsme et christianisme: l'écoute en partage. Patrimoines; 2001 ⇒17,9606; 18,10447. [R]REJ 164 (2005) 316-326 (*Couteau, Élisabeth*).
12066 **Chazan, Robert** Fashioning Jewish identity in medieval western christendom. 2004 ⇒20,10884. [R]ThLZ 130 (2005) 926-927 (*Domhardt, Yvonne*).
12067 **Cohn-Sherbok, Dan; Grey, Mary** Pursuing the dream: a Jewish-Christian conversation. L 2005, Darton L. & T. 269 pp. £16. 0232-5-25404.
12068 **Comeau, Geneviève** Juifs et chrétiens: le nouveau dialogue. Questions ouvertes: 2001 ⇒17,9613. [R]Chemins de Dialogue 25 (2005) 244-246 (*Aveline, Jean-Marc*).
12069 **Cragg, Kenneth** Semitism: the whence and whither, "how dear are your counsels". Brighton 2005, Sussex Academic vii; 214 pp. 1-84-51-9071-8.
12070 *Crüsemann, Frank* Die Kinderfrage und die christliche Identität angesichts des Judentums 5: Mose 6,20-25: Text für die Bibelarbeit des deutschen evangelischen Kirchentages 2005 und für den Eröffnungsgottesdienst. Dialog/59 (2005) 18-33;
12071 "Christen können den Anspruch des jüdischen Volkes auf das Land Israel respektieren". Juden und Christen. 2005 ⇒535. 155-180.
12072 *Cunningham, Philip A.* Covenant and conversion. Seeing Judaism anew. 2005 ⇒618. 151-162.

12073 "Dabru Emet": eine jüdische Stellungnahme zu Christen und Christentum vom 11. September 2000. Juden und Christen. 2005 ⇒535. 39-44 Nationalprojekt jüdischer Gelehrter.

12074 **Dal Bo, Federico** La legge e il volto di Dio: la rivelazione sul Sinai nella letteratura ebraica e cristiana. Ment. *Augustinus*. 2004 ⇒20, 10892. [R]Ter. 56 (2005) 589-590 (*Fornara, Roberto*).

12075 **Detmers, Achim** Reformation und Judentum: Israel-Lehren und Einstellungen zum Judentum von LUTHER bis zum frühen CALVIN. Judentum und Christentum 7: 2001 ⇒17,9621... 20,10894. [R]ZKTh 127 (2005) 139-140 (*Oberforcher, Robert*).

12076 *Deutsch, Celia M.* Ancient rivalries and New Testament interpretation: an example from the Acts of the Apostles. Seeing Judaism anew. 2005 ⇒618. 49-58 [Acts 10,34-43].

12077 *Di Segni, Riccardo* Progressi e difficoltà del dialogo dal punto di vista ebraico. Chiesa ed ebraismo oggi. 2005 ⇒843. 19-29.

12078 Diskussionsbeitrag zur Thesenreihe "Dabru emet (Redet Wahrheit)" des National Jewish Scholars Project (USA): gemeinsamer Ausschuss von EKD, UEK und VELKD "Kirche und Judentum". EvTh 65 (2005) 317-326.

12079 Documenti del Comitato internazionale di collegamento cattolico-ebraico. Chiesa ed ebraismo oggi. 2005 ⇒843. 241-260.

12080 *Dohmen, Christoph* "Juden und Christen stützen sich auf die Autorität desselben Buches". Juden und Christen. 2005 ⇒535. 67-88.

12081 *Dujardin, Jean* Antijudaïsme—antisémitisme (suite). EeV 125 (2005) 1-6.

12082 *Eckardt, Alice L.* Revising christian teaching: the work of the christian scholars group on Christian-Jewish relations. Seeing Judaism anew. 2005 ⇒618. 263-271.

12083 *Ehrlich, Ernst L.* Der christlich-jüdische Dialog aus jüdischer Perspektive. Juden und Christen. 2005 ⇒535. 201-213.

12084 *Ehrlich, Uri; Langer, Ruth* The earliest texts of the Birkat Haminim. HUCA 76 (2005) 63-112.

12085 *Fleischner, Eva* The Shoah and Jewish-Christian relations. Seeing Judaism anew. 2005 ⇒618. 3-14.

12086 *Flusser, David* The Antichrist and 'The house of Israel alone'. Beginnings of christianity. 2005 ⇒786. 349-357.

12087 *Foa, Anna* Il difficile apprendistato della diversità. Chiesa ed ebraismo oggi. 2005 ⇒843. 51-64.

12088 *Foitzik, Alexander* ZdK: Erklärungen zum jüdisch-christlichen Gespräch. HerKorr 59 (2005) 225-227.

12089 *Fonrobert, Charlotte E.* Jewish christians, Judaizers, and christian anti-Judaism. Late ancient christianity. 2005 ⇒517. 234-254.

12090 *Forte, Bruno* Die Katholische Kirche und die Fehler der Vergangenheit. ZMR 89 (2005) 3-11;

12091 Israele e la chiesa, i due esploratori della Terra Promessa: per una teologia cristiana dell'Ebraismo. Chiesa ed ebraismo oggi. 2005 ⇒ 843. 87-109.

12092 *Frankemölle, Hubert* Zum jüdisch-christlichen Dialog in Deutschland nach dem Holocaust bis zu Papst Johannes Paul II. ThG 48 (2005) 76-189 = Juden und Christen. 2005 ⇒535. 9-37;

12093 Die Bedeutung der Christologie im christlich-jüdischen Dialog: bibeltheologische (und päpstliche) Impulse. Studien zum jüdischen Kontext. SBAB 37: 2005 <2002> ⇒210. 292-302.

12094 *Frankfurter, David* Violence and religious formation: an afterword. Violence in the NT. 2005 ⇒439. 140-152.

12095 *Freyer, Thomas* Christologie im Horizont des christlich-jüdischen Gesprächs. ThQ 185 (2005) 15-37.

12096 *Fumagalli, Pier F.* La Commissione per i rapporti religiosi con l'Ebraismo e il Comitato internazionale di collegamento cattolico-ebraico. Chiesa ed ebraismo oggi. 2005 ⇒843. 191-200.

12097 **Galambush, Julie** The reluctant parting: how the New Testament's Jewish writers created a christian book. SF 2005, Harper xxi; 326 pp. $25. 0-06-059636-8. Bibl. 313-320.

12098 *Garber, Z.* An interfaith dialogue on post-Shoah Jewish-Christian scriptural hermeneutics, with a report on the Case Colloquium (April 10, 2005). Council of Societies for the Study of Religion Bulletin [Houston, TX] 34/4 (2005) 76-79 [NTAb 50,233].

12099 *Gargano, Innocenzo* Il dialogo ebraico-cristiano: il cammino fatto, i problemi aperti. AnStR 6 (2005) 473-489.

12100 *Gellman, Yehuda* The *akedah* and covenant today. Two faiths. 2005 ⇒844. 35-42 [Gen 22,1-19].

12101 [E]**Gerhards, Albert; Henrix, Hans Hermann** Dialog oder Monolog?: zur liturgischen Beziehung zwischen Judentum und Christentum. QD 208: 2004 ⇒20,768. [R]FrRu 12 (2005) 211-213 (*Kampling, Rainer*); ThRv 101 (2005) 145-146 (*Richter, Klemens*).

12102 *Gisel, Pierre* Le christianisme face au judaïsme: débat avec Shmuel Trigano. Judaïsme et christianisme. 2005 ⇒12045. 65-97.

12103 *Giuliani, Massimo* Alleanza con Noè: ebraismo e cristianesimo nella teologia ebraica di Irving Greenberg. Studi Fatti Ricerche 112 (2005) 3-7;

12104 La Shoah come ombra sul dialogo ebraico-cristiano e come stimolo ad esso. Chiesa ed ebraismo oggi. 2005 ⇒843. 65-84.

12105 *Goshen-Gottstein, Alon* Das Judentum und die Inkarnationstheologie. FrRu 12 (2005) 242-253.

12106 **Görrig, Detlef** Die Wurzel trägt: Israels 'bleibende Erwählung' und die 'Mission' der Kirche. 2004 ⇒20,10914. [R]ThRv 101 (2005) 480-482 (*Henrix, Hans Hermann*).

12107 *Graetz, Michael* BOSSUETs Schrift 'Politique tirée des propres paroles de l'Ecriture sainte' (1709) und deren Relevanz für das moderne Judentum. Katholizismus u. Judentum. 2005 ⇒596. 102-111.

12108 *Grappe, Christian* La séparation entre juifs et chrétiens à la fin du premier siècle: circonstances historiques et raisons théologiques. ETR 80 (2005) 327-345.

12109 *Grech, Prosper* Il giudeo-cristianesimo: lo stato della questione. Il messaggio biblico. SRivBib 44: 2005 <2003> ⇒216. 237-248.

12110 [E]*Groote, Marc de* Anonyma testimonia adversus Judaeos: critical edition of an antijudaic treatise. VigChr 59 (2005) 315-336.

12111 *Günther, Hartmut* "Die Juden zuerst und ebenso die Griechen" (Röm. 1,16): zur Frage nach den Juden im Zeugnis des Neuen Testaments. LuthBei 10/4 (2005) 235-245.

12112 *Heinz, Hanspeter* Entstehung und Rezeption von Dabru Emet. Juden und Christen. 2005 ⇒535. 45-65.

12113 *Henrix, Hans H.* Katholische Kirche und Judentum: 40 Jahre nach "Nostra Aetate"—am Ende eines bedeutenden Pontifikats. KuI 20 (2005) 162-177.

12114 *Henry, Martin* Christianity and anti-semitism. IThQ 70/4 (2005) 362.

12115 *Heppner, Menachem* Dabru emet und die Juden. FrRu 12 (2005) 33-37.

12116 [E]**Hinze, Bradford E.; Omar, Irfan A.** Heirs of Abraham: the future of Muslim, Jewish, and Christian relations. MKN 2005, Orbis x; 158 pp. 1-570-75585-X. Bibl. 142-148.

12117 *Hofmann, Norbert J.* Un segno di grande speranza: l'avvio del dialogo fra Santa Sede e Gran Rabbinato d'Israele. Chiesa ed ebraismo oggi. 2005 ⇒843. 201-221.

12118 **Holz, Klaus** Die Gegenwart des Antisemitismus: islamistische, demokratische und antizionistische Judenfeindschaft. Ha 2005, Hamburger 113 pp. 3-936096-59-7.

12119 *Høyland, Knut H.* Messianske jøder og misjon for jødene: skal evangeliet forkynnes for Guds folk?. Ung teologi 38/2 (2005) 25-36.

12120 *Hünermann, Peter* La relazione ebraico-cristiana: una scoperta conciliare e le conseguenze metodologiche nella teologia dogmatica. Chiesa ed ebraismo oggi. 2005 ⇒843. 135-150.

12121 **Jaffe, Dan** Le judaïsme et l'avènement du christianisme: orthodoxie et hétérodoxie dans la littérature talmudique $I^{er}$-$II^{e}$ siècle. Patrimoines judaïsme: P 2005, Cerf 484 pp. 2-204-07759-3. [R]REG 118 (2005) 311-312 (*Pouderon, Bernard*); ChDial 26 (2005) 215-234 (*Bony, Paul*).

12122 *Jaffé, Dan* Les mouvements des dissidents aux Sages du Talmud et la rupture entre le judaïsme et le christianisme. FV 104/5 (2005) 7-19.

12123 *Jossa, Giorgio* Giudei o cristiani?. Giudei o cristiani?. 2005 ⇒833. 15-27.

12124 *Kampling, Rainer* "Der Nazismus war kein christliches Phänomen" —wenn die Geschichte der Theologie begegnet. Juden und Christen. 2005 ⇒535. 181-199.

12125 *Kasper, Walter* Percorsi fatti e questioni aperte nei rapporti ebraico-cristiani. Chiesa ed ebraismo oggi. 2005 ⇒843. 7-17.

12126 *Keel, Othmar* Die Heilung des Bruchs zwischen Judentum und Christentum. Vertikale Ökumene. 2005 ⇒590. 27-39.

12127 *Kessler, Edward* Bound by the bible: Jews, christians and the binding of Isaac. Two faiths. 2005 ⇒844. 11-28 [Gen 22,1-19].

12128 [E]**Kessler, Edward; Wenborn, Neil** A dictionary of Jewish-Christian relations. C 2005, CUP xxix; 507 pp. £120. 0-521-82692-6. Bibl. 454-500.

12129 *Klenicki, Leon Ecclesia et synagoga*: a reflection toward the future. ThD 52 (2005) 103-109 <Bulletin of the Central Conference of American Rabbis (Spring 2005) 18-28.

12130 **Klinghoffer, David** Why the Jews rejected Jesus: the turning point in western history. NY 2005, Doubleday 247 pp. $25. 0-385-510-21-7. Bibl. 237-240.

12131 *Kloke, Martin* Endzeitfieber und Pulverfass: Israel und der christliche Fundamentalismus in Deutschland. Dialog/61 (2005) 18-41.

12132 *Kohlschein, Franz* Wo steht der christlich-jüdische Dialog?: die Stellungnahme "Dabru Emet" und die Position von Kardinal Jean-Marie Lustiger. StZ 223 (2005) 401-410.

12133 *Kranemann, Benedikt* "Der ... unüberwindliche Unterschied zwischen Juden und Christen". Juden u. Christen. 2005 ⇒535. 103-29.

12134 *Krasenbrink, Josef* HILDEGARD von Bingen und die Juden: ein kritischer Dialog Hildegards mit den Juden—unser kritischer Dialog mit Hildegard. FSTENDEBACH, F. 2005 ⇒141. 288-296.

12135 **Külzer, Andreas** Disputationes graecae contra judaeos: Untersuchungen zur byzantinischen antijüdischen Dialogliteratur und ihrem Judenbild. 1999 ⇒15,9860; 18,10501. RByZ 98 (2005) 133-135 (*Niehoff-Panagiotidis, Johannes*).

12136 *Laras, Giuseppe* Prospettive ebraiche sul cristianesimo. Chiesa ed ebraismo oggi. 2005 ⇒843. 31-36.

12137 *Lauer, Joachim* Verfeindete Verwandte?: Synagoga und Ecclesia als Motiv in der christlichen Kunst. WUB 38 (2005) 54-62.

12138 **Leffler, William J.; Jones, Paul H.** The structure of religion: Judaism and Christianity. Lanham 2005, University Press of America viii; 117 pp. 0-7618-3315-3.

12139 *Lenzen, Verena* Zum gegenwärtigen Stand des jüdisch-christlichen Dialogs und seinen Perspektiven. Juden und Christen. 2005 ⇒535. 235-247.

12140 *Leonhard, Clemens* Toraschrein und Tabernakel: Berührungspunkte und Unterschiede von Judentum und Christentum. WUB 38 (2005) 49-53.

12141 *Lichtenberger, Hermann* Judaeophobia—von der antiken Judenfeindschaft zum christlichen Antijudaismus. FSTEGEMANN, E. 2005 ⇒139. 168-181.

12142 **Lieu, Judith M.** Image and reality: the Jews in the world of the christians in the second century. 1996 ⇒12,8673... 20,10968. RRBLit 7 (2005) 254-256 (*Arnold, Russell*).

12143 *Lindner, Helgo* Judenmission unter der Lupe: zu einer kirchenhistorischen Neuerscheinung. ThBeitr 36 (2005) 267-271.

12144 *Luomanen, Petri* Nazarenes. A companion to second-century christian 'heretics'. VigChr.S 76: 2005 ⇒567. 279-314.

12145 **Lustiger, Jean-Marie** Die Verheißung: vom Alten zum Neuen Bund. 2003 ⇒19,11442; 20,10970. RFKTh 21 (2005) 63-64 (*Ziegenaus, Anton*).

12146 **Manns, Frédéric** Un père avait deux fils: Judaïsme et christianisme en dialogue. 2004 ⇒20,10971. RSpiritus 179 (2005) 253-254 (*Guillaume, Jean-Marie*); EeV 138 (2005) 25-6 (*Lambert, Pierre*).

12147 *Martini, Carlo M.* Riflessioni sul dialogo ebraico-cristiano. Chiesa ed ebraismo oggi. 2005 ⇒843. 37-47.

12148 *Massonnet, Jean* La triple unité dans la tradition juive: quels échos dans la tradition chrétienne?. Chemins de Dialogue 25 (2005) 145-161.

12149 *Mejía, Jorge M.* La fondazione della Commissione per i rapporti religiosi con l'Ebraismo, e il suo lavoro;

12150 *Melloni, Alberto* Nostra Aetate e la scoperta del sacramento dell'alterità. Chiesa ed ebraismo oggi. 2005 ⇒843. 181-189/153-179;

12151 Synagoge, "Mutter der Kirche"?: vom Versammlungsraum zum Gotteshaus. WUB 38 (2005) 24-25.

12152 *Merkle, John C.* The God of Israel and christian worship. Seeing Judaism anew. 2005 ⇒618. 177-186.

12153 **Mimouni, Simon C.** Les chrétiens d'origine juive dans l'antiquité. Présences du judaïsme: 2004 ⇒20,10978. REeV 138 (2005) 24-25 (*Cothenet, Edouard*); ASEs 22 (2005) 258-9 (*Bernasconi, Rocco*).

12154 *Mitchell, Stephen* An apostle to Ankara from the New Jerusalem: Montanists and Jews in late Roman Asia Minor. SCI 24 (2005) 207-223.

12155 *Mußner, Franz* Der angebliche Hostienfrevel der Juden in Passau 1478: anlässlich der Anbringung einer Tafel an der Salvatorkirche. KuI 20 (2005) 178-180.

12156 *Myllykoski, Matti* Varken judar eller kristna?: tidig kristen identitet utom och inomen judendomen. SEÅ 70 (2005) 339-355.

12157 *Nadeau, Jean-Guy* La mort de Jésus et l'exécution d'un enfant juif au camp de Buna: de l'usage chrétien de la citation. [F]GENEST, O. 2005 ⇒46. 489-502.

12158 *Neusner, Jacob* The kingdom of heaven in kindred systems, Judaic and christian. BBR 15 (2005) 279-305.

12159 **Neusner, Jacob** Judaism when christianity began: a survey of belief and practice. 2002 ⇒18,10519... 20,10983. [R]RBLit 7 (2005) 293-295 (*Garber, Zev*);

12160 Judaism in monologue and dialogue. Lanham 2005, Univ. Press of America viii; 124 pp. 0-7618-3244-0. Bibl.

12161 **Neusner, Jacob; Chilton, Bruce** Jewish-Christian debates: God, kingdom, Messiah. 1998 ⇒14,9008; 15,9882. [R]HeyJ 46 (2005) 232-235 (*McNamara, Martin*).

12162 **Nickelsburg, George W.E.** Ancient Judaism and christian origins: diversity, continuity, and transformation. 2003 ⇒19,11459; 20, 10984. [R]CBQ 67 (2005) 155-157 (*VanderKam, James C.*); JJS 56 (2005) 148-150 (*Carleton Paget, James*); RBLit (2005)* (*Torijano Morales, Pablo*); RBLit 7 (2005) 298-300 (*Van der Horst, Pieter*).

12163 **Novak, David** Talking with christians: musings of a Jewish theologian. GR 2005, Eerdmans 283 pp. $25.

12164 *Osten-Sacken, Peter von der* "Christen kennen und dienen Gott durch Jesus Christus"—Ansätze einer nicht-antijudaistischen Christologie aus der Perspektive des Neuen Testaments. Juden und Christen. 2005 ⇒535. 131-153.

12165 *Pawlikowski, John T.* The challenge of Tikkun Olam for Jews and Christians. Seeing Judaism anew. 2005 ⇒618. 227-238.

12166 *Perry, Yaron* Judeo-Christian disputation in 19th century Palestine. [F]STEGEMANN, E. 2005 ⇒139. 350-361.

12167 *Pesce, Mauro* Come studiare la nascita del cristianesimo?: alcuni punti di vista. Giudei o cristiani?. 2005 ⇒833. 29-51.

12168 **Peters, Francis E.** The children of Abraham: Judaism, christianity, Islam. [2]2004 <1982> ⇒20,10991. [R]Jud. 61 (2005) 167-168 (*Eißler, Friedmann*).

12169 *Peterson, Erik* Judenchristentum. Peterson: Lukasevangelium und Synoptica. 2005 ⇒277. 437-441.

12170 *Petry, Erik* Antisemitismus, das Perpetuum mobile der Gesellschaften am Anfang des 21. Jahrhunderts?: Gedanken über Traditionen, "Innovationen" und Nivellierungen. [F]STEGEMANN, E. 2005 ⇒139. 196-209.

12171 *Petzel, Paul* Erinnern, das der Vesöhnung dient: zur Bedeutung der Studie Erinnern und Versöhnen für die christlich-jüdischen Beziehungen. ZMR 89 (2005) 39-54.

12172 *Pietri, Luce* La place des Juifs dans les cités italiennes de l'antiquité tardive: apports de la prosopographie chrétienne à l'histoire de la diaspora italienne. Prosopographie et histoire religieuse. 2005 ⇒810. 363-378.

12173 *Rappenecker, Monika* Dabru emet—redet Wahrheit: Entstehungsgeschichte und Zielsetzung. FrRu 12 (2005) 30-33.

12174 *Robinson, James M.* Judaism, Hellenism, christianity: Jesus' followers in Galilee until 70 C.E.. The sayings gospel Q. BEThL 189: 2005 <1985> ⇒289. 193-202.

12175 *Ruiz, Jean-Pierre* Ancient Jewish-Christian rivalries in the shadow of empire: the tensions of the past as lessons for the present. Seeing Judaism anew. 2005 ⇒618. 59-69.

12176 *Saggioro, Alessandro* Cristianesimo e giudaismo nel Codice Teodosiano: una disgregazione dell'identità?. ASEs 22/1 (2005) 177-201.

12177 *Saladin, Jean C.* Lire REUCHLIN lire la bible: sur la préface des "Rudimenta hebraica" (1506). RHR 222/3 (2005) 287-320.

12178 *Sander, Hans-Joachim* Identität mit prekärem Plural: eine Ortsbestimmung für die Christen in nachmoderner Zeit. KuI 20 (2005) 4-8.

12179 *Sandmel, D.F.* The christian reclamation of Judaism. Jdm 54 (2005) 251-262 [NTAb 50,240].

12180 *Schulz, Michael* Der Beitrag von Emmanuel LEVINAS zum jüdisch-christlichen Dialog: Menschwerdung Gottes?. MThZ 56 (2005) 148-161.

12181 *Sherman, Franklin* The road to reconciliation: Protestant church statements on Christian-Jewish relations. Seeing Judaism anew. 2005 ⇒618. 241-251.

12182 *Sievers, Joseph* Spiritualità ebraiche e spiritualità cristiane: percorsi diversi—mete comuni?. Nuova Umanità 27 (2005) 589-604 [AcBib 11,148].

12183 **Sievert, Rosemarie** Isaak ben Abraham aus Troki im christlich-jüdischen Gespräch der Reformationszeit. Münsteraner Judaistische Studien 17: Müns 2005, LIT (4) iii; 139 pp. 3-8258-8442-2. Bibl. 134-139.

12184 *Signer, Michael A.* The covenant in recent theological statements. Two faiths. 2005 ⇒844. 111-124.

12185 *Silvestrini, Achille* Il Vaticano e Israele. Chiesa ed ebraismo oggi. 2005 ⇒843. 225-231.

12186 *Sim, D.C.* How many Jews became christians in the first century?: the failure of the christian mission to the Jews. HTSTS 61/1-2 (2005) 417-440 [NTAb 50,369].

12187 *Skarsaune, Oskar* We have found the Messiah: Jewish believers in Jesus in antiquity. Mishkan [J] 45 (2005) 5-122 [NTAb 50,370];

12188 Hvordan oppstod den kristne antijudaismen?. Ung teologi 38/2 (2005) 5-13.

12189 *Soifer, Maya* '*You say that the Messiah has come...*': the Ceuta Disputation (1179) and its place in the christian anti-Jewish polemics of the high middle ages. Journal of Medieval History 31 (2005) 287-307.

12190 *Söding, Thomas* "Für das Volk": die Sendung Jesu und die Hoffnung Israels. Streitfall Christologie. QD 214: 2005 ⇒549. 73-124.

12191 **Spence, Stephen** The parting of the ways: the Roman Church as a case study. 2004 ⇒20,11017. [R]LTP 61 (2005) 187-8 (*Painchaud, Louis*).

12192 *Spillman, Joann* Targeting Jews for conversion: a contradiction of christian faith and hope. Seeing Judaism anew. 2005 ⇒618. 163-174.

12193 *Stenström, Hanna* Respons till Matti Myllikoski: "Varken judar eller kristna?". SEÅ 70 (2005) 357-359.

12194 **Stökl Ben Ezra, Daniel** The impact of Yom Kippur on early christianity: the day of atonement from Second Temple Judaism to the fifth century. WUNT 2/163: 2003 ⇒19,11500; 20,11024. [R]RB 112 (2005) 280-285 (*Nodet, Etienne*).

12195 *Struminski, Wladimir* Die Kippot der Kardinalim: hebräische Wörter für christliche Fachbegriffe. Dialog/60 (2005) 16-18.

12196 **Surall, Frank** Juden und Christen—Toleranz in neuer Perspektive: der Denkweg Franz ROSENZWEIGs in seinen Bezügen zu Lessing, Harnack, Baeck und Rosenstock-Huessy. 2003 ⇒19,11502. [R]Materia giudaica 10 (2005) 430-432 (*Schmahl, Nadine*).

12197 *Tanzarella, Sergio* O il silenzio o l'errore: la nascita del cristianesimo nella manualistica italiana. Giudei o cristiani?. 2005 ⇒833. 167-182.

12198 *Ter Haar Romeny, Bas* Hypotheses on the development of Judaism and christianity in Syria in the period after 70 C.E.. Matthew and the Didache. 2005 ⇒797. 13-33.

12199 *Thachuparamban, Johny* The origin and development of messianic thinking: towards building a bridge between christianity and Judaism on the 40th aniversary of Nostra Aetate. VJTR 69 (2005) 888-903.

12200 *Thoma, Clemens* Juden und Christen beten denselben Gott an: Monotheismus und Trinität. Juden und Christen. 2005 ⇒535. 89-102.

12201 *Trigano, Shmuel* Le judaïsme face au christianisme: questions théologiques et identitaires. Judaïsme et christianisme. 2005 ⇒12045. 15-39.

12202 *Tück, Jan-Heiner* Inkarnierte Feindesliebe: der Messias Israels und die Hoffnung auf Versöhnung. Streitfall Christologie. QD 214: 2005 ⇒549. 216-258.

12203 *Uhlmann, Rainer F.* Messianisches Zeugnis. em 21/1 (2005) 28-34.

12204 *Van de Beek, A.* Mission among the Jews. AcTh(B) 25/2 (2005) 160-176.

12205 *Vischer, Lukas* Erinnern und Versöhnen—der Weg der Ökumene. ZMR 89 (2005) 24-38.

12206 *Williamson, Clark M.* The universal significance of Christ. Seeing Judaism anew. 2005 ⇒618. 138-147.

12207 *Winling, Raymond* Judaïsme et christianisme d'après le *Dialogue avec Tryphon* de JUSTIN. EeV 134 (2005) 12-18.

12208 **Yoder, John Howard** The Jewish-Christian schism revisited. [E]*Cartwright, Michael G.; Ochs, Peter* 2003 ⇒19,297; 20,11048. [R]RRT 12/1 (2005) 136-138 (*Dewey, Brett*); JSJ 36 (2005) 389-392 (*Tomson, Peter J.*); JJS 56 (2005) 156 (*Lieu, Judith*).

12209 *Zenger, Erich* L'alleanza mai revocata: inizi di una teologia cristiana dell'Ebraismo. Chiesa ed ebraismo oggi. 2005 ⇒843. 111-134.

12210 **Zetterholm, Magnus** The formation of christianity in Antioch: a social-scientific approach to the separation between Judaism and christianity. 2003 ⇒19,11521; 20,11051. [R]JSSR 44/1 (2005) 121-122 (*Wortham, Robert A.*); HeyJ 46 (2005) 368-369 (*Taylor, N.H.*).

12211 **Zolli, Eugenio** Prima dell'alba. [E]*Latorre, Alberto*: CinB [2]2004, San Paolo 284 pp.

## XVI. Religiones parabiblicae

### M1.1 Gnosticismus classicus

12212 **Aland, Barbara** Frühe direkte Auseinandersetzung zwischen Christen, Heiden und Häretikern. Hans-Lietzmann-Vorlesungen 8: B 2005, De Gruyter xi; 48 pp. €15. 3-11-018912-7. Bibl.

12213 **Biondi, Graziano** BASILIDE: la filosofia del Dio inesistente. R 2005, Manifestolibri 383 pp €28. 978-88728-54549.

12214 *Bos, Abraham P.* BASILIDES of Alexandria: Matthias (Matthew) and ARISTOTLE as the sources of inspiration for his gnostic theology in HIPPOLYTUS' Refutatio. [F]LUTTIKHUIZEN, G.: AGJU 59: 2005 ⇒93. 397-418.

12215 *Clavier, Paul* Un tournant gnostique de la phénoménologie française?: à propos des paroles du Christ de Michel Henry. RThom 105(2005) 307-315.

12216 *Denzey, Nicola* BARDAISAN of Edessa. A companion to second-century christian 'heretics'. VigChr.S 76: 2005 ⇒567. 159-184;

12217 Stalking those elusive Ophites: the Ophite diagrams reconsidered. Arc 33 (2005) 89-122.

12218 *Desjardins, Michel R.* Rethinking the study of gnosticism. R&T 12 (2005) 370-384.

12219 *Franzmann, Majella* A complete history of early christianity: taking the "heretics" seriously. JRH 29/2 (2005) 117-128.

12220 **García Bazán, Francisco** La gnosis eterna: antología de textos gnósticos, griegos, latinos y coptos, 1: pliegos de Oriente. 2003 ⇒ 20,11056. [R]EstB 63 (2005) 352-353 (*Sen, Felipe*).

12221 *García Bazán, Francisco* Esoterismo, misterio y rituales gnósticos de liberación, 2. Epimelia 14 (2005) 7-22.

12222 **Grypeou, Emmanouela** "Das vollkommene Pascha": gnostische Bibelexegese und Ethik. Orientalia Biblica et Christiana 15: Wsb 2005, Harrassowitz 332 pp. €58. 3-447-05064-0. Bibl. 289-324.

12223 *Jakab, Attila* Le gnosticisme Alexandrin aux premiers temps du christianisme. [F]LUTTIKHUIZEN, G.: AGJU 59: 2005 ⇒93. 365-379.

12224 **King, Karen L.** What is Gnosticism?. 2003 ⇒19,11532; 20, 11061. [R]JEH 56 (2005) 337-338 (*Löhr, Winrich*); LTP 61 (2005) 189-190 (*Painchaud, Louis*); CBQ 67 (2005) 349-351 (*Mirecki, Paul A.*); JThS 56 (2005) 198-202 (*Edwards, M.J.*);

12225 CM 2005 <2003>, Belknap xii; 343 pp. $17. 06740-17625. Pb. ed.

12226 [E]**Marjanen, Antti** Was there a Gnostic religion?. SESJ 87: Gö 2005, Vandenhoeck & R. 151 pp. €26. 3-525-53604-6. SBL Lahti, July 1999; Bibl. 133-145:

12227 *Marjanen, Antti* What is Gnosticism?: from the Pastorals to Rudolph. Was there a Gnostic religion?. 2005 ⇒12226. 1-53.

12228 *Markschies, Christoph* Der religiöse Pluralismus und das antike Christentum—eine Deutung der Gnosis. Querdenker. 2005 ⇒4696. 36-49;

12229 Gnostische und andere Bilderbücher in der Antike. ZAC 9 (2005) 100-121.

12230 **Markschies, Christoph** Gnosis, an introduction. [T]*Bowden, John*: 2003 ⇒19,11537; 20,11064. [R]Neotest. 39 (2005) 199-201 (*Thom, Johan*); RBLit 7 (2005) 467-472 (*Williams, Michael A.*).

12231 **Mastrocinque, Attilio** From Jewish magic to gnosticism. STAC 24: Tü 2005, Mohr S. xv; 244 pp. €59. 3-16-148555-6. Bibl. 223-7.

12232 [T]**Mead, G.R.S.** Pistis sophia: the gnostic tradition of Mary Magdalene, Jesus, and his disciples. Mineola, NY 2005 <1921>, Dover lxix; 325 pp. $16. 0-486-44064-8. Bibl. 1778-1920 [ThD 52,386—W. Charles Heiser].

12233 *Menzago, Cinzia* Gnosi, gnosticismo e nuovi movimenti religiosi: la nascita di un paradigma interpretativo per la 'nuova religiosità'. AnScR 10 (2005) 281-304.

12234 *Meyer, Marvin* Gnosis, Mageia and the Holy Book of the Great Invisible Spirit. [F]LUTTIKHUIZEN, G.: AGJU 59: 2005 ⇒93. 503-517.

12235 *Pearson, Birger A.* BASILIDES the Gnostic. A companion to second-century christian 'heretics'. VigChr.S 76: 2005 ⇒567. 1-31.

12236 *Pouderon, Bernard* La notice d'HIPPOLYTE sur Simon: cosmologie, anthropologie et embryologie. Les Pères de l'Église. ThH 117: 2005 ⇒813. 49-71.

12237 **Scopello, Madeleine** Femme, gnose et manichéisme: de l'espace mythique au territoire du réel. NHMS 53: Lei 2005, Brill xiv; 406 pp. 90-04-11452-1. Bibl. 347-367.

12238 *Scopello, Madeleine* Marie-Madeleine et la tour: πίστις et σοφία. Femme, gnose. NHMS 53: 2005 <1991> ⇒12237. 3-27;

12239 Âme et allégorie chez les gnostiques. Femme, gnose. 2005 <2000> ⇒12237. 179-200.

12240 **Smith, Carl B.** No longer Jews: the search for gnostic origins. 2004 ⇒20,11073. [R]CBQ 67 (2005) 542-543 (*Denzey, Nicola*); RBLit (2005)* (*Tite, Philip*).

12241 **Turner, John D.** Sethian Gnosticism and the Platonic tradition. Bibliothèque copte de Nag Hammadi, Etudes 6: 2001 ⇒17,9737... 20,11077. [R]Or. 74 (2005) 146-151 (*Luisier, Philippe*).

## M1.2 **Valentinus pistis sophia,** *Elchasai*

12242 *Attridge, Harold W.* HERACLEON and John: reassessment of an early christian hermeneutical debate. Biblical interpretation. Ment. *Origenes* SBL.Symp. 26: 2005 ⇒758. 57-72.

12243 *Dehandschutter, Boudewijn* Readers of Luke in the second century: the Valentinian gnostics. [F]DENAUX, A.: BEThL 182: 2005 ⇒34. 49-60.

12244 *Dunderberg, Ismo* The school of VALENTINUS. Companion to second-century christian 'heretics'. VigChr.S 76: 2005 ⇒567. 64-99.

12245 *Létourneau, Pierre* Croyances et contraintes sociales: l'évolution du mouvement valentinien à la lumière du *Traité tripartite* (NH I,5) et du *Dialogue du Sauveur* (NH III,5). Théologiques 13 (2005) 79-94.

12246 *Luttikhuizen, Gerard P.* Elchasaites and their book. A Companion to second-century christian 'heretics'. VigChr.S 76: 2005 ⇒567. 335-364.

12247 *Robinson, James M.* Jesus from Easter to VALENTINUS (or to the Apostles' Creed). The sayings gospel Q. BEThL 189: 2005 <1982> ⇒289. 131-167.

12248 **Thomassen, Elmar** The spiritual seed: the church of the *Valentinians*. NHMS 60: Lei 2005, Brill xvi; 345 pp.

### M1.3 Corpus hermeticum; Orphismus

12249 *Assmann, Jan Periergia*: Egyptian reactions to Greek curiosity. Cultural borrowings. Oriens et Occidens 8: 2005 ⇒652. 37-49.

12250 **Löw, Andreas** Hermes Trismegistos als Zeuge der Wahrheit: die christliche Hermetikrezeption von ATHENAGORAS bis LAKTANZ. Theophaneia 36: 2002 ⇒18,10600. [R]ThLZ 130 (2005) 199-201 (*Ulrich, Jörg*); IJCT 11 (2005) 658-662 (*Moreschini, Claudio*).

12251 [E]**Ramelli, Ilaria** Corpus Hermeticum. [E]*Nock, A.D.; Festugière, A.-J.*: Il pensiero occidentale: Mi 2005, Bompiani 1627 pp. Testo greco, latino e copto a fronte. [R]RFNS 97 (2005) 519-521 (*Radice, Roberto*).

### M1.5 Mani, *dualismus*; Mandaei

12252 *Ataç, Mehmet-Ali* Manichaeism and ancient Mesopotamian 'Gnosticism'. JANER 5 (2005) 1-39.

12253 *Baraniak, Marek* Mandajczycy–ginący świat gnozy [Les mandéistes–univers de la gnose en disparition]. PrzPow 6 (2005) 25-36. **P**.

12254 *BeDuhn, Jason D.* The leap of the soul in Manicheism. Quinto congresso. 2005 ⇒900. 9-26;

12255 AUGUSTINE, Manichaeism, and the logic of persecution. AfR 7 (2005) 153-166.

12256 **Biedenkopf-Ziehner, Anneliese** Mani und ARISTOTELES: das sechste Kapitel der koptischen Kephalaia: Textanalyse und Interpretation. GOF.Ä 42: 2002 ⇒18,10604. [R]OLZ 100 (2005) 402-405 (*Plisch, Uwe-Karsten*).

12257 *Bierbaums, Marcus* Zur Geltung von Freiheit oder Unfreiheit des Willens (Augustinus, *Contra Felicem Manichaeum II*). Quinto congresso. 2005 ⇒900. 27-35.

12258 *Buckley, Jorunn J.* The Mandaean appropriation of Jesus' mother, Miriai. A feminist companion to mariology. 2005 ⇒431. 182-193;

12259 Turning the tables on Jesus: the Mandaean view. Christian origins. A people's history of christianity 1: 2005 ⇒550. 94-109.

12260 *Cirillo, Luigi* From the Elchasaite christology to the Manichaean apostle of light: some remarks about the Manichaean doctrine of the revelation. Quinto congresso. 2005 ⇒900. 47-54.

12261 *Colditz, Iris* Titles of kings and gods in Iranian Manichaean texts. Quinto congresso. 2005 ⇒900. 55-66.

12262 *Colpe, Carsten* Lehr- und Lernbeziehungen zwischen diversen Ostaramäern, westlichen Magiern und frühen Manichäern als dialektisch-historischer Prozess. Quinto congresso. 2005 ⇒900. 67-83.

12263 *Decret, François* En marge du manuscrit manichéen africain de Tébessa: la mission essentielle des auditeurs dans la libération de la lumière. Quinto congresso. 2005 ⇒900. 85-93.

12264 *Demaria, Serena* Die griechischen Entlehnungen in den koptischen manichäischen Texten: Methoden und Ergebnisse. Quinto congresso. 2005 ⇒900. 95-114.

12265 *Esmailpour, Abolqasem* An Iranian cultural approach to Manichaean gnosticism. JDh 30 (2005) 247-259.

12266 *Franzmann, Majella* The Syriac-Coptic bilinguals from Ismant el-Kharab (Roman Kellis): translation process and Manichaean missionary practice. Quinto congresso. 2005 ⇒900. 115-122.

12267 **Franzmann, Majella** Jesus in the Manichaean writings. 2003 ⇒ 19,11566. [R]RRT 12/1 (2005) 146-147 (*Casiday, Augustine*); LTP 61 (2005) 190-192 (*Pettipiece, Timothy*); ThLZ 130 (2005) 1043-1045 (*Lattke, Michael*).

12268 *Gardner, Iain* Some comments on Mani and Indian religions: according to the Coptic Kephalaia. Quinto congresso. 2005 ⇒900. 123-135.

12269 [E]**Gardner, Iain; Lieu, Samuel N.C.** Manichaean texts from the Roman Empire. 2004 ⇒20,11099. [R]RRT 12 (2005) 457-458 (*Casiday, Augustine*); LTP 61 (2005) 193-195 (*Pettipiece, Timothy*).

12270 *Gnoli, Gherardo* Mani, Šabuhr e l'ora di Palmira;

12271 *Gulácsi, Zsuzsanna* Mani's "picture-box"?: a study of a Chagatai textual reference and its supposed pictorial analogy from the British Library (Or. 8212-1691);

12272 *Hunter, Erica C.D.* Theodore bar Kônî and the Manichaeans. Quinto congresso. 2005 ⇒900. 137-148/149-166/167-178.

12273 *Hutter, Manfred* Religionen vergangener Kulturen: manichäische Religion. Handbuch Religionswissenschaft. 2005 ⇒1016. 235-244.

12274 *Iwersen, Julia* The significance of Manichaeism in the history of esotericism. Quinto congresso. 2005 ⇒900. 179-190.

12275 *Kaatz, Kevin W.* What did AUGUSTINE really know about Manichaean cosmogony?. Quinto congresso. 2005 ⇒900. 191-202.

12276 *Khosroyev, Alexander* Zu einem manichäischen (?) Gebet;

12277 *Klein, Wassilios* The epic Buddhacarita by Aśvaghoṣa and its significance for the "life of Mani". Quinto congresso. 2005 ⇒900. 203-222/223-232.

12278 *Koch, Carsten* 'Opfer' und 'Gebet' in der mandäischen Religion. Opfer und Gebet. 2005 ⇒506. 132-145.

12279 *Krause, Martin* Der Stand der Arbeiten an der Arbeitsstelle für Manichäismusforschung in Münster;

12280 *Lieu, Samuel N.C.* Manichaean *technici termini* in the *Liber Scholiorum* of Theodore bar Kônî. Quinto congresso. 2005 ⇒900. 233-243/245-254.

12281 **Lupieri, Edmondo F.** The Mandaeans: the last Gnostics. [T]*Hindley, Charles*: 2002 ⇒18,10611; 19,11570. [R]ThLZ 130 (2005) 378-380 (*Rudolph, Kurt*).

12282 *Mikkelsen, Gunner* Shared features in the terminology of Chinese Nestorian and Manichaean texts. 263-275;

12283 *Morano, Enrico* A Manichaean *oratio dominica*. 277-285;

12284 *Quispel, Gilles* PLOTINUS and the Jewish Gnōstikoi. 287-329;

12285 *Reck, Christiane* The tribulations of human existence: a Sogdian fragment corresponding to a passage of Borzoy's Preface to *Kalilah wa Dimnah*?. 331-341;

12286 *Richter, Siegfried G.* Arbeiten am koptisch-manichäischen Psalmenbuch, Teil 1–ein Zwischenbericht–. Quinto congresso. 2005 ⇒ 900. 343-354.

12287 *Rudolph, Kurt* Der mandäische Priester als Jünger und König. FRIES, J. 2005 ⇒127. 89-98.

12288 *Scopello, Madeleine* Julie, manichéenne d'Antioche (d'après la Vie de Porphyre de Marc le Diacre, ch. 85-91) <1997>;

12289 Bassa la Lydienne <2001>. Femme, gnose. NHMS 53: 2005 ⇒ 12237. 237-291/293-315.

12290 *Sundermann, Werner* ZOROASTRE, prêtre et prophète dans la doctrine des manichéens. FRIES, J. 2005 ⇒127. 59-72;

12291 Was the Ardhang Mani's picture-book?. Quinto congresso. 2005 ⇒ 900. 373-384.

12292 *Tigchelaar, Eibert* Baraies on Mani's rapture, Paul, and the antediluvian apostles. FLUTTIKHUIZEN, G.: AGJU 59: 2005 ⇒93. 429-41.

12293 *Tubach, Jürgen* Die Thomas-Psalmen und der Mani-Jünger Thomas. Quinto congresso. 2005 ⇒900. 397-416.

12294 **Van Oort, Johannes; Quispel, Gilles** De Keulse Mani-Codex. Pimander 11: Amst 2005, Pelikaan 247 pp [ASEs 22,530—Nicklas, Tobias].

12295 *Van Schaik, John* Eén God of twee goden?: vragen bij de vermeende receptie van manichees dualisme bij de katharen. TTh 45 (2005) 240-260.

12296 *Van Tongerloo, Aloïs* The Buddha's first encounter in a Manichaean Old Turkic text. Quinto congresso. 2005 ⇒900. 385-396.

12297 *Wurst, Gregor* L'état de la recherche sur le canon manichéen. Le canon du NT. MoBi 54: 2005 ⇒334. 237-267.

12298 *Wushu, Lin* Notes on the title of the Dunhuang Manichaean Hymnscroll (S.2659 Mo-ni chiao hsia-pu tsan). Quinto congresso. 2005 ⇒900. 255-262.

## M2.1 Nag Hammadi, *generalia*

12299 *Gianotto, Claudio* L'apport des textes de Nag Hammadi à la connaissance des origines chrétiennes. ASEs 22/2 (2005) 397-407.

12300 **Meyer, M.** The Gnostic discoveries: the impact of the Nag Hammadi library. SF 2005, HarperSanFrancisco vii; 239 pp. $22. 00608-21086. Bibl. [NTAb 50,442].

12301 Nag Hammadi Deutsch, 2: NHC V,2-XIII,1, BG 1 und 4. E**Schenke, Hans-Martin; Bethge, Hans-Gebhard; Kaiser, Ursula Ulrike**: GCS 12: Koptisch-Gnostische Schriften 3: 2003 ⇒19,10501; 20,11125. RZRGG 57 (2005) 185-186 (*Beltz, Walter*).

12302 *Perkins, Pheme* A Gnostic gospel?: title and genre in the Nag Hammadi collection. Arc 33 (2005) 6-22.

12303 *Philonenko, Marc* La mystique du char divin, les papyrus démotiques magiques et les textes de Nag Hammadi. CRAI 3 (2005) 983-993.

12304 *Rasimus, Tuomas* Ophite Gnosticism, Sethianism and the Nag Hammadi library. VigChr 59 (2005) 235-263.

12305 *Robinson, James M.* The French role in early Nag Hammadi studies. JCoS 7 (2005) 1-12;

12306 Die Bedeutung der gnostischen Nag-Hammadi Texte für die neutestamentliche Wissenschaft. The sayings gospel Q. BEThL 189: 2005 <1994> ⇒289. 389-404.

12307 *Scopello, Madeleine* Autour de Youel et Barbélo à Nag Hammadi. Femme, gnose. NHMS 53: 2005 <1978> ⇒12237. 49-78;
12308 Un rituel idéal d'intronisation à Nag Hammadi <1978>;
12309 Jewish and Greek heroines in the Nag Hammadi library <1988>;
12310 Titres au féminin dans la bibliothèque de Nag Hammadi <1993>. Femme, gnose. NHMS 53: 2005 ⇒12237. 79-113/155-177/127-53.
12311 [E]**Turner, John D.; McGuire, Anne** The Nag Hammadi library after fifty years. NHMS 44: 1997 ⇒13,341... 20,11127. [R]VigChr 59 (2005) 104-109 (*Scopello, Madeleine*).

## M2.2 *Evangelium etc. Thomae*—**The Gospel of Thomas**

12312 *Arnal, William E.* The rhetoric of social construction: language and society in the *Gospel of Thomas*. Rhetoric and reality. SCJud 16: 2005 ⇒515. 27-47.
12313 *Baarda, Tjitze* "Blessed are the poor ...": concerning the provenance of logion 54 in "Thomas". Arc 33 (2005) 32-51.
12314 *Brankaer, Johanna* L'ironie de Jésus dans le logion 114 de l'*Évangile de Thomas*. Apocrypha 16 (2005) 149-162.
12315 **Davies, Stevan** The gospel of Thomas and christian wisdom. Oregon House, CA 2005 <1983>, Bardic xlii; 204 pp. $20. New Introd. i-xlii + 'Does the *Gospel of Thomas* have a meaning?' pp 148-169.
12316 *DeConick, April D.* Reading the *Gospel of Thomas* as a repository of early christian communal memory. Memory, tradition, and text. SBL.Semeia Studies 52: 2005 ⇒416. 207-220.
12317 **DeConick, April D.** Recovering the original gospel of Thomas: a history of the gospel and its growth. Library of NT Studies 286: L 2005, Clark xvii; 287 pp. $130. 0-567-04342-8.
12318 *Denker, Jürgen* Las relaciones del evangelio de Tomás con otros escritos del cristianismo primitivo. RevBib 67 (2005) 85-102.
12319 *Everhart, Janet S.* Naked Bodies: transgendering the gospel of Thomas. LecDif 1 (2005)*.
12320 *Gianotto, Claudio* Il vangelo secondo Tommaso e la ricerca storica su Gesù. RStB 17/2 (2005) 149-160.
12321 *Hogeterp, Albert L.A.* The gospel of Thomas and the historical Jesus: the case of eschatology. [F]LUTTIKHUIZEN, G.: AGJU 59: 2005 ⇒93. 381-396.
12322 *Klauck, Hans-Josef* The gospel of Thomas: Jesus' secret words?. ThD 52 (2005) 203-209. Summarized from the following:
12323 Geheime Worte Jesu?: das Evangelium nach Thomas aus Nag Hammadi. BiKi 60 (2005) 89-95.
12324 **Klijn, Albertus F.** The Acts of Thomas. NT.S 108: [2]2003 <1962> ⇒19,11589. [R]RBLit (2005)* (*Nicklas, Tobias*).
12325 **Kurikilambatt, James** First voyage of the apostle Thomas to India: ancient christianity in Bharuch and Taxila. Bangalore 2005, Asian Trading xviii; 264 pp. 81-7086-359-7.
12326 **Nordsieck, Reinhard** Das Thomas-Evangelium. 2004 ⇒20,11140. [R]ThR 70 (2005) 384-388 (*Schröter, Jens*); VigChr 59 (2005) 204-205 (*Quispel, Gilles*).
12327 **Pagels, Elaine** Beyond belief: the secret gospel of Thomas. 2003 ⇒19,11601; 20,11142. [R]AThR 87 (2005) 359-360 (*Richards, Bill*);

12328 Das Geheimnis des fünften Evangeliums: warum die Bibel nur die halbe Wahrheit sagt. 2004 ⇒20,11143. [R]Biblos 54 (2005) 154-156 (*Förster, Hans*).
12329 *Pakis, Valentine* (Un)desirable origins: the Heliand and the gospel of Thomas. Exemplaria 17 (2005) 215-253.
12330 *Popkes, Enno E.* Die Umdeutung des Todes Jesu im koptischen Thomasevangelium. Deutungen. WUNT 181: 2005 ⇒392. 513-43.
12331 *Pouderon, Bernard* 'Paysages d'âmes' d'écrits gnostiques: L'Hymne de la perle. Lieux, décors et paysages. CMOM 34: 2005 ⇒889. 337-343.
12332 *Robinson, James M.* On bridging the gap from Q to *The Gospel of Thomas* (or *vice versa*) <1986>;
12333 The pre-Q text of the (ravens and) lilies Q 12:22-31 and P. Oxy. 655 (*Gos. Thom.* 36) <1999>;
12334 A pre-canonical Greek reading in saying 36 of the *Gospel of Thomas* [Lk 12,27]. The sayings gospel Q. BEThL 189: 2005 ⇒289. 203-258/729-775/845-883.
12335 **Roukema, Riemer** Het evangelie van Thomas: vertaald, ingeleid en van aantekeningen voorzien. Ad fontes: Zoetermeer 2005, Meinema 96 pp. €12.50. 90-211-4065-9.
12336 [T]**Rowe, Joseph** The gospel of Thomas : the gnostic wisdom of Jesus. Rochester (Vt.) 2005, Inner Traditions xii, 228 pp. 1-594-77046-8. Introd., commentary by *Jean-Yves Leloup*; Bibl. 227-228.
12337 **Uro, Risto** Thomas: seeking the historical context of the gospel of Thomas. 2003 ⇒19,11607; 20,11149. [R]ThLZ 130 (2005) 492-494 (*Nagel, Titus*).
12338 *Van Aarde, A.G.* Die Griekse manuskrip van die *Kindheidsevangelie van Tomas* in Kodeks Sinaïtikus (Gr 453) vertaal in Afrikaans. HTSTS 61/1-2 (2005) 491-516 [NTAb 50,371];
12339 Die *Kindheidsevangelie van Tomas*—historiese allegorie of mite in die vorm van 'n biografiese diskursiewe evangelie?. HTSTS 61/1-2 (2005) 461-489 [NTAb 50,371];
12340 The infancy gospel of Thomas: allegory or myth—Gnostic or Ebionite?. VeE 26/3 (2005) 826-850.
12341 *Wood, John Halsey* The New Testament gospels and the gospel of Thomas: a new direction. NTS 51 (2005) 579-595.

### M2.3 *Singula scripta*—**Various titles** [⇒K3.4]

12342 *Brankaer, Johanna Marsanes*: un texte Sethien platonisant?. Muséon 118 (2005) 21-41.
12343 *Charron, Régine* The Apocryphon of John (NHC II, 1) and the Graeco-Egyptian alchemical literature. VigChr 59 (2005) 438-456.
12344 [ET]**Kulawik, Cornelia** Die Erzählung über die Seele (Nag-Hammadi-Codex II.6): neu herausgegeben, übersetzt und erklärt. [D]*Bethge, Hans-Gebhard* 2005, Diss. Humboldt [ThLZ 130,881].
12345 *Pouderon, Bernard* "Paysages d'âmes" d'écrits gnostiques: *L'Exégèse sur l'âme*. Lieux, décors et paysages. CMOM 34: 2005 ⇒889. 319-336.
12346 *Scopello, Madeleine* JACQUES de Saroug et l'Exégèse de l'âme (Nag Hammadi II,6). Femme, gnose. NHMS 53: 2005 ⇒12237. 115-23.

## M3.2 Religio comparativa

12347 *Berner, Ulrich* Das Gebet aus der Sicht der analytischen Religionsphilosophie. Opfer und Gebet. 2005 ⇒506. 87-104.

12348 **Borgeaud, Philippe** Aux origines de l'histoire des religions. 2004 ⇒20,11156. [R]AfR 7 (2005) 217-218 (*Dubourdieu, Annie*).

12349 *Figl, Johann* Religionswissenschaft–historische Aspekte, heutiges Fachverständnis und Religionsbegriff. Handbuch Religionswissenschaft. 2005 ⇒1016. 17-61;

12350 Vorstellungen absoluter bzw. göttlicher Wirklichkeit: Gott-monotheistisch. Handbuch Religionswissenschaft. 2005 ⇒1016. 554-58.

12351 *Flasche, Rainer* Opfer und Gebet in der Religionswissenschaft: Versuch einer Vertiefung. Opfer und Gebet. 2005 ⇒506. 107-114.

12352 *Harvey, Susan A.* Locating the sensing body: perception and religious identity in late antiquity. Religion and the self in antiquity. 2005 ⇒818. 140-162.

12353 **Molendijk, Arie L.** The emergence of the science of religion in the Netherlands. SHR 105: Lei 2005, Brill xii; 311 pp. 90-04-14338-6. Bibl. 271-302.

12354 *Muffs, Yochanan* On the demythologizing of religion. Personhood of God. 2005 <1976> ⇒265. 189-193.

12355 *Siegert, Folker* Religionskritik als Mutter der Theologie. [F]STOLLE, V.: Forschung und Wissenschaft 12: 2005 ⇒143. 271-283.

12356 *Tworuschka, Udo* Dimensionen weiterer zentraler religiöser Vorstellungen: heilige Schriften;

12357 *Urban, Otto H.* Religionen vergangener Kulturen: Religion der Urgeschichte. Handbuch Religionswissenschaft. 2005 ⇒1016. 588-611/88-103.

12358 **Wunn, Ina** Die Religionen in vorgeschichtlicher Zeit. Religionen der Menschheit 2: Stu 2005, Kohlhammer x; 496 pp. €89. 31701-6-726X.

## M3.5 Religiones mundi cum christianismo comparatae

12359 **Glaser, Ida** The bible and other faiths: christian responsibility in a world of religions: christian doctrine in a global perspective. DG 2005, InterVarsity 256 pp. $14. 08308-33048 [BiTod 45,54: Dianne Bergant].

12360 **Schmidt-Leukel, Perry** Gott ohne Grenzen: eine christliche und pluralistische Theologie der Religionen. Gü 2005, Gü 536 pp. 3-579-05219-5.

## M3.6 *Sectae*—Cults

12361 **Armstrong, Dave** The catholic verses: 95 bible passages that confound Protestants. 2004 ⇒20,11171. [R]HPR 106/1 (2005) 70-71 (*Miller, Michael J.*).

12362 *Bachmann, Claus* Vom unsichtbaren zum gekreuzigten Gott: die Karriere des biblischen Bilderverbots im Protestantismus. NZSTh 47/1 (2005) 1-34 [Exod 20,4-6].

12363 *Behrens, Achim* Aspekte des Schriftgebrauchs der Lutherischen Bekenntnisschriften: Anmerkungen zum Verhältnis von Bekenntnis und Exegese. LuThK 29/2 (2005) 107-121.

12364 **Clark, David K.; Feinberg, John S.** To know and love God: method for theology. 2003 ⇒19,11662. RRBLit (2005)* (*Dempsey, Carol J.*).

12365 *De Oliveira, Ebenézer A.* Hierarchy of media, but not of sources, truths, or academic disciplines: a rejoinder to Lawson and Wilcox. JPsC 24/3 (2005) 247-253.

12366 **Fath, Sébastien** Militants de la bible aux États-Unis: évangéliques et fondamentalistes du Sud. 2004 ⇒20,11178. RThEv(VS) 4/2 (2005) 88-89 (*Margery, Gordon*).

12367 *Figl, Johann* Religionen der Gegenwart: neue Religionen. Handbuch Religionswissenschaft. 2005 ⇒1016. 457-484.

12368 *Fryer, Kelly A.* The book of Acts in congregational renewal. Word and world 25 (2005) 448-458.

12369 *Gardner, R.B.* Brethren and the bible. BLT 50/3-4 (2005) 103-113 [NTAb 51,4].

12370 **Giussani, Luigi** Teologia protestante americana. Genova 2003, Marietti xxi, 332 pp. 88-211-6960-X. Introd. *Elisa Buzzi*.

12371 **Gundry, Robert Horton** Jesus the Word according to John the Sectarian: a paleofundamentalist manifesto for contemporary evangelicalism, especially its elites, in North America. 2002 ⇒18, 10687; 20,11180. RPSB 26 (2005) 245-248 (*Anderson, Paul N.*).

12372 *Hassey, Janette* Evangelical women in ministry a century ago. Discovering biblical equality. 2005 ⇒387. 39-57.

12373 *Hödl, Hans* Religionen der Gegenwart: alternative Formen des Religiösen. Handbuch Religionswissenschaft. 2005 ⇒1016. 485-524.

12374 **Johnson, Terry L.** The case for traditional Protestantism: the solas of the Reformation. 2004 ⇒20,11182. RSBET 23 (2005) 119-120 (*Van Dixhoorn, Chad B.*).

12375 *Käsemann, Ernst* Was evangelisch "glauben" meint;

12376 Reformatorisches Erbe heute. In der Nachfolge. 2005 ⇒236. 151-163/164-176.

12377 E**Kimbrough, S.T., Jr.** Orthodox and Wesleyan scriptural understanding and practice. Crestwood, NY 2005, St Vladimir's Seminary Pr. 330 pp. $18.

12378 *Klän, Werner* Aspekte lutherischer Identität: eine konfessionelle Sicht. FSTOLLE, V. 2005 ⇒143. 323-338.

12379 *Lawson, David A.; Wilcox, David A.* Philosophical foundations for integration: a response to de Oliveira. JPsC 24/3 (2005) 240-246.

12380 *Lefebvre, Pierre-Louis* La communication apologétique chrétienne évangélique: une avenue de dialogue?. Scriptura(M) 7/2 (2005) 113-124.

12381 *Lougheed, Richard* A primer on evangelicalism. Scriptura(M) 7/2 (2005) 11-28.

12382 *Masenya, Madipoane* The bible and prophecy in African-South African Pentecostal churches. Missionalia 33/1 (2005) 35-45.

12383 **Moyer, R. Larry** Twenty-one things God never said. GR 2004, Kregel 176 pp. $11.

12384 *Patterson, Aimee* Evangelical christians and environmentalism: what deepens the divide. Scriptura(M) 7/2 (2005) 85-94.

12385 *Phelan, Peter* Comparisons: Sabah local culture and the bible. Kota Kinabalu 2005, Key Colour 215 pp.

12386 *Pierce, Ronald W.* Contemporary evangelicals for gender equality. Discovering biblical equality. 2005 ⇒387. 58-75.

12387 *Robitaille, Steve* La fin de la cohésion doctinale évangélique?: les enjeux identitaires de la théologie évangélique post-conservatrice. Scriptura(M) 7/2 (2005) 69-84.

12388 *Rodier, Dany* Pourquoi la controverse créationniste n'est pas près de disparaître: la place de Gn 1,1-3,24 dans la théologie évangélique. Scriptura(M) 7/1 (2005) 129-147.

12389 *Smith, Glenn* Le mouvement 'évangélique' au Québec. Scriptura(M) 7/2 (2005) 29-46.

12390 *Steinacker, Peter* Die Bibel ist nicht Gottes Wort: Interview mit Kirchenpräsident Peter Steinacker über die Bedeutung der Heiligen Schrift für die evangelische Kirche. zeitzeichen 6/11 (2005) 39-42.

12391 *Stiewe, Martin* Die Barmer Theologische Erklärung von 1934 nach mehr als 70 Jahren. WuD 28 (2005) 193-204.

12392 *Vallée, Hélène* La femme dans la famille et le couple évangélique américain: étude, analyse et interprétation. Scriptura(M) 7/2 (2005) 125-141.

12393 *Vincent, Gilbert* Protestantisme libéral, tolérance et esprit laïque: l'interprétation de l'oeuvre de Castellion par Ferdinand Buisson. RHPhR 85 (2005) 253-277.

12394 *Wintle, B.* Evangelicals and the bible. Dharma Deepika [Tamilnadu, India] 9/2 (2005) 9-19 [NTAb 50,243].

12395 **Witherington, Ben, III** The problem with evangelical theology: testing the exegetical foundations of Calvinism, Dispensationalism, and Wesleyanism. Waco, Texas 2005, Baylor xi; 294 pp. $30. 1-932792-42-2. Bibl. 287-294.

12396 **Wolters, Albert M.** Creation regained: biblical basics for a Reformational worldview. GR $^{2}$2005, Eerdmans xi; 143 pp. $12/£7. 0-8028-2969-4.

## M3.8 Mythologia

12397 **Barber, Elizabeth W.; Barber, Paul T.** When they severed earth from sky: how the human mind shapes myth. Princeton 2005, Princeton U.P 312 pp. $40. 06910-99863.

12398 **Blázquez, F.** Diccionario de mitología: dioses, héroes, mitos y leyendas. Estella, Navarra 2005, Verbo Divino 925 pp. 848169-6722.

12399 *Bożyk, Maria M.* Świadomość mityczna [Mythical consciousness as non differentiating consciousness]. StBob 1 (2005) 37-58. **P.**

12400 **Brisson, Luc** Introduction à la philosophie du mythe, 1: sauver les mythes. Essais d'art et de philosophie: P $^{2}$2005 <1996>, Vrin 256 pp. €24. 2-7116-1271-6.

12401 *Brodersen, Kai* "Das aber ist eine Lüge!": zur rationalistischen Mythenkritik des Palaiphatos. Griechische Mythologie. 2005 ⇒542. 44-57.

12402 **Commelin, Pierre; Maréchaux, Pierre** Mythologie grecque et romaine. P 2005, Colin 407 pp. 978-22003-42753.

12403 **Csapo, Eric** Theories of mythology. Ancient Cultures: Oxf 2005, Blackwell xiii; 338 pp. £18. 0631-232486. 10 fig.

12404 **Devinney, Margaret K.; Thury, Eva M.** Introduction to mythology: contemporary approaches to classical and world myths. Oxf 2005, OUP xiv; 722 pp. £30. 01951-5889X.

12405 *Dickson, Keith* Enki and the embodied world. JAOS 125 (2005) 499-515.

12406 *Dresken-Weiland, Jutta* Pagane Mythen auf Sarkophagen des dritten nachchristlichen Jahrhunderts. Griechische Mythologie. 2005 ⇒542. 106-131.

12407 **Frye, Northrop; Macpherson, Jay** Biblical and classical myths: the mythological framework of western culture. 2004 ⇒20,11196. = Frye, Symbolism in the bible; Macpherson, Four ages: the classical myths. RTheoforum 36 (2005) 220-222 (*Laberge, Léo*).

12408 *Fuhrmann, Manfred* Mythen, Fabeln, Legenden und Märchen in der antiken Tradition: mit einer Einleitung: das Märchen von Amor und Psyche im "Goldenen Esel" des APULEIUS. Griechische Mythologie. 2005 ⇒542. 1-20.

12409 **Garbini, Giovanni** Mito e storia nella bibbia. StBi 137: 2003 ⇒ 19,11690; 20,11197. RProtest. 60 (2005) 73-74 (*Noffke, Eric*).

12410 **Girard, René** Miti d'origine: persecuzioni e ordine culturale. E*Antonnello, P.; Fornari, G.*; T*Crestani, E.*: Ancona 2005, Transeuropa 159 pp.

12411 *Heller, Birgit* Vorstellungen absoluter bzw. göttlicher Wirklichkeit: Götter/Göttinnen;

12412 *Hödl, Hans Gerald* Dimensionen weiterer zentraler religiöser Vorstellungen: Mythos. Handbuch Religionswissenschaft. 2005 ⇒ 1016. 530-544/570-587.

12413 **Junker, Klaus** Griechische Mythenbilder: eine Einführung in ihre Interpretation. Stu 2005, Metzler 190 pp. €25. 3-476-01987-X. 36 ill. [EuA 81,336].

12414 *Kunin, Seth* Ideological "destructuring" in myth, history and memory. Writing history. 2005 ⇒523. 179-204 [Judg 9; 11].

12415 **Kunze, Christian** Mythos im Wandel: Studien zur Veränderung des Mythenbildes von der archaischen zur klassischen Zeit. 2005, Diss.-Habil. Bonn [AA 2006/1, 315].

12416 **Lewis-Williams, David; Pearce, David** Inside the neolithic mind: consciousness, cosmos and the realm of the gods. L 2005, Thames & H. 320 pp. 0-500-05138-0. 104 ill.; Bibl. 300-313.

12417 *Luce, J. de* Roman myth. ClW 98/2 (2005) 202-5 [NTAb 49,573].

12418 *Oehl, Benedikt* Mythos und Häresie;

12419 *Rosen, Klaus* Der Mythos von Amor und Psyche in APULEIUS' Metamorphosen. Griechische Mythologie. 2005 ⇒542. 311-38/58-64.

12420 *Van den Heever, Gerhard* Novel and mystery: discourse, myth, and society. Ancient fiction. SBL.Symp. 32: 2005 ⇒721. 89-114.

12421 **Woodford, Susan** Images of myths in classical antiquity. 2003 ⇒ 19,11703; 20,11211. RAJA 109 (2005) 115-117 (*Kilinski, Karl, II*).

12422 *Wyatt, Nick* The mythic mind <2001>;

12423 'Water, water everywhere...': musings on the aqueous myths of the Near East <2004>;

12424 Androgyny in the Levantine world <2004>. Mythic mind. 2005 ⇒ 328. 151-188/189-237/238-255.

12425 *Ziegler, Ruprecht* Der Perseus-Mythos im Prestigedenken kaiserzeitlicher städtischer Eliten Kilikiens. Griechische Mythologie. 2005 ⇒542. 85-105.

## M4.0 **Religio romana**

12426 *Ando, C. Interpretatio Romana.* CP 100/1 (2005) 41-51 [NTAb 49, 572].

12427 *Belayche, Nicole* Realia versus leges?: les sacrifices de la religion d'état au IVe siècle. La cuisine et l'autel. BEHE.R 124: 2005 ⇒539. 343-370.

12428 *Caponera, Annarita* Alcuni aspetti del dibattito 'teologico' del I sec. a.C.: Roma e la crisi religiosa. ConAss 7/1 (2005) 201-212.

12429 *Chaniotis, Angelos* The divinity of Hellenistic rulers. Companion to the Hellenistic world. 2005 ⇒642. 431-445.

12430 *Delplace, Christiane* Entre épigraphie et architecture: aspects du culte impérial à Palmyre. [F]GROS, P. 2005 ⇒51. 311-319.

12431 *Dubourdieu, Annie* Nommer les dieux: pouvoir des noms, pouvoir des mots dans les rituels du *uotum*, de l'*euocatio*, et de la *deuotio* dans la Rome antique. AfR 7 (2005) 183-197.

12432 *Egelhaaf-Gaiser, Ulrike* Sakrallandschaften und Tafelluxus: Adaptation und Naturinszenierung in Bankettträumen pompejanischer Kultgemeinschaften. La cuisine et l'autel. BEHE.R 124: 2005 ⇒ 539. 253-272.

12433 **Fishwick, Duncan** The imperial cult in the Latin West: studies in the ruler cult of the western provinces of the Roman Empire: vol. III: provincial cult, parts 1-3. RGRW 145-7: 2002-2004 ⇒20, 11219. [R]JRS 95 (2005) 260-261 (*Gradel, Ittai*);

12434 vol. III: provincial cult, part 4: bibliography, indices, addenda. RGRW 148: Lei 2005, Brill viii; 256 pp. €105/$142. 978-90-04-1-2807-1.

12435 **Gradel, Ittai** Emperor worship and Roman religion. 2002 ⇒18, 10728... 20,11222. [R]JRS 95 (2005) 259-260 (*Hersch, Karen K.*).

12436 **Haack, Marie-Laurence** Les haruspices dans le monde romain. Scripta Antiqua 6: 2003 ⇒19,11725. [R]AnCl 74 (2005) 420-423 (*Van Haeperen, Françoise*).

12437 *Hemelrijk, Emily A.* Priestesses of the imperial cult in the Latin west: titles and function. AnCl 74 (2005) 137-170.

12438 *Horell, David G.* Introduction. JSNT 27 (2005) 251-255.

12439 **Inwood, Brad** Reading SENECA: Stoic philosophy at Rome. Oxf 2005, Clarendon xvi; 376 pp. 0-19-925089-8. Bibl. 353-362.

12440 **Klauck, Hans-Josef** The religious context of early christianity: a guide to Graeco-Roman religions. [T]*McNeil, Brian* 2003 <2000> ⇒ 16,10191... 20,11225. [R]ArOr 73 (2005) 507-510 (*Břeňová, Klára*); RBLit 7 (2005) 264-266 (*Richey, Lance*).

12441 *Konstan, D.* Clemency as a virtue. CP 100 (2005) 337-346 [NTAb 50,360].

12442 **Krauter, Stefan** Bürgerrecht und Kultteilnahme: politische und kultische Rechte und Pflichten in griechischen Poleis, Rom und antikem Judentum. BZNW 127: 2004 ⇒20,11226. [R]JSJ 36 (2005) 355-358 (*Van der Horst, Pieter W.*).

12443 *Latte, Kurt* Wandel des Glaubens in der Kaiserzeit. Opuscula inedita. 2005 ⇒243. 55-65.

12444 *Lisdorf, A.* The conflict over CICERO's house: an analysis of the ritual element in *De Domo suo*. Numen 52 (2005) 445-464 [NTAb 50,361].

12445 **Martin, Michaël** Magie et magiciens dans le monde gréco-romain. P 2005, Errance 291 pp. 2-87772-309-7.

12446 **Martini, Maria Cristina** Le vestali: un sacerdozio funzionale al 'cosmo' romano. CollLat 282: Bru 2004, Latomus 263 pp. €38. 287-03122-37.

12447 *McLaren, James S.* Jews and the imperial cult: from AUGUSTUS to DOMITIAN. JSNT 27 (2005) 257-278.

12448 *Monaca, Mariangela* Prodigi e profezie nel mondo romano: peculiarità della rivelazione sibillina. Modi di comunicazione. 2005 ⇒858. 311-346.

12449 **Monaca, Mariangela** La Sibilla a Roma: i Libri sibillini fra religione e politica. Hierá 8: Cosenza 2005, Giordano 324 pp. 88-869-19-21-2. Bibl. 285-313.

12450 *Neyrey, Jerome H.* God, benefactor and patron: the major cultural model for interpreting the deity in Greco-Roman antiquity. JSNT 27 (2005) 465-492.

12451 *Oakman, Douglas E.* Culture, society, and embedded religion in antiquity. BTB 35 (2005) 4-12.

12452 **Paschalis, Michael** Roman and Greek imperial epic. Rethymnon Classical Studies 2: Rethymnon 2005, Crete University Pr. xi; 195 pp. 96052-42036.

12453 *Pârvulescu, A.* The golden bough, Aeneas' piety, and the suppliant branch. Latomus 64 (2005) 882-909 [NTAb 50,362].

12454 **Rasmussen, Susanne William** Public portents in Republican Rome. ARID 34: 2003 ⇒19,11745. [R]AnCl 74 (2005) 419-420 (*Van Haeperen, Françoise*).

12455 *Ridley, Ronald T.* The absent Pontifex Maximus. Hist. 54 (2005) 275-300.

12456 **Rieger, Anna-Katharina** Heiligtümer in Ostia. 2004 ⇒20,11230. [R]AnCl 74 (2005) 233-242 (*Van Haeperen, Françoise*).

12457 *Rüpke, Jörg* Divination and political decisions in the Roman Republic. VDI 1 (2005) 34-48. **R**;

12458 Gäste der Götter-Götter als Gäste: zur Konstruktion des römischen Opferbanketts. La cuisine et l'autel. BEHE.R 124: 2005 ⇒539. 227-239.

12459 **Rüpke, Jörg** Die Religion der Römer: eine Einführung. 2001 ⇒17, 9880... 20,11232. [R]HZ 280 (2005) 431-432 (*Bernstein, Frank*);

12460 **Rüpke, Jörg, *al.*,** Fasti sacerdotum: die Mitglieder der Priesterschaften und das sakrale Funktionspersonal römischer, griechischer, orientalischer und jüdisch-christlicher Kulte in der Stadt Rom von 300 v.Chr. bis 499 n.Chr. Potsdamer Altertumswissenschaftliche Beiträge 12/1-3: Stu 2005, Steiner 3 vols; 1860 pp. €141. CD-ROM.

12461 *Santangelo, Federico* The religious tradition of the Gracchi. AfR 7 (2005) 198-214.

12462 *Scheid, John* Manger avec les dieux: partage sacrificiel et commensalité dans la Rome antique. La cuisine et l'autel. BEHE.R 124: 2005 ⇒539. 273-287.

12463 **Scheid, John** Quand faire, c'est croire: les rites sacrificiels des Romains. P 2005, Aubier 348 pp. €26. 2-7007-2298-1. [R]AfR 7 (2005) 219-221 (*Graf, Fritz*).

12464 *Schwabl, Hans* Religionen vergangener Kulturen: griechische und römische Religion. Handbuch Religionswissenschaft. 2005 ⇒1016. 180-197.

12465 *Smadja, Élisabeth* Le culte impérial en Afrique. Pallas 68 (2005) 333-349.

12466 **Van Haeperen, Françoise** Le collège pontifical (3e s. a.C.-4e s. p.C.): contribution à l'étude de la religion publique romaine. 2002 ⇒19,11756. RAnCl 74 (2005) 417-19 (*Estienne, Sylvia*).

12467 *Woolf, Greg* A sea of faith?. Mediterranean paradigms. 2005 ⇒ 669. 126-142.

## M4.5 **Mithraismus**

12468 **Betz, Hans D.** The 'Mithras liturgy': text, translation and commentary. 2003 ⇒19,11760; 20,11240. RRBLit (2005)* (*Gee, John*);

12469 Tü 2005 <2003>, Mohr S. xvii; 274 pp. €39. 31614-8813X. Bibl. [NTAb 50,430].

12470 *Gawlikowski, Michał* Nur aus Bildern bekannt—der Mithraskult: neue Kultstätte in Syrien ausgegraben. WUB 36 (2005) 52-55.

12471 E**Martens, Marleen; De Boe, Guy** Roman Mithraism: the evidence of the small finds. 2004 ⇒20,11245. RRAr (2005/1) 172-175 (*Turcan, Robert*).

12472 *Martin, Luther H.* Performativity, narrativity, and cognition: 'demythologizing' the Roman cult of Mithras. Rhetoric and reality. SCJud 16: 2005 ⇒515. 187-217.

12473 *Sanzi, Ennio* Magia e culti orientali V: che ci fa il dio Mithra in un papiro magico-oracolare?: ovverosia note storico-religiose intorno a PGM V, 1-53. Modi di comunicazione. 2005 ⇒858. 355-383.

12474 *Turcan, Robert* Images et fonctions du "clergé" mithriaque. FRIES, J. 2005 ⇒127. 73-88.

## M5.1 *Divinitates Graeciae*—**Greek gods and goddesses**

12475 *Belayche, Nicole Hypsistos*: une voie de l'exaltation des dieux dans le polythéisme gréco-romain. AfR 7 (2005) 34-55.

12476 *Bendlin, Andreas* Wer braucht "heilige Schriften"?: die Textbezogenheit der Religionsgeschichte und das "Reden über die Götter" in der griechisch-römischen Antike. Heilige Schriften. 2005 ⇒362. 205-228, 251-254.

12477 *Berthiaume, Guy* L'aile ou les mêria: sur la nourriture carnée des dieux grecs. La cuisine et l'autel. 2005 ⇒539. 241-251.

12478 *Blois, François de* New light on the sources of the Manichaean chapter in the Fihrist. Quinto congresso. 2005 ⇒900. 37-45.

12479 **Bowden, Hugh** Classical Athens and the Delphic Oracle: divination and democracy. C 2005, CUP xviii; 188 pp.

12480 *Bremmer, Jan N.* Myth and ritual in ancient Greece: observations on a difficult relationship. Griechische Mythologie. 2005 ⇒542. 21-43;

12481 Canonical and alternative creation myths in ancient Greece. Creation of heaven and earth. 2005 ⇒492. 73-96.

12482 **Bruit Zaidman, Louise** Les Grecs et leurs dieux: pratiques et représentations religieuses dans la cité à l'époque classique. P 2005, Armand Colin 198 pp. 23 fig.

12483 *Bruit-Zaidman, Louise* Offrandes et nourritures: repas des dieux et repas des hommes en Grèce ancienne. La cuisine et l'autel. BEHE. R 124: 2005 ⇒539. 31-46.

12484 *Burkert, Walter* Kritiken, Rettungen und unterschwellige Lebendigkeit griechischer Mythen zur Zeit des frühen Christentums. Griechische Mythologie. 2005 ⇒542. 173-193.

12485 *Busine, Aude* Gathering sacred words: collections of oracles from pagan sanctuaries to christian books. Selecta colligere, II. Hellenica 18: 2005 ⇒681. 39-55.

12486 **Busine, Aude** Paroles d'Apollon: pratiques et traditions oraculaires dans l'antiquité tardive (IIe-VIe siècles). RGRW 156: Lei 2005, Brill xiii; 516 pp. 90-04-14662-8. Bibl. 463-500.

12487 **Currie, Bruno** PINDAR and the cult of heroes. Oxf 2005, OUP xiv; 487 pp. £65. 0-19-9277-249.

12488 **Delattre, Charles** Manuel de mythologie grecque. Rosny-sous-Bois 2005, Bréal 319 pp. 27495-04775.

12489 **Dickie, M.W.** Magic and magicians in the Greco-Roman world. 2001 ⇒17,9897... 20,11256. [R]AnCl 74 (2005) 429-431 (*Parca, Maryline*).

12490 **Dougherty, Carol** Prometheus. L 2005, Routledge xvi; 155 pp. 0-415-32406-8. Bibl. 142-152.

12491 *Duhoux, Yves* Les nouvelles tablettes en linéaire-B de Thèbes et la religion grecque. AnCl 74 (2005) 1-19.

12492 **Ekroth, Gunnel** The sacrificial rituals of Greek hero-cults in the archaic to the early Hellenistic periods. Kernos.S 12: 2002 ⇒18, 10763; 19,11779. [R]SCI 24 (2005) 285-287 (*Lupu, Eran*); AJA 109 (2005) 307-308 (*Dimitrova, Nora*).

12493 *Faraone, Christopher A.* Curses and blessings in ancient Greek oaths. JANER 5 (2005) 139-156.

12494 *Franzmann, Majella, al.*, A living Mani cult in the twenty-first century. RSLR 41 (2005) vii-xi.

12495 *Gebhard, Elizabeth R.* Rites for Melikertes-Palaimon in the early Roman Corinthia. Urban religion in Roman Corinth. HThS 53: 2005 ⇒8093. 165-203.

12496 *Georgoudi, Stella* L'"occultation de la violence" dans le sacrifice grec: données anciennes, discours modernes. La cuisine et l'autel. BEHE.R 124: 2005 ⇒539. 115-147.

12497 *Gnilka, Christian* Wahrheit und Ähnlichkeit. Griechische Mythologie. 2005 ⇒542. 194-226.

12498 **Himmelmann, Nikolaus** Alltag der Götter. Nordrhein-Westfälische Akad. der Wiss. G 385: Pd 2003, Schöningh 124 pp. 47 ill.

12499 **Karageorghis, Jacqueline** Kypris, the Aphrodite of Cyprus, ancient sources and archaeological evidence. Nicosia 2005, Leventis xviii; 269 pp. 329 fig.

12500 *Koch Piettre, Renée* Précipitations sacrificielles en Grèce ancienne. La cuisine et l'autel. BEHE.R 124: 2005 ⇒539. 77-100.

12501 **Kreutz, Natascha** Zeus und die griechischen Poleis. 2005, Diss. Tübingen [AA 2006/1, 312].

12502 *Lanci, John R.* The stones don't speak and the texts tell lies: sacred sex at Corinth. Urban religion in Roman Corinth. HThS 53: 2005 ⇒8093. 205-220.

12503 **Le Bris, Anne** La mort et les conceptions de l'au-delà en Grèce ancienne à travers les épigrammes funéraires. 2001 ⇒17,9906; 18, 10771. [R]REA 107 (2005) 853-854 (*Kolde, Antje*).

12504 **Lefkowitz, M.** Greek gods, human lives: what we can learn from myths. NHv 2005, Yale Univ. Pr. xi; 288 pp. $19. 03001-07692. Bibl. [NTAb 50,630].

12505 *Malkin, Irad* Herakles and Melqart: Greeks and Phoenicians in the middle ground. Cultural borrowings. 2005 ⇒652. 238-257.

12506 *Marabini Moevs, Maria T.* Dionysos at the altar of Rhea: a myth of darkness and rebirth in Ptolemaic Alexandria. [F]MCCANN, A. 2005 ⇒99. 77-88.

12507 *Markschies, Christoph* Odysseus und Orpheus—christlich gelesen. Griechische Mythologie. 2005 ⇒542. 227-253.

12508 **Mikalson, Jon D.** Ancient Greek religion. Blckwell Ancient Religions: Oxf 2005, Blackwell xiv; 225 pp. £17. 0631-232230. 58 fig.

12509 *Motte, André* Figures de prêtre dans la littérature grecque. [F]RIES, J. 2005 ⇒127 1-31.

12510 *Muniz Grijalvo, Elena* Elites and religious change in Roman Athens. Numen 52/2 (2005) 255-282.

12511 **Parker, Robert** Polytheism and society at Athens. Oxford Classical Monographs: Oxf 2005, OUP xxxii; 544 pp. 01992-74835.

12512 *Patrich, Joseph* Was Dionysos, the wine god, venerated by the Nabataeans?. Aram 17 (2005) 95-113.

12513 **Pedley, John Griffiths** Sanctuaries and the sacred in the ancient Greek world. NY 2005, CUP xviii; 272 pp. £45/16. 0-521-80935-5. Bibl. 247-254.

12514 Pettipiece, Timothy A church to surpass all churches: Manichaeism as a test case for the theory of reception. LTP 61 (2005) 247-260.

12515 *Petzl, Georg* Furchterregende Götter?: eine Notiz zu Diogenes von Oinoanda NF 126. ZPE 153 (2005) 103-107.

12516 *Pötscher Walter* Religionen vergangener Kulturen: minoische Religion. Handbuch Religionswissenschaft. 2005 ⇒1016. 156-164.

12517 **Riethmüller, Jürgen W.** Asklepios: Heiligtümer und Kulte. Studien zu antiken Heiligtümern 2/1: Heid 2005, Archäologie und Geschichte 392 pp. 3-935289-308. Diss. Heidelberg 1995.

12518 *Rocchi, Maria* Culti sui monti della Grecia: osservazioni da una lettura di PAUSANIA. AfR 7 (2005) 56-61.

12519 **Rosenzweig, Rachel** Worshipping Aphrodite: art and cult in classical Athens. 2004 ⇒20,11271. [R]AJA 109 (2005) 582-583 (*Lee, Mireille M.*).

12520 *Rudolph, Kurt* Progress of research since the foundation of the I.A.M.S. in 1989. Quinto congresso. 2005 ⇒900. 1-8.

12521 **Schliemann, Alrun** Das Kind im Kult von Athen. 2005, Diss. Salzburg [AA 2006/1, 313].

12522 *Scholten, Helga* Der Demeter- und Persephonemythos in der Auseinandersetzung christlicher Autoren;

12523 *Siegert, Folker* Griechische Mythen im hellenistischen Judentum. Griechische Mythologie. 2005 ⇒542. 268-294/132-152.

12524 *Suárez de la Torre, Emilio* Forme e funzioni del fenomeno profetico e divinatorio dalla Grecia classica al periodo tardo-antico. Modi di comunicazione. 2005 ⇒858. 29-106.

12525 *Svenbro, Jesper* La thusia et le partage: remarques sur la "destruction" par le feu dans le sacrifice grec. La cuisine et l'autel. BEHE.R 124: 2005 ⇒539. 217-225.

12526 *Tahberer, Bekircan; Uzel, İlter* The cult of Asklepios as represented in the ancient coins of Cilicia. BTTK 69 (2005) 9-58.

12527 **Thom, Johan C.** CLEANTHES' hymn to Zeus: text, translation, and commentary. STAC 33: Tü 2005, Mohr S. viii; 244 pp. 3-16-1486-60-9. Bibl. 165-179.

12528 *Valdés Guía, Miriam* The cult of Aglauros (and Aphrodite) in Athens and in Salamis of Cyprus: reflections on the origin of the *genos* of the *Salaminioi*. AWE 4 (2005) 57-76.

12529 *Valditara, Linda M.N. Makariotes*: riflessioni in margine alla beatitudine divina. Hum(B) 60 (2005) 808-843.

12530 *Van Straten, Folkert* Ancient Greek animal sacrifice: gift, ritual slaughter, communion, food supply, or what?: some thoughts on simple explanations of a complex ritual. La cuisine et l'autel. BEHE.R 124: 2005 ⇒539. 15-29.

12531 **Vatin, Claude** Ariane et Dionysos: un mythe de l'amour conjugal. 2004 ⇒20,11277. [R]RAr (2005/2) 396-397 (*Gros, Pierre*).

12532 **Werth, Nina** Hekate: Untersuchungen zur dreigestaltigen Göttin. 2005, Diss. Saarbrücken [AA 2006/1, 314].

12533 *Wickkiser, B.* Asklepios appears in a dream: antiquity's greatest healer. Archaeology Odyssey [Wsh] 8/4 (2005) 14-25, 48-49 [NTAb 49,576].

12534 *Young, Philip H.* The Cypriot Aphrodite cult: Paphos, Rantidi, and Saint Barnabas. JNES 64 (2005) 23-44.

12535 *Zografou, Athanassia* Élimination rituelle et sacrifice en Grèce ancienne. La cuisine et l'autel. BEHE.R 124: 2005 ⇒539. 197-213.

### M5.2 *Philosophorum critica religionis*—**Greek philosopher religion**

12536 *Adinolfi, Marco* PORFIRIO e Giovanni 6,53. Atti del X Simposio di Efeso. Turchia 19: 2005⇒785. 129-133.

12537 [T]**Albrecht, Michael von** JAMBLICH: Περι του Πυθαγορειου βιου: Pythagoras: Legende—Lehre—Lebensgestaltung. 2002 ⇒19, 11810. [R]BZ 49 (2005) 155-157 (*Koskenniemi, Erkki*).

12538 [E]**Amato, Eugenio** FAVORINOS d'Arles: oeuvres, 1: introduction générale–témoignages–discours aux Corinthiens–sur la fortune. [T]*Julien, Yvette*: P 2005, Belles Lettres xiv; 607 pp. €83. 2-251-00528-5.

12539 *Barnhart, J.E.* PLATO's *Symposium* and early christianity. JHiC 11/2 (2005) 12-18 [NTAb 50,554].

12540 *Beatrice, Pier Franco* L'union de l'âme et du corps: NÉMÉSIUS d'Emèse lecteur de PORPHYRE. Les Pères de l'Église. ThH 117: 2005 ⇒813. 253-285.

12541 **Berchman, Robert M.** PORPHYRY: Against the christians. Ancient Mediterranean and Medieval Texts and Contexts 1: Lei 2005, Brill xvi; 243 pp. 90041-48116.

12542 *Berti, Enrico* Il dio di ARISTOTELE. Hum(B) 60 (2005) 732-750.

12543 [E]**Blois, L. de**, *al.*, The statesman in PLUTARCH's works: proceedings of the sixth international conference of the International Plutarch Society, Nijmegen/Castle Hernen, 2002: vol. 2: The statesman in Plutarch's Greek and Roman *Lives*. Mn.S 250/2: Lei 2005, Brill xx; 395 pp. €99/$134. 90041-38080. Bibl. [NTAb 49,433].

12544 *Botter, Barbara* 'Se Dio è incorporeo non è saggio, se Dio è corporeo non è beato, quindi Dio non è'. Ment. *Aristotle*: Hum(B) 60 (2005) 751-785.

12545 *Brenk, Frederick E.* PLUTARCH's Middle-Platonic God: about to enter (or remake) the academy. Gott und die Götter. 2005 ⇒880. 27-49;

12546 O sweet mystery of the *Lives*!: the eschatological dimension of PLUTARCH's Biographies. The statesman in Plutarch's works II. 2005 ⇒12544. 61-74 [AcBib 11,30];

12547 PLUTARCH. Encyclopedia of religion, 11. 2005 ⇒1009. 7199-7202 [AcBib 11,30].

12548 *Campanile, Domitilla* Il sofista allo specchio: FILOSTRATO nelle Vitae Sophistarum. Studi ellenistici XVI. 2005 ⇒698. 275-288.

12549 *Cattanei, Elisabetta* La mantica in PLATONE: tre quadri introduttivi. Hum(B) 60 (2005) 692-707.

12550 *Cazelais, Serge* Quelques remarques sur la réception d'un pseudo-épigraphe: les "Oracles chaldaïques". LTP 61/2 (2005) 273-289.

12551 [ET]**Chaumartin, François-Régis** SÉNÈQUE: De la clémence. P 2005, "Les Belles Lettres" xciv; 124 pp. 2251-01439-X. Bibl. lxvii-lxxxvii.

12552 *Chiesa, Curzio* PORPHYRE et le problème de la substance des *Catégories*. Les *Catégories*. 2005 ⇒624. 81-101.

12553 *D'Ancona, Cristina* Il neoplatonismo alessandrino: alcune linee della ricerca contemporanea. Adamantius 11 (2005) 9-38.

12554 *Dillon, John M.* Design in nature: some comments from the ancient perspective. Creation of heaven and earth. 2005 ⇒492. 263-266.

12555 [T]**Dillon, John M.; Clarke, Emma; Hershbell, Jackson** IAMBLICHUS: On the mysteries. Writings from the Graeco-Roman World 4: 2003 ⇒19,11823. [R]RBLit (2005)* (*Pettipiece, Timothy*).

12556 *Diouf, Eugène* L'*Apologie* d'APULÉE: la rhétorique au secours d'un étranger: *alii orabunt causas melius* (Virgile, *En*., 6, 849) "D'autres feront de meilleures plaidoieries". [F]HEIM, F. 2005 ⇒59. 69-99.

12557 *Drozdek, Adam* Protagoras and instrumentality of religion. AnCl 74 (2005) 41-50.

12558 *Feldmeier, Reinhard* Osiris: der Gott der Toten als Gott des Lebens (*De Iside* Kap. 76-78). Gott und die Götter. Ment. *Plutarch*. 2005 ⇒880. 215-227.

12559 *Fermani, Arianna* Presenza di Dio e condizione umana nelle *Etiche* aristoteliche. Hum(B) 60 (2005) 786-807.

12560 *Ferrari, Franco* Der Gott PLUTARCHs und der Gott PLATONs;

12561 *Frazier, Françoise* Göttlichkeit und Glaube: persönliche Gottesbeziehung im Spätwerk PLUTARCHs. Gott und die Götter. 2005 ⇒ 880. 13-25/111-137.

12562 **Gabaude, Jean-Marc** Pour la philosophie grecque. Ouverture Philosophique: P 2005, L'Harmattan 267 pp. 27475-94208.

12563 *Gaide, Françoise* Le *De magia* d'APULÉE: entre *genus iudiciale* et *genus demonstratiuum*. Pallas 69 (2005) 97-106.

12564 *Gerson, L.* What is Platonism?. JHP 43/3 (2005) 253-276 [NTAb 50,132].

12565 *Gill, C.* Hellenistic and Roman philosophy. Phron. 50/2 (2005) 170-179 [NTAb 49,574].

12566 *Giordano-Zecharya, Manuela* As SOCRATES shows, the Athenians did not believe in gods. Numen 52 (2005) 325-355.

12567 *Gourinat, Jean-Baptiste Explicatio fabularum*: la place de l'allégorie dans l'interprétation stoïcienne de la mythologie. Allégorisme des poètes. 2005 ⇒874. 9-34.

12568 *Görgemanns, Herwig* Eros als Gott in PLUTARCHS 'Amatorius';
12569 *Graf, Fritz* PLUTARCH und die Götterbilder. Gott und die Götter. 2005 ⇒880. 169-195/251-266.
12570 **Hirsch-Luipold, Rainer** PLUTARCHS Denken in Bildern: Studien zur literarischen, philosophischen und religiösen Funktion des Bildhaften. STAC 14: 2002 ⇒18,10798. [R]BZ 49 (2005) 152-154 (*Klauck, Hans-Josef*).
12571 [ET]**Jones, Christopher Prestige** PHILOSTRATUS: The life of APOLLONIUS of Tyana. LCL 16-17: CM 2005, Harvard Univ. Pr. 2 vols. 0-674-99613-5/4-3.
12572 [ET]**Konstan, David; Russell, Donald A.** HERACLITUS: Homeric problems. SBL.Writings from the Greco-Roman World 14: Atlanta, GA 2005, SBL xxx; 144 pp. $21. 1-58983-1225. Bibl. 133-136.
12573 **Lona, Horacio E.** Die "Wahre Lehre" des KELSOS. Kommentar zu frühchristlichen Apologeten, Ergänzungsband 1: FrB 2005, Herder 510 pp. 3-451-28599-1.
12574 **Long, A.A.** Stoic Studies. Hellenistic Culture & Society 36: Berkeley, CA 2001, Univ. of California Pr. xvi, 309 pp. Bibl. 286-294.
12575 *Lucarini, Carlo M.* FILOSTRATO e APOLLONIO di Tiana. Studi ellenistici XVI. 2005 ⇒698. 289-344.
12576 *Majercik, Ruth* PORPHYRY and gnosticism. CQ 55/1 (2005) 277-92.
12577 *Marin, Maurizio* L'ira divina in PLATONE: l'utilizzazione dell'irascibilità umana da parte della sapienza divina. Sal. 67 (2005) 7-25.
12578 *Meinwald, C.* Ignorance and opinion in Stoic epistemology. Phron. 50/3 (2005) 215-231 [NTAb 50,133].
12579 *Mitsis, Phillip* The institutions of hellenistic philosophy. Companion to the Hellenistic world. 2005 ⇒642. 464-476.
12580 *Morlet, Sébastien* PLUTARQUE et l'apologétique chrétienne: la place de la *Préparation évangélique* d'EUSÈBE de Césarée. Pallas 67 (2005) 115-138.
12581 *Natali, Carlo* La religiosità in SOCRATE secondo SENOFONTE. Hum(B) 60 (2005) 670-691.
12582 **Obenga, Théophile** L'Egypte, la Grèce et l'école d'Alexandrie: histoire interculturelle dans l'antiquité: aux sources égyptiennes de la philosophie grecque. P 2005, L'Harmattan 261 pp. 27 pl.
12583 *Opsomer, Jan* Demiurges in early imperial Platonism. Gott und die Götter. 2005 ⇒880. 51-99.
12584 *Perkams, Matthias* Stoische Schicksalslehre und christlicher Monotheismus: KLEANTHES' Schicksalsverse im Spiegel ihrer Überlieferung. Selecta colligere, II. Hellenica 18: 2005 ⇒681. 57-78.
12585 *Pérez Jiménez, Aurelio* 'δικαιοσύνη als Wesenszug des Göttlichen. Gott und die Götter. Ment. *Plutarch*. 2005 ⇒880. 101-109.
12586 [E]**Rabe, Hugo** Invention and method: two rhetorical treatises from the Hermogenic corpus. [T]*Kennedy, George A.*: SBL.Writings from the Ancient World 15; Writings from the Greco-Roman world 15: Atlanta, GA 2005, SBL xix; 267 pp. $33. 1-58983-121-7.
12587 [T]**Ramelli, Ilaria** Anneo Cornuto: compendio di teologia greca. 2003 ⇒19,11835. [R]Aevum 79 (2005) 220 (*Radice, Roberto*).
12588 *Reale, Giovanni* Teologia negativa ed esperienza mistica in PLOTINO. Hum(B) 60 (2005) 859-870.
12589 **Reydams-Schils, Gretchen** The Roman Stoics: self, responsibility and affection. Ch 2005, Univ. of Chicago Pr. xii; 210 pp. $35/ £24.50. 0-226-30837-5.

12590 *Riedweg, Christoph* PORPHYRIOS über Christus und die Christen: *De Philosophia ex oraculis haurienda* und *Adversus Christianos* im Vergleich. L'apologétique chrétienne gréco-latine à l'époque prénicénienne. **Riedweg, C.**, *al.*, Entretiens de la Fondation Hardt 51, Vandœuvres-Genève 2005. 151–203. 978-26000-07511.

12591 **Roskam, Geert** On the path to virtue: the Stoic doctrine of moral progress and its reception in (middle-)Platonism. Ancient and medieval philosophy.1/33: Lv 2005, Leuven University Press viii, 507 pp. 90-5867-476-2. Bibl. 415-442.

12592 **Safty, Essam** La psyché humaine: conceptions populaires, religieuses et philosophiques en Grèce, des origines à l'ancien stoïcisme. 2003 ⇒19,11837. [R]AnCl 74 (2005) 395-400 (*Lefka, Aikaterini*).

12593 *Salles, R.* 'Εκπύρωσις and the goodness of god in CLEANTHES. Phron. 50/2 (2005) 56-78 [NTAb 49,575].

12594 *Schott, Jeremy M.* PORPHYRY on christians and others: "barbarian wisdom", identity politics, and anti-christian polemics on the eve of the great persecution. JECS 13 (2005) 227-314.

12595 *Senković, Željko* Polis i religija [The polis and religion]. Obnovljeni Život 60 (2005) 151-160. **Croatian.**

12596 *Sfameni Gasparro, Giulia* Il sofista e l'"uomo divino": FILOSTRATO e la costruzione della 'vera storia' di APOLLONIO di Tiana. Modi di comunicazione. 2005 ⇒858. 247-309.

12597 *Speyer, Wolfgang* PORPHYRIOS als religiöse Persönlichkeit und als religöser Denker. Griechische Mythologie. 2005 ⇒542. 65-84.

12598 *Stadter, Philip A.* PLUTARCH and Apollo of Delphi. Gott und die Götter. 2005 ⇒880. 197-214.

12599 [E]**Strange, Steven K.; Zupko, Jack** Stoicism: traditions & transformations. C 2004, CUP xi; 295 pp. $70. [R]RBLit (2005)* (*Mason, John*).

12600 *Tieleman, Teun* GALEN and Genesis. Creation of heaven and earth. Themes in biblical narrative 8: 2005 ⇒492. 125-145.

12601 *Toulouse, Stéphane* La théosophie de PORPHYRE et sa conception du sacrifice intérieur. La cuisine et l'autel. BEHE.R 124: 2005 ⇒ 539. 329-341.

12602 *Tulli, Mauro* Investitura e conquista del sapere: la dea nel proemio di PARMENIDE. Hum(B) 60 (2005) 658-669.

12603 *Van den Berg, Robbert M.* God the creator, God the creation: NUMENIUS' interpretation of Genesis 1:2 (Frg.30). Creation of heaven and earth. 2005 ⇒492. 109-123.

12604 *Van der Stockt, Luc* No cause for alarm: chthonic deities in PLUTARCH. Gott und die Götter. 2005 ⇒880. 229-249.

12605 *Zagdoun, Mary-Anne* DION de Pruse et la philosophie stoïcienne de l'art. REG 118 (2005) 605-612.

## M5.3 *Mysteria eleusinia; Hellenistica*—Mysteries; Hellenistic cults

12606 *Benseddik, Nacéra* Esculape et Hygie: les cultes guérisseurs en Afrique. Pallas 68 (2005) 271-288.

12607 *Bernabé, Alberto* La tradizione orfica dalla Grecia classica al Neoplatonismo. Modi di comunicazione. 2005 ⇒858. 107-150.

12608 **Bommas, Martin** Heiligtum und Mysterium: Griechenland und seine ägyptischen Gottheiten. Zaberns Bildbände zur Archeologie: Mainz 2005, Von Zabern vi; 138 pp. €41. 38053-34427. 175 fig.

12609 *Bookidis, Nancy* Religion in Corinth: 146 B.C.E. to 100 C.E. Urban religion in Roman Corinth. HThS 53: 2005 ⇒8093. 141-164.

12610 [E]**Bottini, Angelo** Il rito segreto: misteri in Grecia e a Roma. R 2005, Electa 319 pp. 88370-39131.

12611 *Bricault, Laurent* Les dieux de l'Orient en Afrique romaine. Pallas 68 (2005) 289-309.

12612 **Burkert, Walter** Les cultes à mystères dans l'antiquité. [T]*Segonds, Alain-Philippe*: Vérité des mythes 22: 2003 <1992> ⇒19,11844. [R]SR 34 (2005) 571-574 (*Gaulin, Morgan*);

12613 Cultos mistéricos antiguos. [T]*Tabuyo, María; López, Agustín*: M 2005, Trotta 165 pp. 84-8164-725-X.

12614 *Cosentino, Augusto* Due maghi-illusionisti: Anassilao di Larissa e Marco il Mago. Modi di comunicazione. 2005 ⇒858. 347-354.

12615 *Finkielsztejn, G.* Quelques cultes ayant traversé l'époque perse (Anat-Io, Qôs-Appolon, Phanébal, Asklépios leontoukhos...): ancienneté des cultes du Levant et *interpretatio graeca*. TEuph 30 (2005) 187-188.

12616 [ET]**Gerlaud, Bernard** NONNOS de Panopolis: les dionysiaques, 11: chants XXXIII-XXXIV. CUFr Sér. grecque 443: P 2005, Belles Lettres xi; 266 pp. €47. 2-251-00525-0.

12617 **Jaccottet, A.-F.** Choisir Dionysos: les associations dionysiaques ou la face cachée du dionysisme. 2003 ⇒20,11319. [R]REA 107 (2005) 865-866 (*Mehl, V.*).

12618 **Linssen, Marc J.H.** The cults of Uruk and Babylon: the temple ritual texts as evidence for Hellenistic cult practises [!]. 2004 ⇒20, 11321. [R]BiOr 62 (2005) 298-300 (*Ambos, C.*).

12619 *Martin, Luther H.* Aspects of "religious experience" among the Hellenistic mystery religions. R&T 12 (2005) 349-369.

12620 *Mastrocinque, Attilio* Pregare Ialdabaoth (il dio seduto sul settimo cielo nelle preghiere magiche). Modi di comunicazione. 2005 ⇒ 858. 191-222.

12621 **Morand, Anne-France** Études sur les *Hymnes orphiques*. 2001 ⇒ 17,9935; 19,11850. [R]Gn. 77 (2005) 493-497 (*Graf, Fritz*).

12622 *Pérez Jiménez, Aurelio* Prescrizioni astrologiche relative alla prassi religiosa. Modi di comunicazione. 2005 ⇒858. 151-190.

12623 *Potter, David* Hellenistic religion. Companion to the Hellenistic world. 2005 ⇒642. 407-430.

12624 *Rigoglioso, M.* Persephone's sacred lake and the ancient female mystery religion in the womb of Sicily. JFSR 21/2 (2005) 5-29 [NTAb 50,362].

12625 **Roessli, Jean-Michel** Les Oracles sibyllins: origines païennes et appropriations chrétiennes (livres 6; 7; 8,217-428s). [D]*Wermelinger, Otto*: 2005, Diss. Fribourg [ThRv 102,v].

12626 **Schiano, Claudio** Il secolo della Sibilla: momenti della tradizione cinquecentesca degli 'Oracoli sibillini'. Ekdosis 2: Bari 2005, Pagina 233 pp. €13. 88-7470-016-4.

12627 *Schmitz, Thomas A.* NONNOS und seine Tradition. Die Bibel im Dialog. NET 10: 2005 ⇒333. 195-216.

12628 *Speyer, Wolfgang* Religionen vergangener Kulturen: antike Mysterienreligionen. Handbuch Religionswissenschaft. 2005 ⇒1016. 198-206.

12629 *Struck, Peter T.* The self in Artemidorus' interpretation of dreams. Religion and the self in antiquity. 2005 ⇒818. 109-120.

12630 *Van den Heever, Gerhard* Making mysteries: from the "Untergang der Mysterien" to imperial mysteries; social discourse in religion and the study of religion. R&T 12 (2005) 262-307;

12631 Redescribing Graeco-Roman antiquity: on religion and history of religion. R&T 12 (2005) 211-238 [NTAb 50,559].

12632 *Wellman, Tennyson J.* Ancient "mysteria" and modern mystery cults. R&T 12 (2005) 308-348.

## M5.5 Religiones anatolicae

12633 *Bachvarova, Mary R.* Relations between God and man in the Hurro-Hittite *Song of release*. JAOS 125 (2005) 45-58.

12634 **Balter, Michael** The goddess and the bull. NY 2005, Simon & S. 400 pp. 0-7432-4360-9. Ill. *John-Gordon Swogger*; Bibl. 369-382.

12635 **Bawanypeck, Daliah** Die Rituale der Auguren. Texte der Hethiter 25: Heidelberg 2005, Winter xv; 396 pp. 3-8253-5113-0. Bibl. 380-396.

12636 *Collins, B.J.* A statue for the deity: cult images in Hittite Anatolia. Cult image. ASOR 10: 2005 ⇒801. 13-42.

12637 **Dignas, Beate** Economy of the sacred in Hellenistic and Roman Asia Minor. Oxford Classical Monographs: 2002 ⇒18,10856; 20, 11337. [R]AnCl 74 (2005) 483-485 (*Migeotte, Léopold*).

12638 *Gonnet, Hatice* Analyse étiologique du mythe de Télibinu, dieu fondateur hittite. Anatolica 27 (2001) 145-157.

12639 *Gonzales, M.* The oracle and cult of Ares in Asia Minor. GRBS 45/3 (2005) 261-283 [NTAb 50,132].

12640 **Groddek, Detlev** Eine althethitische Tontafel des KI.LAM-Festes. International Journal of Diachronic Linguistics, Supplements 1: Mü 2005, Peniope 106 pp. 3-936609-15-2. Bibl. 80-88.

12641 **Hazenbos, Joost** The organization of the Anatolian cults during the thirteenth century B.C.: an appraisal of the Hittite cult inventories. 2003 ⇒19,11865; 20,11345. [R]ZA 95 (2005) 308-12 (*Miller, Jared L.*); AWE 3 (2004) 399-402 (*Glatz, Claudia; Matthews, Roger*).

12642 **Hirschmann, V.-E.** Horrenda secta: Untersuchungen zum frühchristlichen Montanismus und seinen Verbindungen zur paganen Religion Phrygiens. Historia, Einzelschriften 179: Stu 2005, Steiner 168 pp. 35150-86757. Bibl.

12643 *Hutter, Manfred* Religionen vergangener Kulturen: Religionen im Hethiterreich. Handbuch Religionswissenschaft. 2005 ⇒1016. 140-155.

12644 *Lebrun, René* Divinités particulières du Tabal. RANT 2 (2005) 419-426.

12645 **Mazoyer, Michel** Télipinu, le dieu au marécage: essai sur les mythes fondateurs du royaume hittite. Kubaba 2: 2003 ⇒19,11871. [R]RHR 222 (2005) 119-120 (*Sergent, Bernard*); BiOr 62 (2005) 96-101 (*Mouton, Alice*).

12646 **Miller, Jared L.** Studies in the origins, development and interpretation of the Kizzuwatna rituals. StBT 46: 2004 ⇒20,11354. [R]WZKM 95 (2005) 435-441 (*Haas, Volkert*).

12647 **Peter, Heike** Götter auf Erden: hethitische Rituale aus Sicht historischer Religionsanthropologie. Sto 2004, Almqvist & W. 288 pp. €34.50/$46.42. Diss. Lund.

12648 *Polvani, Anna Maria* The deity IMIN.IMIN.BI in Hittite texts. Or. 74 (2005) 181-194.

12649 *Popko, Maciej* Der hethitische Gott und seine Kultbilder. JANER 5 (2005) 79-87.

12650 *Rives, J.B.* Phrygian tales. GRBS 45/3 (2005) 223-244 [NTAb 50, 134].

12651 *Singer, Itamar* Sin and punishment in Hittite prayers. FKLEIN, J. 2005 ⇒79. 557-567.

12652 **Singer, Itamar** Hittite prayers. E*Hoffner, Harry Angier*: Writings from the ancient world 11: 2002 ⇒18,10881... 20,11373. RBiOr 62 (2005) 95-96 (*Roos, J. de*); ZA 95 (2005) 312-314 (*Prechel, Doris*); JSSt 50 (2005) 201-202 (*Watson, Wilfred G.E.*); JANER 4 (2004) 155-162 (*Beal, Richard H.*).

12653 **Strauss, Rita** Reinigungsrituale aus Kizzuwatna: ein Beitrag sur Erforschung hithitischer Ritualtradition und Kulturgeschichte. B 2005, De Gruyter xix; 470 pp. 3-11-017975-X. Bibl. 419-447.

12654 *Taracha, Piotr* Zur Entwicklung des offiziellen Pantheons im Staats- und dynastischen Kult der hethitischen Grossreichszeit. JANER 5 (2005) 89-106.

12655 **Taracha, Piotr** Ersetzen und entsühnen: das mittelhethitische Ersatzritual für den Großkönig Tuthalija (CTH *448.4) und verwandte Texte. Culture and history of the Ancient Near East 5: 2000 ⇒16,10204. RJNES 64 (2005) 209-212 (*Mouton, Alice*).

12656 *Yakubovich, Ilya* Were Hittite kings divinely anointed?: a Palaic invocation to the sun-god and its significance for Hittite religion. JANER 5 (2005) 107-137.

## M6.0 Religio canaanaea, syra

12657 **Albertz, Rainer** Storia della religione nell'Israele antico, 1: dalle origini alla fine dell'età monarchica. Introd. allo studio della bibbia, Suppl. 23: Brescia 2005, Paideia 392 pp. €38.60.

12658 *Alegre, Xavier* Per què la bíblia presenta Déu com a gelós dels ídols?: una aproximació a la idolatria ahir i avui des de la perspectiva bíblica. QVC 220 (2005) 7-28.

12659 *Amadasi Guzzo, Maria Giulia; Xella, Paolo* Eshmun-Melqart in una nuova iscrizione fenicia di Ibiza. StEeL 22 (2005) 47-57;

12660 Cultes et épithètes de Milqart. TEuph 30 (2005) 9-18.

12661 *Apicella, Catherine* Das Pantheon wird international: syrische, hellenistische und römische Gottheiten verbinden sich. WUB 36 (2005) 24-28.

12662 **Atwell, James E.** The sources of the Old Testament: a guide to the religious thought of the Hebrew Bible. 2004 ⇒20,11385. RET 117 (2005) 38 (*Carey, Holly J.*).

12663 **Azize, Joseph** The Phoenician solar theology: an investigation into the Phoenician opinion of the sun found in Julian's Hymn to King Helios. Gorgias Dissertations 15: Piscataway, NJ 2005, Gorgias xi; 321 pp. 1-5933-3321-06. Bibl. 267-301.

12664 *Becker, Uwe* Von der Staatsreligion zum Monotheismus: ein Kapitel israelitisch-jüdischer Religionsgeschichte. ZThK 102 (2005) 1-16.

12665 **Belayche, Nicole** Iudaea-Palaestina: the pagan cults in Roman Palestine. Religion der Römischen Provinzen 1: 2001 ⇒17,9957...19, 11887. RSyria 82 (2005) 383-384 (*Bowersock, Glen W.*).

12666 **Brody, Aaron Jed** 'Each man cried out to his God': the specialized religion of Canaanite and Phoenician seafarers. HSM 58: 1998 ⇒ 14,9292; 18,10901. RJNES 64 (2005) 287-290 (*Pardee, Dennis*).

12667 *Budin, Stephanie* Minoan Asherah?. Archaeological perspectives. 2005 ⇒627. 188-197.

12668 *Buttitta, I.E.* Fiamme di vita e sacrifici di infanti;

12669 *Chiodi, S.M.* Dai *rephaim* agli *en-en*. V Congresso di studi fenici. 2005 ⇒959. I, 417-426/139-144.

12670 *Clifford, Richard J.* The Phoenicians: pantheon of gods. Secrets of the bible. 2005 ⇒482. 23-25.

12671 *Cross, Frank Moore* The history of Israelite religion: a secular or theological subject?. BArR 31/3 (2005) 42-45.

12672 **Dever, William G.** Did God have a wife?: archaeology and folk religion in ancient Israel. GR 2005, Eerdmans xvi; 344 pp. $25/ £16. 0-8028-2852-3. Bibl. 318-333.

12673 *Dijkstra, Meindert* The myth of apši 'the (sea)dragon' in the Hurrian tradition: a new join (KBo 27, 180). UF 37 (2005) 315-328.

12674 **Durand, Jean-Marie**, *al.*, Florilegium marianum VIII: le culte des pierres et les monuments commémoratifs en Syrie Amorrite. Mémoires de N.A.B.U. 9: P 2005, SEPOA vii; 215 pp. 0909-5671. Bibl. 187-189. RUF 37 (2005) 823-824 (*Loretz, Oswald*).

12675 *Elayi, J.; Elayi, A.G.* Ba'al Arwad. V Congresso di studi fenici. 2005 ⇒959. I, 129-133.

12676 **Feliu, Lluís** The god Dagan in Bronze Age Syria. T*Watson, Wilfred G.E.*: Culture and History of the Ancient Near East 19: 2003 ⇒19, 11895. RJANER 5 (2005) 213-217 (*Crowell, Bradley L.*).

12677 *Gericke, J.W.* The quest for a philosophical YHWH (Part 1): Old Testament studies and philosophy of religion. OTEs 18 (2005) 579-602.

12678 *Gitin, Seymour* Israelite and Philistine cult and the archaeological record in Iron Age II: the 'smoking gun' phenomenon. BetM 182 (2005) 201-220. Sum 296. **H.**;

12679 **Goldstein, Jonathan A.** Peoples of an Almighty God: competing religions in the ancient world. AncB Reference Library: 2002 ⇒18, 10911... 20,11408. RBZ 49 (2005) 126-128 (*Niehr, Herbert*).

12680 **Grabbe, Lester L.** Judaic religion in the second temple period: belief and practice from the exile to Yavneh. 2000 ⇒16,10227... 20,11409. RRBLit 7 (2005) 202-205 (*Vanderkam, James*).

12681 **Green, Alberto R.W.** The storm-god in the ancient Near East. Biblical and Judaic Studies 8: 2003 ⇒19,11903; 20,11410. RAUSS 43 (2005) 341-345 (*Klingbeil, Martin G.*).

12682 **Hadley, Judith M.** The cult of Asherah in ancient Israel and Judah: evidence for a Hebrew goddess. UCOP 57: 2000 ⇒16,10228 ... 19,11904. RJNES 64 (2005) 281-285 (*Pardee, Dennis*).

12683 **Huber, I.** Rituale der Seuchen- und Schadensabwehr im Vorderen Orient und Griechenland: Formen kollektiver Krisenbewältigung in der Antike. Oriens et Occidens 10: Stu 2005, Steiner 287 pp. 3515-0-80457. Bibl.

12684 **Jericke, Detlef** Regionaler Kult und lokaler Kult—Studien zur Kult- und Religionsgeschichte Israels und Judas im 9. und 8. Jahrhundert v.Chr. [D]*Oeming, Manfred* 2005, Diss.-Habil. Heidelberg [ThLZ 130,886].

12685 *Kaizer, Ted* Leucothea as mater matuta at *Colonia* Berytus: a note on local mythology in the Levant and the hellenisation of a Phoenician city. Syria 82 (2005) 199-206;

12686 Ein Haus der Götter: Kulte und Religion in der Karawanenstadt Palmyra. WUB 36 (2005) 30-35.

12687 **Kaizer, Ted** The religious life of Palmyra: a study of social patterns of worship in the Roman period. Oriens et Occidens 4: 2002 ⇒18,10919... 20,11415. [R]Mes. 40 (2005) 209-210 (*Menegazzi, Roberta*).

12688 *Keel, Othmar* Die Heilung des Bruchs zwischen kanaanäischer und israelitischer Kultur. Vertikale Ökumene. 2005 ⇒590. 11-26.

12689 **Kühn, Dagmar** Totengedenken bei den Nabatäern und im Alten Testament: eine religionsgeschichtliche und exegetische Studie. [D]*Niehr, Herbert*: AOAT 311: Müns 2005, Ugarit-Verlag x; 556 pp. €95.80. 3-934628-48-6. Diss. Tübingen; Bibl. 407-448.

12690 **Lemaire, André** La nascita del monoteismo: il punto di vista di uno storico. StBi 145: Brescia 2005, Paideia 188 pp. €15.70. 88-394-0701-4. [R]Anton. 80 (2005) 743-744 (*Nobile, Marco*).

12691 *Lepore, Luciano* L'umanità in cammino dall'enoteismo al monoteismo: l'evoluzione della religione di Israele. BeO 47 (2005) 23-54.

12692 *Levine, Baruch A.* Assyrian ideology and Israelite monotheism. Iraq 67/1 (2005) 411-427.

12693 *Lewis, T.J.* Syro-Palestinian iconography and divine images. Cult image. ASOR 10: 2005 ⇒801. 69-107.

12694 *Marlasca Martín, R.* La *egersis* de Melqart: una propuesta para su interpretación. V Congresso di studi fenici. 2005 ⇒959. I, 455-61.

12695 **Mettinger, Tryggve N.D.** The riddle of resurrection: "Dying and rising Gods" in the ancient Near East. CB.OT 50: 2001 ⇒17,9987 ... 20,11426. [R]RBLit (2005)* (*Burnett, Joel*).

12696 **Miller, Patrick D.** The religion of ancient Israel. 2000 ⇒16,10238 ... 19,11927. [R]BiblInterp 13 (2005) 327-330 (*Hayward, C.T.R.*).

12697 *Mock, Leo* Religieuze systemen met magische trekjes. ITBT 13/7 (2005) 4-7.

12698 *Muffs, Yochanan* Paganism and biblical religion;

12699 The essence of biblical process. Personhood of God. 2005 ⇒265. 9-17/19-27.

12700 *Münnich, Maciej* Resheph—god of the netherworld?. ArOr 73 (2005) 161-184.

12701 **Nakhai, Beth Alpert** Archaeology and the religions of Canaan and Israel. ASOR 7: 2001 ⇒17,9989. [R]OLZ 100 (2005) 237-239 (*Vieweger, Dieter*).

12702 *Niehr, Herbert* "Der barmherzige Gott, zu dem es gut ist zu beten": Religionen in den aramäischen Königreichen Syriens. WUB 36 (2005) 12-17.

12703 **Niehr, Herbert** Ba'alsamem: Studien zu Herkunft, Geschichte und Rezeptionsgeschichte eines phönizischen Gottes. OLA 123: 2003 ⇒19,11935. [R]WO 35 (2005) 237-239 (*Hutter, Manfred*).

12704 *Niemann, Hermann M.* Altorientalische und Israelitisch-Jüdische Religion (Teil 2). JLH 44 (2005) 71-117.

12705 **Nocquet, Dany** Le "livret noir de Baal": la polémique contre le dieu Baal dans la Bible hébraïque et l'ancien Israël. 2004 ⇒20, 11432. [R]RB 112 (2005) 297-299 (*Tarragon, J.-M. de*).

12706 **Oggiano, Ida** Dal terreno al divino: archeologia del culto nella Palestina del primo millennio. R 2005, Carocci 294 pp. 88-430-3523-1. Bibl. 263-286. RTLu 10 (2005) 511-514 (*Paximadi, Giorgio*); StEeL 22 (2005) 133-134 (*Merlo, Paolo*).

12707 *Ottoson, Magnus* The holy God of Sarepta. SEÅ 70 (2005) 255-64.

12708 *Paul, Shalom M.* 'Emigration' from the netherworld in the ancient Near East. Divrei Shalom. CHANE 23: 2005 <1995> ⇒273. 263-270 [1 Sam 28].

12709 **Penchansky, David** Twilight of the gods: polytheism in the Hebrew Bible. LVL 2005, Westminster xii; 108 pp. $20. 0-664-2288-5-2. Bibl. 93-100.

12710 *Peri, Chiara* The construction of biblical monotheism: an unfinished task. SJOT 19 (2005) 135-142.

12711 **Peri, Chiara** Il regno del nemico: la morte nella religione di Canaan. StBi 140: 2003 ⇒19,11936; 20,11435. [R]RivBib 53 (2005) 91-95 (*Prato, Gian Luigi*).

12712 *Pfälzner, Peter* Syrien: Qatna: Ahnenkult im 2. Jahrtausend v. Chr.. WUB 36 (2005) 56-59.

12713 **Podella, Thomas** Das Lichtkleid JHWHs: Untersuchungen zur Gestalthaftigkeit Gottes im Alten Testament und seiner altorientalischen Umwelt. FAT 15: 1996 ⇒12,1946... 16,10256. [R]ThR 70 (2005) 445-446 (*Reventlow, Henning Graf*).

12714 *Ribichini, S.* 'Interpretazioni' di Astarte. V Congresso di studi fenici. 2005 ⇒959. I, 445-453.

12715 *Salamé-Sarkis, Hassan* Le dieu de Râs ach-Chaqʿa-Théouprosopon. Syria 82 (2005) 173-188.

12716 *Sartre, Maurice* Neue Kleider für alte Götter: Götterwelten im hellenistischen Syrien. WUB 36 (2005) 19-23.

12717 *Schram, Sandra* The lost goddess of Israel. Arch. 58/2 (2005) 36-40.

12718 **Smith, Mark S.** The origins of biblical monotheism: Israel's polytheistic background and the Ugaritic texts. 2001 ⇒17,10001... 20, 11443. [R]HebStud 46 (2005) 397-401 (*Strawn, Brent A.*).

12719 *Sperling, S. David* Monotheism and ancient Israelite religion. Companion to the ancient Near East. 2005 ⇒691. 408-420.

12720 *Strübind, Kim* Monotheismus und Religionsfreiheit in der Bibel. Zeitschrift für Theologie und Gemeinde 10 (2005) 143-161.

12721 *Valkenberg, Pim* Hat das Konzept der "abrahamitischen Religionen" Zukunft?. Conc(D) 41/5 (2005) 553-561.

12722 *Wénin, André* Il serpente, il torello e il Baal. Dalla violenza. 2005 <2003> ⇒323. 53-76.

12723 *Wyatt, Nick* Sea and desert: symbolic geography in West Semitic religious thought. Mythic mind. 2005 <1987> ⇒328. 38-54;

12724 Of calves and kings: the Canaanite dimension in the religion of Israel. Mythic mind. 2005 <1992> ⇒328. 72-91;

12725 Ilimilku the theologian: the ideological roles of Athtar and Baal in KTU 1.1 and 1.6 <2002>;

12726 Ilimilku's ideological programme: Ugaritic royal propaganda, and a biblical postscript <1997>. 'There's such divinity'. 2005 ⇒329. 221-230/133-149.

## M6.5 Religio aegyptia

12727 *Aloise, Agnese* Lo scongiuro: una pratica magica nei testi e nelle iconografie delle sepolture private dell'Antico Regno. Aeg. 85 (2005) 41-51.

12728 *Arafa, Nagwa* Le dieu Igay. DiscEg 63 (2005) 11-22.

12729 *Assmann, Jan* Religionen vergangener Kulturen: ägyptische Religion. Handbuch Religionswissenschaft. 2005 ⇒1016. 104-117.

12730 **Assmann, Jan** Altägyptische Totenliturgien, 2: Totenliturgien und Totensprüche in Grabinschriften des Neuen Reiches. Supplemente zu den Schriften der Heidelberger Akademie der Wissenschaften, Philosophisch-historische Klasse 17: Heidelberg 2005, Winter 635 pp. €79. 3-8253-1583-5;

12731 Death and salvation in ancient Egypt. T*Lorton, David*: Ithaca 2005, Cornell Univ. Pr. xi; 490 pp. 0-8014-4241-9. Bibl. 418-478.

12732 **Backes, Burkhard** Wortindex zum späten Totenbuch (pTurin 1791). Studien zum Altägyptischen Totenbuch 9: Wsb 2005, Harrassowitz xii; 198 pp. €36. 3-447-05258-9.

12733 **Billing, N.** Nut: the goddess of life in text and iconography. Uppsala Studies in Egyptology 5: U 2005, Uppsala Univ. viii; 490 pp. 91-506-16536.

12734 *Bommas, Martin* Sepolture all'interno di corti templari in Egitto: il rinnovamento del rituale di sepoltura all'inizio del 1 millennio a.C. Aeg. 85 (2005) 53-68.

12735 *Bouanich, Catherine* Mise à mort rituelle de l'animal, offrande carnée dans le temple égyptien. La cuisine et l'autel. BEHE.R 124: 2005 ⇒539. 149-162.

12736 *Boulogne, Jacques* Le culte égyptien des animaux vu par PLUTARQUE: une étiologie égyptienne (Isis et Osiris 71-76, 379 D-382 C). Les Grecs de l'antiquité. 2005 ⇒872. 197-205.

12737 *Bremmer, Jan N.* Foolish Egyptians: Apion and Anoubion in the Pseudo-Clementines. FLUTTIKHUIZEN, G.: AGJU 59: 2005 ⇒93. 311-329.

12738 **Bricault, Laurent** Recueil des inscriptions concernant les cultes isiaques. MAIBL 31: P 2005, Inscriptions et Belles Lettres 3 vols; xxxi; 844 pp. €190. 2-87-75-41-56-8. RCRAI (2005/3) 996-997 (*Leclant, Jean*).

12739 **Budge, Ernest A.T.W.** Tutankhamen: amenism, atenism, and Egyptian monotheism. L 2005, Kegan P. 160 pp. 0-7103-1046-3.

12740 *Cooney, Kathlyn M.; McClain, J. Brett* The daily offering meal in the ritual of Amenhotep I: an instance of the local adaptation of cult liturgy. JANER 5 (2005) 41-78.

12741 *Curtis, Neil G.W.; Kockelmann, Holger; Munro, Irmtraut* The collection of Book of the Dead manuscripts in Marischal Museum, University of Aberdeen, Scotland: a comprehensive overview. BIFAO 105 (2005) 49-73.

12742 **Darnell, John Coleman** The enigmatic netherworld books of the solar-osirian unity: cryptographic compositions in the tombs of Tutankhamun, Ramesses VI and Ramesses IX. OBO 198: 2004 ⇒20, 11466. RWO 35 (2005) 22-47 (*Quack, Joachim Friedrich*); DiscEg 61 (2005) 101-113 (*Morenz, Ludwig D.*).

12743 **Dieleman, Jacco** Priests, tongues, and rites: the London-Leiden magical manuscripts and translation in Egyptian ritual (100-300 CE). RGRW 153: Lei 2005, Brill xiv; 342 pp. €90. 90-04-14185-5. Bibl. 317-329.

12744 *Dijkstra, Jitse H.F.* De laatste priesters van Philae en het einde van de oudegyptische religie. Phoe. 51 (2005) 27-37.

12745 *DuQuesne, Terence* The spiritual and the sexual in ancient Egypt. DiscEg 61 (2005) 7-24.

12746 **Duquesne, Terence** The jackal divinities of Egypt, 1: from the archaic period to Dynasty X. Oxfordshire Communications in Egyptology VI: L 2005, Da'th xxii; 566 pp. 1-871266-24-6.

12747 [E]**Enmarch, Roland** The dialogue of Ipuwer and the Lord of all. Oxf 2005, Griffith Institute (8), 84 pp. 0-900416-86-6. Bibl. 11-16.

12748 *Ensoli, Serena* L'Egitto e la Libia: a proposito del culto isiaco nel Mediterraneo e del santuario di Iside e Serapide sull'acropoli di Cirene. RPARA 77 (2004-2005) 137-162.

12749 *Fekri, Magdi* Les attributs de la déesse Hathor. ASAE 79 (2005) 95-106.

12750 [T]**Fischer-Elfert, Hans-W.** Altägyptische Zaubersprüche. Reclams Universal-Bibliothek 18375: Stu 2005, Reclam 187 pp. €5. 3-15-018375-6. Beitr. *Tonio Sebastian Richter*.

12751 *Frankfurter, David* Curses, blessings, and ritual authority: Egyptian magic in comparative perspective. JANER 5 (2005) 157-185.

12752 **Geisen, Chr.** Die Totentexte des verschollenen Sarges der Königin Mentuhotep aus der 13. Dynastie: ein Textzeuge aus der Übergangszeit von den Sargtexten zum Totenbuch. 2004 ⇒20,11479. [R]BiOr 62 (2005) 229-31 (*Meyer-Dietrich, Erika*); JANER 5 (2005) 228-238 (*Quirke, Stephen*).

12753 **Gestermann, Louise** Die Überlieferung ausgewählter Texte altägyptischer Totenliteratur ("Sargtexte") in spätzeitlichen Grabanlagen. ÄA 68: Wsb 2005, Harrassowitz 2 vols; xii; 470 pp. €98. 3-447-05193-0. Teil 1: Text; Teil II: Textanhang; Bibl. 451-470.

12754 *Gozzoli, Roberto B.* La relazione tra dio e faraone nelle stele di Taharqo da Kawa. Aeg. 85 (2005) 161-173.

12755 *Graindorge, Catherine* Le taureau blanc du dieu Min et l'offrande de la gerbe de blé. La cuisine et l'autel. 2005 ⇒539. 47-76.

12756 *Graves-Brown, Carolyn A.* The spitting goddess and the stony divinity and flint in pharaonic Egypt. Current research in egyptology 2003. 2005 ⇒907. 57-70.

12757 **Grimm, A.; Schlögl, H.A.** Das thebanische Grab Nr. 136 und der Beginn der Amarnazeit. Wsb 2005, Harrassowitz 56 + 54 pp. €75. 3-447-05132-9. 54 pp pl.

12758 **Guermeur, Ivan** Les cultes d'Amon hors de Thèbes. BEHE.R 123: Turnhout 2005, Brepols xi; 641 pp. €89. 2-503-51427-8.

12759 **Hart, G.** The Routledge dictionary of Egyptian gods and goddesses. L [2]2005 <1986>, Routledge xv; 170 pp. $87.50/27. 04153-61168/44956. Bibl. [NTAb 50,626].

12760 *Hermsen, Edmund* Opfer und Gebet in der altägyptischen Religion. Opfer und Gebet. 2005 ⇒506. 156-168.

12761 **Hornung, Erik** The secret lore of Egypt: its impact on the West. [T]*Lorton, David*: 2001 ⇒17,10046... 20,11485. [R]AJA 109 (2005) 101-102 (*Mirecki, Paul A.*).

12762 **Jacquet-Gordon, Helen** The graffiti on the Khonsu temple roof at Karnak: a manifestation of personal piety. The Temple of Khonsu 3; UCOIP 123: 2003 ⇒19,12004. [R]BiOr 62 (2005) 252-255 (*Payraudeau, Frédéric*).

12763 *Jansen-Winkeln, Karl* Ein Priester als Restaurator: zu einer ptolemäischen Inschrift am Luxortempel. ZÄS 132/1 (2005) 35-39; Tafel XV-XVI.

12764 **Jasnow, Richard; Zauzich, Karl-Theodor** The ancient Egyptian Book of Thoth: a demotic discourse on knowledge and pendant to the classical hermetica. Wsb 2005, Harrassowitz 2 vols; xx; 581 pp. €178. 3-447-05082-9. 67 pl.; Bibl. 551-568.

12765 **Kaper, Olaf E.** The Egyptian god Tutu: a study of the sphinx-god and master of demons with a corpus of monuments. OLA 119: 2003 ⇒19,12007. [R]OLZ 100 (2005) 30-33 (*Lieven, Alexandra von*).

12766 *Kemboly, Mpay* Iaau and the question of the origin of evil according to ancient Egyptian sources. Current research in egyptology 2003. 2005 ⇒907. 71-103.

12767 *Koemoth, Pierre P.* Byblos, Thessalonique et le mythe hellénisé d'Osiris. DiscEg 61 (2005) 37-47.

12768 *Labrique, Françoise* Le bras de Sekhmet. La cuisine et l'autel. BEHE.R 124: 2005 ⇒539. 163-176.

12769 *Lahn, Kristina Qedeschet*: Genese einer Transfergottheit im ägyptisch-vorderasiatischen Raum. SAÄK 33 (2005) 201-237.

12770 *Laurant, Sophie*, *al.*, Prières d'Égypte. MoBi 167 (2005) 14-42.

12771 *López Grande, M.J.* Western Asiatic winged deities: Egyptian iconographic evidence for the god Horon. V Congresso di studi fenici. 2005 ⇒959. I, 69-78.

12772 *Lucarelli, Rita* I demoni nel Libro dei Morti. Aeg. 85 (2005) 33-39.

12773 *Luiselli, Maria Michela* Fiktionale Dialoge?: zur Interaktion zwischen Gott und Mensch in der altägyptischen Literatur. GöMisz 206 (2005) 39-47;

12774 La partecipazione dell'individuo alla religione: rituali personali tra norma e individualità. Aeg. 85 (2005) 13-31.

12775 **Luiselli, Maria Michela** Der Amun-Re Hymnus des P. Boulaq 17: (P. Kairo CG 58038). KÄT 14: 2004 ⇒20,11499. [R]BiOr 62 (2005) 232-234 (*Manisali, Alexander*).

12776 **Malaise, Michel** Pour une terminologie et une analyse des cultes isiaques. Mémoires de la classe des lettres 35: Bru 2005, Académie royale de Belgique 282 pp. €25. 2-8031-0217-X. Bibl. 231-258.

12777 **Maravelia, Amanda-Alice** Magic in ancient Eygpt: metaphysical quintessence of the land of gods. Athens 2003, Iamblichos 432 pp. 177 fig. **G**.

12778 *Maret, Pierre de* L'oryctérope, un animal 'bon à penser' pour les Africains, est-il à l'origine du dieu égyptien Seth?. BIFAO 105 (2005) 107-128.

12779 *Mastrocinque, Attilio* Le apparizioni del dio Bes nella tarda antichità: a proposito dell'iscrizione di Gornea. ZPE 153 (2005) 243-248.

12780 **Mojsov, Bojana** Osiris: death and afterlife of a god. Malden, MA 2005, Blackwell xx; 150 pp. 1-4051-3179-9. Bibl. 142-144.

12781 **Munro, Irmtraut** Das Totenbuch des Pa-en-nesti-taui aus der Regierungszeit des Amenemope (pLondon BM 10064). Handschriften des altägyptischen Totenbuches 7: 2001 ⇒17,10054... 20,11508.

RBiOr 62 (2005) 466-470 (*Régen, I.*); WZKM 95 (2005) 387-391 (*Haslauer, Elfriede*);

12782 Ein Ritualbuch für Goldamulette und Totenbuch des Month-em-hat. Studien zum altägyptischen Totenbuch 7: 2003 ⇒19,12030; 20, 11507. RJANER 5 (2005) 245-250 (*Stadler, Martin Andreas*); Enchoria 29 (2004-2005) 194-198 (*Lippert, Sandra L.*).

12783 *Neureiter, Sabine* Schamanismus im alten Ägypten. SAÄK 33 (2005) 281-330.

12784 *Poole, Federico* 'All that has been done to the Shabtis': some considerations of the decree for the Shabtis of Neskhons and P.BM EA 10800. JEA 91 (2005) 165-170.

12785 *Ramadan, Wagdy* Les porteurs d'encensoirs de l'Ancien Empire à la Basse époque. DiscEg 63 (2005) 67-83.

12786 *Raven, Maarten J.* Egyptian concepts on the orientation of the human body. JEA 91 (2005) 37-53.

12787 *Ray, John D.* An inscribed linen plea from the sacred animal necropolis, north Saqqara. JEA 91 (2005) 171-179.

12788 E**Redford, Donald B.** The ancient gods speak: a guide to Egyptian religion. 2002 ⇒18,11034; 19,12034. RJNES 64 (2005) 204-206 (*Hays, Harold M.*).

12789 *Rissing, Thilo; Willeke, Michaela* Legende vom Nil: zu Aleida und Jan Assmanns Rehabilitierung Ägyptens. ThPh 80 (2005) 334-366.

12790 *Robins, G.* Cult statues in ancient Egypt. Cult image. ASOR 10: 2005 ⇒801. 1-12.

12791 **Sayed Mohamed, Zeinab** Festvorbereitungen: die administrativen und ökonomischen Grundlagen altägyptischer Feste. OBO 202: 2004 ⇒20,11516. RBiOr 62 (2005) 239-241 (*Spalinger, Anthony*).

12792 *Scandone, Gabriella* Nut a Biblo: un aspetto di Hathor. SMEA 47 (2005) 273-276.

12793 **Servajean, Frédéric** Les formules des transformations du Livre des Morts: à la lumière d'une théorie de la perfomativité: XVIIIe-XXe dynasties. Bibliothèque d'étude 137: 2003 ⇒19,12040; 20, 11519. ROLZ 100 (2005) 147-150 (*Backes, Burkhard*).

12794 **Smith, Mark** On the primaeval ocean. CNI publications 26; Carlsberg papyri 5: K 2002, Museum Tusculanum Pr. 260 pp. Ill.

12795 E**Stadler, Martin A.** Der Totenpapyrus des Pa-Month (P. Bibl. nat. 149). Studien zum altägyptischen Totenbuch 6: 2003 ⇒19,12042; 20,11523. RWO 35 (2005) 188-193 (*Quack, Joachim Friedrich*).

12796 **Stadler, Martin Andreas** Isis, das göttliche Kind und die Weltordnung: neue religiöse Texte aus dem Fayum nach dem Papyrus Wien D 12006 recto. 2004 ⇒20,11524. RAPF 51 (2005) 174-79 (*Quack, Joachim Friedrich*).

12797 *Takács, Sarolta A.* Divine and human feet: records of pilgrims honouring Isis. Pilgrimage. 2005 ⇒958. 353-369.

12798 *Tassie, Geoffrey* Single mother goddesses and divine kingship: the sidelock of youth and the maternal bond. Current research in egyptology II. 2005 ⇒635. 65-73.

12799 *Uranić, Igor Book of the dead* papyrus Zagreb 601. SAÄK 33 (2005) 357-371.

12800 **Wilkinson, Richard H.** The complete gods and goddesses of ancient Egypt. 2003 ⇒19,926; 20,11531. RDiscEg 62 (2005) 103-108 (*Ganley, Andrew H.*).

12801 [E]**Zecchi, Marco** Inni religiosi dell'Egitto antico. Testi del Vicino Oriente antico, 1: Letteratura egiziana classica 5: 2004 ⇒20,11532. [R]RBLit (2005)* (*Mazzinghi, Luca*).

## M7.0 Religio mesopotamica

12802 *Abusch, Tzvi* The promise to praise the God in Šuilla prayer. [M]MORAN, W. BibOr 48: 2005 ⇒107. 1-10.

12803 *Alster, Bendt* Demons in the conclusion of Lugalbanda in Hurrumkurra. Iraq 67/2 (2005) 61-71.

12804 **Annus, Amar** The god Ninurta in the mythology and royal ideology of ancient Mesopotamia. SAAS 14: 2002 ⇒18,11051. [R]BSOAS 68 (2005) 307-309 (*George, Andrew R.*).

12805 *Ataç, Mehemet-Ali* The 'underworld vision' of the Ninevite intellectual milieu. Nineveh. 2005 ⇒901. 67-76.

12806 **Beaulieu, Paul-Alain** The pantheon of Uruk during the Neo-Babylonian period. 2003 ⇒19,12069. [R]BiOr 62 (2005) 293-298 (*Zawadzki, S.*); ZA 95 (2005) 303-306 (*MacGinnis, John*).

12807 **Böck, Barbara** Die babylonisch-assyrische Morphoskopie. 2000 ⇒16,10337...20,11551. [R]OLZ 100 (2005) 257-262 (*Richter, T.*).

12808 **Cohen, Andrew C.** Death rituals, ideology, and the development of early Mesopotamian kingship: toward a new understanding of Iraq's Royal Cemetery of Ur. Ancient magic and divination 7: Lei 2005, Brill xxi; 244 pp. 90-04-14635-0.

12809 *Çiğ, Muazzez I.* Echoes of the Sumerian sacred marriage myth in the Qur'an and bible. [F]KLEIN, J. 2005 ⇒79. 678-684.

12810 *Dick, M.B.* The Mesopotamian cult statue for the deity: a sacramental encounter with the divinity. Cult image. ASOR 10: 2005 ⇒801. 43-67.

12811 **Frechette, Christopher G.** The name of the ritual: investigating ancient Mesopotamian 'hand-lifting' rituals with implications for the interpretation of genre in the Psalms. 2005, Diss. Harvard [HThR 98,496].

12812 **Fritz, Michael M.** "...und weinten um Tammuz": die Götter Dumuzi-Ama'usumgal'anna und Damu. AOAT 307: 2003 ⇒19,12078. [R]AfO 51 (2005-2006) 352-354 (*Alster, Bendt*).

12813 *Glassner, Jean-Jacques* L'aruspicine paléo-babylonienne et le témoignage des sources de Mari. ZA 95 (2005) 276-300.

12814 *Hallo, William W.* Before tea leaves: divination in ancient Babylonia. BArR 31/2 (2005) 32-39.

12815 **Heessel, Nils P.** Pazuzu: archäologische und philologische Studien zu einem altorientalischen Dämon. Ancient Magic and Divination 4: 2002 ⇒19,12082. [R]AfO 51 (2005-2006) 355-8 (*Böck, Barbara*).

12816 **Holloway, Steven W.** Aššur is King! Assur is King!: religion in the exercise of power in the Neo-Assyrian Empire. Culture and history of the Ancient Near East 10: 2002 ⇒18,11066... 20,11555. [R]ZAR 11 (2005) 304-311 (*Otto, Eckart*).

12817 *Jean, Cynthia* Le petit monde des exorcistes de Ninive. Nineveh. 2005 ⇒901. 77-81.

12818 *Karahashi, Fumi* Lugal-e and the Song of Ullikummi: a structural comparison. JEOL 38 (2003-2004) 77-82.

12819 **Katz, Dina** The image of the netherworld in Sumerian sources. 2003 ⇒19,12089; 20,11558. [R]BiOr 62 (2005) 279-286 (*Attinger, Pascal*).

12820 **Koch, Ulla Susanne** Secrets of extispicy: the chapter Multabiltu of the Babylonian extispicy series and Nisirti baruti texts mainly from Assurbanipal's library. AOAT 326: Müns 2005, Ugarit-Verlag x; 630 pp. 3-934628-67-2. Bibl. 624-630.

12821 *Lambert, W.G.* Ištar of Nineveh. Nineveh. 2005 ⇒901. 35-39.

12822 [E]**Mander, Pietro** Canti sumerici d'amore e morte: la vicenda della dea Inanna/Ishtar e del dio Dumuzi/Tammuz. Testi del Vicino Oriente antico 2; Letterature mesopotamiche 8: Brescia 2005, Paideia 201 pp. €21.20. 88-394-0710-3. Bibl. 189-192.

12823 *Mayer, Werner R.* Das Gebet des Eingeweideschauers an Ninurta. Or. 74 (2005) 51-56.

12824 **Ornan, Tallay** The triumph of the symbol: pictorial representation of deities in Mesopotamia and the biblical image ban. OBO 213: FrS 2005, Academic xii; 284 pp. FS87. 3-7278-1519-1. Bibl. 184-220.

12825 *Paul, Shalom M.* Heavenly tablets and the book of life. Divrei Shalom. CHANE 23: 2005 <1973> ⇒273. 59-70.

12826 *Pezzoli-Oligiati, Daria* Erkundungen von Gegenwelten: zur Orientierungsleistung "mythischer" Reisen am Beispiel zweier mesopotamischer Texte. Numen 52/2 (2005) 226-254.

12827 *Pola, Thomas* Welteinheitsideologie: intoleranter Polytheismus bei den Neuassyrern. ThBeitr 36 (2005) 133-151.

12828 *Porter, Barbara N.* Ištar of Nineveh and her collaborator, Ishtar of Arbela, in the reign of Assurbanipal. Nineveh. 2005 ⇒901. 41-44.

12829 [E]**Porter, Barbara Nevling** Ritual and politics in ancient Mesopotamia. AOS 28: NHv 2005, American Oriental Society xi; 120 pp. $42. 0-940490-19-6.

12830 **Radner, Karen** Die Macht des Namens: altorientalische Strategien zur Selbsterhaltung. Santag 8: Wsb 2005, Harrassowitz ix; 341 pp. $147. 3-447-05328-3. Bibl. 303-338.

12831 **Reiner, Erica** Babylonian planetary omens: part four. Cuneiform Monographs 30: Lei 2005, Brill ix; 217 pp. 90-04-14212-6. Collab. *Pingree, David*.

12832 **Rochberg, Francesca** The heavenly writing: divination, horoscopy, and astronomy in Mesopotamian culture. 2004 ⇒20,11575. [R]Isis 96 (2005) 267-268 (*Steele, J.M.*); REA 107 (2005) 862-863 (*Breniquet, Catherine*).

12833 *Sallaberger, W., al.*, Priester. RLA 10/7-8. 2005 ⇒975. 617-648.

12834 *Schwemer, Daniel* Gegründet von den Göttern selbst: Alltag, Religion und Mythos im Babylon des 6. Jahrhunderts v. Chr. WUB 37 (2005) 10-19.

12835 **Schwemer, Daniel** Die Wettergottgestalten Mesopotamiens und Nordsyriens im Zeitalter der Keilschriftkulturen: Materialien und Studien nach den schriftlichen Quellen. 2001 ⇒17,10106... 20, 11578. [R]RA 99 (2005) 185-186 (*Charpin, Dominique*).

12836 *Steinkeller, Piotr* Of stars and men: the conceptual and mythological setup of Babylonian extispicy. [M]MORAN, W.: BibOr 48: 2005 ⇒197. 11-47.

12837 *Trenkwalder, Helga* Religionen vergangener Kulturen: sumerisch-babylonische Religion. Handbuch Religionswissenschaft. 2005 ⇒ 1016. 118-139.

12838 *Van der Stede, Véronique* Le jugement des morts en Mésopotamie: mythe ou réalité. FFINET, A.: Subartu 16: 2005 ⇒40. 153-164.

12839 *Van Koppen, Frans* De kleispijker van Ipiq-Ištar voor het voetlicht. Phoe. 51 (2005) 173-180.

12840 *Villeneuve, Estelle* Les fêtes du renouveau dans l'Orient ancien. MoBi 164 (2005) 18-23.

12841 T**Walker, Christopher; Dick, Michael B.** The induction of the cult image in ancient Mesopotamia: the Mesopotamian *mis pî* ritual. SAA.Literary Texts 1: 2001 ⇒17,10109... 20,11591. RBiOr 62 (2005) 395-409 (*Borger, Rykle*).

12842 *Weaver, Ann M.* The 'sin of Sargon' and Esarhaddon's reconception of Sennacherib: a study in divine will, human politics and royal ideology. Nineveh. 2005 ⇒901. 61-66.

12843 **Zgoll, Annette** Die Kunst des Betens: Form und Funktion, Theologie und Psychagogik in babylonisch-assyrischen Handerhebungsgebeten zu Ištar. AOAT 308: 2003 ⇒19,12117. RThLZ 130 (2005) 620-622 (*Bauks, Michaela*).

## M7.5 Religio persiana

12844 **Foltz, Richard C.** Spirituality in the land of the noble: how Iran shaped the world's religions. 2004 ⇒20,11597. RJAAR 73 (2005) 915-917 (*Buckley, Jorunn J.*).

12845 *Henkelman, Wouter F.M.* De goden van Iran: (breuk)lijnen in een religieus landschap, ca. 4000-330 v.Chr. Phoe. 51 (2005) 130-172.

12846 *Hutter, Manfred* Religionen der Gegenwart: Zoroastrismus. Handbuch Religionswissenschaft. 2005 ⇒1016. 384-394.

12847 *Moazami, Mahnaz* Evil animals in the Zoroastrian religion. HR 44 (2005) 300-317 [NTAb 50,103].

## M8.1 *Religio proto-arabica*—Early Arabic religious graffiti

12848 *Roche, M.-J.* Aspects de ʻAtthar en Arabie du nord aux époques perse et hellénistique. TEuph 30 (2005) 189.

## M8.2 *Muḥammad et asseclae*—Qur'an and early diffusion of Islam

12849 **Aʻzami, Muhammade M. Al-** The history of the Qur'anic text, from revelation to compilation: a comparative study with the Old and New Testaments. 2004 ⇒20,11607. RICMR 16 (2005) 79-80 (*Mullen, Roderic L.*).

12850 *Behr, Harry-Harun* Islamisch-theologisches Nachdenken über Gerechtigkeit. BiHe 41/164 (2005) 22-24.

12851 **Cragg, Kenneth** A certain sympathy of scriptures—biblical and quranic. 2004 ⇒20,11634. RICMR 16 (2005) 81-84 (*Ipgrave, Michael*).

12852 **Déroche, François** Le Coran. QSJ: P 2005, PUF 127 pp [ASSR 131-132,234s—Benkheira, Hocine].

12853 *Eisenman, R.* Who were the Koranic prophets ʻAd, Thamud, Hud, and Salih?. JHiC 11/2 (2005) 96-107 [NTAb 50,563].

12854 [E]**Farid, Malik Ghulam** The holy Quran with English translation and short commentary. 2003 ⇒19,12138. [R]Muslim World Book Review 25/3 (2005) 18-23 (*Kidwai, A.R.*).

12855 *Flaquer, Jaume* Jesús, profeta musulmán de excepción. SelTeol 44 (2005) 165-170 <Religions et histoire 1 (2005) 48-53.

12856 *Fuess, Albrecht* Gotteswort und Prophetenwort: zur Rolle von Koran und Hadith im Islam. Heilige Schriften. 2005 ⇒362. 86-98, 241-242.

12857 **Gallez, Edouard-Marie** Le messie et son prophète: aux origines de l'Islam, 1: de Qumrân à Muḥammad; 2: Du Muḥammad des Califes au Muḥammad de l'histoire. Studia Arabica 1: P 2005, Editions de Paris 524; 582 pp. 2-85162-064-9. Diss. Strasbourg.

12858 *Garsiel, Bat-Sheva* Influence of midrashic bible interpretations on the Quran. BetM 182 (2005) 251-260. Sum 294. **H.**

12859 **Ginaidi, Ahmed** Jesus Christus und Maria aus koranisch-islamischer Perspektive: Grundlagen eines interreligiösen Dialogs. Noëma: Stu 2002, Ibidem 140 pp. 3-89821-237-8.

12860 **Gnilka, J.** Biblia y Corán: lo que nos une, lo que nos separa. Barc 2005, Herder 286 pp.

12861 *Greifenhagen, F.V.* Cooperating revelations?: Qur'an, Bible and intertextuality. Arc 33 (2005) 302-317.

12862 **Khoury, Adel Theodor** Der Koran. Dü 2005, Patmos 352 pp. 3-4-91-72485-6.

12863 *Körner, Felix* Können Muslime den Koran historisch erforschen?: türkische Neuansätze. ThZ 61 (2005) 226-238.

12864 *Leimgruber, Stephan* Was Bibel und Koran erzählen: beide Schriften im Vergleich. [F]LAUB, F. Bibel-Schule-Leben 6: 2005 ⇒87. 195-208.

12865 **Mughal, Aslam** Jesus in Islam. L 2003, Pen xii; 192 pp. 1-904018-48-3.

12866 **Nelson-Pallmeyer, Jack** Is religion killing us? violence in the bible and the Qur'an. NY 2005, Continuum 169 pp. $15 [BiTod 45,193—Dianne Bergant].

12867 *Platti, Emilio* Bible et Islam. Bible et sciences des religions. 2005 ⇒445. 145-162.

12868 **Qarai, Ali Quli** The Qur'ān with a phrase-by-phrase English translation. 2004 ⇒20,11616. [R]Muslim World Book Rview 25/3 (2005) 23-25 (*Kidwai, A.R.*).

12869 [E]**Reeves, John C.** Bible and Qur'an: essays in scriptural intertextuality. SBL.Symposium 24: 2003 ⇒19,2531. [R]Numen 52 (2005) 406-409 (*Schipper, Bernd U.*).

12870 *Robbins, Vernon K.* Lukan and Johannine tradition in the Qur'an: a story of (and program for) *Auslegungsgeschichte* and *Wirkungsgeschichte*. Moving beyond NT theology?. Ment. *Räisänen, H.*: SESJ 88: 2005 ⇒463. 336-368.

12871 *Robinson, Neal* Jesus in the Qur'an, the historical Jesus and the myth of God incarnate. [F]YOUNG, F. 2005 ⇒168. 186-197.

12872 **Wheeler, Brannon M.** Moses in the Quran and Islamic exegesis. 2002 ⇒18,11150; 20,11624. [R]IJMES 37 (2005) 115-117 (*Stewart, Devin*).

12873 [T]**Wheeler, Brannon M.** Prophets in the Quran: an introduction to the Quran and Muslim exegesis. 2002 ⇒18,11151... 20,11625. [R]JR 85 (2005) 350-351 (*GhaneaBassiri, Kambiz*).

12874 **Wimmer, Stefan Jakob; Leimgruber, Stephan** Von Adam bis Muhammad: Bibel und Koran im Vergleich. Stu 2005, Katholisches Bibelwerk 256 pp. €19.90. 3-460-33175-5. Herausgeber Deutscher Katecheten-Verein, München.

### M8.3 **Islam**, *evolutio recentior*—**later theory and practice**

12875 *Prenner, Karl* Religionen der Gegenwart: Islam. Handbuch Religionswissenschaft. 2005 ⇒1016. 436-456.

12876 *Spuler-Stegemann, Ursula* Opfer und Gebet im Islam. Opfer und Gebet. 2005 ⇒506. 61-70.

### M8.4 **Islamic-Christian relations**

12877 [ET]**Amar, Joseph P.** DIONYSIOS bar Salîbî: a response to the Arabs. CSCO 614-615; CSCO.S 238-239: Lv 2005, Peeters 2 vols. 90-429-1567-6/8-4. Bibl.

12878 **Beaumont, Mark** Christology in dialogue with Muslims: a critical analysis of christian presentations of Christ for Muslims from the ninth and twentieth centuries. Oxf 2005, Regnum xxvi; 227 pp. £20. 1842-2712-37.

12879 *Bechmann, Ulrike* Das Eigene des Islam im religiösen Kontext seiner Enstehungszeit: zum Verständnis von erinnerter Trennung und gegenwärtigem Dialog. Vertikale Ökumene. 2005 ⇒590. 40-56.

12880 *Bush, Randall B.* A tale of two scriptures. Jewish-Christian and Islamic paradigms of scripture and their impact on culture. CScR 34 (2005) 309-326.

12881 **Grelot, Pierre** Dialogues avec un musulman. 2004 ⇒20,11635. [R]RICP 94 (2005) 220-222 (*La Hougue, Henri de*).

12882 *Griffith, Sidney H.* Arguing from scripture: the bible in the Christian/Muslim encounter in the middle ages. Scripture and pluralism. 2005 ⇒757. 29-58.

12883 **Hamoneau, D.A.** Moïse, Jésus, Mohamed: les messages de Dieu à travers la Torah, l'évangile et le Coran, l'ancien, le nouveau et le dernier Testament. P 2003, La Ruche 291 pp. €14.

12884 *Holt, David* Notes on Acts 10 from the Middle East studies program. CScR 34 (2005) 519-530.

12885 **Prasetyntha, Yohanes B.** The incarnate Word of God: christian and Islamic doctrine on revelation: a study in comparative theology. R 2005, Pont. Univ. Gregoriana 92 pp. Exc. Diss; Bibl. 73-87.

12886 *Tacchini, Davide* Paolo il falsificatore: l'apostolo di Tarso nella visione dell'Islam radicale. AnScR 10 (2005) 259-280.

12887 *Troll, Christian W.* "Partner und Mitstreiter, nicht Herrscher: ein Gespräch mit Christian W. Troll über Koranexegese, christlich-muslimisches Zusammenleben und die Substanz der Religionen. WUB 35 (2005) 60-64.

### M8.5 **Religiones Indiae**, *Extremi Orientis*; **Africae**

12888 *Derrett, J. Duncan M.* Miracles of feeding: a Biblical-Buddhist dilemma (Mark 11,24). BeO 47 (2005) 89-99.

12889 *Dognini, Cristiano* Tommaso o Bartolomeo: chi evangelizzò l'India?. VP 88/2 (2005) 106-113.
12890 *Hanson, James* Was Jesus a Buddhist?. BudCS 25 (2005) 75-89.
12891 **Nugteren, Albertina** Belief, bounty, and beauty: rituals around sacred trees in India. SHR 108: Lei 2005, Brill x; 509 pp. 90-04-14601-6. Bibl. 445-505.
12892 *Scholz, Susanne* Bible and Yoga: toward an esoteric reading of biblical literature. BudCS 25 (2005) 133-146.
12893 *Schumann, Olaf* Opfer und Gebet in Indonesien. Opfer und Gebet. 2005 ⇒506. 55-60.
12894 *Thiede, Werner* Buday Jesús. SelTeol 44 (2005) 176-184;
12895 Buddha und Jesus: Gemeinsamkeiten und Differenzen. KuD 51/1 (2005) 33-51.
12896 **Uhlig, Helmut** Buda y Jesús: los vencedores del miedo. [T]*Leguillo, Manuel*: Castellón de la Plana 2005, Ellago 309 pp. 84958-81543.
12897 *Wilke, Annette* Opfer, Gebet und Gebetsopfer im Hinduismus. Opfer und Gebet. 2005 ⇒506. 55-60/20-34.
12898 *Wißmann, Hans* Gebet und Opfer bei den Azteken. Opfer und Gebet. 2005 ⇒506. 146-155.
12899 **Zieme, Peter** Magische Texte des uigurischen Buddhismus. Berliner Turfantexte 23: Turnhout 2005, Brepols 237 pp. 2-503-51840-0. Num. ill.

12900 *Adogame, Afeosemime* Prayer as action and instrument in the Aladura churches. Opfer und Gebet. 2005 ⇒506. 115-131;
12901 *Danfulani, Umar H.D.* Affliction, sacrifice and reconciliation: Tok Kum—the theology of the divinatory process among Chadic-speakers of the Jos plateau. Opfer und Gebet. 2005 ⇒506. 35-54.

# XVII. Historia Medii Orientis Biblici

## Q1 *Syria prae-Islamica, Canaan* Israel Veteris Testamenti

12902 **Albertz, Rainer** Die Exilszeit, 6. Jahrhundert v. Chr. 2001 ⇒17, 10163... 19,12197. [R]OLZ 100 (2005) 5-12 (*Pola, Thomas*);
12903 Israel in exile: the history and literature of the sixth century B.C.E. [T]*Green, David*: Studies in Biblical Literature 3: 2003 ⇒19, 12198. [R]JR 85 (2005) 305-307 (*Ahn, John*); JBL 124 (2005) 544-545 (*Grabbe, Lester L.*); RBLit (2005)* (*Grabbe, Lester L.*).
12904 *Bianchi, Francesco* Godolia contro Ismaele: la lotta per il potere politico in Giudea all'inizio della dominazione neobabilonese (Ger 40-41 e 2Re 25,22-26). RivBib 53 (2005) 257-275.
12905 *Carvalho, Corrine L.* The Philistines. BiTod 43 (2005) 159-164.
12906 **Chamaza, Galo W.V.** Die Rolle Moabs in der neuassyrischen Expansionspolitik. AOAT 321: Müns 2005, Ugarit-Verlag viiii; 203 pp. $75. 3-934628-61-3. Bibl. 169-193.
12907 *Chouaya, Mohsen* Les Phéniciens et les Puniques à travers l'historiographie gréco-latine, limites d'une vision variable. OrExp 2 (2005) 39-41.
12908 *Davies, Philip* Crypto-Minimalism. JSSt 50 (2005) 117-136.

12909 **Dever, William G.** What did the biblical writers know and when did they know it?: what archaeology can tell us about the reality of Ancient Israel. 2001 ⇒17,10177... 20,11657. [R]ThZ 61 (2005) 364-368 (*Zehnder, Markus*).

12910 Edom was there: new finds support biblical account. BArR 31/3 (2005) 14 [Gen 36,31; 2 Sam 8,13-4; 1 Kgs 11,15-16; 1 Chr 1,43].

12911 **Elayi, J.** 'Abd'Astart Ier/Straton de Sidon: un roi phénicien entre Orient et Occident. TEuph.S 12: P 2005, Gabalda 192 pp. €54. 2-85021-1631. 5 pl.

12912 *Finkelstein, Israel* (De)formation of the Israelite state: a rejoinder on methodology. NEA 68/4 (2005) 202-208;

12913 Archaeology, bible, and the history of the Levant in the Iron Age. Archaeologies of the Middle East. 2005 ⇒683. 207-222;

12914 A low chronology update: archaeology, history and bible. The bible and radiocarbon dating. 2005 ⇒952. 31-42.

12915 **Fox, Nili Sacher** In the service of the king: officialdom in ancient Israel and Judah. MHUC 23: 2000 ⇒16,10455... 19,12228. [R]JQR 95 (2005) 695-696 (*Brettler, Marc Z.*).

12916 *Gibert, Pierre* L'Ancien Testament troublé par l'histoire et l'archéologie. Études 4035 (2005) 497-508.

12917 *Gitin, Seymour* The Philistines: last days of the Philistines. Secrets of the bible. 2005 ⇒482. 26-32.

12918 *Goldhausen, Marco* Political centralization in the Syrian Jezira during the 3[rd] millennium: a case study in settlement hierarchy. AltOrF 32 (2005) 132-157.

12919 *Görg, Manfred* Philister. RLA 10/7-8. 2005 ⇒975. 526-528.

12920 **Gunneweg, Antonius H.J.** História de Israel—dos primórdios até Bar Kochba e de Theodor HERZL até os nossos días. [T]*Ottermann, Monika;* [E]*Schneider, Nélio*: Biblioteca de estudos do Antigo Testamento: São Paulo 2005, Loyola 392 pp. 85-89067-22-X.

12921 **Isserlin, Benedikt S.J.** Das Volk der Bibel: von den Anfängen bis zum Babylonischen Exil. [T]*Jaros-Deckert, Brigitte*: Kulturgeschichte der antiken Welt 84: 2001 ⇒17,10189. [R]ThLZ 130 (2005) 29-31 (*Dietrich, Walter*);

12922 The Israelites. 2001 ⇒17,10190...19,12239. [R]ThLZ 130 (2005) 29-31 (*Dietrich, Walter*).

12923 *Joannès, Francis* Von der Verzweiflung zum Neuanfang: das Leben der Deportierten in Babylon. WUB 37 (2005) 26-29.

12924 *Killebrew, Ann E.* Cultural homogenisation and diversity in Canaan during the 13th and 12th centuries BC. Archaeological perspectives. 2005 ⇒627. 170-175.

12925 **Kitchen, Kenneth Anderson** On the reliability of the Old Testament. 2003 ⇒19,12242; 20,11666. [R]OLZ 100 (2005) 271-274 (*Rüterswörden, Udo*); BS 162 (2005) 242-244 (*Merrill, Eugene H.*); RB 112 (2005) 267-273 (*Levine, Baruch A.*); BASOR 339 (2005) 117-118 (*Pace, James H.*); SdT 17 (2005) 190 (*Pompili, Marco*); HebStud 46 (2005) 395-397 (*Chavalas, Mark W.*).

12926 *Levy, Thomas E., al.*, Lowland Edom and the high and low chronologies: Edomite state formation, the bible and recent archaeological research in southern Jordan. The bible and radiocarbon dating. 2005 ⇒952. 129-163.

12927 **Lipiński, Edouard** The Aramaeans: their ancient history, culture, religion. OLA 100: 2000 ⇒16,10473...20,11670. [R]OLZ 100 (2005) 657-659 (*Younansardaroud, Helen*).

12928 **Liverani, Mario** Oltre la bibbia: storia antica di Israele. Storia e società: 2003 ⇒19,12245; 20,11672. RProtest. 60 (2005) 76-77 (*Noffke, Eric*); Bib. 86 (2005) 279-283 (*Ska, Jean-Louis*);

12929 Más allá de la biblia: historia antigua de Israel. Barc 2005, Crítica 531 pp. REstAg 40 (2005) 371-372 (*Mielgo, C.*);

12930 Israel's history and the history of Israel. T*Peri, Chiara; Davies, Philip, R.*: L 2005, Equinox xx; 427 pp. $60. 1-904768-76-8. Bibl. 369-406.

12931 **Lods, Adolphe** Israel: from its beginnings to the middle of the eighth century. L 2005, Kegan P. xxiv; 512 pp. 0-7103-1065-X. Bibl. 489-503.

12932 **Maier, Johann** Jüdische Geschichte in Daten. Beck'sche Reihe 1653: Mü 2005, Beck 176 pp. 3-406-52827-9.

12933 *Mattini, Giovanna* Edom e la bibbia. Geo-Archeologia 1 (2005) 117-187.

12934 *Mazar, Amihai* The debate over the chronology of the Iron Age in the southern Levant: its history, the current situation, and a suggested resolution. The bible and radiocarbon dating. 2005 ⇒952. 15-30.

12935 *Momrak, Kristoffer* The Phoenicians in the Mediterranean: trade, interaction and cultural transfer. AltOrF 32 (2005) 168-181.

12936 *Müller, Mogens* Hvad blev Palaestina kaldt i antikken?. DTT 68/2 (2005) 139-144.

12937 *Na'aman, Nadav* Two notes on the history of Ashkelon and Ekron in the late eighth-seventh centuries B.C.E. <1998>;

12938 Population changes in Palestine following Assyrian deportations <1993>;

12939 Province system and settlement pattern in southern Syria and Palestine in the Neo-Assyrian period <1995>;

12940 Rezin of Damascus and the land of Gilead <1995>. Ancient Israel. 2005 ⇒266. 68-75/200-219/220-237/40-55.

12941 *Nápole, Gabriel M.* La historia de Israel en los tiempos bíblicos: *cuestiones disputadas*. La palabra viva. 2005 ⇒746. 37-57.

12942 *Niesiolowski-Spanó, Lukasz* Kiedy napisano historie Izraela?. CoTh 75/4 (2005) 5-16. **P.**

12943 **Provan, Iain; Long, V. Philips; Longman, Tremper, III** A biblical history of Israel. 2003 ⇒19,12261; 20,11680. RBS 162 (2005) 376-377 (*Merrill, Eugene H.*); JETh 19 (2005) 219-221 (*Pracht, Jens*); RBLit 7 (2005) 215-218 (*Grabbe, Lester L*).

12944 **Sacchi, Paolo** The history of the second temple period. JSOT.S 285: 2000 ⇒16,10485... 20,11682. RHeyJ 46 (2005) 358-359 (*Taylor, N.H.*);

12945 Historia del giudaismo en la época del segundo templo. T*Castillo M., Carlos; Sánchez R., Adela; Piñero, Antonio*: 2004 ⇒20,11683. REstAg 40 (2005) 175-176 (*Mielgo, C.*).

12946 *Salamé-Sarkis, Hassan* Le royaume de Sidon au VIIe siècle av. J.-C. Syria 82 (2005) 139-148.

12947 *Schneider, C.E.J.* Marginal kingdoms: the role they played during the Omrid period. JSem 14/1 (2005) 17-39.

12948 *Skaist, Aaron* The order of the rulers of Emar. FKLEIN, J. 2005 ⇒ 79. 568-574.

12949 **Soggin, J. Alberto** Histoire d'Israël et de Juda: introduction à l'histoire d'Israël et de Juda des origines à la révolte de Bar Kokhba.

[T]*Bonnet, Corinne* 2004 ⇒20,11690. [R]Vies consacrées 77 (2005) 206-207 (*Luciani, Didier*); MoBi 163 (2005) 67 (*Boyer, Frédéric*).

12950 *Stieglitz, Robert* The Phoenicians: Early Iron Age geopolitics. Secrets of the bible. 2005 ⇒482. 20-22.

12951 *Sunseri, G. Bruno* I fenici nella storia universale di EFORO di Cuma. V Congresso di studi fenici. 2005 ⇒959. I, 407-415.

12952 **Tanner, Hans Andreas** Amalek: der Feind Israels und der Feind Jahwes: ein Studie zu den Amalektexten im Alten Testament. [D]*Dietrich, Walter*: TVZD: Z 2005, Theologischer 392 pp. $49. 3-2901-7340-2. Diss. Bern.

12953 *Thiel, Winfried* Geschichtliche, innenpolitische und religiöse Entwicklungen in Israel im 9.Jahrhundert v.Chr.;

12954 Israel und die Kulturen des alten Vorderen Orients <1981>. Gedeutete Geschichte. BThSt 71: 2005 ⇒316. 151-167/15-38.

12955 *Tryl, Fabian* Od Otniela do Saula: początki państwowości izraelskiej [From Othniel to Saul: the origins of Israel's state]. RBL 58 (2005) 5-28. **P**.

12956 *Tsirkin, J.B.* Fenicia y los cambios en Asia anterior cerca 1200 a. de C.: cuanto al problema del incio de la historia fenicia. V Congresso di studi fenici. 2005 ⇒959. I, 19-22.

12957 **Tubb, J.N.** Canaanites. People of the past: L 2002, British Museum Pr. 160 pp. 07141-27663. Ill. [R]AWE 2 (2003) 411-413 (*Swinnen, Ingrid*).

12958 *Vasholz, Robert I.* The patriarchs and the Philistines. Presbyterion 31 (2005) 112-113 [OTA 29,137].

12959 **Whitelam, Keith W.** L'invenzione dell'antico Israele: la storia negata della Palestina. [T]*Massardo, Paola*: Genova 2005, ECIG 285 pp. [R]RSO 78 (2004) 286-288 (*Garbini, Giovanni*).

12960 *Wood, Bryant G.* The rise and fall of the 13th-century Exodus-Conquest theory. JETS 48 (2005) 475-489 [OTA 30,21].

## Q2 Historiographia—*theologia historiae*

12961 **Alonso-Núñez, José Miguel** The idea of universal history in Greece: from HERODOTUS to the age of AUGUSTUS. 2002 ⇒18, 11277. [R]AnCl 74 (2005) 498-499 (*Hannick, Jean-Marie*).

12962 *Amherdt, François-Xavier* Bible et histoire selon Paul RICOEUR, 1. CEv 134 (2005) 54-57.

12963 *Anderson, Matthew R.* The reluctant biblical historian: a rhetorical rationale. Arc 33 (2005) 340-355.

12964 *Assmann, Aleida* Geschichte und Gedächtnis: drei Formen von Geschichtsschreibung. Das Alte Testament...Beiträge. ATM 10: 2005 ⇒718. 175-184.

12965 *Becker, Eve-Marie* Historiographieforschung und Evangelienforschung: zur Einführung in die Thematik. Antike Historiographie. BZNW 129: 2005 ⇒348. 1-17.

12966 *Blum, Erhard* Historiographie oder Dichtung?: zur Eigenart alttestamentlicher Geschichtsüberlieferung;

12967 *Cancik, Hubert* Zur Verwissenschaftlichung des historischen Diskurses bei den Griechen. Das Alte Testament...Beiträge. Ment. *Aristoteles; Herodotus; Rad, G. von*: 2005 ⇒718. 65-86/87-100.

[F]CONRAD, J.: Das AT–ein Geschichtsbuch?! 2005 ⇒27.

12968 *Dalley, Stephanie* Semiramis in history and legend: a case study in interpretation of an Assyrian historical tradition, with observations on archetypes in ancient historiography, on Euhemerism before Euhemerus, and on the so-called Greek ethnographic style. Cultural borrowings. Oriens et Occidens 8: 2005 ⇒652. 11-22.

12969 *Dever, William G.* Some methodological reflections on chronology and history-writing. The bible and radiocarbon dating. 2005 ⇒952. 413-421.

12970 *Dijkstra, M.* 'As for the other events...': annals and chronicles in Israel and the ancient Near East. The OT in its world. OTS 52: 2005 ⇒749. 14-44.

12971 **Dreytza, Manfred; Hopp, Traugott** Geschichte als Brücke?: neue Zugänge zum AltenTestament. Gießen 2005, Brunnen 52 pp. €5.

12972 [E]**Enenkel, K.A.E.; Pfeijffer, I.L.** The manipulative mode: political propaganda in antiquity: a collection of case studies. Mn.S 261: Lei 2005, Brill vi; 318 pp. €95/$128. 90041-42916. Bibl. [NTAb 49, 631].

12973 *Frankemölle, Hubert* 'Maranatha—unser Herr ist da!' (Offb 22, 20): die jüdische und christliche Bibel über den Sinn der Geschichte. Studien zum jüdischen Kontext. SBAB 37: 2005 <2000> ⇒210. 91-122.

12974 *Gehrke, Hans-Joachim* Die Bedeutung der (antiken) Historiographie für die Entwicklung des Geschichtsbewußtseins. Antike Historiographie. BZNW 129: 2005 ⇒348. 29-51.

12975 *Gibert, Pierre* Histoire biblique et conscience historienne: de la Genèse au 2e livre des Rois. RSR 93 (2005) 355-380.

12976 *Guillaume, Philippe* New light on the Nebiim from Alexandria: a chronography to replace the deuteronomistic history. JHScr 5/9 (2004)* [Sir 44-49].

12977 *Halpern, Baruch* Biblical versus Greek historiography: a comparison. Das Alte Testament...Beiträge. Ment. *Rad, G. von*: ATM 10: 2005 ⇒718. 101-127.

12978 **Hendel, Ronald** Remembering Abraham: culture, memory, and history in the Hebrew Bible. Oxf 2005, OUP xi; 200 pp. 019-5177-96-7. Bibl. 165-187.

12979 *Henige, David* In good company: problematic sources and biblical historicity. JSOT 30 (2005) 29-47.

12980 [E]**Hogan, Maurice P.** Order and history, 1: Israel and revelation. Collected Works of Eric Voegelin 14: 2001 <1956> ⇒19,12283. [R]IThQ 70 (2005) 92-94 (*McEvoy, James*).

12981 *Hunt, Alice W.* Bringing dialogue from cacophony: can BAKHTIN speak to biblical historiography?. PRSt 32/3 (2005) 325-337.

12982 *Kaiser, Otto* Von den Grenzen des Menschen: theologische Aspekte in HERODOTs Historiai I. [F]CONRAD, J. 2005 ⇒27. 9-36.

12983 **Kofoed, Jens Bruun** Text and history: historiography and the study of the biblical text. WL 2005, Eisenbrauns xiii; 298 pp. €34.50. 1-57506-094-9. Bibl. 249-272. [R]RBLit (2005)* (*Stith, D. Matthew*); SJOT 19 (2005) 111-134 (*Thompson, Thomas L.*).

12984 *Laato, Antti* Making history for Israel—foundation, blocking and policy. SEÅ 70 (2005) 145-176.

12985 *Lemche, Niels P.* Conservative scholarship on the move. SJOT 19 (2005) 203-252.

12986 *Link, Christian* Über den biblischen Umgang mit Geschichte im neuzeitlichen Kontext. Das Alte Testament...Beiträge. ATM 10: 2005 ⇒718. 185-197.

12987 *Loader, James A.* Das Alte Testament—ein Geschichtsbuch?. Das AT und die Kunst. ATM 15: 2005 ⇒711. 31-50.

12988 **Maier, Hans** Cronologia: contare gli anni da cristiano. 2000 ⇒16, 10538; 17,10256. [R]BeO 47 (2005) 277-279 (*Sardini, Davide*).

12989 *Marasco, Gabriele* Storiografia ed agiografia nella tarda antichità: un aspetto dell'incontro fra due culture. Sal. 67 (2005) 639-643.

12990 *Mehl, Andreas* Geschichtsschreibung in und über Rom;

12991 *Meissner, Burkhard* Anfänge und frühe Entwicklungen der griechischen Historiographie. Antike Historiographie. BZNW 129: 2005 ⇒348. 111-136/83-109.

12992 *Meyer, Wilhelm H.* Histories of reading and readings of "history": a study of a group of South African students reading Mark 4:35-41. Neotest. 39 (2005) 141-162.

12993 *Molé Ventura, Concetta* Storia e narrativa nelle storie ecclesiastiche. Sal. 67 (2005) 799-827.

12994 **Morley, Neville** Theories, models, and concepts in ancient history. 2004 ⇒20,11731. [R]ArOr 73 (2005) 363-372 (*Navrátilová, Hana*).

12995 *Mulsow, Martin* Zur Geschichte der Anfangsgeschichten. Antike Historiographie. BZNW 129: 2005 ⇒348. 19-28.

12996 **Na'aman, Nadav** The past that shapes the present: the creation of biblical historiography in the late first temple period and after the downfall. 2002 ⇒18,11299. [R]Zion 70 (2005) 229-236 (*Talshir, Zipora*). **H.**

12997 *Na'aman, Nadav* Habiru-like bands in the Assyrian Empire and bands in biblical historiography. Ancient Israel. 2005 <2000> ⇒ 266. 298-304.

12998 *Nannini, Damián* El exilio de Judá: lectura teológica de una crisis histórica. RevBib 67 (2005) 133-162.

12999 *Nijboer, Albert J.* The Iron Age in the Mediterranean: a chronological mess or 'trade before the flag', Part II. AWE 4 (2005) 255-277.

13000 *Noël, Damien* La recherche de l'historien. CEv 131 (2005) 36-55.

13001 **Organ, Barbara E.** Is the bible fact or fiction?: an introduction to biblical historiography. 2004 ⇒20,11735. [R]RBLit 7 (2005) 511-512 (*Noll, K.L.*).

13002 *Peterson, Erik* Zum urchristlichen Geschichtsverständnis. Peterson: Lukasevangelium und Synoptica. 2005 ⇒277. 427-431.

13003 **Porciani, Leone** Prime forme della storiografia greca: prospettiva locale e generale nella narrazione storica. 2001 ⇒17,10267; 18, 11303. [R]Gn. 77 (2005) 466-468 (*Patzek, Barbara*).

13004 *Rad, Gerhard von* The beginnings of historical writing in ancient Israel. From Genesis. 2005 <1944> ⇒283. 125-153.

13005 *Raurell, Frederic* La noció d'historia en la bíblia hebrea. RCatT 30 (2005) 331-348.

13006 **Reinmuth, Eckart** Neutestamentliche Historik: Probleme und Perspektiven. ThLZ.Forum 8: 2003 ⇒19,12304. [R]ThLZ 130 (2005) 1068-1069 (*Söding, Thomas*).

13007 *Römer, Franz* Biographisches in der Geschichtsschreibung der frühen römischen Kaiserzeit. Antike Historiographie. BZNW 129: 2005 ⇒348. 137-155.

13008 **Scolnic, Benjamin Edidin** If the Egyptians drowned in the Red Sea where are pharaoh's chariots?: exploring the historical dimension of the bible. Lanham 2005, University Press of America (10); 198 pp. 0-7618-3147-9. Bibl. 193-198.

13009 *Seybold, Klaus* Krise der Geschichte: geschichtstheologische Aspekte im Moselied Dt 32. [F]CONRAD, J.: ABIG 17: 2005 ⇒27. 59-80.

13010 *Siegert, Folker* L'antiquité a-t-elle connu la notion de vérité historique?: quelques extraits de POLYBE. ASEs 22/2 (2005) 455-464.

13011 **Siniscalco, Paolo** Il senso della storia: studi sulla storiografia cristiana antica. Armarium 11: 2003 ⇒19,12309. [R]Aug. 45 (2005) 590-592 (*Malaspina, Elena*).

13012 **Stenhouse, William** Reading inscriptions and writing ancient history: historical scholarship in the late Renaissance. BICS.S 86: L 2005, Institute of Classical Studies, University of London School of Advanced Study x; 203 pp. 0-900587-98-9. Bibl. 177-194.

13013 *Thiel, Winfried* Verfehlte Geschichte im Alten Testament. Gedeutete Geschichte. BThSt 71: 2005 <1986> ⇒316. 64-89.

13014 *Timm, Hermann* Ein Geschichtsbuch?. Das AT und die Kunst. Ment. *Rad, G. von*: ATM 15: 2005 ⇒711. 15-29.

13015 *Van Oorschot, Jürgen* Geschichte, Redaktion und Identität—Überlegungen anhand deuterojesajanischer Prophetien. [F]CONRAD, J.: ABIG 17: 2005 ⇒27. 37-57.

13016 **Voegelin, Eric** Ordnung und Geschichte, 2: Israel und die Offenbarung: die Geburt der Geschichte. [E]*Jeremias, J.*; [ET]*Hartenstein, F.*; [T]*Uchegbu, U.; Winkler, N.* Periagoge: Mü 2005, Fink 318 pp. €34.90. 37705-37025;

13017 3: Israel und die Offenbarung: Mose und die Propheten. [E]*Jeremias, J.*; *Hartenstein, F.*; [T]*Uchegbu, U.; Winkler, N.*: Periagoge: Mü 2005, Fink 217 pp. €25.90. 37705-37033.

13018 **Wesselius, Jan-Wim** The origin of the history of Israel: HERODOTUS's Histories as blueprint for the first books of the bible. JSOT.S 345: 2002 ⇒18,11311; 19,12317. [R]HeyJ 46 (2005) 526-27 (*Madigan, Patrick*).

13019 *Wischmeyer, Oda* Orte der Geschichte und der Geschichtsschreibung in der frühjüdischen Literatur;

13020 *Wischmeyer, Wolfgang* Wahrnehmungen von Geschichte in der christlichen Literatur zwischen Lukas und EUSEBIUS: die chronographische Form der Bischofslisten;

13021 *Witte, Markus* Von den Anfängen der Geschichtswerke im Alten Testament—eine forschungsgeschichtliche Diskussion neuerer Gesamtentwürfe. Antike Historiographie. BZNW 129: 2005 ⇒348. 157-169/263-276/53-81.

13022 *Zenger, Erich* Peculiarità e significato delle narrazioni storiche di Israele. Introduzione AT. 2005 ⇒1159. 285-289.

## Q3 *Historia Ægypti*—Egypt

13023 *Ager, S.L.* Familiarity breeds: incest and the Ptolemaic dynasty. JHS 125 (2005) 1-34 [NTAb 50,359].

13024 *Agut-Labordère, D.* Le sens du *Décret de Cambyze*. TEuph 29 (2005) 9-16.

13025 **Baud, Michel** Famille royale et pouvoir sous l'Ancien Empire égyptien. 1999, 2 vols. ⇒15,10460... 19,12324. [R]BiOr 62 (2005) 32-35 (*Gundlach, Rolf*).

13026 *Bourriau, Janine, al.*, The Second Intermediate Period and early New Kingdom at Deir al-Barsha. Ä&L 15 (2005) 101-129.

13027 **Brewer, Douglas J.** Ancient Egypt: foundations of a civilization. L 2005, Longman xvi; 213 pp. 0-582-77253-2. Bibl. 204-208.

13028 *Broekman, Gerard P.F.* The reign of Takeloth II, a controversial matter. GöMisz 205 (2005) 21-35.

13029 **Capponi, Livia** Augustan Egypt: the creation of a Roman province. L 2005, Routledge xiv; 308 pp. £57.

13030 *Carrez-Maratray, J.-Y.* Psammétique le tyran: pouvoir, usurpation et alliances en Méditerranée orientale au IVe siècle av. J.-C. TEuph 30 (2005) 37-63.

13031 **Chadwick, Robert** First civilizations: ancient Mesopotamia and ancient Egypt. L [2]2005, Equinox xviii; 269 pp. $30. 1-904768-77-6. Bibl. 250-261.

13032 [ET]**Eldamaty, Mamdouh** Ein prolemäisches Priesterdekret aus dem Jahr 186 v. Chr.: eine neue Version Philensis II in Kairo. APF.B 20: Mü 2005, Saur xvii; 92 pp. 3-598-77595-4. Bibl. viii-xv.

13033 **Favry, Nathalie** Le nomarque sous le règne de Sésostris Ier. Institutions dans l'Égypte ancienne 1: 2004 ⇒20,11770. [R]BiOr 62 (2005) 464-466 (*Franke, Detlef*).

13034 *Fletcher, Joann* The decorated body in ancient Egypt: hairstyles, cosmetics and tattoos. The clothed body. 2005 ⇒628. 3-13 [Judg 16,1-31].

13035 **Goyon, Jean-Claude** De L'Afrique à l'Orient: l'Égypte des pharaons et son rôle historique 1800-330 avant notre ère. P 2005, Ellipses 382 pp. 2-7298-1944-4. Bibl. 361-363.

13036 **Hawass, Zahi** Tutankhamun and the golden age of the pharaohs. Wsh 2005, National Geographic Society 287 pp. 0-7922-3873-7. Photographs by *Kenneth Garrett*; Bibl. 281-283.

13037 **Homoth-Kuhs, Clemens** Phylakes und Phylakon–Steuer im griechisch-römischen Ägypten: ein Beitrag zur Geschichte des antiken Sicherheitswesens. APF.B 17: Mü 2005, Saur xiii; 222 pp. Bibl. x-xii.

13038 **Höveler-Müller, Michael** Am Anfang war Ägypten: die Geschichte der pharaonischen Hochkultur von der Frühzeit bis zum Ende des Neuen Reiches, ca. 4000-1070 v.Chr.. Kulturgeschichte der antiken Welt 101: Mainz 2005, Von Zabern 303 pp. €40. 3-8053-3444-3. Num. ill.

13039 *Junge, Friedrich* Ägyptische Texte: Hymnus vom Sieg König Ramses' III. über die Seevölker in seinem 8. Jahr. Staatsverträge. TUAT N.F. 2: 2005 ⇒661. 230-245.

13040 **Maree, Marcel** Pharaohs and queens. L 2005, British Museum 48 pp. 0-7141-3109-1.

13041 **Midant-Reynes, Béatrix** Aux origines de l'Egypte: du néolithique à l'émergence de l'état. P 2003, Fayard 441 pp. 2-7028-8447-4. Préf. *Jean Guilaine* et *Nicolas Grimal*; Bibl. 391-418.

13042 *Moeller, Nadine* The First Intermediate Period: a time of famine and climate change?. Ä&L 15 (2005) 153-167.

13043 *Moers, Gerald; Münch, Hans-Hubertus* Kursorisches zur Konstruktion liebender Körper im pharaonischen Ägypten. Perspectives on the Song of Songs. 2005 ⇒401. 136-149.

13044 **Morkot, Robert G.** The Egyptians: an introduction. L 2005, Routledge x; 245 pp. £13. 0-415-27104-9. 24 fig.; Bibl. 231-239.

13045 **Morris, Ellen Fowles** The architecture of imperialism: military bases and the evolution of foreign policy in Egypt's New Kingdom. PÄ 22: Lei 2005, Brill xvii; 891 pp. €229. 90-04-14036-0. Bibl. 829-879.

13046 **Mrsich, Tycho Quirinus** Rechtsgeschichtliches zur Ackerverpachtung auf Tempelland nach demotischem Formular. 2003 ⇒19, 12371. [R]OLZ 100 (2005) 28-30 (*Müller-Wollermann, Renate*); BiOr 62 (2005) 489-495 (*Martin, Cary J.*).

13047 **Muhs, Brian P.** Tax receipts, taxpayers, and taxes in early Ptolemaic Thebes. UCOIP 126: Ch 2005, Oriental Institute xxv; 262 pp. $110. 1-885923-30-9. Bibl. xvii-xxv.

13048 *Müller, Marcus* Die Auswirkungen des Krieges auf die altägyptische Gesellschaft. Krieg–Gesellschaft–Institutionen. 2005 ⇒672. 89-116.

13049 *Nibbi, Alessandra* The Two Lands–again. DiscEg 61 (2005) 67-71.

13050 *Niccacci, Alviero* Egypt and Israel: an overview. BiTod 43 (2005) 147-152.

13051 [E]**Pantalacci, Laure; Berger-El-Naggar, Catherine** Des Néferkarê aux Montouhotep: travaux archéologiques en cours sur la fin de la VIe dynastie et la Première Période Intermédiaire. TMO 40: Lyon 2005, Maison de l'Orient 303 pp. €38. 2-906364-82-1.

13052 *Peeters, Christoph; Verstraeten, Gert; Willems, Harco* Where did Djehutihotep erect his colossal statue?. ZÄS 132/2 (2005) 173-189.

13053 [E]**Pernigotti, Sergio** Scuola e cultura nell'Egitto del Nuovo Regno: le "Miscellanee neo-egiziane". Testi del Vicino Oriente antico, 1: letteratura egiziana classica 6: Brescia 2005, Paideia 147 pp. €15. 80. 88-394-0711-1.

13054 *Quack, Joachim F.* Medien der Alltagskultur in Ägypten und ihre Auswirkungen auf Palästina. Medien im antiken Palästina. FAT 2/10: 2005 ⇒646. 237-268.

13055 **Quirke, Stephen** Titles and bureaux of Egypt 1850-1700 BC. 2004 ⇒20,11803. [R]BiOr 62 (2005) 234-237 (*Doxey, D.M.*).

13056 **Redford, Donald B.** The wars in Syria and Palestine of Thutmose III. Culture and history of the Ancient Near East 16: 2003 ⇒19, 12376. [R]OLZ 100 (2005) 17-23 (*Müller, Marcus*); ArOr 73 (2005) 503-505 (*Mynářová, Jana*);

13057 From slave to pharaoh: the black experience of ancient Egypt. 2004 ⇒20,11804. [R]BASPap 42 (2005) 283-284 (*Verhoogt, Arthur*).

13058 *Rehm, Ellen* 'Auf zu den Ufern des Nils': Vorderasiatica in Ägypten im 1. Jahrtausend v.Chr. UF 37 (2005) 491-516.

13059 **Reiter, Fabian** Die Nomarchen des Arsinoites: ein Beitrag zum Steuerwesen im römischen Ägypten. PapyCol 31: 2004 ⇒20, 11806. [R]CRAI (2005/4) 1348-1352 (*Dentzer, Jean-Marie*).

13060 **Rice, Michael** Egypt's making: the origins of ancient Egypt 5000-2000 BC. 2003 ⇒19,12379. [R]BiOr 62 (2005) 460-463 (*Ciałowicz, Krzysztof*).

13061 **Richards, Janet** Society and death in ancient Egypt: mortuary landscapes of the Middle Kingdom. C 2005, CUP 262 pp. £45. 0-5621-84033-3. Bibl. 221-240.

13062 *Rolandi, Marco* Rapporti fra stato e templi nell'Egitto tolemaico: alcuni esempi. Aeg. 85 (2005) 249-267.

13062 *Rolandi, Marco* Rapporti fra stato e templi nell'Egitto tolemaico: alcuni esempi. Aeg. 85 (2005) 249-267.

13063 *Roth, Ann M.* Gender roles in ancient Egypt. Companion to the ancient Near East. 2005 ⇒691. 211-218.

13064 **Roth, Silke** Die Königsmütter des Alten Ägypten: von der Frühzeit bis zum Ende der 12. Dynastie. ÄAT 46: 2001 ⇒17,10322... 20, 11807. [R]JEA 91 (2005) 207-215 (*Callender, V.G.*).

13065 *Shortland, A.J.* Shishak, King of Egypt: the challenges of Egyptian calendrical chronology. The bible and radiocarbon dating. 2005 ⇒ 952. 43-54.

13066 **Smith, Stuart Tyson** Wretched Kush: ethnic identities and boundaries in Egypt's Nubian empire. 2003 ⇒19,12392. [R]BiOr 62 (2005) 495-499 (*Lohwasser, Angelika*).

13067 *Sternberg-el Hotabi, Heike* Ägyptische Texte: aus den Annalen Thutmosis' III.: erster Feldzug gegen Megiddo;

13068 Ägyptische Texte: eine Beuteliste aus den libyschen Kriegen des Königs Merenptah. Staatsverträge. 2005 ⇒661. 212-220/228-229.

13069 **Straus, Jean A.** L'achat et la vente des esclaves dans l'Égypte romaine. 2004 ⇒20,11813. [R]SCI 24 (2005) 304-310 (*Fikhman, I.F.*).

13070 **Tallet, Pierre** Sésostris III et la fin de la XIIe dynastie. P 2005, Pygmalion 332 pp. 2-85704-851-3. Bibl. 319-329.

13071 *Thijs, Ad* In search of King Herihor and the penultimate ruler of the 20th dynasty. ZÄS 132/1 (2005) 73-91.

13072 **Torallas Tover, Sofía** Identidad lingüística e identidad religiosa en el Egipto grecorromano. Series Minor 11: Barc 2005, Acadèmia de Bones Lletres 116 pp. 84-93328456.

13073 **Veïsse, Anne-Emanuelle** Les 'revoltes égyptiennes': recherches sur les troubles interieurs en Égypte du règne de Ptolémée III à la conquête romaine. StHell 41: 2004 ⇒20,11817. [R]CRAI (2005/4) 1308-1310 (*Desanges, Dehan*).

13074 **Verhoogt, Arthur M.F.W.** Regaling officials in Ptolemaic Egypt: a dramatic reading of official accounts from the Menches Papers (P.L. Bat.32). PLB 32: Lei 2005, xiii; 239 pp. 90-04-14226-6. Bibl. 217-220.

13075 **Vernus, Pascal** Affairs and scandals in ancient Egypt. [T]*Lorton, D.* 2004 ⇒20,11818. [R]AJA 109 (2005) 298-299 (*Wilfong, T.G.*).

13076 **Vittmann, Günter** Ägypten und die Fremden im ersten vorchristlichen Jahrtausend. Kulturgeschichte der Antiken Welt 97: 2003 ⇒ 19,12397. [R]BiOr 62 (2005) 37-39 (*Spalinger, Anthony*).

13077 **Warburton, David** Egypt and the Near East: politics in the Bronze Age. 2001 ⇒17,10334... 20,11820. [R]AfO 51 (2005-2006) 371-373 (*Liverani, Mario*).

13078 **Wedel, Carola** Nofretete und das Geheimnis von Amarna. Zaberns Bildbände zur Archäologie: Mainz 2005, Von Zabern 96 pp. €30. 3-8053-3544-X. Num. ill.

13079 *Weißflog, Kay* Der König als Kind in Altägypten und im Alten Testament. leqach 6 (2005) 115-152.

13080 *Westbrook, Raymond* Patronage in the ancient Near East. JESHO 48 (2005) 210-233 [1 Kgs 17,8-24; 2 Kgs 4,8-37; 8,1-6].

13081 **Wettengel, Wolfgang** Die Erzählung von den beiden Brüdern: der Papyrus d'Orbiney und die Königsideologie der Ramessiden. OBO 195: 2003 ⇒19,10043. [R]BiOr 62 (2005) 219-223 (*Simon, Henrike*); WO 35 (2005) 198-202 (*Quack, Joachim Friedrich*).

13082 **Wilson, Kevin A.** The campaign of Pharaoh Shoshenq I into Palestine. FAT 2/9: Tü 2005, Mohr S. viii; 151 pp. €39. 3-16-148270-0. Diss. Johns Hopkins; Bibl. 135-44. RUF 37 (2005) 838-42 (*Schweitzer, S.D.*).

13083 *Yunusov, M.M.* Baalat Gubl and Hathor: the history of relations between Byblos and Egypt in the periods of the Old and Middle Kingdom. VDI 2 (2005) 3-13. **R**.

## Q4.0 Historia Mesopotamiae

13084 *Arkhipov, I.S.* A palace revolution in Carchemish about 1763 BC. VDI 3 (2005) 236-242. **R**.

13085 **Arnold, Bill T.** Who were the Babylonians?. 2004 ⇒20,11826. RRBLit (2005)* (*Cathey, Joseph*).

13086 E**Averbeck, Richard E.; Chavalas, Mark William; Weisberg, David B.** Life and culture in the ancient Near East. 2003 ⇒19,492. RRStR 31 (2005) 150-151 (*Nakhai, Beth Alpert*).

13087 *Banjevic, Boris* Ancient eclipses and the fall of Babylon. Akkadica 126 (2005) 169-193.

13088 *Breier, Idan* Political factors in the decline of the Neo Assyrian empire. Shnaton 15 (2005) 97-128. **H**.

13089 **Cancik-Kirschbaum, Eva** Die Assyrer. 2003 ⇒19,12411. ROLZ 100 (2005) 47-9 (*Baltrusch, Ernst*).

**Chadwick, R.** First civilizations 2005 ⇒13031.

13090 **Charpin, Dominique; Dietz, Otto Edzard; Stol, Marten** Mesopotamien: die altbabylonische Zeit. Annäherungen 4; OBO 160/4: 2004 ⇒20,11533. RArOr 73 (2005) 259-262 (*Hruška, Blahoslav*); RBLit 7 (2005) 56-60 (*Dahl, Jacob*).

13091 *Charvát, Petr* The ancient Sumerians in the tides of time. Archaeologies of the Middle East. 2005 ⇒683. 271-285.

13092 **Dietrich, Manfried** The Babylonian correspondance of Sargon and Sennacherib. State Archives of Assyria 17: 2003 ⇒19,12417. RBiOr 62 (2005) 82-86 (*Novotny, Jamie R.*).

13093 **Edzard, Dietz Otto** Geschichte Mesopotamiens: von den Sumeren bis zu Alexander dem Grossen. 2004 ⇒20,11839. RHZ 281 (2005) 146-148 (*Meyer, Jan-Waalke*).

13094 *Eph'al, Israel* Esarhaddon, Egypt, and Shubria: politics and propaganda. JCS 57 (2005) 99-111 [OTA 30,19].

13095 *Forest, Jean-Daniel* The state: the process of state formation as seen from Mesopotamia. Archaeologies of the Middle East. 2005 ⇒683. 184-206.

13096 *Foster, Benjamin R.* Shuruppak and the Sumerian city state. MDIAKONOFF, M. 2005 ⇒36. 71-88.

13097 *Freydank, Helmut* Zu den Eponymenfolgen des 13. Jahrhunderts v. Chr. in Dūr-Katlimmu. AltOrF 32 (2005) 45-56.

13098 *Fuchs, Andreas* War das Neuassyrische Reich ein Militärstaat?. Krieg–Gesellschaft–Institutionen. 2005 ⇒672. 35-60.

13099 *Galter, Hannes D.* Textanalyse assyrischer Königsinschriften: der Aufstand des Puzur-Sîn. SAA Bulletin 14 (2002-2005) 1-21.

13100 **Gasche, Hermann** Dating the fall of Babylon: a reappraisal of second-millennium chronology. 1998 ⇒14,9724... 17,10356. RJNES 64 (2005) 214-215 (*Liverani, Mario*).

13101 *Gehlken, Erlend* Childhood and youth, work and old age in Babylonia—a statistical analysis. Approaching the Babylonian economy. AOAT 330: 2005 ⇒915. 89-120.

13102 [T]**Glassner, Jean-Jacques** Mesopotamian Chronicles. [E]*Foster, Benjamin R.* 2004 ⇒20,11844. [R]RBLit (2005)* (*Van der Spek, R.J.*).

13103 *Grayson, A. Kirk* Shalmaneser III and the Levantine states: the "Damascus coalition rebellion". JHScr 5/4 (2004)*.

13104 *Hagens, Graham* The Assyrian king list and chronology: a critique. Or. 74 (2005) 23-41.

13105 *Hecker, Karl* Akkadische Texte. Staatsverträge. TUAT N.F. 2: 2005 ⇒661. 27-93;

13106 'Kundbar werde mir deine Sehnsucht...': Eros und Liebe im Alten Orient. Perspectives on the Song of Songs. 2005 ⇒401. 163-179.

13107 **Heimpel, Wolfgang** Letters to the King of Mari. 2003 ⇒19,12431; 20,11846. [R]JESHO 48 (2005) 326-327 (*Van De Mieroop, Marc*); RBLit 7 (2005) 50-53 (*Wasserman, Nathan*).

13108 **Hilgert, Markus** Drehem administrative documents from the Reign of Amar-Suena. OIP 121: 2003 ⇒19,12432. [R]BiOr 62 (2005) 543-546 (*Bakker, J.A.*).

13109 *Huot, Jean-Louis* Vers l'apparition de l'état en Mésopotamie: bilan des recherches récentes. Annales 60 (2005) 953-973.

13110 *Hurowitz, Victor* Hammurabi in Mesopotamian tradition. [F]KLEIN, J. 2005 ⇒79. 497-532.

13111 *Limet, Henri* La royauté en Mésopotamie: mort et succession du roi. RANT 2 (2005) 295-308.

13112 *Livingstone, Alasdair* Taima' and Nabonidus: it's a small world. [F]MILLARD, A.: LHBOTS 426: 2005 ⇒102. 29-39.

13113 **Luukko, Mikko; Van Buylaere, Greta** The political correspondence of Esarhaddon. State Archives of Assyria 16: 2002 ⇒18, 11395... 20,11858. [R]Or. 74 (2005) 426-434 (*Ponchia, Simonetta*); OLZ 100 (2005) 616-621 (*Oelsner, J.*).

13114 **Mattila, Raija** Legal transactions of the royal court of Nineveh, part II: Assurbanipal through Sin-sarru-iskun. SAA 14: 2002 ⇒18, 11399. [R]BiOr 62 (2005) 68-82 (*Llop, Jaume*).

13115 *Na'aman, Nadav* Sargon II and the rebellion of the Cypriote kings against Shilṭa of Tyre. Ancient Israel. 2005 <1998> ⇒266. 118-28;

13116 The conquest of Yadnana according to Sargon II's inscriptions. Ancient Israel. 2005 <2001> ⇒266. 129-134;

13117 Sennacherib's 'letter to God' on his campaign to Judah. Ancient Israel. 2005 <1974> ⇒266. 135-152;

13118 Esarhaddon's treaty with Ba'al and Assyrian provinces along the Phoenician coast. Ancient Israel. 2005 <1994> ⇒266. 193-199;

13119 The Brook of Egypt and Assyrian policy on the border of Egypt. Ancient Israel. 2005 <1979> ⇒266. 238-264;

13120 An Assyrian residence at Ramat Raḥel?. Ancient Israel. 2005 <2001> ⇒266. 279-297;

13121 Forced participation in alliances in the course of the Assyrian campaigns to the west. Ancient Israel. 2005 <1991> ⇒266. 16-39;

13122 Tiglath-pileser III's campaigns against Tyre and Israel (734-732 BCE). Ancient Israel. 2005 <1995> ⇒266. 56-67;

13123 The historical portion of Sargon II's Nimrud inscription. Ancient Israel. 2005 <1994> ⇒266. 94-97;

13126 **Nagel, Wolfram; Strommenger, Eva; Eder, Christian** Von Gudea bis Hammurapi: Grundzüge der Kunst und Geschichte in Altvorderasien. Köln 2005, Böhlau xiv; 328 pp. €69.90. 3412-143049. 93 ill..

13127 *Neujahr, Matthew* When Darius defeated Alexander: composition and redaction in the dynastic prophecy. JNES 64 (2005) 101-107.

13128 *Neumann, Hans* Texte des 3.Jt. v.Chr. in sumerischer, akkadischer und hurritischer Sprache. Staatsverträge. 2005 ⇒661. 1-26.

13129 [E]**Pettinato, Giovanni** I re di Sumer, 1: iscrizioni reali presargoniche della Mesopotamia. Testi del Vicino Oriente antico 2/5: 2003 ⇒19,12450; 20,11866. [R]RBLit 7 (2005) 54-56 (*Gee, John*).

13130 **Poo, Mu-Chou** Enemies of civilization: attitudes toward foreigners in ancient Mesopotamia, Egypt, and China. Chinese philosophy and culture: Albany 2005, State Univ. of NY Pr. xviii; 211 pp. $30..

13131 *Pruzsinsky, Regine* Ein bibliographischer Wegweiser zur absoluten mesopotamischen Chronologie des 2. Jts. v. Chr.. Ä&L 15 (2005) 181-201;

13132 Zum Verständnis der assyrischen Distanzangaben: Beiträge zur assyrischen Chronologie. SAA Bulletin 14 (2002-2005) 23-31.

13133 [E]**Reynolds, Frances** The Babylonian correspondence of Esarhaddon: and letters to Assurbanipal and Sin-Sarru-Iskun from northern and central Babylonia. State Archives of Assyria 18: 2003 ⇒19, 12455; 20,11871. [R]BiOr 62 (2005) 86-89 (*Novotny, Jaime R.*); OLZ 100 (2005) 616-621 (*Oelsner, J.*).

13134 *Richardson, Seth* Axes against Ešnunna. Or. 74 (2005) 42-50.

13135 **Roux, Georges** Irak in der Antike. [T]*Odenhardt-Donvez, I.*; [E]*Renger, Johannes*: Sonderbände der antiken Welt, Zaberns Bildbände zur Archäologie: Mainz 2005, Von Zabern 292 pp. €50. 3-8053-33-77-3.

13136 **Saggs, Henry W.F.** Völker im Lande Babylon. Stu 2005, Theiss 222 pp. €24.90. 3-8062-1864-1. Num. ill. [ThPQ 153,438].

13137 **Selz, Gebhard J.** Sumerer und Akkader: Geschichte—Gesellschaft —Kultur. Mü 2005, Beck 126 pp. €7.90. 3-406-508-74-X. [R]Mes. 40 (2005) 181 (*Lippolis, Carlo*).

13138 [E]**Seminara, Stefano** Guerra e pace ai tempi di Hammu-rapi. Testi del Vicino Oriente antico, 2: letterature mesopotamiche 7/1: 2004 ⇒20,11876. [R]Sal. 67 (2005) 178-179 (*Marin, Maurizio*).

13139 **Seri, Andrea** Local power in Old Babylonian Mesopotamia. L 2005, Equinox xvi; 240 pp. 18455-30101. Diss. Michigan.

13140 *Sharlach, T.M.* Diplomacy and rituals of politics at the Ur III court. JCS 57 (2005) 17-29 [OTA 30,8].

13141 *Talon, Philippe* Une inscription de Tukulti-Ninurta I. [F]FINET, A.: Subartu 16: 2005 ⇒40. 125-133.

13142 *Tavares, A. Augusto* O ocidente em textos mesopotâmicos e bíblicos. Did(L) 35 (2005) 13-22.

13143 **Van De Mieroop, Marc** A history of the ancient Near East ca. 3000-323 BC. Blackwell History of the Ancient World 1: 2004 ⇒ 20,11880. [R]Or. 74 (2005) 171-173 (*Liverani, Mario*);

13144 King Hammurabi of Babylon: a biography. Blackwell ancient lives: Oxf 2005, Blackwell xii; 171 pp. £45/15. 1-4051-2659-0/60-4. [R]BSOAS 68 (2005) 463 (*George, Andrew R.*).

13145 [T]**Vanstiphout, Herman L.J.** Epics of Sumerian kings: the matter of Aratta. SBL.Writings from the Ancient World 20: 2003 ⇒19, 12470; 20,11883. [R]RBLit 7 (2005) 62-69 (*Hurowitz, Victor A.*).

13146 *Waters, Matthew* Media and its discontents. JAOS 125 (2005) 517-533.
13147 *Wilkinson, T.J., al.*, Landscape and settlement in the Neo-Assyrian Empire. BASOR 340 (2005) 23-56.
13148 **Yamada, Shigeo** The construction of the Assyrian Empire: a historical study of the inscriptions of Shalmanesar III (859-824 B.C.) relating to his campaigns to the west. 2000 ⇒16,10683... 18,11419. [R]AWE 3 (2004) 402-403 (*Glatz, Claudia; Matthews, Roger*).
13149 *Zadok, Ran* On Anatolians, Greeks and Egyptians in 'Chaldean' and Achaemenid Babylonia. TelAv 32/1 (2005) 76-106.

## Q4.5 *Historia Persiae*—**Iran**

13150 **Allen, Lindsay** The Persian Empire:a history. Ch 2005, Univ. of Chicago Pr. 208 pp. $40.
13151 *Baruchi, Yosi* Arsham: a biography of a senior Persian official. Shnaton 15 (2005) 129-164. **H.**
13152 **Briant, Pierre** From Cyrus to Alexander: a history of the Persian Empire. [T]*Daniels, Peter T.* 2002 ⇒18,11423... 20,11895. [R]ZDPV 121 (2005) 86 (*Massmann, L.*);
13153 Darius dans l'ombre d'Alexandre. 2003 ⇒19,12484; 20,11893. [R]Annales 60 (2005) 1071-1072 (*Mossé, Claude*); Or. 74 (2005) 440-442 (*Koch, Heidemarie*).
13154 *Brosius, Maria Pax persica*: königliche Ideologie und Kriegführung im Achämenidenreich. Krieg–Gesellschaft–Institutionen. 2005 ⇒672. 135-161.
13155 **Fried, Lisbeth S.** The priest and the great king: temple-palace relations in the Persian Empire. 2004 ⇒20,11896. [R]JBL 124 (2005) 546-548 (*Ristau, Kenneth A.*).
13156 *Gruen, Erich S.* Persia through the Jewish looking-glass. Cultural borrowings. Oriens et Occidens 8: 2005 ⇒652. 90-104.
13157 *Joannès, Francis* Les relations entre Babylonie et Iran au debut de la période achéménide: quelques remarques. Approaching the Babylonian economy. AOAT 330: 2005 ⇒915. 183-196.
13158 **Jullien, Christelle & Florence** Les *Actes de Mār Māri*. CSCO 602-604: 2003 ⇒19,9899. [R]OrChr 89 (2005) 234-235 (*Rist, Josef*).
13159 **Klinkott, Hilmar** Der Satrap: ein achaimenidischer Amtsträger und seine Handlungsspielräume. Oikumene, Studien zur antiken Weltgeschichte 1: Fra 2005, Antike 578 pp. €69.90.
13160 *Koch, Heidemarie* Achämenidische Verwaltung und Hinweise auf sie in den Randgebieten des persischen Großreiches. ANES 42 (2005) 253-276;
13161 Texte aus Iran. Staatsverträge. TUAT N.F. 2: 2005 ⇒661. 283-306.
13162 *Lincoln, Bruce* Rebellion and treatment of rebels in the Achaemenian Empire. AfR 7 (2005) 167-179.
13163 *Tuplin, Christopher* Darius' accession in (the) Media. [F]MILLARD, A.: LHBOTS 426: 2005 ⇒102. 217-244;
13164 Medes in Media, Mesopotamia, and Anatolia: empire, hegemony, domination or illusion?. AWE 3 (2004) 223-51.
13165 **Wiesehöfer, Josef** Iraniens, Grecs et Romains. StIr 32: P 2005, Association pour l'avancement des études iraniennes 155 pp. 29106-40183.

Q5 *Historia Anatoliae*—**Asia Minor, Hittites** [⇒T8.2]; *Armenia*

13166 *Archi, Alfonso* Remarks on the Early Empire documents. AltOrF 32 (2005) 225-229.

13167 *Bordreuil, Pierre* Tabal sur un sceau-cylindre araméen. RANT 2 (2005) 385-388.

13168 **Brélaz, Cédric** La sécurité publique en Asie Mineure sous le Principat (I^er^-III^ème^ s. ap. J.-C.): institutions municipales et institutions impériales. SBA 32: Ba 2005, Schwabe xi; 530 pp. €82.50. 37965-22009.

13169 **Bryce, Trevor R.** The kingdom of the Hittites. Oxf 2005, OUP xix; 554 pp. £70. 0-19-928132-7. Bibl. 496-535.

13170 *Carruba, Onofrio* Tuthalija 00I. (und Hattusili II.). AltOrF 32 (2005) 246-271.

13171 *Casabonne, Olivier; Vos, Julien de* Chypres, Rhodes et l'Anatolie méridionale: la question ionienne. RANT 2 (2005) 83-102.

13172 *Casabonne, Olivier; Lebrun, René* Le Tabal de la préhistoire au début de l'ère chrétienne. RANT 2 (2005) 383-384.

13173 *Del Monte, Giuseppe F.* The Hittite ḫerem. [M]DIAKONOFF, M. 2005 ⇒36. 21-45.

13174 *Dmitriev, Sviatoslav* The history and geography of the province of Asia during its first hundred years and the provincialization of Asia Minor. At. 93 (2005) 71-133.

13175 *Forlanini, Massimo* Hattušili II.—Geschöpf der Forscher oder vergessener König?: ein Vorschlag zu seiner Stellung in der hethitischen Geschichte. AltOrF 32 (2005) 230-245.

13176 *Freu, Jacques* Des Grands Rois de Taraḫuntašša aux Grands Rois de Tabal. RANT 2 (2005) 399-417;

13177 Les Phrygiens en Tyanide et le problème des Muskis. RANT 2 (2005) 389-398.

13178 *Glatz, Claudia; Matthews, Roger* Anthropology of a frontier zone: Hittite-Kaska relations in Late Bronze Age north-central Anatolia. BASOR 339 (2005) 47-65.

13179 *Gräff, Andreas* Thoughts about the Assyrian presence in Anatolia in the early 2^nd^ millennium. AltOrF 32 (2005) 158-167.

13180 *Günbatti, Cahit* The texts of two treaties found at Kültepe. BTTK 69 (2005) 759-780. **Turkish**.

13181 *Hawkins, John D.* Späthethitische Herrscherinschriften. Staatsverträge. TUAT N.F. 2: 2005 ⇒661. 151-159.

13182 **Healy, Mark** Qadesh 1300 BC: clash of the warriors. Praeger Illustrated Military History: Westport, CT 2005, Praeger 96 pp. $19.

13183 **Jakubiak, Krzysztof** The development of defence system of eastern Anatolia (the Armenian upland) from the beginning of the kingdom of Urartu to the end of antiquity. 2003 ⇒19,12511. [R]OLZ 100 (2005) 249-251 (*Martin, Lutz*).

13184 *Kelder, Jorrit* Greece during the Late Bronze Age. JEOL 39 (2005) 131-179.

13185 *Klengel, Horst* Studien zur hethitischen Wirtschaft: einleitende Bemerkungen. AltOrF 32 (2005) 3-22.

13186 **Klengel, Horst** Hattuschili und Ramses: Hethiter und Ägypter—ihr langer Weg zum Frieden. 2002 ⇒18,11458; 20,11917. [R]OLZ 100 (2005) 53-58 (*Bryce, Trevor*).

13187 *Klinger, Jörg* Staatsverträge mit dem Hethiterreich: der Vertrag Suppiluliumas I. mit Hukkana von Hajasa. 107-112;
13188 Staatsverträge mit dem Hethiterreich: die historischen Einleitungen der Arzawa-Verträge Mursilis II. mit Manapa-Tarhunta von Seha und Kupanta-Kurunta von Mira und Kuwalija. 124-129;
13189 Staatsverträge mit dem Hethiterreich: der Vertrag Tuthalijas von Hatti mit Kurunta von Tarhuntassa. 130-138;
13190 Der sogenannte Anitta-Text. 139-141;
13191 Das Testament Ḫattuşilis I. 142-146;
13192 Der Tatenbericht Şuppiluliumas I. (Auszug). Staatsverträge. TUAT N.F. 2: 2005 ⇒661. 147-150;
13193 Das Korpus der Kaškäer-Texte. AltOrF 32 (2005) 347-359.
13194 *Mazoyer, Michel* Télipinu au Tabal. RANT 2 (2005) 427-438.
13195 [E]**Melchert, H. Craig** The Luwians. HO 1/68: 2003 ⇒19,12514; 20,11921. [R]BiOr 62 (2005) 430-451 (*Singer, Itamar*).
13196 *Mora, Clelia* Grands rois, petits rois, gouvernants de second rang. RANT 2 (2005) 309-314.
13197 *Nemirovsky, A.A.* Mursilis II's 'Comprehensive annals': just a textological conventionality?. VDI 1 (2005) 3-14. **R.**
13198 *Porter, R.M.* Dating the Neo-Hittite kinglets of Gurgum/Maraş. Anatolica 29 (2003) 7-16.
13199 *Ramaekers Hue, Marie-Christine* Les lapicides du Tabal. RANT 2 (2005) 439-448.
13200 *Schwemer, Daniel* Staatsverträge mit dem Hethiterreich: der Vertrag zwischen Tuthalija von Hatti und Sunassura von Kizzuwatna. Staatsverträge. TUAT N.F. 2: 2005 ⇒661. 97-106.
13201 **Schweyer, Anne-Valérie** Les Lyciens et la mort: une étude d'histoire sociale. Varia anatolica 14: 2002 ⇒18,11466. [R]RAr (2005/2) 421-422 (*Le Dinahet, Marie-Thérèse*).
13202 *Skaist, Aaron* When did *Ini-Tešub* succeed to the throne of Carchemish?. UF 37 (2005) 609-619.
13203 *Soysal, Oğuz* Beiträge zur althethitischen Geschichte (III): kleine Fragmente historischen Inhalts. ZA 95 (2005) 121-144.
13204 *Strobel, Karl* State formation by the Galatians of Asia Minor: politico-historical and cultural processes in Hellenistic central Anatolia. Anatolica 28 (2002) 1-46.
13205 *Torri, Giulia* Militärische Feldzüge nach Ostanatolien in der mittelhethitischen Zeit. AltOrF 32 (2005) 386-400.
13206 *Uchitel, Alexander* Land tenure in Mycenaean Greece and the Hittite Empire: Linear B land-surveys from Pylos and Middle Hittite land-donations. JESHO 48 (2005) 473-486.
13207 **Van Dam, Raymond** Families and friends in late Roman Cappadocia. 2003 ⇒19,12519. [R]JR 85 (2005) 319-320 (*McGuckin, J.A.*).
13208 *Wilhelm, Gernot* Zur Datierung der älteren hethitischen Landschenkungsurkunden. AltOrF 32 (2005) 272-279;
13209 Staatsverträge mit dem Hethiterreich;
13210 Staatsverträge mit dem Hethiterreich: der Vertrag Suppiluliumas I. von Hatti mit Sattiwazza von Mitanni;
13211 Staatsverträge mit dem Hethiterreich: der Vertrag Suppiluliumas I. von Hatti mit Tette von Nuhasse. Staatsverträge. TUAT N.F. 2: 2005 ⇒661. 95-96/113-121/122-123.
13212 **Wittke, Anne-Maria** Mušker und Phryger: ein Beitrag zur Geschichte Anatoliens vom 12. bis 7.Jh. v.Chr. BTAVO.B 99: Wsb 2004, Reichert xvi; 389 pp.

## Q6.1 **Historia Graeciae classicae**

13213 **Bernal, Martin** Black Athena writes back: Martin Bernal responds to his critics. [E]*Moore, David Chioni* 2001 ⇒17,9817. [R]JNES 64 (2005) 146-150 (*Joffe, Alexander H.*).

13214 **Brown, John Pairman** Ancient Israel and ancient Greece: religion, politics, and culture. 2003 ⇒19,12522; 20,11932. [R]ArOr 73 (2005) 257-259 (*Břeňová, Klára*).

13215 **Hannah, Robert** Greek and Roman calendars: constructions of time in the classical world. L 2005, Duckworth vi; 170 pp. £17/$31. 07156-33015.

13216 [E]**Hansen, Mogens Herman** The imaginary polis: symposium, January 7-10, 2004. Acts of the Copenhagen Polis Centre 7; DVS.HFM 91: K 2005, Munksgaard 444 pp. 87-7304-310-9. The Royal Danish Academy of Sciences and Letters.

13217 **Hansen, Mogens Herman** The tradition of ancient Greek democracy and its importance for modern democracy. Historisk-filosofiske Meddelelser 93: K 2005, Munksgaard 75 pp. 87-7304-320-6.

13218 **Isaac, Benjamin** The invention of racism in classical antiquity. 2004 ⇒20,11933. [R]SCI 24 (2005) 288-291 (*Jones, Christopher*); JJS 56 (2005) 144-146 (*Williams, Margaret H.*); FrRu 12 (2005) 303 (*Bloch, René*); Zion 70 (2005) 553-558 (*Geiger, Joseph*).

13219 **Llewellyn-Jones, Lloyd** Aphrodite's tortoise: the veiled woman of ancient Greece. 2003 ⇒19,12527. [R]AJA 109 (2005) 117-119 (*Lee, Mireille M.*).

13220 [E]**O'Sullivan, James N.** XENOPHON Ephesius: De Anthia et Habrocome Ephesiacorum Libri V. Lp 2005, Teubner xxxiv; 128 pp. Bibl. xiii-xxix.

13221 **Siapkas, Johannes** Heterological ethnicity: conceptualizing identities in ancient Greece. AUU.Boreas 27: 2003 ⇒19,12530. [R]AJA 109 (2005) 304-305 (*Dakouri-Hild, A.*).

13222 **Zelnick-Abramovitz, R.** Not wholly free: the concept of manumission and the status of manumitted slaves in the ancient Greek world. Mn.S 266: Lei 2005, Brill vii, 385 pp. €119. 9004-145850.

13223 **Zournatzi, A.** Persian rule in Cyprus: source, problems, perspectives. P 2005, De Boccard 88 pp. €24. 96079-05288. Bibl.

## Q6.5 **Alexander, Seleucidae; historia Hellenismi**

13224 *Anson, Edward* Idumaean ostraca and early Hellenistic chronology. JAOS 125 (2005) 263-266;

13225 A note on the first regnal year of Philip III (Arrhidaeus). JCS 57 (2005) 127-128 [OTA 30,18].

13226 *Archibald, Zofia H.* Markets and exchange: the structure and scale of economic behaviour in the Hellenistic Age. Making, moving and managing. 2005 ⇒605. 1-26.

13227 **Barclay, John M.G.** Diaspora: i giudei nella diaspora mediterranea da Alessandro a Traiano (323 a.C.-117 d.C.). 2004 ⇒20,11939. [R]Materia giudaica 10 (2005) 432-437 (*Leoni, Tommaso*).

13228 **Bergmann, Marianne** Die Strahlen der Herrscher: theomorphes Herrscherbild und politische Symbolik im Hellenismus und in der römischen Kaisereit. 1998 ⇒14,9841; 15,10616. RAnCl 74 (2005) 607-608 (*Balty, Jean Ch.*).

13229 *Bloch, René* "Meine Mutter erzählte mir alles": Ezechiel Exagoge 34-35 und der Mythos. Jud. 61/2 (2005) 97-109.

13230 *Brant, Jo-Ann A.* Mimesis and dramatic art in Ezekiel the tragedian's Exagoge. Ancient fiction. SBL.Symp. 32: 2005 ⇒721. 129-47.

13231 *Brown, John P.* The privatization of Greek specialties in the Hellenistic world: drama, athletics, citizenship. RB 112 (2005) 536-66.

13232 *Carney, E.D.* Women and *dunasteia* in Caria. AJP 126/1 (2005) 65-91 [NTAb 49,573].

13233 *Chaniotis, Angelos* Victory' verdict: the violent occupation of territory in Hellenistic interstate relations. La violence dans les mondes grec et romain. 2005 ⇒870. 455-464.

13234 **Chaniotis, Angelos** War in the Hellenistic world: a social and cultural history. Oxf 2005, Blackwell 308 pp. £55/17. 0-631-22-607-9/8-7. 12 fig.

13235 **Clarke, Katherine** Between geography and history: Hellenistic constructions of the Roman world. 1999 ⇒15,10621... 19,12536. RAWE 4 (2005) 188-190 (*Alston, Richard*).

13236 *Collins, John J.* Anti-semitism in antiquity?: the case of Alexandria. Ancient Judaism. JSJ.S 95: 2005 ⇒626. 9-29 = AfR 7 (2005) 86-101.

13237 **Corò, Paola** Prebende templari in età Seleucide. History of the Ancient Near East, Monographs 8: Padova 2005, S.A.R.G.O.N. ix; 513 pp. 88-901286-2-3. Bibl. 505-513.

13238 *Dillery, J.* Greek sacred history. AJP 126 (2005) 505-526 [NTAb 50,359].

13239 *Erskine, Andrew* Approaching the Hellenistic world. Companion to the Hellenistic world. 2005 ⇒642. 1-15.

13240 **Fröhlich, Pierre** Les cités grecques et le contrôle des magistrats (IVe-1e siècle avant J.-C.). HEMGR 33: 2004 ⇒20,11947. RCRAI (2005/1) 440-442 (*Gauthier, Philippe*).

13241 *Gruen, Erich S.* Jews and Greeks. Companion to the Hellenistic world. 2005 ⇒642. 264-279.

13242 **Haag, Ernst** Das hellenistische Zeitalter: Israel und die Bibel im 4. bis 1. Jahrhundert v. Chr. Biblische Enzyklopädie 9: 2003 ⇒19, 12541; 20,11950. RBiLi 78 (2005) 273-275 (*Hieke, Thomas*).

13243 *Hagedorn, A.C.* 'Who would invite a stranger from abroad?': the presence of Greeks in Palestine in Old Testament times. The OT in its world. OTS 52: 2005 ⇒749. 68-93 [1 Kgs 7,13-50].

13244 **Hall, Jonathan M.** Hellenicity: between ethnicity and culture. Ch 2005 <2002>, Univ. of Chicago Pr. xxii; 312 pp. $30/£22.50. 022-63-13301. Bibl. [NTAb 50,437].

13245 **Holt, F.L.** Alexander the Great and the mystery of the elephant medallions. Berkeley 2005 <2003>, Univ. of California Pr. xv; 198 pp. $18/£12. 05202-44834. Bibl. [NTAb 49,634].

13246 *Hoover, Oliver D.* Dethroning Seleucus VII Philometor (Cybiosactes): epigraphical arguments against a late Seleucid monarch. ZPE 151 (2005) 95-99.

13247 E**Karageorghis, Vassos** The Greeks beyond the Aegean: from Marseilles to Bactria. 2003 ⇒19,12548. Symposium New York, 12 October 2002. RRB 112 (2005) 310-311 (*Balandier, Claire*).

13248 *Klumbies, Paul G.* Vorchristliches Erbe in nachchristlicher Zeit: Hellenismus und frühes Christentum von Paul-Gerhard Klumbies. Evangelische Aspekte 15/4 (2005) 7-11.

13249 **Kovelman, Arkady** Between Alexandria and Jerusalem: the dynamic of Jewish and Hellenistic culture. Brill Reference Library of Judaism 21: Lei 2005, Brill xiv; 177 pp. €109/$156. 9004-14402-1.

13250 **Ma, John** Antiochos III and the cities of western Asia Minor. 2002 ⇒19,12553. Rev. ed. $^{R}$IJCT 11 (2005) 463-468 (*Eckstein, A.M.*).

13251 *MacAdam, Henry I.* "Israel and Hellas": the biblical world and the culture of Greece and Rome. PJBR 4/2 (2005) 129-159.

13252 *Modrzejewski, Joseph Mélèze* L'evoluzione del giudaismo ellenizzato. Il mondo della bibbia 77 (2005) 32-37;

13253 Sems Zelte in der Fremde: die Entwicklung des hellenistischen Judentums. WUB 38 (2005) 40-43.

13254 *Ohanian, Laila* Alessandro e l'Egitto: aspetti religiosi nell'ideologia politica. Aeg. 85 (2005) 237-248.

13255 **Queyrel, François** Les portraits des Attalides: fonction et representation. BEFAR 308: 2003 ⇒19,12559. $^{R}$AJA 109 (2005) 317-318 (*Fullerton, Mark D.*).

13256 **Rathmann, Michael** Perdikkas zwischen 323 und 320: Nachlassverwalter des Alexanderreiches oder Autokrat?. DÖAW.PH 724: W 2005, Österr. Akad. der Wissenschaften 100 pp. €29 [HZ 283, 156s—Hans-Ulrich Wiemer].

13257 *Roller, Duane W.* Seleukos and Seleukia. AnCl 74 (2005) 111-118.

13258 $^{E}$**Runia, David T.; Sterling, Gregory E.** The Studia Philonica Annual: studies in Hellenistic Judaism: volume xvi 2004. Providence 2004, Brown University viii; 333 pp. $49. $^{R}$RBLit (2005)* (*Murray, Michele*).

13259 *Scheer, Tanja S.* The past in a Hellenistic present: myth and local tradition. Companion to the Hellenistic world. 2005 ⇒642. 216-231.

13260 Das Sternenverzeichnis des Hipparchos. WUB 38 (2005) 70.

13261 **Vasunia, Phiroze** The gift of the Nile: hellenizing Egypt from AESCHYLUS to ALEXANDER. 2001 ⇒17,10500; 20,11964. $^{R}$Gn. 77 (2005) 421-424 (*Barbantini, Silvia*).

13262 **Virgilio, Biagio** Lancia, diadema e porpora: il re e la regalità ellenistica. Studi ellenistici 14: $^{2}$2002 ⇒19,12566. $^{R}$At. 93 (2005) 327-334 (*Rocchi, Giovanna Daverio*).

13263 **Wiemer, Hans-Ulrich** Alexander der Große. Beck: Mü 2005, Beck 243 pp. 3-406-52887-2.

13264 *Wifstrand, Albert* The Roman Empire from the Greek perspective. Epochs and styles. WUNT 179: 2005 <1961> ⇒325. 151-170.

13265 **Zanker, Graham** Modes of viewing in Hellenistic poetry and art. 2004 ⇒20,11966. $^{R}$AJP 126 (2005) 461-463 (*Elsner, Jaś*).

13266 **Zoumbaki, Sophia B.** Prosographie der Eleer bis zum 1 Jh. v.Chr. Melethmata 40: Athens 2005, National Hellenic Research Foundation 498 pp. €98. 960-7906-20-2 [RB 113,160].

## Q7 Josephus Flavius

13267 *Barclay, John M.G.* Judean historiography in Rome: Josephus and history in Contra Apionem Book 1. Josephus and Jewish history. JSJ.S 104: 2005 ⇒860. 29-43.

13268 *Baumbach, Günther* Die Pharisäerdarstellung des Josephus—propharisäisch oder antipharisäisch? <1997>;

13269 The Sadducees in Josephus <1989>;

13270 Schriftstellerische Tendenzen und historische Verwertbarkeit der Essenerdarstellung des Josephus <1993>. Josephus–Jesusbewegung–Judentum. ANTZ 9: 2005 ⇒182. 21-50/51-72/73-94.

13271 *Begg, Christopher* David's dying directives according to Josephus. Sef. 65 (2005) 271-285 [1 Kgs 2,1-9];

13272 Solomon's installation of the ark in the temple according to Josephus. RCatT 30 (2005) 251-265 [1 Kgs 8,1-11];

13273 David's fourfold escape according to Josephus. Anton. 80 (2005) 433-452 [1 Sam 19];

13274 Ahithophel versus Hushai according to Josephus. ASEs 22/2 (2005) 479-500 [2 Sam 16,15-17,23];

13275 The fall of Jericho according to Josephus. EstB 63 (2005) 323-340 [Josh 6];

13276 The Rahab story in Josephus. LASBF 55 (2005) 113-130 [Josh 2];

13277 The demise of Absalom according to Josephus. OTEs 18 (2005) 482-502 [2 Sam 17,24-18,18];

13278 David's homecoming according to Josephus (part one). PJBR 4/2 (2005) 117-128 [2 Sam 19,9-44];

13279 Joab's murder of Abner according to Josephus. Hermenêutica 5 (2005) 59-94 [2 Sam 3,6-39].

13280 [T]**Begg, Christopher** Josephus Flavius: translation and commentary 4: Judean Antiquities 5-7. [E]*Mason, S.*: Lei 2005, Brill xv; 373 pp. €115/$155. 90-04-11785-7. [R]Faith & Mission 23/1 (2005) 116-119 (*Madden, Shawn C.*).

13281 [T]**Begg, Christopher; Spilsbury, Paul** Josephus Flavius: translation and commentary 5: Judean Antiquities books 8-10. [E]*Mason, S.*: Lei 2005, Brill xiv; 392 pp. €125/$169. 90-04-11786-5.

13282 *Belenkiy, Ari* Der Aufgang des Canopus, die Septuaginta und die Begegnung zwischen Simon dem Gerechten und Antiochus dem Grossen. Jud. 61/1 (2005) 42-54.

13283 *Capponi, Livia* Ecateo di Abdera e la prima *katoikia* di Giudei in Egitto (Giuseppe, *Contro Apione* I 186-9). Materia giudaica 10/2 (2005) 233-240.

13284 **Castelli, Silvia** Il terzo libro delle Antichità giudaiche di Flavio Giuseppe e la bibbia: problemi storici e letterari: traduzione e commento. 2002 ⇒18,11532. [R]JJS 56 (2005) 150-151 (*Rajak, Tessa*).

13285 **Colautti, Federico M.** Passover in the works of Josephus. JSJ.S 75: 2002 ⇒18,11534; 20,11977. [R]ThLZ 130 (2005) 247-249 (*Landau, Tamar*); JSJ 36 (2005) 338-341 (*Castelli, Silvia*); BZ 49 (2005) 295-296 (*Rusam, Dietrich*).

13286 *Dochhorn, Jan* Die phönizischen Personennamen in den bei Josephus überlieferten Quellen zur Geschichte von Tyrus: eine textkritische und semitistische Untersuchung. WO 35 (2005) 68-117.

13287 *Dormeyer, Detlev* The Hellenistic biographical history of King Saul: Josephus, A.J. 6.45-378 and 1 Samuel 9:1-31:13;

13288 *Eberhardt, Barbara* Wer dient wem?: die Darstellung des Flavischen Triumphzuges auf dem Titusbogen und bei Josephus (B.J. 7.123-162). Josephus and Jewish history. JSJ.S 104: 2005 ⇒860. 147-157/257-277.

[E]**Edmondson, J.** Flavius Josephus and Flavian Rome 2005 ⇒938.

13289 *Eilers, Claude* A decree of Delos concerning the Jews? (Jos. AJ 14.231-232). SCI 24 (2005) 65-74.

13290 *Forte, Anthony J.* Translating Book 1 of Josephus' Bellum Judaicum: some critical observations;

13291 *Förster, Niclas* Some observations on Josephus' description of the Essenian morning prayer. Josephus and Jewish history. JSJ.S 104: 2005 ⇒860. 383-403/245-253;

13292 The Prayer of Choni in Josephus Jewish Antiquities XIV 24. Studies in Jewish prayer. JSSt.S 17: 2005 ⇒828. 101-116.

13293 *Galimberti, Alessandro* Flavio Giuseppe e TUCIDIDE. La cultura storica. 2005 ⇒893. 173-188.

13294 *Gruen, Erich* Greeks and Jews: mutal misperceptions in Josephus' Contra Apionem. Ancient Judaism. JSJ.S 95: 2005 ⇒626. 31-51.

13295 *Haaland, Gunnar* Josephus and the philosophers of Rome: does Contra Apionem mirror Domitian's crushing of the "Stoic opposition"?;

13296 *Howell Chapman, Honora* "By the waters of Babylon": Josephus and Greek poetry. Josephus and Jewish history. JSJ.S 104: 2005 ⇒ 860. 297-316/121-146.

13297 *Höffken, Peter* Elischa in seinem Verhältnis zu Elija bei Josephus. EThL 81 (2005) 477-486;

13298 Eine Reichsteilung bei Josephus Flavius: Beobachtungen zu seiner Auffassung von Daniel 5. JSJ 36 (2005) 197-205.

13299 *Inowlocki, Sabrina* 'Neither adding nor omitting anything': Josephus' promise not to modify the scriptures in Greek and Latin context. JJS 56 (2005) 48-65;

13300 La réécriture du mythe de Babel par Flavius Josèphe. [F]FINET, A.: Subartu 16: 2005 ⇒40. 65-78 [Gen 11,1-9].

13301 *Jackson, Bernard S.* The divorces of the Herodian princesses: Jewish law, Roman law or palace law?. Josephus and Jewish history. JSJ.S 104: 2005 ⇒860. 343-368.

13302 *Jones, Kenneth R.* The figure of Apion in Josephus' Contra Apionem. JSJ 36 (2005) 278-315.

13303 *Jonquière, Tessel* Josephus' use of prayers: between narrative and theology. Josephus and Jewish history. JSJ.S 104: 2005 ⇒860. 229-243.

13304 **Jonquière, Tessel** Prayer in Josephus. 2005, vii; 279 pp. 90393-40269. Diss. Utrecht [OTA 29,112].

13305 *Jossa, Giorgio* Jews, Romans, and christians: from the Bellum Judaicum to the Antiquitates. Josephus and Jewish history. JSJ.S 104: 2005 ⇒860. 331-342.

13306 *Kalmin, Richard* Between Rome and Mesopotamia: Josephus in Sasanian Persia. Ancient Judaism. JSJ.S 95: 2005 ⇒626. 205-242.

13307 *Kasher, Aryeh* Josephus in praise of Mosaic laws on marriage (*Contra Apionem*, II, 199-201). [F]STEMBERGER, G.: SJ 32: 2005 ⇒ 140. 95-108.

13308 *Kibbey, D. Marshall* An early fragment of Josephus' Antiquitates Judaicae from Murbach Abbey. New studies on Yale manuscripts. 2005 ⇒606. 23-36 [Scr. 60/1,74*—M. Huglo].

13309 [ET]**Labow, Dagmar** Flavius Josephus, Contra Apionem: Buch I: Einleitung, Text, textkritischer Apparat, Übersetzung und Kommentar. BWANT 167: Stu 2005, Kohlhammer lxxxiv; 395 pp. €50. 3-17-018791-0. Bibl. 343-379.

13310 *Landau, Tamar* Power and pity: the image of Herod in Josephus Bellum Judaicum. Josephus and Jewish history. JSJ.S 104: 2005 ⇒ 860. 159-181.

13311 *Leeming, Henry Josephus slavonice* versus *Josephus graece*: to wards a typology of divergence. SEER 83 (2005) 1-13 [OTA 28, 221].

13312 *Lembi, Gaia* The Latin translation of Josephus' Antiquitates. Josephus and Jewish history. JSJ.S 104: 2005 ⇒860. 371-381.

13313 *Martínez, A.E.* Reevaluación critica del 'testimonio' de Flavio Josefo acerca de Jesús. Apuntes [Dallas, TX] 25/3 (2005) 84-118 [NTAb 50,118].

13314 *Mason, Steve* Of audience and meaning: reading Josephus' Bellum Judaicum in the context of a Flavian audience. Josephus and Jewish history. JSJ.S 104: 2005 ⇒860. 71-100.

13315 **Mason, Steve N.** Josephus and the New Testament. $^{2}$2003 <1992> ⇒19,12586; 20,11995. [R]OCP 71 (2005) 196-199 (*Farrugia, E.G.*); HeyJ 46 (2005) 223-224 (*Madigan, Patrick*); RSR 93 (2005) 614-616 (*Berthelot, Katell*).

13316 *McLaren, James S.* Josephus on Titus: the vanquished writing about the victor. Josephus and Jewish history. 2005 ⇒860. 279-95;

13317 A reluctant provincial: Josephus and the Roman Empire in *Jewish War*. Gospel of Matthew. JSNT.S 276: 2005 ⇒484. 34-48.

13318 *Mendels, Doron* The formation of an historical canon of the Greco-Roman period: from the beginnings to Josephus. Josephus and Jewish history. JSJ.S 104: 2005 ⇒860. 3-19.

13319 [ET]**Nodet, Etienne** Flavius Josèphe: les Antiquités juives, 4: livres VIII et IX. P 2005, Cerf lxxxii; 417 pp. €31. 2-204-07816-6. [R]Gr. 86 (2005) 921-923 (*Sievers, Joseph*); REG 118 (2005) 306-307 (*Pouderon, Bernard*); RBLit (2005)* (*Bloch, René*).

13320 *Oppenheimer, Aharon* Nehardea und Nisibis bei Josephus. Between Rome and Babylon. TSAJ 108: 2005 <1993> ⇒ 356-373.

13321 *Parente, Fausto* The impotence of Titus, or Flavius Josephus's Bellum Judaicum as an example of "pathetic" historiography;

13322 *Price, Jonathan J.* The provincial historian in Rome. Josephus and Jewish history. JSJ.S 104: 2005 ⇒860. 45-69/101-118;

13323 Some aspects of Josephus' theological interpretation of the Jewish War. [F]STEMBERGER, G.: SJ 32: 2005 ⇒140. 109-119.

13324 *Schimanowski, Gottfried* Alexandrien als Drehscheibe zwischen Jerusalem und Rom: die Bedeutung der Stadt im Werk des Josephus. Josephus and Jewish history. JSJ.S 104: 2005 ⇒860. 317-330.

13325 *Schwartz, Daniel R.* Once again: who captured Masada?: on doublets, reading against the grain, and what Josephus actually wrote. SCI 24 (2005) 75-83.

13326 *Semenchenko, L.V.* Were Sadducees Epicureans?: the problem of interrelation of fate, providence and free will in the works of Flavius Josephus. VDI 3 (2005) 125-142. **R.**

13327 **Shahar, Yuval** Josephus Geographicus: the classical context of geography in Josephus. TSAJ 98: 2004 ⇒20,12004. [R]SCI 24 (2005) 318-21 (*Dueck, Daniela*); Sal. 67 (2005) 184-185 (*Vicent, Rafael*).

13328 *Siegert, Folker* Josephus und das Alphabet der Römer: Überlegungen zur Schreibung griechischer Eigennamen in lateinischer Schrift. Josephus and Jewish history. JSJ.S 104: 2005 ⇒860. 405-423;

13329 Concluding remarks. Josephus and Jewish history. JSJ.S 104: 2005 ⇒860. 425-430.

13330 *Sievers, Joseph* What's in a name?: Antiochus in Josephus' 'Bellum Judaicum' JJS 56 (2005) 34-47.

13331 *Spilsbury, Paul* Reading the bible in Rome: Josephus and the constraints of empire. Josephus and Jewish history. JSJ.S 104: 2005 ⇒ 860. 209-227.

13332 *Troiani, Lucio* Il Gesù di Flavio Giuseppe. RStB 17/2 (2005) 137-147;

13333 Le *Antichità giudaiche* e il giudaismo contemporaneo. [F]GHIBERTI, G.: SRivBib 46: 2005 ⇒47. 205-211;

13334 La genèse historique des Antiquités Juives. Josephus and Jewish history. JSJ.S 104: 2005 ⇒860. 21-28.

13335 *Van Henten, Jan W.* Cleopatra in Josephus: from Herod's rival to the wise ruler's opposite. [F]LUTTIKHUIZEN, G.: AGJU 59: 2005 ⇒ 93. 115-134;

13336 Commonplaces in Herod's commander speech in Josephus' A.J. 15. 127-146. Josephus and Jewish history. 2005 ⇒860. 183-206.

13337 **Vidal-Naquet, P.** Flavius Josèphe et la guerre des Juifs. P 2005, Bayard 77 pp. €9. 22274-75311.

## Q8.1 *Roma Pompeii et Caesaris*—**Hyrcanus to Herod**

13338 *Clancy, Frank* DEMETRIUS the Chronographer and 141 BCE. SJOT 19 (2005) 143-145.

13339 **Günther, Linda-Marie** Herodes der Große. Gestalten der Antike: Da:Wiss 2005, 279 pp. €34.90. 3-534-15420-7. Ill. [EuA 82,113s —Benedikt Schwank].

13340 *Heiligenthal, Roman* Herodes: Kindermörder oder weiser Staatsmann?: eine Einführung zur Kontroverse. ZNT 8/16 (2005) 40-41.

13341 *Japp, Sarah* Herodes–ein weiser König: Hintergründe seiner Herrschaftsideologie. ZNT 8/16 (2005) 48-53.

13342 **Knoblet, J.** Herod the Great. Lanham, MD 2005, Univ. Pr. of America xiii; 217 pp. $33. 07618-30871. Bibl. [NTAb 49,636].

13343 **Najman, Hindy** Seconding Sinai: the development of Mosaic discourse in second temple Judaism. JSJ.S 77: 2003 ⇒19,12603; 20, 12011. [R]WThJ 67 (2005) 179-182 (*Dombrowski, Justin*); Bib. 86 (2005) 141-144 (*Labahn, Antje*); RBLit (2005)* (*Römer, Thomas*).

13344 *Retief, Francois; Cilliers, J.F.G.* The illnesses of Herod the Great. Health and healing. AcTh(B).S 7: 2005 <2003> ⇒686. 278-293.

13345 *Schofield, Alison; VanderKam, James C.* Were the Hasmoneans Zadokites?. JBL 124 (2005) 73-87.

13346 *Vogel, Manuel* Herodes: Kindermörder: Hintergründe einer Rollenbesetzung. ZNT 8/16 (2005) 42-47.

13347 *White, L. Michael* Herod and the Jewish experience of Augustan rule. Cambridge companion to the age of Augustus. 2005 ⇒647. 361-387.

13348 *Wilker, Julia* Herodes der Große—Herrschaftslegitimation zwischen jüdischer Identität und römischer Freundschaft. Roms auswärtige Freunde. 2005 ⇒636. 201-223.

### Q8.4 **Zeitalter Jesu Christi**: *particular/general*

13349 [E]**Bock, Darrell L.; Herrick, Gregory J.** Jesus in context: background readings for gospel study. GR 2005, Baker 286 pp. $23. 0-8010-2719-5. Bibl. 265-271.

13350 *Canivet, Pierre* Christianity in the 1st century: the context of the Mediterranean civilizations: Judaic, Greek, Roman and Asian. Christianity. 2005 ⇒607. 47-66.

13351 **Ferguson, William Everett** Backgrounds of early christianity. [3]2003 <1987, 1993> ⇒19,12616; 20,12021. [R]MissTod 7 (2005) 284-286 (*Varickasseril, Jose*); RBLit 7 (2005) 288-291 (*Seesengood, Robert P.*).

13352 *Frevel, Christian* Medien der Alltagskultur in der Antike: eine Einführung. Medien im antiken Palästina. FAT 2/10: 2005 ⇒646. 1-29.

13353 **Hadas-Lebel, Mireille** Hillel: un sage au temps de Jésus. P 2005, Michel 186 pp. €6.

13354 **Hanson, K.C.; Oakman, Douglas E.** La Palestina ai tempi di Gesù: la società, le istituzioni, i suoi conflitti. CinB 2003, San Paolo 308 pp.

13355 **Harland, Philip A.** Associations, synagogues, and congregations: claiming a place in ancient Mediterranean society. 2003 ⇒19, 12508; 20,12023. [R]Interp. 59 (2005) 200-202 (*Ferguson, Everett*); TS 66 (2005) 668-669 (*Harrill, J. Albert*); Bib. 86 (2005) 137-141 (*Runesson, Anders*).

13356 *Herzog, William R., II* Why peasants responded to Jesus. Christian origins. A people's history of christianity 1: 2005 ⇒550. 47-70.

13357 **Hingley, R.** Globalizing Roman culture: unity, diversity and empire. L 2005, Routledge xii; 208 pp. $87.50/30. 04153-51758/6-6. Bibl. [NTAb 50,211].

13358 *Horsley, Richard A.* 'By the finger of God': Jesus and imperial violence. Violence in the NT. 2005 ⇒439. 51-80;

13359 Jesus movements and the renewal of Israel. Christian origins. A people's history of christianity 1: 2005 ⇒550. 23-46.

13360 *Levoratti, Armando J.* L'ambiente storico-culturale del Nuovo Testamento. I vangeli. 2005 ⇒432. 195-338.

13361 *Ostmeyer, Karl-Heinrich* Armenhaus und Räuberhöhle?: Galiläa zur Zeit Jesu. ZNW 96 (2005) 147-170.

13362 [E]**Piétri, Luce** Die Geschichte des Christentums: Religion, Politik, Kultur, 1: die Zeit des Anfangs (bis 250). 2002 ⇒19,12625. [R]SNTU 30 (2005) 251-252 (*Fuchs, Albert*).

13363 *Puigdollers i Noblom, Rodolf* Els grans sacerdots jueus des de l'època d'Herodes el gran fins a la guerra jueva. RCatT 30/1 (2005) 49-89.

13364 **Riedo-Emmenegger, Christoph** Prophetisch-messianische Provokateure der Pax Romana: Jesus von Nazaret und andere Störenfriede im Konflikt mit dem Römischen Reich. NTOA 56: FrS 2005, Academic xxi; 381 pp. €65. 3-7278-1540-X. Bibl. 315-371.

13365 **Schlange-Schöningen, H.** AUGUSTUS. Geschichte kompakt–Antike: Da:Wiss 2005, €15. 35341-65128. Bibl. [NTAb 49,643].

13366 *Scibona, Rocco* Gesù e il giudaismo del suo tempo. Giudei o cristiani?. 2005 ⇒833. 71-81.

13367 **Shotter, David** AUGUSTUS Caesar. Lancaster Pamphlets in Ancient History: L ²2005 <1991>, Routledge ix; 128 pp. $79/18. 0415-319-358/66.

13368 *Silberman, Neil A.* The roots of christianity. Secrets of the bible. 2005 ⇒482. 104-107;

13369 Searching for Jesus. Secrets of the bible. 2005 ⇒482. 91-100.

13370 *Vitelli, Marco* I farisei nel giudaismo palestinese al tempo di Gesù e dei primi cristiani. Giudei o cristiani?. 2005 ⇒833. 53-70.

13371 **Witherington, Ben** New Testament history: a narrative account. 2001 ⇒17,10624... 19,12629. ᴿSBET 23 (2005) 106-107 (*Hardin, Justin K.*); AsbTJ 60/2 (2005) 140-141 (*Reese, Ruth Anne*).

## Q8.7 *Roma et Oriens*, **prima decennia post Christum**

13372 **Andrei, Osvalda** M'. Acilio Glabrione ed il leone: Domiziano tra ebraismo e cristianesimo. Quaderni di Henoch 12: 2002 ⇒18, 11603. ᴿRivCC 81 (2005) 297-299 (*Cesarini, Chiara*).

13373 *Augoustakis, A. Nequaquam historia digna*?: Plinian style in *Ep.* 6. 20. CJ 100/3 (2005) 265-273 [NTAb 49,573].

13374 **Baltrusch, Ernst** Die Juden und das römische Reich: Geschichte einer konfliktreichen Beziehung. 2002 ⇒18,11604... 20,12037. ᴿRSR 93 (2005) 602-603 (*Berthelot, Katell*).

13375 *Baumbach, Günther* Einheit und Vielfalt der jüdischen Freiheitsbewegung im 1. Jh. n.Chr. Josephus–Jesusbewegung–Judentum. ANTZ 9: 2005 <1985> ⇒182. 5-20.

13376 *Bedenbender, Andreas* Kampf der Menschen, Kampf der Götter, 1. Teil: die religiösen und ideologischen Auseinandersetzungen im Umfeld des Jüdischen Krieges. TeKo 28/4 (2005) 26-48.

13377 **Ben Zeev, Miriam Pucci** Diaspora Judaism in turmoil, 116/117 CE: ancient sources and modern insights. Interdisciplinary studies in ancient culture and religion 6: Lv 2005, Peeters xi; 302 pp. €40/ $44. 90-429-1605-2. Bibl. 267-289.

13378 **Blanchetière, François** Les premiers chrétiens étaient-ils missionnaires?: (30-135). 2002 ⇒18,11605... 20,12038. ᴿREJ 164 (2005) 563-565 (*Bobichon, Philippe*).

13379 **Blouin, Katherine** Le conflit judéo-alexandrin de 38-41: l'identité juive à l'épreuve. Judaïsmes: P 2005, L'Harmattan 205 pp. €17.50. 978-27475-83480. Préf. *Joseph Mélèze-Modrzejewski*.

13380 *Gabra, Gawdat* Christianity in the 1st century: the context of the Mediterranean civilizations: Coptic civilization. Christianity. 2005 ⇒607. 67-72.

13381 *Hadas-Lebel, Mireille* Le due rivolte ebraiche contro Roma (66-70/ 133-135). Il mondo della bibbia 77 (2005) 4-11.

13382 *Isaac, Benjamin; Oppenheimer, Aharon* The revolt of Bar Kokhba. Between Rome and Babylon. 2005 <1985> ⇒272. 197-224.

13383 *Laupot, Eric* Rome's invention of Pauline christianity and its responsibility for the Great Fire of Rome in 64 C.E., as part of its backlash against the Jewish guerrilla movement of Jesus and the Nazoreans. REJ 164 (2005) 415-448.

13384 *Lémonon, Jean-Pierre* Der Tempel brennt: Umformungsbewegungen nach der Katastrophe. WUB 38 (2005) 31-33.

13385 **Lémonon, Jean-Pierre** Les débuts du christianisme: de 30 à 135. Tout simplement 38: 2003 ⇒19,12647. [R]POC 55 (2005) 203-204 (*Merceron, R.*).

13386 **Malitz, Jürgen** NERO. [T]*Brown, Allison*: Oxf 2005, Blackwell xi; 174 pp. £15. 1-4051-2178-5. Bibl. 163-164.

13387 [E]*Mantovani, Piera Arata* Gerusalemme: la caduta del tempio 70-135. Il mondo della bibbia 77 (2005) 1-38.

13388 *McKechnie, Paul R.* Judaean embassies and cases before Roman emperors, AD 44-66. JThS 56 (2005) 339-361.

13389 *Michalak, Aleksander* Wojna 66-70, wojna święta?: ideologia wojny świętej w późnym okresie Drugiej Świątyni [Was the war of AD 66-70 a holy war?: the ideology of holy war in the later second temple period]. StBob 2 (2005) 101-130. **P**.

13390 *Oppenheimer, Aharon* Die jüdische Bewohnerschaft Galiläas zur Zeit von Yawne und während des Bar-Kochba-Aufstands. Between Rome and Babylon. TSAJ 108: 2005 <1977> ⇒272. 225-242;

13391 The ban on circumcision as a cause of the revolt. Between Rome and Babylon. TSAJ 108: 2005 <2003> ⇒272. 243-255;

13392 Subterranean hideouts in the Judaean Shephelah. Between Rome and Babylon. TSAJ 108: 2005 <1982> ⇒272. 256-262;

13393 Bar Kokhba and the observance of mitzvot <1984>;

13394 Sabbatheiligung im Bar-Kochba-Aufstand <1993>;

13395 Betar als Zentrum vor dem Bar-Kochba-Aufstand <2004>;

13396 Heiligkeit und Hingabe des Lebens in der Folge des Bar-Kochba-Aufstands <1992>. Between Rome and Babylon. TSAJ 108: 2005 ⇒272. 283-291/292-302/303-319/320-333.

13397 [E]**Schäfer, Peter** The Bar Kokhba War reconsidered: new perspectives on the second Jewish revolt against Rome. TSAJ 100: 2003 ⇒19,541; 20,12049. [R]RSR 93 (2005) 603-605 (*Berthelot, Katell*); ThLZ 130 (2005) 929-931 (*Vogel, Manuel*); CrSt 26 (2005) 557-563 (*Cristofoli, Roberto*).

13398 **Schimanowski, Gottfried** Juden und Nichtjuden in Alexandrien: Koexistenz und Konflikte bis zum Pogrom unter Trajan (117 n. Chr.). Münsteraner Judaistische Studien 18: Müns 2005, LIT 277 pp. €35. 3-8258-8507-0. Bibl. 256-274.

13399 **Shotter, David** NERO. Lancaster Pamphlets in Ancient History: L [2]2005 <1997>, Routledge x; 117 pp. 0-415-31942-0.

13400 *Speidel, Michael Alexander* Early Roman rule in Commagene. SCI 24 (2005) 85-100.

13401 **Vouga, François** Le christianisme à l'école de la diversité: histoire des premières générations. Poliez-le-Grand 2005, Moulin 106 pp. €12. 2-88469-020-4.

### Q9.1 *Historia Romae generalis et* **post-christiana**

13402 *Amata, Biagio* Storia, storiagrafia, agiografia, atti dei martiri. Sal. 67 (2005) 631-637.

13403 *Antonova, Stamenka E.* Barbarians and the empire-wide spread of christianity. Spread of christianity. 2005 ⇒545. 69-85.

13404 *Ashbrook Harvey, Susan* 'Incense in our land': Julian Saba and early Syrian christianity. [F]YOUNG, F. 2005 ⇒168. 120-131.

13405 *Asirvatham, S.R.* Classicism and *romanitas* in PLUTARCH's *De Alexandri fortuna aut virtute*. AJP 126/1 (2005) 107-125 [NTAb 49, 573].

13406 *Ådna, Jostein* The formation of the early church: an introduction. The formation of the early church. WUNT 183: 2005 ⇒708. 1-16.

13407 *Bakker, Henk* Potamiaena: some observations about martyrdom and gender in ancient Alexandria. [F]LUTTIKHUIZEN, G.: AGJU 59: 2005 ⇒93. 331-350.

13408 **Barnett, Paul** The birth of christianity: the first twenty years. After Jesus 1: GR 2005, Eerdmans x; 230 pp. $15. 0-8028-2781-0. [R]RBLit (2005)* (*Albl, Martin; Fairchild, Mark*).

13409 *Batson, D.* Community care and the growth of early christianity. The Fourth R [Santa Rosa, CA] 18/4 (2005) 3-8, 18 [NTAb 50, 136].

13410 *Beckwith, Roger T.* The calendar of the Montanists. Calendar, chronology. AGJU 61: 2005 ⇒184. 99-102.

13411 *Ben Zeev, Miriam P.* Were the Jews accused of roasting their enemies?. [F]STEMBERGER, G.: SJ 32: 2005 ⇒140. 167-170.

13412 *Bennett, Chris* Evidence for the regulation of intercalation under the *Lex acilia*. ZPE 151 (2005) 165-176.

13413 **Bertrandy, François; Coltelloni-Trannoy, Michèle** L'Afrique romaine de l'Atlantique à la Tripolitaine (69-439). P 2005, Colin 256 pp. 2200-26991-9.

13414 *Bodel, J. Caveat emptor*: towards a study of Roman slave-traders. Journal of Roman Archaeology [AA] 18 (2005) 181-195 [NTAb 50,359].

13415 **Boswell, J.** Christianity: social tolerance and homosexuality: gay people in western Europe from the beginning of the christian era to the fourteenth century. Ch 2005 <1980>, Univ. of Chicago Pr. xviii; 424 pp. $23/£16.50. 02260-67114 [NTAb 50,430].

13416 *Branham, Joan R.* Women as objects of sacrifice?: an early christian "chancel of the virgins". La cuisine et l'autel. BEHE.R 124: 2005 ⇒539. 371-386.

13417 *Bregni, Simone* 'Paradisus, locus amoenus': immagini del paradiso nei primi cinque secoli dell'era cristiana. RSLR 41 (2005) 297-328.

13418 **Brown, Peter R.L.** The rise of western christendom: triumph and diversity, A.D. 200-1000. The Making of Europe: ²2003 ⇒19, 12665. [R]JRH 29/1 (2005) 67-76 (*Morehead, J.*).

13419 **Burns, Thomas S.** Rome and the barbarians, 100 B.C. - A.D. 400. 2003 ⇒19,12666. [R]IHR 27 (2005) 106-108 (*Wells, Peter S.*).

13420 *Cameron, Averil* How to read heresiology. The cultural turn. 2005 ⇒670. 193-212.

13421 **Campbell, Brian** War and society in imperial Rome, 31 BC-AD 284. 2002 ⇒19,12667. [R]JRS 95 (2005) 261-263 (*Gulliver, Kate*).

13422 *Carrier, R.C.* Whence christianity: a meta-theory for the origins of christianity. JHiC 11/1 (2005) 22-34 [NTAb 50,137].

13423 *Carter, Warren* Lecture impérialiste: christianisme primitif et monde romain. Guide des nouvelles lectures. 2005 ⇒426. 273-305.

13424 *Clark, Elizabeth A.* Asceticism, class, and gender. Late ancient christianity. 2005 ⇒517. 27-45.

13425 **Cokayne, Karen** Experiencing old age in ancient Rome. 2003 ⇒ 19,12671; 20,12064. [R]SCI 24 (2005) 273-280 (*Suder, Wiesław*); AnCl 73 (2004) 465-466 (*Gourevitch, Danielle*).

13426 **Corbeill, Anthony** Nature embodied: gesture in ancient Rome. 2004 ⇒20,12066. [R]AJP 126 (2005) 143-145 (*Gleason, Maud W.*).

13427 *Cotton, Hannah M.; Eck, Werner* Roman officials in Judaea and Arabia and civil jurisdiction. Law in the documents. JSJ.S 96: 2005 ⇒662. 23-44.

13428 *Cotton, Hannah* Language gaps in Roman Palestine and the Roman Near East. Medien im antiken Palästina. FAT 2/10: 2005 ⇒646. 151-169.

13429 *Cozic, Michel* Présence de PÉLAGE dans le *Liber ad Gregoriam* d'ARNOBE le Jeune. REAug 51 (2005) 77-107.

13430 *Curran, J.* 'The long hesitation': some reflections on the Romans in Judaea. GaR 52/1 (2005) 70-98 [NTAb 50,132].

13431 *Dal Covolo, Enrico* Lo sviluppo del concetto di "pace" nel quadro dei rapporti tra la Chiesa e l'Impero nei primi tre secoli;

13432 "Regno di Dio" nella letteratura cristiana dei primi due secoli. Ricerche teologiche 16 (2005) 71-88/431-451.

13433 **Davidson, Ivor J.** The birth of the church: from Jesus to Constantine A.D. 30-312. Baker History of the Church: GR 2004, Baker 400 pp. $30.

13434 *Duling, Dennis C.* Empire: theories, methods, models. Gospel of Matthew. JSNT.S 276: 2005 ⇒484. 49-74.

13435 *Eck, Werner; Pangerl, Andreas* Neue Konsuldaten in neuen Diplomen. ZPE 152 (2005) 229-262.

13436 **Egea Vivancos, Alejandro** Eufratense et Osrhoene: poblamiento romano en el Alto Éufrates Sirio. Antigüedad y cristianismo 22: Murcia 2005, Universidad de Murcia 791 pp. 84-8371-620-8. Bibl. 737-757.

13437 *Eilers, Claude* A Roman East: Pompey's settlement to the death of Augustus. Companion to the Hellenistic world. 2005 ⇒642. 90-102.

13438 **Ferguson, Thomas C.** The past is prologue: the revolution of Nicene historiography. SVigChr 75: Lei 2005, Brill xiii; 226 pp 90-041-44579.

13439 *Fick, Sabine M.E.* Unreines Land oder Vorort Jerusalems?: jüdische und frühe christliche Gemeinden in Syrien. WUB 36 (2005) 37-42.

13440 [E]**Fiedrowicz, Michael** Christen und Heiden: Quellentexte zu ihrer Auseinandersetzung in der Antike. 2004 ⇒20,12069. [R]FKTh 21 (2005) 62 (*Heid, Stefan*).

13441 *Foxhall, Lin* Cultures, landscapes, and identities in the Mediterranean world. Mediterranean paradigms. 2005 ⇒669. 75-92.

13442 *Frankfurter, David* Beyond magic and superstition. Late ancient christianity. 2005 ⇒517. 255-284.

13443 *Freyburger-Galland, Marie-Laure* DION Cassius et les chrétiens. [F]HEIM, F. 2005 ⇒59. 37-54.

13444 *Fürst, Alfons* Christentum im Trend: monotheistische Tendenzen in der späten Antike. ZAC 9 (2005) 496-523.

13445 *Ghidelli, Carlo* Il cristianesimo come "eresia": alla ricerca dello specifico cristiano. [F]GHIBERTI, G.: SRivBib 46: 2005 ⇒47. 331-40.

13446 *Guijarro Oporto, Santiago* La tradición sobre Jesús y los comienzos del cristianismo en Galilea. EstB 63 (2005) 451-479.

13447 **Guy, Laurie** Introducing early christianity: a topical survey of its life, beliefs and practices. DG 2004, InterVarsity 310 pp. 0-8308-2-698-X.

13448 **Harnack, Adolf von** Mission et expansion du christianisme: aux trois premiers siècles. T*Hoffmann, Joseph*: 2004 ⇒20,12076. ROCP 71 (2005) 206-210 (*Poggi, V.*); RHPhR 85 (2005) 467-468 (*Prieur, J.-M.*); REG 118 (2005) 314-315 (*Pouderon, Bernard*).

13449 *Häkkinen, Sakari* The Ebionites: how the heirs of the earliest christianity became heretics. The Fourth R [Santa Rosa, CA] 18/5 (2005) 5-10, 18 [NTAb 50,367];

13450 Ebionites. A companion to second-century christian 'heretics'. VigChr.S 76: 2005 ⇒567. 247-278.

13451 *Heffernan, Thomas J.* Nomen sacrum: God's name as shield and weapon in the Acts of the christian martyrs. Scripture and pluralism. 2005 ⇒757. 11-28.

13452 *Hester, J.D.* Queers on account of the Kingdom of Heaven: rhetorical constructions of the eunuch body. Scriptura 90 (2005) 809-823 [NTAb 51,352].

13453 *Hezser, Catherine* Towards the study of Jewish popular culture in Roman Palestine. FSTEMBERGER, G.: SJ 32: 2005 ⇒140. 267-297.

13454 **Hill, Robert C.** Reading the Old Testament in Antioch. The Bible in Ancient Christianity 5: Lei 2005, Brill xii; 220 pp. €94/$127. 90-04-14538-9. Bibl. 203-209.

13455 *Hubbard, Moyer V.* Urban uprisings in the Roman world: the social setting of the mobbing of Sosthenes. NTS 51 (2005) 416-428 [Acts 18,12-17].

13456 ET**Jal, Paul** TITE-LIVE: histoire romaine, tome XIV, livre XXIV. CUFr: P 2005, Belles Lettres lii; 112 pp. €45. 2-251-01438-1.

13457 **Jerphagnon, Lucien** Histoire de Rome antique: les armes et les mots. P 42005, Hachette 620 pp. 2-012791-778.

13458 **Johnson, Marguerite; Ryan, Terry** Sexuality in Greek and Roman society and literature: a sourcebook. L 2005, Routledge xxvi; 244 pp. £19. 0-415-17331-0.

13459 **Keller, David G.R.** Oasis of wisdom: the worlds of the desert fathers and mothers. ColMn 2005, Liturgical xii; 181 pp. 0-8146-3034-0. Bibl. 166-168.

13460 **Kleiner, D.E.E.** Cleopatra and Rome. CM 2005, Harvard Univ. Pr. vii; 340 pp. $30/£19. 06740-19059. Bibl. [NTAb 50,629].

13461 **Labriolle, Pierre de** La réaction païenne: étude sur la polémique antichrétienne du 1er au VIe siècle. Patrimoines: P 2005 <1934>, Cerf 519 pp. €40. 2-204-07607-4. Préf. *Jean-Claude Fredouille*; Bibl. 509-511.

13462 *Laes, Christian* A la recherche de la vieillesse dans l'antiquité gréco-romaine. AnCl 74 (2005) 243-255.

13463 **Lampe, Peter** From Paul to VALENTINUS: christians at Rome in the first two centuries. T*Steinhauser, Michael* 2003 ⇒19,12682; 20, 12081. RRRT 12/1 (2005) 145 (*Casiday, Augustine*); JR 85 (2005) 501-503 (*Snyder, Graydon F.*); JJS 56 (2005) 153-4 (*Lieu, Judith*); MillSt 56 (2005) 159-161 (*Byrne, Patrick*); JThS 56 (2005) 655-658 (*Maier, H.O.*).

13464 *Lassère, J.-M.* La christianisation de l'Afrique. Pallas 68 (2005) 311-331.

13465 **Le Bohec, Yann; Le Glay, Marcel; Voisin, Jean-Louis** Histoire romaine. Quadrige: Manuels: P 2005, Presses Universitaires de France xiv; 587 pp. 213-055001-0.

13466 *Levieils, Xavier* Crises dans l'empire romain et lutte contre la superstition chrétienne (I$^{er}$-IV$^{e}$ siècles). RSLR 41 (2005) 1-38.

13467 $^{E}$**Lewin, Ariel** Gli ebrei nell'Impero Romano: saggi vari. 2001 ⇒ 17,415; 18,498. $^{R}$VetChr 42 (2005) 182-184 (*Caruso, Fabio*).

13468 *Lémonon, Jean-Pierre* I cristiani dopo l'incendio del tempio. Il mondo della bibbia 77 (2005) 28-31.

13469 **Lieu, Judith M.** Christian identity in the Jewish and Graeco-Roman world. 2004 ⇒20,12084. $^{R}$RRT 12 (2005) 610-612 (*Bash, Anthony*); SCI 24 (2005) 326-328 (*Ruzer, Serge*); JEH 56 (2005) 543-5 (*Carleton Paget, James*); ThLZ 130 (2005) 1061-1063 (*Niebuhr, Karl-Wilhelm*); BTB 35 (2005) 152-53 (*Harland, Philip A.*).

13470 **Lopez, David A.** Separatist christianity: spirit and matter in the early church fathers. 2004 ⇒20,12085. $^{R}$RBLit (2005)* (*Keough, Shawn; Weedman, Mark*).

13471 *Löhr, Winrich* Die Ausbreitung des antiken Christentums als historiographisches Projekt—Vorschläge, Probleme, Perspektiven. ZNT 8/15 (2005) 22-34.

13472 $^{E}$**Lucarini, Carlo M.** HERODIANUS Syrus: regum post Marcum. Mü 2005, Saur li; 183 pp. 3-598-71282-0. Bibl. xlvii-l.

13473 *Maier, Harry O.* Heresy, households, and the disciplining of diversity. Late ancient christianity. 2005 ⇒517. 213-233.

13474 *Manns, Frédéric* Le judéo-christianisme nazoréen: sources et critique des sources: réalité ou fiction?. EstB 63 (2005) 481-525.

13475 *Mara, Maria G.* Dalla Passio Pionii un cristianesimo differenziato a Smirne. Atti del X Simposio di Efeso. 2005 ⇒785. 173-181.

13476 *Maraval, Pierre* Christianity in the Middle East, in the 2nd and 3rd centuries. Christianity. 2005 ⇒607. 73-92.

13477 *Martin, Luther H.* The Hellenisation of Judaeo-Christian faith or the christianisation of Hellenic thought?. R&T 12 (2005) 1-19.

13478 **Meijering, Eginhard** Geschiedenis van het vroege christendom: van de jood Jezus van Nazareth tot de Romeinse keizer CONSTANTIJN. 2004 ⇒20,12087. $^{R}$KeTh 56 (2005) 251-252 (*Roukema, Riemer*).

13479 **Meyer, Elisabeth A.** Legitimacy and law in the Roman world: *tabulae* in Roman belief and practice. 2004 ⇒20,12088. $^{R}$RBLit (2005)* (*Hagedorn, Anselm C.*).

13480 **Montserrat Torrents, José** La sinagoga cristiana. Trotta $^{2}$2005 <1989>, 380 pp.

13481 *Morris, Ian* Mediterraneanization. Mediterranean paradigms. 2005 ⇒669. 30-55.

13482 **Mullen, Roderic L.** The expansion of christianity: a gazetteer of its first three centuries. SVigChr 69: 2004 ⇒20,12093. $^{R}$RivCC 81 (2005) 371-373 (*Rovidotti, Tatiana*).

13483 **Murray, Michele** Playing a Jewish game: Gentile christian judaizing in the first and second centuries CE. Studies in Christianity and Judaism 13: 2004 ⇒20,12094. $^{R}$TJT 21 (2005) 256-57 (*Chartrand-Burke, Tony*).

13484 *Nodet, Etienne* The origins of christianity: problems of method. Beginnings of christianity. 2005 ⇒786. 45-51.

13485 *North, J.A.* Pagans, polytheists and the pendulum. Spread of christianity. 2005 ⇒545. 125-143.

13486 **Nörr, Dieter** Römisches Recht: Geschichte und Geschichten; der Fall Arescusa et alii (Dig. 19.1.43 sq). Bayerische Akademie der

Wissenschaften: Ph.-hist. Kl. Sitzungsberichte 2005,1: Mü 2005, Bayerische Akademie der Wissenschaften 140 pp. 3-7696-1632-4.

13487 *Oppenheimer, Aharon* The Severan emperors, Rabbi Judah ha-Nasi and the cities of Palestine. [F]STEMBERGER, G.: SJ 32: 2005 ⇒140. 171-181;

13488 Urbanisation and city territories in Roman Palestine. Between Rome and Babylon. TSAJ 108: 2005 <1996> ⇒272. 30-46.

13489 *Osiek, Carolyn* Family matters. Christian origins. A people's history of christianity 1: 2005 ⇒550. 201-220.

13490 **Parkin, Tim G.** Old age in the Roman world: a cultural and social history. 2003 ⇒19,12688; 20,12095. [R]SCI 24 (2005) 273-280 (*Suder, Wiesław*).

13491 **Penrose, Jane** Rome and her enemies: an empire created and destroyed by war. Oxf 2005, Osprey 304 pp. 1-84176-9320.

13492 *Poggi, Vincenzo* Panorama storico delle chiese cristiane in Asia e in Africa: l'Oriente cristiano (1). Sette e religioni 15/1 (2005) 5-133.

13493 **Reff, Daniel T.** Plagues, priests, and demons: sacred narratives and the rise of christianity in the Old World and the New. C 2005, CUP xii; 290 pp. 0-521-84078-3. Bibl. 245-279.

13494 **Rhee, H.** Early christian literature: Christ and culture in the second and third centuries. [D]*Scholer, D.M.*: L 2005, Routledge xiii; 266 pp. £70/$125; £22.50/$40. 04153-54870/89. Diss. Fuller; Bibl. [NTAb 50,221].

13495 **Ritter, Adolf M.** 'L'église et l'état': point de vue du christianisme ancien. [T]*Tolck, Robert*: TC 13: Berne 2005, Lang xl; 279 pp. €67. 70. 3-9067-7070-2;

13496 'Kirche und Staat' im Denken des frühen Christentums: Texte und Kommentare zum Thema Religion und Politik in der Antike. TC 13: Bern 2005, Lang xl; 282 pp. €67.70. 3906-770699.

13497 *Rives, J.B.* Christian expansion and christian ideology. Spread of christianity. 2005 ⇒545. 15-41.

13498 **Rizzo, Francesco P.** Sicilia cristiana dal I al V secolo, vol. I. Testimonia Siciliae antiqua 1/14; Kókalos 17: R 2005, Bretschneider xii; 265 pp. 88-7689-1919.

13499 *Roth, U.* Food, status, and the *peculium* of agricultural slaves. Journal of Roman Archaeology [AA] 18 (2005) 278-292 [NTAb 50, 362].

13500 *Rüpke, Jörg* Bilderwelten und Religionswechsel. Griechische Mythologie. 2005 ⇒542. 359-376.

13501 *Sais i Borràs, Samuel* Identitat i alteritat en els mons grec i romà. La bíblia i els immigrants. 2005 ⇒471. 257-288.

13502 *Sanchez, Sylvain J.G.* L'historiographie du priscillianisme (XIXe-XXIe siècles). RechAug 34 (2005) 195-238.

13503 **Saporetti, Claudio** Schiavi nella Diyala. AIO 158: R 2005, Aracne 191 Pp. 88-548-0244-1.

13504 **Sartre, Maurice** The Middle East under Rome. [T]*Porter, Catherine; Routier-Pucci, Jeanine*: CM 2005, Harvard Univ. Pr. 665 pp. $40. 0-674-01683-1.

13505 *Scheidel, W.* Human mobility in Roman Italy, II: the slave population. Journal of Roman Archaeology [AA] 18 (2005) 64-79 [NTAb 50,363].

13506 *Shaw, Teresa M.* Ascetic practice and the genealogy of heresy: problems in modern scholarship and ancient textual representation. The cultural turn. 2005 ⇒670. 213-236.

13507 *Skarsaune, O.* Jewish believers in Jesus in antiquity—some lessons from a history project. Mishkan [J] 42 (2005) 45-56.

13508 **Smallwood, E. Mary** The Jews under Roman rule: from POMPEY to DIOCLETIAN: a study in political relations. [2]2001 ⇒19,12701. [R]PSB 26 (2005) 236-239 (*Mininger, Marcus A.*).

13509 **Sommer, Michael** Roms orientalische Steppengrenze: Palmyra–Edessa–Dura Europos–Hatra: eine Kulturgeschichte von POMPEIUS bis DIOCLETIAN. Stu 2005, Steiner 454 pp. €48. 3-515-08724-9. 12 pl.; 24 fig.

13510 *Stegemann, Ekkehard W.; Stegemann, Wolfgang* Lief am Anfang etwas falsch?: einige Thesen zur Entstehung des Christentums. KuI 20 (2005) 144-155.

13511 *Strubbe, J.H.M.* Young magistrates in the Greek East. Mn. 68/1 (2005) 88-111 [NTAb 49,549].

13512 *Theißen, Gerd* Kirche oder Sekte?: über Einheit und Konflikt im frühen Urchristentum. ThG 48 (2005) 162-175.

13513 *Van Bremen, Riet* Family structures. Companion to the Hellenistic world. 2005 ⇒642. 313-330.

13514 *Verhoef, E.* The church of Philippi in the first six centuries of our era. HTSTS 61/1-2 (2005) 565-592 [NTAb 50,372].

13515 **Veyne, Paul** L'Empire gréco-romain. P 2005, Seuil 877 pp. 202-0-57798-4.

13516 **Weiler, Ingomar** Die Beendigung des Sklaventums im Altertum: ein Beitrag zur vergleichenden Sozialgeschichte. FASk 36: 2003 ⇒19,12711. [R]AnCl 74 (2005) 495-496 (*Straus, Jean A.*).

13517 **Wilken, Robert Louis** Der Geist des frühen Christentums. 2004 ⇒ 20,12110. [R]ThRv 101 (2005) 20-22 (*Fürst, Alfons*).

13518 **Wilson, Stephen G.** Leaving the fold: apostates and defectors in antiquity. 2004 ⇒20,12111. [R]SR 34 (2005) 603-604 (*Patterson, Dilys*); ET 117 (2005) 122 (*Bellinzoni, Arthur J.*).

13519 *Wlosok, Antonie* Die christliche Apologetik griechischer und lateinischer Sprache bis zur konstantinischen Epoche: Fragen, Probleme, Kontroversen. L'apologétique chrétienne. EnAC 51: 2005 ⇒13520. 1-28.

13520 **Wlosok, Antonie**, *al.*, L'apologétique chrétienne gréco-latine à l'époque prénicénienne: sept exposés suivis de discussions. EnAC 51: Vandoeuvres-Genève 2005, Hardt viii; 316 pp. 2600-00751-2.

13521 *Young, Robin D.* Martyrdom as exaltation. Late ancient christianity. 2005 ⇒517. 70-92.

13522 **Zahran, Yasmine** Zenobia between reality and legend. BAR.Internat. Ser. 1169: 2003 ⇒19,12712. [R]SCI 24 (2005) 301-302 (*Sommer, Michael*).

## Q9.5 Constantine, Julian, Byzantine Empire

13523 *Amerise, Marilena* COSTANTINO il "Nuovo Mosè". Sal. 67 (2005) 671-700.

13524 *Bar, Doron* Roman legislation as reflected in the settlement history of late antique Palestine. SCI 24 (2005) 195-206.

13525 *Criscuolo, Ugo* Biografia e agiografia fra pagani e cristiani fra il IV e il V secolo: le *Vitae* di Eunapio e la *Historia Lausiaca*. Sal. 67 (2005) 771-798.

13526 *Dal Covolo, Enrico* La tradizione storiografica bizantina nella questione dei rapporti tra gli imperatori Severi et il cristianesimo. Sal. 67 (2005) 917-924.

13527 **Davidson, Ivor J.** A public faith: from CONSTANTINE to the medieval world, AD 312-600. Baker history of the church 2: GR 2005, Baker 463 pp. 0-8010-1275-9. Bibl. 411-429.

13528 *Di Santo, Emanuele* GIULIANO l'Apostata nel pensiero di Giovanni CRISOSTOMO: imperatore, filosofo, persecutore. Aug. 45 (2005) 349-387.

13529 *Ducellier, Alain* Autocracy and religion in Byzantium in the 4th and 5th centuries. Christianity. 2005 ⇒607. 93-119.

13530 [T]**Edwards, Mark** CONSTANTINE and christendom: the Oration to the saints; the Greek and Latin accounts of the discovery of the cross; the Edict of Constantine to Pope Silvester. 2003 ⇒19,12717. [R]RivCC 81 (2005) 332-334 (*Heid, Stefan*).

13531 **Gaddis, Michael** There is no crime for those who have Christ: religious violence in the christian Roman Empire. Transformation of the classical heritage 39: Berkeley 2005, University of California Pr. xiv; 396 pp. 0-520-24104-5. Bibl. 343-368.

13532 **Hahn, Johannes** Gewalt und religiöser Konflikt: Studien zu den Auseinandersetzungen zwischen Christen, Heiden und Juden im Osten des Römischen Reiches (von Konstantin bis Theodosius II). 2004 ⇒20,12117. [R]Gn. 77 (2005) 607-611 (*Klein, Richard*).

13533 *Riedweg, Christoph* Mythos mit geheimem Sinn oder reine Blasphemie?: JULIAN über die mosaische Erzählung vom Sündenfall (Contra Galileos fr. 17,10-12 Masaracchia). [F]HURST, A. 2005 ⇒64. 367-375.

13534 *Van Rompay, Lucas* Society and community in the christian east. Cambridge companion to the age of Justinian. 2005 ⇒667. 239-266.

## XVIII. Archaeologia terrae biblicae

### T1.1 General biblical-area archaeologies

13535 [E]**Abulafia, David** The Mediterranean in history. 2003 ⇒19,12723. [R]IJCT 11 (2005) 640-641 (*Rosen, Klaus*).

13536 *Alcock, Susan E.; Gates, Jennifer E.; Rempel, Jane E.* Reading the landscape: survey archaeology and the Hellenistic *oikoumene*. Companion to the Hellenistic world. 2005 ⇒642. 354-372.

13537 *Briend, Jacques* Le travail de l'archéologue. CEv 131 (2005) 4-19.

13538 *Cook, E.M.* The forgery indictments and *BAR*: learning from hindsight. NEA 68/1-2 (2005) 73-75 [NTAb 50,537].

13539 **Currid, John D.** Doing archaeology in the land of the bible: a basic guide. 1999 ⇒15,10818; 17,10705. [R]JETh 19 (2005) 216-217 (*Pehlke, Helmuth*).

13540 *Evans, Craig A.* A fishing boat, a house and an ossuary: what can we learn from the artifacts?. The missions of James. NT.S 115: 2005 ⇒369. 211-231.

13541 *Faust, Avrahama, Safrai, Ze'ev* Salvage excavations as a source for reconstructing settlement history in ancient Israel. PEQ 137 (2005) 139-158.

13542 *Goren, Yuval; Silberman, Neil A.* Faking biblical history. Secrets of the bible. 2005 ⇒482. 188-200.

13543 *Gruson, Philippe* Bulletin: Archéologie et bible. CEv 132 (2005) 53-56.

13544 **King, Philip J.; Stager, Lawrence E.** Life in biblical Israel. Library of Ancient Israel: 2001 ⇒17,10711... 20,12130. [R]RStR 31 (2005) 148-149 (*Nakhai, Beth Alpert*).

13545 Kisten voller Schätze: Afghanistan: Kabul. WUB 35 (2005) 72.

13546 [E]**Koester, Helmut** Cities of Paul: images and interpretations from the Harvard New Testament Archaeology Project. 2005, CD-ROM. [R]Interp. 59 (2005) 432, 434 (*Hultgren, Arland J.*); TrinJ 26 (2005) 353-355 (*Schnabel, Eckhard J.*); OTEs 18 (2005) 940-941 (*Myburgh, J.A.*); RBLit (2005)* (*Carter, Warren; Klein, Ralph*).

13547 *Lernau, O.; Van Neer, W.; Zohar, I.* The emergence of fishing communities in the eastern Mediterranean region: a survey of evidence from pre- and protohistoric periods. Paléorient 31/1 (2005) 131-157.

13548 **Lewin, A.** The archaeology of ancient Judea and Palestine. LA 2005, Getty 204 pp. $40. 08923-68004. Bibl. [NTAb 49,637].

13549 *Liverani, Mario* Imperialism. Archaeologies of the Middle East. 2005 ⇒683. 223-243.

13550 *Millard, Alan* Only fragments from the past: the role of accident in our knowledge of the ancient Near East. [F]MILLARD, A.: LHBOTS 426: 2005 ⇒102. 301-319.

13551 *Nakhai, Beth A.* Daily life in the ancient Near East: new thoughts on an old topic. RStR 31/3-4 (2005) 147-153.

13552 *Niemeyer, H.G.* Phoenicians vs. Greeks: achievements and polemics in archaeological research since the discovery of Al Mina. V Congresso di studi fenici. 2005 ⇒959. I, 11-17.

13553 The other shoe: five accused of antiquities fraud. BArR 31/2 (2005) 58-69.

13554 **Petersen, Andrew** The towns of Palestine under Muslim rule, AD 600-1600. BAR International Ser. 1381: Oxf 2005, Archaeopress xii; 243 pp.£35. 1-84171-821-1. 63 fig.; 44 pl.

13555 *Porath, Renatus* Dois textos, duas leituras: um diálogo crítico entre a exegese e a arqueologia. VoxScr 13/1 (2005) 57-67.

13556 [E]**Richard, Suzanne** Near Eastern archaeology: a reader. 2003 ⇒ 19,12740; 20,12134. [R]OLZ 100 (2005) 468-470 (*Thiel, Winfried*).

13557 *Rollston, Christopher A.; Vaughn, Andrew G.* Fakes, forgeries and biblical scholarship: the antiquities market, sensationalized textual data, and modern forgeries. NEA 68/1-2 (2005) 61-65.

13558 *Rollston, Christopher A.* Navigating the epigraphic storm. NEA 68/1-2 (2005) 69-72.

13559 **Shear, Ione M.** Kingship in the Mycenaean world and its reflections in the oral tradition. Prehistory Monographs 13: Ph 2004, INSTAP A. xii; 233 pp. $40. 11 ill.

13560 *Silberman, Neil Asher* Digging in the land of the bible. Secrets of the bible. 2005 ⇒482. 51-58.

13561 *Steadman, Sharon R.* Reliquaries on the landscape: mounds as matrices of human cognition. Archaeologies of the Middle East. 2005 ⇒683. 286-307.

13562 *Uehlinger, Christoph* "Medien" in der Lebenswelt des antiken Palästina?. Medien im antiken Palästina. FAT 2/10: 2005 ⇒646. 31-61.

13563 Update—finds or fakes?–the other shoe: five accused of antiquities fraud. BArR 31/2 (2005) 58-69 [NTAb 49,550].

13564 *Vieweger, Dieter* Monografien zur Archäologie in Palästina. OLZ 100 (2005) 237-241 [NTAb 50,339].

13565 **Vieweger, Dieter** Archäologie der biblischen Welt. UTB 2394: 2003 ⇒19,12746; 20,12136. RJETh 19 (2005) 218-219 (*Fischer, Stefan*).

13566 *Wenell, Karen J.* The geography, history, and archaeology of the bible. Scripture. 2005 ⇒398. 23-43.

13567 **Wilkinson, Tony J.** Archaeological landscapes of the Near East. 2003 ⇒19,12747; 20,12138. RAntiquity 79 (2005) 224-226 (*Kuzucuoglu, Catherine*).

13568 *Yahya, Adel H.* Archaeology and nationalism in the Holy Land;

13569 *Zimansky, Paul* Archaeology and texts in the ancient Near East. Archaeologies of the Middle East. 2005 ⇒683. 66-77/308-326.

## T1.2 Musea, organismi, *displays*

13570 E**Beck, Herbert; Bol, Peter C.; Bückling, Maraike** Ägypten–Griechenland–Rom: Abwehr und Berührung: Städelsches Kunstinstitut und Städtische Galerie, 26. November 2005 - 26. Februar 2006. Tü 2005, Wasmuth 757 pp. 38030-10578.

13571 E**Berthier, Annie; Zali, Anne** Livres de parole: torah, bible, Coran. P 2005, Bibliothèque nationale de France 231 pp. €39. 2-7177-2338-2. Avant-propos *Dominique Borne* [BCLF 677,11].

13572 *Bogdanos, Matthew* Tracking down the looted treasures of Iraq. BArR 31/6 (2005) 26-39.

13573 **Bogdanos, Matthew; Patrick, William** Thieves of Baghdad: one marine's passion for ancient civilizations and the journey to recover the world's greatest stolen treasures. NY 2005, Bloomsbury 302 pp. 1-582-34645-3. Bibl. 300-302.

13574 **Brehme, Sylvia**, *al.*, Ancient Cypriote art in Berlin. 2001 ⇒17, 10724; 19,12752. RSyria 82 (2005) 367-368 (*Cook, Valérie*).

13575 **Briend, Jacques; Caubet, Annie; Pouyssegur, Patrick** Le Louvre et la bible. P 2005, Bayard 255 pp. €29. 2-227-47138-7. Num. ill. RAkkadica 126 (2005) 97-98 (*Spycket, Agnès*).

13576 E**Caubet, Annie; Pierrat-Bonnefois, Geneviève** Faïences de l'antiquité, de l'Egypte à l'Iran. P 2005, Musée du Louvre 206 pp. €35. 2-35031-019-1. Exp. 2005.

13577 **Cluzan, Sophie** De Sumer à Canaan. P 2005, Musée du Louvre 312 pp. €45. 978-20206-69627. 88 ill.

13578 E**Curtis, John; Tallis, Nigel** Forgotten empire: the world of ancient Persia. Berkeley 2005, Univ. of California Pr. 272 pp. $50. 0-520-24731-0. Num. ill.; Exhib. Brit. Museum 9.9.2005-8.1.2006.

13579 **De Capoa, Chiara** Het Oude Testament. ^T*Salverda, Murk*: Gent 2005, Ludion 351 pp. €19.90. 90-5544-552-5.

13580 *Dlugosz, Dariusz* Qumrân au musée du Louvre. RdQ 22 (2005) 121-129.

13581 *Fassbeck, Gabriele* Deuteronomy in Dixie: Mobile's Gulf Coast Exploreum Science Center brings the Dead Sea scrolls to the Bible belt. NEA 68/4 (2005) 190-192.

13582 *Gigante, L.M.* Death in Louisville, Roman style. Archaeology Odyssey [Wsh] 8/6 (2005) 40-46, 51 [NTAb 50,335].

13583 ^E**Guzzo, Pier Giovanni** Pompeii: stories from an eruption: guide to the exhibition. Mi 2005, Mondadori 207 pp. $32. 8-8370-2363-4. 62 fig.

13584 ^E**Hänggi, Ambros; Maeder, Felicitas; Wunderlin, Dominik** Bisso marino: fili d'oro dal fondo del mare—Muschelseide: goldene Fäden vom Meeresgrund. 2004 ⇒20,12147. ^RUF 37 (2005) 832-833 (*Zwickel, Wolfgang*).

13585 ^E**Herron, Ellen Middlebrook** The Dead Sea scrolls: catalog of the exhibition of scrolls and artifacts from the collections of the Israel Antiquities Authority at the Public Museum of Grand Rapids. 2003 ⇒19,12756. ^RDSD 12 (2005) 363-364 (*Collins, John J.*).

13586 ^E**Hornung, Erik; Bryan, Betsey M.** The quest for immortality: treasures of ancient Egypt. 2002 ⇒19,12757. Denver Museum, Sept. 2004-Jan. 2005 et al. to 2007. ^RAJA 109 (2005) 777-782 (*D'Auria, Sue*).

13587 *Hoss, Stefanie* Niederlande: Nijmegen: das Bijbels Openluchtmuseum. WUB 37 (2005) 68-69.

13588 **Jørgensen, M.** Tomb treasures from ancient Egypt. 2002 ⇒19, 12758. Catalogue exhibition Copenhagen. ^RBiOr 62 (2005) 39-40 (*Podvin, Jean-Louis*).

13589 ^E**Karageorghis, Vassos; Vanchugov, Vladimir P.** Greek and Cypriot antiquities in the archaeological museum of Odessa. 2001 ⇒17,10729; 19,12759. ^RSyria 82 (2005) 366-367 (*Cook, Valérie*).

13590 ^E**Krieg, Martin**, *al.*, Das unsichtbare Bild: die Ästhetik des Bilderverbotes. Z 2004, TVZ 111 pp. €12.20. 32901-73658. Exp. Zurich [Exod 20,4-6].

13591 *Mertin, Andreas* Ansichten Christi: das Christusbild von der Antike bis zum 20. Jahrhundert. KuKi 3 (2005) 198. Ausstellung Köln 2005.

13592 *Moore, Andrew M.T.* A new exhibit on ancient Mesopotamia at the Oriental Institute, University of Chicago. AJA 109 (2005) 281-285.

13593 ^E**Roehrig, Catharine H.; Dreyfus, Renée; Keller, Cathleen A.** Hatshepsut: from queen to pharaoh. NY 2005, Metropolitan Museum of Art xv; 339 pp. $65/50. 0-300-11139-8. Catalog of an exhibition; Bibl. 307-330.

13594 Should the Israel Museum take the Dayan collection off display?. BArR 31/2 (2005) 53-57.

13595 ^E**Simpson, St John** Queen of Sheba: treasures from ancient Yemen. 2002 ⇒18,11712; 19,12762. ^RJRAS 15 (2005) 102-104 (*Maraqten, Mohammed*); AWE 4 (2005) 216-218 (*Overlaet, Bruno*).

13596 *Speiser, Philipp* Zur Entstehungsgeschichte des Museums für Arabische Kunst in Kairo. MDAI.K 61 (2005) 351-360.

13597 **Zuffiano, Stefano** Het NieuweTestament. ^T*Rynck, Patrick de*: Gent 2005, Ludion 383 pp. €19.90. 90-5544-553-3.

## T1.3 *Methodi*—Science in archaeology

13598 *Abay, Eşref; Çevik, Özlem* 'Interaction and migration': issues in archaeological theory. AltOrF 32 (2005) 62-73.

13599 *Bruins, Hendrik J.; Van der Plicht, Johannes* Quality control of Groningen $^{14}$C results from Tel Reḥov: repeatability and intercomparison of proportional gas counting and AMS;

13600 *Bruins, Hendrik J., al.*, The Groningen radiocarbon series from Tel Reḥov: OxCal Bayesian computations from the Iron IB-IIA boundary and Iron IIA destruction events. The bible and radiocarbon dating. 2005 ⇒952. 256-270/271-293.

13601 *Cross, Frank Moore* Statement on inscribed artifacts without provenience. BArR 31/5 (2005) 58-60.

13602 **Davis, Thomas W.** Shifting sands: the rise and fall of biblical archaeology. Ment. *Albright, W.* 2004 ⇒20,12159. [R]PEQ 137 (2005) 79-80 (*Chapman, R.L., III*).

13603 *Ferrara, Enzo* Earth science, soil chemistry, and archaeology. AJA 109 (2005) 87-90.

13604 *Finkelstein, Israel; Piasetzky, Eli* $^{14}$C results from Megiddo, Tel Dor, Tel Reḥov and Tel Hadar: where do they lead us?;

13605 *Higham, Thomas, al.*, Radiocarbon dating of the Khirbat en-Nahas site (Jordan) and Bayesian modeling of the results;

13606 *Kuniholm, Peter I.; Newton, Maryanne W.; Wardle, Kenneth A.* A dendrochronological $^{14}$C wiggle-match for the early Iron Age of north Greece. The bible and radiocarbon dating. 2005 ⇒952. 294-301/164-178/104-113.

13607 *Lehmann, Gunnar* Media and the symbolic texture of material culture: critical theory of practice in archaeology. Medien im antiken Palästina. FAT 2/10: 2005 ⇒646. 63-83.

13608 *Manning, Sturt W., al.*, Radiocarbon calibration in the East Mediterranean region: the East Mediterranean Radiocarbon Comparison Project (EMRCP) and the current state of play. The bible and radiocarbon dating. 2005 ⇒952. 95-103.

13609 *Powers, J., al.*, X-ray fluorescence recovers writing from ancient inscriptions. ZPE 152 (2005) 221-227.

13610 **Rainville, Lynn** Investigating Upper Mesopotamian households using micro-archaeological techniques. BAR Int. Ser. 1368: Oxf 2005, Archaeopress viii; 234 pp. £35. 121 fig.

13611 *Ramsey, Christopher B.* Improving the resolution of radiocarbon dating by statistical analysis. The bible and radiocarbon dating. 2005 ⇒952. 57-64.

13612 Röntgenstrahlen zeigen unsichtbare Inschrift. WUB 38 (2005) 69.

13613 *Shanks, Hershel* Radiocarbon dating—how to find your true love. BArR 31/1 (2005) 50-53.

13614 *Sharon, Ilan, al.*, The Early Iron Age dating project: introduction, methodology, progress report and an update on the Tel Dor radiometric dates. The bible and radiocarbon dating. 2005 ⇒952. 65-92.

13615 *Sherratt, Sue* High precision dating and archaeological chronologies: revisiting an old problem. The bible and radiocarbon dating. 2005 ⇒952. 114-125.

13616 *Steele, Caroline* Who has not eaten cherries with the devil?: archaeology under challenge;

13617 *Verhoeven, Marc* Ethnoarchaeology, analogy, and ancient society. Archaeologies of the Middle East. 2005 ⇒683. 45-65/251-270.

13618 **Warburton, David A.** Archaeological stratigraphy: a Near Eastern approach. 2003 ⇒19,12791; 20,12164. [R]Akkadica 126 (2005) 100-103 (*Tunca, Önhan*).

T1.4 *Exploratores*—**Excavators, pioneers**

13619 **Baikie, James** †1931 A century of excavation in the land of the Pharaohs. L 2005, Kegan P. 252 pp. 0-7103-0985-6.

13620 **Nöldeke, Arnold** Altiki, der Finder: Memoiren eines Ausgräbers. [E]*Weber-Nöldeke, Elisabeth* 2003 ⇒19,12798. [R]OLZ 100 (2005) 41-47 (*Cholidis, Nadja*).

13621 ALBRIGHT W: **Feinman, Peter D.** William Foxwell Albright and the origins of biblical archaeology. Berrien Springs (Mich.) 2004, Andrews Univ. Pr. ix, 250 pp. 1-88392-540-1. Bibl. 203-245.

13622 BANKES W: **Sartre-Fauriat, Annie** Les voyages dans le Hawran (Syrie de Sud) de William John Bankes (1816 et 1818). 2004 ⇒20, 12172. [R]CRAI (2005/1) 140-142 (*Balty, Jean-Charles*);

13623 **Usick, Patricia** Adventures in Egypt and Nubia: the travels of William John Bankes (1786-1855). 2002 ⇒18,11734; 20,12173. [R]JNES 64 (2005) 202-204 (*Peck, William H.*).

13624 BOTHMER B: [E]**Swan, E.** Egypt 1950: my first visit by Bernard V. Bothmer. 2004 ⇒20,12174. [R]BiOr 62 (2005) 214-215 (*Parlasca, Klaus*).

13625 CONDER C: *Cobbing, Felicity; Jacobson, David* "A record of discovery and adventure": Claude Reignier Conder's contributions to the exploration of Palestine. NEA 68/4 (2005) 166-179.

13626 MARIETTE A: *Solé, Robert* Auguste Mariette le pacha de l'égyptologie. MoBi 167 (2005) 64-67.

13627 PETRIE F: [E]**Drower, Margaret S.** Letters from the desert: the correspondence of Flinders and Hilda Petrie. 2004 ⇒20,12182. [R]DiscEg 62 (2005) 109-110 (*Hardwick, Tom*); BiOr 62 (2005) 29-30 (*Patané, Massimo*).

13628 SPYCKET A: **Spycket, Agnès** À temps et à contretemps: un demi-siècle d'archéologie et de contacts dans le domaine du Proche-Orient. 2004 ⇒20,12185. [R]Akkadica 126 (2005) 98-99 (*Vallat, François*).

13629 STÄHLIN F: [E]**Cantarelli, Floriana** L'opera e l'importanza di Friedrich Stählin: (Milano, 13 dicembre 2001). Quaderni di Acme 72: Mi 2005, Cisalpino 184 pp. 88-323-6034-9.

T1.5 *Materiae primae*—**metals, glass**

13630 **Buchwald, Vagn Fabritius** Iron and steel in ancient times. DVS. HFS 29: K 2005, Royal Danish Academy of Sciences and Letters 372 pp. 87-7304-308-7. Bibl. 344-362.

13631 [E]**Hauptmann, Harald; Pernicka, Ernst** Die Metallindustrie Mesopotamiens von den Anfängen bis zum 2. Jahrtausend v. Chr. 2004 ⇒20,12190. [R]Mes. 40 (2005) 194-195 (*Cellerino, Alessandra*).

13632 *Jackson-Tal, Ruth E.* The glass vessels from 'En Gedi. 'Atiqot 49 (2005) 73*-82*. **H.**

13633 [E]**Jennings, Sarah** Vessel glass from Beirut: BEY 006, 007 and 045. Ber. 48-49 (2005) xiv; 1-326.

13634 *Lisella, Anna R.* Glass core pendants from the museum of the Studium Biblicum Franciscanum-Jerusalem. LASBF 55 (2005) 435-456 (Pls. 59-60).

13635 **Saldern, Axel von** Antikes Glas. Handbuch der Archäologie: 2004 ⇒20,12196. [R]Mes. 40 (2005) 207 (*Ponzi, Mariamaddalena N.*).

13636 *Shalev, Sariel; Shilstein, Sana; Yekutieli, Yuval* 'En Yahav—a copper smelting site in the 'Arava. BASOR 340 (2005) 1-21.

13637 **Stern, E.M.** Roman, Byzantine, and early medieval glass: 10 BCE-700 CE. Ernesto Wolf Collection: 2001 ⇒17,10762; 19,12811. [R]BiOr 62 (2005) 144-146 (*Whitehouse, David*).

13638 **Yener, K. Aslihan** The domestication of metals: the rise of complex metal industries in Anatolia. 2000 ⇒16,11009... 18,11751. [R]AWE 4 (2005) 512-514 (*Dolukhanov, P.*).

### T1.7 Technologia antiqua

13639 *Ad, Uzi; Sa'id, 'Abd al-Salama; Frankel, Rafael* Water-mills with Pompeian-type millstones at Naḥal Tanninim. IEJ 55 (2005) 156-171.

13640 **Barber, F.M.** The mechanical triumphs of the ancient Egyptians. L 2005, Kegan P. x; 123 pp. 0-7103-1004-8.

### T1.8 Architectura; *Supellex*; furniture

13641 *Baur, Wolfgang* Auf diese Steine konnten sie bauen ... der Bau mit Ziegeln in vorbiblischer und biblischer Zeit. WUB 37 (2005) 72-5.

13642 **Bernhauer, Edith** Hathorsäulen und Hathorpfeiler: altägyptische Architekturelemente vom Neuen Reich bis zur Spätzeit. Philippika 8: Wsb 2005, Harrassowitz xvi; 132 pp. €48. 978-34470-52146. Vorwort *Christian Loeben*; 45 pl. [LASBF 56,632—A. Niccacci].

13643 *Bretschneider, Joachim* Das Verhältnis von Palast und Tempel im frühen Mesopotamien. UF 37 (2005) 9-25.

13644 **Darcque, Pascal** L'habitat mycénien: formes et functions de l'espace bâti en Grèce continentale à la fin du IIe millénaire avant J.-C. Bibliothèque des Ecoles Françaises d'Athènes et de Rome 319: Athens 2005, Ecole Française d'Athènes 450 pp. €90. 2-86958-18-90. 113 fig.; 163 plans.

13645 *Eck, Werner* Ehret den Kaiser: Bögen und Tore als Ehrenmonumente in der Provinz Iudaea. [F]STEMBERGER, G.: SJ 32: 2005 ⇒ 140. 153-165.

13646 *Faust, Avraham* The Canaanite village: social structure of Middle Bronze Age rural communities. Levant 37 (2005) 105-125.

13647 **Goyon, J.-C.**, *al.*, La construction pharaonique du Moyen Empire à l'époque gréco-romaine: contexte et principes technologiques. 2004 ⇒20,12220. [R]CRAI (2005/2) 707-709 (*Leclant, Jean*).

[F]**GROS, P.** Théorie...pratique de l'architecture romaine 2005 ⇒51.

13648 **Jahn, Beate** Altbabylonische Wohnhäuser, eine Gegenüberstellung philologischer und archäologischer Quellen. Orient-Archäologie 16: Rahden 2005, Leidorf ix; 169 pp. €54.80. 3-89646-646-1. 37 fig.; 40 pl. RMes. 40 (2005) 197-198 (*Lippolis, Carlo*).

13649 **Jones, Mark Wilson** Principles of Roman architecture. 2000 ⇒16, 11029... 18,11776. RRAr (2005/1) 119-122 (*Schmid, Stephan G.*).

13650 *Knauß, Florian S.* Zur eisenzeitlichen Wohnarchitektur Ostgeorgiens. ANES 42 (2005) 187-210.

13651 **Meinecke, Michael; Aalund, Flemming** Bosra: islamische Architektur und Archäologie. Orient-Archäologie 17: Rahden/Westf. 2005, Marie Leidorf x; 199 pp. 3-89646-647-X. Bibl. 177-185.

13652 *Morris, S.P.; Papadopoulos, J.K.* Greek towers and slaves: an archaeology of exploitation. AJA 109 (2005) 155-225.

13653 *Nasrallah, Laura* Empire and Apocalypse in Thessaloniki: interpreting the early christian Rotunda. JECS 13 (2005) 465-508.

13654 **Netzer, Ehud** Nabatäische Architektur: insbesondere Gräber und Tempel. 2003 ⇒19,12854. RAnCl 74 (2005) 650-651 (*Bonato-Baccari, Stéphanie*).

13655 **Nielsen, Inge** Hellenistic palaces: tradition and renewal. 1999 ⇒ 15,10925; 16,11039. RAJA 109 (2005) 315-17 (*Roller, Duane W.*).

13656 **Pilgrim, Cornelius von** Elephantine XVIII: Untersuchungen in der Stadt des Mittleren Reiches und der Zweiten Zwischenzeit. 1996 ⇒ 12,9581; 14,10122. RWZKM 95 (2005) 391-401 (*Eigner, Dieter*).

13657 **Richardson, Peter** City and sanctuary: religion and architecture in the Roman Near East. 2002 ⇒18,11786. RJThS 56 (2005) 652-654 (*Day, Juliette*).

13658 **Rossi, Corinna** Architecture and mathematics in ancient Egypt. 2004 ⇒20,12247. RJAR 61 (2005) 261-262 (*Spence, Kate*); Isis 96 (2005) 268-270 (*Robson, Eleanor*).

13659 **Schmidt-Colinet, Andreas; Plattner, Georg A.** Antike Architektur und Bauornamentik, Grundformen und Grundornamentik. 2004 ⇒20,12249. RRAr (2005/1) 142-144 (*Hellman, Marie-Christine*).

13660 **Seasoltz, R. Kevin** A sense of the sacred: theological foundations of christian architecture and art. NY 2005, Continuum vi; 394 pp. $30. 0-8264-1701-9.

13661 *Sievertsen, Uwe* Frühe Pfeiler-Nischen-Architektur aus Tepe Gawra und Telul Eth-Thalathat. Iraq 67/1 (2005) 399-409.

13662 **Stamper, John W.** The architecture of Roman temples. C 2005, CUP xvi; 287 pp. £50. 0-521-81068-X. 162 ill.

13663 *Takata, Gaku* Problems in the chronology of the Iron Age IIA in Palestine and research on *Bīt Ḫilāni*. Orient 40 (2005) 91-104.

13664 *Thiel, Wolfgang M.* Vom Ornament zum Medium: die kanonischen griechischen Bauordnungen und ihr Beitrag zur Hellenisierung Palästinas im 2. und 1. Jh. v. Chr. Medien im antiken Palästina. FAT 2/10: 2005 ⇒646. 189-235.

13665 **Vomberg, Petra** Das Erscheinungsfenster innerhalb der amarnazeitlichen Palastarchitektur: Herkunft–Entwicklung–Fortleben. Philippika 4: 2004 ⇒20,12254. RBiOr 62 (2005) 480-83 (*Spieser, C.*).

13666 **Wright, George R.H.** Ancient building technology, 2: materials. Technology and change in history 7/1-2: Lei 2005, Brill xxxvi; 316 + xxiv pp. 309 fig.

13667 *Harris, J.* Saved from Vesuvius: rare wooden furniture from Pompeii and Herculaneum. Archaeology Odyssey [Wsh] 8/5 (2005) 24-29 [NTAb 50,105].

13668 *Rehm, Ellen* Assyrische Möbel für den assyrischen Herrscher!. Crafts and images. OBO 210: 2005 ⇒693. 187-206.

## T2.1 *Res militaris*—military matters

13669 *Baker, Patrick* Warfare. Companion to the Hellenistic world. 2005 ⇒642. 373-388.

13670 *Cohen, Susan L.* The spearheads from the 2002-2004 excavations at Gesher. IEJ 55 (2005) 129-142.

13671 **Hamblin, William J.** Warfare in the ancient Near East to 1600 BC: holy warriors at the dawn of history. Warfare and History: L 2005, Routledge 517 pp. €76. 0415255880.

13672 **James, Simon** The excavations at Dura-Europos conducted by Yale University and the French Academy of Inscriptions and Letters, 1928 to 1937: final report 7: arms and armour, and other military equipment. 2004 ⇒20,12262. [R]Antiquity 79 (2005) 723-725 (*Feugere, Michel*).

13673 **Lendon, J.E.** Soldiers & ghosts: a history of battle in classical antiquity. NHv 2005, Yale Univ. Pr. xii; 468 pp. $35. 03001-06637. Bibl. [NTAb 50,631].

13674 **Mayor, Adrienne** Greek fire, poison arrows, and scorpion bombs: biological and chemical warfare in the ancient world. 2003 ⇒19, 12876. [R]SCI 24 (2005) 291-293 (*Shatzman, Israel*).

13675 *Miglus, Piotr A.* Die ankerlose Ankeraxt: Verbreitung und Datierung einer altorientalischen Bronzewaffe. [F]GAWLIKOWSKI, M. 2005 ⇒45. 161-187.

13676 **Morkot, Robert** Historical dictionary of ancient Egyptian warfare. 2004 ⇒20,12265. [R]JAfH 46 (2005) 328-329 (*Brewer, Douglas J.*).

13677 *Patella, Michael* Seers' Corner: embattled Holy Land. BiTod 43 (2005) 96-101.

13678 **Pirson, Felix** Ansichten des Krieges: Kampfdarstellungen klassischer und hellenistischer Zeit im Kulturvergleich. 2005, Diss.-Habil. Leipzig [AA 2006/1, 315].

13679 **Pollard, Nigel** Soldiers, cities, and civilians in Roman Syria. 2000 ⇒16,11070; 18,11811. [R]JNES 64 (2005) 220-222 (*McClellan, Thomas L.*).

13680 **Rehm, Ellen** Waffengräber im Alten Orient: zum Problem der Wertung von Waffen in Gräbern des 3. und frühen 2. Jahrtausends v.Chr. in Mesopotamien und Syrien. BAR Internat. Ser. 1191: 2004 ⇒20,12266. [R]WO 35 (2005) 285-287 (*Novák, Mirko*).

13681 **Sekunda, N.** Hellenistic infantry reform in the 160's B.C.. Studies on the history of ancient and medieval art of warfare 5: 2001 ⇒17, 10801; 19,12881. [R]AJA 109 (2005) 119-121 (*Davies, Gwyn*).

13682 **Shalev, Sariel** Swords and daggers in late Bronze Age Canaan. 2004 ⇒20,12267. [R]AMIT 37 (2005) 443-445 (*Philip, Graham*).

13683 *Stiebel, Guy D.* Scalping in Roman Palestine—'minime Romanum sacrum'?. SCI 24 (2005) 151-162 [2 Macc 7,4].

## T2.2 *Vehicula, nautica*—**transport, navigation**

13684 [E]**Fansa, Mamoun; Burmeister, Stefan** Rad und Wagen: der Ursprung einer Innovation: Wagen im Vorderen Orient und Europa. BAMN 40: 2004 ⇒20,12269. [R]AJA 109 (2005) 798-799 (*Izbitser, Elena*); OLZ 100 (2005) 429-438 (*Jacobs, Bruno*); WO 35 (2005) 280-284 (*Novák, Mirko*).

13685 **Arnaud, Pascal** Les routes de la navigation antique: itinéraires en Méditerranée. P 2005, Errance 248 pp. 2-87772-3143.

13686 *Cohen, Orna* Conservation of the ancient boat from the Sea of Galilee. 'Atiqot 50 (2005) 219-232.

13687 **Fabre, David** Le destin maritime de l'Egypte ancienne. L 2005, Periplus 278 pp. 1902-6991-57. [R]DiscEg 62 (2005) 81-93 (*Vandersleyen, Claude*).

13688 *Friedman, Zaraza* Boats depiction in the 8th century CE nilotic frames mosaic in the church of St. Stephen, Umn al-Rasas, Jordan. LASBF 55 (2005) 595-417 (Pls. 51-56).

13689 **Golvin, Jean-Claude; Reddé, Michel** Voyages sur la Méditerranée romaine. Arles 2005, Actes Sud 137 pp. €39. 28777-23062. Num. ill.

13690 **Kingsley, Sean A.** Shipwreck archaeology of the Holy Land: processes and parameters. L 2005, Duckworth 159 pp. £22. 0-7156-3277-9.

13691 *Pedersen, Ralph K.* Was Noah's ark a sewn boat?. BArR 31/3 (2005) 18-23, 55-56, 58.

13692 **Schulz, R.** Die Antike und das Meer. Da 2005, Primus 256 pp. 3-89678-261-4. Bibl.

13693 *Tammuz, O. Mare clausum*?: sailing seasons in the Mediterranean in early antiquity. Mediterranean Historical Review [TA] 20/2 (2005) 145-162 [NTAb 50,536].

13694 *Werker, Ella* Identification of the wood in the ancient boat from the Sea of Galilee. 'Atiqot 50 (2005) 233-236.

## T2.4 *Athletica*—**sport, games**

13695 [E]**Bell, Sinclair; Davies, Glenys** Games and festivals in classical antiquity: proceedings of the conference held in Edinburgh 10-12 July 2000. BAR International Series, 1220: Oxf 2004, Archaeopress vi; 153 pp. $28. 1-84171-580-8. Num. ill.

13696 **Bohne, Anke** Untersuchungen zum Sport in der römischen Kaiserzeit–Darstellungen sportlicher Thematik und ihr Kontext. 2005 Diss. Bonn [AA 2006/1, 309].

13697 *Bosman, P.R.* Meat, muscle and mind: DIOGENES and the athletes. Scriptura 90 (2005) 660-669 [NTAb 51,351].

13698 *Castelli, Elizabeth A.* Persecution and spectacle: cultural appropriation in the christian commemoration of martyrdom. AfR 7 (2005) 102-136.

13699 *Juschka, D.* Spectacles of gender: enacting the masculine in ancient Rome and modern cinema. RStT 24/1 (2005) 75-110 [NTAb 50, 133].

13700 [E]**Knauß, Florian; Wünsche, Raimund** Lockender Lorbeer: Sport und Spiel in der Antike. Mü 2004, Staatliche Anitkensammlungen 503 pp. Ausstellungskatalog; Num. ill.

13701 **König, J.** Athletics and literature in the Roman Empire. C 2005, CUP xix; 398 pp. £55. 0-521-83845-2. 12 fig.

13702 *Marzahn, Joachim* Spielbretter aus Berlin. [M]DIAKONOFF, M. 2005 ⇒36. 149-164.

13703 **Newby, Zahra** Greek athletics in the Roman world: victory and virtue. Oxford studies in ancient culture and presentation: Oxf 2005, OUP xiv; 314 pp. £80. 0-19-927930-6. Num. ill.

13704 **Sinn, Ulrich** Das antike Olympia: Götter, Spiel und Kunst. 2004 ⇒ 20,12282. [R]HZ 280 (2005) 146-147 (*Mann, Christian*).

### T2.5 *Musica, drama, saltario*—**music, drama, dance**

13705 **Basurko, Xabier** O canto cristão na tradição primitiva. [T]*Teixeira, Celso Márcio*: Liturgia e música: São Paulo 2005, Paulus 254 pp.

13706 *Brummitt, Mark* Hand(e)ling the Messiah. ET 117 (2005) 95-99.

13707 *Cappellini, Maria R.* La bibbia a passo di danza: alcune considerazioni rabbiniche contemporanee sulla danza biblica nella tradizione ebraica. StPat 52 (2005) 575-588.

13708 *Couture, Pamela* Bible, music and pastoral theology. Bible in pastoral practice. 2005 ⇒341. 286-295.

13709 *Dienst, Karl* "Unendlichkeit" als theologisch-philosophische Kategorie im Kirchenlied des Barockzeitalters: eine Skizze. [F]BÖCHER, O. 2005 ⇒14.368-380.

13710 *Downey, Charles T.; Fleming, Keith A.* Some multiple-melody communions with texts from the gospels. EtGr 33 (2005) 5-74.

13711 **Flynn, William T.** Medieval music as medieval exegesis. 1999 ⇒ 15,10966... 18,11834. [R]Spec. 80 (2005) 222-223 (*Hiley, David*).

13712 *Garfinkel, Y.* Dancing scenes in early rural societies. Qad. 38 (2005) 66-80. **H.**

13713 [E]**Gilmour, Michael J.** Call me the seeker: listening to religion in popular music. NY 2005, Continuum 310 pp. $32. 978-0826-4171-38.

13714 *Goecke-Seischab, Margarete L.* Von der Macht der Musik und der Psychologie der Farben. KatBl 130 (2005) 440-449.

13715 **Habinek, T.** The world of Roman song: from ritualized speech to social order. Baltimore 2005, Johns Hopkins Univ. Pr. vii; 329 pp. $52. 08018-81056. Bibl. [NTAb 50,209].

13716 *Hagel, Stefan* Is *nīd qabli* Dorian?: tuning and modality in Greek and Hurrian music. BaghM 36 (2005) 287-348.

13717 *Kubies, Grzegorz* Orkiestra króla Nabuchodonozora II czy zespół Antiocha IV Epifanesa?: kilka uwag muzykologa [The orchestra of the king Nebuchadnezzar II or the band of Antiochus IV Epiphanes?: a few remarks made by a musicologist]. RBL 58 (2005) 135-150. **P.**

13718 **Labie, Jean-François** Le visage du Christ dans la musique des XIXe et XXe siècles. P 2005, Fayard 460 pp. €25.

13719 **Lockyer, Herbert, Jr.** All the music in the bible: an exploration of musical expression in scripture and church hymnody. Peabody, MA

2004, Hendrickson 209 pp. £10. 1-56563-5310. [R]ET 117 (2005) 121-122 (*Ortlund, Eric*).

13720 *Marchesin, Isabelle* Les images musicales occidentales aux VIIIe et IXe siècles: une exégèse visuelle. Biblical studies. 2005 ⇒773. 259-282 [Scr. 60/1,86*—G. Michiels].

13721 *Müßgens, Bernhard* Chaos, Angst und Ordnung durch Musik und Tanz?: zum Beispiel Jericho .... Das Buch. Vechtaer Beiträge zur Theologie 11: 2005 ⇒487. 9-22 [Josh 6].

13722 *Nieten, Ulrike-Rebekka* Die griechische Ethoslehre und ihr Einfluß auf den Orient. [F]VOIGT, R. AOAT 317: 2005 ⇒158. 269-282.

13723 *O'Donovan, Matthew; O'Donovan, Oliver* BACH's musical treatment of Jesus' baptism. Com(US) 32/1 (2005) 119-127 [Mt 3,13-17]; IKaZ 34 (2005) 68-75.

13724 **Onstine, Suzanne L.** The role of the chantress (sm'yt) in ancient Egypt. BAR intern. ser. 1401: Oxf 2005, Archaeopress iv; 164 pp. 1841718408. Bibl. 151-64. [R]DiscEg 63 (2005) 97-103 (*DuQuesne, Terence*).

13725 **Perez Arroyo, Rafael** Egypt: music in the age of the pyramids. 2003 ⇒19,12920. [R]WO 35 (2005) 209-212 (*Lieven, Alexandra von*); ArOr 73 (2005) 501-502 (*Vachala, Břetislav*).

13726 *Puaud, Gaëtan* Olivier MESSIAEN ou les couleurs musicales de la Jérusalem céleste. Graphè 14 (2005) 145-153.

13727 **Schauensee, Maude de** Two lyres from Ur. 2002 ⇒18,11841. [R]BASOR 340 (2005) 81-82 (*Lawergren, Bo*); JNES 64 (2005) 313-314 (*Biggs, Robert D.*).

13728 **Schuol, Monika** Hethitische Kultmusik: eine Untersuchung der Instrumental- und Vokalmusik anhand hethitischer Ritualtexte und von archäologischen Zeugnissen. 2004 ⇒20,12302. [R]Mes. 40 (2005) 187-189 (*Martino, Stefano de*).

13729 *Stutz, Justin R.* The Reformers and church music: a biblical analysis of their philosophies. Faith & Mission 22/3 (2005) 3-16.

13730 Tempelmusik [Die vorliegende CD entstand für die Hörstation der Ausstellung "Salomons Tempel" des Projekts Bibel+Orient Museum] = Musique de temple. FrS 2005, 1 CD, 12 cm, 1 Begleitheft.

## T2.6 *Vestis*, **clothing**; *ornamenta*, **jewellry**

13731 *Pasquali, Jacopo* Remarques comparatives sur la symbolique du vêtement à Ébla. [M]DIAKONOFF, M. 2005 ⇒36. 165-184.

13732 **Scheele, Katrin** Die Stofflisten des Alten Reiches: Lexikographie, Entwicklung und Gebrauch. MENES 2: Wsb 2005, Harrassowitz ix; 171 pp. €58. 3-447-05092-6. Bibl. 157-166. [R]ArOr 73 (2005) 505-507 (*Vymazalová, Hana*).

13733 **Schmidt-Colinet, Andreas; Stauffer, Annemarie**, *al.*, Die Textilien aus Palmyra—neue und alte Funde. Damaszener Forschungen 8: 2000 ⇒16,11119... 20,12315. [R]IEJ 55 (2005) 246-247 (*Merker, Gloria S.*).

13734 *Hirschfeld, Yizhar; Peleg, Orit* An early Roman gemstone depicting Apollo found at Ramat ha-Nadiv. ZDPV 121 (2005) 59-66.

13735 *Paul, Shalom M.* Jerusalem of gold—revisited. Divrei Shalom. CHANE 23: 2005 ⇒273. 333-342.

## T2.8 **Utensilia**

13736 *Ariel, Donald T.* Stamped amphora handles amd unstamped amphora fragments from Acre (‘Akko). ‘Atiqot 50 (2005) 181-193.

13737 **Bignasca, Andrea M.** I kernoi circolari in Oriente e in Occidente: strumenti di culto e immagini cosmiche. OBO.A 19: 2000 ⇒16, 11122; 18,11852. [R]OLZ 100 (2005) 180-185 (*Hausleiter, Arnulf*); Gn. 77 (2005) 248-252 (*Scheibler, Ingeborg*).

13738 *Hartmann, Rita; Hartung, Ulrich* Zwei vermutlich aus der Westwüste stammende Gefäße im prädynastischen Friedhof U in Abydos. MDAI.K 61 (2005) 211-218; Taf. 36.

13739 *Kashani, Natascha Bagherpour* The ‘cultic vessel’ from Inandiktepe: was it used for alcohol?. Aram 17 (2005) 211-220.

13740 **Khodzhash, Svetlana Izmailovna** Ancient Egyptian vessels in the State Pushkin Museum of Fine Art, Moscow. Baltimore, MD 2005, Halgo vii; 150 pp. 1-89284-003-0. Bibl. 143-150.

13741 **Kristakis, Konstandinos S.** Cretan Bronze Age pithoi: tradition and trends in the production and consumption of storage containers in Bronze Age Crete. [D]*Warren, Peter*: Prehistory Monographs 18: Ph 2005, INSTAP Academic xvi; 111 pp. $60. 1-931534-152. Diss. Bristol; 45 fig.; 28 pl.

13742 *Mazzoni, Stefania* Pyxides and hand-lion bowls: a case of minor arts. Crafts and images. OBO 210: 2005 ⇒693. 43-66.

13743 *Piccirillo, Michele* Una macina per il grano ad uso di una famiglia cristiana di Madaba. LASBF 55 (2005) 498 (Pls. 70).

13744 *Ramadan, Wagdy* Les sortes et noms de l’encensoir dans l’Egypte ancienne. DiscEg 61 (2005) 73-80.

13745 *Scigliuzzo, Elena* La produzione di beni di lusso nel Levante dell’Età del Ferro: il ruolo socio-culturale degli artigiani. EVO 28 (2005) 255-267.

13746 *Zimmermann, Thomas* Perfumes and policies—a ‘Syrian bottle’ from Kinet Höyük and Anatolian trade patterns in the advanced third millennium BC. Anatolica 31 (2005) 161-169.

## T2.9 *Pondera et mensurae*—**weights and measures**

13747 *Hafford, William B.* Mesopotamian mensuration: balance pan weights from Nippur. JESHO 48 (2005) 345-387.

13748 **Michailidou, A.** Weight and value in pre-coinage societies: an introduction. Melethmata 42: P 2005, De Boccard 173 pp. €40. 960-7905-237. Bibl.

13749 **Payne, Margaret** Urartian measures of volume. ANESt.S 16: Lv 2005, Peeters xv; 387 pp. 90-429-1483-1.

13750 **Pommerening, Tanja** Drei altägyptische Hohlmaße. SAÄK.B 10: Hamburg 2005, Buske xiii; 503 pp. Bibl. 425-454.

13751 *Sader, H.* An inscribed weight from Byblos. V Congresso di studi fenici. 2005 ⇒959. I, 47-51.

13752 *Schmitt, Götz* Zum altägyptischen Hohlmaßsystem. ZÄS 132/1 (2005) 55-72.

### T3.0 **Ars antiqua**, *motiva, picturae* [icones T3.1 infra]

13753 *Albenda, Pauline* The "Queen of the Night plaque"—a revisit. JAOS 125 (2005) 171-190.

13754 **Albenda, Pauline** Ornamental wall painting in the art of the Assyrian Empire. Cuneiform Monographs 28: Lei 2005, Brill xiii, 148 pp. 90-04-14154-5. Bibl. 137-144.

13755 *Albersmeier, Sabine* Griechisch-römische Bildnisse der Isis (Kat. 200-214). Ägypten–Griechenland–Rom. 2005 ⇒13570. 310-314.

13756 *Amedick, Rita* "Iesus Nazarenus Rex Iudaiorum": hellenistische Königsikonographie und das Neue Testament;

13757 *Balch, David L.* Zeus, vengeful protector of the political and domestic order: frescoes in dining rooms N and P of the house of the Vettii in Pompeii, Mark 13:12-13, and I Clement 6:2. Picturing the New Testament. WUNT 2/193: 2005 ⇒396. 53-66/67-95.

13758 **Biaggio, Monica** I gesti della seduzione: tracce di comunicazione non-verbale nella ceramica greca tra VI e IV sec. a.C. 2004 ⇒20, 12330. [R]RAr (2005/2) 386-387 (*Cassimatis, Hélène*).

13759 *Brier, Bob; Wilkinson, Caroline* A preliminary study on the accuracy of mummy portraits. ZÄS 132/2 (2005) 107-111; Pl. XXIII-XXIX.

13760 *Buchholz, H.-G.* Beobachtungen zur nahöstlichen, zyprischen und frühgriechischen Löwenikonographie. UF 37 (2005) 27-215.

13761 **Capriotti Vittozzi, Giuseppina** L'arte egizia: il potere dell'immagine. R 2005, ARACNE 71 pp. 88-548-0311-1. Bibl. 67-69.

13762 *Cecchini, Serena M.* The 'suivant du char royal': a case of interaction between various genres of minor art. Crafts and images. OBO 210: 2005 ⇒693. 243-264.

13763 **Clarke, John R.** Art in the lives of ordinary Romans: visual representation and non-elite viewers in Italy, 100 B.C.-A.D. 315. 2003 ⇒19,12954. [R]AJP 126 (2005) 623-626 (*D'Ambra, Eve*).

13764 **Collon, Dominique** The Queen of the Night. British Museum Objects in Focus: L 2005, British Museum Pr. 47 pp. 0-7141-5043-6. 19 ill.

13765 **Croisille, Jean-Michel** La peinture romaine. Manuels d'art et d'archéologie antique: P 2005, Picard 375 pp.

13766 [E]**Davies, W.V.** Colour and painting in Ancient Egypt. 2001 ⇒17, 10872... 19,12958. [R]JNES 64 (2005) 121-123 (*Hill, Marsha*).

13767 [E]**Donohue, A.A.; Fullerton, M.D.** Ancient art and its historiography. 2003 ⇒19,12961; 20,12338. [R]AWE 4 (2005) 191-192 (*Boardman, John*).

13768 *Dorn, Andreas* Men at work: zwei Ostraka aus dem Tal der Könige mit nicht-kanonischen Darstellungen von Arbeitern. MDAI.K 61 (2005) 1-11; Taf. 1-4.

13769 **Ewald, Björn Christian** Der Philosoph als Leitbild: ikonographische Untersuchungen an römischen Sarkophagreliefs. 1999 ⇒15, 11016...18,11890. [R]AnCl 74 (2005) 635-636 (*Balty, Jean Ch.*).

13770 *Fazzini, Richard; Josephson, Jack A.; O'Rourke, Paul* The Doha head: a late period Egyptian portrait. MDAI.K 61 (2005) 219-241; Taf. 37-41.

13771 *Fendrich, Herbert* Himmelhoch!: der babylonsiche Turm und seine Bilder. WUB 37 (2005) 58-65.

13772 *Fick, Sabine M.E.* Jupiter Optimus Maximus Heliopolitanus. WUB 36 (2005) 29.
13773 **Fiechter, J.J.** Faux et faussaires en art égyptien. Brepols 2005, Turnhout xii; 318 pp. €79. 978-25035-15847.
13774 *Fine, Steven* Liturgy and the art of the Dura Europos synagogue. Liturgy in the life of the synagogue. Duke Judaic Studies 2: 2005 ⇒848. 41-71.
13775 **Fischer, Erika** Die Elfenbeinschnitzerei in Syrien-Palästina während der Späten Bronzezeit. 2005, Diss. Halle Wittenberg [AA 2006/1, 310].
13776 [E]**Giuliani, Luca** Meisterwerke der antiken Kunst. Mü 2005, Beck 185 pp. €24.90. 3406-53094X. 77 fig.
13777 **Giuliani, Luca** Bild und Mythos: Geschichte der Bilderzählung in der griechischen Kunst. 2003 ⇒19,12965; 20,12343. [R]RAr (2005/2) 393-396 (*Siebert, Gérard*).
13778 *Grimm, Alfred* Imagines Aegypti—varia ikonologica: ein Mykerinos-Bildnis in Privatbesitz. ZÄS 132/1 (2005) 12-34; Tafel VI-XIV.
13779 *Gubel, Eric* Phoenician and Aramean bridle-harness decoration: examples of cultural contact and innovation in the eastern Mediterranean. Crafts and images. OBO 210: 2005 ⇒693. 111-148.
13780 *Haase, Mareile* Etruskische Tieropferdarstellungen: Bild und Handlung. La cuisine...l'autel. BEHE.R 124: 2005 ⇒539. 291-307.
13781 *Hoffman, Gail L.* Defining identities: Greek artistic interaction with the Near East. Crafts and images. OBO 210: 2005 ⇒693. 351-390.
13782 **Junker, Klaus** Griechische Mythenbilder: eine Einführung in ihre Interpretation. Stu 2005, Metzler 190 pp. €25. 3-476-01987-X. 36 ill. [EuA 81,336].
13783 *Keel, Othmar, al.*, Les belles images du monde oriental éclairent le texte biblique. MoBi 167 (2005) 50-53.
13784 **Keel, Otmar; Schroer, Silvia** Eva—Mutter alles Lebendigen: Frauen- und Göttinnenidole aus dem Alten Orient. 2004 ⇒20, 12356. [R]JNSL 31/2 (2005) 129-130 (*Cornelius, Sakkie*).
13785 *Lagarce, J.; Puytison-Lagarce, E. du* Quelques aspects de l'iconographie royale et divine dans le royaume d'Ugarit à l'âge du Bronze récent. V Congresso di studi fenici. 2005 ⇒959. I, 53-67.
13786 **Le Quellec, Jean-Loïc; Flers, Philippe de; Flers, Pauline de** Du Sahara au Nil: peintures et gravures d'avant les pharaons. Études d'égyptologie 7: P 2005, Fayard 382 pp. 2-213-62488-7. Préf. *Nicolas Grimal*; Bibl. 356-369.
13787 **Leach, Eleanor W.** The social life of painting in ancient Rome and on the Bay of Naples. 2004 ⇒20,12359. [R]AJP 126 (2005) 626-629 (*Lorenz, Katharina*).
13788 *Lurson, Benoît* Un topos iconographique de l'époque ramesside: l'encadrement du dieu ithyphallique: à propos des scènes du péristyle sud de la deuxième cour du Grand Temple de Medinet Habou. ZÄS 132/2 (2005) 123-137.
13789 *Matthäus, Hartmut* Toreutik und Vasenmalerei im früheisenzeitlichen Kreta: minoisches Erbe, lokale Traditionen und Fremdeinflüsse. Crafts and images. OBO 210: 2005 ⇒693. 291-350.
13790 **Metzger, Martin** Vorderorientalische Ikonographie und Altes Testament. [E]*Pietsch, Michael; Zwickel, Wolfgang* 2004 ⇒20,242. [R]OLZ 100 (2005) 625-629 (*Schroer, Silvia*).

13791 *Millard, Alan* Makers' mark, owners' names and individual identity. Crafts and images. OBO 210: 2005 ⇒693. 1-10.

13792 *Minas, Martina* Macht und Ohnmacht: die Repräsentation ptolemäischer Königinnen in ägyptischen Tempeln. APF 51/1 (2005) 127-154.

13793 **Moorey, Peter** Idols of the people: miniature images of clay in the ancient Near East. 2003 ⇒19,12986. [R]CamArchJ 15 (2005) 120-122 (*Garfinkel, Yosef*).

13794 *Muth, Susanne* Die Sicht der Sieger: Bilder vom Krieg im antiken Griechenland und Rom. BiKi 60 (2005) 221-226.

13795 **Padgett, J. Michael**, *al.*, The centaur's smile: the human animal in early Greek art. 2003 ⇒19,12991. [R]RAr (2005/1) 156-157 (*Isler-Kerényi, Cornelia*).

13796 *Pino, Cristina* The market scene in the tomb of Khaemhat (TT 57). JEA 91 (2005) 95-105.

13797 **Porter, Barbara** Trees, kings, and politics: studies in Assyrian iconography. OBO 197: 2003 ⇒19,257; 20,12372. [R]OLZ 100 (2005) 424-29 (*Faist, Bettina*); Mes. 40 (2005) 200-201 (*Lippolis, Carlo*).

13798 **Schachner, Andreas** Bilder eines Weltreichs: kunst- und kulturgeschichtliche Untersuchungen zu den Verzierungen eines Tores in Balawat (Imgur-Enlil) aus der Zeit von Salmanassar III, König von Assyrien. 2005, Diss.-Habil. München [AA 2006/1, 315].

13799 **Schroer, Silvia; Keel, Othmar** Die Ikonographie Palästinas/Israels und der Alte Orient: eine Religionsgeschichte in Bildern, 1: vom ausgehenden Mesolithikum bis zur Frühbronzezeit. FrS 2005, Academic 392 pp. €44. 3-7278-1508-6.

13800 *Sole, L.* Iconografie religiose fenicie nelle emissioni di *Melite* (Malta). TEuph 29 (2005) 171-187; Pls. V-VII.

13801 **Stockfisch, Dagmar** Untersuchungen zum Totenkult des ägyptischen Königs im Alten Reich: die Dekoration der königlichen Totenkultanlagen. Antiquitates 25: 2003 ⇒19,13004. [R]OLZ 100 (2005) 14-16 (*Landgráfová, Renata*).

[E]**Suter, C.** Crafts and images in contact 2005 ⇒693.

13802 *Uehlinger, Christoph* Die Elfenbeinschnitzereien von Samaria und die Religionsgeschichte Israels: Vorüberlegungen zu einem Forschungsprojekt. Crafts and images. OBO 210: 2005 ⇒693. 149-86.

13803 *Vázquez Hoys, A.M.* La magia de la Gorgona Medusa: serpientes, nudos, mal de ojo y Oriente. TEuph 30 (2005) 149-171.

13804 *Watanabe, Chikako E.* The 'continuous style' in the narrative scheme of Assurbanipal's reliefs. Nineveh. 2005 ⇒901. 103-114.

13805 *Wicke, Dirk* "Roundcheeked and ringletted": gibt es einen nordwestsyrischen Regionalstil in der altorientalischen Elfenbeinschnitzerei?. Crafts and images. OBO 210: 2005 ⇒693. 67-110.

13806 *Winter, Irene* Establishing group boundaries: toward methodological refinement in the determination of sets as a prior condition to the analysis of cultural contact and/or innovation in first millennium BCE ivory carving. Crafts and images. 2005 ⇒693. 23-42.

## T3.1 *Icones*—**ars postbiblica**

13807 **Achkarian, Hovsep** Manuale di iconografina armena. Catanzaro 2005, Rubbettino 155 pp.

13808 *Alcoy i Pedros, Rosa* Les illustrations recyclées du Psautier anglo-catalan de Paris: du douzième siècle anglais à l'italianisme pictural de Ferrer Bassa. Manuscripts in transition. 2005 ⇒935. 81-92 [Scr. 60/1,3*—A. Dubois].

13809 *Allen, Anthony* El Cristo de VELÁZQUEZ. Eccl(R) 19/1 (2005) 89-96.

13810 **Andreopoulos, Andreas** Metamorphosis: the Transfiguration in Byzantine theology and iconography. Crestwood, NY 2005, St. Vladimir's Seminary Pr. 286 pp. $26. 088141-2953 [ThD 52,365—W. Charles Heiser] [Mt 17,1-9].

13811 *Augustyn, Wolfgang* Zur Illustration von Psalterien und Psalmenkommentaren in Italian vom frühen 11. bis zum ausgehenden 13. Jahrhundert;

13812 *Backhouse, Janet* The psalter of Henry VI (London, BL, ms. Cotton Dom[itian] A XVII). Illuminated psalter. 2005 ⇒3817. 165-180/329-386 [Scr. 60,142*—M. Huglo].

13813 *Baur, Wolfgang* Wenn Steine reden: ein jüdischer Prophet im Ulmer Münster. WUB 38 (2005) 63.

13814 *Beall, Barbara A.* The tabernacle illumination in the Codex Amiatinus reconsidered. Biblical studies. 2005 ⇒773. 29-40 [Scr. 60/1,9* —G. Michiels].

13815 *Beckett, Wendy* Sister Wendy's top twenty biblical paintings. BiRe 21/1 (2005) 15-35.

13816 *Bertoldi, Anita* Con GEROLAMO 'nella pace silenziosa dello "studio" invaso dal sole': BALTHASAR interpreta DÜRER. Hum(B) 60 (2005) 1296-1313.

13817 **Brambilla, Gaetano** Volti di Gesù dal medioevo al rinascimiento: per la contemplazione, la preghiera et la catechesi. Leumann 2005, Elledici 184 pp. €14. 88-0103-1831.

13818 **Braun-Niehr, Beate** Das Brandenburger Evangelistar. Schriften des Domstifts Brandenburg 2: Rg 2005, Schnell & S. 104 pp. €15. 3-7954-1698-1. Ill. [Scr. 60/1,26*s—J. Hamburger].

13819 *Bräm, Andreas* Neapolitanische Trecento-Psalterien. Illuminated psalter. 2005 ⇒3817. 193-209 [Scr. 60,150*—M. Huglo].

13820 **Bulgakov, Sergius** The friend of the bridegroom: on the Orthodox veneration of the forerunner. [T]*Jakim, Boris*: 2003 ⇒19,13022; 20, 12386. [R]HPR 105/7 (2005) 72-73 (*Meconi, David*).

13821 *Camille, Michael* Bodies, names and gender in a Gothic psalter (Paris, BNF, ms. Lat. 10435). Illuminated psalter. 2005 ⇒3817. 377-386 [Scr. 60,157*—M. Huglo].

13822 **Cartlidge, David R.; Elliott, J. Keith** Art and the christian apocrypha. 2001 ⇒17,10917... 19,13027. [R]HeyJ 46 (2005) 229-230 (*McNamara, Martin*).

13823 [E]**Cassanelli, Roberto; Guerriero, Elio** Iconografia e arte cristiana. 2004 ⇒20,12388. [R]StPat 52 (2005) 682-684 (*Corsato, Celestino*).

13824 **Cavarnos, Constantine** Guide to Byzantine iconography, 1-2. 1993-2001 ⇒10,11863... 17,10918. [R]Logos 46/1-2 (2005) 245-247 (*Tribe, Shawn*).

13825 *Chazelle, Celia* Christ and the vision of God: the biblical diagrams of the Codex Amiatinus. The mind's eye. 2005 ⇒512. 84-111 [Scr. 60,160*—G. Hendrix];

13826 Violence and the virtuous ruler in the Utrecht Psalter. Illuminated psalter. 2005 ⇒3817. 445-46, 449-450 [Scr. 60,161*—M. Huglo].

13827 *Crippa, Maria Antonietta Il battesimo di Cristo* di PIERO della Francesca. Com(I) 199 (2005) 55-61.

13828 *Crossan, J. Dominic* A woman equal to Paul: who is she?. BiRe 21/3 (2005) 29-31, 46, 48 [NTAb 50,138] [Theocleia, mother of Thecla in Cave of St Paul at Ephesus. Contrast *Acts of Paul*].

13829 *Dekeyzer, Brigitte* From word to image: the illustration of 'religious' manuscripts throughout the Middle Ages. Manuscripts in transition. 2005 ⇒935. 7-21 [Scr. 60/1,38*—A. Dubois].

13830 *Dufrenne, Suzy* L'image dans les psautiers byzantins à illustrations intégrales Scr. 60, 169*—M. Huglo];

13831 *Engelhart, Helmut* Der Hornplatteneinband: eine charakteristische Form der Einbandgestaltung illuminierter Psalterhandschriften des 13. Jahrhunderts [Scr. 60,172*—M. Huglo];

13832 *Euw, Anton von* Die Darstellungen zum 90. (91.) Psalm in der frühmittelalterlichen Psalter- und Evangelienillustration mit Ergänzungen und Kommentarien. Ill. 406-417 [Scr. 60,266*—M. Huglo]. Illuminated psalter. 2005 ⇒3817. 157-163/441-456/405-411.

13833 *Fendrich, Herbert* Lesemutter Anna. BiHe 41/162 (2005) 22-23.

13834 *Feuchtwanger-Sarig, Naomi* "May he grow to the Torah ...": the iconography of Torah reading and Bar Mitzvah on Ashkenazi Torah binders. Liturgy in the life of the synagogue. Duke Judaic Studies 2: 2005 ⇒848. 161-176.

13835 **Folda, Jaroslav** Crusader art in the Holy Land, from the Third Crusade to the fall of Acre, 1187-1291. C 2005, CUP 714 pp. 978-0521-835831. Num. ill.; supplementary CD-ROM with 501 ill.

13836 *Freeman-Sandler, Lucy* Word imagery in English Gothic psalters: the case of the Vienna Bohum manuscript (ÖNB, cod 1826*). Illuminated psalter. 2005 ⇒3817. 387-395 [Scr. 60,178*—M. Huglo].

13837 **Gallino, Oreste Mendolia** La vita di Gesù a tre dimensioni. Mi 2005, Paoline 48 pp. €9.50 [CiVi 61/1,96].

13838 [E]**Geddes, Jane** Der Albani-Psalter: eine englische Prachthandschrift des 12. Jahrhunderts für Christina von Markyate. Rg 2005, Schnell & S. 136 pp. €29.80. 3-7954-1751-1. 89 ill.;

13839 The St. Albans psalter: a book for Christina Markyate. L 2005, British Library 136 pp. Ill. [RBen 118,165–P.-M. Bogaert].

13840 **Gerits, Huub** CHAGALL vertelt/vertaalt: de bijbel in kleur. Averbode 1999, Altiora 168 pp. €18,10. 90-317-1507-7.

13841 **Grün, Anselm** Nuovi volti di Gesù. [T]*Ruzzon, Alessandro*: CinB 2003, San Paolo 231 pp.

13842 **Gulácsi, Zsuzsanna** Mediaeval Manichaean book art: a codicological study of Iranian and Turkic illuminated book fragments from 8th-11th century east central Asia. NHMS 57: Lei 2005, Brill xvi; 240 pp. 90-04-13994-X. Bibl. 223-233.

13843 [E]**Hall, Marcia** MICHELANGELO's 'Last Judgement'. Masterpieces of western painting: C 2005, CUP 194 pp. $24. 0-521-783-68-2.

13844 *Hamarneh, Basema* Icona plumbea inedita con l'effige di Cristo nimbato e di Maria orante. LASBF 55 (2005) 501-504 (Pls. 76).

13845 *Hamburger, Jeffrey F.* Rewriting history: the visual and the vernacular in late medieval history bibles. ZDP Sonderheft 124 (2005) 260-308 [Scr. 60/1,61*—B. Gullath].

13846 **Hamburger, Jeffrey F.** St. John the Divine: the deified evangelist in medieval art and theology. 2002 ⇒18,11948... 20,12416. [R]CHR 91 (2005) 357-358 (*O'Reilly, Jennifer*).

13847 *Hartmann, Winfried* "Der Glanz der Seele": Beobachtungen zu einem Bildnis des Kardinals Albrecht von Brandenburg. [F]STENDEBACH, F. 2005 ⇒141. 181-197.

13848 *Häusl, Maria* Das atl. Bildungsrepertoire der Altäre in der Pfarrkirche St. Johannes d. Täufer, Petting. [F]SEIDL, T.: ATSAT 75: 2005 ⇒137. 225-252.

13849 **Hornik, Heidi J.; Parsons, Mikeal C.** Illuminating Luke: the public ministry of Christ in Italian Renaissance and baroque painting. NY 2005, Clark xiii; 177 pp. $35. 0-567-02820-8.

13850 **Jensen, Robin Margaret** Face to face: portraits of the divine in early christianity. Mp 2005, Fortress 252 pp. $20. 0-8006-3678-3.

13851 *Jordan-Ruwe, Martina* "Er wird verspottet, misshandelt und angespuckt werden, und man wird ihn geißeln und töten (Lk 18,32): zu einer Darstellung der Arma Christi in der Michaelskirche zu Fulda. [F]ZMIJEWSKI, J. BBB 151: 2005 ⇒172. 289-306.

13852 *Kahsnitz, Rainer* Frühe Initialpsalter. Illuminated psalter. 2005 ⇒ 3817. 137-155 [Scr. 60,202*—M. Huglo].

13853 *Kaiser, Helga* Schätze vom Sinai: Ikonen aus dem Katharinenkloster. WUB 35 (2005) 2-7.

13854 *Kawtaria, Nino* Die künstlerische Gestaltung der im Skriptorium des Klosters Kalipos bebilderten Evangelienhandschriften (A-484, S-962, K-76). Georgica 28 (2005) 192-202.

13855 **Kidd, Richard; Sparks, Graham** God and the art of seeing: visual resources for a journey of faith. 2003 ⇒19,13055. [R]Interp. 59 (2005) 326, 328 (*Towner, W. Sibley*).

13856 *Klemm, Elisabeth* Die Darstellung der Heiligen als Thema der Psalterillustration. Illuminated psalter. 2005 ⇒3817. 361-376 [Scr. 60, 204*—M. Huglo].

13857 **Kraus, Jeremia** Worauf gründet unser Glaube?: Jesus von Nazaret im Spiegel des Hitda-Evangeliars. [D]*Verweyen, Hans-Jürgen*: FThSt 168: FrB 2005, Herder 431 pp. €48. 3-451-28653-X. Diss. Freiburg/Br.; Num. ill.

13858 [E]**Krischel, Roland; Morello, Giovanni; Nagel, Tobias** Ansichten Christi: Christusbilder von der Antike bis zum 20. Jahrhundert. Köln 2005, Du Mont 295 pp. €29. 3-8321-7565-2. Ausstellung Köln 2005. [R]Volto dei volti 8/2 (2005) 71.

13859 *Kuder, Ulrich* Illuminierte Psalter von den Anfängen bis um 800. Illuminated psalter. 2005 ⇒3817. 107-35 [Scr. 60,207* M. Huglo].

13860 *Luz, Ulrich* Keimenike hermeneia kai eikonographia. DBM 23/2 (2005) 151-173 [Mt 26-27]. **G.**

13861 *Malinski, Martine* Les enluminures de la Jérusalem céleste dans quelques manuscrits monastiques du haut moyen âge. Graphè 14 (2005) 77-101 [Rev 21].

13862 *Mann, Vivian B.* Between worshipper and wall: the place of art in liturgical spaces. Liturgy in the life of the synagogue. Duke Judaic Studies 2: 2005 ⇒848. 109-119.

13863 *Marti, Susan* Assoziative Kompilation—Psalterminiaturen von Ordensfrauen. Manuscripts in transition. 2005 ⇒935. 193-201 [Scr. 60/ 1,87*—A. Dubois].

13864 *Menges, Thomas* Wie Bildwerke die Geschichte von Abraham und Isaak deuten. KatBl 130 (2005) 106-110 [Gen 22].

13865 [E]**Metzsch, Friedrich-A. von** Bild und Botschaft: biblische Geschichten auf Bildern der Alten Pinakothek München. 2002 ⇒18, 11980. [R]ThR 70 (2005) 248-249 (*Lindemann, Andreas*).

13866 *Meyer, Holt* Das Buch (in) der Verkündigung an Maria: Zeugenaussagen der Ikonographie und deren Spuren in der Schrift. Heilige Schriften. 2005 ⇒362. 132-158, 244-245.

13867 **Michaels, Daniel** 'Imago ut Verbum Dei': medieval exegesis and the frescoes of the basilica of Saint Francis of Assisi. [D]*Hellmann, J.A.W.* 2005, Diss. St. Louis [RTL 37,622].

13868 **Milstein, Rachel** La bible dans l'art islamique. Islamiques: P 2005, Presses universitaires de France 155 pp.

13869 **Morgan, David** The sacred gaze: religious visual culture in theory and practice. Berkeley 2005, Univ. of California Pr. 318 pp. £14.

13870 **Muzi, Maria Giovanna** Un maître pour l'art chrétien: André Grabar: iconographie et théophanie. Histoire: P 2005, Cerf 289 pp. €49. 2-204-07485-3.

13871 **Nes, Solrunn** The mystical language of icons. GR ²2005, Eerdmans 112 pp. $30. 0-8028-29163 [ThD 52,381—W. Charles Heiser].

13872 [E]**O'Malley, John W.; Bailey, Gauvin A.** The Jesuits and the arts, 1540-1773. Ph 2005, St Joseph's Univ. Pr. 447 pp. $50. 0-916101-52-5. Bibl. 427-442.

13873 *O'Kane, Martin* The artist as reader of the bible: visual exegesis and the adoration of the magi. BiblInterp 13 (2005) 337-373 [Mt 2, 1-12].

13874 *Oliver, Judith* A primer of thirteenth-century German convent life: the psalter as office and mass book (London, BL, ms. Add. 60629). Illuminated psalter. 2005 ⇒3817. 259-70 [Scr. 60,229* M. Huglo].

13875 *Ovadiah, Asher* Symbolic aspects of early christian art. Beginnings of christianity. 2005 ⇒786. 315-322.

13876 *Peterson, Elisabeth A.* Scholastic hermeneutics in historical initials of 13th century French psalters. Illuminated psalter. 2005 ⇒3817. 349-359 [Scr. 60,232*—M. Huglo].

13877 [E]**Petrowa, Ewgenia; Solowjowa, Irina** Nowgorod—das goldene Zeitalter der Ikonen. Mü 2005, Hirmer 223 pp. €39.90. 3-7774-25-95-8. Num. ill. [EuA 81,339].

13878 *Pfändtner, Karl G.* Zwei Bologneser Psalter des 13. Jahrhunderts und ihr Illustrationssystem (Bologna, Bibl. univ. cod 346 und Paris, BNF, Ms Smith-Lesouëf 219. Illuminated psalter. 2005 ⇒3817. 181-192 [Scr. 60,233*—M. Huglo].

13879 *Pindel, Roman* 'Da gingen ihnen die Augen auf und sie erkannten ihn': die Analyse Lk 24,13-35 und die Wirkungsgeschichte anhand der Werke REMBRANDTs van Rijn. ACra 37 (2005) 309-339.

13880 **Rachiteanu, Eugen** L'icona nella vita della chiesa: tre rappresentazioni dell'ultima cena. Dissertationes ad Lauream 108: R 2005, Seraphicum 76 pp. Bibl. 69-74.

13881 *Raeber, Judith* Illuminierte Psalterien aus den Innerschweizer Doppelklöstern Muri und Engelberg vom 12. bis 14. Jahrhundert. Illuminated psalter. 2005 ⇒3817. 223-238 [Scr. 60,236*—M. Huglo].

13882 *Raguse, Hartmut* Moses im Angesicht seines Todes?: zu zwei neuen Büchern über den Moses des MICHELANGELO. ThZ 61 (2005) 162-170.

13883 *Reilly, Diane* The roots of Capetian royalty and the Saint-Vaast Bible. Manuscripts in transition. 2005 ⇒935. 31-39 [Scr. 60/1,106* —A. Dubois].

13884 *Reveyron, Nicolas* Sources orientales dans l'iconographie lyonnaise de l'époque romane: l'incrédulité de Salomé et le premier bain de l'enfant à la cathédrale de Lyon (XIIe siècle). MUSJ 58 (2005) 211-226.

13885 *Ricciuti, Gail* The bible and the arts. Bible in pastoral practice. 2005 ⇒341. 296-304.

13886 **Saracino, Francesco** Pittori di Cristo. 2004 ⇒20,12455. RVolto dei volti 8/2 (2005) 69-70.

13887 *Scillia, Diane G.* Composing the 'Raising of Lazarus', ca. 1495. Manuscripts in transition. 2005 ⇒935. 399-405 [Scr. 60/1,113*—A. Dubois] [John 11].

13888 **Seraïdari, Katerina** Le culte des icônes en Grèce. Anthropologiques: Toulouse 2005, Presses universitaires du Mirail 256 pp.

13889 **Soltes, Ori Z.** Our sacred signs: how Jewish, christian, and Muslim art draw from the same source. Boulder 2005, Westview xi; 275 pp. 0-8133-4297-X.

13890 **Sörries, Reiner** Daniel in der Löwengrube: zur Gesetzmäßigkeit frühchristlicher Ikonographie. Wsb 2005, Reichert 215 pp. €72. 978-38950-04698. 26 pl.

13891 *Stahl, Harvey* Bathsheba and the kings: the Beatus initial in the psalter of Saint Louis (Paris, BNF ms lat. 10525). Illuminated psalter. 2005 ⇒3817. 427-434 [Scr. 60,248*—M. Huglo].

13892 *Steenbock, Frauke* Psalterien mit kostbaren Einbänden. Illuminated psalter. 2005 ⇒3817. 435-440 [Scr. 60,248*—M. Huglo].

13893 *Stirnemann, Patricia* The Copenhagen Psalter (Kongel. Bibl., ms Thott 143 2°) reconsidered as a coronation present for Canute VI. Illuminated psalter. 2005 ⇒3817. 323-8 [Scr. 60,248*: M. Huglo].

13894 *Stock, Alex* Der Vogel, die Hand und der Mann im Wasser: zur Ikonographie der Taufe Jesu. IKaZ 34 (2005) 56-67 [Mt 3,13-17].

13895 **Suarès, André** Passion: eaux-fortes originales en couleurs et bois dessinés par Georges Rouault. P 2005, Cerf 154 pp. €39 [EeV 116/1,26s—Robert Pousseur].

13896 *Suckale, Gude* Zwei Bilderpsalter für Frauen aus dem frühen 13. Jahrhundert. Illuminated psalter. 2005 ⇒3817. 249-258 [Scr. 60, 249*—M. Huglo].

13897 *Theißen, Henning* Das Antlitz Jesu: zur theologischen Würdigung künstlerischer Christusdarstellung. ThZ 61 (2005) 143-161.

13898 *Tiffany, Tanya J.* Visualising devotion in early modern Seville: VELÁZQUEZ's *Christ in the house of Martha and Mary*. SCJ 36 (2005) 433-453.

13899 **Török, László** After the pharaohs, treasures of the Coptic art from Egyptian collections, Museum of Fine Arts, Budapest, 18 March-18 May 2005. Budapest 2005, Museum of Fine Arts 278 pp. 96395-5-2569. Num. ill.

13900 *Tripps, Johannes* From singing saints to descending angels: medieval ceremonies and cathedral façades as representations of the heavenly Jerusalem. ACr 93/1 (2005) 1-13.

13901 *Van den Hoek, Annewies* Peter, Paul and a consul: recent discoveries in African red slip ware. ZAC 9 (2005) 197-246.

13902 *Vasiliu, Anca* Entre *muses* et *logos*: invention de l'allégorie et naissance de l'icône (*Sophistes* et *Pères* à la fin de l'antiquité). Allégorisme des poètes. 2005 ⇒874. 149-193.

13903 **Verkerk, Dorothy** Early medieval bible illumination and the Ashburnham pentateuch. 2004 ⇒20,12466. RCHR 91 (2005) 135-138 (*Nees, Lawrence*); ChH 74 (2005) 353-355 (*Corrie, Rebecca W.*).

13904 *Villeneuve, Estelle* Türkei: Ephesus: unveröffentlichte Gemälde in der Paulushöhle. WUB 37 (2005) 66-67.

13905 *Watson, Janell* The face of Christ: Deleuze and Guattari on the politics of word and image. BiCT 1/2 (2005)*.

13906 *Weissenrieder, Annette; Wendt, Friederike* Phänomenologie des Bildes: ikonographische Zugänge zum Neuen Testament. ZNT 8/16 (2005) 3-12;

13907 Images as communication: the methods of iconography. Picturing the New Testament. WUNT 2/193: 2005 ⇒396. 3-49.

13908 *Wheelock, A.K.*, *al.*, Saints as men: REMBRANDT's New Testament portraits. BiRe 21/2 (2005) 26-31 [NTAb 49,472].

13909 *Wittekind, Susanne* Verum etiam sub alia forma depingere: illuminierte Psalmenkommentare und ihr Gebrauch. Illuminated psalter. 2005 ⇒3817. 271-280 [Scr. 60,271*—M. Huglo].

13910 **Zell, Michael** Reframing REMBRANDT: Jews and the christian image in seventeenth-century Amsterdam. Berkeley 2002, Univ. of California Pr. xix; 264 pp. [R]JQR 95 (2005) 742-45 (*Cahn, Walter*).

13911 **Zibawi, Mahmoud** Images de l'Égypte chrétienne: iconologie copte. 2003 ⇒19,13092. [R]BiOr 62 (2005) 530-532 (*Martens-Czarnecka, Malgorzata*).

13912 [T]**Zucker, Arnaud** Physiologos: le bestiaire des bestiaires. Atopia: Grenoble [2]2005, Million 328 pp. €33. 28413-71719.

## T3.2 Sculptura

13913 **Albersmeier, Sabine** Untersuchungen zu den Frauenstatuen des ptolemäischen Ägypten. Aegyptiaca Treverensia 10: 2002 ⇒18, 12025. [R]WO 35 (2005) 225-228 (*Höckmann, Ursula*).

13914 *Bartl, Peter V.* Layard's drawings of the incised decorations on the Nimrud reliefs compared with the originals. Iraq 67/2 (2005) 17-29.

13915 *Berlejung, Angelika* Gewalt ins Bild gesetzt: Kriegsdarstellungen auf neuassyrischen Palastreliefs. BiKi 60 (2005) 205-211.

13916 [E]**Bol, Peter C.**, *al.*, Die Geschichte der antiken Bildhauerkunst, 1: frühgriechische Plastik. 2002 ⇒18,12030; 20,12476. [R]AnCl 74 (2005) 275-281 (*Duplouy, Alain*).

13917 **Bolshakov, Andrey O.** Studies on Old Kingdom reliefs and sculpture in the Hermitage. ÄA 67: Wsb 2005, Harrassowitz (8); 279 pp. 3-447-05184-1. Bibl. 241-271. 42 pl.

13918 *Bonatz, Dominik* Ninurtas Gaben: assyrische Kriegsideologie und ihre Bilder. Krieg–Gesellschaft–Institutionen. 2005 ⇒672. 61-88.

13919 *Booth, Charlotte* A Ptolemaic terracotta head in the Petrie Museum. JEA 91 (2005) 197-200.

13920 **Bovot, Jean-Luc** Les serviteurs funéraires royaux et princiers de l'Ancienne Égypte. 2003 ⇒20,12478. [R]JEA 91 (2005) 220-224 (*Schneider, H.D.*).

13921 **Böhm, Stephanie** Klassizistische Weihreliefs: zur römischen Rezeption griechischer Votivbilder. 2004 ⇒20,12479. [R]RAr (2005/2) 413-414 (*Zagdoun, Mary-Anne*).

13922 **Brand, Peter James** The monuments of Seti I: epigraphic, historical and art historical analysis. PÄ 16: 2000 ⇒16,11284... 19, 13099. [R]JNES 64 (2005) 113-115 (*Peck, William H.*).

13923 *Danrey, V.* Winged human-headed bulls of Nineveh: genesis of an iconographic motif. Nineveh. 2005 ⇒901. 133-139.

13924 **Downey, Susan B.** Terracotta figurines and plaques from Dura-Europos. 2003 ⇒19,13103; 20,12490. RRAr (2005/2) 422-425 (*Martinez-Sève, Laurianne*).

13925 **Englund, Klaudia** Nimrud und seine Funde: der Weg der Reliefs in die Museen und Sammlungen. 2003 ⇒19,13104. ROr. 74 (2005) 135-136 (*Pinnock, Frances*).

13926 *Erlich, A.* Persian and Hellenistic terracotta figurines from Maresha: aspects of succession and modification. TEuph 30 (2005) 186.

13927 *Espinel, Andrés D.* A newly identified stela from Wadi el-Hudi (Cairo JE 86119). JEA 91 (2005) 55-70.

13928 *Faegersten, Fanni* Ivory, wood, and stone: some suggestions regarding the Egyptianizing votive sculpture from Cyprus. Crafts and images. OBO 210: 2005 ⇒693. 265-290.

13929 *Feldman, Marian H.* Nineveh toThebes and back: art and politics between Assyria and Egypt in the seventh century BCE. Nineveh. 2005 ⇒901. 141-150.

13930 E**Hainaut-Zveny, Brigitte d'** Miroirs du sacré: les retables sculptés à Bruxelles XVe-XVIe siècles: production, formes et usages. Lieux de Mémoire: Bru 2005, CFC 254 pp. €36. 2-930018-55-0.

13931 **Hallett, Christopher H.** The Roman nude: heroic portrait statuary 200 BC-AD 300. Oxford studies in ancient culture and presentation: Oxf 2005, OUP xxii; 391 pp. £80. 0-19-9240-493. 160 pl.

13932 **Hill, Marsha** Royal bronze statuary from ancient Egypt: with special attention to the kneeling pose. Egyptological Memoirs 3: 2004 ⇒20,12497. RBiOr 62 (2005) 483-487 (*Raven, Maarten J.*).

13933 **Hölzl, Regina** Reliefs und Inschriftensteine des Alten Reiches II. CAA Wien 21: 2000 ⇒16,11293... 19,13112. RJNES 64 (2005) 115-116 (*Papazian, Hratch*).

13934 *Incordino, Ilaria* Il significato dei santuari nei bassorilievi regali della III dinastia. Aeg. 85 (2005) 185-197.

13935 *Jean, Cynthia* Des rapaces dévoreurs d'ennemis: un symbole de la victoire royale. FFINET, A. Subartu 16: 2005 ⇒40. 85-97.

13936 **Keesling, Katherine** The votive statues of the Athenian acropolis. 2003 ⇒19,13117; 20,12500. RAJA 109 (2005) 114-115 (*Perry, Ellen*).

13937 *Kohlmeyer, Kay* Syrien: Aleppo: Aufsehen erregende Reliefs auf der Zitadelle. WUB 36 (2005) 60-61.

13938 **Kosmopoulou, Angeliki** The iconography of sculptured statue bases in the archaic and classical periods. 2002 ⇒18,12056; 20, 12502. RAnCl 74 (2005) 598-599 (*Prost, Francis*).

13939 *Kousser, Rachel* Creating the past: the Vénus de Milo and the Hellenistic reception of classical Greece. AJA 109 (2005) 227-250.

13940 **Koutsogiannis, Charissios** Untersuchungen zu griechischen Weihreliefs an Artemis aus klassischer Zeit. 2005, Diss. Heidelberg [AA 2006/1, 312].

13941 *Lobell, J.A.* Myth in marble. Arch. 58/4 (2005) 26-29 [NTAb 50, 107].

13942 **Martin, Geoffrey T.** Stelae from Egypt and Nubia in the Fitzwilliam Museum, Cambridge. C 2005, CUP ix; 202 pp. £100. 0-521-84290-5. Bibl. viii-xi. RBiOr 62 (2005) 487-488 (*Meulenaere, H.J.A. de*).

13943 *Müller-Kessler, Christa* Zwei palmyrenische Relieffragmente. [M]HILLERS, D. 2005 ⇒61. 130-136.

13944 *Nadali, Davide* Sennacherib's siege, assault, and conquest of Alammu. SAA Bulletin 14 (2002-2005) 113-128.

13945 *Ornan, Tallay* Expelling demons at Nineveh: on the visibility of benevolent demons in the palaces of Nineveh. Nineveh. 2005 ⇒901. 83-92.

13946 *Parlasca, Klaus* Varianten palmyrenischer Grabreliefs. [F]GAWLIKOWSKI, M. 2005 ⇒45. 203-212.

13947 **Perry, Ellen** The aesthetics of emulation in the visual arts of ancient Rome. C 2005, CUP 208 pp. $75. 0-521-83165-2.

13948 **Regier, Willis** Goth Book of the Sphinx. 2004 ⇒20,12516. [R]AJA 109 (2005) 800-801 (*Katz, Joshua T.*).

13949 *Rolley, Claude* Les bronzes grecs et romains: recherches récentes. RAr 2 (2005) 339-364.

13950 **Rolley, Claude** La sculpture grecque, 2: la période classique. 1999 ⇒15,11143...19,13136. [R]AnCl 74 (2005) 600-02 (*Prost, Francis*).

13951 *Ross, Jennifer C.* Representations, reality, and ideology. Archaeologies of the Middle East. 2005 ⇒683. 327-350.

13952 *Sader, Hélène* Iron Age funerary stelae from Lebanon. Cuadernos de Arqueología Mediterránea [Univ. Pompeu Fabra, Barcelona] 11 (2005) 5-159. 118 fig.

13953 *Schmidt-Colinet, Andreas* Stuck und Wandmalerei aus dem Areal der 'hellenistischen Stadt' von Palmyra. [F]GAWLIKOWSKI, M. 2005 ⇒45. 225-241;

13954 *Schmidt-Colinet, Constanze* König und Nachfolger: zu den Löwenjagd-Reliefs aus Raum S des Nordpalasts in Ninive und noch einmal zur Bankettszene Assurbanipals. Mes. 40 (2005) 31-79.

13955 *Scigliuzzo, Elena* The 'wig and wing workshop' of Iron Age ivory carving. UF 37 (2005) 557-607.

13956 **Stewart, Peter** Statues in Roman society: representation and response. 2003 ⇒19,13141. [R]AnCl 74 (2005) 631-3 (*Balty, Jean C.*).

13957 *Stokkel, Peter J.A.* A new perspective on Hittite rock reliefs. Anatolica 31 (2005) 171-188.

13958 *Stucky, Rolf A.* Prêtres syriens III: le relief votif du prêtre Gaïos de Killiz et la continuité des motifs proche-orientaux aux époques hellénistique et romaine. [F]GAWLIKOWSKI, M. 2005 ⇒45. 277-284.

13959 *Sugimoto, David T.* Female figurines with a disk from Palestine: an analysis of their distribution patterns. AJBI 30-31 (2004-5) 61-97.

13960 *Summerer, Lâtife* Achämeniden am Schwarzen Meer: Bemerkungen zum spätarchaischen Marmorkopf aus Herakleia Pontike. ANES 42 (2005) 231-252.

13961 *Thomason, Allison K.* From Sennacherib's bronzes to Taharqa's feet: conceptions of the material world at Nineveh. Nineveh. 2005 ⇒901. 151-162.

13962 **Tomoum, Nadja S.** The sculptors' models of the late and Ptolemaic periods: a study of the type and function of a group of ancient Egyptian artefacts. [T]*Siller, Brenda*: Cairo 2005, National Center for Documentation 265 pp. 97730-58166. 102 pp of pl. Bibl. 251-264.

13963 **Vachala, Břetislav** Die Relieffragmente aus der Mastaba des Ptahschepses in Abusir. Abusir 8: 2004 ⇒20,12522. [R]BiOr 62 (2005) 472-474 (*Hölzl, Regina*).

13964 *Vittozzi, Giuseppina C.* Una statuetta della dea ippopotamo all'Università di Roma 'La Sapienza'. Aeg. 85 (2005) 219-235.

13965 *Wielgosz, Dagmara* La présence de marbres précieux à Palmyre. FGAWLIKOWSKI, M. 2005 ⇒45. 303-323.

13966 **Wrede, Nadja** Uruk: Terrakotten I: von der 'Ubaid- bis zur altbabylonischen Zeit. ADFGUW.Endberichte 25: 2003 ⇒19,13146. RMes. 40 (2005) 196-197 (*Menegazzi, Roberta*).

13967 *Yalçin, Ansu B.* Sculture bizantine conservate nel museo del Castello di Bodrum. Atti del X Simposio di Efeso. 2005 ⇒785. 327-345.

13968 E**Zimmer, Gerhard** Neue Forschungen zur hellenistischen Plastik. 2003 ⇒19,13148. RRAr (2005/1) 103-106 (*Marcadé, Jean*).

## T3.3 *Glyptica*; **stamp and cylinder seals**; *scarabs, amulets*

13969 *Amiet, Pierre* Les sceaux de l'administration princière de Suse à l'époque d'Agadé. RA 99 (2005) 1-12.

13970 *Amorai-Stark, Shua; Minster, Tsevi; Rosenfeld, Ammon* Seals of the 11th-9th century BCE from Israel made of oil shale. LASBF 55 (2005) 419-434 (Pls. 57-58).

13971 *Ben Guiza, R.* A propos des décans égyptiens et de leur réception dans le monde phénicien et punique. TEuph 29 (2005) 49-81; Pls. I-IV.

13972 *Berlin, Andrea; Herbert, Sharon* Life and death on the Israel-Lebanon border: excavation yields thousands of seal impressions. BArR 31/5 (2005) 34-43.

13973 **Beyer, Dominique** Emar IV: les sceaux: mission archéologique de Meskéné-Emar: recherches au pays d'Astata. OBO.A 20: 2001 ⇒ 17,11027... 20,12528. RJNES 64 (2005) 68-70 (*Garrison, M.B.*).

13974 *Charvát, Petr* The backs of some sealings from Nineveh 5. Iraq 67/1 (2005) 391-397.

13975 **Collon, Dominique** First impressions: cylinder seals in the ancient Near East. L 22005 <1987>, British Museum 208 pp. £15. 0-7141-1136-8. Bibl. 198-204.

13976 **Dusinberre, Elspeth R.M.** Gordion seals and sealings: individuals and society. Univ. Museum Monographs 124; Gordion Special Studies 3: Ph 2005, Univ. of Pennsylvania Museum xvi; 179 pp. $60. 237 fig.; incl. CD-ROM.

13977 **Garrison, Mark B.; Root, Margaret C.** Seals on the Persepolis fortification tablets: images of heroic encounter. 2001 ⇒17,11040 ... 20,12535. RZA 95 (2005) 155-159 (*Seidl, Ursula*).

13978 *Heeßel, Nils P.* Zu dem verschollenen Kudurru des Marduk-aḫḫē-erība. BaghM 36 (2005) 225-233.

13979 *Heltzer, M.* A Moabite seal with a unique iconography. FKLEIN, J. 2005 ⇒79. 738-741.

13980 **Herbordt, Suzanne** Die Prinzen- und Beamtensiegel der hethitischen Grossreichszeit auf Tonbullen aus dem Nisantepe-Archiv in Hattusa. Bogazköy-Hattusa 19: Mainz 2005, Von Zabern xv; 443 pp. €92.50. 3805333110. Kommentare *J.D. Hawkins*; Bibl. xiii-xiv.

13981 E**Invernizzi, Antonio**, *al.*, Seleucia al Tigri: le impronte di sigillo dagli archivi. 2004 ⇒20,12544. RMes. 40 (2005) 205-207 (*Callieri, Pierfrancesco*).

13982 *Kaoukabani, Ibrahim* Les estampilles phéniciennes de Tyr. Archaeology and History in Lebanon 21 (Spring 2005) 8-79 [UF 36,652—Heltzer, M.].

13983 **Kaptan, Deniz** The Daskyleion bullae: seal images from the western Achaemenid Empire. Achaemenid History 12: 2002 ⇒18, 12100; 20,12546. [R]AJA 109 (2005) 791-792 (*Gates, Charles*).

13984 **Keel-Leu, Hildi; Teissier, Beatrice** Die vorderasiatischen Rollsiegel der Sammlungen "Bibel+Orient" der Universität Freiburg Schweiz. OBO 200: 2004 ⇒20,12548. [R]BiOr 62 (2005) 343-349 (*Ottol, Adelheid*); OLZ 100 (2005) 451-454 (*Klengel-Brandt, E.*); WZKM 95 (2005) 432-434 (*Bleibtreu, Erika*).

13985 **Krsyszkowska, Olga** Aegean seals: an introduction. BICS 85: 2004 ⇒20,12550. [R]SMEA 47 (2005) 353-59 (*Weingarten, Judith*).

13986 *Kyriakidis, E.* Unidentified floating objects on Minoan seals. AJA 109 (2005) 137-154.

13987 **Lindström, Gunvor** Uruk: Siegelabdrücke auf hellenistischen Tonbullen und Tontafeln. 2003 ⇒19,13179; 20,12553. [R]Or. 74 (2005) 434-436 (*Rossi, Marco*); Mes. 40 (2005) 125-144 (*Messina, Vito*); Syria 82 (2005) 375-377 (*Martinez-Sève, Laurianne*).

13988 *Mazzoni, Stefania* Les sceaux d'Emar. Syria 82 (2005) 331-336.

13989 **Merrillees, Parvine H.** Catalogue of the western Asiatic seals in the British Museum: cylinder seals VI: pre-Achaemenid and Achaemenid periods. L 2005, British Museum x; 161 pp. €90. 0-7141-11-58-9. 35 pl.

13990 *Münger, Stefan* Medien und Ethnizität: das Beispiel einer tanitischen Stempelsiegel-Gruppe der frühen Eisenzeit. Medien im antiken Palästina. FAT 2/10: 2005 ⇒646. 85-107.

13991 *Münger, Stefan* Stamp-seal amulets and early Iron Age chronology. The bible and radiocarbon dating. 2005 ⇒952. 381-404.

13992 [E]**Pini, Ingo** Corpus der minoischen und mykenischen Siegel, 5: kleinere griechische Sammlungen Suppl. 3: Neufunde aus Griechenland. 2004 ⇒20,12559. [R]AJA 109 (2005) 575-576 (*Younger, John G.*).

13993 *Staubli, Thomas* Schutz, Schmuck und Unterschrift: Stempelsiegelamulette in Israel/Palästina. WUB 35 (2005) 73-75.

13994 **Teeter, Emily** Scarabs, scaraboids, seals, and seal impressions from Medinet Habu. UCOIP 118: 2003 ⇒19,13196. [R]BiOr 62 (2005) 44-47 (*Stoof, Magdalena*); BASOR 339 (2005) 114-117 (*Ben-Tor, Daphna*); JEA 91 (2005) 226-228 (*Martin, Geoffrey T.*).

13995 *Wimmer, Stefan Jakob* Byblos vs. Ugarit: the Alalakh seal impression 194 once again. Levant 37 (2005) 127-132.

13996 *Yalali, Serap* An Old Babylonian cylinder seal from Daskyleion in northwestern Anatolia. ANES 42 (2005) 299-311.

13997 *Zamora López, José-Ángel* Un bollo punico da Puig de la Nau de Benicarló (Castellón) e la questione della stampigliatura anforica nell'occidente mediterraneo. StEeL 22 (2005) 59-77.

## T3.4 **Mosaica**

13998 *al-As'ad, Khaled; Briquel-Chatonnet, Françoise; Yon, Jean-Baptiste* The sacred banquets at Palmyra and the function of the *tesserae*: reflections on the tokens found in the Arṣu temple;

13999 *al-As'ad, Khaled; Schmidt-Colinet, Andreas* A new *tessera* from Palmyra: questions of iconography and epigraphy. [M]HILLERS, D.: 2005 ⇒61. 1-10/166-180.

14000 **Bleiberg, Edward** Tree of paradise: Jewish mosaics from the Roman Empire. Brooklyn 2005, Brooklyn Museum 66 pp. $18. 08-72-73-1553. Num. ill.; Exhib. Oct. 2005-June 2006.

14001 *Cousland, J.R.C.* The much suffering eye in Antioch's *House of the evil eye*: is it Mithraic?. RStT 24/1 (2005) 61-74 [NTAb 50,132].

14002 **Ferdi, Sabah** Corpus des mosaïques de Cherchel. Etudes d'antiquités africaines: P 2005, CNRS 256; xci pp. €39. 9782-2710-63595. Préf. *M. Blanchard-Lemée*; Ill.

14003 *Gawlikowsky, Michal* L'apothéose d'Odeinat sur une mosaïque récemment découverte à Palmyre. CRAI 4 (2005) 1293-1304.

14004 *Lindgård, Fredrik* The mosaics of the house of Aion in Paphos, Cyprus. [F]AEJMELAEUS, L. SESJ 89: 2005 ⇒1. 528-545.

14005 *Merrony, Mark W.* The mosaic pavements of Khirbet el-Jiljil. BAIAS 23 (2005) 91-100.

14006 [E]**Morlier, Hélène** La mosaïque gréco-romaine: actes du IXe colloque international pour l'étude de la mosaïque antique et médiévale, Rome, nov. 2001. Coll. EFR 352: Rome 2005, EFR 398 pp.

14007 *Piccirillo, Michele* Un nuovo volto per la Terra nel mosaico superiore nella cappella del Prete Giovanni al Nebo. LASBF 55 (2005) 498-500 (Pls. 70).

14008 *Sudilovsky, Judith* Better late than never: Caesarea mosaic uncovered—again. BArR 31/6 (2005) 17.

14009 **Talgam, Rina; Weiss, Zeev** The mosaics of the house of Dionysos at Sepphoris. Qedem 44: 2004 ⇒20,12577. [R]SCI 24 (2005) 321-323 (*Millar, Fergus*); Qad. 38 (2005) 61-63 (*Hachlili, Rachel*); BASOR 340 (2005) 95-97 (*Parrish, David*).

14010 *Waliszewski, Tomasz* Some remarks on the Okeanos from Petra. [F]GAWLIKOWSKI, M. 2005 ⇒45. 285-301.

## T3.5 *Ceramica*, **pottery**

14011 [E]**Al-Maqdissi, Michel; Matoian, Valérie; Nicolle, Christophe** Céramique de l'âge du Bronze en Syrie, 1: la Syrie du Sud et la vallée de l'Oronte. BAH Beyr. 161: 2002 ⇒18,12137... 20,12579. [R]BiOr 62 (2005) 50-354 (*Duistermaat, Kim*).

14012 **Avissar, Miriam; Stern, Edna J.** Pottery of the crusader, Ayyubid, and Mamluk period in Israel. IAA Reports 26: J 2005, Israel Antiquities Authority vii; 177 pp. 965-406-180-5. Bibl. 173-177.

14013 *Badre, Leila, al.*, The provenance of Aegean- and Syrian-type pottery found at Tell Kazel (Syria). Ä&L 15 (2005) 15-47.

14014 *Barnard, H.; Dooley, A.N.; Faull, K.F.* New data on the Eastern Desert ware from Sayala (Lower Nubia) in the Kunsthistorisches Museum, Vienna. Ä&L 15 (2005) 49-64.

14015 *Beit-Arieh, Itzhaq; Karasik, Avshalom; Smilansky, Uzy* New typological analyses of early Bronze Age holemouth jars from Tel Arad and southern Sinai. TelAv 32/1 (2005) 20-31.

14016 **Bergoffen, Celia J.** The Cypriot Bronze Age pottery from Sir Leonard WOOLLEY's excavations at Alalakh (Tell Atchana). Contributions to the chronology of the eastern Mediterranean 5: W

2005, Verlag der Österreichischen Akademie der Wissenschaften 158 pp. €49. 3-7001-3245-X.. 50 pl.

14017 **Beuger, Claudia** Keramik der spätfrühdynastischen bis spätassyrischen Zeit aus Assur: eine Bearbeitung unter chronologischen Gesichtspunkten. 2005, Diss. Freie Univ., Berlin [AA 2006/1, 309].

14018 **Bourriau, Janine**, *al.*, The Memphite tomb of Horemheb commander-in-chief of Tutʿankhamun, 3: the New Kingdom pottery. L 2005, Egypt Exploration Society xvii; 115 pp. £35. 0-85698-167-2.

14019 **Dolinka, Benjamin J.** Nabataean Aila (Aqaba, Jordan) from a ceramic perspective: local and intra-regional trade in Aqaba ware during the first and second centuries A.D. 2003 ⇒19,13216. [R]BASOR 340 (2005) 97-99 (*Schmid, Stephan G.*).

14020 *Doumet-Serhal, C.* Tell Rachidieh: le Black on red local. V Congresso di studi fenici. 2005 ⇒959. I, 79-86.

14021 **Faiers, Jane**, *al.*, Late Roman pottery at Amarna and related studies. MEES 72: L 2005, Egypt Exploration Society 283 pp. £60. 0-85698-162-1.

14022 **Fortner, Sandra** Hellenistische und frührömische Keramik und Kleinfunde von Julias/Betsaida am See Gennesaret. 2005, Diss. München [AA 2006/1, 310].

14023 **Güntner, Wolfgang** Figürlich bemalte mykenische Keramik aus Tiryns. 2000 ⇒17,11104; 19,13223. [R]BiOr 62 (2005) 354-356 (*Van Wijngaarden, Gert Jan*).

14024 *Jamieson, Andrew S.* A painted eye-vase from Tell Ahmar and the Syro-Cilician painted ceramic tradition. [F]FINET, A. 2005 ⇒40. 79-83.

14025 *Johnston, Alan W.* Kommos: further Iron Age pottery. Hesp. 74 (2005) 309-393.

14026 *Klinger, Sonia* Observations on the range and nature of Attic black and red figure pottery in Israel: the Yavneh-Yam contribution. AWE 2 (2003) 135-145.

14027 *Kourou, N.* Horse-bird *askoi* from Carthage and central Mediterranean: a case study of cultural interrelations in early Iron Age Mediterranean. V Congresso di studi fenici. 2005 ⇒959. I,247-58.

14028 **Loffreda, Stanislao** Holy Land pottery at the time of Jesus: early Roman period 63 BC-70 AD. Studium Biblicum Franciscanum, Museum 15: 2002 ⇒18,12166. [R]BiOr 62 (2005) 601-2 (*Ortiz, S.*).

14029 *Ludwig, Nadine* Die kachetische Keramik des I. Jts. v. Chr.—eine Einführung. ANES 42 (2005) 211-230.

14030 *Magee, Peter* The production and function of Iron Age bridge-spouted vessels in Iran and Arabia: results from recent excavations and geochemical analysis. Iran 43 (2005) 93-115.

14031 *Martin, S. Rebecca; Stewart, Andrew* Attic imported pottery at Tel Dor, Israel: an overview. BASOR 337 (2005) 79-94.

14032 *Mlynarczyk, Jolanta* The pottery from Khirbet el-Jiljil (second season). BAIAS 23 (2005) 139-166.

14033 **Pinnock, Frances** La ceramica del palazzo settentrionale del Bronzo Medio II. Materiali e studi archeologici di Ebla (MSAE) 6: R 2005, "La Sapienza" 171 pp. 88882-33032. 118 pl.; Bibl. 156-168.

14034 **Postgate, Carolyn; Oates, David; Oates, Joan** The excavations at Tell al Rimah: the pottery. 1997 ⇒13,10466... 17,11114. [R]JNES 64 (2005) 65-68 (*Ur, Jason*).

14035 **Rotroff, Susan I.; Oliver, Andrew, Jr.** The Hellenistic pottery from Sardis: the finds through 1994. Mon. 12: 2003 ⇒19,13244. [R]BASOR 338 (2005) 102-104 (*Slane, Kathleen Warner*).

14036 [E]**Rouillard, Pierre; Verbanck-Piérard, Annie** Le vase grec et ses destins. 2003 ⇒19,13245. [R]AJA 109 (2005) 113-4 (*Lyons, Claire*).

14037 *Rubinson, Karen S.* Second millennium B.C. painted potteries and problems of terminologies. AMIT 37 (2005) 133-138.

14038 **Van Wijngaarden, Gert Jan** Use and appreciation of Mycenaean pottery in the Levant, Cyprus and Italy (1600-1200 BC). Amsterdam archaeological studies 8: 2002 ⇒18,12178. [R]BiOr 62 (2005) 140-143 (*Iamoni, M.*); BASOR 338 (2005) 100-2 (*Rutter, Jeremy*).

14039 *Vincenz, Anna de* The pottery from Khirbet el-Jiljil (first season). BAIAS 23 (2005) 111-138.

14040 [E]**Warden, P. Gregory** Greek vase painting: form, figure and narrative: treasures of the National Archaeological Museum in Madrid. 2004 ⇒20,12612. [R]AJA 109 (2005) 312-314 (*Padgett, J. Michael*).

14041 *Yannai, Eli* Late Bronze Age pottery from tombs 12 and 13 at Tell Jatt, Sharon plain. 'Atiqot 49 (2005) 13*-30*. **H.**

## T3.7 *Cultica*—**cultic remains**

14042 *Atiat, Taysir M.* A Nabataean sanctuary at al-Mujib nature reserve: a preliminary notice. Levant 37 (2005) 163-168.

14043 *Avner, R.* The Kathisma church on the road from Jerusalem to Bethlehem. Qad. 38 (2005) 117-121. **H.**

14044 *Aydingün, Şengül; Rose, Mark* Saving a fabled sanctuary. Secrets of the bible. 2005 ⇒482. 139-146. Justinian's great church in Istanbul.

14045 *Barringer, Judith M.* The temple of Zeus at Olympia, heroes and athletes. Hesp. 74 (2005) 211-241.

14046 *Becking, B.* Temple, marzeaḥ, and power at Elephantine. TEuph 29 (2005) 37-47.

14047 **Bénichou-Safar, Hélène** Le tophet de Salammbô à Carthage: essai de reconstitution. CEFR 342: R 2004, Ecole française de Rome 217 pp. 54 pl.

14048 **Bonnet, Charles** Le temple principal de la ville de Kerma et son quartier religieux. 2004 ⇒20,12621. [R]BiOr 62 (2005) 500-504 (*Zibelius-Chen, K.*).

14049 *Bonnet, Corinne* Entre terre et ciel: parcours historiographique en 'hauts-lieux' sur les traces de Franz Cumont et d'autres historiens des religions. AfR 7 (2005) 5-19.

14050 *Briquel Chatonnet, Françoise* Les cités de la côte phénicienne et leurs sanctuaires de montagne. AfR 7 (2005) 20-33.

14051 **Cauville, Sylvie** Le temple de Dendara: la porte d'Isis. 1999 ⇒15, 11254...20,12627. [R]OLZ 100 (2005) 381-385 (*Waitkos, Wolfgang*).

14052 *Cazanove, Olivier de* Mont et citadelle, temple et *templum*: quelques réflexions sur l'usage religieux des hauteurs dans l'Italie républicaine. AfR 7 (2005) 62-82.

14053 *Ciampini, Emanuele M.* L'accesso al tempio nel I millennio tra linguaggio monumentale e modelli popolari. Aeg. 85 (2005) 103-134.

14054 *Contessa, A.* Synagogue (cont.). DBS 13/75. 2005 ⇒970. 770-785.

14055 **Da Riva, Rocío** Der Ebabbar-Tempel von Sippar in frühbabylonischer Zeit (640-580 v. Chr.). AOAT 291: 2002 ⇒18,12192; 20, 12630. [R]Or. 74 (2005) 129-132 (*Dandamayev, M.A.*).

14056 *Durand, Caroline; Tholbecq, Laurent* A Nabatean rock-cut sanctuary in Petra: preliminary report on three excavation seasons at the "Obodas chapel", Jabal Numayr (2002-2004). ADAJ 49 (2005) 299-311.

14057 *Dvorjetski, E.* The synagogue-church at Gerasa in Jordan: a contribution to the study of ancient synagogues. ZDPV 121 (2005) 140-167.

14058 *Eichner, Ina; Fauerbach, Ulrike* Die spätantike/koptische Klosteranlage Deir el-Bachit in Dra' Abu el-Naga (Oberägypten), zweiter Vorbericht. MDAI.K 61 (2005) 139-152; Taf. 21-26.

14059 *Ferrary, Jean-Louis* Les mémoriaux de délégations du sanctuaire oraculaire de Claros et leur chronologie. CRAI 2 (2005) 719-765.

14060 [E]**Figueras, Pau** Horvat Karkur 'Illit: a Byzantine cemetery church in the northern Negev: final report of the excavations 1989-1995. 2004 ⇒20,12635. [R]BASOR 340 (2005) 99-100 (*Lawlor, John I.*).

14061 *Fine, Steven* The temple menorah—where is it?. BArR 31/4 (2005) 18-25, 62-63.

14062 *Gass, E.; Zissu, B.* The monastery of Samson up the Rock of Etham in the Byzantine period. ZDPV 121 (2005) 168-183.

14063 *Gilli, Barbara* Templi e spazi sacri nelle zone di cave e miniere: forme di adattamento all'ambiente naturale. Aeg. 85 (2005) 149-60.

14064 **Gonnella, Julia; Khayyata, Wahid; Kohlmeyer, Kay** Die Zitadelle von Aleppo und der Tempel des Wettergottes–neue Forschungen und Entdeckungen. Mü 2005, Rhema 120 pp. 3-930454-44-0.

14065 *Groenewoud, E.M.C.* Water in the cultic worship in Phoenician sanctuaries. V Congresso di studi fenici. 2005 ⇒959. I, 149-155.

14066 *Hassell, Jonathan* A re-examination of the cuboid incense-burning altars from Flinders PETRIE's Palestinian excavations at Tell Jemmeh. Levant 37 (2005) 133-162.

14067 **Held, Winfried** Milesische Forschungen, 2: das Heiligtum der Athena in Milet. 2000 ⇒16,11410; 18,12209. [R]AWE 4 (2005) 202-205 (*Nicholls, Richard*).

14068 **Holtzmann, Bernard** L'Acropole d'Athènes: monuments, cultes et histoire du sanctuaire d'Athèna Polias. 2003 ⇒19,13285. [R]AnCl 74 (2005) 610-611 (*Esposito, Arianna*).

14069 **Hölbl, Günther** Altägypten im römischen Reich: der römische Pharao und seine Tempel, 3: Heiligtümer und religiöses Leben in den ägyptischen Wüsten und Oasen. Zaberns Bildbände zur Archäologie: Mainz 2005, Von Zabern 116 pp. €37.90. 3-8053-3512-1. Num. ill.

14070 **Hölzl, Regina** Ägyptische Opfertafeln und Kultbecken: eine Form- und Funktionsanalyse für das Alte, Mittlere und Neue Reich. 2002 ⇒18,12211...20,12641. [R]JEA 91 (2005) 215-218 (*Martin, Karl*).

14071 *Khalil, Lutfi* The western basilica church at Khirbat Yajuz. ADAJ 49 (2005) *53-*63. **A**.

14072 **Kockelmann, Holger** Die Toponymen- und Kultnamenlisten zur Tempelanlage von Dendera nach den hieroglyphischen Inschriften von Edfu und Dendera. [E]*Kurth, Dieter*: 2002 ⇒18,12213... 20, 12643. [R]JEA 91 (2005) 229-232 (*Leitz, C.*).

14073 **Kohlmeyer, Kay** Der Tempel des Wettergottes von Aleppo. 2000 ⇒16,11413...19,13292. [R]BiOr 62 (2005) 342-343 (*Meijer, D.J.W.*).

14074 *Krumeich, Kirsten* Von Hauskirchen und Wallfahrtsorten: frühe christliche Sakralbauten. WUB 36 (2005) 45-50.

14075 *Laurent, Sophie* Ein Kloster ersteht aus dem Sand: Ägypten: Baouit. WUB 35 (2005) 71.

14076 **Lepage, Claude; Mercier, Jacques** Art éthiopien: les églises historiques du Tigray. [T]*Williams, Sarah*: P 2005, Études et Recherche sur les Civilisations 247 pp. €30. 2-8653-82990. Édition bilingue français-anglais. [R]CRAI (2005/3) 1036-1037 (*Lepage, Claude*).

14077 **Leypold, Christina** Das Bankett im Heiligtum: Identifizierung, Gestalt und Funktion saktaler Bankettgebäude und Klinenräume in Griechenland von archaischer bis hellenistischer Zeit. 2005, Diss. Würzburg [AA 2006/1, 312].

14078 *Lurson, Benoît* La conception du décor d'un temple au début du règne de Ramsès II: analyse du deuxième registre de la moitié sud du mur ouest de la grande salle hypostyle de Karnak. JEA 91 (2005) 107-124.

14079 *Magness, Jodi* The date of the Sardis synagogue in light of the numismatic evidence. AJA 109 (2005) 443-475.

14080 *Maher, Edward F.* A Hippopotamus tooth from a Philistine temple: symbolic artefact or sacrificial offering?. NEA 68/1-2 (2005) 59-60.

14081 *Mohamed Ahmed, Salah; Anderson, Julie* Le temple d'Amon à Dangeil (Soudan). BSFÉ 162 (2005) 10-27.

14082 *Mouton, Jean M.; Popescu-Belis, Andrei* La fondation du monastère Sainte-Catherine du Sinaï selon deux documents de sa bibliothèque: Codex Arabe 692 et rouleau Arabe 955. CCO 2 (2005) 141-205.

14083 [E]**Neils, Jenifer** The Parthenon: from antiquity to the present. C 2005, CUP xvi; 430 pp. 0-521-82093-6. Bibl. 397-422.

14084 *Nuzzolo, Massimiliano* I templi solari della V dinastia: significato e pratiche cultuali. Aeg. 85 (2005) 75-101.

14085 *On, A.; Weksler-Bdolah, S.* Khirbet Um el-Umdan—a Jewish village with a synagogue from the second temple period at Modiin. Qad. 38 (2005) 107-116. **H.**

14086 *Ornan, Tallay* A complex system of religious symbols: the case of the winged disc in Near Eastern imagery of the first millennium BC. Crafts and images. OBO 210: 2005 ⇒693. 207-242.

14087 *Ovadiah, Asher* Liturgical modifications in the early Byzantine church in Eretz Israel: the architectural and epigraphic evidence. LASBF 55 (2005) 363-376 (Pls. 39-50).

14088 **Parenti, Stefano** Il Monastero di Grottaferrata nel Medioevo (1004-1462): segni e percorsi di una identità. OCA 274: R 2005, Pontificio Istituto Orientale 570 pp. 88-7210-349-5.

14089 *Peri, C.* La roccia e il diluvio: considerazioni sul tempio siropalestinese. V Congresso di studi fenici. 2005 ⇒959. I, 145-148.

14090 *Piccirillo, Michele* Una cappella nella regione di Suf-Jerash (Pls. 65). LASBF 55 (2005) 490 (Pls. 65);

14091 Copia dell'ambone della Chiesa dei Leoni a Umm al-Rasas-Kastron Mefaa. LASBF 55 (2005) 500-501 (Pls. 74-75).

14092 *Reade, Julian* The Ishtar temple at Nineveh. Iraq 67/1 (2005) 347-390.

14093 *Rose, Mark* Early church at Aqaba. Secrets of the bible. 2005 ⇒ 482. 101-103.

14094 *Shanks, Hershel* Scholars fear to publish ancient house shrine. BArR 31/6 (2005) 20-25.

14095 *Shaya, Josephine* The Greek temple as museum: the case of the legendary treasure of Athena from Lindos. AJA 109 (2005) 423-442.

14096 **Solima, Isabella** Heiligtümer der Artemis auf der Peloponnes. 2005, Diss. Heidelberg [AA 2006/1, 313].

14097 *Sotinel, Claire* Les lieux de culte chrétiens et le sacré dans l'Antiquité tardive. RHR 222/4 (2005) 411-434.

14098 **Stucky, Rolf A.**, *al.*, Das Eschmun-Heiligtum von Sidon: Architektur und Inschriften. Antike Kunst.B 19: Ba 2005, Vereinigung der Freunde antiker Kunst 332 pp. 3-909064-19-1. 58 pp of pl. RSyria 82 (2005) 369-371 (*Apicella, Catherine*).

14099 **Thiers, Christophe; Volokhine, Youri** Ermant I: les cryptes du temple ptolémäque: étude épigraphique. MIFAO 124: Le Caire 2005, Institut Français d'Archéologie Orientale x; 120 pp. £210. 2-7247-0412-6. Bibl. 111-120.

14100 *Troupeau, Gérard* Les églises et les monastères de Syrie dans l'oeuvre d'Abu al-Makarim. MUSJ 58 (2005) 573-586.

14101 *Van der Steen, Eveline J.* The sanctuaries of Early Bronze IB Megiddo: evidence of a tribal polity?. AJA 109 (2005) 1-20.

14102 **Van Ess, Margarete** Uruk: Architektur II: von der akkad- bis zur mittelbabylonischen Zeit, Teil 1: das Eanna-Heiligtum zur Ur III- und altbabylonischen Zeit. ADFGUW.Endberichte 15/1: 2001 ⇒ 17,11157...20,12666. RAntiquity 79 (2005) 703-4 (*Roaf, Michael*).

14103 *Vezzani, Irene* I guardiani del tempio: leoni e sfingi custodi del sacro. Aeg. 85 (2005) 199-218.

14104 *Villeneuve, Estelle* Le sinagoghe si trasformano. Il mondo della bibbia 77 (2005) 16-21.

14105 **Weiss, Ze'ev**, *al.*, The Sepphoris synagogue: deciphering an ancient message through its archaeological and socio-historical contexts. 2004 ⇒20,12668. RSCI 24 (2005) 323-324 (*Millar, Fergus*). **H.**

### T3.8 Funeraria; *Sindon*, the Shroud

14106 *Akdeniz, Engin* Chalcolithic urn burials at Pirot Höyük, eastern Turkey: an assessment. ANES 42 (2005) 277-298.

14107 *Alexanian, Nicole; El-Ghandour, Magdy* An Old Kingdom cemetery in southern Dahshur. MDAI.K 61 (2005) 191-206; Pl. 28-35.

14108 *Al-Shiyab, Atef M.; Perry, Megan A.* A late Roman tomb near Quaṣr ar-Rabba. ADAJ 49 (2005) 81-87.

14109 *Aubet, M.E.* Scavi nella necropoli di Tiro-Al Bass. V Congresso di studi fenici. 2005 ⇒959. I, 87-92.

14110 *Bareš, Ladislav; Smolárikovā, Kveta; Strouhal, Eugen* The Saite-Persian cemetery at Abusir in 2003. ZÄS 132/2 (2005) 95-106; Pl. XVII-XXII.

14111 **Berman, Rochel U.** Dignity beyond death: the Jewish preparation for burial. J 2005, Urim 223 pp. 965-7108-66-7. Foreword by *Irving Greenberg*; Bibl. 218-219.

14112 *Bilgi, Önder* Distinguished burials of the Early Bronze Age graveyard at Ikiztepe in Turkey. AnaAra 18/2 (2005) 15-113.

14113 *Břeňová, Klára* Secondary burial in ancient Israel. ArOr 73 (2005) 1-12.

14114 [E]**Brodbeck, Andreas; Wiese, André B.** Tutanchamun: das goldene Jenseits: Grabschätze aus dem Tal der Könige. 2004 ⇒20, 12682. [R]WO 35 (2005) 223-225 (*Gamer-Wallert, Ingrid*).

14115 *Buckley, Ian M.; Buckley, Peter; Cooke, Ashley* Fieldwork in Theban tomb KV 39: the 2002 season. JEA 91 (2005) 71-82.

14116 *Burke, Brendan* Materialization of Mycenaean ideology and the Ayia Triada sarcophagus. AJA 109 (2005) 403-422.

14117 *Cartwright, Caroline* The Bronze Age wooden tomb furniture from Jericho: the microscopical reconstruction of a distinctive carpentry tradition. PEQ 137 (2005) 99-138.

14118 **Castel, Georges**, *al.*, Balat VII: les cimitières est et ouest du mastaba de Khentika: oasis de Dakhla. FIFAO 52: Cairo 2005, Institut Français d'Archéologie Orientale vi; 584 pp. 2-7247-0378-2. Bibl. v-vi.

14119 *Cilliers, Louise; Retief, François P.* Burial customs, the afterlife and the pollution of death in ancient Greece <2000>;

14120 Burial customs and the pollution of death in ancient Rome: procedures and paradoxes <2002>. Health and healing. AcTh(B) 7: 2005 ⇒686. 44-61/128-146.

14121 **Dayagi-Mendels, Michal** The Akhziv cemeteries: the Ben-Dor excavations, 1941-1944. 2002 ⇒18,12266. [R]BASOR 337 (2005) 99-101 (*Brody, Aaron*).

14122 **Der Manuelian, Peter** Slab stelae of the Giza necropolis. 2003 ⇒ 20,12691. [R]JEA 91 (2005) 201-202 (*Altenmüller, Hartwig*).

14123 *Druks, Adam* Late Roman-period burial complexes at Ẓippori. 'Atiqot 49 (2005) 105*-106*. **H.**

14124 *Dugay, Laurinda* Early Bronze Age burials from Tell Ahmar. [F]FINET, A. Subartu 16: 2005 ⇒40. 37-49.

14125 **Dunand, Françoise**, *al.*, La nécropole de Douch: exploration archéologique, II, Monographie des tombes 73 à 92: structures sociales, économiques, religieuses de l'Égypte romaine. DFIFAO 45: Le Caire 2005, Institut Français d'Archéologie Orientale du Caire vii; 225 pp.

14126 **Evans, Craig A.** Jesus and the ossuaries. 2003 ⇒19,5211; 20, 12695. [R]ArOr 73 (2005) 148-150 (*Břeňová, Klára*); RBLit 7 (2005) 295-297 (*Nicklas, Tobias*).

14127 *Frendo, A.J.; De Trafford, A.; Vella, N.C.* Water journeys of the dead: a glimpse into Phoenician and Punic eschatology. V Congresso di studi fenici. 2005 ⇒959. I, 427-443.

14128 *Gal, Zvi; Zori, Nehemya* A Middle Bronze Age IIB—Late Bronze Age I burial cave at 'En Nashab, in the Bet She'an Valley. 'Atiqot 49 (2005) 17-31.

14129 **Gallou, Chrysanthi** The Mycenaean cult of the dead. BAR-IS 1372: Oxf 2005, Archaeopress vi; 240 pp. £36. 18417-18149. 90 fig.

14130 *Gawlikowski, Michal* The city of the dead. [M]HILLERS, D.: Culture and History of the ancient Near East 22: 2005 ⇒61. 44-73.

14131 *Gershuny, Lilly; Eisenberg, Emanuel* A Middle Bronze Age burial cave at Tur'an. 'Atiqot 50 (2005) 1-17.

14132 **Ghiberti, Giuseppe** Dalle cose che patí (Eb 5,8): evangelizzare con la Sindone. 2004 ⇒20,207. [R]ATT 11 (2005) 207-208 (*Casale, Umberto*).

14133 **Gophna, Ram; Van den Brink, Edwin C.**, *al.*, Shoham (North): late Chalcolithic burial caves in the Lod Valley, Israel. IAA Reports 27: J 2005, Israel Antiquities Authority 207 pp. 96540-61848.

14134 **Grajetzki, Wolfram** Burial customs in ancient Egypt: life in death for rich and poor. 2003 ⇒19,13353. [R]OLZ 100 (2005) 241-246 (*Schiestl, Robert*).

14135 **Hachlili, Rachel** Jewish funerary customs, practices and rites in the second temple period. JSJ.S 94: Lei 2005, Brill xli; 588 pp. €179. 90-04-12373-3. Bibl. 545-571. [R]BiLi 78 (2005) 147-148 (*Schipper, Friedrich*); Qad. 38 (2005) 124-126 (*Magness, J.*); LASBF 55 (2005) 558-563 (*Manns, Frédéric*).

14136 *Hudec, Jozef, al.*, A new Egyptian human mummified head in the Slovak National Museum, Bratislava. JEA 91 (2005) 190-197.

14137 **Jánosi, Peter** Giza in der 4. Dynastie: die Baugeschichte und Belegung einer Nekropole des alten Reiches, I: die Mastabas der Kernfriedhöfe und Felsgräber. DÖAW 30; Untersuchungen der Zweigstelle Kairo des Österreichischen Archäologischen Institutes 24: W 2005, Verlag der ÖAW 459 pp. 37001-3244-1. Bibl. 19-26; 124 Ill.

14138 **Kanawati, Naguib**, *al.*, Deir el-Gebrawi. Warminster 2005, Aris & P. 416 pp. $130. 0-85668-807X. Australian Centre for Egyptology.

14139 *Kloner, Amos* Reconstruction of the tomb of the Rotunda of the Holy Sepulchre according to the archaeological finds and Jewish burial customs of the first century CE. Beginnings of christianity. 2005 ⇒786. 269-278.

14140 *Kormysheva, E.Y.* On the semantics of the ancient Egyptian tomb: or some reflections about how to study Egyptology. VDI 2 (2005) 131-145. **R.**

14141 **Köhler, E. Christiana** Helwan I: excavations in the Early Dynastic cemetery: season 1997/98. Studien zur Archäologie und Geschichte Altägyptens 24: Heid 2005, Orientverlag xii; 86 pp. €40. 3-927552-42-9. 69 pl.; Bibl. ix-xvii.

14142 **Labrousse, Audran; Lauer, Jean-Philippe** Les complexes funéraires d'Ouserkaf et de Néferhétepès. Bibliothèque d'étude 130,1-2: 2000 ⇒16,11467. [R]OLZ 100 (2005) 23-28 (*Bárta, Miroslav*).

14143 *Levy, Thomas E., al.*, Iron Age burial in the lowlands of Edom: the 2004 excavations at Wadi Fidan 40, Jordan. ADAJ 49 (2005) 443-487.

14144 **Lewartowski, Kazimierz** Late Helladic simple graves: a study of Mycenaean burial customs. BAR international series 878: 2000 ⇒ 16,11470. [R]AJA 109 (2005) 297-298 (*Thomas, Patrick M.*).

14145 **Lilyquist, Christine** The tomb of three foreign wives of Tuthmosis III. 2003 ⇒20,12714. [R]BiOr 62 (2005) 237-239 (*Dodson, Aidan*); Antiquity 79 (2005) 720-721 (*Snape, Steven*); PEQ 137 (2005) 80-82 (*Uphill, E.P.*); DiscEg 61 (2005) 95-100 (*Hardwick, Tom*).

14146 *Maaß-Lindemann, G.* Tyre-Al Bass and the western colonies: a comparison of funeral offerings and burial customs. V Congresso di studi fenici. 2005 ⇒959. I, 107-114.

14147 **Maier, Aren** Bronze and Iron Age tombs at Tel Gezer, Israel: finds from Raymond-Charles Weill's excavations in 1914 and 1921. 2004 ⇒20,12716. [R]BASOR 337 (2005) 97-98 (*Ortiz, Steven M.*).

14148 **McKane, Byron R.** Roll back the stone: death and burial in the world of Jesus. 2003 ⇒19,13369; 20,12720. [R]HeyJ 46 (2005) 366-368 (*Taylor, N.H.*); RBLit (2005)* (*Van der Watt, Jan G.*).

14149 **Merthen, Claudia** Beobachtungen zur Ikonographie von Klage und Trauer: griechische Sepulkralkeramik vom 8. bis 5. Jahrhundert v. Chr. 2005, Diss. Würzburg [AA 2006/1, 312].
14150 *Mouritsen, H.* Freedman and decurions: epitaph and social history in imperial Italy. JRS 95 (2005) 38-63 [NTAb 50,361].
14151 *Muhly, James D.* Mycenaeans were there before the Israelites: excavating the Dan tomb. BArR 31/5 (2005) 44-51.
14152 *Núñez Calvo, F.J.* Tyre-Al Bass '97: the pottery evidence. V Congresso di studi fenici. 2005 ⇒959. I, 93-106.
14153 *Olyan, Saul M.* Some neglected aspects of Israelite interment ideology. JBL 124 (2005) 601-616.
14154 *Ökse, A.* Tuba Early Bronze Age chamber tomb complexes at Gre Virike (period IIA) on the Middle Euphrates. BASOR 339 (2005) 21-46.
14155 **Papadopoulos, John K.** The Early Iron Age cemetery at Torone. Monumenta Archaeologica 24: LA 2005, Corsen xliv; 1281 pp. $200. 1-931745-161. 245 fig.; 540 pl.
14156 *Piacentini, Danila* The Palmyrene attitudes towards death. Aram 17 (2005) 245-258.
14157 *Pury, Albert de* Le tombeau des Abrahamides d'Hébron et sa fonction au début de l'époque perse (résumé). TEuph 30 (2005) 183-84.
14158 *Raven, Maarten J., al.*, Preliminary report on the Leiden excavations at Saqqara, season 2003: the tomb of Meryneith;
14159 Preliminary report on the Leiden excavations at Saqqara, season 2004: the tomb of Horemheb. JEOL 38 (2003-2004) 5-23/25-44;
14160 Preliminary report...season 2005: the tombs of Horemheb and Meryneith. JEOL 39 (2005) 5-17.
14161 **Raven, M.J.; Taconis, W.K.** Egyptian mummies: radiological atlas of the collections in the National Museum of Antiquities in Leiden. Turnhout 2005, Brepols 335 pp. €55. 978-25035-17018.
14162 *Raya, Rafeh Abu; Zissu, Boaz* A second temple period burial cave from the Mount of Olives, Jerusalem. 'Atiqot 49 (2005) 33-37.
14163 *Reader, Colin* The age of the sphinx and the development of the Giza necropolis. Current research in egyptology II. 2005 ⇒635. 47-56.
14164 **Riggs, Christina** The beautiful burial in Roman Egypt: art, identity, and funerary religion. Oxford Studies in Ancient Culture and Representation: Oxf 2005, OUP xxiv; 334 pp. £80. 0-19-927665-X.
14165 *Rowland, Joanne* The transition to state society in Egypt: problems and possibilities of applying mortuary evidence. Current research in egyptology II. 2005 ⇒635. 57-63.
14166 *Saito, Kiyohide* Palmyrene burial practices from funerary goods. [M]HILLERS, D.: 2005 ⇒61. 150-165.
14167 *Shirai, Yayoi* Royal funerary cults during the Old Kingdom. Current research in egyptology 2003. 2005 ⇒907. 71-103.
14168 **Smith, Grafton Elliot** Tutankhamen and the discovery of his tomb. L 2005 <1923>, Kegan P. 133 pp. 0-7103-1005-6.
14169 **Sora, Steven** Treasures from heaven: relics from Noah's Ark to the Shroud of Turin. Hoboken (N.J.) 2005, Wiley 250 pp. 0-471-4623-2-2. Bibl. 235-239.
14170 *Stuart, B.* Iron Age tombs in Beirut. V Congresso di studi fenici. 2005 ⇒959. I, 115-120.

14171 *Tal, Oren* On the origin and concept of the loculi tombs of Hellenistic Palestine. AWE 2 (2003) 288-307.

14172 *Tenu, Aline; Bachelot, Luc* Tell Shiukh Fawqani (Syrie): la campagne de sondage 2003 dans la nécropole à incinération. Akkadica 126 (2005) 159-168.

14173 *Thomas, Christine* Placing the dead: funerary practice and social stratification in the early Roman period at Corinth and Ephesos. Urban religion in Roman Corinth. HThS 53: 2005 ⇒8093. 281-304.

14174 *Torge, Hagit; Badhi, Radwan* A burial cave from the Roman period at Shoham (East). ʿAtiqot 49 (2005) 31*-39*. **H.**

14175 **Turcan, Robert** Études d'archéologie sépulcrale: sarcophages romains et gallo-romains. 2003 ⇒19,290. [R]RAr (2005/2) 426-428 (*Gaggadis-Robin, Vassiliki*).

14176 **Ubertini, Christian** Elephantine XXXIV: restitution architecturale à partir des blocs et fragments épars d'époque ptolemaïque et romaine. Archäologische Veröffentlichungen 120: Mainz 2005, Von Zabern 87 pp. 3-8053-3349-8. Bibl. 9.

14177 **Valloggia, Michel** Le monument funéraire d'Ima-Pepy/Ima-Meryrê: Balat IV. DFIFAO 38,1-2: Le Caire 1998, Institut Français d'Archéologie Orientale du Caire 2 vols; 227; 10 pp. 27247-02182. 118 pl.; Bibl. v.1, 195-201. [R]JEA 91 (2005) 204-205 (*Strudwick, Nigel*).

14178 *Walbank, Mary* Unquiet graves: burial practices of the Roman Corinthians. Urban religion in Roman Corinth. 2005 ⇒ 8093. 249-80.

14179 **Washbourne, Rose M.** Out of the mouth of pots: towards an interpretation of the symbolic meaning of Cypriot Bronze Age funerary artifacts including...the Univ. of Canterbury's Logie Collection. 2000 ⇒17,11223. [R]JNES 64 (2005) 144-145 (*Rutter, Jeremy B.*).

14180 *Wenning, Robert* "Medien" in der Bestattungskultur im eisenzeitlichen Juda?. Medien im antiken Palästina. FAT 2/10: 2005 ⇒646. 109-150.

14181 **Worschech, Udo** A burial cave at Umm Dimis north of el-Bālūʿ. Beiträge zur Erforschung der antiken Moabitis (Ard El-Kerak) 3: 2003 ⇒19,13401. [R]BASOR 340 (2005) 92-94 (*Mattingly, Gerald*).

14182 **Zanker, Paul; Ewald, Björn C.** Mit Mythen leben: die Bilderwelt der römischen Sarkophage. 2004 ⇒20,12748. [R]JRS 95 (2005) 303-304 (*Huskinson, Janet*); RAr (2005/1) 79-87 (*Turcan, Robert*).

14183 *Zelinger, Yehiel; Golani, Amir* Rock-cut shaft tombs from the Intermediate Bronze Age near the Holyland Hotel, Jerusalem. ʿAtiqot 49 (2005) 1-7.

14184 *Zingale, Livia M.* In tema di clausole funerarie: osservazioni sui testamenti romani d'Egitto. Aeg. 85 (2005) 269-278.

14185 *Zissu, Boaz* A burial cave with a Greek inscription and graffiti at Khirbat El-ʿEin, Judean Shephelah. ʿAtiqot 50 (2005) 27-36.

## T3.9 *Numismatica*, coins

14186 *Ariel, Donald T.; Hirschfeld, Yizhar* A coin assemblage from the reign of Alexander Jannaeus found on the shore of the Dead Sea. IEJ 55 (2005) 66-89.

14187 *Ariel, Donald T.* Coins from the excavations in the village at 'En Gedi: 1993-1995. 'Atiqot 49 (2005) 83*-88*. **H.**

14188 *Arslan, Ermanno A.* The coins from Khirbet el-Jiljil. BAIAS 23 (2005) 107-110.

14189 *Barag, D.* Coins of the Crusader Kingdom and the defeat at the Horns of Hattin. Qad. 38 (2005) 43-44.

14190 Bollettino di numismatica. Bollettino di numismatica, supplemento al n. 44-45: R 2005, Istituto Poligrafico dello Stato 330 pp.

14191 *Cahill, Nicholas; Kroll, John H.* New archaic coin finds at Sardis. AJA 109 (2005) 589-617.

14192 **Duyrat, Frédérique** Arados hellénistique: étude historique et monétaire. BAHI 173: Beyrouth 2005, Institut Français d'Archéologie du Proche-Orient 433 pp. Diss.; 17 fig.; 50 pl.

14193 *Elayi, A.G.; Elayi, J.* La scène du char sur les monnaies de Sidon à l'époque perse. TEuph 30 (2005) 185.

14194 *Goodwin, Tony* Seventh-century coins in the Palestine Exploration Fund collections. PEQ 137/1 (2005) 65-76.

14195 **Guest, Peter S.W.** The late Roman gold and silver coins from the Hoxne treasure. L 2005, British Museum Press 160 pp. 0-7141-18-10-9. Bibl. 157-160.

14196 **Houghton, A.; Lorber, C.** Seleucid coins: a comprehensive catalogue, 1: Seleucus through Antiochus III, vols 1-2. 2002 ⇒19, 13420. [R]VDI (2005/1) 200-203 (*Koschelenko, G.A.*); Syria 82 (2005) 377-378 (*Duyrat, Frédérique*).

14197 [E]**Howgego, Christopher; Burnett, Andrew** Coinage and identity in the Roman provinces. Oxf 2005, OUP xv; 228 pp. £80. 0-19-92-6526-7. 32 pl.

14198 *Hübner, Ulrich* Tradition und Innovation: die Münzprägungen der Hasmonäer des 2. und 1. Jahrhunderts v. Chr. als Massenmedien. Medien im antiken Palästina. FAT 2/10: 2005 ⇒646. 171-187.

14199 *Kind, Hans D., al.*, Coins from Faynan, Jordan. Levant 37 (2005) 169-195.

14200 **Knapp, Robert C.; Mac Isaac, John D.** Excavations at Nemea III: the coins. Berkeley 2005, University of California Press xxxi; 290 pp. 0-520-23169-4. 32 pl.

14201 **Marcellesi, Marie-Christine** Milet des Hécatomnides à la domination romaine: pratiques monétaires et histoire de la cité du IVe au IIe siècle av. J.-C. Milesische Forschungen 3: 2004 ⇒20,12767. [R]CRAI (2005/1) 268-275 (*Picard, Olivier*).

14202 Ein neuer römischer Kaiser. WUB 35 (2005) 72.

14203 **Ostermann, Siegfried** Die Münzen der Hasmonäer: ein kritischer Bericht zur Systematik und Chronologie. NTOA 55: FrS 2005, Academic viii; 89 pp. 3-7278-1499-3. Bibl. 60-69.

14204 **Schaps, David M.** The invention of coinage and the monetization of ancient Greece. AA 2004, Michigan UP xvii; 293 pp. $48. 13 ill.

14205 *Schwentzel, Christian-Georges* Les thèmes du monnayage royal nabatéen et le modèle monarchique hellénistique. Syria 82 (2005) 149-166.

14206 Il "Tesoro" dell'Agorà di Iasos: un archivio d'argento dell'epoca di PLOTINO. Bollettino di numismatica 40-43: R 2005, Istituto Poligrafico dello Stato 16 pp.

14207 *Vargyas, Peter* Moneybags in Neo-Babylonian texts. [F]KLEIN, J. 2005 ⇒79. 587-592.

14208 *Vismara, N.* Ritratti umani o teste divine nella monetazione arcaica della Lycia: manifestazione della potestà d'imperio od espressione del sentimento religioso?. TEuph 30 (2005) 173-181; pls. I-III.

### T4.3 Jerusalem, *archaeologia* et historia

14209 [E]**Arubas, Benny; Goldfus, Haim** Excavations on the site of the Jerusalem International Convention Center (Binyanei Ha'uma): a settlement of the late first to second temple period, the tenth legion's kilnworks, and a Byzantine monastic complex: the pottery and other small finds. Journal of Roman Archaeology.S 60: Portsmouth, Rhode Island 2005, Journal of Roman Archaeology 296 pp. 1-887829-60-1.

14210 *Avni, G.* The urban limits of Roman and Byzantine Jerusalem: a view from the necropoleis. Journal of Roman Archaeology [AA] 18 (2005) 373-396 [NTAb 50,333].

14211 *Baert, Barbara* The pool of Bethsaïda: the cultural history of a holy place in Jerusalem. Viator 36 (2005) 1-22.

14212 *Barker, Margaret* Jerusalem the golden: vision and memory of the church. IJSCC 5 (2005) 1-10.

14213 **Bartolini, E.L.** Per amore di Tzion: Gerusalemme nella tradizione ebraica. Studi giudaici 2: Cantalupa (TO) 2005, Effatà 109 pp. €10.50. 88-740-21852. Postf. *R.Fontana*. [R]Teol(Br) 30 (2005) 226-227 (*Ubbiali, Sergio*); Il Regno 50 (2005) 546-547 (*Stefani, Piero*).

14214 **Ben-Dov, Meir** Historical atlas of Jerusalem. [T]*Louvish, David* 2002 ⇒18,12372; 20,12781. [R]JSSt 50 (2005) 370-71 (*Prag, Kay*).

14215 **Binz, Stephen J.** Jerusalem, the holy city. Threshold bible study: New London, CT 2005, Twenty-Third ix; 128 pp. $13 [BiTod 43, 200—Donald Senior].

14216 *Bloedhorn, Hanswulf* Die Wasserversorgung Jerusalems in der Bronze- und Eisenzeit. AA 2 (2005) 103-119.

14217 *Broshi, Magen; Eshel, Hanan; Jull, Timothy A.J.* Four Murabba'at papyri and the alleged capture of Jerusalem by Bar Kokhba. Law in the documents. JSJ.S 96: 2005 ⇒662. 45-50.

14218 *Buber, Martin* Die Frage nach Jerusalem: aus einer auf einer deutschen Konferenz für das arbeitende Palästina gesprochenen Rede. Schriften zu Jugend. 2005 <1929> ⇒196. 171-172.

14219 *Cignelli, Lino* Our Lady's tomb in the Apocrypha. Holy Land (Spring 2005) 2-9.

14220 **Clark, Victoria** Holy fire: the battle for Christ's tomb. L 2005, Macmillan xviii; 293 pp. £20.

14221 *Dauphin, Claudine* Sainte-Anne de Jérusalem: le projet Béthesda;

14222 The Bethesda Project at St Anne's in the Old City of Jerusalem. POC 55 (2005) 254-262/263-269.

14223 **David, Abraham** Reflections on Jewish Jerusalem: an anthology of Hebrew letters from the Mamluk age. 2003 ⇒19,13442. [R]REJ 164 (2005) 383-384 (*Nahon, Gérard*).

14224 *Du Toit, J.S.* Jerusalem, "as Englishmen suppose": imperialism and the reconstruction of sacred space. JSem 14/2 (2005) 306-322.

14225 **Edelman, Diana Vikander** The origins of the 'second' temple: Persian imperial policy and the rebuilding of Jerusalem. L 2005, Equinox xvii; 440 pp. 1-8455-3017-9. Bibl. 378-405.

14226 **Eliav, Yaron Z.** God's mountain: the Temple Mount in time, place, and memory. Baltimore 2005, Johns Hopkins University Press xxxv; 353 pp. $40. 0-8018-8213-3. Bibl. 303-337.

14227 *Faust, A.* The settlement of Jerusalem's western hill and the city's status in Iron Age II revisited. ZDPV 121 (2005) 97-118.

14228 **Franken, H.J.** A history of potters and pottery in ancient Jerusalem: excavations by K.M. KENYON in Jerusalem 1961-1967. L 2005, Equinox xvi; 216 pp. £85. 81 fig.; 37 tables.

14229 *Garbarino, Osvaldo* Il Santo Sepolcro di Gerusalemme: appunti di ricerca storico-architettonica. LASBF 55 (2005) 239-314.

14230 [E]**Geva, Hillel** Jewish Quarter excavations in the Old City of Jerusalem: conducted by Nahman Avigad. 2000-2003 ⇒16,11563... 20, 12787. [R]OLZ 100 (2005) 69-71 (*Vieweger, Dieter*).

14231 *Gibson, S.* The pool of Bethesda in Jerusalem and Jewish purification practices of the second temple period. POC 55 (2005) 270-93.

14232 **González Echegaray, J.** Pisando tus umbrales, Jerusalén: historia antigua de la ciudad. Estella 2005, Verbo Divino 412 pp. 84-8169-684-6. Ill.

14233 *Groot, A. De* Excavations in the south of the city of David—reinterpretation of former excavations. Qad. 38 (2005) 81-86. **H**.

14234 *Himmelfarb, Elizabeth J.* The gospel's holiest sanctum. Secrets of the bible. 2005 ⇒482. 164-169. Church of the Holy Sepulchre.

14235 **Hjelm, Ingrid** Jerusalem's rise to sovereignty: Zion and Gerizim in competition. JSOT.S 404: 2004 ⇒20,12793. [R]SJOT 19 (2005) 290-301 (*West, Jim*); RBLit (2005)* (*West, James*).

14236 Israel: Jerusalem: Tempelberg-Rampe vor Einsturz. WUB 36 (2005) 64.

14237 Israel: Jerusalem: Archäologen wollen den Palast König Davids entdeckt haben. WUB 38 (2005) 66.

14238 *Kaiser, Helga* Entdeckung in Jerusalem: der alte und der neue Teich Schiloach. WUB 38 (2005) 2-7.

14239 **Kaufman, Asher Selig** The Temple Mount: where is the Holy of Holies?. 2004 ⇒20,3322. [R]CBQ 67 (2005) 321-3 (*Ritmeyer, Leen*).

14240 *Kjaer-Hansen, K.* First 'organized' bible work in 19[th] century Jerusalem (1816-1831): part III: James Connor in Jerusalem. Mishkan [J] 44 (2005) 62-75 [NTAb 50,17].

14241 **Kohler, Oliver** Zwischen christlicher Zionssehnsucht und kaiserlicher Politik: die Entstehung von Kirche und Kloster Dormitio Beatae Mariae Virginis in Jerusalem. St Ottilien 2005, EOS xxi; 637 pp. 3-8306-7181-4.

14242 *Küchler, Max* Meine Augen haben ihr Heil gesehen (fast Lk 2,30): das Mariengrab im Kedrontal als Ausdruck des christlichen Paradoxes vom Glauben aus dem Sehen des Abwesenden. [F]SCHENKER, A.: OBO 214: 2005 ⇒134. 160-182.

14243 *Lewy, Mordechay* An unknown view of Mt. Zion monastery by the Flemish old master Pieter Coecke van Aelst (1502-1550) as evidence to his pilgrimage to Jerusalem. LASBF 55 (2005) 315-326 (Pls. 1-10).

14244 **Lipschits, Oded** The fall and rise of Jerusalem: Judah under Babylonian rule. WL 2005, Eisenbrauns xiv; 474 pp. $47.50. 1-57506-0-95-7. Diss.; Bibl. 383-447.

14245 *Livne-Kafri, Ofer* On Muslim Jerusalem in the period of its formation. LASBF 55 (2005) 203-216.

14246 *Lohse, Eduard* Nächstes Jahr in Jerusalem: die deutsche Benediktinerabtei am Zionstor lädt Studierende der Theologie ein. zeitzeichen 6/4 (2005) 58-59.

14247 *Marguerat, Daniel* Gerusalemme brucia. Il mondo della bibbia 77 (2005) 22-27.

14248 **Mazar, Eilat** The complete guide to the Temple Mount excavations. 2002 ⇒18,12406. [R]RB 112 (2005) 470-72 (*Murphy-O'Connor, Jerome*);

14249 **Mazar, Eilat**, *al.*, The Temple Mount excavations in Jerusalem 1968-1978 directed by Benjamin Mazar: final reports vol. 2: the Byzantine and early Islamic periods. Qedem 43: 2003 ⇒19,13475. [R]RB 112 (2005) 126-130 (*Murphy-O'Connor, Jerome*); BASOR 337 (2005) 104-106 (*Magness, Jodi*).

14250 *Mongin, Olivier* Jérusalem, la ville lumière, en noir et blanc. Esprit 313 (2005) 271-272. Prés. exposition de dessins de *Fanny Rabut*, 1.3-12.4.2005, Paris.

14251 **Morris, Colin** The sepulchre of Christ and the medieval west: from the beginning to 1600. Oxf 2005, OUP 456 pp. £55. 0-1982-6928-5. Bibl. 384-409. [R]Tablet (25 June 2005) 29-30 (*Riley-Smith, Jonathan*); ChH 75 (2005) 183-184 (*Kieckhefer, Richard*).

14252 *Murphy-O'Connor, Jerome* Grób św. Jakuba (the tomb of St. James). Roczniki Teologiczne 52/1 (2005) 175-84 [NTAb 50,538]. **P.**

14253 *Oppenheimer, Aharon Ḥavurot* in Jerusalem at the end of the second temple period. Between Rome and Babylon. TSAJ 108: 2005 <1980> ⇒272. 102-114.

14254 *Oredsson, Dag* Mishneh, Jerusalems Östermalm eller Rinkeby?. SEÅ 70 (2005) 247-253.

14255 *Paczkowski, Mieczyslaw C.* Gerusalemme-"ombelico del mondo" nella tradizione cristiana antica. LASBF 55 (2005) 165-202.

14256 **Peri, Oded** Christianity under Islam in Jerusalem: the question of the holy sites in early Ottoman times. 2001 ⇒17,11286... 19, 13478. [R]IJSCC 5 (2005) 208-209 (*O'Mahony, Anthony*).

14257 *Petrozzi, Maria Tereza* The place of Mary's Dormition. Holy Land (Spring 2005) 20-27.

14258 *Puech, Émile; Zias, Joe* The tomb of Absalom reconsidered. NEA 68/4 (2005) 148-165.

14259 *Regev, Eyal* The ritual baths near the Temple Mount and extra-purification before entering the temple courts. IEJ 55 (2005) 194-204.

14260 *Reich, R.; Shukron, E.* The Shiloah pool during the second temple period. Qad. 38 (2005) 91-96. **H.**

14261 **Ritmeyer, Leen; Ritmeyer, Kathleen** Jerusalem in the time of Nehemiah. J 2005, Carta 71 pp. 965-220-556-7.

14262 *Saddington, Denis* A note on the number of troops stationed in the Antonia in Jerusalem. ET 116 (2005) 431.

14263 *Sahm, Ulrich W.* Archäologen haben biblischen Siloah-Teich entdeckt: so groß wie ein olympisches Schwimmbecken. HlL 137/1 (2005) 22-23.

14264 *Scham, Sandra* A fight over sacred turf. Secrets of the bible. 2005 ⇒482. 151-158. Temple Mount.

14265 *Shanks, Hershel* Sifting the Temple Mount dump: finds from first temple period to modern times. BArR 31/4 (2005) 14-15;

14266 The Siloam pool: where Jesus cured the blind man. BArR 31/5 (2005) 16-23 [John 9,1-11].

14267 [E]**Shanks, Hershel** The City of David: revisiting early excavations. 2004 ⇒20,12816. [R]RB 112 (2005) 472-474 (*Murphy-O'Connor, Jerome*).

14268 *Söllner, Peter* Jerusalem in neutestamentlicher Zeit. [F]STOLLE, V.: Theologie: Forschung und Wissenschaft 12: 2005 ⇒143. 285-302.

14269 [T]*Terian, Abraham* Letter from Jerusalem to the Armenians: regarding the feast of the Presentation of the Lord: by Grigor Bishop of the Arcrunis (6th century). Saint Nersess theological review 10 (2005) 39-49.

14270 **Tilly, Michael** Jerusalem—Nabel der Welt: Überlieferung und Funktionen von Heiligtumstraditionen im antiken Judentum. 2002 ⇒18,12426... 20,12818. [R]RBLit (2005)* (*Ehrlich, Carl; Hieke, Thomas*).

14271 *Ussishkin, David* Big city, -few people: Jerusalem in the Persian period. BArR 31/4 (2005) 2635.

14272 [E]**Vaughn, Andrew G.; Killebrew, Ann E.** Jerusalem in bible and archaeology: the first temple period. SBL.Symposium 18: 2003 ⇒ 19,829. [R]OLZ 100 (2005) 482-485 (*Thiel, Winfried*); BASOR 337 (2005) 98-99 (*Zorn, Jeffrey R.*); NEA(BA) 68 (2005) 197-199 (*Gilmour, Garth*).

14273 *Veinstein, Gilles* Le rôle des tombes sacrées dans la conquête ottomane. RHR 222/4 (2005) 509-528.

## T4.4 **Judaea, Negeb**; *situs alphabetice*

14274 *Gruson, Philippe, al.*, La Judée. MoBi (2005) 42-52.

14275 **Hirschfeld, Yizhar** Longing for the desert: the Dead Sea valley in the second temple period. 2004 ⇒20,12823. [R]Qad. 38 (2005) 58-60 (*Meshel, Z.*).

14276 ***Ashdod***: **Dothan, Moshe; Ben-Shlomo, David** Ashod VI: the excavations of Areas H and K (1968-1969). IAA Reports 24: J 2005, Israel Antiquities Authority vi; 310 pp. $36. 965-406-178-3;

14277 *Kogan-Zehavi, E.* An Assyrian building south of Tel Ashdod. Qad. 38 (2005) 87-90. **H.**

14278 ***Ashkelon***: *Master, Daniel M.* Iron I chronology at Ashkelon: preliminary results of the Leon Levy expedition. The bible and radiocarbon dating. 2005 ⇒952. 337-348.

14279 ***Beer-Sheba***: *Panitz-Cohen, Nava* A salvage excavation in the new market in Beer-Sheba: new light on Iron Age IIB occupation at Beer-Sheba. IEJ 55 (2005) 143-155.

14280 ***Benei Beraq***: *Oppenheimer, Aharon* Tannaitic Benei Beraq: a peripheral centre of learning. Between Rome and Babylon. TSAJ 108: 2005 <1996> ⇒272. 66-82.

14281 ***Bet-Eglayim***: *Sparks, Rachael T.* The lost loci of Tell el-ʿAjjul: Petrie's Area C. PEQ 137/1 (2005) 23-29.

14282 ***Beth Shemesh***: *Strus, Andrzej; Gibson, Shimon* New excavations at Khirbet el-Jiljil (Bet Gamal) near Beth Shemesh. BAIAS 23 (2005) 29-89.

14283 ***Bethel***: **Köhlmoos, M.** Erinnerungen an eine Stadt: Perspektiven der alttestamentlichen Bet-El-Überlieferung. [D]*Spieckermann, Hermann* 2005, Diss.-Habil. Göttingen [ThLZ 131,336].

14284 ***'Ein Feshkha***: *Netzer, Ehud* Did any perfume industry exist at 'Ein Feshkha?. IEJ 55 (2005) 97-100.

14285 ***Ekron***: *Dothan, Trude; Gitin, Seymour; Naveh, Joseph* The Philistines: Ekron identity confirmed. Secrets of the bible. 2005 ⇒482. 33-36;

14286 *Gitin, Seymour* Excavating Ekron: major Philistine city survived by absorbing other cultures. BArR 31/6 (2005) 40-56, 66-67;

14287 *Ussishkin, David, al.*, The fortifications of Philistine Ekron. IEJ 55 (2005) 35-65.

14288 ***Elusa***: *Christopherson, Gary L.; Saidel, Benjamin A.* Four days at Khalasa: using aerial photography and GIS analysis to reappraise Woolley and Lawrence's survey of Byzantine Elusa in the western Negev desert. PEQ 137/1 (2005) 53-63.

14289 ***'En Gedi***: *Carmi, Israel; Segal, Dror* Radiocarbon dating of samples from the village at 'En Gedi. 'Atiqot 49 (2005) 103*-104*. **H.**;

14290 *Hadas, Gideon* Excavations at the village of 'En Gedi: 1993-1995. 'Atiqot 49 (2005) 41*-71*. **H.**;

14291 *Hirschfeld, Yizhar* En-Gedi: "a very large village of Jews". LASBF 55 (2005) 327-354 (Pls. 11-34);

14292 *Melamed, Yoel; Kislev, Mordechai* Remains of seeds, fruits and insects from the excavations in the village of 'En Gedi. 'Atiqot 49 (2005) 89*-102*. **H.**;

14293 *Porath, Yosef* Survey of ancient agricultural systems at the 'En Gedi oasis. 'Atiqot 50 (2005) 1*-20*. **H.**

14294 ***Gath***: *Maeir, Aren M.; Uziel, Joe* Scratching the surface at Gath: implications of the Tell eṣ-Ṣafi/Gath surface survey. TelAv 32/1 (2005) 50-75.

14295 ***Gaza***: [E]**Saliou, Catherine** Gaza dans l'antiquité tardive: archéologie, rhétorique et histoire. CARDO 2: Salerno 2005, Helios xvi; 240 pp. €38. 88-88123-09-1. Coll. Univ. de Poitiers.

14296 ***Gezer***: **Dever, William G.** Gezer: a crossroad in ancient Israel. TA 1998, Hakibbutz Hameuchad 203 pp. NIS72. Num. ill. [IEJ 50, 147s—Katzenstein, Hannah].

14297 ***Goren***: *Villeneuve, Estelle* Israel: Tel Goren: babylonische Objekte in Judäa. WUB 38 (2005) 67.

14298 ***Herodium***: *Netzer, E.; Kalman, Y.; Laureys-Chachy, R.* New discoveries at the excavations of Lower Herodium. Qad. 38 (2005) 30-42. **H.**

14299 ***Jericho***: **Nigro, Lorenzo**, *al.*, Tell Es-Sultan/Gericho alle soglie della prima urbanizzazione: il villaggio e la necropoli del Bronzo Antico I (3300-3000 a.C.). "La Sapienza" studies on the archaeology of Palestine & Transjordan 1 (ROSOPAT 1): R 2005, Università di Roma "La Sapienza" viii; 211 pp. 88-88438-02-5.

14300 ***Kadesch-Barnea***: *Ben-Gad Hacohen, David* Kadesh: the hidden toponym. Shnaton 15 (2005) 3-19 [Deut 1,40; 1,46]. **H.**

14301 ***Lachisch***: *King, Philip J.* Why Lachish matters: a major site gets the publication it deserves. BArR 31/4 (2005) 36-47;

14302 **Ussishkin, David** The renewed archaeological excavations at Lachish (1973-1994). 2004 ⇒20,12859. [R]BASOR 340 (2005) 83-86 (*Dever, William G.*).

14303 ***Maresha***: *Kloner, A.* Evidence of an Idumean presence at Maresha in the 5th-4th centuries BCE. TEuph 30 (2005) 188-189.

14304 ***Masada***: *Rose, Mark* The history and legends of Masada. Secrets of the bible. 2005 ⇒482. 76-78.
14305 ***Mo'a***: *Shamir, Orit* Textiles, basketry, cordage and whorls from Mo'a (Moje Awad). 'Atiqot 50 (2005) 99-152.
14306 ***Modi'in***: *Golani, Amir* Salvage excavations in the Modi'in landscape. 'Atiqot 50 (2005) 73-97.
14307 ***Motza***: *Thiede, Carsten P.; Lass, Egon H.E.; Lewis, Rafael* The excavation of a crusader building at Motza. BAIAS 23 (2005) 9-27.
14308 ***Nahas***: *Finkelstein, Israel* Khirbet en-Nahas, Edom and biblical history. TelAv 32/1 (2005) 119-125.
14309 ***Ono***: *Gophna, Ram; Taxel, Itmar; Feldstein, Amir* A new identification of ancient Ono. BAIAS 23 (2005) 167-176.
14310 ***Rekhes Nafha***: *Saidel, Benjamin Adam* On the periphery of an agricultural hinterland in the Negev Highlands: Rekhes Nafha 396 in the sixth through eighth centuries C.E. JNES 64 (2005) 241-255.
14311 ***Shihor; Shur***: *Na'aman, Nadav* The Shihor of Egypt and Shur that is before Egypt. Ancient Israel. 2005 <1980> ⇒266. 265-278.
14312 ***Timnah***: **Mazar, Amihai; Panitz-Cohen, Nava** Timnah (Tel Batash) II: the finds from the first millennium BCE. 2001 ⇒17,11327; 19,13575. [R]IEJ 55 (2005) 241-244 (*Wolff, Samuel R.*).
14313 ***Yotvata***: *Davies, Gwyn; Magness, Jodi* The Roman fort at Yotvata, 2004. IEJ 55 (2005) 227-230.
14314 ***Ziklag***: *Borowski, Oded* Tel Halif: in the path of Sennacherib. BArR 31/3 (2005) 24-35 [2 Kgs 18,13; 2 Chr 32,1].

## T4.5 Samaria, Sharon

14315 *Gophna, Ram; Tsuk, Tsvika* Chalcolithic settlements in the western Samaria foothills. TelAv 32/1 (2005) 3-19.
14316 *Gruson, Philippe* La Samarie. MoBi (2005) 38-41.
14317 *Tal, Oren* Some remarks on the coastal plain of Palestine under Achaemenid rule—an archaeological synopsis. L'archéologie de l'empire achéménide. Persika 6: 2005 ⇒926. 71-96.
14318 *Acco*: *Oppenheimer, Aharon* Das Verhältnis der Stadt Akko zum Land Israel und zu Galiläa. Between Rome and Babylon. TSAJ 108: 2005 <1991> ⇒272. 83-92.
14319 ***Bethel***: **Koenen, Klaus** Bethel: Geschichte, Kult und Theologie. OBO 192: 2003 ⇒19,13580; 20,12875. [R]BiOr 62 (2005) 101-102 (*Tromp, Joh.*); OLZ 100 (2005) 495-500 (*Pfeiffer, Henrik*) [Ps 20].
14320 ***Caesarea M***: **Ayalon, Etan** The assemblage of bone and ivory artifacts from Caesarea Maritima, Israel 1st-13th centuries CE. BAR International Ser. 1457: Oxf 2005, Archaeopress ix; 396 pp. 18417-18955. Diss. Bar-Ilan.
14321 ***Dothan***: [E]**Master, Daniel** Dothan I: remains from the tell (1953-1964). Excavations of Joseph P. Free at Dothan (1953-1964): WL 2005, Eisenbrauns xiv; 186 pp. 1-57506-115-5. Bibl. 179-186.
14322 ***Fattir; Bet Gemal***: **Strus, Andrzej** Khirbet Fattir—Bet Gemal: two ancient Jewish and christian sites in Israel. 2003 ⇒19,13587; 20, 12881. [R]Asp. 52 (2005) 443-444 (*Di Palma, Gaetano*).
14323 ***Geulah***: *Monchot, H.* Un assemblage original au Paléolithique moyen: le repaire à hyènes, porcs-épics et hominidés de la grotte Geula (Mont Carmel, Israël). Paléorient 31/2 (2005) 27-42.

14324 ***Kabri***: **Kempinski, Aharon** Tel Kabri: the 1986-1993 excavation seasons. [E]*Scheftelowitz, N.; Oren, R.* 2002 ⇒19,13593; 20,12884. [R]IEJ 55 (2005) 120-121 (*Stern, Ephraim*).

14325 ***Krokodeilonpolis***: *Gorzalczany, Amir* Shuni: a new Middle Bronze IIA domestic site on the northern bank of Naḥal Tanninim. TelAv 32/1 (2005) 32-49.

14326 ***Lod***: *Oppenheimer, Aharon* Jewish Lydda in the Roman era. Between Rome and Babylon. TSAJ 108: 2005 <1988> ⇒272. 47-65.

14327 ***Mazor-El'ad***: *Zilberbod, Irina; Golani, Amir; Amit, David* A tumulus at Mazor-El'ad (Site 96). 'Atiqot 49 (2005) 9-15.

14328 ***Megiddo; Reḥov***: *Finkelstein, Israel* High or low: Megiddo and Tel Reḥov. The bible and radiocarbon dating. 2005 ⇒952. 302-309.

14329 ***Megiddo; Samaria***: *Franklin, Norma* Correlation and chronology: Samaria and Megiddo Redux. The bible and radiocarbon dating. 2005 ⇒952. 310-322.

14330 ***Michal***: **Grossmann, Eva** Maritime Tel Michal and Apollonia: results of the underwater survey 1989-1996. 2001 ⇒17,11343; 19, 13596. [R]IEJ 55 (2005) 237-241 (*Fischer, Moshe*).

14331 ***Nahal Oren***: *Ashkenazy, H.; Belfer-Cohen, A.; Grosman, L.* The Natufian occupation of Nahal Oren, Mt. Carmel–Israel—the lithic evidence. Paléorient 31/2 (2005) 5-26.

14332 ***Neapolis***: *Fabbrini, Michelangelo* Reperti archeologici nella città vecchia di Nablus. LASBF 55 (2005) 355-362 (Pls. 35-38).

14333 ***Ramat Hanadiv***: *Feinberg Vamosh, Miriam; Hirschfeld, Yizhar* A country gentleman's estate. BArR 31/2 (2005) 18-31.

14334 ***Reḥov***: *Mazar, Amihai, al.*, Ladder of time at Tel Reḥov: stratigraphy, archaeological context, pottery and radiocarbon dates. The bible and radiocarbon dating. 2005 ⇒952. 193-255.

14335 ***Shechem***: *Finkelstein, Israel; Na'aman, Nadav* Shechem of the Amarna period and the rise of the Northern Kingdom of Israel. IEJ 55 (2005) 172-193.

14336 ***Tanninim***: *Sieglman, Azriel; Yanklevitz, Shalom* Tel Tanninim. 'Atiqot 49 (2005) 119*-127*. **H.**

14337 ***Umm Kalkha***: *Dagot, Angelina* Khirbat Umm Kalkha—a rural settlement from the Middle Bronze Age IIA in the Shephelah. 'Atiqot 49 (2005) 5*-11*. **H.**

### T4.6 **Galilaea**; *Golan*

14338 **Chancey, Mark A.** The myth of a gentile Galilee. MSSNTS 118: 2002 ⇒18,12492... 20,12896. [R]ThLZ 130 (2005) 35-37 (*Schröter, Jens*);

14339 Greco-Roman culture and the Galilee of Jesus. MSSNTS 134: C 2005, CUP xvii; 285 pp. $90. 0-521-84647-1. Bibl. 236-274.

14340 *Debergé, Pierre, al.*, La Galilée. MoBi (2005) 14-29.

14341 *Garfinkel, Yosef* Sha'ar ha-Golan, 2004. IEJ 55 (2005) 107-110.

14342 *Gruson, Philippe, al.*, Les pays voisins. MoBi (2005) 30-37.

14343 **Lichtenberger, Achim** Kulte und Kultur der Dekapolis: Untersuchungen zu numismatischen, archäologischen und epigraphischen Zeugnissen. ADPV 29: 2003 ⇒19,13609. [R]OLZ 100 (2005) 462-468 (*Japp, Sarah*); Syria 82 (2005) 374-375 (*Sartre, Maurice*).

14344 *Meyers, Eric M.* Galilee in the time of Christ. Secrets of the bible. 2005 ⇒482. 108-110

14345 *Rumple, J.* Galilee and Jewish resistance movements. Stone-Campbell Journal [Joplin, MS] 8 (2005) 55-72 [NTAb 49,566].

14346 *Zarzecki-Peleg, Anabel* Trajectories of Iron Age settlement in North Israel and their implications for chronology. The bible and radiocarbon dating. 2005 ⇒952. 367-378.

14347 ***'Akko***: *Vitto, Fanny* Hellenistic and Crusader remains at Montmusard, Acre ('Akko). 'Atiqot 50 (2005) 153-179.

14348 ***Bet She'arim***: *Levine, Lee I.* Bet Šeʿarim in its patriarchal context. [F]STEMBERGER, G.: SJ 32: 2005 ⇒140. 183-225.

14349 ***Bet Yerah***: *Greenberg, Raphael; Paz, Yitzhak* The Early Bronze Age fortifications at Tel Bet Yerah. Levant 37 (2005) 81-103.

14350 ***Beth Shearim***: *Tepper, Yigal; Tepper, Yotam* Beit Shearim, the village and nearby burials. 2004 ⇒20,12905. [R]Qad. 38 (2005) 123-124 (*Hachlili, Rachel*).

14351 ***Bethsaida***: [E]**Arav, Rami; Freund, Richard A.** Bethsaida: a city by the north shore of the Sea of Galilee, 3. Bethsaida Excavations Project: Kirksville 2004, Truman State University Press xxv; 310 pp. $30. 40 fig. [R]RBLit (2005)* (*Fairchild, Mark*);

14352 *Arav, Rami* Bethsaida, 2003. IEJ 55 (2005) 101-106.

14353 ***Capernaum***: *Hoppe, Leslie J.* Peter's house in Capernaum. BiTod 43 (2005) 244-249;

14354 **Loffreda, Stanislao** Cafarnao V: documentazione fotografica degli scavi (1968-2003). SBF.CMa 44: J 2005, Franciscan 245 pp. 965-516-069-6. Bibl. 9-10.

14355 ***Dan***: *Bruins, Hendrik J.* Iron-Age $^{14}$C dates from Tel Dan: a high chronology. The bible and radiocarbon dating. 2005 ⇒952. 323-336.

14356 ***'Ein Gev***: *Tomotoshi, Sugimoto* When was the city at Tel 'Ein Gev established?: a study in Iron Age chronology. Orient 48/2 (2005) 1-27. **J.**

14357 ***Gamla***: *Syon, Danny; Yavor, Zvi* Gamla 1997-2000. 'Atiqot 50 (2005) 37-71.

14358 ***Gennesaret***: [E]**Faßbeck, Gabriele** Leben am See Gennesaret: kulturgeschichtliche Entdeckungen in einer biblischen Region. 2003 ⇒19,511. [R]NT 47 (2005) 397-399 (*Stenschke, Christoph*).

14359 ***Hazor***: *Ben-Tor, Amnon* Tel Hazor, 2005. IEJ 55 (2005) 209-216;

14360 *Finkelstein, Israel* Hazor at the end of the Late Bronze Age: a reassessment. UF 37 (2005) 341-349;

14361 *Laurant, Sophie* Visite du site d'Haçor, la plus grande cité cananéenne. MoBi 168 (2005) 44-45;

14362 *Rabinovich, Abraham; Silberman, Neil A.* The burning of Hazor. Secrets of the bible. 2005 ⇒482. 59-65.

14363 ***Hippos-Sussita***: *Segal, A.; Eisenberg, M.* Hippos-Sussita of the Decapolis—first five years of excavation. Qad. 38 (2005) 15-29. **H.**

14364 ***Khirbet el-Minya***: *Rosen-Ayalon, Myriam; Cytryn-Silverman, Katya* Khirbet el-Minya. IEJ 55 (2005) 216-219.

14365 ***Magdala***: *Patella, Michael* Seers' Corner: Magdala: the town. BiTod 43 (2005) 300-303.

14366 ***Megiddo***: *Hancock, R.G.V.; Harrison, T.P.* Geochemical analysis and sociocultural complexity: a case study from early Iron Age Meggido (Israel). Archaeometry 47 (2005) 705-722;

14367 **Harrison, Timothy P.**, *al.*, Megiddo, 3: final report on the Stratum VI excavations. OIP 127: 2004 ⇒20,12921. [R]Syria 82 (2005) 349-350 (*Margueron, Jean-Claude*);

14368 *Silberman, Neil A.*, *al.*, Digging at Armageddon. Secrets of the bible. 2005 ⇒482. 79-87.

14369 ***Qarqur***: [E]**Lapp, Nancy** Preliminary excavation reports and other archaeological investigations: Tell Qarqur, Iron I sites in the north-central highlands of Palestine. AASOR 56: 2003 ⇒19,13658; 20, 12926. [R]OLZ 100 (2005) 64-66 (*Vieweger, Dieter*).

14370 ***Qashish***: **Ben-Tor, Amnon; Bonfil, Ruhama; Zuckerman, Sharon** Tel Qashish: a village in the Jezreel Valley: final report of the archaeological excavations (1978-1987). Qedem Reports 5: 2003 ⇒19,13659. [R]BASOR 338 (2005) 94-97 (*Schaub, R. Thomas*).

14371 ***Sepphoris***: *Weiss, Zeev* Sepphoris (Ṣippori), 2005. IEJ 55 (2005) 219-227.

14372 ***Shelomit***: *Getzov, Nimrod* Settlement remains from the Intermediate Bronze Age at Shelomit. 'Atiqot 49 (2005) 1*-4*. **H.**

14373 ***Tiberias***: **Stacey, David** Excavations at Tiberias, 1973-1974: the early Islamic periods. IAA Reports 21: 2004 ⇒20,12932. [R]PEQ 137 (2005) 182 (*McQuitty, Alison*);

14374 *Zangenberg, Jürgen* Neue Ausgrabungen in Tiberias. WUB 35 (2005) 68-69;

14375 Israel: Tiberias: Palast des Herodes Antipas gefunden?. WUB 37 (2005) 70.

14376 ***Tyre***: *Oppenheimer, Aharon* Tyrus, Phönizien und Galiläa. Between Rome and Babylon. TSAJ 108: 2005 <1991> ⇒272. 93-101.

14377 ***Yin'am***: **Liebowitz, Harold A.** Tel Yin'am I: the Late Bronze Age: excavations at Tel Yin'am, 1976-1989. Studies in Archaeology 42: 2003 ⇒19,13670. [R]BASOR 338 (2005) 98-100 (*Cohen, Susan L.*).

14378 ***Yoqne'am***: **Avissar, Miriam** Tel Yoqne'am excavations on the Acropolis. IAA Reports 25: J 2005, Israel Antiquities Authority viii; 132 pp. 965-406-179-1. Bibl. 117-122.

### T4.8 *Transjordania*: (East-)Jordan

14379 **Abujaber, Raouf S.; Cobbing, Felicity** Beyond the river: Ottoman Transjordan in original photographs. L 2005, Stacey 239 pp. £25. 978-19009-88827.

14380 *Bazzoni, Serena* L'archeologia di Edom;

14381 *Boccalaro, Giorgio* Sela', la terra di Edom, la strada dei re nella geologia dell'Arabia. Geo-Archeologia 1 (2005) 29-116/13-27.

14382 *Cobbing, Felicity J.* The American Palestine Exploration Society and the survey of eastern Palestine. PEQ 137/1 (2005) 9-21.

14383 *Fujii, Sumio* Wadi Burma north, Tal'at'Ubyda, and Wadi al-Qusayr: a preliminary report of the Jafr Basin prehistoric project, 2004. ADAJ 49 (2005) 17-55.

14384 Harrat al-Juhayra pseudo-settlement: a preliminary report of the Jafr Basin prehistoric project, 2004. ADAJ 49 (2005) 57-70.

14385 *Herr, Larry G.*, *al.*, The Ayl To Ras An-Naqab archaeological survey, southern Jordan–phase 1 (2005): preliminary report. 277-298;

14386 *Holmgren, Richard; Kaliff, Anders* The hermit life on al-Lisan peninsula—results of the Swedish Dead Sea expedition: a preliminary report. 167-176;

14387 *Kaptijn, Eva, al.*, Dayr ʿAlla regional project: settling the steppe (first campaign 2004). 89-99;

14388 *Lovell, J.L., al.*, The first preliminary report of the Wadi ar-Rayyan archaeological project: the survey of al-Khawarij. ADAJ 49 (2005) 189-200.

14389 *MacDonald, Burton* The Ayl to Ras an-Naqb archaeological survey, southern Jordan-first season, 2005;

14390 *Naghaway, Aida* Jordan Archaeological museum, as a prototype for other museums in Jordan. ADAJ 49 (2005) *7-*10. **A.**

14391 *Piccirillo, Michele* Aggiornamento delle liste episcopali delle diocesi in territorio transgiordanico. LASBF 55 (2005) 377-394.

14392 **Routledge, Bruce Edward** Moab in the Iron Age. 2004 ⇒20, 12956. [R]BASOR 340 (2005) 90-92 (*Herr, Larry G.*).

14393 *Savage, Stephen H.; Zamora, Kurt A.; Keller, Donald R.* Archaeology in Jordan, 2004 season. AJA 109 (2005) 527-555.

14394 *Schmid, Stephan G.* The international Wadi Farasa Project (IWFP): preliminary report on the 2004 season. ADAJ 49 (2005) 71-79.

14395 **Van der Steen, Eveline** Tribes and territories in transition: the central East Jordan Valley in the late Bronze Age and early Iron Ages: a study of the sources. OLA 130: 2004 ⇒20,12961. [R]BASOR 339 (2005) 113-114 (*MacDonald, Burton*).

14396 *Wasse, Alexander; Rollefson, Gary* The Wadi Sirhan project: report on the 2002 archaeological reconaissance of Wadi Hudruj and Jabal Tharwa, Jordan. Levant 37 (2005) 1-20.

14397 **Worschech, U.** Das Land jenseits des Jordan: biblische Archäologie und Zeitgeschichte, 1: Jordan. Giessen 2004, Brunnen 240 pp.

14398 ***Abila***: *Fayyad, Salameh; Karasneh, Wajeh* Abila between the local community and public awareness. ADAJ 49 (2005) 521-529.

14399 ***al-Basatin***: *Banning, Edward B.; Gibbs, Kevin; Kadowaki, Sejii* Excavations at late neolithic al-Basatin in Wadi Ziqlap, northern Jordan. ADAJ 49 (2005) 229-243.

14400 ***Al-Khazna***: *Zayadine, Fawzi* Al-Khazna, the treasury re-visited a forgotten document of Leon de Laborde. ADAJ 49 (2005) 395-401.

14401 ***al-ʿUmayri***: *Clark, Douglas R.; Herr, Larry G.* Madaba plains project: excavations at Tall al-ʿUmayri, 2004. ADAJ 49 (2005) 245-260;

14402 Madaba plains project—Tall al-ʿUmayri, 2004. AUSS 43 (2005) 229-246.

14403 ***ʿAmman***: *Mansour, Sahar* Figurines and Iron Age objects from ʿAmman citadel. ADAJ 49 (2005) 541-555.

14404 ***as-Sakhina***: *Harun, Jihad* Tall as-Sakhina/northern al-Aghwar. ADAJ 49 (2005) *11-*14. **A.**

14405 ***Ayla***: *Niemi, Tina M.; Rucker, John D.* New excavations of the city wall at Islamic Ayla in ʿAquaba, Jordan. ADAJ 49 (2005) 501-508.

14406 ***'Ayn Jadidah***: *Mortensen, Peder* Archaeological investigations of "Conder's circle" at 'Ayn Jadidah near Mount Nebo. LASBF 55 (2005) 488-489 (Pls. 63-64)/485 (Pls. 61-62).

14407 ***Banyas; Petra***: *Uri Maʿoz, Zvi* Al-Madras-Petra and the paneion at Banyas: the Operosa Antra. ADAJ 49 (2005) 531-539.

14408 ***Bayḍa***: *Bikai, Patricia M.; Kanellopoulos, Chrysanthos; Saunders, Shari L.* Bayḍa documentation project. ADAJ 49 (2005) 339-344.

14409 ***Bayt Ras***: *Fayyad, Salama; Karasneh, Wajih* The theatre of Bayt Ras. ADAJ 49 (2005) *39-*45. **A.**;

14410 *Jumʿa al-Shami, Ahmad* A new discovery at Bayt Ras/Capitolias-Irbid. ADAJ 49 (2005) 509-519.

14411 ***Bâb edh-Drâʾ***: **Rast, Walter; Schaub, Thomas,** *al.*, Bâb edh-Dhrâʾ: excavations at the town site (1975-1981). 2003 ⇒19,537; 20,12974. [R]BASOR 340 (2005) 77-79 (*Philip, Graham*).

14412 ***Bethany***: *Khouri, Rami* Where John baptized: Bethany beyond the Jordan. BArR 31/1 (2005) 34-43;

14413 *Mkhjian, Rustom* Preliminary report Rhetorius monastery Bethany beyond the Jordan. ADAJ 49 (2005) 403-410;

14414 *Waḥeeb, M.* Mosaic floors in the baptism site (Bethany beyond the Jordan). ADAJ 49 (2005) 345-349.

14415 ***Bir Madhkur***: *Smith, Andrew M.* Bir Madhkur project: a preliminary report on recent fieldwork. BASOR 340 (2005) 57-75.

14416 ***Busayra***: **Bienkowski, Piotr** Busayra: excavations by Crystal-M. Bennett 1971-1980. British Academy Monographs in Archaeology 13: 2002 ⇒18,12565; 20,12978. [R]AJA 109 (2005) 107-108 (*Ortiz, Steven M.*); BASOR 337 (2005) 101-103 (*Mattingly, Gerald L.*).

14417 ***Chirbet Dharih***: *Villeneuve, Estelle* Jordanien: Chirbet Dharih: Neuigkeiten rund um den nabatäischen Opferaltar. WUB 38 (2005) 70.

14418 ***Dhiban***: *Porter, Benjamin, al.*, Tall Dhiban 2004 pilot season: prospection, preservation, and planning. ADAJ 49 (2005) 201-216.

14419 ***Gadara***: *Dijkstra, Jan, al.*, Regionaal archeologisch onderzoek nabij Umm Qes (ant. Gadara): de opgravingen op Tell Zera'a en de ligging van laatbrons Gadara. Phoe. 51 (2005) 5-26;

14420 *Dijkstra, Jan; Dijkstra, Meindert; Vriezen, Karel J.H.* The Gadara-Region-Project: preliminary report of the sondage on Tall Zarʿa (2001-2002) and the identification of late Bronze Age Gadara. ADAJ 49 (2005) 177-188;

14421 **Weber, Thomas Maria** Gadara—Umm Qês, 1: Gadara decapolitana. ADPV 30: 2002 ⇒18,12574... 20,12983. [R]RB 112 (2005) 311-312 (*Murphy-O'Connor, Jerome*); OLZ 100 (2005) 414-423 (*Kose, Arno*).

14422 ***Ghawr Aṣ-Ṣafi***: *Politis, Konstantinos D., al.*, Survey and excavations in the Ghawr Aṣ-Ṣafi 2004. ADAJ 49 (2005) 313-326.

14423 ***Ḫirbet ez-Zeraqon***: *Leiverkus, Patrick, al.*, Geophysikalische Prospektion in *Ḫirbet ez-Zeraqon*, 2003 und 2004. ZDPV 121 (2005) 31-38.

14424 ***Jabal Al-Muṭawwaq***: *Fernández-Tresguerres Velasco, Juan A.* Jabal Al-Muṭawwaq. ADAJ 49 (2005) 365-372.

14425 ***Jawa***: **Daviau, Paulette M.** Excavations at Tall Jawa, Jordan, 1: the Iron Age town. Culture and history of the Ancient Near East 11/1: 2002 ⇒18,12586. [R]OLZ 100 (2005) 66-69 (*Jericke, Detlef*).

14426 ***Kallirrhoë***: *Strobel, August; Wimmer, Stefan, al.*, Kallirrhoë (ʿĒn ez-Zāra): Dritte Grabungskampagne des Deutschen Evangelischen Instituts für Altertumswissenschaft des Heiligen Landes... ADPV 32: 2003 ⇒19,13710. [R]OLZ 100 (2005) 165-171 (*Japp, Sarah*).

14427 ***Khirbat Adh-Dhariḥ***: *Al-Muheisen, Zeidoun; Villeneuve, François* Archaeological research at Khirbat Adh-Dhariḥ;

14428 ***Khirbat al-Mamariyah***: *Ninow, Friedbert* Soundings at Khirbat al-Mamariyah in the Wadi al-Mujeb area. LASBF 55 (2005) 486-488.

14429 ***Khirbat Iskandar***: *Long, Jesse C., Jr.; Richard, Suzanne* Three seasons of excavations at Khirbat Iskandar, 1997, 2000, 2004;

14430 ***Khirbat Kazun***: *Kelly, Amanda M.; Politis, Konstantinos D.; Usman, Lisa* Survey and excavations at Khirbat Kazun 2004;

14431 ***Khirbat Marbaṭ Badran***: *Abu Shmais, Adeib* Khirbat Marbaṭ Badran/Rujum Abu Nuṣayr: industrial and agricultural production center preliminary study of the excavations during 2003-2005. ADAJ 49 (2005) 489-499/261-275/327-337/411-416.

14432 ***Khirbat Shuwayka***: *Abu Khalaf, Marwan* The archaeological excavations at Khirbat Shuwayka, eighth season 2004. ADAJ 49 (2005) *15-*27. **A.**

14433 ***Madaba***: *Barlow, Celeste; Harrison, Timothy P.* Mesha, the mishor, and the chronology of Iron Age Mādabā. The bible and radiocarbon dating. 2005 ⇒952. 179-190.

14434 ***Pella***: **Lilimbaki-Akamati, M.** To hiero tes meteras ton theon kai tes Aphrodites sten Pella. Thessaloniki 2000, xiii; 429 pp. 96021-4-2812. Num. ill. [R]AWE 4 (2005) 491-4 (*Kathariou, Kleopatra*). **G.**

14435 ***Petra***: **Amadasi Guzzo, Maria Giulia; Equini Schneider, Eugenia** Petra. [T]*Cochrane, Lydia G.* 2002 ⇒19,13716. [R]JNES 64 (2005) 212-213 (*Fiema, Zbigniew T.*);

14436 **Bedal, Leigh-Ann** The Petra pool complex: a Hellenistic paradeisos in the Hellenistic capital: results from the Petra 'Lower Market' survey and excavations, 1998. 2004 ⇒20,12993. [R]BASOR 339 (2005) 118-120 (*Nielsen, Inge*);

14437 **Crawford, Gregory A.** Petra and the Nabataeans: a bibliography. ATLA.BS 49: Lanham 2003, Scarecrow xii; 274 pp. $65;

14438 *Farajat, Suleiman; Nawafleh, Sami* Report on the Al-Khazna courtyard excavation at Petra (2003 season). ADAJ 49 (2005) 373-393;

14439 *Graf, David F., al.*, The Hellenistic Petra project: excavations in the civic center, preliminary report of the first season, 2004. ADAJ 49 (2005) 417-441;

14440 *Joukowsky, Martha S.* Brown University archaeological research at the Petra great temple. ADAJ 49 (2005) 147-165;

14441 [E]**Markoe, Glenn** Petra rediscovered: lost city of the Nabataeans. 2003 ⇒19,13725. [R]AJA 109 (2005) 783-787 (*Downey, Susan B.*);

14442 **McKenzie, J.** The architecture of Petra. Oxf 2005 <1990>, Oxbow xxii; 209 + 245 pp. £40. 1-84217-164-X. 245 pp of pl.;

14443 *Ortloff, Charles R.* The water supply and distribution system of the Nabataean city of Petra (Jordan), 300 BC-AD 300. CamArchJ 15 (2005) 93-109;

14444 **Taylor, Jane** Petra and the lost kingdom of the Nabataeans. 2001 ⇒17,11449. [R]IJCT 11 (2005) 460-463 (*Kühn, Dagmar*);

14445 **Zayadine, Fawzi; Larché, François; Dentzer-Feydy, Jacqueline** Le Qasr al-Bint de Pétra: l'architecture, le décor, la chronologie et les dieux. 2003 ⇒19,13726; 20,13005. [R]RAr (2005/2) 425-426 (*Gawlikowski, Michel*).

14446 ***Qaṣr Al-Uṣaykhim***: *Al-Khouri, Maysoun; Infranca, Giuseppe C.* The archaeological site of Qaṣr Al-Uṣaykhim. ADAJ 49 (2005) 351-364.

14447 ***Ṣabra***: *Lindner, Manfred* Water supply and water management at ancient Sabra (Jordan). PEQ 137/1 (2005) 33-52.

14448 ***Shakarat al-Musay'is***: *Jensen, C.H., al.*, Preliminary report on the excavations at Shakarat al-Musay'is, 1999-2004. ADAJ 49 (2005) 115-134.

14449 ***Umm Saysaban***: *Gunsam, E.; Lindner, M.; Schreyer, E.* Early Bronze Age Umm Saysaban excavation continued in 2001: insights and conjectures. ADAJ 49 (2005) 217-227.

14450 ***Umn al-Rasas***: *Abela, J.; Pappalardo, C.; Piccirillo, Michele* Umn al-Rasas 2005, excavation report. LASBF 55 (2005) 491-498 (Pls. 66-69).

14451 ***'Uyun al-Hammam***: *Maher, Lisa A.* Recent excavations at the middle epipaleolithic encampment of 'Uyun al-Hammam, northern Jordan. ADAJ 49 (2005) 101-114.

14452 ***Zera'a***: *Häser, Jutta; Vieweger, Dieter* Preliminary report on the archaeological investigations of the Wadi al-'Arab and the Tall Zar'a, 2003 and 2004. ADAJ 49 (2005) 135-146;

14453 Der *Tell Zera'a* im *Wadi el-'Arab*: das 'Gadara region project' in den Jahren 2001 bis 2004. ZDPV 121 (2005) 1-30;

14454 *Vieweger, Dieter* Jordanien: Tell Zera'a: eine antike Siedlung—Schicht für Schicht. WUB 36 (2005) 62-64.

14455 ***Zizia***: *Villeneuve, Estelle* Jordanien: Zizia: die Schlafstörungen des Priesters Kamason. WUB 37 (2005) 71.

### T5.1 **Phoenicia**—*Libanus*, **Lebanon**; *situs mediterranei*

14456 [TE]**Bierling, Marilyn R.** The Phoenicians in Spain: an archaeological review of the eight-sixth centuries B.C.E. 2002 ⇒18,449. [R]CBQ 67 (2005) 165-167 (*Aznar, Carolina A.*); OLZ 100 (2005) 438-445 (*Zamora, José A.*).

14457 *Bikai, Patricia M.* The Phoenicians: rich and glorious traders of the Levant. Secrets of the bible. 2005 ⇒482. 3-9.

14458 *Fantar, M.H.* L'archéologie punique en Tunisie (1995-2000). V Congresso di studi fenici. 2005 ⇒959. I, 201-206.

14459 *Garrard, Andrew; Yazbeck, Corine* The revival of prehistoric field research in Lebanon: the Qadisha Valley prehistoric project. NEA 68/4 (2005) 193-194.

14460 *Gilboa, Ayelet* Sea peoples and Phoenicians along the southern Phoenician coast—a reconciliation: an interpretation of Šikila (SKL) material culture. BASOR 337 (2005) 47-78.

14461 *Markoe, Glenn* The Phoenicians: a nation of artisans;

14462 *McGovern, Patrick E.* The Phoenicians: a dye for god and king. Secrets of the bible. 2005 ⇒482. 10-15/16-19.

14463 **Nordiguian, Lévon** Temples de l'époque romaine au Liban. Beyrouth 2005, Presse de l'Université Saint Joseph 231 pp. 99534-556-27. Ill.

14464 **Sagona, Claudia** The archaeology of Punic Malta. Ancient Near Eastern Studies, Supplement 9: 2002 ⇒18,12630. [R]AWE 4 (2005) 503-506 (*Termini, A.*).

14465 ***Arwad; Simirra***: *Briquel Chatonnet, F.* Arwad et Simirra: problèmes géostratégiques de la Phénicie du nord;

14466 ***Beirut***: *Curvers, H.H.* The lower town of Beirut (600-300 BC): urban planning?. V Congr. di studi fenici. 2005 ⇒959. I, 23-6/121-7;

14467 *Vidal, Jordi* The political decadence of Beirut ($14^{th}$-$7^{th}$ centuries BCE). UF 37 (2005) 643-651.

14468 ***Sidon***: *Sader, H.* Les fouilles de Tell el-Buraq-Liban: lumière sur le royaume de Sidon à l'époque perse. TEuph 30 (2005) 190.

## T5.3 **Carthago**

14469 *Aznar, C.* Cerámica fenicia en el área alrededor de Cartago: un análisis petrográfico y sus implicaciones. I, 285-292;

14470 *Bénichou-Safar, H.* Une alliance hommes-dieux dans la religion des Carthaginois?. I, 315-323;

14471 *Debergh, J.* Jean Emile Humbert et les premières découvertes puniques à Carthage: stèles et inscriptions funéraires et votives. I, 293-302;

14472 *Docter, R.F.* The *koprologoi* of Carthage: on the scarcity of settlement finds in Carthage between c. 550 and 480 BC. I, 269-276;

14473 *Gorokhovskaia, L.P.; Tsirkin, J.B.* Carthage and the north Black Sea area. I, 195-197;

14474 *Mansel, K.* Una contribución a la formación social del Cartago arcáico: la cerámica a mano de los s. VIII y VII a.C. V Congresso di studi fenici. 2005 ⇒959. I, 259-268.

14475 *Minunno, Giuseppe* La crocifissione cartaginese. StEeL 22 (2005) 79-93.

14476 *Sammartano, R.* Λιβύν περίρρυτος: ERODOTO e le informazioni cartaginesi sulla geografia africana. I, 221-229;

14477 *Sznycer, Maurice* Les Phéniciens et les Puniques vus à travers les études classiques (gréco-romaines): le cas de Carthage. I, 207-220;

14478 *Vegas, M.* L'influsso della ceramica greca sul vasellame di Cartagine. V Congresso di studi fenici. 2005 ⇒959. I, 277-283.

## T5.4 **Ugarit**—*Ras Šamra*

14479 *Calvet, Yves* L'environnement antique d'Ougarit. [M]CAQUOT, A. 2005 ⇒22. 45-66.

14480 **Cornelius, Izak; Niehr, Herbert** Götter und Kulte in Ugarit: Kultur und Religion einer nordsyrischen Königsstadt in der Spätbronzezeit. Zaberns Bildbände zur Archäologie: 2004 ⇒20,13023. [R]WZKM 95 (2005) 428-430 (*Jaroš, Karl*).

14481 *Devolder, Maud* Distribution sociale de l'architecture domestique à Ougarit. RANT 2 (2005) 237-263.

14482 *Dietrich, Manfried; Loretz, Oswald* Der Begriff *editio princeps* in der Ugaritologie. UF 37 (2005) 217-219.

14483 *Healey, John F.* More than marginal: Ugarit in its eastern Mediterranean setting. [F]ULLENDORFF, E.: SStLL 47: 2005 ⇒154. 181-188.

14484 *Heltzer, M.* Some thoughts about the last days of Ugarit. UF 37 (2005) 371-373.

14485 *Lackenbacher, Sylvie; Malbran-Labat, Florence* Ugarit et les Hittites dans les archives de la 'Maison d'Urtenu'. SMEA 47 (2005) 227-240.

14486 *Michaud, Jean-Marc* Ougarit et la genèse de la Bible hébraïque. [M]CAQUOT, A. 2005 ⇒22. 3-25.

14487 *Olmo Lete, Gregorio del Ḫalma* of Emar and *Ġlmt* of Ugarit: a 'dark' deity. [M]DIAKONOFF, M. 2005 ⇒36. 47-57.

14488 *Pardee, Dennis* Defense de la grammaire ougaritique: le cas de RS 15.053. StEeL 22 (2005) 13-18;
14489 Dresser le boeuf à Ougarit. [F]MILLARD, A.: LHBOTS 426: 2005 ⇒102. 41-47;
14490 La pratique de la religion à Ougarit d'après les textes. [M]CAQUOT, A. 2005 ⇒22. 115-144;
14491 G. del Olmo Lete's views on Ugaritic epigraphy and religion. UF 37 (2005) 767-815.
14492 *Roche, Carol* Introduction à la civilisation d'Ougarit. [M]CAQUOT, A. 2005 ⇒22. 29-44.
14493 *Smith, Mark S.* Ugaritic literature. BiTod 43 (2005) 165-169.
14494 **Smith, Mark S.** Untold stories: the bible and Ugaritic studies in the twentieth century. 2001 ⇒17,12603... 20,13035. [R]Kerux 20/3 (2005) 42-6 (*Smith, Scobie P.*); AsbTJ 60/1 (2005) 131-4 (*Strawn, Brent A.*).
14495 *Tsumura, David T.* 'Misspellings' in cuneiform alphabetic texts from Ugarit: some cases of loss or addition of signs. [F]MILLARD, A.: LHBOTS 426: 2005 ⇒102. 143-153.
14496 **Van Soldt, Wilfred Hugo** The topography of the city-state of Ugarit. AOAT 324: Müns 2005, Ugarit-Verlag vi; 253 pp. 3-9346-28-64-8. Bibl. 194-205. [R]UF 37 (2005) 836-837 (*Müller, G.G.W.*).
14497 *Vidal, Jordi* Beirut and Ugarit in the 13th century BCE. SMEA 47 (2005) 291-298;
14498 Ugarit at war (1): the size and geographical origin of the *ḫrd*-militia. UF 37 (2005) 653-672.
14499 *Vita, Juan-Pablo* Ougarit entre la guerre et la paix. [M]CAQUOT, A. 2005 ⇒22. 67-98.
14500 *Wyatt, Nicolas* The religious role of the king at Ugarit. UF 37 (2005) 695-727;
14501 Who killed the dragon?. Mythic mind. 2005 <1987> ⇒328. 18-37;
14502 The vocabulary and neurology of orientation: the Ugaritic and Hebrew evidence. Mythic mind. 2005 <1996> ⇒328. 125-150;
14503 Le mariage et le meurtre: stratégies royales au Levant. [M]CAQUOT, A. 2005 ⇒22. 213-244 [Gen 9,20-25].
14504 [E]**Yon, Marguerite; Arnaud, Daniel** Études ougaritiques I: travaux 1985-1995. 2001 ⇒17,11482... 20,13039. [R]Or. 74 (2005) 136-145 (*Márquez Rowe, Ignacio*); JNES 64 (2005) 125-6 (*Biggs, Robert*); WO 35 (2005) 235-6 (*Tropper, Josef*); JSSt 50 (2005) 202-5 (*Watson, Wilfred G.E.*); Syria 82 (2005) 350-52 (*Butterlin, Pascal*).

### T5.5 Ebla

14505 **Mander, Pietro** Le religioni del Vicino Oriente antico, 1: la religione di Ebla (xxv-xxiv sec. a.C.). Quaderni napoletani di assiriologia 5: R 2005, Aracne 129 pp. €9. 88-548-0280-8.
14506 **Pasquali, Jacopo** Il lessico dell'artigianato nei testi di Ebla. QuSem 23: F 2005, Univ. di Firenze, Dipartimento di Linguistica 212 pp. 88-901340-2-X. Bibl. 187-212.
14507 *Tonietti, Maria V.* Symbolisme et mariage à Ébla: aspects du rituel pour l'intronisation du roi. [M]DIAKONOFF, M. 2005 ⇒36. 245-261.

## T5.8 Situs efossi Syriae in ordine alphabetico

14508 Orte & Zeiten: 25 Jahre archäologische Forschung in Syrien: 1980-2005. Damaskus 2005, Deutsches Archäologisches Institut 179 pp. 3-00-016309-3 [UF 36,701s–M. Dietrich].

14509 **Akkermans, Peter M.M.G.; Schwartz, Glenn M.** The archaeology of Syria: from complex hunter-gatherers to early urban societies (c. 16,000-300 BC). 2003 ⇒19,13797; 20,13045. [R]AJA 109 (2005) 303-304 (*Marchetti, Nicolò*); Antiquity 79 (2005) 972-973 (*Semple, Miranda J.*); BiOr 62 (2005) 589-592 (*Becker, J.*).

14510 **Butcher, Kevin** Roman Syria and the Near East. 2003 ⇒19,13799. [R]BASOR 337 (2005) 103-104 (*Downey, Susan B.*); AWE 4 (2005) 482-484 (*Kaizer, Ted*).

14511 [E]**Geyer, Bernard; Monchambert, Jean-Yves** La basse vallée de l'Euphrate Syrien du Néolithique à l'avènement de l'Islam: géographie, archéologie et histoire. 2003 ⇒19,13803-4; 20,13050. [R]Mes. 40 (2005) 192-193 (*Lippolis, Carlo*).

14512 [E]**Iwasaki, Takuya; Tsuneki, Akira** Archaeology of the Rouj Basin, 1. Al Shark 2: 2003 ⇒19,13805; 20,13051. [R]Syria 82 (2005) 345 (*Contenson, Henri de*).

14513 [E]**Klengel-Brandt, Evelyn; Kulemann-Ossen, Sabina; Martin, Lutz** Tall Knédig: die Ergebnisse der Ausgrabungen des Vorderasiatischen Museums Berlin in Nordost-Syrien von 1993 bis 1998. WV.DOG 113: Saarbrücken 2005, Saarbrücker xxxiv; 404 pp. €88. 3-930843-97-8. Bibl. xx-xxxiv.

14514 ***Al Umbashi***: [E]**Braemer, Frank; Échallier, Jean-Claude; Taraqji, Ahmad** Khirbet Al Umbashi: villages et campements de pasteurs dans le 'désert noir' (Syrie) à l'âge du Bronze. BAH 171: 2004 ⇒20,13054. [R]Syria 82 (2005) 346-347 (*Margueron, Jean-Claude*); Paléorient 31/2 (2005) 187-189 (*Betts, Alison*).

14515 ***Alalaḫ***: *Dassow, Eva von* Archives of Alalaḫ IV in archaeological context. BASOR 338 (2005) 1-69.

14516 ***Al-Rawda***: *Castel, Corinne, al.*, Rapport préliminaire sur les activités de la mission archéologique franco-syrienne dans la micro-région d'Al-Rawda (Shamiyeh): deuxième et troisième campagnes (2003 et 2004). Akkadica 126 (2005) 51-95.

14517 ***Amarna (Syria)***: [E]**Molist, Miquel; Tunca, Öhnan** Tell Amarna (Syrie) I: la période de Halaf. Publications de la Mission archéologique de l'Univ. de Liège en Syrie: Lv 2004, Peeters viii; 283 + 11 pp en arabe. 90429-14246.

14518 ***Beydar***: *Lebeau, Marc* Eau et sanitaires à l'étage. [F]FINET, A.: Subartu 16: 2005 ⇒40. 99-105;

14519 **Lebeau, Marc; Suleiman, Antoine,** *al.*, Tell Beydar / Nabada: une cité du Bronze ancien en Jezireh syrienne: 10 ans de travaux (1992-2002) = an early Bronze age city in the Syrian Jezirah: 10 years of research (1992-2002). Documents d'archéologie syrienne 6: Damas 2005, Ministère de la culture 107, 64 pp; 102 pp of pl.;

14520 [E]**Lebeau, Mark; Suleiman, Antoine** Tell Beydar, the 1995-1999 season of excavations: a preliminary report. Subartu 10: Turnhout 2003, Brepols 567 pp. 2-503-99117-3. 37 plans; num. ill.

14521 **Van Lerberghe, Karel; Voet, Gabriella** Tell Beydar: environmental and technical studies. Subartu 6: 2001 ⇒17,11623 [!]. [R]OLZ 100 (2005) 159-162 (*Kulemann-Ossen, Sabina*).

14522 ***Boueid***: [E]**Nieuwenhuyse, Olivier; Suleiman, Antoine** Tell Boueid II: a late neolithic village on the middle Khabur (Syria). Subartu 11: Turnhout 2002, Brepols vi; 193 pp. 2503513441. Bibl. 179-87.

14523 ***Brak***: **Oates, David; Oates, Joan; McDonald, Helen** Excavations at Tell Brak, vol. 2: Nagar in the third millennium BC. 2001 ⇒17, 11500; 20,13062. [R]Antiquity 79 (2005) 704-705 (*Roaf, Michael*).

14524 ***Damascus***: **Burns, Ross** Damascus: a history. L 2005, Routledge xx; 386 pp. £60. 0-415-27105-3. 14 maps; 82 ill. [R]Syria 82 (2005) 373 (*Sartre, Maurice*).

14525 ***Dura-Europos***: *Scholten, Helga* Akkulturationsprozesse in der Euphrat-Region am Beispiel der griechisch-makedonischen Siedlung Dura-Europos. Hist. 54 (2005) 18-36.

14526 ***Emar***: **Mori, Lucia** Reconstructing the Emar landscape. Quaderni di geografia storica 6: 2003 ⇒19,13818. [R]Or. 74 (2005) 128-129 (*Van De Mieroop, Marc*).

14527 ***Ḥalaf***: *Kaiser, Helga* Boten aus tiefer Vergangenheit: das Tell Halaf-Projekt des Vorderasiatischen Museums Berlin. WUB 36 (2005) 2-7.

14528 ***Hauran***: [E]**Dentzer-Feydy, Jacqueline & Jean-Marie; Blanc, Pierre-Marie** Hauran II: les installations de SIʿ 8: du sanctuaire à l'établissement viticole. 2003 ⇒19,13821. [R]Antiquity 79 (2005) 725-6 (*Genequand, Denis*); Mes. 40 (2005) 208-9 (*Lippolis, Carlo*).

14529 ***Homs***: *Philip, Graham, al.*, Settlement and landscape development in the Homs region, Syria: report on work undertaken during 2001-2003. Levant 37 (2005) 21-42.

14530 ***Kazel***: *Capet, Emmanuelle* Tell Kazel (Syrie), rapport préliminaire sur les $9^{e}$-$17^{e}$ campagnes de fouilles (1993-2001) du musée de l'université Américaine de Beyrouth, chantier II. Berytus 47 (2003) 63-128. Corrected reprint.

14531 ***Mari***: *Anbar, Moshé* Ḫanûm: nom ethnique ou nom générique?. [F]KLEIN, J. 2005 ⇒79. 446-461;

14532 **Fleming, Daniel E.** Democracy's ancient ancestors: Mari and early collective governance. 2004 ⇒20,13075. [R]BTB 35 (2005) 40 (*Eddinger, Terry W.*); JESHO 48 (2005) 325-326 (*Van De Mieroop, Marc*);

14533 **Margueron, Jean-Claude** Mari: métropole de l'Euphrate, au IIIe et au début du IIe millénaire av J.C. 2004 ⇒20,13077. [R]RA 99 (2005) 188-189 (*Charpin, Dominique*); CRAI (2005/1) 350-351 (*Leclant, Jean*).

14534 ***Muṣur***: *Makinson, Martin* Muṣru, Maṣuwari and MṢR: from Middle Assyrian frontier to Iron Age City. SAA Bulletin 14 (2002-2005) 33-62.

14535 ***Palmyra***: *Cussini, Eleonora* Beyond the spindle: investigating the role of Palmyrene women. [M]HILLERS, D.: Culture and History of the ancient Near East 22: 2005 ⇒61. 26-43;

14536 *Delplace, Christiane* Quelques remarques sur les 'salles de banquet' à Palmyre. [F]GAWLIKOWSKI, M. 2005 ⇒45. 43-52;

14537 *Rey-Coquais, Jean-Paul* De Tyr à Palmyre. [F]GAWLIKOWSKI, M. 2005 ⇒45. 213-224;

14538 [E]**Schmidt-Colinet, Andreas** Palmyra: Kulturbegegnung im Grenzbereich. Bildbände zur Archäologie: Mainz $^{3}$2005 <1995>, Von Zabern iv; 99 pp. €34.80. 3-8053-3557-1. 150 ill.;

14539 *Seigne, Jacques; Yon, Jean-Baptiste* Documents nouveaux de la grande colonnade de Palmyre. [F]GAWLIKOWSKI, M. 2005 ⇒45. 243-261;

14540 *Teixidor, Javier* Palmyra in the third century. [M]HILLERS, D.: Culture and History of the ancient Near East 22: 2005 ⇒61. 181-225;

14541 *Żuchowska, Marta* Palmyre—cité caravanière?. [F]GAWLIKOWSKI, M. 2005 ⇒45. 325-347.

14542 ***Qarqur***: [E]**Lapp, Nancy** Preliminary excavation reports and other archaeological investigations: Tell Qarqur, Iron I sites in the north-central highlands of Palestine. AASOR 56: 2003 ⇒19,13658; 20, 12926. [R]OLZ 100 (2005) 64-66 (*Vieweger, Dieter*).

14543 ***Ras Ibn Hani***: **Bounni, Adnan; Lagarce, Elisabeth; Lagarce, Jacques** Ras Ibn Hani, 1: le palais nord du Bronze Récent: fouilles 1979-1995, synthèse préliminaire. BAH 151: 1998 ⇒14,10941... 17,11512. [R]BiOr 62 (2005) 341-342 (*Meijer, D.J.W.*).

14544 ***Sam'al***: **Wartke, Ralf-B.** Sam'al: ein aramäischer Stadtstaat des 10. bis 8. Jhs. v.Chr. und die Geschichte seiner Erforschung. Mainz 2005, Von Zabern 96 pp. €20.50. 3-8053-2918-0. Num. ill.

14545 ***Tuttul***: **Miglus, Peter A.; Strommenger, Eva** Tall Bi'a/Tuttul, VIII: Stadtbefestigungen, Häuser und Tempel. WVDOG 103; Ausgrabungen in Tall Bi'a/Tuttul 8: 2002 ⇒18,12700. [R]OLZ 100 (2005) 156-159 (*Werner, Peter*).

## T6.1 **Mesopotamia**, *generalia*

14546 *Amiet, Pierre* L'effigie royale aux origines de la civilisation mésopotamienne. RB 112 (2005) 5-19.

14547 **Bertman, Stephen** Handbook to life in ancient Mesopotamia. NY 2005, OUP 416 pp. $22. 01951-83649. Num. ill.

14548 [E]**Chavalas, Mark William; Younger, K. Lawson** Mesopotamia and the bible: comparative explorations. JSOT.S 341: 2002 ⇒18, 458... 20,13088. [R]TrinJ 26 (2005) 133-134 (*Graves, David G.*).

14549 *Crawford, Harriet* Mesopotamia and the Gulf: the history of a relationship. Iraq 67/2 (2005) 41-46.

14550 *Ducène, Jean-Charles* La Mésopotamie ancienne chez les géographes arabes médiévaux: entre mythe et mémoire. [F]FINET, A. Subartu 16: 2005 ⇒40. 31-36.

14551 *Fiorina, Paolo; Bombardieri, Luca; Chiocchetti, Lucia* Kalḫu-Kaḫat: elementi di continuità attraverso il periodo neoassiro finale e l'età neobabilonese caldea in Mesopotamia settentrionale. Mes. 40 (2005) 81-102.

14552 *Hieke, Thomas* Die Bibel—ein babylonischer Text?: der Babel-Bibel-Streit. WUB 37 (2005) 57.

14553 **Matthews, Roger** The archaeology of Mesopotamia: theories and approaches. 2003 ⇒19,13854; 20,13098. [R]CamArchJ 15 (2005) 125-127 (*Watkins, Trevor*).

14554 **Nemet-Nejat, Karen R.** Daily life in ancient Mesopotamia. 2001 ⇒17,11529...20,13101. [R]RStR 31 (2005) 149-150 (*Nakhai, Beth*).

14555 **Oates, David** Studies in the ancient history of northern Iraq. L 2005 <1968>, British School of Archaeology in Iraq 192 pp. £30. 0-903472-198. Pref. *Joan Oates*.

14556 *Quenet, Philippe* The diffusion of the cuneiform writing system in northern Mesopotamia: the earliest archaeological evidence. Iraq 67/2 (2005) 31-40.

14557 *Steele, J.M.* A new scheme from Uruk for the retrograde arc of Mars. JCS 57 (2005) 129-133 [OTA 30,8].

14558 [E]**Steele, John M.; Imhausen, Annette** Under one sky: astronomy and mathematics in the ancient Near East. AOAT 297: 2002 ⇒18, 9014. [R]AfO 51 (2005-2006) 350-352 (*Hunger, Hermann*).

14559 *Ur, Jason* Sennacherib's northern Assyrian canals: new insights from satellite imagery and aerial photography. Iraq 67/1 (2005) 317-345.

14560 *Van de Mieroop, Marc* A tale of two cities: Nineveh and Babylon. Nineveh. 2005 ⇒901. 1-5.

### T6.5 Situs effossi Iraq *in ordine alphabetico*

14561 **Bernhardsson, Magnus Thorkell** Reclaiming a plundered past: archaeology and nation building in modern Iraq [1900-1941]. Austin, TX 2005, Univ. of Texas Pr. xi; 327 pp. £29; $34. 0-292-70947-1. Diss. 1999; Bibl. 285-311.

14562 **Canby, Jeanny Vorys** The "Ur-Nammu" stela. 2001 ⇒17,11545. [R]AJA 109 (2005) 301-303 (*Suter, Claudia E.*).

14563 *Laurent, Sophie* Das irakische Kulturerbe bewahren. WUB 35 (2005) 66-67.

14564 [E]**Root, Margaret Cool** This fertile land: songs + symbols in the early arts of Iran and Iraq. Kelsey Museum publication 3: AA 2005, Kelsey Museum of Archaeology viii; 192 pp. 0-9741873-2-1. Bibl. 175-189.

14565 ***al-Ḥamidiya***: **Wäfler, Markus** Tall al-Ḥamidiya, 4: Vorbericht 1988-2001. OBO.A 23: 2003 ⇒19,13861. [R]OLZ 100 (2005) 408-409 (*Martin, Lutz*).

14566 ***Assur***: [E]**Marzahn, Joachim; Salje, Beate** Wiedererstehendes Assur: 100 Jahre deutsche Ausgrabungen in Assyrien. 2003 ⇒19, 13862; 20,13104. [R]OLZ 100 (2005) 609-611 (*Radner, Karen*).

14567 ***Babylon***: Der Wiederaufbau Babylons unter Saddam Hussein: ein neuer Nebukadnezzar. WUB 37 (2005) 30-31;

14568 *Glassner, Jean-Jacques* Die Bürde der Entdeckungen: Auswirkungen auf die Bibelwissenschaft. WUB 37 (2005) 54-56;

14569 *Kaiser, Helga* Die Göttertürme: die Bedeutung der Zikkurats. WUB 37 (2005) 20-21;

14570 *Röwekamp, Georg* "... dort kann man innerhalb der Mauern auf Reisen gehen": antike Texte zu Babylon. WUB 37 (2005) 22-24.

14571 ***Babylon; Nineveh***: *Vlaardingerbroek, Menko* The founding of Nineveh and Babylon in Greek historiography. Nineveh. 2005 ⇒901. 233-241.

14572 ***Brak***: [E]**Matthews, Roger** Excavations at Tell Brak 4: exploring an Upper Mesopotamian regional centre, 1994-6. 2003 ⇒19,13866; 20,13106. [R]Mes. 40 (2005) 195-196 (*Cellerino, Alessandra*).

14573 ***Chagar Bazar***: *McMahon, Augusta; Colantoni, Carlo; Semple, Miranda* British excavations at Chagar Bazar, 2001-2. Iraq 67/2 (2005) 1-16.

14574 ***Haradum***: *Kepinski, Christine* Material culture of a Babylonian commercial outpost on the Iraqi middle Euphrates: the case of Haradum during the Middle Bronze Age. Akkadica 126 (2005) 121-131.

14575 ***Lagash***: **Huh, Sa Kyung** Studien zur Genese und Entwicklung der Region Lagasch: von den Anfängen bis zur altbabylonischen Zeit. 2005, Diss. Münster [AA 2006/1, 311].

14576 ***Mashkan-shapir***: **Stone, Elizabeth Caecilia; Zimansky, Paul E.** The anatomy of a Mesopotamian city: survey and soundings at Mashkan-shapir. 2004 ⇒20,13109. [R]BASOR 340 (2005) 79-81 (*Matthews, Roger*); Akkadica 126 (2005) 99-100 (*Pons, Nina*).

14577 ***Nimrud***: *Herrmann, Georgina* Naming, defining, explaining: a view from Nimrud. Crafts...images. OBO 210: 2005 ⇒693. 11-22.

14578 ***Nineveh***: *Foster, Karen P.* The hanging gardens of Nineveh. Nineveh. 2005 ⇒901. 207-220;

14579 *Frame, Grant; George, Andrew* The royal libraries of Nineveh: new evidence for their formation. Iraq 67/1 (2005) 265-284;

14580 *Pickworth, Diana* Excavations at Nineveh: the Halzi gate. Iraq 67/1 (2005) 295-316;

14581 *Rivaroli, Marta* Nineveh: from ideology to topography;

14582 *Tenu, Aline* Ninive et Aššur à l'époque médio-assyrienne. Nineveh. 2005 ⇒901. 199-205/27-33.

14583 ***Nippur***: **Cole, Steven William** Nippur IV: the early Neo-Babylonian governor's archive from Nippur. 1996 ⇒12,10398; 14,10967. [R]RA 99 (2005) 180-182 (*Joannès, F.*).

14584 ***Nuzi***: [E]**Owen, David I.; Wilhelm, Gernot** General studies and excavations at Nuzi 11/1. Studies on the civilization and culture of Nuzi and the Hurrians 15: Bethesda, MD 2005, CDL viii, 261 pp. 1-883053-897.

14585 ***Sippar***: *Fadhil, Abdullah; Al-Samarraee, Zuhair R.A.* Ausgrabungen in Sippar (Tell Abu Habbah)—Vorbericht über die Grabungsergebnisse der 24. Kampagne 2002. BaghM 36 (2005) 157-224.

14586 ***Tepe Gawra***: **Rothman, Mitchell S.** Tepe Gawra: the evolution of a small, prehistoric center in northern Iraq. 2002 ⇒18,12728. [R]Antiquity 79 (2005) 973-974 (*Oates, Joan*).

14587 ***Uruk***: **Boehmer, Rainer Michael** Uruk: früheste Siegelabrollungen. Ausgrabungen in Uruk-Warka Endberichte 24: 1999 ⇒15, 11733...20,13125. [R]AJA 109 (2005) 300-301 (*Porter, Barbara A.*).

## T6.7 **Arabia; Iran; Central Asia**

14588 **Farès-Drappeau, Saba** Dédan et Liḥyān: histoire des Arabes aux confins des pouvoirs perse et hellénistique (IV$^{e}$-II$^{e}$ s. avant l'ére chrétienne). TMO 42: Lyon 2005, Maison Orient Mediterranéen 325 pp. €30.40. 29032-64848. Diss. Aix-en-Provence 1999; Préf. *C. Robin*; 10 fig.; 32 pl.

14589 **Hoyland, Robert G.** Arabia and the Arabs: from the Bronze Age to the coming of Islam. 2001⇒17,11547; 19,13876. [R]AnCl 74 (2005) 591-592 (*Sartre, Maurice*).

14590 *Kaiser, Helga* Saudi-Arabien: Tayma: Karawanenoase an der Weihrauchstraße. WUB 38 (2005) 64-66.

14591 *Laurant, Sophie* Hegra, ein zweites Petra: die nabatäische Stadt Hegra in Saudi-Arabien. WUB 37 (2005) 2-7.

14592 *Azarnoush, Massoud; Helwing, Barbara* Recent archaeological research in Iran—prehistory to Iron Age. AMIT 37 (2005) 189-246.

14593 *Fazeli, Hassan; Potts, Daniel T.; Wong, Edna H.* The Qazvin plain revisited: a reappraisal of northwestern central plateau, Iran, in the 6th to the 4th millennium BC. ANES 42 (2005) 3-82.

### T7.1 **Ægyptus**, *generalia*

14594 *Adly, Emad; Grimal, Nicolas* Fouilles et travaux en Égypte et au Soudan, 2003-2004. Or. 74 (2005) 195-314; Tab. IX-XXVII.

14595 Ägypten: Kairo: Ägypten fordert Stein von Rosette zurück. WUB 38 (2005) 68.

**Bickel, S.** In ägyptischer Gesellschaft 2004 ⇒614.

[E]**Cooke, A.** Current research in egyptology II 2005 ⇒635.

14596 *Depauw, Mark; Hoffmann, Friedhelm* Demotische Literaturübersicht XXIX. Enchoria 29 (2004/2005) 119-181.

14597 **Duhoux, Yves** Des minoens en Egypte?: "Keftiou" et "les îles au milieu du Grand Vert". PIOL 52: 2003 ⇒19,13893. [R]AJA 109 (2005) 295-297 (*Barber, E.J.W.*).

14598 **Gillam, Robyn** Performance and drama in ancient Egypt. L 2005, Duckworth x; 182 pp. £17. 07156-34046.

14599 **Grieshaber, Frank** Lexikographie einer Landschaft: Beiträge zur historischen Topographie Oberägyptens zwischen Theben und Gabal as-Silsila anhand demotischer und griechischer Quellen. 2004 ⇒20,13137. [R]DiscEg 61 (2005) 119-120 (*Warburton, David A.*).

14600 **James, Thomas G.H.** Ancient Egypt: the British Museum concise introduction. L 2005, British Museum Pr. 208 pp. €15. 0-7141-1966-0. Bibl. 202.

14601 **Meskell, Lynn** Private life in New Kingdom Egypt. 2002 ⇒18, 12750; 19,13907. [R]RStR 31 (2005) 150 (*Nakhai, Beth Alpert*).

14602 Mitteilungen des Deutschen Archäologischen Instituts Abteilung Kairo, Band 61 (2005). Mainz 2005, Von Zabern 402 pp. 3-8053-3496-6. 56 pl.

14603 *Muskett, Georgina* Egypt and Mycenaean Greece: a Mycenaean perspective. Current research in egyptology II. 2005 ⇒635. 39-46.

14604 **Rawnsley, Hardwicke D.** †1920 Notes for the Nile: together with a metrical rendering of the hymns of ancient Egypt and of the precepts of Ptah-Hotep. L 2005, Kegan P. xv; 324 pp. 07103-0983X.

14605 **Schmelz, Georg** Kirchliche Amtsträger im spätantiken Ägypten: nach den Aussagen der griechischen und koptischen Papyri und Ostraka. APF.B 13: 2002 ⇒18,8387. [R]BiOr 62 (2005) 526-530 (*Wilfong, T.G.*).

14606 **Toivari-Viitala, Jaana** Women at Deir El-Medina: a study of the status and roles of the female inhabitants in the workmen's community during the Ramesside period. 2001 ⇒17,11573; 19,13919. [R]JESHO 48 (2005) 459-461 (*Sweeney, Deborah*).

14607 **Valloggia, Michel** Les oasis d'Egypte dans l'antiquité: des origines au IIe millénaire avant J.-C. 2004 ⇒20,13158. [R]CRAI (2005/1) 257-258 (*Leclant, Jean*).

14608 [E]**Vermeulen, Urbain; Van Steenbergen, J.** Egypt and Syria in the Fatimid, Ayyubid, and Mamluk eras IV: proceedings of the 9th and 10th International Colloquium organized at the Katholieke Universiteit Leuven in May 2000 and May 2001. OLA 140: Lv 2005, Peeters xii; 496 pp.

14609 **Versluys, M.J.** Aegyptiaca Romana: Nilotic scenes and the Roman views of Egypt. RGRW 144: 2002 ⇒18,12760... 20,13159. [R]AWE 4 (2005) 221-223 (*Vout, Caroline*).

14610 *Wikgren, Heidi* The festival calendar at Deir el-Medina. Current research in egyptology 2003. 2005 ⇒907. 179-200.

14611 **Wilkinson, Toby A.H.** The Thames & Hudson dictionary of ancient Egypt. L 2005, Thames & H. 272 pp. 0-500-05137-2. Bibl. 270-271.

14612 **Willeitner, Joachim** Die ägyptischen Oasen: Städte, Tempel und Gräber in der Libyschen Wüste. 2003 ⇒19,13922. [R]WO 35 (2005) 218-220 (*Fritz, Ulrike*).

14613 *Wilson, Penelope, al.*, Fieldwork, 2004-05: Sais, Memphis, Saqqara bronzes project, Tell el-Amarna, Tell el-Amarna glass project, Qasr Ibrim. JEA 91 (2005) 1-36.

## T7.2 *Luxor*; **Karnak** [East Bank]—**Thebae** [West Bank]

14614 **Azim, Michel; Réveillac, Gérard** Karnak dans l'objectif de Georges Legrain–catalogue raisonné des archives photographiques. 2004 ⇒20,13163. [R]CRAI (2005/1) 258-259 (*Leclant, Jean*).

14615 **Cabrol, A.** Les voies processionnelles de Thèbes. OLA 97: 2001 ⇒17,11579; 18,12764. [R]OLZ 100 (2005) 34-5 (*Lieven, Alexandra von*).

14616 **Jacquet, Jean** Karnak-Nord IX: le trésor de Thoutmosis Ier. 2001 ⇒17,11577. [R]OLZ 100 (2005) 142-147 (*Luiselli, Maria Michela*).

14617 *Muhs, Brian* The girls next door: marriage patterns among the mortuary priests in early Ptolemaic Thebes. JJP 35 (2005) 169-194.

14618 **Seiler, A.** Tradition & Wandel: die Keramik als Spiegel der Kulturentwicklung Thebens in der zweiten Zwischenzeit. Mainz 2005, Von Zabern xiv; 265 pp. €51. 38053-35032.

14619 Sensationsfund in Theben. WUB 35 (2005) 70.

## T7.3 **Amarna**

14620 Akhénaton et l'époque amarnienne. P 2005, Khéops 318 pp. €24. 29504-36862.

14621 *Artzi, Pinhas* EA 42, the earliest known case for Parṣu, 'correct international custom'. [F]KLEIN, J. 2005 ⇒79. 462-479.

14622 **Giles, Frederick J.** The Amarna Age: Egypt. 2001 ⇒17,11582... 20,13168. [R]JNES 64 (2005) 305-307 (*Dorman, Peter F.*).

14623 [T]**Kochavi-Rainey, Z.** למלך אדוני (To the King my Lord: letters from el-Amarna, Kumidu, Taanach and other letters from the fourteenth century BCE). Biblical Encyclopaedia Library 20: J 2005, Bialik xxx; 346 pp. 965-342-886-1. **H.**

14624 *Mynářová, Jana* 'Akissi of Qaṭna—a case of a diplomatic *faux pas*?'. UF 37 (2005) 445-459.

14625 *Mynářová, Jana* A comment on the opening passages of the Amarna Letters—its structure and its address [!]. ArOr 73 (2005) 397-406.
14626 *Nemirovsky, A.A.* 'Let the gods know it!': EA 43 and the political history of the Amarna age. VDI 4 (2005) 108-127. **R.**
14627 **Smith, Wendy** Archaeobotanical investigations of agriculture at late antique Kom el-Nana (Tell el-Amarna). Excavation Memoir 70: 2003 ⇒19,13943. [R]BiOr 62 (2005) 47-48 (*Germer, Renate*).
14628 *Vita, Juan-Pablo* The town of Mušiḫuna and the cities of the 'Beqaʿ alliance' in the Amarna Letters. StEeL 22 (2005) 1-7.

### T7.4 **Memphis,** *Saqqara*—**Pyramides,** *Giza* (Cairo); **Alexandria**

14629 *Bárta, Miroslav* Location of the Old Kingdom pyramids in Egypt. CamArchJ 15 (2005) 177-191.
14630 **Brovarsky, Edward** The Senedjemib Complex part I: the Mastabas of Senedjemib Inti (G 2370), Khnumenti (G 2374), and Senedjemib Mehi (G 2378). Giza Mastabas 7: 2001 ⇒17,11596. [R]BiOr 62 (2005) 40-43 (*Van Walsem, René*); JEA 91 (2005) 202-204 (*Altenmüller, Hartwig*).
14631 **Haase, Michael** Eine Stätte für die Ewigkeit: der Pyramidenkomplex des Cheops aus baulicher, architektonischer... kulturhistorischer Sicht. 2004 ⇒20,13179. [R]WO 35 (2005) 216-8 (*Fritz, Ulrike*).
14632 *Kashiwagi, Hiroyuki; Kawai, Nozomu; Yoshimura, Sakuji* A sacred hillside at northwest Saqqara: a preliminary report on the excavations 2001-2003. MDAI.K 61 (2005) 361-402; Pl. 51-56.
14633 **Polz, Daniel; Seiler, Anne** Die Pyramidenanlage des Königs Nub-Cheper-Re Intef in Draʿ Abu el-Naga: ein Vorbericht. 2003 ⇒19, 13955. [R]WO 35 (2005) 212-215 (*Fritz, Ulrike*).
14634 **Raven, Maarten J.,** *al.*, The tomb of Pay and Raia at Saqqara. The Egypt Exploration Society.Memoir 74: Lei 2005, National Museum of Antiquities xxiv; 171 pp. £95. 0-85698-164-8. Num ill.; Bibl. xvi-xix.
14635 **Schoch, Robert M.; McNally, Robert Aquinas** Pyramid quest: secrets of the great pyramid and the dawn of civilization. NY 2005, Tarcher 368 pp. 1-585-42405-6. Bibl. 340-362.

14636 [E]**Hirst, A.; Silk, M.** Alexandria: real and imagined. 2004 ⇒20, 13191. Conf. 1997. [R]BiOr 62 (2005) 509-512 (*Tkaczow, Barbara*).
14637 *McKechnie, Paul* Beau monde and demi-monde in Alexandria, 323-116 BC. AnCl 74 (2005) 69-82.

### T7.6 *Alii situs Ægypti* **alphabetice**

14638 ***Bakchias***: *Pernigotti, Sergio* La cronologia di Bakchias. REAC 7 (2005) 37-72.
14639 ***Dachla***: *Riemer, Heiko, al.*, Zwei pharaonische Wüstenstationen südwestlich von Dachla. MDAI.K 61 (2005) 291-350.
14640 ***Deir el-Medina***: **Häggman, Sofia** Directing Deir el-Medina: the external administration of the necropolis. Uppsala Studies in Egyptology 4: 2002 ⇒20,13206. [R]JEA 91 (2005) 224-226 (*Exell, K.M.*);

14641 **Janssen, Jack J.; Frood, Elizabeth; Goecke-Bauer, Maren** Woodcutters, potters and doorkeepers: service personnel of the Deir-El-Medina workmen. Egyptologische uitgaven 17: 2003 ⇒19, 13978. RBiOr 62 (2005) 477-480 (*Häggman, Sofia*).

14642 ***Edfu***: *Gascoigne, Alison L.* Dislocation and continuity in early Islamic provincial urban centres: the example of Tell Edfu. MDAI.K 61 (2005) 153-189; Pl. 27;

14643 **Kurth, Dieter** Edfou VII. Inschriften des Tempels von Edfu, 1: Übersetzungen 2: Wsb 2004, Harrassowitz xviii; 865 pp. €128. CD-ROM RLASBF 55 (2005) 532-534 (*Niccacci, Alviero*);

14644 *Moeller, Nadine* Les nouvelles fouilles de Tell Edfou. BSFÉ 164 (2005) 29-46.

14645 ***el-Dabʿa***: *Bietak, Manfred* Ausgrabungen eines Palastbezirkes der Tuthmosidenzeit bei Ezbet Helmi/Tell el-Daba, Vorbericht für Herbst 2004 und Frühjahr 2005. Ä&L 15 (2005) 65-100.

14646 ***El-Dabʿa; Qantir***: **Habachi, Labib** Tell El-Dabʿa I: the site in connection with Qantir. 2001 ⇒19,13981. RBiOr 62 (2005) 471-472 (*Hoffmeier, James K.*).

14647 ***Elephantine***: *Bommas, Martin, al.*, Stadt und Tempel von Elephantine, 31./32: Grabungsbericht. MDAI.K 61 (2005) 13-138;

14648 *Raue, Dietrich* Éléphantine: cinq campagnes de fouilles dans la ville du IIIe millénaire avant J.-C. BSFÉ 163 (2005) 8-26;

14649 **Rodziewicz, Mieczyslaw D.** Elephantine XXVII: early Roman industries on Elephantine. Archäologische Veröffentlichungen 107: Mainz 2005, Von Zabern 257 pp. 3-8053-3266-1. Bibl. 233-245.

14650 ***Tanis***: *Brier, Bob* Treasures of Tanis. Arch. 58/3 (2005) 18-25;

14651 *Devauchelle, D.* Tanis–Tell Sân el-Hagar. DBS 13/75. 2005 ⇒970. 908-918.

## T7.7 Antiquitates Nubiae et alibi

14652 **Bonnet, Charles; Valbelle, Dominique** Des pharaons venus d'Afrique: la cachette de Kerma. P 2005, Citadelles 216 pp. €52. RCRAI (2005/3) 1027-1028 (*Leclant, Jean*).

14653 **Edwards, David N.** The Nubian past: an archaeology of the Sudan. 2004 ⇒20,13217. RJAfH 46 (2005) 330-331 (*Fattovich, Rodolfo*); ArOr 73 (2005) 141-143 (*Smoláriková, Květa*).

14654 *Glück, Birgit* Zur Frage der Datierung der früheren C-Gruppe in Unternubien. Ä&L 15 (2005) 131-151.

14655 **Lobban, Richard A., Jr.** Historical dictionary of ancient and medieval Nubia. 2004 ⇒20,13220. RJAfH 46 (2005) 328-330 (*Brewer, Douglas J.*).

14656 *Rose, M.* Return to Cyrene. Arch. 58/5 (2005) 16-23 [NTAb 50, 108].

14657 *Shaw, Ian* Sudan's ancient treasures: an exhibition of recent discoveries. AJA 109 (2005) 81-86.

14658 E**Shinnie, Peter L.; Anderson, Julie R.** The capital of Kush, 2: Meroë excavations 1973-1984. Meroitica 20: 2004 ⇒20,13221. RBiOr 62 (2005) 504-508 (*Edwards, David N.*).

14659 E**Welsby, Derek A.; Anderson, Julie R.** Sudan: ancient treasures. 2004 ⇒20,13225. RBiOr 62 (2005) 255-258 (*Fitzenreiter, M.*).

### T7.9 Sinai

14660 **Beit-Arieh, Itzhaq** Archaeology of Sinai: the Ophir expedition. Mon. Ser. 21: TA 2003, Institute of Archaeology xvi; 452 pp. $65. 248 fig.

14661 *Bruins, Hendrik J.; Van der Plicht, Johannes* Desert settlement through the Iron Age: radiocarbon dates from Sinai and the Negev Highlands. The bible and radiocarbon dating. 2005 ⇒952. 349-66.

### T8.1 Anatolia *generalia*

14662 *Bartl, Peter V.* The Middle Bronze Age on the upper Tigris: new evidence from the excavations at Giricano and Ziyaret Tepe. AMIT 37 (2005) 153-162.

14663 **Brandt, Hartwin; Kolb, Franz** Lycia et Pamphylia: eine römische Provinz im Südwesten Kleinasiens. Zaberns Bildbände zur Archäologie: Mainz 2005, Von Zabern iv; 146 pp.

14664 **Casabonne, Olivier** La Cilicie à l'époque achéménide. Persika 3: 2004 ⇒20,13233. [R]AJA 109 (2005) 789-790 (*Gates, Charles*).

14665 **Cavalier, L.** Architecture romaine d'Asie Mineure: les monuments de Xanthos et leur ornementation. Scripta Antiqua 13: Bordeaux 2005, Ausonius 324 pp. 29100-2363X. Pl.; Bibl.

14666 *Di Nocera, Gian M.* Mobility and stability: preliminary observations on Early Bronze Age settlement organisation in the Malatya Plain. AMIT 37 (2005) 63-70.

14667 *Dömez, Şevket* The Iron Age settlements in Amasya province: surveyed results 1997-1999. BTTK 69 (2005) 425-465.

14668 *Neumann, G., al.*, Phrygien, Phryger. RLA 10/7-8. 2005 ⇒975. 543-555.

14669 *Ökse, A. Tuba* Early Bronze Age settlement pattern and cultural structure of the Sivas region. AMIT 37 (2005) 35-51.

14670 *Özfirat, Aynur* Transhumance on the eastern Anatolian high plateau in the 2[nd] mill. B.C. AMIT 37 (2005) 139-152.

14671 [E]**Sagona, Antonio; Sagona, Claudia** Archaeology at the north-east Anatolian frontier, I: an historical geography and a field survey of the Bayburt province. ANESt.S 14: 2004 ⇒20,627. [R]Paléorient 31/2 (2005) 177-179 (*Marro, Catherine*).

14672 *Uggeri, Giovanni* La Ionia meridionale nella descrizione di PLINIO (N.H., V, 112-115). Atti del X Simposio di Efeso. Turchia 19: 2005 ⇒785. 217-252.

### T8.2 Boğazköy—*Hethaei*, the Hittites

14673 **Czichon, Rainer Maria** Studien zur Regionalgeschichte von Ḫattuscha/Bogazköy vom Chalkolithikum bis zur Byzantinischen Zeit. 2005, Diss.-Habil. Würzburg [AA 2006/1, 315]

14674 **Ehringhaus, Horst** Götter, Herrscher, Inschriften: die Felsreliefs der hethitischen Grossreichszeit in der Türkei. Bildbände zur Archäologie: Mainz 2005, Von Zabern 124 pp. €37.90. 3-8053-3469-9. Ill. [RB 112,638]

14675 **Neve, Peter** Die Oberstadt von Hattusa: die Bauwerke: I, die Bastion des Sphinxtores und die Tempelviertel am Königs- und Löwentor. Bogazköy-Hattusa 17: 2001 ⇒17,11652. [R]AWE 3 (2004) 167-169 (*Mielke, Dirk P.*).

## T8.3 Ephesus; Pergamon

14676 **Hofbauer, Martin** Zum Theater von Ephesus. 2005, Diss. Wien [AA 2006/1, 311].

14677 **Koester, Helmut** Ephesos, metropolis of Asia: an interdisciplinary approach to its archaeology, religion, and culture. HThS 41: 2004 ⇒20,13250. [R]RAr (2005/2) 417-421 (*Chaisemartin, Nathalie*).

14678 [E]**Lang-Auinger, Claudia** Hanghaus 1 in Ephesos. Forschungen in Ephesos 8/4: 2003 ⇒19,14012. [R]Gn. 77 (2005) 702-705 (*Strocka, Volker Michael*); BTTK 69 (2005) 1053-1055 (*Öztepe, Erhan*).

14679 *Orselli, Alba M.* Efeso nelle fonti del tardoantico latino. Atti del X Simposio di Efeso. Turchia 19: 2005 ⇒785. 205-216.

14680 **Scherrer, Peter** Studien zur Topographie und Baugeschichte von Ephesos. 2005, Diss.-Habil. Salzburg [AA 2006/1, 315].

14681 **Trebilco, Paul** The early christians in Ephesus from Paul to IGNATIUS. WUNT 166: 2004 ⇒20,13253. [R]RSR 93 (2005) 388-389 (*Aletti, Jean-Noël*); TrinJ 26 (2005) 331-4 (*Schnabel, Eckhard J.*); ScC 133 (2005) 732-4 (*Manzi, Franco*); ZRGG 57 (2005) 274-276 (*Horn, Friedrich W.*); Bib. 86 (2005) 290-293 (*Manzi, Franco*); RBLit 7 (2005) 271-274 (*Kaler, Michael*); ET 116 (2005) 412-414 (*Foster, Paul*); BTB 35 (2005) 112-113 (*Witulski, Thomas*).

14682 **Halfmann, Helmut** Städtebau und Bauherren im römischen Kleinasien: ein Vergleich zwischen Pergamon und Ephesos. IM.B 43: 2001 ⇒17,11654. [R]AJA 109 (2005) 325-328 (*Ratté, Christopher*).

14683 [E]**Hoffmann, Adolf** Ägyptische Kulte und ihre Heiligtümer im Osten des Römischen Reiches. BYZAS 1: Istanbul 2005, Deutsches Archäologisches Institut 282 pp. 975807105X. Koll. Sept. 2003, Bergama.

14684 **Kranz, Peter** *Pergameus Deus*: archäologische und numismatische Studien zu den Darstellungen des Asklepios in Pergamon während Hellenismus und Kaiserzeit mit einem Exkurs zur Überlieferung statuarischer Bildwerke in der Antike. Möhnesee 2004, Bibliopolis 189 pp. 93 ill.

14685 **Mania, Ulrich** Die Rote Halle in Pergamon und ihre figürliche Ausstattung. 2005, Diss. Halle-Wittenberg [AA 2006/1, 312].

14686 **Qeyrel, François** L'autel de Pergame: images et pouvoir en Grèce d'Asie. Antiqua 9: P 2005, Picard 207 pp. Num. ill. [R]CRAI (2005/3) 1029-1035 (*Marcadé, Jean*).

## T8.6 *Situs Anatoliae*—Turkey sites; *Armenia*

14687 [E]**Yener, Kutlu Aslihan** The Amuq Valley regional project, 1: surveys in the plain of Antioch and Orontes Delta, Turkey, 1995-2002. OIP 131: Ch 2005, Oriental Institute xli; 293 pp. £40. 1-885923-32-5. 8 pl.; Bibl. xxiii-xli.

14688 ***Çatalhöyük***: [E]**Hodder, I.** Changing materialities at Çatalhöyük: reports from the 1995-99 seasons by members of the Çatalhöyük teams. Çatalhöyük Research Project 5; BIAA Monograph 39: L 2005, British Institute of Archaeology at Ankara xviii; 395 pp. £59. 19029-37287;

14689 Çatalhöyük perspectives: reports from the 1995-99 seasons by members of the Çatalhöyük teams. Çatalhöyük Research Project 6; BIAA Monograph 40: L 2005, British Institute of Archaeology at Ankara xii; 245 pp. £39. 19029-37295.

14690 ***Gordion***: [E]**Kealhofer, Lisa** The archaeology of Midas and the Phrygians: recent work at Gordion. Ph 2005, Univ. of Pennsylvania Museum of Archaeology and Anthropology 258 pp. $50. 1-931-707-76-6. Num. ill.;

14691 *Keenan, Douglas J.* Radiocarbon dates from Iron Age Gordion are confounded. AEW 3 (2004) 100-103;

14692 *Muscarella, Oscar W.* The date of the destruction of the Early Phygian period at Gordion. AWE 2 (2003) 225-252.

14693 ***Hassek Höyük***: **Gerber, J.C.** Hassek Höyük III: die frühbronzezeitliche Keramik. IF 47: Tü 2005, Wasmuth xii; 356 pp. €57.80. 38030-17688.

14694 ***Karatepe-Aslantaş***: **Çambel, H.; Özyar, A.** Karatepe-Aslantaş: Azatiwataya: die Bildwerke. 2003 ⇒19,14016; 20,13261. [R]BiOr 62 (2005) 124-128 (*Bonatz, Dominik*); OLZ 100 (2005) 410-414 (*Gilibert, Alessandra*).

14695 ***Sardis***: **Dusinberre, Elspeth R.M.** Aspects of empire in Achaemenid Sardis. 2003 ⇒19,14018. [R]AJA 109 (2005) 790-791 (*Gates, Charles*).

14696 ***Tilbeshar***: *Kepinski, Christine* Tilbeshar—a Bronze Age city in the Sajur Valley (southeast Anatolia). Anatolica 31 (2005) 145-159.

14697 *Areshian, Gregory E.* Early Bronze Age settlements in the Ararat Plain and its vicinity. AMIT 37 (2005) 71-88.

## T9.1 Cyprus

14698 **Bekker-Nielsen, T.** The roads of ancient Cyprus. K 2004, Museum Tusculanum 308 pp. 87728-99565. Ill.; Bibl.

14699 **Bolger, Diane** Gender in ancient Cyprus: narratives of social change on a Mediterranean island. 2003 ⇒19,14020; 20,13274. [R]NEA(BA) 68 (2005) 200-201 (*London, Gloria*).

14700 **Given, Michael; Knapp, A. Bernard** The Sydney Cyprus Survey Project. 2003 ⇒19,14026; 20,13278. [R]IEJ 55 (2005) 235-7 (*Maeir, Aren M.*).

14701 *Hermary, A.* Scènes de culte originales sur un vase chypriote archaïque. V Congresso di studi fenici. 2005 ⇒959. I, 171-179.

14702 *Iacovou, Maria* Cyprus at the dawn of the first millennium BC: cultural homogenisation versus the tyranny of ethnic identifications. Archaeological perspectives. 2005 ⇒627. 125-134.

14703 **Karageorghis, J.** Kypris: the Aphrodite of Cyprus, ancient sources and archaeological evidence. Nicosia 2005, Leventis xviii; 269 pp. CYP30. 9963-560-67-9. 329 fig.

14704 **Karageorghis, Vassos**, *al.*, Ancient art from Cyprus: the Cesnola Collection of the Metropolitan Museum of Art. 2000 ⇒16,12069; 17,11678. [R]Syria 82 (2005) 355-357 (*Cassimatis, Hélène*).

14705 **Karageorghis, Vassos** Ancient Cypriote art in Copenhagen. 2001 ⇒17,11681; 18,12885. [R]Syria 82 (2005) 354-355 (*Hermary, Antoine*);

14706 Ancient Cypriot art in the National Archaeological Museum of Athens. 2003 ⇒19,14029. [R]Gn. 77 (2005) 735-737 (*Höckmann, Ursula*).

14707 [E]**Karageorghis, Vassos** Ancient Cypriote art in the Musée d'Art et d'Histoire, Geneva. 2004 ⇒20,13281. [R]RAr (2005/2) 370-371 (*Fourrier, Sabine*);

14708 Ancient Cypriote art in Russian museums. Nicosia 2005, Leventis xii; 168 pp. CYP20. 9963-560-65-2 [RB 113,157].

14709 **Karageorghis, Vassos** Excavations at Kition VI: the Phoenician and later levels, I. Nicosia 2005, Dept of Antiquities xix; 134 pp. Contrib. *Olivier Callot*; Num. ill.

14710 **Keswani, Priscilla** Mortuary ritual and society in Bronze Age Cyprus. 2004 ⇒20,13283. [R]Antiquity 79 (2005) 706-7 (*Crewe, Lindy*).

14711 *Keswani, Priscilla Schuster* Death, prestige, and copper in Bronze Age Cyprus. AJA 109 (2005) 341-401.

14712 **Malmgren, Kjell** Klavdhia-Tremithos: a Middle and Late Cypriote Bronze Age site. 2003 ⇒19,14033; 20,13285. [R]AJA 109 (2005) 104-106 (*Iacovou, Maria*).

14713 **Palaima, Thomas** The triple invention of writing in Cyprus and written sources for Cypriote history. Annual lecture in memory of Constantine Leventis, 6 Nov. 2004: Nicosia 2005, Leventis 64 pp. CYP3. 9963-560-88-D.

14714 [E]**Peltenburg, E.; Wasse, A.** Neolithic revolution: new perspectives on southwest Asia in light of recent discoveries on Cyprus. Levant Suppl. Ser. 1: 2004 ⇒20,13288. [R]BiOr 62 (2005) 133-136 (*Aurenche, Olivier*); BASOR 338 (2005) 93-94 (*Twiss, Katheryn*).

14715 [E]**Peltenburg, Edgar** The colonisation and settlement of Cyprus: investigations at Kissonerga-Mylouthkia, 1976-1996. Lemba Archaeological Project 3/1; Studies in Mediterranean Archaeology 70/4: 2003 ⇒19,14036; 20,13289. [R]Antiquity 79 (2005) 450-452 (*Jones, Paula Louise*).

14716 *Petit, T.* Les origines du royaume d'Amathonte (Chypre) et les Phéniciens. V Congresso di studi fenici. 2005 ⇒959. I, 165-170.

14717 [E]**Smith, Joanna S.** Script and seal use on Cyprus in the Bronze and Iron Ages. Colloquia and Conference Papers 4: 2002 ⇒18,12886; 19,14037. [R]JNES 64 (2005) 215-219 (*Younger, John G.*).

14718 **Steel, Louise** Cyprus before history: from the earliest settlers to the end of the Bronze Age. 2004 ⇒20,13291. [R]AJA 109 (2005) 578-80 (*Knapp, A. Bernard*); Antiquity 79 (2005) 705-706 (*Crewe, Lindy*).

14719 *Tatton-Brown, V.* Cyprus and Phoenicia. V Congresso di studi fenici. 2005 ⇒959. I, 157-164.

14720 *Ulbrich, Anja* The worship of Anat and Astarte in Cypriot Iron Age sanctuaries. Archaeological perspectives. 2005 ⇒627. 198-206.

14721 **Yon, Marguerite** Kition-Bamboula V: Kition dans les textes. 2004 ⇒20,13296. [R]RAr (2005/2) 368-369 (*Cayla, Jean-Baptiste*).

### T9.3 *Graecia*, **Greece**

14722 *Carile, Antonio* San Cristodulo fondatore di Patmos. Atti del X Simposio di Efeso. Turchia 19: 2005 ⇒785. 301-312.

14723 *Ducrey, Pierre* Quarante années de fouilles suisses à Erétrie (Grèce) 1964-2004: bilan et perspectives. CRAI 2 (2005) 553-578.

14724 *Elliger, Winfried* Korinth. RAC 165/166. 2005 ⇒973. 579-605.

14725 **Evely, R.D.G.** Minoan crafts: tools and techniques: an introduction. Studies in Mediterranean Archaeology 92/2: Sto 2000, Aström 517 pp. $126. 91708-11555. [R]Gn. 77 (2005) 529-534 (*Müller, Walter*).

14726 **Kyrieleis, Helmut**, *al.*, XII. Bericht über die Ausgrabungen in Olympia: 1982-1999. 2003 ⇒19,14042. [R]Antiquity 79 (2005) 956-958 (*Spivey, Nigel*).

14727 *Patitucci, Stella* Patmos rivisitata: contributo per la carta archeologica dell'isola. Atti del X Simposio di Efeso. 2005 ⇒785. 253-300.

14728 **Roland, Étienne** Athènes, espaces urbains et histoire, des origines à la fin du IIIe siècle apr. J.-C. Carré Histoire: 2004 ⇒20,13308. [R]RAr (2005/1) 94-96 (*Mossé, Claude*).

14729 *Romano, David Gilman* A Roman circus in Corinth. Hesp. 74 (2005) 585-611.

14730 *Sakel, Dean* Codex Patmiacus Graecus 132 and the chronicle of Scutariotes. Atti del X Simposio di Efeso. Turchia 19: 2005 ⇒785. 313-326.

14731 *Salt, Alun; Boutsikas, Efrosyni* Knowing when to consult the oracle at Delphi. Antiquity 79 (2005) 565-572.

14732 *Whitley, J.* Archaeology in Greece 2004-2005. ArRep 51 (2005) 1-118 [NTAb 50,339].

14733 [E]**Williams, Charles K., II; Bookidis, Nancy** Corinth, the centenary, 1896-1996. 2003 ⇒19,14050. [R]AnCl 74 (2005) 615-617 (*Prost, Francis*); AWE 4 (2005) 511-512 (*Salmon, J.*).

### T9.4 **Creta**

14734 **Alexiou, Stylianos; Warren, Peter** The Early Minoan tombs of Lebena, southern Crete. SIMA 30: Sävedalen 2004, Åströms 223 pp. $158. 91708-11377. Num. ill.

14735 *Coldstream, J.N.* Phoenicians in Crete, north and south: a contrast. V Congresso di studi fenici. 2005 ⇒959. I, 181-187.

14736 *Erickson, Brice* Archaeology of empire: Athens and Crete in the fifth century B.C. AJA 109 (2005) 619-663.

14737 **Haggis, Donald C.** Kavousi 1: the archaeological survey of the Kavousi region. Prehistory Monographs 16: Ph 2005, Academic xxxii; 242 pp. $60. 1-931534-187. 71 fig.; 41 pl.

14738 **Hakulin, Lena** Bronzeworking on late Minoan Crete: a diachronic study. BAR-IS 1245: 2004 ⇒20,13320. [R]AJA 109 (2005) 576-578 (*Gillis, Carole*).

14739 **Hatzaki, Eleni M.** Knossos: the Little Palace. ABSA.S 38: L 2005, British School at Athens xi; 221 pp. 0-904887-50-2. Bibl. 205-211.

14740 **Kyriakidis, Evangelos** Ritual in the Bronze Age Aegean: the Minoan peak sanctuaries. L 2005, Duckworth x; 202 pp. £45. 0-7156-3248-5. 50 fig.; 29 tables.

14741 *Mantzourani, Eleni; Vavouranakis, Giorgos; Kanellopoulos, Chrysanthos* The Klimataria-Manares building reconsidered. AJA 109 (2005) 743-776.

14742 **Prent, Mieke** Cretan sanctuaries and cults: continuity and change from late Minoan IIIC to the archaic period. RGRW 154: Lei 2005, Brill xviii; 737 pp. 90-04-14236-3. Bibl. 655-699.

14743 **Shaw, Joseph** Kommos: a Minoan harbour and Greek sanctuary in southern Crete. Princeton 2005, American School of Classical Studies at Athens 171 pp. 087661-6600. Bibl.

### T9.6 Urbs Roma

14744 **Allison, Penelope E.** Pompeian households: an analysis of the material culture. Monumenta Archaeologica 20: 2004 ⇒20,13323. [R]AJA 109 (2005) 323-324 (*Richardson, L., Jr.*).

14745 **Benoist, Stéphane** Rome, le Prince et la Cité: pouvoir impérial et cérémonies publiques (1er s- av.-début du IVe siècle ap. J.-C.). Le noeud gordien: P 2005, PUF xi; 397 pp. €32. 2-13-053909-2.

14746 **Connolly, Peter** Colosseum: Arena der Gladiatoren. Stu 2005, Reclam 224 pp. 3-15-010551-X. 213 fig.

14747 **Cooley, Alison E.** Pompei. 2003 ⇒19,14061. [R]AJA 109 (2005) 322-323 (*Richardson, L., Jr.*).

14748 [E]**Edwards, Catharine; Woolf, Greg** Rome the cosmopolis. 2003 ⇒19,508. [R]IHR 27 (2005) 108-110 (*Talbert, Richard J.A.*).

14749 *Elliott, Neil* Disciplining the hope of the poor in ancient Rome. Christian origins. A people's history of christianity 1: 2005 ⇒550. 177-197.

14750 *Esler, Philip F.* Rome in apocalyptic and rabbinic literature. Gospel of Matthew. JSNT.S 276: 2005 ⇒484. 9-33.

14751 **Faas, P.** Around the Roman table. [T]*Whiteside, S.*: Ch 2005 <2003>, Univ. of Chicago Pr. xi; 371 pp. $18. 02262-33472. Bibl.; [NTAb 50,435].

14752 *Fantham, E.* Liberty and the people in Republican Rome. T(P)APA 135/2 (2005) 209-229 [NTAb 50,360].

14753 **Grandazzi, Alexandre** Les origines de Rome. QSJ 216: 2003 ⇒ 19,14065. [R]RAr (2005/1) 118-119 (*Bourdin, Stéphane*).

14754 **Heiken, G.; Funiciello, R.; De Rita, D.** The seven hills of Rome: a geological tour of the eternal city. Princeton 2005, Princeton Univ. Pr. 288 pp. £19. 0-691-06995-6.

14755 *Howe, T.N.* Power houses: the seaside villas of Stabiae. Archaeology Odyssey [Wsh] 8/1 (2005) 16-27, 50-51 [NTAb 49,333].

14756 *Jones, Rick; Robinson, Damian* Water, wealth, and social status at Pompeii: the house of the Vestals in the first century. AJA 109 (2005) 695-710.

14757 **Lancaster, Lynne C.** Concrete vaulted construction in imperial Rome: innovations in context. NY 2005, CUP xxii; 274 pp. $85. 0-521-84202-6. 146 fig.

14758 *Lefkowitz, M.* Using ancient texts in translation to teach women's life in Greece and Rome. ClB 81/2 (2005) 165-75 [NTAb 50,558].

14759 **Lott, J. Bert** The neighborhoods of Augustan Rome. C 2004, CUP xiii; 262 pp. $70. [R]RBLit (2005)* (*Seesengood, Robert*).

14760 *Nolan, L.A.* Emulating AUGUSTUS—the Fascist-era excavation of the Emperor's peace altar in Rome. Archaeology Odyssey [Wsh] 8/3 (2005) 38-47 [NTAb 49,553].

14761 *Oakes, Peter* A state of tension: Rome in the New Testament. Gospel of Matthew. JSNT.S 276: 2005 ⇒484. 75-90.

14762 **Ricci, Cecilia** Orbis in urbe: fenomeni migratori nella Roma imperiale. R 2005, Quasar 106 pp. €12.90.

14763 *Rose, C.B.* The Parthians in Augustan Rome. AJA 109 (2005) 21-75.

14764 **Veyne, Paul** Sexe et pouvoir à Rome. P 2005, Tallandier 208 pp. 2-84734-244-3. Préface de *Lucien Jerphagnon*; Bibl. 201-204.

14765 *Witcher, R.* The extended metropolis: *urbs, suburbium* and population. Journal of Roman Archaeology [AA] 18 (2005) 120-138 [NTAb 50,363].

## T9.7 Catacumbae

14766 *Bisconti, Fabrizio* L'arcosolio di Celerina in Pretestato: fasi e significati della decorazione pittorica. RivCC 81 (2005) 21-52.

14767 **Ghilardi, Massimiliano** Subterranea civitas: quattro studi sulle catacombe romane dal medioevo all'età moderna. 2003 ⇒20, 13346. [R]RivCC 81 (2005) 285-287 (*Baruffa, Antonio*).

14768 *Minasi, Mara* L'affresco di *Cristo tra santi* della catacomba di Generosa alla Magliana: revisione critica e nuove ipotesi interpretative. RivCC 81 (2005) 53-98.

14769 *Proverbio, Cecilia* Nuove osservazioni su un affresco nella regione e dell'ex vigna Chiaraviglio in S. Sebastiano. RivCC 81 (2005) 99-128.

## T9.8 *Archaeologia paleochristiana*—early Christian archaeology

14770 [E]**Bitton-Ashkelony, Brouria; Kofsky, Arieh** Christian Gaza in late antiquity. Jerusalem Studies in Religion and Culture 3: 2004 ⇒ 20,555. [R]SCI 24 (2005) 324-326 (*Ben Ezra, Daniel Stökl*).

14771 *Brandt, Olof* Deer, lambs and water in the Lateran baptistery. RivCC 81 (2005) 131-156.

14772 **Heinz, Werner** Der Aufstieg des Christentums: Geschichte und Archäologie einer Weltreligion. Stu 2005, Theiss 126 pp. €25. 144 ill.

14773 **Monelli, Nanni; Santarelli, Giuseppe** L'altare degli apostoli nella Santa Casa di Loreto. Loreto 2005, Lauretane 101 pp. €6.50. 88-8-7651-15-9. Ill.

14774 **Rebillard, E.** Religion et sépulture: l'église, les vivants et les morts dans l'antiquité tardive. 2003 ⇒20,13357. [R]RivCC 81 (2005) 235-253 (*Guyon, Jean*).

14775 **Volp, Ulrich** Tod und Ritual in den christlichen Gemeinden der Antike. SVigChr 65: 2002 ⇒19,12943; 20,13360. [R]RSR 93 (2005) 155-157 (*Sesboüé, Bernard*); ThLZ 130 (2005) 1200-1202 (*Bergjan, Silke-Petra*).

### T9.9 Rome western empire, Europe

14776 *Wilkes, J.J.* The Roman Danube: an archaeological survey. JRS 95 (2005) 124-225 [NTAb 50,339].

## XIX. Geographia biblica

### U1.0 Geographica

14777 [T]**Amato, E.** DIONISIO di Alessandria: Descrizione della terra abitata. Testi a fronte 93: Mi 2005, Bompiani 374 pp. 88452-33723. Bibl.

14778 [T]**Auberger, Janick** PAUSANIAS: Description de la Grèce, 4: livre IV: la Messénie. [E]*Casewitz, M.*: CUFr: P 2005, Belles Lettres lxxv; 272 pp. €65. 2-251-00523-4. Texte établi *Michel Casevitz*.

14779 *Ortiz, Pedro* Geografia del Nuovo Testamento. I vangeli. 2005 ⇒432. 184-194.

14780 [ET]**Radt, Stephan** STRABONs Geographika, 1: Buch I-IV: Text und Übersetzung. Gö 2002, Vandenhoeck & R. xxvi; 563 pp. €141. 978-35252-59504;

14781 3: Buch IX-XIII: Text und Übersetzung. Gö 2004, Vandenhoeck & R. 681 pp. €192. 978-35252-59528;

14782 4: Buch XIV-XVII: Text und Übersetzung. Gö 2005, Vandenhoeck & R. iv; 574 pp. €169. 35252-59535.

14783 [E]**Radt, Stephan** Strabons Geographika. 2002-2003 ⇒19,14091. [R]AnCl 74 (2005) 314-315 (*Mund-Dopchie, Monique*).

14784 **Tristram, Henry Baker** Bible places; or, the topography of the Holy Land: a succinct account of all places, rivers, and mountains of the land of Israel, mentioned in the bible, so far as they have been identified: together with their modern names and historical references. Piscataway, NJ 2005 <1884>, Gorgias xvi; 382 pp. 1-5-93-33142-8.

14785 *Winn, Robert E.* The natural world in the sermons of EUSEBIUS of Emesa. VigChr 59 (2005) 31-53.

### U1.2 Historia geographiae

14786 *Faust, Avraham* On the use of 'land of Israel', 'Palestine' and other terms in the study of 'western Asia': a comment on a review by C. Dauphin. BAIAS 23 (2005) 177-183.

14787 **Gordon, Robert P.** Holy Land, Holy City: sacred geography and the interpretation of the bible. 2004 ⇒20,13362. [R]JThS 56 (2005) 512-514 (*Walker, Peter*).

14788 *Helwing, Barbara; Özgen, Engin* On the shifting border between Mesopotamia and the west: seven seasons of joint Turkish-German excavations at Oylum Höyük. Anatolica 29 (2003) 63-85.

14789 *Maeda, Tohru* Royal inscriptions of Lugalzagesi and Sargon. Orient 40 (2005) 3-30.

14790 **Magnani, Stefano** Geografia storica del mondo antico. Itinerari, Storia: Bo 2003, Mulino 173 pp. €12. 12 ill.

14791 *Miroschedji, Pierre de* The frontier of Egypt in the Early Bronze Age: preliminary soundings at Tell es-Sakan (Gaza Strip). Archaeological perspectives. 2005, 155-169.

14792 *Patella, Michael* Seers' Corner: The ancient Near East. BiTod 43 (2005) 170-175.

14793 *Woudhuizen, Fred C.* The Luwian hieroglyphic contribution to Anatolian geography. Anatolica 29 (2003) 1-6.

14794 *Yamada, Keiko* 'From the upper sea to the lower sea': the development of the names of seas in the Assyrian royal inscriptions;

14795 *Yamada, Shigeo Kārus* on the frontiers of the Neo-Assyrian Empire. Orient 40 (2005) 31-55/56-90.

### U1.4 Atlas— maps; photographiae

14796 **Alai, Cyrus** General maps of Persia: 1477-1925. HO 1/80: Lei 2005, Brill xv; 317 pp. 90-04-14759-4. Bibl. 287.

14797 **Anastasio, Stefano; Lebeau, Marc; Sauvage, Pierre** Atlas of preclassical Upper Mesopotamia. Subartu 13: Turnhout 2004, Brepols ii; 420 pp. 2-503-99120-3. Contrib. *Alexander Pruss*; CD.

14798 [E]**Bolen, Todd** Survey of western Palestine: the maps. Historic views of the Holy Land (1870s): 2004, $35. CD-ROM; electronic address: BiblePlaces.com.

14799 **Bruce, Frederick Fyvie** Bible history atlas: study edition. J 2005, Carta 93 pp.. 965-220-554-0.

14800 **Galbiati, Enrico; Serafini, Filippo** Atlas histórico de la biblia. 2004 ⇒20,13371. [R]Alpha Omega 8 (2005) 333-334 (*Furlong, Jude*); EstTrin 39 (2005) 137-138 (*Miguel, José María de*); EstJos 59 (2005) 147-148 (*Llamas, Román*).

14801 **Gavish, Dov** A survey of Palestine under the British Mandate, 1920-1948. L 2005, RoutledgeCurzon 256 pp. £65. 02033-3955-X.

14802 **Har-El, Menashe** Understanding the geography of the bible: an introductory atlas. [E]*Wright, Paul H.*: J 2005, Carta 40 pp. 965-220-588-5.

14803 *Nasrallah, Laura* Mapping the world: JUSTIN, TATIAN, LUCIAN, and the Second Sophistic. HThR 98 (2005) 283-314.

14804 **Ohler, Annemarie** dtv-Atlas Bibel. 2004 ⇒20,13375. [R]ThRv 101 (2005) 28-29 (*Dormeyer, Detlev*).

14805 **Olami, Y.; Sender, S.; Oren, E.** Map of Dor (30). J 2005, Israel Antiquities Authority 65 Eng.; 75 Hebr. pp. $15. 978-96540-61827 [PEQ 139,62s—Sean Kingsley].

14806 [E]**Parpola, Simo; Porter, Michael** The Helsinki Atlas of the Near East in the Neo-Assyrian Period. 2001 ⇒17,11764; 19,14099. [R]JSSt 50 (2005) 197-198 (*Millard, Alan*).

### U1.5 Photographiae

14807 [E]**Denise, Fabrice; Nordiguian, Lévon** Une aventure archéologique: Antoine POIDEBARD, photographe et aviateur. Beirut 2004, Presses de l'Univ. Saint-Joseph 333 pp. 28636-41255. 156 pl.

14808 [E]**Nollé, Johannes; Schwarz, Hertha** Mit den Augen der Götter: Flugbilder des antiken und byzantinischen Griechenland. Zaberns Bildbänder zur Archäologie: Mainz 2005, Von Zabern 204 pp. €44.90. 978-38053-33795. 111 ill.; Fotogr. *Georg Gerster*.

14809 Pictorial library of bible lands. 2004 ⇒20,13378. 10 CDs; compatible with Windows 95 or higher...with Macintosh using PowerPoint 98 or higher. [R]TrinJ 26 (2005) 165-7 (*Schnabel, Eckhard J.*).

14810 **Shalev-Khalifa, Nirit** A locked garden. Or Yehuda 2005, Kinneret 224 pp. NIS128. Phot. *Baruch Gian*. **H.**

14811 **Taylor, Jane** Jordan: images from the air. Jordan 2005, Al-Uzza Books 160 pp. £16. 99574-51073.

## U1.6 Guide books, *Führer*

14812 **Bruneau, Pilippe; Ducat, Jean** Guide de Délos. Sites et monuments 1: Athènes [4]2005 <1965, 1983>, Ecole française d'Athènes 339 pp. 28695-82102

14813 **Burns, Ross** Monuments of Syria: an historical guide. [2]1999 <1992> ⇒15,11937. [R]JNES 64 (2005) 219-220 (*McClellan, Thomas L.*).

14814 **Cignelli, L.** La grazia dei luoghi santi. J 2005, Franciscan 105 pp. [CDios 219/1,332—Gutiérrez, J].

14815 **Cimok, Fatih** Biblical Anatolia: from Genesis to the Councils. Stanbul 2005, A Turizm Yayinlari 203 pp.

14816 **Zambon, Maria G.** Antiochia sull'Oronte. Parma 2005, Eteria 135 pp. Ill.

## U1.7 Onomastica

14817 **Elitzur, Yoel** Ancient place names in the Holy Land: preservation and history. 2004 ⇒20,13383. [R]RBLit (2005)* (*Krieger, William*).

14818 *Gass, Erasmus* Biblische Ortsnamen mit theophoren Elementen: Beiträge zu einer Religionsgeographie Palästinas. [F]SEIDL, T.: ATSAT 75: 2005 ⇒137. 42-82.

14819 **Kaswalder, Pietro A.** Onomastica biblica: fonti scritte e ricerca archeologica. SBF.CMi 40: 2002 ⇒18,12966; 19,14103. [R]PEQ 137 (2005) 82-83 (*Taylor, Joan*).

14820 [T]**Notley, R. Steven; Safrai, Ze'ev** EUSEBIUS, Onomasticon: the place names of divine scripture, including the Latin edition of JEROME, translated into English and with topographical commentary. Jewish and Christian Perspectives 9: Lei 2005, Brill xxxvii; 212 pp. €125. 0-391-04217-3.

## U2.1 Geologia

14821 [E]**Foulon, E.** Connaissance et représentation des volcans dans l'antiquité. ERGA 5: 2004 ⇒20,13385. [R]REG 118 (2005) 279-283 (*Le Blay, Frédéric*).

14822 *Korjenkov, Andrey M.; Mazor, Emanuel* Diversity of earthquakes destruction patterns: the Roman-Byzantine ruins of Haluza, Negev Desert, Israel. AA 2 (2005) 1-15.

14823 *Lancel, Serge* Les hommes de l'antiquité face aux séismes. CRAI 4 (2005) 1281-1289.

14824 *Lebreton, Stéphane* Le Taurus en Asie Mineure: contenus et conséquences de représentations stéréotypées. REA 107 (2005) 655-674.

14825 **Nützel, Werner** Einführung in die Geo-Archäologie des Vorderen Orients. 2004 ⇒20,13388. [R]OLZ 100 (2005) 262-271 (*Schachner, Andreas*); Mes. 40 (2005) 191 (*Lippolis, Carlo*).

### U2.2 *Hydrographia*; **rivers, seas, salt**; *Clima*, **climate**

14826 *Döring, M.* Römische Wasserversorgungstunnel im Norden Jordaniens: eine Vorerkundung. ZDPV 121 (2005) 130-139.

14827 *Shemesh, Abraham Ofir* Water sources in the bible proprietorship, drawing rights and allotment. BetM 181 (2005) 99-108 Sum 200. **H.**

14828 [E]**Cusset, Christophe** La météorologie dans l'antiquité, entre science et croyance. Mémoire 25: 2003 ⇒19,14115. [R]REG 118 (2005) 283-285 (*Le Blay, Frédéric*).

14829 **Fitzgerald, Aloysius** The Lord of the east wind. CBQ.MS 34: 2002 ⇒18,12992...20,13405. [R]WThJ 67 (2005) 182-84 (*Estelle, Bryan*).

14830 *Moeller, Nadine* The First Intermediate Period: a time of famine and climate change?. Ä&L 15 (2005) 153-167.

14831 *Wilson, James Kinnier* On the ud-šu-bala at Ur towards the end of the third millennium BC. Iraq 67/2 (2005) 47-60.

### U2.5 *Fauna*, **animalia**

14832 **Amar, Zohar** הארבה במסורת ישראל [Le criquet dans la tradition juive]. 2004 ⇒20,13408. [R]REJ 164 (2005) 366-68 (*Lacombe-Hagaï, Gabriel*). **H.**

14833 *Clark, David* Red and green horses?. BiTr 56 (2005) 67-71 [Zech 1,8; 6,2-7; Rev 6,2-8; 19,11-14].

14834 [E]**Collins, Billie Jean** A history of the animal world in the ancient Near East. HO 1/64: 2002 ⇒18,12995; 20,13413. [R]OLZ 100 (2005) 446-451 (*Vila, Emmanuelle*).

14835 **Davies, Sue; Smith, H.S.** The sacred animal necropolis at North Saqqâra: the fąlcon complex and catacomb: the archaeological report. Egypt Exploration Society Excavation memoir 73: L 2005, Egypt Exploration Society xxi; 158 pp. 0-85698-165-6. Plans and drawings by *Kenneth J. Frazer*.

14836 *Dohmen, Christoph* Mitgeschöpflichkeit und Tierfriede. BiKi 60 (2005) 26-31.

14837 *Driesch, Angela von den*, *al.*, Mummified, deified and buried at Hermopolis Magna—the sacred birds from Tuna el-Gebel, Middle Egypt. Ä&L 15 (2005) 203-244.

14838 *Furlanetto, Alberto* I linguaggi degli animali in storie di iniziazione. Animali. 2005 ⇒14847. 155-163.

14839 [E]**Giacomuzzi, Luigi** Gli animali e il sacro nell'antico Egitto e nell' interpretazione di maestri dell'arte moderna. Viadana 2005, Arti Grafiche Castello 348 pp.

14840 **Giebel, Marion** Tiere in der Antike: von Fabelwesen, Opfertieren und treuen Begleitern. 2003 ⇒19,14127. [R]AnCl 74 (2005) 432-435 (*Fögen, Thorsten*).

14841 **Gransard-Desmond, Jean-Olivier** Etude sur les Canidae des temps pré-pharaoniques en Egypte et au Soudan. BAR Intern. Ser. 1260: 2004 ⇒20,13415. [R]DiscEg 62 (2005) 95-98 (*DuQuesne, Terence*).

14842 *Horne, Milton* From ethics to aesthetics: the animals in Job 38:39-39:30. RExp 102 (2005) 127-142.

14843 [E]**Ikram, Salima** Divine creatures: animal mummies in ancient Egypt. Cairo 2005, American University in Cairo Press xxi; 257 pp. 977-424-858-9. Bibl. 230-257.

14844 **Jankovic, Bojana** Vogelzucht und Vogelfang in Sippar im 1. Jahrtausend v. Chr. AOAT 315: 2004 ⇒20,13420. [R]AfO 51 (2005-2006) 318-321 (*MacGinnis, John*).

14845 *Janowski, Bernd* Noahs Erbe: Tiere als Opfer und Mitgeschöpfe im Alten Testament. BiKi 60 (2005) 32-37 [Gen 9; Lev 16-17].

14846 **Janssen, Jack J.** Donkeys at Deir El-Medîna. Egyptologische uitgaven 19: Lei 2005, Nederlandsch Instituut voor Het Nabije Oosten xi;127 pp. €39.22. 90-6258-219-2.

14847 [E]**Milano, Lucio; Ghersetti, Antonella; Cingano, Ettore** Animali tra zoologia, mito e letteratura nella cultura classica e orientale: atti del convegno, Venezia, 22-23 maggio 2002. Padova 2005, S.A.R. G.O.N. 373 pp. 88-901-2869-0.

14848 *Reuter, Eleonore* Der Zoo als Arche Noah: Zooführungen als bibelpastorales Projekt. Diak. 36 (2005) 177-180.

14849 [E]**Vagnetti, Lucia; Damiani, Isabella; Bettelli, Marco** L'avorio in Italia nell'età del bronzo. Incunabula Graeca 102: R 2005, CNR 135 pp. 88-87345-13-9. Bibl.

14850 *Vila, Emmanuelle; Besso, Mussab El* Rapport préliminaire de l'étude de la faune d'Al-Rawda (campagnes 2002 à 2004). Akkadica 126 (2005) 111-119.

14851 **Watanabe, Chikako Esther** Animal symbolism in Mesopotamia: a contextual approach. Wiener Offene Orientalistik 1: 2002 ⇒18,13068. [R]Mes. 40 (2005) 198-200 (*Lippolis, Carlo*).

14852 *Whitekettle, Richard* Bugs, bunny, or boar?: identifying the Zîz animals of Psalms 50 and 80. CBQ 67 (2005) 250-264 [Ps 50,10-11; 80,9-14];

14853 The raven as kind and kinds of ravens: a study in the zoological nomenclature of Leviticus 11,2-23. ZAW 117 (2005) 509-528.

## U2.6 *Flora*; **plantae biblicae et antiquae**

14854 *Abouzayd, Shafiq* The prohibition and the use of alcohol in the Syrian ascetic tradition and its biblical and spiritual origins;

14855 *Al-Salameen, Zeyad* Nabataean winepresses from Bayda, southern Jordan. Aram 17 (2005) 135-156/115-127.

14856 *Baruch, Uri* Identification of charred wood remains from 'En Gedi. 'Atiqot 49 (2005) 43-48.

14857 *Brock, Sebastian* Sobria ebrietas according to some Syriac texts. Aram 17 (2005) 185-191.

14858 *Broshi, Magen* Ladanum at 'En Gedi?. IEJ 55 (2005) 94-96.

14859 *Deckers, K.* Anthracological research at the archaeological site of Emar on the Middle Euphrates, Syria. Paléorient 31/2 (2005) 153-167.

14860 *Derfler, Steven* The wine industry, the Sharon plain and Tel Michal. Aram 17 (2005) 83-94.

14861 **Dobat, Klaus; Habrich, Christa; Kowalski, Michael** Pflanzen der Bibel: Begleitheft zur Sonderausstellung im Deutschen Medizinhistorischen Museum Ingolstadt...Juni-Sept. 2005... Kataloge des Deutschen Medizinhistorischen Museums Ingolstadt 27: Ingolstadt $^{3}$2005, Deutsches Medizinhist. Museum Ingolstadt 206 pp.

14862 *Du Toit, J.S.; Naudé, J.A.* Lost in translation: designation, identification and classification of flora in translated Biblical Hebrew texts. JNSL 31/2 (2005) 33-58.

14863 *Dzierzbicka, Dorota* Wineries and their elements in Graeco-Roman Egypt. JJP 35 (2005) 9-91.

14864 *Hein, Kristina* Die Besonderheiten der Verbindung von Weintrauben und Feigen. GöMisz 205 (2005) 67-69.

14865 Israel: Ketura: 2000 Jahre alter Dattelpalmenkeimling. WUB 38 (2005) 68.

14866 *Knauf, Ernst Axel* Wer könnte leben ohne den Trost der Bäume?: Wald und Bäume im Leben und in der Religion Israels und seiner Nachbarn. BiKi 60 (2005) 23-25.

14867 "Das Land lasse junges Grün wachsen": der Berchinger Bibelgarten. BiHe 41/164 (2005) 28-29.

14868 *Lenchak, Timothy A.* What's biblical about... incense?. BiTod 43 (2005) 387-388.

14869 **McGovern, Patrick E.** Ancient wine: the search for the origins of viniculture. 2003 ⇒19,14151. $^{R}$AJA 109 (2005) 106-107 (*Palmer, Ruth*).

14870 *Nelson, Max* Divine or godless drink?: ancient Greek notions concerning the origins of beer and wine. Aram 17 (2005) 129-134.

14871 *Pasqualetti, Tito* Lettura "botanica" dei vangeli. RivBib 53 (2005) 191-210.

14872 *Paul, Shalom M.* Classifications of wine in Mesopotamian and rabbinic sources. Divrei Shalom. 2005 <1975> ⇒273. 71-74.

14873 *Reid, Barbara E.* What's biblical about... drinking wine?. BiTod 43 (2005) 314-316.

14874 *Staubli, Thomas* Zur Realität und Symbolik der Pflanzenwelt in der südlichen Levante. BiKi 60 (2005) 10-15;

14875 Land der sprießenden Zweige. BiKi 60 (2005) 16-22.

14876 *Suderman, W. Derek* Modest or magnificent?: lotus versus lily in Canticles. CBQ 67 (2005) 42-58 [Cant 2,1-2; 2,16].

14877 *Viviani, Maria Teresa* The role of alcoholic beverages in Sumer and Akkad: an analysis of iconographic patterns (4000-2000 B.C.). Aram 17 (2005) 1-50.

## U2.8 Agricultura, alimentatio

14878 **Bellwood, Peter** First farmers: the origins of agricultural societies. Malden, Mass. 2005, Blackwell xix; 360 pp. 0-631-20566-7.

14879 **Borowski, O.** Agriculture in Iron Age Israel. 2002 <1987> ⇒19, 14159. $^{R}$IEJ 55 (2005) 116-120 (*Ayalon, Etan*).

14880 **Brun, Jean-Pierre** Archéologie du vin et de l'huile en Gaule romaine. Hesperides: P 2005, Errance 268 pp. €29. 2-87772-304-6. 195 fig.; 13 maps.

14881 **Carroll, Maureen** Earthly paradises: ancient gardens in history and archaeology. 2003 ⇒20,13459. $^{R}$NEA(BA) 68 (2005) 138 (*Miller, Naomi E.*).

14882 **Dalby, Andrew** Food in the ancient world from A to Z. 2003 ⇒19, 14161. $^{R}$Gn. 77 (2005) 641-643 (*Fellmeth, Ulrich*).

14883 *Dirven, Lucinda* Banquet scenes from Hatra. Aram 17 (2005) 61-82.

14884 **Dunbabin, Katherine M.D.** The Roman banquet: images of conviviality. 2003 ⇒19,14163; 20,13462. $^{R}$AJA 109 (2005) 816-817 (*Curtis, Robert I.*); RAr (2005/1) 170-172 (*Hesberg, Henner von*).

14885 **Furger, Andreas** Übrigens bin ich der Meinung... der römische Politiker und Landmann Marcus CATO zu Olivenöl und Wein. Mainz 2005, Von Zabern 147 pp. €26. 3-8053-3523-7.

14886 *Gubler, Marie-Louise* Vom Hunger in der Wüste zum Mahl im Namen Jesu: Essen und Trinken in der Bibel. Diak. 36 (2005) 15-19.

14887 $^{ET}$**Guillaumin, Jean-Yves** Sextus Iulius FRONTINUS: Les arpenteurs romains, 1: Hygin le gromatique. P 2005, Belles Lettres 265 pp. 2-251-01440-3.

14888 *Jüngling, Hans-Winfried* Erziehungsreden über das Mahl und beim Mahl. $^{F}$ZMIJEWSKI, J.: BBB 151: 2005 ⇒172. 131-150 [Sir 32,1-3; Lk 14,1-24; 22,1-38].

14889 *Koslova, Natalia V.* Feld oder Gerste?: zur Versorgung der landwirtschaftlichen Arbeiter in Umma der Ur III-Zeit. $^{M}$DIAKONOFF, M.: 2005 ⇒36. 703-712.

14890 *Kron, G.* Anthropometry, physical anthropology, and the reconstruction of ancient health, nutrition, and living standards. Hist. 54 (2005) 68-83 [NTAb 49,548].

14891 *Lernau, Omri* Fish remains from 'En Gedi. 'Atiqot 49 (2005) 49-56.

14892 *Mirković, Miroslava* Child labour and taxes in the agriculture of Roman Egypt: ΠΑΙΣ and ΑΦΗΔΙΞ. SCI 24 (2005) 139-149.

14893 *Price, Simon; Nixon, Lucia* Ancient Greek agricultural terraces: evidence from texts and archaeological survey. AJA 109 (2005) 665-694.

14894 **Sharon, Diane M.** Patterns of destiny: narrative structures of foundation and doom in the Hebrew Bible. 2002 ⇒18,13090; 19,14171. $^{R}$BiOr 62 (2005) 103-104 (*Holman, Jan*).

14895 **Stein-Hölkeskamp, Elke** Das römische Gastmahl: eine Kulturgeschichte. Mü 2005, Beck 364 pp. €29.90. 3-406-52890-2.

14896 **Vamosh, Miriam F.** Essen und Trinken in biblischer Zeit. $^{T}$*Frisch, Hermann-Josef*: Dü 2005, Patmos 104 pp. €19.90. 3-491-79741-1. Num. ill.

14897 *Verardi, Virginia* Le rôle du banquet en Mésopotamie. $^{F}$FINET, A.: Subartu 16: 2005 ⇒40. 165-174.

14898 *Zwickel, Wolfgang* Salz: lebensfeindlich, aber schmackhaft. WUB 38 (2005) 73-75.

## U2.9 **Medicina** *biblica et antiqua*

14899 **Allen, James P.** The art of medicine in ancient Egypt. NY 2005, Metropolitan Museum of Art 115 pp. 978-03001-07289. 104 ill.; Essay by *David T. Mininberg*; Bibl.

14900 **Andorlini, Isabella; Marcone, Arnaldo** Medicina, medico e società nel mondo antico. F 2004, Le Monnier Univ. viii; 268 pp. €17. 50. [R]ASEs 22 (2005) 255-257 (*Mazza, Roberta*).

14901 *Brock, Sebastian* The instructions of Anton, PLATO's physician. Studia semitica. JSSt.S 16: 2005 ⇒603. 129-138.

14902 *Casaburi, Maria Cristina* Early evidences of astrological aspects in a Neo-Assyrian medical hemerology. SAA Bulletin 14 (2002-2005) 63-88.

14903 *Cilliers, Louise; Retief, François P.* HIPPOCRATES: facts and fiction. Health and healing. AcTh(B) 7: 2005 <2000> ⇒686. 1-13;

14904 The death of Alexander the Great <1999> 14-28;

14905 The army of Alexander the Great and combat stress syndrome (326 BC) <2000> 29-43;

14906 The death of Cleopatra <1999> 79-88;

14907 Causes of death among the Caesars (27 BC-AD 476) <2000> 89-106;

14908 The eruption of Vesuvius in AD 79 and the death of Gaius PLINIUS Secundus <1997> 107-114;

14909 The epidemic of Justinian (AD 542): a prelude to the Middle Ages <2000> 115-127;

14910 Lead poisoning in ancient Rome <2000> 147-164;

14911 The healing hand: the role of women in ancient medicine <1999> 165-188;

14912 Snake and staff symbolism and healing <2002> 189-199;

14913 Tumours and cancers in Graeco-Roman times <2001> 200-212;

14914 The evolution of hospitals from antiquity to the Renaissance <2002> 213-232;

14915 Diseases and causes of death among the Popes <2000> 233-246;

14916 The influence of christianity on Graeco-Roman medicine up to the Renaissance <2001> 259-277;

14917 *Cilliers, Louise* Where were the doctors when the Roman Empire died? <1993>. Health and healing. AcTh(B) 7: 2005 ⇒686. 62-78.

14918 **Dörnemann, Michael** Krankheit und Heilung in der Theologie der frühen Kirchenväter. STAC 20: 2003 ⇒19,14178; 20,13491. [R]RivCC 81 (2005) 334-335 (*Heid, Stefan*).

14919 [ET]**Garofalo, Ivan**; [T]**Debru, Armelle** Galenus: Les os pour les débutants: l'anatomie des muscles. P 2005, Belles Lettres xii; 211 pp. 2-251-00524-2.

14920 **Geller, Markham J.** Renal and rectal disease texts. Die babylonisch-assyrische Medizin in Texten und Untersuchungen 7: B 2005, De Gruyter viii; 284 pp. €112. 31101-79644.

14921 **Haas, Volkert** Materia magica et medica hethitica: ein Beitrag zur Heilkunde im Alten Orient. 2003 ⇒19,14182. [R]JANER 5 (2005) 218-227 (*Hutter, Manfred*).

14922 *Heeßel, Nils P.* Stein, Pflanze und Holz: ein neuer Text zur 'medizinischen Astrologie'. Or. 74 (2005) 1-22.

14923 [E]**King, Helen** Health in antiquity. L 2005, Routledge xxii; 292 pp. £50. 0-415-22065-3. 25 fig.

14924 [E]**Leven, Karl-Heinz** Antike Medizin: ein Lexikon. Mü 2005, Beck xliv; 867 col. €50. 3-406-52891-0.

14925 **Massar, Natacha** Soigner et servir: histoire sociale et culturelle de la médecine grecque à l'époque hellénistique. ULB Culture et cité 2: P 2005, De Boccard 338 pp. €33. 2-7018-01850.

14926 **Nutton, Vivian** Ancient medicine. 2004 ⇒20,13503. RRSIt 117 (2005) 360-363 (*Mazzarello, Paolo*); AnCl 74 (2005) 439-440 (*Gourevitch, Danielle*);

14927 Ancient medicine. Sciences of Antiquity: L 2005 <2004>, Routledge xiv; 486 pp. $35. 0415-368480. Bibl. [NTAb 50,218].

14928 **Samama, E.** Les médecins dans le monde grec: sources épigraphiques sur la naissance d'un corps médical. HEMGR 31: 2003 ⇒ 19,14191; 20,13505. RAnCl 74 (2005) 257-266 (*Massar, N.*).

14929 *Scholten, Clemens* Welche Seele hat der Embryo?: Johannes PHILOPONOS und die Antike Embryologie. VigChr 59 (2005) 377-411.

14930 **Scurlock, Jo Ann; Andersen, Burton R.** Diagnoses in Assyrian and Babylonian medicine: ancient sources, translations, and modern medical analyses. Urbana 2005, Univ. of Illinois Pr. xxiii; 879 pp. 0-252-02956-9. Bibl. 765-778.

14931 **Van der Eijk, Philip J.** Medicine and philosophy in classical antiquity: doctors and philosophers on nature, soul, health and disease. C 2005, CUP xii; 404 pp. £55. 0-521-81800-1.

14932 **Verhey, Allen** Reading the bible in the strange world of medicine. 2003 ⇒19,14195. RCTJ 40 (2005) 123-126 (*Groenhout, Ruth*); TS 66 (2005) 214-215 (*Martone, Marilyn*); ThLZ 130 (2005) 564-566 (*Riha, Ortrun*).

14933 *Wifstrand, Albert* Sidelights on Greek culture from a Greek medical writer. Epochs and styles. Ment. *Galen*: WUNT 179: 2005 <1955> ⇒325. 213-236.

### U3 *Duodecim tribus*; **Israel tribes**; *land ideology; adjacent lands*

14934 *Berger, Ulla* De naam Israël in de godsdienstles. ITBT 13/1 (2005) 29-31.

14935 **Brueggemann, Walter** The land: place as gift, promise, and challenge in biblical faith. Overtures to Biblical Theology: ²2002 ⇒18, 13110. RTJT 21 (2005) 227-228 (*Idestrom, Rebecca G.S.*).

14936 *Chouraqui, Jean* Terre promise, terre permise?. FV 104/5 (2005) 48-56.

14937 *Evans, Bryan* A theology of folklands?. Evangel 23 (2005) 79-86.

14938 **Grant, Asahel** The Nestorians, or, The lost tribes: containing evidence of their identity, an account of their manners, customs and ceremonies: together with sketches of travel in ancient Assyria, Armenia, Media and Mesopotamia, illustration of Scripture prophecy, and appendices. Gorgias reprint 22: Piscataway N.J. 2002 <1841>, Gorgias iii; x; 338 pp. 1-931956-07-3. Introd. *Hendrika L. Murre-van den Berg*.

14939 *Naor, Arye* 'Behold, Rachel, behold': the Six Day War as a biblical experience and its impact on Israel's political mentality. TA 24 (2005) 229-250.

14940 **Holes, Clive** Dialect, culture, and society in eastern Arabia, 2: ethnographic texts. HO 1/51.2: Lei 2005, Brill 90-04-14494-3.

### U4.5 *Viae*, **roads, routes**

14941 **Nicholson, J.** The Hejaz railway. L 2005, Stacey xiii; 193 pp. £29. 50. 1-9009-8881-X.

14942 *Roll, Israel* Imperial roads across and trade routes beyond the Roman provinces of Judaea-Palaestina and Arabia: the state of research. TelAv 32/1 (2005) 107-118.

14943 *Smith, Andrew M.* Pathways, roadways, and highways: networks of communication and exchange in Wadi Araba. NEA 68/4 (2005) 180-189.

## U5.0 *Ethnographia*, **sociologia**; *servitus*

14944 **Agosto, Efrain** Servant leadership: Jesus and Paul. St. Louis, MO 2005, Chalice viii; 248 pp. $30. 0-8272-3463-5. Bibl. 232-240.

14945 *Aguirre, Rafael* Los evangelios y los emigrantes y extranjeros. ResB 46 (2005) 21-28.

14946 [E]**Balch, David L.; Osiek, Carolyn** Early christian families in context: an interdisciplinary dialogue. 2003 ⇒19,657; 20,13529. Conf. Brite Divinity School. [R]ThLZ 130 (2005) 667-669 (*Omerzu, Heike*); HeyJ 46 (2005) 542-543 (*Taylor, N.H.*); TJT 21 (2005) 219-221 (*Campbell, Joan*).

14947 **Balla, Peter** The child-parent relationship in the New Testament and its environment. WUNT 155: 2003 ⇒19,14221; 20,13530. [R]NT 47 (2005) 186-189 (*Burke, Trevor J.*); De Processibus matrimonialibus 12 (2005) 281-285 (*Müller, Christoph G.*);

14948 Peabody, MA 2005 <2003>, Hendrickson xii; 279 pp. $30. 15985-60344. Diss.-Habil. Evangelical-Lutheran Theol. Univ., Budapest.

14949 *Baumbach, Günther* Die Anfänge der Kirchwerdung im Urchristentum. Josephus–Jesusbewegung. 2005 <1982> ⇒182. 118-133.

14950 **Blenkinsopp, Joseph** Sapiente, sacerdote, profeta. StBi 146: Brescia 2005, Paideia 286 pp. €26.80. 88-394-0702-2.

14951 *Boer, Roland* Woman first?: on the legacy of 'primitive communism'. JSOT 30 (2005) 3-28.

14952 **Borowski, Oded** Daily life in biblical times. SBL.Archaeology and Biblical Studies 5: 2003 ⇒19,14227; 20,13534. [R]CBQ 67 (2005) 108-109 (*Smith-Christopher, Daniel L.*); OLZ 100 (2005) 470-472 (*Zwickel, Wolfgang*); RStR 31 (2005) 148 (*Nakhai, Beth Alpert*); TJT 21 (2005) 224-225 (*Irwin, Brian P.*).

14953 **Buell, Denise K.** Why this new race: ethnic reasoninig in early christianity. NY 2005, Columbia University Press xiv; [2], 257 pp. $45/£29.50. 0-231-13334-0. Bibl. 233-250.

14954 *Cardona Ramírez, Hernán* La comunidad como nueva familia. El grano. 2005 ⇒197. 175-190.

14955 **Cook, Stephen L.** The social roots of biblical Yahwism. 2004 ⇒ 20,13546. [R]RBLit (2005)* (*Sparks, Kenton*).

14956 *Crook, Zeba A.* Reflections on culture and social-scientific models. JBL 124 (2005) 515-520.

14957 *Crüsemann, Frank* Der Glaube an den einen Gott und die Entstehung einer kollektiven Identität Israels. KuI 20 (2005) 120-129.

14958 **Destro, Adriana; Pesce, Mauro** Forme culturali del cristianesimo nascente. Scienze umane n.s. 2: Brescia 2005, Morcelliana 202 pp. 88-372-2084-7. Bibl. 175-192.

14959 *Dorey, P.J.* Diakroniese perspektiewe op die huwelik: kultuurhistoriese gesigspunte vanuit verskillende tye en omstandighede (2112 vC-1753 nC). OTEs 18 (2005) 542-566.

14960 **Dunning, Benjamin Harrison** Aliens and sojourners: self as other in the rhetoric of early christian identity. 2005, Diss. Harvard [HThR 98,493].

14961 **Fischer, James A.** Leaders and people in biblical stories. 2004 ⇒ 20,13553. [R]RBLit (2005)* (*Feinman, Peter*).

14962 **Flemming, Dean E.** Contextualization in the New Testament: patterns for theology and mission. GR 2005, Brazos 344 pp. $26. 0-8-308-2831-1. Bibl. 323-330.

14963 *Friesen, Steven J.* Injustice or God's will: explanations of poverty in proto-christian communities. Christian origins. A people's history of christianity 1: 2005 ⇒550. 240-260.

14964 **Gehring, Roger W.** House church and mission: the importance of household structures in early christianity. 2002 ⇒19,14238. [R]CBQ 67 (2005) 528-530 (*Ascough, Richard S.*).

14965 *George, P.G.* 'Immigrant Abraham' on the move: towards an immigrant theology. BiBh 31 (2005) 18-26 [Gen 11,31-12,9].

14966 *Georgi, Dieter* Socioeconomic reasons for the "divine man" as propagandistic pattern. The city in the valley. Studies in biblical literature 7: 2005 ⇒214. 11-23.

14967 *Gerstenberger, Erhard S.* Pluralism in theology?: an Old Testament inquiry part 1: *sojourners we are*: social rootings of biblical witnesses. Scriptura 88 (2005) 64-72 [OTA 29,82];

14968 part 2: *that all may become one*: global responsibility in christian thinking. Scriptura 88 (2005) 73-84 [OTA 29,82].

14969 *Gillmayr-Bucher, Susanne* Selbstbewusstsein und Identität im Spiegel des Fremden. ThG 48 (2005) 190-199.

14970 **Glancy, Jennifer A.** Slavery in early christianity. 2002 ⇒18,13152 ... 20,13556. [R]IJCT 11 (2005) 471-473 (*Harrison, J.R.*).

14971 **Goldenberg, David M.** The curse of Ham: race and slavery in early Judaism, christianity and Islam. 2003 ⇒19,14243; 20,13557. [R]Journal of Social History 38 (2005) 831-833 (*Miller, Dean A.*) [Gen 9,18-25].

14972 *Guenther, Allen* A typology of Israelite marriage: kinship, socio-economic, and religious factors. JSOT 29 (2005) 387-407.

14973 *Hamilton, Mark W.* Critiquing the sovereign: perspectives from Deuteronomy and Job. RestQ 47/4 (2005) 237-249.

14974 **Hanson, Paul D.** The people called: the growth of community in the bible. 2001 <1986> ⇒17,11886. [R]BiOr 62 (2005) 317-325 (*Holman, Jan*).

14975 *Harrison, Peter* 'Fill the earth and subdue it': biblical warrants for colonization in seventeenth-century England. JRH 29/1 (2005) 3-24.

14976 *Hentschel, Georg* Israel als Modell eines universalen Gottesvolkes. ThG 48 (2005) 200-210.

14977 *Hieke, Thomas* Endogamy in the book of Tobit, Genesis, and Ezra-Nehemiah. Book of Tobit. JSJ.S 98: 2005 ⇒3620. 103-119.

14978 **Hiltbrunner, Otto** Gastfreundschaft in der Antike und im frühen Christentum. Da:Wiss. 2005, 224 pp. €34.90. 3-534-18383-5.

14979 *Horsley, Richard A.* Prominent patterns in the social memory of Jesus and friends. Memory, tradition, and text. SBL.Semeia Studies 52: 2005 ⇒416. 57-78.

14980 **Horsley, Richard A.; Silberman, Neil A.** The message and the kingdom: how Jesus and Paul ignited a revolution and transformed the ancient world. 2002 ⇒18,13165... 20,13568. ^R HeyJ 46 (2005) 73-74 (*Taylor, N.H.*); RBLit 7 (2005) 453-458 (*Nicklas, Tobias*);

14981 La revolución del reino: cómo Jesús y Pablo transformaron el mundo antiguo. Panorama 9: Sdr 2005, Sal Terre 283 pp. 84293-16035.

14982 *Hurtado, Larry W.* To live and die for Jesus: social and political consequences of devotion to Jesus in earliest christianity. SEÅ 70 (2005) 309-331 = How on earth. 2005 ⇒227. 56-82;

14983 Religious experience and religious innovation in the New Testament. How on earth. 2005 <2000> ⇒227. 179-204.

14984 **Johnson-DeBaufre, Melanie** Jesus among her children: Q, eschatology, and the construction of christian origins. HThS 55: CM 2005, Harvard University Pr. xvi; 233 pp. 0674-01899-0.

14985 **Jossa, Giorgio** Giudei o cristiani?: i seguaci di Gesù in cerca di una propria identità. StBi 142: 2004 ⇒20,13571. ^R CBQ 67 (2005) 348-349 (*Bernas, Casimir*); Asp. 52 (2005) 572-575 (*Castello, Gaetano*).

14986 *Kalluveettil, Paul* From inculturation dynamics to conservative nationalism: the Old Testament perspectives. ThirdM 8/1 (2005) 7-37.

14987 *Kanjamala, Augustine* Inculturation: a biblical model. VSVD 46 (2005) 163-178.

14988 *Kazen, Thomas* Response to Larry Hurtado: "To live and die for Jesus ....". SEÅ 70 (2005) 333-338.

14989 *Kelber, Werner H.* The works of memory: christian origins as mnemohistory—a response. Memory, tradition, and text. SBL.Semeia Studies 52: 2005 ⇒416. 221-248.

14990 **Killebrew, Ann E.** Biblical peoples and ethnicity: an archaeological study of Egyptians, Canaanites, Philistines, and early Israel, 1300-1100 B.C.E. SBL.Archaeology and Biblical Studies 9: Atlanta 2005, SBL xx; 362 pp. $164/40. 15898-30970. Bibl. 253-334.

14991 *Kleinig, J.W.* Ordered community: order and subordination in the New Testament. LTJ 39/2-3 (2005) 196-209 [NTAb 50,91].

14992 **Koch, Stefan** Rechtliche Regelung von Konflikten im frühen Christentum. WUNT 2/174: 2004 ⇒20,13575. ^R ThLZ 130 (2005) 1323-1326 (*Omerzu, Heike*).

14993 *Landgrave G., Daniel R.* La biblia, vertebrada socialmente (primera parte). EfMex 67 (2005) 3-40.

14994 **Lartigolle, Jean** Préhistoire de la foi chrétienne: de l'animisme à l'incarnation. Initiations bibliques: 2004 ⇒20,13578. ^R EeV 137 (2005) 28 (*Cothenet, Édouard*).

14995 *Loubser, J.A.* Invoking the ancestors. some socio-rhetorical aspects of the genealogies in the gospels of Matthew and Luke. Neotest. 39 (2005) 127-140 [Mt 1,1-17; Lk 3,23-38].

14996 *Lourenço, João* Mundo bíblico e estruturas sociais. Theologica 40 (2005) 13-32.

14997 *Martin, Clarice J.* The eyes have it: slaves in the communities of Christ-believers. Christian origins. A people's history of christianity 1: 2005 ⇒550. 221-239.

14998 *Monera, Arnold T.* The christian's relationship to the state according to the New Testament: conformity or non-conformity?. AJTh 19/1 (2005) 106-142.

14999 *Morra, Stella* Lo straniero nella bibbia/1: non c'è più straniero né ospite. Presbyteri 39 (2005) 207-211.

15000 *Moxnes, Halvor* From theology to identity: the problem of constructing early christianity. Moving beyond NT theology?. Ment. *Räisänen, H.*: SESJ 88: 2005 ⇒463. 264-281.

15001 *Muffs, Yochanan* Family and nation: two versions of national formation. Personhood of God. 2005 ⇒265. 45-51.

15002 **Otto, Eckart** Max WEBERs Studien des antiken Judentums: historische Grundlegung einer Theorie der Moderne. 2002 ⇒18,13189; 20,13598. [R]ThLZ 130 (2005) 252-254 (*Kessler, Rainer*).

15003 **Penna, Romano** Il DNA del cristianesimo: l'identità cristiana allo stato nascente. Guida alla Bibbia 103: 2004 ⇒20,13599. [R]ATT 11 (2005) 455-457 (*Ghiberti, Giuseppe*).

15004 *Perrot, Charles* Les premières communautés chrétiennes au sein du judaïsme: diversité et unité. EeV 123 (2005) 5-11.

15005 *Rodríguez, Lidia* La memoria, fundamento de la acogida al emigrante. ResB 46 (2005) 13-20.

15006 **Römer, Thomas; Bonjour, Loyse** L'homosexualité dans le Proche-Orient ancien et la bible. Essais bibliques 37: Genève 2005, Labor et F. 124 pp. €29. 2-8309-1165-2.

15007 *Rusam, Dietrich* "... der soll das Herz der Väter bekehren zu den Söhnen und das Herz der Söhne zu ihren Vätern": alttestamentliche Beobachtungen zum Spannungsverhältnis der Generationen. Evangelische Aspekte 15/2 (2005) 37-41.

15008 **Sadler, Rodney Steven, Jr.** Can a Cushite change his skin?: an examination of race, ethnicity, and othering in the Hebrew Bible. JSOT.S 425; LHBOTS 425: NY 2005, Clark xii; 175 pp. $115. 97-80-5060-7080-917. Bibl. 153-165.

15009 **Saldarini, Anthony J.** Farisei, scribi e sadducei nella società palestinese: ricerca sociologica. Intro. allo studio della bibbia, suppl. 14: 2003 ⇒19,14282; 20,13606. [R]RivBib 53 (2005) 116-120 (*Jossa, Giorgio*); Asp. 52 (2005) 600-601 (*Di Palma, Gaetano*).

15010 *Schwartz, Barry* Christian origins: historical truth and social memory. Memory, tradition, and text. SBL.Semeia Studies 52: 2005 ⇒416. 43-56.

15011 *Simkins, Ronald A.* Family in the political economy of monarchic Judah. BiCT 1/1 (2004)*.

15012 *Sivertsev, Alexei* Sects and households: social structure of the proto-sectarian-movement of Nehemiah 10 and the Dead Sea sect. CBQ 67 (2005) 59-78.

15013 *Snyman, Gerrie* Constructing and deconstructing identities in post-apartheid South Africa: a case of hybridity versus untainted Africanicity?. OTEs 18 (2005) 323-344.

15014 **Spina, Frank A.** The faith of the outsider: exclusion and inclusion in the biblical story. GR 2005, Eerdmans x; 206 pp. $16. 0-8028-2864-7. [R]RBLit (2005)* (*Kraus, Thomas*).

15015 **Stegemann, Ekkehard W.; Stegemann, Wolfgang** The Jesus movement: a social history of its first century. 1999 ⇒15,12141... 18,13209. [R]JRH 29 (2005) 178-180 (*Crotty, Robert*);

15016 História social do protocristianismo: os primórdios no judaísmo e as comunidades de Cristo no mundo mediterrâneo. [T]*Schneider, Nélio* 2004 ⇒20,13614. [R]Estudos Bíblicos 87 (2005) 113-115 (*Orofino, Francisco*).

15017 *Strong, John T.* Israel as a testimony to Yhwh's power: the priests' definition of Israel. [F]McBride, D. 2005 ⇒98. 89-106.

15018 *Svartnik, Jesper* How Noah, Jesus and Paul became captivating biblical figures: the side effects of the canonization of slavery metaphors in Jewish and christian texts. JGRChJ 2 (2005) 168-227.

15019 *Tellbe, Mikael* "Vi är dom vi inte är!"—identitet och exklusivitet bland de tigida kristna i Efesos. SEÅ 70 (2005) 361-387.

15020 **Tenhafen, Heinz** Das neue Gottesvolk: die Anfänge des Christentums und der antike Ethnizitäts-Diskurs. [D]*Stegemann, Wolfgang* 2005, Diss. Augustana [ThLZ 130,889].

15021 *Towner, W. Sibley* Beyond the blue horizon: the polity of Israel and the nations yet to come. [F]McBride, D. 2005 ⇒98. 295-312.

15022 *Treiber, Hubert* Anmerkungen zu Max Webers Charismakonzept. ZAR 11 (2005) 195-213.

15023 *Tuell, Steven S.* The priesthood of the 'foreigner': evidence of competing polities in Ezekiel 44:1-14 and Isaiah 56:1-8. [F]McBride, D. 2005 ⇒98. 183-204.

15024 **Vartejanu-Joubert, Madaline** Folie et société dans l'Israël antique. Théologie plurielle: P 2004, L'Hartmattan 331 pp. €29. [R]RBLit (2005)* (*Vogels, Walter*).

15025 **Weber, Cornelia** Altes Testament und völkische Frage: der biblische Volksbegriff in der alttestamentlichen Wissenschaft der nationalsozialistischen Zeit, dargestellt am Beispiel von Johannes Hempel. FAT 28: 2000 ⇒16,12371; 17,11929. [R]BiOr 62 (2005) 105-108 (*Holman, Jan*).

15026 **Yamauchi, Edwin** Africa and the bible. 2004 ⇒20,13621. [R]RRT 12 (2005) 355-8 (*Ngong, David T.*); CBQ 67 (2005) 331-32 (*Morschauser, Scott*); AThR 87 (2005) 722-723 (*LeMarquand, Grant*); JETh 19 (2005) 221-223 (*Pracht, Jens*).

15027 **Zehnder, Markus** Umgang mit Fremden in Israel und Assyrien: ein Beitrag zur Anthropologie des Fremden im Licht antiker Quellen. BWANT 168: Stu 2005, Kohlhammer 613 pp. €45. 3-17-0189-97-2. Diss.-Habil. Basel; Bibl. 559-599.

## U5.3 Commercium, oeconomica

15028 **Abraham, Kathleen** Business and politics under the Persian Empire: the financial dealings of Marduk-nasir-apli of the House of Egibi (521-487 B.C.E.). 2004 ⇒20,13622. [R]ArOr 73 (2005) 381-383 (*Pečirková, Jana*).

15029 **Braun-Holzinger, Eva A.; Rehm, Ellen** Orientalischer Import in Griechenland im frühen 1. Jahrtausend v. Chr. AOAT 328: Müns 2005, Ugarit-Verlag vi; 208 pp. 3-934628-72-9. Bibl. 185-192.

15030 *Charpin, Dominique* Chroniques bibliographiques 5, économie et société à Sippar et en Babylonie du Nord à l'époque paléo-babylonienne. RA 99 (2005) 133-176.

15031 *Faust, Avraham; Weiss, Ehud* Judah, Philistia, and the Mediterranean world: reconstructing the economic system of the seventh century B.C.E.. BASOR 338 (2005) 71-92.

15032 *Fletcher, Richard* Sidonians, Tyrians and Greeks in the Mediterranean: the evidence from Egyptianising amulets. AEW 3 (2004) 51-77.

15033 **Goddeeris, Anne** Economy and society in northern Babylonia in the early Old Babylonian Period (ca. 2000 - 1800 BC). OLA 109: 2002 ⇒18,13235; 19,14301. [R]JNES 64 (2005) 127-128 (*Van de Mieroop, Marc*).

15034 *Graslin, Laetitia* Les théories économiques du commerce international et leur usage pour l'étude des échanges à longue distance à l'époque néo-babylonienne. Approaching the Babylonian economy. AOAT 330: 2005 ⇒915. 121-136.

15035 *Jasmin, Michaël* Les conditions d'émergence de la route de l'encens à la fin du IIe millénaire avant notre ère. Syria 82 (2005) 49-62.

15036 *Kristiansen, Kristian; Larsson, Thomas B.* L'âge du Bronze, une période historique: les relations entre Europe, Méditerranée et Proche-Orient. Annales 60 (2005) 975-1007.

15037 [E]**Manning, J.G.; Morris, Ian** The ancient economy: evidence and models. Stanford 2005, Stanford Univ. Pr. xi; 258 pp. $60.

15038 [E]**Milano, Lucio; Parise, Nicola** Il regolamento degli scambi nell' antichità: (III-I millennio a.C.). 2003 ⇒19,14306. [R]JESHO 48 (2005) 328-332 (*Seri, Andrea*).

15039 *Reger, Gary* The economy. Companion to the Hellenistic world. 2005 ⇒642. 331-353.

15040 **Rosenfeld, Ben-Zion; Menirav, Joseph** Markets and marketing in Roman Palestine. [T]*Cassel, Chawa*: JSJ.S 99: Lei 2005, Brill xii; 281 pp. $137. 90-04-14049-2. Bibl. 235-259.

15041 *Şahin, H. Ali* Interest payment procedures applied by Assyrian merchants during the first quarter of the second millennium B.C. in Anatolia. BTTK 69 (2005) 425-465. **Turkish**.

15042 *Schmidt, Conrad* Überregionale Austauschsysteme und Fernhandelswaren in der Ur III-Zeit. BaghM 36 (2005) 7-155.

15043 **Van Driel, Govert** Elusive silver: in search of a role for a market in an agrarian environment. 2002 ⇒18,13246; 20,13651. [R]BiOr 62 (2005) 64-66 (*Vargyas, Péter*).

15044 **Warburton, David A.** Macroeconomics from the beginning: the *General theory*, ancient markets, and the rate of interest. 2003 ⇒ 19,14316. [R]JESHO 48 (2005) 118-122 (*Hudson, Michael*).

15045 *Widell, Magnus* Some reflections on Babylonian exchange during the end of the third millennium BC. JESHO 48 (2005) 388-400.

15046 *Yamada, Shigeo Kārus* on the frontiers of the Neo-Assyrian Empire. Orient 40 (2005) 56-90.

## U5.8 **Urbanismus**

[E]**Cunliffe, B.** Mediterranean urbanization 2005 ⇒638.
[E]**Falk, H.** Wege zur Stadt 2005 ⇒644.

15047 *Foxhall, Lin* Village to city: staples and luxuries?: exchange networks and urbanization. Mediterranean urbanization. 2005 ⇒638. 233-248.

15048 **Gates, Charles** The archaeology of urban life in the ancient Near East and Egypt, Greece, and Rome. 2003 ⇒19,14323. [R]ANESt 42 (2005) 356-358 (*Çevik, Özlem*).

**Georgi, D.** The city in the valley 2005 ⇒214.

15049 **Hansen, Mogens H.; Nielsen, Thomas H.** An inventory of archaic and classical poleis: an investigation conducted by the Copenhagen Polis Centre for the Danish National Research Foundation. Oxf 2004, OUP xv; 1396 pp. 0-19-814099-1.

15050 [E]**Luce, Jean-Marc** Habitat et urbanisme dans le monde grec de la fin des palais mycéniens à la prise de Milet (494 av. J.-C.). 2003 ⇒19,14328. [R]RAr (2005/2) 378-381 (*Siard, Hélène*).

15051 *Negbi, Ora* Urbanism on Late Bronze Age Cyprus: LC II in retrospect. BASOR 337 (2005) 1-45.

15052 **Novak, M.** Herrschaftsform und Stadtbaukunst. 1999 ⇒15,12180. [R]Or. 74 (2005) 132-134 (*Pucci, Marina*).

15053 **Pezzoli-Olgiati, Daria** Immagini urbane: interpretazioni religiose della città antica. OBO: 2002 ⇒18,13256. [R]Mes. 40 (2005) 181-182 (*Liverani, Mario*).

15054 *Purcell, Nicholas* Statics and dynamics: ancient Mediterranean urbanism. Mediterranean urbanization. 2005 ⇒638. 249-272.

15055 [E]**Reddé, Michel** La naissance de la ville dans l'antiquité. De l'archéologie à l'histoire: 2003 ⇒19,14333. [R]RAr (2005/1) 165-169 (*Greco, Emanuele*).

15056 **Smith, Adam T.** The political landscape: constellations of authority in early complex polities. 2003 ⇒19,14336. [R]CamArchJ 15 (2005) 269-270 (*Saitta, Dean J.*).

15057 **Yoffee, Norman** Myths of the archaic state: evolution of the earliest cities, states, and civilizations. C 2005, CUP 291 pp. £45/20; $75/35. 0-521-81837-0/52156-4. Num. ill. [R]CamArchJ 15 (2005) 251-254, 266-268 (*Yoffee, Norman*); 254-256 (*Matthews, Roger*); 256-258 (*Trigger, Bruce G.*); 259-260 (*Kohl, Philip L.*); 260-264 (*Webster, David*); 264-266 (*Schreiber, Katharina*).

## U6 Narrationes peregrinorum et exploratorum; *loca sancta*

15058 *Alturo, Jesús* Deux nouveaux fragments de l'"Itinerarium Egeriae" du IXe-X[e] siècle. RBen 115 (2005) 241-250.

15059 **Bitton-Ashkelony, Brouria** Encountering the sacred: the debate on christian pilgrimage in late antiquity. Berkeley 2005, Univ. of California Pr. xv; 254 pp. $45.

15060 [E]**Boadt, Lawrence; Di Camillo, Kevin** John Paul II in the Holy Land in his own words. Mahwah, NJ 2005, Paulist 17; 156 pp.

15061 [ET]**Cachey, Theodore J.** PETRARCH's guide to the Holy Land: itinerary to the sepulcher of our Lord Jesus Christ. 2002 ⇒18, 13263. [R]RHE 100 (2005) 958-961 (*Cannuyer, Christian*).

15062 **Chareyron, Nicole** Pilgrims to Jerusalem in the Middle Ages. [T]*Wilson, W. Donald*: NY 2005, Columbia Univ. Pr. 287 pp. £29.50.

15063 *Classen, Albrecht* Imaginary experience of thre divine: Felix Fabri's *Sionspilger*—late-medieval pilgrimage literature as a window into religious mentality. StSp(K) (2005) 109-128.

15064 **Coffey, Andrew** Camel trails, spice markets, journeys through the lands of the bible. Gt. Yarmouth 2005, Araxa 350 pp. £8.

15065 **Dietz, Maribel** Wandering monks, virgins, and pilgrims: ascetic travel in the Mediterranean world, A.D. 300-800. University Park, PA 2005, Pennsylvania State University Press ix; 270 pp. 0-271-02677-4. Bibl. 221-257.

15066 *Elsner, Jaś* Piety and passion: context and consensus in the audiences for early christian pilgrimage. Pilgrimage. 2005 ⇒958. 411-434.

15067 *Geus, C.H.J. de* Eeuwenlang geboeid en betoverd door het Heilige Land. Phoe. 51 (2005) 38-52.

15068 [E]**Herz, Randall** Die 'Reise ins Gelobte Land' Hans Tuchers des Älteren (1479-1480): Untersuchungen zur Überlieferung und kritische Edition eines spätmittelalterlichen Reiseberichts. Wsb 2002, Reichert xvii; 792 pp. €63. 38950-02540.

15069 *Jacoby, D.* Bishop Gunther of Bamberg, Byzantium and christian pilgrimage to the Holy Land in the eleventh century. [F]PRINZING, L. 2005 ⇒124. 267-285.

15070 *Kuelzer, A.* Byzantine and early post-Byzantine pilgrimage to the Holy Land and to Mount Sinai. Travel in the Byzantine world. [E]**Macrides, Ruth**: Aldershot 2002, Ashgate. 149-61. 07546-07687.

15071 *Lang, Bernhard* Der Orientreisende als Exeget, oder Turban und Taubenmist: Beiträge der Reiseliteratur zum Verständnis der Bibel im 18. und 19.Jh.. ZDPV 121 (2005) 67-85.

15072 [E]**Paoletti, Anna** Viaggio a Gerusalemme di Pietro Casola. Viaggiatori italiani dal Medioevo al Rinascimento, Oltramare 11: Alessandria 2001, Orso 345 pp.

15073 *Prousis, Theophilus C.* The holy places: a Russian travel perspective. SVTQ 49 (2005) 271-296.

15074 *Pullan, Wendy* 'Intermingled until the end of time': ambiguity as a central condition of early christian pilgrimage. Pilgrimage. 2005 ⇒ 958. 387-409.

[E]**Rutherford, I.** Pilgrimage in...christian antiquity 2005 ⇒958.

15075 **Serra, Armando** Pellegrinaggio al Monte Sinai dal IV s. al 2001. 2003 ⇒19,14357. [R]OCP 71 (2005) 249-251 (*Poggi, V.*).

15076 **Wolff, Anne** How many miles to Babylon?: travels and adventures to Egypt and beyond, from 1300 to 1640. 2003 ⇒19,14364. [R]IJMES 37 (2005) 133-134 (*Williams, Caroline*).

## U7 *Crucigeri*—**The Crusades**

15077 *Hillenbrand, Carole* The evolution of the Saladin legend in the west. MUSJ 58 (2005) 497-510.

15078 **Lower, Michael** The barons' crusade: a call to arms and its consequences. Ph 2005, U. of Pennsylvania 256 pp. £32.50.

15079 *Richard, Jean* Les mercenaires francs dans les armées musulmanes au temps des croisades. MUSJ 58 (2005) 227-237.

15080 *Scham, Sandra* Legacy of the Crusades. Secrets of the bible. 2005 ⇒482. 175-181.

15081 [T]**Sweetenham, Carol** ROBERT the Monk's History of the first crusade. Crusade Texts in Translation 11: Aldershot 2004, Ashgate ix; 243 pp.

15082 *Voisin, Jean-Claude* Les échanges Orient-Occident au Moyen Âge: les Thuringiens en Terre sainte. MUSJ 58 (2005) 239-268.

## U8 Communitates Terrae Sanctae

15083 **Anderson, Irvine** Biblical interpretation and Middle East policy: the promised land, America, and Israel, 1917-2002. Gainesville, Fla. 2005, Univ. Press of Florida x; 187 pp. $40. 08130-27985.

15084 *Brocke, Edna* Israel—Zivilgesellschaft und Religion. KuI 20 (2005) 156-161.

15085 *Buey, Félix del; Alvi, Cristóforo* Origenes de la custodia de Tierra Santa: ayuda de los reinos de Aragón, Nápoles y Castilla (capítulo reabierto). AIA 65 (2005) 7-96.

15086 *Hoppe, Leslie J.* The Middle East: then and now. BiTod 43 (2005) 141-146.

15087 **Kirchhoff, Markus** Text zu Land—Palästina im wissenschaftlichen Diskurs 1865-1920. Schriften des Simon-Dubnow-Instituts 5: Gö 2005, Vandenhoeck & R. 425 pp.

15088 **Krupp, Michael** Die Geschichte des Staates Israel: von der Gründung bis heute. [2]2004 ⇒20,13697. [R]Bibel und Liturgie 78 (2005) 48-49 (*Schipper, Friedrich*).

15089 *McGarry, Michael B.* The land of Israel in the cauldron of the Middle East: a challenge to Christian-Jewish relations. Seeing Judaism anew. 2005 ⇒618. 213-224.

15090 **O'Mahony, Anthony** Christian communities of Jerusalem and the Holy Land: studies in history, religion and politics. 2003 ⇒19, 14391. [R]JRH 29 (2005) 197-198 (*Masters, Bruce*); JRAS 15 (2005) 220-224 (*Freeman-Grenville, G.S.P.*).

15091 *Scham, Sandra* Hope amid the carnage. Secrets of the bible. 2005 ⇒482. 159-163. Palestinians & Israelis protect endangered sites.

15092 **Terra, João E.M.** A questão da Palestina. 2003 ⇒19,14393. [R]REB 65 (2005) 499-502 (*Pereira, Ney Brasil*).

15093 *Watzman, Haim* Biblical iconoclast. Secrets of the bible. Ment. *Finkelstein, Israel* 2005 ⇒482. 182-187.

# XX. Historia scientiae biblicae

## Y1.0 History of exegesis: General

15094 *Abouzayd, Shafiq* Ascetic movement in the east: origins, development and dissemination: in Syria, Iraq and Palestine. Christianity. 2005 ⇒607. 385-411.

15095 *Agosti, Gianfranco* Interpretazione omerica e creazione poetica nella tarda antichità. [F]HURST, A. 2005 ⇒64. 19-32.

15096 *Ayres, Lewis* The patristic hermeneutic heritage. Bible in pastoral practice. 2005 ⇒341. 25-41.

15097 **Badilita, Cristian** Métamorphoses de l'Antichrist chez les Pères de l'Eglise. ThH 116: P 2005, Beauchesne (8) 557 pp. 2-7010-1454-9. Bibl. 533-557. [R]REG 118 (2005) 312-314 (*Pouderon, Bernard*).

15098 *Bonney, Gillian* May bible scholars and fathers never meet?: a proposal for use in teaching. Sal. 67 (2005) 255-297.

15099 **Breck, John** Scripture in tradition: the bible and its interpretation in the Orthodox Church. 2001 ⇒17,12004; 20,13705. [R]OCP 71 (2005) 193-195 (*Farrugia, E.G.*).

15100 *Brock, Sebastian* The rise of christian thought: the theological schools of Antioch, Edessa and Nisibis. Christianity. 2005 ⇒607. 143-160.

15101 **Clark, Elizabeth A.** History, theory, text: historians and the linguistic turn. 2004 ⇒20,13706. [R]JBL 124 (2005) 582-584 (*Otten, Willemien*); RBLit (2005)* (*Otten, Willemien*).

15102 **Cook, John Granger** The interpretation of the Old Testament in Greco-Roman paganism. STAC 23: 2004 ⇒20,13708. [R]VigChr 59 (2005) 465-467 (*Van der Horst, Pieter W.*); ThLZ 130 (2005) 1167-1169 (*Dochhorn, Jan*).

15103 *Dal Covolo, Enrico* La *Lectio divina* nei padri della chiesa dalla 'svolta origeniana' alle regole monastiche, fino a Giugo II. Lectio divina. 2005 ⇒437. 97-111.

15104 **Daley, Brian** The hope of the early church: a handbook of patristic eschatology. [2]2003 <1991> ⇒19,14403; 20,13710. [R]ThLZ 130 (2005) 963-965 (*Ruge, Susanne*).

15105 *Escribano, Victoria* Heresy and orthodoxy in fourth-century Hispania: Arianism and Priscillianism. Hispania. 2005 ⇒617. 121-149.

15106 *Gahbauer, Ferdinand R.* Die Jakobsleiter, ein aussagenreiches Motiv der Väterliteratur. ZAC 9 (2005) 247-278 [Gen 28,12].

15107 *Gila, Angelo M.* Mariologia patristica. Maria madre del Signore. DSBP 41: 2005 ⇒579. 16-229.

15108 *Horne, Simon* 'These then let us emulate': the early church illuminates two gospel impairment encounters. [F]YOUNG, F. JSNT.S 295: 2005 ⇒168. 10-25 [Mt 9,1-8; Lk 13,11-16; John 5,2-18].

15109 **Kannengiesser, Charles** Handbook of patristic exegesis: the bible in ancient christianity, 1-2. The bible in ancient christianity 1: 2004 ⇒20,375. [R]Faith & Mission 22/2 (2005) 149-150 (*Nixon, John Ashley*); TrinJ 26 (2005) 338-340 (*Schnabel, Eckhard J.*); AUSS 43 (2005) 353-355 (*Martens, Peter*); REG 118 (2005) 316-317 (*Pouderon, Bernard*); TJT 21 (2005) 291-292 (*Keough, Shawn W.J.*); Bijdr. 66 (2005) 344-346 (*Koet, Bart J.*).

15110 **Laporte, Jean** Los padres de la iglesia: padres griegos y latinos en sus textos. Monumenta: 2004 ⇒20,13718. [R]EstJos 59 (2005) 153-154 (*Egido, Teófanes*).

15111 *Laurence, Patrick* La faiblesse féminine chez les Pères de l'Église. Les Pères de l'Église. ThH 117: 2005 ⇒813. 351-377.

15112 *Malaty, Tadros Y.* The rise of christian thought: theological thought in the school of Alexandria. Christianity. 2005 ⇒607. 121-141.

15113 **Mattei, Paul** Le christianisme antique (Ier-V[e] siècle). L'antiquité: une histoire: 2003 ⇒19,14413; 20,13721. [R]ASSR 130 (2005) 192-193 (*Gounelle, Rémi*).

15114 *Miller, Patricia C.* Shifting selves in late antiquity. Religion and the self in antiquity. 2005 ⇒818. 15-39.

15115 *Miller, Robert D., II* Reading scripture in communion with the church fathers. DR 432 (2005) 205-209.

15116 **Moreschini, Claudio; Norelli, Enrico** Early christian Greek and Latin literature: a literary history, 1: from Paul to the age of Constantine; 2: from the Council of Nicea to the beginning of the medieval period. Peabody, MA 2005, Hendrickson 455 + 754 pp. $100. 1-56563-606-6.

15117 **O'Keefe, John J.; Reno, Russel R.** Sanctified vision: an introduction to early christian interpretation of the bible. Baltimore 2005, Johns Hopkins xiii; 156 pp. $45/17. 0-8018-8087-4/8-2. Bibl. 149-152. [R]RBLit (2005)* (*Nicklas, Tobias; Sigismund, Marcus*).

15118 **Sandys-Wunsch, John** What have they done to the bible?: a history of modern biblical interpretation. ColMn 2005, Liturgical 378 pp. $40. 0-8146-5028-7. Bibl. 341-362.

15119 *Stroumsa, Guy G.* From master of wisdom to spiritual master in late antiquity. Religion and the self in antiquity. 2005 ⇒818. 183-196.

15120 **Tábet, Miguel Angel** Le trattazioni teologiche sulla bibbia: un approccio alla storia dell'esegesi. Parola di Dio 22: 2003 ⇒19,14418; 20,13729. [R]Asp. 52 (2005) 281-282 (*Rolla, Armando*).

15121 **Trevijano Etcheverria, Ramón** La bibbia nel cristianesimo antico: esegesi prenicena, scritti gnostici, apocrifi del Nuovo Testamento. [E]*Zani, Antonio*: Introduzione allo studio della Bibbia 10: 2003 ⇒19,14421. [R]RBLit (2005)* (*West, James E.*).

15122 *Vercruysse, Jean-Marc* Voir le diable derrière l'idole à l'époque patristique. L'idole dans l'imaginaire occidental. 2005 ⇒524. 117-28.

15123 *Vian, Giovanni M.* Filología e historia de los textos cristianos. M 2005, Cristiandad 471 pp.

15124 *Wallraff, Martin* Von der antiken Historie zur mittelalterlichen Chronik: die Entstehung christlicher Universalgeschichtsschreibung. Welt-Zeit. 2005 ⇒597. 1-19.

15125 *Watts, Edward* The student self in late antiquity. Religion and the self in antiquity. 2005 ⇒818. 234-251.

15126 **Wilken, Robert Louis** The spirit of early christian thought: seeking the face of God. 2003 ⇒19,14423; 20,13731. [R]JThS 56 (2005) 207-208 (*Casiday, A.M.C.*);

15127 NHv 2005 <2003>, Yale Univ. Pr. xxii; 367 pp. $19. 03001-53983.

### Y1.4 *Patres apostolici et saeculi II*—**First two centuries**

15128 *Aasgaard, Reidar* Brothers and sisters in the faith: christian siblingship as an ecclesiological mirror in the first two centuries. The formation of the early church. WUNT 183: 2005 ⇒708. 285-316.

15129 *Alexander, Loveday* The Four among pagans. [F]STANTON, G. Ment. *Celsus* 2005 ⇒138. 222-237.

15130 *Bellinzoni, Arthur J.* The gospel of Luke in the Apostolic Fathers: an overview. Trajectories. 2005 ⇒753. 45-68.

15131 *Birley, Anthony R.* Attitudes to the state in the Latin Apologists. L'apologétique chrétienne. EnAC 51: 2005 ⇒13520. 249-277.

15132 *Brent, Allen* IGNATIUS and POLYCARP: the transformation of New Testament traditions in the context of mystery cults. Trajectories. 2005 ⇒753. 325-349.

15133 **Daniélou, Jean** Teología del judeocristianismo. [T]*Esquivias Villalobos, A.* 2004 ⇒20,13740. [R]EstB 63 (2005) 348-352 (*Sen, Felipe*).

15134 *Ehrman, Bart D.* Textual traditions compared: the New Testament and the apostolic fathers. The reception of the NT. 2005 ⇒752. 9-27.

15135 [ET]**Ehrman, Bart D.** The Apostolic Fathers. LCL 24-25: 2003 ⇒ 19,14429. [R]AnCl 74 (2005) 367-368 (*Schamp, Jacques*).

15136 *Filoramo, Giovanni* La falsità della profezia e la costruzione della comunità cristiana. Modi di comunicazione. 2005 ⇒858. 223-246.

15137 *Grech, Prosper* Agli inizi della teologia cristiana. Il messaggio biblico. SRivBib 44: 2005 <1993> ⇒216. 23-88.

15138 *Gregory, Andrew F.* Reflections on method: what constitutes the use of the writings that later formed the New Testament in the apostolic fathers?. The reception of the NT. 2005 ⇒752. 61-82.

15139 *Haehling, Raban von* Voraussehung und Willensfreiheit: die geistige Auseinandersetzung der frühen Christen mit dem Erzählgut der griechischen Tragödie. Griechische Mythologie. 2005 ⇒542. 339-358.

15140 **Jefford, Clayton N.** The Apostolic Fathers: an essential guide. Nv 2005, Abingdon 133 pp. $15. 0-687-34204-X. Bibl. 131-133.

15141 *Koester, Helmut* Gospel and gospel traditions in the second century. Trajectories. 2005 ⇒753. 27-44.

15142 *Lindemann, Andreas* Paul's influence on 'CLEMENT' and IGNATIUS. Trajectories. 2005 ⇒753. 9-24.

15143 *Lombino, Vincenzo* Male–Maligno–peccato nei padri greci dei primi due secoli. Male. DSBP 39: 2005 ⇒580. 27-121.

15144 *Löhr, Winrich A.* Deutungen der Passion Christi bei Heiden und Christen im zweiten und dritten Jahrhundert. Deutungen. WUNT 181: 2005 ⇒392. 545-574.

15145 **Middleton, Paul** Radical martyrdom and cosmic conflict in early christianity. [D]*Hurtado, L.* 2005, 300 pp. Diss. Edinburgh [RTL 37, 616].

15146 **Muradyan, Gohar** Physiologus: the Greek and Armenian versions with a study of translation technique. Hebrew University Armenian Studies 6: Lv 2005, Peeters v; 215 pp. 90429-16575.

15147 *Petersen, William L.* Textual traditions examined: what the text of the apostolic fathers tells us about the text of the New Testament in the second century. The reception of the NT. 2005 ⇒752. 29-46.

15148 **Pouderon, Bernard** Les apologistes grecs du IIe siècle. Initiations aux Pères de l'église 18: P 2005, Cerf 355 pp. €35. 2-204-07531-0. Bibl. 323-345 [BCLF 677,14].

15149 *Ramelli, Ilaria* Gesù tra i sapienti greci perseguitati ingiustamente in un antico documento filosofico pagano di lingua siriaca. RFNS 97 (2005) 545-570.

15150 *Stewart-Sykes, Alistair* Prophecy and patronage: the relationship between charismatic functionaries and household officers in early christianity. Trajectories. 2005 ⇒753. 165-189.

15151 **Susini, Mirella** Il martirio cristiano esperienza di incontro con Cristo: testimonianze dei primi tre secoli. Teologia viva 46: 2002 ⇒ 19,14435. [R]StPat 52 (2005) 657-658 (*Corsato, Celestino*).

15152 *Trevett, Christine* The church before the bible. Bible in pastoral practice. 2005 ⇒341. 5-24.

15153 **Uthemann, Karl-Heinz** Christus, Kosmos, Diatribe: Themen der fruehen Kirche als Beitraege zu einer historischen Theologie. B 2005, De Gruyter xii; 665 pp. 3-11-018428-1. Bibl. 557-561, Uthemann 563-570.

[E]**Wlosok, A.** L'apologétique chrétienne 2005 ⇒13520.

15154 *Wright, David F.* The Apostolic Fathers and infant baptism: any advance on the obscurity of the New Testament?. Trajectories. 2005 ⇒753. 123-133.

15155 *Wyrwa, Dietmar* Religiöses Lernen im zweiten Jahrhundert und die Anfänge der alexandrinischen Katechetenschule. Religiöses Lernen. WUNT 180: 2005 ⇒384. 271-305.

15156 *Young, Frances* Wisdom in the Apostolic Fathers and the New Testament. Trajectories. 2005 ⇒753. 85-104.

15157 ARISTIDES A: [ET]**Pouderon, Bernard; Pierre, Marie-Joseph**, *al.*, Aristide: Apologie. SC 470: 2003 ⇒19,14439. [R]RSR 93 (2005) 110-112 (*Sesboüé, Bernard*).

15158 BARNABAS: *Carleton-Paget, James* The *Epistle of Barnabas* and the writings that later formed the New Testament. The reception of the NT. 2005 ⇒752. 229-249.

15159 BASILIDES: *Kelhoffer, James A.* Basilides's gospel and Exegetica (Treatises). VigChr 59 (2005) 115-134.

15160 CLEMENS A: *Bianco, Maria G.* Male–Maligno–peccato in Clemente Alessandrino. Male. DSBP 39: 2005 ⇒580. 205-220;

15161 *Brown, Michael J.* Jewish salvation in Romans according to Clement of Alexandria in Stromateis 2 [Rom 10-11];

15162 *Gaca, Kathy L.* A response: is Clement of Alexandria a supersessionist? [Resp. to Brown];

15163 Response: elucidating Romans in *Stromateis* 2 [Resp. to Welborn]. Early patristic readings. 2005 ⇒393. 42-62/63-65/84-86;

15164 *Herrmann, John; Van den Hoek, Annewies* The sphinx: sculpture as a theological symbol in PLUTARCH and Clement of Alexandria. [F]LUTTIKHUIZEN, G.: AGJU 59: 2005 ⇒93. 285-310;

15165 *Merino, Marcelo* El Stromata VIII de Clemente de Alejandría. ScrTh 37 (2005) 13-51;

15166 **Osborn, Eric Francis** Clement of Alexandria. C 2005, CUP xviii; 324 pp. $85. 0-521-83753-7. Bibl. 293-304;

15167 *Rizzerio, Laura* Le "prêtre véritable" chez Clément d'Alexandrie. [F]RIES, J. 2005 ⇒127. 143-155;

15168 [E]**Van den Hoek, Annewies** Clément d'Alexandrie: les Stromates: Stromate IV. [T]*Mondésert, Claude*: SC 463: 2001 ⇒17,12051; 19, 14444. [R]REAug 51 (2005) 187-192 (*Rizzi, Marco*);

15169 *Van den Hoek, Annewies* Apologetic and protreptic discourse in Clement of Alexandria. L'apologétique chrétienne. EnAC 51: 2005 ⇒13520. 69-93;

15170 *Vanderheijden, Stephanie* Mythos zwischen Aberglaube und Philosophie in den Stromateis des Clemens von Alexandrien. Griechische Mythologie. 2005 ⇒542. 295-310;

15171 *Welborn, L.L.* The soteriology of Romans in Clement of Alexandria's *Stromateis* 2: faith, fear, and assimilation to God. Early patristic readings. 2005 ⇒393. 66-83.

15172 CLEMENS R: *Amsler, Frédéric* Les citations évangéliques dans le roman pseudo-clémentin: une tradition indépendante du Nouveau Testament?. Le canon du NT. MoBi 54: 2005 ⇒334. 141-167;

15173 Les Homélies du Pseudo-Clement ou comment justifier l'octroi d'une chaire d'enseignement à un croyant d'origine païenne. Analyse narrative. BEThL 191: 2005 ⇒742. 337-350;

15174 **Bakke, Odd Magne** "Concord and peace": a rhetorical analysis of the first letter of Clement with an emphasis on the language of unity and sedition. WUNT 2/143: 2001 ⇒17,12053... 19,14446. [R]ThLZ 130 (2005) 265-8 (*Löhr, Hermut*); RSR 93 (2005) 108-9 (*Sesboüé, Bernard*);

15175 *Gregory, Andrew F.* 1 Clement and the writings that later formed the New Testament. The reception of the NT. 2005 ⇒752. 129-57;

15176 *Gregory, Andrew F.; Tuckett, Christopher M.* 2 Clement and the writings that later formed the New Testament. The reception of the NT. 2005 ⇒752. 251-292;

15177 *Jones, F. Stanley* Jewish christianity of the Pseudo-Clementines. A companion to second-century christian 'heretics'. VigChr.S 76: 2005 ⇒567. 315-334;

15178 *Kelley, Nicole* Problems of knowledge and authority in the Pseudo-Clementine romance of Recognitions. JECS 13 (2005) 315-348;

15179 **Löhr, Hermut** Studien zum frühchristlichen und frühjüdischen Gebet: Untersuchungen zu 1 Clem 59 bis 61 in seinem literarischen, historischen und theologischen Kontext. WUNT 160: 2003 ⇒19, 14456; 20,13763. [R]RSR 93 (2005) 109-110 (*Sesboüé, Bernard*);

[E]**Luisier, P.** Studi su Clemente Romano 2003 ⇒850.

15180 *Pratscher, Wilhelm* Die theologische Reflexion im 2. Clemensbrief. [F]NIEDERWIMMER, K. Gutachten und Studien 2: 2005 ⇒112. 81-96.

15181 DIDACHE: *Claussen, Carsten* The eucharist in the gospel of John and in the *Didache*. Trajectories. 2005 ⇒753. 135-163;

15182 **Del Verme, Marcello** Didache and Judaism: Jewish roots of an ancient Christian-Jewish work. 2004 ⇒20,13765. [R]RBLit (2005)* (*Van de Sandt, Huub*);

15183 *Draper, Jonathan A.* First-fruits and the support of prophets, teachers, and the poor in *Didache* 13 in relation to New Testament parallels. Trajectories. 2005 ⇒753. 223-243;

Didache...Matthew...Judaism? 2005 ⇒5663;

15184 *Jefford, Clayton N.* Social locators as a bridge between the *Didache* and Matthew. Trajectories. 2005 ⇒753. 245-264;

15185 *Kloppenborg, John S.* Didache 1.1-6.1, James, Matthew, and the Torah. Trajectories. 2005 ⇒753. 193-221;

15186 The use of the synoptics or Q in *Did.* 1:3b-2:1. Matthew and the Didache. 2005 ⇒797. 105-129;

15187 *Milavec, Aaron* The Didache: a window on Gentile christianity before the written gospels. The Fourth R [Santa Rosa, CA] 18/3 (2005) 7-11, 15-16 [NTAb 50,142];

15188 A rejoinder. JECS 13 (2005) 519-523 [Resp. to Tuckett];

15189 When, why, and for whom was the Didache created?: insights into the social and historical setting of the Didache communities. Matthew and the Didache. 2005 ⇒797. 63-84;

15190 **Milavec, Aaron** The Didache: faith, hope, & life of the earliest christian communities, 50-70 C.E. 2003 ⇒19,14469; 20,13767. [R]AThR 87 (2005) 154-155 (*Vivian, Tim*); Neotest. 39 (2005) 203-207 (*Draper, Jonathan A.*); Theoforum 36 (2005) 226-228 (*Coyle, J. Kevin*); RBLit (2005)* (*Bredin, Mark; Nicklas, Tobias*);

15191 The Didache: text, translation, analysis, and commentary. 2004 ⇒ 20,13767. [R]Worship 79 (2005) 185-187 (*Johnson, Maxwell E.*); RBLit 7 (2005) 458-460 (*Peerbolte, Bert J.L.*);

15192 *Öhler, Markus* Die Didache und antike Vereinsordnungen—ein Vergleich. [F]NIEDERWIMMER, K. 2005 ⇒112. 35-65;

15193 *Rouwhorst, Gerard* Didache 9-10: a litmus test for the research on early christian liturgy eucharist;

15194 *Syreeni, Kari* The Sermon on the Mount and the two ways teaching of the Didache [Mt 5-7];

15195 *Tomson, Peter J.* The halakhic evidence of Didache 8 and Matthew 6 and the Didache community's relationship to Judaism. Matthew and the Didache. 2005 ⇒797. 143-156/87-103/131-141;

15196 *Tuckett, Christopher* The Didache and the Synoptics once more: a response to Aaron Milavec. JECS 13 (2005) 509-18 [⇒19,14466];

15197 The Didache and the writings that later formed the New Testament. The reception of the NT. 2005 ⇒752. 83-127;

*Tuilier, A.* Les charismatiques dans la Didachè 2005 ⇒5723;

15198 *Van de Sandt, Huub* The Egyptian background of the 'ointment' prayer in the eucharistic rite of the Didache (10.8). [F]LUTTIKHUIZEN, G.: AGJU 59: 2005 ⇒93. 227-245;

15199 Two windows on a developing Jewish-Christian reproof practice: Matt 18:15-17 and *Did.* 15:3. Matthew and the Didache. 2005 ⇒ 797. 173-192;

15200 **Van de Sandt, Huub; Flusser, David** The Didache: its Jewish sources &...place in early Judaism & Christianity. 2002 ⇒18,13361 ...20,13769. [R]BiblInterp 13 (2005) 333-336 (*Draper, Jonathan*);

15201 *Varner, W.* The Didache's use of the Old and New Testaments. MastJ 16/1 (2005) 127-151 [NTAb 50,144];

15202 *Verheyden, Joseph* Eschatology in the Didache and the gospel of Matthew. Matthew and the Didache. 2005 ⇒797. 193-215;

15203 *Wolmarans, Johannes L.* The semiotics of the ritual meal in the "Didache". APB 16 (2005) 308-324.

15204 DIOGNETUS: *Pouthier, Jean-Luc* Die Christen sind die Seele der Welt: die Apologie an Diogenet. WUB 38 (2005) 38-39.

15205 HERMAS: [TE]**Mangoni, Maria B.** Erma: Il pastore. 2003 ⇒19, 14481; 20,13775. [R]Alpha Omega 8 (2005) 334-35 (*Furlong, Jude*);

15206 *Verheyden, Joseph* The *Shepherd of Hermas* and the writings that later formed the New Testament. The reception of the NT. 2005 ⇒ 752. 293-329.

15207 HIPPOLYTUS R: **Bradshaw, Paul F.; Johnson, Maxwell E.; Phillips, Edward** The Apostolic tradition: a commentary. [E]*Attridge, Harold W.* 2002 ⇒18,13330... 20,13778. [R]JEH 56 (2005) 547-548 (*Brent, Allen*); VigChr 59 (2005) 337-340 (*Rouwhorst, Gerard*); ThQ 185 (2005) 323-326 (*Winkler, Gabriele*);

15208 *Nicolotti, Andrea* Che cos'è la *Traditio apostolica* di Ippolito?: in margine ad una recente pubblicazione. RiSCr 2/1 (2005) 219-237.

15209 IGNATIUS A: *Foster, Paul* The epistles of Ignatius of Antioch and the writings that later formed the New Testament. The reception of the NT. 2005 ⇒752. 159-186;

15210 *Hill, Charles E.* Ignatius, 'the gospel', and the gospels. Trajectories. 2005 ⇒753. 267-285;

15211 *Isacson, Mikael* Follow your bishop!: rhetorical strategies in the letters of Ignatius of Antioch. The formation of the early church. WUNT 183: 2005 ⇒708. 317-340;

15212 **Isacson, Mikael** To each their own letter: structure, themes, and rhetorical strategies in the letters of Ignatius of Antioch. CB.NT 42: 2004 ⇒20,13782. [R]RBLit (2005)* (*Tite, Philip*);

15213 *Maier, Harry O.* The politics and rhetoric of discord and concord in Paul and Ignatius. Trajectories. 2005 ⇒753. 307-24 [1 Cor 1-4].

15214 *Marshall, John W.* The objects of Ignatius' wrath and Jewish angelic mediators. JEH 56 (2005) 1-23;

15215 *Myllykoski, Matti* Wild beasts and rabid dogs: the riddle of the heretics in the letters of Ignatius. The formation of the early church. WUNT 183: 2005 ⇒708. 341-377;

15216 *Reis, David M.* Following in Paul's footsteps: *mimēsis* and power in Ignatius of Antioch. Trajectories. 2005 ⇒753. 287-305;

15217 *Weinandy, Thomas G.* The apostolic christology of Ignatius of Antioch: the road to Chalcedon. Trajectories. 2005 ⇒753. 71-84.

15218 IRENAEUS L: **Aróztegui Esnaola, Manuel** La amistad del verbo con Abraham según San Ireneo de Lyon. AnGr 108: R 2005, E.P. U.G. 293 pp. 88-7839-008-9 [Gen 12,1];

15219 *Bassler, Jouette M.* A response to Jeffrey Bingham and Susan Graham: networks and Noah's sons, Early patristic readings. 2005 ⇒ 393. 133-151 [Rom 8-11];

15220 *Bendinelli, Guido* Fede e gnosi nel cristianesimo primitivo: Ireneo e Clemente Alessandrino a confronto. DT(P) 108/41 (2005) 13-54;

15221 *Bingham, D. Jeffrey* Irenaeus reads Romans 8: resurrection and renovation. Early patristic readings. 2005 ⇒393. 114-132;

15222 *Graham, Susan* Irenaeus as reader of Romans 9-11: olive branches;

15223 *Markschies, Christoph* A response to Jeffrey Bingham and Susan Graham [Rom 8-11]. Early patristic readings. 2005 ⇒393. 87-113/ 152-158;

15224 **Mutschler, Bernhard** Irenäus als johanneischer Theologe: Studien zur Schriftauslegung bei Irenäus von Lyon. STAC 21: 2004 ⇒20, 13787. [R]ThRv 101 (2005) 227-229 (*Gemeinhardt, Peter*);

15225 **Osborn, Eric Francis** Irenaeus of Lyons. 2001 ⇒17,12108... 20,13791. [R]JR 85 (2005) 312-313 (*Grant, Robert M.*);

15226 *Perrone, Lorenzo* Eine 'verschollene Bibliothek'?: das Schicksal frühchristlicher Schriften (2.-3. Jahrhundert)—am Beispiel des Irenäus von Lyon. ZKG 116 (2005) 1-29;

15227 *Steenberg, Matthew C.* To test or preserve?: the prohibition of Gen 2.16-17 in the thought of two second-century exegetes. Gr. 86 (2005) 723-741. Irenaeus; Theophilus of Antioch.

15228 JUSTINUS M: **Allert, Craig D.** Revelation, truth, canon and interpretation: studies in Justin Martyr's Dialogue with Trypho. SVigChr 64: 2002 ⇒18,13384. [R]ThLZ 130 (2005) 665-667 (*Ulrich, Jörg*); RSR 93 (2005) 117-118 (*Sesboüé, Bernard*); JThS 56 (2005) 210-213 (*Lieu, Judith*);

15229 *Bobichon, Philippe* Justin martyr: étude stylistique du *Dialogue avec Tryphon* suivie d'une comparaison avec l'*Apologie* et le *De resurrectione*. RechAug 34 (2005) 1-61;

15230 [ET]**Bobichon, Philippe** Justin Martyr, Dialogue avec Tryphon. Paradosis 47/1-2: 2003 ⇒19,14503; 20,13799. [R]EeV 134 (2005) 20-21 (*Winling, Raymond*); ThLZ 130 (2005) 669-671 (*Ulrich, Jörg*);

15231 **Granados, José** Los misteros de la vida de Cristo en Justino Mártir. AnGr 296: R 2005, E.P.U.G. 599 pp. €40. 88-7839-048-8.

15232 **Heimgartner, Martin** Pseudojustin—über die Auferstehung: Text und Studie. PTS 54: 2001 ⇒17,12114... 20,13804. [R]RSR 93 (2005) 115-117 (*Sesboüé, Bernard*);

15233 **Horner, Timothy** "Listening to Trypho": Justin Martyr's Dialogue reconsidered. CBET 28: 2001 ⇒17,12116...20,13805. [R]ThLZ 130 (2005) 406-409 (*Skarsaune, Oskar*); REJ 164 (2005) 571-573 (*Bobichon, Philippe*); RHE 100 (2005) 852-6 (*Sanchez, Sylvain J.G.*);

15234 **Kibangu Malonda, Denis Benjamin** Revelation et cultures chez Saint Justin martyr. R 2005, Pontificia Universitatis Lateranensis 125 pp. Extrait de thèse; Bibl. 103-120;

15235 *Manns, Frédéric* Justin's Dialogue with Trypho. Beginnings of christianity. 2005 ⇒786. 359-378;

15236 [E]**Marcovich, Miroslav** Iustinus Martyr: Apologiae pro christianis —Dialogus cum Tryphone. PTS 38/47: B 2005, De Gruyter xi; 211 pp / xv; 399 pp. €128. 3-11-018541-5. 1994; 1997;

15237 *Nigro, Giovanni* L'esegesi del Salmo 21 in Giustino. VetChr 42 (2005) 73-102;

15238 **Sanchez, Sylvain J.G.** Justin apologiste chrétien: travaux sur le *Dialogue avec Tryphon* de Justin Martyr. CRB 50: 2000 ⇒16,12554 ... 20,13810. [R]ThLZ 130 (2005) 58-60 (*Skarsaune, Oskar*);

15239 *Ulrich, Jörg* Innovative Apologetik: Beobachtungen zur Originalität Justins am Beispiel der Lehre vom Logos spermatikos und anderer Befunde. ThLZ 130 (2005) 1-16.

15240 MARCION: *Ardovino, Adriano* "Der fremde Gott": aspetti della ricezione del "Marcione" di HARNACK e trasformazioni storiche della categoria di "marcionismo". AnStR 6 (2005) 99-134;

15241 *Bloth, Peter C.* Beobachtungen und Fragen zur Edition von Adolf HARNACKs erster 'Marcion'-Schrift. ZKG 116 (2005) 79-89;

15242 *Detering, H.* Is LUCIAN's 'On the death of Perigrinus' a satire on Marcion?. JHiC 11/1 (2005) 69-94 [NTAb 50,138];

15243 **Harnack, Adolf von** Marcion: l'évangile du Dieu étranger: une monographie sur l'histoire de la fondation de l'église catholique. [T]*Lauret, Bernard*: 2003 <1921> ⇒19,14515; 20,13813. [R]RSR 93 (2005) 112-115 (*Sesboüé, Bernard*); VigChr 59 (2005) 103-104 (*Meijering, E.P.*); OrChr 89 (2005) 227-230 (*Possekel, Ute*);

15244 Marcion: der moderne Gläubige des 2. Jahrhunderts, der erste Reformator. [E]*Steck, Friedemann*: TU 149: 2003 ⇒19,14516. [R]ThLZ 130 (2005) 185-187 (*Greschat, Katharina*);

**May, G.** Markion: gesammelte Aufsätze 2005 ⇒256;

15245 *Räisänen, Heikki* Marcion. A companion to second-century christian 'heretics'. VigChr.S 76: 2005 ⇒567. 100-124;

15246 [E]**Steck, Friedemann** Adolf HARNACK: Marcion: der moderne Gläubige des 2. Jahrhunderts, der erste Reformator. [D]*Barth, Ulrich*: TU 149: 2003, xlvii; 446 pp. €128. 3-11-0175-339. Diss. Halle-Wittenberg. [R]ZKG 116 (2005) 79-89 (*Bloth, Peter C.*);

15247 *Stern, Jean* Marcionisme, néo-marcionisme et tradition de l'église. RThom 105 (2005) 473-506;

15248 *Tardieu, Michel* Markion, der radikale Bruch: zwei Götter und zwei Testamente?. WUB 38 (2005) 34-37.

15249 MELITO S: *Wifstrand, Albert* The homily of Melito on the Passion. Epochs and styles. WUNT 179: 2005 <1948> ⇒325. 111-132.

15250 MONTANUS: *Marjanen, Antti* Montanism: egalitarian ecstatic 'new prophecy'. A companion to second-century christian 'heretics'. VigChr.S 76: 2005 ⇒567. 185-212.

15251 PAPIAS: *Gundry, Robert H.* The apostolically Johannine pre-Papian tradition concerning the gospels of Mark and Matthew. The old is better. WUNT 178: 2005 ⇒220. 49-73;

15252 *Norelli, Enrico* Papias de Hiérapolis a-t-il utilisé un recueil "canonique" des quatre évangiles?. Le canon du NT. MoBi 54: 2005 ⇒ 334. 35-85;

15253 ET**Norelli, Enrico** Papias di Hierapoli: esposizione degli oracoli del Signore: i frammenti. Mi 2005, Paoline 596 pp. €34. 88315-27525.

15254 POLYCARPUS S: *Dehandschutter, Boudewijn* The New Testament and the *Martyrdom of Polycarp*;

15255 *Hartog, Paul A.* The opponents of Polycarp, *Philippians*, and 1 John;

15256 *Holmes, Michael W.* The *Martyrdom of Polycarp* and the New Testament passion narratives. Trajectories. 2005 ⇒753. 395-405/ 375-391/407-432;

15257 Polycarp's *Letter to the Philippians* and the writings that later formed the New Testament. The reception of the NT. 2005 ⇒752. 187-227.

15258 TATIANUS: **Hunt, Emily J.** Christianity in the second century: the case of Tatian. 2003 ⇒19,14524; 20,13820. RAnCl 74 (2005) 368-370 (*Schamp, Jacques*); JR 85 (2005) 662-663 (*Droge, A.J.*);

15259 *Petersen, William L.* Tatian the Assyrian. A companion to second-century christian 'heretics'. VigChr.S 76: 2005 ⇒567. 125-158.

15260 THEOPHILUS A: ET**Martín, José Pablo** Teófilo de Antioquía: a Autólico. Fuentes patrísticas 16: 2004 ⇒20,13821. REstTrin 39 (2005) 113-114 (*Silanes, N.*); StPat 52 (2005) 653-655 (*Corsato, Celestino*).

## Y1.6 **Origenes**

15261 *Agosti, Gianfranco* Origenis, *In Gen.* 1.14 (MS 2634/2). Greek Papyri, Volume I. 2005 ⇒682. 73-75.

15262 ET**Amacker, René; Junod, Éric** PAMPHILUS Caesariensis—EUSEBIUS Caesariensis: Apologie pour Origène: suivi de RUFIN d'Aquilée: Sur la falsification des livres d'Origène. SC 464-465: 2002 ⇒ 18,13419. RRSR 93 (2005) 122-123 (*Sesboüé, Bernard*).

15263 *Bastit, Agnès* Typologie des prologues aux commentaires des évangiles. Commento a Giovanni di Origene. 2005 ⇒789. 83-115.

15264 *Bendinelli, Guido* Male–Maligno–peccato nell'opera di Origene. Male. DSBP 39: 2005 ⇒580. 221-264;

15265 Il *Commento a Giovanni* e la tradizione scolastica dell'antichità. Commento a Giovanni di Origene. 2005 ⇒789. 133-156.

15266 *Bennett, Byard* The soiling of sinful flesh: primordial sin, inherited corruption and moral responsibility in DIDYMUS the Blind and Origen. Adamantius 11 (2005) 77-92.

15267 *Buchinger, Harald* Towards the origins of paschal baptism: the contribution of Origen. StLi 35 (2005) 12-31.

15268 **Buchinger, Harald** Pascha bei Origenes, 1: diachrone Präsentation; 2: systematische Aspekte. [D]*Auf der Maur, Jörg; Lies, Lothar*: IThS 64: Innsbruck 2005, Tyrolia 2 vols; 1038 pp. €98. 3-7022-25-42-0. Diss. Wien 2001.

15269 *Bumazhnov, Dmjtrij F.* Towards a better understanding of the identity of the 'simple people': some remarks concerning Origen's treatment of previous exegetical traditions: CIo XIII,325-337. Commento a Giovanni di Origene. 2005 ⇒789. 413-422.

15270 [E]**Castagno, Adele M.** La biografia di Origene fra storia e agiografia. Villa Verucchio 2004, Pazzini 332 pp. VI Conv. Gruppo di ricerca su Origene...

15271 *Cattaneo, Enrico* L'episodio della Samaritana (Gv 4,1-42) come paradigma di conversione dallo gnosticismo. Commento a Giovanni di Origene. 2005 ⇒789. 537-553;

15272 La dottrina dei "sensi spirituali" in Origene: nuovi apporti. Adamantius 11 (2005) 101-113.

15273 *Ciner, Patricia A.* Misterio, esoterismo e iniciación en la teología de Orígenes. Epimelia 14 (2005) 65-80.

15274 *Clark, Elizabeth A.* Origen, the Jews, and the Song of Songs: allegory and polemic in christian antiquity. Perspectives on the Song of Songs. 2005 ⇒401. 274-293.

15275 *Clements, Ruth* Origen's readings of Romans in *Peri Archon*: (re)-constructing Paul. Early patristic readings. 2005 ⇒393. 159-179 [Rom 2,28-29; 1 Cor 10,18].

15276 *Cocchini, Francesca* Origene e la lavanda dei piedi nel commentario al vangelo di Giovanni. Atti del X Simposio di Efeso. Turchia 19: 2005 ⇒785. 119-128 [John 13];

15277 La chiesa nel *Commento a Giovanni*. Commento a Giovanni di Origene. 2005 ⇒789. 333-360.

15278 *Contreras, Enrique; Peña, Roberto* Orígenes: Homilía XXVII sobre el libro de los Numeros. Soleriana 30/1 (2005) 37-138.

15279 *Cosgrove, Charles H.* A response to Ruth Clements and Sze-kar Wan: will the real Paul please stand up!. Early patristic readings. 2005 ⇒393. 195-205.

15280 *Dal Covolo, Enrico* Argomentazioni patristiche sulla verità: "Ego sum via et veritas" (cf. Gv 14,6) in Origene e in AGOSTINO. [F]GHIBERTI, G.: SRivBib 46: 2005 ⇒47. 309-321;

15281 La lectio divina nei padri della chiesa: dalla 'svolta origeniana' alle regole monastiche, fino a Guigo II. Ripartire da Cristo. 2005 ⇒ 800. 73-85.

15282 **Dawson, John David** Christian figural reading and the fashioning of identity. 2002 ⇒18,13429... 20,13830. [R]PSB 26 (2005) 241-243 (*Parsenios, George*).

15283 **Dively Lauro, Elizabeth Ann** The soul and spirit of scripture within Origen's exegesis. BAChr 3: Lei 2005, Brill xii; 250 pp. 0-391-04199-1. Bibl. 241-245.

15284 *Drecoll, Volker H.* Giuda Iscariota nel *Commento a Giovanni*. Commento a Giovanni di Origene. 2005 ⇒789. 555-570 [John 13].

15285 *Dunn, Matthew W.* Origen reconsidered as an exegete of scripture. TJT 21/2 (2005) 153-168.

15286 *Georgi, Dieter* IRENAEUS's and Origen's treatment of Paul's epistle to the Romans: an assessment;

15287 *Gorday, Peter* A response: Origen's Christian Platonist readings of Romans. Early patristic readings. 2005 ⇒393. 206-212/180-183.

15288 *Grech, Prosper* Justification by faith in Origen's *Commentary on Romans*. Il messaggio biblico. SRivBib 44: 2005 <1996> ⇒216. 259-276.

15289 *Heine, Ronald E.* The testimonia and fragments related to Origen's commentary on Genesis. ZAC 9 (2005) 122-142.

15290 **Henne, Philippe** Introduction à Origène: suivie d'une anthologie. Initiations aux pères de l'église: 2004 ⇒20,13833. [R]Brot. 160 (2005) 409-410 (*Silva, Isidro Ribeiro da*); LTP 61 (2005) 179-181 (*Bélanger, Steve*); RHPhR 85 (2005) 470-471 (*Gounelle, R.*); SR 34 (2005) 584-586 (*Zamagni, Claudio*); POC 55 (2005) 490-491 (*Attinger, D.*).

15291 *Heyer, René* Sacrificier la promesse?: le sacrifice d'Isaac dans la lecture d'Origène. RevSR 79 (2005) 408-416 [Gen 22].

15292 *Hirshman, Marc* Origen and the rabbis on Leviticus. Adamantius 11 (2005) 93-100.

15293 *Junod, Eric* Origène face au problème du désaccord (διαφωνία) entre les évangiles (CIo X, 3-36). Commento a Giovanni di Origene. 2005 ⇒789. 423-439.

15294 *Le Boulluec, Alain* De Paul à Origène: continuité ou divergence?. Allégorisme des poètes. 2005 ⇒874. 113-132;

15295 La foi (*pistis*) entre croyance et savoir selon Origène dans le *Contre Celse*. Théologiques 13 (2005) 59-78.

15296 *Lettieri, Gaetano* Il νοῦς mistico: il superamento origeniano dello gnosticismo nel *Commento a Giovanni*. Commento a Giovanni di Origene. 2005 ⇒789. 177-275.

15297 **Lubac, Henri de** Histoire et Esprit: l'intelligence de l'écriture d'après Origène. Oeuvres complètes 16: 2002 <1950> ⇒18,13418; 19,14567. [R]RSR 93 (2005) 127-128 (*Sesboüé, Bernard*).

15298 *Markschies, Christoph* Der Heilige Geist im Johanneskommentar: einige vorläufige Bemerkungen. Commento a Giovanni di Origene. 2005 ⇒789. 277-299;

15299 Die Origenes-Editionen der Berliner-Akademie: Geschichte und Gegenwart. Adamantius 11 (2005) 39-49.

15300 *Mazzucco, Clementina* L'Apocalisse nel *Commento a Giovanni*. Commento a Giovanni di Origene. 2005 ⇒789. 571-611.

15301 [E]**McGuckin, John Anthony** The Westminster handbook to Origen. 2004 ⇒20,13839. [R]AThR 87 (2005) 357-358 (*Vivian, Tim*); CTJ 40 (2005) 368-370 (*Payton, James R., Jr.*); TJT 21 (2005) 297-298 (*Keough, Shawn W.J.*); JThS 56 (2005) 217-218 (*Widdicombe, Peter*).

15302 *Metzler, Karin* Weitere Testimonien und Fragmente zum Genesis-Kommentar des Origenes. ZAC 9 (2005) 143-148;

15303 Genesiskommentierung bei Origenes und PROKOP von Gaza. Adamantius 11 (2005) 114-123.

15304 **Moser, Maureen** Teacher of holiness: the Holy Spirit in Origen's *Commentary on the epistle to the Romans*. Gorgias Diss. 17; Early Christian Studies 4: Piscataway, NJ 2005, Gorgias xii; 231 pp. 1-593-33149-5. Bibl. 205-225.

15305 *Navascués, Patricio de* La ciudad de Cafarnaún: notas de topografía teológica en HERACLEÓN y Orígenes. Commento a Giovanni di Origene. 2005 ⇒789. 519-535.

15306 *Nesterova, Olga* Les interprétations modernes de la doctrine origénienne des "trois sens" de l'Écriture: examen critique. Adamantius 11 (2005) 184-210.

15307 *Noce, Carla* Cristo gran sacerdote secondo l'ordine di Melchisedech nel *Commento a Giovanni*;

15308 *Norelli, Enrico* La profezia nel *Commento a Giovanni*;

15309 *Pazzini, Domenico* Considerazioni sulla lingua del *Commento a Giovanni*;

15310 *Pennacchio, Maria C.* Da Okeanos al Logos: trasformazioni esegetiche di un fiume cosmico: la simbologia del Giordano nel *Commento a Giovanni* [Josh 3-4];

15311 *Perrone, Lorenzo* Il profilo letterario del *Commento a Giovanni*: operazione esegetica e costruzione del testo. Commento a Giovanni di Origene. 2005 ⇒789. 449-461/301-331/117-131/463-482/43-81;

15312 Tradizione alessandrina e studi origeniani: prospettive della ricerca. Adamantius 11 (2005) 7-8;

15313 Fra silenzio e parola: dall'apologia alla testimonianza del cristianesimo nel *Contro Celso* di Origene. L'apologétique chrétienne. EnAC 51: 2005 ⇒13520. 103-141.

15314 [E]**Perrone, Lorenzo** Origeniana Octava: Origen and the Alexandrian tradition. BEThL 164: 2003 ⇒19,699. [R]StPat 52 (2005) 655-657 (*Corsato, Celestino*); ZKG 116 (2005) 256-258 (*Gemeinhardt, Peter*); JThS 56 (2005) 664-667 (*Gould, Graham*).

15315 *Pietras, Henryk* Dio d'elezione (CIo II, 24);

15316 *Piscitelli Carpino, Teresa* L'esegesi di Gv 1,29b "Ecco l'agnello di Dio che prende su di sé il peccato del mondo": dalla conoscenza del Battista al sacrificio di Cristo. Commento a Giovanni di Origene. 2005 ⇒789. 441-448/483-517 [John 1,15-37].

15317 [E]**Pizzolato, Luigi F.; Rizzi, Marco** Origene maestro di vita spirituale: Origen: master of spiritual life. SPMed 22: 2001 ⇒18,653... 20,13841. [R]RSR 93 (2005) 128-129 (*Sesboüé, Bernard*).

15318 *Prinzivalli, Emanuela* L'uomo il suo destino nel *Commento a Giovanni*. Commento a Giovanni di Origene. 2005 ⇒789. 361-379.

15319 *Rizzi, Marco* Un'ipotesi sulla provenienza dell'*Encomio di Origene* attribuito a GREGORIO il Taumaturgo. Adamantius 11 (2005) 124-132.

15320 **Röwekamp, Georg** Streit um Origenes: eine theologiegeschichtliche Untersuchung zur Apologie für Origenes des PAMPHILUS von Caesarea. 2005, Diss. Paderborn [ThRv 102,x].

15321 [E]**Simonetti, Manlio** Origene: omelie sulla Genesi. 2002 ⇒18, 13448; 19,14595. [R]Asp. 52 (2005) 285-286 (*Longobardo, Luigi*);

15322 Origene: omelie sull'Esodo. [T]*Danieli, Maria I.*: Opere di Origene 2: R 2005, Città N. 438 pp. €55. 88-311-9523-9.

15323 **Simonetti, Manlio** Origene esegeta e la sua tradizione. 2004 ⇒20, 13845. [R]ASEs 22 (2005) 257-258 (*Villani, Andrea*).

15324 *Simonetti, Manlio* Su un passo della traduzione latina del *Commento a Matteo* di Origene (12,9-14). Aug. 45 (2005) 265-294 [Mt 16, 13-20];

15325 Il *Commento a Giovanni* tra esegesi e teologia;

15326 *Somos, Róbert* Elements of the theory of scientific knowledge in the *Commentary on John*. Commento a Giovanni di Origene. 2005 ⇒789. 15-41/157-175.

15327 *Torjesen, Karen Jo* The enscripturation of philosophy: the incorporeality of God in Origen's exegesis. Biblical interpretation. SBL. Symp. 26: 2005 ⇒758. 73-84.

15328 *Van der Horst, Pieter W.* 'The God who drowned the king of Egypt': a short note on an exorcistic formula. [F]LUTTIKHUIZEN, G.: AGJU 59: 2005 ⇒93. 135-139 [Exod 15,4; Deut 11,3-4].

15329 *Van Nuffelen, Peter* Two fragments from the *Apology for Origen* in the *Church history* of SOCRATES Scholasticus. JThS 56 (2005) 103-114.

15330 *Wan, Sze-kar* Jews and gentiles in Origen's *Commentarii in epistulam Pauli ad Romanos*. Early patristic readings. 2005 ⇒393. 184-194 [Rom 2,9-10; 2,17-24; 3,29; 11,25].

## Y1.8 Tertullianus

15331 **Alexandre, Jérôme** Le Christ de Tertullien. CJJC 88: 2004 ⇒20, 13853. [R]Gr. 86 (2005) 189-190 (*Ladaria, Luis F.*); TS 66 (2005) 672-674 (*Efroymson, David P.*).

15332 *Chapot, Frédéric, al.*, Chronica Tertullianea et Cyprianea 2004. REAug 51 (2005) 375-413;

15333 Langue du droit et littérature: à propos de quelques mots du vocabulaire de la propriété chez Tertullien. [F]HEIM, F. 2005 ⇒59. 3-24.

15334 *Dunn, Geoffrey D.* Rhetoric and Tertullian's *De virginibus velandis*. VigChr 59 (2005) 1-30.

15335 **Dunn, Geoffrey D.** Tertullian. 2004 ⇒20,13858. [R]Theoforum 36 (2005) 228-238 (*Coyle, J. Kevin*).

15336 **Foster, Edgar G.** Angelomorphic christology and the exegesis of Psalm 8:5 in Tertullian's *Adversus Praxean*: an examination of Tertullian's reluctance to attribute angelic properties to the Son of God. Lanham 2005, University Press of America xxiv; 101 pp. 0-7618-3314-5. Bibl. 93-98 [Ps 8,5].

15337 *Fredouille, Jean-Claude* Réflexions de Tertullien sur l'allégorie. Allégorisme des poètes. 2005 ⇒874. 133-148;

15338 Notes sur Tertullien, An., 53,4 et Res., 8,2. REAug 51 (2005) 9-19;

15339 Observations sur la terminologie anthropologique de Tertullien: constantes et variations. Les Pères de l'Église. ThH 117: 2005 ⇒ 813. 321-334.

15340 *Gallon-Sauvage, Anne-Laure Delphines Neptuno uomunt*: Tertullien et les dauphins du Cirque. [F]HEIM, F. 2005 ⇒59. 25-36.

15341 **Hunink, Vincent** Tertullian: De Pallio. Amst 2005, Gieben 332 pp. 90-5063-4397.

15342 **Rambaux, Claude** L'accès à la vérité chez Tertullien. CollLat 293: Bru 2005, Latomus 264 pp. 2-87031-2342.

15343 *Scopello, Madeleine* Femme et societé dans les polémiques contre les gnostiques: quelques notes sur IRÉNÉE et Tertullien. Femme, gnose. 2005 <1989> ⇒12237. 203-235.

15344 *Vicastillo, Salvador* El pecado original en el pensamiento de Tertuliano. RevAg 46 (2005) 277-295.

15345 *Zanetti, Paolo S.* Note su Tertulliano e FILONE d'Alessandria. Imitatori di Gesù Cristo. 2005 <1959> ⇒330. 37-61;

15346 Avulsi sumus in eis (Ez. 37,11 ap. Tert. *Resurr.* 29,12). Imitatori di Gesù Cristo. 2005 <1990> ⇒330. 477-482.

15347 **Zilling, Henrike Maria** Tertullian: Untertan Gottes und des Kaisers. 2004 ⇒20,13866. [R]EstAg 40 (2005) 184-185 (*De Luis, P.*); HZ 281 (2005) 156-158 (*Klein, Richard*).

Y2.0 *Patres graeci*—**The Greek Fathers**—*in ordine alphabetico*

15348 *Carrara, Paolo* Male–Maligno–peccato nei padri antiocheni. Male. DSBP 39: 2005 ⇒580. 289-305.

15349 *Frede, Michael* Les *Catégories* d'ARISTOTE et les Pères de l'Église grecs. Les *Catégories* et leur histoire. 2005 ⇒624. 135-173.

15350 *Geerlings, Wilhelm* Das Bild des Sängers Orpheus bei den griechischen Kirchenvätern. Griechische Mythologie. 2005 ⇒542. 254-267.

15351 *Girardi, Mario* 1 Cor 7 nell'esegesi di BASILIO e GREGORIO di Nazianzo: l'economia salvifica fra matrimonio e verginità;

15352 Gli "sciti" fra mito e storia nei Cappadoci [Col 3,11]. VetChr 42 (2005) 59-72/275-287.

15353 **Russell, Norman** The doctrine of deification in the Greek patristic tradition. Oxf 2004, OUP xiv; 418 pp. 01992-65216. Bibl. 345-80.

15354 *Trisoglio, Francesco* Il male, il peccato, il Maligno nei padri cappadoci. Male. DSBP 39: 2005 ⇒580. 265-288.

15355 *Uthemann, Karl-Heinz* Dritter Bericht zur griechischen Patristik: über Editionen und Textkritik, Handschriften, Instrumente und Verwandtes (1998-2001) (3. Teil). ZAC 9 (2005) 3-50.

15356 ASTERIUS S.: [T]**Kinzig, Wolfram** Asterius Sophistas: Psalmenhomilien. BGrL 56-57: 2002 ⇒18,13468; 19,14621. [R]ThLZ 130 (2005) 400-402 (*Vinzent, Markus*); RSR 93 (2005) 132-133 (*Sesboüé, Bernard*); VigChr 59 (2005) 93-102 (*Leonhard, Clemens*).

15357 ATHANASIUS A: *Aragione, Gabriella* La lettre festale 39 d'Athanase: présentation et traduction de la version copte et de l'extrait grec. Le canon du NT. MoBi 54: 2005 ⇒334. 197-219;

15358 **Ernest, James D.** The bible in Athanasius of Alexandria. TBAC 2: 2004 ⇒20,13875. [R]RBLit (2005)* (*Zamagni, Claudio*);

15359 *Marasco, Gabriele* Atanasio fra storia ed agiografia. Sal. 67 (2005) 829-859.

15360 BASILIUS C: [T]**Harrison, Nonna Verna** St. Basil the Great: On the human conditio. Crestwood, NY 2005, St. Vladimir's Seminary Press 126 pp. 0-88141-294-5. Bibl. 125-126.

15361 CHRYSOSTOMUS: **Amirav, Hagit** Rhetoric and tradition : John Chrysostom on Noah and the Flood. 2003 ⇒19,14628; 20,13884. [R]RHE 100 (2005) 549-551 (*Petit, Françoise*) [Gen 6-9];

15362 *Barone, Francesca P.* Per un'edizione critica delle omelie *De Davide et Saule* di Giovanni Crisostomo. Aug. 45 (2005) 231-258;

15363 **Brottier, Laurence** L'appel des "demi-chrétiens" à la "vie angélique": Jean Chrysostome prédicateur entre idéal monastique et réalité mondaine. P 2005, Cerf 421 pp. 2-204-07478-0. Bibl. 389-394;

15364 *Hall, Christopher A.* John Chrysostom. Reading Romans. 2005 ⇒400. 39-57;

15365 [T]**Hill, Robert C.** St. John Chrysostom: eight sermons on the book of Genesis. 2004 ⇒20,13890. [R]EThL 81 (2005) 533-534 (*Leemans, Johan*);

15366 **Mayer, Wendy** The homilies of St John Chrysostom, provenance: reshaping the foundations. OCA 273: R 2005, Pontificio Istituto Orientale 570 pp. 88-7210-347-9. Bibl. 15-19;

15367 *Miranda, Americo* La definizione di 'uomo spirituale' nell'esegesi alla *Prima ai Corinzi* di Giovanni Crisostomo. BeO 47 (2005) 169-184;

15368 *Mondet, Jean-Pierre* Le sacerdoce ministériel dans le *Commentaire sur l'épître aux Hébreux* de S. Jean Chrysostome. FRIES, J. 2005 ⇒ 127. 157-176;

15369 **Naidu, Ashish** The doctrine of Christ as it relates to the christian life in John Chrysostom's Homilies on the gospel of John and Hebrews. D*McFarland, I.* 2005, Diss. Aberdeen [RTL 37,620];

15370 **Roten, Philippe de** Baptême et mystagogie: enquête sur l'initiation chrétienne selon S. Jean Chrysostome. LWQF 91: Müns 2005, Aschendorff xlv; 498 pp. 3-402-04070-0. Bibl. xv-xxx;

15371 TE**Zincone, Sergio** Giovanni Crisostomo: omelie sul vangelo di Matteo: introduzione, traduzione e note. CTePa 170-172: 2003 ⇒ 19,14636. RSal. 67 (2005) 595-598 (*Pasquato, Ottorino*).

15372 CYRILLUS A: E**Weinandy, Thomas G.; Keating, Daniel A.** The theology of St Cyril of Alexandria: a critical appreciation. 2003 ⇒ 19,14644; 20,13904. RHeyJ 46 (2005) 387-388 (*Hill, Robert C.*).

15373 CYRILLUS H: *Kalleres, Dayna S.* Cultivating true sight at the center of the world: Cyril of Jerusalem and the Lenten Catechumenate. ChH 74 (2005) 431-459;

15374 *Stewart-Sykes, Alistair* The anaphora of *Catecheses mystagogicae* 5 and the *Birkath ha-mazon*: a study in development. Aug. 45 (2005) 309-347;

15375 **Yarnold, Edward** Cyril of Jerusalem. 2000 ⇒16,12634; 18, 13488. RIThQ 70 (2005) 81-82 (*Lang, Uwe M.*).

15376 DIDYMUS C: **Layton, Richard A.** Didymus the Blind and his circle in late-antique Alexandria: virtue and narrative in biblical scholarship. 2004 ⇒20,13908. RCHR 91 (2005) 513-4 (*O'Keefe, John J.*);

15377 T**Prinzivalli, E.** Didimo il Cieco: lezioni sui salmi. LCPM 37: Mi 2005, Paoline 900 pp. RVetChr 42 (2005) 175-177 (*Aulisa, Immacolata*);

15378 **Steiger, Peter** Theological anthropology in the Commentary on Genesis by Didymus the Blind. D*Young, R.D.* 2005, 414 pp. Diss. Catholic Univ. of America [RTL 37,621].

15379 DIO P: *Moles, J.* The thirteenth oration of DIO Chrysostom: complexity and simplicity, rhetoric and moralism, literature and life. JHS 125 (2005) 112-138 [NTAb 50,361].

15380 EPIPHANIUS C: *Bumazhnov, Dmitrij F.* Einige Aspekte der Nachwirkung des Ancoratus und des Panarion des hl. Epiphanius von Salamis in der früheren monastischen Tradition. Adamantius 11 (2005) 158-178;

15381 **Osburn, Carroll D.** The text of the Apostolos in Epiphanius of Salamis. The NT in the Greek Fathers 6: 2004 ⇒20,13910. RRBLit (2005)* (*Wasserman, Tommy; Williams, Peter*).

15382 EUSEBIUS C: **Carriker, Andrew** The library of Eusebius of Caesarea. SVigChr 67: 2003 ⇒19,14657; 20,13912. RThLZ 130 (2005)

404-406 (*Winkelmann, Friedhelm*); VigChr 59 (2005) 462-465 (*Inowlocki, Sabrina*);

15383 *Jacobson, Howard* Eusebius, Polyhistor and Ezekiel. JSPE 15/1 (2005) 75-77;

15384 **Kofsky, Arieh** Eusebius of Caesarea against paganism. Jewish and Christian Perspectives 3: Lei 2000, Brill xiii; 337 pp. €118/$148. 90041-16427. RVigChr 59 (2005) 209-212 (*Johnson, Aaron P.*);

15385 *Morgan, Teresa* Eusebius of Caesarea and christian historiography. At. 93 (2005) 193-208;

15386 *Pierri, Rosario* La preposizione πρὸς nell'Onomastico di Eusebio di Cesarea (III-IV sec.). LASBF 55 (2005) 141-164;

15387 *Pinzone, Antonino* Eusebio e la storiografia profana: il caso della *Praeparatio Evangelica*. Sal. 67 (2005) 645-669;

15388 E**Timm, Stefan** Eusebius Caesariensis: das Onomastikon der biblischen Ortsnamen: Edition der syrischen Fassung mit griechischem Text, englischer und deutscher Übersetzung. TU 152: B 2005, De Gruyter viii; 253 pp. €98. 3-11-018191-6;

15389 *Ulrich, Jörg* Eusebius als Kirchengeschichtsschreiber. Antike Historiographie. BZNW 129: 2005 ⇒348. 277-287;

15390 **Zamagni, Claudio** Eusebii Caesarensis Quaestionum concordantia: textus iuxta Vat. Pal. AlOm 245: Hildesheim 2005, Olms 426 pp. 3487-13074-2.

15391 EUSTATIUS A.: E**Declerck, José H.** Eustatius, Antiochenus: opera quae supersunt omnia. CChr.SG 51: 2002 ⇒18,13498. RJThS 56 (2005) 219-221 (*Ward, Robin*).

15392 EVAGRIUS P: *Brakke, David* Making public the monastic life: reading the self in Evagrius Ponticus' talking back. Religion and the self in antiquity. 2005 ⇒818. 222-233;

15393 **Dysinger, Luke** Psalmody and prayer in the writings of Evagrius Ponticus. Oxford Theological Monographs: Oxf 2005, OUP ix; 245 pp. £55. 0-19-927320-0. Diss.; Bibl. 217-235.

15394 GREGORIUS NAZ: *Bezarashvili, Ketevan* The significance of Gregory the theologian's works for the Georgian literary tradition. Muséon 118 (2005) 269-297;

15395 *Elm, Susanna* Hellenism and historiography: Gregory of Nazianzus and JULIAN in dialogue. The cultural turn. 2005 ⇒670. 258-277;

15396 *Gautier, Francis* À propos du témoignage de Grégoire de Nazianze sur le concile de Constantinople (mai-juillet 381) aux vers 1750-1755 du *De uita sua*. REAug 51 (2005) 67-76;

15397 E**Haelewyck, Jean-Claude** Sancti Gregorii Nazianzeni opera: versio syriaca, 3: orationes XXVII, XXXVIII, XXXIX. CChr.SG 53; Corpus Nazianzenum 18: Turnhout 2005, Brepols lxxxii; 193 pp. 2-503-40531-2;

15398 **McGuckin, John** Saint Gregory of Nazianzus: an intellectual biography. 2001 ⇒19,14666; 20,13928. RCrSt 26 (2005) 569-572 (*McLynn, Neil*);

15399 E**Moreschini, Claudio** Gregorio di Nazianzo: Tutte le orazioni. T*Sani, Chiara; Vincelli, Maria*: Mi 22002, Bompiani cv; 1420 pp. 88-452-9034-4. Pref. *Carmelo Crimi; Chiara Sani*; Bibl. xxix-xxxv.

15400 GREGORIUS NYS: [T]**Albl, Martin C.** Pseudo-Gregory of Nyssa: Testimonies against the Jews. WGRW 5: 2004 ⇒20,13932. [R]RBLit (2005)* (*Stander, Hennie*);

15401 *Ayres, Lewis* Deification and the dynamics of Nicene theology: the contribution of Gregory of Nyssa. SVTQ 49 (2005) 375-394;

15402 *Bonato, Antonio* La conoscenza mistica nelle *Omelie sul Cantico* di Gregorio di Nissa. Teol(Br) 30 (2005) 49-74;

15403 *Dal Bosco, Flavio* In viaggio verso l'ἀρετή: ἄσκησις ed ἐπιθυμία nel pensiero di Gregorio di Nissa. StPat 52 (2005) 771-816;

15404 *Daniélou, Jean* La typologie biblique de Grégoire de Nysse. Bulletin des amis du Cardinal Daniélou 31 (2005) <1967> 48-58 < SMSR 38,185-196;

15405 *Geljon, Albert-Kees* Divine infinity in Gregory of Nyssa and PHILO of Alexandria. VigChr 59 (2005) 152-177;

15406 **Laird, Martin** Gregory of Nyssa and the grasp of faith: union, knowledge, and divine presence. 2004 ⇒20,13939. [R]WThJ 67 (2005) 184-187 (*Fairbairn, Donald*);

15407 *Lallemand, Annick* Références médicales et exégèse spirituelle chez Grégoire de Nysse. Les Pères de l'Église. ThH 117: 2005 ⇒ 813. 401-426;

15408 **Lilla, Salvatore Romano Clemente** Neuplatonisches Gedankengut in den 'Homilien über die Seligspreisungen,' Gregors von Nyssa. [E]*Drobner, Hubertus R.*: SVigChr 68: 2004 ⇒20,13940. [R]ThLZ 130 (2005) 1078-1079 (*Zachhuber, Johannes*);

15409 **Pachas Zapata, José Antonio** El misterio de Dios y su comunicación gratuita en el *In inscriptiones psalmorum* de Gregorio de Nisa. AFTC 56/1: Santiago 2005, Pont. Univ. Católica de Chile 316 pp;

15410 [ET]**Reynard, Jean** Grégoire de Nysse: sur les titres des Psaumes. SChr 466: 2002 ⇒18,13514... 20,13943. [R]ScEs 57 (2005) 181-184 (*Cazelais, Serge*);

15411 *Simonelli, Cristina* Conformati dalla grazia dello Spirito Santo (Gregorio di Nissa, *In Cant VII*). Teol(Br) 30 (2005) 75-91;

15412 *Zachhuber, Johannes* Once again: Gregory of Nyssa on universals. JThS 56 (2005) 75-98.

15413 HIPPOLYTUS R.: **Cerrato, John A.** Hippolytus between East and West: the commentaries and the provenance of the corpus. OTM: 2002 ⇒18,13518; 20,13944. [R]JR 85 (2005) 504-505 (*Johnson, Maxwell E.*); SVTQ 49 (2005) 353-355 (*Stewart-Sykes, Alistair*); VigChr 59 (2005) 85-92 (*Scholten, Clemens*); RivCC 81 (2005) 331-332 (*Heid, Stefan*);

15414 *Nicolotti, Andrea* Che cos'è la "Traditio apostolica" di Ippolito?: in margine ad una recente pubblicazione. RiSCr 2/1 (2005) 219-237.

15415 MAXIMUS C: **Kattan, Assaad Elias** Verleiblichung und Synergie: Grundzüge der Bibelhermeneutik bei Maximus Confessor. SVigChr 63: 2003 ⇒19,14679; 20,13947. [R]RSR 93 (2005) 146-148 (*Sesboüé, Bernard*).

15416 MELITO S: [⇒15249] *Broadhurst, Laurence* Melito of Sardis, the Second Sophistic, and 'Israel'. Rhetoric and reality. SCJud 16: 2005 ⇒515. 49-74.

15417 NONNOS P: *Lozza, Giuseppe* Postille al Canto XI della *Parafrasi* di Nonno di Panopoli. Nuovo e antico. 2005 ⇒634. 527-541.

15418 PHILOPONUS J: [E]**Congourdeau, Marie-Hélène** Jean Philopon: La création du monde. [T]*Rosset, Marie-Claude*: Les pères dans la foi 87: 2004 ⇒20,13949. [R]LTP 61 (2005) 198-200 (*Dritsas-Bizier, Moa*); ETR 80 (2005) 137-138 (*Molac, Philippe*).

15419 SEVERUS A: **Allen, Pauline; Hayward, Robert** Severus of Antioch. L 2004, Routledge vii; 200 pp. 0-415-23401-8. Bibl. 185-192.

15420 SOZOMENUS: **Festugière, André-Jean; Grillet, Bernard; Sabbah, Guy** Sozomène: Histoire ecclésiastique: livres V-VI. SC 495: P 2005, Cerf 489 pp. 2204-07918-9. Texte grec de l'édition J. Bidez–G.C. Hansen (GCS).

15421 THEODORE M: **Thome, Felix** Historia contra Mythos: die Schriftauslegung DIODORS von Tarsus und Theodors von Mopsuestia im Widerstreit zu Kaiser JULIANS und SALUSTIUS' allegorischem Mythenverständnis. Hereditas 24: 2004 ⇒20,13956. [R]CHR 91 (2005) 131-132 (*Bowersock, G.W.*); EThL 81 (2005) 531-533 (*Auwers, Jean Marie*); RHE 100 (2005) 179-182 (*Petit, Françoise*); JThS 56 (2005) 675-676 (*Lössl, Josef*).

15422 THEODORETUS C: *Guinot, Jean-Noël* Doit-on glorifier le Christ ou le Fils Monogène?: la défense par Théodoret de Cyr d'une doxologie incriminée (*ep.* 147). REAug 51 (2005) 327-356;

15423 *Martin, Annick* RUFIN et Théodoret: deux mal aimés de l'historiographie. [F]THELAMON, F. 2005 ⇒148. 135-147;

15424 [E]**Petit, Françoise** Autour de Théodoret de Cyr: la Collectio Coisliniana sur les derniers livres de l'Octateuque et sur les Règnes; le Commentaire sur les Règnes de PROCOPE de Gaza. 2003 ⇒19, 14688. [R]Muséon 118 (2005) 171-174 (*Auwers, Jean-Marie*).

15425 THEODORUS M: *Flores, Daniel E.* Thomas on the problem of Theodore of Mopsuestia, exegete. Thom. 69 (2005) 251-277;

15426 *Pappas, Harry S.* Theodore of Mopsuestia's *Commentary on Psalm 44*: a study of exegesis and christology. DBM 23/1 (2005) 77-96. **G**.

### Y2.4 Augustinus

15427 [E]**Van Geest, P.; Van Oort, J.** Augustiniana neerlandica: aspecten van Augustinus' spiritualiteit en haar doorwerking. Lv 2005, Peeters vii; 539 pp. €45. 90-429-1627-3.

15428 **Akamine, Julio Endi** 'Non enim misit Deus Filium in mundum, ut iudicet mundum, sed ut salvetur mundus per ipsum' (Io 3,17): o Pai como origem das missões salvíficas nos: *Tractatus CXXIV In Iohannis evangelium* de Santo Agostinho de Hipona. [D]*Pastor, Félix*: R 2005, 116 pp. Extr. Diss. Gregoriana; Bibl. 97-110.

15429 [T]**Alici, Luigi; Pizzani, Ubaldo; Di Pilla, Alessandra** Sant'Agostino: Contro Fausto Manicheo (libri 20-33). Nuova Biblioteca Agostiniana 14/2: 2004 ⇒20,13960. [R]RTE 9/1 (2005) 323-325 (*Scimè, Giuseppe*).

15430 *Alvarez Maestro, Jesús* San Agustín y el pensamiento hebreo. Augustinus 50 (2005) 11-27.

15431 [T]**Andigné-Kfouri, Marie-Hélène d'** Saint Augustin: de consensu euangelistarum, livre III, commentaire et traduction. [D]*Fredouille, Jean-Claude* 2005, 2 vols; 157 + 160 pp. Diss. Paris IV-Sorbonne.

15432 **Berrouard, Marie-François** Introduction aux homélies de saint Augustin sur l'évangile de saint Jean. Coll. EAug.Antiquité 170: 2004 ⇒20,13963. RVetChr 42 (2005) 177-178 (*Maselli, Maria*).

15433 *Blanchard, Yves-Marie* Le Christ médecin et la relecture augustinienne du prologue johannique [John 1,13];

15434 *Bochet, Isabelle* Maladie de l'âme et thérapeutique scripturaire selon Augustin. Pères de l'Église. 2005 ⇒813. 477-495/379-400.

15435 **Bochet, Isabelle** 'Le firmament de l'Ecriture': l'herméneutique augustinienne. 2004 ⇒20,13964. RREAug 51 (2005) 461-2 (*Bouton-Touboulic, Anne-Isabelle*).

15436 *Bouton-Touboulic, Anne-Isabelle* La voix de la vérité, un élément de démonstration chez saint Augustin. Pallas 69 (2005) 179-193.

15437 *Bright, Pamela* Augustine. Reading Romans. 2005 ⇒400. 59-80.

15438 **Brown, Peter** Santo Agostinho—uma biografia. T*Ribeiro, Vera*: Rio de Janeiro 2005, Record 669 pp.

15439 *Bruns, Peter* Augustinus von Hippo. Grosse Gestalten. 2005 ⇒623. 21-28.

15440 Bulletin augustinien pour 2004/2005 et compléments d'années antérieures. REAug 51 (2005) 415-499.

15441 **Burnell, Peter** The Augustinian person. Wsh 2005, Catholic University of America Pr. 218 pp. 0-8132-1418-1. Bibl. 205-208.

15442 *Caltabiano, Matilde* Agostino e i suoi libri: dalla composizione alla diffusione. Aug. 45 (2005) 519-537.

15443 *Chase, Michael* PORPHYRE et Augustin: des trois sortes de "visions" au corps de résurrection. REAug 51 (2005) 233-256.

15444 **Clark, Gillian** Augustine: the Confessions. Exeter 2005, Bristol Phoenix xvi; 104 pp. 1-904675-40-9. Bibl. 97-101.

15445 E**Daur, Kl.D.** Sancti Aurelii Augustini epistulae LVI-C. CChr.SL 31 A; Aurelii Augustini opera 3/2: Turnhout 2005, Brepols xvii; 266 pp. 2-503-00313-3.

15446 *Dodaro, Robert* Cristo, eucaristia e fame dell'essere umano nella teologia di Agostino d'Ippona. Conc(I) 41 (2005) 247-254; Conc(D) 41,172-177.

15447 *Dolbeau, François* Une citation non reconnue de Job 31,11 (LXX) dans un sermon d'Augustin. Augustin et la prédication en Afrique;

15448 Une citation d'Isaïe (57,8 LXX), non reconnue dans les éditions d'Augustin. Augustin et la prédication en Afrique. 2005 ⇒15450. 157-159/155-156 [RBen 116,155—P.-M. Bogaert];

15449 Une compilation morale africaine formée d'extraits de saint Augustin. RechAug 34 (2005) 143-193.

15450 E**Dolbeau, François** Augustin et la prédication en Afrique: recherches sur divers sermons authentiques, apocryphes ou anonymes. EAug.Antiquité 179: LvN 2005, Brepols viii; 687 pp. €69. 19. 2-85121-210-9.

15451 *Doyle, Daniel E.* Spread throughout the world: hints on Augustine's understanding of Petrine ministry. JECS 13 (2005) 233-246.

15452 *Drobner, Hubertus R.* Augustinus als Redner und Prediger in Theorie und Praxis. WuD 28 (2005) 361-372.

15453 T**Drobner, Hubertus R.** Augustinus von Hippo: Predigten zum Buch Genesis. 2000 ⇒16,12698. RVigChr 59 (2005) 341-6 (*Bastiaensen, Antoon*);

15454 Predigten zu den Büchern Exodus, Könige und Job ('Sermones' 6-12). 2003 ⇒19,14698. RAnCl 74 (2005) 377-378 (*Savon, Hervé*);

15455 Predigten zum Buch der Sprüche und Jesus Sirach (Sermones 35-41). Patrologia 13: 2004 ⇒20,13973. RRBen 115 (2005) 441-442 (*Baise, Ignace*); REAug 51 (2005) 443-444 (*Dolbeau, François*).

15456 *Dulaey, Martine* L'apprentissage de l'exégèse biblique par Augustin (3): années 393-394. REAug 51 (2005) 21-65.

15457 *Eguiarte Bendímez, Enrique A.* 'Spiritus rectus, spiritus sanctus, spiritus principalis': la triple epíclesis de 'en. Ps.' 50. Augustinus 50 (2005) 91-105.

15458 **Ellingsen, Mark** The richness of Augustine: his contextual and pastoral theology. LVL 2005, Westminster xiv; 216 pp. £14. 0-664-22618-3.

15459 **Evans, Chris** Augustine's theology of divine inspiration in the production and reading of ecclesiastical writings. D*Steinhauser, K.B.* 2005, Diss. St. Louis [RTL 37,620].

15460 *Flores, Miguel* La comunidad cristiana de Jerusalén en san Agustín: estudio exegético-teológico. Augustinus 50 (2005) 303-395 [Acts 2,42-45; 4,32-35].

15461 *François, Wim* Johannes DRIEDO's *De ecclesiasticis scripturis et dogmatibus* (1533) on scripture, Augustine, and the catholic tradition. Augustiniana neerlandica. 2005 ⇒15427. 427-466 [VigChr 59,472 —J. van Oort]. '**Netherlandic**'.

15462 **Fuhrer, Therese** Augustinus. 2004 ⇒20,13979. RThLZ 130 (2005) 1077-1078 (*Mühlenberg, Ekkehard*).

15463 **García Grimaldos, M.** El nuevo impulso de San Agustín a la antropología cristiana. R 2005, Inst. Patristicum Augustinianum 532 pp.

15464 **Genovese, Armando S.** Agostino e il Cantico dei Cantici: tra esegesi e teologia. SEAug 80: 2002 ⇒18,13551; 19,14712. RTer. 56 (2005) 306-307 (*Sánchez, Manuel Diego*).

15465 *Georgi, Dieter* Should Augustine have the last word on urban theology?. The city in the valley. 2005 ⇒214. 195-220.

15466 *Gnilka, Christian* Bemerkungen zum Text der Confessionen Augustins. VigChr 59 (2005) 178-186.

15467 *Grech, Prosper* L'ermeneutica agostiniana: il terzo libro del *De doctrina christiana*. Il messaggio biblico. SRivBib 44: 2005 <1995> ⇒216. 163-177.

15468 *Greer, Rowan A.* Sighing for the love of truth: Augustine's quest. God, truth, and witness. 2005 ⇒532. 13-34.

15469 *Grossi, Vittorino* La problematica del male–Maligno–peccato in s. Agostino. Male. DSBP 39: 2005 ⇒580. 366-388.

15470 *Harkins, Franklin* Nuancing Augustine's hermeneutical Jew: allegory and actual Jews in the bishop's sermons. JSJ 36 (2005) 41-64.

15471 *Kamimura, Naoki* Augustine's first exegesis and the divisions of spiritual life. AugSt 36 (2005) 421-432.

15472 **Kapusta, Pawel** Articulating creation, articulating kerygma: a theological interpretationof evangelisation and Genesis narrative in the writings of Saint Augustine of Hippo. EHS.T 804: Fra 2005, Lang 296 pp. $58. 3-6315-3368-3.

15473 *Kloos, Kari* Seeing the invisible God: Augustine's reconfiguration of theophany narrative. AugSt 36 (2005) 397-420.

15474 *Kotzé, Annemaré Confessiones* 13: Augustine, the Manichaeans, and the creation narrative. Augustiniana neerlandica. 2005 ⇒

15427. 149-161 [VigChr 59,472—J. van Oort] [Gen 1-2]. **'Netherlandic'**.

15475 *Lam Cong Quy, Joseph* Religionsbegriff bei Augustinus und Kant: Augustinus von Hippo und Immanuel KANT zum 1650. Geburtstag bzw. 200. Todestag. Aug. 45 (2005) 549-570.

15476 *Leijendekkers, Hélène* Idithun: a new suggestion for a spiritual reading of some of Augustine's commentaries on the Psalms. Augustiniana neerlandica. 2005 ⇒15427. 225-238 [VigChr 59,472—J. van Oort] [Ps 38; 61; 76]. **'Netherlandic'**.

15477 *Lévy, Carlos* L'Académicien et le Cynique: Augustin et la négation de l'altérité. Pallas 69 (2005) 195-205.

15478 *Massin, Marianne* L'esthétique augustinienne. LTP 61 (2005) 63-75.

15479 **Matthews, Gareth B.** Augustine. Oxf 2005, Blackwell x; 148 pp. $55. [R]IPQ 45 (2005) 417-418 (*Evans, G.R.*).

15480 [E]**Mayer, Cornelio** CAG 2. Corpus Augustinianum Gissense: die elektronische Edition der Werke des Augustinus von Hippo. 2004 ⇒20,13993. [R]ThGl 95 (2005) 397-399 (*Fischer, Norbert*).

15481 *McCarthy, Michael C.* An ecclesiology of groaning: Augustine, the psalms, and the making of church. TS 66 (2005) 23-48.

15482 **O'Donnell, James J.** Augustine: a new biography. NY 2005, HarperCollins 396 pp. $27. 0-0605-3537-7. [R]America 193 (2005) 23-24 (*Hunter, David G.*); SvTK 81 (2005) 184-185 (*Fredriksen, Paula*); Augustinus 50 (2005) 458-459 (*Silva, Álvaro*); AugSt 36 (2005) 447-452 (*Van Fleteren, Frederick*).

15483 *Partoens, Gert* Augustine on Ephesians 3,13-18: a reading of *sermo* 165. Augustiniana neerlandica. 2005 ⇒15427. 255-273 [VigChr 59,472—J. van Oort]. **'Netherlandic'**;

15484 Le sermon 163 de saint Augustin: introduction et édition. RBen 115 (2005) 251-285.

15485 **Pauliat, Patrice** Le décalogue ou 'Les dix paroles' dans l'éthique théologique de Saint Augustin d'Hippone (usage—interpretation—rayonnement): obstacle et chemin vers Dieu. [D]*Schmitz, Philipp:* R 2005, 144 pp. Extr. Diss. Gregoriana; Bibl. 20-31 [Exod 20,1-17].

15486 [E]**Ramsey, Boniface** Letters 211-270, 1*-29* (*Epistulae*). [T]*Teske, Roland*: Works of Saint Augustine 2/4: NY 2005, New City 350 pp. 1-56548-209-3;

15487 On christian belief. Works of Saint Augustine 1/8: NY 2005, New City 372 pp. 1-56548-233-6.

15488 *Ries, Julien* La conversion de saint Augustin du manichéisme au catholicisme: controverses anciennes et positions récentes. Quinto congresso. 2005 ⇒900. 355-371.

15489 *Rouanet Bastos, Luciano* 'Io. eu. tr.' 20-22: sentido de la segunda exégesis agustiniana de Jn 5,19-30. Augustinus 50 (2005) 107-192.

15490 *Rutten, Thijs* Augustine and the spirituality of the Psalms: the *Confessions* as a role play deduced from the Psalms. Augustiniana neerlandica. 2005 ⇒15427. 113-129 [VigChr 59,472—J. van Oort]. **'Netherlandic'**.

15491 *Santi, Giorgio Verum* et *veritas* in Agostino. Aquinas 48 (2005) 199-224.

15492 *Schrama, Martijn* 'As you did it to one of the least of these, you did it to me': Augustine on Matthew 25. Augustiniana neerlandica.

2005 ⇒15427. 289-307 [VigChr 59,472—J. van Oort]. **'Netherlandic'**.

15493 *Stepantsov, S.A.* Anti-Donatist tendency as an exegetical factor in St. Augustine's 'Tractates on the first epistle of John'. VDI 1 (2005) 153-167. **R.**;

15494 'Sicut torrens in austro': Ps 125:4b in St. Augustine's interpretation. VDI 3 (2005) 143-151. **R.**

15495 *Studer, Basil* Augustins *De Trinitate*, eine christliche Botschaft. Aug. 45 (2005) 501-517.

15496 *Svartvik, Jesper* Ordets hydda i Babel, Alexandria, Hippo och Lissabon: om teodicén som hermeneutisk metod. SvTK 81/1 (2005) 29-39.

15497 *Tilley, Maureen A.* No friendly letters: Augustine's correspondence with women. The cultural turn. 2005 ⇒670. 40-62.

15498 *Trego, Kristell* De l'éthique de la sagesse à l'éthique de la liberté: la doctrine de la liberté d'Augustin à la lumière de ses sources philosophiques antiques. RSPhTh 89 (2005) 641-653.

15499 *Van der Meeren, Sophie Rationale* et *rationabile* dans le *De ordine* de saint Augustin: ou comment Augustin fait d'une distinction lexicale un outil à la fois philosophique et pédagogique. Kairos 25 (2005) 235-278.

15500 *Van Reisen, Hans* AMBROSE and Augustine on Peter's denial. Augustiniana neerlandica. 2005 ⇒15427. 239-253 [VigChr 59,472—J. van Oort] [Mt 26,69-75]. **'Netherlandic'**.

15501 *Vannier, Marie A.* Augustin et la Jérusalem céleste. Graphè 14 (2005) 41-53;

15502 Augustin prédicateur dans les *Homélies sur l'évangile de S. Jean*. ConnPE 99 (2005) 69-74.

15503 [E]**Vannier, Marie-Anne** Encyclopédie saint Augustin: la Méditerranée et l'Europe IV$^{e}$-XXI$^{e}$ siècle. P 2005, Cerf 1489 pp. €114. 978-22040-73394.

15504 *Vessey, Mark* History, fiction and figuralism in Book 8 of Augustine's Confessions. The cultural turn. 2005 ⇒670. 237-257.

15505 *Wohlmuth, Josef* Augustins *De magistro* und das inspirierte Subjekt bei Emmanuel LÉVINAS: Inszenierung eines Dialogs. Religiöses Lernen. WUNT 180: 2005 ⇒384. 307-320.

### Y2.5 **Hieronymus**

15506 **Adkin, Neil** Jerome on virginity: a commentary on the *Libellus de virginitate servanda* (Letter 22). 2003 ⇒19,14750. [R]Gn. 77 (2005) 594-599 (*Paschoud, François*); AnCl 74 (2005) 381-383 (*Savon, Hervé*).

15507 *Breukelman, Frans* De kerkvader Hiëronymus en het grondbeginsel van bijbelvertaling: 'De optimo genere interpretandi,' over de beste wijze van (bijbel) vertalen. [F]HOOGEWOUD, F. 2005 ⇒63. 43-56 [OTA 29,8].

15508 *Bruin, Wim M. de* Traces of a Hebrew text division in the bible commentaries of Jerome. Layout markers. Pericope 5: 2005 ⇒422. 21-39.

15509 *Cain, Andrew* In AMBROSIASTER's shadow: a critical evaluation of the last surviving letter exchange between Pope Damasus and Jerome. REAug 51 (2005) 257-277.

15510 *Courtray, Régis* La réception du *Commentaire sur Daniel* de Jérôme dans l'Occident médiéval chrétien (VII^e-XII^e siècle). SE 44 (2005) 117-187.

15511 *Duval, Yves-Marie* Diététique et médecine chez Jérôme. Les Pères de l'Église. ThH 117: 2005 ⇒813. 121-139.

15512 [ET]**Duval, Yves-Marie** La décrétale *Ad Gallos Episcopos*: son texte et son auteur: texte critique, traduction française et commentaire. SVigChr 73: Lei 2005, Brill x; 177 pp [RBen 116,158—P.-M. Bogaert].

15513 *Feiertag, Jean-Louis* VIGILANCE et Jérôme sur la lecture d'ORIGÈNE dans un florilège du XI^e siècle. REAug 51 (2005) 279-296.

15514 [E]**Feiertag, Jean-Louis** S. Hieronymi presbyteri opera III, opera polemica 5: adversus Vigilantium. CChr.SL 79 C: Turnhout 2005, Brepols clxxvi; 58 pp. 2-503-00797-X.

15515 **Fürst, Alfons** Hieronymus: Askese und Wissenschaft in der Spätantike. 2003 ⇒19,14759. [R]Bijdr. 66 (2005) 346-47 (*Koet, Bart J.*).

15516 **González Salinero, Raúl** Biblia y polémica antijudía en Jerónimo. TECC 70: 2003 ⇒19,14760. [R]JThS 56 (2005) 227-9 (*Lössl, Josef*).

15517 [T]**Gourdain, Jean-Louis** Jérôme: homélies sur Marc. SC 494: P 2005, Cerf 232 pp. €27. 2-204-07928-6. Texte latin de *Germain Morin*.

15518 *Gutowska, Emilia* Demonologia alegoryczna?: uwagi na marginesie Hieronimowego komentarza do 34 rozdz księgi Izajasza [Allegorical demonology?: some remarks on Saint Jerome's commentary on ch. 34 of the book of Isaiah]. STV 43/2 (2005) 67-78. **P.**

15519 [ET]**Herrera García, Rosa María** San Jerónimo, obras completas IV: cuestiones relativas al Antiguo Testamento: cuestiones hebreas sobre el Génesis; libro de la interpretación de los nombres hebreos; fragmentos selectos del salterio; comentario al Eclesiastés. 2004 ⇒ 20,14021. Ed. bilingüe. [R]Studium 45/1 (2005) 149-150 (*López, L.*).

15520 [T]**Jeanjean, Benoît; Lançon, Bertrand** Saint Jérôme: Chronique. [E]*Helm, R.* 2004 ⇒20,14022. Continuation de la *Chronique* d'EUSÈBE années 326-378. [R]RHPhR 85 (2005) 477-478 (*Prieur, J.-M.*).

15521 *Kamesar, Adam S.* Gerolamo, la valutazione stilistica dei profeti maggiori ed i *genera dicendi*. Adamantius 11 (2005) 179-183.

15522 *Manns, Frédéric* Les traditions targumiques dans le commentaire de Qohelet de St Jérôme. Did(L) 35 (2005) 65-83.

15523 *Messina, Marco T.* Nuove tracce di ORIGENE nel *Commento ad Osea* di Girolamo?. Nuovo e antico. 2005 ⇒634. 417-446.

15524 *Moran, Michael L.* Nazirites and Nazarenes: the meaning of Nazaraeus in Saint Jerome. ZAC 9 (2005) 320-366 [Mt 2,23].

15525 *Rico, Christophe* L'art de la traduction chez saint Jérôme: la Vulgate à l'aune de la Néovulgate: l'exemple du quatrième évangile. REL 83 (2005) 194-218.

15526 [T]**Risse, Siegfried** Hieronymus: Commentarioli in Psalmos, Anmerkungen zum Psalter. FC 79: Turnhout 2005, Brepols 268 pp. 2-503-52154-1. Lateinischer Text von *G. Morin* (CChr.SL 72).

15527 *Šanjek, Franjo* À la recherche de Stridon, lieu de naissance de Saint Jérôme. RHE 100 (2005) 146-151.

15528 *Wallraff, Martin* Die Chronik des Hieronymus und ihre frühen Drucke. Welt-Zeit. 2005 ⇒597. 63-67.

15529 **Weingarten, Susan** The saint's saints: hagiography and geography in Jerome. Ancient Judaism & Early Christianity 58; AGJU 58: Lei 2005, Brill xv; 317 pp. 90-04-14387-4. Bibl. 273-298.

15530 *Zanetti, Paolo S.* Sul criterio e il valore della traduzione per CICERONE e S. Gerolamo. Imitatori di Gesù Cristo. 2005 <1961> ⇒330. 63-113;

15531 Una note sul 'mysterium' dell'"ordo verborum" nelle scritture. Imitatori di Gesù Cristo. 2005 <1985> ⇒330. 363-374;

15532 Hieronymus: liber de optimo genere interpretandi (epistula 57). Imitatori di Gesù Cristo. 2005 <1986> ⇒330. 375-380.

### Y2.6 **Patres Latini** *in ordine alphabetico*

15533 *Consolino, Franca E.* Il senso del passato: generi letterari e rapporti con la tradizione nella 'parafrasi biblica' latina. Nuovo e antico. 2005 ⇒634. 447-526.

15534 *Dolbeau, François* A propos d'un agraphon: réflexions sur la transmission de l'homilétique latine antique, avec l'édition du sermon 'sermo sacerdotis Dei'. Augustin et la prédication en Afrique. 2005 <2003> ⇒15450. 458-472 [RBen 116,162—P.-M. Bogaert].

15535 *Kenny, Anthony* Les Catégories chez les Pères de l'Eglise latins. Les *Catégories* et leur histoire. 2005 ⇒624. 121-133.

15536 *Peretto, Elio* Male–Maligno–peccato nei padri occidentali del II-III secolo. Male. DSBP 39: 2005 ⇒580. 122-204.

15537 *Pesthy, Monika* 'Mulier est instrumentum diaboli': women and the desert fathers. [F]LUTTIKHUIZEN, G.: AGJU 59: 2005⇒93. 351-362.

15538 *Rossi, Alessandro* Fabio Vittore: dal sangue dei martiri nascono i padri?: per una rilettura degli "Acta Maximiliani". AnScR 10 (2005) 181-218.

15539 AMBROSIASTER: *Bray, Gerald* Ambrosiaster. Reading Romans. 2005⇒400. 21-38;

15540 *Pollastri, Alessandra* L'Apocalisse nell'Ambrosiaster: una lettura millenarista nella Roma del IV secolo?. [F]VANNI, U. 2005 ⇒156. 703-733.

15541 AMBROSIUS M: *Bonato, Antonio* Antropologia teologica e soteriologia: presenza del Maligno e conseguenze della colpa d'origine nell'opera di s. Ambrogio. Male. DSBP 39: 2005 ⇒580. 306-365;

15542 **Colish, Marcia L.** Ambrose's patriarchs: ethics for the common man. ND 2005, University of Notre Dame Press viii; 193 pp. $35/ 15. 0-268-02364-6. Bibl. 159-175;

15543 *Coraluppi, Luigi F.* Uso retorico del lessico giuridico nel *De Tobia* di Ambrogio: considerazioni preliminari. Nuovo e antico. 2005 ⇒ 634. 685-730;

15544 Indagine sull'uso retorico del linguaggio giuridico in Ambrogio: "consors naturae, coheres gratiae". AnScR 10 (2005) 27-38;

15545 *Cutino, Michele* Per una lettura del 'De Joseph' di Ambrogio di Milano. AnScR 10 (2005) 53-97;

15546 La tripartizione del sapere in Ambrogio. Nuovo e antico. 2005 ⇒ 634. 561-631;

15547 *Guinot, Jean-Noël* La recente pubblicazione della cronologia e della bibliografia santaambrosiane e il progetto di "Sources Chrétiennes" sulle opere di sant'Ambrogio. ScC 133 (2005) 711-719;

15548 **Maschio, Giorgio** La figura di Cristo nel 'Commentario al Salmo 118' di Ambrogio di Milano. SEAug 88: 2003 ⇒19,14769; 20, 14040. [R]Sal. 67 (2005) 600-602 (*Poblano, Gregorio*);

15549 *Nauroy, Gérard* Ambroise de Milan face à l'*Ennéade* I, 4 de PLOTIN et l'esquisse d'un eudémonisme chrétien. [F]HEIM, F. 2005 ⇒59. 137-161;

15550 **Nauroy, Gérard** Ambroise de Milan: Écriture et esthétique d'une exégèse pastorale. 2003 ⇒19,464. [R]REAug 51 (2005) 200-204 (*Lanéry, Cécile*); JAC 47 (2004) 178-181 (*Dassmann, Ernst*).

15551 **Novo Cid-Fuentes, A.** Los misterios de la vida de Cristo en Ambrosio de Milán. 2003 ⇒19,14771. [R]Teol. 42 (2005) 215-218 (*De Fina, Darío*);

15552 *Passarella, Raffaele* Le spalle di Sichem (Ambr. *Interpell.* 4.4.16). Nuovo e antico. 2005 ⇒634. 731-739;

15553 Semi ciceroniani, fioriture ambrosiane: appunti sulla presenza del "Cato maior" nell'opera di Ambrogio. AnScR 10 (2005) 39-52;

15554 *Raschle, Christian R.* Ambrosius' Predigt gegen Magnus Maximus: eine historische Interpretation der *explanatio in psalmum* 61 (62). Hist. 54 (2005) 49-67;

15555 *Roques, Martine* La tradition manuscrite de l'*Apologia Dauid altera* attribuée à Ambroise. RechAug 34 (2005) 239-297;

15556 *Wilken, Robert L.* A Constantinian bishop: St. Ambrose of Milan. God, truth, and witness. 2005 ⇒532. 73-87.

15557 AVITUS A: [ET]**Hecquet-Noti, Nicole** Avit de Vienne: Histoire spirituelle, 1: chants I-III; 2: chants IV-V. SC 444; 492: P 1999-2005, Cerf 2 vols; 344 + 254 pp. €27 + 27. 2-2040-63215/7925-1.

15558 CAESARIUS A: *Mayeski, Marie A.* An urban bishop in a changing world: the exegesis of Caesarius of Arles. PRSt 32 (2005) 401-419.

15559 CASSIANUS J: **Reedijk, Wim** Zuiver lezen, de lectio divina van Johannes Cassianus en de bijbelse hermeneutiek. 2003 ⇒19,14774. [R]KeTh 56 (2005) 70 (*Kooijman, Arie C.*).

15560 CASSIODORUS: [E]**Caruso, Antonio** Flavio Magno Aurelio Cassiodoro: spaccati di vita, 1: i salmi di Gesù. Tradizione e Vita 15: Monopoli 2005, Vivere In 204 pp. €18.50. 88-7263-245-5.

15561 CHRYSOLOGUS: [T]**Palardy, William B.** St. Peter Chrysologus: selected sermons, 3. FaCh: Wsh 2005, Catholic Univ. of America xviii; 372 pp. 0-8132-0110-1.

15562 CYPRIANUS C: *Dunn, Geoffrey D.* Widows and other women in the pastoral ministry of Cyprian of Carthage. Aug. 45 (2005) 295-307;

15563 *Noll, Raymund* Doctor Sacrae Scripturae—Schrifthermeneutik und Lehren anhand der Heiligen Schrift bei Cyprian von Karthago. "Lebendige Gemeinde". ESt 54: 2005 ⇒578. 254-283;

15564 *Zanetti, Paolo S.* Osservazioni su Proverbi 19,17a in Cipriano. Imitatori di Gesù Cristo. 2005 <1988> ⇒330. 437-446.

15565 EUCHERIUS L: **Antulov, Marco** Die exegetischen Schriften des Eucherius von Lyon–ein historisch-theologischer Kommentar. [D]*Kriegbaum, Bernhard* 2005, Diss. Innsbruck [ThRv 102,vii];

15566 *Dulaey, Martine* Eucher exégète: l'interprétation de la bible en Gaule du Sud dans la première moitié du Ve siècle. Mauritius. 2005 ⇒966. 67-93.

15567 FACUNDUS H.: [E]**Clément, Jean-Marie; Vander Plaetse, R.** Facundus Hermianensis: défense des trois chapitres (à Justinien), 1: livres I-II. [T]*Fraïsse-Bétoulières, Anne*: Ment. *Theodorus Mopsuestia; Theodoretus*: SC 471: 2002 ⇒18,13626. [R]REAug 51 (2005) 208-210 (*Weiss, Jean-Pierre*).

15568 GREGORIUS E: *Heintz, Michael* Gregory of Elvira *On Noah's ark*. Antiphon 9/1 (2005) 65-76 [Gen 6,13-16; 8,10-11].

15569 GREGORIUS M: **Crivello, Fabrizio** Le 'Omelie sui vangeli' di Gregorio Magno a Vercvelli: le miniature del ms. CXLVIII/8 della Biblioteca Capitolare. Archivum Gregorianum 6: F 2005, SISMEL xiv; 151 pp. €77. Num. ill.;

15570 **D'Imperio, Francesca S.** Gregorio Magno: bibliografia per gli anni 1980-2003. Archivum Gregorianum 4: F 2005, SISMEL xvii; 353 pp. 88-8450-1687;

15571 [ET]**Etaix, Raymond; Judic, Bruno; Morel, Charles** Grégoire le Grand: Homélies sur l'évangile: livre I (homélies I-XX). SC 485: P 2005, Cerf 482 pp. €41. 2-204-07691-0;

15572 *Jurasz, Isabelle* La figure de la femme de Job selon Grégoire le Grand dans *Morales sur Job*—étude de l'exégèse patristique. L'eredità spirituale di Gregorio Magno. 2005 ⇒831. 67-86 [Job 2,9];

15573 **Moorhead, John** Gregory the Great. L 2005, Routledge 177 pp. $32. 0-415-23390-9. Bibl. 169-173;

15574 *Salati, Stefano* Rilevanza teologica della presenza/assenza di S. Gregorio Magno nel VI cap. della *Dei verbum*: 'La sacra scrittura nella vita della chiesa'. L'eredità spirituale. 2005 ⇒831. 361-381;

15575 *Simón, Alfredo* Il metodo teologico di Gregorio Magno: il processo plurisemantico della analogia metaesegetica. L'eredità spirituale di Gregorio Magno. 2005 ⇒831. 153-180 = RET 65 (2005) 5-29.

15576 HILARIUS P: **Descourtieux, Patrick** Saint Hilaire de Poitiers, premier exégète latin des Psaumes: les Tractatus super Psalmos: introduction, traduction et notes de commentaire. [D]*Reale, V.*: R 2005, 131 pp. Diss. Santa Croce; Bibl. 111-131;

15577 *Kamesar, Adam* Hilary of Poitiers, Judeo-Christianity, and the origins of the LXX: a translation of Tractatus Super Psalmos 2.2-3 with introduction and commentary. VigChr 59 (2005) 264-285;

15578 *Meyer, John R. Assumptio Carnis* and the ascent to God: Hilary's revision of Irenaeus' doctrine of *Salus Carnis*. ZAC 9 (2005) 303-319;

15579 *Turek, Waldemar* I figli di Zebedeo (cf Mt 20,20-23) nell'esegesi di Ilario di Poitiers. Atti del X Simposio di Efeso. Turchia 19: 2005 ⇒785. 135-148.

15580 LACTANTIUS: *Heck, Eberhard* Defendere-instituere: zum Selbstverständnis des Apologeten Lactanz. L'apologétique chrétienne. EnAC 51: 2005 ⇒13520. 205-240;

15581 Lactantius, *De falsa religione*: Textkritisches zum 1. Buch der *Diuinae institutiones*. [F]HEIM, F. 2005 ⇒59. 55-67;

15582 [E]**Heck, Eberhard; Wlosok, Antonie** L. Callius Firmianus Lactantius: Divinarum institutionum libri septem, Fasc. 1: libri I et II. BSGRT: Mü 2005, Saur lvi; 200 pp. 3-598-71265-0;

15583 [T]**Spinelli, Mario** Lattanzio: come muoiono i persecutori. CTePa 180: R 2005, Città N 149 pp. 88-311-3180-X;

15584 *Van der Meeren, Sophie Recta ratio vivendi*: sur une définition sénéquienne de la philosophie, rapportée et critiquée par Lactance. REL 83 (2005) 154-178.

15585 LEO M: *Caruana, Salvino 'Scripturarum capere sacramentum...'*: scripture as sacrament in *Sermon* 66,1 of Pope St. Leo the Great. MTh 56/1 (2005) 61-92.

15586 PAULINUS N: *Grottanelli, Cristiano* Tuer des animaux pour la fête de Saint Félix. La cuisine et l'autel. BEHE.R 124: 2005 ⇒539. 387-407.

15587 PELAGIUS: *Dupont, Anthony* Pelagius: just an ethicist or also a theologian?: a reading of Pelagius' commentary on Romans. Augustiniana neerlandica. 2005 ⇒15427. 355-363 [VigChr 59,472—J. van Oort]. **'Netherlandic'**.

15588 POTAMIUS L: *González Salinero, Raúl* Exégesis antiarriana y polémica antijudía en Potamio de Lisboa. ASEs 22/2 (2005) 465-477.

15589 RUFINUS A: **Fedalto, Giorgio** Rufino di Aquileia tra Oriente e Occidente. R 2005, Città N. 209 pp. [R]LASBF 55 (2005) 564-565 (*Piccirillo, Michele*).

15590 SEVERINUS: *Régerat, Philippe* Bible et prédication dans la *Vita Severini*. ConnPE 99 (2005) 91-102.

15591 TYCONIUS: [T]**Vercruysse, Jean-M.** Tyconius: le livre des règles. SC 488: 2004 ⇒20,14072. [R]RHPhR 85 (2005) 476-77 (*Gounelle, R.*).

15592 VICTORINUS P: *Pani, Giancarlo* L'Anticristo nel commento all' Apocalisse di Vittorino di Petovio. [F]VANNI, U. 2005 ⇒156. 677-701;

15593 Le sette chiese nel commento all'Apocalisse di Vittorino di Petovio. Atti del X Simposio di Efeso. 2005 ⇒785. 149-171 [Rev 2-3].

## Y2.8 **Documenta orientalia**

15594 *Ashbrook Harvey, Susan* Gendered words in Syriac Marian tradition. The cultural turn. Ment. *Ephrem* 2005 ⇒670. 63-86.

15595 *Baarda, Tjitze* Luke 2,14 and Luke 19,38: EPHRAEM'S commentary on the Diatessaron Ch. II: 14-15. [F]DENAUX, A:. BEThL 182: 2005 ⇒34. 93-112.

15596 *Brock, Sebastian P.* The Syriac Orient: a third "lung" for the church?. OCP 71 (2005) 5-20.

15597 **Burkitt, Francis C.** Early eastern Christianity: St. Margaret's lectures, 1904, on the Syriac-speaking church. Piscataway (N.J.) 2004 <1904>, Gorgias viii; 228 pp. 1-593-33101-0.

15598 [T]**Isebaert-Cauuet, Isabelle** JACQUES de Saroug: La fin du monde: homélies eschatologiques. CPF 91: P 2005, Migne 225 pp. €15. 2-908587-52-1. Bibl. 215-217.

15599 *Janse, S.* Een vervangingstheologie uit het oude Perzië: APHRAHAT over het Joodse volk. KeTh 56/2 (2005) 127-142;

15600 De joodse achtergrond van het gebed in APHRAHATs "Demonstrationes" 23.53-59. NedThT 59/1 (2005) 41-59.

15601 *Kofsky, Aryeh; Ruzer, Serge* Christology and hermeneutics in PHILOXENUS' commentary on John 1:14. OCP 71 (2005) 343-362.

15602 **Manikulam, Shaji Thomas** The nativity of Our Lord: a study based on the writings of St. EPHREM the Syrian. R 2002, Pontificium Institutum Orientale l; 111 pp. Bibl. xiii-l; Exc. Diss.

15603 *Russell, Paul S.* St EPHRAEM'S *Carmina Nisibena 33*: a hymn on paganism's place in the world. SVTQ 49 (2005) 395-415;

15604 Nisibis as the background to the life of Ephrem the Syrian. Hugoye 8/2 (2005)*.

## Y3.0 **Medium aevum**, *generalia*

15605 *Albert, B.-S.* Anti-Jewish exegesis in the Carolingian period: the commentaries on Lamentations of HRABANUS Maurus and PASCHASIUS Radbertus. Biblical studies in the early middle ages. Millennio Medievale 52; Atti di convegni 16: 2002 ⇒773. 175-192.

15606 *Alcázar, Luis del* In evangelium Joannis praefatio. ATG 68 (2005) 153-220 [John 1,1-18].

15607 **Ara, Alberto** Angeli e sostanze separate: l'idea di materia spiritualis tra il secolo XII e il secolo XIII: ricognizione storico-testuale—valutazione teoretica. F 2005, Facoltà Teologica dell'Italia Centrale pag. varia. Bibl. 771-820.

15608 *Bataillon, Louis-Jacques* Chronique de doctrines médiévales: philosophie, exégèse et théologie. RSPhTh 89 (2005) 575-589.

15609 *Bentzinger, Rudolf* Historienbibeln als Gebrauchsliteratur: Edition mit Quellenerschließung und Dokumentation rezeptionbezogener Varianz. Deutsche Texte des Mittelalters zwischen Handschriftennähe und Rekonstruktion. [E]**Schubert, Martin J.**: Tü 2005, Niemeyer €112. 269-285. 3-484-29523-6 [Scr. 60,146*—G. Hendrix].

15610 *Berndt, Rainer* Neue Forschungen zur Glossa der Bibel. Archa Verbi 2 (2005) 177-182 [Scr. 60,147*—G. Hendrix].

15611 *Burkitt, Francis C.* †1935. Literatura cristiana palestinense. CCO 2 (2005) 327-340.

15612 *Dahan, Gilbert* L'allégorie dans l'exégèse chrétienne de la bible au moyen âge. Allégorisme des poètes. 2005 ⇒874. 205-230;

15613 L'Ecclésiaste contre ARISTOTE?: les commentaires de Eccl 1,13 et 17-18 aux XIIe et XIIIe siècles. [F]PACHECO, M. 2005 ⇒118. 205-233.

15614 [E]**Dinkova-Bruun, Greti** The ancestry of Jesus. excerpts from Liber generationis Iesu Christi filii David filii Abraham (Matthew 1:1-17). TMLT 28: Toronto 2005, Pont. Inst. of Mediaeval Studies viii; 133 pp. CAN$8. 0-88844-478-8. Edited from Heidelberg, Universitätsbibliothek, MS Salem IX 15.

15615 *Dolso, Maria Teresa* La parabola della zizzania e il problema ereticale tra XII e XIII secolo. CrSt 26 (2005) 225-264 [Mt 13,24-30].

15616 *Dronke, Peter* Les conceptions de l'allégorie chez Jean Scot ÉRIGÈNE et HILDEGARDE de Bingen. Allégorisme des poètes. 2005 ⇒ 874. 231-244.

15617 *Ellis, Roger* The medieval experience. Bible in pastoral practice. 2005 ⇒341. 59-77.

15618 *Faes de Mottoni, Barbara* Mosè e Paolo figure della contemplazione e del rapimento nelle teologie del secolo XIII. MEFRM 117 (2005) 83-113.

15619 **Gatti, Roberto** Ermeneutica e filosofia: introduzione al pensiero ebraico medioevale (secoli XII-XIV). 2003 ⇒19,14813. [R]Hum(B) 60 (2005) 639-642 (*Tonelli, Ivano; Ghia, Francesco*).

15620 *Georgi, Dieter* The religious dimensions of the world market: a farewell to the Middle Ages. The city in the valley. Studies in biblical literature 7: 2005 ⇒214. 255-282.

15621 *Gorman, Michael M.* Frigulus: Hiberno-Latin author or pseudo-Irish phantom?: comments on the edition of the *Liber questionvm in evangeliis* (CCSL 108F). RHE 100 (2005) 425-456.

15622 *Gow, Andrew* Challenging the Protestant paradigm: bible reading in lay and urban contexts of the later middle ages. Scripture and pluralism. 2005 ⇒757. 161-191.

15623 *Groote, Marc* De Alttestamentliche Passionsprophezeiungen in einem Vatikaner Codex. SE 44 (2005) 227-239.

15624 **Hazard, Mark** The literal sense and the gospel of John in late-medieval commentary and literature. Ment. *Nicolaus of Lyra* 2002 ⇒18,13659. ^R JR 85 (2005) 114-115 (*Klepper, Deeana C.*).

15625 *Hughes, Christopher* Typology and its uses in the moralized bible. The mind's eye. 2005 ⇒512. 133-150 [Scr. 60,195*—G. Hendrix].

15626 **Hughes, Kevin L.** Constructing antichrist: Paul, biblical commentary, and the development of doctrine in the early middle ages. ^D *McGinn, B.*: Wsh 2005, Catholic University of America xxi; [2], 278 pp. $60. 0-8132-1415-7. Diss. Chicago; Bibl. 251-269. ^R ChH 75 (2005) 176-177 (*Lerner, Robert E.*).

15627 *Lipton, Sara* The sweet lean of his head: writing about looking at the crucifix in the High Middle Ages. Spec. 80 (2005) 1172-1208 [Scr. 60,211*—A. Smets].

15628 **Lobrichon, Guy** La bible au Moyen Âge. Médiévistes français 3: 2003 ⇒19,227; 20,14100. ^R JEH 56 (2005) 351-352 (*McGurk, Patrick*); RMab 16 (2005) 286-287 (*Morard, Martin*); BECh 163 (2005) 318-319 (*Giraud, Cédric*).

15629 *Mairey, Aude* Pratiques de l'allégorie dans la poésie anglaise du XIV^e siècle. Allégorisme des poètes. 2005 ⇒874. 266-288.

15630 **Marschler, Thomas** Auferstehung und Himmelfahrt Christi in der scholastischen Theologie bis zu THOMAS von Aquin. BGPhMA 64/ I-II: 2003 ⇒19,14821; 20,14101. ^R TS 66 (2005) 189-191 (*O'Collins, Gerald*).

15631 *Mews, Constant J.* The world as text: the bible and the book of nature in twelfth-century theology. Scripture and pluralism. 2005 ⇒ 757. 95-122.

15632 *Miller, E.P.* The political significance of Christ's kingship in the biblical exegesis of HRABANUS Maurus and ANGELOMUS of Luxeuil. Biblical studies in the early middle ages. Millennio Medievale 52; Atti di convegni 16: 2002 ⇒773. 193-213.

15633 *Obrist, Barbara* Alchimie et allégorie scripturaire au moyen âge. Allégorisme des poètes. 2005 ⇒874. 245-265.

15634 **Ocker, Christopher** Biblical poetics before humanism and Reformation. 2002 ⇒18,13662; 20,14106. ^R SCJ 36 (2005) 514-16 (*Hansen, Gary Neal*).

15635 *Olsen, G.W.* The *ecclesia primitiua* in John CASSIAN, the Ps. Jerome commentary on Mark and BEDE;

15636 *Orlandi, G.* Scriptores celtigenae I-III and textual criticism. Biblical studies in the early middle ages. 2002 ⇒773. 5-27/309-321.

15637 *Otten, Willemien* Reading creation: early medieval views of Genesis and PLATO'S Timaeus. Creation of heaven and earth. Themes in biblical narrative 8: 2005 ⇒492. 225-243.

15638 **Pavlidou, Kleoniki** Ein frühbyzantinisches Glossar zu den Briefen des Apostels Paulus: handschriftliche und kritische Ausgabe. Serta Graeca 22: Wsb 2005, Reichert xxiv; 332 pp. 38950-04677. Diss. Hamburg.

15639 *Pelletier, Anne M.* Le désir de Dieu, porte de Jérusalem dans la littérature monastique du XI siècle. Graphè 14 (2005) 55-75.

15640 **Pletl, Renate** Irdisches regnum in der mittelalterlichen Exegese: ein Beitrag zur exegetischen Lexikographie und ihren Herrschaftsvorstellungen (7.-13. Jahrhundert). EHS.G 881: 2000 ⇒19,14829. [R]Francia 32/1 (2005) 225-227 (*Veyrard-Cosme, Christiane*).

15641 *Puig i Oliver, Jaume de* La *Vida de Crist* de Francesc Eiximenis i el *Flos Sanctorum* castellà. RCatT 30/1 (2005) 91-116 [Gen 1,26].

15642 *Reinink, G.J.* The lamb on the tree: Syriac exegesis and anti-Islamic apologetics. Syriac christianity. 2005 <2002> ⇒284. xv; 109-124 [Gen 22].

15643 *Savigni, Raffaele* La parabola della zizzania (Mt 13,24-30 e 36-43) nei commenti biblici altomedievali (secc. VI-X). CrSt 26 (2005) 189-223.

15644 *Signer, Michael A.* Consolation and confrontation: Jewish and christian interpretation of the prophetic books. Scripture and pluralism. 2005 ⇒757. 77-93.

15645 *Stotz, P.* Zwei unbekannte metrische Psalmenparaphrasen wohl aus der Karolingerzeit. Biblical studies in the early middle ages. Millennio Medievale 52; Atti di convegni 16: 2002 ⇒773. 239-257.

15646 *Taguchi, Mayumi* A Middle English penitential treatise on Job 10: 20-22, Dimitte me, Domine .... MS 67 (2005) 157-217.

15647 *Van Liere, Frans* ANDREW of St. Victor, JEROME, and the Jews: biblical scholarship in the twelfth-century Renaissance. Scripture and pluralism. 2005 ⇒757. 59-75.

Y3.4 **Exegetae mediaevales** [Hebraei ⇒K7]

15648 AELRED R: [E]**Briey, G. de** Aelred de Rievaulx: sermons pour l'année, 4, collection de Durham, sermons 47 à 64. Pain de Cîteaux 23: Oka 2005, Abb. Notre-Dame du Lac 261 pp. €19. 29215-92290;

15649 Sermons pour l'année, 5, sermons 65 à 84, collection de Durham (2e partie): sermon conservé par Matthieu de Rievaulx, sermons de Lincoln; Prière d'un pasteur. Pain de Cîteaux 24: Oka 2005, Abb. Notre-Dame du Lac 295 pp. €19. 29215-92312;

15650 [E]**Raciti, Gaetano** Aelredi Rievallensis: homeliae de oneribus propheticis Isaiae. CChr.CM II D; Aelredi Rievallensis opera omnia 5: Turnhout 2005, Brepols xxi; 393 pp. €185. 2-503-03029-7.

15651 ALBERTUS M: *Aris, Marc-Aeilko* Apothecarius gratiarum: Albertus Magnus und der Evangelist Lukas. [F]ZMIJEWSKI, J.: BBB 151: 2005 ⇒172. 277-288.

15652 ALCUIN: *Guglielmetti, R.* Il commento al Cantico dei Cantici di Alcuino di York: appunti per un'edizione. Biblical studies in the early middle ages. Millennio Medievale 52: 2002 ⇒773. 143-153.

15653 ALEXANDER H: *Lluch-Baixauli, Miguel* La trinidad y el decálogo: los preceptos de la primera tabla en la escuela de ALEJANDRO de Hales. ScrTh 37 (2005) 99-140.

15654 AQUINAS: *Ashley, Benedict M.* The extent of Jesus' human knowledge according to the fourth gospel. Reading John. 2005 ⇒727. 241-253;

15655 *Baglow, Christopher T.* Rediscovering St. Thomas Aquinas as biblical theologian. L&S 1 (2005) 137-146;

15656 *Bauerschmidt, Frederick C.* 'That the faithful become the temple of God': the church militant in Aquinas's *Commentary on John.* Reading John. 2005 ⇒727. 293-311;
15657 *Biffi, Inos* L'Eucaristia e la divinizzazione nella Lectura super Ioannem di San Tommaso. DT(P) 108/42 (2005) 111-146;
15658 *Boguslawski, Steven* Thomas Aquinas. Reading Romans. 2005 ⇒ 400. 81-99;
15659 *Bonino, Serge-Thomas* The role of the apostles in the communication of revelation according to the *Lectura super Ioannem* of St. Thomas Aquinas. Reading John. 2005 ⇒727. 318-346;
15660 *Boyle, John F.* Authorial intention and the *Divisio textus*;
15661 *Brown, Stephen F.* The theological role of the fathers in Aquinas's *Super evangelium S. Joannis lectura*;
15662 *Burrell, David B.* Creation in St. Thomas Aquinas's *Super Evangelium S. Joannis lectura.* Reading John. 2005 ⇒727. 3-8/9-20/115-126.
15663 *Castro, Michel* Tradition biblique et tradition hellénique dans la doctrine chrétienne de Dieu chez Saint Thomas d'Aquin: présentation, texte et bref commentaire d'un inédit de Henri Bouillard. RSR 93 (2005) 55-63.
15664 *Dauphinais, Michael* 'And they shall all be taught by God': wisdom and the eucharist in John 6. Reading John. 2005 ⇒727. 312-7;
[E]**Dauphinais, M.** Reading John with St. Thomas 2005 ⇒727;
15665 **De Bertolis, Ottavio** Origine ed esercizio della potestà ecclesiastica di governo in San Tommaso. TGr.Diritto Canonico 70: R 2005, E.P.U.G. 210 pp. 88-7839-033-X.;
15666 *Emery, Gilles* Biblical exegesis and the speculative doctrine of the Trinity in St. Thomas Aquinas's *Commentary on St. John*;
15667 *Gondreau, Paul* Anti-docetism in Aquinas's *Super Ioannem*: St. Thomas as defender of the full humanity of Christ. Reading John. 2005 ⇒727. 23-61/254-276;
15668 **Guggenheim, Antoine** Jésus-Christ, grand prêtre de l'Ancienne et de la Nouvelle Alliance: étude théologique et herméneutique du commentaire de saint Thomas d'Aquin sur l'épître aux Hébreux. 2004 ⇒20,14131. [R]NRTh 127 (2005) 479-480 (*Tourpe, Emm.*); ETR 80 (2005) 570-572 (*Molac, Philippe*);
15669 *Jordan, Mark D.* CICERO, AMBROSE, and Aquinas "On duties" or the limits of genre in morals. JRE 33 (2005) 485-502 [Mt 7,12];
15670 **Kostko, Giovanni** Beatitudine e vita cristiana nella Summa Theologiae di s. Tommaso d'Aquino. SacDo.M 50,3-4: Bo 2005, Studio Domenicano 394 pp. 88-7094-575-8. Bibl. 385-394;
15671 *Lamb, Matthew L.* Eternity and time in St. Thomas Aquinas's lectures on St. John's gospel. Reading John. 2005 ⇒727. 127-139;
15672 *Leget, Carlo* The concept of 'life' in the *Commentary on St. John*;
15673 *Levering, Matthew* Does the paschal mystery reveal the Trinity. Reading John. 2005 ⇒727. 153-172/78-91.
15674 **Levering, Matthew** Scripture and metaphysics: Aquinas and the renewal of trinitarian theology. 2004 ⇒20,14133. [R]ProEc 14 (2005) 108-110 (*Hütter, Reinhard*); RRT 12 (2005) 331-337 (*McCosker, Philip*); JThS 56 (2005) 285-288 (*Horne, Brian*).
15675 *Levering, Matthew* Participation and exegesis: response to Catherine Pickstock. MoTh 21 (2005) 587-601;

15676 **Livi, Antonio** L'epistemologia di Tommaso D'Aquino e le sue fonti. N 2005, Comunicazioni Sociali 37 pp. 88-900-0768-6-0. Pont. Fac. Teologica dell'Italia Meridionale; Sez. S. Tommaso D'Aquino;

15677 *Long, Steven A.* Divine providence and John 15:5. Reading John. 2005 ⇒727. 140-150;

15678 **Maillard, Pierre-Yves** La vision de Dieu chez Thomas d'Aquin: une lecture de l'*In Ioannem* à la lumière de ses sources augustiniennes. Bibliothèque thomiste: 2001 ⇒19,14855. [R]REAug 51 (2005) 227-230 (*Berceville, Gilles*).

15679 *Marshall, Bruce D.* What does the Spirit have to do?. Reading John. 2005 ⇒727. 62-77;

15680 *Mróz, Mirosław* "Non repulit Deus plebem suam": wykład św. Tomasza z Akwinu na temat miary Bozej madrości wzgledem gens Iudaeorum w świetle Expositio super Epistolam ad Romanos (cap. IX-XI). CoTh 75/2 (2005) 57-82. **P.**;

15681 **Paillerets, Michel de** Santo Tomás de Aquino. Retratos de bolsillo: M 2005, San Pablo 143 pp. 84-2852-734-2;

15682 *Pazdan, Mary* Thomas Aquinas and contemporary biblical interpreters: 'I call you friends' (*John 15:15*). NBl 86 (2005) 465-477;

15683 **Perillo, Graziano** Teologia del *Verbum*: la *Lectura super Ioannis evangelium* di Tommaso d'Aquino. Eccedenza del passato, studi e testi 11: 2003 ⇒19,14858; 20,14138. [R]RFNS 97 (2005) 531-533 (*Rossi, Margherita Maria*);

15684 **Reinhardt, Elisabeth** La dignidad del hombre en cuanto imagen de Dios: Tomás de Aquino ante sus fuente. Pamplona 2005, Eunsda 244 pp. Diss. [Gen 1,26-27];

15685 **Rickmann, Osanna** La struttura trinitaria della morale di S. Tommaso. Vaduz 2005, Pont. Univ. S. Thoma 321 pp. Bibl. 308-321; Diss. Pont. Univ. S. Thoma;

15686 [T]**Saint-Eloi, Jean-Eric de** Thomas d'Aquin: commentaire de la première épître aux Corinthiens. 2002 ⇒18,13676... 20,7599. [R]IThQ 70 (2005) 291-292 (*O'Reilly, Kevin*);

15687 *Schenk, Richard* And Jesus wept: notes towards a theology of mourning. Reading John. 2005 ⇒727. 212-237;

15688 *Sherwin, Michael* Christ the teacher in St. Thomas's *Commentary on St. John*. Reading John. 2005 ⇒727. 173-193;

15689 *Smith, Janet* 'Come and see'. Reading John. 2005 ⇒727. 94-211;

15690 **Torrell, Jean-Pierre** Saint Thomas Aquinas, 2: spiritual master. [T]*Royal, Robert* 2003 ⇒19,14861. [R]TS 66 (2005) 204-205 (*McDermott, John M.*);

15691 [E]**Torrell, J.-P.** Saint Thomas d'Aquin: la prophétie: Somme théologique, $2^a$-$2^{ae}$: questions 171-178. [T]*Synave, Paul; Benoit, Pierre*: P [2]2005, Cerf 133* + 403 pp. €45. 2-204-038903-X;

15692 *Valkenberg, Pim* Aquinas and Christ's resurrection: the influence of the *Lectura super Ioannem* 20-21 on the *Summa theologiae*;

15693 *Waldstein, Michael* The analogy of mission and obedience: a central point in the relation between *Theología* and *Oíkonomía* in St. Thomas Aquinas's *Commentary on John*. Reading John. 2005 ⇒ 727. 277-289/92-112;

15694 **Wawrykow, Joseph P.** The Westminster handbook to Thomas Aquinas. LVL 2005, Westminster 190 pp;

15695 The SCM Press A-Z of Thomas Aquinas. L 2005, SCM 190 pp. £23. 9780-3340-40125;

15696 [E]**Weinandy, Thomas G.; Keating, Daniel A.; Yocum, John P.** Aquinas on scripture: an introduction to his biblical commentaries. E 2005, Clark xii; 257 pp. $30. 0-567-08474-4. Bibl. 245-251.

15697 ARNALDUS V: [E]**Perarnau, Josep** Arnaldi de Villanova: Introductio in librum [Ioachim] 'De semine scripturarum' e Allocutio super significatione nominis tetragrammaton. Arnaldi de Villanova opera theologica omnia III: 2004 ⇒20,14145. [R]Cart. 21 (2005) 249 (*Hernández Valenzuela, J.*); AFH 98 (2005) 825-7 (*Mensa i Valls, Jaume*); EstFr 106 (2005) 447-451 (*Requesens i Piquer, Joan*); Ter. 56 (2005) 316-8 (*Giordano, S.*); CFr 75 (2005) 406-8 (*De Armellada, Bernardino*); Archa Verbi 2 (2005) 210-212 (*Gerwing, Manfred*).

15698 BALIANITES L: *Giannouli, Antonia* Die exegetischen Didaskalien des Leon Balianites. Wiener Byzantinistik und Neogräzistik... Gedenken an Herbert HUNGER. [E]**Hörandner, W.**, *al.*, W 2004, ÖAW. 143-158. 3-7001-32697.

15699 BEDA V: *Brown, George Hardin* Le commentaire problématique de Bède sur le premier livre de Samuel. Bède le Vénérable. 2005 ⇒ 849. 87-96;

15700 Bede's commentary on I Samuel. Biblical studies in the early middle ages. Millennio Medievale 52: 2002 ⇒773. 77-90;

15701 [E]**Crépin, André** Bède le Vénérable: Histoire ecclésiastique du peuple anglais (Historia ecclesiastica gentis anglorum), 1: Livres I-II; 2: Livres III-IIII. [T]*Monat, Pierre; Robin, Philippe*: SC 489; 490: P 2005, Cerf 433 + 423 pp. €33+35. 2-2040-78492/80128. Introd., notes *A. Crépin*; Texte critique *M. Lapidge*;

15702 3: Livre V. [T]*Monat, P.; Robin, P.*: SC 491: P 2005, Cerf 251 pp. €22. 22040-80454. Introd., notes *Crépin*; Texte critique *Lapidge*.

15703 *Davril, Anselme* Bède et la Saint-Benoît du 21 mars;

15704 *DeGregorio, Scott* Bede, the monk, as exegete: evidence from the Commentary on Ezra-Nehemiah. RBen 115 (2005) 27-32/343-369.

15705 *Dolbeau, François* Epilogue: travaux récents sur Bède: le point de vue d'un philologue. Bède le Vénérable. 2005 ⇒849. 321-329;

15706 *Foley, W.T.* Bede's exegesis of passages unique to the gospel of Mark;

15707 *Holder, A.* The Anti-Pelagian character of Bede's commentary on the Song of Songs. Biblical studies in the early middle ages. Millennio Medievale 52: 2002 ⇒773. 105-124/77-103;

15708 *Meyvaert, Paul* The date of Bede's *In Ezram* and his image of Ezra in *Codex Amiatinus*. Spec. 80 (2005) 1087-1133 [RBen 116,136—P.-M. Bogaert].

15709 BERNARDUS C: [T]**Callerot, Françoise; Miethke, Jürgen; Jaquinod, Christiane** Bernardus Claraevallensis: le précepte et la dispense; la conversion. SC 457: Paris 2000, Cerf 466 pp. 2-204-065-86-2. Texte latin des S. Bernardi opera, par *J. Leclerq, H. Rochais* et *Ch. H. Talbot*; introduction, traduction et notes par *F. Callerot, Jürgen Miethke* et *Christiane Jaquinod*; Bibl. 138-140;

15710 [T]**Fassetta, Raffaele**, *al.*, Bernard de Clairvaux: sermons sur le Cantique, 3: sermons 33-50. [E]*Leclercq, Jean, al.*, SC 452: 2000 ⇒16, 12878... 19,14866. [R]ScEs 57 (2005) 177-178 (*Cazelais, Serge*);

15711 *Gómez, Pedro Edmundo* La teología monástica como 'eructatio scripturae' en San Bernardo. CuMon 40 (2005) 317-331.

15712 BONAVENTURA: *Damiata, Marino* L'ultimo Bonaventura VII: Collationes de decem praeceptis. StFr 102 (2005) 119-142;

15713 **Raurell, Frederic** Ermeneutica biblico-bonaventuriana. 1998 ⇒ 19,14875. [R]EstFr 106 (2005) 431-435 (*Bosch i Veciana, Antoni*);

15714 *Poppi, Antonino* L'itinerario bonaventuriano alla *plenitudo sapientiae* tra sant'ANTONIO e DUNS SCOTO nelle *Collationes in Hexaëmeron*. [F]PACHECO, M. 2005 ⇒118. 235-253.

15715 CHRISTIAN DE S: *Huygens, R.B.C.* À propos de Christian dit de Stavelot et son explication de l'évangile selon Matthieu. SE 44 (2005) 247-273.

15716 CLAUDIUS T: *Boulhol, P.* Esegesi compilativa a propaganda iconoclastica: Claudio di Torino in bilico tra ossequio alle autorità patristiche e voglia di autogiustificazione. Biblical studies in the early middle ages. Millennio Medievale 52: 2002 ⇒773. 155-174.

15717 DIONYSIUS BAR SALIBI: **Ryan, Stephen Desmond** Dionysius Bar Salibi's factual and spiritual commentary on Psalms 73-82. CRB 57: 2004 ⇒20,14158. [R]OLZ 100 (2005) 507-510 (*Vincent, Jean Marcel*); RBLit (2005)* (*Pentiuc, Eugene*); LASBF 55 (2005) 563-4 (*Pazzini, Massimo*); JThS 56 (2005) 723-26 (*Arthur, Rosemary*).

15718 ECKHART M: *Chardonnens, Denis* La personne du Saint-Esprit dans le commentaire de Maître Eckhart sur l'évangile de saint Jean. Ter. 56 115 (2005) 55-81.

15719 EUGENIUS T: [E]**Alberto, Paulo F.** Eugenii Toletani opera omnia. CChr.SL 114: Turnhout 2005, Brepols 480 pp. 2-503-01141-1. Bibl. 27-32.

15720 FIORE G: *Ford, Josephine M.* L'Anticristo e la nuova Gerusalemme negli scritti di Gioacchino da Fiore. [F]VANNI, U. 2005 ⇒156. 735-752 [Rev 21,1-22,5].

15721 FRANCISCUS A: **Stadler, Volker** 'Ich kenne Christus, den Armen, den Gekreuzigten': paulinische Rezeption in den Schriften des Franziskus von Assisi. [D]*Winkler, Gerhard B.*: Veröffentlichungen der Duns-Skotus Akademie 20: Mönchengladbach 2005, Kühlen 191 pp. €26.80. 3-87448-261-8. Diss. Salzburg.

15722 FRANCISCUS M: *Karris, Robert J.* Francis of Meyronnes' Sermon 57 on the parable of the prodigal son (Luke 15:11-32). FrS 63 (2005) 131-158.

15723 GREGORIUS T: *Ferrarini, E. Cibus, solidus scripturarum sanctarum*: Gregorio di Tours e la bibbia. Biblical studies in the early middle ages. Millennio Medievale 52: 2002 ⇒773. 41-60.

15724 GULIELMUS S.THEODORICI: [E]**Verdeyen, Paul**, *al.*, Meditationes devotissimae. CChr.CM 89: Turnhout 2005, Brepols xix; 142 pp. 2-503-03891-3.

15725 HAIMO A: *Gorman, M.* The commentary on the gospel of John by Haimo of Auxerre. RBen 115 (2005) 61-111;

15726 *Savigni, R.* Il commentario a Isaia di Aimone d'Auxerre e le sue fonti. Biblical studies in the early middle ages. Millennio Medievale 52; Atti di convegni 16: 2002 ⇒773. 215-238.

15727 HEIMERIC C: *Kałuża, Zenon* Brèves remarques sur le triple commentaire du *Pater noster* de Heimeric de Campo (1395-1460). Acta Mediaevalia 18 (2005) 237-252.

15728 HERMANNUS W: [E]**Schmidt, Paulus Gerhardus** Hermanni Werdinensis: Hortus deliciarum. CChr.CM 204: Turnhout 2005, Brepols xix; 489 pp. 2-503-05049-2. Collab. *Mundt, H.; Weber, M.-L.*

15729 HILDEGARD B: *Góngora D., María E.* Escritura e imagen visionaria en el Liber divinorum operum de Hildegard de Bingen. TyV 46 (2005) 374-388.

15730 HUGH S-C: [E]**Bataillon, Louis-J.; Dahan, Gilbert; Gy, Pierre-M.** Hugues de Saint-Cher († 1263), bibliste et théologien. Bibliothèque d'histoire culturelle du Moyen Âge 1: 2004 ⇒20,742. [R]Ang. 82 (2005) 503-4 (*Zambruno, Pablo*); RHEF 91 (2005) 438-9 (*Longère, Jean*); RThom 105 (2005) 661-664 (*Boning, Serge-Thomas*).

15731 ISIDORUS S: *Elfassi, Jacques* Genèse et originalité du style synonymique dans les *Synonyma* d'Isidore de Séville. REL 83 (2005) 226-245.

15732 JOHANNES A: [ET]**Roberto, Umberto** Ioannis Antiocheni fragmenta ex Historia chronica. TU 154: B 2005, De Gruyter ccxi; 661 pp. 3-11-018687-X.

15733 JOHANNES D: [T]**Migliarini, Margherita** Johannes Damascenus: disputatio christiani et saraceni: controversia tra un saraceno e un cristiano. [E]*Rizzi, Giovanni*: Ecumenismo e dialogo: Mi 1998, Centro Ambrosiano 76 pp. 88-8025-108-2.

15734 JOHN OF FORD: [TE]**Emery, Pierre-Yves** Jean de Ford: sermons sur le Cantique des cantiques, 2-3. 2000 ⇒16,12890; 17,12467-8. [R]Mar. 67 (2005) 687-688 (*Gharib, Georges*).

15735 JUAN S: *Wolf, Anne M.* Precedents and paradigms: Juan de Segovia on the bible, the church, and the Ottoman threat. Scripture and pluralism. 2005 ⇒757. 143-160.

15736 JUNILLUS A: [T]**Maas, Michael** Exegesis and empire in the early Byzantine Mediterranean: Junillus Africanus and the Instituta regularia divinae legis. STAC 17: 2003 ⇒19,14898; 20,14178. [R]JThS 56 (2005) 236-238 (*Lössl, Josef*).

15737 LAURENTIUS D: **Daub, Susanne** Von der Bibel zum Epos: poetische Strategien des Laurentius am geistlichen Hof von Durham. Köln 2005, Böhlau 283 pp. €29.90. 3-412-14005-8.

15738 LOVE N: [E]**Sargent, Michael G.** Nicholas Love: the mirror of the blessed life of Christ: a full critical edition based on Cambridge University Library Additional MSS.6578 and 6686. Exeter Medieval Texts and Studies: Exeter 2005, Univ. of Exeter Pr. xviii; 433 pp. £60. 08598-97400.

15739 LUIS DE L: [E]**Barrientos García, José** Fray Luis de León: Tratado sobre la ley: introducción, transcripción y notas. [T]*Fernández Vallina, Emiliano*: Monasterio de El Escorial 2005, Escurialenses 581 pp. [R]RevAg 46 (2005) 632-635 (*Lazcano, Rafael*).

15740 LULLUS R: [T]**Domínguez Reboiras, Fernando** Ramon Llull: das Buch über die heilige Maria/Libre de sancta Maria: katalanisch-deutsch. *Padrós* [T]*Wolff, Elisenda*: MyGG.Abt. I. Christliche Mystik 19: Stu 2005, Frommann-H. xlvii; 379 pp. 3-7728-2216-9;

15741 [E]**Medina, Jaume** Raimundus Lullus: in Cypro, alleas in Cilicia deque Transmarinis veniente annis MCCCI-MCCCII compilata. CChr.CM 184; Raimundi Lulli opera latina 30: Turnhout 2005, Brepols xli; 248 pp. 2-503-04841-2. Opera et catalogi xxxvi-xli.

15742 MAXIMUS C: *Benevich, Grigory* The sabbath in St. Maximus the Confessor. Studi sull'Oriente Cristiano 9/1 (2005) 63-81;

15743 **Cooper, Adam G.** The body in St. Maximus the Confessor: holy flesh, wholly deified. Oxf 2005, OUP xii; 287 pp. 0-19-927570-X. Bibl. 255-276;

15744 **Renczes, Philipp Gabriel** Agir de Dieu et liberté de l'homme: recherches sur l'anthropologie théologique de saint Maxime le Confesseur. CFi 229: 2003 ⇒19,14903. [R]RSR 93 (2005) 144-146 (*Sesboüé, Bernard*); RHE 100 (2005) 185-187 (*Larchet, Jean-Claude*); JThS 56 (2005) 239-240 (*Louth, Andrew*).

15745 NICHOLAS L: [E]**Krey, Philip D.W.; Smith, Lesley J.** Nicholas of Lyra: the senses of scripture. SHCT 90: 2000 ⇒16,1466... 18, 13717. [R]ThR 70 (2005) 84-87 (*Obst, Martin*).

15746 PETRUS C: [E]**Sylwan, Agneta** Petrus Comestoris Scolastica Historia: liber Genesis. CChr.CM 191: Turnhout 2005, Brepols lxxxix; 227 pp. 2-503-04911-7. Bibl.

15747 RICHARD C : **Carpin, Attilio** I sacramenti nelle "Costituzioni Sinodali" di Richard "the Poor". SacDo.M 50/1: Bo 2005, Studio Domenicano 157 pp.

15748 RUPERTUS T: [ET]**Magoga, Alessio** Ruperto di Deutz: Mite e umile di cuore: i libri XII et XIII del 'De gloria et honore Filii hominis: super Matthaeum'. Sapientia 13: Mi 2004, Glossa xiii; 288 pp. €28. 978-88710-51680. Ed. biling.

15749 SCOTUS D: *Pickstock, Catherine* Duns Scotus: his historical and contemporary significance. MoTh 21 (2005) 543-574.

15750 WILLIAM A: *Smith, Lesley* William of Auvergne and the law of the Jews and the Muslims. Scripture and pluralism. 2005 ⇒757.123-142.

15751 WILLIAM S-T: *Partoens, Gert* La présence d'AUGUSTIN dans l'*Expositio super epistolam ad Romanos* de Guillaume de Saint-Thierry. SE 44 (2005) 285-300.

15752 WYCLIF J: [E]**Brocchieri, M. Fumagalli Beonio; Simonetta, S.** John Wyclif: logica, politica, teologia. Impruneta 2003, Sismel 195 pp. ⇒19, 14916. [R]Il Pensiero Politico 38 (2005) 316-318 (*Scichilone, G.*);

15753 **Evans, G.R.** John Wyclif: myth and reality. DG 2005, Intervarsity 320 pp. $25;

15754 **Levy, Ian Christopher** John Wyclif: scriptural logic, Real Presence, and the parameters of orthodoxy. 2003 ⇒19,14917; 20, 14193. [R]ChH 74 (2005) 364-365 (*Jeffrey, David Lyle*);

15755 **Zamagni, Gianmaria** Scrittura, verità, domini: bibbia, metafisica e politica nell'ermeneutica di John Wyclif tra la 'Postilla in totam bibliam' e il 'Tractatus de veritate sacre Scripture' (1372-1378). 2005, Diss. Bologna [ASEs 23,558—Mauro Pesce].

### Y4.1 Luther

15756 *Arnold, Matthieu* La christologie de Martin Luther d'après sa correspondance. RHPhR 85 (2005) 151-169.

15757 *Asendorf, Ulrich* Schrift und Dogma: zur Systematik in Luthers Theologie [Scripture and dogma: regarding the systematic aspect of Luther's theology]. Luther Digest 13 (2005) 10-11 <KuD 48 (2002) 301-318.

15758 *Bell, Theo M.M.A.C.* Man is a microcosmos: Adam and Eve in Luther's "Lectures on Genesis" (1535-1545). CTQ 69/2 (2005) 159-184 [Gen 2,4-3,24].

15759 E**Beutel, Albrecht** Luther Handbuch. Tü 2005, Mohr S. 537 pp. €44. 3-16-148267-0.
15760 *Birmelé, André* De Luther à Leuenberg. RHPhR 85 (2005) 137-50.
15761 **Burgwald, Christopher T.** The sinfulness of the justified in Lutheran-Catholic dialogue in the United States of America. Siouxormen 2005, n.p. iv; 169 pp. Bibl. 152-169.
15762 *Chen, Kuan-Shian* The teaching of the Lord's Supper in Luther's *Confession concerning Christ's Supper*. ThLi 28 (2005) 187-206 Sum. 205s.
15763 *Christensen, Carl C.* Luther and the woodcuts to the 1534 Bible. LuthQ 19/4 (2005) 392-413.
15764 *Forsberg, Juhani* Die finnische Lutherforschung seit 1979. LuJ 72 (2005) 147-182.
15765 *Frankemölle, Hubert* Völker-Verheißung (Gen 12-18) und Sinai-Tora im Römerbrief: das "Dazwischen" (Röm 5,20) als hermeneutischer Parameter für eine lutherische oder nichtlutherische Paulus-Auslegung. Lutherische und neue Paulusperspektive. WUNT 182: 2005 ⇒339. 275-307.
15766 *George, Timothy* Martin Luther. Reading Romans. 2005 ⇒400. 101-119.
15767 *Hartweg, Frédéric* Luther et le livre. RHPhR 85 (2005) 125-135.
15768 *Hofmann, Frank* Christus als Mitte der Schrift: eine Erinnerung an Martin Luthers Umgang mit der Bibel. Luther-Bulletin 14 (2005) 10-26.
15769 *Jensen, Finn G.* Om Martin Luthers oversaettelse af Det Nye Testamente: med et sideblik til ERASMUS af Rotterdams "Novum instrumentum". DTT 68/2 (2005) 97-108.
15770 *Jones, Ken S.* The apocalyptic Luther. Word and world 25 (2005) 308-316.
15771 *Junghans, Helmar* Martin Luther und die Welt der Reformation. LuJ 72 (2005) 183-198.
15772 *Junghans, Helmar*, *al.*, Lutherbibliographie 2005. LuJ 72 (2005) 199-260.
15773 *Junghans, Helmar* Bibelhumanistische Anstöße in Luthers Entwicklung zum Reformator. RHPhR 85 (2005) 17-42.
15774 **Kaufmann, Thomas** Luthers "Judenschriften" in ihren historischen Kontexten. NAWG I. Phil.-hist. Kl. 2005,6: Gö 2005, Vandenhoeck & R. 108 pp.
15775 *Koch, Ernst* Ecclesia peccatrix: Beobachtungen zur Auslegung des Gleichnisses Matthäus 13,24-30 bei Martin Luther und einigen seiner Zeitgenossen. FSTOLLE, V. 2005 ⇒143. 111-125.
15776 *Kreuzer, Siegfried* Die Botschaft von der Rechtfertigung im Alten Testament [The message of justification in the Old Testament]. Luther Digest 13 (2005) 12-14 ⇒18,7870.
15777 E**Lull, Timothy F.** Martin Luther's basic theological writings. Mp 22005 <1989>, Fortress xxviii; 489 pp. $39. 0-8006-3680-5. Foreword *Jaroslav Pelikan*; CD-ROM ed. by *William R. Russell* [ThD 52,174—W. Charles Heiser].
15778 **Mannermaa, Tuomo** Christ present in faith: Luther's view of justification. E*Stjerna, Kirsi*: Mp 2005, Fortress xx; 136 pp. $18. 0-800-6-3711-9 [ThD 52,176—W. Charles Heiser].
15779 Martin Luther's tabletalk: Luther's comments on life, the church and the bible. 2003 ⇒19,14936. RSBET 23 (2005) 217-219 (*Thomas, Geoffrey*).

15780 **Marty, Martin** Martin Luther: a penguin life. 2004 ⇒20,14209. [R]AThR 87 (2005) 505-507 (*Carty, Jarrett*).

15781 [E]**McKim, Donald K.** The Cambridge companion to Martin Luther. 2003 ⇒19,14939; 20,14212. [R]Luther-Bulletin 14/Nov. (2005) 98-99 (*Zwanepol, Klaas*).

15782 *Meyer zu Helligen, Klaus-Peter* Martin Luther, wie er sich selbst verstanden hat. WuD 28 (2005) 139-156.

15783 **Mullett, Michael A.** Martin Luther. 2004 ⇒20,14214. [R]RRT 12/1 (2005) 1-2 (*Wollaston, Isabel*).

15784 **Nicolaus, Georg** Die pragmatische Theologie des Vaterunsers und ihre Rekonstruktion durch Martin Luther. Lp 2005, Evangelische 384 pp. 3-374-02251-0.

15785 **Öberg, Ingemar** Bibelsyn och bibeltolkning hos Martin Luther. 2002 ⇒18,13751; 20,14217. [R]ThLZ 130 (2005) 1083-1085 (*Johansson, Torbjörn*).

15786 **Parsons, Michael** Luther and CALVIN on Old Testament narratives: Reformation thought and narrative text. TSR 106: 2004 ⇒20, 14218. [R]SCJ 36 (2005) 592-594 (*MacGregor, Kirk R.*).

15787 *Pilvousek, Josef* Martin Luther, Erfurt und die Scherflein der armen Witwe. ThG 48 (2005) 148-149 [Mark 12,42; Lk 21,2].

15788 *Posset, Franz* BERNHARD von Clairvauxs Meditation zu Psalm 31,2 bei Martin Luther [Martin Luther's reference to Bernard of Clairvaux's meditation on Psalm 31:2]. Luther Digest 13 (2005) 15 <LuJ 69 (2002) 71-78.

15789 **Schneider, Florian** Christus praedicatus et creditus: die reformatorische Christologie Luthers in den Operationes in Psalmos (1519-1521). 2004 ⇒20,14221. [R]EstAg 40 (2005) 183-184 (*Garrido, A.*).

15790 **Schulken, Christian** Lex efficax: Studien zur Sprachwerdung des Gesetzes bei Luther im Anschluß an die Disputationen gegen die Antinomer. HUTh 48: Tü 2005, Mohr S. xi;, 450 pp. 3-16-148638-2. Bibl. 427-441.

15791 *Stolle, Thomas* Weil es um Menschen geht: Luthers Ansicht zur Bedeutung der Vermittlung bei tiefgreifenden Reformvorhaben. [F]STOLLE, V. 2005 ⇒143. 143-150.

15792 *Stolle, Volker* Nomos zwischen Tora und Lex: der paulinische Gesetzesbegriff und seine Interpretation durch Luther in der zweiten Disputation gegen die Antinomer vom 12. Januar 1538. Lutherische und neue Paulusperspektive. WUNT 182: 2005 ⇒339. 41-67;

15793 'Von der Freiheit eines Christenmenschen' (1520): ein exemplarisches Selbstporträt Luthers mit paulinischen Zügen. LuJ 72 (2005) 13-48.

15794 **Thompson, Mark D.** A sure ground on which to stand: the relation of authority and interpretive method in Luther's approach to scripture. 2004 ⇒20,14226. [R]TrinJ 26 (2005) 337-38 (*Gazal, Andre A.*).

15795 *Westhelle, V.* Luther on the authority of scripture. LuthQ 19 (2005) 373-391 [NTAb 50,243].

15796 *Windhorst, Christof* Theologie mit Herz bei Martin Luther und "Herzensfrömmigkeit" im Pietismus. WuD 28 (2005) 157-181.

15797 *Wolff, Jens* 'Die größten Worte der gesamten Schrift': der gottverlassene Christus laut Psalm 22 aus Luthers Sicht. Luther 76 (2005) 101-107.

15798 **Wolff, Jens** Metapher und Kreuz: Studien zu Luthers Christusbild. HUTh 47: Tü 2005, Mohr S. xxiii; 677 pp. 3-16-148605-6. Bibl. 609-640.

15799 *Yang, Andrew S.* Abraham and Isaac, child abuse and Martin Luther. LuthQ 19/2 (2005) 153-166 [Gen 22,1-19].

15800 [E]**Zschoch, Hellmut** Das Wort Gottes zwischen Mystik und Politik: Martin Luthers Predigt über Lk 7,11-17 vom 2. Oktober 1530 auf der Veste Coburg. Luther 76 (2005) 3-10.

## Y4.3 Exegesis et controversia saeculi XVI

15801 *Arnold, Matthieu; Philonenko, Marc* La réformation, un temps, des hommes, un message: hommage à Marc Lienhard à l'occasion de son soixante-dixième anniversaire. RHPhR 85 (2005) 3-4.

15802 *Bräuer, Siegfried* Umgestaltung und Übergänge: Beobachtungen zu den Anfängen des reformatorischen Gottesdienstes. RHPhR 85 (2005) 51-71.

15803 *Bühler, Pierre* La réception de la parabole du blé et de l'ivraie dans la période de la Réforme. CrSt 26 (2005) 265-278 [Mt 13,24-30; 13,36-43].

15804 *Elwood, Christopher* A singular example of the wrath of God: the use of Sodom in sixteenth-century exegesis. HThR 98 (2005) 67-93 [Gen 19].

15805 *Jung, Martin H.* Die Bibel im Streit zwischen den Konfessionen. Das Buch. Vechtaer Beiträge zur Theologie 11: 2005 ⇒487. 79-86.

15806 *Matter, E. Ann* Religious dissidence and the bible in sixteenth-century Italy: the idiosyncratic Bible of Lucia Brocadelli da Narni. Scripture and pluralism. 2005 ⇒757. 193-207.

15807 *Millet, Olivier* Propagande catholique, convictions protestantes et duplicité textuelle: la paix de Dieu (1685/1690) du compte Gédéon de Reffuge, nouveau converti. RHPhR 85 (2005) 73-87.

15808 *Neumann, Klaus* "Was Gott zusammengefügt hat, das soll der Mensch nicht scheiden": Recht, Ritual, Romantik—Kontexte des Schriftwortes Mt 19,6 und seiner Interpretation in der Reformationszeit und im bürgerlichen Zeitalter. [F]STEGEMANN, W. 2005 ⇒ 139. 83-106.

15809 *Tozzini, Cinzia* La bibbia nel cinquecento: un sito web dedicato alle edizioni e alle interpretazioni della sacra scrittura. Rinasc. 45 (2005) 399-411.

15810 *Trueman, Carl* The impact of the Reformation and emerging modernism. Bible in pastoral practice. 2005 ⇒341. 78-96.

15811 **Zwaan, Johan; Vree, Jasper** Abraham KUYPER'S Commentatio (1860): the young Kuyper about CALVIN, a Lasco, and the Church. Brill's series in church history 24: Lei 2005, Brill 2 vols; 664 pp. 90-04-14940-6.

## Y4.4 Periti aetatis reformatoriae

15812 BUCER M: *Greschat, Martin* Vielgestaltigkeit und Geschlossenheit im Kirchenverständnis Martin Bucers. RHPhR 85 (2005) 103-114;

15813 *Noblesse-Rocher, Annie* La prédication prophétique selon le réformateur Martin Bucer (1491-1551). ConnPE 99 (2005) 103-110;

15814 Bucer et les juifs. FV 104/5 (2005) 21-35.

15815 BULLINGER H: *Scharf, Greg R.* Was Bullinger right about the preached word?. TrinJ 26 (2005) 3-10.

15816 CALVIN J: **Boer, E.A. de** John Calvin on the visions of Ezekiel. 2004 ⇒20,14243. RSCJ 36 (2005) 845-846 (*Balserak, Jon*).

15817 *Demson, David* John Calvin. Reading Romans. 2005 ⇒400. 137-148;

15818 *Edmondson, S.* Christ and history: hermeneutical convergence in Calvin and his challenge to biblical theology. MoTh 21/1 (2005) 3-35 [NTAb 49,235];

15819 E**McKim, Donald K.** The Cambridge companion to John Calvin. 2004 ⇒20,507. RRRT 12 (2005) 539-542 (*Fout, Jason A.*); Neotest. 39 (2005) 201-203 (*Coetzee, C.F.C.*); RHE 100 (2005) 997-999 (*Gilmont, Jean-François*);

15820 *Schützeichel, Heribert* Der eine Gott genügt: Calvins Auslegung des 16. Psalmes. TThZ 114 (2005) 46-61;

15821 **Schützeichel, Heribert** Der Herr mein Hirt: Calvin und der Psalter. Trier 2005, Paulinus 112 pp. €14.90. 3-7902-0221-5.

15822 E**Selderhuis, Herman J.** Calvini opera database 1.0. Apeldoorn 2005, Instituut voor Reformatienonderzoek [Kerux 21/2,45s—J.T. Dennison, Jr.].

15823 **Tourn, Giorgio** Giovanni Calvino: il riformatore di Ginevra. T 2005, Claudiana 100 pp;

15824 **Walker, Williston** John Calvin: revolutionary, theologian, pastor. Fearn 2005 <1906>, Christian Focus 342 pp.

15825 CAPITO W: *Brady, Thomas A.* Wolfgang Capito's in-laws: the Roettels of Strasbourg. RHPhR 85 (2005) 43-50.

15826 ERASMUS: **Christ-von Wedel, Christine** Erasmus von Rotterdam: Anwalt eines neuzeitlichen Christentums. 2003 ⇒19,14962. RHZ 280 (2005) 172-173 (*Mörke, Olaf*);

15827 *François, Wim* La condamnation par les théologiens parisiens du plaidoyer d'Érasme pour la traduction de la bible dans la langue vulgaire (1527-1531). Aug(L) 55 (2005) 357-405;

15828 **Mansfield, Bruce** Erasmus in the twentieth century: interpretations c. 1920-2000. 2003 ⇒19,2160; 20,14262. RJR 85 (2005) 316-317 (*Kooistra, Milton*);

15829 E**Minnich, Nelson H.** Erasmus: Controversies: Responsio ad epistolam paraeneticam Alberti Pii Apologia adversus rhapsodias Albert Pii Brevissima scholia. T*Sheerin, Daniel*: Collected works of Erasmus 84: Toronto 2005, Univ. of Toronto Pr. cxli; 483 pp. 0-80-20-4397-6. Bibl. 406-419 [Ps 22; 28; 33; 85];

15830 E**Pabel, Hilmar Matthias; Vessey, Mark** Holy Scripture speaks: the production and reception of Erasmus' 'Paraphrases on the New Testament'. Erasmus Studies 14: 2002 ⇒18,13785; 20,14263. RZwingliana 32 (2005) 162-164 (*Christ-von Wedel, Christine*);

15831 **Rummel, Erika** Erasmus. 2004 ⇒20,14264. RZwingliana 32 (2005) 161-162 (*Christ-von Wedel, Christine*).

15832 IGNATIUS L: *Gabel, H.* Ignatian contemplation and modern biblical studies. Way 44/2 (2005) 37-49;

15833 **Mendiboure, Bernard** Lire la bible avec Ignace de Loyola. P 2005, L'Atelier 252 pp. €23.

15834 JOHN C: *Girón Negrón, Luis M.* 'Mi alma tuvo sed de ti...': San Juan de la Cruz y sus dos versiones del psalmo 62:2. San Juan de la Cruz 21 (2005) 131-152.

15835 LATIMER H: *Zschoch, Hellmut* Hugh LATIMER als Prediger auf dem Weg zur Reformation. WuD 28 (2005) 117-138.

15836 MELANCHTHON P: *Büttgen, Philippe* Doctrine et allégorie au début de la Réforme: Melanchthon. Allégorisme des poètes. 2005 ⇒874. 289-322;

15837 *Pérès, Jacques-Noël* Melanchthon, par les pères le retour à l'écriture. ConnPE 100 (2005) 31-36.

15838 MONTAIGNE M DE: *Vignolo, Roberto* Michel de MONTAIGNE, utente ottimale dell'Ecclesiaste. Teol(Br) 30 (2005) 377-398.

15839 SOTO D DE: *Artola, Antonio M.* Domingo de Soto pionero de la propedéutica bíblica. CTom 132 (2005) 265-294.

15840 TYNDALE W: *Greenman, Jeffrey P.* William Tyndale. Reading Romans. 2005 ⇒400. 121-136;

15841 *Snare, Gerald* Reading Tyndale's bible. JMEMS 35 (2005) 289-325.

15842 WITZEL G: *Kathrein, Werner* Eine Auslegung von Lk 2,1-14 durch den Fuldaer Theologen Georg Witzel (1501-1573). [F]ZMIJEWSKI, J.: BBB 151: 2005 ⇒172. 307-319.

## Y4.5 *Exegesis post-reformatoria*—Historical criticism to 1800

15843 *Chédozeau, Bernard* Lectures port-royalistes de la parabole de l'ivraie. CrSt 26 (2005) 279-295 [Mt 13,24-30].

15844 **Sheehan, Jonathan** The Enlightenment Bible: translation, scholarship, culture. Princeton 2005, Princeton Univ. Pr. 273 pp. $35. 0-691-11887-6.

## Y4.7 Auctores 1600-1800 alphabetice

15845 BAYLE P: *Gros, Jean-Michel* La parabole de la zizanie chez Pierre Bayle. CrSt 26 (2005) 297-319 [Mt 13,24-30].

15846 EDWARDS J.: **Brown, Robert E.** Jonathan Edwards and the bible. 2002 ⇒18,13802...20,14274. [R]MoTh 21/1 (2005) 183-185 (*Chamberlain, Ava*); RBLit (2005)* (*Clark, Ronald*).

15847 HAMANN J: *Levy, Ze'ev* Hamanns Gegenüberstellung von Abraham, Moses und Jesus. Die Gegenwärtigkeit. 2005 ⇒830. 467-474;

15848 *Lindner, Helgo* Hören auf Johann Georg Hamann in der Auseinandersetzung um die Wahrheit der Bibel: die bleibende Bedeutung der Hamann-Rezeption im Hallenser Biblizismus. Die Gegenwärtigkeit. 2005 ⇒830. 441-453.

15849 LAURENTIUS B: [E]**Tombeur, Paul**, *al.*, Thesaurus Laurentii a Brundusio, 1: opera theologica et exegetica, series A—formae: enumeratio formarum. CChr.Thesaurus Patrum Latinorum: Turnhout 2005, Brepols xlvii; 386 pp.

15850 LOCKE J: **Parker, Kim Ian** The biblical politics of John Locke. 2004 ⇒20,14288. [R]JThS 56 (2005) 776-781 (*Pailin, David A.*).

15851 MEIJER L: **Meijer, Lodewijk** Philosophy as the interpreter of Holy Scripture (1666). [T]*Shirley, Samuel*: Marquette studies in philosophy 43: Milwaukee, WI 2005, Marquette Univ. Pr. vi, 291 pp. 087-4626668. Introd., notes: *Lee C. Rice*; *Francis Pastijn*; Bibl. 271-91.

15852 NEWTON I: *Lucci, Diego* Filosemitismo e apocalittica nell'ermeneutica biblica di Isaac Newton. Materia giudaica 10/1 (2005) 135-150.

15853 SIMON R: **Müller, Sascha** Richard Simon (1638-1712): Exeget, Theologe, Philosoph und Historiker: eine Biographie. Wü 2005, Echter 160 pp. €14.80/15.30. 3-429-02399-8.

15854 SPINOZA B: *Lötzsch, Frieder* Spinozas "Theologisch-politischer Traktat" oder die Kunst, auf theologische Weise "untheologisch" zu sein. [F]STOLLE, V. 2005 ⇒143. 29-39.

15855 SWEDENBORG E; SKOVORODA H: *Scherer, Stephen P.* A comparison of Swedenborg and Skovoroda's biblical thought. Logos 46/1-2 (2005) 45-71.

15856 TIRSO DE M: *Eguiarte Bendímez, Enrique* El "Pentateuco" tirsiano: en torno las obras del ciclo bíblico de Tirso de Molina. Mayéutica 31/71 (2005) 5-33.

15857 WESLEY J: *Shepherd, Victor* John Wesley. Reading Romans. 2005 ⇒400. 149-168.

Y5.0 *Saeculum XIX*—**Exegesis—19th century**

15858 **Baird, William** History of New Testament research, 2: from Jonathan EDWARDS to Rudolf BULTMANN. 2003 ⇒19,14997; 20,14296. [R]JRH 29 (2005) 310-312 (*Kloppenborg, John*); Neotest. 39 (2005) 434-439 (*Stenschke, Christoph*).

15859 *Fessenden, Tracy* The nineteenth-century bible wars and the separation of church and state. ChH 74 (2005) 784-811.

15860 *Finlay, Hueston* From SCHLEIERMACHER to BARTH: meeting the challenge of critical scholarship. Bible in pastoral practice. Ment. *Newman, J.*: 2005 ⇒341. 97-116.

15861 *Negri, Rosalba* Far festa in Quaresima: la Samaritana nella tradizione popolare in Brianza. Acme 58/2 (2005) 159-195 [John 4,1-42].

15862 **Whelan, Irene** The bible war in Ireland: the 'Second Reformation' and the polarization of Protestant-Catholic relations, 1800-1840. Dublin 2005, Lilliput 384 pp.

15863 **Wintzek, Oliver** Mythos und Offenbarung: David Friedrich STRAUSS und Friedrich Wilhelm Joseph SCHELLING. [D]*Salmann, Elmar*: R 2005, 152 pp. Extr. Diss. Gregoriana; Bibl. 119-144.

15864 COLENSO J: *Larsen, Timothy* John William Colenso. Reading Romans. 2005 ⇒400. 187-204.

15865 FICHTE J: *Grätzel, Stephan* Verkündigung in Übereinstimmung mit der Vernunft: Fichtes Auslegung des Johannesevangeliums;

15866 HEGEL G: *Ringleben, Joachim* Die Dialektik von Freiheit und Sünde: Hegels Interpretation von Genesis 3. Biblical interpretation. SBL.Symp. 26: 2005 ⇒758. 103-112/133-139.

15867 HODGE C: *Noll, Mark* Charles Hodge. Reading Romans. 2005 ⇒ 400. 169-186.

15868 HUPFELD H: **Kaiser, Otto** Zwischen Reaktion und Revolution: Hermann Hupfeld (1796-1866)—ein deutsches Professorenleben.

AAWG.PH 268: Gö 2005, Vandenhoeck & R. 304 pp. €74.90. 35-258-25408.

15869 KIERKEGAARD S: *Klauck, Hans-Josef* Abraham and Kierkegaard: a reading of *Fear and trembling*. ThD 52 (2005) 303-320 [Gen 22].

15870 RENAN E: **Rétat, Laudyce** L'Israël de Renan. Recherches en littérature et spiritualité 9: Bern 2005, Lang xv; 208 pp. €42.80. 3-039-10-646-5.

15871 SCHELLING F: *Gräb, Wilhelm* Anerkannte Kontingenz: Schellings existentiale Interpretation des Johannesprologs in der Philosophie der Offenbarung [John 1,1-18];

15872 SCHLEIERMACHER F: *Helmer, Christine* The consummation of reality: soteriological metaphysics in Schleiermacher's interpretation of Colossians 1:15-20. Biblical interpretation. SBL.Symp. 26: 2005 ⇒758. 141-154/113-131.

[E]**Mariña, J.** Cambridge companion to Schleiermacher 2005 ⇒566.

15873 VAN ESS L: **Altenberend, Johannes** Leander van Eß (1772-1847). SQWFG 41: 2001 ⇒17,12590. [R]TThZ 114 (2005) 341-342 (*Meier, Johannes*); ZKG 116 (2005) 417-419 (*Hauzenberger, Hans*).

## Y5.5 *Crisi modernistica*—The Modernist Era

15874 [E]**Chauvin, Ch.** A. LOISY: Ecrits évangéliques: un siècle après les 'petits livres rouges'. 2002 ⇒18,13823. [R]RB 112 (2005) 308-309 (*Nodet, Etienne*).

15875 **Goichot, Émile** Alfred LOISY et ses amis. 2002 ⇒18,13826. [R]RB 112 (2005) 306-308 (*Nodet, Etienne*).

15876 *Joassart, Bernard* Figures du modernisme: Eudoxe Irénée MIGNOT et Marie-Joseph LAGRANGE: à propos de livres récents. NRTh 127 (2005) 615-622.

15877 *Pym, David* How Edwardian Modernists read the canon: a short study of Hastings Rashdall, Hensley Henson and Charles Gore. MoBe 46/3 (2005) 6-14.

## Y6.0 *Saeculum XX-XXI*—20th-21st Century Exegesis

15878 *Boisclair, Regina* Developments in catholic biblical studies reflected in three 20th century 'Catholic encyclopedias'. JRTI 7/1 (2005) 57-72.

15879 **Chalamet, Christophe** Dialectical theologians: Wilhelm HERRMANN, Karl BARTH and Rudolf BULTMANN. Z 2005, Theologischer 327 pp. 3290-17324-0.

15880 *Eder, Manfred* Hitler und die Bibel: Anmerkungen zu einem merkwürdigen Verhältnis. Das Buch. Vechtaer Beiträge zur Theologie 11: 2005 ⇒487. 130-162.

15881 [E]**Ford, David F.; Muers, Rachel** The modern theologians: an introduction to christian theology since 1918. Oxf 2005, Blackwells xxi; 819 pp. £20. 1-4051-02772 [RRT 13,263s—Philip McCosker].

15882 **Harrington, Daniel J.** How do catholics read the bible?. Lanham 2005, Rowman & L. xv; 159 pp. $16. 0-7425-4870-8. Bibl. 133-35.

15883 **Hoppe, Leslie J.** New light from old stories: the Hebrew scriptures for today's world. NY 2005, Paulist x; 192 pp. 0-8091-41167. Bibl. 192.

15884 *Léon-Dufour, Xavier* Che cosa aspettarsi da un esegeta?. Un biblista cerca Dio. Collana biblica: 2005 <1967> ⇒245. 15-30.

15885 *Matand Bulembat, Jean-Bosco* From text to meaning: the itinerary of an exegete and the task of inculturation. African christian studies 21/3 (2005) 5-34.

15886 *Merk, Otto* 'Viele waren Neutestamentler': zur Lage neutestamentlicher Wissenschaft 1933-1945 und ihrem zeitlichen Umfeld. ThLZ 130 (2005) 106-120.

15887 **Myre, André** Maintenant la parole: propos inspirés de la bible. 2004 ⇒20,14315. [R]Theoforum 36 (2005) 247-48 (*Vogels, Walter*).

15888 *Rogerson, John* The gifts and challenges of historical and literary criticism. Bible in pastoral practice. 2005 ⇒341. 121-134.

15889 **Savran, George W.** Encountering the divine: theophany in biblical narrative. JSOT.S 420: L 2005, Clark viii; 280 pp. £75. 0-567-043-91-6. Bibl. 254-262.

15890 [E]**Sozzi Manci, Maria Assunta** Le figlie di Abramo: donne, sessualità e religione. Percorsi dell'identità femminile nel Novecento 5: Mi 1998, Guerini 94 pp. 88-7802-867-3. Bibl.

15891 **Wersinger, Jacques** Lire la bible avec P. RICOEUR et P. BEAUCHAMP. [D]*Chauvet, Louis-Marie* 2005, Diss. Institut catholique de Paris.

15892 [E]**Yarbrough, Robert W.** The salvation historical fallacy: reassessing the history of New Testament theology. 2004 ⇒20,14319. [R]Theol. 108 (2005) 357-358 (*Marshall, I. Howard*).

15893 ALLEGRO J: **Brown, Judith Anne** John Marco Allegro: the maverick of the Dead Sea scrolls. GR 2005, Eerdmans xvi; 288 pp. $25/€16. 0-8028-2849-3. [R]OTEs 18 (2005) 930-932 (*Naudé, J.A.*).

15894 ALLIS O: *Wood, John H.* Oswald T. Allis and the question of Isaianic authorship. JETS 48 (2005) 249-261 [OTA 30,354].

15895 BAGATTI B: *Rees, Elizabeth* A great scholar: Bellarmino Bagatti. Holy Land (Winter 2005) 5-6.

15896 BALTHASAR H VON: *Bramwell, Bevil* Hans Urs von Balthasar's theology of scripture. NBl 86 (2005) 308-322;

15897 [E]**Capol, Cornelia; Müller, Claudia** Hans Urs von Balthasar: Bibliographie 1925-2005. FrB 2005, Johannes 223 pp. €24. 3-89411-029-5;

15898 **Dickens, William Thomas** Hans Urs von Balthasar's theological aesthetics: a model for post-critical biblical interpretation. 2003 ⇒ 19,15062. [R]ThTo 62 (2005) 99-100 (*Steck, Christopher*); JThS 56 (2005) 281-283 (*Horne, Brian*);

15899 *Löser, Werner* Wort und Wort Gottes in der Theologie Hans Urs von Balthasars. ThPh 80 (2005) 225-248.

15900 BARTH K: **Aguti, Andrea** La questione dell'ermeneutica in Karl Barth. 2001 ⇒17,12606; 18,13846. [R]RSR 93 (2005) 434-437 (*Holzer, Vincent*);

15901 *Baumbach, Günther* Was ich bei Karl Barth gelernt habe: Anmerkungen eines Exegeten zu Barths Umgang mit der Heiligen Schrift. Josephus–Jesusbewegung. 2005 <1987> ⇒182. 221-232;

15902 **Bourgine, Benoît** L'herméneutique théologique de Karl Barth: exégèse et dogmatique dans le quatrième volume de la Kirchliche Dogmatik. 2003 ⇒19,15064; 20,14323. [R]Gr. 86 (2005) 190-191

(*Hercsik, Donath*); RSR 93 (2005) 437-440 (*Holzer, Vincent*); Iren. 78 (2005) 295-298; EThL 81 (2005) 545-550 (*Cardon, P.*);

15903 **Burnett, Richard** Karl Barth's theological exegesis: the hermeneutical principles of the Römerbrief period. WUNT 2/145: 2001 ⇒ 17,12608...20,14324. [R]SBET 23 (2005) 103-4 (*Gignilliat, Mark*);

15904 **Gallas, Alberto** Il giovane Barth: fra teologia e politica. 2004 ⇒ 20,14327. [R]Il Regno 50 (2005) 545-546 (*Potestà, Gian Luca*);

15905 **Müller, Denis** Karl Barth. Initiation aux Théologiens: P 2005, Cerf 372 pp. €32. 2-204-07913-8;

15906 *Rostagno, S.* Karl Barth (1886-1968). CredOg 25/2 (2005) 33-42;

15907 *Stegemann, Ekkehard W.* Israel in Barths Erwählungslehre: zur Auslegung von Röm 9-11 in KD II, 2, § 34. KuI 20 (2005) 19-42;

15908 *Webster, John* Karl Barth. Reading Romans. 2005 ⇒400. 205-223;

15909 **Webster, John** Karl Barth. 2000 ⇒16,13015... 20,14334. [R]ThLZ 130 (2005) 310-311 (*Drewes, Hans-Anton*);

15910 Karl Barth. [2]2004 <2000> ⇒20,14334. [R]SBET 23 (2005) 124-125 (*McDivitt, Heather Paige*).

15911 *Wood, Donald* 'Ich sah mit Staunen': reflections on the theological substance of Barth's early hermeneutics. SJTh 58 (2005) 184-198.

15912 BELTZ W: Bibliographie Walter Beltz. HBO 40 (2005) 1-14.

15913 BENEDICT XVI: *Kaczorowski, Robert* Kardynała Ratzingera teoria sztuki i muzyki biblijnej [Cardinal Ratzinger's theory of biblical art and music]. RBL 58 (2005) 291-300. **P.**

15914 BONHOEFFER D: [E]**Bethge, Renate; Gremmels, Christian** Dietrich Bonhoeffer: Bilder eines Lebens. Gü [3]2005, Gü 160 pp. 3-579-071-13-0. Zahlr. Fotos.

15915 BÖCHER O: *Himmighöfer, Traudel* Bibliographie Otto Böcher [in Auswahl; ohne Buchbesprechungen]. [F]BÖCHER, O. 2005 ⇒14. 433-460.

15916 BROOKE G: *Schuller, Eileen* George J. Brooke and the Dead Sea scrolls. BJRL 86/3 (2004) 175-196.

15917 BROWN R: *Barré, Michael L.* A bibliography of the publications of Raymond E. Brown, S.S. [M]BROWN, R. 2005 ⇒15. 259-289;

15918 *Witherup, Ronald D.* The incarnate word revealed: the pastoral writings of Raymond E. Brown. [M]BROWN, R. 2005 ⇒15. 238-252;

15919 Biography of Raymond E. Brown, S.S. [M]BROWN, R. 2005 ⇒15. 254-258.

15920 BRUCE F: *Oakes, Peter* F.F. Bruce and the development of evangelical biblical scholarship. BJRL 86/3 (2004) 99-124.

15921 BRUEGGEMANN W: *Brueggemann, Walter* Concluding reflections. [F]BRUEGGEMANN, W.—COUSAR, C. 2005 ⇒16. 157-163.

15922 BUBER M: [E]**Friedenthal-Haase, Martha; Koerenz, Ralf** Martin Buber: Bildung, Menschenbild und hebräischer Humanismus. Pd 2005, Schöningh xiv; 264 pp. €29.90. 3-506-71790-1;

15923 *Jacobi, Juliane* Einleitung. Buber, Martin: Werkausgabe, 8: Schriften zu Jugend, Erziehung und Bildung. 2005 ⇒196. 11-76.

15924 BULTMANN R: *Boff, G.* Rudolf Bultmann (1884-1976). CredOg 25/2 (2005) 23-32;

15925 **Bultmann, Rudolf** Wachen und Träumen: Märchen. [E]*Zager, Werner*: B 2005, Wichern 80 pp. 3-88981-171-X;

15926 **Dreher, Matthias** Rudolf Bultmann als Kritiker in seinen Rezensionen und Forschungsberichten: kommentierte Auswertung. D*Merk, Otto*: Beiträge zum Verstehen der Bibel 11: Müns 2005, LIT 504 pp. €40. 3-8258-8545-3. Diss. Erlangen-Nürnberg;

15927 *Gibson, Michael D.* Does Jesus have a say in the kerygma?: a critical remembrance of Bultmann. SJTh 58 (2005) 83-103;

15928 *Hammann, Konrad* Rudolf Bultmanns Begegnung mit dem Judentum. ZThK 102 (2005) 35-72;

15929 **Jaspers, Karl** Myth & christianity: an inquiry into the possibility of religion without myth. Amherst, NY 2005, Prometheus 109 pp. 1-591-02291-6;

15930 Moon, Byeung-Goo Rudolf Bultmanns Ausführungen zum ersten Korintherbrief: Beiträge zur Rekonstruktion seiner Vorlesung. D*Merk, O.* 2005, Diss. Erlangen-Nürnberg [ThLZ 131,336].

15931 CONGAR Y: *Lécrivain, Philippe* Yves Congar (1904-1995): une vie toute imprégnée par les Écritures. BLE 106 (2005) 39-50.

15932 CULLMANN O: *De Rosa, M.* Oscar Cullmann (1902-1999). CredOg 25/2 (2005) 61-74.

15933 DEISSMANN A: *Markschies, C.* Adolf Deissmann—ein Heidelberger Pionier der Ökumene. ZNTG 12/1 (2005) 47-88 [NTAb 50, 250].

15934 DELITZSCH F; KITTEL R; LEIPOLDT J: *Arndt, Timotheus* Bemerkungen zum Studium des Judentums unter Franz Delitzsch, Rudolf Kittel und Johannes Leipoldt: ein Zwischenbericht. leqach 6 (2005) 153-172.

15935 DELORME J: *Panier, Louis* Jean Delorme. SémBib 119 (2005) 3-8;

15936 *Thériault, Jean-Yves* Bibliographie de Jean Delorme (révisée fin août 2005). SémBib 119 (2005) 50-67.

15937 DENAUX A: *Neirynck, Frans* Adelbert Denaux's triple interest. FDENAUX, A. BEThL 182: 2005 ⇒34. 345-50 [Mt 28,9-10; Lk 24,12];

15938 *Van Belle, Gilbert* Bibliographia academica A. Denaux. FDENAUX, A. BEThL 182: 2005 ⇒34. xi-xxiv.

15939 DODD C: *Dunn, James D.G.* C.H. Dodd and New Testament studies. BJRL 86/3 (2004) 55-76.

15940 FIORENZA E: **Green, E.** Elisabeth Schüssler Fiorenza. Novecento teologico 13: Brescia 2005, Morcelliana 151 pp. €14. 8837219865.

15941 FLUSSER D: *Gager, J.G.* Scholarship as moral vision: David Flusser on Jesus, Paul, and the birth of christianity. JQR 95 (2005) 60-73 [NTAb 49,250].

15942 FRANKL V: *Batthyany, Alexander* Viktor E. Frankl: Leben und Werk. Gottsuche. 2005 ⇒536. 9-21.

15943 FREI H; AUERBACH E: *Vidu, Adonis* Frei and Auerbach on the meaning of the gospel narratives. TrinJ 26 (2005) 245-265.

15944 GADAMER H: **Grondin, Jean** Hans-Georg Gadamer: a biography. T*Weinsheimer, Joel* 2003 ⇒19,15098. RScEs 57 (2005) 184-186 (*Peddle, Francis K.*).

15945 GHIBERTI G: *Passoni Dell'Acqua, Anna* Date di una biographia;

15946 Bibliografia di Giuseppe Ghiberti. FGHIBERTI, G.: SRivBib 46: 2005 ⇒47. 9-10/11-21.

15947 GIRARD R: **Kirwan, Michael** Discovering Girard. 2004 ⇒20, 14359. RWay 44/3 (2005) 101-102 (*Hewett, Billy*); RRT 12 (2005) 596-598 (*Hovey, Craig*);

15948 **Mancinelli, Paola** Cristianesimo senza sacrificio: filosofia e teologia in René Girard. 2001 ⇒19,15100. [R]RFNS 97 (2005) 356-359 (*Gamba, Alessandro*);

15949 **Palaver, Wolfgang** René Girard's mimetische Theorie: im Kontext kultur-theoretischer und gesellschaftspolitischer Fragen. 2003 ⇒ 19,15101; 20,14362. [R]ThPh 80 (2005) 132-133 (*Kirwan, M.*);

15950 **Ruiz Lozano, Pablo** Antropología y religión en René Girard. BTGran 36: Granada 2005, Univ. Granada 416 pp. 84-9216-2375. [R]ATG 68 (2005) 227-228.

15951 HONEYCUTT R: *Tate, Marvin E.* Roy Lee Honeycutt as a biblical scholar. RExp 102 (2005) 647-669.

15952 IRSIGLER H: *Irsigler, Hubert* Bibliographie. [F]IRSIGLER, H. ATSAT 76: 2005 ⇒67. 207-210.

15953 JOHANNES PAULUS II: *Varickasseril, Jose* Looking at John Paul II through biblical spectacles. MissTod 7 (2005) 220-231.

15954 JUNCO GARZA C: *Cepeda Salazar, Antonino* Carlos Junco Garza, maestro y pedagogo de la sagrada escritura: más que una fría bibliografía, una cálida biografía. [F]JUNCO GARZA, C.: Estudios Bíblicos Mexicanos 4: 2005 ⇒74. 27-46.

15955 KUSS O: *Ernst, Josef* Gedanken über Otto Kuss, den Hundertjährigen. MThZ 56 (2005) 176-183.

15956 LAGRANGE M: *Gilbert, Maurice* Il padre Lagrange: l'esegesi scientifica al servizio della chiesa. RTE 9 (2005) 461-476;

15957 *Montagnes, Bernard* Le P. Lagrange: la critique historique au service de la bible. EeV 115/139 (2005) 16-22 [NTAb 51,243];

15958 Marie-Joseph Lagrange: une biographie critique. Histoire: P 2005, Cerf 626 pp. €49. 2-204-07228-1. [R]NRTh 127 (2005) 619-622 (*Joassart, Bernard*); AnBoll 123 (2005) 217-219 (*Joassart, Bernard*); RHEF 91 (2005) 472-473 (*Moulinet, Daniel*);

15959 *Vesco, Jean-Luc* Le Père Lagrange et l'exégèse du psautier. [F]SCHENKER, A.: OBO 214: 2005 ⇒134. 410-417.

15960 LAPIDE P: *Lapide, Ruth* Pinchas Lapide: Leben und Werk. Gottsuche. 2005 ⇒536. 23-31.

15961 LEVINE A: *Graham, Helen* Amy-Jill Levine. Ethical dimensions. 2005 ⇒739. 51-53.

15962 LÉON-DUFOUR X: **Léon-Dufour, Xavier** Un bibliste cherche Dieu. Parole de Dieu: 2003 ⇒19,224; 20,14369. [R]Gr. 86 (2005) 408-409 (*Farahian, Edmond*).

15963 LÉVINAS, E: [E]**Eskenazi, Tamara; Jobling, David; Phillips, Gary** Levinas and biblical studies. SBL.Semeia 43: 2003 ⇒19,338; 20, 14373. [R]CBQ 67 (2005) 167-168 (*Beach, Dennis*); SvTK 81 (2005) 142-143 (*Alfort, Sara*); RBLit (2005)* (*Landy, Francis*).

15964 LIENHARD, MARC: *Arnold, Matthieu* Bibliographie de Marc Lienhard. RHPhR 85 (2005) 171-190.

15965 LINDARS B: *Evans, Craig A.* Barnabas Lindars and the Semitic context of scripture. BJRL 86/3 (2004) 125-140.

15966 LOHMEYER E: **Köhn, Andreas** Der Neutestamentler Ernst Lohmeyer: Studien zu Biographie und Theologie. WUNT 2/180: 2004 ⇒20,14378. [R]TrinJ 26 (2005) 147-148 (*Yarbrough, Robert W.*); SNTU 30 (2005) 276 (*Fuchs, Albert*); ZNTG 12 (2006) 346-347 (*Graf, Friedrich Wilhelm*);

15967 **Kuhn, Dieter** Metaphysik und Geschichte: zur Theologie Ernst Lohmeyers. [D]*Bayer, Oswald*: TBT 131: B 2005, De Gruyter xiii; 197 pp. €74. 3-11-018379-X. Diss. Tübingen.

15968 LUBAC H DE: *D'Ambrosio, Marcellino* The spiritual sense in De Lubac's hermeneutics of tradition. L&S 1 (2005) 147-157.
15969 LUST J: *García Martínez, Florentino* Johan Lust: academic bibliography. [F]LUST, J.: BEThL 192: 2005 ⇒92. xvii-xliii;
15970 *Lamberigts, Mathijs* Johan Lust: academic biography. [F]LUST, J.: BEThL 192: 2005 ⇒92. xiii-xvi.
15971 LÜTGERT W: *Schirrmacher, Thomas* Wilhelm Lütgert und seine Studien zu den Gegnern der Apostel. JETh 19 (2005) 139-166.
15972 MACHEN J: *Jipp, J.W.* The quest for the historical Machen. Themelios 30/3 (2005) 59-68 [NTAb 50,20].
15973 MANSON T: *Hooker, Morna D.* T.W. Hanson and the twentieth-century search for Jesus. BJRL 86/3 (2004) 77-98.
15974 MARQUARDT F: *Stöhr, Martin* Auf einem Schul-Weg mit Israel: F.-W. Marquardts Neubestimmung der christlichen Theologie. FrRu 12 (2005) 87-93.
15975 MARTINI, C: **Ravasi, Gianfranco** Martini: mis tres ciudades: un coloquio revelador. 2003 ⇒19,15122; 20,14379. [R]EfMex 67 (2005) 125-128 (*Landgrave G., Daniel R.*).
15976 MEDALA S: *Bartnicki, Roman* Sylwetka naukowa ks. prof. dr. hab. Stanislawa Medali CM. CoTh 75/3 (2005) 7-16. **P.**
15977 MOLTMANN J: *Ferraro, F.* Jürgen Moltmann (1926-). CredOg 25/2 (2005) 107-116.
15978 NEVES, J: *Lourenço, João Duarte* Joaquim Carreira das Neves: uma vida em prol da bíblia. Did(L) 35 (2005) 1-12. Bibl. 7-12.
15979 NIDA E: **Stine, Philip C.** Let the words be written: the lasting influence of Eugene A. Nida. SBL.Biblical Scholarship in North America 21: 2004 ⇒20,14382. [R]RBLit (2005)* (*Shepherd, David*).
15980 NORTH R: *North, Robert* Biblical scholarship as pilgrimage. BiTod 43 (2005) 304-308.
15981 ORBE A: *Bastit, Agnès* Antonio Orbe (1917-2003) ou les deux sources du christianisme ancien. REAug 51 (2005) 3-8. Bibl. Orbe 7-8 [NTAb 50,19].
15982 PEAKE A: *Larsen, Timothy* A.S. Peake, the Free Churches and modern biblical criticism. BJRL 86/3 (2004) 23-53.
15983 PETERSON E: *Bendemann, Reinhard von* Zur Edition und Einführung in Petersons Auslegung des Lukasevangeliums und seine weiteren Synoptica;
15984 *Nichtweiß, Barbara* Nachwort. Peterson: Lukasevangelium und Synoptica. 2005 ⇒277. xvii-xcvi/442-445.
15985 PFITZNER V: Literary activity of Victor C. Pfitzner. LTJ 39/2-3 (2005) 243-247 [NTAb 50,18].
15986 PIPER O: *Black, C. Clifton* Remembering Otto Piper. PSB 26 (2005) 310-327 [NTAb 50,471].
15987 PRIOR M: *Macpherson, Duncan* Rev. Professor Michael Prior, CM. ScrB 35 (2005) 1-4.
15988 RAD G. VON: *Böhm, Susanne* Gerhard von Rad in Jena. [F]*Conrad, J.*: ABIG 17: 2005 ⇒27. 203-240.
15989 RADERMAKERS J: **Radermakers, Jean** Ta parole, ma demeure: entretiens avec Fernand Colleye. Namur 2005, Fidélité 240 pp. 2-873-56324-9.
15990 RAHNER K: [E]**Schöndorf, Harald** Die philosophischen quellen der Theologie Karl Rahners. QD 213: FrB 2005, 200 pp. 3451-022133.

15991 RÄISÄNEN H: *Levine, Amy-Jill* Homeless in the global village. Moving beyond NT theology?. SESJ 88: 2005 ⇒463. 179-196;
15992 *Penner, Todd* The challenge from within: reading Räisänen against dominant methodological discourse;
15993 *Räisänen, Heikki* What I meant and what it might mean... an attempt at responding;
15994 *Scholz, Susanne* Standing at the crossroads with Räisänen's *Program*: toward a future of biblical studies in post-biblical societies;
15995 *Strecker, Christian* New Testament research: theological or atheological?: some observations on Heikki Räisänen's two-stage program. Moving beyond NT theology?. SESJ 88: 2005 ⇒463. 1-31/ 400-443/161-178/243-263.
15996 RENDTORFF R: *Zenger, Erich* Ein großer Ausleger der Hebräischen Bibel: Laudatio zum 80. Geburtstag von Rolf Rendtorff. KuI 20 (2005) 99-108.
15997 RICCIOTTI G: *Marconi, Nazzareno* L'Abate Ricciotti, un pioniere italiano dell'esegesi letteraria. ConAss 7/1 (2005) 215-224;
15998 *Michelini, Giulio* La vita di Gesù Cristo di Giuseppe Ricciotti;
15999 RICCIOTTI G; BUONAIUTI E: *Cesarini, Dante* Ricciotti e Buonaiuti: incontri e scontri. ConAss 7/1 (2005) 225-238/239-257.
16000 RICOEUR P: *Amherdt, François-Xavier* Théologiens, exégètes et prédicateurs à l'école de Paul Ricoeur. Theoforum 36/3 (2005) 279-291;
16001 **Amherdt, François-Xavier** L'herméneutique philosophique de Paul Ricoeur et son importance pour l'exégèse biblique. La nuit surveillée: 2004 ⇒20, 14399. [R]RThPh 137 (2005) 70-2 (*Schouwey, Jacques*); ETR 80 (2005) 287-289 (*Muller, Marc*); CEv 132 (2005) 58-59 (*Noël, Damien*); EThL 81 (2005) 217-9 (*Vandecasteele, P.*);
16002 *Bertoletti, Ilario* Ricoeur pensatore dialettico?: in memoriam. Hum(B) 60 (2005) 1343-1346;
16003 *Grampa, Giuseppe* 'Uditore della parola': il contributo di Paul Ricoeur all'interpretazione della Scrittura. RCI 86 (2005) 802-812;
16004 RICOEUR P: **Kearney, Richard** On Paul Ricoeur. 2004 ⇒20, 14401. [R]RThPh 137 (2005) 69-70 (*Schouwey, Jacques*);
16005 [E]**Revault d'Allonnes, Myriam; Azouvi, François** Ricoeur. 2004 ⇒20,14403. [R]RThPh 137 (2005) 66-68 (*Schouwey, Jacques*);
16006 *VanDenHengel, John W.* In memory of Paul Ricoeur, 1913-2005. Theoforum 36/3 (2005) 267-277;
16007 *Vanhoozer, K.J.* The joy of yes: Ricoeur: philosopher of hope. CCen 122/17 (2005) 27-28 [NTAb 50,22];
16008 **Vela Valldecabres, Daniel** Del simbolismo a la hermenéutica: Paul Ricoeur (1950-1985). Anejos de Revista de Literatura 67: M 2005, Consejo Superior de Investigaciones Científicas 192 pp.
16009 ROBINSON J: *Wright, N.T.* Doubts about doubt: *Honest to God* forty years on. JAnS 3/2 (2005) 181-195 [NTAb 50,251].
16010 ROSENZWEIG F: [E]**Brasser, Martin** Rosenzweig als Leser: kontextuelle Kommentare zum 'Stern der Erlösung'. Tü 2004, Niemeyer 606 pp. €98. 34846-5144X. [R]Bijdr. 66 (2005) 119-120 (*Adriaanse, H.J.*);
16011 **Casper, Bernhard** Religion der Erfahrung: Einführung in das Denken Franz Rosenzweigs. Pd 2004, Schöningh 212 pp. €19.80. 3-50-67-0138X;

16012 *Fraisse, Otfried* Die exegetische Form von Franz Rosenzweigs Stern der Erlösung-oder (Bild)Sprache und "performative Hermeneutik". Jud. 61 (2005) 252-267, 337-350;

16013 *Fricke, Martin* Unausgeschöpfte Impulse des neuen Denkens von Franz Rosenzweig für Kirche und Theologie. KuI 20 (2005) 60-72;

16014 **Malka, Salomon** Franz Rosenzweig, le cantique de la révélation. La nuit surveillée: P 2005, Cerf 132 pp. €17. 22040-79103;

16015 **Rühle, Inken** Gott spricht die Sprache der Menschen: Franz Rosenzweig als jüdischer Theologe—eine Einführung. 2004 ⇒20, 14407. [R]Jud. 61 (2005) 282-283 (*Dober, Hans Martin*);

16016 *Vinci, Daniele* 'Il nome non è rumore e fumo, ma parola e fuoco': Franz Rosenzweig nella lettura di Hans Urs von Balthasar. Hum(B) 60 (2005) 1275-1295.

16017 SCHLATTER A: **Hägele, Clemens** Die Schrift als Gnadenmittel: Adolf Schlatters Lehre von der Schrift in ihren Grundzügen. [D]*Bayer, O.* 2005, Diss. Tübingen [ThLZ 131,342].

16018 SCHÜRMANN H: *Ruberti, Andrea* Gesú e il suo agire profetico in Heinz Schürmann. StPat 52 (2005) 215-231.

16019 SCHWEITZER A: [E]**Brabazon, J.** Albert Schweitzer: essential writings. Modern Spiritual Masters: Mkn 2005, Orbis 165 pp. $16. 15-7075-6023. Bibl. [NTAb 50,156].

16020 SMITH M: *Sievers, Joseph* Smith, Morton. Encyclopedia of religion, 12. 2005 ⇒1009. 8448-8450 [AcBib 11,33].

16021 STEGEMANN E: *Gelardini, Gabriella* Schriftenverzeichnis von Ekkehard W. Stegemann (1974-2005);

16022 Einleitung. [F]STEGEMANN, E. 2005 ⇒139. 464-491/9-24.

16023 STEGEMANN W: *Neumann, Klaus* Schriftenverzeichnis Wolfgang Stegemann (Stand: 2005). [F]STEGEMANN, W. 2005 ⇒139. 455-466.

16024 STENDEBACH F: *Beyer, Stephanie* Der Besucher des Monats: Prof. P. Dr. Franz-Josef Stendebach;

16025 *Gaidetzka, Petra* Familienspuren;

16026 *Heinrichs, Norbert* Mensch, wo bist du? (Gen 3,9);

16027 *Jagelki, Jürgen* Ein Mann für jede Bibelstelle. [F]STENDEBACH, F. 2005 ⇒141. 349-351/352-356/357-359/360-362.

16028 STOLLE V: *Schwertner, Siegfried M.* Bibliographie Volker Stolle;

16029 *Stolle-Spies, Katja; Stolle, Peter* Lebenslauf Dr. Volker Stolle. [F]STOLLE, V. 2005 ⇒143. 533-609/531-532.

16030 SYE P: *An, Theresa* Paul Sye. SémBib 119 (2005) 9.

16031 TUCKETT C: *Cotter, Wendy* Christopher Tuckett and the question of Q. BJRL 86/3 (2004) 141-173.

16032 VAN ESBROECK M: *Samir, S.K.* Michel van Esbroeck, SJ (1934-2003), le collègue et l'ami. CCO 2 (2005) 409-440 [NTAb 50,21].

16033 VAN TILBORG S: *Berges, Ulrich; Counet, Patrick C.* Sjef van Tilborg: a short biography. [M]VAN TILBORG, S.: 2005 ⇒155. 351-355;

16034 *Counet, Patrick C.* Bibliography of Sjef van Tilborg. [M]VAN TILBORG, S.: 2005 ⇒155. 357-360.

16035 VANNI U: *Martini, Carlo M.* Ugo Vanni e l'Apocalisse. [F]VANNI, U. 2005 ⇒156. 11-16.

16036 VOS G: [E]**Olinger, Danny** A Geerhardus Vos anthology: biblical and theological insights alphabetically arranged. Phillipsburg, NJ 2005, Presbyterian & R. xxii; 375 pp. $20 [CTJ 40,376: John Bolt].

16037 WEBER M: *Ghosh, P.* The place of Judaism in Max Weber's *Protestant ethic.* ZNTG 12/2 (2005) 208-261 [NTAb 50,545].

16038 WRIGHT N: *Bandy, Alan S.* Eschatology and restoration: the relationship between theology and eschatology in the writings of N.T. Wright. Faith & Mission 22/2 (2005) 56-84;

16039 *Ruiz, J.* N.T. Wright ou la recatholicisation de la pensée protestante. Résister et Construire [Lausanne] 55-56 (2005) 36-62 [NTAb 50,21].

16040 YOUNG F: *Williams, Rowan* Profile: Frances Young. FYOUNG, F. JSNT.S 295: 2005 ⇒168. 1-7.

## Y6.3 *Influxus Scripturae saeculis XX-XXI*—Survey of current outlooks

16041 *Abadie, Philippe; Artus, Olivier* Bulletin d'Ancien Testament (I et II). RSR 93 (2005) 571-596.

16042 **Bach, Alice** Religion, politics, media in the broadband era. 2004 ⇒ 20,14419. RBiCT 1/3 (2005)* (*Walsh, Richard*).

16043 **Barton, John; Bowden, Julia** The original story: God, Israel and the world. 2004 ⇒20,14421. RTheol. 108 (2005) 205-206 (*Moore, Elizabeth*).

16044 *Baum, Armin D.* Neutestamentliche Wissenschaft in Deutschland: Beobachtungen und Fragen. ThBeitr 36 (2005) 152-157.

16045 *Bennett, Zoë; Rowland, Christopher* Contextual and advocacy readings of the bible;

16046 *Brueggemann, Walter* The re-emergence of scripture: post-liberalism. Bible in pastoral practice. 2005 ⇒341. 174-190/153-173.

16047 *Ericsson, B.* Religious studies in Sweden during the 20th century. PJBR 4/2 (2005) 161-165 [NTAb 50,19].

16048 *Farkaš, Pavol* Minulosť a prítomnosť biblických vied v slovenskom kontexte [The past and present of the biblical sciences in the Slovakian context]. SBSl (2005) 11-16. **Slovak.**

16049 *Greenspoon, Leonard J.* What America believes about the bible. BiRe 21/5 (2005) 27-29 [OTA 29,117].

16050 *Harrington, Daniel J.* The bible and history. America [NY] 192/9 (2005) 26-30.

16051 *Jeremias, Jörg* Vier Jahrzehnte Forschung am Alten Testament—ein Rückblick. VF 50/1/2 (2005) 10-25.

16052 *MacDonald, Patricia M.* With a little help from my friends: "interfaces" and college biblical studies: review essay. Horizons 32 (2005) 398-403.

16053 *Martens, Klaus* Let us now praise famous men: zur Bedeutung der Religion in den USA. Zwischen Bibel und Wissenschaft. Glauben und Leben 31: 2005 ⇒407. 89-98.

16054 *Mathys, Hans-Peter* Gesammelte Studien zum Alten Testament. ThR 70/2 (2005) 217-227.

16055 *Naudé, Piet* Can we still hear Paul on the Agora?: an outsider perspective on South African New Testament scholarship. Neotest. 39/2 (2005) 339-358.

16056 *Nel, Philip* The study of Hebrew and the Old Testament in Africa. BOTSA 18 (2005) 2-10.

16057 **Ostwalt, Conrad** Secular steeples: popular culture and the religious imagination. 2003 ⇒20,14430. RRBLit 7 (2005) 530-536 (*Ruprecht, Louis A., Jr.*).

16058 *Reventlow, Henning Graf* Biblische, besonders alttestamentliche Theologie und Hermeneutik I: Forschungsgeschichte und Gesamtdarstellungen. ThR 70 (2005) 1-43;

16059 II: gesamtbiblische Theologie: Alttestamentliche Ethik. ThR 70 (2005) 137-173;

16060 III: Kanonproblem; christlich-jüdisches Gespräch; biblische Hermeneutik. ThR 70 (2005) 279-337;

16061 IV: alttestamentliche Theologie und/oder israelitische Religionsgeschichte; biblischer Monotheismus; alttestamentliche Theologie als Rede von Gott. ThR 70 (2005) 408-454.

16062 *Sæbø, Magne* Zur neueren Interpretationsgeschichte des Alten Testaments. ThLZ 130 (2005) 1033-1044.

16063 *Sesboüé, Bernard* Bulletin de théologie patristique grecque. RSR 93 (2005) 107-160.

16064 *Wénin, André* Des outils de travail en français pour (re)découvrir le Premier Testament. RTL 36 (2005) 539-553.

Y7.2 *Congressus biblici*: **nuntii,** *rapports, Berichte*

16065 *Ahl, Ruth* Die Weisheit hat sich ein Haus gebaut: christlich-jüdische Bibelwoche im Bildungshaus Mariatrost in Graz. FrRu 12 (2005) 67-69.

16066 *Alzati, Cesare* San Luca evangelista testimone della fede che unisce: presentazione del vol. III degli Atti del Congresso internazionale di Padova. StPat 52 (2005) 615-627.

16067 *Banaszek, Andrzej* Konferencja dyrektorów katolickich ośrodków apostolatu biblijnego regionu Europy Środkowej, Dolany (Czechy), 6-9 IX 2004. CoTh 75/1 (2005) 209-217.

16068 *Barrado, Pedro* XVII jornadas de la Asociación Bíblica Española. ResB 48 (2005) 68-69. 'Los orígenes del cristianismo', Orense, 13-15 sept. 2005.

16069 *Cartledge, M.J.* Conference report: *Why did Christ die?: a symposium on the theology of atonement*, sponsored by the Evangelical Alliance and the London School of Theology, 6-8th July 2005. Anvil 22/3 (2005) 213-220 [NTAb 50,259].

16070 *Cifrak, Mario* XIII. Colloquium Biblicum Vindobonense. BoSm 75 (2005) 953-954. **Croatian**.

16071 *Ebner, Martin; Schreiber, Stefan* 59th. General Meeting der Studiorum Novi Testamenti Societas vom 3.-7. August 2004 in Barcelona. BZ 49 (2005) 158-159.

16072 *Farisani, Elelwani B.* African biblical hermeneutics, Society of Biblical Literature, Philadelphia, USA, November 2005. BOTSA 19 (2005) 18-19.

16073 *François, W. Biblia sacra* at the Sixteenth Century Society and Conference, Atlanta, Oct. 2005. EThL 81 (2005) 613-614.

16074 *Horvat, Mladen* Simpozij katolickih biblicara Starog zavjeta njemackoga govornog podrucja u Olomoucu. BoSm 75 (2005) 631-633. **Croatian**.

16075 *Jędrzejewski, Sylwester* V Międzynarodowy Kongres Associazione Biblica Salesiana (Kraków, 27 grudnia 2004 - 4 stycznia 2005). RBL 58 (2005) 67-69. **P**.

16076 *Kot, Anna* 'Gdzie jest Abel, brat twój?': premoc w biblii sympozjum biblijne, Warszawa, 12 IV 2005. CoTh 75/3 (2005) 207-10. **P**.
16077 *Leemans, J.* Themes in biblical narrative: Balaam and his speaking ass. EThL 81 (2005) 611-612.
16078 *Marchadour, Alain* Comment la bible saisit-elle l'histoire?. CEv 134 (2005) 50-53.
16079 *Maritz, Petrus; Verhelst, Nele* Symposium on 'Imagery in John' (Eisenach, 30 July-1 August 2005). EThL 81 (2005) 580-586.
16080 *Matand Bulembat, Jean-Bosco* Sagesses bibliques vues d'Afrique. CEv 134 (2005) 57-58;
16081 Le 12ème congrès de l'APECA, Centre catholique Nganda, Kinshasa, R.D. Congo, Septembre 2005. BOTSA 19 (2005) 15-17.
16082 *Nazarczuk, Maria* Report of the sixty-eighth international meeting of the Catholic Biblical Association of America. CBQ 67 (2005) 662-670.
16083 *Niebuhr, Karl-Wilhelm* 'Einheit und Vielfalt der neutestamentlichen Ekklesiologie': 3. Ost-Westliches Symposium europäischer Bibelwissenschaftler, Sankt Petersburg, 24.-31. August 2005. ThLZ 130 (2005) 1386-1387.
16084 *Van Belle, Gilbert* De dood van Jezus in het vierde evangelie: verslag van het 54ste Colloquium Biblicum Lovaniense. Coll. 35/4 (2005) 425-434;
16085 De onbekennde Jezus van de apocriefe geschriften (K.U. Leuven aug. 2005). EThL 81 (2005) 599-600;
16086 The death of Jesus in the fourth gospel: Colloquium Biblicum Lovaniense LIV (2005). EThL 81 (2005) 567-579;
16087 Studiorum Novi Testamenti Societas: 60th general meeting, Halle, Aug. 2005. EThL 81 (2005) 610-611.
16088 *Wojciechowski, Michał* 59. Zjazd Societas Novi Testamenti Studiorum Barcelona, 3-7 VIII 2004. CoTh 75/1 (2005) 205-207. **P**.;
16089 60. Zjazd Societas Novi Testamenti Studiorum Halle, 2-6 VIII 2005. CoTh 75/3 2005, 219-221. **P**.
16090 *Yorke, Gosnell L.* Bible interpretation and translation in Africa, University of KwaZulu-Natal, Pietermaritzburg, September 2005. BOTSA 19 (2005) 11-14.

## Y7.4 *Congressus theologici*: **nuntii**

16091 *Di Girolamo, Luca M.; Maggiani, Silvano M.* XV simposio mariologico internazionale (Roma 4-7 ottobre 2005). Mar. 67 (2005) 655-666.
16092 *Fernández Sagrador, Jorge Juan* XXXIV incontro di studiosi dell' antichità cristiana, Roma 5-7 de mayo de 2005: pagani e cristiani alla ricerca della salvezza (I-III sec.). RevAg 46 (2005) 185-188.
16093 *Haquin, André* Conférences Sedes Sapientiae: le mal, qu'en faire? (Louvain-La-Neuve, fév.-mars 2005). EThL 81 (2005) 591-594;
16094 Conférences Sedes Sapientiae: le mal, qu'en faire?. RTL 36 (2005) 440-443. Fév.-mars 2005.
16095 *Lieggi, Jean Paul* Il giorno del Signore: prospettive bibliche e patristiche. Rivista di science religiose 19/1 2005, 119-131. Convegno di studi, Pont. Fac.Teol. dell'Italia Meridionale.

16096 *Llamas, Enrique* LVII Semana de 'Estudio marianos' (León 8-11 giugno 2005). Mar. 67 (2005) 648-654.
16097 *Miguel González, José María de* XL simposio de teología trinitaria. EstTrin 39 (2005) 103-112.
16098 *Sanders, H.* Mariage, divorce et remariage (Leuven avril 2005). EThL 81 (2005) 595-598.
16099 *Spieß, Christian* Religion als Brennstoff und Terror als Gottesdienst: die 4. Internationale Theologische Studienwoche in Münster. ThRv 101 (2005) 21-24.
16100 *Tomaino, Maria Gemma* IV Incontro di studi di mariologia medievale (Parma 21-22 maggio 2004). Mar. 67 (2005) 639-647.
16101 *Torresin, Antonio* La figura di Gesù. Il Regno 50 (2005) 191-194. Conv. della fac. teologica di Milano.

## Y7.8 Reports of archaeological meetings

16102 *Cifrak, Mario* Arheologija i tekst: zasjedanje radne zajednice profesora Novoga zavjeta njemačkog govornog područja, Fribourg, 21.-25. veljače 2005. BoSm 75 (2005) 407-409. **Croatian**.
16103 *Shanks, Hershel* Roundup of annual meetings. BArR 31/2 (2005) 41-51 [NTAb 49,554].
16104 Tagung zur Zukunft der Biblischen Archäologie. WUB 38 (2005) 69.
16105 The thirty-first archaeological conference in Israel. IEJ 55 (2005) 111-112.

## Y8.0 *Periti*: Scholars, personalia, organizations

16106 Amir Drori, 1937-2005: from general to antiquities director. BArR 31/3 (2005) 16.
16107 *Bachtin, Michail M.* Bakhtin and the bible: a select bibliography. PRSt 32/3 (2005) 339-345.
16108 *Bodner, Keith; Dempster, Stephen G.; Tull, Patricia K.* Bakhtin in recent biblical studies: book reviews. PRSt 32/3 (2005) 347-353.
16109 *Buber, Martin* 13 Jahre Hebräische Universität Jerusalem. Schriften zu Jugend. 2005 <1938> ⇒196. 299-302.
16110 *Buffon, Giuseppe* Les Franciscains en Terre Sainte au 19e siècle: de l'espace au territoire, entre opposition et adaptation. RHE 100 (2005) 797-845.
16111 **Buffon, Giuseppe** Les franciscains en Terre sainte: religion et politique: une recherche institutionnelle (1869-1889). 2004 ⇒20, 14487. RPOC 55 (2005) 497-498 (*Attinger, D.*); AFH 98 (2005) 841-843 (*Dedieu, Hugues*); Carthaginensia 21 (2005) 517-519 (*Riquelme Oliva, P.*).
16112 *Buzzetti, Carlo; Bachelet, Giovanni* La spiritualità 'interconfessionale': storia e ispirazione delle società bibliche. RCI 86 (2005) 53-62, 156-164.
16113 *Carmesund, U.* Motsatta förväntningar på 'Guds folk' i Palestina. SvTK 81/4 (2005) 169-182. Swedish Theological Institute, Jerusalem [NTAb 50,249].

16114 *Dolman, R.* Profile: Ivor Harold Jones. EpRe 32/1 (2005) 16-26 [NTAb 49,476].

16115 *Ferrary, Jean-Louis* Rapport général sur la vie et les activités de l'École française de Rome pour l'année 2004-2005. CRAI 4 (2005) 1357-1381.

16116 *García-Plaza, A.* Erik Peterson: una fe escatológica y sobrenatural, pero en viva tensión dialéctica. Burg. 46 (2005) 511-526 [NTAb 50,471].

16117 *Garrone, Daniele* La facoltà valdese di teologia. CredOg 25/2 (2005) 129-134.

16118 *Gauthier, Philippe* Rapport général sur l'état et les activités de l'École française d'Athènes pendant l'année 2004. CRAI 4 (2005) 1211-1231.

16119 *Gelin, Mathilde* L'Institut français d'Archéologie de Beyrouth 1946-1977. Syria 82 (2005) 279-330.

16120 *Green, Barbara* Mikhail Bakhtin and biblical studies. PRSt 32/3 (2005) 241-248.

16121 *Guthrie, S.* Wycliffe in overdrive. ChrTo 49/2 (2005) 74-75 [NTAb 49,246].

16122 *Homan, Michael* Happy birthday, BR!. BiRe 21/1 (2005) 12-14.

16123 *Mettinger, Tryggve N.D.* Stig I.L. Norin: an appreciation. SEÅ 70 (2005) 9-10.

16124 **Moscrop, John J.** Measuring Jerusalem: the Palestine Exploration Fund and British interests in the Holy Land. 2000 ⇒16,13166; 20, 14509. [R]BAIAS 23 (2005) 185-187 (*Jacobson, David M.*).

16125 **Nida, Eugene** Fascinated by languages. 2003 ⇒19,15235. [R]BiTr 56 (2005) 58-59 (*Stine, Philip C.*).

16126 *Palm, Jonas* Eulogy for Albert Wifstrand. Epochs...styles. WUNT 179: 2005 ⇒325. 9-13.

16127 [E]**Pantalacci, Laure** Travaux de l'Institut français d'archéologie orientale en 2004-2005. BIFAO 105 (2005) 405-543.

16128 *Philonenko, Marc* Rapport sur la vie et les activités de l'École biblique et archéologique française de Jérusalem. CRAI 4 (2005) 1179-1182.

16129 *Porter, Stanley E.* Eugene Nida and translation. BiTr 56 (2005) 8-19;

16130 *Porter, Wendy J.* A brief look at the life and works of Eugene Albert Nida. BiTr 56 (2005) 1-7.

16131 *Richardson, M.E.J.* The Journal of Semitic Studies: the first fifty years and their background. Studia semitica. JSSt.S 16: 2005 ⇒ 603. 1-37.

16132 *Robinson, James M.* Theological autobiography. The sayings gospel Q. BEThL 189: 2005 ⇒289. 3-34.

16133 *Rogerson, J.W.* The Manchester faculty of theology 1904: beginnings and background. BJRL 86/3 (2004) 9-22.

16134 *Rosenthal, David* Tribute to Professor David Flusser on his eightieth birthday. Beginnings of christianity. 2005 ⇒786. 15-20.

16135 *Schäfer, Peter* Martin Hengel at seventy. Beginnings of christianity. 2005 ⇒786. 21-34.

16136 *Schorsch, I.* Coming to terms with biblical criticism. Conservative Judaism [NY] 57/3 (2005) 3-22. Jewish Theological Seminary of New York [NTAb 50,22].

16137 *Spangenberg, Sakkie; Strydom, Gerrie* In celebration of James Alfred Loader's sixtieth birthday (12 July 1945-12 July 2005). OTEs 18 (2005) 165-171.

16138 *Statham, Nigel* Nida and 'functional equivalence': the evolution of a concept, some problems, and some possible ways forward. BiTr 56 (2005) 29-43.

16139 *Varickasseril, Jose* Looking at John Paul II through biblical spectacles. MJOHN PAUL II. 2005 ⇒72. 24-36.

16140 *Villiers, Pieter G.R. de* Turbulent times and golden years: the first twenty five years of the New Testament Society of South Africa (1965-1990). Neotest. 39 (2005) 75-110, 229-253.

16141 *Watt, Jonathan M.* The contributions of Eugene A. Nida to sociolinguistics. BiTr 56 (2005) 19-29.

16142 Životné jubileum prof. Jozefa Heribana [The jubilee of Prof. Jozef Heriban]. SBSl (2005) 98. **Slovak**.

### Y8.5 *Periti*: **in memoriam**

16143 Ackroyd, Peter Runham 15.9.1917-23.1.2005. RPEQ 137 (2005) 5 (*Coggins, Richard*).

16144 Adinolfi, Marco 10.6.1919-29.8.2005. RAnton. 80 (2005) 751-753; (*Barbagallo, Salvatore*); LASBF 55 (2005) 457-472 (*Bottini, Giovanni C.*).

16145 Akurgal, Ekrem 30.3.1911-1.11.2002 ⇒19,15249; 20,14527. RAJA 109 (2005) 561-563 (*Greenwalt, Crawford H., Jr.*).

16146 Alonso Díaz, José †8.6.2005.

16147 Amiran, Ruth 1915-15.12.2005 [Qad. 131,63s—M. Sabban].

16148 Ardusso, Franco 14.7.1935-14.4.2005.

16149 Best, Ernest 23.5.1917-1.10.2004 ⇒20,14529. RIBSt 26 (2005) 58-59 (*Ker, Donald*).

16150 Betz, Otto 8.6.1917-27.5.2005. RThLZ 130 (2005) 1027 (*Hengel, Martin*); PJBR 4 (2005) 108-116 (*Kapera, Z.J.; Lichtenberger, Hermann; Hengel, Martin*).

16151 Bourke, Myles M. 30.1.1917-13.11.2004 ⇒20,14532. RCBQ 67 (2005) 102-103 (*Meier, John P.*).

16152 Buis, Pierre 1929-2005. RCEv 134 (2005) 63.

16153 Burger, Hilde 1952-20.9.2005. RITBT 13/7 (2005) 21 (*Parlevliet, Leendeert-Jan*).

16154 Caquot, André 24.4.1923-31.8.2004 ⇒20,14538. RREJ 164 (2005) 1-3 (*Hadas-Lebel, Mireille*); REJ 164 (2005) 5-8 (*Lemaire, André*); JA 293 (2005) 1-10 (*Bordreuil, Pierre*); RdQ 22 (2005) 3-5 (*Puech, Émile*); FV 104/4 (2005) 89-91 (*Robert, Philippe de*); Megillot 3 (2005) xxi-xxiv [Bibl. Caquot on Qumran Scrolls & related lit. יג-יז by *Devorah Dimant & Ariel Feldman*] (*Bar-Asher, Moshe*).

16155 Carpi, Daniel 3.8.1926-3.12.2005. RMateria giudaica 10/2 (2005) 221-232 [incl. bibl.] (*Zorattini, Pier C.I.; Perani, Mauro*).

16156 Ceresko, Anthony Raymond 20.8.1942-13.8.2005. RITS 42 (2005) 231.

16157 Cisterna, Félix E. 13.10.1942-11.10.2005.

16158 Craig, Barbara 22.10.1915-25.1.2005. RPEQ 137 (2005) 6-7 (*Dauphin, Claudine*).

16159 De Haes, René 9.9.1933-7.5.2005.
16160 Deissler, Alfons 2.4.1914-10.5.2005. RFrRu 12 (2005) 316-317 (*Renker, Alwin*).
16161 Delorme, Jean 17.6.1920-30.8.2005. RCEv 133 (2005) 87.
16162 Derrida, Jacques 15.7.1930-8.10.2004 ⇒20,14546. RNBl 86 (2005) 1-2 (*Kerr, Fergus*).
16163 Drori, Amir 1937-2005. RQad. 38 (2005) 127-128 (*Tsafrir, Yoram*).
16164 Dupuis, Jacques 5.12.1923-28.12.2004 ⇒20,14547. RIl Regno 50/2 (2005) 63-65 (*Egaña, Francisco Javier*); ZMR 89 (2005) 58-59 (*Waldenfels, Hans*); REB 65 (2005) 414-417 (*Gibellini, Rosino*); VJTR 69 (2005) 84-86 (*Amaladoss, Michael*); VJTR 69 (2005) 449-459 (*O'Collins, Gerald*).
16165 Durrwell, François-Xavier 26.1.1912-15.10.2005.
16166 Edzard, Dietz Otto 28.8.1930-2.6.2004 ⇒20,14548. RZA 95 (2005) 1-6 (*Krebernik, Manfred*).
16167 Franken, Hendricus Jacobus 4.7.1917-18.1.2005. RPEQ 137 (2005) 7-8 (*Vilders, Monique*); Phoe. 51 (2005) 3; Levant 37 (2005) vii-viii (*Van As, Abraham; Steiner, Margreet*); ADAJ 49 (2005) 11-13 (*Van der Kooij, Gerrit*).
16168 Freeman-Grenville, Greville Stewart Parker 1919-2005. RPEQ 137 (2005) 8 (*Day, Stephen*).
16169 Friedlander, Albert 10.5.1927-8.7.2004 ⇒20,11896. RFrRu 12 (2005) 73-74 (*Henrix, Hans Hermann*).
16170 Funk, Robert Walter 18.7.1926-3.9.2005. RBiRe 21/5 (2005) 8-9 (*Patterson, S.J.*); Fourth R 18/5 (2005) 2-3.
16171 Griffiths, Gwyn 7.12.1911-15.6.2004 ⇒20,14556. RJEA 91 (2005) 181-185 (*Lloyd, Alan B.*).
16172 Gullini, Giorgio 13.8.1923-13.10.2004. RADAJ 49 (2005) 15-16 (*Parapetti, Roberto*).
16173 Jameson, Michael H. 1924-2004. RAJA 109 (2005) 77-80 (*Dengate, J.A.*).
16174 JOHANNES PAULUS II 18.5.1920-2.4.2005.
16175 Katzenstein, Hannah 1908-2004 ⇒20,14562. RQad. 38 (2005) 64; IEJ 55 (2005) 1-2.
16176 Kehl, Nikolaus 26.12.1914-3.11.2005.
16177 Korfmann, Manfred Osman 26.4.1942-11.8.2005. RAMIT 37 (2005) 457-462 (*Özdoğan, Mehmet*).
16178 Lane, David J. 1935-9.1.2005. ROrChr 89 (2005) 225 (*Kaufhold, Hubert*).
16179 Langlamet, François 17.5.1931-28.2.2005. RCEv 132 (2005) 63.
16180 Leeming, Henry 1920-2004. RSEER 83 (2005) 493-494 (*Stone, Gerald*).
16181 Lewis, Naphtali 14.12.1911-11.9.2005.
16182 Lichtheim, Miriam 3.5.1914-27.3.2004 ⇒20,14567. RZÄS 132 (2005) III-IV (*Shirun-Grumach, Irene*).
16183 Maass, Fritz 15.2.1910-11.03.2005.
16184 Mateos Álvarez, Juan José 15.1.1917-23.9.2003 ⇒19,15280; 20,14571. ROCP 71 (2005) 265-297 [incl. bibl.] (*Taft, Robert F.*).
16185 Mayer, Günter 6.4.1936-29.12.2004 ⇒20,14573. RThLZ 130 (2005) 344-345 (*Dietz, Walter*).
16186 McPolin, James 4.6.1931-9.10.2005.

16187 Meshorer, Ya'akov 1935-23.6.2004 ⇒20,14575. [R]SCI 24 (2005) 339-340 (*Gitler, Haim*).

16188 Millet, Nicholas B. 28.6.1934-19.5.2004. [R]JSSEA 32 (2005) v-vi (*Shaw, Roberta*).

16189 Moorey, P. Roger S. 30.5.1937-23.12.2004 ⇒20,14577. [R]AJA 109 (2005) 565-566 (*Muscarella, Oscar White*); Iraq 67/2 (2005) vii-x (*Potts, Timothy*); PEQ 137 (2005) 93-97 (*Dauphin, Claudine*): Levant 37 (2005) v-vi (*Prag, Kay*).

16190 Mopsik, Charles 1956-13.6.2003; aet. 46 ⇒19,15282; 20,14578. [R]REJ 164 (2005) 547-552 (*Goetschel, Roland*).

16191 Müller, Hans-Peter 21.2.1934-18.10.2004 ⇒20,14582. [R]ThLZ 130 (2005) 120-122 (*Reuter, Hans-Richard; Albertz, Rainer*).

16192 Negev, Avraham 1923-28.11.2004 ⇒20,14583. [R]Qad. 38 (2005) 126-127 (*Rosenthal-Heginbottom, R.*).

16193 O'Callaghan Martínez, José 7.10.1922-15.12.2001 ⇒17,12800; 18, 14060. [R]RCatT 30/1 (2005) 215-216 (*Oriol Tuñí, Josep*).

16194 Özgüç, Tahsin 20.3.1916-28.11.2005. [R]Akkadica 126 (2005) 105-106 (*Hrouda, Barthel*).

16195 Pépin, Jean 1924-10.9.2005.

16196 Ponthot, Joseph 6.3.1924-25.5.2005. [R]RTL 36 (2005) 437-439 (*Focant, Camille*); EThL 81 (2005) 603-605 (*Focant, Camille*).

16197 Potocki, Stanisław 1928-2004 ⇒20,14586. [R]RBL 58 (2005) 233-238 [incl. bibl.] (*Haręzga, Stanisław*).

16198 Quast, Udo 18.4.1939-30.12.2005.

16199 Randellini, Lino 4.2.1904-31.12.2003 ⇒19,15286. [R]VivH 16 (2005) 361-372 (*Faggioni, Maurizio*).

16200 Reiner, Erica 4.8.1924-31.12.2005. [R]Akkadica 126 (2005) 107-109 (*Spycket, Agnès*).

16201 Ricoeur, Paul 27.2.1913-20.5.2005. [R]ThRv 101 (2005) 177-178 (*Werbick, Jürgen*); QVC 220 (2005) 100-107 (*Marquès, Andreu*); EstFil 54 (2005) 533-539 (*López Santamaría, Justino*); EThL 81 (2005) 586-590 (*Vansina, Frans D.*); CEv 132 (2005) 63.

16202 Robertson, Charles Martin 11.9.1911-26.12.2004 ⇒20,14593. [R]AJA 109 (2005) 557-559 (*Ridgway, Brunilde Sismondo*).

16203 Saggs, Henry W.F. 2.12.1920-31.8.2005. [R]Iraq 67/2 (2005) vi (*Millard, Alan*).

16204 Sandevoir, Pierre 1947-2005. [R]CEv 133 (2005) 87.

16205 Sarna, Nahum 27.3.1923-23.6.2005. [R]BArR 31/6 (2005) 18-19.

16206 Schille, Gottfried 6.8.1929-23.2.2005. [R]ThLZ 130 (2005) 584-585 (*Niebuhr, Karl-Wilhelm*).

16207 Schofield, Elizabeth 1935-2005 [AJA 110,157ss–Cadogan, G.].

16208 Segert, Stanislav 4.5.1921-30.9.2005. [R]CV 47 (2005) 234-235 (*Sláma, Petr*); ArOr 73 (2005) 497-500 (*Oliverius, Jaroslav; Zemánek, Petr*); UF 37 (2005) ix-x (*Dietrich, Manfried; Loretz, Oswald*).

16209 Stefanini, Ruggero 11.7.1932-6.5.2005.

16210 Stegemann, Hartmut 18.12.1933-22.8.2005 [ThLZ 131,336].

16211 Stricker, Bruno Hugo Ob. 18.9.2005, aet. 95. [R]Phoe. 51 (2005) 127.

16212 Strus, Andrzej 16.4.1938-13.6.2005.

16213 Style, Peter 3.1934-8.2.2005. [R]BAIAS 23 (2005) 198 (*Rosenberg, Stephen G.; Jones, Ashley*).

16214 Suhl, Alfred 27.1.1934-22.4.2005. [R]ThLZ 130 (2005) 585 (*Reuter, Hans-Richard*).
16215 Tadmor, Haim 18.11.1923-11.12.2005 [Qad. 131,62s].
16216 Taeger, Jens-W. 16.2.1945-7.12.2004 ⇒20,14603. [R]ThLZ 130 (2005) 345-346 (*Reuter, Hans-Richard*).
16217 Thiede, Carsten Peter 8.8.1952-14.12.2004 ⇒20,14604. [R]BAIAS 23 (2005) 195-197 (*Sahm, Ulrich; Lass, Egon H.E.*).
16218 Touati, Charles 1.2.1925-15.3.2003 ⇒19,15298. [R]REJ 164 (2005) 539-546 (*Nahon, Gérard*).
16219 Tsereteli, Konstantin 4.2.1921-27.2.2004 ⇒20,14605. [R]OrChr 89 (2005) 221-224 (*Gamkredlize, Thomas V.; Chikovani, Guram*).
16220 Van der Ploeg, Johannes Petrus Maria 4.7.1909-4.8.2004 ⇒20, 14607. [R]OrChr 89 (2005) 224-225 (*Kaufhold, Hubert*).
16221 Varro, Roger 1931-2005. [R]CEv 134 (2005) 63.
16222 Veijola, Timo 25.4.1947-1.8.2005.
16223 Weitemeyer, Mogens 26.5.1922-15.4.2005.
16224 Wiles, Maurice 17.10.1923-3.6.2005.
16225 Wölfle, Meinrad 12.11.1913-8.5.2005. [R]BVLI 49 (2005) 9-10.

# Index Alphabeticus

## Auctorum

[D]dir. dissertationis [E]editor [F]Festschrift [M]mentio [R]recensio [T]translator/vertens

## Situs

## Voces

### Akkadicae



### Aramaicae



### Emar

**Graecae**

**Hebraicae**

# Sacra Scriptura

**Exodus**

**Joannes**

END

STAMPA: Ottobre 2008

presso la tipografia
"Giovanni Olivieri" di E. Montefoschi
ROMA • info@tipografiaolivieri.it